INTRODUCTION TO BASIC LEGAL PRINCIPLES

1994 Edition

Benjamin N. Henszey
John W. Bagby
Reed T. Phalan
Barry L. Myers
Jeffery Sharp

KENDALL/HUNT PUBLISHING COMPANY
4050 Westmark Drive   Dubuque, Iowa 52002

CONTENTS

Contents

Chapter 2: Administrative Law

Contents

Chapter 5: The Basic Law of Contracts: Offer and Acceptance

Contents

Chapter 7: Legal Capacity to Make a Contract

Chapter 8: Reality of Consent

Contents

Contents

  C. Duty to Bargain in Good Faith 379
   1. Subjects of Bargaining 380
  D. Impasse 381
  E. Union Security Agreements 381
   1. Right to Work Laws 382
 VII. Union Concerted Activities 383
  A. Regulation of Strikes 383
   1. Types of Strikes 383
   2. No Strike Clauses 384
   3. National Emergency Strikes 385
  B. Picketing 385
  C. Secondary Pressure 385
 VIII. Labor Arbitration and Grievance Settlement 386
  A. Union Democracy 387
  B. Labor's Bill of Rights 387
  C. Trusteeship 387
  Problems 388

Chapter 14: Employment Law

 I. Occupational Safety and Health 392
  A. The OSHA Administration 392
  B. Employer's Duty of Safety 393
   1. Design vs. Performance Standards 393
   2. Health and Safety Rulemaking Process 394
  C. Variances 394
  D. OSHA Enforcement Procedures 395
   1. Recordkeeping and Reporting Requirements 395
   2. OSHA Administration Inspections 396
   3. OSHA Violations 396
  E. State Occupational Safety Laws 397
 II. Workers' Compensation 397
  A. Workers' Compensation Administration 397
  B. Benefits 398
  C. Compensable Injuries 398
 III. Equal Employment Opportunities 399
  A. Equal Pay Act 400
   1. Comparable Worth 400
  B. Civil Rights Act of 1964 400
   1. Theories of Discrimination 401
   2. Protected Classes 402
   3. Statutory Exceptions 404
  C. Sexual Harassment 406
  D. Equal Employment Opportunity Commission 407
  E. Affirmative Action 407
  F. Executive Order Program 407
 IV. Employment Compensation 408

Contents

Chapter 16: Securities Regulations

Contents

Chapter 17: Environmental Law

Chapter 18: Agency

Contents

Chapter 19: Partnerships

Chapter 20: Corporations

Chapter 21: The Sale and Lease of Goods: Contract Formation

Contents

Chapter 22: The Sale and Lease of Goods: Contract Performance and Remedies

Contents

Chapter 23: Commercial Paper: Negotiability

Contents

Chapter 25: Banks, Checks and Electronic Funds Transfers

Contents

Chapter 26: Bailments, Documents of Title and Investment Securities

Chapter 27: Secured Transactions

Contents

Chapter 28: Debtor–Creditor Relations

Contents

Chapter 29: Bankruptcy

Chapter 30: Real Property

Contents

Chapter 31: Gifts and Inheritance

Appendices

PREFACE

There is unanimous agreement that college education for business should include some study of law, legal reasoning, and legal institutions. Courses designed to meet this need, usually titled with some variation of the term "business law," have long been included in business administration curricula. In more recent years, a further need for basic law courses has been developing. Recognizing that the law is one of the most important of the social sciences, more and more educators are seeking a basic law course for undergraduates as a social science or general education elective, a course for students in all curricula.

Basic survey courses offered for students from other specialties are an essential part of the college scene, and the general purpose of such survey courses is well understood—namely, to *show how the discipline under study* (physics, chemistry, geology, economics, law, or some other course) *fits into and affects the social order, thus enabling the student, as an educated person, to better understand, adjust to, and contribute to his social environment.* No one will claim that completion of a basic physics course will make the student a scientist or enable him to carry on scientific research. A person does not become an economist with one course in economics or a historian after having a survey course in history. Equally limited in purpose and effect are basic law courses offered to college undergraduates, whether business administration majors or not. Such courses, therefore, should be general education or social science courses, rather than sets of rules for "do-it-yourselfers." The primary purpose is not to teach rules of law or to enable students to handle their own legal affairs, but rather to introduce the law as a social institution.

When it comes to determining the course content for an undergraduate survey course in law, the following factors provide helpful guidelines:

1. The law is the chief agency for social control.

2. The law achieves social control through weighing and adjusting the conflicting interests of individuals and of groups, and then recognizing and defining legal rights and enforcing legal obligations.

3. The conduct of business—the buying and selling of goods, land, and services is the principal nonpolitical activity of society.

4. The bases for most private or nonpolitical legal rights and obligations involve two main fields of the law, torts and contracts.

Therefore, for a basic law course to adequately picture the law and legal reasoning in action, it should briefly describe courts and lawsuits, and then consider some of the basic policy factors which have shaped the law and continue to shape it in the fields of torts, crimes, contracts, and general business operations and transactions.

If a survey course in any field is to achieve its proper objectives, the manner in which the course is presented is of vital importance. A student taking a basic physics course will not concentrate on memorizing formulas for momentum, falling bodies, intensity of light, and so on. Rather, he will examine the basic principles from which the formulas are derived. Such an approach is especially necessary for an undergraduate law course in order to emphasize clearly the most important feature of the law as a social institution—namely, that a rule of law is a statement of what is considered to be sound, wise policy (fair, reasonable, and practical) under certain particular circumstances.

We should like to outline the manner in which this book attempts to achieve the foregoing objectives.

1. The book begins with a general introduction to the nature of law, to legal systems and courts, and to basic legal procedure, followed by a general introduction to the basic principles involved in the fields of tort, crimes and contract law.

2. Following this general introduction, certain specific topics are presented to introduce students to the general plan of the law as applied in greater detail to common business operations and transactions.

3. When applicable, the basic policy decisions written into the Uniform Commercial Code are indicated and illustrated.

4. A considerable amount of case material is included in the examples and problems. The examples demonstrate the interplay of policy factors and the application of legal principles in resolving disputes. The problems stimulate the student in analyzing fact situations, recognizing legal issues, thinking in terms of basic legal factors, and applying fundamental principles to resolve disputes.

5. On the whole, the approach for most topics is *analytical* rather than merely *descriptive*, emphasizing the policy factors which underlie the basic rules of law. We believe that by means of this "policy" approach, not only will a student become somewhat familiar with the basic everyday rules under which society operates, but, what is more important, he will observe the legal process in action--the weighing of conflicting interests in the determination and formulation of what are believed to be the soundest policies and the wisest rules.

Our selection of legal topics and the space allocated to each has been guided by the objectives for which this book has been prepared. Admittedly, certain topics are very briefly referred to; others are covered in summary fashion. Even the discussions which go into greater detail make no pretense of covering topics in every detail or providing solutions for all conceivable situations. We are confident, however, that with our general objectives in mind, our reader will be misled into taking our discussions for more than they are intended to be--basic surveys of some of the more important legal topics which affect the day-to-day activities of society.

During the last decade, the law applicable to commercial transactions has been substantially modernized by the adoption of the Uniform Commercial Code in every state. In order to better understand the meaning and application of this important body of law, we have integrated non-Code and Code rules of law throughout the text. By doing this, as opposed to isolating Code law in a separate chapter or section as many texts do, we hope to emphasize the importance of the Code as well as facilitate the student's understanding of its relationship to non-Code legal principles.

Many popular texts in the field devote sections, sometimes large sections, of each chapter to reproducing court opinions in some form or another. We have not chosen to follow this popular method of case presentation anywhere in the text. Court opinions are written as cohesive wholes and do not lend themselves to the drastic surgery performed upon them by many authors. The real purpose of encouraging students to explore court opinions is to better understand judicial logic and to develop comparative analytical skills. Current works in the field merely create an appearance of meeting these goals by their token case presentations. The cases are either pared down too much or are too few to illustrate the important text points. They amount to awkward text appendages. The fact is that there is no requirement that basic law courses include token cases. It is the judicial logic and comparative analysis which needs development.

We have chosen to develop examples and problems which achieve the clear, analytical thought that the true case method, which law schools employ, is designed to achieve. Yet we have endeavored to avoid the pitfalls of the "token case" authors. Each of our chapters contain strategically placed examples within the body of the text to illustrate interesting or difficult points of law and to provide the basis for comparative analysis and understanding of judicial thought. Also, each chapter contains a section of thought-provoking problems to challenge the student and provide the basis for extended discussions.

The authors have combined teaching experience of over four decades. They have developed the materials in this book while teaching both large and small classes and the materials have been used by both two-year and four-year students. It is believed that this text provides excellent up-to-date materials of great versatility which can be used by teachers in both junior and community colleges as well as the four-year college or major university.

For those who desire a text for the first course in business law, the first seventeen chapters can serve this purpose by covering the legal system, torts and business ethics, administrative law, constitutional law, contracts, labor law, and government regulation of business. An expanded first course could include Chapters 18, 19, 20, 30, or 31, agency, partnerships, corporations, real property, estates and gifts. A second course can be developed around Chapters 21 through 29 by covering the U.C.C. and sales, commercial paper, and debtor-creditor relations.

DEDICATION

To Emmett Ellis, Lucinda, Robin Sue, Julia Marie, & John Robert.

JOHN W. BAGBY

To my children, Alex, Melissa, & Rebekah.

BENJAMIN N. HENSZEY

To my grandparents, Eugene V. and Julia M. Harris, for their lifelong love and encouragement; and for their demonstration that a rewarding life is a quest for wisdom and knowledge liberally seasoned with laughter.

JEFFERY M. SHARP

1

The Legal System

CHAPTER OUTLINE

The Legal System

I. Law

A. A General Definition and Historical Background

In any society persons can be expected to act primarily for their own interests, with friction and conflict resulting from the competition of various self-interests. To restrain such friction and conflict within tolerable limits, rules for the control of people have been essential from the very dawn of civilization, rules which set the framework or pattern within which all human activity is carried on. The chief repository for such rules is the law. The *law* can be defined, therefore, as a body of rules for human conduct, enforced by a governing power, as the means by which the control of society is achieved. (The term *society* includes the neighborhood, town, state, nation, and, to the extent control among nations is achieved through law, the world.)

The rules of law that exist today are the result of a process of gradual evolution over centuries of social progress, a process which continues unabated. The remote roots of any legal system can be traced back to early tribal life. As disputes arose within a tribe, rules for the conduct of the tribal members were gradually formulated. In a primitive hunting society disputes like that given in the following example probably arose frequently.

At first the Roman law underwent such a gradual evolution. Then with the Roman penchant for centralized government and for de-tailed logical classification, various codifications and texts appeared, culminating finally in the sixth century with the promulgation by the Roman Emperor Justinian of a complete code of law, frequently referred to as the Justinian Code. By this time however, the breakup of the Roman Empire had already begun. With the further disintegration of the Empire, together with the breakdown of trade and commerce that followed the Moslem conquest of Northern Africa and Spain, Europe regressed to a disorganized, rural society, and the Roman Code, no longer necessary, sank into obscurity. Europe's emergence from the Dark Ages spurred interest in the study of Roman law. As Europe developed economically and politically and centralized governments began to emerge, the Roman Code provided the framework for the expanding legal systems needed by the increasingly complex society. Various revisions of the Roman Code were made, and finally in 1804 the most famous recodification was promulgated by Emperor Napoleon. The Napoleonic Code (also called the French Civil Code or Code Napoleon) has become the basis of the legal systems in the countries of continental Europe, and in areas settled under continental European influence—including all of the nations on the American continents, except the United States and Canada; in these two nations, only the state of Louisiana and the province of Quebec, both settled by the French, base their legal systems on the Napoleonic Code.

Example. A and B, both members of the same tribe, were hunting separately. B grievously wounded an animal and was in pursuit when A, not seeing B nearby, intercepted the animal, killed it, and took possession of it. Tribal rules forbade combat within the tribe. Therefore, to settle the disputed ownership, A and B requested a decision from the chief.

Whichever way the chief decided, he would necessarily be stating a rule that would apply in the future should the same kind of dispute arise again. Through the process of deciding day-to-day disputes, rules for conduct were gradually built up.

It is interesting to note that the primitive rule favored the party who first took possession of an animal; during centuries of social progress in conceptions of justice, methods of proof, and knowledge of mortal and nonmortal wounds, the rule gradually changed. In a case which arose in 1914, the Wisconsin Supreme Court said:

> "It is conceded that if the plaintiffs had substantially permanently deprived the wolf of his liberty— had him so in their power that escape was highly improbable, if not impossible, before defendant appeared on the scene, and, with his gun pointed so as to reach within some 3 feet of the animal, delivered a finishing shot, it had become the property of plaintiffs, and was wrongfully appropriated by appellant [the defendant]. Such is according to the prevailing rule. The instant a wild animal is brought under the control of a person, so that actual possession is practically inevitable, a vested property interest in it accrues, which cannot be divested by another's intervening and killing it.... Such is the law of the chase by common-law principles, differing from the more ancient civil law which postponed the point of vested interest to that of actual taking."[1]

The legislature of some states have felt that a codification (definite statutory rule) either repeating or changing the common-law rule is desirable. For example, the Pennsylvania statute deviates from the modern common-law rule and returns somewhat to the ancient rule, saying: "When a mortal wound has been lawfully inflicted on any game, but the same is not killed immediately and continues in flight, and is thereafter lawfully shot by another hunter who inflicts a mortal wound, thereby stopping the flight of such game and killing it, enabling such hunter to take possession of the carcass, the ownership of the carcass shall be deemed to be in the hunter whose fatal wound stopped the flight of such game and enabled him to take possession of the carcass." Apparently the legislature believes that a rule awarding game to the person who delivers the killing blow and takes possession is simpler and easier to apply than the common-law rule and therefore a more desirable rule. ▢

1. *Liesner v. Wanie*, 156 Wis. 16, 50 L.R.A.N.S. 703 (1914)

No such complete codification occurred in England. Although the Norman Conquest of 1066 brought centralization of government at a much earlier date than on the continent, the Norman political system had not yet developed the concept of detailed legislation. Instead, beginning in the twelfth century, centralization of justice was begun by the King's improving and expanding the jurisdiction and authority of the King's Court. The judges of the King's Court, whether holding central court at Westminster, or traveling on circuit and holding court throughout the country, formulated the legal principles which they felt should be applied to the controversies brought before them. These principles were based largely on the customs and rules that had gradually evolved over the centuries. When these customs differed among the various communities, as they frequently did, the King's judges decided which should stand as the common law of the land, thus gradually developing the English common-law system. Even as late as the thirteenth century the quantity of legislative or enacted law in England was very slight. Most of the legal principles were formulated by the judges in the process of settling controversies brought before them. Such judicial lawmaking is the chief characteristic of the English legal system from which the American common-law system developed, as opposed to the Roman code-law system (also called the civil-law system) which is based on legislative law.

B. The Law Broadly Classified

I. LEGISLATIVE AND DECISIONAL LAW

As indicated by the foregoing discussion, rules of law can be broadly classified into legislative law and decisional law. *Legislative law* consists of rules enacted and promulgated for the future conduct of all persons, according to the legislative authority's conception of the public good. A *decisional rule of law* is a rule formulated by the decisional authority (usually a court) in the course of settling a particular dispute between two parties. In deciding the outcome of a particular dispute, a court may simply be required to select the proper legislative rule and apply it to the facts of the dispute. Frequently under the common-law system, however, no applicable legislative rule exists. Since the dispute must be resolved, the court must function as a lawmaker, determining and formulating what it feels to be the proper rule to apply from the standpoint of sound public policy. The American legal system today consists of legislative law (constitutions, statutes enacted by legislatures, and regulations and ordinances promulgated under statutory authority) and also of a considerable body of decisional law.

It should be emphasized that rules of law, whether legislative or decisional, are reflections of what is considered sound public policy, from the standpoint of fairness, reasonableness, practicality, and consistency with previously declared rules. As Justice Holmes has written in his memorable book, THE COMMON LAW:

The life of the law has not been logic: it has been experience. The felt necessities of the time, the prevalent moral and political theories, intuitions of public policy, avowed or unconscious, even the prejudices which judges share with their fellow-men, have had a good deal more to do than the syllogism in determining the rules by which men should be governed. The law embodies the story of a nation's development through many centuries, and it cannot be dealt with as if it contained only the axioms and corollaries of a book of mathematics. In order to know what it is, we must know what it has been, and what it tends to become. We must alternately consult history and existing theories of legislation. But the most difficult labor will be to understand the combination of the two into new products at every stage. The substance of the law at any given time pretty nearly corresponds, so far as it goes, with what is then understood to be convenient; but its form and machinery, and the degree to which it is able to work out desired results, depend very much upon its past....

A very common phenomenon, and one very familiar to the student of history, is this. The customs, beliefs, or needs of a primitive time establish a rule or a formula. In the course of centuries the custom, belief, or necessity disappears, but the rule remains. The reason which gave rise to the rule has been forgotten, and ingenious minds set themselves to inquire how it is to be accounted for. Some ground of policy is thought of, which seems to explain it and to reconcile it with the present state of things; and then the rule adapts itself to the new reasons which have been found for it, and enters on a new career. The old form receives a new content, and in time even the form modifies itself to fit the meaning which it has received....

The very considerations which judges most rarely mention, and always with an apology, are the secret root from which the law draws all the juices of life. I mean, of course, considerations of what is expedient for the community concerned. Every important principle which is developed by litigation is in fact and at a bottom the result of more or less definitely understood views of public policy; most generally, to be sure, under our practice and traditions, the unconscious result of instinctive preferences and inarticulate convictions, but none the less traceable to views of public policy in the last analysis.[2]

In short, legislative and decisional law is determined by policy. Conceptions of policy and circumstances which shape policy change over time. If a rule of law is a viable rule today, it must have sound, present-day policy reasons for its existence. In seeking present-day reasons, one should bear in mind that the promotion of certainty and stability in the law is itself a desirable and necessary objective. The law must not only determine the effect of past conduct but must also give assurances as to a person's future rights and obligations. A necessary legal principle therefore is expressed by the term *stare decisis*, Latin for "let the decision stand." Under this principle, once a decisional rule of law has been formulated, it is applied to similar disputes in the future, until the court is clearly convinced that the rule has become obsolete or is wrong.

An excellent example of the common-law system in operation, with the court reasoning from prior decisional law to form new decisional law, is provided by the case of *Summit Hotel Co. v. National Broadcasting Co.*, 336 Pa. 182 (1939). The citation for this case shows that the lawsuit was brought by the hotel as the plaintiff against (versus) the broadcasting company as the defendant, and that the court's written *opinion*—statement of the court's conclusion and its reasons for reaching that conclusion—is published in volume

---

2. Holmes, Oliver Wendell, Jr., THE COMMON LAW (1881; Cambridge: Harvard University Press, 1963), pp. 5, 8, 31-32.

336 of the Pennsylvania Supreme Court reports at page 182.

2. CIVIL AND CRIMINAL LAW

Rules of law formulated by the legislative and decisional processes are generally either civil or criminal in nature. Civil rules of law have as their purpose the protection of private rights and the providing of redress for private wrongs. On the other hand, criminal rules of law, which are primarily legislative, have as their purpose the protection of public rights and the providing of redress for the public wrongs. The distinction between civil and criminal law, therefore, is based upon whose rights are affected. If, for example, a contract is breached, the offended party would look to civil rules of law for redress since the contract is of interest only to the contracting parties and not to the public in general. However, if an individual is severely beaten by another, not only have his individual rights been infringed upon, giving rise to a remedy under civil rules of law, but the rights of the public or society as a whole have been affected in the sense that such conduct is clearly anti-social. Such actions have fallen below legislative standards of conduct to which all persons should adhere. The second example illustrates an important concept—depending upon the facts and circumstances, rules of civil law or criminal law or both can be used to redress the wrong committed. They are not mutually exclusive.

3. SUBSTANTIVE AND PROCEDURAL LAW

Legislative and decisional rules of law have been stated to be generally civil or criminal in nature. Civil and criminal rules of law can be further classified as being either substantive or procedural in nature. Substantive rules of law create, define and regulate rights. On the other hand, procedural rules of law set forth the methods of enforcing rights or of obtaining redress for their invasion. Every state, for example, statutorily provides that the opera-

Example. The lawsuit in the Summit Hotel case developed from a statement made during a radio broadcast. In 1935 the Shell Oil Company sponsored an NBC radio program starring Al Jolson. One program featured Jolson interviewing a golf champion. The prepared script, which was followed exactly during rehearsal, had Jolson asking, "But tell me, Sam, what did you do after you got out of college?" and the golf champion answering, "I turned golf professional and in 1932 I got a job at the Summit Golf Club in Uniontown, Pennsylvania." During the actual broadcast, Jolson at this point ad libbed, "That's a rotten hotel." The Summit Hotel Company sued NBC for $15,000 damages for the defamation.

The question was whether a radio company should be held liable for a performer's unexpected remark. This exact question had never before been litigated, and at that time no applicable legislative law existed. The closest analogies which had already developed in the courts involved newspaper publishers and owners of public halls. In reference to these, Jolson of course would be liable for his slanderous statement. If Jolson as a columnist had made the statement in a newspaper column, the newspaper publisher would be liable. In some states the decisional rule is that a newspaper publisher is absolutely liable for defamatory statements, the rule in some other states is that a publisher is liable if he has failed to take all reasonable measures to assure that a published statement is true. Under either rule, the publisher's liability is based upon his opportunity to control what is printed. On the other hand, if the owner of an auditorium with a public address system rents it to a lecturer, the owner is not liable for defamatory statements which the lecturer is able to spread through use of the hall and equipment.

The court decided, from the standpoint of fairness, reasonableness, and practicality, that the radio case more nearly resembled the auditorium case. Although the radio broadcaster had a control booth, the sound engineer with his switches and dials was merely assuring the technical quality of the broadcast and was not in the position of a censor. He had no opportunity to cut off Jolson's remark; it was made and broadcast before the engineer could act, unlike the publisher who has ample opportunity during the preparation of a newspaper to delete defamatory material. ▭

tor of a motor vehicle must be licensed. Presumably, if not licensed, an operator would be a threat to society. Motor vehicle licensing statutes, therefore, are, by definition, legislative rules of substantive criminal law. When an operator of a motor vehicle is found to be in violation of the substantive rule of law in that he is not a licensed driver, a citation is issued to him in accordance with legislative rules of criminal procedural law. Accordingly, the citation will instruct the motor vehicle operator procedurally what to do. He can pay the fine and costs or appear before the issuing authority and argue his case. The process by which cases, either civil or criminal, are brought to trial and the procedure for conducting the trial are purely procedural in na-

ture as shown in subsequent parts of this chapter.

4. CONSTITUTIONAL LAW

The Federal Constitution is the highest law in the United States to which all other law must conform, including state legislation and constitutions. The various state constitutions represent the highest law of a state to which all other law in that particular state must conform. Constitutional law therefore deals directly with each of the broad classifications of law discussed immediately above. For example, a state *legislative law* stating that it is a crime to shout obscenities in public places would certainly be challenged under the Federal Constitution. The *substance* of the state *legislative* act is *criminal* in nature and may violate First Amendment Freedom of Speech rights under the Federal Constitution. The state law must pass Constitutional scrutiny.

Because of its importance to a free society, constitutional law is discussed in more detail in Chapter 3.

5. NATIONAL AND INTERNATIONAL LAW

In the last decade, commerce and business has become increasingly multinational in character. There is little doubt that this trend will continue with even greater rapidity in subsequent decades. The multinational economic impact of world events in the 1990s is not clearly known at this point; nevertheless, current political events provide clear signals that existing and proposed changes will be significant and lasting. For example, the merger of West and East Germany and the attempt of the European Common Market to remove all trade barriers by the end of 1992 has major implications to the world economy. Japan's continued economic growth and restrictive trade practices pose significant problems to businessmen in the United States as well as other countries. As Russia moves towards democracy and free trade and China attempts to modernize its industries, additional international trade problems will be superimposed on an already complicated and highly competitive multinational scene. These and other events have given rise to an increased need for businessmen to understand the nature and implications of national and international law.

Simply stated, national law is law (legislative and decisional, civil and criminal, substantive and procedural and constitutional) which applies to a nation. For example, if a United States corporation does business in another country, it will have to know how the particular transaction is taxed in two nations, the United States and the foreign country. Each country has its own national tax law which is applicable only to persons or things subject to

its jurisdiction. On the other hand, international law consists of a body of law which affects two or more nations who, by mutual consent, agree to be bound by its dictates. For example, to facilitate business and commerce, the United States has entered into double taxation treaties with countries such as England and West Germany that prevents income earned and taxed in one country from being taxed a second time to another country. A United States Corporation, therefore, is subject to the national tax law of the United States and international treaties that exist between the United States and other countries where it does business.

International law is developed in three fundamental ways: by treaty, through various organizational structures and custom. A treaty is an agreement or contract between or among nations. An example is the U.S.–Canada Free Trade Agreement which went into effect in 1989. It removes import duties on various goods which has resulted in a significant increase in cross-border trade between the two nations. The Constitution gives the president power to make treaties which must be ratified by two-thirds of the Senators present to be valid. (See Chapter 3.)

International organizations through conventions and meetings have developed what might be termed international law. They develop standards for nations that have the effect of influencing economic and other behavior. For example, in 1947 the General Agreement on Tariffs and Trade (GATT) resulted in a de facto international trade organization whose primary goal was to liberalize international trade. In part, it accomplished that goal by member nations agreeing to be bound by a series of published tariff schedules. An example of a regional organization is the Organization of Petroleum Exporting Countries (OPEC) where several oil producing countries agreed to establish the price of petroleum. An example of a truly international organization is the United Nations where the General Assembly has adopted numerous resolutions that bind member nations. International customs, like the common law, is based upon a course of dealing over many years.

International custom, like the common law, has resulted in the acceptance of certain practices that have occurred over a long period of time. For example, for years it was the custom in many countries not to assert criminal or civil jurisdiction over ambassadors. Like many common law rights and duties, custom with respect to ambassadors has been formalized in legislation or a treaty.

C. Enforcement

An essential part of the concept of law is enforcement by a governing power. Without enforcement a rule actually is not law. Force is obvious in a criminal law action; after being apprehended and adjudged guilty, a wrongdoer is punished by the imposition of a fine or imprisonment or both. Force is equally a part of civil law. For example a seller sells and delivers certain goods to a buyer who promises to pay $500 in thirty days. The goods are of proper quality but the buyer fails to pay. The seller sues the buyer and the court determines that the buyer owes the seller $500 and has no valid excuse for not paying. The court's conclusion is called the *judgment* in the case, and in effect is the court's stamp of approval on the seller's claim for $500. If the buyer fails to pay the amount of the judgment, the court will at the seller's request, order the sheriff to seize property belonging to the buyer, sell it at public auction sale (sheriff's sale), and turn over to the seller the proceeds, up to $500 plus certain expenses; any money remaining is paid to the buyer. This force which can be used if necessary—in this example seizure and sale of the buyer's property—stands behind every civil dispute.

D. Conflict of Laws

I. BETWEEN AND AMONG STATE AND FEDERAL LAW

As discussed in greater detail in Chapter 3, the United States Constitution grants to the Federal government the general power to regulate businesses and commerce which cross state lines (generally termed *interstate commerce*) or which affect interstate commerce. This means that the Federal government has the power to establish rules of law applying to most businesses. This power extends even to businesses which do not themselves sell and ship across state lines, because although not directly a part of interstate commerce, the activities of such business may nevertheless "affect" interstate commerce. The Federal government has exercised its power by establishing rules of law for working conditions in businesses which affect interstate commerce (minimum wages, maximum hours, labor relations, etc.), and by establishing freight rates and other rules for transportation affecting interstate commerce.

Congress has not yet considered it desirable as a matter of policy for the Federal government to exercise completely its powers over matters affecting interstate commerce. Rather, Congress has left to the states the function of declaring and enforcing rules of law for many matters involving the conduct of business. Particularly, the information and enforcement of agreements or contracts are still ruled by state law, even though many of the contracts involve the sale and shipment of goods across state lines.

There is a tendency for rules of law to vary somewhat from one state or country to another. These variations are the result both of varying economic, geographic, social, and political conditions, and also of varying opinions as to desirable policy from the standpoint of fairness, reasonableness, and practicality. Such variations appear both in legislative law and in decisional law. When a business transaction involves persons and businesses in more than one state, the substantive rules of law which will apply are generally those of the state in which the contract is formed and is to be carried out, even though these rules may differ from those of the state in which a lawsuit is brought to enforce the contract. The procedural rules of law which will apply are those of the state in which the lawsuit is brought. Thus if a contract formed and to be performed in Michigan is sued on in Ohio, the Ohio court will apply Michigan substantive and Ohio procedural law to the dispute. Suppose that a buyer in Pennsylvania orders goods from separate sellers in New York, Ohio, and Michigan. Usually each seller's shipment of the goods will form a contract and begin performance. Each of the buyer's three contracts therefore will be controlled by the substantive law of a different state. If the states were to have differing rules of law, a cautious buyer would want to familiarize himself with all of the varying rules before entering into the contracts. An immense saving of time and of money results when rules of law are made uniform so that the same rules apply regardless of the state in which contracts are made and are to be performed. Smooth, efficient conduct of business requires that rules of law be stable and uniform throughout the multistate business community.

Several organizations, composed of prominent lawyers, judges, and law teachers, and aided by many businesses, have been working for some time to promote uniformity of state laws, both legislative and decisional laws. The two most important and effective of these organizations are the National Conference of Commissioners on Uniform State Laws, and the American Law Institute. The National Conference, composed of members from all states (usually appointed by the governors) was first organized in the 1890s. It determines topics upon which uniform statutes among the states seem desirable, studies and discusses drafts of such statutes, and recommends the completed drafts to the state legislatures. In this way, uniform statutes covering various phases of business transactions have been prepared and enacted into law by the legislatures in most of the commercial states. The most important of these uniform statutes are the Negotiable Instruments Law (covering checks, notes, and drafts), the Sales Act (covering sales of goods), the Conditional Sales Act (covering installment purchasing by consumers), the Trust Receipts Act (covering credit purchases of inventory by dealers), the Bills of Lading Act, the Warehouse Receipts Act, and the Stock Transfer Act. The American Law Institute was organized in the 1920s by a number of prominent lawyers, judges, and law teachers, aided by grants of money from charitable foundations and other sources. It has been mainly concerned with nonstatutory or decisional rules of law. The Institute studies, consolidates, and publishes concise statements of decisional rules of law, using the title, "Restatement of the Law." Topics covered by such studies include contracts, agency, torts, property, and many others. These restatements are very often used by courts as convenient and authoritative sources of decisional rules of law.

Both of these organizations have cooperated in the preparation of the *Uniform Commercial Code*, a complete restatement and codification of the rules of law applying to commercial transactions. The objectives of the Code are to modernize the rules of commercial law and to present them as a unified whole, rather than in a series of separate statutes. The Conference and the Institute both felt that just as a business transaction is a unified whole, involving the interrelation of sale, shipment, financing, payment by check (or note or draft), etc., so too should the rules of law be unified and interrelated. The Code was recommended to the state legislatures for enactment into law, replacing all of the previous uniform commercial statutes.

All the states except one have adopted the Code, usually with minor variations. (Although Louisiana has not adopted the Code in its entirety, it has adopted substantial parts of it.) Sometimes the Code rules are the same as the rules under the uniform statutes; sometimes the Code makes changes and additions.

Preparation of the Code took a number of years, cost hundreds of thousands of dollars, and involved thousands of hours of study and conferences by a number of legal and business groups. The history of the common law has never before seen anything like such a sweeping codification and rewriting of the law. As can be expected with such a sizable undertaking, involving policy decisions on numerous controversial points, the Code has both advocates and opponents.

On the side of the Code's advocates, the late Judge Herbert F. Goodrich, chairman of the entire project, has written his forward to the 1957 Official Edition of the Code:

> Neither the Institute nor the Commissioners can claim perfection for this Code. No group of people, however careful, can use words that will be perfectly clear in their meaning to all other people. No group can make rules for the whole broad field of commercial law and have every rule which is written completely satisfactory to all who read it. There are interests to be balanced between parties whose desires conflict. What can be said for the Code is that the language has been worked over with care and the ideas embodied in the rules likewise worked over with care to get a fair balance of interests for all concerned.

Opponents have challenged some of the policy decisions embodied in the Code as being unfair, unreasonable, impractical, or overly partial to certain business interests, and also have argued that some of the language is so general as to be confusing and ambiguous, inviting differing interpretations by courts in various states, and thus actually reducing the desired uniformity of commercial laws. Obviously the best measure of the Code is how it works in actual practice. The consensus is that it is working very satisfactorily. As an indication of its acceptance, every state has adopted it entirely or in a modified version.

The Code is divided into twelve Articles entitled as follows:

Article 1	General Provisions
Article 2	Sales
Article 2A	Leases
Article 3	Commercial Paper
Article 4	Bank Deposits and Collections
Article 4A	Funds Transfers
Article 5	Letters of Credit
Article 6	Bulk Transfers
Article 7	Warehouse receipts, Bills of Lading and Other Documents of Title
Article 8	Investment Securities
Article 9	Secured Transactions; Sales of Accounts, Contract Rights and Chattel Paper
Article 10	Effective Date and Repealer

2. BETWEEN NATIONAL AND INTERNATIONAL LAW

Just as laws between and among states may differ, conflicts arise between national and international laws. Two important principles that help to regulate such conflicts are the Act of State Doctrine and the Principle of Comity.

The *act of state doctrine* provides that "[e]very sovereign state is bound to respect the independence of every other sovereign state, and the courts of one country will not sit in judgment of another government's acts done within its own territory."[3] The public acts committed by a foreign nation in its own territory are presumed to be valid. For example, Cuba's expropriation of a United States corporation's property and rights could not be interfered with by a United States court.

---

3. *Underbill v. Hernandez,* 168 U.S. 250, 252, 18 S.Ct. 83, 84, 42 L.Ed. 456 (1897).

The *principle of comity* arises when one nation recognizes and gives effect to the laws and policies of another nation. The principle applies where the act of the foreign government purports to have an extraterritorial effect. For example, if a foreign government stopped payment on debt obligations owed to a United States corporation, United States law and policy would be considered because the act of the foreign government has the effect of interfering with a property right located in the United States. The extraterritorial nature of the problem removes it from the act of state doctrine.

II. The Courts

A. Purpose and General Structure

Rules of law established through the legislative and decision making processes take on meaning only when they are applied to actual situations. The ideal situation occurs when two parties can resolve their differences by agreement. Frequently, however, the parties cannot reach such an agreement. They may irreconcilably disagree over the facts in controversy or the law applicable to the facts, or both. At this point, the courts may be called upon, for it is their function to resolve differences between parties. To illustrate how factual and legal controversies arise and often intertwine, suppose, for example, that a Seller wrote to a Buyer and offered to sell him "my house located at 100 Spring Street for $25,000, acceptance to be made within ten days of the date of this letter." Fifteen days later, Seller called Buyer and informed him that since he never received an acceptance, the offer was no longer open (under general contract principles, an offer must be accepted within the period stated therein for a valid and binding contract to exist). Whereupon Buyer told Seller that he had accepted Seller's offer by return mail within the requested ten-day period, but apparently the acceptance letter was lost in the mails. If Seller and Buyer disagreed over the existence of a contract, the obvious factual issue in controversy is whether or not Buyer ever dispatched an acceptance. The legal issue in controversy is more subtle. If it was factually determined that an acceptance letter was dispatched, would it become legally effective when received or when dispatched. (The purpose here is not to resolve the factual and legal issues. This will be done in subsequent chapters dealing with contract law.) The point is that if Seller and Buyer cannot resolve their factual and legal differences, they can turn to the appropriate court whose function is to resolve such differences by the meshing of fact and rules of law through a process called *adjudication*.

In the English and American legal systems, a lawsuit is conducted as a debate. Each side of a legal dispute is represented by a lawyer whose duty is not to be impartial, but rather, in an entirely partisan manner, to present and argue his client's side as vigorously and skillfully as he can. The decision is then made by an impartial court (judge and jury, judge alone, or group of judges) on the basis of the evidence and arguments produced and developed by the partisan lawyers. The manner of deciding disputes, frequently referred to as the *adversary system*, has been described and explained in the following manner by Professor Lon Fuller of Harvard Law School:

> The philosophy of adjudication that is expressed in "the adversary system" is, speaking generally, a philosophy that insists on keeping distinct the function of the advocate, on the one hand, from that of the judge, or of the judge from that of jury, on the other. The decision of the case is for the judge, or for the judge and jury. That decision must be as objective and as free from bias as it possibly can. The Constitution of Massachusetts provides in language that in its idiom calls at once to mind the spirit of a great age, the Age of the Enlightenment and of the American and French Revolutions—that "It is the right of every citizen to be tried by judges as free, impartial and in-

dependent as the lot of humanity will admit." If the judge is to perform that high function— a function which the Constitution recognizes may put human nature to a severe test then the rules of procedure that govern a trial must be such that they do not compel or invite him to depart from the difficult role in which he is cast. It is not his place to take sides. He must withhold judgment until all the evidence has been examined and all the arguments have been heard.

The judge and jury must, then, be excluded from any partisan role. At the same time, a fair trial requires that each side of the controversy be carefully considered and be given its full weight and value. But before a judge can gauge the full force of an argument, it must be presented to him with partisan zeal by one not subject to the restraints of judicial office. The judge cannot know how strong an argument is until he has heard it from the lips of one who has dedicated all the powers of his mind to its formulation.

This is the function of the advocate. His task is not to decide but to persuade. He is not expected to present the case in a colorless and detached manner, but in such a way that it will appear in that aspect most favorable to his client. He is not like a jeweler who slowly turns a diamond in the light so that each of its facets may in turn be fully revealed. Instead the advocate holds the jewel steadily, as it were, so as to throw into bold relief a single aspect of it. It is the task of the advocate to help the judge and jury to see the case as it appears to interested eyes, in the aspect it assumes when viewed from that corner of life into which fate has cast his client.

This is in general what we mean by the adversary system when we apply that phrase to the trial of controversies before courts....

Let me begin with that aspect of the adversary philosophy which is most puzzling— not to say, most offensive to the layman....

The rule I am discussing is one which says that without impropriety a lawyer may, if he sees fit, defend a man he knows to be guilty. Not only that, but the lawyer may render this service for a fee; he may, without qualms of conscience, accept compensation for appearing in court to plead the cause of a man he knows to be guilty....

The purpose of the rule is not merely to protect the innocent person against the possibility of an unjust conviction, precious as that objective is. The purpose of the rule is to preserve the integrity of society itself. It aims at keeping sound and wholesome the procedures by which society visits its condemnation on an erring member.

Why have courts and trials at all? Why bother with judges and juries, with pleas and counterpleas? When disputes arise or accusations are made, why should not the state simply appoint honest and intelligent men to make investigations? Why not let these men, after they have sifted the evidence and resolved apparent contradictions, make their findings without the aid of advocates and without the fanfare and publicity of a trial?

Arrangements tending in this direction are not unknown historically. One of them has at various times and in various forms been familiar in the European continent. This is the institution of the investigation magistrate, *le juge d'instruction*. . .

No such office or institution exists in the countries of the common law, including the United States. Why do we reject an arrangement that seems so reasonable in its quiet efficiency? In answer I might simply draw on the European experience and quote a French observer who remarked that in cases where the *juge d'instruction* reaches the conclusion that no prosecution should be brought, it is usually with a tinge of regret that he signs the necessary documents. European experience also suggests that political interests are often involved in charges of crime and that it is desirable in order to prevent abuse that every fact bearing on guilt be tried in courts open to the public.

But publicity is not of itself a guarantee against the abuse of legal procedures. The public trials of alleged traitors that nearly always follow violent revolutions are a sufficient testimonial to this fact. What is essential is that the accused have at his side throughout a skilled lawyer, pledged to see that his rights were protected. When the matter comes for final trial in court, the only participation accorded to the accused in that trial lies in the opportunity to present proofs and reasoned arguments on his behalf. This opportunity cannot be meaningful unless the accused is represented by a professional advocate. If he is denied his representation the processes of public trial become suspect and tainted. It is for this reason that I say that the integrity of society itself demands that the accused be represented by counsel. If he is plainly guilty this representation may become in a sense symbolic. But the symbolism is of vital importance. It marks society's determination to keep unsoiled and beyond suspicion the procedures by which men are condemned for a violation of its laws.

The lawyer appearing on behalf of an accused person is not present in court merely to represent his client. He represents a vital interest of society itself, he plays an essential role in one of the fundamental processes of an ordered community. The rules that govern his conduct make this clear.

It is a fundamental principle of the lawyer's canons of ethics that he may not state to the judge or jury that he personally believes in the innocence of his client. He may say, for example, "I submit that the evidence fails to establish the guilt of my client." But he may not say, "I personally know my client to be innocent," just as he may not be asked why the judge or jury whether he believes his client to be guilty.

These rules concerning the lawyer's conduct in court are not only important in themselves, but also for the spirit that lies back of them. They make it clear that the lawyer is present, not as an individual with all of his likes and dislikes, beliefs and disbeliefs, but as one who plays an important role in the process of social decision. At no time is the lawyer a mere agent of his client. If he disapproves of his client's conduct during the trial, he may though this is often a painfully difficult decision—withdraw from the case. Obviously, he may not participate in the fabrication of testimony, just as he may not, to free his client, cast suspicion on innocent persons....

I have so far emphasized chiefly the role of the lawyer in the defense of criminal cases. But the need for an adversary presentation, with both sides vigorously upheld, is also present in civil suits. For one thing, there is an element of social condemnation in almost all adverse legal judgments, so that the considerations that apply to criminal cases are also relevant to civil controversies. To be found guilty of negligent driving or of breaking a contract does not carry the stigma of a criminal conviction, but in these cases, too, society must be concerned that even the qualified condemnation implied in an adverse civil judgment should not be visited on one who has not had a chance to present his case fully.

More important in complicated controversies is the contribution that an adversary presentation makes to a properly grounded decision, a decision that takes account of all the facts and relevant rules. In a statement issued recently by a committee of the American Bar Association, it was pointed out how, in the absence of an adversary presentation, there is a strong tendency by any deciding official to reach a conclusion at an early stage and to adhere to that conclusion in the face of conflicting considerations later developed. In the language of the committee:

"What generally occurs in practice is that at some early point a familiar pattern will seem to emerge from the evidence; an accustomed label is waiting for the case and, without waiting further proofs, this label is promptly assigned to it. It is a mistake to suppose that this premature cataloguing must necessarily result from impatience, prejudice or mental sloth. Often it proceeds from a very understandable desire to bring the hearing into some order and coherence, for without some tentative theory of the case there is no standard of relevance by which testimony may be measured. But what starts as a preliminary diagnosis designed to direct the inquiry tends, quickly and imperceptibly, to become a fixed conclusion, as all that confirms the diagnosis makes a strong imprint on the mind, while all that runs counter to it is received with diverted attention.

An adversary presentation seems the only effective means for combating this natural human tendency to judge too swiftly in terms of the familiar that which is not yet fully known. The arguments of counsel hold the case, as it were, in suspension between two opposing interpretations of it. While the proper classification of the case is thus kept unresolved, there is time to explore all of its peculiarities and nuances...."

I have only a few minutes to touch on an expanded sense of the adversary system that applies its philosophy to decisions reached by less formal procedures, let us say, decisions reached in the course of operating an industrial or educational enterprise. In the conduct of any human enterprise, collective decisions must always involve a compromise of interests that are at least partially divergent. For example, in the operation of a factory one may distinguish among the following groups: (1) those whose primary objective is to produce a maximum of goods, (2) those whose primary interest is in developing a satisfied work force, working under conditions of complete dignity and impartial justice, and (3) those whose main urge is to improve the product, even at the cost of some present inefficiency. Each of these interests is a legitimate and proper one, yet each must be qualified by a recognition of the legitimate demands of the others.

An effective consensus cannot be reached unless each party understands fully the position of the others. This understanding cannot be obtained unless each party is permitted to state fully what its own interest is and to urge with partisan zeal the vital importance of that interest to the enterprise as a whole. At the same time, since an effective consensus requires an understanding and willing cooperation of all concerned, no party should so abandon himself in advocacy that he loses the power to comprehend sympathetically the views of those with different interests. What is required here is a spirit that can be called that of tolerant partisanship. This implies not only tolerance for opposing viewpoints, but tolerance for a partisan presentation of those viewpoints, since without that presentation they may easily be lost from sight....

In the end, the justification for the adversary system lies in the fact that it is a means by which the capacities of the individual may be lifted to the point where he gains the power to view reality through eyes other than his own, where he is able to become as impartial, and as

free from prejudice, as "the lot of humanity will admit."[4]

B. Court Systems— State and Federal

Within any state in the United States, two court systems have jurisdiction: (1) the courts of that particular state, and (2) the Federal courts. Although the courts in the various states differ somewhat among themselves and also from the Federal courts in the names by which they are known, they all follow the same general pattern, classifiable into trial courts and appeal courts.

I. STATE COURTS

Trial Courts

Most states have two types of trial courts: (1) courts of limited jurisdiction, for the trial of less significant cases and cases involving smaller amounts of money, and (2) courts of unlimited, general jurisdiction.

Courts Of Limited Jurisdiction. A typical state court at the lower end of the hierarchy of trial courts is the justice of the peace court. In larger communities, courts of limited jurisdiction are frequently called magistrates' courts, small claims court, or municipal or city courts. Very often justices of the peace and magistrates are not required to have legal training. This is a holdover from much earlier times when there was a shortage of men schooled in the law, and travel was slow and difficult. To settle minor local disputes it was necessary to vest judicial authority in men whose lack of legal knowledge, it was hoped, could be compensated for by sound judgment and common sense. While justices of the peace served usefully under these early conditions, experts in judicial administration feel that since such conditions no longer ex-

---

4. Reprinted with permission from Harold J. Berman (ed.), TALKS ON AMERICAN LAW, (New York: Vintage, 1961), Chap. 3.

ist, any system which vests judicial functions in persons without legal training should be discarded. However, although they have become quite obsolete, justice of the peace court cannot be easily or quickly abolished, both because the incumbents have political strength, and also because the court systems of many states are prescribed by their constitutions, and constitutional amendment is slow and difficult.

Frequently a jury is not used in a trial before a justice of the peace or similar judicial official, both the determination of facts and the application of law to the facts being made by the justice or magistrate. Also, procedure is much less formal than in trials conducted before legally trained judges. Although a person has the right to be his own lawyer in any case, considerable knowledge of law and legal procedure is required for adequate presentation of a case in the more formal trial courts, while less technical knowledge is required for simpler cases before a justice of the peace or magistrate. Nevertheless, a litigant before one of these minor courts is well advised to seek legal assistance if he is the defendant, or if the dispute is at all complex or involves more than an insignificant amount of money.

Frequently, no word-for-word record is made of the testimony of witnesses during a justice of the peace trial. Because of this, an appeal from the decision of a justice court is frequently not merely a review of the previous trial but instead involves a new, full-scale lawsuit and trial in the next higher court.

Some states have small claims courts where a litigant is not permitted to be represented by a lawyer. The rationale for this is that there is an absolute right to appeal the case to higher court and, possibly, neither party could gain an advantage by having a lawyer when the other does not have one.

Some states have made provision for compulsory arbitration courts, another type of court with limited jurisdiction. Pennsylvania, for example, provides that where the amount in dispute is less than a specified dollar amount (the range can vary between $10,000 and $20,000 depending upon county classification) either party can elect compulsory arbitration. Under this plan, a lawsuit is initiated in the usual way. Then, when the case is ready for trial, instead of going to a court trial, the case is referred to a board of arbitrators consisting of three lawyers selected by the clerk of court from an alphabetical list. A separate board is appointed for each case. The board holds a hearing, considers the evidence, and reaches a conclusion deciding the dispute. This decision becomes the binding judgment in the case unless the losing party promptly files an appeal in court. The compulsory-arbitration system is in effect in most of the more populous counties under a Pennsylvania statute which authorizes all county courts at their option to adopt the system. Since the inauguration of the compulsory arbitration system, relatively few arbitration decisions have been appealed; the system has been quite successful and is popular with lawyers, judges, and litigants alike.

Arbitration can also occur by agreement, a practice which is growing in favor with many businesses. To settle a dispute in this way, the parties agree to submit their dispute to an arbitrator (or group of arbitrators) for decision, *and* to abide by the decision. Such an agreement for arbitration can be entered into after a dispute arises, or it can be included as a contract provision when the parties are negotiating their contract. Such an arbitration agreement will be enforced by the courts. If a plaintiff starts a lawsuit in violation of his agreement to have disputes arbitrated, the court will grant the defendant's motion to dismiss the action; the plaintiff must comply with the agreed arbitration procedure if he wishes to have the dispute settled. If, after completion of an arbitration proceeding, the losing party refuses to abide by the decision or award, the winning party may obtain a court judgment

15

based on the award, without the necessity of a court trial of the dispute.

For many business disputes, arbitration offers various advantages over court settlement including the following:

1. The formality of court procedure and overcrowded court calendars frequently combine to cause considerable delay in court actions. Appeals increase the delay so that it is not unusual for a year or two to pass between the start of a lawsuit and final satisfaction of the judgment thereby obtained. On the other hand, arbitration can be quite speedy.

2. Technical knowledge is often required in deciding a business dispute. Technical words in a contract, trade practices and customs, or particular production and operational techniques may be involved. In such a case a court trial is further delayed by the need to impart the necessary technical knowledge to the judge and jury, and sometimes their lack of technical background may result in an inaccurate consideration of the entire problem. However, arbitrators are usually selected from men already quite familiar with the techniques of the particular trade involved.

3. Discontinuance of further business relations between the parties is frequently an outcome of a dispute which goes into a lawsuit, whereas this is not as likely to follow a dispute settled by arbitration.

4. Court proceedings are public, whereas arbitration proceedings can be private, avoiding public disclosure of operations and information which businesses might prefer to keep private. (See pages 37-38 for additional discussion on arbitration.)

Courts of Unlimited Jurisdiction. Cases before trial courts of general or unlimited jurisdiction are easily classifiable into three types. In many states separate courts are provided for each type. Although known by a variety of names in the different court systems, these courts, *in function*, are: (1) criminal courts, (2) estate courts (having jurisdiction over the estates of deceased persons, the guardian of minors, and the like), and (3) general civil courts.

Appellate Courts

Every court system has an appellate court which hears appeals from the decisions of the various trial courts. Because of the great number of appeals, many states, in addition to a final appellate court, have one or more intermediate appellate courts to consider appeals in specialized or less important cases. However, even if a state has both an intermediate appellate court and a final appellate court, a litigant usually has a right to only *one* appeal. He has no *right* to have a second appeal in the final appellate court. The latter court may, at its discretion, allow a further appeal if the court feels the case warrants it, but the decision as to whether or not to hear a second appeal is entirely up to the higher appellate court.

It is important for the trial attorney to present as complete a case as possible at the trial court level, because, on appeal, only the record is brought up for review. It is upon this record that the appellate court will, in part, base its decision.

2. FEDERAL COURTS

National

The Federal district courts are the trial courts in the Federal system. The appellate courts include the courts of appeal (of which there are thirteen for the entire country) and the United States Supreme Court.

The Federal courts have *exclusive* jurisdiction of crimes punishable under Federal statutes and of cases arising on navigable waters, or under bankruptcy, postal, or Federal banking laws. *Concurrent* with state courts, the Federal courts have jurisdiction in cases in which (1) a Federal question is involved, that is, a question under the United States Constitution, laws or treaties or (2) the amount in dispute exceeds $50,000 and there is diversity of citizenship, that is, a dispute between citizens of different states. For example, if a seller in Chicago has a $52,000 claim against a buyer in Philadelphia, the seller can at his option sue in the Federal District Court for the Eastern District of Pennsylvania, or in the state trial court of general civil jurisdiction for Philadelphia County. If the amount claimed is less than $50,000, the seller has no choice—he can bring the action only in the state court. Whether the action is brought in a state or in a Federal court, the same rules will be applied in deciding the dispute.

The United States Constitution provides that Federal laws are the supreme law of the land, and that the Federal judicial power extends to all cases arising under the United States Constitution or laws. One result of these provisions is that while a state court has no power over a case properly in Federal court, a Federal court can take control over some types of cases in the state courts. This supremacy of Federal courts appears mainly in three types of situations.

1. Before trial, a lawsuit begun in a state court may be transferred to a Federal district court upon prompt request by the defendant, if (a) the case involves a right arising under Federal laws or Constitution, or (b) the case involves an amount in excess of $50,000 and the parties are citizens of different states, with the defendant being a nonresident of the state in which the case starts.

2. After trial and appeal in the proper state courts the losing party may request the United States Supreme Court to hear a further appeal if the case involves a right arising under the United States Constitution or statutes. Whether or not it will hear such an appeal is left to the discretion of the United States Supreme Court; it may grant or deny the requested appeal. One of the most important provisions in the United States Constitution in regard to federal–state relationships is the guaranty to a person that no state shall deprive him of life, liberty, or property without due process of law. For example, if it is

claimed that a state criminal conviction is based upon a confession forced involuntarily from the accused, a Federal question is raised upon which the accused may request an appeal to the United States Supreme Court. If a dispute in a state court does not involve Federal rights, there is no basis upon which to request an appeal to the United States Supreme Court. Most civil disputes in state courts do not involve Federal laws or issues. If a state court follows proper judicial procedure but the losing party claims that the court's decision is erroneous because of a mistake as to applicable state law, a Federal issue is not raised. The losing party is considered to have had the benefit of proper judicial due process as guaranteed to him by the United States Constitution. The interpretation and application of state law is left to the state courts, the United States Supreme Court having no general right to supervise such local matters.

3. After exhausting all available rights of appeal, a person imprisoned under state authority may ask a Federal district court to inquire into his imprisonment and order his release, if shown to be in violation of his rights under the United States Constitution.

The general structure of the State and Federal Court System is summarized in Figure 1.1.

Foreign Nations

The *doctrine of sovereign immunity* generally provides that a foreign nation is not subject to the jurisdiction of United States courts unless a claim arises from commercial activity of the foreign nation in the United States or the foreign nation has waived its immunity. The doctrine was codified in 1976 in the Foreign Sovereign Immunities Act (FSIA)[5] which is the primary source of United States jurisdiction over foreign nations. For example, because the commercial activity exception does not exist under FSIA, a United States court would

---

5. 28 U.S.C. Sec. 1602-11.

not have jurisdiction over a matter involving the sinking of a foreign owned oil tanker off the coast of a foreign country. If the owner of the tanker carried on commercial activity in the United States, jurisdiction could be obtained by a United States court.

In addition, FSIA provides that property of a foreign nation used for commercial activity in the United States is not immune from seizure to a judgment.

C. Use of the Courts

1. CAUSE TO SUE— LEGAL RIGHTS AND DUTIES

Control of society is achieved through the creation of rules of civil and criminal law wherein various legal rights and duties are delineated. For every legal right, there is a corresponding legal duty. The driver of an automobile has the right to be secure from injury caused by the careless acts of other drivers. All drivers have the duty to act carefully so as not to cause injury. If carelessness causes injury, the injured person has as a legal remedy a procedure to recover money from the careless person, money for his expense (for hospital and doctor, repair of damaged property, etc.), money to make up for lost or reduced income (for time from work, temporary or permanent disability, etc.), and money to compensate for any pain suffered. A lawsuit or legal action between parties in their private capacities is called a *civil action*. Its main purpose is to compensate for injury sustained through the violation of an individual legal right. Generally, punishment of a wrongdoer is not a proper objective of a civil action.

Society (that is, the community—city, county, state, and nation) has the right to remain at peace, undisturbed by wrongful conduct. To continue the example used in the preceding paragraph, careless driving may be so reckless as to be considered a disturbance of the peace—a crime. Society has, as a legal reme-

dy, a procedure to punish the wrongdoer, by fine, imprisonment, or some other deprivation of rights—for example, a reckless driver may have his driver's license suspended or revoked. A lawsuit or legal action brought by society (State, Commonwealth, or United States) against a wrongdoer is called a *criminal action*. Generally its main purpose is to punish, not to compensate an injured person. Any fine that is collected goes to society as a whole and cannot be used for the benefit of the injured person. The proper objectives of punishment are to deter both the wrongdoer and others from committing such acts, to reform the wrongdoer, and when necessary for the protection of society, to segregate the wrongdoer from society either for a time or permanently.

As pointed out earlier in this chapter, if certain conduct violates both individual and community rights, both a civil action (to compensate the injured person) and a criminal action (to punish the wrongdoer) may be brought.

Individual rights are of two main types:

1. Rights possessed by all persons in society. These include the rights to be secure or free from wrongful injuries to the body, to property (both personal property and real estate), to reputation, etc. A violation of such a right is called a *tort* (discussed in Chapter 4).

2. Rights arising out of agreement or contract. Consider a typical sales contract in which a seller agrees to sell and deliver certain described standardized goods, and a buyer agrees to receive the goods and to pay $500 as the purchase price. The law accomplishes enforcement by recognizing that, arising from the agreement, the seller has a right to receive $500 in exchange for the goods (and the buyer a corresponding duty to pay), and the buyer a legal right to receive the goods in exchange for his money (and the seller a corresponding duty to deliver). If the seller fails to deliver, the buyer can recover the money loss he sustains from the seller's wrongful act.

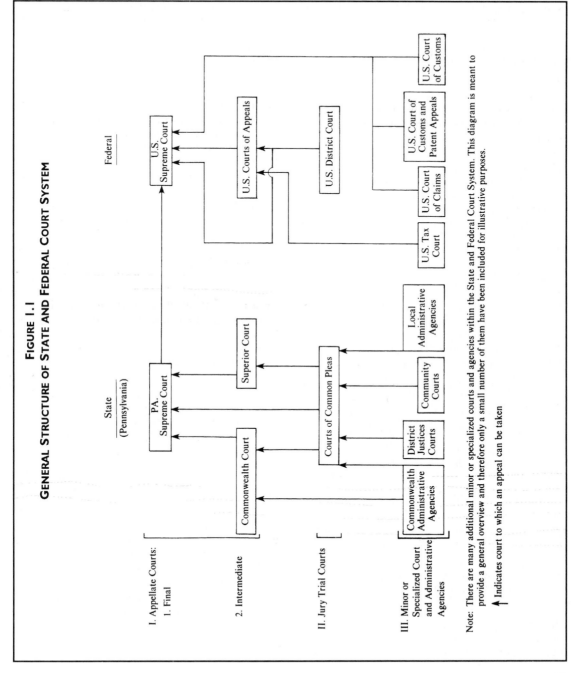

FIGURE 1.1
GENERAL STRUCTURE OF STATE AND FEDERAL COURT SYSTEM

State
(Pennsylvania)

Federal

I. Appellate Courts:
1. Final

2. Intermediate

II. Jury Trial Courts

III. Minor or
Specialized Court
and Administrative
Agencies

PA.
Supreme Court

Commonwealth Court

Superior Court

Courts of Common Pleas

Commonwealth
Administrative
Agencies

District
Justices
Courts

Community
Courts

Local
Administrative
Agencies

U.S.
Supreme Court

U.S. Courts of Appeals

U.S. District Court

U.S. Tax
Court

U.S. Court
of Claims

U.S. Court of
Customs and
Patent Appeals

U.S. Court
of Customs

Note: There are many additional minor or specialized courts and agencies within the State and Federal Court System. This diagram is meant to
provide a general overview and therefore only a small number of them have been included for illustrative purposes.

↑ Indicates court to which an appeal can be taken

Likewise, should the buyer default, the seller can recover his resulting money loss from the buyer.

2. PARTIES

In a civil action, the individual who commences an action or law suit in a court of law is known as the plaintiff. The individual against whom the action or law suit is commenced is known as the defendant. Therefore, the caption or title of a civil action will, in part, read: *F. Smith, Plaintiff, v. J. Doe, Defendant*. On the criminal side, society, in the form of the federal or state governmental unit, is the plaintiff, so that the caption or title of a criminal action instituted against an individual will read, for example, Commonwealth v. J. Doe, defendant.

In most cases, when a decision is reached by a trial court, either at the state or federal level, the parties will abide by the finding of the court. If, however, one of the parties disagrees with the decision, one alternative, given the proper circumstances, is to appeal to an appropriate appellate court. The party who takes the appeal is known as the appellant, and the party against whom the appeal is taken is known as the appellee. The caption or title at the appellate level would then be *F. Smith, Appellant, v. J. Doe, Appellee*. Most state appellate courts will retain the order of the parties as they existed at the lower court level even though the appellant may be the defendant. However, in the federal courts, the appellant's name always appears first; therefore, it would be impossible to determine who was the plaintiff and who was the defendant in the lower court by simply looking at the caption of the appellate court case.

3. BASIS FOR SELECTION OF COURT— JURISDICTION AND VENUE

For a court to have power to validly settle a dispute, the court in front of which an action is commenced must have jurisdiction, the legal power to act over (1) the subject matter of

the case and (2) the parties involved. A court obtains jurisdiction over the subject matter when the facts presented are ones which, by legislatively established rules of procedure, the court is permitted to act upon. For example, a Federal district court does not have jurisdiction over the subject matter of a case involving a simple sale of goods contract where the amount involved is less than $50,000. And, on a broader level, a civil court does not have the power or authority to decide cases involving crimes. Each type of court, then, is legislatively designed to hear certain specific types of cases exclusively. Perhaps the broadest range of cases, according to subject matter, are heard by the general state trial courts.

A court obtains power over the plaintiff's rights in a dispute when the plaintiff brings the lawsuit in that court. Usually the court obtains power to adjudge the defendant's rights in a dispute when an officer of the court (usually the sheriff, a deputy sheriff, or a comparable official) gives to the defendant a written notice of the general nature of the lawsuit and of the time within which the defendant must present in court any defense he may have. Such a notice is frequently called a summons. With some exceptions the summons must be served on the defendant while he is within the geographical area (usually a particular county) over which the court has the power to operate. Cases in which it is possible for a court to obtain power over a defendant without a summons being served within its territorial jurisdiction (under long-arm statutes) include:

1. Accident claims against nonresident motorists. A court in the state where an auto accident occurs can obtain jurisdiction over a nonresident driver even though he is not served with a summons within that state; usually this is accomplished by serving the summons on a state official designated by statute, and sending a certified mail notice to the nonresident defendant.

2. Claims against nonresident owners of local property. If a plaintiff sues in a county where some of a nonresident defendant's property is located (either personal property or real estate) the plaintiff may have that property attached and subjected to his claim even though no summons is served on the defendant within that state.

3. Claims arising out of business transactions. A nonresident who engages in business in a state gives his consent to be sued in that state based on a claim arising out of any business transacted in the state.

If, after a court obtains jurisdiction over a defendant, he thereafter fails to appear before the court and present his defense, the court may enter a judgment by default against him and in favor of the plaintiff. Such a default judgment is just as effective as a judgment after a full-scale trial.

Not only must a court have jurisdiction over the subject matter and the parties involved, but venue must be proper. Venue designates the physical locale in which a court with jurisdiction may hear and determine the case. For example, even though the court in one county had jurisdiction over the subject matter and the parties, venue might be improper if the case was concerned with title to land located in another county. (The general procedural rule of law here is that where matters affecting ownership of real property or land are concerned, only the appropriate court where the land is located can hear the case.) Venue problems have been popularized in notorious criminal cases where defendant's counsel moves for a change in venue based upon the claim that his client could not get a fair trial in the instant court.

Jurisdiction and venue are often confused. Simply remember that jurisdiction means that a court has the inherent power to decide a case and venue isolates the particular geographic location in which a court with jurisdiction may hear and determine the case.

4. AVAILABLE REMEDIES AT LAW AND IN EQUITY

The usual individual remedies available in a lawsuit are:

1. An action for money damages; or
2. An action for the owner of certain property to recover its possessions when it is wrongfully withheld from him.

At an early date in the development of the English law, situations arose in which the law-court remedies were not adequate. Aggrieved persons appealed directly to the king for special relief, the king referred these petitions to one of his advisers, called the chancellor, and eventually a system of courts was set up called chancery or equity courts. Their purpose was to give remedies when ordinary remedies available in the law courts were not adequate, and otherwise to handle matters not considered by the law courts.

The legal system known as *equity* is, therefore, a system of remedies available for situations where the ordinary legal remedies (available through law procedure as distinguished from equity procedure) are not adequate. Originally the equity system was administered through separate equity courts. In most states the law system and the equity system are now both administered by the same courts. Whichever remedy is appropriate for the dispute determines which system—law or equity—is to be applied.

The principal (but not the only) equity remedies are: (1) an injunction, (2) a decree of specific performance, and (3) a decree ordering rescission or cancellation of a contract. Note that the equitable remedies are available *only* when the ordinary remedies available in a law action are not adequate.

5. PLEADINGS

The pleadings are the formal written statements which the parties file with the court, alleging what each party believes to be the true factors upon which he bases his claim or defense. By comparing the plaintiff's and the defendant's statements, it is then possible to isolate the fact questions upon which the parties are in dispute and avoid wasting time on points that are not disputed.

The primary pleading is the *complaint* which is prepared by the plaintiff and served upon the defendant. Although the scope of the complaint differs somewhat under state and federal rules of procedure, it serves in both cases to set forth generally those facts upon which plaintiff relies to support his demand for a remedy. If the complaint does not clearly set forth the cause of action, the defendant may, in the form of a preliminary objection, move the court to require the plaintiff to file a more specific pleading. After the complaint has been served and its contents clarified, if necessary the defendant, within a statutorily specified period of time, must prepare and serve upon the plaintiff a responsive pleading called an *answer*. The answer responds to the statements made in plaintiff's complaint and, in addition, may set forth affirmative defenses such as contributory negligence, consent and assumption of the risk under *new matter*. Under the heading *counterclaim*, the defendant may set forth in the *answer* any causes of action he may have against the plaintiff.

An example of a complaint and answer is shown on pages 25-26. Notice that the caption of each pleading identifies the court (Pennsylvania trial court), the nature of the action (civil action law), the parties involved (plaintiff and defendant) and the number of the case on the docket or calendar.

6. PRETRIAL PROCEDURES AND JURY SELECTION

After the pleadings are closed, the general position of each party with respect to the facts and the law should be ascertainable. It might, at this point, appear to either party that he is entitled to a judgment based upon the statements made in the pleadings alone. If, for example, the defendant admits to virtually every allegation contained in the complaint, it would appear to be senseless to waste the court's time by proceeding to trial; therefore, the plaintiff would make a pretrial motion called a *motion for judgment on the pleadings*. Either party can make such a motion, and if allowed, a judgment would be obtained without the necessity of proceeding to trial.

In preparing for a trial, a skilled trial attorney will naturally attempt to present the facts of the case in a manner which is most favorable to his client. The attorney's task is to ascertain what the facts are prior to trial, particularly as viewed by adverse witnesses. Procedurally, therefore, discovery procedures in the form of depositions and interrogatories help insure the fairness of a trial by allowing each

Example. By written contract, a seller agreed to sell and a buyer to buy 1,000 bushels of a specified grade of potatoes at $2 a bushel, to be delivered on a specified date. Without excuse the seller refused to deliver on that date. To obtain the same grade of potatoes on the market, the buyer had to pay $2.50 per bushel. He bought 1,000 bushels, paying $500 more than he would have paid if he could have obtained the potatoes from the seller according to the contract.

The buyer could sue the seller and recover $500 as damages suffered through the seller's breach of contract. The $500 would compensate the buyer for the seller's breach of contract. It would put the buyer in about as good a position as he would have been in if the seller had performed as agreed. Should the seller refuse to pay the judgment, the buyer could obtain the $500 through a sheriff's seizure and sale of the seller's property. The buyer's remedy in this example is obtainable in a law action rather than through an equity action. □

Example. By written contract a seller agreed to sell and a buyer to buy a described plot of land at a stated price. The seller thereafter refused to transfer the land.

Land is different from the potatoes of the preceding example inasmuch as the same plot of land cannot be procured elsewhere. Therefore money damages ordinarily will not compensate a land-contract buyer; he wants the described plot of land, not another. Since the ordinary legal remedies would not be adequate, the buyer could seek relief in equity. He could ask the court to decree or order the seller to carry out the contract, that is, to specifically perform the contract (the equity remedy of specific performance). If the seller still refused, he would be disobeying a direct order of the court, would be guilty of contempt of court, and could be punished by fine, imprisonment, or both. And if his refusal persisted, the court could transfer the land to the buyer who would obtain the seller's title by authority of the court proceeding. This would be an equity action.

* * *

Example. The owner of an auto, driving negligently, ran into and injured a pedestrian who had been walking carefully. The pedestrian incurred hospital and doctor bills, lost time from work, suffered pain, and sustained a permanent disability. The pedestrian could sue the driver and recover money damages to compensate for his injuries. So far as the pedestrian can be compensated at all, money will do it. This would be a law action.

* * *

Example. As part of the written agreement for the sale of a grocery business and its goodwill, a seller agreed with a buyer not to open a similar business within a radius of one mile during the next five years. A few months after making the agreement, the seller began preparations to open another grocery store within the prescribed area.

The amount of loss sustained by the buyer as a result of the seller's competition would be speculative, since the profits of a business are affected by many factors. Also, if the buyer sued for money damages, he would have to estimate into the future, bring a series of lawsuits, or wait until expiration of the five years. An action for money damages for breach of the contract, therefore, would not give adequate relief. The buyer could ask for an equitable remedy—a court order or decree prohibiting the seller from opening the competing business; this would be an injunction. A person who disobeys an injunction can be punished for contempt of court, and other means of enforcement are available. This would be an equity action.

party to ascertain from the other that which he previously did not know. A *deposition* is an out-of-court oral examination of a witness or other individual before an authorized agent of the court whose function it is to take down in writing the questions and answers thereto.

On the other hand, *interrogatories* are out-of-court written questions addressed to a witness or other individual who responds with written answers. Not only do discovery procedures allow the parties to ascertain the facts, but they can be used later at trial to impeach a witness if his testimony at trial is in conflict

with that given in the deposition or interrogatory.

After each party has prepared his case, and if a jury trial is impending, a jury must be selected prior to trial. The jurors carry a heavy burden, since it is their function, after listening to all the testimony, to decide the facts of the case. Initially, the jury is selected at random, perhaps from the tax rolls of the locality. Then, in order to obtain as impartial- a jury as possible, the parties are permitted to have any number of jury members removed for a specific prejudicial reason. These are called *challenges for cause* and often are the reason why,

Example. A landowner procured a quantity of dirt and had it dumped on his land to bring it up to street level so that he could have a driveway constructed. The owner did not have a retaining wall built and every time it rained some of the loose dirt washed down onto his neighbor's adjoining land.

What the owner did (or hired to be done) was wrongful and constituted a trespass to his neighbor's land. (A trespass is a wrongful entry or intrusion upon another's land.) The neighbor could sue for damages but after he recovered a sum of money for restoration of his property, future rains would bring more of the loose dirt. To require the neighbor to wait until he suffered damages and then to bring a series of lawsuits would not afford the neighbor a complete and adequate remedy for the owner's wrong. The neighbor could sue in equity and, in addition to recovering the damage already done, he could obtain an order or decree requiring the owner to stop his wrongful act by having a retaining wall constructed. This would be an equity action. ☐

in controversial cases, it takes many days to select a jury.

A limited number of jury members can be removed arbitrarily. These are called *peremptory challenges*. Of course, as jury members are successfully challenged, their places are taken by other randomly selected individuals who in turn are subject to challenge.

7. TRIAL

The purpose of a trial is to determine the facts in the case, to decide from the evidence what actually occurred as to the point or points upon which the parties are in dispute. If the parties to a lawsuit are in agreement as to the facts, but disagree as to what legal rights and liabilities result from the facts, no trial is necessary. Instead, the lawyers for the parties present to the judge oral and written arguments concerning the disputed legal question, and the judge then reaches a conclusion as to the correct rule of law and gives judgment accordingly. If facts are in dispute so that a trial is necessary, the parties sometimes agree to have the judge determine the facts. Otherwise, the facts are decided by a jury (except in equity cases) with the conduct of the trial refereed by the judge. The referee is nec-

essary to assure that the parties comply with the standard rules prescribed for the presentation of evidence, rules which are designed for more quickly and accurately deciding disputed facts.

During the course of the trial it is not unusual that the testimony of one person will differ in certain respects from that of another. This does not necessarily mean that one or the other is deliberately lying; not infrequently a person is honestly mistaken in his recollection of events.

At the end of the trial, after all of the evidence is seen and heard by the jury, the judge instructs the jury as to the rules of law which apply to the dispute. The jurors go off by themselves, discuss the evidence as they remember it, and vote to determine their conclusion on the disputed fact or facts. When they all agree, they report their verdict to the judge. A jury does not often fail to reach an agreement. However (under the common-law rules which still prevail in most states) if the jury cannot agree unanimously one way or the other, they so report to the judge, and if the failure to agree persists, the judge will declare the trial ended with no settlement of the dispute. To obtain what he is seeking the

IN THE COURT OF COMMON PLEAS OF CENTRE COUNTY, PENNSYLVANIA
CIVIL ACTION—LAW

SAM SELLER, INC. Plaintiff	: No. 94- XXXX
	:
	:
Caption vs.	:
	:
	:
BEN BUYER Defendant	:
	:

COMPLAINT

AND NOW COMES SAM SELLER, INC., Plaintiff in the above captioned matter, and represents the following:

Alleged facts on which claim is based

1. The Plaintiff is SAM SELLER, INC., a business entity having offices at 100 Jones Street, Smithville, Pennsylvania.
2. The Defendant is BEN BUYER, an individual having offices at 310 E. Hamilton Avenue, State College, Pennsylvania.
3. At all times material to the matters stated herein, SAM SELLER, INC. was engaged in the business of distributing, selling and supplying items of electronic equipment and accessories to retail establishments.
4. At all times material to the matters stated herein, BEN BUYER was engaged in the business of retailing items of electronic equipment and accessories.
5. On or about January 1, 1991, SAM SELLER, INC. sold a quantity of Zenith Color Television sets to BEN BUYER, pursuant to an agreement to purchase said goods entered into by the parties hereto.
6. Copies of the invoices relating to the transaction described in the preceding paragraph are attached hereto as Exhibits A and B.
7. Despite due demand, the Defendant has refused to make full payment with respect to the sales of goods described herein and the outstanding account balance is $5,000.00.
8. The price charged for the goods described herein was fair and reasonable and in accordance with the terms of the agreement of the parties.

Request for Damages

WHEREFORE, it is respectfully requested that judgment be entered in favor of BEN BUYER in the amount of $5,000.00 plus interest or delay damages and costs.

JONES & SMITH

By:_____
John Jones, Esq.
Attorney for Plaintiff

IN THE COURT OF COMMON PLEAS OF CENTRE COUNTY, PENNSYLVANIA
CIVIL ACTION—LAW

Caption

SAM SELLER, INC.	:	No. 94- XXXX
Plaintiff	:	
	:	
vs.	:	
	:	
BEN BUYER	:	
Defendant	:	

ANSWER

Response to alleged facts in complaint

1. Admitted
2. Admitted
3. Admitted
4. Admitted
5. Admitted
6. Admitted
7. Admitted in part and denied in part. It is admitted that Defendant failed to make full payment after due demand. It is denied, however, that the outstanding balance is $5,000,00. To the contrary, the balance is $2,000.00, which Defendant previously tendered to Plaintiff.
8. Admitted in part and denied in part. It is admitted that the price charged for the goods were fair and reasonable. It is denied, however, that the terms of the agreement were that Defendant pay such sum. To the contrary, Defendant was entitled to credit for its cooperative advertising in the sum of $2,000, which Defendant previously submitted to Plaintiff.

WHEREFORE, Defendant respectfully requests the entry of judgment in its favor.

_____
James Lawyer
Attorney for Defendant

plaintiff will then have to bring the dispute to another trial with a new jury.

If the jurors agree on a verdict which in the opinion of the judge is supported by believable evidence, the judge enters a judgment accordingly. A decision of the disputed facts in favor of the defendant and a judgment to that effect expresses the court's conclusion that the defendant is not liable to the plaintiff. On the other hand, if the jury and the court decide that the defendant owes the plaintiff a certain amount of money, the judge will enter a judgment in favor of the plaintiff for that amount, plus interest and court costs.

The court costs usually do not include the expenses of the plaintiff's lawyer. Suppose that a plaintiff has a legal right to collect $2,000 from a defendant and that because of the defendant's refusal to pay, the plaintiff has to spend $500 in lawyer fees to obtain a $2,000 judgment against the defendant. It is certainly arguable that the plaintiff should have the right to collect $2,500 from the defendant, the original obligation plus the expense of obtaining the judgment. Likewise, if after initiating a lawsuit a plaintiff is unable to prove his case so that judgment is entered in favor of the defendant, it is arguable that the plaintiff should compensate the defendant for the lawyer expenses which the plaintiff's lawsuit required the defendant to incur in defending the action. Whether the losing party should be required to pay the fees of the winning party's lawyer is entirely a question of policy as to what society considers to be fair, reasonable, and practical under the circumstances. Early in its development the English common law system began the practice of permitting the winning party to recover reasonable lawyer fees from the losing party, and the English courts have continued the practice. After the American Revolution, the practice was not considered to be desirable policy in the United States and was gradually abandoned, so that in most cases under the present American system lawyer fees in any substantial

amount cannot be collected by the winning party. The chief reasons given for the American view can be summarized as follows:

1. The purpose of a civil lawsuit is to compensate a plaintiff for the damages he sustains as the result of the defendant's wrongful act.

(a) Litigation expenses are indirect. Even though the defendant may be guilty of the alleged wrong, the expenses of the plaintiff's attorney are not a direct result of the defendant's wrong. In the words of the Connecticut Supreme Court:

> Now the expenses of litigation are never damages sued for in any case when the action is brought for the wrong itself, not even if the tort (wrongful conduct) be wanton or malicious. They are not the "natural and proximate consequence of the wrongful act, . . . but are remote, future and contingent."[6]

(b) Engaging in litigation is not of itself wrongful. If there is reason to be doubtful of a defendant's actual liability, it should not be considered wrongful for a person, either as plaintiff or defendant, to insist upon a lawsuit to determine this doubtful question. Since, therefore, bringing or defending a reasonably disputed lawsuit is not wrongful conduct in itself, no damages should be awarded either way for the expenses required by the litigation.

2. Under the constitutional provision that no person can be deprived of his property without due process of law, a person clearly has the right of access to the courts for a determination of his legal rights and liabilities. Certainly a person should not be penalized for exercising a constitutional right, and it is arguable that to require a litigant to pay for his opponent's lawyer as well as for his own would in a sense be penalizing him for bringing about the litigation.

3. The time, effort, training, and experience required of a trial lawyer varies so considerably from one lawsuit to another that no

---

6. *St. Peter's Church v. Beach*, 26 Conn. 355 (1857).

fixed scale of fees can be drawn up with any accuracy or fairness. On the other hand, granting the winning party a right to be reimbursed for his lawyer fees without any restraint on the amount of the fees would in effect be giving the winning party's attorney a blank check at the expense of the losing party. Therefore any system for recovering lawyer fees would require court supervision of the fees in each individual case, increasing the time and effort involved in each lawsuit, and imposing on lawyers some of the restraints which result from any system of price regulation

The American rule developed during what was primarily a frontier era, when ready access to the courts was considered highly desirable. Present-day society, organized about a metropolitan rather than a frontier economy, is much more complex, and overcrowded court calendars delay the settlement of disputes. Some legal scholars suggest that, in order to encourage compromises and diminish litigation, the American rule and the factors supporting it should be reexamined alongside the experience and practice of the English system in which the recovery of reasonable lawyers fees is permitted.

Even under the American rule, when a lawsuit is brought about through the serious and intentional wrong of one party, the policy picture changes, and a more persuasive argument can be made in favor of the innocent party's recovering his lawyer fees. Under such circumstances statutes in some states permit at least a limited recovery of lawyer fees as do certain federal laws.

8. JUDGMENT

After a jury has heard the relevant facts as presented by the opposing parties' attorneys, and has received instructions from the court concerning the applicable law, it will make a decision (verdict) resolving the factual and legal matters submitted to it. This decision is reported to the court where it becomes official in the form of the court's judgment. When the party against whom the verdict was rendered thinks the verdict was contrary to the weight of evidence, he can among other choices, move the court for a new trial or ask the court to take matters into its own hands by granting a judgment to the losing party notwithstanding the verdict reached by the jury (sometimes called *judgment n.o.v.* or *judgment notwithstanding the verdict*). Unless the jury was obviously lax in the performance of its duties, courts will generally not grant such motions, thereby forcing the losing party to appeal if he wishes to proceed further.

Appeal. Just as a person is entitled to a court hearing before a decision is made concerning his rights and liabilities, so too he is usually entitled to have the conduct and result of that hearing reviewed by another court called an appeal or appellate court. Because this is not a second trial, a jury is unnecessary. In an appeal, the several judges of the appellate court read the written record of what was done and said in the trial court, consider the oral and written arguments of the lawyers representing the litigants, and determine as a matter of law whether or not there was error in the trial and judgment. An appeal in a civil case is usually so expensive in lawyer and court costs that a losing party will take an appeal only if he firmly believes: (1) that the trial judge through error permitted certain evidence to be presented which under the established rules for trials was very misleading to the jurors and should not have been considered by them, or (2) that the rule of law applied by the trial judge was not the correct rule of law, or (3) that the verdict of the jury is not supported by any believable evidence.

When the appellate court judges finish considering and discussing the appealed case among themselves, they vote as to their conclusion. If a majority believe that prejudicial error occurred during the trial, they declare that the judgment of the trial court is canceled or reversed. With the reversal, if it is clear that all evidence has been presented and only one conclusion may properly be reached, the appellate court will enter judgment for the other party. This is the final judgment of the dispute, unless in turn reversed by a higher appellate court. If the appellate court feels that the evidence must be reweighed before the dispute can be settled, it will send the case back to the trial court for a new trial. The plaintiff can then quit; if he still feels he is entitled to a judgment against the defendant, he can obtain it only by initiating and winning another trial. If the appellate court concludes that no prejudicial error was involved and that the judgment of the trial court is correct and binding, the appellate court will affirm the judgment.

The party against whom a decision was rendered by an intermediate appellate court can, in many circumstances, appeal to the state's highest appellate court, known in most states as the Supreme Court. The supreme courts of the various states generally have supervisory and administrative authority over all the other courts in the state. In addition, the Supreme Courts have original jurisdiction over certain types of cases and exercise general appellate jurisdiction as provided under constitutional and statutory provisions of the various states.

Once a judgment becomes final, a party against whom it was rendered usually satisfies the judgment on a voluntary basis. If he does not, as indicated in a previous section of this chapter, his property can be sold by an officer of the court, usually the sheriff, under the authority of a writ of execution, and the proceeds therefrom applied toward the judgment.

Judgment by Confession

Unless a claimant has a lien (such as an ownership interest, a mortgage, or some other security interest) on some item of his debtor's property, the claimant usually has no right personally to take any of the debtor's property, or to interfere with it in any way. As an unsecured creditor, the claimant has only the usual collection remedy—namely, to sue and obtain a judgment against the debtor, and after obtaining the judgment to have the sheriff attach and sell property belonging to the debtor. Note that to obtain satisfaction the creditor must first obtain a judgment against the debtor. A creditor usually obtains a judgment in the manner previously described and illustrated—by commencing and successfully completing a full-scale lawsuit against the debtor. However, if before trial a debtor should voluntarily admit or confess to the court that he is liable for the amount claimed by the plaintiff, further litigation would become superfluous, and a judgment could be entered against the debtor without a trial. If a defendant wishes to confess his liability, he can do so personally, or instead through an agent whom he authorizes to act for him, and for whose authorized act the defendant would therefore be bound. As the practice of judgment by confession has developed at common law, such an authorization can be given to a certain named attorney or instead can be given to any person in general, or to any person of a certain class (such as any lawyer); and the authorization to confess liability in the defendant's name is effective whether the authority is granted before or after the start of a lawsuit against the defendant.

In states in which this common-law practice is still followed, confession of judgment provisions are frequently included in many types of standard form contracts, such as promissory notes and contracts for either purchasing or leasing real estate or goods. The following promissory notes illustrate simplified versions of authorizations to confess judgment.

Form 1

Philadelphia, Pa., [Date]

Two years after date I promise to pay to the order of Charles Carter $1,000.

And further, if this note is not paid at maturity, I authorize any attorney of any court of record of the

United States or elsewhere, to appear for me and confess judgment against me for the above sum.

(signed) Donald David

Form 2

Philadelphia, Pa., [Date]

Two years after date I promise to pay to the order of Charles Carter $1,000.

And further I do hereby authorize any attorney of any court of record of the United States or elsewhere, to appear for me and confess judgment against me for the above sum.

(signed) Donald David

Pursuant to such an authorization, any attorney (usually the same one who is serving as the plaintiff's attorney) can submit the defendant to the jurisdiction of the court (without the necessity of service of summons on the defendant even if the defendant is a nonresident) and in the defendant's name admit or confess his liability for the stated or claimed sum. The judgment which is thereupon automatically entered is as effective as one obtained after a full-scale lawsuit; it can form the basis for a sheriff's attachment and sale, and must be accepted as a valid judgment by the courts of other states. By having a confession-of-judgment paragraph inserted in the debtor's contract, a creditor is able to obtain a quick and inexpensive judgment against his debtor.

There are two types of confession of judgment provisions in common use:

1. A provision authorizing confession of judgment if the specified obligation is not paid when due, as in Form 1 above.

2. A provision authorizing confession of judgment at any time, even before the specified obligation comes due. Usually this latter type of provision is written in one of two ways. The authorization to confess judgment may expressly state that it can be exercised at any time; a common phrasing for this is "as of any term." Or instead, the authorization to confess judgment may be expressed in the present tense with no time stated. In Form 2

above, while the obligation evidenced by the note does not come due until the time stated (two years), the creditor can obtain judgment against the debtor as soon as the note is signed or any time after that.

If a creditor has a judgment confessed and entered before maturity of the related obligation, he cannot collect on the judgment (through sheriff's levy and sale) until the obligation matures. Nevertheless many creditors desire such a provision because as soon as a judgment is entered on the record (even though the related obligation is unmatured) the judgment is a lien on real estate owned by the defendant in that county. The effective date of the lien is the date the judgment is entered rather than the date the related obligation matures.

Sometimes, as illustrated in the following example, creditors have misused the power to obtain judgments by confession.

The legislatures of a number of states feel that the practice of obtaining judgments by confession gives too much power to creditors or is otherwise unfair, and should be restricted or abolished. Many states have altogether abolished judgments by confession, while other states restrict the use of such judgments. In some states the restrictions are minor; some other states impose major restrictions. One common type of minor restriction attempts to warn a debtor of the presence of a confession of judgment provision by requiring the provision to be written or printed separate from other parts of the contract and separately signed. A common major restriction voids confession of judgment provisions in contract forms, by providing that such a provision is not effective unless signed *after* maturity of the obligation to which it relates. On the other hand, some states place no restrictions at all on confessed judgments. In these states confession of judgment provisions are commonly included in most standard contract forms.

Example.   The above procedures involving use of courts are summarized, in part, in the case that follows:

A buyer in Erie, Pennsylvania, wrote a letter ordering from a seller in Chicago, Illinois, a stated quantity of a specified kind, grade, and size of lumber for $2,000, payable thirty days after shipment. The lumber which the seller promptly shipped in response to the order was delivered at the railroad siding in the buyer's lumber yard. After inspecting the shipment, the buyer notified the seller that the lumber was not of proper contract quality, that the buyer did not want to keep it, and that the seller should make arrangements to take the lumber away. The seller's answering letter asserted that the lumber did conform to the buyer's order. About a week later, while the parties were still haggling, a fire and explosion occurred in an adjoining factory and the flames quickly spread to the buyer's lumber yard, destroying a quantity of lumber, including the railroad cars and lumber received from the seller. The seller demanded that the buyer pay $2,000. When the buyer refused, the seller sued the buyer. For the sake of this example, assume that the buyer did all he reasonably could to prevent the destruction of the lumber and that it was customary for the buyer's fire-insurance coverage not to extend to lumber as yet unloaded from railroad cars. The seller's lawsuit would involve the following basic steps:

1. *Commencement of the Lawsuit.* Assuming that the buyer did no traveling and owned no property away from Erie, the seller plaintiff would have a lawyer file a lawsuit in the Court of Common Pleas of Erie County, Pennsylvania, and have the sheriff (or his deputy) serve a summons on the buyer as defendant.

2. *Pleadings.* The plaintiff frequently combines his pleading with the first step. The seller's statement would describe the buyer's order, the seller's alleged shipment in conformity with the order, and the buyer's failure to pay. The buyer's statement would describe the alleged defective quality of the lumber, the buyer's offer to return the lumber, and its accidental destruction. The pleadings would thus disclose the fact question in dispute to be whether or not the lumber was of contract quality.

3. *Trial.* Assuming that the parties did not agree to waive a jury trial, a jury would be called together to decide the disputed fact in question. Under oath to tell the truth, the seller would present to the jury the buyer's written order and describe the lumber that he shipped in response to the order. Any of the seller's employees who worked on the shipment could also testify under oath. Upon completion of the seller's evidence, the buyer, under oath to tell the truth, would describe to the jury the lumber received from the seller. Any employees of the buyer could also testify. If the buyer had an impartial inspector examine the lumber (a wise precaution when a dispute concerning quality arises), the inspector would testify. When both parties finished presenting their witnesses, the judge would summarize the evidence for the members of the jury and instruct them that if they believed the lumber to have been of contract quality the seller should collect the agreed price plus interest, but that if they believed that the lumber was not of contract quality, the seller should not collect anything.

4. *Verdict and Judgment.* Assume that after considering the evidence the jury decided that the lumber did conform to the contract. On the basis of this verdict the judge would announce judgment for the seller and against the buyer for $2,000, plus interest and court costs (which would not include the expense of the seller's lawyer).

5. *Appeal.* Assume that the buyer believed the verdict and judgment to be erroneous. The buyer could have his lawyer file and appeal with the Pennsylvania Superior Court for the conduct and result of the trial to be reviewed. In actual practice, usually the buyer's lawyer would first urge or make a motion that the trial judge enter judgment in favor of the buyer, notwithstanding the verdict, or that the trial judge grant a new trial; upon the trial judge's refusal to grant either motion, the appeal could be taken.

Example (continued)

6. *Enforcement of the Judgment*. Assume that the seller won the appeal but that the buyer still refused to pay. The seller would have his lawyer obtain a court order directing the sheriff to seize or levy on property belonging to the buyer, and (after proper time and notice) put the property up for public auction (sheriff's sale). After deducting the costs of the sale, the sheriff would pay to the seller the proceeds received from the sale, up to the amount of the judgment and interest. Any balance remaining would be returned to the buyer. ▢

Since confession of judgment in effect eliminates the possibility of having the case heard in open court in some situations decisional law has recognized that it may be altogether unconstitutional as resulting in a denial of due process of law. Therefore, confessed judgments cannot be relied upon as being absolute. It appears that they are headed for extinction.

Finality of Judgments

In most cases the time for taking an appeal or otherwise correcting the action of a trial court varies from a few weeks to a few months, depending upon the type of lawsuit. If the proper time has passed without a reversal or correction, a civil judgment is usually considered final and conclusive as to the rights and liabilities involved in the dispute, and usually will not be dissolved or changed by later action, either of the same court or of some other court. This is a policy rule, necessary for the protection of honest litigants. Suppose that long after a trial and decision the losing party was able to have the issue reopened by claiming that he had newly discovered evidence not available to him at the time of the previous trial, or by claiming that the previous judgment was obtained by perjured testimony. Such claims might be false but the successful party might be unable to disprove them, if his witnesses had forgotten or died or certain essential documents had been lost or destroyed. Also (even more than is regrettably true at present) ultimate victory might go to the litigant able and willing to spend the most money on litigation. The fact that in a few cas-

es the rule of conclusiveness of judgments will reward a perjurer is usually considered as overbalanced by the protection which the rule gives to honest litigants. Accordingly in most states cancellation of a judgment is usually limited to the rare situations in which the court process itself has been tampered with in such a way as to completely prevent it from functioning fairly—as for example when the winning party bribed a juror or bribed the losing party's attorney to "throw" the case, or through a trick the winning party kept the losing party from attending the trial.

Generally a judgment is conclusive not only in the state where it was obtained but also in all other states. The United States Constitution expressly requires that each state give full faith and credit to the judicial acts of other states. If a New York court, with proper jurisdiction over the parties and over the matter in dispute enters a judgment in favor of a plaintiff, that judgment will have the same effect in California as it has in New York. If the defendant owns property in California, the plaintiff through the simple procedure of suing for a California judgment on the basis of the New York judgment, can in effect have the judgment transferred to California, and can proceed to have the defendant's California property levied on, without the needless burden of retrying the merits of the case in California.

Use of the State and Federal Court Systems is generally summarized in Figure 1.2.

D. International Implications

Preparing a case for trial in a state or federal trial court can be a complex, time consuming and costly endeavor as can be easily under stood from the previous discussion. Preparing a case with international implications adds to the burden. However, to assist in the processing and preparation of a case with international overtones, a number of international agreements have been reached by participating countries to facilitate the process. For example, the Hague Convention on Service Abroad of Judicial and Extrajudicial Documents in Civil and Commercial Matters, which became operative in the United States in 1969, facilitates the service and processing of various legal documents by requiring each participating nation to maintain a Central Authority for that purpose. The Hague Convention on the Taking of Evidence Abroad in Civil or Commercial Matters, which became operative in the United States in 1972, attempts to facilitate the discovery process and make it easier to obtain evidence for use in international litigation. Pretrial discovery in foreign countries is more limited than in the United States.

After a judgment has been rendered against a United States defendant by a foreign court, the question is whether it will be enforced in the United States. On the Federal level, there is no statutory authority which controls the issue; therefore, the courts generally will enforce a foreign judgment if there has been an opportunity for a full and fair hearing before a court of competent jurisdiction. On the state level, a number of states have adopted the Uniform Foreign Court Money Judgments Recognition Act. On the regional level, the European Economic Community (EEC) recognizes and enforces judgments of EEC member nations.

III. Alternative Dispute Resolution

A. Introduction and General Definition

Resolving disputes by use of the traditional litigation process as described earlier in this chapter has come under attack during the past decade. The primary objections are based upon prohibitive costs (lawyer and witness fees), time consumption (procedural and other delays in using the courts), and complexity (a plethora of available causes of action, remedies and procedural rules). Other but less emphasized objections include the adversarial nature of the litigation process which tends to polarize the parties rather than resolve differences, the rigidity of the process, lack of judicial expertise since the judge is in reality a generalist and the difference in abilities of competing advocates (lawyers). Because of these and other objections, an innovative but not necessarily new approach called Alternative Dispute Resolution (ADR) has emerged.

As the name indicates, ADR is an alternative to litigation or the traditional court system of resolving disputes. It is less costly and faster-hence arguably better.[7] In addition, depending upon the method used, ADR tends to be less complex (formal rules of evidence and other procedural rules are not applied), more tailored towards the subject matter in dispute (an expert, independent, third-party arbitrator is chosen) and may be binding (not appealable to a higher body).

---

7. Although ADR may be faster and less costly, the jury is still out with respect to the comparative quality of justice dispatched. Edwards, "Alternative Dispute Resolution: Panacea or Anathema," 99 *Harv. L. Rev.* 668 (1986); Enslen, "ADR. Another Acronym, Or A Viable Alternative To The High Cost Of Litigation And Crowded Court Dockets? The Debate Commences", 18 *N.M.L. Rev.* I (1988).

Example. Through fraudulent misrepresentation a dealer induces a buyer to purchase certain goods, and has the buyer sign a written contract, agreeing to pay the purchase price of $500 at a stated future time and authorizing a confession of judgment for that amount. When the buyer discovers the fraud, he tenders return of the goods. When the dealer refuses to take back the goods, the buyer says that he thereafter holds the goods for the dealer, makes no further use of them, and upon contract payment date, refuses to pay.

The buyer would have a good defense should the dealer sue for the agreed $500. However with the confession of judgment provision, the dealer can obtain a judgment without giving the buyer an opportunity to present his defense. The buyer would then have to initiate a legal proceeding to have the judgment canceled on the ground of fraud. The burden of starting a lawsuit is thus shifted. Instead of waiting for the dealer to sue and then presenting his defense in the dealer's lawsuit, the buyer must take the initiative in starting a lawsuit.☐

Arguably, any method that does not follow the adversarial path of formal court room litigation falls under the definition of ADR. For example, administrative agencies as described in Chapter 2 could fall under the rubric of ADR. However, the remainder of this chapter will consider only those methods which seem to have strongly emerged in ADR literature. Specifically, old methods to which new applications have been extended include negotiation, mediation and arbitration. New methods include the minitrial, summary jury trial and rent–a–judge.

B. Negotiation

Negotiation deals with direct bargaining between or among two or more parties for the purpose of arriving at a mutually satisfactory solution to a problem. It is separate from, complementary to and a part of the formal adjudication process. For example, when a seller and buyer negotiate to establish a purchase price, they attempt to create rights and duties without use of the legal system. Those rights are not determined by an independent judge through the adjudicatory process, but by the give and take of negotiation. If the result of the negotiation is the creation of legal rights and duties as formalized in the written agreement, and a subsequent dispute arises between the parties as to the meaning of certain terms, the parties can "negotiate" to have the matter resolved in a "mini-trial" by an independent third-party judge or any other appropriate method. Or if the dispute goes to court, they might through negotiation resolve the matter at a pretrial conference. Negotiation, therefore, can take place before, during and after the formal adjudicatory process. It is both an "alternative" and a supplement to adjudication. It has existed for as long as the people have been selling, buying and exchanging goods and services.

What is new is that negotiation as an alternative to formal litigation is being increasingly encouraged by the legal system. It continues to be applied to old situations such as labor negotiations. It is being applied to new and different types of situations such as domestic relations, personal injury and criminal law cases. In some cases, negotiation is compelled. For example, the National Labor Relations Act provides that "It shall be an unfair labor practice for a labor organization or its agents . . . to refuse to bargain collectively with an employer...."[8] In most cases negotiation is either voluntary or encouraged. For ex-

---

8. 29 U.S.C. Sec.158(b)(3).

Example. A seller sold and delivered certain goods to a buyer on credit. After making various payments from time to time, the buyer contended that he had paid the price in full and refused to pay anything further. The seller contended that a balance of $800 remained unpaid and sued the buyer to recover that amount. At the trial the buyer and a witness for the buyer both testified that the buyer had made payments in addition to those admitted by the seller. The jury returned a verdict in favor of the buyer and judgment was entered for the buyer and against the seller—in other words, the seller lost the lawsuit. About two months later the witness signed a confession that he had testified falsely. The buyer and the witness were both indicted for the perjury involved in having given false testimony in the seller's lawsuit. The witness pleaded guilty, the buyer was tried and convicted, and both were sentenced to prison. The seller then brought an action to cancel the judgment previously entered against his $800 claim.

In a similar case, the Pennsylvania Superior Court [9] held that since the time for correction had passed, the seller was not entitled to have the adverse judgment canceled. The Court pointed out that during the original trial the seller had full opportunity to challenge the buyer's testimony and to disprove his defense of alleged payments. Since the issue of the alleged extra payments was tried and decided, the court felt that as a matter of policy the dispute should be considered settled.

---

9. *Powell v. Doyle*, 77 Pa. Super. 520(1921).

ample, in a 1983 Amendment to the Federal Rules of Civil Procedure, Rule 16(c)(7) provides for "the possibility of settlement or the use of extrajudicial procedures to resolve the dispute." By way of explanation, the Advisory Committee's Note to Rule 16(c)(7) explains that:

> Clause (7) explicitly recognizes that it has become commonplace to discuss settlement at pretrial conferences. Since it obviously eases crowded court dockets and results in savings to the litigants and the judicial system, settlement should be facilitated at as early a stage of the litigation as possible. Although it is not the purpose of Rule 16(b)(7) to impose settlement negotiations on unwilling litigants, it is believed that providing a neutral forum for discussing the subject might foster it. (citation omitted) [10]

Whether negotiating for the creation or resolution of rights and duties, legal implications aside, the procedure and strategies involved have come under close scrutiny for the obvious reason that important advantages can be gained by being familiar with the intricacies of the process. For example, one author who gives an overview of legal negotiation behavior notes that "[m]ost lawyers not only change their tactics from one negotiation to another, but also use a combination of varying tactics . . . within a single negotiation."[11]

C. Mediation

Mediation generally is defined as a process where an independent third party assists two or more persons in resolving a dispute. A mediator does not impose a decision upon the parties, rather he facilitates the negotiating process by helping competing parties to focus

---

10. 28 U.S.C.A. Rule 16(c)(7) Notes Of Advisory Committee On Rules.

11. D. Gifford, Legal Negotiation Theory And Applications (1989).

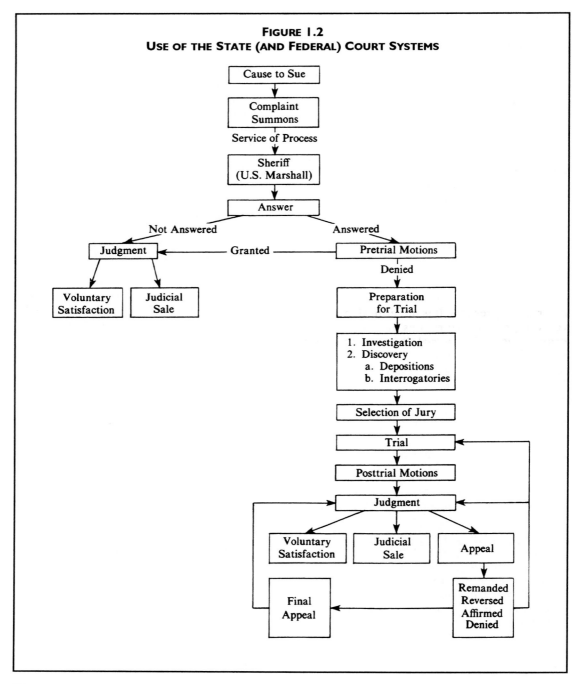

FIGURE 1.2
USE OF THE STATE (AND FEDERAL) COURT SYSTEMS

on their differences and by suggesting solutions. Its most recognized use has been in the area of labor-management and public interest disputes. More recently, it has gained wide acceptance in the domestic relations area. California law, for example, requires mandatory mediation for child custody cases in divorce. The stated rationale is to "reduce acrimony which may exist between the parties and to develop an agreement assuring the child . . . close and continuing contact with both parents after the marriage is dissolved."[12]

Mediation invariably has legal implications. In the divorce example above, custody and visitation rights and duties are established or resolved within the framework of established legal principles. Because of their legal training, lawyers are being increasingly called upon to act as mediators in domestic relation and other cases. However, ethical questions exist if a lawyer mediates between two parties he or she represents. It is not ethical for a lawyer to represent two parties in an adversarial proceeding such as a trial. But it is ethical for him or her to mediate where two parties are working towards the resolution of a dispute. The ethical guideline that a lawyer must follow in dual representation and mediation situations are established in the Model Rules of Professional Conduct as adopted by the American Bar Association in 1983. Rule 2.2 provides that a lawyer may act as an intermediary between clients if:

> (1) the lawyer consults with each client concerning the implications of the common representation, including the advantages and risks involved, and the effect on the attorney-client privileges, and obtains each client's consent to the common representation;
> (2) the lawyer reasonably believes that the matter can be resolved on terms compatible with the client's best interests, that each client will be able to make adequately informed decisions in the matter and that there is little risk of prejudice to the interests of any of the cli-

ents if the contemplated resolution is unsuccessful; and
> (3) the lawyer reasonably believes that the common representation can be undertaken impartially and without improper effect on other responsibilities the lawyer has to any of the clients.

The key is full disclosure to each client. The Comments to Rule 2.2 state that where a lawyer is not representing a client, he is free to act as a mediator between or among parties to a dispute.

D. Arbitration

I. NATIONAL

Arbitration is a process where a dispute is submitted to a neutral party or parties who, based upon the submitted evidence, resolves the dispute and renders a decision. The decision is either binding or non-binding. As the name implies, binding arbitration means that the decision of the arbitrators is final. It cannot be appealed to a higher authority. Conversely, if the decision is non-binding, it can be appealed to a higher authority for a de novo (new) hearing or trial.

Binding arbitration compares to the traditional litigation process in the sense that it results in a final conclusion to a dispute. It has several advantages over the traditional litigation process. It tends to be more informal because the rules of evidence are relaxed. The arbitrators are usually experts in the field which leads to a better understanding and resolution of the issues. The atmosphere surrounding the proceedings are less adversarial which promotes a continuing relationship between the parties. The proceedings, if agreed upon by the parties, can be kept confidential as opposed to taking place in a large, public court room. And, like most ADR methods, binding arbitration is faster and less costly than the formal litigation process.

Non-binding arbitration is more closely analogous to mediation than is binding ar-

---

12. CAL.CIV. Code Sec. 4607(a).

bitration. As the name implies, the decision reached by the arbitrators is meaningless (non-binding), unless agreed upon by the parties. Non-binding arbitration therefore is more closely tied to mediation than binding arbitration. As a practical matter, it has proved to be eminently successful in many states in expediting the trial and disposition of civil cases. The reason undoubtedly is that it has all the advantages of binding arbitration and where the dollar amount involved is small, the economics of appeal are not attractive. As discussed earlier in this chapter, Pennsylvania, for example, has a compulsory arbitration statute in which one or both parties can submit their civil claims of up to $20,000 to arbitration. Procedurally, three members of a local bar association are selected as members of an arbitration board who decide the dispute. Written testimony does not have to be taken and the award does not have to specify exact legal rationale. Even though either party is entitled to a de novo trial, the Pennsylvania experience has been quite successful.

Arbitration clauses are often inserted in domestic relations (pre and post nuptial), commercial, labor and other written agreements in an effort to better resolve potential problems and head off costly litigation. The validity of such agreements has been recognized on both state and federal levels. For example, the Federal Arbitration Act[13] provides that written agreements to arbitrate disputes arising out of contract "shall be valid, irrevocable, and enforceable, save upon such grounds as exist at law or in equity for the revocation of any contract." Many states have similar statutes. An example of an arbitration clause in an international contract that was approved by the Supreme Court is as follows:

ARBITRATION OF CERTAIN MATTERS

All disputes, controversies or differences which may arise between MMC and BUYER out of or in relation to Articles I-B through V of this Agreement or for the breach thereof, shall be finally settled by arbitration in Japan in accordance with the rules and regulations of the Japan Commercial Arbitration Association.[14]

2. INTERNATIONAL

In the context of international business, arbitration clauses such as appears in the example immediately above are frequently used to resolve disputes. In 1970, the United States made a commitment to enforce private agreements to arbitrate disputes by acceding to the Convention on the Recognition and Enforcement of Foreign Arbitral Awards. The purpose of the Convention which was originally adopted in 1958 was to "encourage the recognition and enforcement of commercial arbitration agreements in international contracts and to unify the standards by which agreements to arbitrate are observed and arbitral awards are enforced in the signatory countries." The Convention states that each contracting country shall recognize arbitration awards as binding and shall enforce them unless the award is contrary to the public policy of a country or is not capable of being settled by arbitration in that country.

Settling international commercial disputes by arbitration has become so popular that a number of organizations have established procedures to follow. For example, in the example immediately above, the parties chose to follow the rules and regulations of the Japan Commercial Arbitration Association. Two other organizations are the International Chamber of Commerce and the American Arbitration Association.

E. Mini-Trial

A mini-trial is a new ADR procedure. The term "mini-trial" is deceiving because it does not relate to a true trial. Rather it is a voluntary, private, proceeding usually arranged to assist in

---

13. U.S.C. Sec. 2.

14. *Mitsubishi Motors Corp. v. Soler Chrysler-Plymouth*, 473 U.S. 614, 105 S.Ct. 3346, 87 L.Ed.2d 444 (1985).

resolving complex corporate disputes. Although there is no set format for a mini-trial, typically, a mutually selected neutral adviser, often an expert in the Geld, acts as "judge" in conjunction with CEOs or other senior corporate officers. After the evidence has been presented in the manner agreed upon, the parties will attempt to negotiate a settlement. If settlement cannot be reached, the neutral adviser will be asked to render an "opinion." The opinion will be binding or nonbinding at the option of the parties.

The advantage of the mini-trial lies in the fact that it exposes both the strengths and weaknesses of the parties which allows them to realistically assess the costs/benefits of litigation. There are a number of format variations of the mini-trial. For example, the neutral adviser could be eliminated and the CEOs could act as "judge." But no matter what format is agreed upon, the key ingredient is cooperation between and among the various parties. Although there appears to be no empirical evidence on the subject, the literature indicates that most mini-trials lead to successful settlement.

F. Summary Jury Trial

Similar to the mini-trial, a summary jury trial is a fairly recent ADR settling device that more closely resembles a traditional trial than does a mini-trial. It takes place in a courtroom where a judge or magistrate presides over the case. A mock jury is selected; evidence is briefly presented by lawyers representing the disputing parties; instructions relative to the law (charges) are given by the court to the jurors who then deliberate and announce a decision. The important part follows. The jurors are given an opportunity to discuss the strengths and weaknesses of the case with the lawyers for each party. The facts are now "on the table," the rationale for a decision delivered and an opportunity or setting for continued negotiation and ultimate settlement provided. Similar to the mini-trial, if the jury

decision is not acceptable by either party, a trial de novo can take place.

Although some states provide for summary jury trials in their statutory rules of court, because it is merely part of the settlement process, it can be ordered by the court. In his 1985 Year End Report of the Judiciary, then Chief Justice Burger recommended it. One author suggests that use of summary jury trials should extend to cases that fall into one or a combination of the following categories:

(1) where there are substantial discrepancies between the opposing attorneys' evaluation of unliquidated damages such as "pain and suffering";

(2) where the lawyers disagree sharply as to how the jury will apply the facts to nebulous legal concepts such as "reasonableness";

(3) where one of the parties lacks a realistic view of the value of the case; or

(4) where one of the parties strongly desires to have his "day in court" or to have his case heard by an impartial jury.[15]

G. Rent–a–Judge

A third new development as an alternative to traditional litigation is rent-a-judge. Just as the name indicates, parties to a dispute rent or pay for the services of a judge who is usually a retired judge or lawyer. Two states have statutory rules which control the process. For example, Indiana requires such qualifications (retired judge or lawyer) whereas California does not. The parties name the person they wish to serve as judge then, whether by court appointment or strictly private arrangement, the person selected agrees to act in that capacity. A date is set for the proceedings and the rented judge conducts it much like a traditional trial. In Indiana, the procedural rules state that the parties waive their right to a trial by jury, but following the rented judge's deci-

---

15. D. Gifford, *supra* note 11, at 216-17.

sion, either party has the right to appeal to an intermediate court of appeals.

Reportedly, the California experience with a rent-a-judge has resulted in substantial savings in time and money (lawyer fees). Comparable with other ADR procedures, the parties have the added advantage of being able to select a judge who is familiar with similar cases. Thus, there is less likelihood that an appeal will be taken since the judge's knowledge helps to instill in the parties a feeling of equity and fairness.

* * *

Problems

1. What is the difference between legislative and case law and how do they interrelate?

2. Suppose you read or heard the following statement: The doctrine of stare decisis is archaic, smacks of ancestor worship, and should have little application in today's modern, rapidly changing society. Would you agree with the statement? Explain.

3. In many states any number of persons, or only one person, may lawfully own all the stock of a business corporation. In such a state the stock of a particular corporation was owned by three persons, B, C, and S, with B owning 45 percent, C 47 percent and S 8 percent. S entered into a legally binding contract with B under which S agreed to sell and deliver his stock to B and B agreed to pay a certain stated price. When the time came for performance of the contract, B tendered the agreed amount of money to S, but S said he had changed his mind and refused to take the money or to transfer his stock to B. Explain what legal remedy or remedies B would have. If you were B, what would you do? (Modified from A.I.C.P.A., Nov. 40-12 and May 56-3.)

4. A produce dealer in Buffalo, New York, ordered in writing from a New York City produce wholesaler 500 crates of apples at $10 per crate, the order specifying grade and shipment date. The wholesaler promptly accepted the order in writing and promised to ship the goods as ordered. However, when the shipment date arrived, the market price was such that the same grade of apples purchased elsewhere would cost the dealer $1,000 more than the contract price. The dealer learned that the wholesaler had on hand more than a sufficient quantity of the proper grade of apples to fill the dealer's contract and that the wholesaler was retaining them, hoping for an additional increase in the market price. The dealer sued the wholesaler for specific performance and requested the court to order the wholesaler to ship the agreed apples to the dealer. Should the court decree that the wholesaler specifically perform the contract? Explain.

5. Determining the inferences which may properly be drawn from certain evidence often involves consideration of the rules of law and of logic. Some persons suggest that in this modern age of specialization, the jury system should be abolished and that instead cases should be tried and facts determined by trained legal logicians. What do you think of such a suggested change?

6. B, owner of a large business in Cleveland, Ohio, operated a small branch in Erie, Pennsylvania. For the Erie branch, B ordered and received a certain specially designed machine from S of Erie, B agreeing to pay $6,000 in 30 days. Shortly thereafter B complained to S of unsatisfactory operation, discontinued use of the machine, and offered to return it to S. S refused to accept the return of the machine, asserting that it was not defective, and when B refused to pay for the machine, S sued B in the Erie County court. The court instructed the jury that if the machine was defective as B claimed, B could return it and have no liability to pay S anything; but that if the machine was of contract quality, S could recover the agreed purchase price. From conflicting evidence as to the condition of the machine, the jury returned a verdict that the machine conformed to the contract, and the court entered judgment for S and against B for $6,000 plus interest and costs. B appealed the judgment to the Pennsylvania Supreme

Court. There being sufficient evidence to sustain the jury's verdict, and the trial judge's statement of the applicable rule of law being correct, the Supreme Court found no reason to reverse the judgment and therefore affirmed it. Upon being advised of the outcome of the appeal, B resumed use of the machine and shortly it broke down completely. A thorough inspection conclusively showed that the cause of the breakdown was the very weakness about which B had complained. An inspection thorough enough to disclose this type of weakness could not previously have been made without wrecking the machine. B refused to pay the $6,000 judgment. Each of the following is a separate fact situation.

(a) B promptly brought an action in the Erie County court to have the judgment canceled, and offered as evidence the thorough inspection described above (conclusively showing that the machine had been defective ever since received). Should the judgment be canceled? Explain.

(b) The assets of the branch not being sufficient for collection of the judgment (assume that B made no attempt to have the judgment canceled by the court which entered it), S sued B in Cuyahoga County, Ohio (Cleveland area), on the Pennsylvania judgment. B offered as evidence the thorough inspection described above (conclusively showing that the machine had been defective ever since received). Was S entitled to recover in the Ohio lawsuit? Explain.

7. B of Philadelphia purchased and received certain goods from S of Chicago, for which B promised to pay a certain price in thirty days. After unpacking and inspecting the goods, B decided that they were defective, put them aside, and never used them. He advised S that he would not pay and asked for instructions as to how S wished to have the goods returned. S refused to permit return, asserted that the goods were not defective, and when B still refused to pay, sued B for $55,000 damages.

(a) S started the lawsuit in the Federal District Court for the Philadelphia area. Explain whether this court would be a proper court for S's lawsuit.

(b) Assume that S brought the lawsuit in the proper state trial court for the Philadelphia area. After a close trial involving conflicting expert testimony, the jury concluded that the goods conformed to B's order and returned a verdict in favor of S and against B for $55,000. The trial court entered judgment accordingly, and on appeal the Pennsylvania Supreme Court affirmed the trial court's judgment. B then asked his lawyer about further appealing the case to the United States Supreme Court. On these facts, explain whether any basis existed upon which the United States Supreme Court could be requested to consider a further appeal.

8. This chapter discussed at least four ways by which a judgment can be obtained. Identify them and state why you would prefer to obtain a judgment in one way rather than another.

9. Sun Company was organized under the law of a foreign country. It was licensed to do business and in fact was conducting business in the state of California. Beta Corporation was a California corporation that conducted business only in that state. If Beta was interested in entering into a purchase agreement with Sun Company, would Beta be concerned about the Act of State Doctrine, the Principle of Comity or Sovereign Immunity? What suggestions might you give to Beta in drafting its agreement with Sun Company.

10. What prevents a corporation doing business in several different countries from being taxed on the same income in each country?

11. Why do the decisions reached by alternative dispute resolution techniques tend to be final, i.e. the parties will not appeal even though the decision is non-binding?

12. In your opinion, what is the single most important characteristic that is common to all forms of alternative dispute resolution?

13. What is the difference between: mediation and arbitration, arbitration and a summary jury trial and a summary jury trial and rent-a-judge?

Administrative Law

Administrative Law

(Agency)

THE PERVASIVE REGULATION of business is the most significant legal and economic development of the twentieth century. Regulation has some impact on nearly every aspect of business activity. Although, the trend toward *deregulation* caused some pullback in new regulatory programs during the 1980s, regulation continues to impose significant constraints on business activities. In order for business to effectively manage it's regulatory environment, managers must understand the public policy pressures for re-regulation, the substance of existing and proposed regulations, and the administrative processes agencies use. This chapter focuses on the influences and processes which shape the regulation of business by local, state, and federal administrative agencies.

I. Enabling Legislation

Administrative agencies begin life in an *enabling* statute which is passed by Congress, a state legislature, or a local government entity. Enabling acts usually create the agency and then *delegate* certain powers to it. Typically, Congress first recognizes the existence of a social, economic, health, or safety problem. If the subject matter to be regulated is too complex or technical for constant Congressional oversight, an agency may be created. Theoretically, agencies acquire specialized talent by hiring scientific and other experts to conduct the regulatory program. The agency's continued exposure to the regulated activity allows

it to be flexible to the changing needs of the regulatory environment. This adjustment process is necessary before the agency will be acceptable as a legitimate institution and have success gaining compliance. In most instances, administrative regulation is more efficient than if such decisions were made by the judiciary.

A. Agency Functions

Agencies have three basic functions which parallel the three branches of government. *Executive* powers enable the agency to set policy, gather information, and then investigate or prosecute violations of statutes or regulations. *Legislative* power is delegated to agencies by Congress within narrow guidelines to promulgate rules (i.e. pass regulations). Finally, *judicial* power is used to adjudicate controversies. These three separate functions are housed within nearly every agency. Most federal agencies are subject to direct managerial control by the Presidential administration. Similar executive controls may exist over state agencies by the governor. This structure raises questions of *separation of powers*, the Constitutional concept that constrains the design of government to avoid the tyrannical rule of a small group. The system of *checks and balances* between the branches of government is a fundamental method to keep governmental powers separate. As long as agency prosecutors and judges maintain some independence from each other, there is a separation of intra-agency powers. There are many other checks and balances applicable to agencies, between agencies, and within agencies.

The primary function of agencies today is the promulgation and enforcement of its own rules or regulations. Most agencies' law enforcement processes are defined by statute, executive order, and by the agency's own policies. However, some enabling acts provide for special procedures, like the Food and Drug Administration's procedures for testing and licensing of new food additives or therapeutic drugs.

Most agencies have similar procedures because these are prescribed in the Administrative Procedure Act of 1946 (APA). When agencies legislate with new regulations, they generally must publish notice in the *Federal Register*. The Federal Register is a chronological collection published every weekday that includes all agency proposals, rules, notices, and Presidential proclamations. Each year the newly published regulations are reorganized and added to the *Code of Federal Regulations* (CFR). The CFR is organized by agency and by subject matter (e.g. securities, banking, labor) as a set of paperback regulation books. The CFR contains all the presently effective regulations except for those which were added, revised, or deleted since the last CFR publication. While most regulations have the force of law, courts may invalidate them if they conflict with the Constitution, a statute, or an executive order.

B. Agency Acronyms

Most of the agencies encountered by business managers are referred to by an acronym taken from the first letter of each word in the agency's official title. While this seems like an esoteric exercise in alphabet soup, it is advisable to be familiar with some of the better known agencies' acronyms. Figure 2.1 lists many of the better known federal administrative agencies with an impact on business.

C. State Administrative Agencies

Most of the states have several administrative agencies. Although many states' administrative procedures vary considerably, there are many similarities due to the trends set by the federal administrative procedure law. The states' administrative agencies commonly license professionals, regulate banking institutions, set utility rates, regulate the sale of insurance and claims processing, regulate land use (e.g., zoning), collect taxes, administer prisons, regulate environmental and labor matters, and support education. Although, the primary focus here is on federal regulation, most of the issues and procedures are similar at the state level.

II. Reasons for Regulating

The American political system is premised on the economic theory of *laissez faire*, so government intervention into economic activity is resisted. Therefore, an understanding of the justifications for regulation are useful. Laissez-faire assumes that the best allocation for goods and services in an economy results from primary reliance on the market system. Competition prevents excessive use of private economic power. As long as competition provides choices to economic actors, producers are motivated to be efficient. This should result in an optimal allocation of capital to the most deserving businesses and provide optimal choices in goods and services. This free market theory is premised on rational actors who seek to maximize their own per-sonal utility (e.g. wealth). Firms likewise seek to maximize their profits or market forces motivate firms to behave like profit-maximizers.

However, experience with laissez-faire has illustrated that market imperfection and other side-effects are regularly produced. In a democracy, a regulatory response to these imperfections is a natural and apparently inevitable political reaction to market imperfections. Therefore, regulation is justified by the

FIGURE 2.1: SELECTED FEDERAL ADMINISTRATIVE AGENCIES

FTC   *Federal Trade Commission*
Enforces anti-trust and trade laws

NLRB *National Labor Relations Board*
Enforces labor law to preserve fair
bargaining between employers and
employees

SEC   *Securities and Exchange Commission*
Enforces securities laws to protect investors
and instill confidence in the capital
markets

ICC   *Interstate Commerce Commission*
Sets rates and fosters competition in
transportation industry, reduced under
deregulation

FCC   *Federal Communications Commission*
Licenses broadcasters and guides fairness,
access, and responsiveness of programs

Fed.   *Federal Reserve System*
(FRB) Nation's central bank sets monetary and
financial policies

DOJ   *Department of Justice*
Enforces federal criminal law under the
Attorney General

CIA   *Central Intelligence Agency*
Provides for national security

DOT   *Department of Transportation*
Sets transportation policies

EEOC *Equal Employment Opportunity
Commission*
Regulates employment practices

EPA   *Environmental Protection Agency*
Sets and enforces pollution standards

SBA   *Small Business Administration*
Promotes small business development
with loans and consulting

CPSC *Consumer Product Safety Commission*
Sets and enforces design standards for
the safety of consumer products

NRC   *Nuclear Regulatory Commission*
Licenses nuclear power plants and
promotes nuclear power safety

CBO   *Congressional Budget Office*
Assists Congress in budget and
appropriations matters

OMB   *Office of Management and Budget*
Assists the President in budgeting and
coordinating all agency activities

FAA   *Federal Aviation Administration*
Oversees aircraft safety; licenses pilots, air
traffic controllers, and new airplane design

FBI   *Federal Bureau of Investigation*
Investigates federal and multi-state
criminal activities

FERC *Federal Energy Regulatory Commission*
Regulates oil and gas industries

IRS   *Internal Revenue Service*
Collects federal income taxes

OSHA *Occupational Safety and Health
Administration*
Promotes work place safety

USDA *United States Department of Agriculture*
Promotes farming and regulates food purity

FDA   *Food and Drug Administration*
Licenses food additives and drugs

GAO   *General Accounting Office*
Audits federal agencies and programs

GSA   *General Services Administration*
Acquires and manages federal government
property, facilities, and services

failure of the market mechanisms to make optimal protection of and representation of the public interest. Government or private regulation motivates economic actors to move toward fulfilling responsibility to cure market imperfections. There are four basic market failure commonly addressed through regulation: natural monopolies, externalities, destructive competition, and social policies.

A. Natural Monopolies

Natural monopolies arise where economies of scale are so large that the market is best served by one producer or supplier. Usually the marginal costs of producing extra units decreases over the whole range of the quantity demanded. However, experience shows that monopolists pursuance of the profit maximization goal leads them to make pricing and production quantity decisions based on the point where marginal revenue equals marginal cost. This usually results in production of an insufficient quantity to satisfy demand. The good or service is usually priced higher than under competition. Most utilities and some transportation firms have a natural monopoly position. There would be significant societal inefficiencies if the pipeline or wiring networks of utilities were duplicated by several competitors. Typically, the states regulate the maximum price which can be charged by natural monopolies. This permits maintenance of the economies of scale but without the negative impact of a monopolist's reduced production or increased price.

B. Externalities

Externalities arise when a firm does not pay all the costs or receive all the benefits from its activities. Firms that generate side-effects on society are shifting their costs to others. Examples include: pollution, unsafe products, and health hazards because society bears these costs. Business activity can also produce beneficial externalities that benefit society.

For example, there is often regional prosperity when a new firm begins business. Regulation often intervenes when externalities are discovered that impose costs on society. The tort law system compensates victims after the effects of negative externalities arise. By contrast, modern regulation theory seeks to prevent negative externalities *before* damage occurs.

C. Destructive Competition

Destructive competition can arise in industries with excessive supply capacity. Sometimes existing firms cut their prices to capture larger market shares forcing competitors to either cut costs or go bankrupt. If several competitors cease business, the survivor may be left with a monopoly or the nation may lose all its production capacity in some strategic product. Additionally, cost cutting may adversely affect the quality or safety of the goods or services.

Government has experimented with the prevention of destructive competition by establishing minimum prices or rates. For example, price regulation in the transportation and milk industries is often intended to prevent destructive competition. Such regulations have arisen on the federal, state, and local levels to protect producers, customers, productive capacity, and the health and safety of consumers. However, rate regulation encourages inefficiency so most of the deregulation efforts have targeted rate regulation.

D. Social Policies

Regulation has been a favored tool of social policy makers. For example, many observers believe that discrimination in housing, voting, selling practices, and employment has not adequately been remedied by the market as quickly or efficiently as under regulation. Another area of social policy adjustment is wealth redistribution usually effected through taxation, welfare systems, or the regulation of maximum or minimum prices. In times of unanticipated scarcity, regulation has been used to readjust the allocation of goods by removing the market pricing mechanism as the primary basis for allocation. For example, fairness is often cited to justify food rationing during wartime or the control of petroleum prices during the oil embargo.

III. Control Of Agency Actions

Administrative agencies' significant powers present a potential for abuse. Many agencies have some independence from direct political pressures to prevent their misuse by politicians. However, regulatory agencies left unchecked could become despotic. In order to monitor and prevent these natural tendencies, the public and the three branches of government exercise certain control over agencies. The following section discusses how the President, the Congress, the Judiciary, the press, and the public impact administrative agencies' actions.

A. Judicial Controls

The courts bear the ultimate responsibility to determine when agencies abuse their powers through judicial review. This involvement begins with application of the *delegation* doctrine that prohibits the legislature from abdicating its legislative responsibilities. Many agencies are responsible to the executive branch yet possess executive, legislative, and judicial powers, the combination of which arguably frustrates the balance envisioned by the separation of the powers. The delegation is illegitimate when such legislative grants of power to agencies are excessive.

Congress has designed various regulatory systems. Several poorly designed regulatory programs were passed by Congress in the panic to restore the economy during the Great Depression. Excessive power was delegated to agencies allowing them to act as "roving commissions to inquire into evils and

upon discovery, correct them." When such an enabling statute fails to announce a clear policy objective, it grants power that is "not canalized within banks that keep it from overflowing."

Excessive delegations may arise where the enabling act contains conflicting policies so there are no standards provided to the agency. In other instances legislation can fail to provide sufficient accountability or the rudiments of due process. In these instances the courts have declared the regulatory scheme unconstitutional as an excessive delegation.

Today, the Congress and most state legislatures are more careful in designing regulatory programs. Few delegations are successfully challenged as excessive. The delegation doctrine requires the enabling
act provide both substantive and procedural controls to limit the overexercise of agency powers. Agencies may have broader powers where technical expertise is necessary or there are rapidly changing conditions in the regulated industry.

B. Legislative Controls

Congress has initial control over administrative agencies through passage of the enabling legislation. In many instances enabling statutes: (1) create the agency, (2) define its policies and mission, (3) design the agency's organization and structure, (4) provide for special procedures, and (5) pass the laws and/or delegate rulemaking power for the agency to enforce. Congress can expand or contract these powers with supplemental legislation as the agency's performance is monitored.

Automatic periodic review of agencies is required in some states and for some federal agencies under sunset legislation. At regular intervals, particular agencies which are not renewed with a new enabling statute are dissolved. This forces the legislature, regulated entities, and other constituencies to re-examine the agency's record and project its future contributions. Pennsylvania's sunset law re-

Example. The Environmental Protection Agency (EPA) established a plan to control ambient air quality standards for airborne pollutants, photochemical oxidants, and carbon monoxide in Massachusetts. The Clean Air Act empowered the EPA to establish and implement nationwide air-quality standards for those pollutants with an adverse affect on public health and welfare. When Massachusetts failed to propose a plan, the EPA Administrator proposed one as he was obligated under the enabling act. The plan proposed to discourage private vehicle use by freezing the number of available parking spaces, creating special bus and car pool lanes, establishing a car pool computer matching system, and requiring emissions testing, among other provisions. Several affected parties challenged the EPA's action as an overbroad and unconstitutional delegation of legislative power.

The exercise of EPA power here is not "unconfined and vagrant" because it has a well-defined task to reduce pollution levels for protection of the public health. The Clean Air Act prescribes the EPA's approach and details its powers. Even though there are complexities in the trade-offs between various methods for pollution abatement, definitive benchmarks exist to guide the EPA. The EPA's prescribed methods and the eventual results can be measured scientifically. In highly technical regulatory areas such as pollution control, the legislature is not well suited to micromanagement of complex pollution abatement. Therefore, it is not an unlawful delegation of legislative power for Congress to delegate the details of pollution control to the EPA. ☐

quires a staggered review of all agencies every ten years.

Funding of agency operations is an important control device. Though the initial *authorization* for budget lines and the annual *appropriation* of specific budget allotments, Congress provides for each agency's spending on staff, equipment, and supplies. Particular agency activities may be supported with specific additional funds or extinguished by the removal of funding. Typically, the agency compiles a budget request based on its projection of activity and associated costs. At the federal level, the President's Office of Management and Budget (OMB) reviews the request and may make alterations. All agency and federal program budgets are consolidated into the Presidents budget proposal which is transmitted to Congress for approval. The appropriations committees of both houses hold hearings and Congress approves the final revisions. The President may sign or veto the budget bill and occasionally has withheld

the expenditure of funds after they were appropriated. Certain annual expenditures for *entitlement* programs (e.g. social security, welfare) are fixed by statutory formulas so they are not subject to the regular budgeting process.

Several forms of indirect control by Congress allow for a more subtle impact on agency actions. Congressional oversight committees have "watchdog" authority over the agencies through investigations and the hearings process. These proceedings are designed to gather data to decide if new or revised legislation is necessary. This threat of legislative action coupled with political and public pressure is often sufficient to pressure the agency to modify its behavior. Studies by special Congressional agencies such as the General Accounting Office (GAO), Congressional Research Service (CRS), the Congressional Budget Office and the Administrative Conference highlight the strengths and weaknesses of regulatory programs. This review and evaluation is enhanced with annual self-reports from each agency highlighting its accomplishments and activities.

Although the President usually selects department heads and regulatory commissioners, the Senate must approve these appointments with its power of advice and consent. Middle level agency personnel, known as "inferior officers," are political appointees selected at the discretion of the President or the agency heads. The civil service system was established by Congress to insulate the majority of the bureaucracy from political pressure. However, because Congress can modify this system, lower echelon agents must follow the policy directives received from upper-level agency heads.

Congress has attempted to preserve some direct legislative control over the broad rule-making power delegated to several agencies. Typically, this has been accomplished with a *legislative veto* power that could be exercised by either house of Congress to effectively nullify an administrative regulation or ruling. However, serious violations of the separation of powers doctrine have arisen with legislative vetoes. For example, the lobbying strength of the used car industry was evidenced by the pressure placed on the FTC. Congress eventually cast a legislative veto over the FTC's revised used car disclosure rule.

The abuse of the *legislative veto* power led to a Supreme Court finding which appears to invalidate all Congressional uses of the device. While many states apply the separation of powers concept, not all have followed the Supreme Court's lead by invalidated their state legislative veto powers.

C. Executive Controls

Although administrative agencies are often referred to as the "fourth branch" of government, the executive branch has the clearest line of authority over most agencies. Most agency heads are political appointees who are ideologically and directly responsible to the President's Administration. The President has the ultimate law enforcement and policy making responsibility. This arises from the Constitutional charge to assure that the laws are "faithfully executed." The President may issue *Executive Orders* which have the force of law unless Congress supersedes them by later passing a statute, a court interpretation overrides, or another executive order changes it. In this way, the President commonly implements regulatory policy either from power conferred by Congress or the inherent powers of the office.

The inherent managerial power of the Presidency usually includes the power to hire and fire administrative agents at will. The chairs of independent commissions are routinely appointed by the President. Subject to the civil service system and Senate approval, the President can control attitudes, abilities, and political loyalties of the policymakers in most agencies. However, Congress intended that certain agencies maintain some independence from such executive domination. For example, the SEC, CPSC, FTC, ICC, FCC, CFTC, NRC, Federal Reserve Board, and any Congressional agency (e.g. Library of Congress, CBO, Copyright Office) are quasi-independent agencies. The policies of independent agencies are protected from political pressure by fixed terms of office, political party balance, staggered terms for commissioners, and removal-for-cause statutes. Agency heads may not be removed except for *cause* which is usually defined as "inefficiency, neglect of duty, or malfeasance in office." Although the heads of dependent agencies may be removed for any reason at the President's discretion, independent agency heads may not.

The President has control over the department level agencies. For example, the President's control over the Department of Justice (DOJ) adds to the President's practical control over regulatory agencies. The power to

Example. Chadha was a foreign (alien) student who remained in the U.S. after his visa expired. An immigration judge suspended his deportation but the U.S. House passed a resolution (legislative veto) overriding the suspension, effectively ordering Chadha's deportation. This raised the question whether the legislative veto power of either house of the U.S. Congress was constitutional under the separation of powers doctrine in light of the valid delegation by Congress to the Immigration and Naturalization Service (INS).

The records of the Constitutional conventions that drafted the U.S. Constitution indicate that all legislation must be presented to the President for approval or veto before becoming law. This presentment power was designed to become a major check on the rather extensive legislative power of the Congress by giving the President a role in disapproving oppressive, improvident, or ill-conceived legislation. The President's review of prospective legislation gives a national perspective to the legislative process.

Another principle of constitutional government is violated by the legislative veto. The Constitutional framers sought to permit the passage of legislation only after consideration by all officials elected to national office. Legislatures may come under the dominion of strong passions and excitements, impatience, irritability, and impetuousness. Additionally, the two houses of Congress permit some proportional representation (in the House) and some equal representation (in the Senate) from the states. Except in narrowly defined areas where a single house acts alone, the bicameralism principle requires that both houses of Congress consider any law. Because the legislative veto failed to receive presentment to the President or consideration by both houses, it violates the separation of powers. While these two additional processes may not always be efficient, the Constitutional framers considered other values to be paramount. □

conduct criminal investigations and prosecutions rests solely with Justice Department. The Attorney General is directly responsible to the President and usually anticipates the President's political policy emphasis. Although many agencies have separate powers to bring civil actions seeking injunctions, orders, civil fines, and damages, all criminal cases must be referred to prosecution by the Justice Department. The prosecutorial intent, emphasis, as well as many law and policy determinations are ultimately dependent on Justice Department philosophy. The executive's influence in criminal law enforcement predominates their prosecutions.

Agencies may be reorganized by the President with Congressional consent. Under the *Reorganization Act* the President may transfer functions and powers among existing agencies or to newly created agencies. For example, the EPA and the FERC received regulatory powers previously held by other agencies and departments. Reorganization should be performed to consolidate functions in the hands of experts, coordinate conflicting policies, and reduce the inefficient duplication of functions.

Occasionally, other agencies exercise oversight and control over each other. For example, EPA rule proposals were routinely circulated among interested agencies under the "quality of life review" procedure used during the Nixon Administration. Often the Commerce Department challenged the EPA's assumptions and policies. This process delayed new regulations until EPA submitted modifications accommodating the objections of other agencies. Today, OMB has pervasive over-

51

Example. President Franklin D. Roosevelt fired Humphrey, a FTC commissioner who held different political views from the administration. After Humphrey died his executor sued the government for the salary owed due during the remainder of the commissioner's unexpired term after dismissal by FDR. The question raised concerned the FTC as an independent agency and the President's power to remove an independent commissioner without proof of good cause.

The Federal Trade Commission Act that created the FTC provides for seven year terms of office for each of the five commissioners. While each commissioner is initially appointed by the President, with advice and consent of the Senate, the term of some commissioners may extend into the next elected Presidential Administration. The FTC Act provided for political balance, no more that three members may be from one political party. Any commissioner may be removed by the President for inefficiency, neglect of duty or malfeasance in office, essentially for cause. The Congressional debates over the FTC Act indicated it was designed to be politically insulated from the Presidential Administration except in their selection. They are to exercise independent expertise. The President's exercise of removal power without good cause frustrates this political independence that Congress intended for the FTC. ☐

sight in agency rule-making since President Reagan issued Executive Orders #No. 12291 (1981) and No. 12498 (1985) discussed later.

D. Indirect Controls

The influence of pluralist interest groups often exerts significant pressure on agencies. Public interest groups, such as the Sierra Club, have brought problems to the attention of agencies or have litigated questions directly without the assistance of the agencies. Lobbyists influence Congress and regulatory policy makers in similar ways. Publicity, about the public acceptance or rejection of the legitimacy of regulatory programs can also place practical limits on an agency's success. For example, the press often mobilizes support for or pressure on administrative agencies, Congress, and on the President's Administration to pursue or change policies.

Two statutes facilitate the indirect public control of agencies. The *Freedom of Information Act* (FOIA), discussed later, opens much of an agency's inner workings to public scrutiny. The *Government in the Sunshine Act* opens up to public scrutiny many of the meet-

ings of the independent agencies. However, most staff level meetings are not subject to the "sunshine"; instead, only the meetings in which official policy-making actions must be made public. A one week's notice is required for these official meetings. The Federal Reserve Board commonly held highly secretive meetings to make monetary policy decisions until it was forced into the "sunshine." However, there are exceptions for the exercise of enforcement related powers and it is easy to circumvent this "open meeting" law.

IV. Information

Securing information is critical to the efficiency and effectiveness of the regulatory process. Agencies acquire information through: (1) direct observation of regulated activities, (2) public complaints and comments, (3) inspections of private areas, (4) *subpoenas* directing witness testimony and (5) *subpoena duces tecum* requiring the production of documents. The Constitution protects individuals and regulated entities from unreasonable searches and seizures in the 4th Amendment and from self-incrimination in the 5th Amendment.

A. Subpoena Enforcement

Most administrative agencies may not enforce subpoenas immediately after issue. Administrative subpoenas are not self-executing, which means a subpoena recipient may refrain from testifying until a court orders compliance. To gain a court ordered enforcement, the agency must demonstrate the investigation is fair and it needs the information sought.

The level of formality in an administrative subpoena enforcement proceeding varies. The recipient must be afforded an opportunity to object at a hearing where evidence may be offered, oral arguments taken, or affidavits filed, and pre-hearing discovery may be appropriate. To sustain the initial burden of proof, the agency need only make a superficial recital of its jurisdiction and a statement of the basis for enforcement. Thereafter, the burden of proof shifts to the subpoena recipient who must show that the agency is abusing its authority.

The subpoena recipient must have standing to challenge the agency, a recognizable stake in the outcome. Taxpayers lack standing to restrain the IRS from enforcing a subpoena directed towards a tax preparer who possesses the taxpayer's documents. Similarly, bank customers have no standing to deny the IRS access to the bank's records of the customer's account. The *Powell* standards for subpoena enforcement apply equally to all administrative subpoenas. These standards: (1) a *legitimate purpose*, (2) *relevant inquiry*, (3) *agency's possession*, and (4) proper *administrative steps* will now be examined.

It is *illegitimate* for agencies to use the subpoena power to harass and pressure regulated entities to settle matters. Subpoena enforcement has been denied where the agency's illegitimate purpose was evident. For example, illegitimate purposes have arisen where the agency: (1) used a defamatory and adverse publicity campaign against a regulated business, (2) retaliated for aiding a Congressional investigation of the agency, or (3) inherited the bad faith of an informant. The agency must have the statutory authority to investigate the matter and a reasonable expectation of obtaining a valid conviction.

The information sought in the subpoena must be *relevant* to the legitimate investigatory purpose. As long as the information sought might "throw light" on suspected wrongdoing and the request is not unreasonably burdensome, the subpoena is relevant. For example, internal budgets and an auditor's procedural program are considered irrelevant to the IRS's tax collection purposes.

The information sought must not already be in the *agency's possession*. Duplicative production of identical materials is harassment and may be used to harass to induce the target's settlement of charges. The agency must follow its own procedures and *administrative steps* in issuing the subpoena. Harassment by lower echelon agents or only part of the agency deprives the subpoena recipient of the accountability inherent in coordinated agency efforts.

B. Privileges

There are two narrow privileges which shield certain information from investigating agencies. The first privilege is derived from the Fifth Amendment. This protects criminal suspects from being compelled to testify against themselves. This privilege is available only in criminal prosecutions. However, the privilege does not apply in the majority of administrative actions because they are typically noncriminal. Only natural persons may assert the privilege, it is not available to corporations or other organizations (e.g. labor unions). Documents which are required to be kept for governmental purposes are not privileged. The privilege protects against oral testimony and not incriminating writings. Finally, several im-

Example. Max Powell, as corporate president, refused to produce corporate records subpoenaed by the IRS. The IRS claimed these were necessary to verify that certain deductions the corporation took on its tax return were legitimate. The IRS had previously examined certain corporate records but the statute of limitations had expired so the IRS was prohibited from assessing any tax deficiency against the corporation. This subpoena enforcement action raised the question whether the IRS must prove that it has probable cause of criminal fraud before it could subpoena the documents. The statute of limitations does not prohibit enforcement of the subpoena if criminal tax fraud was involved.

Congress decided that investigatory powers of lower echelon tax agents must be curbed. Repetitive re-examination of taxpayer records must be cleared with a superior officer within the IRS. However, there is no need to require the IRS to prove probable cause of criminal activity every time it seeks to re-examine taxpayer records. Most administrative agencies have an inquisitorial power to investigate whenever it has a reasonable suspicion of wrongdoing, analogous to the Grand Jury's powers. The IRS and other agencies must prove that it has a legitimate purpose in investigating, the inquiry is relevant to that purpose, the agency does not already possess the information sought, and is following its own administrative steps to acquire the information. The investigatory target may challenge the subpoena on these bases at an enforcement hearing. ▢

munity statutes remove the privilege if the person receives immunity from prosecution.

The second privilege arises under state law. These have developed around the relationships between several classes of persons to encourage frank and open disclosure and to foster the relationships. The privilege has developed to protect conversations between attorney and client, priest and penitent, spouses, and accountant and client. However, federal law recognizes only the attorney-client privilege as a bar to agency investigations. The privilege is available if (1) information passes, (2) from client to practicing attorney, (3) in confidence, (4) not from some other source, (5) for the purpose of receiving professional advice. In the corporate context there are additional requirements: (1) the employee must be ordered to communicate, (2) information gained within the employee's duties, (3) which is not immediately available to upper management. The Supreme Court has observed that the potential for expanding the attorney-client privilege to idle communi-

cations is too great. Unprivileged idle communications are those not made in confidence or not seeking legal advice. Additionally, the strict privilege requirements enumerated above are designed to prevent misuse of the privilege. Thereby, communications with corporate attorneys cannot be made intentionally to shield information if the purpose is not primarily for professional advice.

C. Inter-Agency Exchange of Information

Agencies often save considerable investigatory expense by securing information held by another agency. However, there may be constitutional problems with certain inter-agency transfers of evidence. Specifically, the scope of criminal discovery might be expanded impermissibly and the integrity of the grand jury process could be compromised. The sharing of SEC investigatory files with the Justice Department is permissible because concurrent or *parallel investigations* may be necessary

Example. Several persons were targeted by the SEC for investigation of trading violations of the securities laws. The SEC had issued a Formal Order of Investigation, it followed the internal administrative steps required to authorize the use of the subpoena power. The financial records of the targets were sought from third parties such as the target's stock broker. However, the targets of the investigation were not informed of the subpoenas. This raised the question of whether the target of an administrative investigation has any right to receive notice that a subpoena is issued to a third party holding the target's documents. Without such notice the target could become unable to challenge whether the subpoena was properly authorized or for its legitimacy, relevance, or duplication.

Most agencies, like the SEC, have broad investigatory powers. Subpoenas issued to third parties without notifying the target do not violate the Constitution's due process, confrontation, or self-incrimination protections. Absent some privilege (e.g., attorney-client) there is no confidentiality from government investigators for information communicated to a third party. Notice given to a target would raise the probability that targets with something to hide would impede legitimate investigations. For example, the target could urge the third party to refuse to comply, or delay disclosure, destroy or alter documents, and intimidate witnesses. While the SEC may choose to inform targets of a pending investigation, there is no duty to do so. □

to protect the integrity of the public securities markets. However, in the federal tax context the IRS may not validly issue a civil summons after it has referred a criminal case to the Justice Department.

Documents, transcripts, and exhibits are pieces of evidence often in the hands of the federal grand jury. The Federal Rules of Criminal Procedure prohibit regulatory agencies from gaining access to this evidence if it involves "matters occurring before the grand jury." This policy is intended to maintain confidentially for witnesses, encourage their testimony, and minimize their fear of reprisals by defendants.

There are two narrow exceptions permitting access to grand jury files. First, "an attorney for the government for use in the performance of such attorney's duty" may have access. However, only Justice Department attorneys are "government attorneys," administrative agency attorneys are not. Second, access to grand jury files may be permitted "when so directed by a court preliminarily to

or in connection with a judicial proceeding." For this "judicial proceeding exception" to apply, the agency must be directly involved in identifiable litigation. Access to grand jury files is denied if the agency's action does not require litigation to accomplish its goal. For example, some agencies like the IRS or the SEC may use several forms of process which are not directly connected to litigation. The IRS may levy on property, garnish wages, or assess a deficiency. The SEC may issue a *stop order* to halt distribution or trading in securities. As the likelihood that nonjudicial enforcement increases, the availability of grand jury files decreases.

D. Warrantless Inspections

Some statutory schemes allow agencies to search private areas of personal or business premises without a warrant. These intrusions may involve illegal unreasonable searches or seizures unless certain conditions are met. Some industries have experienced a long history of close and pervasive regulation, there-

Example. As part of a routine audit of the Amerada Hess Corp.'s 1972-1975 tax returns, the IRS sought tax accrual workpapers held by Arthur Young & Co., the auditor. The IRS had discovered questionable payments made from a "special disbursement account." Tax accrual workpapers are necessary to a financial audit to verify the accuracy of the income tax expenses claimed for financial reporting purposes. Such workpapers are helpful to the IRS in discovering any questionable tax treatments claimed by the taxpayer. An administrative summons was issued to Arthur Young. The appeals court applied the state accountant-client privilege to this federal investigation preventing the IRS from securing the papers it sought from Arthur Young. This raised the question of whether the accountant-client privilege is available to resist an IRS subpoena for materials held by a third party.

The internal revenue code permits the IRS to obtain items that have potential relevance to its investigation. Because the tax collection system is based on self-reporting it demands that taxpayers be forthright in disclosing their activities. Congress intended to favor disclosure rather than secrecy. The possibility of chilling open discussions between the accountant and client does not outweigh the tax collection objective. Accountants stand in a different relation to their clients than do attorneys. Independent auditors perform a public watchdog function while attorneys must be loyal advocates for their clients. Although approximately 20 states recognize such a privilege, there is no accountant-client privilege under federal law. ☐

fore they cannot reasonably expect total privacy. For example, in the sales of firearms, liquor, food and drugs, the public's interest in safety outweighs the individual business' right to privacy. Additionally, in *emergency* situations, where *consent* is given, or where the regulated activities are in open and plain view, agencies may conduct surprise warrantless inspections.

In most other situations an agency must secure a warrant from a federal magistrate before commencing a search. The warrant should be issued only on the agency's showing of *administrative* probable cause. There are three factors which can form the basis for the grant of an *ex parte* warrant (the target is not present at the hearing): (1) "specific evidence of existing violations," (2), employee complaints, or (3) "reasonable legislative or administrative standards" (i.e., random, regular, and routine inspections, re-inspections or follow-up inspections). The surprise element may be necessary to avoid the destruction of

evidence, intimidation of witnesses, or the correction of the violation.

V. Hearings

While the vast majority of administrative actions are processed informally, in some instances a *hearing*, a form of adjudication, is used. Administrative hearings are not identical to court trials, there are many variations with some similarities to judicial trials.

A. Due Process

Due process prohibits government from depriving a person of life, liberty, or property without due process of law. Due Process protects regulated business entities from the inadequacy of regulatory hearing procedures. The individual or business must be given adequate *notice*, a meaningful *opportunity to be heard*, and *fair trial procedures*. However, due to the wide variation in administrative responsibilities and the liberty and property interests they affect, the precise type of due process protections can vary considerably.

Life interests are generally not affected by regulatory actions. However, the discontinuation of welfare benefits could be life threatening. In the business regulation context, due process violations usually involve liberty and property interests. *Liberty* usually includes the right to work, move about freely, contract, marry, have children, worship, and learn. In the administrative context, liberty interests are affected by the denial of a security clearance, parol decisions, institutionalization of mentally ill, revocation of prisoner's good time credits, corporal punishment, or the stigma arising from public accusation or defamation. However, the existence of a tort remedy (e.g. suit for libel or slander) may be a sufficient "after-the-fact" protection.

Property interests are the most common due process object, because administrative adjudication usually has an economic impact. Property deprivations may require that adequate administrative processes be provided if the action involves: (1) an entitlement to government benefits (e.g. welfare or disability benefits, aid to dependent children), (2) licenses revocation, (3) tenure or job status, (5) the right to sue, (6) or academic dismissal. A court considering the deprivation of due process by regulatory agencies must weigh the interests of the government against the individual's interest. Some types of government interests may take precedence over private rights. For example, interests where the need for immediate protection of the public outweigh private rights, including public health emergencies or bank seizures which are usually effected through summary and immediate administrative action.

B. Form of Hearing

The precise form for the administrative hearing may also vary greatly among various agencies and between particular types of actions brought by a particular agency. Procedures may include: adequate notice of the hearing, an impartial tribunal, preservation of the hearing record for appeal purposes, oral hearings, the right to cross-examine witnesses, presentation of evidence, representation by counsel, written decision of findings and conclusions, public or private hearing, procedural and evidentiary rules, other parties participation, and an appeal.

The APA requires that "persons entitled to notice of an agency hearing shall be timely informed." This means "notice reasonably calculated to apprise interested parties of the pendency of the action and afford them an opportunity to present their objections." However, the APA fails to identify all interested parties. Clearly the individual or regulated entity which is directly affected must be notified. Often other parties may be indirectly interested in the outcome of the hearing. For example, many drug producers may have property interests in FDA approval or denial of a new drug application. Competing broadcasters must be allowed a *comparative* hearing to have their mutually inconsistent interests determined in the FCC's assignment of a single broadcast frequency or TV channel. Often the same factors for determination of standing are considered in allowing indirect parties to *intervene* in a hearing. If the intervenor has a sufficient "stake in the outcome" and could suffer "injury in fact" if not notified, then the additional complexity and costs of the intervention should be allowed.

C. Presentation of Proof

The typical order of a court trial is often followed in administrative hearings. The parties file pleadings or motions and may attend prehearing conferences to crystallize the issues. Counsel usually introduces exhibits, examines witnesses, and makes closing arguments. The parties also submit legal briefs and proposed findings to the Administrative Law Judge (ALJ). When regulated entities are

Example. The Occupational Safety and Health Act (OSHA) authorizes personnel from the OSHA Administration to inspect work areas of any facility covered by the Act. An inspector visited the Barlow's factory for a randomly chosen inspection for worker safety violations. The inspector had received no employee complaints and had no search warrant so the business owner denied him access to the non-public areas of the facility. The case raises the question whether an OSHA inspector must secure a warrant to search regulated premises if administrative probable cause is absent.

The Fourth Amendment's provision requiring warrants for searches applies to commercial premises as well as private dwellings. It was drafted in response to the English practice of using "general warrants" or "writs of assistance" to search the business premises of merchants during colonial times. Warrantless searches are unreasonable except for pervasively regulated businesses with a history of close regulation. Surprise inspections necessary to preserve evidence of violations are still possible but must be based on administrative probable cause from evidence of an existing violation or based on reasonable legislative or administrative standards for conducting an inspection on the subject premises. Administrative efficiency is an insufficient reason to ignore the constitutional protection against unreasonable searches and seizures. □

sued, the complainant, usually a lawyer working for agency, acts like a civil prosecutor. The agency must usually satisfy the burden of proof by initially going forward with allegations and presenting convincing evidence. Most administrative cases are determined by the ALJ using the preponderance of the evidence standard as the point of persuasion.

The form of evidence at administrative hearings is somewhat different than at a judicial trial. Although a witness's oral testimony is often taken, the APA provides that written statements may replace direct testimony if no prejudice results. Written affidavits, questions, and answers are often appropriate. Some agencies allow the parties to make brief oral summaries of written testimony.

The use of written evidence raises constitutional questions of confrontation and cross-examination. Judicial hearings usually involve limited policy determinations but are focused on the determination of facts. By contrast administrative hearings are somewhat less concerned with the determination of specific past events and are more concerned with policy

and the opinions of expert witnesses. Cross-examination is an efficient process for testing the credibility, accuracy, and completeness of witnesses testimony of past facts. Confrontation of adverse witnesses by cross-examination usually allows the fact finder to observe the witness' demeanor and assess the witnesses' memory, objectivity, financial or ideological bias, or competence. While the opinions of experts and non-experts may need probing in administrative hearings, direct attacks on their credibility are rarely useful. Although the credentials, data, assumptions, methodology, or value judgments of expert witnesses are important, their demeanor on the witness stand is usually of little value. As a result, Congress intended that administrative hearings draw a balance between the costly and complex trial-like procedures and efficiency. Most agencies limit oral testimony and cross-examination, substantially reducing hearing time.

The distinction between adjudicative facts and legislative facts is related to the cross-examination policy mentioned above. *Adjudicative facts* involve particular individuals or past events and call for confrontation or cross-examination. *Legislative facts* are policy determinations and are general principles that are derived from research or general knowledge. Only limited confrontation is allowed in the presentation of legislative facts. Some matters are so widely recognized that their proof is excused. In such cases the ALJ may simply assume these facts through a process known as taking *official notice* in administrative hearings. It is called *judicial notice* in the courts. For example, information from medical treatises or engineering principles are so well settled that the hearing should not be burdened with the additional costs of proving them.

The judicial rules of evidence are largely inapplicable in administrative hearings. The APA allows agencies discretion in the admission of oral or documentary evidence and the power to exclude "irrelevant, immaterial or unduly repetitions evidence." Generally, the judicial evidence rules concerning hearsay, privilege, or incompetence do not apply in administrative hearings. These principles apply in judicial trials because jurors tend to overestimate the probative value of hearsay. These risks of inaccurate results are reduced when expert ALJ's perform the fact-finding. ALJ's may conduct physical inspections and admit statistical data into evidence.

D. The Decision Process

In many agencies there are lower levels of review and determination before any formal hearing is held. For example, an Internal Revenue agent often gathers evidence and makes an initial determination of tax liability. Most agencies have a formal level (trial-type) where the ALJ, also know as a *hearing examiner*, determines facts and applies law and policy to particular controversies. The agency's heads (e.g. commissioners) need only be aware of ALJ decisions to maintain constitutionality of these decisions. ALJ's are independent presiding officers who are assigned cases by rota-

tion. They maintain independence from the agency's hierarchy to provide checks and balances. An ALJ may be removed only for cause and does not serve at the pleasure of agency heads. ALJ's are civil servants compensated independently of agency recommendations and are appointed through a professional merit selection system. The ALJ may not supervise or be supervised by any agency personnel who prosecute or investigate the cases adjudicated by the ALJ.

While the ALJ performs a function somewhat similar to a judge, administrative hearings are somewhat less adversarial than trials at law. The ALJ is not a passive referee like judges usually are, but often actively question witnesses.

The ALJ's may issue an *initial decision* on routine matters by applying law to the facts determined. This initial decision may become the agency's *final decision* unless it is appealed. *Recommended decisions* by ALJ's are always overseen by either the agency's intermediate appeal board or by the agency's head(s). Recommended decisions usually involve novel matters that develop policy. Although ALJ decisions typically carry great weight with agency heads and appeals courts, sometimes their decisions are overturned. The *findings and conclusions* of the ALJ must be included in the record. The quality and accuracy of the decision is enhanced by this discipline which forces the ALJ to justify conclusions and consider all the evidence. Review of the decision is more accurate if the whole record is available.

It is illegal to bring improper influence on a decision at any agency level. These influences may come from outsiders, litigants, both from within and without the agency and from the ALJ's bias. This rule is balanced against the practicalities of agency action. Agencies possess considerable expertise on highly technical issues which may require intra-agency communication. The accuracy and quality of a decision will be directly effected by the ALJ's access to expertise often found within the agency. Investigators and prosecutors may not participate in hearing decisions except as witnesses or counsel.

The APA provides for the consideration of bias in the determinations of an ALJ. Although ALJs are free to have ideological and generalized views on law or policy, a fixed opinion concerning a particular litigant would be prejudicial and require disqualification of the ALJ. The test is whether prior exposure to the evidence makes it virtually impossible to sway the ALJ's mind. Clearly, the ALJ's financial stake or direct pecuniary interest in the outcome would make it improper for participation in the decision. For example, a state optometrist board made up of sole practitioners were financially biased against optometrists working for corporations. The board members had a financial stake in restricting the entry of chain-store optometrists into the state and were illegally biased. Pressure brought on savings and loan regulators to overlook solvency problems is also illegal.

Another source of improper influence may be felt from excessive Congressional or Executive pressure. Where the SEC conducted a negative publicity campaign against a registered issuer at the insistence of an influential Senator, the pressure was considered improper. In another case, the FTC was harassed by a Congressional committee investigation and were disqualified from making a decision concerning the regulated entity.

E. Ex Parte Contacts

Ex Parte communications are "oral or written communications not on the public record with respect to which reasonable prior notice to all parties is not given." Off-the-record communications from regulated entities and regulators are considered unsavory. Particularly where an adjudicatory decision is affected by an ex parte contact, any other interested parties are deprived of an opportunity to refute the information in the contact.

The APA prohibits ex parte contracts in formal adjudication and in rulemaking. The adjudicatory or rulemaking record is considered incomplete and unreviewable if substantial ex parte contacts are made. They taint the proceeding and may unduly influence the decision maker. Where the person who made the contact clearly benefited by the contact and the opponent had an inadequate opportunity to respond, the contact may require that the agency's action be reversed on judicial review. However, ex parte contacts are not illegal in informal adjudication or if they are made by the president or other agencies in executive branch.

VI. Rulemaking

Congress often provides agencies with the applicable substantive law. However, many regulatory details require experience and expertise that Congress does not have. Consequently, enabling statutes often delegate rulemaking authority to agencies, and some provide for special agency rulemaking processes. If special processes are not provided, the APA, presidential executive orders, and judicial interpretations establish rulemaking procedures. Although rulemaking has been a source of legislation since the early 19th Century, the greatest increase in administrative regulations resulted from the New Deal and from the environmental, safety, consumer, and equal opportunity legislation of the 1970s.

Rulemaking has certain advantages over adjudication. Rules apply equally to all persons or businesses making them a clearer and more legitimate source for policy making than a precedent produced by adjudication against a single party. All affected parties have an opportunity to participate in rulemaking while outsiders are usually denied any meaningful participation in adjudication. Additionally, a single rulemaking may be more efficient than a case by case or piecemeal approach to policy making. The disadvantages of rulemaking are evident when affected parties become united in strong opposition to it and the public interest is overpowered. Additionally, it is difficult to clearly draft a general rule which does not eventually have an unintended impact.

Rules are "the whole or part of an agency statement of general or particular applicability and future effect designed to implement, interpret, or prescribe law or policy." The term *regulation* should be considered synonymous with rule. Rules apply generally to future behaviors of groups rather than to isolated individuals. Sanctions may be levied only after prosecution and adjudication of a rule violation.

Rules are based on legislative rather than adjudicative facts. There are three basic rulemaking processes, exempted, formal and informal. These processes vary in the type and amount of public participation afforded. Additionally, Congress and the courts have modified the standard processes to make hybrid rulemaking procedures.

A. Exempted Rulemaking

The APA allows the agencies to determine whether any public participation at all is desirable in certain sensitive areas. There is no requirement for notice and comment periods or for a hearing if the rulemaking involves: (1) "a military or foreign affairs function," (2) "agency management or personnel" functions, (3) "public property, loans, grants, benefits, or contracts," (4) "interpretative rules, general statements of policy, or rules of agency organization, procedure, or practice," or (5) where public procedures are "impracticable, unnecessary, or contrary to the public interest." Rules may be interpretative or substantive. *Substantive* rules are legislative with a substantial impact directly on affected parties. *Interpretive* rules are intended by the agency to explain the meaning of the terms and procedures it uses.

B. Informal Rulemaking

Informal rulemaking is the most predominant type of rulemaking. It utilizes the public *notice and comment* form of participation. The agency must publish notice in the Federal Register of "either the terms or substance of the proposed rule or a description of the subjects and issues involved." The legal authority relied on must be stated and the agency usually solicits comments from any *interested persons*. A contact person at the agency is provided to obtain further information. Most information submitted to the agency is placed in the public record and becomes available for public inspection. These items include the "submission of written data, views, or arguments with or without the opportunity for oral presentation."

After the agency has considered the comments of interested persons and has decided to issue a *final rule*, it must publish the final rule at least 30 days before it becomes effective. The publication of a final rule must include "a concise general statement of their basis and purpose." Agencies are not bound to follow comments, criticisms, or views submitted by the public. However, the agency must consider the "relevant matter presented." This process is considered a shortcoming of informal rulemaking so that more *formal rulemaking* is necessary in certain instances if required by statute.

C. Formal Rulemaking

Adjudicative or *formal* rulemaking is required where enabling statues envision the need for interactive participation by constituencies. After notice of *formal rulemaking* is made in the Federal Register, a formal hearing is held *on the record*. Trial-type proceedings allow the opportunity for testimony and cross-examination of witnesses. The agency issues its findings as a formal rule which can be judicially overturned if it is not supported by substantial evidence. Formal rulemaking is extremely costly and time consuming, sometimes generating thousands of pages of exhibits and testimony. The process is usually used in economic determinations where licenses or ratemaking is envisioned.

D. Hybrid Rulemaking

There are rulemakings where some particular feature of either formal or informal rulemaking would be useful. For example, where the high costs of formal rulemaking should be avoided but greater personal involvement is desirable the courts and Congress have combined features of both rulemaking forms. An agency may need to state its methodology if it concludes that rulemaking is necessary. An agency may need to publish notice if it intends to rely on specific studies or data. In other instances, an agency may need to respond to *cogent comments* made in the record. However, the Supreme Court has halted all judicially imposed hybrid rulemaking. New initiatives in the redesign of hybrid procedures must emanate from Congress or the agencies themselves.

E. Modifications of the Rulemaking Process

In recent years the President and other executive offices have had an increasing impact on the mechanics of rulemaking. Concern over the inflationary impact of regulations prompted the Ford Administration to require agencies to publish economic impact statements. President Carter expanded this process under Executive Order No. 12,044. The Reagan Administration again revised the economic justification process with Executive Order No. 12,291 and instituted policy conformance with Executive Order No. 12,498. Although several presidential administrations have sought to exercise greater coordination over regulatory actions, the Reagan initiatives are the most pervasive. Congress has also sought to modify regulatory policy making. The Reg-

ulatory Flexibility Act is designed to reduce the unnecessary negative impact of regulations on small businesses through procedures similar to Executive Order No. 12,291. However, legislative attempts at further regulatory reforms have been unsuccessful.

F. Executive Order No. 12,291

Executive Order No. 12,291 provides for the evaluation of *major rules* on a cost-benefit basis. Major rules are regulations likely to have a significant financial effect on the economy. This is typically determined by the finding that a recurring $100 million annual effect on the economy will arise. However, the existence of major increases in costs or prices, or significant adverse effects on particular segments of the economy may also require analysis by an agency. The Office of Management and Budget (OMB) has considerable oversight powers in all phases of this economic justification process. However, the independent regulatory agencies are not bound to follow these procedures, although there is some voluntary compliance.

All regulations must comply with the policies contained in the enabling legislation and with the following five principles of rational regulation. First, agencies must consider adequate information in formulating rules. Second, initial cost-benefit/analyses must be performed on *all* rule proposals to determine whether a *major rule* is present. Third, regulatory objectives should maximize net benefits to society and regulatory action taken only if societal benefits outweigh the costs. Fourth, alternative proposals must be considered. Fifth, all regulatory proposals should be correlated to reduce conflicts. Each *major rule* must be subjected to extensive cost-benefit/analysis and a *Regulatory Impact Analysis* prepared to justify the rulemaking.

Sixty days prior to publication of rulemaking proposal in the Federal Register, the agency must transmit a *preliminary impact analysis* to OMB. A period of informal consultation between OMB and the agency may follow and result in modification of the proposal. After publication and the opportunity for public comments, the rule may again be revised. The agency must then prepare a *final impact analysis* and transmit it to OMB for regulatory review. If OMB has conflicting *views* about the rule or the *impact analysis*, the agency must respond to it on the record. Final publication and the effective date follow this economic consultation and justification process.

Some problems exist with economic justification of regulation. First, ex parte contacts occur and are not usually recorded making it difficult for interested parties to respond to the contact or for courts to review the whole record. Second, Executive Order No. 12,291 is not judicially reviewable, so the methodologies used to justify regulations are not open to public scrutiny or effective expert criticism. Third, there are no time constraints on the OMB review and clearance procedures which allows OMB discretion to slow or halt rulemaking. Fourth, tangible or immediate costs are much easier to quantify than intangible or future costs or benefits. This reduces the accuracy of cost-benefit/analyses. For these reasons it is important for regulated entities and the public affected by rule proposals to participate in the process. For example, the submission of comments and the criticism of assumptions, methodologies, and projections could help refine the impact analyses.

G. Executive Order No. 12,498

The unified policy conformance directive in Executive Order No. 12,498 (E. O. #12,498) is designed to complement the economic justification procedures in Executive Order No. 12,291. Several of the procedural steps are combined into comprehensive Presidential oversight conducted by OMB. Under E. O. #12,498 the heads of agencies must strive to conform the regulatory programs overseen by their agencies to the specific policies of the President's Administration. E. O. #12,498 is designed to increase the accountability of agencies, minimize duplication and conflicts in regulation and enhance the public and Congressional understanding of Administration Policies.

The order requires an annual publication of a coordinated Administration Regulatory Program in May. This program describes the expected *significant regulatory actions* which will be taken by all agencies which are directly responsible to the President. This includes all department level agencies (i.e. Agriculture, Commerce, Education, Energy, Health and Human Services, Housing and Urban Development, Interior, Justice, Labor, Transportation, Treasury) as well as the EPA, EFOC, GSA, SBA, VA, and the Office of Personnel Management. A two-step process is created for (1) clearance of each agency's regulatory program and (2) public notification of the Administration's program. Each agency head must compile all expected *significant regulatory actions* into a *draft regulatory program* and transmit it to OMB. *Ex parte* discussions between the agency and OMB or other administration entities may result in revisions of the regulatory program consistent with the prevailing view of Administration policy. A *final regulatory program* is prepared for inclusion in the Administration's overall plan.

Agencies must report expected *significant regulatory actions* which are steps towards adoption of a rule. These include *pre-rulemaking actions* which are in consideration of rulemaking, publication of notices, seek comments, initiate research or information gathering, preliminary policy proposals, or otherwise might lead to rulemaking. *Rulemaking actions* are also significant regulatory actions taken after rules are drafted and lead toward the actual "notice and comment" processes. Together with the biannual *unified agendas* outlining expected rulemaking, the regulatory program outlined in E. O. #12,498 puts regulated entities on notice of the likely regulatory actions which may affect them.

VII. Agency Disclosures Under the Freedom of Information Act

The pervasive investigatory powers of most regulators provides access to considerable private information. Prior to the passage of the Freedom of Information (FOIA) in 1966 it was widely felt that agencies acted too secretively. Agency processes were generally closed to public scrutiny so they appeared unresponsive to the public will. Congress intended the FOIA to increase agency accountability by opening agency files to public interest groups, scholars, and journalists. Public monitoring by outsiders arguably enhances agency fairness.

Every president since George Washington has claimed a constitutional right to exempt sensitive information from public disclosure. This doctrine of *executive privilege* has been used to withhold information from the public and from Congress. Until 1966 most federal agencies made similar claims to withhold information from the public. However, the FOIA mandates convenient disclosure of all agency files unless a specific exemption shields the information from disclosure. The FOIA was passed as an amendment to the APA. It is organized into three sections. Subsection (a) mandates disclosure and the process for accessing information. Subsection (b) exempts disclosure of certain types of agency files at the agency's discretion. Subsection (c) denies use of the exemptions in (b) when Congress is seeking information.

The FOIA requires all agencies, departments, and independent commissions to publish their organization, functions, and decisions. Agencies must index all these matters so that the public may locate them and rely on the agencies opinions and findings. All reasonably well-described requests for records from whatever internal agency source must be disclosed, if the request is made in accordance with the agency's published rules. The agency may charge reasonable fees for document search and photocopying. The agency may decline to charge a fee when it decides that free or reduced fee disclosure is in the public interest.

When agencies are reluctant to provide information, a complaint can be made to the United States District Courts seeking a injunction against the agency's withholding of records. Agencies must respond with a notice of intent to comply to information requests within 10 working days of its receipt. An appeal may be made to the agency's head when a lower echelon official withholds disclosure. These appeals must be processed within 20 working days. The agency or the courts may extend the time if *unusual circumstances* arise such as voluminous requests or the need for consultation with other agencies with a substantial interest in the matters to be disclosed. The United States District Court may issue contempt citations against agency personnel for refusing to comply with court ordered disclosure.

A. FOIA Exemptions

On first examination, it appears that the FOIA opens all government records to public scrutiny. However, both executive privilege and the ten major FOIA exemptions permit agencies to withhold many documents. First, disclosure is excused where the President issues an Executive order to keep secret any matter of *national defense* or *foreign policy*. Many foreign governments, acting through intermediaries, use the FOIA to access agency data. Therefore, this exemption is crucial for national security.

The second exemption shields the *internal personnel rules and practices* of an agency. For example, the sick leave, vacation, or parking policies of agencies are considered irrelevant to monitoring agencies' public policy activities. The third exemption recognizes exemptions contained in other *statutes*. The fourth exempts *trade secrets, commercial, or financial* information which are privileged or confidential concerning regulated entities. However, this exemption simply permits the agency to protect confidential information, it does not require confidentiality. Therefore, the individual or business who could be damaged by disclosure has no right to halt the disclosure.

The fifth exemption protects the disclosure of *inter-agency* or *intra-agency* memoranda or letters which represent the agency's internal deliberative process. Without this exemption there would be a chilling effect on the frank policy discussions and enforcement priorities among agency personnel. The sixth exempts *personnel or medical files* because their disclosure would invade the privacy of agency personnel. The seventh exempts *investigatory* files compiled for law enforcement purposes. Their disclosure should be withheld if it would (a) interfere with enforcement proceedings, (b) deprive a person of a fair trial, (c) disclose a confidential source or investigatory techniques, or (d) endanger the safety of law enforcement officials.

The eighth exempts *condition reports* of financial institutions. This exemption supports the bank secrecy ethic which developed after the Great Depression. It is believed that confidence in the banking system is fragile and crucial to the health of the economy. Loss in confidence may result in a destructive run on a bank. This FOIA exemption restricts public access to sensitive bank condition information. The ninth exempts geological and geophysical information concerning oil and gas wells because it is proprietary information. The final exemption protects the disclosure of trade secrets to competitors.

The selective release of information by agencies may represent an abuse of its discretion. If an agency publicly discloses or leaks information, a private entity's trade secrets may be lost destroying a competitive advantage. An agency that threatens disclosure of confiden-

tial information to force settlement or compliance is clearly abusing its discretion. In such cases, the information supplier may sue for a protective order. The Justice Department may prosecute disclosures that are illegal under the Trade Secrets Act. However, such issues are not ripe for adjudication until after the disclosure is made and the damage may already be done. In the alternative, regulated entities may seek judicial review of an agency's decision to release information. However, many agencies do not notify the suppliers of information before disclosing confidences.

VIII. Judicial Review

When regulated entities are dissatisfied with agency decisions, the courts may intervene. However, there are a group of technical defenses that may prevent judicial review because of efficiency and separation of powers. The party seeking court reversal of an administrative determination may be required to show that: (1) all administrative remedies have been exhausted, (2) the issue is ripe for judicial determination, (3) the party has standing to appeal, (4) the agency does not have primary jurisdiction over the matter, (5) the suit is not barred by immunity, or (6) the agency exceeded its authority or acted unreasonably.

A. Jurisdiction
The availability of judicial review depends on the enabling legislation or a related statute that provides for specific procedures. Where no specific statutory provision exists, the *common law writs* are available for partial relief. For example, an *injunction* may be issued to restrain an agency from taking an action which would cause irreparable harm. A *declaratory judgment* may pronounce the legality of an agency's action. A writ of *mandamus* orders an agency official to perform a non-discretionary act or perhaps to exercise its discretion.

Example. As a government contractor, the Chrysler Corporation was required to report on the affirmative action procedures it employs to avoid discrimination. The Department of Labor's Office of Federal Contract Compliance Programs requires defense contractors to submit the details of their affirmative action programs to the Defense Logistics Agency. Regulations also require these submissions be made public under the FOIA. However, Chrysler claimed the methods it developed in its affirmative action program were unique, providing it a competitive advantage. Chrysler instituted a "reverse-FOIA" suit to enjoin the agency from publicly disclosing its affirmative action compliance methods. This raised the question whether a regulated entity that provides information to a agency has standing to enforce the FOIA exemption for trade secrets and commercial or financial information.

The FOIA is a disclosure statute that attempts to open up the workings of government. The FOIA exemption simply states the materials specified may be withheld in the agency's discretion. It is up to the agency to determine whether confidentiality would further the regulatory program. Congress did not design the FOIA exemptions to become mandatory bars against disclosure to be invoked by the regulated entity submitting the information. Chrysler and other regulated entities have no right to halt FOIA disclosures. ☐

A companion concept to jurisdiction is the *statutory preclusion* of judicial review in which APA denies judicial review in two situations. Judicial review is precluded if a statute precludes review or the matter is committed to agency discretion. Most agency actions are reviewable unless there is clear and convincing Congressional intent to bar judicial review. Courts often go to great lengths to permit at least some limited review. For example, the denial of veterans benefits is precluded from review, but the statutory classification of which veterans are denied benefits may be reviewed if they are unconstitutional. Military draft and dishonorable discharge matters are generally precluded from review. However, in one instance the pre-induction behavior of some recruits was illegally considered by their draft board, so judicial review was permitted.

Agency decisions which are committed to agency discretion are often considered non-reviewable such as political matters. Matters affecting national defense or foreign policy are generally unreviewable. For example, the President's decision to modify the licensing of air routes to foreign nations is a political rather than judicial matter. Judicial review is also precluded where agency discretion is given to managerial matters.

B. Standing

The Constitution grants judicial power to the courts only in "cases or controversies." This is a limitation on access to the courts to assure the parties have genuine adverse interests providing sufficient incentive to gather facts and fully argue the facts and law. Collusive suits between non-adversarial parties are likely to produce poorly reasoned precedent. Any person seeking judicial review must be a real party in interest to sufficiently identify their affected interest to the outcome of the litigation. The APA provides standing to any person "adversely affected or aggrieved by agency action."

The modern test for standing requires the plaintiff to show that the agency's action caused injury in fact. Injuries may be economic, environmental, or aesthetic. In one case the Sierra Club sought to halt the development of a ski resort which would have cut through the Sequoia National Forest. Threats to aesthetic, recreational, and environmental interests could confer sufficient standing to sue. However, the Sierra Club failed to allege any direct impact on its membership so it was denied standing. The plaintiff must not only allege injury to protected interests, but must be among those who are injured.

C. Exhaustion of Administrative Remedies

The exhaustion doctrine appears on first blush to be the essence of administrative "red tape." Judicial review is postponed until all administrative procedures are pursued completely. This prevents a plaintiff from short circuiting the agency's internal process. In most cases an agency's final order must be issued before judicial review is allowed.

The exhaustion doctrine serves a legitimate purpose of permitting full development of the facts and expertise from within the agency before the courts step in. The agency's expertise and discretion should be exercised completely and entered on the record to facilitate accurate decisions. This permits the agency to correct its own mistakes eliminating unnecessary judicial review. An agency's autonomy is undermined by excessive judicial review, so the courts initially defer until the agency's internal procedures have run their course.

Exceptions to the exhaustion doctrine have developed where the agency efficiency is not critical. If the agency becomes deadlocked or further proceedings would be futile judicial review may interrupt incomplete agency process. For example, the selective service (military draft) system announced that it would not grant student deferments for anti-war demonstrators. Judicial review was permitted because exhaustion would be futile given the agency's announced attitude. Additionally, where agency actions are not authorized by statute or where Constitutional questions arise, judicial review may precede an exhaustion of remedies.

D. Primary Jurisdiction

The doctrine of primary jurisdiction is similar to the exhaustion doctrine in that the courts must defer to agency action. However, primary jurisdiction recognizes the agency's special expertise or competence. Courts interpretations of regulations can lead to inconsistent results. An agency with some special expertise is best suited to make the initial factual determinations. Primary jurisdiction does not apply if the matter is non-technical or there are other legal issues. The primary jurisdiction doctrine has been applied primarily in transportation, labor, and antitrust contexts. These areas combine expert influence and policy considerations best instituted by the agency. After a full record is compiled, the courts may then review the agency's discretion for conformity with legal standards.

E. Ripeness

Ripeness of an issue for appeal focuses on the fitness of the issues themselves for judicial determination at the time of suit. An issue is not ripe for review unless the issues are fit for immediate review and the parties will suffer hardship if the agency's decision is not immediately reviewed. Issues that are factual, require expertise, or are policy determinations are usually unfit for judicial review. Where the potential harm to the parties is great, the court should consider the issue as ripe.

Most ripeness cases arise where the agency has not yet taken any action against the plaintiff. Instead the plaintiff expects to be affected sometime in the future and seeks to truncate agency action. For example, in two cases the ripeness of challenges of FDA decisions were considered. In the first, the FDA determined that drug labels must include the generic name of the drug. The issue was ripe where one plaintiff questioned the FDA's power to require labeling. However, where FDA inspectors went prospecting for the misuse of color additives in cosmetics, the cosmetic

Example. The Bureau of Public Roads and the Federal Highway Administration approved the location of a six-lane interstate highway, Interstate 40, to run through Overton Park in Memphis, Tenn. Overton Park is the city's big park with 342 acres, a zoo, municipal golf course, outdoor theater, nature trails, bridle path, art academy, picnic areas, and 170 acres of forest. The proposed interstate would sever the zoo from the rest of the park and destroy 26 acres of Overton Park. Federal funding for construction of the roadway could not be released until the U.S. Secretary of Transportation determined that there was no feasible and prudent alternative to use of existing parkland and the program includes all possible planning to minimize harm to parkland used in a right of way. This raised the question whether the agencies determination was subject to judicial review under the arbitrary, unreasonable, and abuse of discretion standard.

An agency must have considered the relevant factors required by the law. If there is no abuse of discretion, the agency followed the prescribed procedures, and there was no clear error of judgment, the courts are not permitted to simply substitute their judgment for that of the agency. However, the absence of an adequate record of the agency's deliberations requires re-examination of that issue. □

producers had not yet been affected so their suit was premature until charged by the FDA of the misuse. The issue must be ripe in the sense that legal issues are presented and potential harm to the plaintiff is imminent.

F. Immunity

In early history, governments were headed by persons of royal bloodline. Often monarchs were considered divine so they were incapable of doing any wrong. Indeed, the sovereign immunity doctrine prohibits suit against the government or its officials because "the king can do no wrong." Today the fallibility of government is apparent so new justifications for sovereign immunity have developed: suit against governments impose an intolerable financial burden and the threat of suit unduly limits the discretion of leaders. In most cases, damages arising out of discretionary policy actions of the federal and local governments are barred by discretionary immunity.

No immunity exists where government perform acts that a private person could be held liable for. Statutes and court decisions expose most governments to negligence suits. For example, the Federal Tort Claims Act waives the sovereign immunity of the United States government. Private plaintiffs injured by federal conduct that is negligent or involves intentional assault, battery, false imprisonment, false arrest or abuse of process may sue the federal government. However, no suit may be brought against the United States on any of the following theories: strict liability for ultrahazardous activities, defamation, misrepresentation, trespass, or interference with contract relations. The APA allows suit against the United States if money damages are not sought and no person suffers wrong due to an agency action.

G. Scope of Review

An aggrieved party able to overcome the constraints of jurisdiction, standing, ripeness, exhaustion, primary jurisdiction, or sovereign immunity, face one final issue. The court must decide *how* to review the administrative agency's action. There are two primary standards for the *scope of review* of agency decisions: substantial evidence or arbitrary, capricious or an abuse of discretion.

The *substantial evidence* test is used in both state and federal court reviews of administrative fact finding. An agency's fact determinations should be set aside on judicial review if they are unsupported by substantial evidence. Substantial evidence is satisfied if sufficient evidence exists so that a reasonable mind might accept it as adequate to support a conclusion. Substantial evidence requires that there be at least some evidence supporting the agency's conclusion. However, this amount of evidence may be far less convincing than the evidence required for a criminal conviction (beyond a reasonable doubt), for significant deprivations (clear and convincing evidence), or for civil damage judgments (preponderance of the evidence or greater weight of evidence). The court need only find that there is some evidence supporting the agency's decision and that the agency considered the evidence offered by both sides in the case.

A different standard applies in cases where agencies dictate policy or exercise discretion such as in informal rulemaking, investigations, or prosecutions. Discretionary agency decisions will be overturned on review only where they are made arbitrarily, capriciously, or with an abuse of discretion. A reviewing court may overturn an agency's discretionary decision if inappropriate factors were considered, appropriate factors were not considered, or clear errors of judgment were made. This review standard gives agencies broad discretion in most policy matters.

* * *

Problems

1. What are the basic justifications offered for government regulation of business activity? What type of regulatory activities do these justifications suggest?

2. The administrator of the National Tourist Board (NTB) has decided to attract Japanese travelers to U.S. vacation sites. The administrator has established a three part regulatory system de-

signed to give Japanese visitors preference in several desirable vacation areas: the Colorado Rockies, the Miami Beach area, the Blue Ridge Mountains, and the Oregon coastal area. The administrator promulgates three regulations applicable to all lodging and restaurant establishments in the areas mentioned. First, reservations made by U.S. citizens must be cancelled if necessary to make room for Japanese visitors. Second, all restaurants must carry at least 50% Japanese food items on their menus. Third, these establishments may advertise only in Japanese magazines, newspapers, and television. What legislative controls might Congress exercise over the NTB to prevent implementation of these regulations? What other controls might be effective in eliminating these regulations?

3. In the problem above, who might have standing to attack the NTB regulations? What arguments might be offered against judicial review of the NTB regulations? What standard of judicial review would be used?

4. During World War II Congress established price controls to permit a fair distribution of goods while rationing existed. The Office of Price Administration (OPA) was created to establish and enforce maximum "fair" prices. Merchants convicted of selling above the maximum prices established by OPA regulations sued the agency claiming the enabling act was an unconstitutional delegation of the legislature's responsibility to oversee prices. Does the delegation doctrine apply to the actions of this agency?

5. A university rule permits instructors who suspect students of cheating to summarily dismiss them from their programs without a hearing. What argument does a student dismissed under this rule have concerning the legality of this process?

6. The federal Mine Safety and Health Act of 1977 requires the inspection of all underground mine facilities at least four times each year to determine compliance with the Act's health and safety standards. Surprise inspections are authorized. The Secretary of Labor may seek an injunc-

tion requiring inspection if a mine operator refuses access to the inspector. Does the rule requiring the inspector to obtain a warrant based on administrative probable cause apply here? Would the answer be different if the problem involved a state day-care center regulation statute?

3 Constitutional Law

Constitutional Law

I. General Framework

A. Introduction

1. FEDERALISM

Following the Revolutionary War, the original thirteen states did not have a central form of government. Under the Articles of Confederation, they operated as closely knit but sovereign, independent units. It soon became apparent, particularly in the area of business and commerce, that they would have to cooperate to deal with common problems. At the same time, the states wanted to be free to act independently in matters that did not affect the whole. The method chosen to accomplish this objective is called Federalism, generally defined as the division of authority between and among two or more governing units. The United States Constitution, ratified on September 17, 1787 by representatives of the thirteen original states, is the document through which the principles of Federalism were established. Professor Mary A. Hepburn, University of Georgia and Director of the Constitution 200 Project, summarizes the concept of federalism as follows:

> Perhaps the most fundamental question that the Framers had to decide was the power relationship between the national government and the states. At the Philadelphia convention, some delegates proposed a nation where the states would hold the greatest power. Others, led by James Madison, argued for a supreme national government with power to overrule the states. The result is a government in which the *Constitution and the laws of the United States which shall be made in pursuance thereof . . . shall be the supreme law of the land* (Article VI). It is, however, also a government in *which the powers not delegated to the United States by the Constitution, nor prohibited by it to the States, are reserved to the State respectively, or to the people* (Tenth Amendment). This system of shared power between the federal government and the states has come to be called "federalism." Although clearly stated, this concept leaves room for disagreement regarding the scope of national power and ultimate sovereignty, implying an ongoing tension between state and federal governments as major public issues arise.[1]

B. Constitutional Overview— Separation and Division of Powers and Individual Liberties

The Constitution can be divided into two parts. First, creation, separation and division of powers which is contained in Articles I through III. Article I creates and defines legislative power. Article II creates and defines executive power. Article III creates and defines judicial power. As a fundamental principle of constitutional law, it is important to recognize that although these powers are separate and apart, they are internally subject to a system of check and balances. For example, Arti-

---

1. Constitution 200 A Bicentennial Collection of Essays 1 (M. Hepburn ed. (1988).

cle 1, Section 7 gives the executive the power to veto all legislation; Article II, Section 2 allows the Senate to detain confirmation of Presidential appointees; and most importantly for purposes of this chapter, Article III the federal courts the power of judicial review.

The remaining Articles, IV through VII, generally do not receive the same attention as the first three; however, a number of them are deserving of brief comment so that a more complete general understanding of the Constitution can be gained. Article IV, Section 2 contains the Privileges and Immunities Clause which provides for equality of treatment of the citizens of all states. That is, when a state confers benefits on its own citizens, citizens of other states are entitled to the same benefits unless there is substantial justification for different treatment. Article V deals with the process of Constitutional Amendment. Article VI contains the Supremacy Clause which provides that the Constitution, laws made pursuant thereto and treaties are the supreme law of the land. Furthermore, state judges are bound by the United States Constitution even if state law is to the contrary. Article VII no longer has any applicability since it deals with ratification of the Constitution by nine of the original thirteen states.

Second, basic individual rights and liberties are initially contained in the first ten amendments, known as the Bill of Rights, adopted in 1791. (As noted above, Article V establishes the amendment process.) Subsequently, sixteen amendments have been adopted. The last or XXVI Amendment was adopted in 1971. It deals with the right of citizens who are eighteen years of age or older to vote and reflects the continuing concern of Congress for individual rights. Amendment activity continues to the present day. For example, in 1971-72 Congress overwhelmingly passed the Equal Rights Amendment (ERA) which was not ratified by the states before the end of the seven year period ended in 1979 as provided

for in the amendment. It stated: "Equality of rights under the law shall not be denied or abridged by the United States or by any state on account of sex." Most recently, in light of increasingly frequent flag burning incidents and the refusal of the Supreme Court to decide against it, a number of politicians have argued that an amendment should be added which prohibits it.

C. Scope of Chapter

One chapter in a business law textbook cannot begin to do justice to the subject of United States Constitutional law. Brief as the Constitution may be, its construction and interpretation is much too complex. Nevertheless, this chapter will deal with a number of general, broad ranging principles of constitutional law that have an impact upon business and society and specific sections of the constitution that directly affect the conduct and regulation of local, state, national and international business. To that end, and within the framework of the first three Articles of the Constitution as outlined above, this chapter will first examine the concept of national and state legislative, executive and judicial power. It will then examine the Commerce Clause and Taxing Power contained in Article I, Section 8 of the Constitution because of their continuing and significant impact upon the business community. Lastly, this chapter will focus upon a number of important individual freedoms, in particular those provisions of the Fifth and Fourteenth Amendments dealing with due process and equal protection, the provision of the First Amendment dealing with freedom of speech, and the provision of the Fourth Amendment dealing with search and seizure.

II. Legislative, Judicial and Executive Power

A. Legislative Power

Constitutional authority for Congress to legislate is specifically granted in Article 1, Section 1. The scope of legislation is regulated by Section 8 of the same Article which, among many other specific provisions, expressly grants Congress the power to "lay and collect Taxes . . . regulate Commerce with foreign Nations, and among the several States . . . coin Money . . . constitute Tribunals inferior to the supreme Court . . . and To make all Laws which are necessary and proper for carrying into Execution the foregoing Powers." This final provision in Section 8 is known as the Necessary and Proper clause.

In the landmark case of *McCulloch v. Maryland*[2] the Supreme Court interpreted the Necessary and Proper clause to give Congress broad implied powers to implement the express powers enumerated in Section 8. The fundamental question in the case was whether the legislative power given to Congress authorized it to incorporate a national bank. Even though no express provision existed, Chief Justice Marshall concluded that by combining express powers with the Necessary and Proper clause, Congress had broad implied powers to legislate. Hence, the bank was allowed to incorporate not because of an expressly stated Section 8 power, but because a connection existed between the express powers to "lay and collect taxes; to borrow money; to regulate commerce; to declare and conduct a war, and to raise and support armies and navies"[3] and the bank. In a famous statement from the case, Chief Justice Marshall said the test for federal power to legislate is as follows:

Let the end be legitimate, let it be within the scope of the constitution, and all means which are appropriate, which are plainly adapted to that end, which are not prohibited, but consist with the letter and spirit of the constitution, are constitutional.[4]

B. Executive Power

Although Article II creates an executive branch of government by vesting executive power in a President, it does not directly give the President legislative power. The President's legislative influence stems primarily from the political process of legislative recommendations and veto power. Article I, Section 7, for example, requires every bill passed by Congress to be signed by the President. His veto can be overridden by a two thirds vote of Congress. The President also has a direct impact upon legislation through political appointments (for example appointment of members to the Nuclear Regulatory Commission and Federal Trade Commission), executive orders and proclamations.

In the foreign arena, under Article II, Section 2., an important power given by the Constitution to the President is to make treaties with the advice and consent of two thirds of the Senators present. Article VI provides that treaties enjoy supremacy over state law to the extent an inconsistency exists. Undoubtedly, the President, through his constitutional power to enter into treaties and agreements with foreign nations is going to have increasing influence over international business ventures as the United States works outs its relationships with the European Common Market in the mid 1990s.

---

2. 17 U S. (4 Wheat.) 316, 4 L Ed. 579 (1819)
3. 17 U.S. (4 Wheat.) at 407.

---

4. 17 U.S. (4 Wheat.) at 421.

C. Judicial Power

1. FEDERAL JURISDICTION

Article III vests judicial power "in one su-preme Court, and in such inferior Courts as the Congress may from time to time ordain and establish." Article III, Section 2 further provides that those courts have jurisdiction only over certain constitutionally defined "cases" or "controversies." The two most well-know situations are those arising under the Constitution and between citizens of differ-ent states. With respect to disputes between citizens of different states, as seen in Chapter 1., Congress decides the amount ($50,000) that must be controversy for federal jurisdic-tion to arise. The Article III case or controver-sy requirement has been interpreted by the Supreme Court to mean that in addition to meeting the constitutionally mandated juris-dictional requirements, the matter presented to the court must be adversarial in nature and capable of judicial resolution. Thus, the juris-diction of federal courts does not extend to advisory opinions.

Section 2 further provides that the Supreme Court has original jurisdiction in all cases af-fecting ambassadors, public ministers and consuls and those where a state is a party. In all other applicable cases, the Supreme Court has appellate jurisdiction. Appeals can be tak-en from the various courts shown in the dia-gram below directly to the Supreme Court.

2. JUDICIAL REVIEW

One of the crucial questions raised by the Constitution is the relationship between the Constitution itself and law enacted by Con-gress, state governments and acts of the exec-utive. This question was answered in the famous case of *Marbury v. Madison*[5] where the Supreme Court unequivocally held that the Courts have a duty to determine whether

5. U.S. (1 Cranch) 137, 2 L. Ed. 60 (1803)

or not a legislative act violates any provisions of the Constitution, and if it does, the man-dates of the Constitution control. In support of its conclusion, the Court, in part, stated:

Certainly all those who have framed written constitutions contemplate them as forming the fundamental and paramount law of the na-tion, and consequently, the theory of every such government must be, that an act of the legislature, repugnant to the constitution, is void.

This theory is essentially attached to a writ-ten constitution, and, is consequently to be considered, by this court, as one of the funda-mental principles of our society. It is not, therefore, to be lost sight of in the further con-sideration of this subject.

If an act of the legislature, repugnant to the constitution, is void, does it, notwithstanding its invalidity, bind the courts, and oblige them to give it effect? Or, in other words, though it be not law, does it constitute a rule as opera-tive as if it was a law? This would be to over-throw in fact what was established in theory; and would seem, at first view, an absurdity too gross to be insisted on....

It is emphatically the province and duty of the judicial department to say what the law is. Those who apply the rule to particular cases, must of necessity expound and interpret that rule. If two laws conflict with each other, the courts must decide on the operation of each.

So if a law be in opposition to the constitu-tion; if both the law and the constitution apply to a particular case, so that the court must ei-ther decide that case conformably to the law, disregarding the constitution; or conformably to the constitution, disregarding the law; the court must determine which of these conflict-ing rules governs the case. This is of the very essence of judicial duty.

If, then, the courts are to regard the consti-tution, and the constitution is superior to any ordinary act of the legislature, the constitution and not such ordinary act, must govern the case to which they both apply.

Those then, who controvert the principle that the constitution is to be considered, in court, as a paramount law, are reduced to the necessity of maintaining that courts must

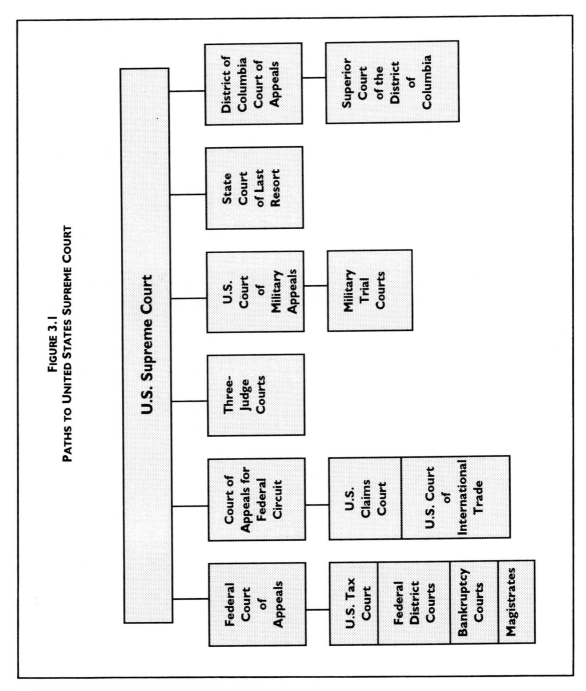

FIGURE 3.1
PATHS TO UNITED STATES SUPREME COURT

close their eyes on the constitution, and see only the law.

This doctrine would subvert the very foundation of all written constitutions. It would declare that an act which, according to the principles and theory of our government, is entirely void, is yet, in practice, completely obligatory. It would declare that if the legislature shall do what is expressly forbidden, such act, notwithstanding the express prohibition, is in reality effectual.... It is prescribing limits, and declaring that those limits may be passed at pleasure.... The judicial power of the United States is extended to all cases arising under the constitution. Could it be the intention of those who gave this power, to say that in using it the constitution should not be looked into? That a case arising under the constitution should be decided without examining the instrument under which it arises? This is too extravagant to be maintained.[6]

Due in part to scarce judicial resources, the maintenance of judicial independence and integrity, the avoidance of sensitive political issues and the need for flexibility, the scope of judicial review has been limited by the application of so-called "gatekeeping rules." Courts can choose to ignore them or apply them in a way as to reach a desired result. Several of these rules or doctrines are as follows: (1) There must be standing to sue. This means that not only must a party who invokes judicial review be able to demonstrate that a statute is unconstitutional, but also that he suffered or was threatened with personal injury. For example, in a well publicized environmental law case from the 1970's, the Supreme Court held that the Sierra Club had no standing to prevent a proposed ski area development because the Sierra Club failed to allege that it or its members would be effected in any of their activities by the development.[7] (2) There must be mootness. This means that a court must have a means of

granting relief. Standing to sue might exist at the outset, but subsequent events could make the issue moot. For example, the states failure to ratify the Equal Rights Amendment made pending law suits based upon extending the ratification deadline from 1979 to 1982 moot. (3) There must be ripeness. This means that the case must not be premature. There must be a present injury or the threat of injury. For example, in a leading case dealing with the ripeness doctrine, plaintiff-employees sought to prevent enforcement of the Hatch Act which prohibited federal employees from engaging in political activity. At the time the law suit was brought, they had not engaged in any political activities. The Court concluded that "A hypothetical threat is not enough. We can only speculate as to the kinds of political activity the appellants desire to engage in or as to the contents of their proposed public statements or the circumstances of their publication."[8]

III. The Commerce Clause and Taxing Power

A. Regulation of Interstate Commerce

I. COMMERCE DEFINED

One would expect the early view of commerce to differ markedly from the modern view where telecommunications, Concord jet travel and multinational corporations are a standard, twentieth century fact of business life. Insurance represents a classic example of the two points of view. In 1868,[9] the Supreme Court sustained a tax on a foreign insurance company as a condition of doing business in a state when no comparable tax was imposed

---

6. U.S. (1 Cranch) at 177-78.
7. *Sierra Club v. Morton*, 405 U.S. 727, 92 S.Ct. 1361, 31 L. Ed.2d 636 (1972).

8. *United Public Workers v. Mitchell*, 330 U.S. 75, 89, 67 S Ct. 556, 564, 91 L.Ed. 754 (1947).
9. *Paul v. Virginia*, 75 U.S. (8 Wall.) 168, 19 L.Ed. 357 (1868).

on local insurance companies. The Commerce Clause did not apply because insurance was not commerce. The Court concluded that:

> The policies are simple contract of indemnity against loss by fire, entered into between the corporations and the assured, for a consideration paid by the latter. These are not articles of commerce in any proper meaning of the word. They are not subjects of trade and barter offered in the market as something having an existence and value independent of the parties to them. They are not commodities to be shipped or forwarded from one State to another, and then put up for sale. They are like other personal contracts between parties which are completed by their signature and the transfer of the consideration. Such contracts are not inter-state transactions, though the parties are domiciled in different States. The policies do not take effect—are not executed contracts—until delivered by the agent in Virginia. They are, then, local transactions, and are governed by the local law. They do not constitute a part of the commerce between the States....[10]

Under the modern view, commerce deals not only with the purchase, sale and exchange of tangible "articles of commerce in any proper meaning of the word," but also with the instrumentalities and agencies used to foster them. Commerce has come to be broadly defined. The business of insurance, therefore, is now clearly commerce within the meaning of the Commerce Clause as is the performance of a service. Interstate commerce is commerce between or among two or more states including all the component parts of commercial intercourse such as entering another state to make a sale, making a telephone call, sending letters or reports and advertising among the various states.

---

10. Id. 75 U.S. (8 Wall.) at 183.

2. STATE REGULATION OF INTERSTATE COMMERCE

One of the inherent weaknesses of the Articles of Confederation was the inability to regulate interstate and foreign commerce.[11] The result was harmful trade wars among the states and the failure to present a united front in foreign commerce. The need to eliminate this problem was an important incentive for including in the Constitution Article I, Section 8, Clause 3 which gives Congress the power "To regulate Commerce with foreign Nations, and among the several States...."

Supreme Court interpretation of Commerce Clause application was substantially divided until the mid-1800s. One view was that regulation of commerce was exclusively a federal power, hence any state regulation thereof was invalid. Another view was that commerce power was concurrent or shared between Congress and the states. Under this view, states were free to regulate if Congress had not already acted in the same area. The turning point came in 1851 with the formulation of the *Cooley* doctrine.[12] Under this doctrine, if the subject of the regulation was national in scope, congressional power was exclusive. But if the subject of the legislation was local, concurrent power existed providing congress had not preempted the area. The concurrent power approach was now firmly established. More importantly, a standard based upon the scope of the subject was developed to judge a challenged state regulation. The major criticisms of the *Cooley* doctrine were that it focused on the subject and not the nature of the state regulation and that it provided no clear criteria for differentiating between legislation that was national or local in character. Finally, in 1945 the Court discarded the Cooley doctrine subject matter test for a balancing ap-

---

11. THE FEDERALIST No. 42 (J. Madison).
12. The Cooley doctrine was first enunciated by the Supreme Court in *Cooley v. Board of Wardens*, 53 U.S. (12 How.) 299, 13 L.Ed. 996 (1851).

Example. Based upon a safety rationale, the state of Arizona passed a law that prohibited trains with more than fourteen passenger cars or seventy freight cars from operating within the state. The law applied to over ninety percent of all freight and passenger train traffic in Arizona since it was interstate in nature. To comply with the law, Southern Pacific Co. had to make over thirty percent more train trips in Arizona than would otherwise be necessary, the practical effect being that a heavier burden was placed on interstate commerce than was placed upon intrastate commerce. Safety data showed that the increased safety resulting from shorter trains was more than offset by the increased number of trips required to carry the same number of passengers or amount of freight.

The court concluded that the Train Limit Law should be stricken since the burdens on interstate commerce outweighed the state's evidence of safety. In essence, by carefully examining the facts of the case, the court balanced the national and state interest in making a choice as to which should prevail. □

proach. Instead of inquiring into the national scope of the challenged regulation, it inquires into the nature or impact of the state regulation balancing local interests against the national interest in maintaining free and open interstate commerce. The balancing approach was first applied by the Supreme Court in *Southern Pacific Co. v. Arizona*[13] where its function as arbiter of the validity of state law affecting interstate commerce was firmly established. The facts in the following example are patterned after the *Southern Pacific Co.* case.

3. THE MODERN COMMERCE CLAUSE

Commerce power is both exclusive and concurrent. It is exclusive under the Supremacy Clause (Article VI) when federal and state commerce legislation conflict. It is concurrent in the sense that states are permitted to legislate in areas not preempted by Congress. Under the modern test, state commerce legislation will be upheld if (1) it does not arbitrarily discriminate against interstate commerce; (2) a legitimate public interest is involved; (3) the effects on interstate commerce

are only incidental; and (4) the incidental burdens are not excessive in relation to the putative local benefits. The Supreme Court explicitly stated the modern rule as follows:

Although the criteria for determining the validity of state statutes affecting interstate commerce have been variously stated, the general rule that emerges can be phrased as follows: Where the statute regulates evenhandedly to effectuate a legitimate local public interest, and its effect on interstate commerce are only incidental, it will be upheld unless the burden imposed on such commerce is clearly excessive in relation to the putative local benefits. If a legitimate local purpose is found, then the question becomes one of degree. And the extent of the burden that will be tolerated will of course depend on the nature of the local interest involved, and on whether it could be promoted as well with a lesser impact on interstate activities. Occasionally the Court has candidly undertaken a balancing approach in resolving these issues, but more frequently it has spoken in terms of "direct" and "indirect" benefits.[14]

---

13. 325 U.S. 761, 65 S.Ct. 1515, 89 L.Ed. 1915 (1945).

14. *Pike v. Bruce Church, Inc.*, 397 U.S. 137, 142, 90 S. Ct. 844, 847, 25 L. Ed. 174 (1970).

Example. State X, a dairy state, passed a law which required milk dealers in State X to pay a minimum price for milk no matter where it was purchased. As a result of State X's minimum price law, dealers in State X obviously would receive no benefit from buying out-of-state. City Y in State X passed a law which, for purported health reasons and reasons related to the convenience, economy and efficiency of inspection of the pasteurization plants, required pasteurized milk to be sold in a radius of no more than five miles from the plant.

Clearly, State X's law violates Commerce Clause standards. Its clear purpose is to discriminate against sellers of milk in other states who may be willing to sell at lower prices than local sellers in State X. It essence, it attempts to legislate milk prices in other states. City Y's law also violates Commerce Clause standards. Similar to the law of State X, it discriminates against interstate commerce. City Y's attempt to justify its law based upon local health interests would be rejected because reasonable, local, nondiscriminatory methods could be used to accomplish the same thing. City Y could, for example, have its own personnel inspectors for pasteurization and assess the cost to the seller. Similar to the *Southern Pacific Co*. case, the burden on interstate commerce outweighs the City's evidence of health and safety. □

4. A RELATED JURISDICTIONAL ISSUE—TAX NEXUS

Increased pressure on the states to find additional revenue sources has in part caused them to look towards revenues derived from interstate commerce. The modern rule is that assessment of state or local taxes on interstate commerce is permissible as long as the activity taxed has a substantial nexus with the taxing state, the tax is fairly apportioned, the tax does not discriminate against interstate commerce, and the tax is fairly related to the services provided by the state. Commerce clause requirements focus on fair apportionment and undue burden. Similarly, due process limitations focus upon nexus.

Relative to state and local taxation, nexus refers to the level of activity that must exist within a taxing jurisdiction before it can impose a tax. It requires some definite link, some minimum connection between the state and the property or transaction it seeks to tax. Nexus clearly exists where a business is incorporated and headquartered in a state. Nexus may not exist where a business does not have a clear physical presence in the state. Consider the business problems raised by the use tax collection issue in the booming mail order business. An order is mailed by a resident of State X to a mail-order company headquartered in State Z. If a use tax cannot be collected by State X from the buyer, local (State X) merchants would not be protected from out-of-state mail-order competitors since the product they sell will be subject to a sales tax, but the product ordered through the mails will not be subject to a corresponding use tax. Furthermore, even though use taxes are Constitu-tional, their collection is for all practical purposes impossible unless, similar to sales taxes, they are collected and remitted by the seller. There is, therefore, a direct relationship between the Commerce Clause and nexus. The courts generally agree in this situation that where there is a clear physical presence in the taxing state, jurisdictional nexus exists.

Another contemporary nexus issue deals with state income taxation of transportation.

The Commerce Clause, similar to the use tax example, will not prevent assessment of an income tax on interstate transportation. Nexus is the real issue since a number of states have accepted the argument that pass-through use of a state's highways, without additional contact, is sufficient to establish nexus. States believe that interstate motor carriers who use their highways derive some benefit or economic advantage from them. At the very least, the state has provided a bridge from one point to another. Therefore, the states have by case, statute, regulation, ruling or policy concluded that nexus exists even for limited use of their highways.

As interstate commerce becomes an increasingly integral part of doing business, the protection provided by the Commerce Clause takes on new importance. However, it does not provide full protection. Taxation is a prime example. Therefore, modern business by necessity is concerned with the close interplay between the Commerce Clause and jurisdictional nexus.

B. Taxing Power

No power given by the Constitution to Congress has a greater impact upon business and the economy than the power to tax as provided in Article 1, Section 8, clause I of the Constitution. Because Constitutional principles applicable to this power have been firmly established, the remaining discussion will briefly focus upon the source of federal tax law and the avenue taxpayers take to contest unfavorable tax decisions.

As enacted by Congress, federal tax statutes are incorporated into one document called the Internal Revenue Code which addresses income, estate and gift, employment, and a variety of excise taxes including alcohol and tobacco. In an administrative capacity (see Chapter 2), the Treasury Department issues Regulations as explanations and interpretations of the complex statutory language. Some Regulations have the same force and ef-

fect as legislation. In addition to the Code and Regulations, judicial decisions constitute an important source of tax law. Taxpayers can begin an action related to federal tax law in one of three federal courts, the U.S. Tax Court, the U.S. Claims Court or the U.S. District Court. Which court a taxpayer chooses depends upon a number of factors including precedents established in the various courts and timing of payment. If the taxpayer wants to start his action in the U.S. District Court or U.S. Claims Court, he is required to pay the contested tax and sue for a refund. If the taxpayer begins his action in the Tax Court, payment of any deficiency need not be made until the case is decided. Appeal from a decision of any one of these courts follows the route indicated in Figure 3.2.

IV. Individual Freedoms

A. Due Process of Law

I. GENERAL MEANING (FIFTH AND FOURTEENTH AMENDMENTS)

In addition to being protected by Constitutional separation of powers, individual rights and liberties are protected from interference by governmental power under the Fifth and Fourteenth Amendments. The Fifth Amendment limits the powers of the federal government by stating that no person shall be "deprived of life, liberty or property without due process of law." The Fourteenth Amendment, where the various fundamental guarantees contained in the Bill of Rights are selectively made applicable to the states, sets forth the same due process limitation on the powers of the states by stating that "nor shall any state deprive any person of life, liberty or property without due process of law."

The term due process of law generally has three different meaning s or applications. The first meaning relates to due process in the jurisdictional sense. If a state regulates or inter-

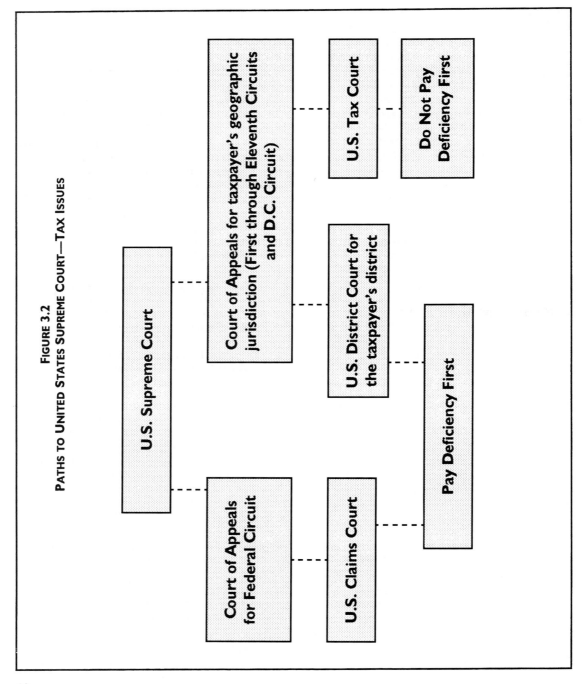

FIGURE 3.2
PATHS TO UNITED STATES SUPREME COURT—TAX ISSUES

feres with one's person or property which is outside its jurisdiction, it deprives that person of his individual liberties or property without due process of law. In the preceding section of this chapter, an example was given where a state attempted to impose an income tax on interstate motor carriers whose only connection with the state was that of passing through it. The question there, in part, was whether such a tax would violate the motor carrier's due process rights. Did the taxing state have the requisite jurisdiction or control over the motor carrier? The answer given was that there was sufficient nexus (connection) to give the taxing state jurisdiction and the right to assess an income tax. The second meaning, discussed below, relates to due process in the substantive sense. The third meaning, also discussed below, relates to due process in the procedural sense.

2. SUBSTANTIVE DUE PROCESS

Generally, due process of law in the substantive sense requires that state or federal legislation imposing a restraint on liberty or property have some rational basis grounded in public policy. There must be some reasonable connection between the restraint and the government's policy it is designed to foster. Substantive due process, therefore, prohibits arbitrary governmental action. To reiterate the discussion from chapter 1, it deals with the substance of the law rather than the procedures employed.

Until the mid-1930s, applying the reasonableness standard, the Court acted like a "super legislature" invalidating or supporting social welfare or economic legislation that came before it. Clear Constitutional guidelines did not exist for its action. For example, freedom of contract was thought to be an individual liberty protected by the Fourteenth Amendment; therefore, a state law setting maximum hours of employment for certain employees was invalidated because it unreasonably inter-

fered with the employer-employee right to contract.

Under modern law, with respect to social and economic legislation, the Court applies a "rational basis" test involving minimal judicial scrutiny. The state law will be upheld unless no reasonable set of facts could establish a rational relationship between the challenged law and a legitimate end of government. On the other hand, under modern law a different standard of review is applied where legislation invades a "fundamental right" which primarily includes freedom of association, voting, interstate travel, fairness in the criminal process and in claims against governmental deprivations of life, liberty, or property and privacy.

The "fundamental rights" standard of review is much stricter than the "rational basis" standard of review. It necessitates "strict scrutiny" to determine if questioned legislation is necessary to promote a compelling or overriding state interest. In *Roe v. Wade*,[15] a case that still divides large segments of the population, the Supreme Court found that a Texas law prohibiting abortion except to save the life of the mother was unconstitutional. The Court expanded the concept of personal privacy to include a woman's right to have an abortion. The Court went on to state:

> With respect to the State's important and legitimate interest in the health of the mother, the "compelling" point, in light of present medical knowledge, is at approximately the end of the first trimester. This is so because of the now-established fact, . . ., that until the end of the first trimester mortality in abortion cases may be less than mortality in normal childbirth. . .
>
> This means, . . . that, for the period of pregnancy prior to this "compelling" point, the attending physician, in consultation with his patient, is free to determine, without regulation by the State, that, in his medical judgment, the patient's pregnancy should be terminated. If

---

15. 410 U.S. 113, 93 S. Ct. 705, 35 L.Ed.2d 147 (1973).

Example. Suppose a state statute prohibited anyone from possessing a red jacket. Having a suspicion that D possessed a red jacket and had it hanging in his apartment clothes closet, the municipal police came to the apartment building, borrowed the manager's master key, and in D's absence, entered D's apartment and seized the red jacket from the clothes closet. D was charged with illegal possession of the red jacket.

D would protest that the search and seizure was in violation of Fourth Amendment rights and therefore constituted a procedural deprival of due process of law in violation of the Fourteenth Amendment. ☐

that decision is reached, the judgment may be effectuated by an abortion free of interference by the State.[16]

3. PROCEDURAL DUE PROCESS

Due process in the procedural sense means that a person's "life, liberty, or property" cannot be taken without the chance to be heard by a fair, impartial decision maker. Simply stated, a person is entitled to his day in court. Contrasted with substantive due process which relates more to the creation of property and liberty interests, procedural due process provides safeguards against their deprivation by requiring: (1) notice of the applicable proceeding, (2) a reasonable opportunity for a fair and impartial hearing, and (3) an impartial tribunal adjudicating the matter.

The average citizen tends to associate procedural due process with the bodily restraints imposed by the criminal process. The rules are similar in that procedural due process is denied if the process of obtaining evidence is not fair, that is in accordance with established policies and procedures.

Nevertheless, "liberty" and "property" interests have a broader meaning than that which is applied by the criminal process. A liberty interest can include the right to contract and the right to reputation. For example, a defamatory statement that results in loss of an employment opportunity deprives the defamed

person of a liberty interest. A property interest includes more than the actual ownership of real or personal property. For example, if a state statute creates an employment opportunity where the employee can be terminated only for cause, a property interest has been created by the contract.

The nature of the notice given and the scope of the hearing required to satisfy procedural due process need not always be as strict as that required in a formal court proceeding. It is much more flexible and depends upon (1) the nature of the interest involved, (2) the risk of depriving a person of the interest, and (3) the fiscal and administrative burdens imposed by the government following a set of prescribed procedures. For example, in a case dealing with dismissal of a student for academic reasons, the Supreme Court observed that there is a significant difference between procedural due process requirements in cases dealing with academic dismissal of a student than there is in disciplinary action against a student for violation of rules of conduct. Determination of a rule violation requires a hearing where the student can present his side of the factual issue. Dismissal for academic reasons does not require a hearing; therefore, procedural due process requirements are not nearly as strict.

Under the circumstances, we decline to ignore the historic judgment of educators and thereby formalize the academic process by requiring a hearing. The educational process is

---

16. 410 U.S. at 163, 93 S.Ct. at 731-32.

not by nature adversary; instead it centers around a continuing relationship between faculty and students.... We recognize ... that a hearing may be "useless or harmful in finding out the truth as to scholarship." (citation omitted)[17]

To summarize, jurisdictional due process requires that a court must have in some way acquired jurisdiction or control over the person or subject matter before the court. The rules relative to service of process as discussed in Chapter 1 are not the same as those necessary to satisfy the requirements of substantive and procedural due process. Simply stated, substantive due process requires that legislation be reasonable and not arbitrary whereas procedural due process requires that a defendant receive proper notice under the circumstances thus giving him an opportunity for his day in court.

B. Equal Protection

I. GENERAL MEANING (FOURTEENTH AMENDMENT)

In addition to the due process language, the Fourteenth Amendment, Section 1 states that "No state shall . . . deprive any person within its jurisdiction of the equal protection of the laws." Its purpose is to prohibit arbitrary governmental legislation by providing a guarantee that similar people will be treated in a similar manner. The equal protection provision does not prevent a government from classifying persons, but it does guarantee those classifications will not be based upon arbitrary standards or impermissible criteria. There is no equivalent language in the Fifth Amendment applicable to the federal government. However, it is implicit that if a federal law is arbitrary and unreasonable, it may violate the due process clause of the Fifth

Amendment on the theory that there is no rational policy reason for its existence. Hence, constitutional equal protection is applicable directly to state law and indirectly to federal law.

There is a close connection between substantive due process and equal protection. Both deal with the substance of the law and not the procedure employed to enforce it. Where a law limits the rights of all people to engage in a particular activity, it may be a substantive due process question. Where the law limits the rights of some people to engage in a particular activity, it may be an equal rights question. For example, if a state law prohibits the sale of beer to anyone in the state, it raises a substantive due process question. But if a state law prohibits the sale of beer to women only, it raises an equal protection problem based upon gender classification. Similarly, the tests or standards for determining whether an equal protection guarantee has been violated parallels the tests or standards applied in substantive due process cases.

2. STANDARDS OF REVIEW

Under modern law, two standards of review similar to those applicable to substantive due process cases have been developed by the Supreme Court in equal protection cases, "minimal scrutiny" or "rational basis" and "strict scrutiny" or "compelling interest." The traditional "rational basis" test applies where it is conceivable that the classification bears some rational relationship to a governmental interest which is not prohibited by the Constitution. It is applied only to classifications which relate to matters of economic and social welfare and not "fundamental rights." For example, state X passed a law that imposed higher income taxes on out-of-state corporations than on in-state corporations. If the only purpose of the law was to improve the local economy in state X, it clearly violates the equal protection clause because it does not satisfy a legitimate governmental interest. The state X

---

17. *Bd. Of Curators Of University Of Mo. v. Horowitz*, 435 U.S. 78, 90, 98 S.Ct. 948, 955, 55 L.Ed.2d 1-24 (1978).

tax law has no rational relationship to a legitimate state interest. It is given "minimal scrutiny." But if the state X income tax law was designed to accomplish a goal other than to discriminate against out-of-state competition, such as the operation and maintenance of a building to disseminate information on out-of-state businesses to in-state consumers, it would stand a better chance of passing the "rational basis" test.

The "strict scrutiny" standard applies when a law relates to a "suspect classification" (such as race or national origin) or burdens the exercise of a "fundamental right" in which case the law must be such that it promotes a "compelling" governmental interest. A compelling interest exists when its value justifies the limitation of fundamental constitutional rights. For example, in *Regents Of University Of California v. Bakke*,[18] a case where a white male successfully challenged the legality of a medical school's special admissions program under which 16 of the 100 positions in the class were reserved for "disadvantaged" minority students, Justice Powell applied the "strict scrutiny" test to a "suspect classification" based upon race. By carefully examining the purposes served by the special admissions program, he concluded that it violated Fourteenth Amendment Equal Protection. One of those purposes dealt with "obtaining the educational benefits that flow from an ethically diverse student body." Justice Powell viewed the attainment of a diverse student body as being closely tied to academic freedom which in turn is viewed as a special concern of the First Amendment. However, since the admissions program was based solely on race, it was not seen as sufficiently compelling. Justice Powell concluded with respect to this point:

> Ethnic diversity . . . is only one element in a range of factors a university properly may consider in attaining the goal of a heterogeneous student body. Although a university must have

wide discretion in making sensitive judgments as to who should be admitted, constitutional limitations protecting individual rights may not be disregarded. Respondent urges and the courts below have held that petitioner's dual admissions program is a racial classification that impermissibly infringes upon his rights under the Fourteenth Amendment. As the interest of diversity is compelling in the context of a university's admissions program, the question remains whether the program's racial classification is necessary to promote this interest.[19]

Although the other Justices did not join with Powell on the Equal Protection issue, the medical student prevailed because the admissions program violated Title VI of the 1964 Civil Rights Act.

3. CLASSIFICATION—RACE, ALIENAGE AND GENDER

Race

Cases can be factually classified based upon the type of traits involved. Common classifications relate to race or national origin, alienage and gender. If a classification is based upon race or national origin, it is "suspect" and courts apply the strict scrutiny test. As a consequence, the law is not valid under Equal Protection Clause unless it is necessary to a compelling objective. Typically, a compelling interest is not found and the law is invalidated. It is unclear, however, whether the laws fostering "benign" discrimination (classifications that discriminate in of favor racial minorities) must undergo the same standard of review. Remember in the *Bakke* case immediately above, Justice Powell used the "strict scrutiny" standard arguing that the "interest of diversity is compelling in the context of a university's admissions program," but standing alone, not sufficiently compelling. On the other hand, Justice Brennan used an intermediate or less severe standard of review. He

---

18. 438 U.S. 309, 98 S.Ct. 2733, 57 L.Ed.2d 750 (1978).

19. 438 U.S. at 314 15, 98 S.Ct. at 2760-1.

supported his conclusion that the admissions program was valid under the Equal Protection Clause by reasoning that a valid benign racial classification program was based upon a two-part test: (1) an important and articulated purpose for its use must be shown, and (2) it must stigmatize any group or single out those least well represented in the political process to bear the brunt of a benign program. The important and articulated purpose that was found to be sufficient was to remedy past societal discrimination. It did not stigmatize Bakke or any other white person because he was not "stamped as inferior by their rejection."

Alienage

If a classification is based upon alienage, the equal protection question is whether any proper governmental purpose is served by differentiating United States citizens from aliens. The Supreme Court has not established a definite standard of review. However, alienage appears to fall into the "sometimes suspect" category in the sense that courts do not always apply strict scrutiny. Strict judicial scrutiny applies when a state or local law distributes economic benefits or relates to a private sector economic activity. For example, a state law that limited admission to practice a profession such as law or medicine to United States citizens would not under the strict scrutiny test furnish the compelling interest needed by a state to pass the equal protection barrier. The same conclusion would be reached if a state law based the receipt of welfare benefits on residency or citizenship. But if a state law deals with governmental appointments, the "mere rationality" test applies. For example, law dealing with the appointment of policemen or teachers was found to be constitutional because they directly or indirectly participate in public policy.

Gender

If a classification is based upon gender, the Supreme Court treats it as being "almost suspect" and applies an intermediate standard of scrutiny. For example, in considering whether an Oklahoma statute that prohibited the sale of 3.2% beer to males under the age of 21 and to females under the age of 18 was constitutional under the Equal Protection Clause, the Supreme Court said the test should be: "To withstand constitutional challenge, previous cases establish that classifications by gender must serve important governmental objectives and must be substantially related to achievement of those objectives."[20] The Court concluded that the gender based statute constituted a denial of equal protection for males aged 18-20 there being no important governmental objective satisfied. Using the same argument, the Supreme Court concluded that a Federal Act which provided for the registration of males but not females into the armed services was an "important government interest" hence constitutional.[21]

C. Freedom of Speech

I. RATIONALE (FIRST AMENDMENT)

The First Amendment states that "Congress shall make no law . . . abridging freedom of speech...." It is widely agreed that this freedom is fundamental to the survival of democracy which feeds on the free interchange of ideas and thoughts. The general philosophy and principles of free speech were eloquently expressed by Justice Brandeis in 1927 when, in a concurring opinion, he expressed what he thought those who won our independence believed.

> They believed that freedom to think as you will and to speak as you think are means indis-

---

20. *Craig v. Boren* 429 U.S. 190 at 197, 97 S.Ct. 451 at 457, 50 L.Ed. 2d 397 (1976).
21. *Rostker v. Goldberg*, 453 U.S. 57, 101 S.Ct. 2646, 69 L.Ed. 2d 478 (1981).

pensable to the discovery and spread of political truth; that without free speech and assembly discussion would be futile; that with them, discussion affords ordinarily adequate protection against the dissemination of noxious doctrine; that the greatest menace to freedom is an inert people; that public discussion is a political duty; and that this should be a fundamental principle of the American government. They recognized the risks to which all human institutions are subject. But they knew that order cannot be secured merely through fear of punishment for its infraction; that it is hazardous to discourage thought, hope and imagination; that fear breeds repression; that repression breeds hate; that hate menaces stable government; that the path of safety lies in the opportunity to discuss freely supposed grievances and proposed remedies; and that the fitting remedy for evil counsels is good ones. Believing in the power of reason as applied

through public discussion, they eschewed silence coerced by law - the argument of force in its worst form. Recognizing the occasional tyrannies of governing majorities, they amended the Constitution so that free speech and assembly should be guaranteed.[22]

2. REGULATION

The First Amendment has never been interpreted to confer an absolute right of free speech to anyone at any time. To do so would be to give up total governmental control over its citizens. To permit parades or public processions without a license, to permit sound trucks from blaring loud and raucous noises, to permit speeches in the middle of a busy street, to permit the interruption of public

------

22. *Whitney v California*, 264 U.S. 357 at 375-76, 47 S.Ct. 641 at 648, 71 L.Ed. at 1095 at 1106 (1927).

Example. A local criminal ordinance made it unlawful and a breach of peace for any person to "curse or revile or to use obscene or opprobrious language toward any police officer during the performance of his or her duties." Although the Supreme Court constitutionally approves of laws banning "fighting words" (defined as personally abusive language that is sufficient to incite physical retaliation in a reasonable person in the position of the hearer), in this case it could be argued that words such as "opprobrious" do not tend to incite physical retaliation. In any event, the ordinance is overbroad and vague since it does not attempt to limit or define the meaning of "opprobrious" or for that matter any other term. ☐

* * *

Example. The Flag Protection Act of 1989 criminalized the conduct of anyone who "knowingly mutilates, defaces, physically defiles, burns, maintains on the floor or ground, or tramples upon" a United States flag. A person prosecuted for burning a United States flag argued that the Act was unconstitutional on the grounds that it violated the First Amendment. The Supreme Court in United States v. Eichman et al, [23] agreed. There was no question about the act of burning the flag being a First Amendment issue. It is clear that the government's asserted "interest" in protecting the "physical integrity" of a privately owned flag in order to preserve the flag's status as a symbol of the Nation is related to suppression of freedom of expression. The constitutional shortcoming was based upon the content of the Act. Its "restriction on expression cannot be justified without reference to the content of the regulated speech. ☐

23. _____ U.S. _____, 110, S.Ct. 2404, _____LEd.2d _____ (1990).

meetings are obvious examples of speech related activities that may have to be regulated or controlled to protect other societal interests. The question is to what extent government can regulate these and other activities involving speech. There is no easy answer because the Supreme Court often develops different tests for the various categories and types of speech. However, there are several well-established techniques that the Supreme Court has used to judge the validity of freedom of speech cases including, but not limited to, the Overbreadth and Vagueness Doctrines, the Clear and Present Danger Doctrine and the Commercial Speech Doctrine.

The basic test is that governmental regulation is permissible if it (1) furthers an important or substantial governmental interest unrelated to the suppression of free expression and (2) the restriction of alleged First Amendment freedoms is "narrowly tailored," i.e. no greater than is essential to the furtherance of the interest. Within the scope of this test are issues that are dealt with by applying the doctrines and tests specified above.

Overbreadth and Vagueness Doctrines

In the context of free speech, a law is overbroad if it is designed to provide redress for activities that are not protected by the First Amendment, but the possibility exists that it may affect activities which are protected by the First Amendment. For example, if a statute required a person to apply for and obtain a permit before holding a religious meeting on the street, the statute would not pass First Amendment scrutiny if it was totally void of appropriate standards to determine whether a permit should or should not be issued. It is too broad in the sense that it has the clear potential of interfering with free speech. But if the statute was narrowly drawn, that is strict standards such as those relating to public health, safety and welfare were specified, it could have been adjudged constitutional. Similarly, if a law is vague in the sense that it has the potential for deterring constitutionally protected free speech, it will not be upheld. The vagueness doctrine applies to all criminal laws including those that relate to free speech.

Clear and Present Danger Doctrine

If there is a clear and present danger that speech has the potential of leading to or producing unlawful criminal conduct, government regulation that relates to it may be Constitutional. Under the modern clear and

Example. Defendant was arrested and charged under a state syndicalism statute which punishes an individual for "advocat[ing] *** the duty, necessity, or propriety of crime, sabotage, violence, or unlawful methods of terrorism as a means of accomplishing industrial or political reform" and for "voluntarily assembl[ing] with any society, group, or assemblage of persons formed to teach or advocate the doctrine of criminal syndicalism." Defendant's conduct that initiated the arrest consisted of attending an organizational meeting and rally of the Klu Klux Klan where he, among other things, stated that "there might have to be some revengeance taken." The case against Defendant would have to be dismissed because the statute by its own words and as applied purports to punish mere advocacy and not, as required under the modern clear and present danger test, incitement to imminent lawless action. Even if the statute was more narrowly drawn to include incitement language, it is questionable under the facts whether Defendant's conduct and language was sufficient to produce incitement to imminent lawless action.[24] ☐

24. *Brandenburg v. Ohio*, 395 U.S. 444, 89 S.Ct. 1827, 23 L.Ed.2d 430 (1969)

present danger test, speech may be suppressed if it is (1) intended to incite (not advocate) unlawful conduct, (2) likely to produce "imminent lawless action," and (3) objectively encouraging incitement.

Commercial Speech Doctrine

The free speech doctrines relating to overbroadness, vagueness and clear and present danger apply to many different types of situations. There are a variety of other doctrines that are more specific in nature. One of these which is of interest to the business sector is the Commercial Speech Doctrine. Generally, commercial speech is that which advertises a product or service for profit. Historically, all commercial speech, including advertising, has not received the protection of the First Amendment. But under modern law, commercial speech or advertising is protected. The rule that has been developed generally states that commercial speech is protected under the First Amendment if it (1) concerns a lawful activity and is not misleading and (2) the asserted governmental interest is not substantial or if it is substantial, the governmental interest is too broadly defined. In one case, a state Public Utility Commission regulation banned all public utility advertising promoting the use of electricity. The Commission's argument was that such promotional advertising was contrary to national energy conservation policy therefore its regulation did not violate First Amendment rights. Applying the modern two-step rule, (1) commercial speech (promotional advertising) is lawful and in this case is not misleading, and (2) the governmental interest in energy conservation is substantial, but the banning of all advertising is too excessive; therefore, the regulation is not valid. The commercial speech in this case is protected.[25] Obviously, it is not protected from false or deceptive advertising or from advertisements relating to illegal goods or services such as the sale of marijuana or the performance of a crime.

D. Search and Seizure

I. RATIONALE (FOURTH AMENDMENT)

In achieving social control by means of the criminal law, society acts much more directly and forcefully than with the civil law. For this reason, it is essential, if society is to remain

---

25. *Central Hudson Gas & Electric Corporation v. Public Service Commission,* 447 U.S. 557, 100 S.Ct. 2343, 65 L.Ed.2d 341 (1980).

Example. Philadelphia law enforcement officers had information that untaxed liquor was being brought into Philadelphia from Camden, New Jersey, in a dark, late model sedan. Watching the Benjamin Franklin Bridge leading from Camden to Philadelphia, the officers saw a dark, late model sedan approaching from Camden, riding quite low in the rear. They stopped the car. Upon lifting the tarp that covered the rear area, they found both the rear seat and rear back rest had been removed, and that the rear and trunk of the car contained 375 bottles of whiskey and wine, none of which bore Pennsylvania tax seals. D was prosecuted for bringing untaxed liquor into Pennsylvania.

Even if the officers had probable cause to believe that the information they had received was credible and reliable, they had no probable cause to believe that the load carried by Defendant's car was untaxed liquor. That it was carrying something was clear, but the officers could not look at the car and reasonably conclude that it was more probable than not that the load was untaxed liquor. Since the officers did not have probable cause, the seizure was in violation of Fourth Amendment rights and therefore a denial of due process under the Fourteenth Amendment. ☐

free, that the power of the government to directly regulate and prohibit conduct be effectively restrained.

> The basic political problem of a free society is the problem of controlling the public monopoly of force. All other freedoms, freedom of speech, of assembly, of religion, of political action, presuppose that arbitrary and capricious police action has been restrained. Security in one's home and person is the fundamental without which there can be no liberty.[26]

The principal (but not the only) restraint on governmental power in the criminal law area is found in the Fourth Amendment. It provides that people have the right to be "secure in their persons, houses, papers, and effects, against unreasonable searches and seizures" and that "no Warrant shall issue, but upon probable cause." It places certain procedural obstacles in the way of law enforcement officers in order in insure a freer society whereas law enforcement under a totalitarian government (police state) sacrifices efficiency for security and freedom.

Applying previous concepts stated in this chapter, the Fourth Amendment restraint is imposed on state governments by the Fourteenth Amendment in accordance with the concepts of "due process of law" and "equal protection of the laws." If a state or city police officer conducts a search and seizure which would be a violation of the Fourth Amendment if conducted by a Federal officer, the state action constitutes a deprival of due process of law in violation of the Fourteenth Amendment.

2. PROCEDURE

The language of the Fourth Amendment prohibits unreasonable searches and seizures and prohibits issuance of a warrant unless

---

26. Paulsen, *The Exclusionary Rule and Misconduct by the Police,* 52 J Crim. Law, Crim & Police Sci. 255 (1961).

there is probable cause and specificity. As interpreted and applied, this means that for a search or seizure to be valid under the constitution, there must be (1) probable cause and (2) either a warrant (a judicial decision that probable cause exists) or urgency (under the circumstances it is impractical to delay in order to obtain a warrant.) The key element is probable cause which means that, based upon the quality and quantity of the evidence, an officer has probable cause to believe that a certain thing exists or is true.

In order to make a full seizure (an arrest), probable cause must exist. In a variety of suspicious situations which police encounter, a need frequently arises to make a limited, temporary seizure while further inquiry is made. The Supreme Court has recognized that even in the absence of probable cause, a limited seizure (stop and temporary detention) can be reasonable and therefore justified under the Fourth Amendment. For example, assume a police officer observed a man and a woman at a street corner. The man walked to a store window, paused, then rejoined the woman with whom he conferred. The woman then walked to the same store window, paused, then rejoined the man at the street corner. This routine was repeated alternately six times by each person. This activity would not give probable cause, but it would justify a limited seizure since the officer had reasonable cause to suspect that a crime was being contemplated. The officer could, therefore, temporarily detain the man and woman and ask them for identification.

* * *

Problems

1. A Missouri statute includes a list of twelve categories of medical services that are not eligible for Medicaid funding. The twelfth statutory category states: "(12) Family planning services as defined by federal rules and regulations; provided,

however, that such family planning services shall not include abortions unless such abortions are medically indicated." Two Missouri based physicians challenged the constitutionally of this statute. Without considering the substance of the statute, what argument can be made for dismissing the case and with what effect?

2. The Pennsylvania capital stock tax grants an election to domestic corporations to apportion the value of their capital stock by one of two methods (the traditional single factor asset method or a three factor formula based upon property, payroll and sales within and without the state. Only the three factor formula was available to foreign corporations. What constitutional objection could be made to this version of the Pennsylvania capital stock tax?

3. An ordinance governing disorderly conduct and loitering provided as follows: Any person persisting in loitering upon a public highway or street corner, or in front of any store, shop, place of business, place of amusement, or place of worship, after being requested by a police officer to vacate such place or places and move on, shall be guilty of an offense. Would this ordinance pass constitutional scrutiny?

4. The California statutory rape law defines unlawful intercourse as "an act of sexual intercourse accomplished with a female not the wife of the perpetrator, where the female is under the age of 18 years." Defendant was charged with violating this provision of the California statutory rape law. What might his constitutional defenses be and with what success? What arguments can be made in support of the law?

5. Iowa law prohibits the use of 65-foot double-trailer trucks within its borders. It allows the use of 55-foot single-trailer trucks and 60-foot double trailer trucks. A trucking company argued that Iowa's law unconstitutionally burdened interstate commerce because it could not use its 65-foot doubles to move goods through Iowa. It had to use either shorter truck units or divert its 65-foot doubles around Iowa. Iowa defended the law

based upon a safety interest claiming in part that single trucks take less time to pass and clear inspection and that shorter trucks are less likely to jackknife. Is Iowa's truck law constitutional? Give the constitutional and policy reasons for your answer.

6. A Kansas statute made it a misdemeanor for any person to engage "in the business of debt adjustment" except for lawyers. The statute defined "debt adjusting as "the making of a contract, express or implied with a particular debtor whereby the debtor agrees to pay a certain amount of money periodically to the person engaged in the debt adjusting business who shall for a consideration distribute the same among certain specified creditors in accordance with a plan agreed upon." A lower court found that debt adjusting by those other than lawyers was unlawful. Do you agree? Explain the constitutional foundation for your arguments. Why or why not?

7. Defendant was arrested and convicted for disorderly conduct when he shouted "we'll take the fucking street later" during an antiwar demonstration. During the course of trial, two witnesses testified that defendant's tone of voice was not louder than others in the crowd and that the statements he made did not appear to encourage anyone in the crowd into action. What arguments can be made in support of the conviction or for reversing it?

8. A police officer on patrol in a marked car saw two cars parked in the middle of a dark, abandoned, private parking lot of a swimming pool which was being salvaged. The two cars were parked parallel to each other and were facing the street. Dora and Mary were seated in the front of one of the cars and John was standing next to it. In view of the late hour and the occasional burglaries in the area the police officer decided to ask the three people for identification. The officer parked his patrol car next to Dora and Mary's car and asked the three persons what they had been doing. They responded that they had been talking. He then requested identification. As Dora opened her purse, the officer shinned his flashlight into the

purse and saw a small plastic bag containing a substance he reasonably believed to be marijuana. Could the marijuana be used as evidence against Dora in a criminal case for illegal possession of a dangerous substance?

9. Suppose that Jane Doe, a minor, was voluntarily admitted to a mental hospital over her objection. What constitutional basis would she have for making the objection?

10. What is the connection between the Fourth and Fourteenth Amendments?

Torts and Business Ethics

Torts and Business Ethics

1. General Definition and Historical Background

A tort can be defined as a civil wrong, other than a breach of contract, for which a court will provide a remedy.[1] It is a wrong which arises from the violation of a duty owing to the plaintiff where the duty exists because the law has held one to exist, not merely because a duty is created by agreement between the parties. This definition appears to provide a Pandora's box from which nearly all human problems might flow. Indeed it does. A tort might arise from a punch in the mouth, a defamatory statement appearing in a newspaper, pollution from a smokestack, an error during a surgical operation, poor advice from a lawyer, electronic eavesdropping, carelessly driving an automobile, a dog bite, making noise in a residential neighborhood, or failing to remove ice from a sidewalk. Tort liability is limited only by the genius of man and the willingness of a court to fashion a remedy.

Tort law then is an area of the law for redressing wrongs and breaches of duties which arise between persons, businesses, associations, corporations, and government units acting in their private capacities. Breaches of public duties and commissions of *public* wrongs are dealt with by the criminal law.

In redressing private wrongs, the tort law makes the determination of whether a loss or

injury will be allowed to remain where it has fallen or whether it should be shifted from the injured party to the injuring party by means of compensation. In formulating any rule of law, courts and legislatures balance conflicting interests and weigh various factors to determine, from the standpoint of fairness, reasonableness, and practicality, what seems to be the best policy to follow. This interplay of various factors is especially apparent with the rules of law pertaining to torts. If a person is obliged to compensate for injuries which his conduct causes, then to that extent such conduct, is made more costly and sometimes is discouraged altogether. What conduct should in this way, be prohibited, somewhat restricted, or totally uninhibited (in other words, which injuries are compensable and which are not) constitutes the policy question to be decided according to what is best for the individuals involved and for society as a whole.

The control of traffic in play areas presents a simple example of this balancing of interests. Many children, in the excitement of play, thoughtlessly run into the street and are injured or killed by carefully driven cars. The number of such accidents would be considerably reduced if all automobiles were required to have governors preventing speeds in excess of 15 miles per hour. In modern society such an overall restriction on speed would result in incalculable harm both to individual drivers and to society as a whole, harm which would not be justified even by the injuries

---

1. Prosser, *Law of Torts*, p. 2.

ing interests are balanced and a compromise is reached with the rule that drivers must slow down in school and play areas.

The policy factors most important in the formulation of the rules of tort law include the following:

1. The social value or utility of the particular activity in question.
2. The intent or mental attitude of the doer of the act.
3. The likelihood that the act will cause injury.
4. The possibility of avoiding injury while still substantially accomplishing the purpose of the act.
5. The type or nature of the injury threatened.
6. The ease or difficulty of supervising or enforcing a restraint upon the particular activity.

During its centuries of evolution, tort law did not develop as a unified system. Rather, until relatively modern times, the rules pertaining to different torts developed somewhat independently from each other in connection with the varying procedural rules that were applicable in different types of lawsuits and in connection with the different factual and historical settings of the evolutionary development. Originally the criminal and tort remedies were administered by the same court in the same action, and both the criminal punishment and civil damage award were made together. Because of this common origin of the early torts and crimes these torts went by the same name as their kindred crimes and this similarity survives today. Accordingly, there is a tort called *assault* and one called *battery*. Others include trespass, libel, slander and false imprisonment. More modern torts have developed totally independent of the criminal law. Such torts as negligence, invasion of privacy and strict liability are torts of more independent origin.

The heavy hand of the past still survives in the tort law though in the area of damage awards. Earlier it was noted that the substantive aspect of the tort law was to determine when compensation would be awarded to an injured party. But in circumstances where the wrongdoer displays malice in his acts, it is sometimes considered sound policy in assessing damages to take into account the wrongdoer's maliciousness. This element of recoverable money damages, called "exemplary" or "punitive" damages, is admittedly for the purpose of punishing the wrongdoer and deterring him and others from committing similar acts. Punitive damages in an amount reasonably related to the wrong can usually be awarded for acts done with a bad motive or with reckless indifference to the rights of others, or where elements of aggravation, outrage or spite exist.

Since tort and criminal law were once joined together, the question occurs, now that they are separate, as to which legal action, the criminal or the civil, can or should be used for an act which might transcend both areas of the law. If an individual intentionally strikes another with his fist and thereby commits a battery, is it a criminal battery, a civil battery, or perhaps both? Since the objects and purposes of the criminal and civil law are different, pursuing a remedy under one does not accomplish the purpose of the other. Determining, under the criminal law, that the person inflicting the battery should be punished by fine or imprisonment for his harm to the tranquility of society (which is one objective of the criminal law) does not aid the victim who has sustained a broken nose and the resultant pain, suffering, medical expenses, loss of wages and other personal and financial harm. Such aid is available in a civil suit for battery asking for monetary compensation from the wrongdoer for the harm he has caused.

The fact that two actions, one civil and one criminal, can emanate from the same act gives rise to two common questions: (1) Need the verdicts in the two trials be consistent, and (2) Is it not a violation of constitutional guaranties to try a person twice for the same act?

The answer to both questions is "no."

The two trials are conducted based upon two separate bodies of law, criminal and civil. Each has different rules concerning procedures and degree of proof required. Accordingly, it is quite possible to have verdicts which appear inconsistent. The fact that the defendant loses the civil tort case but is acquitted in his criminal trial is not really an inconsistency so much as a faulty comparison. Furthermore, since the cases are about different aspects of the event, they may be tried either concurrently or consecutively with the decision in one case not in any way conclusive for the other. In fact, in some states the result of the one case is not admissible as evidence in the other.

As to the second question, it can be noted that the Fifth Amendment to the Federal Constitution states that no person shall " . . . be subject for the same offense to be twice put in jeopardy of life or limb...." The general interpretation of this provision is that a civil suit, arising out of an act which might also be criminal, does not subject one to jeopardy of life or limb. Its object is financial compensation. Accordingly, it is outside the protection of that clause.

II. Bases of Tort Liability

A. Multiple Torts Arising from a Single Incident

A tort is a civil wrong, but it is the type and nature of the wrong which fixes the various definitions of specific torts. A certain type of act, such as the swinging of a baseball bat, might, depending on the facts and circumstances, be no tort at all when it is done in proper context in the course of a baseball game, even though someone is struck by it.

On the other hand, if done in a crowd of people with an intent to strike someone, it might constitute a *battery* if the intent to strike is carried out. If the attempt to strike is made but fails, an *assault* might result. Alternatively, if the bat is swung off of the baseball field near other people, but with no intent to strike anyone, the inadvertent hitting of another person might be considered the tort of negligence. The context of the act, the intent of the perpetrator, the knowledge or consent of the victim and the interest of the public all interact through the definitions which exist for the different torts. It is these definitions of particular torts which have evolved through the past, and which continue to evolve, which provide the yardstick for gauging a given incident to determine whether a tort or torts have been committed.

It is especially significant to note that, in the course of occurrence of any given incident, any number of torts can be committed. The question to ask is: With what tort definitions does a given act coincide? True, some torts are mutually exclusive; a single act cannot be both negligently done and intentionally done. But others are not. A defendant becomes liable for all torts which he commits so long as the elements of the torts alleged can be proven. Therefore, the question to be asked if it is suspected that a tort has occurred is: Are the definitional elements of the tort present'? If that question can be answered in the affirmative, a remaining question is: What are the damages?

B. Classifying the Bases of Liability

Torts can be classified in various ways. Generally they are divided and labeled by the type of interest they invade (e.g., persons or property), by the state of mind of the actor (e.g., intentional or unintentional), or by the legal policy of liability (e.g., strict liability, nuisance, invasion of privacy). Table 4.1 presents illustrative examples of this classification scheme. It is not exhaustive.

TABLE 4.1: GENERAL CLASSIFICATION OF TORTS

TYPE OF INTEREST INVADED	State of Mind	
	INTENTIONAL TORTS	NON-INTENTIONAL TORTS
1. Property	Trespass Conversion	Negligence Strict Liability
2. Person a. Physical Well Being	Battery False Imprisonment	Negligence Strict Liability
b. Mental Well Being	Assault Infliction of Mental Distress Defamation* Invasion of Privacy*	Negligence Strict Liability Defamation Invasion of Property

* Defamation or invasion of privacy could ultimately affect property values

III. Intentional Torts

Any system of classifying torts usually starts by considering the intent of the wrongdoer and subdividing torts into those which are intentional and those which are unintentional. The concept of intent as developed in tort law goes beyond the malicious or evil motives usually looked for in criminal law. It is possible for a defendant's act to be classified as intentional even though he neither desires nor reasonably expects that his act will interfere with the legal interests of another. On the other hand, a defendant's act can be unintentional even though it occurs as a result of his intentional conduct. If a defendant strikes a plaintiff with a baseball bat, clearly the defendant's act should be classified as intentional if his desire or purpose is to strike the plaintiff. If the defendant is merely swinging the bat for exercise, without any desire or expectation of hitting anyone, then, although the defendant's act of swinging the bat is a voluntary and intentional act, his striking the plaintiff should clearly be classified as unintentional.

Suppose that a farmer, mistaken about his boundary line, cuts down his neighbor's tree, honestly and reasonably believing it to be his own tree. Although the farmer does not intend to trespass on his neighbor's property, his purpose is to cut down that particular tree. Since cutting the tree is an intentional act, the farmer would be classified as an intentional wrongdoer. Suppose further that the farmer cuts up the tree into a load of fireplace logs, which he sells to a householder. The householder's burning of the logs is an intentional act. Without the original owner's permission, it is a wrongful act. Although wholly innocent of any malice and therefore not guilty of any crime, the householder would nevertheless be classified by tort law as an intentional wrongdoer.

The intent with which tort liability is concerned is not then necessarily a hostile intent or a desire to do harm or injury, but rather it is the intent to bring about a result which will invade another person's property or personal interests in a way that the law will not sanction. Following are some explanations of commonly occurring intentional torts. They are representative of the group, not exhaustive.

A. Battery

The tort of battery occurs when there is an intentional infliction of a harmful or offensive bodily contact upon another without his or her consent. This definition has three major parts: the intentional infliction, the bodily contact, and the lack of consent.

To satisfy the requirement of "intentional infliction" it is not sufficient, as discussed above, that the act itself is an intentional act. It must be an intentional act which has as its purpose an unpermitted contact. This type of intent can be actual, in that it is provable what the defendant's thoughts were, or it can be implied by the conduct of the defendant which was such that a reasonable person would have known that his act would cause the unauthorized contact. For example, if someone is staying in a hotel on a street in New York City, and he is aware that large crowds are usually present during the late afternoon hours, and at 5:00 p.m. on such a day he throws a trash can out of a window above that street, it matters not if he took careful aim at a particular pedestrian or merely indiscriminately let the can go. In the first instance intent to cause an unauthorized contact is obvious; in the second instance, intent exists because a reasonable person would have known to a substantial certainty that a pedestrian would be struck under those circumstances. Accordingly, yelling to a crowd of people to "get out of the way" before intentionally driving an automobile toward the spot where they are standing is insufficient to show that one lacked the intent to strike

them. Intent need not be directed toward the person contacted to be sufficient to satisfy the definition. If you make a paper airplane and throw it at A, but instead it strikes B in the eye, it will not be a defense to claim that you intended only to strike A. The intent to strike A will be transferred to B. Likewise, the intent to merely swing your fist at A but not hit him will not help in your argument that no intent existed when your near-miss turned out to be a hit because of an inaccurate swing.

The bodily contact involved need not be harmful, to be merely offensive is sufficient. Whether a contact is offensive is determined by referring to the reasonable person's sense of personal dignity. For a man to come up to his wife and give her a hug and a kiss would certainly be a reasonable act; for a drunken stranger to do the same act would be considered an offensive contact.

The bodily contact need not actually touch the skin or exposed portions of the plaintiff's body, the touching of anything closely connected with one's body is sufficient to constitute a "bodily contact." Accordingly, a store manager who grabs a customer by the coat collar has made a bodily contact. Similarly, one who throws an object at A but hits A's dog instead might be held to have contacted A. The question here would be how closely connected to A's body was the dog. If the animal was on a short leash being held by A, closeness is established; if, however, the dog is running free five paces in front of A, no contact has probably occurred.

It is also true that the defendant's act need not be carried out by his own hand. It can be accomplished by setting an object in motion such as throwing a rock, shooting a gun, driving an automobile or using duress to force another to do the act.

Consent to a battery can arise by the plaintiff agreeing to the infliction of the bodily contact. The consent can be either expressed or implied. An expressed consent might be verbal or written. A verbal consent might occur

2. Ibid.

where two friends agree to punch each other in the arm to see who has the more powerful swing. A written consent form might be presented for signing in a more formal or institutionalized setting such as when someone enrolls in a self-defense course or enters a hospital for tests or surgery. An implied consent would occur where one acts in such a manner as to lead others to believe he is consenting to the contact. A person entering upon a football field during a game and dressed in a football uniform would be implying his consent to contacts to be expected in the course of such a game. The "course of the game" concept is an important one in limiting the scope of the consent. Accordingly, if one hockey player strikes another player over the head with his hockey stick, not while legitimately pursuing the game, but in the course of starting an altercation, such an antagonist cannot claim the other player's consent to play the game as consent to the intentional strike on the head.

Consent must also be an "informed" consent. In order for one to give an effective consent one needs to have knowledge of the pertinent facts and his consent must not be elicited by withholding such facts or through fraud or deceit. A surgeon who operates without obtaining specific consent after an explanation of risks and alternatives may find himself liable in battery where he operates on a different bodily part than intended or expands the scope of the original operation even though the result was beneficial to the patient.

Someone suffering under a legal incapacity must understand the nature, extent and consequences of his consent, or a parent or guardian must consent on his behalf.

B. Assault

The tort of assault occurs when one intentionally creates an apprehension that a harmful or offensive bodily contact is imminent upon the plaintiff without his or her consent. An assault is an invasion of one's mental tranquility as contrasted with a battery which offers redress for an invasion of one's physical integrity.

The intent required is not limited to the intent to create a mental apprehension in itself but also extends to those acts of intentional personal invasion which would reasonably lead to the creation of such apprehension. If one intends to commit a battery by swinging a club and striking the plaintiff and prior to the actual contact the plaintiff perceives the threat in the form of the swing of the club in close proximity to his head, the tort of assault is present. That the club proceeds to strike its target and result in a battery does not serve to eradicate the assault, but merely to add the commission of a second tort, the battery, to the list of wrongful acts committed. The fact that the defendant does not intend to strike the plaintiff by his swing, and he does not strike the plaintiff, is immaterial if the intent is to make the plaintiff apprehensive that a contact will occur, for that is the essence of the tort of assault whereas the contact is the essence of the battery.

The apprehension created must be reasonably based. The plaintiff must reasonably believe that the defendant appears to have the ability to inflict the contact. So that if a defendant stands across a room with a real-looking toy gun and threatens to shoot the plaintiff, an assault has occurred if the plaintiff believed the gun to be real. On the contrary, however, is the case where the defendant says, "I will get a gun next week and shoot you," because the defendant does not have the ability to inflict the contact on the present occasion. Verbal threats, like these, by themselves will usually not constitute an assault. Such threats if coupled with other acts or circumstances might give rise to the tort. Furthermore, a conditional threat, if coupled with the present ability to carry it out, would be sufficient to constitute an assault. A large, burly store manager who threatens a suspicious customer by saying, "I promise you will not get hurt if you open your purse," while menacing a clenched fist, has committed an assault even though he has provided the means for the plaintiff to avoid the potential contact. The apprehension must be created for an assault to occur; if the threat is not perceived—for example when, from a concealed and distant position, a defendant aims a rifle at plaintiff—no assault occurs. Care should be taken here to note that such an act, while not a civil wrong, is nevertheless considered an offense under the criminal law in many jurisdictions.

Except for the differences in the interest invaded, the torts of assault and battery are virtually the same with the principles discussed above concerning contacts and consent in battery equally applicable to assault.

C. Infliction of Mental Distress
Whereas the tort of assault is aimed at redressing intentional inflictions of mental distress, it is limited in scope to those actions which threaten physical contact as the source of the distress created. Without an additional remedy, mental distress created by circumstances manipulated by a defendant but not threatening physical contact would go unredressed.

Such situations could arise through intentionally telling a person that a loved one is seriously injured or dead as a result of an automobile accident when in fact the story has been fabricated by the teller, or through a credit or collection agency employing high-pressure techniques such as threatening arrest and ruination of credit, telephone calls around the clock, or calling neighbors and employers. Liability has also been imposed upon the operators of common carriers, public utilities and operators of public accommodations for use of profane language to their patrons or language indecent or grossly insulting to people of ordinary sensibilities.

The tort generally requires three elements to be present: that the mental distress be inflicted intentionally, that the mental distress in fact exists and is severe; and that the distress is such that one of "ordinary sensibilities" would experience it in a similar situation.

Looking at the first element, it can be observed that the intent here is an intent to do an act calculated to cause the mental distress or doing an act knowing to a substantial certainty that mental distress will follow from the act. Some cases have lowered the intent requirement to encompass wanton, willful and even reckless conduct. It is also required that the distress in fact occur and be substantial in nature. Under this requirement, mere annoyance would not qualify, nor would it be sufficient that one of ordinary sensibility would have suffered severe distress under the circumstances. The plaintiff must actually sustain the distress. If unusual distress results which is greater than what one of ordinary sensibilities would experience in a similar situation, the perpetrator will not be held responsible for the unusual distress unless the perpetrator knew of some special circumstances affecting the plaintiff which would cause an unusual amount or type of distress to result from the inflicting act.

D. False Imprisonment
This tort occurs when one intentionally confines another, either directly or indirectly without consent, and the person confined is conscious of the confinement or is harmed by it. The intent must be to confine substantially, not merely to hold for a brief and harmless period. The cause of the confinement may vary from actual enclosures from which escape is not possible to threats which elicit an invalid consent to the confinement. Non-physical confinements brought about by threats present the greatest difficulty to prove because if the threat is vague or not operable in the present or immediate future, it may be deemed insufficient to persuade a person of reasonable determination to submit himself

to the confinement. Circumstances and knowledge of the confined person may reflect upon the coerciveness of the threat. It has been held that an old and sickly woman who was told she was not allowed to leave the hospital until she paid her bill and who stayed an extra day believing she could not leave unless she performed the demanded act, could bring an action for false imprisonment. Had the person been aware that the hospital could bring suit for the bill owed but not prevent a patient from leaving, then the threat alone would not carry coercive value and a confinement would not occur. A threat which employs a purported legal authority to overcome a person's will to escape or leave can also constitute a confinement. A mere transitory event is usually insufficient for the tort.

A confinement, whether physical or nonphysical, must be complete. The erection of a mere obstacle which plaintiff need only circumvent in order to escape is not a complete confinement. However, if the circumvention route involves a risk of harm or if the route itself is unknown the confinement is complete.

The person confined must be aware of the confinement or be harmed by it. Generally, if a person is in a room, working with the door closed, and another comes along and locks the door from the outside with the intent to confine the individual in the room, but the person in the room is unaware of the door having been locked, false imprisonment does not occur until the one inside the room becomes aware of the confinement. Therefore, if the person in the room does not try to leave for three hours and after two hours the confiner has come back and unlocked the door, no false imprisonment has occurred because when the one in the room goes to leave he may do so unhampered and gains no knowledge during the time of confinement that it has in fact occurred. However, there are some exceptional cases where knowledge has not been required where harm has occurred, as with an imprisoned infant.

Consent to false imprisonment is governed by the same consent rules as were explained in relation to the tort of battery.

E. Trespass to Land

Trespass to land is often referred to as *trespass q.c.f.* The initials *q.c.f.* stand for the Latin words *quare clausum fregit* which mean "trespass wherefore he broke the close," that is, the real or imaginary structure enclosing the land. A trespass to land occurs when one intentionally intrudes upon the land in possession of another. Land in this context actually means real property and includes houses, apartments, stores, and mobile homes as well as vacant land.

The intent required is the intent to do the act which results in the intrusion, not the intent to intrude itself. Accordingly, by intentionally driving one's car around a hold in a road, a trespass could occur if in doing so the car was driven over someone's land which abutted the road. The fact that the driver did not intend to go off the public right of way is not of import. With regard to public highways, a privilege does exist to trespass upon abutting land if the road is impassable and the trespass is necessary to continue the journey. The trespass must be to a reasonable extent and done in a reasonable manner.

Trespass is a tort against possession, not ownership. As a result, a tenant could sue a landlord in trespass if the landlord wrongfully entered on the premises of the tenant. Trespassers are liable for all harm done while on the premises of another, however, no damage needs to be shown in order to successfully sue for this tort. If no actual damages are shown, nominal damages will be awarded.

Some intrusions, while constituting trespass, are privileged and hence cannot serve as the basis for a cause of action. The public highway privilege is discussed above. Other privileged intrusions include reasonable overflights by aircraft, necessity resulting from the need to avert imminent public disaster, reasonable reclamation of one's private property, service of legal process and, under certain circumstances, abatement of a private nuisance.

F. Trespass to Chattels

Trespass to chattels is often referred to as *trespass d.b.a.* The initials *d.b.a.* stand for the Latin words *de bonis asportatis* which mean "trespass for goods carried away." Originally, the tort applied only to situations involving asportation, or carrying off, of the property. This was later expanded to include any damage to personal property.

Accordingly, this form of trespass can now be defined as the intentional interference with the right of possession of personal property. Possession, or a right to future possession, must reside in the plaintiff and there must be some actual deprivation of the article's use or impairment of its condition, quality or value.

G. Conversion

If the interference with personal property is significant, rather than suing in trespass, the greater tort of conversion is charged. This implies that there was an intentional exercise of control over personality which seriously interfered with the right of the plaintiff to control or possession of it. The remedy for conversion is full payment for the value of the article involved.

Originally only a tangible chattel could be converted, but the tort has developed to include many intangibles of the type where a document had been merged with other intangible rights. Such documents capable of being converted can include stock and bond certificates, promissory notes, savings bank books, policies of insurance, bills of lading, checks and the like.

The tort requires an intentional exercise of control but not the intent to deprive one of possession. Cases where one has wrongfully

taken possession such as through trespass, fraud or theft are not difficult to deal with since the taking itself is wrongful. However, where one acquires the property in good faith from a wrongful taker, the question arises as to whether such good faith purchaser can acquire possession properly. Since, however, the essence of the tort is the wrongful exercise of control, the good faith of the holder is not generally relevant. The Uniform Commercial Code has made alterations in this concept with regard to negotiable instruments and entrusting concepts.[3]

H. Defenses

It is a defense to an intentional tort for the defendant to prove that a particular element of the tort is missing and thereby show that the tort itself was not committed. For instance, if the defendant can show that the plaintiff consented to the act then the tort cannot be made out against the defendant. There are other defenses which present circumstances that in some way justify the fact that the defendant actually did commit the tort alleged. These defenses are such that if they can be proved, social policy dictates that the committed tort be excused.

I. DEFENSE OF SELF, OF OTHERS, AND OF PROPERTY

Self-defense can be an excuse to the commission of an intentional tort. It is not an absolute defense, rather it must be exercised in a reasonable fashion. One can use reasonable force to repel threatened harm which is likely to occur in the immediate future. Such is the case where a fist is thrown to repel a threatened assault or battery. In such instances there is no duty to retreat before employing the physical force. Should the defense require the use of force which is likely to cause serious bodily harm or death, there is first a duty

---

3. See U.C.C. §2-403, 7-205, 3-305, and 3-419.

to retreat if such a retreat would remove the need to use such a harsh defense. Generally, however, if one is in his home or place of business, he need not retreat before employing this type of force. If one is reasonably placed in fear of grave bodily harm or death, one is usually justified in using deadly force.

In situations where a third person is the one endangered, another can defend that third person as he could himself provided he reasonably believes that the third person has the right of self-defense and if the defense is necessary to protect the third person.

It should be noticed that in discussing self-defense, the right is bound up with the concept of protecting one's person, but not one's property. The law does allow one to defend one's property, but the amount of force allowable in defense of property differs from that allowable for defense of one's person. In protecting one's property reasonable force can be used; that is, force short of that which can cause serious bodily harm or death. Usually a request must be made for the intruder to cease, unless such request would be futile. The mere threat to cause death or serious bodily harm, in itself, is usually considered reasonable force. The use of mechanical devices, animals, or other traps or deterrents must adhere to these standards. Since an owner of property has the right to do what is reasonably necessary to protect his property, a retail store owner has the right to detain a customer for investigation if the retailer has reasonable grounds to believe that the customer is guilty of shoplifting. That the investigation which follows the detention proves the customer innocent does not retroactively nullify the right which the retailer exercised in detaining the customer, provided (1) the retailer had reasonable grounds to be suspicious, and (2) the detention was reasonable in manner and extent. Since a jury can be expected to sympathize with an insulted and humiliated customer, a retailer should be extremely cautious.

2. ARREST AND DISCIPLINE

A police officer is entitled to make an arrest by the use of reasonable force if he possesses an arrest warrant. If he is without a warrant he may use reasonable force to make an arrest for a misdemeanor if he observes its commission or if he reasonably believes a felony to have been committed and that the plaintiff is the felon. Private individuals are also entitled to use reasonable force to make an arrest, however, the arrest must be under circumstances where a felony has actually been committed and the private person reasonably believes the plaintiff to be the felon.

A parent or one *in loco parentis* may use reasonable force to control one's child or to control children in one's charge. Many states have specific provisions in statutes or administrative regulations for school authorities to use corporal punishment as a discipline method. Such discipline must be used in a reasonable manner and under reasonable circumstances. Some regulations may provide for a parent's written exception to the policy as a means of withdrawing the privilege.

Officials of prisons, military organizations, detention facilities, psychiatric facilities, and other such institutions often possess specialized disciplinary rights as well.

3. EMERGENCY

In situations where actual bona fide emergencies exist, and the defendant is justified in the belief that the plaintiff would consent to the action of the defendant, one can proceed, without such consent, to commit a tort in a reasonable manner as necessitated by the emergency. Such situations could arise where one commits trespass by entering another's land and breaking in a door in order to remove a plaintiff from a burning building, or where a doctor ministers emergency first aid to an unconscious person.

I. Damages

An intentionally wrongful act is more reprehensible than an act which is careless but not intended, and as a matter of policy should be attended with greater liability. Thus the victim of an intentional wrong can recover for all his actual injuries, even those that are quite unusual and could not have been anticipated. In addition, the plaintiff can recover for his pain, suffering, humiliation, and any other emotional distress. Naturally, no definite price can be placed on pain, suffering, or emotional disturbances, just as no money value can be placed on sight or hearing. However, to the extent that an injured plaintiff can be compensated in any way for pain and emotional disturbances, money will do it. He is, therefore, entitled to recover a sum of money reasonably related to the degree of his pain, suffering, humiliation, and any other emotional distress. Furthermore, when a defendant is guilty of intentional misconduct, the plaintiff is permitted to recover for humiliation or shock even though he sustains no real injuries. For example, a person who without justification is intentionally struck and knocked down may sustain no actual injuries, perhaps not even be bruised. Nevertheless, most courts consider it sound policy for the plaintiff to have a right to recover money damages from the wrongdoer in an amount commensurate with the plaintiff's humiliation and indignity.

IV. Negligent Torts

A. Elements of Negligence

Negligence, the antithesis of intentional misconduct, is inattention or carelessness. As a general proposition it seems fair to say that a careless person should be required to compensate for injuries which his carelessness causes to other persons. However, various factors argue that a defendant's liability for negligence should be limited to some extent. Some of these factors are:

1. In comparison with cases involving intentional misconduct, evidence of whether or not a defendant has been careless is frequently less clear-cut, with a proportionate increase in the possibility of mistaken and faked claims.

2. Jurors often tend to favor a seriously injured plaintiff even though the question whether or not the defendant exercised adequate care is arguable.

3. The seriousness of a plaintiff's injury may be unexpectedly enhanced by his peculiar characteristics and weaknesses. While it seems quite clear that an intentional wrongdoer should be liable for *all* injuries that result, it is not so clear that a negligent defendant (whose only wrong is his inattention or neglect to use sufficient care) should be liable for highly unusual injuries which could not reasonably have been foreseen.

4. A single careless act may set in motion a lengthy chain of events. Here again the policy question arises whether it is fair to hold a negligent defendant to the same liability as an intentional wrongdoer for remote injuries which could not reasonably have been foreseen. Suppose that a defendant is driving carelessly and, as a result, collides with a properly driven car. Certainly the careless defendant should be held liable for damages to the other car and for injuries to its occupants. Suppose, further, that the defendant's car rams the other car into a pole, knocking the pole over and causing it, or some wires, to fall on a nearby pedestrian. It seems fair to hold that the careless defendant should be liable to the pedestrian also. But suppose that the collision with the pole causes an electric wire to fall on a hunter 500 yards away from the scene of the collision. Should the defendant be held liable to the hunter? Suppose that the electric shock causes the hunter (through no fault of his) to discharge his rifle and, by rare chance, the bullet injures a pas-

senger riding in the car with which the defendant originally collided. While it is fair to hold the defendant liable for injuries caused by the collision of the cars, is it fair to hold him liable for the totally unexpected gunshot wound of one of the passengers?

The question of when a person should be held liable for injuries resulting from his carelessness and when liability should not be imposed requires (as with all law) the legislatures, and especially the courts, to decide and declare what they consider to be sound policy from the standpoint of fairness, reasonableness, and practicality. In a case before the Wisconsin Supreme Court, the question was whether a driver who carelessly ran down and killed a little girl should be held liable for physical injuries sustained by the girl's mother as a result of witnessing the accident. In deciding against liability the court explained that its decision was entirely one of policy, saying:

> Human wrongdoing is seldom limited in its injurious effects to the immediate actors in a particular event. More frequently than not, a chain of results is set up that visits evil consequences far and wide. While from the standpoint of good morals and good citizenship the wrongdoer may be said to violate a duty to those who suffer from the wrong, the law finds it necessary . . . to attach practical and just limits to the legal consequences of the wrongful act.... The answer to this question cannot be reached solely by logic, nor is it clear that it can be entirely disposed of by a consideration of what the defendant ought reasonably to have anticipated as a consequence of his wrong. The answer must be reached by balancing the social interests involved in order to ascertain how far defendant's duty and plaintiff's right may justly and expediently be extended.[4]

In determining whether one is liable for conduct resulting from carelessness or inattention, courts will generally conclude that one

who conducts himself without exercising reasonable care, or who fails to adhere to statutorily defined conduct for the protection of others is negligent and, consequently, liable for the results of his acts.

The tort of negligence is generally conceptualized as containing three or four elements. These are (1) a duty to use reasonable care, (2) the breach of that duty, (3) harm which is (4) proximately caused by the breach. Some authorities combine the first two elements and refer to them as "negligent conduct." These elements and their relationships are presented in Figure 4.1.

1. DUTY OF CARE

A person should always be attentive and careful in his associations with others. In attempting to define more particularly the degree of care which a person should exercise, the law creates a hypothetical "reasonable man" as its standard. The English wit and playwright, A. P Herbert, has written the following humorous and picturesque description of the role which the reasonable man plays in the common-law system:

> The Common Law of England has been laboriously built about a mythical figure—the figure of "The Reasonable Man." In the field of jurisprudence, this legendary individual occupies the place which in another science is held by the Economic Man and in social and political discussions by the Average or Plain Man. He is an ideal, a standard, the embodiment of all those qualities which we demand of the good citizen. No matter what may be the particular department of human life which fails to be considered in these Courts, sooner or later we have to face the question: Was this or was it not the conduct of a reasonable man? Did the defendant take such care to avoid shooting the plaintiff in the stomach as might reasonably be expected of a reasonable man? . . . Did the plaintiff take such precautions to inform himself of the circumstances as any reasonable man would expect of an ordinary person having the ordinary knowledge of an ordinary

---

4. *Waube v. Warrington,* 216 Wis. 603, 258 N.W. 497, 98 A.L.R. 394 (1935).

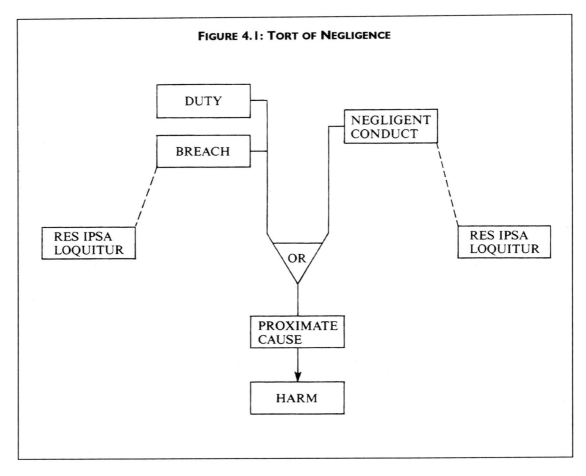

FIGURE 4.1: TORT OF NEGLIGENCE

person of the habits of wild bulls when goaded with gardenfolks and the persistent agitation of red flags?

I need not multiply examples. It is impossible to travel anywhere or to travel for long in that confusing forest of learned judgments which constitutes the Common Law of England without encountering the Reasonable Man. He is at every turn, ever-present help in time of trouble, and his apparitions mark the road to equity and right. There has never been a problem, however difficult, which His Majesty's judges have not in the end been able to resolve by asking themselves the simple question, "Was this or was it not the conduct of a reasonable man?" and leaving that question to be answered by the jury.

This noble creature stands in singular contrast to his kinsman, the Economic Man, whose every action is prompted by the single spur of selfish advantage and directed to the single end of monetary gain. The Reasonable Man is always thinking of others; prudence is his guide, and "Safety First" . . . is his rule of life. All solid virtues are his, save only that peculiar quality by which the affection of other men is won. For it will not be pretended that socially he is much less objectionable than the

Economic Man. While any given example of his behavior must command our admiration, when taken in the mass, his acts create a very different set of impressions. He is one who invariably looks where he is going and is careful to examine the immediate foreground before he executes a leap or bound; who neither stargazes nor is lost in meditation when approaching trapdoors or the margin of a dock . . . who never mounts a moving omnibus and does not alight from any car while the train is in motion; who investigates exhaustively the bona fides of every mendicant before distributing alms and will inform himself of the history and habits of a dog before administering a caress . . . who never drives his ball till those in front of him have definitely vacated the putting-green which is his own objective . . . who in the way of business looks only for that narrow margin of profit which twelve men such as himself would reckon to be "fair," and contemplates his fellow merchants, their agents and their goods, with that degree of suspicion and distrust which the law deems admirable; who never swears, gambles, or loses his temper; who uses nothing except in moderation and even while he flogs his child is meditating only on the golden mean. Devoid, in short, of any human weakness, with not one single saving vice, sans prejudice, procrastination, ill nature, avarice, and absence of mind, as careful for his own safety as he is for that of others, this excellent but odious character stands like a monument in our Courts of Justice, vainly appealing to his fellow citizens to order their lives after his own example.

I have called him a myth; and insofar as there are few, if any, of his mind and temperament to be found in the ranks of living men, the title is well chosen. But it is a myth which rests upon solid and even, it may be, upon permanent foundations. The Reasonable Man is fed and kept alive by the most valued and enduring of our juridical institutions—the common jury. Hateful as he must necessarily be to any ordinary citizen who privately considers him, it is a curious paradox that where two or three are gathered together in one place they will with one accord pretend an admiration for him; and when they are gathered together in the formidable surroundings of a British jury, they are easily persuaded that they themselves are, each and generally, reasonable men. And without stopping to consider how strange a chance it must have been that has picked fortuitously from a whole people no fewer than twelve examples of a species so rare, they immediately invest themselves with the attributes of the Reasonable Man and are, therefore, at one with the Courts in their anxiety to support the tradition that such a being in fact exists. Thus it is that while the Economic Man has under the stress of modern conditions almost wholly disappeared from view his Reasonable cousin has gained in power with every case in which he has figured.[5]

Writing in a more serious vein, Justice Holmes says in his book, THE COMMON LAW:

The ideal average prudent man, whose equivalent the jury is taken to be in many cases and whose culpability or innocence is the supposed test, is a constant; and his conduct under given circumstances is theoretically always the same....

The standards of the law are standards of general application. The law takes no account of the infinite varieties of temperament, intellect, and education which make the internal character of a given act so different in different men. It does not attempt to see men as God sees them for more than one sufficient reason. In the first place, the impossibility of nicely measuring a man's powers and limitations is far clearer than that of ascertaining his knowledge of law, which has been thought to account for what is called the presumption that every man knows the law. But a more satisfactory explanation is that when men live in society a certain average of conduct, a sacrifice of individual peculiarities going beyond a certain point, is necessary to the general welfare. If, for instance, a man is born hasty and awkward, is always having accidents and hurting himself or his neighbors, no doubt his congenital defects will be allowed for in the courts of Heav-

---

5. Reprinted from the fictitious case of *Fardell v. Potts*, published in A. P. Herbert's, THE UNCOMMON LAW (London: Methuen, 1952), with permission of the author, the Proprietors of PUNCH, and the publisher.

en; but his slips are no less troublesome to his neighbors than if they sprang from guilty neglect. His neighbors accordingly require him, at his proper peril, to come up to their standard; and the courts which they establish decline to take his personal equation into account.[6]

In short, a person should exercise the care expected of an average, normal person under like circumstances. If a person is handicapped (blind, deaf, etc.), he must use care sufficient to compensate for his disability. However, the law allows for the immaturity of children. A child is expected to use the care of an average child of like age, intelligence, and experience. A limited number of states use arbitrary ages as milestones to delimit the increasing duty of care that advances with age. These states will consider a child below the age of five (some states as high as seven) to be incapable off intentional or negligent torts; and children from about seven to fourteen, to be presumed incapable; whereas those over fourteen, but less than full legal age, are to be presumed capable, but the contrary may be shown.

2. DUTY OF CARE—SPECIAL CASES

The duty of care varies with circumstances both of the individuals involved and the situation.

Foreseeability of Plaintiff

This is a disputed requirement with regard to negligence and is articulated in the famous case of *Palsgraf v. Long Island Railroad Co.*[7] The essential facts of this case are as follows:

After a train which had been stopped at a station began to move, a man ran across the station platform and jumped onto the moving car. The man was carrying a small package wrapped in a newspaper. The package contained fireworks, but its appearance gave no notice of its dangerous contents. After jumping onto the car, the man seemed unsteady, as if about to fall. A trainman who was holding the car door open reached forward lo help the man and a station employee pushed the man from behind. The pulling and pushing knocked the package from the man's hand. When the package fell on the rails, it exploded. The concussion of the explosion caused some scales stacked at the other end of the platform to fall on a woman who was standing beside the scales, injuring her. The injured woman sued the railroad for damages.

This classic case in the law of negligence was decided by the New York Court of Appeals in 1928 with the court's opinion written by Justice Benjamin Cardozo, an outstanding and widely respected legal scholar. In the course of the opinion, which denied the woman's right to recover, Justice Cardozo, wrote:

The conduct of the defendant's guard, if a wrong in its relation to the holder of the package, was not a wrong in its relation to the plaintiff, standing far away. Relatively to her it was not negligence at all. Nothing in the situation gave notice that the falling package had in it the potency of peril to persons thus removed.... One who jostles one's neighbor in a crowd does not invade the rights of others standing at the outer fringe when the unintended contact casts a bomb upon the ground. The wrongdoer as to them is the man who carries the bomb, not the one who explodes it without suspicion of the danger. Life will have to be made over, and human nature transformed, before prevision so extravagant can be accepted as the norm of conduct, the customary standard to which behavior must conform....

The argument for the plaintiff is built upon the shifting meanings of such words as 'wrong' and 'wrongful,' and shares their instability. What the plaintiff must show is 'a wrong' to herself, i.e., a violation of her right, and not merely a wrong to someone else, nor conduct 'wrongful' because unsocial, but not 'a wrong' to anyone.... One who seeks redress at law does not make out a cause of action by showing without more that there has been damage

---

6. Holmes, Oliver Wendell, Jr., The COMMON LAW (1881; Cambridge: Harvard University Press, 1963), pp. 86, 89.
7. 248 N.Y. 339, 162 N.E. 99, 59 A.L.R. 1253 (1928), noted 29 *Col. L. Rev.* 53, 37 *Yale L.J.* 1002.

damage to his person. If the harm was not willful, he must show that the act as to him had possibilities of danger so many and apparent as to entitle him to be protected against the doing of it though the harm was unintended....

Another court has summarized Justice Cardozo's reasoning in the following language: "The defendant's act cannot be negligent as to the plaintiff unless some harm to the plaintiff or the class to which he belonged was foreseeable; the orbit of danger as disclosed to the eye of reasonable vigilance is the orbit of the duty, and no duty is owed to one who is outside such orbit of danger."[8] Accordingly, the Palsgraf Rule can be viewed as defining to whom a duty is owed. While a majority of states had followed the rule for a number of years, the more recent trend has been away from the conceptualization of the foreseeable plaintiff serving to delimit the scope of one's duty in favor of asking the question of whether there is a close connection between the defendant's conduct and the plaintiff's harm. This trend toward viewing the problem as one of proximate cause is now followed by a majority of states.

Type of Injury

If the injury which a defendant's carelessness inflicts upon a plaintiff within the zone of danger is of the general type threatened by the defendant's conduct, the plaintiff should be able to recover even though the exact manner in which the injury occurs may be unexpected or unusual.

On the other hand, even though a plaintiff is within the zone of danger, and, therefore, a person to whom the defendant owes a duty to use proper care, the plaintiff cannot recover for a particular injury resulting from the defendant's carelessness if it was *highly extraordinary* that such a type of injury

would result. In the hypothetical case of the power line and the hunter, it is arguable that a bullet wound as a result of careless driving is so unusual that the defendant would not be liable for such an injury. (The wounded passenger, of course, could not recover from the hunter either, since the hunter was not at all careless or at fault.)

Statutory Duties

Legislation, or regulations issued pursuant to legislation, may by their terms create civil duties and tort liabilities. If the statute or regulation in question does not create civil liability courts may nonetheless adopt the standard of conduct provided in the statute or regulation as the basis for one's duty. Usually courts will make such an adoption if the statute or regulation is designed to protect the class of persons and particular interests involved in the case before it and it is aimed at the type of harm or hazard which the case presents.

Trespassers

A *trespasser* is a person who comes onto another's property without express or implied permission. A trespasser is not completely outside the protection of the law—there is never an "open season" on trespassers—but he is entitled to less protection than is accorded an invitee. In most states the possessor of a tract of land is not liable for negligent injuries sustained by a trespasser, but he is liable for intentional injuries and injuries resulting from the possessor's willful, wanton, or reckless conduct. Even though prior experience would reasonably lead a possessor to expect trespassers on his property, he generally owes no duty to take affirmative steps to make the premises reasonably safe, unless the trespassers are children. The law recognizes children's consuming curiosity, their delight in playing with unusual devices and in unusual places, their inattention to their surroundings while playing, and their inability to recognize many possible dangers.

---

8. *Dahlstrom v. Shrum.* 368 Pa. 423, 84 A.2d 289 (1951).

Example. A mining company owned and operated a private, narrow-gauge railroad line. The narrow-gauge track crossed the tracks of the Pennsylvania Railroad company (PRR), curved in a semicircle, and recrossed the PRR tracks again, the two intersections being about 650 feet apart. On one occasion, an inexperienced engineer was operating the narrow-gauge engine, backing toward one of the crossings, pushing a loaded car. Because of large slag piles, it was impossible for anyone nearing this crossing on the narrow-gauge line to see trains approaching on the PRR line. The narrow-gauge engineer failed to sound the whistle and failed to have an adequate watch at the crossing. When the narrow-gauge engine had almost reached the crossing, the engineer saw, for the first time, a PRR train already at the crossing. The narrow-gauge engineer applied his brakes, then reversed his engine; and when he saw he would be unable to avoid a collision, he shut off the steam and jumped. The narrow-gauge car collided with the rear car of the PRR train, derailing one set of the latter car's wheels. The PRR train made an emergency stop, at which time it was partly across the second narrow-gauge crossing. The impact of the collision jarred the narrow-gauge engine, opening the throttle. With the controls already in reverse and nobody in the cab to change the controls, the narrow-gauge engine ran around the semicircle of track and struck the middle coach of the PR train at the second crossing, injuring a passenger. The passenger sued the mining company.

The passenger could recover damages. Careless operation of the narrow-gauge engine constituted an unreasonable risk of injury to anyone on the PRR train or any person or property near the crossings. The injured person was within the zone of foreseeable danger, and his injury through a collision of the trains was not unexpected, even though the exact manner in which the accident occurred was quite unusual. ☐

On the other hand, the law wishes to avoid imposing unreasonably burdensome duties on property owners and possessors. As a compromise (sometimes referred to as the "attractive nuisance" doctrine), the courts feel that it is sound policy to hold a property possessor liable for injuries to trespassing children if all the following conditions are present:

1. The possessor knows or reasonably should know that children are likely to trespass,

2. The possessor maintains a structure or device which he realizes or should realize offers an unreasonable risk of serious injury to children,

3. The children, because of their youth, are unaware of the danger, and

4. The cost of removing the danger or of rendering the structure or device rea-

sonably safe is slight when compared with the risk to young children.

Business Premises

The obligation of a businessman to exercise reasonable care and thereby to keep his premises in reasonably safe condition extends not only to his building and equipment but also to all other conditions on the premises, including the behavior and conduct of other persons. If a businessman knows of a disturbance or of the dangerous conduct of other persons, or if in the exercise of reasonable supervision over his establishment he should know of the disturbance or danger, he is obliged to take reasonable steps to correct the condition. He is expected to try to stop a fight and to call for police assistance, when necessary. If the businessman fails to do what he reasonably can to quell the disturbance and as a result an innocent bystander is injured, the businessman is liable for the injuries.

3. BREACH OF DUTY

Here the question is whether or not the defendant observed the standard of care required of him under the circumstances. If an individual receives medication and is cautioned that the drug might lead to dizziness or fainting and he is further cautioned not to drive or operate machinery while taking the drug, but in disregard of these instructions, he drives his car, it could be said that he has breached his duty of care and if he passes out from the drug and causes an accident he should be held liable. However, if an individual is not on medication and is in good health the fact that he unexpectedly faints while driving, resulting in an accident, will not lead to the conclusion that he breached his duty.

4. PROXIMATE CAUSE

The fact that one has conducted himself negligently by breach of an established duty does not render him liable for the plaintiff's harm unless it can be shown that the harm which the plaintiff sustained was caused by the defendant's breach. The question of causation is legally analyzed by asking if the negligence was a substantial factor in bringing about the plaintiff's harm. How much is a "substantial factor" can be evaluated by asking three questions: (1) How many other factors were involved and how extensive was their contribution to the harm? (2) Did the defendant's conduct set in motion forces which were continuous and active in producing the harm? (3) How much time elapsed between the defendant's act and the plaintiff's harm? The closer the connection between act and harm the more likely a conclusion of legal causation.

Another way of looking at the question of proximate cause is to ask if the plaintiff's harm would have resulted even if the defendant had not been negligent. If so, then the defen-

dant is not the causal agent. It should be noted though that where one has caused initial harm, liability will attach for harm resulting from reasonable attempts by others to render aid or to illness or accident occurring as a result of the initial harm.

5. HARM

The injury for which a careless defendant is liable generally must be an actual physical injury or actual property damage. When a defendant is a careless wrongdoer rather than an intentional wrongdoer, a plaintiff usually cannot recover for fright, shock, or other emotional disturbance which does not result in harmful physical consequences to the plaintiff.

In addition to actual injury, courts in a few states also require that the injury be associated in some way with an actual physical contact with the plaintiff or his property. In the absence of such a contact, these courts hold that the defendant is not liable for a physical injury resulting solely from the plaintiff's emotional disturbance. The policy reasons followed by these courts to permit a plaintiff to recover for physical injury not associated with physical contact, would produce a multitude of lawsuits and often would raise evidence questions which would be very difficult to supervise and too easily faked. Especially in recent years, most courts in which the question has arisen have concluded that the drawbacks are not overwhelming and have permitted recovery for actual injuries, in spite of a lack of physical contact, if all of the other negligence elements are present.

B. Proof of Negligence—Res Ipsa Loquitur

In most negligence lawsuits, the burden is on the plaintiff to present sufficient evidence to prove that the defendant has been negligent. If the plaintiff fails to do so, he will lose the lawsuit and judgment will be given in favor of the defendant. In other words, the law will not presume or infer that the defendant is guilty of negligence or of any other wrongful conduct merely because an accident occurs in which the plaintiff is injured. However, under circumstances where the plaintiff cannot prove negligent conduct on the part of the defendant, but the plaintiff can show that (1) the result that happened generally does not occur except through negligent action, (2) the harm was caused by an agency or instrumentality within the exclusive control of the defendant with there being no contribution to the harm on the part of the plaintiff, and (3) the indicated negligence is within the scope of the defendant's duty to the plaintiff, then the plaintiff can shift the burden of proof to the defendant. The result of this doctrine, known as *res ipsa loquitur,* is that a presumption of negligence is raised and the burden of proving that proper care was used is placed upon the defendant.

C. Defenses

As a defense to the tort of negligence, as was the case with intentional torts, a defendant may show that one or more of the necessary elements of the tort is missing or unproved, and thereby show that the tort itself was not committed. There are other defenses which present circumstances showing that the plaintiff in some way was responsible, at least in part, for his own injury. In these situations, social policy has allowed the plaintiff a recovery of less than full damages or no recovery at all.

1. CONTRIBUTORY AND COMPARATIVE NEGLIGENCE

Even though a defendant's negligence causes an accident resulting in an injury to a plaintiff, the injured person generally cannot recover if his own failure to use proper care is a contributing cause of the accident. Many legal writers and judges have, with good reason, soundly criticized this contributory negligence rule.

Suppose that a careless driver runs into a careless pedestrian, resulting in damages in the amount of $10,000 to the pedestrian (medical expenses and lost and impaired income) and damages in the amount of $100 to the driver's car (bent fender and broken headlight). In some states the pedestrian's contributory negligence will prevent him from recovering anything at all. Since both are at fault, it certainly does not seem fair that the pedestrian should bear the full $10,000 loss while the driver bears only his $100 loss. One suggestion is that the entire damages be totaled and split equally. This would permit the pedestrian to recover $4,950 from the driver. An objection frequently raised to this solution is that in many cases the parties are not equally at fault. Accordingly, another suggestion is that the total loss be adjusted in proportion to the relative degree of the negligence of each.

This concept of relative adjustment is called *comparative negligence.* However, degrees of negligence (such as slight, ordinary, and gross) are difficult to define and still more difficult for juries to apply in the multitude of varying factual situations that commonly arise in negligence cases. Moreover, accidents—especially automobile mishaps—frequently involve more than two participants and often include several victims, further complicating any formula for sharing losses. The well-known tendency of juries to sympathize with grievously injured persons is also an important factor, throwing doubt on a jury's ability to administer or apply any formula for sharing losses. While the civil-law system (as distinguished from the common-law system) and the English and American admiralty-law systems, which are derived largely from the civil law, do not hold that contributory negligence bars recovery, any relaxation of the contributory negligence theory in common-law jurisdictions has been generally by statute. More and more states have been adopting such statutes. In some states the contributory-negli-

Example. The defendant's automobile skidded and collided with the plaintiff's auto, causing a total of $5,000 damages to the plaintiff and to his car. The plaintiff sued the defendant for that amount.

These facts alone would not be sufficient to show that the defendant was at fault. Unless the plaintiff introduced evidence from which it could be fairly concluded that the skidding was caused by the defendant's negligent driving, judgment would be given in favor of the defendant.☐

* * *

Example. The plaintiff, a passenger in a railway coach, was injured in a train wreck and sued the defendant railway company. The only evidence the plaintiff presented was the fact of the train wreck and the extent of his injuries.

Unless the defendant railroad presented evidence showing that the accident was not caused by any negligence of the railway, the plaintiff would be entitled to recover for his damages. For this type of accident, the burden of presenting evidence of what happened would be on the defendant. ☐

gence theory remains quite inflexible; even though a plaintiff is only a little careless while a defendant is extremely careless, these courts will not attempt to compare the relative degrees of negligence, but instead will rule that the plaintiff cannot recover from the defendant at all.

It should be noted, however, that a plaintiff will not be classed as contributorily negligent unless he is guilty of negligence in the eyes of the law. Thus an extremely young child can recover from a negligent defendant even though the child's injury is caused not only by the defendant's negligence but also by the child's conduct—conduct which in an older child or in an adult would be classed as contributory negligence sufficient to prevent the older child or adult from recovering from the negligent defendant. Also, although the courts generally reject comparative negligence theory, the plaintiff's negligence will not cancel a defendant's liability if the defendant's misconduct is worse than carelessness. If a defendant is guilty of reckless indifference to consequences (sometimes called willful and wanton misconduct) or of intentional wrongdoing, the injured plaintiff can recover

even though his own negligence contributed to the happening of the incident which caused his injury. In defining wanton misconduct, the Pennsylvania Supreme Court has said:

> It must be understood, of course, that wanton misconduct is something different from negligence however gross different not merely in degree but in kind and evincing a different state of mind on the part of the tortfeasor [person guilty of a tort]. Negligence consists of inattention or inadvertence, whereas wantonness exists where the danger to the plaintiff, though realized, is so recklessly disregarded that even though there be no actual intent there is at least a willingness to inflict injury, a conscious indifference to the perpetration of the wrong.[9]

2. LAST CLEAR CHANCE

Many states ease the strictness and rigidity of the contributory negligence rule by allowing a plaintiff to recover full damages if the plaintiff's negligence preceded that of the defendant by a sufficient interval of time so that,

---

9. *Kasanovich v. George.* 348 Pa. 199, 34 A.2d 523 (1943).

Example. A customer in a supermarket was pushing a shopping cart through the aisles of the store. At one point, she was walking beside the cart while scanning the tops of the shelves for a particular commodity. Suddenly she tripped and fell over a full bucket of scrub water, which was on the floor near the shelves. One of the employees had been using the scrub bucket while cleaning some shelves and had been called away to assist another customer. The injured customer sued the owner of the market for injuries sustained in the fall. The store owner was not liable if contributory negligence theory is applied. A person in business is required to keep his premises in reasonably safe condition for persons whom he can expect will enter to trade. However, although the store owner (through his employee, for whose acts he was responsible) was negligent, the customer was contributorily negligent in not looking where she was walking, and therefore could not recover. ▢

* * *

Example. P, driving north on North Street, approached the intersection of North and West Streets, where a police officer was directing traffic. The officer made the proper hand signals to stop vehicles on West Street and permit vehicles on North Street to move through the intersection. At the officer's signal, the driver ahead of P drove through the intersection. Dividing his attention between watching the traffic officer and the car ahead, P drove into the intersection. Suddenly D, driving west on West Street, entered the intersection on P's right, completely disregarding the traffic officer's signals, and collided with P, damaging P's car and injuring P. P sued D for damages.

P was held guilty of contributory negligence and barred from recovering even though D was negligent. A person is justified in assuming that others will act carefully and properly. However, this assumption should not be made blindly; a person is careless if he fails to give even cursory attention to the possible carelessness of others. Even though P had been signaled ahead by the traffic officer, he should have looked for oncoming traffic before committing himself to the intersection. With a brief glance, P could have noticed that D was not preparing to stop and could have and should have avoided the collision. Therefore, P could not recover. ▢

after discovering the position of peril into which the plaintiff has negligently placed himself, the defendant, through the exercise of reasonable care, could have avoided injuring the plaintiff. This rule is usually called the "last clear chance doctrine" or the "doctrine of discovered peril." Some states limit this rule considerably or refuse to follow it altogether.

3. ASSUMPTION OF THE RISK

When an individual intentionally exposes himself to a danger that is known to him, and he appreciates the quality of danger, he assumes the risks of injury which attends the danger. The concept is akin to the element of consent discussed in relation to intentional torts. A person may assume a risk expressly or by implication.

It is imperative that the plaintiff himself, not a reasonable person in the plaintiff's position, know of and understand the risk and that he freely and voluntarily chooses to incur it. Age, experience, and information available will be considered in assessing one's knowledge and consent.

Agreements which expressly state that one party is assuming a risk are valid unless there is obvious disparity in bargaining power between the parties. Persons may not contract away the performance of public responsibilities. Such agreements are void. This concept is further discussed in Chapter 10 on illegal agreements.

V. Strict Liability

A. Common Law Application

The usual grounds or bases for legal liability are either agreement (contract) or wrongdoing (tort). If a person's conduct is not in violation of any agreement and he is not committing a tort, he usually is not liable, no matter how much he injures others. However, in a few limited situations the law considers it sound policy to hold a person liable for damages which he causes, even though he is not at all blameworthy or at fault in causing the damages. The use of explosives is one of the most common examples. No matter how carefully explosives are used, the results are not fully predictable and may cause injury to adjoining property owners. On the other hand, prohibiting their use would be very unwise; they are necessary to accomplish purposes highly useful to society. The law, therefore, makes a policy compromise. Engaging in such ultrahazardous activities is not prohibited, but one engaging in such activities is liable for *all* damages which may result from the hazard which makes the activity abnormally dangerous, regardless of one's care or lack of fault.

Strict liability has been applied, through case law, not only to ultrahazardous or abnormally dangerous activities but also to the keeping of wild animals outside of their natural habitat, to the dangerous propensities of domestic animals and to the trespasses of livestock. More recent application has occurred in the field of products liability. It has been held that one in the business of selling a product will be liable to the user for physical harm and property damage if the product is defective and unreasonably dangerous. The questions of care or lack of privity of contract are not considered.

B. Statutory "No-Fault"

The theory of liability regardless of fault, which the common law applies to a limited number of situations, has in most states been extended to industrial accidents by workmen's compensation statutes. These statutes provide an excellent illustration of the continuing evolution of the law to reflect changing conceptions of public policy. After more than a century of industrial development, the conviction spread that the conventional tort rules were hopelessly inadequate for the mounting toll of industrial accidents. Under the conventional rules, the liability of employers to injured employees was based upon fault. An employer was not liable unless the injured employee could prove (1) that his injury was caused by his employer's negligence, (2) that the employee was not himself guilty of contributory negligence, and (3) that the injury was not associated with risks which theoretically the employee was being paid to assume, including the risk of the ordinary hazards involved in the type of work undertaken and the risk of possible negligent conduct of fellow employees. Most workmen's compensation statutes abandon the conventional theory that liability should be based on fault, and instead adopt a policy of compensation regardless of fault. Under these statutes, which have been adopted in all fifty states, the employer (and through him, society) is liable for industrial injuries, regardless of the care or lack of care shown by the employer, by the injured employee, or by fellow workers. Compensation payments are made from insurance funds, the premiums for which are paid by employers, who in turn pass the cost along to the consuming public. In the early days of workmen's compensation statutes, many state appellate courts, and the United States Supreme Court as well, were called upon to consider the purpose and theory of such statutes and invariably upheld the statutes as a valid exercise of the governmental power to legislate for the public welfare. In 1916 the Montana Supreme Court wrote:

> With the increased hazards consequent upon the use of high explosives, complicated and dangerous machinery, the powerful agencies of steam and electricity, the percentage of injured employees having justifiable claims rapidly increased until relief was sought in liability statutes which modified or eliminated some or all of the common-law defenses. But whether remedy was sought at common law or under an employer's liability statute, the actionable wrong . . . for which the master was liable . . . was the gist of the claim for damages and the basis of any right to recover. Experience demonstrated that more than one-half of all industrial injuries resulted from inevitable accident or from the risks of the business for which no one could be held responsible; that neither the common law nor employers' liability statutes furnished any measure of relief to more than 12 or 15 percent of the injured and that further appreciable improvement from the modification of existing laws could not be expected so long as the element of negligence was the foundation of legal liability.

Workingmen's insurance and compensation laws are the products of the development of the social and economic idea that the industry which has always borne the burden of depreciation and destruction of the necessary machinery shall also bear the burden of repairing the efficiency of the human machines without which the industry itself could not exist. The economic loss from vocational disease, industrial accident, old age, and unemployment was a subject of serious inquiry among the constituent German states before the days of the Empire, but the credit for crystallizing the sentiment into workable laws will always remain with Bismarck. From the enactment of the sick insurance statute in Germany in 1883 and the fundamental law in 1884, the idea of compensation based only upon the risks of the business and the impairment of earning efficiency spread to other European states, and finally penetrated to this country.... The fundamental difference between the conception of liability and compensation is found in the presence in the one, and the absence from the other, of the element of actionable wrong. The common law and liability statutes furnished an uncertain measure of relief to the limited number of workmen who could trace their injuries proximately to the master's negligence. Compensation laws proceed upon the theory that the injured workingman is entitled to pecuniary relief from the distress caused by his injury, as a matter of right, unless his own willful act is the proximate cause, and that it is wholly immaterial whether the injury can be traced to the negligence of the master, the negligence of the injured employee or a fellow servant, or whether it results from an act of God, the public enemy, an unavoidable accident, or a mere hazard of the business which may or may not be subject to more exact classification; that his compensation shall be certain, limited by the impairment of his earning capacity, proportioned to his wages, and not dependent upon the skill or eloquence of counsel or the whim or caprice of a jury; that as between workmen of the same class who suffer like injuries, each shall receive the same compensation and that, too, without the economic waste incident to protracted litigation, and without reference to the fact that the injury to the one may have been occasioned by the negligence of the master and to the other by reason of his own fault.[10]

Some feel that, in the present motor age, the numerous and costly injuries inflicted upon persons and property through the operation of millions of motor vehicles should be treated the same as industrial injuries; that, instead of liability dependent upon fault, the theory of recovery should be changed to one allowing compensation regardless of fault; and that all persons suffering injuries or damages from motor-vehicle accidents should be compensated according to a statutory scale, regardless of who was at fault in causing the accident and even though no one was at fault. In 1946 the Canadian province of Sas-

10. *In re Application of Lewis and Clark County,* 52 Mont. 6, 155 P. 268, L.R.A. 1916 D 628 (1916).

katchewan made a limited beginning in this direction by requiring compulsory insurance and providing for a scale of varying payments to be made to all who suffer injuries from auto accidents, without regard to fault. The Saskatchewan plan, however, supplements rather than replaces the conventional tort approach which ties liability to fault; although an injured person will receive a payment according to the statutory scale, his conventional tort remedies remain.

During the late 1960s and early 1970s, no-fault automobile insurance gained considerable favor among consumer groups in the United States and a number of states have enacted laws in this field. While differing, most abolish the right to sue for negligence in connection with certain types of injuries resulting from motor vehicle accidents. These statutes are in some instances limited in application to only bodily injury and not property damage or only to smaller claims such as injuries where the amount claimed is less than $10,000. An important feature is the restriction or elimination of pain and suffering as a compensable element of damage. In conjunction with the elimination of the requirement to prove legal fault, these acts make the carrying of designated insurance coverages mandatory. No fault automobile insurance statutes have been, in some states, suffering from lack of confidence during the 1980's, with repeal occurring in some states.

C. Defenses

While contributory negligence on the part of the plaintiff is not a defense to a strict liability case, voluntary assumption of the risk generally is a good defense. Additionally, statutory recognition of an otherwise hazardous activity as a desirable social benefit may create a privilege to conduct the activity without incurring strict liability. Furthermore, specific statutes may do away with the action altogether in certain specific instances and require at least the showing of negligence in order to effect recovery.

VI. Nuisances

If a defendant comes onto a plaintiff's land without permission, he violates the plaintiff's legally protected right to have exclusive and undisturbed possession of his land and is guilty of the tort known as trespass to land. A defendant's nontrespassing conduct (acts which the defendant performs on his own land) may also interfere with a plaintiff's use and enjoyment of his land. Examples include air pollution, water pollution, and vibration. All such disturbances are not necessarily wrongful. What a defendant should be permitted to do on his own land without incurring liability for disturbing his neighbor is, like other aspects of tort law, a question of policy. If a particular act of the defendant's is considered wrongful, his tort is termed a *nuisance*.

Factors important in determining what a defendant is permitted to do on his own land and at what point he incurs liability for disturbing his neighbor include the tort policy factors discussed at the beginning of this chapter; most important are the following factors:

1. The nature and extent of the harm threatened by the defendant's act.
2. The social utility of the defendant's act and its suitability to the particular locality.
3. The expense or burden of performing the act in a way that will eliminate or reduce disturbance to others.

VII. Defamation

A. Libel and Slander

Just as the law has opposed physical violence since early in the evolution of legal rights (and therefore has recognized that a person has a legal right to be free from injury or distur-

Example. A homeowner lived in an area partly devoted to manufacturing operations. A manufacturer bought the vacant corner lot adjoining the homeowner's house and constructed a manufacturing plant. Heavy machinery was installed on the side of the plant nearest the homeowner's land. When production began, the machinery caused considerable vibration to the homeowner's land and house and interfered with his rest and sleep. When the homeowner complained, the manufacturer offered to buy the homeowner's property. The homeowner refused to sell and sued for relief. In the lawsuit, the evidence conclusively showed that neither in the construction nor in the operation of the factory was it important that the machinery be located along one side rather than another.

Under the circumstances, the manufacturer's conduct was considered unreasonable and he was held responsible for maintaining a nuisance. The homeowner recovered money damages and obtained a court order requiring the manufacturer to move his machinery to the other side of his building, even though the evidence also showed that moving the machinery would cost more than the value of the homeowner's property and would force suspension of manufacturing operations for several weeks.

If the position of the machinery where originally installed had been a significant factor in the efficient operation of the manufacturing plant, the court might have awarded money damages to the homeowner for the reduction in value to his property as a result of the vibration but refused to issue an injunction requiring the factory owner to remedy the situation. Or, it is possible that no nuisance would be found and the homeowner would be denied any recovery.

bance through the wrongful, unjustified physical acts of others), so also has it opposed intentional or unjustifiable injuries to reputations. The tort involved is called *defamation*.

There are two types of defamation: *slander* and *libel*. Slander is the publication of defamatory matter by spoken words or gestures, whereas libel is publication of defamatory matter by permanent visual form, usually writing, printing or pictures, but it also includes any defamation capable of injuring similar to a written or printed statement. Accordingly, radio and television broadcasts have been held to be libel, not slander.

In defining the legally protected right to be secure in reputation, the law has developed certain policy rules, principally the following:

1. There is no defamation unless the defendant communicates the defamatory words to one or more third persons. What the defendant thinks of the plaintiff, or tells, or writes to him, cannot affect the plaintiff's reputation unless the defendant permits his words to be heard or read by some third person. No particular number of third persons is required; the tort of defamation is committed whether the defendant libels the plaintiff in a newspaper article read by thousands or in a letter addressed to the plaintiff's business office, which, as the defendant has reason to expect, is opened and read by the plaintiff's secretary. The number of persons to whom the defendant spread the defamatory words is merely a factor in determining the extent of injury to the plaintiff and the amount of damages he can recover.

2. The words used must actually injure the plaintiff's reputation or have a strong likelihood of doing so. In many states, the law of defamation makes a distinction between an impermanent, oral statement and a more lasting written statement. If the oral statement falsely accuses the plaintiff of committing a crime or of having a loathsome disease, or is

such as to injure the plaintiff in his business, trade, or profession, the plaintiff can recover commensurate damages without proving actual injury to his reputation. For other oral statements the plaintiff can collect substantial damages only if he can prove some actual injury to his reputation. No such distinction is made with written defamation; the plaintiff is entitled to recover commensurate damages in any case. Of course, the reputation protected is only that to which the plaintiff is entitled. Generally, telling or writing the truth about a person is not defamation, although such conduct may constitute another tort (invasion of the right of privacy).

B. Defenses

While proving the statement to be true generally acts as an absolute defense, some states require not only that the statement be true, but that it is made with good motive or other justifiable ends. Consent is generally an absolute defense, as is privilege. Privileges arise through existence of the right to make defamatory statements because to restrict such a right would be to hamper the workings of society or the right to free expression. Based on this policy, judges, lawyers and jurors involved in judicial proceedings enjoy this privilege, as do legislators involved in legislative proceedings and government executives exercising their duties. Husbands and wives enjoy the privilege with respect to one another. And, of significant import for freedom of the press, a qualified privilege exists to print material regarding public officials or public figures if the publication is not made maliciously.

VIII. Invasion of Privacy

In fairly recent years the law has recognized that a person has a right to have certain of his acts and circumstances kept private. This right does not extend to circumstances or incidents which are of legitimate public inter-est (such as news stories) or to persons who strive to catch the public eye (such as politicians and theatrical stars). It should be emphasized that no attempt is made here to cover completely, or even in a general way, the activities or incidents which the law encloses within the protective curtain of the right of privacy.

IX. Business Torts

A number of torts have grown up in the specific context of the business situation. The torts involve the elements of intent or negligence discussed above, some relate directly to a contract that has been entered into, while others have to do with methods of doing business or employee-employer relations. Some of these torts are briefly noted here.

A. Interference with Business Relations

When one intentionally interferes with the business or jobs of another for a malicious purpose, this tort will be found.

B. Interference with Contractual Relations

If one intentionally induces or causes another to break or dishonor his contract with a third person, this tort can be found. Raiding of another's employees who are under contract or holding over on a lease to prevent the new tenant to occupy would be examples of this tort.

C. Injurious Falsehood or Disparagement

This tort lies for the publication of a matter derogatory to plaintiff's title to his property or to its quality, or to his business. The matter must be of a kind calculated to prevent third persons from dealing with him. Also, the plaintiff must prove the falseness of the mat-

Example. Davis owed a garageman a past-due debt. After unsuccessfully attempting to collect the obligation and warning that publicity would be given to unpaid bills, the garageman placed the following sign in his show window:

> NOTICE: Davis owes an account here of $49.67, and if promises would pay an account, this account would have been settled long ago. This account will be advertised as long as it remains unpaid.

For emotional distress and humiliation resulting from the sign, Davis sued the garageman and recovered a verdict for $1,000 damages.

On appeal, the Kentucky Court of Appeals held that the defendant was guilty of a tort, namely, an invasion of the plaintiff's right of privacy.[11]

---

11. *Brents v. Morgan*, 221 Ky. 765, 299 S.W. 967, 55 A.L.R. 964 (1927).

D. Unfair Competition

It is held to be tortious to compete by the use of methods the law holds to be unfair. Such methods include imitating another's sign, advertisements, or the like, or by appropriating another's trade name, or by combining with others to eliminate competing enterprises. The misappropriation of trade secrets is also actionable. These matters are discussed more fully in Chapter 10.

E. Misrepresentation

If a person causes another to act or refrain from acting in his interest by the making of a misrepresentation, he may be liable in tort, if the misrepresentation is reasonably relied upon, and it was made intentionally or negligently. These problems are discussed in Chapter 8.

X. Business Ethics

A. Introduction

As discussed in this chapter, most of the well-defined principles of tort law had their origins in the Common Law. Rules and standards did not appear over night. Rather, as the need arose, they were developed and refined over a period of years and eventually codified or firmly established by case. The law relating the "reasonable man" standard in negligence is a classic example. On the other hand, the law relating to business ethics is of comparatively recent origin. Indeed, one could easily argue that general principles of law related to business ethics do not exist or, at best, are vague. However, based in large part upon the technological advances in doing business, rules and principles (codes of conduct) relating to the 'rightness' or 'wrongness' (ethics) of the actions of business managers and professionals are by necessity currently being scrutinized and developed. Many of the rules that are developed as standards of conduct may become law (legislative or case).

Internally developed standards or codes of conduct tend to set minimum requirements of behavior. Ethically developed standards tend to be stricter although they clearly can be identical. Neither may be law in the technical sense, but may become law if codified or resolved through the formal litigation process. In any event, ethics, standards or codes of conduct, and the law, although separate concepts, are fast becoming interwoven and increasingly important in the modern business world. The remainder of this chapter will discuss each concept and their interrelationships.

B. Codes (Standards) of Professional Conduct

Codes of conduct developed by the different professions (lawyers, accountants, doctors, engineers etc.) are perhaps the earliest, best known, most comprehensive and most often applied business standards of behavior. For example, in 1908 the American Bar Association adopted the original Canons of Professional Ethics applicable to the practice of law. Change has been continual. Most recently, in 1977 the American Bar Association appointed the Commission on Evaluation of Professional Standards which, after months of careful consideration, had its final draft of the Model Rules Of Professional Conduct adopted by the Association in 1983. The Rules represent a list of 'black-letter' regulatory provisions which help to prescribe a lawyer's professional responsibilities. But, as noted in the Preamble to the Rules, "a lawyer is also guided by personal conscience." Furthermore, as also noted in the Preamble, the Rules do not "exhaust the moral and ethical consideration that should inform a lawyer, for no worthwhile activity can be completely defined by legal rules. The Rules simply provide a framework for the ethical practice of law."

Similarly, the American Institute of Certified Public Accountants (AICPA) has developed a comprehensive *Code of Professional Conduct* that consists of general statements of ideal professional conduct for certified public accountants and specific rules that set forth unacceptable behavior. There are four parts to their code: ethical principles which create ideal standards of conduct, rules of conduct which create minimum standards, interpretations of the rules by the AICPA Division of Professional Ethics and ethical rulings which are published explanations to questions about the rules of conduct. Similar to a lawyer's or other professional's code of conduct, only the rules of conduct creating minimum standards are enforceable. Among other requirements, the rules require a CPA's independence, integrity, objectivity, compliance with general accounting standards and maintenance of confidentiality.

C. Codes (Standards) of Business Conduct

In the business sector, many corporations have addressed the issue of business standards of ethical conduct by establishing in-house ethics programs. General Dynamics, for example, has developed an ethics program "to provide guidance to all employees on matters of ethics and business conduct." Typically, conduct that has the greatest potential of producing unethical behavior is addressed. Such conduct would include inside information, conflicts of interest, antitrust, gifts and entertainment, pricing and selling, political activity etc. Similar to rules of professional ethics, such programs merely provide guidance to employees in the conduct of business. They do not have the same force and effect as statutory, case or regulatory law. Nevertheless, as issues dealing with violations of these and other standards arise, they may eventually become law.

Although not law in the technical sense, it has been noted that business codes of ethical conduct have had at least three effects:

❑ Standards that may have been unstated or unclear are now explicit. There is a sharper distinction between what is permissible and what is not.

❑ Employees are on notice as to what actions will land them in trouble. Misdeeds that were due to ignorance or false assumptions are less likely to occur.

The third effect is not salutary, and therefore is not talked about very much:

Example. A good argument can be made that the conduct of management in many insolvent savings and loan institutions was not ethical even though it may not have violated an existing industry code of conduct or a law. Whether their actions are lawful remains to be seen, but certainly the ethics of the situation will help to mold whatever standards are subsequently developed.

* * *

Most would agree that television shows depicting acts of sex and violence have marginal value to society. Nevertheless, many of them are protected under the Bill of Rights. Law and ethics come into conflict. Even though management may have a legal right to show such programs, for ethical reasons it may choose not to.

* * *

A company's code of conduct towards its employees states that at least one year's notice must be given prior to termination of employment unless the area of operation ceases to be profitable. The company hired an employee knowing that the employee's area of operation would be terminated within six months. Even though the company code of conduct did not require disclosure of this fact, an ethical argument can be made that such a fact should be disclosed prior to hiring the employee.

The third effect is not salutary, and therefore is not talked about very much:

- A code of ethics shifts the blame for bad conduct from the company to the individual. In that sense, a code of ethics can be a way for a company to wash its hands publicly of responsibility for the evils its employees commit.[12]

However, codes of business conduct have not addressed many important questions that relate directly to management and operation policy and governmental intervention. Several recent cases illustrate the point. For example, should Ford Motor Company be allowed to lobby Congress for legislation that eliminates compliance with safety standards that may reduce rear end gas tank explosions? Should Nestle Company be allowed to sell infant formula to Third World babies? Should drug testing be permitted in the work place? Should American corporations be required to divest their South African assets? These are a few of the many ethical questions that go beyond existing internal standards and codes of conduct that relate primarily to employee behavior. They relate to issues that have been litigated but for which no hard and fast rules or laws exist. In short, corporations as a whole do not have well defined codes of conduct, and external codes such as that developed by the United Nations' World Health Organization (as it relates to the sale of infant formula) have no direct impact on corporate behavior.

The question remains from a legal point of view: where do we go from here? Will minimum standards developed by codes of professional and business conduct rise to a higher ethical plane and eventually be codified? In all likelihood the answer is yes because, analogous to the doctrine of stare decisis, conditions in society are changing and from all appearances a need has been recognized to develop a body of law that addresses the eth-

12. Gellerman, S. W., *Managing Ethics from the Top Down,* SLOAN MANAGEMENT REVIEW 73, (Winter 1989).

Example. Rule 1.1 states: A lawyer shall provide competent representation to a client. Competent representation requires the legal knowledge, skill, thoroughness and preparation reasonably necessary for the representation.

Rule 1.3 states: A lawyer shall act with reasonable diligence and promptness in representing a client.

Suppose W, a wealthy actress, comes into John Lawyer's office and tells John that H, her husband, has threatened her life on repeated occasions. She tells John that she is afraid of H and wants a divorce as soon as possible. John tells W that he is a corporate attorney and is working on an important international corporate merger. He also tells her he will study the matter and get back to her soon. One month later, having not acted on W's information, John read a newspaper account of the severe beating of W by H. An argument can be made that John did not violate Rule 1.1 because he explained to W that he was not a domestic relations or criminal lawyer but he would study the matter. An argument can be made that John did not violate Rule 1.3 because one month is a reasonable time to act when representing a client in this kind of situation, especially when he told W that he had to dispose of impending business first. However, a good argument can also be made that from an ethical point of view, given the apparent need to act immediately, John should have refused W as a client and advised her to immediately seek appropriate legal help. Even if the rules of professional conduct were not technically violated, moral and ethical considerations might demand different conduct by John. □

ical and moral issues involved in doing business.

XI. Parties

As was observed earlier, some allowance will be made if the person committing the tort is a child. Other special allowances or exceptions either exist in the law or are commonly believed to exist in connection with responsibility for one's torts.

Under the common-law rule followed in many states, a parent is not liable for injuries caused by his child's torts unless the parent's connection with the child's wrongful act involves more than merely being the parent of the child and the owner of the property being used by the child. For a parent to be liable, usually either of the following situations must exist:

1. The parent himself is guilty of a tort which is a substantial factor in causing the injury in question. Thus a parent will be liable if he puts a dangerous object into the hands of his child, knowing that the child will not use proper care, or if the parent fails to use proper care to supervise and control his child.

2. The child's tort which causes the injury in question is associated with a master-servant relationship existing between the parent and the child *at that time*. The relationship between an employer and his employee is commonly termed by the law a master-servant relationship. Although a parent has the general right to control and discipline his child, a master-servant relationship does not exist between the parent and child except when the child is performing some service not, for his parent and under the parent's control. When a master-servant relationship does exist (either between a parent and child or between an employer and employee), the law considers that as a matter of fairness the master should be held liable for the torts which are committed by the servant while he is engaged in advancing the interests of his mas-

ter. In connection with automobile accidents, for example, a master-servant relationship arises if an owner permits someone to drive his car while the owner rides as a passenger; the presence of the owner in the car usually gives him the right to control the manner of driving, regardless of who is being benefited by the trip, and thus makes the driver the owner's servant, with the result that the owner is liable for the driver's negligence. If an owner permits another person to drive his car and the owner is not present in the car, a master-servant relationship exists only if the driver is on an errand for the owner. Compulsory insurance statutes in effect in many states usually do not change the ordinary master-servant rules. The typical statute will usually provide that in case of an accident caused by a person driving with the owner's consent, if the owner does not have insurance (or a statutory equivalent) covering the accident, his auto registration will be suspended for a time while the possibility of an actual master-servant relationship can be litigated. However, unless an actual master-servant situation is found to exist, the owner will not be liable for the driver's negligence.

In some states the rules for liability in automobile accidents have been extended beyond the ordinary master-servant rules, either (1) by permissive driving statutes, or (2) by the family-purpose doctrine.

Permissive Driving Statutes. Statutes in New York and some other states provide that if the owner of a car permits another to drive, the owner is liable for the driver's negligence even though (I) the owner is not present at the time of an accident, and (2) the driver is not on an errand for the owner. It should be noted that liability is determined according to the law of the place where an auto accident occurs. If an auto owned and registered in Pennsylvania is involved in an accident in New York State, New York substantive law will apply in the accident. The owner with whose permission it is being driven will be liable for the driver's negligence, even though the circumstances are such that the owner would not be liable had the accident occurred in Pennsylvania.

Family-Purpose Doctrine. In some states the courts consider that it is sound policy in connection with automobiles to broaden the ordinary master-servant rules by a theory called the family-purpose doctrine. Usually a family automobile is purchased and intended for use by the family while title is taken in the name of the head of the family or parents. The family-purpose doctrine provides that the head of the family is liable for any negligent driving which occurs while the car is being used for the usual family purposes. A son's taking of his girl friend to a dance is a common use of the family car. In some of the states which follow this doctrine, the parent-owner would be liable for the son's negligent driving while on his date. Some other states, even though following the family-purpose doctrine, would not extend it to the son's using the car for his dance date. In many other states the courts feel that the family-purpose doctrine is not desirable policy and do not follow it.

While minority will possibly affect one's liability for tort, mental incapacity of an adult will not alter the degree of care required for negligence nor lessen liability for intentional torts. However, it may be used to show lack of ability to form the requisite intent for such torts.

If the party to a suit is the government itself, an instrumentality of the government or a public official, such party may enjoy immunity or partial immunity from suit. The common law doctrine of sovereign immunity prevented tort claims from being pursued against the government or governmental agencies or instrumentalities. This immunity has been abolished in about half of the states and restricted in others. As to the federal government, it has been restricted under the Federal Tort Claims Act. High public officials enjoy similar immunity within the scope of their authority and judicial officers and public employees enjoy it in regard to negligence in discretionary acts within the scope of their employment duties. In a minority of jurisdictions, charitable organizations still enjoy the common law immunity from tort liability, too.

All persons who, in pursuit of a common plan or design, actively take part in the commission of a tortious act will be considered as parties defendant. Also liable are those who further such acts by cooperation, who lend aid or encouragement to the actor or ratify and adopt his acts done for their benefit. Such *joint-tortfeasors* need not cooperate based on an expressed agreement, only tacit understanding is required. For example, where two drivers suddenly and without consultation decide to race their automobiles on a public highway, both will be liable if one or the other alone causes harm to a third person.

* * *

Problems

1. After D, a retailer, conducted an advertising campaign to introduce a new type of product into his community, P, the owner of a competing store, acquired some similar items which he advertised at a lower price. Although P's advertising in no way misled customers into confusing the item P was selling with the item D had advertised, it was clear that P was taking advantage of the market demand which D had developed by his advertising campaign. Quite angered, D wrote to P saying among other things, "Your practices are fraudulent and dishonest, and you are not better than a thief." P sued D for damages for defamation.

(a) No one other than P (and, of course, D) read the letter. What should be the result of P's lawsuit against D? Explain.

(b) P was the first person (other than D) to read the letter. After reading it, P gave it to his secretary to read and had her send it to P's lawyer.

What should be the result of P's lawsuit against D? Explain.

(c) D dictated the letter to his secretary. After she had typed the letter, D signed it and had her mail the letter. After the letter left D's office, no one other than P read it. What should be the result of P's lawsuit against D? Explain.

(d) As D knew, P's standard office practice was for his secretary to open all mail not marked "personal." Personal mail the secretary would put on P's desk unopened. No one (other than D) read the letter before it arrived in P's office. (1) D did not mark the envelope "personal," and P's secretary opened and read the letter before giving it to P. What should be the result of P's lawsuit against D? Explain. (2) Although D marked the envelope "personal," P's secretary overlooked that notation and opened and read the letter before giving it to P. What should be the result of P's lawsuit against D? Explain.

2. On the way home from school, an eleven-year-old girl stopped in the book department of a large department store. The girl was carrying a briefcase in one hand and a box of popcorn in the other hand. While looking at some books, she put the box of popcorn in her briefcase. After spending a few minutes at the book department, the girl went to the ladies' rest room. A woman detective employed by the store, having noticed the girl putting something in her briefcase, followed the girl into the ladies' rest room and asked the girl where she had put the books she had taken from the book counter. When the girl began to cry, the detective took hold of the girl's arm with one hand and took her briefcase in the other hand. Two women shoppers who were also in the rest room protested the detective's actions and all four (the girl, the detective, and the two shoppers) went to the manager's office. When it was ascertained that the girl had not taken any books, she was escorted to a bus stop and put on the bus which she usually used to go home. The girl was quite nervous, upset, and became ill, and through her parents sued the store for damages.

(a) On what grounds could the lawsuit be brought? Explain.

(b) What would be the result of the lawsuit? Explain.

3. The trustees of a nonprofit hospital decided to establish a nursing school to be operated in conjunction with the hospital. A fund-raising campaign was initiated, appealing to all persons and businesses in the community for contributions for the nursing school. A number of businessmen signed pledges agreeing to pay amounts ranging from $100 to $5,000, payments to be completed by the middle of the year. In the fall, the nursing school began operation. Shortly thereafter a full-page newspaper advertisement was published by the trustees in space donated by the local newspaper. The advertisement read in part:

> We acknowledge with justifiable pride in our community the generous support given our community hospital nursing school. The nursing school, which will be of inestimable value to the community, would not have been possible without the generous support of the following community-spirited business establishments:

Name of Business	Immediate Payments and/or Pledges Payable by June 30 of this year	Total Payments Actually Made up to October 1
Ace Athletic Store	$1,000	$1,000
Barton Bakery	$500	None
Carter Car Sales	$750	$600

[The advertisement continued in the same way, listing the names of about forty other businesses.]

A further report will be made to the community at the end of the year.

Board of Trustees
Community Hospital

(a) The information concerning Barton Bakery was true. Nevertheless, Barton Bakery sued the trustees for damages. On what grounds and with what result? Explain.

(b) A business in the community, known as the Allen Auto Sales, had declined to contribute anything to the nursing school fund, and the preceding advertisement made no mention of the Allen Auto Sales. The Allen Auto Sales sued the trustees for damages. On what grounds and with what results? Explain.

4. One evening a woman was annoyed by her neighbor's loud playing of his radio and complained to the police. The following day the woman was sitting on the back porch of her home with a friend and the friend's two children when the neighbor came home from work. Seeing the woman, the neighbor came to the fence between the two properties and in a loud voice profanely called the woman various abusive names. The woman was considerably shocked, upset, and humiliated, and remained nervous and physically upset for several days. The woman sued the neighbor for damages. Assume that under the circumstances it was clear to any hearer that the words used by the neighbor were not intended to have their literal meaning and that the neighbor therefore was not guilty of slander. Do you think the neighbor committed a tort for which the woman should be able to recover damages? Briefly state a few policy arguments on both sides of the question, and explain your decision whether or not the woman should collect.

5. A bill collector called at a woman's home to collect a $10 debt she owed his employer. The woman was alone at the time, and when she truthfully said that she was unable to pay at the moment but would be able to pay a few days later, the bill collector profanely called the woman abusive names. The woman was considerably shocked, upset, and humiliated, and remained nervous and physically upset for several days. The woman sued the bill collector. Would your policy arguments in this case be any different from your arguments in Problem 4? Explain.

6. While driving north on a through highway at a moderate rate of speed, D slowed, upon approaching an intersection. As a result of an incident [described in Parts (a) and (b)] occurring at the intersection, D's car went out of control. After his car was out of control, D did all he reasonably could to bring it under control. In spite of D's efforts, the car mounted the curb, striking and seriously injuring P, a pedestrian, who was using

proper care when he was injured. P sued D and proved damages of $5,000. D did not have any liability insurance.

(a) D's car went out of control as a result of a collision with another car. Although using proper care, D was unable to avoid the collision. The other car was driven by a person who, without stopping at the stop sign, entered the intersection from D's left. Following the collision, while D was still dazed, the other driver drove away and the police were unable to locate or identify him. Was P entitled to judgment against D? Explain.

(b) D's car went out of control as a result of skidding on some spots of oil on the road. D did not see the oil at the intersection, and a driver exercising reasonable care could not have seen the oil in time to avoid skidding on it. Was P entitled to judgment against D? Explain.

(c) Other facts remaining the same, assume that at the time of the accident, D had an insurance policy under which the insuring company agreed to pay any amount, up to $10,000, for which D might become legally obligated because of personal injuries to others resulting from D's operation of an automobile. With the fact of D's insurance added to the previously mentioned facts: (1) Would your answer to the situation in Part (a) now be the same as, or different from, the answer you had given? Explain. (2) Would your answer to the situation in Part (b) now be the same as, or different from, the answer you had given? Explain.

7. On June 1, S, a retail appliance dealer, entered into a written contract with B, a customer, under which (1) S sold and delivered a described TV set to B for $400, (2) $50 of the price was payable upon signing of the agreement, the balance in monthly installments of $50 each, starting July 1, (3) until the entire $400 was paid, title to the TV set was to remain with S, and (4) if B defaulted in the agreed payments, S was to have the right to repossess the set from B's home at any time. B made the $50 down payment and the July 1 payment, but by the middle of August had paid nothing further. S called on B at his home, and when B said

he was then unable to pay anything further but would be able to pay $100 on September 1, S said he intended to repossess the TV set. When B protested, asking for more time, S swung his arm in a backhand motion against B's head, pushing B out of the doorway. S, thinking B was feigning when he seemed to sustain great pain from the push, entered the house and removed the TV set. S's backhand motion was more of a push than a blow. However, the impact on B's ear was sufficient to aggravate and spread an ear infection, causing a more serious infection and a partial loss of hearing in that ear. B's wife, who was seven months pregnant, was also present. S did not threaten her in any way or come near her, but her fright and shock at seeing S's conduct caused her to collapse in a hysterical condition and to suffer a miscarriage.

(a) B sued S for a substantial amount for the serious results sustained from S's backhand motion. S conclusively proved that he had no knowledge of B's ear infection and, through the exercise of reasonable care, could not have suspected the existence of the infection. S also proved that, under ordinary circumstances, his backhand motion would have caused no injury to B at all. What should be the result of B's lawsuit? Explain.

(b) B's wife sued S for the damages which she sustained. What should be the result of the wife's lawsuit? Explain.

8. (a) D, a former resident of a small town, returned to that town for a short visit after an absence of several months. When D resided there, Sassafras Street, running north and south, was a two-way, through street with stop signs to halt traffic before entering Sassafras Street. During D's absence from the town, Sassafras Street was made a one-way through street for southbound traffic only. The first day of his visit, D (with a new, quietly operating car) drove west on 25th Street, stopped at the intersection, and then, not noticing the small one-way sign with an arrow pointing south, turned north (the wrong way) on Sassafras Street. As D, driving north on Sassafras Street, approached the intersection of 24th Street, D saw P, a pedestrian on the sidewalk walking west toward

Sassafras Street. When P reached the intersection of 24th and Sassafras Street, he stopped at the curb for a moment and then suddenly stepped into the street only 10 feet in front of D's car. Although D was driving at a reasonable speed, he could not avoid hitting P. P sued D for the injuries sustained. At the trial, P testified that, before stepping off the curb, he had looked toward the north (looking for southbound traffic) but had not looked toward the south and therefore did not see D's car. Explain (1) the reasoning upon which P might attempt to collect, (2) the reasoning upon which D might attempt to defend, and (3) who should win the lawsuit.

(b) Other facts remaining the same, assume the following changed facts: At the time of the accident, Sassafras Street was, and always had been, a two-way street. P, looking toward the north but not toward the south, did not see D approaching from the south. Because D was driving unreasonably, but not recklessly, fast, he could not avoid hitting P. P sued D. Answer the same questions asked in Part (a).

9. A merchant owned and operated a small two-story department store, the second floor being reached by a staircase at the rear of the store. When the building was constructed, there were railings on each side of the staircase. After a time, the railings became loose and the railings and brackets were removed. One day a woman customer was shopping on the second floor. As she was going down the stairs, the heel of one of her shoes came off. As the woman felt herself falling, she grabbed for the wall. Because there was no railing and the wall was smooth, she was unable to avoid falling. This was the first time the heel had come off; it had not previously appeared loose. The woman sued the merchant for damages for injuries which resulted from the fall.

(a) Explain (1) the reasoning upon which the woman might attempt to recover, (2) the reasoning upon which the merchant might attempt to defend, and (3) which party should be given judgment.

(b) Would your answers be the same if the staircase had never been equipped with railings? Explain.

10. P was driving slightly over 40 miles per hour along a two-lane, concrete highway when he was unexpectedly blinded by the bright headlights of an oncoming car. Because the other driver failed at any time to switch his lights to the lower beam, P's vision remained obscured until the other car passed, during which time P's car traveled about 150 feet. Immediately after the blinding lights had passed, P saw, for the first time, the rear of a truck 30 feet ahead. P had not seen the truck sooner because the truck body was dark in color and had no rear lights and no illumination or reflectors of any kind. The truck was heavily loaded with coal and moving at a very slow speed, whereas P's car was traveling about 40 miles per hour. After seeing the truck, P did all he reasonably could, but was unable to swerve sufficiently and crashed into the rear of the truck, causing considerable damage to his own car. P sued the truck driver. What would be the result of the lawsuit? Explain.

11. State Street was a one-way street for westbound traffic only; North Street was a north-south street open to two-way traffic; and East Street, one block (200 yards) east of North Street, ran parallel to North Street. D, driving north on North Street in a negligent manner, collided with M, who was driving west on State Street with proper care. The force of the collision knocked M's car into the porch of A's frame house located on the northeast corner of the intersection. A fire immediately broke out in M's car. M managed to struggle clear from his car before the gas tank exploded, spraying burning gasoline onto A's porch. A's porch quickly joined the conflagration. The fire spread to the remainder of A's house and, in spite of firemen's efforts, to B's house just east of A's house. The draft created by the growing fire accelerated its spread and all the buildings in the block were destroyed or badly damaged by the fire before it was finally put out. Included, in addition to a number of intervening buildings, was C's retail store

building on the northwest corner of State Street and East Street. A, B, and C each filed a separate lawsuit against D. Explain (1) the reasoning upon which the plaintiff in each lawsuit might attempt to collect, (2) the reasoning upon which D might attempt to defend the lawsuits, and (3) which party should be given judgment in each lawsuit.

12. A construction company was under contract to install curbs and sidewalks and repave a certain street. Alongside the street ran the tracks to the Community Transit Company. The tracks were embedded in concrete and the company's streetcars were of a new type, relatively noiseless in operation. P, an employee of the construction company, on an errand to the toolhouse, was walking west along the westbound track not more than 18 inches from the north rail. P was negligent in walking with his back toward the east, the direction from which streetcars would come on the westbound track. (This was so clearly negligence that a jury could not reasonably conclude otherwise). A streetcar motorman, a little behind schedule, was taking advantage of the slight downgrade and driving his westbound streetcar about 30 to 35 miles per hour. The motorman first saw P walking beside the track when the streetcar was about 200 feet away from P. Although P continued to be clearly visible to the motorman from that time on, the motorman did not sound his bell, slow down, or apply the brakes until after the right front of the streetcar struck P a severe and crippling blow. P sued the transit company for damages. Explain (1) the reasoning upon which P could attempt to recover, (2) the reasoning upon which the transit company could attempt to defend, and (3) which party should be given judgment.

13. A manufacturer owned a piece of land upon which was a factory and along the edge of which was a small, unused, brick stable, one and one-half stories high. The east wall of the stable was three feet from the west wall of a factory located on an adjoining property. Desiring to construct an addition to his factory, the manufacturer contracted with a builder for demolition of the stable and construction of a new building. Since the

stable and the land immediately surrounding it had not been previously used by the manufacturer, children had always used the premises as a playground. During demolition of the stable, children gathered to watch. On the third day of demolition, a heavy rain began about 3 p.m., forcing the builder's workmen to quit work. The rain lasted an hour, after which the builder decided to do nothing more that day and sent his men home. At that time, all that remained standing of the stable was a section of the east wall about 10 to 15 feet high. During the process of demolition, bricks had fallen or been thrown into the narrow space between the east wall of the stable and the west wall of the adjoining factory. When the rain stopped, a number of children returned to the area to play. After they had been playing awhile, three boys were standing on the top of the section of wall which had not been demolished; P, 14 years old, was standing at the bottom of the wall. Suddenly the wall collapsed, almost burying P in a mass of bricks. P sustained serious and permanent injuries and through his father sued the builder for damages. Experts on building demolition testified that the wall collapsed because of a combination of the following factors: (1) the builder's workmen had already chipped and weakened the wall near the bottom, (2) rain water was absorbed by the bricks piled in the narrow space between the wall and the adjoining factory, causing them to exert pressure against the wall, and (3) the rain had weakened the exposed mortar in the wall. The experts also testified that the presence of the three boys on top of the wall had nothing to do with the collapse of the wall. Explain (1) the reasoning upon which P could attempt to collect, (2) the reasoning upon which the building could attempt to defend, and (3) which party should be given judgment.

14. The plaintiff complained to his neighbor, the defendant, about the latter's dumping trash at the back of his property in such a careless manner that some fell onto the plaintiff's property. The defendant became angered and without justification hit the plaintiff, knocking him to the ground and breaking his glasses (costing $25) and a dental

plate (costing $75). The plaintiff was not other-wise injured. The plaintiff swore out a warrant against the defendant for the crime of assault and battery. The defendant was arrested, tried, and convicted as charged. He was sentenced to pay a fine of $100 and court costs, which he paid. The plaintiff then demanded that the defendant pay for replacing the plaintiff's glasses and dental plate, and when the defendant refused, the plaintiff sued the defendant for $100. In defense the defendant protested that he had already been tried and had fully paid for his wrongful act. Would the defendant's defense be effective to prevent the plaintiff from recovering a judgment for $100? Explain.

15. Arriving before game time to participate in inaugural ceremonies for a new baseball stadium scheduled to precede the game plaintiff was hit by a baseball during batting practice, which had commenced a little earlier than usual to accommodate the pregame activities. At the time she was hit by the baseball, plaintiff was behind a four foot wall on an interior walkway above the bull pen and immediately within the right field foul territory area. On what basis could plaintiff sue and how could defendant contest the suit. (Jones v. Three Rivers Management Corp. and Pittsburgh Athletic Co. 1978)

16. Describe the difference between law and ethics and give comparative examples of each.

The Basic Law of Contracts: Offer & Acceptance

CHAPTER OUTLINE

The Basic Law of Contracts: Offer and Acceptance

I. The Nature of a Contract

A. A General Definition

Briefly stated, under Common Law, a *contract* is an agreement involving a promise or a set of promises which the law will enforce. While modern society is absolutely dependent upon the making and performing of promises, no legal system in the world enforces *all* promises which people make. The task of the law therefore is not only to enforce promises (that is, to provide adequate remedies to persons who are injured when others fail to perform their promises) but also to formulate rules for determining as a matter of public policy, just when, under what circumstances, and to what extent promises should be enforced.

The Uniform Commercial Code applies this definition but generally limits its applicability to transactions pertaining to the sale of goods. Under the Code, " 'goods' means all things (including specially manufactured goods) which are movable at the time of identification to the contract for sale other than the money in which the price is to be paid, investment securities . . . and things in action."[1] This definition would, of course, exclude

such things as land, buildings, and permanently attached fixtures.

In recent years, there has been an effort on the part of lawyers to apply Code pro-visions to certain nonsale transactions such as leases, bailments, and service contracts. Similarly, an effort has been made to apply Code provisions to sales of things other than "goods," such as the application of implied warranty principles to the sale of houses. These efforts have met with some success; however, the primary function of the Code continues to be that of controlling the sale of goods.

B. Classification of Contracts

1. EXPRESS OR IMPLIED CONTRACTS

An express contract arises when the parties state the terms of their agreement or understanding either in written or spoken words. However, in certain instances, the parties need not expressly state in written or spoken words all the terms of their con-tract. Terms can be implied from the conduct of the parties, and the actual making of the entire agreement itself can be implied from the conduct of the parties. Thus, an implied contract can arise where the agreement is inferred from the conduct of the parties alone, without the necessity of written or spoken words.

---

1. U.C.C. Sec. 105(1).

Example. S said to B: "I hereby offer to sell you the following goods (describing them) for $100." B promptly replied, "I accept your offer," thus forming an enforceable express contract.

Since neither party expressly stated otherwise, it would be presumed (or implied) that both parties intended delivery and payment to be made in the usual or customary manner. Delivery and payment at the customary time and place would, therefore, be enforceable obligations, undertaken by the parties when they formed their agreement without specifying other terms. □

* * *

Example. Wishing to buy bread, a buyer went to a grocery store where he had a charge account. Seeing that the grocer was busy waiting on another customer, the buyer picked up a loaf of bread, and waved it at the grocer. The grocer nodded his head and the buyer left the store.

The grocer and the buyer thus entered into a contract under which the buyer agreed to pay the usual price at the usual time. Since nothing was stated expressly in words, the contract would be classified as an implied contract, both the formation of the agreement and its terms being implied from the conduct of the parties. □

* * *

Example. S promised B that he would give B $5 if B delivered a package to the post office by a certain date. It's possible that if B made a return promise to deliver the package, a bilateral contract would arise. A promise is given for a promise. But, if B said nothing and delivered the package to the post office, a unilateral contract arises. A promise is given for an act. □

2. BILATERAL AND UNILATERAL CONTRACTS

A bilateral contract arises when a promise is given in exchange for another promise. A unilateral contract, on the other hand, arises where a promise is given in exchange for a requested performance. The promise made by one party is framed in such a way that an act is required before the contract is formed. However, it is not unusual for a promise to form the basis of an agreement where the response can be either a return promise (bilateral contract) or an act (unilateral contract).

The distinction between bilateral and unilateral contracts, as they specifically relate to the acceptance and consideration elements in contract formation, will be discussed in greater depth in Part II of this chapter and in Chapter 6.

3. QUASI-CONTRACTS

In addition to determining the existence and scope of contractual promises, the law finds it useful to borrow from contract rules and apply their ideas in certain situations, even though an actual contract does not exist. The theory, called quasi-contract, is one of the most common examples.

The Latin term *quasi* means "as if" or "analogous to." The term *quasi-contract* is a tag or label for a theory which provides for recovery in a situation in which, although there is no actual agreement between parties, not even an implied agreement, it would be unfair and unjust to deny recovery. In the early development of the law, the form in which a lawsuit was brought was of vital importance. If a plaintiff could not fit his case into one of the

Example. From time to time Davis incurred obligations to Carter. On one occasion when Davis was paying various of his creditors, he erroneously thought that he owed Carter $200 and paid him that amount. Although Davis was not indebted to Carter at that time, Carter honestly thought that there was an outstanding obligation and accepted the payment.
When the parties discovered their mistake, Davis demanded return of the money and upon Carter's refusal, sued Carter to recover $200.

When cases such as this first arose, tort law had not developed to the point of considering that Carter's retention of the payment might constitute a tort. However the law permitted Davis to recover on the theory that, to prevent unfairly and unjustly enriching Carter at Davis' expense, the situation should be treated "as if" there were a promise by Carter to repay the $200 to Davis. ▢

* * *

Example. When a bus was involved in an accident, a passenger suffered a serious head injury, and was rushed to a hospital in an unconscious condition. A surgeon performed an emergency operation in a reasonable attempt to save the injured person's life, but the patient died without regaining consciousness.

Since the passenger was unconscious all of the time, he was unable to form an actual contract with the surgeon. Nevertheless, a patient of sufficient means is expected to pay for medical services. When the injured passenger was found to have left a sizable estate, the surgeon was able to recover from the estate for the reasonable value of his medical services—on the theory of quasi-contract, "as if" there were a contract. ▢

* * *

Example. On January 30, S promised in writing to sell to B two residential building lots for $3,000 per lot, and B accepted in writing. At this point in time, the S-B contract was wholly executory since neither land nor money had been exchanged by the parties. By February 15, S had delivered to B title to one of the lots and B had paid S $3,000. Now the contract is partially executed and partially executory since both parties had performed in part. On March 1, S delivered title to the remaining lot to B and B paid S the remaining $3,000. At this point in time, the contract is executed since performance has taken place in full. ▢

recognized forms, he might be unable to obtain relief. If it seemed too unfair to deny recovery, the law would grant relief to a plaintiff by pretending that he was a party to a contract, permitting him to recover in a quasi-contract action, "as if" there were a contract.

4. EXECUTED AND EXECUTORY CONTRACTS

An executed contract is one where full performance has taken place under the terms of the contract. An executory contract is one where compliance with the contract is not complete. Some future act has to take place before the contract terms are fulfilled. A contract can be executed in part and executory in part.

C. Parties to a Contract

1. PROMISOR AND PROMISEE

In the example immediately above, with respect to S's promise to sell, S is promisor, or one who makes a promise, and B is a promisee, or one to whom a promise is made. On the other hand, with respect to B's promise to accept, B is a promisor and S is a promisee. Whether a party to a contract is labeled as a promisor or promisee depends upon whose promise is being considered. This distinction is particularly relevant to the study of consideration in Chapter 6.

2. OFFEROR AND OFFEREE

Using the same S-B contract as an example, S is also an offeror, or one who makes a proposal wherein another is given the power to create a legally enforceable obligation. No matter how the relationship between the contracting parties is viewed, there is generally only one offeror and one offeree to a contract. Identifying the offeror and offeree becomes important in establishing the offer element of a contract which is considered in detail in Part II of this chapter.

3. SELLER AND BUYER

Under the Uniform Commercial Code, the parties to a contract are identified as the Seller and Buyer. Simply stated, a seller is one who sells goods and a buyer is one who buys goods.[2] The Code frequently has special rules applicable to sellers and buyers who are merchants or where the transaction is between merchants. The Code definition of a merchant is a person who deals in or holds himself out as having knowledge of the goods involved in the transaction.[3] Since merchants in a sense are considered to be professionals with respect to their goods, they are held to a higher degree of care and responsibility than are nonmerchants.

II. Formation of Contracts

A. The Basic Elements

In order for a contract at common law to be legally enforceable, various elements must be taken into account as follows (not necessarily in terms of their relative priority, but as they will be sequentially discussed in this and subsequent chapters): (1) mutual manifestation

2. U.C.C. Secs. 2-103(1) (a) and (d).
3. U.C.C. Secs. 2-104(1) and (3).

of intent (Chapter 5); consideration (Chapter 6); capacity (Chapter 7); reality of consent (Chapter 8); legality of purpose (Chapter 10); and compliance with the statute of frauds (Chapter 9). The relationship of these elements is shown in Figure 5.1.

Generally, therefore, in analyzing the validity of a contract, four questions must be addressed: (1) has an offer been made which is legally capable of being accepted; (2) has the offer been properly accepted; (3) is the consideration or its equivalent legally recognized; (4) do the parties have the capacity to contract.

B. Mutual Manifestation of Intent

For a legally enforceable contract to be formed, two (or more) persons must indicate that they are in agreement on a certain proposition—they must mutually consent or assent to something which binds or commits them in some definite way. The mechanics by which two persons form a contractual agreement is, almost invariably, for one person to make a definite proposal or offer to the other and for the other to acquiesce in or accept the offer. Suppose that the owner of a rare book remarks to a companion, "I'm thinking of selling this book. I'd like to get $300 for it," to which the companion promptly replies, "I'll give you $300 for it." Suppose further that after thinking a moment the owner answers, "No, I've changed my mind. I guess I won't sell now," where-upon the companion insists that a legally enforceable contract has already been formed. The question thus raised is whether or not the parties have mutually assented to a binding commitment. Clearly the answer is not to be found by asking either the owner or his companion what he actually intended or what he believes the rights of the parties should be. Any system for deciding

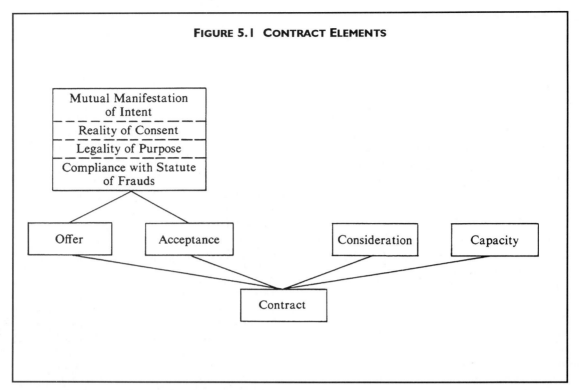

FIGURE 5.1 CONTRACT ELEMENTS

disputes must utilize provable and impartial measuring devices. In contract law as in tort law—in fact for all human activity—the law's chief yardstick is "the reasonable man." In the above-described rare-book dispute, the companion certainly agreed to commit or bind himself to something definite—to buy the book for $300. The only question is whether the owner bound himself to sell—whether a reasonable man would conclude from what was said that the owner intended to be committed as soon as the companion might acquiesce and without any chance to bargain or discuss the matter further. Analyzed in this way, the owner's statement clearly does not form a sound basis for considering him legally bound. The law expresses this conclusion by saying that the owner did not make an offer,

and therefore, although the companion acquiesced, no contract was formed. The minds of the parties had not met. In this manner the law uses the concepts of offer and acceptance as the measuring instruments for analyzing a fact situation and determining, from the stand-point of the reasonable man, whether a contractual agreement has been formed. In summary, a contract cannot be formed until there is a mutual manifestation of intent as expressed through an offer and its acceptance.

III. Offer

As previously stated, a person who makes an offer is usually referred to as the offeror, while the person to whom the offer is made is the offeree. When a person makes a proposal ex-

Example. A few days after an old harness owned by the defendant and worth about $15 disappeared from the defendant's barn, a boy found a portion of the harness in the plaintiff's berry patch. The defendant and the plaintiff recovered that part and brought it to the plaintiff's blacksmith shop, where the defendant gave the boy a quarter and promised him a dollar if he found the remainder of the harness. At the same time, the defendant angrily exclaimed to the plaintiff and other men who had gathered around, "I'll give $100 to any man who will find out who the thief is and $100 to a lawyer for prosecuting him, and I won't get a cheap lawyer but a good one," accompanying his statement with rough language and epithets concerning the thief. Shortly afterwards, a neighbor told the plaintiff about seeing Smith, who was the village halfwit, carrying a harness on the day of the theft. The plaintiff watched Smith that night and saw him hiding the remainder of the harness. When the plaintiff told the defendant of this, they obtained a search warrant and recovered the remainder of the harness from Smith's house. The plaintiff then demanded the $100 reward and sued when the defendant refused to pay.

The plaintiff could not recover. On similar facts, the Appellate Court of Illinois said[4] that under the circumstances (swearing and boasting, the trifling amount paid and promised to the boy, great disproportion between the amount-of the "reward" and the value of the harness), a reasonable man in the position of the plaintiff would not have been justified in believing that the owner seriously intended to offer a $100 reward. ☐

* * *

Example. A man and his wife lived on the fourth floor of an apartment hotel. At a time when the husband was away but the wife was known to be in the building, a fire started. After the fire had been raging for about thirty minutes, the husband arrived on the scene in great excitement and declared, "I will give $5,000 to any person who will bring the body of my wife out of that building, dead or alive." Hearing this statement, the plaintiff entered the building at great personal risk and brought out the dead body of the wife. When the husband later refused to pay the promised reward, the plaintiff sued for $5,000. ☐

---

4. *Higgins v. Lessig*, 49 Ill. App. 459 (1893).

---

pressing an intent as to the kind of contract he is willing to make and the terms by which he is willing to be legally bound, the expression of intent is an offer if it would lead a reasonable man in the position of the offeree to believe that the one who is expressing his intent means to be bound or committed to the stated proposition as soon as the offeree indicates his consent, without any further bargaining or discussion of the matter. If a reasonable person would not conclude that the maker of the statement is making such a commitment, no offer is made. This question whether a statement of intent is or is not an offer most commonly arises in connection with statements made in jest or under strong emotion (such as anger or fear) and with statements made to invite or attract persons to buy or to deal.

A. Manner in which Offer was Made

I. JOKING AND EMOTIONAL EXCLAMATIONS

A statement of intent may appear to be seriously meant and therefore may constitute an offer even though the maker of the statement is excited, angry, fearful, or joking. Such agitation or jocularity is merely a circumstance to be considered with all of the other surrounding circumstances in determining whether a reasonable person would be justified in believing that the statement is seriously meant.

Whether a reasonable person would be justified in believing that an offer was really intended would depend upon all of the surrounding circumstances, including the husband's manner of speaking, his seeming ability to pay such a sum (judging from his appearance and the type of residence involved), etc. In the case upon which this example is based, the jury concluded that under the circumstances, as disclosed by the evidence presented during the trial, the husband reasonably appeared to have a serious intent, and therefore an enforceable contract was formed.

2. INVITATIONS TO DEAL

Statements intended to invite or to attract persons to buy or to deal are made in circular letters, advertisements, catalog listings, and other announcements concerning items for sale. Again the reasonable person serves as the guide for determining whether or not such statements are offers. The statement is an offer only if, under all of the circumstances, a reasonable person would be justified in concluding that the one making the particular statement intends to be bound or committed as soon as the offeree indicates his consent and without any further bargaining or discussion. Factors important in resolving this question include the following:

1. The definiteness of the language used:

a. As to the *when, where*, and *what* of the contract terms.

b. As to the person to whom the statement is made.

c. As to the quantity of the commodity available.

2. Otherwise (in addition to definiteness or indefiniteness), the appropriateness of the language to indicate or express a commitment.

3. The customs of business.

The terms of an agreement must be reasonably definite or certain in order for the agreement to be considered an enforceable contract. This does not mean that all of the terms must be expressly stated. When the parties to an agreement do not expressly indicate otherwise, it is presumed that they are contracting according to the usual or customary terms, and such terms therefore become an actual part of their contract. However, if the parties show that they are not following the pattern of what is usual or customary, and at the same time they fail to indicate the essential terms of the agreement with reasonable clearness, no enforceable contract is formed.

Practically all contracts involve a sale for a price—a sale of goods, of lands, or of services. The elements of a contractual agreement consist of what each is to give or to do under the agreement, and when and where the contract is to be performed. Usually no difficulty arises when an agreement is silent as to the "when" or the "where." *As to when*: it is presumed that the seller is to deliver or to perform at the usual time (that is, within a reasonable time), and that the buyer is to pay at the usual time (on delivery or completion of performance). *As to where*: with sales of goods not involving a shipment, the usual place of delivery is the seller's place of business, or his home if he has no place of business. In service contracts, the place of performance is usually determined by the nature of the services to be performed.

As to what: if an agreement is silent as to how much a buyer is to pay, it is presumed that he is to pay the usual or reasonable charge. If, however, the parties expressly exclude reasonableness as the measure of an indefinite bargain, they never form an enforceable agreement. For ex-ample, an employment agreement which provided for a specified salary plus "a liberal share of profits" was held to be too indefinite for the employee to collect more than the specified salary. On the other hand, an agreement for cost plus "a reasonable profit" did not exclude reasonableness as the test, and so constituted an enforceable agreement for whatever the court determined to be a reasonable profit under the circumstances.

Sometimes when entering into an agreement the parties expressly state that omitted details will be supplied by a later agreement. At common law an enforceable contract does not exist until the later agreement is entered into, and if the parties are unable to agree at the specified later time, no contract ever exists. For sales-of-goods contracts, however, the Uniform Commercial Code rejects this common-law view that "an agreement to agree is never enforceable." Instead, the Code attempts to give greater effect to the intent of the parties. If the parties show an intent to form an actual contract, the law will cooperate as much as it can in defining and enforcing their intent. In accomplishing this liberalization of contract theory, the Code provides:

> Even though one or more terms are left open a contract for sale does not fail for indefiniteness if the parties have intended to make a contract and there is a reasonably certain basis for giving an appropriate remedy.[5]

5. U.C.C. Sec. 2-204.

In partial explanation of this provision, the authors of the Code have written:

> If the parties intend to enter into a binding agreement, this subsection recognizes that agreement as valid in law, despite missing terms, if there is any reasonably certain basis for granting a remedy. The test is not certainty as to what the parties were to do nor as to the exact amount of damages due the plaintiff. Nor is the fact that one or more terms are left to be agreed upon enough of itself to defeat an otherwise adequate agreement. Rather, commercial standards on the point of "indefiniteness" are intended to be applied, this Act making provision elsewhere for missing terms needed for performance, open price, remedies and the like.[6] [Emphasis added.]

As the authors point out in the last sentence just quoted, the Code goes on to draw various guidelines for interpreting the meaning of an agreement in which certain terms are left open, (both the commonly omitted terms such as time and place for delivery, and time, place, and manner of payment, and also terms such as price, duration of a contract, and to some extent quantity), as in output and requirements contracts or in contracts giving a buyer some choice as to quantity.

For example, in respect to an open price term, the Code provides (in part):

(1) The parties if they so intend can conclude a contract for sale even though the price is not settled. In such a case the price is a reasonable price at the time for delivery if
(a) nothing is said as to price; or
(b) the price is left to be agreed by the parties and they fail to agree; or
(c) the price is to be fixed in terms of some agreed market or other standard as set or recorded by a third person or agency and it is not so set or recorded.

6. Comment to Sec. 2-204.

Example. A seller agreed to sell and a buyer to buy 5,000 gallons of a specified brand of motor oil, with the buyer to specify from SAE 10 to SAE 70 weight at stated future delivery dates, and with the price to vary from 21 cents to 31 cents per gallon depending upon the viscosity of oil selected by the buyer.

Before the Code, some courts said that such an agreement was not definite enough to be enforced, while other courts (taking the view now written into the Code) decided more reasonably that since the parties manifested an intent to form a contract, and since there was a reasonably certain basis for estimating damages (that is, the buyer was obliged to take at least the lowest-priced item or pay damages for not doing so), there would be an enforceable contract. ▢

(2) A price to be fixed by the seller or by the buyer means a price for him to fix in good faith.

(3) When a price left to be fixed otherwise than by agreement of the parties fails to be fixed through fault of one party the other may at his option treat the contract as cancelled or himself fix a reasonable price.[7]

Notice how this provision clarifies the status of agreements which state that the price is to be the seller's list price on the date of shipment. Under the Code, if the parties intend to be *presently bound*, their agreement forms an enforceable contract for a price reasonably and in good faith fixed by the seller at the stated future time.

The Code's liberalized approach also clarifies the law with respect to another fairly common type of contract, one in which a buyer is given a choice within stated limits, with the price to vary according to the buyer's choice.

Suppose that a retailer displays in his store window a radio bearing the tag, "For Sale, $95." Rather than being directed to any particular person, this statement is made to anyone who happens to look into the window. Two or more persons might simultaneously enter the store and, speaking to different clerks, each say that he will buy the radio displayed in the window. If the window display is considered to be an offer, then a contract would arise as soon as each customer agreed to buy. If the retailer's supply were limited, he could become bound by more contracts than he would be able to fill. It would not be reasonable, therefore, to say that when the retailer displayed the radio, he was committing himself to sell without any further expression of assent on his part. Unless a retailer clearly indicates that he intends to commit himself, his window display is not an offer but rather is an invitation for customers to enter his store and offer to buy. The retailer can then accept or reject such offers as he wishes. Although retailers will usually sell according to their published advertisements in order to maintain customer goodwill, a retailer does not owe potential customers any legally enforceable obligation to sell even one advertised or displayed item. Such a retailer may, however, incur a criminal liability. Although the courts have uniformly held that false advertising statutes do not apply to "come-on" advertisements, a few state statutes go further. For example, one such statute provides that a person is guilty of a misdemeanor punishable by not more than six months' imprisonment, $1,000 fine, or both, if by any means he adver-

7. U.C.C. Sec. 2-305.

Example. A wholesale salt dealer wrote to a quantity salt buyer: "In consequence of a break in the salt trade, we are able to offer Michigan fine salt in full carload lots of 80 to 95 barrels, delivered at your city, at 85 cents per barrel, to be shipped per the C&NW Railroad only. At this price it is a bargain. We shall be pleased to receive your orders." On receipt of this letter, the buyer promptly telegraphed to the dealer: "You may ship me 2,000 barrels of Michigan fine salt as offered in your letter." Two thousand barrels was a reasonable quantity for the buyer to order, and not in excess of what the dealer, from his knowledge of the buyer's business, might reasonably expect to be ordered. The dealer refused to ship and the buyer sued for damages for breach of contract.

Under similar facts, the Wisconsin Court held[8] that no contract was formed and that therefore the buyer could not recover. Although the word "offer" was used, the indefiniteness of quantity made it unreasonable to assume that the dealer was committing himself to sell any quantity that might be ordered, or even any quantity he might reasonably expect would be ordered. The indefiniteness of quantity also indicated that probably the same communication was sent to a number of potential buyers. The dealer's letter was a circular-type letter, inviting buyers to offer to buy; a dealer could reject any or all such offers, without any liability. ☐

8. *Moulton v. Kershaw*, 59 Wis. 316, 18 N.W. 172(1884).

tises something for sale to the general public with no intent to sell at the advertised price. The statute adds that unless the price is erroneously stated (through a typographical error or some other innocent mistake), a refusal to sell at an advertised price is prima-facie evidence (that is, sufficient evidence without the necessity of more proof) of such an intent not to sell, unless the advertisement also states the limited quantity that is available for sale. Note that although this statute prohibits conduct which the legislature feels constitutes an unfair business practice, the statute *does not* create a contract where one would not otherwise exist, nor in any other way change the *civil* effect of the retailer's conduct.

Just as it is unreasonable to conclude from a window display that a seller intends to bind himself to an unlimited number of persons, so also is it unreasonable to assume that, without any further expression of assent on his part, a seller who announces goods for sale intends to bind himself to sell an unlimited quantity. It is possible for a seller to commit himself to sell whatever quantity a buyer may order, but this is so unusual that such an intent must be clearly stated.

A statement concerning the price of certain described goods may be definite both as to the person to whom made and as to the quantity of goods, but nevertheless business custom may weigh against the statement being construed as an offer. A common example is a price quotation in response to an inquiry. Sellers frequently receive letters asking for their prices for certain quantities of goods. It is a common business practice for a potential buyer to send the same inquiry to several different sellers. Moreover, it is not unusual for the one who makes such an inquiry to decide not to purchase from anyone. For these reasons, a seller who answers such an inquiry is not expected to set the described goods aside or to hold them available on the slim chance that the inquirer might order. Therefore, although a seller's reply to an inquiry is definite both as to person and quantity, it is usually not reasonable to consider it an offer.

Example. On December 15, a buyer wrote to the owner of a vacant lot, saying: "If you have not sold, I of course am the logical purchaser, as your lot is worth more to me than to anyone else. I hope I shall have the pleasure of hearing from you shortly." On December 16, the owner wrote to the buyer: "If you should be interested in this lot, I would be glad to hear from you. Size of lot, 20 feet by 100 feet, price, $1,000." Two days later the buyer telegraphed to the owner: "Will accept your proposition of $1,000." However, the owner decided to sell the lot to another person and so notified the buyer on December 23. The buyer thereupon sued for a decree of specific performance to require the owner to transfer the lot to the buyer.

Under similar facts, a New York court held[9] that the buyer could not recover. Generally a mere statement of the price at which property is held for sale is not a commitment or offer to sell at that price. ☐

* * *

Example. On April 20 a buyer wrote to a seller: "Please advise us the lowest price you can make us on our order for ten carloads of Mason green jars complete with caps, packed one dozen in a case, either delivered here or f.o.b. cars your place as you prefer. State terms and cash discount." On April 23, the seller wrote to the buyer: "Replying to your letter of April 20, we quote you Mason fruit jars complete in one-dozen boxes, f.o.b. cars at our plant, as follows: pints $4.50, quarts $5, half-gallons $6.50, per gross, for immediate acceptance and shipment not later than May 15; sixty days credit or two percent off for cash in ten days. Please note that we make all quotations and contracts subject to the contingencies of agencies or transportation, delays or accidents beyond our control." On April 24, the buyer wired the seller: "Your letter 23d received. Enter order ten carloads as per your quotation. Letter specifying sizes follows." The seller wired the following reply on the same day: "Impossible to book your order. Output all sold." When the seller refused to deliver the ordered jars, the buyer sued for damages for breach of contract.

The Kentucky Court of Appeals[10] concluded that seller's reply was an offer and that the buyer's order was an acceptance, thus forming a contract. This is a borderline case; another court could easily have decided just the opposite, and said that the seller's reply was not an offer.

Argument for the Buyer: By using the expression "for immediate acceptance" the seller showed an intent to be bound upon the buyer's immediate or prompt acceptance. Therefore since person and quantity were sufficiently definite, the seller's reply constituted an offer. Although quantities for various sizes were not fixed, the seller's reply could be construed as an offer to sell the stated quantity in whatever assortment of the three specified sizes the buyer might later select.

Argument for the Seller: The word "quote" is usually not considered as expressing a commitment to sell. Likewise a reply to a price inquiry is usually not construed as an offer. Although the total quantity was definite, the quantity of each size to be delivered was indefinite. The phrase "for immediate acceptance" was merely a form expression meaning that the stated price was a current price quotation. The seller did not offer to sell; rather, the buyer's order was an offer to buy. The buyer's offer was rejected and no contract was formed. ☐

---

9. *Patrick v. Kleine*, 215 N.Y.S. 305 (1926).
10. *Fairmount Glass Works v. Crunden-Martin Woodenware Co.*, 106 Ky. 659, 51 S.W. 196 (1899).

Example. D, a friend of P, promised to give P $500 when P attained the age of eighteen. At age eighteen, P demands that D pay him the $500. Under most circumstances, a reasonable man would construe D's promise as being gratuitous in nature and hence not binding. Similarly, if D advised P to buy a house and promised to pay $500 of the down payment, the law is to the effect that assurances of assistance accompanied by kind advice are not to be considered as binding offers. ☐

* * *

Example. Bernard Barton writes to a seller: "Please ship to me the following goods [describing them] for which I will pay you $500 one month after delivery. (signed) Bernard Barton." When the seller promptly ships the requested goods, a unilateral agreement is formed. The agreement consists of the promise of the buyer to pay $500 for the goods which the seller, in accepting the offer, has shipped. ☐

* * *

Example. Barton writes to a seller: "Please enter my order for the following goods [describing them] to be shipped to me two months from this date, for which I will pay you $500 one month after delivery. (signed) Bernard Barton."

When the seller promptly writes to the buyer promising to ship the ordered goods, a contract is formed. The contract consists of promises by both parties, the promise of the seller to ship and that of the buyer to pay. ☐

When a businessperson is involved in a legal dispute, he incurs expenses and loses goodwill even if he wins the lawsuit. Certainly he should do all he reasonably can to prevent disputes from arising. In connection with his invitations to deal (that is, advertisements, circular letters, catalog listings, price quotations, and the like) a businessperson can minimize the possibility of disputes by including a provision clearly showing that he is not making an offer. Such expressions as the following are commonly used: "This is not an offer," "All quotations are subject to prior sale," "All prices are subject to change without notice."

3. AS A GRATUITY

Promises made to bestow a gift upon the happening of some future event are generally not considered to be binding offers. However, it is often a close and difficult question of fact as to whether or not a promise to make such a gift could reasonably be construed as a mere gratuitous statement or as an offer to enter into a contract. Again, it depends upon a reasonable man interpretation of the promise.

The above example also relates to the question of consideration which will be discussed in detail in Chapter 6.

B. Effective Date of Offer

Since an offer cannot be accepted without knowledge of its existence, it follows that an offer becomes effective when it is received by the offeree or his agent.

IV. Acceptance

An offer can be called a conditional commitment—that is, a commitment which is conditioned or dependent upon the offeree's expressing his acquiescence by accepting in the

Example. Desiring to build a warehouse adjacent to his factory, a manufacturer advertised for bids for construction according to certain written plans and specifications. Several builders submitted written bids and were present when the bids were opened. When he determined which bidder had submitted the lowest bid, the manufacturer said to that builder that the contract was his, asked him to start work at once, and instructed him to have the formal contract written, sign it, and send it to the manufacturer for signature. The builder accordingly began construction, including subletting a portion of the work, and had a contract drawn embodying the plans and specifications and the agreed price. The builder signed the contract but the manufacturer refused to sign, saying that he had changed his mind and that the builder should proceed no further with the work. The builder sued for damages for breach of contract. Since the manufacturer had not signed the contract form, he argued that an enforceable contract had not yet been formed between the parties, and that his only liability was on a quasi-contract theory for expense incurred by the builder at the manufacturer's request prior to the stop-work order.

There was an enforceable contract between the parties. If all essential terms are agreed upon and all that remains is to incorporate the agreement into a formal writing, an enforceable contract is formed when the parties first reach their agreement, unless they also manifest an intent that they not be bound until the formal writing is signed. ☐

manner requested by the offer. If the offer requests an act in exchange for the offered promise, the offer is accepted and a contract is formed when the offeree performs the requested act (a unilateral contract situation).

If an offer requests a promise from the offeree in exchange for the promise offered by the offeror, the offeree accepts by making the requested promise (a bilateral contract situation).

It is not unusual that after one party makes a proposal, the other party replies suggesting certain changes, to which the first party suggests further changes, and so on until they finally reach an agreement. In such a case there are a series of offers, with each party in turn being an offeror until one party finally expresses satisfaction with and thus accepts the other party's latest proposal. Negotiating back and forth in this way while bargaining over a myriad of details can become quite involved. The terms of the offer that are finally accepted may be spread over several communications, so that all of them must be read together to determine exactly what the parties have agreed to. Sometimes the parties expect that after they finally reach an agreement a single contract form will be prepared and signed by both parties. This is usually intended to provide convenient evidence of the agreement; unless it is clear that the parties do not intend to be bound until this contract form is prepared and signed, they form a binding contract as soon as they reach an agreement, even before preparation and signing of the formal contract.

Example. M, a manufacturer, in a newspaper advertisement, offered to give anyone $5,000 who could suggest an appropriate name for his new product. P submitted a name which was adopted for use by M. After M adopted the name supplied by P, M's sales escalated tremendously. If it can be shown that M intended the offer to be binding, it was open to P since P was a member of the public and P's submission of an appropriate name constituted his acceptance thus forming a valid contract. ☐

A. Person Entitled to Accept an Offer

I. ADDRESSEE

Since an offeror has a right to contract with an offeree of his choice, the general rule is that the only one who has the power to accept an offer is the person to whom the offer is addressed. Thus, if S offers to sell his automobile to B for $1,000, and B tells C, C cannot accept S's offer because it was not addressed specifically to him. This conclusion could also be reached by stating that there was no mutual manifestation of intent, that is, the minds of the parties never met, since S never intended the offer to extend to C.

2. PERSONAL REPRESENTATIVE OF DECEASED OR INCOMPETENT OFFEREE

When a person dies, his estate, in most cases, is represented by an administrator or executor. When an individual is incompetent, due, perhaps, to poor health or advancing age, a guardian will usually act on his behalf. Therefore, since the only one who has power to accept an offer is the offeree to whom it is addressed, it follows that the administrator or executor of an estate or the guardian of an incompetent individual acting in the capacity of a personal representative has no power to accept an offer addressed to an offeree who dies or becomes incompetent before accepting the offer.

This general rule does not apply in the case of a valid option agreement or a firm offer situation both of which are explained later in this chapter.

3. MEMBER OF THE PUBLIC

The general rule that an offer can be accepted only by the person to whom it is addressed is modified to some extent where the offer is made to the public in general. Where such an offer is appropriately worded, there is nothing to prevent any member of the public from accepting it, even when the offeree learned of the offer from sources independent of the offeror. An important point to remember here is that the original offer must be intended by the offeror to be one which any member of the public can accept.

B. Requirements for Valid Acceptance

For an offeree's response to an offer to constitute a binding acceptance, his response must comply with certain requirements which can be summarized as follows:

1. The offeree must have knowledge of the offer.
2. The offeree's response must manifest unequivocal agreement with the offer.
3. The offeree's response must become effective while the offer is still open.

Example. An owner who lost a wallet containing considerable money, cards, and valuable papers advertised a $100 reward for its return. The person who found the wallet ascertained the owner's name and address from the cards and returned the wallet and contents to the owner. The owner said, "That's fine. I guess you're entitled to the reward I advertised." The finder replied, "Oh, was there a reward? I didn't see the ad." The owner then refused to pay and the finder sued.

The finder could not recover. The finder could not accept an offer and become a party to an agreement if he was ignorant of the offer. Therefore no contract was formed and the owner would have no obligation to pay the advertised reward to the finder. □

4. The offeree's response must comply with the terms of the offer.

I. KNOWLEDGE OF OFFER

Obviously a person cannot accept an offeror's proposition unless he knows of the offer at the time of his alleged acceptance. Furthermore, no offer exists in respect to a particular offeree (and thus he has no power to accept and form a contract) unless and until the offer is communicated to him by the offeror or by the offeror's authorized agent.

2. UNEQUIVOCAL AGREEMENT

In order to form a contract, an offeree's acceptance must indicate that he clearly and definitely agrees to the offer. If the offeror intends a bilateral contract, the offeree's acceptance must manifest a commitment sufficient to bind the offeree himself to an enforceable obligation. In other words, the acceptance must be clear and definite enough to justify a reasonable person in concluding that the offeree is in full agreement with the offer, and is committing himself as requested in the offer, without reservation and without any intent to delay final commitment until some further expression of assent by the offeree. Thus a reply, "We have received your order and it will receive our prompt and careful attention," has been held not to be an acceptance. The offeree is really only saying, "We will think about

it," and not necessarily saying, "We will ship the ordered goods."

3. EXISTENT OFFER

Certainly no agreement can arise through an offer and an acceptance if the offer has ended or terminated before the offeree tries to accept it. An offer will terminate or come to an end in any of a variety of ways, the most common of which are: (1) lapse of time, (2) revocation by the offeror, (3) rejection by the offeree, and (4) death or insanity of either party before acceptance.

Termination by Lapse of Time

It is quite unreasonable to assume that an offeror intends the conditional commitment he makes in his offer to bind him for an extended period. Therefore the law concludes that an offer will end upon the expiration of the time specified in the offer, or if no time is specified, upon the expiration of a reasonable time.

Expressly Stated Duration. Sometimes the duration of an offer is indicated by a request for a reply by "return mail." This expression should be given a reasonable interpretation. It does not necessarily mean the very next mail which leaves after the offeree receives the offer. In a large city with mails leaving frequently it might be impossible for an offeree to get a reply on the very next mail train. Usually the term "return mail" means that the re-

Example. On May 4, B sent to S a written order for 8 carloads of lumber. The order specified grade, size, price, and delivery in stated installments beginning June 15. By letter of May 9, S acknowledged receipt of the order but instead of accepting it, wrote: "This being our first business with you, it is only proper for us to have an understanding as to terms." S then stated his terms for time and manner of payment, and listed certain contingencies (such as rail strike and the like) which would excuse S from any contract obligation to deliver. S concluded his letter by writing: "If the above conditions are satisfactory, we will be glad to begin shipment as requested in your order. Please let us hear from you on the subject." On May 15, B wrote S: "We have for acknowledgment your letter of May 9 regarding our order for 8 cars to be delivered as specified in our order, beginning June 15, all of which is in order." On May 24, S wrote to B: "We have previously written you on the subject of terms and manner in which we wish the stock to be paid for and not hearing from you in reply to our letter, we take for granted that you do not wish the material and are therefore canceling your order." B in turn wrote to S: "Replying to your letter of the 24th, we refer to our letter of the 15th replying to yours of May 9, in which we advise that the terms, etc., as given in your letter were all in order." When S refused to ship, having canceled the order and sold the goods elsewhere, B sued S for damages for breach of contract.

On somewhat similar facts, the Pennsylvania Superior Court held[11] that no contract was formed between the parties, and that therefore B could not recover. S made a counteroffer in stating the terms under which he was willing to contract. The expression B used in referring to S's counteroffer, "all of which is in order," was not a clear-cut expression of acceptance sufficient to bind S to his proposal.

One judge dissented, stating that in his opinion B's May 15 letter was a sufficient agreement to S's proposed terms.

Whichever view is taken of B's reply, it certainly violates a cardinal principle of good letter writing—that a business letter should state clearly, simply, and exactly the meaning and intent of the writer. 🗅

11. *Coastwise Lumber Supply Co. v. Stitzinger*, 81 Pa. Super. 554(1923).

ply should be on its way the same day that the offer is received; if there is no mail shipment which the offeree can reasonably reach that day, then the reply is sufficiently prompt if it is in the first reasonably available mail shipment the following day.

If an offeror requests a reply within a specified number of days, a question will sometimes arise as to when the specified period should begin. Suppose that a seller offers to sell a described plot of land for a stated price, and in his offering letter to the buyer says, "You have ten days in which to accept." Under

the standard "reasonable man" test, the offeror should be bound by what a reasonable man in the position of the offeree would assume is the offeror's intent, regardless of what the offeror actually means.

. Under this approach there are three possible theories as to when the ten-day period begins to run:

1. Since the offeror has no way of knowing exactly when the offeree receives the offering letter, it is reasonable to assume (unless clearly stated otherwise) that the offeror intends

the ten-day period to start from the date of his offering letter.

2. Since no offer is actually in existence until it has been communicated to the offeree, the ten days begins to run from the date upon which the offeree receives the offering letter.

3. The third theory is a modification of the second. If the offeree knows or has reason to know of some unusual delay in the delivery of the offering letter, the ten-day period should be counted from the time when the offeree would ordinarily have received the offering letter.

Surprisingly few cases have involved this point. While it is arguable that the first theory is the most reasonable, one of the few courts faced with the question (the West Virginia Supreme Court) adopted[12] the second theory, even though in the case before the court, an error of the postal authorities delayed delivery of the offering letter for three days beyond normal delivery time. If an offeror wishes to specify a duration for his offer, he should avoid ambiguity by indicating a certain date by which the offeree must accept. For example, instead of saying, "You have ten days in which to accept," the offeror should say, "This offer is subject to your acceptance by [a specified date]," or "This offer is subject to my receipt of your acceptance by [specified date]."

Implied Duration. If an offeror fails to specify a time period for his offer, the offer will be considered as lapsing after the expiration of a reasonable time. The duration of this "reasonable time" will depend upon the circumstances of each case, with the following factors being particularly important:

1. The time needed to do whatever is indicated as an acceptance. If an offer calls for an act as acceptance, the expected duration of

the offer will at least be long enough for performance of that act.

2. The method used to communicate the offer. Sending an offer by telegraph indicates urgency; if an offering telegram is received near the close of business hours, an attempt to accept early the following day will usually be too late. Likewise, if an offer is made orally during a conversation, it will not extend beyond that immediate conversation unless the offeror expressly agrees to a longer time.

3. The stability in value of the subject matter involved. If an offer concerns a commodity whose value fluctuates rapidly on the market, the duration of the offer will be much shorter than for an offer concerning an item of stabilized value.

4. The customs of the particular business involved.

The Uniform Commercial Code generally follows the same reasonable man standards that apply above. The Code specifically states, with respect to a unilateral contract, that "where the beginning of a requested performance is a reasonable mode of acceptance, an offeror who is not notified of acceptance within a reasonable time may treat the offer as having lapsed before acceptance."[13]

Termination by Revocation

The word *revocation* is applied to the termination of an offer by the offeror's with-drawing it. While a revocation is usually accomplished by a direct notice to the offeree, an indirect revocation is possible. Suppose that after offering to sell certain land to an offeree, the offeror sells and transfers the same land to someone else. The offeror's disposal of the offered property does not automatically terminate the offer. If the offeree accepts before he

---

12. Caldwell v. Cline, 109 W. Va. 553, 156 S.E. 55, 72 A.L.R. 1211(1930).

13. U.C.C. Sec. 2-206(2).

Example. On June 3 a buyer received from a seller a letter dated June 1 stating: "I hereby offer to sell you the following land [describing it] for $20,000 and agree that this offer will remain open until June 30. To be effective your acceptance must reach me by June 30." On June 22 the buyer received from the seller a letter dated June 20, stating, "I hereby withdraw my offer of June 1." On June 27 the seller received from the buyer a letter dated June 25, stating, "You agreed that your June 1 offer would remain open and I hereby accept it."

The offeror could terminate his offer anytime before acceptance. Since the offer was revoked, the attempted acceptance would not form a contract. ▢

* * *

Example. On June 3, after preliminary negotiations, a seller signed and gave to a buyer a letter dated June 1, stating: "In consideration of your payment to me of $1, receipt of which I hereby acknowledge, I offer to sell you the following land [describing it] for $20,000 and agree that this offer will remain open until June 30. To be effective your acceptance must reach me by June 30." Assume that revoking and accepting letters were written and received just as in the preceding example.

A contract would be formed on June 27 when the seller received the buyer's accepting letter. In this type of offer or option the agreed money is paid for the offeror's holding the offer open for the time stated and makes the offer irrevocable for that period. (The money paid and received for an option is not considered as a part payment of the purchase price, unless the parties expressly so agree; therefore, if the offeree decides not to accept he is not entitled to return of the money he paid for the option.) ▢

learns of the sale, the offeror will be bound by a contract, and since he can no longer perform the contract, he will be liable for damages for breach of contract. However, if before the offeree tries to accept he learns of the offeror's disposal of the land, the offeree's knowledge of the offeror's change of mind would serve to terminate the offer. Obviously, it is risky for an offeror to rely on the uncertainty of an indirect revocation to terminate his offer.

Time of Revocation. Usually a revocation notice becomes effective either when it is received by the offeree, or when it is received at the place to which the original offer was sent, whichever occurs first. If an offeree denies ever receiving a revocation, it may be difficult (but not impossible if the jury believes the offeror's testimony) for the offeror to prove that

he revoked the offer if all he has is his own testimony, plus the presumption that if a letter is mailed with correct address and postage it is usually delivered. In matters of any importance it would be wise for the offeror to revoke by a means which would be easier to prove, such as telegraph or certified mail.

Right to Revoke—In General. By its very nature a contract is considered a two-sided proposition. This is not inconsistent with the idea of unilateral contracts. Although a unilateral contract consists of a promise on one side only, it is given in ex-change for the other party's performance of an act. The promise is legally enforceable because the promisee has already done something or given something which is binding upon him. On the other hand, if nothing is done or given in exchange for a promise, the promise is not legally enforceable, unless some other factor is present which makes it desirable policy for society to enforce the promise. This legal principle—that usually both parties must in some way be bound or obligated or no contract exists—is customarily expressed in terms of *consideration* and *equivalents of consideration*, which are further discussed in the next chapter.

While by definition an offer is an expression of a binding commitment, it is a conditional commitment. The offeror is not bound to anything until the offeree agrees and binds himself by accepting the offer. Since an offeror is not bound before acceptance, it logically follows that the offeror can withdraw his offer at any time before the offeree accepts it. Sometimes, however, in addition to making an offer, an offeror also agrees or promises that he will not withdraw the offer for a certain period of time. Following the reasoning that an offeror is not bound until the offeree binds himself in some way, the common law has formulated the generally accepted rule that despite an offeror's promise to hold his offer open, he can nevertheless withdraw the offer anytime before it is accepted. If on the other hand the offeree binds himself in some way, for example by paying to hold the offer open, then the offeror is also bound and cannot terminate his offer. This type of transaction is usually called an *option agreement*.

Sometimes an offeree will sustain a monetary loss if an offeror is permitted to renege on his promise to keep his offer open. For example, in order to decide whether or not to accept, an offeree may have to make some preliminary surveys or research, and he may be willing to undertake this expense only because of the offeror's assurance that the offer will remain open. Or in reliance on an offer, an offeree may make a further contractual commit-

ment to some third person. While an offeree can make an offer irrevocable by entering into an option agreement with the offeror, this is not always convenient or even practical. A number of years ago, therefore, some businessmen began to think and speak of certain offers as being "firm" and irrevocable. Following the lead of the business world in recognizing a need for irrevocable offers other than options, the New York legislature adopted a "firm offer" statute in 1941, and the Uniform Commercial Code contains a similar provision. Writing about the Code provision, Professor Corbin has said:

> This section recognizes a growing custom among merchants in both Britain and America to differentiate between two kinds of offers. Knowing that offers are generally revocable by notice, at the will of the offeror, there is a felt need for a type of offer on which the offeree can rely, for a reasonable time or for a definitely stated time. More and more frequently, offerors are making what they describe as a "firm offer," understanding by that term that the offer so described shall be irrevocable for a limited time. Sometimes the offer is made in this form at the special request of the offeree, and sometimes by the offeror's own motion in order to make it more attractive to the offeree and to induce his serious consideration. Unless the law gives effect to the intention of the parties in these cases, an offer represented to be "firm" and "irrevocable" becomes a trap to the offeree and a special advantage to those offerors who are willing to be guilty of bad faith.
>
> It is only three-quarters of a century since a very learned author could write that "an irrevocable offer is a legal impossibility." No doubt, the statement was incorrect when made; but theory and practice alike have grown continually more opposed to it.[14]

The Code provision states: "An offer by a merchant to buy or sell goods in a signed writ-

---

14. 59 *Yale L. J.* 821 (1950).

Example. On June 3 a buyer received a letter dated June 1, written by a seller who was a businessman, stating: "I hereby make a firm offer to sell you the following goods [describing them] for $1,000. To be effective your acceptance must reach me by June 30." On June 22 the buyer received from the seller a letter dated June 20, stating, "I hereby withdraw my offer of June 1." On June 27 the seller received from the buyer a letter dated June 25, stating, "You agreed that your June 1 offer would remain open and I hereby accept it."

There would be a contract between the parties. □

* * *

Example. On June 3 a buyer received a letter dated June 1, written by a seller who was a businessman, stating: "I hereby offer to sell you the following goods (describing them) for $1,000 and agree that this offer will remain open for six months from the date of this letter To be effective your acceptance must reach me by December 1 of this year."

Since no payment or equivalent of payment was made to hold the offer open, the offer would be an irrevocable firm offer for only three months and, until accepted, could be revoked any time after expiration of the three-month period. □

ing which by its terms gives assurance that it will be held open is not revocable, for lack of consideration,[15] during the time stated or if no time is stated for a reasonable time, but in no event may such period of irrevocability exceed three months....[16]

In summarizing the legal pattern which has developed in regard to the right to revoke offers, it will be helpful to distinguish between

---

15. The term "consideration" refers to the concept, explained in Chapter 6, that a promise is not legally enforceable unless something is given in exchange for the promise or unless there is some other good reason for enforcing the promise.

16. U.C.C. Sec. 2-205. A basic tenet of the Code is that, for certain situations, greater business competency and a higher standard of reliability are expected from merchants than from nonmerchants. Accordingly, although Article 2 of the Code applies to all sales-of-goods transactions whether the parties are merchants or not, some special rules are expressly stated as applying only to merchants. Some of these special rules (like the one involving firm offers) apply to merchants in general— meaning any person, partnership, or corporation engaged in business to such an extent as to be presumed to be familiar with common, nonspecialized business practices—while a few of the special rules are expressly limited to merchants who are dealers in goods of the kind involved in the transaction in question.

bilateral and unilateral contract offers and then to consider offers for auction sales separately.

Revocability of Offers for Bilateral Contracts. Initially a distinction must be made between (1) offers which say nothing as to their duration, and (2) offers which expressly state that they are irrevocable or firm, or which otherwise indicate that they will be held open. Clearly, offers of the first type can be revoked at any time before acceptance. On the other hand, the revocability of offers of the second type depends on additional facts, which can be summarized as follows:

1. If the offer involves something other than the sale of goods, it can be withdrawn at any time before acceptance, even though the offeror has assured the offeree that the offer will remain open for a longer period (unless the promise to keep the offer open is paid for or supported by a recognized equivalent of payment as explained in Chapter 6).

2. If the offer involves the sale or purchase of goods, then:

(a) If the offer is made by a nonmerchant, or is made by a merchant whose assurance to keep the offer open is oral, the offeror's right to revoke is the same as for an offer which does not involve the sale of goods.

(b) If the offer is made by a merchant who in a signed writing assures that the offer will remain open, the offer is irrevocable for the duration stated (but not exceeding three months), even though the offeree pays nothing to hold the offer open. Should the specified duration exceed three months, the offer is irrevocable for only three months (unless the offeree makes a payment or its equivalent to hold the offer open). If the merchant's written assurance that the offer will remain open specifies no time period but merely states that the offer is irrevocable or firm, the offer will be irrevocable for a reasonable time—which of course would never exceed three months and usually would be considerably shorter than that.

Revocability of Offers for Unilateral Contracts. An offer for a unilateral contract is one which is to be accepted by the offeree's performing a certain act. If such an offer is a firm offer under the Uniform Commercial Code, it is irrevocable. As to offers which do not come under the Code's firm offer theory, a very vexing problem is presented when the offeree, intending to accept, begins performance of the requested act, and then before completion of the offeree's performance, the offeror gives notice revoking his offer. To hold that there is no contract would deprive the offeree of compensation for what he has already done; on the other hand to argue that there is a contract suggests that the offeror should be bound before he receives what he requested as an acceptance.

It is certainly sound policy for the law to avoid this vexing dilemma, if possible. There-fore if an offer does not clearly indicate that it can be accepted only by performance of a certain act, the courts will usually interpret it as acceptable either by the offeree's performance of the act or by his promise to perform the act. The Uniform Commercial Code expressly adopts this view for sales-of-goods offers.[17]

If the offer is not ambiguous, if it clearly specifies that it can be accepted only by performance of a specified act, many courts use some variation of the irrevocable offer concept to prevent the unfairness which would result from a revocation after partial performance. Basically, these courts hold that unless an offer expressly states other-wise, the act of the offeree in promptly beginning performance, with reasonable notice thereof to the offeror, has the effect of making the offer irrevocable for the time reasonably necessary for completion of the performance. In applying this theory, the courts will distinguish between preparation to begin performance and the actual commencement of performance; thus, if an offer specifies the payment of a stated sum of money as the acceptance, the offeree's assembling the necessary currency, and even starting toward the offeror's place of business with the money, would usually be classed as preparatory only, rather than commencement of performance.

Revocability in Auction Sales. As the law in regard to auction sales gradually evolved from early common law days, two rules emerged as expressions of what society considered to be sound policy.

The first auction rule is that neither an announcement (or advertisement) that certain property will be sold at auction to the highest bidder, nor putting the property up for auc-

---

17. U.C.C. Sec. 2-206.

Example. A seller wished to have an old building removed from his land to make way for a new structure. The seller advertised that the old building would be sold at public auction, the successful bidder to remove the building within a stated time. On the day of the auction sale, bidding progressed until the amount of $675 was bid by A. B then bid $680. The auctioneer told B that $5 was too small an increase for his bid to be considered.When B failed to make a higher bid, the auctioneer announced that the building was sold to A for $675. B protested and tendered $680 to the seller. The seller refused the tender and made out a written contract of sale to A for $675. B then sued the seller for damages for breach of contract.

Since the auction was not announced as being "without reserve," the seller (through the auctioneer as his agent) was free to reject B's bid. Thus no contract was formed with B, and B was not entitled to recover. ☐

tion and receiving bids, should be construed as an offer on the part of the seller or auctioneer. This rule is based on the general policy conclusion that although there is definiteness both as to the property to be auctioned and also as to the manner for determining the person to whom the property will be sold (namely the highest bidder), there nevertheless appears little reason for treating either the advance announcement or the commencement of the auction as any different from a retailer's advertisement or window display. Therefore when the auctioneer asks, "What am I bid?" he is not offering to sell to the highest bidder but rather is inviting offers. A bid is an offer to buy. The first time that an offer appears in the transaction is when a bid is made, and no binding contract is formed until the auctioneer announces that he accepts a particular bid, either by the fall of his hammer, by saying "sold," or by other customary manner.

The second auction rule is that if the auctioneer expressly states that the auction is "without reserve" (meaning that the auctioneer relinquishes both the right to set a certain minimum price and also the right to withdraw an item from the sale after bidding begins) the auctioneer binds himself to sell to the highest bidder. The "without reserve" term therefore is a firm or irrevocable commitment to sell to the highest bidder. Under the generally accepted common law theory, a without-reserve auction is just like a with-reserve auction except that the auctioneer has a binding obligation to accept the highest bid. Thus each bid is an offer and no contract is formed until, upon completion of the bidding, the auctioneer accepts the highest bid. Some legal scholars have suggested a different theory, arguing that a without-reserve auction should be considered as involving a series of contracts successively formed and canceled. Under this proposed theory, putting goods up for sale in a without-reserve auction would be construed as an irrevocable, firm offer, and a bid would be an acceptance, thus forming a contract conditioned, however, on no higher bid being made. Each time a higher bid would be made the contract with the previous bidder would be automatically canceled and a new contract would be formed with the new bidder. Although an earlier, tentative version of the Uniform Commercial Code adopted this suggested theory, the common law theory won out in the final draft of the Code, in the absence of any sound policy reason for making the change or for having the rule which applies to goods different from the common

Example. Assume that each letter in this example was delivered the day after it was written. On June 1 a seller wrote to a buyer: "I hereby offer to sell you my land [describing it] for $20,000. You have thirty days from the date hereof to accept. To be effective your acceptance must reach me by June 30."

1. Assume that on June 5 the buyer wrote to the seller, "I do not want to buy your land for $20,000." To this the seller made no reply and on June 10 the buyer wrote again to the seller, saying, "I have changed my mind and will buy your land for $20,000 as offered in your letter of June 1." The seller however had changed his mind and refused to sell.

There would be no contract. When the buyer rejected the offer, the seller was reasonably justified in concluding that the buyer was no longer interested. The rejection terminated the offer.

2. Assume that on June 5 the buyer wrote to the seller, "In reply to your letter of June 1, I'll give you $17,000 for your land." To this the seller made no reply and on June 10 the buyer wrote again to the seller, saying, "I have changed my mind and will buy your land for $20,000 as offered in your letter of June 1." The seller refused to sell.

There would be no contract. From the buyer's counteroffer of June 5, the seller would be reasonably justified in assuming that the buyer was not interested in buying for $20,000. The counteroffer therefore implied a rejection and terminated the original offer.

3. Assume that on June 5 the buyer wrote to the seller, "In regard to your June 1 letter, will you take $17,000 for your land?" On June 6, the seller replied by letter, "In reply to your June 5 letter, I will not sell for $17,000." On June 10 the buyer wrote again to the seller, "I will buy your land for $20,000 as offered in your letter of June 1." The seller however refused to sell.

There would be a contract. The buyer's June 5 letter was not a counteroffer; the buyer was inquiring about possible better terms but was not offering to buy for $17,000. Since the buyer did not clearly indicate that he was no longer interested in the seller's June 1 offer, the offer was still open when the buyer accepted with his June 10 letter.

4. Assume that on June 5 the buyer wrote to the seller, "In regard to your June 1 offer, I'll think about it but if you wish to close the deal immediately, I'll give you $17,000 for your land." On June 6 the seller replied by letter, "In reply to your June 5 letter, I will not sell for $17,000." On June 10 the buyer wrote again to the seller, "I will buy your land for $20,000 as offered in your letter of June 1." The seller refused to sell.

There would be a contract. Although the buyer made a counteroffer, he indicated that he was still considering the seller's original offer. Therefore the seller's June 1 offer was still open when the buyer accepted with his June 10 letter. ▢

law rule which still applies to land-auction sales.

Thus, the Uniform Commercial Code provides:

A sale by auction is complete when the auctioneer so announces by the fall of the hammer or in other customary manner....

Such a sale is with reserve unless the goods are in explicit terms put up without reserve. In an auction with reserve the auctioneer may withdraw the goods at any time until he announces completion of the sale. In an auction without reserve, after the auctioneer calls for bids on an article . . . that article . . . cannot be withdrawn unless no bid is made within a reasonable time. In either case a bidder may retract his bid until the auctioneer's announcement of completion of the sale, but a bidder's retraction does not revive any previous bid.

If the auctioneer knowingly receives a bid on the seller's behalf or the seller makes or procures such a bid, and notice has not been given that liberty for such bidding is reserved, the buyer may at his option avoid the sale or take the goods at the price of the last good faith bid prior to the completion of the sale. This subsection shall not apply to any bid at a forced sale.[18]

Notice that a seller's secretly having someone bid an item up is considered dishonest and the usual common law remedies are restated in the Code.

Rejection

Different from a revocation (which is a withdrawal of an offer by the offeror), a *rejection* is a refusal or turning down of an offer by the offeree. If the offeree reasonably leads the offeror to understand or assume that the offeree does not intend to accept and is no longer considering the offer, the offer is terminated, and the offeree cannot afterwards change his mind and accept the offer. Suppose that upon receiving an offer the offeree promptly replied that he was not interested in buying. If the offeror should afterwards change his mind about selling, he would not consider it necessary to give notice of revocation to the offeree, who had already said that he was not interested. It would not be fair, therefore, to consider an offer still open after the offeree rejects it, even though time remains during which the offer would still be open had it not been rejected.

Termination by Death

A person's death does not automatically cancel all of his existing contracts; only those con-

tracts that require his personal performance are affected. For example, sup-pose that B engages A to perform services which depend upon A's special abilities or qualifications. Since B cannot without his consent be required to accept performance by some person other than A, such a contract would be classified as requiring personal performance by A. In other words, the continuation of A's ability to perform would be a necessary condition for enforcement of the contract. Should A die, the contract would be considered as automatically canceled.

Most contracts do not require personal performance. Thus, in a contract for the sale of either land or goods, it is usually immaterial who actually makes delivery, so long as the buyer obtains the land or the goods described in the contract. Likewise, to whom the property is delivered is immaterial so long as the seller receives the agreed price. In such an impersonal contract, death of one of the parties or of both parties will have no effect on the continued enforceability of the contract. When a party to a contract dies, a court will appoint a personal representative (an administrator or executor) for the decedent's estate. The administrator or executor takes over the decedent's property in order to collect obligations owed to the decedent and to complete the decedent's outstanding commitments.

Even though the death of either party or of both parties *after* the formation of an impersonal contract will have no effect on the life of the contract, sometimes the death of a party *before* an offer has been accepted will automatically terminate the offer and prevent a contract from being formed. Usually the effect that death will have on an unaccepted offer depends upon whether the offer is revocable or irrevocable. If an offer is irrevocable (either

18. U.C.C. Sec. 2-328.

Example. A publisher advertised a contest in which he offered a prize of $1,000 to the person submitting a list containing the greatest number of words which could be made from the letters in the word "determination." Among the published rules for the contest was the following: "Do not use obsolete or foreign words, abbreviations, contractions, reformed spelling, prefixes and suffixes, or proper nouns or adjectives." The two contestants submitting the largest number of words were A and B. A submitted a list of 3,938 words, B 1,428 words. Of A's words 2,481 violated the above quoted rule, leaving 1,457 correct words. The publisher awarded the prize to B. A sued the publisher, contending that since he submitted the largest number of correct words he was entitled to the prize.

In a case presenting substantially these facts, the Iowa court held[19] that since the publisher's offer specified certain terms and conditions, a contestant's entry could not be an acceptance if it failed to comply with the stated conditions. ☐

19. *Scott v. People's Monthly Co.*, 209 Iowa 503, 228 N.W. 263, 67 A.L.R. 413(1929).

because contained in an option agreement or made as a firm offer), it is considered as vesting in the offeree a legally enforceable right to form a contract by accepting within the irrevocable period. This right is something of value which the offeree owns, in much the same way as he owns his car or his house. It cannot be taken away from him without his consent, and like most of his other impersonal rights, it can be transferred by him to someone else, who thereby obtains a right to accept the offer and form a contract with the offeror. Since the offeree's right to accept is not personal to the offeree, and cannot be affected by any act of the offeror, the offer is not affected by the death of either the offeror or the offeree. Therefore (assuming, of course, that the offer contemplates an impersonal contract) if an offeree has an irrevocable right to accept, he can still accept and form a contract after the offeror dies. Likewise, if the offeree dies, his personal representative can accept and form a contract binding upon the offeror (or upon the offeror's estate if the offeror is also dead).

On the other hand, if an offer is revocable so that it can be taken away from the offeree at any time without his consent, he cannot be considered as having an ownership interest in the offer. Without an ownership interest there is nothing which the offeree can transfer or which will remain after his death. All that the offeree has is a power to form a contract by accepting while the offer is still open. The exercise of this power is dependent upon the offeror's continuing intent to form a contract, an intent which he manifests by refraining from withdrawing the offer. After an offeror dies he cannot be said to continue to manifest any intent. Therefore most courts hold that if an offer is revocable, the death of either the offeror or the offeree will automatically and immediately terminate the offer so that it cannot afterwards be accepted.

Termination by Insanity

An offeror or offeree's becoming mentally incompetent to handle his own affairs, has the same effect on an outstanding offer as the incompetent party's death would have.

4. COMPLIANCE WITH OFFER

An offer states the terms and conditions upon which the offeror is willing to contract.

Since different terms cannot be imposed upon him without his consent, an enforceable contract can be made only on the offeror's terms and conditions.

Offers for Unilateral Contracts

In a unilateral contract situation, sometimes the act performed by an offeree in apparent acceptance of an offer fails to comply exactly with what the offeror has requested. The common law has adopted the policy view that usually no contract rights or obligations can arise except on the offeror's exact terms, that any deviation in the offeree's performance from what the offeror requests will prevent a contract from being formed.

When this fundamentally sound common law rule is applied to modern commercial transactions, the results are sometimes unfair. Suppose that in response to a buyer's order for certain first-quality goods, a seller shipped the correct quantity of what appeared to be first-quality goods; however, in due course the buyer discovered the goods to be of second quality rather than of first quality. If the buyer sued the seller for breach of contract, the seller could point out that since the only communications between the parties consisted of the buyer's order and the seller's shipment, the only acceptance could be the seller's act of shipping. From this the seller could argue that if the goods which were shipped were actually not first quality, then under the common law rule the seller never accepted the buyer's order, and no contract was ever formed between the parties. On the other hand, the buyer could argue that the seller manifested an intent to accept the offer, when he made a shipment without advising the buyer that the shipment differed from the order; that in doing so the seller reasonably led the buyer to believe that a contract was formed; and that therefore it would be unfair to permit the seller to deny the existence of a contract. Under circumstances such as these, it seems fair and reasonable to decide that a contract exists and to hold the seller liable for breach of contract. The task of the law is to formulate a practical and workable rule to reach this desired conclusion, without undermining, unduly weakening, or confusing the whole structure of admittedly sound and desirable contract rules.

To resolve such situations, the authors of the Uniform Commercial Code have formulated the following rule, which (with the economy of words characteristic of the Code) is combined with the rule relating to offers which are ambiguous as to the method for accepting:

> Unless otherwise unambiguously indicated by the language or circumstances . . . an order or other offer to buy goods for prompt or current shipment shall be construed as inviting acceptance either by a prompt promise to ship or by the prompt or current shipment of conforming or non-conforming goods, but such a shipment of non-conforming goods does not constitute an acceptance if the seller seasonably notifies the buyer that the shipment is offered only as an accommodation to the buyer.[20]

This is certainly a model of brevity; some people feel that here the authors of the Code have been too stingy with words. However, stating the rule with greater exactness would be quite difficult and perhaps unnecessary. Certainly if a seller ships five refrigerators when a buyer has ordered five stoves, no one should contend that the seller is manifesting any agreement concerning the order for stoves. If a seller ships glass tumblers when a buyer has ordered plastic tumblers, any question as to whether the seller is thus forming a contract

---

20. U.C.C. Sec. 2-206

Example. A seller was unwilling to extend credit to Bernard Brown. At Brown's request, G, on June 1, signed and mailed to the seller the following: "[Date] If you will sell goods to Bernard Brown on sixty days' credit, I will guaranty his payment up to $500." The seller received the guarantying letter on June 2 and on the same day sold and delivered certain goods to Brown for $475 due in sixty days. On June 3, the seller received a letter from G revoking his letter of June 1. Although the seller had not previously intended to notify G of the sale, he immediately replied to G's revoking letter, telling of the June 2 sale to Brown. When Brown defaulted in payment, the seller sued G.

The seller could recover. When the seller made the June 2 sale to Brown, he performed the requested act, thus accepting G's offer and forming a contract with G. The seller's June 3 letter was notice within a reasonable time and prevented the contract from lapsing. ☐

for the plastic tumblers ordered by the buyer would seem fairly to depend upon a number of variable factors concerning the buyer's needs, expectations, and subsequent conduct. Suppose that knowing of the seller's shipment but unaware that the tumblers are glass instead of plastic, the buyer makes further plans or commitments on his own part in the expectation of receiving plastic tumblers. The one who creates the problem is the seller when, without disclosing the fact, he ships something different from what has been ordered. Fairness dictates that the burden should be on the seller to absolve himself, to show that under all of the surrounding circumstances a reasonable person in the position of the buyer would not be justified in assuming that his order has been accepted.

Regardless of whether this Code provision should be interpreted broadly or narrowly, it certainly serves as a warning to sellers in respect to substitute shipments. Some sellers, when they are unable to ship goods which have been ordered but have similar goods on hand, occasionally (to increase customer goodwill or sometimes merely to make a sale) will ship the similar goods without first ascertaining if the buyer is willing to accept the substitute. Under this Code provision, unless

the seller explains that his act means something else, his act of shipping goods in response to the order will sometimes be considered as an acceptance of the order and an agreement to be bound by its terms. If so construed, the buyer not only could reject the substitute goods (since they fail to conform exactly to his order) but also could hold the seller to a contract to deliver as ordered. If a seller does not wish his shipping substitute goods to obligate him to deliver as ordered, the seller should, with the shipment or in advance of it, explain to the buyer that it is a substitute shipment sent as an accommodation to the buyer. If the seller so explains, then his act of shipping does not form a contract between the parties, but merely makes a counteroffer. If the buyer rejects the counteroffer, the only loss to the seller will be his own shipping and handling expenses; he will not be obliged to ship the originally ordered goods.

Notice of Acceptance. If an offer requests performance of an act as the acceptance, a contract is formed as soon as the offeree performs the requested act, even though the offeror is unaware of the offeree's performance. It is not fair, however, for the offeror to be kept in ignorance of the acceptance. Therefore if the act which has been performed is

Example. A seller wrote to a buyer offering to sell a described plot of land for $2,000. The buyer promptly wrote to the seller, "I accept your offer on condition that you can convey good title to me."

 If an offer to sell property says nothing about any mortgages or other liens against it, it is assumed that what is offered is a good title clear of all liens. Therefore the buyer's reply, "on condition that you can convey good title to me," merely expressed what was already implied, did not add or change any terms, and so was an unconditional acceptance and would form a contract between the parties.

* * *

Example. S offered to sell B "500 bottles of Brand X cola for $.07 per bottle." B replied: "I accept your offer, but in addition send 200 bottles of Brand Y cola at $.07 per bottle." A valid contract exists for the Brand X cola since B unconditionally accepted S's offer. An offer exists with respect to the Brand Y cola.

* * *

Example. In a letter to B, S made the following proposal: "S hereby offers to sell to B 100 school desks at $20 per desk. This offer will remain open if B should care to submit a counteroffer."

 From the language used in the offer, it appears obvious that any counteroffer made by B would not terminate the offer. If, however, S omitted the provision with respect to the counteroffer, the only way for B to reply with a counteroffer and still keep the original offer open is for him to indicate that he still has the original offer under consideration.

not likely soon to come to the offeror's attention, the offeree must notify the offeror within a reasonable time that the accepting act has been performed. Otherwise the contract formed upon performance of the act will automatically lapse or terminate.

Offers for Bilateral Contracts

Deviation from Requested Promise. If an offer requests a certain promise as an acceptance, obviously a different promise will not constitute an acceptance and there-fore will not form a contract. Where the offeree's return promise changes the key terms of the offer, generally the promisee has made a counteroffer which, as previously noted, operates as a rejection. However, in determining the effect of a reply which includes terms not expressed in an offer, it should be borne in

mind that an offer may not state all of the terms and provisions which are intended to apply to the proposed contract. For example, an offer to sell certain described goods at a certain price may say nothing about the time for delivery and payment. The offeror is presumed to intend the customary terms and provisions when he does not state otherwise. Delivery within a reasonable time and payment upon delivery are therefore implied terms of the offer. If in reply the offeree says, "I accept provided delivery is to be within a reasonable time and payment is to be made upon delivery," the offeree is merely expressing what is already implied by the offer. Since the offeree's reply neither changes nor adds to any of the offered terms, the reply would be a valid acceptance and would form a contract.

It would not be considered a counteroffer and hence a rejection.

Other circumstances can arise where an offeree's return promise is not construed as a counteroffer with respect to the original offer. For example, where the offeree makes an unconditional acceptance of the offer and accompanies it with a request for modification, the contract will be enforceable with respect to the original promise, but the modification will be treated as an offer.

The same reasoning can be applied when there has been an unconditional acceptance accompanied by a gratuitous promise to do something else. If, in the example immediately above, B replied, "I accept your offer and in addition I promise to buy all my cola needs in the future from you," a valid contract would be formed with respect to the 200 bottles of Brand X cola, but the remaining promise would be treated as a mere gratuity.

Finally, a counteroffer will not operate as a rejection of the original offer where the offeror is willing to hold his offer open during which time he will accept counteroffers. Similarly, the offeror's offer would remain open where the offeree in submitting the counteroffer states that he still is considering the offer.

Sometimes an offeree's reply in response to an offer is so ambiguous that it is difficult to determine exactly what intent the offeree means to express. Suppose that a seller offers to sell certain property to a buyer for $1,000, payable on delivery, and that the buyer replies: "I accept your offer and will buy the property for $1,000. I will pay $500 on delivery and the balance one month after delivery." This ambiguous reply raises a question as to the buyer's intent—or, more accurately, as to what a reasonable man would be justified in concluding is the buyer's intent. Is the buyer primarily interested in buying for $1,000, and willing to pay on delivery if he has to, or instead is he primarily interested in deferring a portion of the payment and definitely not agreeable to paying the entire price in cash? The rule which gradually evolved at common law is a fairly simple and clear-cut rule, related to the policy view that if an offeree wants to accept and form a contract with an offeror, the offeree must clearly and unequivocally indicate that he is in complete agreement with the offer. Thus under the common law rule, the legal effect of an offeree's reply is determined by the total intent which he expresses. If in its totality, the offeree's reply differs from the offer, the offeree's reply is not an acceptance and no contract is formed. In the above-quoted reply ("I will accept your offer and will buy the property for $1,000. I will pay $500 on delivery and the balance one month after delivery.") the total intent expressed by the buyer differs from the seller's terms. Under the common law rule, therefore, the reply is not an acceptance but rather a counteroffer, and no contract would be formed unless the seller in turn accepts the counteroffer.

However, when this fundamentally sound common law rule is applied to modern commercial transactions, the results are not always satisfactory, especially in the type of situation which is frequently dubbed "the battle of the forms." Large business establishments commonly use printed forms in ordering and in accepting or acknowledging orders. The forms used by each business are prepared with the help of its legal staff and incorporate the terms and conditions under which the business intends to make its contracts. As can be expected the terms stated in one form will frequently differ from those in the form used by another business. Sometimes the differences are trivial, sometimes substantial. Employees who use such forms usually do not diligently compare, item for item, the form received from another business establishment with the form sent or being sent out by their own establishment. Confusion also may arise when representatives of businesses negotiate a sales agreement through a number of oral conferences or by a series of letters and then, as frequently occurs, one (or both) of them sends a formal acknowledgment or memorandum stating the agreement. Especially when the acknowledgment or memorandum has gone through the legal office of the sender, it may include some added items that were not previously discussed; again the employees involved may not diligently compare the formal writing with the previous negotiations. In most such cases the goods in question are shipped and paid for and no question is raised. If, however, a dispute arises and the common law rule is applied, the legal staffs of the businesses, and the courts as well, have a vexing problem in determining whether a contract actually exists, and if so what its terms are.

Additional Terms in Acceptance or Confirmation Under the UCC. The authors of the Uniform Commercial Code felt that for sales-of-goods transactions, the common law rule should be somewhat modified into a more modern rule which they state as follows:

> 1. A definite and seasonable expression of acceptance or a written confirmation which is sent within a reasonable time operates as an acceptance even though it states terms additional to or different from those offered or agreed upon, unless acceptance is expressly made conditional on assent to the additional or different terms.
>
> 2. The additional terms are to be construed as proposals for addition to the contract. Between merchants such terms become part of the contract unless:

> (a) the offer expressly limits acceptance to the terms of the offer;
>
> (b) they materially alter it; or
>
> (c) notification of objection to them has already been given or is given within a reasonable time after notice of them is received.
>
> 3. Conduct by both parties which recognizes the existence of a contract is sufficient to establish a contract for sale although the writings of the parties do not otherwise establish a contract. In such case the terms of the particular contract consist of those terms on which the writings of the parties agree, together with any supplementary terms incorporated under any other provision of this Act.[21]

This Code rule reflects the willingness and ability of the more mature legal system of modern times to undertake complex tasks of analysis and interpretation. In distinction to the common-law "total intent" rule, the Code rule can be called a "principal intent" rule. If the main or primary intent which the offeree expresses is to accept and form a contract as offered, the offeree's reply has the desired effect; it is an acceptance and forms a contract on the offeror's terms, even though the reply includes different or changed terms. On the other hand, if the offeree's principal intent is to form no contract except on his own terms, then the offeree's reply is a counteroffer and not an acceptance. Note that the determinant is the principal intent of the offeree as disclosed in the language he uses, without regard to the importance or unimportance of the changes suggested by the new or changed terms. If the offeree's principal intent is to accept, a contract is formed on the offeror's terms; in also adding new or changed terms to his acceptance, the offeree is offering or proposing an amendment to the contract which the principal part of his reply has already formed. The original offeror can in turn ac-

---

21. U.C.C. Sec. 2-207.

Example. On June 1 B sent S a written order for certain described goods costing $800, one-half of the order to be shipped on the following August 1, the remainder on September 1; terms for payment were stated as 2/20, net 60 (meaning 2 percent discount for payment within 20 days after shipment, the net amount due in 60 days).

1. On June 2 S replied in writing: "I hereby accept your order of June 1 and agree to ship at the times stated. Terms for payment: net 20 days." B did not reply and on August 1, S made the first shipment which B received without complaint or qualification. At the expiration of 20 days, S demanded payment. B refused, asserting that he had an additional 40 days in which to pay. On September 1 S refused to ship the second installment of goods, contending that he was excused from shipping because of B's continuing failure to pay for the first shipment. B assured S that payment would be made within the 60-day period, and when S persisted in demanding payment before making the September 1 shipment, B sued S for damages.

It is strongly arguable that the contract between the parties gave B 60 days in which to pay, and that therefore(1) B was not in default for refusing to pay within 20 days, (2) S was not excused from making the second shipment, and (3) B could recover damages for S's refusal to ship on September 1. The principal intent of S's June 2 reply (it is strongly arguable) was to accept B's offer on B's terms, and at the same time to further offer to amend the contract thus formed, in order to change the terms for payment from "2/ 20, net 60," to "net 20." This would be a material change. Even if B were a merchant, his failure to object to the change would not make it a part of the contract. His acceptance of the shipment would not show that he was agreeable to S's terms because (as is strongly arguable) there was already a contract on B's terms.

2. On June 2 S replied in writing: "Subject to your agreement to the terms and conditions on the reverse side hereof, I hereby accept your order and agree to ship at the time stated...." On the reverse side of S's communication was written (or printed): "Terms for payment: net 20 days." The principal intent of S's June 2 reply was not to accept, but rather to make a counteroffer; no contract would arise between the parties unless B in turn agreed to the counteroffer.

3. Suppose other facts as in Part 2 of this example, except that S's June 2 communication read: "Subject to the terms and conditions on the reverse side hereof . . .," omitting the phrase "your agreement to" which appears in Part 2 immediately after the words, "Subject to."

It is arguable that without the omitted phrase ("Your agreement to") S's reply would not be (in the language of the Code) ". . . expressly made conditional on assent to the additional or different terms," (emphasis added), and that therefore S's reply would be an acceptance on B's terms. Although this argument is weak, it would be unwise for S to omit some statement requiring B's agreement to the new terms.

4. Assume the same facts as in Part 2 of this example, plus the following: B never replied to S's June 2 communication, and on August 1, S shipped one-half of the ordered goods. B received and retained the goods without any comment. Twenty days later S demanded that B pay.

The principal intent of S's June 2 letter was to make a counteroffer. B's failure to reply to the counteroffer would usually not be construed as an acceptance. However, S's shipment was a renewal of his counteroffer to sell on S's terms, and B's retention of the goods was an acceptance; a contract was thereby formed, and the terms would be S's terms. □

Example. Upon opening a package received by a messenger, the recipient found a book which he had not ordered or requested. Included with the book was a letter identifying the sender, describing the book, stating the price, and adding, "If you do not wish to buy this book, return it to us and you will have no further obligation." The recipient put the book aside, and did not use it, pay for it, return it, or communicate with the sender in any way.

The recipient did not accept the offer and no contract was formed. If the recipient had used the book (more than merely for examination) or otherwise had acted as an owner toward it (even by giving or throwing it away when he had sufficient storage space) he would be doing something more than merely remaining silent and his conduct would constitute acceptance. ☐

* * *

Example. A seller says to a buyer, "I'll sell you this book for $5. It is such a good bargain that unless you say 'no' in ten seconds I'll assume that you accept."

1. The buyer says nothing, but does not intend to accept. There is no acceptance and no contract. Usually a person cannot be forced to reply at the risk that if he does not, he will be assumed to have accepted a certain proposition.

2. Intending to accept, the buyer makes no reply. Although the offeree's remaining silent is doing exactly what the offeror requests as an acceptance, some courts tend toward the view that since the offeree's remaining silent is not a definite manifestation of an intent to bind himself, his mere silence is not sufficient to bind the offeror on the offeror's promise; and that therefore even though an offeror specifies silence as an acceptance, an offer for a bilateral contract is incapable of being accepted by the offeree's silence, unless accompanied by some additional conduct manifesting the offeree's intent to be bound. ☐

cept or reject the offeree's proposed amendment. If the offeror makes no reply to the proposed changes, only then does the importance of the changes become relevant. If the original offeror and offeree are both merchants, and also if the proposed changes are minor, then if the offeror fails to write to the offeree rejecting the changes, the offeror's silence constitutes an acceptance of the change. If the proposed changes are material, or if one or both parties are not merchants, the offeror's failure to object is not an acceptance of the changes. The authors of the Code suggest that changes in terms are material if they would cause surprise or objection, or would result in hardship if considered a part of the contract without both parties being expressly aware of them. Examples include negating a standard warranty, or requiring 100 percent deliveries when some deviation is usual in the type of commodity and trade involved. Minor differences are such as would cause no undue surprise. Examples include: fixing within customary limits a certain time for return of defective items with no claim or return permitted after such time; providing for interest to accrue on overdue money obligations, stating situations under which a seller would be excused from performing and including only those which customarily excuse a party, or only slightly enlarge on the customary excuses.

5. METHOD OF ACCEPTANCE—IN GENERAL

Certainly a legally enforceable obligation cannot arise from a person's making an uncom-

Example. On June 25, a man signed an application directed to the X Insurance Company, applying for a 20-payment $2,000 life insurance policy payable to the applicant's estate, and paid $4 as a deposit on the first premium. The agent to whom the application and money were given was not authorized to issue insurance policies, not even temporary binding agreements; he was merely an agent to solicit applications. The applicant was thereafter contacted by agents from other life insurance companies but was not interested in their proposals because of his application to the X company. On August 24 the applicant was accidentally killed. Up to that time the X Company had failed to give notice of its action on the application. The applicant's administrator sued the company for the amount of the policy, contending that by holding the application for so long a period, the company had accepted it. The company in turn tendered return of the applicant's $4 initial payment.

Under somewhat similar facts the Pennsylvania Supreme Court said[22] (as would courts in many other states) that the failure to reject was not an acceptance and that the company's only obligation was to return the $4. Which party took the initiative was immaterial—whether the company's agent first contacted the applicant and induced him to apply for the insurance, or whether the applicant sought out the agent. ☐

* * *

Example. During the seven-month period preceding August 23, a wholesale grocer gave a series of orders to the district salesman of a meat packing company. The orders were accepted and the goods shipped not later than one week after the date of each order. On August 23 the wholesaler gave the salesman an order calling for the prompt shipment of a certain quantity of shortening at 7 1/2 cents per pound. As had the previous order forms, this form stated: "This order is subject to acceptance by the packer at the point of shipment." Not receiving the shortening nor hearing from the packer within one week, the wholesaler inquired as to when the shipment would be made. In a reply received by the wholesaler on September 4, the packer said that the order was rejected. By that time the price of shortening had risen to 9 cents per pound, and the wholesaler sued the packer for damages for refusal to ship at 7 1/2 cents per pound.

The Mississippi Supreme Court said[23] that there was an enforceable contract at 7 1/2 cents per pound, that through his past conduct the offeree led the offeror to reasonably assume that silence or inaction following receipt of an offer was intended as acceptance, and that therefore failure to promptly reject the August 23 order constituted an acceptance. Courts in some states would agree with this conclusion, while courts in some other states would not. ☐

22. *Zayc v. John Hancock Mut. Life Ins. Co.*. 338 Pa. 426, 12 A.2d 34(1940).
23. *Ammons v. Wilson & Co.*, 176 Miss. 645, 170 S. 227(1936).

municated promise to himself. Thus for an offeree to make a promissory commitment requires some kind of communication, some conduct which as a matter of policy will be considered sufficient to manifest the offeree's commitment to the offeror. In addition to a promise made in the usual way through spoken or written words, a promise to the offeror may, under certain circumstances, be made by the offeree–promisor's conduct, and occasionally by his inaction or remaining silent.

Promise Communicated Through Conduct

Even though an offer requests a promise rather than an act as an acceptance, it frequently is possible for the offeree to make the requested promise by conduct instead of by words. If the conduct of the offeree reasonably leads the offeror to believe that the offeree is agreeable to the offer and is committing himself accordingly, the offeree's conduct makes and communicates the requested promise and forms a contract. Thus if an offeree accepts goods which he should reasonably know are not intended as a gift, the offeree by his conduct of accepting the goods makes a promise to pay the requested price according to the stated terms. If no price is stated, the offeree is obligated to pay a reasonable price on customary terms. An example of a contract formed in this way is shown in Part 4 of the preceding example. A person who continues to accept delivery of a periodical after his subscription has expired is likewise, through his conduct, promising to pay.

Promise Communicated Through Failure to Act

Usually it is not fair to assume that a person is agreeing to a certain proposition merely because he remains silent or inactive after learning of the proposal. Therefore silence is usually not construed as an acceptance.

Suppose, however, that not only does an offer indicate silence or inaction as the method by which it is to be accepted, but in addition the offeree remains silent with an intent to accept. If thereafter, contrary to the offeree's expectation, the offeror should assert that no contract has been formed, persuasive arguments can be made for either side of the dispute. It is not surprising, therefore, that in the few cases which have involved this point, the court decisions are not in agreement.

Admittedly some other conduct on the part of the offeree, when added to his silence, may constitute a sufficient manifestation of the offeree's intent to bind himself, and thus also serve to bind the offeror. The courts are not in agreement as to what such "other conduct" may consist of. Only a few courts have said that if an offeree induces the offeror to make an offer, the offeree's remaining silent and failing to promptly reject the offer thus solicited by him constitutes an acceptance. On the other hand, many courts have held that if through prior dealings the offeree has led the offeror reasonably to believe that the offeree will respond promptly to an offer, then the offeree's failure to act promptly is sufficient to constitute an acceptance and to form a contract binding on both parties.

Promise Communicated Through Words

Federal law is clear with respect to unsolicited goods sent through the mails. Not only will silence not operate as acceptance, but the addressee can use the goods without undergoing the risk of contractually binding himself.

Although the offeree can make his acceptance promise by conduct or occasionally through silence, an offeree usually makes the requested promise in words (such as "I accept"), which indicate that he is agreeing to the offeror's proposal and willing to be bound by it. If the parties are not talking directly to each other, either face-to-face or by telephone, but instead the offeree expresses his acceptance by letter or telegram, there is a delay or time lag between the offeree's expression of his intent and the offeror's receiving and learning of the acceptance. If during this time lag the offeror attempts to revoke his offer, or if one of the parties dies (automatically revoking unaccepted offers), it immediately becomes essential to know at what point of time the acceptance becomes effective, if at

Example. A nonmerchant offeror sent an offer by regular mail, giving ten days to accept, not specifying a medium for replying, and not stating that the acceptance would be effective only when received. In reply the offeree mailed an acceptance on the sixth day, properly addressed and stamped.

1. Assume that the offeree's accepting letter was received by the offeror on the eighth day. The contract would be considered as formed on the sixth .

2. Assume that the offeree's accepting letter was delayed in transit (through no fault of the offeree) and not delivered until the fifteenth day. The contract would be considered as formed on the sixth.

3. Assume that the offeree's accepting letter was lost in the mail (through no fault of the offeree). If the offeree's testimony that he properly mailed an acceptance on the sixth is believed, a contract would be considered as formed on the sixth.

4. Assume that the offeree changed his mind and (as is possible under postal regulations) obtained return of his accepting letter from the postal system so that it never was delivered to the offeror. If the offeror could prove these facts, a contract would be considered as formed on the sixth.

5. Assume that the offeree's accepting letter was mailed on the sixth and received by the offeror on the eighth day, but that on the seventh day, the offeree had received from the offeror a communication revoking the offer. The contract would be considered as formed on the sixth. Since the offeree effectively accepted before receiving the revocation, the revocation would not be effective.

6. Assume that after mailing his acceptance on the sixth, the offeree, on the seventh, telegraphed that he had changed his mind and that his accepting letter should be ignored; the offeror received the telegraph on the seventh, and the accepting letter on the eighth. The contract would be considered as formed on the sixth, and the offeree could not undo or cancel the contract without the offeror's consent. The telegram of the seventh would be construed as an offer to cancel, and the recipient's failure to reply usually would not be construed as an acceptance of this proposal. ☐

all, so as to know whether or not there is a contract.

Since the offeror is initiating the proposed offer, he may specify whatever he wishes as an acceptance. He may, for example, specify that the acceptance must be communicated in a certain way or delivered to a certain place, and the offeree cannot accept unless he meets these conditions. Most offers, however, fail to specify particular conditions for acceptance; for such offers reasonable rules have evolved as to when an acceptance is considered communicated and effective. The chief fact situations can be classified as to whether transmis-

sion is (1) through the offeror's personal agent or (2) through an independent agency.

1. **Transmission Through Offeror's Personal Agent**. If the offeree delivers his acceptance to the offeror's personal agent who is authorized to receive such communi-cations, the acceptance should certainly be considered communicated and effective when given to the agent. For example, if the offeree takes his written acceptance to the offeror's office, the acceptance is considered as communicated and effective when the offeree gives it to a suitable employee in the offeror's office, even though the offeror himself is not available. Likewise, suppose that in communicating an

Example. A nonmerchant offeror sent an offer by regular mail, giving ten days to accept, not specifying a medium for replying, and not stating that the acceptance would be effective only when received. On the fifth day the offeree mailed a letter rejecting the offer, but on the sixth day, the offeree changed his mind and mailed a letter (properly addressed and stamped) accepting the offer. The offeree's rejecting letter was received on the seventh, his accepting letter on the eighth. When the offeror denied that there was a contract, the offeree sued, arguing that since a rejection is not effective until received, the offer was still open on the sixth and that therefore a contract was formed on the sixth when the accepting letter was mailed.

To avoid such an unfair result, the law would say that the offeree's conduct suspended the ordinary rule of an acceptance being effective when mailed. If an offeree sends both an acceptance and a rejection, knowing that the rejection might arrive first (and the rejection contains no reference to any previous acceptance), then the acceptance will be effective only if the offeror actually receives it before he receives the rejection. If the rejection arrives first (and contains no reference to any previous acceptance), the acceptance arriving later will not be effective to form a contract. ☐

* * *

Example. A nonmerchant offeror sent an offer by regular mail, giving ten days to accept, not specifying a medium for replying, and not stating that the acceptance would be effective only when received. In reply, the offeree telegraphed an acceptance on the ninth day, properly addressed and with charges prepaid. Transmission of the telegram was delayed through fault of the telegraph company and the telegram was not delivered to the offeror until the twelfth.

1. Assume that the offer concerned the sale of goods. Under the Uniform Commercial Code, if reply by telegram was reasonable (as it usually would be), it was an authorized medium of communication, and a contract would be considered as formed on the ninth.

2. Assume that the offer concerned something other than sale of goods—such as land, personal services, or a loan. Some courts would say that the use of the telegraph was unauthorized, that the acceptance could not be effective until received (on the twelfth) by which time the offer had expired, and that therefore no contract was formed. Other courts would follow the same rule as the Code adopts for sales-of-goods offers. ☐

offer the offeror uses his own employee as a messenger, instructing him not only to deliver the offer but also to wait for an answer; the offeree's acceptance in reply to the offer would be communicated and effective as soon as given to the offeror's messenger, although the messenger would still be on the offeree's premises.

2. **Transmission Through Independent Agency.** Usually the offeree delivers his acceptance to some independent transmission system, such as the postal system or the telegraph company, for transmittal to the offeror.

To have a workable rule, the law must indicate some pinpoint of time as the moment when an acceptance can be said to become effective. There are two possible choices: either the time when the acceptance is delivered to the transmission system, or the time when the transmission system delivers the acceptance to the offeror's address. Which of these two the law should select is entirely a matter of policy of fairness, reasonableness, and practicality under the circumstances. In deciding the question, the law has concluded that although the postal or telegraph system is not actually a personal messenger employed by the offeror, it is sufficiently similar to justify applying the personal messenger rule. The chief policy factors leading to this conclusion are demonstrated by comparing the results of each of the two possible choices. If the acceptance is effective when mailed, then sometimes the offeror will be unaware of when he becomes bound by a contract or whether there is a contract at all. The offeror could avoid this disadvantage by specifying in his offer that an acceptance will not be effective until received. On the other hand, if the acceptance is effective only when received, then sometimes the offeree will have the disadvantage of not knowing when he becomes bound by a contract or whether there is a contract at all. The offeree could reduce this disadvantage by using a means of transmission, such as a telegram or certified mail, which would enable him more easily to determine the time his acceptance has been delivered. Thus whichever rule is followed—acceptance effective when sent or not until received—one or the other party will sometimes be at a disadvantage. The law considers it fair to pick the offeror as the one to bear this disadvantage since he can so easily avoid it when he initiates the offer (by specifically requiring receipt of the acceptance), and since by selecting a certain medium for transmission he to some extent assumes the risks which that medium entails, such as loss or delay in transit, etc.

As a matter of policy, therefore, the rule has become well established that if an offer does not specifically require that the acceptance must be received to be effective, an acceptance sent in a way authorized by the offeror is effective when started on its way (that is, depending on which means is authorized, when dropped in a mail box or given to a clerk in a telegraph office properly addressed, with charges prepaid. On the other hand, if an acceptance is sent in an unauthorized way, it is not effective until received—provided the offer is still open at that time. The medium that is authorized for transmitting an acceptance is the way specified in the offer. If none is specified, the medium used to transmit the offer is, by implication, authorized for transmitting the acceptance. If the medium which the offeree selects for transmitting his acceptance is not expressly specified in the offer and also is different from the medium used to transmit the offer, but is nevertheless reasonable under the circumstances, then (1) if the offer concerns something other than sale of goods, some courts say that the different but reasonable medium is not authorized, some say that it is authorized; (2) if the offer concerns a sale of goods, the Uniform Commercial Code states[24] that in the absence of a contrary express requirement, any medium reasonable in the circumstances is authorized. A medium of communication is reasonable if it is in common use and also is as fast or faster than the medium used to transmit the offer.

V. Summary of Differences Between Common Law and U.C.C. Offer and Acceptance

Throughout this Chapter, it has been emphasized that the U.C.C. tends to liberalize the formation of contracts to reflect modern methods of doing business. Table 5.1 serves to summarize some of the major differences between the common law and U.C.C. law of contracts that were discussed in this Chapter.

---

24. U.C.C. Sec. 2-206.

TABLE 5.1: DIFFERENCES BETWEEN COMMON LAW AND U.C.C. CONTRACTS

	Common Law	U.C.C.
Parties identified as	offeror, offeree; promisor, promisee; etc.	seller, buyer; merchant
where offer is indefinite	reasonableness standards applied	commercial standards applied
Where offeror terminates offer before acceptance	offer cannot be accepted unless it is in the form of an option	offer can be accepted if it is "firm "
Where acceptance is by shipment of nonconforming goods	acceptance is not good, but operates as a counteroffer	acceptance is good if not accompanied by an accommodation notice
Where additional terms are included in the acceptance offeror, offeree; promisor, promisee; etc.	acceptance is good if "total intent" established	acceptance is good if "principal intent" established

Problems

1. A construction company was building an Army camp, and in a nearby town, the plaintiff operated a dormitory for workmen. In November the personnel manager of the construction company called the plaintiff to the camp, said that he had more men coming and didn't know where to put them, and asked how many additional men the plaintiff could accommodate. The plaintiff replied that his first floor was about filled, but that if he could obtain pipe to extend heat to the second floor of his building, he could take care of about 50 additional men. The personnel manager replied, "I would like to reserve that upstairs for us," to which the plaintiff answered, "O.K." The personnel manager helped the plaintiff to obtain the nec-essary pipe from the construction company's supplies, and the plaintiff extended heat to his second floor and installed beds. About the middle of December the plaintiff notified the personnel manager that the accommodations were ready. However, the construction company never used or paid for the second-floor accommodations. The following March the plaintiff received from the construction company a bill for the pipe which the plaintiff had used. The plaintiff thereupon sent the construction company a bill for $3,000, as the charge for the second-floor accommodations from the middle of December to March, and when the company failed to pay, the plaintiff sued the company. Explain (1) the reasoning upon which the construction company might attempt to defend, (2) the reasoning upon which the plaintiff might

attempt to recover, and (3) which party should be given judgment.

2. B. Brown, a wholesaler, entered into the following written agreement with S. Smith, a miller:

> S. Smith hereby agrees to sell and B. Brown to buy the following commodities, f.o.b. car of initial carrier at shipping point, freight allowed to Chicago, Ill.
>
> *Time of shipment*: December 1 of this year, unless ordered out sooner.
>
> *Destination:* Track, Chicago, Ill.
>
> *Terms of payment*: 2/10 net 30 from date of each shipment.
>
> *Quantity:* 630 barrels
>
> *Shipping dates:* to follow. [Date]
>
> | Brand of flour | Price per barrel |
> |---|---|
> | Confidence | 6.65 |
> | Harvester | 6.45 |
> | De Luxe Pastry | 6.40 |
> | Sierra Pastry | 5.90 |
>
> (*signed*) S. Smith (*signed*) B. Brown

In accordance with the contract and at B's direction, S milled and delivered to B 210 barrels of Confidence brand flour on April 15, for which B paid according to contract. B refused to order any more flour and after December 1, S sued B for damages. Explain (1) the reasoning upon which B might attempt to defend, (2) the reasoning upon which S might attempt to collect, and (3) which party should be given judgment.

3. In writing S agreed to sell and B to buy 10,000 bushels of a specified kind and type of grain, to be delivered in installments of 2,000 bushels by the tenth of each month for five successive months, beginning on a specified month. The only provision as to price read: "The price B is to pay for each installment shall be the Chicago market price on the date of shipment f.o.b. Chicago, payable within ten days after delivery." When S tendered delivery of the first installment according to contract, B refused to accept. S sued B for damages. Explain (1) the reasoning upon which B might attempt to defend, (2) the reasoning upon

which S might attempt to collect, and (3) which party should be given judgment.

4. Martin Stores, Inc., decided to sell a portion of its eight-acre property. Consequently, the president of Martin wrote several prospective buyers the following letter:

> Dear Mr. Smith: We are sending this notice to several prospective buyers because we are interested in selling four acres of our property located in downtown Metropolis. If you are interested, please communicate with me at the above address. Don't bother to reply unless you are thinking in terms of at least $100,000.
>
> James Martin, President.

One day after Mr. Smith received Martin's letter, he responded by letter:

> Enclosed is my signed check for $100,000. Please mail deed for said four acres as soon as possible.

Upon Martin's refusal to send a deed, Smith sued Martin for specific performance. Would Smith's suit be successful? (Modified from A.I.C.P.A. November 78-27.)

5. In response to an advertisement in a newspaper, O, the owner of a factory in a small town, met with S to discuss the availability of O's factory for assembling storm windows from materials to be furnished by S. After inspecting O's plant, S said that if O would make certain specified alterations and install certain specified equipment, S would supply O with sufficient material for assembling 1,000 to 3,000 storm windows per day, under an agreement whereby O would pay for the material received at a price to be fixed between the parties and thereafter, upon delivery of the assembled storm windows to S or to a designated customer of S, S would pay O a price sufficient to cover all of O's costs plus a reasonable profit. It was agreed that the final terms, including the duration of the arrangement, would be determined and a formal written contract prepared when O's factory was ready to go into operation. With frequent consultation with S, O promptly made the necessary alterations and purchased and installed the necessary equipment. In the meantime, however, S made other arrangements and refused to have any

further dealings with O. The alterations and special equipment cost O $3,000 and were of use only for the specified purpose. O sued S for $3,000. Explain (1) the reasoning upon which S might attempt to defend, (2) the reasoning upon which O might attempt to collect, and (3) which party should be given judgment.

6. A retail clothier contracted with the publisher of a newspaper for the following advertisement: "Special in furs. Large animal scarfs, taupe, brown, and black. Satin lined. For three days only. Special price, $15." When the advertisement appeared in the newspaper, it erroneously stated the price as $5. Since no proof sheet of the advertisement was submitted to the retailer, he did not see the error until the newspaper was published. The retailer sued the publisher for $480 damages for breach of contract and proved that after the advertisement was published, 48 persons came to the retailer's store, mentioned seeing the advertisement, and demanded and were each sold a scarf for $5.

(a) Was the retailer entitled to judgment against the publisher for $480? Explain.

(b) Suppose that the advertisement reading $5 was what the retailer had ordered published, but that the retailer had thereafter changed his mind and did not want to sell for less than $15. Unaware of the retailer's change of mind, a customer who had read the advertisement came to the store and told the retailer that he wanted to buy for $5. When the retailer refused to sell for less than $15, the customer accused the retailer of breaking a contract. Was the customer correct? Explain.

7. B. Brown received the following typewritten letter, dated February 2, from S. Smith: "Dear Mr. Brown: We have Mason green jars of one quart capacity complete with caps that we can offer you at this time for immediate acceptance at $8 per gross, delivered in your city. Terms 60 days or less, 2 percent for cash in 10 days. Awaiting your orders we are yours truly, (signed) S. Smith." B promptly replied by telegraph as follows: "Your February 2 letter just arrived. Enter order for 500 gross complete

goods." The February 2 letter had not been in response to any inquiry from B. Five hundred gross was a reasonable quantity for B to order and not in excess of what S, from his knowledge of the business of B, might reasonably expect B to order. S answered by telegraph: "We can enter order for only 250 gross." B sued for breach of contract for S's refusal to ship 500 gross of jars.

(a) Was B entitled to judgment? Explain.

(b) Explain how, if at all, S could have avoided the possibility of this dispute arising, without further limiting his freedom of action.

(c) Other facts remaining the same, assume the February 2 letter was printed and the salutation read: "Dear Customer." Was B entitled to judgment against S for refusing to ship 500 gross? Explain.

8. On March 10, Brown Seed Company received the following letter from S. Smith, a farmer residing at Lowell, Nebraska: "Brown Seed Co., Omaha, Nebraska. Gentlemen: I have for sale about 1800 bu. of millet seed of which I am mailing you a sample enclosed with this letter. This millet is recleaned and was grown on sod and is good seed. I want $2.25 per hundredweight for this seed, f.o.b. Lowell. (signed) S. Smith." The same day B Company sent S the following telegram: "S. Smith, Lowell, Nebraska. Sample and letter received.

Accept your offer. Millet like sample two twenty-five per hundred. (signed) Brown Seed Co." S received the telegram the same day it was sent. S refused to sell, having found another buyer and B Company sued S for damages.

(a) Explain (1) the reasoning upon which B Company could attempt to collect, (2) the reasoning upon which S could attempt to defend, and (3) which party should be given judgment.

(b) Explain how, if at all, S could have avoided the possibility of this dispute arising, without limiting his freedom of action.

19. S of Detroit, Michigan, was the owner of a piece of property, well known as the Table property, located in Sharon, Pennsylvania. B of Sharon told S's sister that he was considering purchasing the property for $40,000. S's sister told S of this conversation and on July 11 S wrote B: "In reference to the offer you recently quoted to my sister ($40,000 cash) for the sale of the Table property, I am pleased to accept your offer. Please write me and let me know when it would be convenient for us to get together in Sharon to close the deal." In reply, B wrote S, July 13: "I am enclosing an option which you are to sign in which you agree to sell this property, clear of all liens, for $40,000. I want the sixty days mentioned in the option in order to try to raise enough money to purchase the property myself. If I am unable to do so, I feel certain I can interest somebody in Sharon at this price." In reply to this letter, S wrote B, July 18: "I am returning the option which I do not care to sign. However, if at any time you have raised the money and wish to close the deal, 1 shall be glad to do 80. Let me hear from you soon." On August 21, B wrote S: "I hereby accept your written offer of July 18 to sell me the Table property for $40,000." When S refused to sell, B sued S for a decree of specific performance which would order S to transfer his interest in the property to B for $40,000. S contended that there was no offer which B could accept by his August 21 letter, because (a) any offer S had made had lapsed, and (b) S really had made no offer. Was B entitled to the requested decree? Explain.

10. B was in the business of exporting crude petroleum to France, his trade amounting to about 100,000 barrels a year. S, an oil refiner, contacted B, suggesting that B purchase his requirements of oil from S and further suggesting that B attempt, by a visit to Paris, to increase his export trade. To assist B on his trip, S on March 1 signed and gave B a letter reading in part: "In accordance with our interview, I am willing to enter into a contract with you for the furnishment of Pennsylvania crude oil for a term of two years in the amount of 400,000 barrels of 42 gallons each, per year, at the following price . . . [specifying a price and details

of transportation and handling charges]. 1 extend to you a refusal of making the contract on the above basis for the term of four months from this date. Should it not be accepted in writing on or before that time the above is to become null and void and without effect between us." B traveled to Paris at his own expense and after some negotiations succeeded in entering into contracts with various French refiners to supply them with crude petroleum totaling 400,000 barrels a year.

(a) Thereafter, S sent B the following: "May 23. I wish to advise you that I withdraw my offer of March 1. You will therefore consider the same canceled." To this B replied: "May 24. 1 hereby notify you that I accept and will fully carry out the option and contract you gave me by your letter of March 1. I hereby repudiate your attempted withdrawal of said option." Each letter was received by the respective addressee the day following the date of mailing. Upon S's refusal to deliver oil to B, B sued for damages for breach of contract. Was B entitled to judgment against S? Explain.

(b) Assume facts the same as in Part (a) of this problem, except that the date of S's letter to B was June 23 and the date of B's answering letter to S was June 24. Was B entitled to judgment against S? Explain.

11. A state government advertised for bids for the construction of a public building. A merchant sent an employee to the state capitol to look over the building plans and specifications and calculate the total amount of linoleum required for the building. The employee underestimated the total yardage by about one-half the proper amount. On December 24, in ignorance of the mistake, the merchant sent to about thirty builders likely to bid on the job, an offer to supply at a specified price all the linoleum required in the specifications for this particular building. The offering letters concluded saying: "We are offering this price for reasonably prompt acceptance after the general contract has been awarded." B, a builder, received one of the offering letters on December 28, used the linoleum figure in calculating his bid, and the same day submitted the bid to the proper state office to-

Problems

gether with the usual money deposit. On December 29 the merchant discovered the error and telegraphed all the builders to whom the offering letters had been sent, withdrawing the offer and saying that a new offer would be sent at about double the amount of the old one. Upon receiving the telegram, B did not withdraw his bid because there was not sufficient time to submit another bid, the linoleum was a trifling part of the cost of the whole building, and withdrawal of the bid would have resulted in forfeiture of the money deposit. On December 30 the state awarded the contract to B. On January 2 B sent to the merchant an acceptance of his December 24 offer. When the merchant refused to supply linoleum at that price, B sued for damages. Explain (1) the reasoning upon which the merchant might attempt to defend, (2) the reasoning upon which B might attempt to recover, and (3) which party should be given judgment.

12. On December 8, in reply to an inquiry S telegraphed to B: "Will sell you 2,000-5,000 tons of 50 pound iron rails for $54 per gross ton, cash, f.o.b. cars our mill, March delivery. If offer accepted, expect to be notified of same prior to December 20." Assume that under the particular circumstances this constituted an offer. On December 16 B telegraphed S: "Enter order 1,200 tons rails as per your wire of December 8." On December 18 S telegraphed B: "Cannot book your order of 16th at that price." On December 19 B telegraphed S: "Enter order 2,000 tons as per your wire of December 8." S received this telegraph on December 19 but did not reply until January 19 when, after repeated inquiries from B, S stated that he would not ship the rails. B sued S for damages for breach of contract. Explain (1) the reasoning upon which B might attempt to collect, (2) the reasoning upon which S might attempt to defend, and (3) which party should be given judgment.

13. On February 1, B, a manufacturer of refrigerator cases, sent to S, a supplier, a written order for 300 latches of a certain style called "spring lock" at $2 per latch, f.o.b. shipping point, 2/10 net 30. This was S's first order from B, and S desired to obtain B as a customer. However, S had no spring lock latches on hand and could procure them only at a price which, with S's normal markup, would make S's selling price $3 per latch. S had on hand a quantity of "roll-lock" latches on which S's normal selling price was $2.15 per latch. As S knew, many manufacturers had found the roll-lock latch as satisfactory as or superior to the spring lock latch. In response to B's order and without any further communication, S, on February 3, shipped to B 300 roll-lock latches invoiced to B at $2 apiece. On tender of delivery B noticed that the latches were roll-lock latches and refused to receive delivery. The railroad returned them to S on S's payment of the freight charges. B demanded but S refused to ship any other latches.

(a) If S sued B for the loss resulting from B's refusal to receive delivery, could S recover? Explain.

(b) If B sued S for the loss resulting from S's refusal to ship other latches, could B recover? Explain.

(c) How if at all could S have shown that he desired to serve B promptly and still have avoided the dispute and lawsuit? Explain.

14. Brown ordered 100 cases of Delicious Brand peas at list price from Smith Wholesaler. Immediately upon receipt of Brown's order, Smith sent Brown an acceptance which was received by Brown. The acceptance indicated that shipment would be made within ten days. On the tenth day, Smith discovered that all of its supply of Delicious Brand peas had been sold. Instead Smith shipped 100 cases of Lovely Brand peas, stating clearly on the invoice that the shipment was sent as an accommodation only. Was a contract formed between Brown and Smith? (Modified from A.I.C.P.A. May 81-15.)

15. S wrote to B: "I hereby offer to sell you my land [describing it] for $2,000, transfer to be made in one month." Assume that under the circumstances this constituted an offer. B promptly replied in writing: "I hereby accept your offer and agree to buy your land for $2,000, on condition that you can convey to me a good title. Terms shall

175

be $500 on delivery of deed, the balance in two months." S did not reply. The following day, still within a reasonable time, B wrote S: "I accept your offer and will pay $2,000 on transfer of the property." S did not reply within a reasonable time.

(a) Assume that B changed his mind and decided he did not want to buy. Was there a contract which S could enforce against B and if so what were its terms? Explain.

(b) Assume that S changed his mind and decided he did not want to sell. Was there a contract which B could enforce against S and if so what were its terms? Explain.

(c) Other facts remaining the same, assume that the subject matter of S's offering letter was certain described goods, and that after B's second communication, S decided he did not want to sell. Was there a contract which B could enforce against S and if so what were its terms? Explain.

16. B Company sent to S Company a signed printed purchase order form reading in part: "Please enter our order for the following described goods," followed by a typewritten description of the goods ordered and prices. The form contained no reference to strikes. In reply S Company sent to B Company a signed printed form titled "Purchase Memo," the pertinent part of the printed form reading: "This acknowledges receipt of your order for the following described goods, which we accept, subject to the terms and conditions on the reverse side hereof." The description of goods and prices were typewritten on the S Company form, as copied from the B Company's purchase order. On the reverse side of S Company's purchase memo form, among other things, was printed: "S Company will not be liable for any delay in delivery or failure to deliver, resulting from labor trouble or strike." B Company did not reply.

(a) Before S Company could ship the ordered goods, its plant was closed by a strike. B Company sued S Company for damages for nondelivery. Assume that the ordinary rule concerning strikes (see Chapter 12) would apply, that is, that a seller's labor trouble will not excuse him from his contract obligation to deliver unless his contract expressly contains a strike excuse or escape provision. Explain (1) the reasoning upon which B Company might attempt to win the lawsuit, (2) the reasoning upon which S Company might attempt to defend, and (3) which party should be given judgment.

(b) Receiving no reply from B Company, S Company shipped the ordered goods with reasonable promptness. B Company had decided not to purchase (without informing S Company of this fact), and refused the shipment. S Company sued B Company for damages for breach of contract. What result? Explain.

17. On November 9 B wrote to S, a manufacturer, ordering certain described packing materials, at a stated price, one-tenth of the total quantity ordered to be shipped as soon as possible, and the remainder to be retained by S until requested by B, since B had no storage space; the goods were to be billed only when and as shipped on B's instructions and B was to give shipping instructions for all the ordered goods within the next four months. On November 12 S replied that he could not store and ship in that way without charging an extra 5 percent for the accommodation. On November 15 B wrote S refusing to pay an extra 5 percent, stating that B had dealt under those terms with other manufacturers, and hoping that S would reconsider and enter B's November 9 order. Without further correspondence, S began to manufacture the described material and on December 15 shipped the one-tenth portion requested in B's November 9 letter, billed "as per your November 9 order," at the price in the original order. Assume that under the circumstances this shipment was "as soon as possible," within the meaning of B's November 9 order.

(a) B refused the shipment and S sued B for damages for breach of contract. Explain (1) the reasoning upon which S might attempt to recover, (2) the reasoning upon which B might attempt to defend, and (3) which party should be given judgment.

(b) B accepted delivery and paid as billed. Shortly afterwards B wrote to S that no further shipments would be accepted. By that time the manufacture of all of the packing material was completed. After repeated vain attempts during the next four months to induce B to accept more of the packing materials, S sued B for breach of contract. Answer the same questions as are asked in Part (a).

18. Jane Anderson offered to sell Richard Heinz a ten-acre tract of commercial property. Anderson's letter indicated the offer would expire on March 1, at 3:00 p.m. and that any acceptance must be received in her office by that time. On February 29, Heinz decided to accept the offer and posted an acceptance at 4:00 p.m. Heinz indicated that in the event the acceptance did not arrive on time, he would assume there was a contract if he did not hear anything from Anderson in five days. The letter arrived on March 2. Anderson never responded to Heinz's letter. Heinz claims a contract was formed between himself and Anderson. Is Heinz correct? (Modified from A.I.C.P.A. May 80-3B.)

19. Effective April 1, an insurance company issued a $25,000 one-year policy of fire insurance to a businessman covering certain described buildings owned by the businessman. This was the first insurance the businessman ever obtained from this particular company. On March 15 of the following year, the businessman received a letter from the company saying that the policy would be renewed for the same buildings and amount, for a further term of one year from April 1, and that the company would bill the businessman for the annual premium on May 1, unless the businessman notified the company that he did not want the insurance renewed. Intending to have the insurance renewed, the businessman filed the letter and made no reply. On April 20 the buildings were totally destroyed by an accidental fire. When the businessman filed a claim with the insurance company for $25,000, the company asserted that the buildings were not insured. The businessman sued the company for $25,000. Explain (1) the reasoning upon which the businessman could attempt to collect, (2) the reasoning upon which the company could attempt to defend, and (3) which party should be given judgment.

20. On April 7 S mailed a letter to B, offering to sell two carloads of specified goods for a stated price, and saying nothing as to the method of replying to the offer. The letter containing the offer was delivered to B in due course at 10 a.m., April 9. B replied as described in (a) or (b) below. At 9:30 a.m. on April 9, S dispatched a telegram to B reading "Disregard my letter of April 7. Have sold goods elsewhere." B received this telegram at 10:55 a.m., April 9. B maintained that there was a contract. S denied this and refused to deliver. The market price for such goods having gone up, B sued S for damages for breach of contract.

(a) Assume that at 10:30 a.m., April 9, B mailed to S a letter of acceptance. The letter was postmarked 11 a.m., April 9 and delivered to S. 10 a.m., April 11. Was B entitled to judgment in his lawsuit against S? Explain.

(b) Assume that at 10:30 a.m., April 9, B dispatched to S a telegram of acceptance. The telegram was delivered to S, 11:30 a.m., April 9. Was B entitled to judgment in his lawsuit against S? Explain. Would your answer be different if through the sole fault of the telegraph company, the telegram was delayed and not delivered to S until 5 p.m., April 12? Explain.

(c) Explain how, if at all, S could have phrased his letter to avoid the possibility of such a dispute as arose here.

21. At 10 a.m., March 10, S of Philadelphia sent an air-mail letter to B of Portland, Oregon. Under the circumstances, the letter constituted an offer to sell certain described goods to B at a stated price f.o.b. Philadelphia. The letter concluded by saying: "You have three days in which to accept." B received the letter in due course at 10 a.m., March 12. At 4 p.m. March 14, B mailed by regular mail a letter accepting S's offer. S received the accepting letter in due course of mail at 10 a.m., March 17. Learning of a chance to sell to someone else at a

higher price, S refused to ship to B and B sued S for damages. Explain (1) the reasoning upon which S might attempt to defend, (2) the reasoning upon which B might at-tempt to collect, and (3) which party should be given judgment.

22. S decided to replace a machine in his factory with one of more modern design. Re-calling interest in the machine previously expressed by his friend B, owner of a small ma-chine shop, S, on a Wednesday, dictated a letter to his secretary offering to sell the described machine to B for $400. After the letter was typed, S sent his secretary out to deliver a folder in another building, and before she returned S had to leave for a business conference. He signed the letter containing the offer to B and left it on his secretary's desk, together with a separate note that he would be out the remainder of the day. After the secretary returned, she began working on some files in an adjoining room. A few minutes later B came into the office to see S. Noticing that the letter on the secretary's desk was addressed to him, B read it. Also seeing the note that S would not be back, B left without seeing S's secretary.

(a) Before leaving, B wrote on the bottom of S's letter, "Accepted. Thanks a lot" and signed it. Was a contract formed and if so, when? Explain.

(b) Assume that although B read S's letter, he wrote nothing on it. At 5 p.m. S's secretary mailed the letter and it was delivered to B the following morning (Thursday) at 10 a.m. Late Wednesday afternoon B wrote a letter to S accepting the offer made in the letter B had seen in S's office. B mailed his accepting letter at 6 p.m. and it was delivered to S Thursday morning at 11 a.m. By this time S had changed his mind and at 11:30 a.m. Thursday he phoned B that the deal was off. B sued S for breach of contract. Was a contract formed, and if so, when? Explain.

23. S offered by mail to sell B a described farm for $10,000. S's letter was mailed on July 5 and received by B on July 8.

(a) Assume that B wrote S on July 9, inquiring: "Won't you take less?" S replied by letter on July 13, "No." B then mailed a letter to S on July 14, stating "I accept your offer of July 5." S refused to have any further dealings with B. Assuming that July 14 was (under the particular circumstances) a reasonable time within which to have replied to the offer of July 5, was there a valid contract between S and B for the sale of the farm? Explain.

(b) Assume that B, on July 9, sent a telegram to S in which B accepted the offer of July 5. S never received the telegram. Was a valid contract formed between S and B for the sale of the farm? Explain.

(c) Assume that B was not interested in S's offer and gave S's letter to P telling P to accept it if he were interested. P sent a letter to S in which he said, "I accept your offer of July 5." When S refused to transfer the property to P, P sued S. Was P entitled to recover? Explain. (Modified from A.I.C.P.A., Nov. 52-3.)

(d) Assume that on July 10, B mailed a letter to S in which B accepted the offer of July 5. Unknown to B, S had suffered a heart attack on July 9 and died the same day. When B's letter arrived, it was turned over to the executor appointed for S's estate. The executor refused to transfer the land to B and B sued S's estate and the executor. What result? Explain.

(e) Assume that on July 10, B mailed a letter to S in which B accepted the offer of July 5. Unknown to B, S suffered a heart attack on July 12 and died the same day. When B's letter arrived on July 13, it was turned over to the executor appointed for S's estate. The executor refused to transfer the land to B and B sued S's estate and the executor. What result? Explain.

24. After exchanging telegrams not constituting offers, relative to the price of Puerto Rico potatoes for prompt shipment, B, on Friday, February 2, sent to S, an importer, a telegram reading "Ship 150 barrels Puerto Rico today at your quoted price. Wire car number." S replied by telegram the same day, "Will ship Monday." The potatoes were not shipped on Monday, and B wired S on Wednesday, February 7, "When are you going to ship potatoes? Booked shipment. Answer quick."

By "booked shipment" B meant that he had in turn already entered into a contract to sell the potatoes to someone else. Upon receiving this wire on February 7, S did not reply, inasmuch as he had written and mailed a letter to B on February 6, explaining that he was unable to ship on account of weather conditions. Assume that this reason would not excuse a person from performing any contract he may have entered into. S shipped the potatoes on February 10 and wired B at the time of shipment, giving the car number. On February 14, when the potatoes arrived in due course, B refused to accept them. S sued for damages for breach of contract. Was S entitled to judgment against B? Explain.

25. Describe several similarities and differences between offers and acceptances under Common Law and Uniform Commercial Code principles. What do you think the policy reasons are for these differences?

Consideration and Equivalents of Consideration

Consideration and Equivalents of Consideration

THE MERE FACT that two parties have reached an agreement one party making a proposal and the other party accepting the proposal does not necessarily mean that the parties have formed a legally enforceable contract. One outstanding type of promise which the law will almost invariably refuse to enforce is a social arrangement. Suppose, for example, that the annual golf tournament of a county real estate association has been scheduled for a certain afternoon, and that realtor Davis has promised that he will stop at realtor Porter's house right after lunch and give him a ride to the golf course. Suppose further that Davis forgets, and it being too late for Porter to make other arrangements, he has to take a taxi to the golf course. Should Davis be required to pay Porter's taxi fare? Although admittedly the parties reached an agreement, it seems clear that the agreement should not be treated as a legally binding, contractual agreement. Even if he had given Porter the promised ride, Davis could not reasonably expect to be compensated. Would it be fair to hold Davis legally obligated to perform a favor for which he would have no legal right to be paid? It seems better policy to say that if a person is not entitled to payment for some promised performance, he should not be obligated to render the performance—unless something else is present of sufficient importance to justify legal enforcement of the promise. Of the multitude of legal scholars who have expressed this concept in various ways, the following is a limited sample:

There can be no doubt from an empirical or historical point of view, the ability to rely on the promises of others adds to the confidence necessary for social intercourse and enterprise. But as an absolute proposition this is untenable. The actual world . . . is not one in which all promises are kept, and there are many people—not necessarily diplomats—who prefer a world in which they and others occasionally depart from the truth and go back on some promise. It is indeed very doubtful whether there are many who would prefer to live in an entirely rigid world in which one would be obliged to keep all one's promises instead of the present more viable system, in which a vaguely fair proportion is sufficient.

Many of us indeed would shudder at the idea of being bound by every promise no matter how foolish, without any chance of letting increased wisdom undo past foolishness. Certainly, some freedom to change one's mind is necessary for free intercourse between those who lack omniscience.[1]

When one receives a naked promise [that is, a promise for which nothing is given in exchange] and such a promise is broken, he is no worse off than he was. He gave nothing for it, he has lost nothing by it, and on its breach he has suffered no damage cognizable by courts. No benefit accrued to him who made the promise, nor did any injury flow to him who received it. Such promises are not made within the scope of transactions intended to confer rights enforceable at law.

1. Cohen, "The Basis of Contract," 46 *Harv. L. Rev.* 553 (1933).

They are lightly made, dictated by generosity, courtesy, or impulse often by ruinous prodigality. To enforce them by a judgment in favor of those who gave nothing therefor would often bring such imperfect obligations into competition with the absolute duties to wife and children, or into competition with debts for property actually received, and make the law an instrument by which a man could be forced to be generous before he was just.[2]

There is a social interest in being able to rely upon any promise that any person may make. Our social order would be a better social order if people could always rely upon every statement that others might make. Human beings would be happier if all of them always told the truth. Under these circumstances it may be wondered why the law has not made contracts out of all promises. The reason why it has not is probably a reason of public policy. Some promises are not of enough importance to make it worthwhile to make contracts out of them. The legal enforcement of all promises is expensive. No more expense should be incurred for the enforcement of promises than the needs of our social order make imperative. There is a social interest in personal liberty; and personal liberty, even the personal liberty to lie, ought not to be delimited unless the social interests of other people are thereby injured enough so as to warrant the delimitation of personal liberty. Self-control is also a matter in which there is a social interest. If social control was applied to all promises there would be very little opportunity left for self-control. So far as it is possible the making and performance of promises should, therefore, be left to personal liberty.

Yet some promises are of such importance that social control must be applied to them. Not all promises can be left to self-control. Wealth in a commercial age is largely made up of promises. An important part of everyone's substance consists of advantages promised by others. There is a demand of society that some promises, at least, be kept. Hence,

our Anglo-American law, much as all systems of law have done, has compromised between enforcing all promises and enforcing no promises, and as a result we have special classes of promises to which this form of social control is applied and which are contracts. Our problem, therefore, simmers down to a problem of determining these different classes of promises.[3]

Through centuries of evolution in which the mechanics of the English legal procedure were gradually adapted to meet the needs of a growing commercial economy, a rule termed the *consideration rule* was forged as the chief measuring device with which the Anglo-American law separates agreements into those which are legally binding and those which are not. The word consideration, as it is popularly used by nonlawyers, has various, somewhat related, but different meanings. One meaning refers to "thoughtful contemplation or meditation," another meaning to "thoughtfulness or kindness," and still another to "the reason or basis for a conclusion or action." The law of contracts uses the word in this last sense.

It cannot be too strongly emphasized that the rule of consideration is entirely a rule of policy. It is felt to be sound public policy that every promise which a person makes should not necessarily be legally enforceable, that there must be "something" in addition to the fact that a promise is made and an agreement reached, for the promise to be deemed enforceable in the courts. This "something" which policy indicates should be present to make a promise legally enforceable, usually (but not always) consists of an exchange given or received for the promise. Modern theory applies the term *consideration* to this exchange. In addition, it is also felt to be sound public policy that certain other circumstances should be deemed sufficient to justify legal enforcement of promises, even though con-

---

2. *Davis & Co. v. Morgan*, 117 Ga. 504, 43 S E 732, 61 L.R.A. 148, 97 Am. St. Rep. 171 (1903).

3. Willis, "Rationale of the Law of Contracts," 11 *Indiana L. J.* 227 (1936).

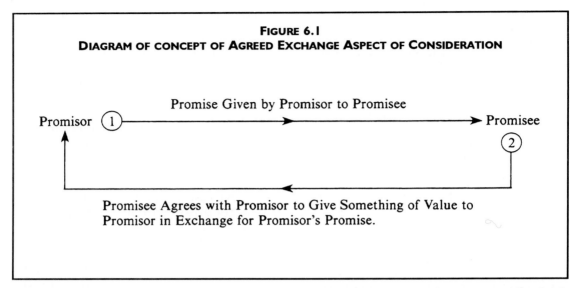

FIGURE 6.1
DIAGRAM OF CONCEPT OF AGREED EXCHANGE ASPECT OF CONSIDERATION

Promise Given by Promisor to Promisee

Promisor ① ⟶ Promisee ②

Promisee Agrees with Promisor to Give Something of Value to Promisor in Exchange for Promisor's Promise.

sideration in the usual, exchange sense is not present. These other circumstances are frequently referred to as "equivalents of consideration." To summarize, therefore, unless a promise is accompanied either by consideration in the exchange sense, or by a legally recognized equivalent of consideration, the promise is not legally enforceable. The task, then, is to define "consideration" and to spell out the special circumstances which should be accepted as "equivalents of consideration."

I. Consideration

Consideration can be conceptualized as the price paid for a promise. Courts evaluate consideration by looking for two main ingredients: agreed exchange and legal benefit or detriment. In order for something to be construed as legally sufficient consideration for a promise, it must be given or received as the agreed exchange for the promise (that is, as the price bargained for and paid for the promise), and also it must involve either a legal benefit acquired by the promisor or a legal detriment sustained by the promise. While

detriment and benefit are usually both present in an enforceable agreement, both are not necessary; either legal detriment *or* legal benefit will be sufficient to constitute consideration. Additionally, the thing to be construed as legally sufficient consideration must consist of something the law regards as consisting of value.

A. Agreed Exchange

When consideration is defined as the *agreed exchange* for a promise, both of these words are meaningful.

I. AGREEMENT

Something upon which the parties have not agreed cannot be consideration for a promise. Since the agreement of the parties is expressed by one party making an offer and the other party accepting the offer, the consideration is necessarily a part of the offer and acceptance. For example, if consideration is present in a unilateral agreement, it is found in the performance of the act which the offered promise requests as an acceptance.

Example. A tramp came to a householder's front door asking for something to eat. The householder said, "If you go around to the back door, I'll give you a piece of pie and a cup of coffee." The tramp promptly went around to the rear of the house, but in the interim the householder decided to discourage vagrancy, and upon reaching the back door told the tramp, "Beat it or I'll call a cop." If the tramp should sue for the value of the promised food, he would not recover because there was no consideration for the householder's promise. Under the circumstances, a reasonable man would not be justified in concluding that the requested act was the price or exchange for the promise. The tramp's going to the rear of the house was not an agreed exchange for the promise, but instead was merely a condition for the promised gift. The fact that a condition was stated and performed did not change the promise from what it essentially was, a promise to make a gift. □

2. EXCHANGE

Something done by a promisee, even if requested by the promisor, cannot be consideration unless it appears to have been given or paid for the promise. As Justice Benjamin Cardozo has said:

> "Nothing is consideration" it has been held, "that is not regarded as such by both parties...." The fortuitous presence in a transaction of some possibility of detriment, latent but unthought of, is not enough.... Promisor and promisee must have dealt with it as the inducement to the promise.[4]

Elaborating on this same point, Justice Holmes has written in his book, THE COMMON LAW:

> But although the courts may have sometimes gone a little far in their anxiety to sustain agreements, there can be no doubt of the principle which I have laid down, that the same thing may be a consideration or not, as it is dealt with by the parties. This raises the question how a thing must be dealt with, in order to make it a consideration.
>
> It is said that consideration must not be confounded with motive. It is true that it must not be confounded with what may be the prevailing or chief motive in actual fact. A man may promise to paint a picture for five hundred dollars, while his chief motive may be a desire for fame. A consideration may be given and accepted, in fact, solely for the purpose of making a promise binding. But, nevertheless, it is the essence of a consideration, that, by the terms of the agreement, it is given and accepted as the motive or inducement of the promise. Conversely, the promise must be made and accepted as the conventional motive or inducement for furnishing the consideration. The root of the whole matter is the relation of reciprocal conventional inducement, each for the other, between consideration and promise....
>
> Both sides of the relation between consideration and promise, and the conventional nature of that relation, may be illustrated by the case of the cask. Suppose that the truckman is willing to carry the cask, and the owner to let him carry it, without any bargain, and that each knows the other's state of mind; but that the truckman, seeing his own advantage in the matter, says to the owner, "In consideration of your delivering me the cask, and letting me carry it, I promise to carry it," and that the owner thereupon delivers it. I suppose that the promise would be binding. The promise is offered in terms as the inducement for the delivery, and the delivery is made in terms as the inducement for the promise. It may be very probable that the delivery would have been made without a promise, and that the promise would have been made without a promise, and that the promise would have been in gratuitous form if it had not been accepted upon consider-

---

4. *McGovern v. New York*, 234 N.Y. 377, 138 NE. 26,25 A.L.R. 1442 (1923).

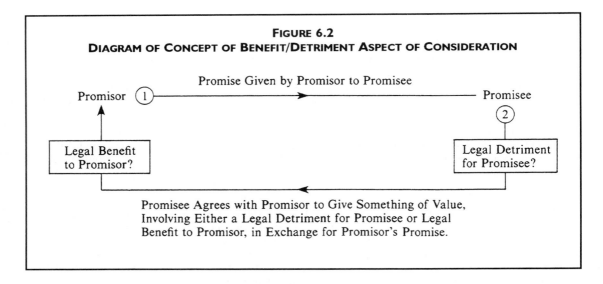

FIGURE 6.2
DIAGRAM OF CONCEPT OF BENEFIT/DETRIMENT ASPECT OF CONSIDERATION

ation; but this is only a guess after all. The delivery need not have been made unless the owner chose, and having been made as the term of a bargain, the promisor cannot set up what might have happened to destroy the effect of what did happen. It would seem therefore that the same transaction in substance and spirit might be voluntary or obligatory, according to the form of words which the parties chose to employ for the purpose of affecting the legal consequences.[5]

The thing given as value and hence the thing which constitutes the legal benefit or legal detriment must have been agreed upon by the promisor and promisee as the thing to be exchanged for the promise. If a bargain is intended, the fact that what is given is of little value will not defeat the bargained exchange requirement. On the other hand, if a gift, rather than a bargain is intended, stating the transaction in terms of a bargain will not satisfy the bargained exchange requirement unless

something of actual value is agreed to be exchanged.

B. Legal Detriment and Legal Benefit

The benefit or detriment involved need not be what one might think of in terms of some actual benefit or detriment. The words are used in a technical legal sense. Accordingly, a legal benefit arises if, as the result of a request or statement attached to one's promise, he receives something to which he previously was not legally entitled to receive, such as a return promise, an act or a forbearance. Similarly, a legal detriment occurs if, in response to a promise, he does something or promises to do something which he was not previously obligated to do. Only a legal benefit or a legal detriment need be found, not both. However, in most cases both will be present, since the thing given as consideration will usually move from the promisee to the promisor.

In a unilateral contract a promisee's doing something (consisting of either legal detriment to the promisee or legal benefit to the

5. Oliver Wendell Holmes, Jr., THE COMMON LAW (1881; Cambridge: Harvard University Press, 1963), pp. 230-232.

Example. An uncle promised to pay his nephew $500 if the nephew obtained a grade of "A" in his basic law course. The nephew applied himself and earned an "A" (it is possible). The uncle however refused to pay and the nephew sued.

The uncle asserted that his promise was not enforceable because it lacked consideration, and supported his assertion with two arguments:

1. The nephew did not sustain a detriment, but instead really acquired a benefit in developing better study habits, increasing his knowledge, and obtaining an excellent grade on his record.

Answer to the Argument: The nephew was under no legal duty to the uncle or to anyone else to work harder for the excellent grade or even to pass the course. Even though he may have acquired an actual benefit, the nephew sustained a legal detriment in doing something he was not previously legally bound to do.

2. The nephew was a good student and would have worked hard and obtained the excellent grade anyway.

Answer to the Argument: For the performance of an act to constitute consideration for a promise, it is not necessary that the promise be the sole motive or only reason for performance of the act. If the parties bargain or agree on the act in exchange for the promise, and if in performing the act the promisee is doing something he previously was not legally bound to do, the act is consideration for the promise.

Therefore the nephew could recover the promised $500. ▢

promisor) as the agreed exchange for a promise, constitutes the consideration necessary to make the promise enforceable. In a bilateral contract the promisee's legally binding promise to do the agreed thing can be just as effective as his actual doing of the thing to constitute the necessary consideration for the promisor's promise.

Suppose that a seller delivers a requested book to a buyer and in exchange the buyer promises to pay the price of $5 in seven days. The seller's act of delivering the book, which he was not previously obligated to do, is a legal detriment and constitutes consideration for the buyer's promise to pay. If instead of delivering the book immediately, the seller promises to deliver the book in thirty days and the buyer promises to pay $5 within seven days from the date of the contract, each promise is given for the other. The buyer is promising to pay in advance of time for delivery, and in exchange for his promise he obtains the seller's promise to deliver the book

in thirty days. Previous to making the agreement the seller had no obligation to deliver the book. When the seller assumes such an obligation, the buyer acquires a legal right which constitutes consideration sufficient to make the buyer's promise enforceable. Therefore, the seller can collect from the buyer after expiration of the seven-day period. Should the seller promise to deliver in seven days and the buyer to pay in thirty days, then the buyer could enforce the seller's promise to deliver, even though (as provided in the agreement) the buyer would not yet be required to pay anything.

Note that the requirement of consideration does not mean that unless some money is paid a sales contract is not enforceable. If so agreed, a legally binding promise to pay is just as effective a consideration as an actual payment would be.

Example. On June 1, without any exchange bargained for, an uncle promised that he would pay his nephew $500 on the following July 1. The nephew expressed full agreement with the idea. When the uncle defaulted on his promise, the nephew sued.

The nephew argued that his acquiring $500 would be a legal benefit to which he was not previously legally entitled, and that the uncle's paying would be a legal detriment, the uncle doing something he was not previously legally obliged to do.

The nephew could not recover. There are two fallacies in the nephew's argument:

1. The argument goes around in a closed circle, it declares that if a certain promise is enforced, then its performance constitutes the act sufficient to make it enforceable. Under this argument all promises would be enforceable without anything more. Consideration for a promise must be something separate from the promise itself.

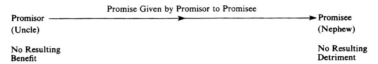

2. The argument reverses the direction in which benefit and detriment must go. The following diagram shows that the promise is out from the promisor and in to the promisee, and in exchange for the promise there must be something in to the promisor or out from the promisee—an in for an out. Of course the same thing can be and usually is both detriment to the promisee and benefit to the promisor. ☐

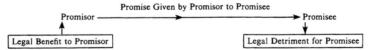

C. Adequacy of Consideration

To say that consideration is something given in exchange for a promise does not mean that the value of what is given must be substantially equal to the value of the promise. If anything regardless of how small its value is actually bargained for and given in exchange for a promise, this will usually be sufficient. In bargaining, the parties express their conclusion as to the value of what is given, and the courts will usually not attempt to usurp the opinion of the parties. The fact that one party receives inordinately more or less than the other in the agreed exchange is legally irrelevant. The requirement is that there be some value to the thing exchanged, for if there were no value, no legal benefit or legal detriment would exist. The value can be an expected value or possibility of value occurring or developing in the future.

I. GROUPS OF PROMISE

If several items or promises are involved, the courts will usually not inquire into adequacy of consideration by attempting to allocate or divide portions of consideration among the items or promises. What is given is consideration for all that is received, what is received is consideration for all that is given.

Example. A debtor owed his creditor a past due debt of $1,000. A guarantor wrote to the creditor, "If you will give the debtor six months longer on his $1,000 debt owed to you, I will guaranty payment." The creditor replied that he agreed and waited six months without trying to collect from the debtor. After expiration of the six months, the debt was still unpaid and the creditor was unable to collect from the debtor because he had become insolvent. The creditor demanded payment from the guarantor and on his refusal to pay, sued the guarantor.

The guarantor argued that he had received nothing in exchange for his promise. Whether or not the guarantor received any benefit is immaterial. Either detriment or benefit is sufficient to constitute consideration. In waiting six months the creditor did something he was not legally obliged to do in exchange for the guarantor's promise, and the creditor thus sustained a legal detriment. This constituted consideration for the guarantor's promise and the guarantor's promise would be enforceable. ☐

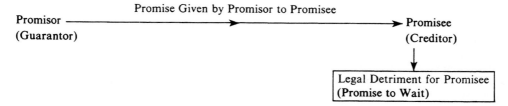

2. POSSIBILITY OF VALUE

If the bargained-for act or promise is without value in the legal sense of benefit and detriment, the consideration is inadequate. If, however, there is a possibility of value, because of the passage of time or events, the consideration is adequate.

3. FORBEARANCE AND EXPECTATIONS

Where one exchanges his forbearance from a legally allowable act for a promise, the length of time of the forbearance is not material to determine if it is adequate, the value of the forbearance being left to the parties to decide. If something to be given as consideration declines in value or becomes worthless prior to the time it is actually given, this later value is irrelevant. The value of importance is the value at the time of the agreed exchange.

4. EXCHANGE OF IDENTICAL ITEMS

There is an exception to the rule that the courts will not inquire into the relative value of what is given in exchange for one or more promises. If a bargain concerns things identical in nature (especially money for money) to be exchanged at the same time and place, value is already so fixed and clear that the bargain cannot be said to involve any individual opinion of the parties. The identical items will be canceled out; something additional must be given for any additional promise. Contract forms used by some businesses and even by some lawyers begin: "In consideration of $1 each to the other in hand paid, receipt of which is hereby acknowledged, the following agreement is hereby made...." The swapping of dollar bills even if actually done is ridiculous and not consideration for anything. If nothing further is given by one party, there is no consideration for anything further promised by the other party.

Example. An owner owned a vacant lot across which his neighbor habitually drove as a shortcut, ignoring the owner's frequent requests to desist. Hoping to break the habit, the owner said to the neighbor, "If you will refrain from driving across my lot for one month, I'll pay you $10." The neighbor ceased his trespassing for one month, claimed $10, and sued when the owner refused to pay.

Since there was no consideration for the promise, the neighbor could not recover. Although the neighbor sustained an actual detriment in exchange for the promise, it was not a legal detriment—he did only what he was already legally obliged to do. Although the owner acquired an actual benefit, it was not a legal benefit; he acquired nothing more than he was already legally entitled to—that is, to have the neighbor cease trespassing. ▢

* * *

Example. An owner sent ten shirts to a laundry and in due course received them back together with a bill for the usual charges. Printed on the bill was the statement, "All claims for damages must be made within ten days after return of goods." The owner read this statement and then paid his bill without protest. This was the owner's first experience with that laundry.

Two weeks later when the owner for the first time unfolded the tenth shirt in the pile, he discovered that it had been badly torn through negligence of the laundry. When the owner notified the laundry and claimed payment or replacement, the laundry refused to make any adjustment because the owner had not presented his claim within ten days. The owner sued.

The owner could collect. Since the owner had no prior dealings with the laundry he was unfamiliar with the ten-day limitation until his shirts were returned. Therefore it was not an implied term of his original contract.

The laundry would argue that since the owner knew of, and acquiesced in, the time limitation when he accepted return of his shirts, he thereupon agreed to the limitation. This is correct, but there was no consideration for the owner's agreement. The laundry was already under a legal duty to return the shirts. It sustained no legal detriment, the owner acquired no legal benefit, thus there was no consideration, and the owner's agreement to the ten-day limitation was not enforceable.

If the laundry wished to hold customers to the ten-day limitation it should have made the limitation part of its original contracts. Added afterwards, it would have to be supported by additional consideration in order to be enforceable. ▢

5. EQUITABLE RELIEF

Although something inadequate in value can be sufficient consideration for a promise, a court may refuse equitable remedies if the disproportion in value is considerable. A person has no *right* to equity remedies, he may obtain relief in equity only if fairness and justice so indicate.

D. Situations Lacking Consideration

1. MUTUALITY OF OBLIGATION

In a bilateral contract the promise of each party is given in exchange for, and constitutes consideration for, the promise of the other party. For this reason, there must be mutuality of obligation, each party must be bound to something which involves legal detriment, or

Example. A buyer (B. Brown) paid a seller $1 and the seller signed and gave to the buyer the following: "In consideration of $1 in hand paid, receipt of which is hereby acknowledged, I hereby offer to sell to B. Brown my land [describing it] for $25,000 and agree that this offer shall remain open for six months." A few days later the seller notified the buyer that the option was terminated and tendered return of the buyer's $1. The buyer refused the $1 and sent a written acceptance of the seller's offer. When the seller refused to transfer the land on the buyer's tender of $25,000, the buyer sued.

The buyer could recover. The seller might argue that $1 was ridiculously inadequate for a six-month option on property worth $25,000. Nevertheless that was the price the parties had placed on the option, there was consideration, and the offer would be irrevocable. ☐

* * *

Example. A creditor (C. Carter) refused to make a requested $1,000 six-month loan to a debtor (D. Davis) unless someone with a good credit rating guaranteed the debtor's repayment. Accordingly a guarantor dated, signed, and gave to the creditor the following: "In consideration of C. Carter's loaning D. Davis $1,000 due six months from date, I promise that if Davis does not repay the loan when due, I will pay Carter." At the same time the creditor loaned $1,000 to the debtor, the latter dated, signed, and gave to the creditor the following: "Six months from date I promise to pay C. Carter $1,000," When the debtor defaulted, the creditor sued the guarantor.

The guarantor argued that the creditor's loan was consideration for the debtor's promise and that there was no additional consideration for the guarantor's promise. However, the creditor bargained for both promises. What the creditor gave was consideration for all of the bargained exchange, and the creditor could recover from the guarantor. ☐

neither party is bound. Whether or not there is mutuality of obligation becomes a pertinent question if the promise of one of the parties is to do one of two or more things in the alternative, with the promisor reserving to himself the right to choose which alternative he will perform. If any one of such alternatives does not involve legal detriment, then the promise of that party is not consideration for the promise of the other party, and therefore the promise of the other party is not enforceable.

The principal types of contracts in which the question of mutuality has arisen are (1) contracts which provide that one party has a right to cancel the contract, and (2) contracts which provide for delivery of an indefinite quantity of goods.

a. Right to Cancel

If a contract expressly gives one party an unlimited right to cancel, then in reality that party is not binding himself to do something involving legal detriment, and there is no consideration for the other party's promise. If, however, a party's right to cancel is limited to certain conditions or can be exercised only in a certain way, then that party is limiting his freedom of action to some extent and is thus sustaining some legal detriment, which constitutes consideration for the other party's promise.

b. Indefinite Quantity

Sometimes an agreement is entered into under which a seller promises to sell and deliver whatever quantity of certain described goods the buyer may order, up to a stated maximum.

Example. Wishing to bind himself to give his nephew (N. Norton) $1,000 in one year, an uncle requested and received $1 from the nephew and dated, signed, and gave to the nephew the following promissory note: "In consideration of $1 in hand paid, receipt of which is hereby acknowledged, I promise to pay N. Norton $1,000 one year from date." Upon maturity of the note the uncle defaulted and the nephew sued.

There was consideration for the uncle's promise. This is a promise of money for money, but not at the same time and place. The parties in effect have valued the use of $1 for one year at $999, and the court will not usurp the parties' judgment as to value. The uncle's promise however might not be enforceable for another reason—interest at an excessive rate is usury and cannot be collected (see Chapter 10). □

Whether there is consideration for the seller's promise depends upon whether or not the buyer binds himself to do something involving legal detriment. The reverse type of agreement also is possible, with a buyer promising to buy whatever quantity the seller delivers, up to a stated maximum.

2. PREEXISTING DUTIES

Sometimes a party to an existing contract makes a new promise adding to or modifying his obligation under the existing contract. If what the promisee of such a promise does or promises to do in exchange for the new promise is no more than what he is already obliged by the existing contract to do, there is usually no consideration for the new promise. Some common situations involving the relationship between contractual duties previously in existence and new promises related to these preexisting duties follow.

a. Prior Promises Between the Parties

A modification of a contract already in existence requires that the rights and obligations of each party be altered in order for there to be consideration for the modification. Cancellation of a contract where both parties have a right to further performance includes consideration. And, once released, the parties can enter into a new agreement which is similar to the old agreement except for a change in the

right of one party. Each party is also free to refuse to deal further with the other.

An agreement modifying a contract for the sale of goods needs no consideration to be binding. The Code considers[6] the existence of the original contract a sufficient equivalent of consideration to make enforceable any agreed modification of the contract.

Transactions to which the Code does not apply include contracts involving the sales of land, construction of buildings, performance of services by employees and others, and loans of money (unless the loan happens to be evidenced by a negotiable promissory note).

Generally if a debt for a definite amount is matured, not reasonably in dispute, and not evidenced by a negotiable promissory note, the creditor's promise to accept a smaller sum as payment in full is not supported by consideration and is not enforceable.

If a debtor makes a payment prior to the date his obligation comes due, the debtor is doing something he is not legally obliged to do, and the creditor is obtaining money before he is legally entitled to it. The early payment therefore will be consideration for the creditor's promise to accept a smaller sum as payment in full, if the earliness of the payment is agreed to by both parties as the exchange for

_____
6. U.C.C Sec.2-209.

Example. A decedent was survived by his wife, an adult son, and other relatives: The decedent's will was probated and the court appointed an executor to take over the decedent's assets, pay his debts, and distribute the remainder according to the will. The decedent's assets included a $900 judgment against the son, and the decedent's will left a bequest of $1,300 to the wife. After some negotiations involving the executor and all of the heirs, the wife and the executor reached an agreement, the executor agreeing to transfer the $900 judgment to the wife and the wife agreeing that $900 be deducted from her $1,300 bequest. A few months later the executor prepared the papers which had to be filed in court to carry out this agreement. When the wife refused to sign, the executor brought an action in the name of the decedent's estate against the wife for a decree of specific performance, to require the wife to sign the papers necessary to effectuate the agreement. Evidence in the lawsuit showed that the son was completely insolvent, his debts considerably exceeding the total value of his assets, so that there were no assets from which the $900 judgment could be collected at that time.

The Pennsylvania Superior Court refused to issue a decree of specific performance, saying: "We must not lose sight of the fact that this is not an action at law for damages for breach of the contract, nor is it a distribution of the estate . . . in the orphans' court; it is a proceeding in equity to specifically enforce the contract according to its very terms.... There was no question that the consideration was sufficient to support the contract as a binding obligation in a court of law.... We are of the opinion that this contract was upon the part of the widow so exceedingly improvident that a chancellor [that is, the judge in the equity lawsuit] ought not to be called upon to enforce it according to its terms; the parties should be left to their remedy at law." □

the creditor's promise, or at least if the earliness of the payment appears presumably to be in the contemplation of both parties as a significant element of the new agreement.

b. Disputes Between Parties

A debt is indefinite in amount if the debtor has engaged work to be done without any agreement, either express or implied, as to the price he will pay. The debtor's resulting obligation is to pay the reasonable charge for the work done. If the parties cannot agree, a court must eventually determine what amount is reasonable.

A debt may be disputed even though a definite amount has been agreed upon by the parties. If goods shipped under a sales contract fail to conform to the contract, the buyer can either reject them altogether, or, if he wishes, retain them. If he retains the goods, his obligation is to pay the contract price less damages resulting from the failure of the goods to conform to the contract. If a buyer honestly and reasonably believes that goods do not conform to his contract, then, whether he rejects or retains them, his obligation to pay is "reasonably in dispute," even though court action might later determine that the goods exactly conform to the contract.

If the amount is either indefinite or reasonably in dispute, a debtor is not obliged to pay any specific sum until a court determines whether he has any obligation at all, and if so, the exact amount of his obligation. In paying anything at all in advance of such a court determination, the debtor is doing something which he is not at that time legally obliged to do. Such a payment therefore constitutes legal detriment and is consideration for any promise made by the creditor.

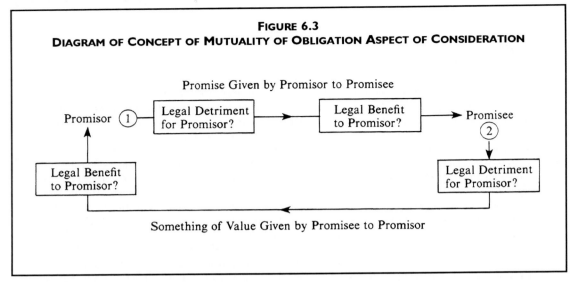

FIGURE 6.3
DIAGRAM OF CONCEPT OF MUTUALITY OF OBLIGATION ASPECT OF CONSIDERATION

c. Prior Promises to Third Parties

Suppose that at a time when a debtor's obligation to his creditor is past due, a third person promises to give the debtor some specified item if the debtor will pay this debt. Courts of the various states are not agreed as to whether the debtor's paying (or promising to pay if a promise is what the third person requests) can be consideration for the third person's promise. Some argue that in paying his creditor, the debtor is doing only what he is already legally obliged to do and thus is giving no consideration for the third person's promise. Others argue that the obligation is owed to the creditor not to the third person, and that if for the third person or at his request the debtor makes payment to his creditor (or promises to do so), the third person is obtaining something to which he himself was not previously legally entitled; and that the third person thus obtains a legal benefit which is sufficient consideration to make his promise enforceable.

d. Unilateral Release

A unilateral release contains no consideration and hence is unenforceable (unless a consideration equivalent is present). However, the Code provides an exception to this rule.

In addition to sales of goods, transactions to which the Code applies include storage and shipment of goods, borrowing on goods, negotiable commercial paper (checks, notes, and drafts), issuance and sale of stocks, and some other types of transactions. As to any such transaction, the Code provides:

> Any claim or right arising out of an alleged breach can be discharged in whole or in part without consideration by a written waiver signed and delivered by the aggrieved party.[7]

The preexisting obligation together with putting the waiver of renunciation in writing constitute an equivalent of consideration sufficient to make the waiver or renunciation enforceable without actual consideration.

---

7. U.C.C. Sec. 1-107.

Example. A contract for the sale and purchase of certain described goods at a stated price expressly gave the seller a right to cancel, the cancellation provision reading as quoted below. Although the seller did not cancel, the buyer repudiated the contract and refused to receive the goods or to pay when the seller tendered delivery according to the contract. The seller thereupon sued for damages for breach of contract.

1. The cancellation provision read: "The seller reserves the right to cancel this contract at any time the seller may deem proper, by giving ten days written notice thereof to the buyer."

The seller would have a right to recover damages for the buyer's breach of contract. According to the contract, the seller could perform either (1) by delivering goods according to the contract, or (2) by giving to the buyer the described notice of cancellation. The first alternative would obviously involve legal detriment. So also would the second alternative—before making the contract the seller had no legal obligation to write the described notice to the buyer. Since even the second alternative involved legal detriment, its value (that is, the value or worth of the seller writing a letter ten days before delivery time) would be immaterial. This was the exchange agreed upon between the parties for the buyer's promise. The buyer's promise therefore was supported by consideration and would be enforceable.

2. The cancellation provision read: "The seller reserves the right to cancel this contract at any time the seller may deem proper."

Some courts would say that if the seller decided to cancel, he could do so by taking no action whatsoever, that by doing nothing at all the seller could fully perform his promise, and that therefore since the seller could select an alternative which would not involve legal detriment, his promise would not be consideration for the buyer's promise and the buyer's promise would not be enforceable. Some other courts would say that any cancellation provision implies the affirmative act of giving notice and that therefore this cancellation provision should have the same effect as that quoted in Part 1 of this example. ☐

II. Equivalents of Consideration

An *equivalent of consideration* is a fact situation which, as a matter of policy, is felt to justify the legal enforcement of a promise without actual consideration. Amendments or waivers involving contracts under the Uniform Commercial Code, and compositions of creditors are two equivalents of consideration which have already been referred to. In addition to these two situations, the principal equivalents of consideration are found in connection with promises made for past obligations or performances, promises upon which promises rely, promises under seal, and promises expressly stated to be legally binding. While all such promises are not automatically enforceable, some of these types of promises are, under certain circumstances, deemed to be enforceable without actual consideration.

A. Promises for Past Acts

After one person has completely performed an act, another person will sometimes make a promise to pay a certain amount to the one who has performed. Since the act has already been performed, there is, of course, no exchange of the act for the promise, and therefore the past act cannot be actual consideration for the present promise. However, un-

Example. On March 1 a seller dated, signed, and sent to a buyer two copies of the following: "I hereby offer to sell to you all the wheat (specifying the grade) that you choose to order at $3 a bushel, not to exceed 10,000 bushels. If you wish to accept this offer, sign and return one copy of this letter. Upon your acceptance of this offer, the contract will continue in effect for six months from date hereof." On the same day the buyer wrote "Accepted" at the bottom of one copy, signed it, and returned it to the seller. During the next four months the buyer ordered, received, and paid for 5,000 bushels. At the beginning of the fifth month the buyer ordered 1,000 bushels. The seller promptly replied rejecting the order and stating that he canceled the March 1 agreement. The buyer protested and ordered an additional, 2,000 bushels. When the seller refused to deliver any of the 3,000 bushels, the buyer sued for damages for breach of contract.

The buyer could recover damages for nondelivery of 1,000 bushels but would not have an enforceable contract for the other 2,000 bushels. All that the buyer gave in exchange for the seller's promise to sell for six months was a promise to buy what he chose to order. The buyer's promise would not be broken if he chose to order nothing or bought elsewhere. Since the buyer's promise contained an alternative which did not involve legal detriment, it was not consideration for the seller's promise, and therefore the seller's promise to sell at $3 for six months was not an enforceable contract. The seller's promise was merely an offer which the seller stated would remain open for six months. As a firm offer under the Uniform Commercial Code, the offer would be irrevocable for three months and revocable afterwards. The buyer ordered 1,000 bushels before the seller revoked the offer and thus formed an enforceable contract for 1,000 bushels. The seller then terminated his offer so that no contract was formed when the buyer ordered 2,000 bushels.

If as the requested exchange for the seller's promise, the buyer had promised to buy all of the wheat he needed in his established milling business for the next six months, the buyer's commitment not to buy his requirements elsewhere would be consideration for the seller's promise and the seller's promise would be fully enforceable.

Or, if as the requested exchange for the seller's promise, the buyer had agreed to buy some specified quantity (for example 1,000 bushels), the buyer's promise would be consideration for the seller's promise to sell all that the buyer chose to order, up to 10,000 bushels. An enforceable maximum-minimum contract would thus be formed, with the buyer obliged to buy at least the minimum (1,000 bushels) and the seller obliged to sell any additional quantity the buyer wished to purchase, up to the agreed maximum. ☐

der certain circumstances it is felt to be sound policy to enforce such a promise even though there is no actual consideration. The principal fact situations involving present promises for past acts may be classified as follows:

I. STATUTE OF LIMITATIONS AND DISCHARGE IN BANKRUPTCY

These situations occur when the promisor was at one time legally obligated on a debt but

Example.   The owner of a plot of land contracted with a builder for construction of a house according to certain plans and specifications for $25,000. When the house was partially completed, labor and material costs increased. The builder said he could not finish unless the owner would agree to pay $2,000 more.

The owner promised that upon completion he would pay $2,000 in addition to the original contract price. However, when the building was completed, the owner refused to pay more than the original price, and the builder sued for the additional $2,000.

Courts in most states would hold that the builder could not recover. In exchange for the owner's promise, the builder did only what he was already under contract obligation to do. Therefore the builder sustained no legal detriment, the owner acquired no legal benefit, there was no consideration, and the owner's promise would not be enforceable. ☐

* * *

Example. The parties in the example above entered into a second contract expressly canceling all prior agreements, and agreeing that the builder would build according to stated plans and specifications (identical with those of the original contract) and the owner would pay $27,000 ($2,000 more than in the original contract). When the building was completed the owner refused to pay more than the original price and the builder sued for the additional $2,000.

1. The question is whether there was consideration for the owner's agreement to pay the additional $2,000. The builder would argue that the old contract was canceled and a new, enforceable contract formed. The theory of canceling the old contract and substituting a new contract would apply if the parties actually did just that—that is, if they actually canceled the old contract so that both, even for a moment, were free from any contract obligation. If both were freed, if the builder could then have refused to sign the new contract and walked off with no further obligation to continue building, then the builder's promise to build would be consideration for the owner's promise to pay the price in the second contract. However, parties will seldom wish to risk fully releasing each other. Here, since the cancellation provision was a part of the new contract, neither party was free at any time from the obligation of the first contract. Therefore, whatever the parties would call it a promise to pay additional compensation or a cancellation of the old contract and the formation of a new one—there would be no consideration for the additional $2,000, because the builder was agreeing to do only what he was already bound to do.

2. In requesting the additional $2,000, the builder offered to add a breezeway not included in the original plans if the owner would agree to pay the additional $2,000. The owner agreed and the builder completed the building according to the original plans and also added the agreed breezeway. The owner paid only $300 more than the original contract price and when the builder sued for the remaining $1,700, the owner presented evidence conclusively showing that the breezeway increased building costs by not more than $300.

The builder would collect the $1,700 for which he sued. The builder was not previously obliged to include a breezeway. His doing so in exchange for the owner's promise would be sufficient consideration to bind the owner on his promise to pay the additional $2,000, regardless of the actual cost or value of the breezeway. ☐

Example. In an obligation not coming under the Uniform Commercial Code, a debtor named D. Davis owed his creditor, C. Carter, $2,000 due February 1.

Part I. On February 7 the debtor paid the creditor $1,500, in exchange for which the creditor dated, signed, and gave to the debtor the following: "Received from D. Davis $1,500 which I hereby accept as payment in full of his $2,000 debt owed to me, which came due February 1." A month later the creditor changed his mind and sued the debtor for the $500 balance of the debt.

The creditor could collect the $500 for which he was suing. The debtor would argue that the creditor had promised to accept the part payment as payment in full. However, in exchange for this promise the creditor received nothing more than he was already legally entitled to receive and the debtor paid no more (in fact $500 less) than he was already legally obliged to pay. Thus there was no legal benefit or detriment, no consideration, and the creditor's promise would not be enforceable.

Part II. On February 7 the debtor sent to the creditor a check for $1,500, payable to the creditor; on the check the debtor wrote, "Payment in full of all claims to date." The creditor crossed out this statement, indorsed and cashed the check, receiving $1,500, and then sued the debtor for $500 as the balance claimed due on the debt.

The creditor could collect the $500 for which he was suing. The check was an offer by the debtor to settle the debt for $1,500. As the offeree, the creditor could not use the check and refuse the conditions under which it was tendered. Although the creditor was attempting to reject the offer by crossing out the statement, his conduct of cashing the check constituted his acceptance. By cashing the check the creditor in effect promised to accept the $1,500 as payment in full. However there was no more consideration for this promise than there was in Part I of this example. Therefore, the creditor's promise would not be enforceable.

Part III. On February 7 the debtor signed and gave to the creditor a one-month negotiable promissory note in the amount of $1,500 naming the creditor as payee, and the creditor agreed to accept the note as full satisfaction for the $2,000 debt. A few weeks later the creditor changed his mind and sued for the full $2,000. (Since the debt had not previously been evidenced by a negotiable promissory note, the creditor agreeing to release the debtor from a portion of the debt would not be a release of rights arising under the Uniform Commercial Code and therefore would not come under the provision, that such a waiver can be enforced without consideration.)

The courts of the various states do not agree as to this type of situation:

1. Courts in some states would say that the creditor could recover nothing until maturity of the note and then only the face amount of the note ($1,500). The note was itself something of value; it is easier to sue on an obligation when it is evidenced by a negotiable note, and a negotiable note can more easily be transferred than can a debt not evidenced by a note. Under this view, when the creditor received the $1,500 note, he received something to which he was not previously legally entitled (legal benefit), the debtor gave something he was not previously obligated to give (legal detriment), there was consideration for the creditor's promise, and the promise to accept the note as full payment would be enforceable. This reasoning—concerning the debtor's giving a negotiable note—is not inconsistent with the reasoning in Part II of this problem which involves the debtor's giving a negotiable check for a lesser amount. A note is used when the parties intend to delay payment, and therefore is a contract separate and different from payment itself, while a check is merely a way to make a present payment of money. (*continued on next page*)

Example (*continued from previous page*)

2. Courts in some states would say that there is no difference between a debtor's note for $1,500 and his cash (or check) payment in that amount, that the giving of the note would not be consideration for the creditor's promise to accept its amount as full payment, and that therefore the creditor would be entitled to collect the full $2,000 debt.

Part IV. On February 7 the debtor and creditor dated and signed the following agreement: "C. Carter hereby agrees to extend for six months the $2,000 debt owed to Carter by D. Davis, which originally came due February 1, and Davis hereby agrees to pay the debt six months from date hereof, with interest at the rate of 6 percent per year." Several weeks later the creditor changed his mind, decided not to wait the full six months, and on April 1 sued the debtor for $2,000 with interest to that date.

The courts of the various states do not agree as to the solution of this situation.

Creditor's Argument: Even if the original debt does not provide for interest, interest accrues and is payable at the legal rate (for example, 6 percent per year in some states) on any overdue obligation. Since the debtor was already bound to pay interest until the debt was paid, his promise to pay interest imposed no additional legal obligation on him. There was no legal detriment or benefit, no consideration, and the creditor's promise would not be enforceable. The courts of some of the states have adopted this view.

Debtor's Argument: It is true that interest accrues and is due at the legal rate on any overdue obligation. However, unless he agrees otherwise a debtor may at anytime stop further interest from accruing by paying his overdue obligation. In the quoted agreement the debtor bound himself to pay interest for six months longer, thus surrendering his right to terminate his interest obligation by paying before then. Thus the debtor was undertaking an additional legal obligation and the creditor was acquiring an additional legal right (namely interest for the six-month period, not subject to reduction by the debtor's paying earlier), there was consideration, and the creditor's promise would be enforceable. This seems to be a sounder argument and is followed by a majority of the state courts.

Part V. The debtor was indebted to various other creditors in addition to Carter and was unable to pay them all in full. On February 7 the debtor explained his financial situation to Carter, and Carter dated, signed, and gave to the debtor the following: "To Whom It May Concern: This is to certify that in consideration of $1,500 to be paid to me by D. Davis three months from date, I will accept said sum in full satisfaction of his $2,000 debt owed to me which originally came due February 1." The debtor showed this writing to some of his other creditors and obtained their agreements to settle for part payment. When the three-month period expired, Carter changed his mind, refused the debtor's tender of $1,500, and sued for the entire $2,000.

Carter would not be able to recover. A creditor who joins in such an agreement (called a composition of creditors) does so because other creditors have joined or are expected to join in similar agreements. This mutual action, or expectation of mutual action, is a recognized equivalent of consideration and makes each participating creditor's promise enforceable without actual consideration, even though the arrangement does not include all creditors. The form of the composition agreement is not material. Frequently all joining creditors sign one paper; sometimes a condition is stated that the agreement does not become effective until a stated number of creditors join. See Section II, B, 3 later in this chapter. ▢

Example. A seller sold, indorsed, and delivered to a buyer (B. Burns) a certificate for ten shares of stock in a certain corporation, for which the buyer paid to the seller $200 and agreed to pay the seller $1,000 more in sixty days. After the obligation was overdue, the buyer paid the seller $750 and the seller signed and gave to the buyer the following: "Received from B. Burns $750 in full satisfaction of the $1,000 still owed to me for the purchase of stock, and I hereby release him from said debt." The seller afterwards changed his mind and sued for the $250 balance due.

The seller could not recover. His waiver of rights would be enforceable without consideration. ☐

its enforcement is barred by a statute of limitation[8] or by the promisor being discharged from his obligation through a bankruptcy proceeding. The fact that there once existed a legally enforceable obligation is recognized as an equivalent of consideration, so that a new promise to pay the obligation is legally enforceable without any new consideration. With regard to the statute of limitations this new promise may be made at any time. This also used to be true with regard to discharges in bankruptcy but under the bankruptcy act such an affirmation must be done at the time of discharge and with court approval.

2. UNREQUESTED BENEFIT

If the recipient of certain, nongratuitous performance has requested the performance, he certainly has an actual contractual obligation to pay. On the other hand, if he does not request or permit the performance, no actual contract arises. The classic example is the case of the painter who mistakenly paints the wrong house. If the homeowner is aware of the painter's mistake and stands by without

saying anything, when he reasonably should know that the paint job is no gift, the homeowner's conduct amounts to an acceptance of the painter's offer and forms a contract. If, however the house is painted in the owner's absence, no actual contract ever arises. If such an unrequested act is of necessary or vital importance to a person, some courts have found a quasi-contractual obligation to pay. But if an act has not been requested or voluntarily accepted, and is not of vital importance, the recipient of the performance is not bound to pay; he has neither a contractual nor a quasi-contractual obligation. Suppose, however, that such a person agrees to pay a certain amount for what has been done for him. In many states the promise will not be legally enforceable against the promisor. In some states, however, if an unrequested benefit is substantial, it will be deemed an equivalent of consideration, sufficient to make a promise to pay enforceable without actual consideration. Note that this equivalent of consideration applies only when the promisor was not previously under a contractual obligation; the theory, therefore, cannot be stretched to cover a promise to pay more than had been originally agreed for certain contracted performance.

3. ENFORCEABLE, UNLIQUIDATED LIABILITY

An unliquidated or indefinite liability can arise in a number of ways. For example, if nongratuitous services are performed at the request of a person who has not in advance agreed on the amount of compensation to be

---

8. A statute of limitations is a statute fixing a period of time within which a lawsuit must be brought. Its purpose is to prevent enforcement of stale claims after passage of so long a period of time that proof of any defense could become impossible through loss of evidence and witnesses. Under the Uniform Commercial Code, for example, lawsuits must be brought within four years (unless the time is shortened by the contract of the parties) for claims involving sales of goods (U.C.C. Sec. 2-725). Statutes of limitation are further discussed in Chapter 10.

paid, the recipient of the services will be obliged to pay whatever amount the court may determine to be the reasonable value of the services. Suppose that before court action the recipient promises to pay a specific amount for the services, later reneges on his promise, and the resulting lawsuit determines that the reasonable value is less than the promised amount. Courts in some states say that the promisor is obliged to pay the promised amount, that the existence of the enforceable but unliquidated liability is sufficient as an equivalent of consideration to make the promise to pay the specified amount enforceable. The Uniform Commercial Code adopts[9] this view if the promise to pay the specific sum is evidenced by a negotiable promissory note. If a negotiable note is not used, some courts hold that the promisor is only obliged to pay the reasonable value of the services, that the promise to pay a specific sum is evidence of value but is not itself an enforceable promise without additional consideration.

B. Detrimental Reliance or Promissory Estoppel

In practically every contract lawsuit which is brought following a defendant's failure to perform his promise, the plaintiff has sustained the damages for which he is suing only because he has to some extent relied on the defendant's promise. To say that such reliance should automatically make the defendant's promise enforceable would completely reverse the policy of the law so long recognized as sound, that consideration or other good reason is necessary for a promise to be legally enforceable. On the other hand there is a limit to how far society can permit a promisor to mislead others. It is certainly sound policy for some promises to be declared enforceable solely because promisees have sub-

---

9. U.C.C. Sec. 3-408.

stantially relied on them. This policy view has given rise to a theory, usually called the *promissory estoppel* or *detrimental reliance* theory. Under this theory, the combination of the following three conditions will constitute an equivalent of consideration, sufficient to make a promise enforceable without actual consideration:

1. From the nature of the promise in question and the circumstances under which it is made, the promisor should reasonably expect that the promisee will rely on the promise and act in some definite and substantial way (or to a substantial degree give up or refrain from some definite action).
2. The promisee does so act (or refrain from acting).
3. Substantial unfairness or injustice will result unless the promise is declared enforceable.

1. CHARITABLE OR GIFT PROMISES

When a promise to contribute to a charitable institution is deemed to be enforceable, it is usually on the basis of the detrimental reliance theory. If the institution relies on a promise and makes binding commitments (for building, expansion, or whatever is contemplated), the promise is enforceable. That other persons contribute (or promise to contribute), induced by the promise of an earlier contributor, is held by courts in some states to be sufficient to make the earlier promise enforceable, even before the charity takes any action. Courts in some other states however say that the promise is not enforceable until the charity itself acts in reliance on it.

One distinguished court has suggested that the detrimental reliance theory applies only to gift promises, that is, promises (like charitable subscriptions) for which no exchange is expected. Another court has doubted that the theory should be restricted only to donative promises. However, even if not limited to donative promises, the detrimental reliance theory does *not* apply to the majority of promises that are made. Notice especially the terms used in stating the detrimental reliance theory: "reasonable expectation," "substantial action," "substantial unfairness and injustice." Such vague, flexible terms, incapable of exact definition, should warn a person that he is taking a great chance on his promisor's good faith if he relies on a promise not otherwise enforceable against the promisor.

2. CONTRACT MODIFICATION

Where parties agree to a one-sided change in a contract and one party allows the other to make a substantial change in position relying on the agreed change, estoppel will sometimes allow the enforcement of the modification.

3. COMPOSITION AGREEMENTS

Where several creditors of a debtor agree to accept a percentage of their due in full payment of a debt, the agreement will be enforced based on mutual reliance.

C. Promises Under Seal

Under the common law, a written promise to which the promisor has added his seal needs no consideration to be enforceable. Thus a seal is deemed to be an equivalent of consideration, making the promise enforceable without actual consideration. No particular form is required for a seal. A seal can be any mark the signer uses for that purpose. Nowadays usually only corporations have distinctive seals and even some corporations dispense with the formality. In most sealed documents, the seal consists of the word "seal", or the letters "L.S." (abbreviation for a Latin term meaning "place of seal"), and a person (or corporation acting through its agent) who signs beside the word "seal" or the letters "L.S." is deemed to adopt the word or letters as his personal seal.

The historical reason for this common law rule goes back hundreds of years and no longer prevails. When an ordinary person signs a contract form, it is usually immaterial to him whether the line on which he signs is followed by the word "seal" or is blank. If the average person who signs beside the word "seal" does not attach any significance to the word, it is certainly arguable that the law should not assume otherwise and therefore should not treat a sealed contract as any different from an unsealed one. Pursuant to this reasoning, the legislatures in most states have completely abrogated the common law rule, and the Uniform Commercial Code does likewise with respect to negotiable commercial paper (notes, drafts, and checks), and sales-of-goods offers and contracts.[10]

Also, courts of equity have usually required actual consideration, rather than a mere seal, before allowing the issuance of equitable relief.

D. Firm Offers—U.C.C.

The U.C.C. has specifically provided for a merchant to make a firm offer without the need for consideration. The firm offer must be in writing and signed and it will last for the time stated, or if none is stated, for a reasonable time, but in no event may any such period exceed three months. This Code section is discussed more fully in Chapter 5.

E. Uniform Written Obligations Act

Sometimes a person who promises to make a gift, desires to make the promise legally binding upon himself or upon his estate after his death. Some legal scholars believe that as a matter of policy the law ought to provide a way for this to be done, and several states have adopted statutes accordingly. One such statute is the Uniform Written Obligations Act (drafted under the auspices of the Commis-

---

10. U.C.C. Secs. 2-203, 3-113.

sioners on Uniform State Laws), which has been adopted by a few states. Under this statute, a promise or release is binding without consideration if all of the following three conditions are present:

1. The promise or release is in writing.
2. The writing is signed by the one promising or releasing.
3. *In addition* to the promise or release, the writing contains (in any form of language) an express statement that the signer *intends to be legally bound.*

* * *

Problems

1. S. Smith advertised that he wished to sell a plot of vacant land known as the Smith Farm for $25,000. B. Brown wrote to S, "I would like a three-month option to buy the Smith Farm for $25,000." In reply S wrote to B, "July 1. To B. Brown: I hereby give you a three-month option to buy the Smith Farm for $25,000. If you choose to exercise this option, I shall expect to hear from you by October 1." On July 9 B wrote to S, "Enclosed is my check for $100 which I feel is a fair price for the three-month option you gave me in your letter of July 1." On July 16 S wrote to B, "I have decided not to sell the Smith Farm and therefore hereby return your $100 check sent to me on July 9, and withdraw the option previously given you." On July 27 B wrote to S, "Enclosed is the $100 check you returned to me with your letter of July 26. You gave me a three-month option on the Smith Farm and I hereby give notice that I am taking up the option. I hereby agree to buy the Smith Farm for $25,000, which I will pay you upon delivery to me of the deed." When S tendered return of the $100 check and refused to sell, B refused the check and sued for a decree of specific performance. The evidence showed that $100 was a fair price for such an option. Assume that each of the above letters was properly addressed and signed, and received by the respective addresses on the day following the date of the letter.

(a) What would be the result of the lawsuit? Explain.

(b) Other facts remaining the same, assume that starting with B's July 9 letter, the parties were dealing with $100 in cash. Explain whether your answer would be the same as in Part (a).

2. On July 1 B, a doctor, signed in duplicate a printed order form furnished by S. Smith, a car dealer, reading in part: "To S. Smith: I hereby order you to equip and deliver to me at Scranton, Pennsylvania, as soon as reasonably possible, the following described motor vehicle which I agree to accept at the price and according to the terms set forth below and on the reverse side hereof." Appropriate spaces on the front of the order form were filled in with the make, model, and price of the car B wanted. On the reverse side was printed: "It is agreed that the seller will not be held liable for any delay or failure to make delivery through any cause whatsoever." On the same day, S dated and signed both copies of the form after the printed word, "Accepted," and delivered one copy to B. On July 10, before S had tendered any car to B, B notified S to cancel the order. On July 15, which was a reasonable time for delivery of a car ordered on July 1, S tendered to B a car exactly complying with the description in the order form. When B refused to accept delivery, S sued B for damages for breach of contract. Explain (1) the reasoning upon which B might attempt to defend, (2) the reasoning upon which S might attempt to collect, and (3) which party should be given judgment.

3. (a) A trucker who owned and operated several trucks for short distance hauling was negotiating with a distributor of petroleum products. On January 28 the distributor wrote to the trucker the following, which under the circumstances legally constituted an offer: "I hereby offer to sell you Star Brand Motor Oil, SAE 20 at 60 cents a gallon and Star Brand Regular Gasoline at 15 cents a gallon, in such quantities as you may order, delivery to be made within 5 days after order, payment within 30 days after delivery, 2 percent off for ten days. Upon acceptance by you of this offer, the agreement will

continue in effect for six months from February 1." Receiving two copies, the trucker wrote on the bottom of one copy, "Accepted, January 30," signed it, and returned it to the distributor. During February, March, and the first part of April the trucker ordered, received, and paid for various quantities of gas and oil from the distributor. On April 15 the trucker sent an order, received by the distributor April 16, for 5,000 gallons of gasoline. On April 17 the distributor wrote a letter received by the trucker April 18, saying: "I regret I will be unable to deliver your April 15 order or any further orders at the previous prices. Our costs have advanced sharply and I'm sure you will understand my position. I shall be happy to fill your April 15 order and any further orders in any quantities you wish, at my current prices of $1 a gallon for oil and 25 cents a gallon for gasoline of the grades you have previously been buying." The trucker protested but the distributor remained firm and refused to deliver at the January prices. On April 22 the trucker sent an order received by the distributor April 23 for 1,000 gallons of oil, the trucker specifying that he was ordering under the January agreement. The distributor refused to deliver. On May 6 the trucker sent an order, received by the distributor May 9, for 3,000 gallons of gasoline, the trucker specifying that he was ordering under the January agreement. The distributor refused to deliver. These three orders conformed in quantity and frequency with the trucker's orders during the previous two and a half months. Each time the distributor refused to deliver, the trucker purchased the same grade elsewhere at the lowest obtainable prices of 80 cents a gallon for oil and 20 cents a gallon for gasoline. The trucker sued the distributor for damages consisting of the amounts the trucker had to pay over the prices in the January agreement, namely (1) $250 on the April 15 order, (2) $200 on the April 22 order, and (3) $150 on the May 6 order. Disregarding court costs and interest, state how much, if anything, the trucker was entitled to recover. Explain.

(b) Other facts being the same, assume that the three orders were dated May 15, May 22, and June 6 and that the distributor's letter first giving notice of the price increase was dated May 17, received May 18. Disregarding court costs and interest, state how much, if anything, the trucker was entitled to recover. Explain.

4. On May 16 a salesman for a manufacturer of farm machinery solicited an order from a farmer for a certain type of farm machine at a stated price. The order form signed in duplicate by the farmer concluded by stating: "This order is not subject to countermand. No verbal understanding of the agent is to affect this order, all conditions under which this order is given are specified herein. All orders are subject to approval of the manufacturer." The order form contained no warranty of any kind. The salesman sent the signed copies of the order form to the manufacturer. On May 23, before anything further had been done about the order, the farmer notified the manufacturer canceling the order and stating that he would not accept the machine. On May 26 the manufacturer wrote on both copies of the order form: "Accepted, will ship today, May 26," signed both copies, and mailed one copy to the farmer. Assume that under the circumstances this was within a reasonable time. The manufacturer shipped the machine to the farmer on May 26, but the farmer refused to receive it from the carrier. The carrier returned the machine to the manufacturer, who again reshipped it back to the farmer. The salesman then on June 30 induced the farmer to receive delivery and permit the machine to be installed, the salesman expressly warranting in the manufacturer's name that the machine would operate in a certain way. The machine did not perform as warranted and the farmer demanded that the manufacturer remove it. The manufacturer refused and sued the farmer for the purchase price.

(a) Was an enforceable contract between the manufacturer and farmer formed on May 26? Explain.

(b) Was an enforceable contract between the manufacturer and farmer formed on June 30? Explain.

(c) Was the manufacturer entitled to recover the purchase price from the farmer? Explain.

5. S sold and delivered a certain machine to B. S expressly warranted satisfactory operation for six months and B promised to pay the agreed price in twelve equal monthly installments. Eight months later the machine broke down, and B, who had been paying according to the agreement, refused to pay any more. S proposed that if B would pay the remainder of the price at once, S would repair the machine at no cost to B. B agreed and paid S the balance of the price. S then refused to repair the machine, and B sued S for damages. Explain (1) the reasoning upon which S could attempt to defend and (2) whether B should recover from S. (Hint: Draw a diagram showing promisor, promisee, benefit and detriment, if any).

6. D owed C $1,000 in a transaction that did not come under the Uniform Commercial Code. On the due date, February 1, C requested payment from D. D said he was unable to pay the entire debt but would pay $300 if C would extend the balance six months longer. C said he would not extend the debt unless another person guaranteed payment. D suggested G, a friend of his, and C acknowledged that G's credit was satisfactory. On February 6 the three parties got together. As a favor to D and without compensation, G signed and delivered to C the following writing, dated February 6: "To C: If you will agree with D to give him six months longer on his debt to you, not to exceed $700, will guaranty his payment." D paid C $300, and C signed and delivered to D and G the following writing, dated February 6: "At the request of D and G, I hereby agree to extend until next August 6, D's obligation to pay the $700 balance of his debt to me." (Hint: Draw a diagram as suggested in problem 5).

(a) Assume the following additional facts: D failed to pay on August 6, or thereafter, and C, unsuccessful in attempting to collect from D, demanded payment from G. G refused to pay on the ground that he had received nothing for his promise. Could C recover from G? Explain.

(b) Instead of (a) above, assume the following additional facts: On April 6, C changed his mind about waiting until August for his money and sued D for the $700 balance. Could C recover from D in the April lawsuit? Explain.

7. A mare named Grace, owned by O, was entered in the Kentucky Futurity Race to be held in connection with the meeting of the Kentucky Trotting Horse Breeders Association in Lexington, Kentucky. The mare was to be driven by D, a driver of great skill and experience, who was then in the employ of O. This race was one of the most noted races among trotting horsemen in the United States, and the winning of it greatly increased the value of the sire, dam, and brother and sisters of the winning horse. The purse offered in the race was $14,000, division of which included $10,000 to the owner of the winner and $300 to the owner of the dam of the winner. At this time and for many years prior, F owned and managed a stock farm near Lexington. Among the race horses owned by F were the sire, dam, and brothers of the mare Grace. Before the race, F agreed with D to give D $1,000 if, with him as driver, the mare Grace should win the race. D agreed and the mare driven by D won the race. Thereafter F paid D $200 but failed to pay the balance and D sued F for $800. Explain (1) the reasoning upon which F could attempt to defend, (2) the reasoning upon which D could attempt to collect, and (3) which party should be given judgment.

8. On June 22 a retailer orally ordered from a manufacturer 60 dozen shirts of stated sizes, colors, and styles at $4.75 per dozen, and the manufacturer orally accepted the order. On August 11 the manufacturer wrote to the retailer: "Due to labor increases as effected by a new contract signed by the garment industry with the clothing workers' union, we are compelled to add a surcharge of $2.50 per dozen on existing shirt orders now in the process of manufacture, among which yours is included. We ask your permission to add the surcharge as listed above to existing orders, and will await billing any additional merchandise for your account until we receive your permission to do so.

If you are unwilling to pay this additional charge which is right and proper from every angle, we will be willing to accept cancellation on that portion of your order to which the surcharge would be applicable. In view of the replacement costs which are much higher than our price plus surcharges, we would strongly advise that you accept the merchandise under these conditions." On August 14 the retailer replied by letter: "In answer to your letter of August 11, we ask that you please rush the shirts on back order, and add the $2.50 surcharge." On August 18 the manufacturer shipped the 60 dozen shirts which the retailer had ordered. The retailer paid $285 (the price of 60 dozen at $4.75 per dozen). When the retailer refused to pay any more, the manufacturer sued for $150 as balance due. Assume that under the circumstances a shipment on August 18 was reasonably prompt for the June 22 order.

(a) Explain (1) the reasoning upon which the manufacturer might attempt to recover, (2) the reasoning upon which the retailer might attempt to defend, and (3) which party should be given judgment.

(b) Would your answer be different if the retailer's reply of August 14 had been made orally by long-distance phone? Explain.

9. A debtor sends a $100 check to his creditor with a letter stating, "This is payment in full," and the creditor cashes the check. Later if the creditor sues the debtor to recover a balance allegedly still due, it will be important for the trial court to determine whether the original debt was liquidated or unliquidated. Explain concisely why this is to. (Modified from A.I.C.P.A., Nov. 55-6a).

10. A homeowner engaged a plumber to do certain work, with no agreement as to the amount to be charged for the work. Upon satisfactory completion of the work, the plumber sent the homeowner a bill for $163. The homeowner objected that the bill was too high and requested an itemized bill. The itemized bill the plumber sent to the homeowner totaled $175.06. A few weeks later, the homeowner phoned and told the plumber that he was going to send a check for $100 in full settlement. The plumber replied that he was unwilling to settle for that amount. Nevertheless, the homeowner sent the plumber a check for $100 marked on the face and back "Payment in full for all claims to date." The plumber crossed out the quoted words and indorsed and cashed the check, receiving $100. The plumber then sued the homeowner to recover $75.06 as the balance due. The court concluded that the reasonable charge for the work was $170.

(a) Did the plumber make a promise to accept $100 as payment in full? Explain.

(b) How much could the plumber recover from the homeowner? Explain.

11. M. Morton desired to have his auto engine overhauled, including reboring cylinders, reseating valves, and replacing piston rings. M discussed what he wanted with a garageman. At M's request, the garageman prepared a written statement detailing all that would be done, and stating that the job would cost $350. The garageman prepared the statement in duplicate, signed both copies, gave one copy to M and retained the other copy after having M write on the bottom of the paper, "I hereby engage the above-named garageman to do the work described above and agree to pay the above price within 30 days after completion of the work. (signed) M. Morton." The garageman completed the work satisfactorily and returned the care to M on June 1. About two weeks later M's neighbor had the same work done on his car by another serviceman for $250. The neighbor's car was the same make, model, and year as M's, and had been in approximately the same condition. When M questioned the garageman about the amount of his bill, the garageman replied that his price for the work done was as stated, $350. Thereupon, on the date stated below, M wrote to the garageman that he thought he had been overcharged, would not pay $350, but was willing to pay $275 for the work, and enclosed his check for $275 marked, "In full payment for all work done on my car to date." The garageman crossed out this statement, cashed the check, and sued M for $75 as the balance

claimed due. In the lawsuit it was proven through impartial witnesses that the work done on the two cars (the neighbor's and M's) was exactly the same in kind and quality. In the lawsuit for $75, explain (1) the reasoning upon which M might attempt to defend, (2) the reasoning upon which the garageman might attempt to collect, and (3) which party should be given judgment, if:

    (a) The date of M's letter and check was July 25.

    (b) The date of M's letter and check was June 25.

12. A public accountant rendered professional services to a businessman, without advance agreement as to the amount of the fee. Upon completion of the work, the accountant told the businessman that the fee for the work was $2,000, which according to local custom was payable in thirty days. The businessman accordingly signed and gave the accountant a thirty-day note for $2,000, naming the accountant as payee. Two weeks later the businessman had the accountant's work appraised by three disinterested experts, all of whom agreed that the fair value of the services was $500. When the businessman offered this amount as full payment, the accountant refused the offer and sued the businessman on the note. What defense could the businessman present, and would the defense be good if (1) the note was negotiable in form? (2) if the note was nonnegotiable in form? (Modified from A.I.C.P.A., Nov. 30-3.)

13. A number of identical new homes were built fronting on Roger Road. T, owner of a newly constructed house at 1452 Roger Road, obtained a quotation of $500 from P. Porter, owner and operator of the Porter Paving Company, for blacktop paving of T's driveway and breezeway area. After obtaining other quotations, T phoned the Porter Company giving his name and address and requesting that the paving be done immediately. In the absence of the regular secretary, one of the field men took the message, writing on a slip of paper which he turned over to one of the paving foremen. The address was so sloppily written that

it looked like 1462 Roger Road. At that address was another new home recently purchased by D who had not yet moved in. D had also obtained a quotation from Porter for similar paving but had done nothing further. After checking the file copy of Porter's estimate for 1462 Roger Road, the foreman took his men, materials, and equipment and paved the driveway and breezeway area at 1462 Roger Road. Upon discovering the error, Porter wrote to D explaining what had happened and saying that he thought as a matter of fairness D should pay at least $250 for the job.

    (a) D refused to pay anything and Porter sued D. What result? Explain.

    (b) D replied by letter that he believed $250 a fair price and would pay Porter that amount within sixty days. When D failed to pay, Porter sued D. What result? Explain.

14. A public accountant was engaged by a businessman to make an audit of the latter's books, at specified per diem rates. During the course of the audit, the accountant uncovered a defalcation whereby the businessman saved $25,000. After the audit was concluded and the accountant rendered his report, the businessman promised to pay the accountant an additional fee of $5,000 for uncovering the defalcation. Later the businessman paid only the specified per-diem charge for the audit and refused to pay more. The accountant sued for the additional $5,000 promised. Could the accountant recover? Explain. (Modified from A.I.C.P.A., Nov. 30-6.)

15. The trustees of the Presbyterian Church in a small town planned to have a new church constructed. To raise the necessary funds, they prepared and circulated the following subscription paper written on the church letterhead paper: "I, the undersigned, hereby subscribe and promise to pay to the trustees of the above-named Presbyterian Church the sum set opposite my name, for the purpose of raising $50,000 for the building fund of the new Presbyterian Church which the trustees are to have erected at the corner of Beaver Avenue and Frazier Street. Said sum is to be paid within

one month after the trustees give notice that at least $50,000 has been promised by the signers hereto." C and D were early signers, each agreeing to contribute $1,000. Before the subscription list was completed, C became a Catholic and notified the trustees that he withdrew his subscription, and D died. After more than $50,000 was subscribed, the trustees had the new church constructed and brought lawsuits against C and against D's estate.

(a) What result? Explain.

(b) Could the trustees have worded the subscription promise differently to make collection easier? Explain.

16. D and B were partners operating a clothing store in a building leased from L, landlord, for a term of four years at a stated monthly rental. Two years later D desired to withdraw from the clothing business and start a different kind of business in another locality, but only if he could be free from all obligations of the clothing business. D explained his desire to L. L said, "So long as you are withdrawing from the business, I release you and am satisfied to look to B alone for the remaining payments under the lease." D and B then entered into an agreement under which B bought out D's interest in the partnership, B agreed to be solely liable for the remainder of the lease, and the partnership was terminated. D notified L of the agreement, B continued operating the clothing store, and D started a restaurant in the same town. A year later the clothing store began falling behind in rent payments, and upon expiration of the lease period owed $1,500 overdue rent. It is a rule of law that a person who was a partner at the time an obligation was undertaken continues to be personally liable on that obligation even after termination of the partnership, unless the creditor makes an enforceable agreement releasing such a person. L sued D and B.

(a) Explain (1) the reasoning upon which L might attempt to hold D liable, along with B, (2) the reasoning upon which D might attempt to defend the action, and (3) whether L should obtain judgment against D as well as against B.

(b) Briefly explain how, if at all, D could best have prevented this dispute from arising.

(c) Other facts remaining the same, would it make any difference if L had said to D: "If you withdraw from the business, I will release you"? Explain.

17. A debtor borrowed $5,000 from a creditor, promised to repay the loan in five years, and, as security, gave the creditor a mortgage on certain property belonging to the debtor, consisting of a house (valued at $15,000) and the land on which erected (valued at $2,000). The debtor had a fire insurance policy covering the house. At the debtor's request the insurance company added a mortgagee provision to the policy, so that, in case of fire loss, the proceeds of the policy would first be paid to the creditor to the extent of his interest, and then the remainder paid to debtor. A few years later the debtor sold the house and lot to a buyer. The premises remained subject to the mortgage, but since the buyer did not specifically promise to pay the amount of the mortgage debt, he did not become personally liable to the creditor for the debt. The buyer took out a fire insurance policy payable entirely to the buyer. The policy did not mention the mortgage. The creditor also took out a $5,000 fire insurance policy on the house, payable to himself. Shortly afterwards the creditor and buyer met on the street. During their conversation the buyer mentioned having fire insurance on the house. The creditor said that the policy should have a mortgagee provision. The buyer replied that on the following day he would have the creditor's name as mortgagee added to the policy. After this conversation the creditor canceled his own policy. Unknown to the creditor, the buyer neglected to have the mortgagee provision added. About a month later the house was completely destroyed by fire, through no fault of the buyer. When the proceeds from the buyer's fire insurance were paid entirely to the buyer, the creditor sued the buyer claiming the amount of the mortgage as damages for the buyer's failure to have a mortgagee provision added. Explain (1) the reasoning upon which the buyer might attempt to defend,

(2) the reasoning upon which the creditor might attempt to collect, and (3) which party should be given judgment.

18. M. Martin, the owner of a small manufacturing business, did not have a pension plan and had never mentioned any arrangements for retired employees. However, when E. Edwards, one of M's long and faithful employees reached the age of 65 years and retired, M promised E to pay him $100 per month for the remainder of his life. The promise was made in the manner described below. After continuing such payments for three years, M ceased further payments although E was still alive and not gainfully employed in any manner. E sued M for the promised pension.

(a) M made the promise to E during a conversation between the two in M's office. Explain (1) the reasoning upon which M might attempt to defend, (2) the reasoning upon which E might attempt to collect, and (3) which party should be given judgment.

(b) M made the promise to E at the conclusion of a speech at a banquet given in E's honor by M and attended by all of M's employees. Explain whether your answers in Part (a) will also apply here.

(c) M dated, signed, and gave E the following writing: "To E. Edwards: In consideration of and appreciation for your long and faithful service in my business, I hereby agree to pay you $100 per month for the remainder of your life, payments to begin one month after date hereof. (signed) M. Martin." Explain whether your answers in Part (a) will also apply here. (Modified from A.I.C.P.A. May 33- 1.)

19. After several years employment by a manufacturing company, F was promoted to the position of a department foreman at a salary of $125 per week, and D was promoted to the position of chief draftsman at an annual salary of $8,500 payable in monthly installments. As was also true with F's former positions with the company, no particular period of time for F's employment as a department foreman was named. D's employment was on a one-year contract running from May 1. On June 1, the company obtained an important defense contract, to be completed by January 1, of the following year, and on June 15 announced to all employees: "The Board of Directors has decided that for the purpose of inducing employees to continue with the company and refrain from accepting employment elsewhere until after completion of the current defense contract, the company promises all employees now in its employment that upon completion of the defense contract the company will pay to each employee as a bonus a sum of money equal to one month's salary of each such employee who continues in the company's employment until completion of the said defense contract." The defense contract was completed on time, but shortly thereafter the company began to feel the pinch of a recession and was unable to pay the announced bonus without borrowing money, an act which the directors wished to avoid. The company therefore announced: "Because of present economic conditions, the company cannot at this time pay the bonus announced on last June 15." F and D each sued the company for the promised bonus. In each lawsuit impartial witnesses proved that the salaries paid to F and D were reasonable and fair compensation for the type of work they were hired to perform.

(a) As to F's lawsuit, explain (1) the reasoning upon which the company might attempt to defend, (2) the reasoning upon which the plaintiff might attempt to collect, and (3) which party should be given judgment.

(b) As to D's lawsuit, would any of the answers be different than the answers given in Part (a)? Explain.

20. L. Lucas and T. Thomas, as landlord and tenant respectively, entered into a written lease agreement under which L leased certain described premises to T for one year from June 1, of a specified year, and as rental for that period T agreed to pay L the sum of $600, payable monthly in advance. The lease agreement also provided: "During the duration of this lease, L. Lucas hereby gives T. Thomas an option to purchase the rented pre-

mises for $20,000." On the following February 1, L notified T in writing that L no longer wished to sell the property and that the option was terminated as of that date. On March 1, along with his March rental payment, T notified L that T wished to exercise the option and purchase the property. On March 15, T tendered $20,000 to L and demanded a deed for the property. When L refused to deliver a deed, T sued for a decree of specific performance.

(a) What result? Explain.

(b) Other facts being the same assume that the conclusion of the lease agreement read: "In witness whereof the parties have hereunto set their hands and seals on the date above written. (signed) L. Lucas SEAL (signed) T. Thomas SEAL." The word "seal" was typed twice as indicated when the lease agreement was being prepared for the signatures of the parties. How would your answer compare with the answer in Part (a) above? Explain. (Modified from A.I.C.P.A., May 47-1.)

Legal Capacity to Make a Contract

Legal Capacity to Make a Contract

BASICALLY ALL PERSONS should be considered as having equal rights and equal obligations. Equality under the law is certainly an essential concept for any system worthy of being called a system of justice. However, the concept must conform to reality; the law cannot validly require a standard of conduct which is an absolute impossibility. Therefore, although a person is entitled to full legal protection from the moment of his birth, a tiny baby obviously cannot be held legally responsible for his conduct. The law delays holding persons legally responsible until they can be considered actually aware of the nature of their acts. What age this should be depends upon the act in question and the needs of society.

In a very simple, primitive society, persons were considered adult members at a fairly young age, sometimes as soon as they had reached the age of puberty. As society became more complex, it was necessary gradually to delay the age of full maturity. The introduction of heavy armor in the days of knighthood forced considerable delay in contrast with other notions of maturity current at that time. Necessarily, knighthood (and the burden of a hundred pounds of sheet metal) could not be conferred on a young man until he had reached his full physical growth and strength, and as the eminent historians of English law, Pollock and Maitland, point out:

> . . . here again we have a good instance of the manner in which the law for the gentry becomes English common law. The military tenant is kept in ward until he is twenty-one years old; . . . gradually . . . the knightly majority is becoming the majority of the common law.[1]

Thus the rule developed under the English common law system that a person is not considered a mature, adult member of society until he reaches the age of twenty-one years. With the advent of the 18-year-old franchise in America, many states have, by statute, reduced the age of legal maturity to 20, 19, and 18 years. Persons of less than legal age are sometimes referred to under the law as *infants*. The term *minor* is also used to denote a person of less than legal age, and this term is perhaps more acceptable to nonlawyers and seems more appropriate. A discussion of the role of age as it relates to tort liability was presented in Chapter 4. The factor of age will be considered here in relation to capacity to enter into binding contracts.

Age relates to mental development, maturity of judgment and experience, but so do other factors relate to these qualities. Such factors could include insanity, mental incompetency, stupefaction by drugs or intoxicating drink, as well as special legal disabilities as might attach to conviction of a serious crime. All of these factors, including age, can affect one's ability to develop the level of intent which the law considers desirable for the meeting of minds necessary to form a binding agreement. Ac-

---

1. Sir Frederick Pollock and F. W. Maitland, HISTORY OF ENGLISH LAW BEFORE THE TIME OF EDWARD 1, Vol. 2 (2d ed.: Boston: Little. Brown. 1899). D. 438.

cordingly, persons who are considered not to possess sufficient capacity are protected by law from full legal consequences attaching to their attempts to form contracts. It is the purpose of this chapter to explore the situations where capacity is limited and the effect of such limitations.

I. Contracts of Minors

Because a minor frequently lacks the experience and sound judgment necessary to protect himself from unwise and wasteful agreements, the law considers it desirable policy to afford minors some protection. Prohibiting all minors from making contracts or declaring their contracts completely void would be too extreme and unnecessary a remedy. Instead, the protection takes the form of recognizing the validity of minors' contracts, but at the same time permitting minors to disaffirm (that is to cancel or avoid) most of their contracts.

In thus protecting minors, the law recognizes an exception to the usual requirement (see Chapter 6) that contract obligations must be mutual, that usually both parties must be bound or neither is bound. Unless a minor is guilty of dishonestly inducing an adult to enter into a contract by fraudulently misrepresenting his age, the minor may, as he wishes, either disaffirm the contract or enforce it against the adult. And even in some cases of misrepresentation of age, the minor can still disaffirm.

To spare the courts the impossible task of attempting to appraise the competency of each individual and analyze every agreement, the law extends its protection *generally*—to *all* minors and for *all* contracts (with some exceptions). Therefore a minor's right to disaffirm a contract is not dependent on proof that the particular agreement is unfair or unwise, nor that the particular minor lacks sound judgment. The degree of a minor's independence is not important; a minor freed from

parental control, even one married and supporting his own family, is protected.

But, a dissenter might object, if the protection is applied generally, is it not possible for a minor who is a shrewd bargainer to speculate as to future business conditions or prices, enjoy all the advantages of a fair and reasonable contract, and at the same time shift the risk of possible loss to the adult contracting party? The answer is yes. Admittedly the protection which the law extends to minors is at the expense of adult parties to contracts, and at times will be quite unfair to the adults. This is another instance in which the law balances conflicting interests and, entirely as a matter of policy, decides to throw a loss upon one of two equally innocent parties. Once society decides as a matter of basic policy (1) that while it is socially desirable for minors to be free to enter into contracts, it is equally socially desirable to protect them in their contracts, and (2) that it is impossible as a practical matter to administer protection by testing each individual minor and appraising each individual contract, then the result is unavoidable—there will be a certain amount of unfairness and injustice to adults. How much unfairness should be tolerated, what price adult society should pay for protecting minors or in other words, how much protection should be given minors—is entirely a question of policy, in which the need for protecting minors and the desirability of having a workable rule of general application is weighed against the resulting unfairness to adults. And as with almost any question of policy, the courts and legislatures of the different states have reached varying conclusions, some states giving only limited protection and other states giving fairly extensive protection.

In discussing the status of minors' contracts, it is helpful to classify the contracts into three types: nonvoidable contracts, voidable contracts, and contracts for necessaries.

A. Nonvoidable Contracts

Certain contracts are considered of such social significance that the enforceability of the contract is deemed more important than is the policy of protecting the minor party. Such contracts include contracts of enlistment in the armed forces, marriage contracts and certain loans guaranteed by the federal government. If a minor enters into such a contract the fact of his minority will not provide a defense to an attempt to enforce the contract nor may he validly claim disaffirmance.

B. Voidable Contracts

A voidable contract is enforceable until it has been disaffirmed by the minor. Upon reaching majority, a former minor is able to ratify his contracts; once he does so his right to disaffirm later is terminated.

1. RATIFICATION

Affirmance or ratification of a contract consists of any manifestation by a contracting party, *after* he comes of age, that he considers the agreement binding. After an ex-minor effectively ratifies his contract, he cannot disaffirm it. An effective ratification can be either expressly stated, or instead implied from conduct. Thus an ex-minor by implication ratifies his contract if (*after* coming of age), he sells or uses the item obtained under the contract or otherwise accepts a benefit under the contract, or even if he retains the item without use for longer than is considered reasonable for giving notice of disaffirmance. Some states have statutes which require the ratification to be in writing. Ratification should be recognized as a situation where the question of a lack of consideration might arise. However, it is generally held that no new consideration is needed as the past consideration is sufficient to make the new promise binding.

Sometimes an ex-minor may be unaware of his right to disaffirm contracts. This is entirely immaterial. If the enforcement of legal rights and obligations were made dependent upon actual proof that the parties involved were aware of the applicable rules of law, the legal system would be entirely unworkable. In recognition of this, courts frequently repeat the well-known axioms, "Ignorance of the law is no excuse," and "Every person is presumed to know the law." Thus an ex-minor's words or conduct can form a binding ratification, even though at the time he spoke or acted he was unaware of his legal right to disaffirm.

2. AVOIDANCE

A contract can be disaffirmed only by the minor party; an adult party is fully bound to the contract. The adult is unable to escape contractual responsibility based upon the minority of the other party even though the adult was unaware that the other party was a minor. The fact that the minor deceived the adult or lied about his age does not provide the adult with a reason for refusing to honor the contract either although it may, in some states, restrict the minor's right to disaffirm.

a. Timing

The time at which a contract may be disaffirmed can depend upon the stage of completion of the contract. An executory contract (one where there has been an exchange of promises, but no performance) can be disaffirmed during either minority or majority. With such an unperformed contract, the mere lapse or passage of time after reaching majority will not prevent later disaffirmance. A few states have, by statute, changed this rule by requiring disaffirmances to occur within a reasonable time after minority ends. A contract which has been executed (fully performed) may be disaffirmed under the same rules which apply to executory contracts if the executed contract involved personality. With regard to real property contracts, though, an executed contract can generally be disaffirmed only after minority ends.

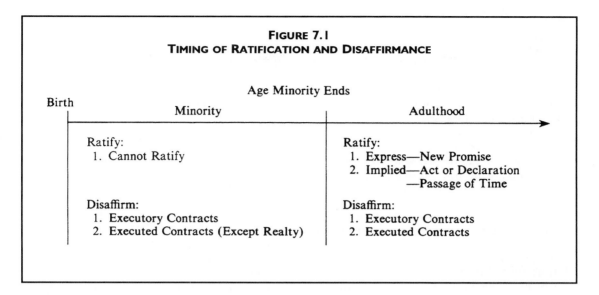

FIGURE 7.1
TIMING OF RATIFICATION AND DISAFFIRMANCE

The timing of disaffirmance and ratification may be summarized as in Figure 7.1.

b. Return of Benefits and Age Misrepresentation

In a majority of jurisdictions, a minor's right to disaffirm is given extensive protection. These, so-called *extensive-protection states*, allow a minor to cancel or avoid his contractual obligations and allow the minor to recover whatever he gave or paid to the adult party under the contract, or its value; but, these states do not require as any kind of condition to the disaffirmance that the minor return any of the benefits he received from the adult party to the contract.

The only obligation imposed upon the minor or ex-minor is to return what he received under the contract, if he still has it, in whatever condition it is in at the time he disaffirms. He is not liable for depreciation, wear and tear, damages, or the value of his use. If whatever the minor or ex-minor received under the contract is no longer in his possession, if he has consumed, discarded, or sold it, he can still disaffirm and is not required to account for any proceeds received from his disposal of the item. A minor's failure voluntarily to disclose his age is not dishonesty or fraud, and he can still disaffirm. In extensive-protection states, a minor's lying about his age has no effect on his right to disaffirm his contract nor on his right to recover what he paid. However, a minor who fraudulently misrepresents his age is committing a crime equal in gravity to stealing, and, through a criminal prosecution, he can be punished with a substantial fine, jail sentence, or both.

Other states also provide protection to minors, but the protection is less broad. These states are referred to as *limited-protection states*. The usual limitation affects the amount which a disaffirming minor or ex-minor can recover. In some states, if the contract was fair and reasonable, the value of the minor's (or ex-minor's) use of the item he is returning, or the amount of damages or depreciation, will be deducted from what the minor paid or gave, and he can only recover the difference. For example, in many limited–

Example.   A seller sold a horse, harness, and wagon to a minor who was 17 years old, was married, and had one child. The minor had no use for the outfit except driving for pleasure. He disposed of the harness and wagon, and the horse became so emaciated and disabled, either by disease or neglect, that it was shot on order of agents for the Society for Prevention of Cruelty to Animals. When the seller sued for the unpaid balance of the purchase price, the minor disaffirmed the contract and sued for the amount already paid to the seller.

In approving the trial court's decision in favor of the minor, the Rhode Island Supreme Court applying the minority rule said: "The law gives to a minor the right to disaffirm his contracts on the ground of the disability of infancy. This has been provided as a protection to him from the consequences of his own improvidence and folly. It is the same lack of foresight that in most instances leads to his dissipation of the proceeds of his voidable contracts. To say that he shall not have the protection of disaffirmance with which the policy of the law seeks to guard him, unless he has had sufficient prudence to retain the consideration of the contract he wishes to avoid, would in many instances deprive him, because of his indiscretion, of the very defense which the law intended that he should have against the results of his indiscretion.... Not infrequently, even in cases where the infant still has the consideration and returns it to the other party to the contract, such other party is far from being placed in status quo [the status he was in before entering into the contract]. It has been said that the right of an infant to avoid his contract is absolute and paramount to all equities."[2]

A different result would be reached under the majority rule which states that a minor who is married is treated as an adult. ☐

2. *McGuckian v. Carpenter*, 43 R.I. 94, 110 A. 402 (1920)

protection states if a minor buys and pays $100 for a radio, but after the radio has depreciated to $60 disaffirms the contract and returns the radio, he can recover only $60 rather than the $100 which he originally paid. Some states which grant extensive protection to honest minors limit the protection if a minor has dishonestly lied about his age. Some of these states prohibit disaffirmance altogether, some other states permit the dishonest minor to disaffirm his contract but require him to pay for damages or depreciation or deduct this amount from what he can recover.

At first glance it may seem only fair that a disaffirming minor or ex-minor should be charged for depreciation, damages, or use. However, a strong argument can be made for the view of the extensive-protection states, in

which a minor can recover all that he paid without any deduction. The granting of any protection at all to minors is based on society's conviction that, as a result of their lack of experience, maturity, and sound judgment, they may enter into unwise and wasteful agreements. To the extent that a minor who has purchased an item is charged for use, depreciation, or damage, to that extent he is being charged for the exercise of his immature judgment, the very thing against which society has decided to protect him.

But how about the dishonest minor who lies about his age? Certainly a system of justice should never deliberately prefer a dishonest defrauder over the innocent victim of the fraud. Nevertheless, a strong policy argument can be made to support the rule in the extensive-protection states that a minor's fraud should not effect his right to disaffirm and to recover all that he paid. When a court in an extensive-protection state permits a defrauding minor to disaffirm his contract and make full recovery, the court is not saying that society should overlook the minor's dishonesty or that society should protect the minor from the consequences of his deliberate lie. If the defrauded adult will swear out a warrant against the minor, the court will, in a *criminal* action, have the minor prosecuted and, if convicted, fined or jailed for his crime. The law's paying no attention to the minor's fraud in a *civil* action is largely a result of the law's taking a practical and realistic view of people, both jurymen and litigants. A rule of law may actually be sound and wise, and may clearly be the best policy rule to follow when considered within the entire framework or pattern of society, yet at the same time the rule may seem unreasonable and unfair if considered alone, separated from this societal pattern, and divorced from related fact situations. More specifically, some persons, especially if they are adult businesspersons, may take a narrow view, condemn as archaic the rule protecting minors, and strongly believe that minors should be bound by their fair and reasonable contracts. Suppose that a group of such persons form the jury when a minor disaffirms his contract and sues to recover what he paid. So long as the facts are undisputed, the judge can direct a verdict and prevent the jurors from ignoring the accepted rule of law. However, if the defendant-seller sees a way of beating the case and saving himself a substantial sum of money, he may be the type of person (of which unfortunately too many exist) who is willing to lie under oath if he thinks he can "get away" with it. The seller will be tempted to testify falsely that the minor lied about his age, if under the law of that state the minor's dishonesty would affect his right to recover. This would then raise a question of fact upon which the jury would have to decide. The jurors might actually believe that the minor was honest and did not lie about his age, but if the jurors also stubbornly insist that a minor should not be able to recover, in spite of what the judge tells them is the correct rule of law, the jurors are offered an easy way to achieve their desired result. They can pretend that the minor lied about his age and thereby prevent the minor from recovering. The ease with which jurors who disapprove of certain rules of law are able surreptitiously to ignore them, has been described by Professor Henry J. Abraham, who writes:

> On the basis of the somewhat questionable assumption that the jury fully comprehends the judge's instructions concerning the applicable substantive legal rules, it is usually required to return a *general or over-all* verdict in favor of one party or another. Theoretically . . . this jury verdict is based on the *facts* of the case, the judge himself having determined the rules of *law*—although it is not always possible to separate facts and law. In practice, however, the general verdict permits the jury to do what it pleases; it gives no details, simply reports its decision, and no one either really knows or may safely predict just what facts a jury found from the evidence.[3]

Thus to the extent that the state law limits the right of a defrauding minor to recover, adult parties are tempted to perjure themselves and make fraud an issue in every case, and jurors (who, of course, are always adults), even though unconvinced of a minor's dishonesty, are enabled to tamper with the law and illegally restrict the rights of minors to recover. In extensive-protection states the *criminal* law is used to control dishonest minors; dishonest litigants and stubborn jurors are not enabled to subvert the protection which society believes should be accorded to minors.

---

3. Henry J. Abraham, THE JUDICIAL PROCESS, (New York: Oxford U.P., 1962), p. 117.

C. Contracts for Necessaries

While a minor can disaffirm even his contracts for necessaries, he will generally be liable in quasi-contract for the reasonable value of necessaries received. A minor is also liable for necessaries supplied to his wife (arguably also one's husband) and in some states, his dependent children.

The rule as to contracts not involving necessaries and the rule as to necessaries are both based on the welfare of the minor. Usually protection of the minor is accomplished by permitting him to avoid his contracts fully. But in some situations it is of more benefit to the minor that he be able to bind himself. Suppose a minor supporting and maintaining his own home and family buys and pays for a loaf of bread which he and his family eat. If he could then recover his money from the grocer, most grocers would be unwilling to undertake the risk and would refuse to sell food to the minor. Thus the minor is benefited by being able to bind himself for the reasonable value of his necessaries.

I. NECESSARIES DEFINED

Necessaries are those things which, as a matter of policy, are considered essential or of sufficient benefit to the minor in question, that the law will help him to obtain them. The position and station in life of a particular minor are considered in determining what are necessaries for him. Even if an item is of a type considered essential (which would certainly include food, clothing, shelter, medical services, and elementary or vocational education), it is not a necessary if the particular minor already has a sufficient supply or has a parent or guardian able and willing to supply him with his needs. Necessaries are usually limited to the person of the minor (and of spouse and children if any). Items considered useful or even essential for the maintenance of a minor's property or for the operation of his business, are usually not necessaries, even if the business is the minor's sole support.

2. THING OF RESPONSIBILITY

If a contract for necessaries is wholly executory, it can be avoided by the minor, as can other voidable contracts, since the minor has received nothing for which he must pay the reasonable value. If the contract is executed, the minor may disaffirm it. He will, after disaffirmance, beheld responsible in quasi-contract and be required to pay the reasonable value for the goods, not the agreed upon contract price.

In a few states, if he disaffirms within a reasonable time after receiving the necessaries, he may return the goods and have no further liability. After a reasonable time he must pay the reasonable value of the goods, not the agreed upon contract price.

D. Contracts Between Minors

If both contracting parties are minors, either one or both may disaffirm the contract. Relatively few cases have litigated the point, but the practical effect of a double disaffirmance would seem to be that (1) either party can avoid his further obligation under the contract, and (2) either party can recover whatever property or money he gave or paid under the contract, but only to the extent such property or money is still in the other party's possession. A minor who is no longer in possession of what he received under a contract has no obligation to repay its value. This has been held to apply to money, with the result that if a minor-buyer pays for goods received from the minor seller, the buyer can recover what he paid only if the seller has the identical pieces of currency that he received from the buyer.

E. Parent's Liability

As a general rule, it can be stated that a parent is not liable for contracts made by his children. But, there are exceptions. If a parent has breached his obligation of support to his minor child, he may be liable for the reason-

TABLE 7.1
EFFECT OF DISAFFIRMANCE OF A CONTRACT
FOR NECESSARIES ON MINOR'S LIABILITY

Action by Minor	Status of Contract			
	Executory	Partially Executed *(minor has performed)*	Partially Executed *(adult has performed)*	Executed
Disaffirmance	No liability	No liability (Minor entitled to return of value of his performance	Liability in quasi-contract for value of adult's performance	1. Liability in quasi-contract in most states 2. No liability in some states if disaffirmance within a reasonable time and minor returns adult's performance

able value of necessaries supplied to such child. Also, as with any adult, a parent can voluntarily assume liability for his child's contract by becoming a co-signer or other form of guarantee or suretyship. Additionally, an adult may have a minor act as his agent thereby allowing the minor to make a binding contract on behalf of the adult or parent. This concept is dealt with more extensively in Chapter 18.

F. Contract Related Torts

As was explained in Chapter 4, a minor can be held fully liable for his torts. However, if a contract is so closely connected with a tort so that allowing recovery for the tort would be tantamount to allowing recovery on the contract, no recovery may be held against the minor.

G. Protecting the Adult Party

In view of a minor's limited liability both for contracts and also for torts related to contracts, the practical question arises as to what an adult should do in dealing with a minor or with a youthful-appearing person. Relying on the minor's word is not safe since he may be lying about his age. If an adult wants to avoid the risk of possibly sustaining a loss should a youthful person actually be a minor and later disaffirm a contract, the adult could do either of the following:

1. Refuse to deal with the youthful person. Instead, have him bring in a person known to be an adult with whom the other adult may then safely contract. Whether the adult promptly gives the purchased item to the minor is of no concern to the seller, since the adult cannot disaffirm his contract.

Example. Falsely saying that he was twenty-two years old, a minor induced a seller to sell and deliver certain goods to the minor, which the minor agreed to pay the purchase price of $200 in thirty days. Through the minor's fault the goods were destroyed. When the obligation matured, the minor refused to pay and disaffirmed his contract. The seller sued the minor for damages resulting from his tort of fraudulently misrepresenting his age.

The seller could not recover in an extensive-protection state. However, although the minor would have no civil liability, he could be punished in a criminal proceeding. In a limited protection state, where the tort is misrepresentation of minority status, as is the case in this example, recovery is sometimes allowed for the tort of deceit. ▢

2. Accept the minor or youthful person as a customer only after he brings in an adult of satisfactory credit, who will sign a guaranty agreeing to pay the other adult party the amount of his loss if the minor later fails to pay or disaffirms the contract.

II. Contracts of the Insane or Mentally Incompetent

A. Voidable Nature

Generally speaking, contracts made by persons who are insane or mentally incompetent are voidable as are contracts of minors. Such a contract may be disaffirmed by the person suffering the disability when he reacquires his mental health or, during the period of disability, by his legal guardian or representative.

It is more difficult to deal with such a contract than one involving a minor because the minor's legal disability ends at an easily measurable point in time. With mental incompetency, not only does the disability not end at a given time, but the nature of the disability varies from one individual to another. One person may manifest a severe case of mental disease while another only slight symptoms. To constitute a basis for disaffirmance the infirmity need not amount to an entire lack of reason; it must be such as to render one incapable of comprehending the subject, nature and probable consequences of the contract at the time it is made. The cause of the mental condition is not material unless it is a mere temporary stupefaction caused by drug or drink. This disability is discussed below.

A contract involving mental incapacity may be disaffirmed under the same conditions under which it may be ratified: by the incapacitated person during periods of health, by his guardian during times of incapacity, or by his heirs or legal representatives after death.

A majority of courts, while allowing disaffirmance, require return of the consideration as a condition to avoidance if the other party entered into the contract in good faith and was ignorant of the other party's disability. In some states, a return of benefits is not considered a condition to avoidance.

In a situation where a person is legally adjudged as insane, and a guardian appointed, any contract subsequently made by such insane person is not voidable but totally void.

B. Contracts for Necessaries

A person suffering mental incapacity can disaffirm contracts for necessaries as can a minor. But, as with a minor, he or his estate will be held liable in quasi-contract for the reasonable value of the necessaries received by him, his wife, or children.

III. Contracts of Those Temporarily Incompetent Or under Special Disabilities

Contracts made by a person who becomes stupefied by the taking of drugs or intoxicating drink are valid and enforceable against such persons unless it can be shown that such person was incapable of understanding the nature and effect of such contract when it was made. If that is the case, some states will allow the person stupefied, upon recovering his judgment, to disaffirm such contracts. The right may be limited, however, by imposing a quasi-contractual responsibility to pay the reasonable value for necessaries furnished and, in some states, by preventing any disaffirmance if the other party dealt in good faith without knowledge of the disability.

Other special disabilities apply, in various states, to persons convicted of major crimes, rendering them incapable of making certain types of contracts, to married women, rendering their contracts void (but this disability has now been removed in most states by statute) and to corporations, with regard to acts or contracts not authorized by their corporate charters.

* * *

Problems

1. B, a minor, without misrepresenting his age, entered into a written contract with S, an adult, under which S agreed to sell to B, and B to buy at a stated price, certain described merchandise not constituting necessaries. When the time came for performance, B, still a minor, tendered the price but S refused to deliver on the ground that B was a minor.

(a) S was aware of B's age at the time of entering into the contract but was not cognizant of the law pertaining to minor's contracts. B sued S for damages resulting from S's refusal to deliver. Was B entitled to judgment against S? Explain.

(b) After entering into the contract, S for the first time learned that B was a minor. B sued S for damages resulting from S's refusal to deliver. Was B entitled to judgment against S? Explain. (Modified from A.I.C.P.A., Nov. 37-5.)

2. B, who had just celebrated his seventeenth birthday, bought and received from S, an appliance dealer, a stereo radio-phonograph for $300. B paid the entire price in cash upon receiving the instrument. B made no statement as to his age, and since it was S's practice to require proof of age from youthful-appearing customers only in credit sales, S did not hesitate selling the instrument to B. After six months B tendered return of the instrument, stated that he was disarming his contract, and demanded return of the $300 he had paid. S refused and B sued S for $300. S proved that the value of the instrument had depreciated to $100. Was B entitled to judgment against S, and if so, for how much? Explain. (Assume legal age = 18.)

3. B who looked older than his actual age, lived with his parents but had a full-time job and was permitted to retain all his earnings. B's birthday was June 18. On April 1, B, then seventeen years old, falsely stated that he was twenty-four years old, and entered into a contract with S, an adult, under which S sold and delivered to B a certain car, not a necessary, for $800, B paying $200 in cash and signing a two-month note for the balance of $600. (Assume legal age = 18.)

(a) On April 3 S learned of B's actual age, offered to return to B $200 in cash and his note, and demanded return of the car. When B refused, S sued B to recover possession of the car. What result?

(b) Assume that the facts under (a) above did not occur. Two and a half months after purchasing the car, B, on June 15, considerably damaged the car by carelessly driving into a concrete abutment. After the collision the fair value of the car was $100. (1) B offered to return the car to S, said that he was disaffirming the contract, and demanded return of his $200. When S refused, B sued S. What result? (2) Assume that after the June 15 collision B did not return the car to S but instead, on the date stated below, sold and delivered it to P for $100, its fair value. On June 22 S who had heard nothing concerning the car since selling it to B, demanded payment of B's $600 note, then three weeks overdue. B in turn told S that he was disaffirming the contract and demanded return of $100 of the $200 he had paid, saying that as a matter of fairness he would consider the $100 received from P as for the benefit of S. When S refused this arrangement, B sued S for $200. S filed a counterclaim against B for $600, the amount of B's note. (a) The date of B's sale and delivery of the car to P was June 16. (1) What would be the result of B's lawsuit and S's counterclaim? (2) Suppose S sued B's parents. What result? (b) the date of B's sale and delivery of the car to P was June 20. What would be the result of B's lawsuit and S's counterclaim?

4. M who looked older than his actual age of twenty years owned an automobile which was not a necessary. M lived with his parents but had a full-time job and was permitted to retain all that he earned. Falsely stating that he was twenty-two years old, M left his car with a garageman for a complete motor overhaul, including grinding valves and reboring cylinders When the work was completed and the bill submitted to M for the reasonable value of the work, M refused to pay and demanded return of his car. The garageman refused to surrender the car and cited the following state statute: "When, pursuant to a valid contract with the owner of goods, a repairman takes possession of and performs work upon said goods, and the contract between the repairman and the owner contains no provision for the extension of credit to the owner, the repairman shall have the right under said contract to retain possession of the said goods until the owner shall have paid to the repairman the contracted price for the work or if no price shall have been agreed upon, the reasonable value of the contract work." M sued to recover possession of the car and proved that he was

only 20 years old. What result? (Assume legal age = 21.)

5. B looked older than his actual age of nineteen years. Falsely stating that he was twenty-two years old, B entered into a contract with S, an adult, to buy a radio from S for $400. B paid $25 at the time of the purchase and agreed to pay the balance in monthly installments of $50 each. After B used the radio for two weeks, it was accidently broken, through no fault of B's, so that it no longer worked. B returned the damaged radio to S and asked for return of his $25. S refused and sued B for damages for tort. S proved that when returned, the radio had a fair value of $50. (Assume legal age = 20.)

(a) Did B commit a tort against S? Explain.

(b) Could S recover tort damages from B and if so, how much? Explain.

6. A seventeen-year-old self-supporting orphan was employed as a bookkeeper. He subscribed for a noncancellable correspondence course in accountancy for which he agreed to pay a stipulated amount. He completed half of the course, paid one-quarter of the stipulated amount and thereupon, at the age of eighteen years, refused to continue the course or to make further payments. What were the rights of the parties? Explain. (Assume legal age = 18.) (Modified from A.I.C.P.A., Nov. 35-3).

7. An adult merchant sold a suit of clothing to a buyer who said he was twenty-two years old when in fact he was only seventeen. The agreed price for the suit was $100, payable in thirty days. However, the fair market value of the suit was only $75. After the thirty days had expired, the buyer refused to pay, offered to return the suit, and said he was disaffirming his contract. Since a used suit was of no value to the dealer, he refused to accept the return of the suit and sued the buyer. What result? Explain. (Assume legal age = 18.) (Modified from A.I.C.P.A., Nov. 50-1.)

8. B, twenty years old, owned and operated a lumber yard by means of which he supported him-

self, his wife, and his one-year-old baby. B regularly purchased lumber from S on thirty days' credit and regularly paid promptly. The price of lumber suddenly dropped at a time when B still had intact in his yard the last carload of lumber obtained from S. Since B had not yet paid for this lumber, he notified S that he was disaffirming the contract because of his minority and offered to return the lumber to S. S refused to take back the lumber, and sued B for the agreed price. Explain (1) the reasoning upon which S might attempt to collect, (2) the reasoning upon which B might attempt to defend, and (3) which party should be given judgment. (Assume legal = 21.)

9. D, seventeen years old and a high-school senior living with and supported by his parents, had a date for the senior prom. F, D's father, consented to D's using F's car the night of the prom. While returning from the dance late that night, D, driving negligently, ran into the car of T. Although he was using proper care, T was unable to avoid the accident. The next morning, after D told F of the accident, D, F, and T went to the garage to which T's car had been towed. T did not threaten arrest or suit, but asked F what he was going to do. F said, "Have your car repaired and I'll pay the cost of the repairs." Later the same day, and before T had ordered work to begin on his car, F called T and said that he had changed his mind, did not consider himself responsible, and would not pay for any damage. F had no liability insurance. T had his car repaired and, upon completion, sued F for the expense of the repairs. (Assume legal age = 18.)

(a) Was F liable for D's tort? Explain.

(b) Was F liable on his promise? Explain.

Reality of Consent

CHAPTER OUTLINE

Reality of Consent

DURING THE OFFER and acceptance stage of a contract, a common understanding must have been reached by the parties relative to the key terms of the agreement. If a common understanding is not reached, the consent expressed during the offer and acceptance stage is not *real* and, hence, society may not be willing to enforce the agreement. In other words, the minds of the parties must meet with respect to material or key terms for reality of consent to exist. Reality of consent may be lacking for a variety of reasons, the principal of which are as follows:

1. Mistake;
2. Fraud in the inducement; and,
3. Duress.

I. Mistake

Sometimes a person's decision to enter into an agreement is based largely on a mistaken assumption or understanding concerning something connected with the agreement. When the mistake is discovered, if the other person nevertheless wants to enforce the agreement while the mistaken party wants to cancel it, society must then decide what effect the mistake in question should have on the validity of the agreement. All mistaken agreements are not automatically invalid. When persons enter into agreements, they are frequently taking chances or making assumptions concerning possible existing facts or future expectations. To permit an agreement to be canceled every time one party makes a mistaken assumption would unduly weaken the stability of contracts. On the other hand, justice requires that some mistaken agreements be canceled. The effect which a particular mistake should have on the validity of an agreement is, therefore, entirely a matter of policy—of what seems fair, reasonable, and practical under the circumstances.

The chief types of mistakes which may possibly affect the validity of agreements can be broadly classified as mistakes of fact, mistakes of law, and mistakes by a scrivener.

A. Mistakes of Fact

1. KEY TERMS

Key terms are those that go to the very root or substance of a contract such as those relating to price, quantity, delivery or the subject matter of the agreement. It is not unusual for either one or both of the parties entering into a contract to do so under a mistaken conception of certain key terms relating to the subject matter or the actual or intended meaning of those terms. The effect of such mistakes depends upon whether or not it was a bilateral mistake (both parties were mistaken) or a unilateral mistake (one of the parties was mistaken).

If the mistake was bilateral, the general rule is that the contract can be rescinded by the party who was injured by the mistake.

Example. S wanted to sell and B to buy a tract of mountain land owned by S. S told B that he would have the land surveyed and sell it to B for $100 per acre. Subsequently, based upon the surveyor's statement that S's mountain land contained 100 acres, a price of $10,000 was agreed upon and reproduced in a written contract. Just before the closing date (when S would receive $10,000 from B and B would receive a deed to the land), B discovered the tract of land was 50 acres in size.

Since the price was specifically fixed at $100 per acre, the bilateral mistake pertains to a key term. Therefore, under the general rule relating to bilateral mistake of facts pertaining to key terms in a contract, B, the injured party, could rescind or reform the S-B contract. ☐

* * *

Example. A seller owned Lots 2 and 3 in Block 1 in a certain residential area. On Lot 2 was the seller's house. Lot 3 was vacant. Deciding to sell Lot 3, the seller advertised and interested a buyer who agreed to buy the vacant lot for $4,000. A written contract was typed but the typist struck the wrong key so that the contract read "Lot 2, Block 1" instead of "Lot 3, Block 1." Without noticing the error the parties signed the contract form. When the error was discovered the buyer tendered $4,000 and insisted on a literal enforcement of the written agreement.

Since $4,000 would obviously not be the price for the lot upon which the house was erected, the seller could prove what the parties actually had intended, and the court would correct the written contract accordingly. ☐

If the mistake is unilateral, the general rule is that the injured or mistaken party cannot rescind as long as the other party to the contract acted in good faith and without knowledge of such mistake. This general rule is subject to two important exceptions: (1) where the key terms used are reasonably subject to two meanings; or (2) where the mistake made by one party is induced by the fraud or negligence of the other party, the contract can be rescinded by the injured party.

First, since many words have varying shades of meaning, the courts are frequently called upon to interpret the meaning of certain key terms used in an agreement. The best guide is reasonableness. If the parties to an agreement do not expressly define the meaning of their key terms, they are presumed to be using words in their customary manner. If the parties are not both members of a particular trade or vocation, the customary meaning of the words in question is taken to be the meaning commonly given such words by the gen-

eral public. On the other hand if both parties to an agreement are members of a certain trade or vocation, they are presumed to be using whatever particular meaning such words usually have in that trade or vocation.

Before entering into an agreement a person should request an explanation of any words or terms which he does not understand. He will not be excused from an agreement merely because he assumed in his own mind that certain words had a different meaning than their customary meaning, or merely because he was ignorant of the customary meaning of such words.

Sometimes certain words used in an agreement are capable of different meanings or applications, each of which is equally reasonable under the circumstances. If one party has one such meaning in mind and the other party is using the other meaning, they never actually reach an agreement at all and therefore no enforceable contract is formed.

Example. A seller and a buyer contracted for the sale and purchase at a stated price of 125 bales of a specified grade of cotton which was to arrive in Liverpool on the ship "Peerless" from Bombay. Unknown to the parties at the time of their agreement, there were two ships by that name both carrying cotton from Bombay, one to arrive in October the other in December. The buyer was thinking of the October ship, while the seller's cargo was on the December ship. When the October ship arrived, the buyer demanded that the seller deliver the agreed cotton. The seller refused since none of that cargo belonged to him. When the December ship arrived with the seller's cargo, the buyer refused to accept the cotton tendered by the seller, and the seller sued the buyer for damages for breach of contract.

The seller could not recover. Since the seller attached one meaning to the word "Peerless," and the buyer another meaning, and since both meanings were equally reasonable, there was no agreement and no enforceable contract between the parties. ☐

* * *

Example. S knew that B wanted to buy an authentic, original Kentucky rifle to hang over his fireplace. S also knew that B had no knowledge of Kentucky rifles. Therefore, in an attempt to take advantage of B's lack of expertise, S offered to sell B "an original Kentucky rifle for $1,000." B accepted, but later discovered that the rifle he purchased from S was in reality a reproduction worth $300.

B's unilateral mistake was induced by S's deception since S knew of B's desire to purchase and his lack of expertise on the subject. Therefore, B could rescind or reform the contract. ☐

Second, it would be unfair to apply the general rule with respect to unilateral mistake of fact where the mistake was induced by the fraud or negligence of the other party. In such a case, the defrauded party can rescind the contract.

2. EXTRINSIC FACTS

Extrinsic facts are facts which are collateral to the key terms or substance of a contract. Such a fact does not go to the essence of the agreement.

Although an agreement correctly states the intent of the parties with respect to key terms, one party or both parties will sometimes be mistaken as to certain extrinsic facts concerning the subject matter of the contract, the mistake being such that had the truth been known the mistaken party or parties would not have consented to the agreement. When litigation arises because of the mistake, a very basic policy question is presented. To what

extent can relief from mistakes be given without unduly weakening the stability of contracts? For contracts to have any value in society, they must be quite stable, not easily changed to overturned. It is not unusual for one party to a contract to become disappointed and dissatisfied, and wish to cancel his contract. Many people are not above pretending that they made some mistake if doing so would help them to escape from a burdensome contract. The overall stability of contracts would be seriously jeopardized if people could easily cancel contacts with which they had become displeased. On the other hand it would be quite unfair to rigidly enforce all contracts regardless of very serious mistakes which the parties may have made. In weighing (on one side) the desirability that contracts be stable, against (on the other side) considerations of fairness and reasonableness, one of the chief guides used by the courts is to evaluate the relationship which the particular mistake in question bears to the

Example. A seller sold a certain tract of land to a buyer for $5,000 which the buyer paid upon receiving the deed. Unknown to the seller, oil had been discovered on adjoining land and the actual value of the tract at the time of the sale was $10,000. When the seller learned of this, he sued to have the transfer canceled.

1. Assume that at the time he purchased, the buyer was also unaware of the oil discovery.

In estimating value each party assumed the risk of error. That the assumed risk occurred would not be reason to cancel.

2. Assume that at the time he purchased, the buyer was aware of the discovery of oil and knew that the seller was ignorant of the presence of oil.

So long as the buyer was not guilty of any actual misrepresentation or misstatement of fact, the seller could not cancel. ☐

risk of misjudgment present, at least to some extent, in every contract. Another factor also considered is the severity of the loss threatened by the mistake and the possibility of avoiding such loss.

Risk Evaluation

When entering into any contract both parties are guessing or estimating as to the value of what each is to give in exchange for what he will obtain. Since value is based on a number of variable factors, it seems fair to say that each party is assuming (consciously or unconsciously) the risk of possible error in his opinion as to value. Certainly the occurrence of the very error upon which a party takes a chance should not justify canceling his contract, whether the mistake is unilateral or bilateral. Also (different from knowingly taking advantage of another's mistaken expression of intent, which is clearly unfair), it is usually not unfair for a nonmistaken party to take advantage of the other's unilateral mistake or ignorance concerning value. Parties to sales contracts are said to be dealing at "arm's length," meaning that usually neither party is obliged to share all that he knows with the other party. However, if one person induces a mistake through misrepresentations, the picture changes. A person should not be permitted to take advantage of a mistake which

he himself has caused. Mistakes caused by one party's misrepresentations, therefore, are classified differently from other mistakes and will be discussed later.

During the process of evaluating the relative risks which contracting parties assume, some courts rather needlessly involve themselves in semantical difficulties. These courts say that a mistake in the *value* of the subject matter of a contract is not grounds for canceling the contract while a mistake as to the *existence* or *nature* of the subject matter is grounds for canceling a contract. When the rule is stated in this way, there remains the very difficult problem of distinguishing between the "value" of the subject matter and its "nature" or "existence," since a mistake can directly affect value and nevertheless seem to justify canceling the contract. It is easier and more accurate, therefore, to state this policy factor simply in terms of assumed risk. Thus even though a mistake affects value, if it concerns a matter totally unexpected, a matter assumed by the parties to be stable and not subject to variation, it is a matter regarding which they are not assuming the risk of error. Stability of contracts is not too greatly weakened when relief from such mistakes is permitted.

229

Example. A seller agreed to sell and a buyer to buy for $10,500 a tract of land described by its exact boundaries. Both parties believed that the described tract contained about 200 acres. When the parties later learned that the tract actually contained 175 acres, the buyer attempted to cancel the contract.

The contract would be enforceable as made. Since the agreement did not call for a survey, size as well as other factors affecting value was something both parties were estimating. That they might be in error was a risk both were assuming, and therefore not grounds to cancel the contract.

* * *

Example. A seller and a buyer had a tract of land surveyed. The surveyor reported that the tract contained 200 acres. The seller and buyer then contracted for the sale and purchase of the specified tract at $30 per acre. The buyer paid the agreed down payment of $100, gave his note for $5,900 (the balance of the purchase price), and received a deed for the land. Later the parties learned that the surveyor had made a mistake, and that the tract contained only 175 acres. The buyer paid $5,150 which added to his down payment paid for 175 acres at $30 per acre. When the seller demanded the remaining $750 due on the buyer's note, the buyer refused to pay, proposing that the seller should either consider the land fully paid for or instead return the buyer's money and cancel the transfer. The seller refused both suggested alternatives and sued to collect the $750 unpaid balance of the buyer's note.

The seller could not recover. In entering into the contract the parties believed that the survey was accurate. The mistake in size was totally unexpected and unforeseeable, and not a risk that the parties were assuming. For such a mistake the original contract could be canceled. □

Loss Evaluation

In addition to considering the risks assumed by contracting parties, some courts also consider (1) the loss which would result from enforcement of the contract as compared with the loss if the contract is canceled (disregarding of course any gain resulting solely from the mistake itself), and (2) the possibility of restoring the status quo—that is, considering the particular mistake in question and the time it is discovered, whether it is possible to prevent a substantial loss by restoring the parties to the positions they were in before making the contract. If a mistake is unilateral, the courts in some states give little weight to the possibility of restoring the status quo and instead say rather rigidly that a mistake of one party only is never (or almost never) grounds for canceling a contract.

The entire field of extrinsic mistake is quite complex and fixed guidelines cannot be found which will apply with equal effect in all cases. The ultimate objective is to achieve justice while at the same time maintaining stability of contracts, but both of these are variable concepts. While the two most important factors to be considered are the risks assumed and the losses threatened, these factors must in some cases be further subdivided and other factors also considered. From the standpoint of risks assumed, some risks are more consciously and completely assumed than are certain other risks. To illustrate, consider the following example of builders A and B.

In summary, the general rule is that a mistake of extrinsic or collateral fact will not allow the person prejudiced by such mistake to rescind the contract, unless the mistake results from a risk which is not assumed or a loss which is extraordinary. Since the mistake pertains to a wholly collateral or extrinsic fact, it cannot be

Example. Builder A contracted to construct a certain building for $48,000, and builder B a different building for the same price. Before entering into their respective contracts, A and B each calculated construction costs at $40,000 and added 20 percent for profit and overhead depreciation of equipment, etc.).

A's Contract. From the normal test boring pattern, A assumed the existence of a certain underground rock formation. However, on the day after A entered into the contract an accidentally heavy dynamite explosion occurred on a nearby road construction job. The resulting surface subsidence of nearby land disclosed the existence of an unsuspected underground rock cavern, a portion of which extended under the lot where A was to build. This would increase A's costs to $50,000, and A requested cancellation of his contract.

B's Contract. In calculating his costs, B mistotaled a column of figures, putting down $40,000 instead of the correct total of $50,000. On the day after B entered into the contract he discovered his error in arithmetic, and requested cancellation.

Clearly A's mistake would be classified as an extrinsic mistake, and so would B's. B made no mistake in expressing his intent. At the time he expressed his intent, he intended to build for $48,000, he said what he meant and meant what he said. Although both contracts involve extrinsic mistake, B's argument for cancellation would be stronger than A's. A's mistake was so clearly the very type of risk that any builder is assuming that his argument would arouse little sympathy. On the other hand. while B's mistake was his own fault, it is not so obviously the type of risk which a builder consciously assumes or should be considered as assuming. A builder takes a chance on increased material and labor costs, on bad weather, and on a myriad of other conditions and occurrences that might adversely affect construction—including the subsurface land pattern. Any such event usually will not excuse the builder from his contract. But a builder does not to the same extent assume the risk of clerical or computational errors, and if such an error causes no loss to the other party, why should not the builder be relieved from it? Although B's argument is strong, this does not mean that he should be excused or that most courts would excuse him. Other factors are also involved. For example, in approaching such cases the law can never lose sight of the possibility that B found his contract unprofitable for some reason, and made up the appealing story of being a good-faith contractor who was just poor in arithmetic, in order to escape from his contract. Some courts would excuse B, some other courts would not. The latter courts would argue that merely because a contract has recently been formed and performance not yet begun is no reason to permit the contract to be canceled, and that to excuse a person on the ground of computational error would undermine the practice of awarding contracts by secret bids. It would tempt a builder to shave his costs very closely and then, should he find his bid substantially lower than all the rest, claim mistake and excuse, thus almost completely defeating the purpose of having sealed bids submitted.

regarded as going to the essence of the agreement.

B. Mistakes of Law

All too often, in an effort to save lawyers' fees, parties will enter into a homemade agreement which appears to set forth their full understanding; however, in many cases, had the parties understood the law as it affected their agreement, they would not have entered into it. In such a situation, the law adopts the same general attitude as it did for mistakes of ex-

Example. S owned and lived on a one-acre tract of land along a major highway on which he and his family had built a residential house many years ago. Wishing to move into a quieter neighborhood with less traffic, S entered into a contract with B wherein B agreed to buy S's land and house for $150,000. The price was established between S and B based on the assumption that the R-6 zone in which the tract was located permitted sixty apartment units. In fact, under the zoning ordinance, 60 units could be built in an R-6 zone, as long as the land area exceeded two acres. Both S and B had overlooked the area requirements under the applicable ordinance. After B had demolished the residential house in preparation for construction, he discovered he was limited to building 30 units. B then sought to rescind the contract based on a mistake of law.

Since the residential house had been destroyed, it would work an undue hardship on S to permit B to rescind the contract. Under the general rule, a mistake of law will not allow recision unless the status quo can be restored without undue hardship. In this example, after the house was demolished, it would be obviously impossible to restore the status quo. ☐

trinsic facts. The rule here is that where parties enter into a contract as the result of a mistake of law, the courts will refuse to permit either party to rescind if such recision would work an injustice or undue hardship on the other party.

C. Mistakes Caused by Scrivener

Sometimes although there is no misunderstanding concerning the meaning of words, a mistake arises through the selection or use of wrong or inaccurate words in expressing an agreement. If both parties make the same mistake in expressing their agreement, as previously seen, the case is relatively simple.

A much more difficult case arises if only one of the two parties to an agreement inadvertently uses the wrong word and mistakenly expresses his intent. Of course, if the other party knows of the error before a contract is formed—knows, for example, that the offer he has received is not the sender's actual intent—then certainly the erroneous communication cannot form the basis of an enforceable contract. Proof of actual knowledge is often difficult, sometimes impossible. Therefore, even though the recipient of a communication may deny knowing of an error, the fairest approach is to assume that all persons are rea-

sonable, and possess the knowledge and form the conclusions of reasonable people. If under the circumstances the error in question would have been apparent to a reasonable person, then the recipient is treated as though he had actual knowledge of the error—and he cannot form a contract on the basis of the erroneous communication. If, on the other hand, the recipient is unaware of the error, an enforceable contract will *sometimes* be formed. Situations involving this type of error—that is, an erroneous expression of one party's intent can be subdivided into (1) those in which the error arises through the fault of the sender of the erroneous communication or through the fault of his employee for whose acts it is fair to hold the sender responsible, and (2) those in which the error arises through the fault of an independent transmission agency.

1. Mistake by Sender or His Employee. Frequently the courts will hold a sender to what he personally, or through his employee, leads the other party reasonably to understand is meant. Thus if an offeror misstates his price and the offeree accepts without knowing of the error, many courts will hold that an enforceable contract exists from that moment on. On the other hand, some courts have

Example. A lumber dealer in Bangor, Maine, delivered to the telegraph office in Bangor a message addressed to a buyer in Philadelphia, containing the following offer: "Will sell you 500 M laths delivered at your wharf two ten net cash. July shipment. Answer quick." When the message was delivered to the buyer it read, ". . . two net cash . . ." the "ten" having been omitted through the telegraph company's negligent transmission of the message. The buyer was unaware of the error and under the circumstances a reasonable person would not have suspected the error. The buyer immediately replied by telegraph, "Accept your telegraph offer on laths." Through subsequent correspondence the parties learned of the error before the laths were shipped, and the question immediately arose as to whether or not a contract had actually been formed.

Argument for the Buyer: The seller knew that his message would be recopied in the course of its transmission by telegraph, and in selecting the telegraph system he assumed the risks involved in that medium of transmission. Generally an offeror is bound by what he leads the offeree reasonably to understand is meant, and no sound reason is present to deviate from this general rule here. Some courts therefore would hold that an enforceable contract was formed for the sale of the laths at $2 per thousand.

Argument for the Dealer: Since the dealer had no control over the selection of telegraph company personnel and no right to supervise their work, there was no master-servant relationship between the dealer and the telegraph company. The message delivered to the buyer was not the message sent by the dealer. Neither the dealer nor a person for whose conduct he was responsible led the buyer to believe that the offered price was $2 per thousand. Therefore, many courts would hold that the exchange of the quoted telegrams did not form a contract.

Regardless of which view a particular court might follow, the telegraph company would be liable to whichever of the parties sustained damages as a result of the company's failure to transmit the message correctly. However, recoverable damages might be inadequate, inasmuch as a contract between a sender and a telegraph company usually contains a provision limiting the company's liability. For example, one standard form of telegraph blank in common use states on the reverse side: "The Company shall not be liable for mistakes or delays in the transmission or delivery . . . of any message received for transmission at the unrepeated message rate beyond the sum of five hundred dollars. . . ." ☐

shown a tendency to permit a contract to be canceled if the error is quite substantial and is discovered early enough so that canceling the contract will restore both parties to the position they were in before forming their contract.

2. Mistake by Independent Transmission Agency. If an error is made by an independent transmission agency, the courts in some states hold that the erroneous communication will nevertheless form the basis of an enforceable contract, but the courts in most states have reached the opposite conclusion.

II. Misrepresentation

During contract negotiations, parties often make various statements of fact concerning the matters being negotiated. A statement of fact which is influential in bringing about an agreement is called a *representation*. A false statement is called a *misrepresentation*. A person who is induced to enter into a contract through a misrepresentation is acting under a mistake of fact caused directly by the other party to the contract, that is, by the representer who made the misrepresentation. The fact that the representer has led the other

Example. A seller owned a block of 100 shares of stock in the Star Corporation. In inducing a buyer to buy, the seller said, "Dividends you will receive for this stock in the next five years will equal what you are paying for the stock."

Although the seller's statement was an expression of opinion, it implied that he was unaware of any fact which would make the occurrence of what he predicted practically impossible. Suppose that the buyer could prove that when the seller made the quoted statement, he knew that the corporation was hopelessly insolvent. In such a case, the seller could be found guilty of misrepresenting a fact. ☐

* * *

Example. While attempting to sell a suburban lot, a salesman was asked by a prospective buyer whether the city water main had been extended to the area. Although the salesman did not know, he answered. "Yes" instead of saying, "I don't know but will check and find out." Actually city water was not available in the area. The salesman would be guilty of a dishonest or fraudulent misrepresentation. ☐

party into mistakenly entering into the agreement is certainly sufficient reason to cancel or invalidate the agreement, without further inquiry into the relative risks assumed by the parties or the other factors previously discussed in this chapter.

In connection with the effect of misrepresentations, the law makes an important distinction between face and opinion. A person forms a variety of opinions as a result of many influences, including intangible feelings and personal idiosyncrasies; persons can be expected to hold radically different opinions on the same thing. Usually it is not considered sound policy, therefore, to hold a person legally liable for entertaining erroneous opinions, nor for expressing them, and a mistake as to another's opinion is usually not considered sufficiently important to affect the validity of a contract. Thus, for a misrepresentation to justify the cancellation of a contract, it must concern some actual fact rather than the representer's opinion as to a certain fact.

The law sometimes encounters difficulty in classifying a certain statement as to whether it concerns fact or opinion. A statement describing past occurrences is usually a statement of fact, while a statement of what can be expected to occur in the future is usually merely the representer's opinion. However, a statement of future expectations or an expression which the representer clearly states is only his opinion, may nevertheless imply the existence of certain facts. To that extent, such a statement constitutes a representation of certain facts, although it may be expressed in the form of an opinion.

Suppose that when a person enters into a contract with a representer he is acting on the faith of a statement of fact which the representer previously made to someone else. In order to avoid the unacceptable proposition that a person can be held liable to everybody, everywhere, and for any amount, the courts have usually limited cancellation or other liability for misrepresentation to situations in which the representer *directly* misleads another person into making a contract. In other words, usually the only person who can hold a representer liable for a misrepresentation of fact is the person to whom he has directly made the misrepresentation in question, plus the other persons (if any) whom he actually intended would rely on the misrepresentation.

Example. A seller moved to a town about 300 miles away from a 160-acre plot of land which he owned. When the seller moved, there were several producing oil wells in the neighborhood. About two years after the seller moved, a new deeper well was drilled on adjoining land and began producing oil in considerably greater quantities than the previous wells. A buyer called on the seller and offered to buy the 160-acre tract. During the course of their conversation the buyer told the seller how the existing wells were producing and of various neighborhood occurrences, but the buyer said nothing about the new oil strike, of which the buyer knew the seller was ignorant. The seller agreed to sell and delivered a deed for the land to the buyer. A few days later the seller learned of the new oil discovery and sued to cancel the sale because of fraud.

The transfer could be canceled. The buyer was not obliged to give the seller any information, but once he started to tell of happenings, he was obliged to give a complete picture. The buyer was guilty of fraud in deliberately omitting one important fact while appearing to tell about all of the important occurrences since the seller moved away. ☐

Misrepresentations of fact can be classified in the following way, according to what the representer indicates is his intent or state of mind:

1. Dishonest Misrepresentations (otherwise known as "fraudulent misrepresentations"). This type of misrepresentation is a tort and usually also a crime. It occurs when the representer does not honestly believe that the fact represented is true, either because he knows that his statement is false or because he is aware that he lacks the knowledge which he manifests in making the statement.

2. Honest Misrepresentations. This type occurs when the representer honestly believes that the fact he states is true. Such misrepresentations can be further subdivided according to whether the representer's belief is reasonable or not. To say that his belief is not reasonable is another way of saying that the representer has failed to use reasonable care to assure the accuracy of his representation. This is sometimes called a negligent misrepresentation.

A. The Element of Fraud and Types of Fraud

Fraudulent misrepresentations can be made in several ways, principally by an express lie,

by giving partial information, by conduct, and sometimes by nondisclosure of facts.

I. EXPRESS LIE

The representer states in words that a certain fact exists, when he knows either that the fact does not exist or that he has no knowledge as to whether or not the fact exists.

2. PARTIAL INFORMATION

While appearing to state all of the facts pertaining to a certain matter, the representer states only a part of the facts and deliberately refrains from disclosing the remainder of the facts.

3. ACTS OR CONDUCT

Sometimes a person will act in a certain way in order to assert that a certain fact situation exists when actually the true facts are otherwise. For example, although he says nothing, a used-car dealer who daubs grease over a crack in the engine block before showing a car to a prospective buyer is through such conduct asserting a fact which is not true.

4. NONDISCLOSURE

Everyone has a natural inclination to try to obtain the best bargain he can for himself. It is usually considered better overall social policy to leave this natural inclination fairly unrestricted, and to accord to each person full freedom to negotiate advantageous contracts, so long as he avoids actual dishonesty. Usually therefore, a person with certain knowledge concerning the subject matter of an agreement, is not required to disclose what he knows to the other party, and his nondisclosure does not constitute fraud. As the Georgia Court of Appeals has remarked:

> We are aware that neither courts of law nor courts of equity maintain as high a standard of business and commercial integrity and honesty as is demanded by moral obligation. The doctrine of the Roman law, strongly approved by that great orator and lawyer, Cicero, that it is the duty of every man to disclose all facts to another with whom he is dealing which are material to his interest (Cic. de Offic. Lib. 3, Ch.13),[1] is not generally enforced in courts of justice, either in England or America.... While principles of justice and sound morals may require the most scrupulous good faith, candor, and truth, in all dealings whatsoever, the courts of law and equity take a more practical and commercial view of the question, and assign limits to the exercise of their jurisdiction, short of these principles. The well-established rule of the common law, that men who trade at arm's length, is applicable to business transactions, in the absence of any special fiduciary relations between the parties. This rule is not based on a high standard of business morality, but appears to be the outgrowth of practical business exigency.[2]

And as the Kentucky Court of Appeals has said:

> If any other rule were adopted, it would have a depressing tendency on trade and commerce by removing the incentive to speculation and profit that lies at the foundation of almost every business venture.[3]

At an earlier date the same court said:

> From those who have reason to expect information from us the truth should not be withheld, but such as look not to us for information and expect no disclosure from us, have no cause to complain of our silence, and to reproach us for not speaking, with having suppressed the truth.[4]

If a certain specialized fact situation exists, the courts follow a different rule and impose upon a person a legal obligation to make a full disclosure of facts. The most important of these special situations include the following:

1. When the undisclosed fact involves a matter concerning which the contracting parties are not assuming the risk of error: in other

---

1. Cicero wrote (to quote from the Walter Miller translation, 1913):

"The following are problems of this sort: Suppose, for example, a time of death and famine at Rhodes, with provisions at fabulous prices; and suppose that an honest man has imported a large cargo of grain from Alexandria and that to his certain knowledge also several other importers have set sail from Alexandria, and that on the voyage he has sighted their vessels laden with grain and bound for Rhodes; is he to report the fact to the Rhodians or is he to keep his own counsel and sell his own stock at the highest market price: I am assuming the case of virtuous, upright man, and I am raising the question how a man would think and reason who would not conceal the facts from the Rhodians if he thought that it was immoral to do so, but who might be in doubt whether such silence would really be immoral.

"In deciding cases of this kind Diogenes of Babylonia, a great and highly esteemed Stoic, consistently holds one view; his pupil Antipater, a most profound scholar, holds another. According to Antipater all the facts should be disclosed, that the buyer may not be uninformed of any detail that the seller knows; according to Diogenes the seller should declare any defects in his wares, in so far as such a course is prescribed by the common law of the land; but for the rest, since he has goods to sell, he may try to sell them to the best possible advantage, provided he is guilty of no misrepresentation."

Cicero then summarizes what Diogenes and Antipater might say to each other if they were discussing this case, and as his own opinion writes:

"I think, then, that it was the duty of that grain dealer not to keep back the facts from the Rhodians.... At all events he would be no candid or sincere or straightforward or upright or honest man, but rather one who is shifty, sly, artful, shrewd, underhand, cunning, one grown old in fraud and subtlety. Is it not inexpedient to subject oneself to all these terms of reproach and many more besides?"

words, the undisclosed fact is such that a contract would be cancellable if both contracting parties were mistaken concerning the fact. If the fact is of this type, a party who knows the truth concerning the fact in question is obliged to disclose what he knows to the other party, and his failure to make a full disclosure constitutes fraud.

2. When the nondisclosing party is already under an obligation to be loyal to the interests of the other contracting party, as for example when the nondisclosing party is an agent for the other party or when the parties are copartners.

3. When the failure to warn of hidden conditions unreasonably jeopardizes the health or physical safety of the other contracting party.

4. When the nondisclosing party goes further than merely remaining silent and actively attempts to conceal a fact. Such a case is more properly classified as a species of misrepresentation by act or conduct.

A person who is induced by a fraudulent misrepresentation to enter into a contract usually has a choice between either of two remedies, namely:

1. **Rescission.** The defrauded party can rescind or cancel the contract, return the property he received under the contract, and recover what he gave or paid. Also he can usually recover for any consequential damages he has sustained, such as personal injuries or actual expenses.

2. **Affirmance and Recovery of Damages.** Instead of rescinding, the defrauded party can affirm the contract (that is, retain what he received under the contract) and recover as damages the loss sustained as a result of the fraud. In measuring the amount of this loss,

the courts in the various states use either of two theories: (1) the out–of–pocket rule, or (2) the loss–of–bargain rule. Under the out–of–pocket rule, the loss recoverable by the defrauded party is determined by subtracting the actual value of the purchased property from the contract price the defrauded party was induced to pay. The loss–of–bargain rule is the same rule that is applied in measuring damages for breach of warranty, discussed later in this chapter. Under this rule, the amount of recoverable loss is determined by subtracting the actual value of the purchased property from the value it would have had if the representation had been true.

As discussed in the chapter on torts (Chapter 4), a plaintiff's contributory negligence does not bar him from recovering if a defendant is guilty of an intentional tort. By definition fraud is an intentional tort. Therefore the fact that a defrauded party has relied on a misrepresentation instead of making his own investigation of facts certainly should not bar him from recovering, nor should a defrauded party's failure to use proper care to protect his own interests (contributory negligence) bar him from recovering.

B. Uniform Commercial Code Approach

The Uniform Commercial Code provides that "Every contract or duty within this Act imposes an obligation of good faith in its performance or enforcement."[5] "Good faith" is defined, in the case of a merchant, to mean "honesty in fact and the observance of reasonable commercial standards of fair dealing in the trade."[6] Merchants, therefore, have the added duty of abiding by commercial standards of fair dealing as a measure of their honesty and integrity as well as the common law duties of not making fraudulent misrepresentations in a contract situation.

---

2. *Marietta Fertilizer Co. v. Beckwith*, 4 Ga. App. 245, 61 S.E. 149 (1908).
3. *Hays v. Meyers*, 32 Ky. 832, 107 S.W. 287, 17 L.R.A.N.S. 284 (1908).
4. *Taylor v. Bradshaw*, 6 T. B. Monroe (Ky.) 145, 7 Am. Dec. 132 (1827).

---

5. U.C.C. Sec. 1-203.
6. U.C.C. Sec. 2-103(b).

Example. Through fraudulent misrepresentations a seller induced a buyer to purchase a tract of land for $10,000. Upon discovering that he had been defrauded, the buyer decided to retain the property and sue the seller for damages. The evidence showed that the actual value of the land at the time of the purchase was $8.000. and that if the seller's misrepresentations had been true, the land would have been worth $13,000.

The out-of-pocket damages would be $2,000—the $10,000 paid by the buyer minus $8,000, the actual value.

The loss-of-bargain damages would be $5,000—$13,000, the value if the misrepresentation had been true, minus $8,000, the actual value. ☐

C. Negligent Misrepresentations

Before discussing the status of contracts obtained by means of negligent misrepresentations, it will be helpful to consider the general overall liability of negligent informants.

I. GENERAL LIABILITY FOR DAMAGES

Chapter 4 discusses the way in which the law interposes certain policy limitations on a person's liability for careless conduct. Beyond such limits a careless person is not held liable even though his carelessness does cause additional damages. Such policy limitations apply whether the defendant is driving a car without proper care or is giving information without taking proper care to assure its truth and accuracy.

The results of applying such policy limitations to negligent misrepresentation cases can be summarized by classifying the cases according to the relationship between the parties (whether personal or impersonal), and also according to the type of harm threatened (whether bodily or merely monetary). A relationship is impersonal when an informant makes a negligent misrepresentation to the general public; the relationship is personal if the negligent misrepresentation is made to a specific person. If an informant is under contract to supply information to a specific person, certainly the informant should be held liable for losses which that person sustains as a

result of negligently erroneous information. The courts are reluctant to extend liability much further than this. Thus a negligent informant will usually not be held liable to a person with whom he has no contract to supply information, if nothing more than money or property loss is involved. On the other hand, even when the relationship is impersonal, if bodily injury is foreseeable as a result of erroneous information, liability is frequently extended to any person who is thus threatened with injury.

2. VALIDITY OF CONTRACTS

Suppose that through a represener's negligent misrepresentation, a person is induced to enter into a contract with the representer. Usually a distinction is made between the two standard misrepresentation remedies—(1) affirmance of the contract and recovery of damages, and (2) rescission of the contract.

1. Affirmance and Recovery of Damages. As previously indicated in discussing overall liability for negligent misrepresentations, the expresser's liability for damages is a question of policy, depending upon whether, under the circumstances, the representer should be considered as owing to the injured party a duty to use proper care. At the present stage of legal evolution such a duty is usually not recognized (and therefore a negligent misrepresenter is not liable for damages), unless the misrepresentation involves either an unrea-

Example. Through a jeweler's carelessness, a clock in his window labeled "Correct Time" is thirty minutes slow. A person relies on the clock and misses an important appointment (or misses a train or the like) and sustains a loss. The jeweler would not be liable. □

* * *

Example. Through a publisher's carelessness, information given in a newspaper is erroneous (but not defamatory). A person sustains a loss through relying on such information. The publisher would not be liable. □

* * *

Example. An accountant was engaged by a businessman to conduct a complete audit of the latter's business and to submit a report to the businessman. Because of the accountant's carelessness, his audit report inaccurately pictured the business as being in good financial condition when actually it was practically insolvent. The businessman showed the audit report to a bank and obtained a substantial loan. When the businessman became insolvent and unable to repay the loan, the bank investigated, discovered the inaccuracy of the audit report and sued the accountant for the amount of the loan.

The accountant would not be liable to the bank. If an informant's carelessness does not threaten possible bodily injury, it is usually not considered sound policy to hold the careless informant liable to an unlimited number of persons for an infinite variety of kinds and amounts of money or property loss.

If an accountant's misstatement is intentional or reckless (as, for example, when he certifies something as true of his own knowledge although he fails to make an investigation) courts have held the accountant liable to a third party for money loss sustained in relying on the erroneous audit. □

* * *

Example. A manufacturer engaged a boiler inspector to inspect the factory's steam boiler. The inspector was careless in his inspection and gave to the manufacturer a report inaccurately certifying the boiler as safe to a certain pressure. Shortly afterwards, while under pressure much less than that certified as safe, the boiler exploded, injuring a homeowner who resided near the factory. The injured homeowner sued the boiler inspector.

Since the inspector's carelessness threatened a foreseeable risk of bodily injury to third persons, the court held the boiler inspector liable to the injured homeowner, both for bodily injury and also for property damage. □

sonable risk of bodily harm, or a contract obligation to give information to the injured party.

2. Rescission. Regardless of whether or not the represener would be liable for damages, the misled party will usually have the right to rescind the contract and recover all that he paid or gave, if the misrepresented fact was at all material in his deciding to enter into the contract; the represener should not be permitted to retain a benefit obtained through a mistake which he has induced.

D. Innocent Misrepresentations

An innocent misrepresentation differs from a negligent misrepresentation in that not only does the represener honestly believe the truth of the fact he represents or expresses, but also his belief is reasonable. Nevertheless, since the representation is not true, it is classed as a misrepresentation. Again a distinction is made between the two standard misrepresentation remedies.

1. Affirmance and Recovery of Damages. A person who makes an innocent misrepresentation is not guilty of wrongdoing and has no tort liability for damages, although—as is discussed in the next chapter—the expresser may under certain circumstances have a contract (breach of warranty) liability for damages.

2. Rescission. If the misrepresented fact is at all material to the contract the misled person usually has the right to cancel the contract; the representer should not be permitted to retain the benefit of the other party's mistake when the representer, however innocently, has caused that mistake. Note, however, that the qualification in regard to certain written contracts, discussed in Chapter 9 applies here; under the circumstances indicated in that discussion, a misled person may have no right to cancel at all.

III. Duress

Under sufficient torture, most people can be induced to agree to practically anything. Obviously an agreement obtained through wrongful pressure (duress) should not be considered as legally enforceable. On the other hand, it is equally obvious that *every* type of pressure should not be condemned and considered as sufficient reason to excuse a person from an agreement which he is thereby induced to make. Most people live under a variety of economic and social pressures which shape, direct, or influence their conduct. Only if the pressure to which a person is subjected is *wrongful* will it constitute duress.

If an agreement is obtained under duress, it is not enforceable. The victim of the duress can avoid (that is cancel or disaffirm) any such agreement, and he can also recover whatever he has been forced to pay or give provided he

paid more than he actually owed. As to this proviso even though a payment is obtained by duress, a debtor cannot recover his payment if it is made for a definite, undisputed, legally enforceable obligation. Permitting recovery of such a payment would accomplish nothing; the creditor could still enforce his claim and reobtain the amount paid. However even if the debtor is for this reason unable to recover the amount he is forced to pay, he can still recover damages for any tort the creditor may commit in wrongfully inducing the payment.

The word "pressure" in reference to duress means any act or threatened act which causes a person to agree to a proposition to which he otherwise would not have agreed. Pressure which is considered as wrongful usually involves either (1) personal violence, (2) criminal prosecution, or (3) interference with property or contract rights.

A. Personal Violence

Actual or threatened violence either to the person who is thus induced to enter into an agreement, or to a close relative of his, is clearly wrongful pressure.

B. Criminal Prosecution

Sometimes a person is induced to enter into an agreement because of threats that he or a close relative will be criminally prosecuted. The criminal law is for the protection of society as a whole. In a few exceptional situations, criminal proceedings may properly be threatened to assist the collection of civil claims. Except for such situations, an individual who uses or threatens to use the criminal process to induce settlement of a civil claim, is misusing the criminal process, and thereby exerting wrongful pressure or duress. Threatening criminal proceedings for personal gain would seem to be a misuse of the criminal process (except for the situations noted), regardless of the guilt or innocence of the threatened

Example. A landlord, owner of a house in Philadelphia, leased it to a tenant for one year at a yearly rental of $6,000, payable in monthly installments of $500 on the first of each month. In the latter part of the leasehold year, the tenant fell behind in his rental payments. He began paying smaller amounts on account whenever he was able, but he failed to keep an accurate record of his payments. A few days before the expiration of the leasehold year, the tenant went to the landlord to make another partial payment on his overdue rent obligation. When the tenant told the landlord that he intended to move the following day, the landlord demanded that the entire balance of overdue rent be paid immediately and asserted that the amount still owed was $1,500. When the tenant replied that he was unable to pay the entire sum, the landlord asked the tenant to sign a one-year note for $1,500. The landlord threatened that if the tenant refused to sign, the landlord would have all of the tenant's household belongings seized the following morning before the tenant could move out. As the landlord knew, the tenant's wife had been sick for some time. The tenant signed the note because of the landlord's threatened action and its possible adverse effect on his wife's health. When the tenant failed to pay the note upon its maturity, the landlord sued for $1,500, the amount of the note. The landlord could, of course, recover whatever amount of rent was still due; the question raised was whether the landlord could recover the specific amount of the note.

Under the common law remedy for overdue rent, a landlord has the right, without a prior lawsuit, to seize goods on the premises and have them sold in order to secure the rental money due him. Since the landlord was merely threatening to do what he had the legal right to do, he was not exerting wrongful pressure. His demand that the tenant sign the note before moving his household effects from the premises was not oppressive, not an abuse of the landlord's rights, and therefore not duress. The note could be enforced under common law.

person. However, courts in some states hold that such a threat is duress only if the threatened person is actually innocent of the crime for which imprisonment is threatened.

In addition to the risk that his threat constitutes duress, there are further reasons for a creditor to be extremely wary (and to seek legal advice) before threatening criminal proceedings in order to induce a civil settlement. By making such a threat, a creditor may himself incur a civil liability for the tort of malicious prosecution, and he may incur criminal liability for extortion and/or for compounding a crime. A creditor's attempt to collect by threatening to accuse his debtor of a crime has been held by courts in some states to constitute the crime of extortion or blackmail, even though the debt involved is definite, undisputed, and past due, and even though the debtor is actually guilty of the crime which the creditor threatens to expose. As to the possible offense of compounding a crime: a creditor is guilty of this offense when he agrees to accept something of value for stifling information concerning the "compounded" crime.

C. Interference with Property or Contract Rights

Taking, retaining, or injuring a person's property or threatening to do so:

1. Is wrongful if done without legal process or right. Interfering with another's property without legal process or right is clearly wrongful; it is tortious and frequently criminal;

2. Is wrongful if done under legal process or right but in such a way or under such circumstances as to constitute a misuse of the process or right. A claimant who threatens an or-

Example. A corporation's business included dealing in trading-stamp books. The treasurer's daughter was employed by the corporation as a clerk. One day the treasurer was called to the office of the corporation's president where he found, in addition to the president, the corporation's lawyer, and three directors.

The lawyer told the treasurer that his daughter was accused of stealing trading-stamp books. After some discussion the lawyer demanded $2,500 from the treasurer as settlement for his daughter's theft. After further discussion, the lawyer reduced his demand to $1,500 and said that if the treasurer failed to pay within a week his daughter would be arrested and put in jail. The demand and warning were repeated during the week. The treasurer was considerably upset and agitated for the next few days, and was seen actually to be crying at various times. During the week the treasurer paid $200, and by the end of the week an additional $500 which he obtained by borrowing on his life insurance. For the $800 balance the treasurer signed a promissory note. When the note came due, the treasurer refused to pay and asserted that his signature had been obtained through duress.

Some courts have said that vague, indefinite references to the possibility of arrest will usually not constitute duress. In the case upon which this example is based,[7] although criminal action had not been started, the threat was clear that such an action would immediately result if the treasurer failed to make the demanded settlement. The court held that the note was signed under duress and therefore was not enforceable against the treasurer. □

7. *Ortt v. Schwartz,* 62 Pa. Super. 70 (1916).

dinary lawsuit is bringing some pressure on the other party to induce him to settle or compromise in order to avoid the various detrimental results (expense, inconvenience, and adverse publicity) which frequently accompany a lawsuit, even a lawsuit which the defendant ultimately wins. Such pressure is not duress. Even greater pressure is exerted if the lawsuit is the unusual type which can be initiated by attaching some of the defendant's property at the start of the lawsuit, as, for example, when the lawsuit is initiated in the state where the property is situated, and the defendant is a nonresident of that state. This pressure is usually not duress, even though the plaintiff attempts to induce a settlement by securing a court attachment of the defendant's property in an amount which clearly exceeds what is reasonably necessary for the plaintiff to pursue his proper legal remedies. Usually a grossly excessive attachment does not of itself constitute duress, because the de-

fendant is considered sufficiently protected by his usual legal remedy, namely applying for a release from the attachment. However if a plaintiff deliberately has a grossly excessive attachment made when the defendant has insufficient time to secure relief through legal process, when any such delay will result in irreparable loss to the defendant, the plaintiff will be considered guilty of misusing the legal process and exerting wrongful pressure.

Sometimes after a contract has been formed, one party attempts to force the other to agree to an amendment by threatening to breach the contract if it is not amended. Usually the ordinary legal remedies for breach of contract are considered sufficient to protect the innocent party from any threatened loss. Therefore (and consistent with the general policy of not interfering with the freedom of contract unless clearly necessary), a threat to breach a

Example. For steel previously sold and delivered, the seller (a steel producer) had a claim against the buyer (a steel distributor) for the agreed purchase price. However, because of alleged defects in the shipment, the distributor reasonably disputed the amount of this obligation. To avoid litigation, the parties agreed to compromise the disputed obligation for a lesser sum, which the distributor then fully paid. Sometime afterwards the producer and distributor entered into another contract for the sale of a certain quantity of steel to the distributor, to be shipped by a certain date. The distributor in turn contracted with a refrigerator manufacturer to sell and deliver this steel to him. However, on the date agreed upon for shipment to the distributor, the producer refused to ship unless the distributor would pay the full amount which the producer had claimed in their prior dispute. The producer persisted in his refusal even after the distributor explained that he had already contracted to resell the steel. Because of an unusual demand for steel at the time, there was a reasonable likelihood that the distributor could not obtain steel elsewhere in time to perform his resale contract. Therefore, to obtain the steel he needed for his other contract the distributor, under protest, paid the producer the amount he demanded. After obtaining the steel and filling his resale contract, the distributor sued the producer.

In a somewhat similar case a court held that the producer was guilty of duress and permitted the distributor to recover the additional payment. The case presented these unusual circumstances:

1. The producer's demand was oppressive. Because of the prior compromise agreement, the producer knew that he had no grounds whatsoever for his claim.

2. The producer knew of the distributor's urgent need to obtain prompt shipment in order to avoid liability for substantial damages on his resale contract.

3. The producer knew that it was practically impossible for the distributor to obtain the needed steel elsewhere.

4. At the time he made his involuntary payment the distributor could reasonably fear that his ordinary court remedies would not be adequate to save him from sustaining a substantial loss. ☐

contract is usually not considered wrongful pressure. However, under special circumstances such a threat may be so oppressive that it will be considered as wrongful pressure and therefore duress.

* * *

Problems

1. A builder entered into a written contract with a landowner under which (1) the builder was to construct 90 dwelling houses on the owner's land, according to stated plans and specifications, (2) the buildings were to be completed within one year, and (3) the owner was to pay $26,000 per house payable in stated installments at specified times as the work progressed. Two months later the builder had 50 houses at the point in their construction when, according to the contract, the owner was to pay the builder the first 30 percent of the contract price for each of the 50 houses. On this date the builder received a notice that the owner wished to modify their contract. When the builder refused, the owner refused to make any payment, saying that he would abandon the entire project unless the builder would agree to amend the original contract, reducing to 50 the total number of houses to be built and reducing the total price per house to $25,000. The builder owed subcontractors and suppliers for work already done and faced financial ruin if he could not obtain the amount of money due from the owner under the contract. In order to obtain the needed money, the builder agreed to a written amendment of the original contract. The owner thereupon paid the

installment then due. After completing the construction of the 50 houses and receiving $25,000 per house from the owner, the builder sued the owner for an additional $1,000 for each of the 50 completed houses.

(a) Was there consideration for the amendment to the original contract?

(b) Explain (1) the reasoning (other than lack of consideration) upon which the builder could attempt to collect an additional $50,000, (2) the reasoning upon which the owner could attempt to defend, and (3) which party should be given judgment in the builder's lawsuit for $50,000.

2. D, who owned and operated a certain business, owed various sums of money to a number of creditors, including a debt of $6,000 owed to a local bank. D went through a bankruptcy proceeding under which the bank was paid $500 on its $6,000 claim. Upon completion of the bankruptcy proceeding D obtained a discharge as to all his unpaid debts. (This meant that after such discharge, none of the creditors including the bank had any legal remedy or right to collect from D for any of the unpaid debts incurred before the bankruptcy proceeding.) Shortly after completion of the bankruptcy proceeding, D started a different kind of business in the same community. An official of the bank called on D and said that unless D would sign a note promising to pay the bank the balance of the unpaid debt ($5,500) the bank would consider D an unsatisfactory credit risk and so report in response to any inquiries concerning D's credit. Needing a favorable credit rating to start his new business, D signed a note promising to pay the bank $5,500 within six months. When the note came due, D refused to pay and the bank sued. D's defenses were: lack of consideration, and duress.

(a) Explain whether the first defense was good.

(b) Explain whether the second defense was good.

3. In transcribing her notes, an accountant's secretary erroneously wrote to a prospective client that the per diem charge for a senior accountant

was $25 (instead of $35 which had been dictated to her), and as the accountant had instructed her to do, she then signed the accountant's name and mailed the letter. The client immediately wrote to the accountant engaging him "at the rates specified in your letter." The accountant satisfactorily performed the work and billed the client at the rate of $35 per day. As the client was fully aware at all times, $35 per day was the prevailing rate. Could the accountant collect $35 per day from the client? Explain. (Modified from A.I.C.P.A., Nov. 38-4.)

4. On June 6 a New York City importer and seller of souvenir postal cards sent a letter to a Washington, D.C., dealer, enclosing a sample of a new card showing various Washington views. The letter stated that the regular price of the cards was $15 per thousand but that the seller was making a price to jobbers of $10 per thousand. This letter was typed by the seller's stenographer from a circular letter which stated a price of $10 per thousand. She erroneously typed "$1" instead of "$10." The dealer replied by letter: "This is in reply to your letter of the 7th. Your sample card sent us is very good and owing to the price you quote us, the stock must be faulty in some way or your stenographer made a mistake in the price. If the stock is good and the price correct as quoted, we will take several thousand." The seller looked up a copy of the circular letter from which the letter sent to the dealer had been typed (no carbon copy of the letter sent having been retained) and replied by letter that the cards were first class in every respect, that they were being sold at cost, and that the seller would guaranty them in every respect. On receipt of this letter, the dealer wrote ordering "25,000 cards as per sample at price quoted in your letter of the 7th." The seller shipped the ordered cards and mailed a bill to the dealer, billing the cards at $10 per thousand. The dealer received the cards the following day, unpacked them and placed them on his shelves. Later the same day the dealer received the bill and immediately wrote: "We have just received your bill for postal cards and return it for correction. The price of these cards is $1 instead of $10 as you bill them. We refer to your let-

ter of the 7th when you sent us sample and price." The seller replied: "There is evidently an error some place. The price of the cards as quoted you was $10 per thousand and not $1. The import duty alone on these cards costs us $2.25 per thousand, and you can readily understand that it would be impossible for us to sell them at any such price as $1 per thousand. If the price of $10 per thousand is not satisfactory, we request that you send us the cards immediately. Kindly return to us the letter in which you state that you are quoted $1 per thousand." The dealer refused to return the cards and tendered $25 plus shipping charges as payment in full. The seller refused and sued for $250. Explain (1) the reasoning upon which the seller might attempt to collect, (2) the reasoning upon which the dealer might attempt to defend, and (3) which party should be given judgment.

5. On June 13 R. Roger, a retailer in Chicago, telegraphed M. Martin, a manufacturer in New York City, "I can use one hundred children's and juniors' dresses at close-out price." The same day M gave to the telegraph once in New York for transmission to R, the following telegram, "To R. Roger, Chicago. Can ship two hundred junior dresses in linen, silkette, dotted plain and fancy voile at $2.75 net, also six dozen children's dresses, cotton shantungs, voile, poplins, and linens at $16.50 net dozen, advise all close-out prices wonderful opportunity for a big sale. (signed) M. Martin." Because of negligence in transmission, the telegram delivered to R read as to the first price "twenty seventy-five net" instead of $2.75. R assumed that this meant $20.75 per dozen, and on the same day wired M, "Send entire lot of dresses as per your telegram." On the next day M shipped the described dresses to R and mailed an invoice calculated at $2.75 for each junior dress. Two days later R wired M, "Invoice received does not agree with your telegram of the 13th, will not accept merchandise unless billed as bought wire answer."

(a) Explain the legal effect of each telegram.

(b) Was there a contract between the parties, and if so what were the terms? Explain.

6. On October 3, S. Smith of New York City sent to B. Brown of Chicago a letter which, under the circumstances, constituted an offer to sell to B certain described goods at a stated price. Receiving the letter on October 5, B immediately dispatched a telegram accepting the offer. The message B gave to the telegraph office in Chicago was addressed to S and read: "Your offer of October 3 accepted. (signed) B. Brown." Through negligence of the telegraph company, the message was garbled in transmission so that the telegram delivered to S in New York on October 5 read: "Your offer of October 3 rejected. (signed) B. Brown." After S sold the goods to another purchaser, the above facts were discovered, and B sued S for damages for breach of contract. Explain (1) the reasoning upon which B might attempt to collect, (2) the reasoning upon which S might attempt to defend, and (3) which party should be given judgment.

7. S sold to B ten shares of stock of the Carter Corporation for $1,360. At the time of the sale, the books of the corporation showed that the shares of stock, which were originally issued at the par value of $100 per share, had a book value of $136 per share. S and B assumed that the true condition of the corporation was accurately described in the books. Unknown to them at that time, some of the corporation's employees had kept the books in such a manner as to conceal defalcations of which they were guilty; actually the assets of the corporation at the time of the sale were so depleted that the stock was worth only $60 per share. Upon discovering these facts a month after the sale, B offered to return the stock to S and demanded return of his purchase price. S refused and B sued to rescind. At the trial S proved that he had made no representations and was not guilty of any fraud. Explain (1) the reasoning upon which B might attempt to recover, (2) the reasoning upon which S might attempt to defend, and (3) which party should be given judgment.

8. The owner of a plot of land contracted with a builder for construction of an office building on the owner's land according to certain stated specifications, at a cost of $190,000. A few days later

and before any work had been done under the contract, the builder discovered that he had made a $15,000 error in his calculations. Could the builder have his contract rescinded because of this mistake? Explain. (Modified from A.I.C.P.A., May 51-4.)

9. S owned a stationery business which for a number of years had earned a net profit of $6,000. By falsely stating that the net profit had been $20,000, S induced B to purchase the business. When B discovered the true facts, he sued S to rescind the contract. At the trial, S conclusively proved that if B had made inquiries of other persons or if B had used ordinary diligence, he could have discovered the truth. For whom should judgment be given? Explain. (Modified from A.I.C.P.A., May 31-3.)

10. S was the secretary of a corporation that had been in existence for a number of years, and was duly authorized to solicit subscriptions for unissued capital stock, the par value of which was $100 per share. On July 1, S induced B to subscribe for 100 shares at a total price of $50 per share by telling B (1) that the corporation's gross sales for that July were certain to exceed $40,000, (2) that the certificate of incorporation expressly empowered the corporation to conduct certain activities, and (3) that B would not be liable to the corporation or to any other person or corporation for any amount in excess of the subscription price of $50 per share. B agreed to pay for the stock on the following September 1. On the following August 16, however, B ascertained that the gross sales for the previous July had been slightly less than $10,000, and that the certificate of incorporation did not grant the corporate power stated by S. Also, B was informed by his attorney that according to law, if a corporation should become insolvent, any person to whom par value stock was issued for less than par value can be required to pay to the corporation for the benefit of creditors the difference between what he paid for his stock and its par value. Could B immediately cancel his subscription agreement? Explain. (Modified from A.I.C.P.A., Nov. 37-9.)

11. B, a violin expert, ascertained that S owned an old violin of famous make, worth many thousands of dollars. In talking with S, B found that the violin had been in S's family for many years but that S had no knowledge of its true value. After some persuasion and by offering what to S seemed an excessive price ($350), B succeeded in buying the instrument. Later S learned the true facts and, tendering return of the purchase price, sued B to recover the violin .

(a) Was S entitled to judgment against B? Explain.

(b) Other facts remaining the same, assume that B was not an expert and was unaware of the actual value of the violin until after buying it. Would this change the answer given in Part (a) of this problem? Explain. (Modified from A.I.C.P.A., May 29-8.)

12. As B was well aware, his business had become insolvent. However, B hoped to earn sufficient profit to restore the business to solvency if he could operate for another month or so. B ordered certain goods from S at a stated price, the terms of payment being 2/10 net 30, and S shipped the goods. At no time did B make any statements to S concerning his financial condition. After a month the business was hopelessly insolvent and a receiver was appointed by the court to take over and liquidate the assets of the business. Included among the assets were the goods S had sold and delivered to B. S realized that if he filed a claim along with all of B's other creditors, he would receive only a fraction of what was due him. Since S had not retained title or an interest in the goods, he had no right to repossess them. However, if he could cancel the contract, he could reclaim the goods. S therefore notified the receiver that he rescinded the sale because of fraud and wished to take back the goods. The receiver refused and S sued. Explain (1) the reasoning upon which S might attempt to cancel and recover possession of the goods, (2) the reasoning upon which the receiver might attempt to defend, and (3) which party should be given judgment.

13. In December, the owner of a nightclub was solicited for advertising by an agent who represented the publisher of a weekly magazine known as *Nightlife*. When the owner expressed reluctance to obligate himself for a year's advertising, the agent said that the contract form permitted an advertiser to cancel at will. Relying upon the agent's statement, and without reading the agent's printed order form, the owner signed a subscription for advertising in 52 weekly issues at $ 15 per issue. The printed order form stated, "Oral agreements will not be recognized," and contained no provision regarding cancellation. The publisher accepted the subscription and the advertising began in the January 1 issue. In February the owner told the publisher that he wished to cancel the advertising. When the publisher objected, the owner told the publisher of what the agent had said. This was the first that the publisher knew of the agent's statement. The publisher explained that the agent had no authority to say that advertising contracts could be cancelled, but offered that if the owner would continue to advertise, the publisher would release him from the written contract if the owner was still dissatisfied, and the owner could then terminate the advertising at will. The owner agreed and continued to pay for advertising until April, when he notified the publisher to cancel his advertising for the remainder of the year. The publisher refused to permit cancellation, and sued the owner for damages. The owner raised two defenses: (1) that he was induced to sign the December contract through the agent's fraud and (2) that the December contract was superseded by the February agreement under which the publisher had said that the owner could cancel at will. Explain (1) the reasoning upon which the publisher could attempt to answer the first defense, (2) the reasoning upon which the publisher could attempt to answer the second defense, and (3) which party should be given judgment in the lawsuit.

14. S, for many years, owned and operated a used car lot from which he sold used cars. On January 1, 1982, S purchased, sight unseen, a used 1975 Chevrolet sedan from D for $400. On January 2, 1982, B saw the same automobile on S's lot and asked S if it was in good condition. Although S had not had time to inspect the car, he told B that it was in good condition and that it was for sale for $750. B paid S $750, drove the car from S's lot and on January 3, 1982, discovered that the entire body was nearly rusted through from underneath. Could B return the car to S and demand his money back?

15. Master Corporation, a radio and television manufacturer, invited Darling Discount Chain to examine several odd lots of discontinued models and make an offer for the entire lot. The odd lots were segregated from the regular inventory but inadvertently included 15 current models. Darling was unaware that Master did not intend to include the 15 current models in the group. Darling made Master an offer of $9,000 for the entire lot, which represented a large discount from the normal sales price. Unaware of the error, Master accepted the offer. Master would not have accepted had it known of the inclusion of the 15 current models. If Darling sued Master for breach of contract after Master refused to deliver, would Master have a good defense? (Modified from A.I.C.P.A., Nov., 78-7.)

Writings: Requirements and Evidence

Writings: Requirements and Evidence

ORAL AGREEMENTS are, as a general rule of law, as valid and enforceable as written agreements. Verbal contracts do, however, suffer from the practical problem of being difficult to prove. Because of this, and other policy considerations, some types of contracts are required, by *statutes of frauds*, to be in writing or evidenced by a written memorandum. All other contracts may, at the parties' choice, be reduced to writing as a practical expedient. If a contract is reduced to writing either voluntarily or because required by law, evidence of prior or contemporaneous statements may be excluded from a case by operation of the *parol evidence rule*.

I. Statutes of Frauds

The term "statutes of frauds" is a generic term for a number of statutes, which have as their purpose protecting persons from being unjustly deprived of their rights through false testimony. The need for protection is great. Just how frequently the testimony of witnesses is inaccurate or even completely wrong comes as a considerable surprise to many people. A brief discussion of the fallibility of witnesses, therefore, will be quite helpful.

Most of the uncertainty regarding the outcome of lawsuits is the result of uncertainty concerning the disputed facts of the cases. If conflicting evidence of equal credibility is presented in a lawsuit, it will often be impossible to predict what the court will decide to be the true fact situation. Actually the expression "true fact situation" is a misnomer. As has been quipped, the true facts are known only to God, and He is reserving judgment until a later time. When facts are disputed, the outcome of a lawsuit depends upon the facts that can be satisfactorily proven, rather than on the abstract, elusive notion of a "true" fact situation. Lawyers frankly admit that a person's case is no stronger than his proofs. As Judge Jerome Frank has written:

> The facts of a case, remember, are not what actually happened but, at best, what the trial courts says it thinks happened. [1]

Evidence consisting of a document or some other tangible item gives relatively little difficulty. Usually, however, most of the evidence in a case will consist of the testimony of persons. Sometimes when there are no impartial witnesses, a litigant's own testimony is all the evidence he has; and the testimony of one litigant may conflict with the testimony of the other. If testimony is conflicting, the court (jury, or judge if trial is without a jury) must make the best guess it can as to what the actual facts are.

Because the outcome of most lawsuits is based largely on oral testimony, the courts and honest litigants are to a great extent at the mercy of clever, convincing liars. Perjury (tes-

---

1. Jerome Frank, COURTS ON TRIAL (Princeton, N.J.: Princeton U. P., 1949); Atheneum paperback ed., 1963 p. 326.

tifying falsely under oath) is a serious offense, it is a grave moral wrong, and its punishment is severe. Unfortunately, moral restraints are insufficient for a number of people; if they think they can "get away with it," they will lie without hesitation. Very often they *do* get away with it. Society must necessarily make criminal convictions of perjurers quite difficult to obtain. Otherwise the entire trial system would be fatally throttled, because honest witnesses would be afraid to testify for fear of retaliation in the form of perjury prosecutions, however unjustified. Therefore, merely because in a civil dispute the court decides that the facts are different from the testimony of one party does not mean that the party who was not believed can automatically be found guilty of perjury. To convict a person of perjury requires proof not only that he testified falsely but also that he *knew* his testimony was false. For the further protection of honest witnesses, the law usually requires evidence of two witnesses in order to prove perjury or the evidence of one witness plus additional circumstances indicating perjury. And since criminal guilt is in issue, the evidence must be sufficient to leave no reasonable doubt of guilt.

Although perjurers have been soundly cursed as serious obstructions to the fair operation of any judicial system, many legal scholars believe that an even greater obstacle to the determination of truth is the honestly mistaken witness, so often present in lawsuits. As Judge Frank has written:

> Sir William Eggleston, a noted lawyer . . . expresses the opinion that "no witness can be expected to be more than 50 percent correct, even if perfectly honest and free from preconception."
>
> The axiom or assumption that, in all or most trials, the truth will out, ignores, then, the several elements of subjectivity and chance. It ignores perjury and bias; ignores the false impression made on the judge or jury by the honest witness who seems untruthful because he is frightened in the courtroom or because he is irascible or overscrupulous or given to exaggeration. It ignores the mistaken witness who honestly and convincingly testifies that he remembers acts or conversations that happened quite differently than he narrates them in court. It neglects, also, the dead or missing witness without whose testimony a crucial fact cannot be brought out, or an important opposing witness cannot be successfully contradicted. Finally it neglects the missing or destroyed letter, or receipt, or cancelled check.[2]

Another legal scholar has written:

> Once the evidence is received, there is the difficult problem of analyzing it and determining its weight. There are legal rules which act as a check, but the task of sifting truth from falsehood, of inferring the known from the unknown, is determined mainly by the common sense, experience, and subtlety of the tribunal.... The fallibility of human testimony is a well-recognized fact today. Apart altogether from perjury and the unconscious twist to our recollection which bias gives, great inaccuracies exist even in the evidence of disinterested third parties.... Scientific research into the nature of the eye has shown how comparatively easy it is for vision to be mistaken; lack of observation and faulty memory add to the difficulties. Experiments by criminologists have shown the high percentage of error in the reports of a class of students witnessing an unexpected incident.... In the hands of an experienced practitioner, cross-examination is a valuable weapon to sift out the truth, but it cannot always be relied on to defeat either a skillful perjurer, or one who has formed a wrong conclusion as to what he saw and with honest stubbornness sticks to his story.[3]

Professor Hugo Munsterberg, one-time Harvard psychology professor, was one of the leaders in proposing that the courts seek the help of psychology in evaluating the tes-

---

2. *Op. cit.*, 18, 20.
3. Paton, A Textbook of Jurisprudence, 2d ed., (London: Oxford U. P., 1951), pp. 487 488.

timony of witnesses. In his book, On the Witness Stand, Professor Munsterberg describes numerous instances of mistaken observation and recollection, including a dramatic incident deliberately staged as a complete surprise during a scientific association meeting of about forty jurists, psychologists, and physicians. Not only were there numerous omissions in the forty written reports by the "eye witnesses," but,

> . . . there were only six among the forty which did not contain positively wrong statements; in twenty-four papers up to ten percent of the statements were free inventions, and in ten answers—that is, in one-fourth of the papers,—more than ten percent of the statements were absolutely false, in spite of the fact that they all came from scientifically trained observers.... The scientific commission which reported the details of the inquiry came to the general statement that the majority of the observers omitted or falsified about half of the processes which occurred completely in their field of vision.[4]

And Professor Munsterberg himself willingly confessed to the same fallibility, writing:

> Last summer I had to face a jury as witness in a trial. While I was with my family at the seashore my city house had been burglarized and I was called upon to give an account of my findings against the culprit whom they had caught with a part of the booty. I reported under oath that the burglars had entered through a cellar window, and then described what rooms they had visited. To prove, in answer to a direct question, that they had been there at night, I told that I found drops of candle wax on the second floor. To show that they intended to return, I reported that they had left a large mantle clock, packed in wrapping paper, on the dining room table. Finally, as to the amount of clothes they had taken, I asserted that the burglars did not get more than a specified list which I had given the police.

Only a few days later I found that every one of these statements was wrong. They had not entered through the window, but had broken the lock of the cellar door; the clock was not packed by them in wrapping paper, but in a tablecloth; the candle droppings were not on the second floor, but in the attic; the list of lost garments was to be increased by seven more pieces; and while my story under oath spoke always of two burglars, I do not know that there was more than one. How did all these mistakes occur? . . .

Of course, I had not made any careful examination of the house. I had rushed in from the seashore as soon as the police notified me, in the fear that valuable contents of the house might have been destroyed or plundered. When I saw that they had treated me mildly, inasmuch as they had started in the wine cellar and had forgotten under its genial influence, on the whole, what they had come for, I had taken only a superficial survey. That a clock was lying on the table, packed ready to be taken away, had impressed itself clearly on my memory; but that it was packed in a tablecloth had made evidently too slight an impression on my consciousness. My imagination gradually substituted the more usual method of packing with wrapping paper, and I was ready to take an oath on it until I went back later, at the end of the summer vacation. In the same way I got a vivid image of the candle droppings on the floor, but as, at the moment of perception, no interest was attached to the peculiar place where I saw them, I slowly substituted in my memory the second floor for the attic, knowing surely from strewn papers and other disorder that they had ransacked both places. As to the clothes, I had simply forgotten that I had put several suits in a remote wardrobe; only later did I find it empty. My other two blunders clearly arose under the influence of suggestion. The police and every one about the house had always taken as a matter of course that the entrance was made by a cellar window, as it would have been much more difficult to use the locked doors. I had thus never examined the other hypothesis, and yet it was found later that they did succeed in removing the lock of a door. And

---

4. Hugo Munsterberg, ON THE WITNESS STAND (New York: Clark Boardman, Ltd., 1908); reprint, 1933, p. 52.

finally, my whole story under oath referred to two burglars, without any doubt at the moment. The fact is, they had caught the gentleman in question when he, a few days later, plundered another house. He then shot a policeman, but was arrested, and in his room they found a jacket with my name written in it by the tailor. That alone gave a hint that my house had also been entered; but from the first moment he insisted that there had been two in this burglary and that the other man had the remainder of the booty. The other has not been found . . . but I never heard any doubts as to his existence, and thus, in mere imitation, I never doubted that there was a companion, in spite of the fact that every part of the performance might just as well have been carried out by one man alone; and, after all, it is not impossible that he should lie as well shoot and steal.

In this way, in spite of my best intentions, in spite of good memory and calm mood, a whole series of confusions, of illusions, of forgetting, of wrong conclusions, and of yielding to suggestions were mingled with what I had to report under oath, and my only consolation is the fact that in a thousand courts at a thousand places all over the world, witnesses every day affirm by oath in exactly the same way much worse mixtures of truth and untruth, combinations of memory and of illusion, of knowledge and of suggestion, of experience and wrong conclusions.... Of course, judge and jury and later, the newspaper reader try their best to weigh the evidence. Not every sworn statement is accepted as absolute reality. Contradictions between witnesses are too familiar. But the instinctive doubt refers primarily to veracity. The public in the main suspects that the witness lies, while taking for granted that if he is normal and conscious of responsibility he may forget a thing, but it would not believe that he could remember the wrong thing. The confidence in the reliability of memory is so general that the suspicion of memory illusions evidently plays a small role in the mind of the juryman, and even the cross-examining lawyer is mostly dominated by the idea that a false statement is the product of intentional falsehood.

All this is a popular illusion against which modern psychology must seriously protest. Justice would less often miscarry if all who are to weigh evidence were more conscious of the *treachery of human memory.*[5] [Emphasis added.]

Because of the all-too-frequent presence of deliberate perjurers and of honestly mistaken witnesses, people are constantly warned by their lawyers that all important agreements should be in writing or evidenced by written memoranda.

At a fairly early date (1677) in the development of rules of law, of trial procedure, and of commerce, the English Parliament decided as a matter of policy that perjurers and honestly mistaken witnesses constituted sufficient of a threat to require some remedial action. A statute was passed, entitled "An Act for the Prevention of Frauds and Perjuries" (which is commonly shortened to "Statute of Frauds"). In essence the statute provided that:

1. Certain types of agreements [chiefly, (1) a lease of real estate for more than three years, (2) a transfer or contract to transfer real estate, (3) a promise to pay the debts of another person, (4) an agreement not to be performed within one year from formation] could not be enforced unless put in writing or evidenced by a written memorandum signed by the party transferring or promising.

2. Agreements for the sales of goods for ten pounds sterling or more could not be enforced unless evidenced by a writing signed by the party to be bound by the agreement, or unless the goods or a portion of them were delivered or paid for.

Ever since its adoption and continuing to the present day, the wisdom of statutes of frauds has been the subject of vigorous argument. As one writer has noted:

The appraisals of the Statute's value in modern society range from Llewellyn's "After two centuries and a half the statute stands in

---

5. *Op. cit.,* pp. 39-44.

essence better adapted to our need than when first passed," to Ireton's observation that the Statute "has proved to be ambiguous, archaic, arbitrary, uneven, unwieldy, unnecessary and unjust."[6]

The original statute of frauds accomplished its purpose—preventing false testimony from foisting nonexistent contracts upon courts and honest defendants—by requiring (in most cases) written evidence in order for contracts covered by the statute to be enforced. Many lawyers and judges feel that the statute has generated as many frauds as it prevents, since it affords many persons who no longer wish to perform their contracts an easy escape, merely because the evidence of formation of the contract happens not to satisfy the statute of frauds. This objection to the general philosophy of statutes of frauds is quite persuasive. If a person must have written evidence of the principal details of a contract in order to bring a lawsuit to enforce it, it is in a sense almost like requiring the state to prove an accused guilty beyond a reasonable doubt in order to have him held for trial, when the purpose of the trial itself is to determine whether or not he is guilty beyond a reasonable doubt. In criminal procedure an accused person's rights are satisfied and he can be held for trial if the state presents enough evidence at the preliminary hearing to show reasonable grounds for suspecting him. The modern thinking on statutes of frauds tends to the view that a plaintiff's initiation of a breach-of-contract lawsuit certainly should not be more difficult than the state's initiation of a criminal prosecution. "All that is required," write the authors of the Uniform Commercial Code,[7] "is that the writing [to satisfy the statute of frauds] afford a basis for

believing that the offered oral evidence rests on a real transaction." The modern view as written into the Code applies to sales-of-goods contracts, while the older, more strict view, applies to other types of contracts covered by statutes of frauds.

A. Effect Upon Contracts

The effect of the statute of frauds may generally be likened to a gate across the courtroom door. For certain types of contracts the gate may be kept locked by the defendant; in order to gain entrance to the courtroom and pursue his suit of the alleged contract, the plaintiff must possess the proper key. That key is the written and signed material required by the statute of frauds or presentment of circumstances which allow for exception from the statute's requirements in the particular case. It is important to keep in mind though, that possession of the key does not assure victory in the case, but merely allows the case into the courtroom to be heard. The specific allegations of fact must still be proved and the assertions of law must still be convincing.

In most states the statute of frauds is viewed as a *procedural device* and operates generally in the manner described above. That is, the statute does not prevent the formation of a valid contract but merely allows for a type of procedural disaffirmance by the defendant. In a given case, a defendant can compel, as a condition precedent to plaintiff's suit and as a procedural defense, that the plaintiff satisfy the statute of frauds requirements. Under these circumstances, however, if an oral contract, which should otherwise have been in writing, is fully performed by both parties, no writing is necessary because the parties have, by their behavior, evidenced the existence of a contract. Accordingly, the procedural effect of the statute does not apply to fully performed contracts.

About one-third of the states consider the statute of frauds to be *substantive* in nature, rather than merely procedural. These sub-

---

6. 40 *Cornell L. Q.* 531 (1955), the quoted references being taken from Llewellyn, "What Price Contract? An Essay in Perspective," 40 *Yale L J.* 704 (1931) and Ireton, "Should We Abolish the Statute of Frauds?" 72 U.S. L. Rev. 195 (1938.)

7. Comment to U.C.C. Sec. 2-201.

stantive statutes are identified by language which states that a contract covered by the statute is void or invalid unless the writing requirement is satisfied. As a result, such a statute makes a writing a necessary element of a contract equal in stature to the need for an offer, acceptance, and consideration.

B. General Requirements

1. WRITING

There are two primary requirements of the statute of frauds. One is that there be some written evidence of the transaction, and a second is that the written evidence be signed. It is usually not required that the contract itself be in writing, but merely that there be written documentation of the agreement. The documentation may, in fact, be the entire contract, or it may be a memorandum of the agreement or a collection of correspondence (letters, telegrams, sales slips, order forms, confirmation slips or the like) or a single piece of correspondence.

The statutes which apply to transactions other than for the sale of goods (non-U.C.C. transactions) generally require that the writing must contain the terms sufficient to show an enforceable contract. Such terms should, as a minimum, identify the contracting parties, describe the property or subject of the agreement, and state the price.

Sales of goods transactions are covered by the more liberal Code requirements which state that the written documentation need merely be sufficient to indicate that a contract for sale has been made between the parties. Also, under the Code, the writing is not rendered insufficient nor inadequate because it omits or incorrectly states a term agreed upon; however, under such circumstances, the contract will not be enforceable for a greater quantity of goods than is shown in the writing.

2. SIGNATURE

Often what is required as corroboration is either a written contract or a written memorandum of a contract, signed sometimes by one party, sometimes by both parties. The term "signed" is not restricted in meaning to a manually handwritten signature at the bottom or end of a paper. A valid and binding signature may be typed, printed, or stamped. A printed name on a letterhead may constitute a signature. In general, a name anyplace on the writing, and in any form, is the signature of the one whose name it is if so intended by that person or his authorized agent. Unless required by statute for particular situations, a typed, printed, or stamped signature needs no further authentication. However, as an aid in proving genuineness or authority if either is later questioned, it is wise for a party entering into a contract to request that whoever applies a stamp or uses a document with a typed or printed signature, add his own handwritten signature or initials to aid in later identifying the one making out the writing. Although desirable, witnesses to a signature are not necessary unless required by some special statute. However, if a person unable to write his name signs by making his mark ("X" is a commonly used mark), usually there must be two witnesses to the making of the mark and they must also sign the paper stating that they were witnesses.

C. Applicable Transactions

Practically all states have statutes of frauds covering certain types of contracts. Although varying somewhat in coverage and details, most of the states to some extent follow the pattern of the English Statute of Frauds. Thus the principal types of contracts in which the law requires additional evidence to corroborate a plaintiff's oral testimony in order for the contract to be provable and enforceable can be classified as follows: (1) guaranties of debt, (2) promises in consideration of marriage, (3) contracts for the sale or transfer of real property, (4) contracts not to be performed within one year, and (5) sales of goods.

I. GUARANTIES OF DEBT

Most states have guaranty-of-debt statutes of frauds which usually provide something like the following:

> No action shall be brought to charge a person upon any promise to answer for the debt or default of another person, unless the agreement upon which such action shall be brought, or some memorandum of it, shall be in writing and signed by the party to be charged or by his duly authorized agent.

The agent's authority is usually not required to be in writing.

A guarantor is a person (or business) who agrees to pay a debt which is not primarily his own debt. The one primarily liable for the debt is usually called the principal debtor. A guarantor promises that he will pay the amount of the debt to the principal debtor's creditor if the debtor himself should fail to pay. If the principal debtor does default so that the guarantor is forced to make good on his promise to pay the creditor, the guarantor will succeed to the creditor's rights and in turn be entitled to recover from the principal debtor.

Sometimes the term "guarantor" is used in a narrower sense, in contradistinction to the term "surety." The distinction is a procedural one. A surety promises to pay if the principal debtor *does not* pay when due, and a guarantor (when the term is used in its narrower sense) promises to pay if the principal *cannot* pay. Therefore, to collect from a guarantor (narrower sense) the creditor usually must first sue the debtor, attempt to collect, and by reason of the debtor's insolvency be unsuccessful. In contrast, a creditor has a right to collect from a surety as soon as the principal debtor defaults, without the necessity of first attempting to collect from the debtor. A number of states declare by statute that a person

promising to pay the debt of another is a surety unless the agreement specifies otherwise. The indorser of a check, note, or draft under the Uniform Commercial Code[8] can indicate his intent with respect to this procedural distinction by writing "payment guaranteed," and become a surety, or "collection guaranteed," and become a guarantor in the narrower sense, as distinguished from a surety. In the present discussion, the term guarantor (except when specified otherwise) is used in its broader sense, including both guarantors (in the narrower sense) and sureties.

There must of course be consideration, or a recognized equivalent of consideration (see Chapter 6) in order for a guarantor's promise to be legally enforceable. If a guaranty promise is made either prior to or at the same time the principal debt arises the act of the creditor in extending credit to the debtor is usually the agreed consideration for the guarantor's promise. On the other hand, if a guaranty promise is made after the principal debt is already in existence, separate consideration is necessary, such as the creditor's giving the debtor more time on the debt, or the guarantor's being paid a sum of money for his guaranty promise.

The general philosophy of guaranty-of-debt statutes of fraud is quite sound. Suppose that a seller is claiming a right to recover $500 from a guarantor for certain goods which were sold and delivered to a buyer on thirty days' credit. If the seller were suing the buyer, the fact that the seller delivered the goods to the buyer would tend to corroborate the seller's testimony, showing at least that some transaction involving the delivered goods had occurred between the parties. However, the seller's making a delivery to the buyer is not an act which necessarily involves the guarantor at all. An unpaid seller might conceivably pick any name from the telephone book and

---

8. U.C.C. Sec.. 3-416.

Example. A builder contracted with a landowner to build a house on the latter's lot. A supplier who had previously been extending credit to the builder, refused to make any further deliveries until the builder paid for his prior purchases of materials which he had used in other of construction jobs. The landowner who was well known to the supplier, called him on the telephone and said: "If you will let the builder have the materials he needs for use in the house he is buildingfor me, I'll guaranty his payment for such materials."

Many courts would enforce the oral guaranty. ☐

dishonestly allege that that person had guaranteed the buyer's payment. Since an ordinary guarantor derives no direct benefit from an extension of credit and is not otherwise brought into the picture by the facts, the basic policy of guaranty-of-debt statutes of frauds is to require that a plaintiff have something more than oral testimony and the fact that credit was extended to a debtor, in order to hold a guarantor liable. The statutes uniformly require a signed writing for this purpose. In some guaranty situations, however, special facts are present which afford some corroboration without written evidence. For such special situations, statute-of-frauds protection is unnecessary, and most courts accordingly hold that in such situations the statutes of frauds do not apply. These special situations in which the courts are usually willing to enforce oral promises to pay the debts of other persons include the following:

1. Guarantor Receiving Direct Benefit. If (different from the customary guaranty transaction) the facts in a particular case show that a guarantor himself was directly benefited by the extension of credit to the debtor, this tends to corroborate the creditor's testimony that the guarantor actually did promise to guaranty the debtor's repayment. Under such circumstances oral guaranties have frequently been enforced.

2. **Guarantor Undertaking Direct Obligation.** Sometimes a promisor enters into a contract with a debtor under which (for a certain consideration) the promisor agrees that he will pay an obligation which the debtor owes to some third party. In making such a promise, the promisor is not really guaranteeing the debtor's obligation but rather is undertaking a direct obligation on his own part. Thus the courts in most states hold that while a guaranty-of-debt statute of frauds will apply to a promise which the promisor makes to a *creditor* (promising to pay the debt which the debtor owes to the creditor), the statute does not apply to a promise which the promisor makes to a debtor, to the effect that the promisor will pay the debtor's obligation. The contract between the promisor and the debtor is an independent, third-party-beneficiary contract upon which the creditor can recover (as discussed in Chapter 11), even though the promise is oral.

Similarly, a promisor is considered as undertaking a direct obligation of his own rather than merely guaranteeing another's prior obligation when, at a debtor's request or with his authorization, the promisor makes a promise to a creditor to the effect that the promisor will pay the debtor's obligation out of funds which belong to the debtor and which the promisor has or will acquire for that purpose. For example, suppose a debtor delivers certain goods to a factor with oral instructions to sell the goods and to use the proceeds to pay an obligation which the debtor owes to a certain creditor. If the factor notifies the creditor of the arrangement, and orally assures him that he will pay the debtor's obligation from the proceeds of the sale, the factor is in a sense orally promising the creditor that he will pay the debtor's debt. However, the factor is really promising nothing more than he has already undertaken to do in his agreement with the debtor. The creditor is a third-party beneficiary of the factor-debtor contract and courts in most states hold that the creditor can enforce this contract against the factor.

2. PROMISES IN CONSIDERATION OF MARRIAGE

While a promise to marry another person need not be in writing to be binding, promises concerned with a property settlement or arrangement which is given as a part of an agreement to marry is covered by the statute of frauds.

3. CONTRACTS FOR THE SALE OR TRANSFER OF REAL PROPERTY

When purchases are quite costly, and especially when real estate is purchased, a transfer is usually made in two steps. First the parties enter into a contract by which they agree that at a stated future date the seller will transfer the described property and the buyer will pay the stated price; then later, at the agreed time, they complete the transaction, transferring title and paying the price. In most states neither a contract to transfer real estate nor an actual transfer of real estate will be effective unless evidenced by a written memorandum which identifies or describes the parties, the price, and the real estate involved. In some states the memorandum must be signed by the party against whom an attempt is being made to enforce the agreement—that is, it must be signed by the buyer if the seller is suing to enforce the alleged agreement against the buyer, or it must be signed by the seller if the buyer is suing the seller. In other states the memorandum only needs to be signed by the seller. In such states a seller can enforce an oral land-purchase contract against a buyer, but the buyer cannot enforce the oral agreement against the seller.

In interpreting and applying real estate statutes of frauds, the courts are ever mindful of the reason for the statutes. If a buyer sufficiently relies on a seller's oral transfer or contract to transfer in a way that clearly corroborates the existence of such an agreement, many courts will enforce the agreement against the seller even in the absence of a written memorandum. In defining the limits of this "exception" to the real estate statutes of frauds, the courts weigh principles of fairness and justice on one side against the policy reasons for statutes of frauds on the other side, with some reference to the ancient common law method of transferring real estate—by going on the land and handing the buyer a lump of earth (or some other appropriate symbol) while stating words of transfer. As can be expected in matters of policy, the courts in different states vary somewhat in their opinions as to exactly what conduct will be sufficient to make a seller's oral transfer or contract to transfer enforceable without a writing. In many states, the following conditions must all be present. (1) the terms of the oral contract must be clear and definite, (2) the buyer must take exclusive possession under the agreement, and (3) there must be some additional circumstances making it extremely unfair to the buyer not to enforce the agreement. For example, many courts have held a seller's oral agreement enforceable if (the first two conditions also being present) the buyer has paid the seller the entire purchase price, or the buyer has constructed substantial, permanent improvements on the premises.

Whether a particular case can be brought under the exception will usually be uncertain until litigated. It is, therefore, unwise for a buyer to rely on this exception. He should insist upon having all real estate agreements put in writing and signed by the seller.

The provisions covering real property interests are actually broader in coverage than might at first be surmised from the above statement. Real property interests not only include sale contracts for lands and buildings but also for condominiums and leases for apartments as well as land and buildings. Also included are mortgages, expectant interests and estates, easements, covenants and naturally occurring minerals or vegetation to be transferred in place.

Leases are generally treated somewhat specially.

The usual statute provides in substance:

A lease of real property to extend for not more than three years (the period varies, many statutes saying one year) from the agreement date may be in writing, or may be oral, but a lease to extend for more than the statutory period from the agreement date, to be effective for the full term, must be in writing and signed by the parties or by their agents whose authority must be in writing.

The typical statute also applies to assignments and cancellations of written leases which are for longer than the statutory period.

In many states an oral lease which is to extend for more than the statutory period is considered to be a lease at will during the first year, terminable by either party at any time; after the first year of occupancy, the tenancy usually becomes a year-to-year periodic tenancy. The main features of the latter type of tenancy are:

1. The tenant has the right to occupy for the entire leasehold year. (The leasehold year starts at the time stated in the agreement, and does not necessarily coincide with the calendar year.)

2. The landlord has the right to receive rent for the entire leasehold year.

3. Unless the agreement expressly provides otherwise, the tenancy automatically renews itself for another year and continues to do so, until one party gives the other advance notice that he wishes to terminate the tenancy. The notice must be given a certain time in advance of the end of the current leasehold year; how much in advance is generally regulated by

statutes in the different states and usually varies from one month in some states to three months in others. In some states the automatic renewal upon failure to give advance notice is in favor of the tenant only. In these states if the tenant moves out before expiration of his leasehold year, he has no liability after expiration of the year, even though he gives the landlord no previous notice of his intent to move (unless the agreement expressly requires such notice). In most states, however, either party, landlord or tenant, who wishes to stop the automatic renewal of a year-to-year tenancy must give proper notice to the other.

4. CONTRACTS NOT TO BE PERFORMED WITHIN ONE YEAR

The original English Statute of Frauds provided:

. . . from and after the said fower and twentyeth day of June noe action shall be brought . . . upon any agreement that is not to be performed within the space of one yeare from the making thereof unlesse the agreement upon which such action shall be brought or some memorandum or note thereof shall be in writeing and signed by the partie to be charged therewith or some other person thereunto by him lawfully authorized.

The results of this provision are sometimes as odd as the seventeenth-century spelling. Suppose an oral contract is formed hiring someone for a year and a day. Even though the employment contract would impliedly be subject to the employee's continuing to live, the terms of the contract express no such qualification. By the terms of the contract it is not to be performed within one year and, therefore, if not in writing, the contract would be unenforceable. On the other hand, an oral contract to hire someone for life would be perfectly valid. By its terms it is possible to perform it within one year from the time it is made, since the employee might die at any time. Therefore, even though he continues to live for fifty years longer, the contract would continue to be fully enforceable.

It is understandable that this provision of the original Statute of Frauds has provoked considerable criticism. In fact, while preserving in other more modern statutes most of the effect of the original Statute of Frauds, the English Parliament has repealed the original Statute and by doing so has abandoned any attempt to draw a one-year time-line between oral and written contracts. Some states also make no distinction, but the statutes of frauds in many states still draw the one-year line.

5. SALES OF GOODS

The Uniform Commercial Code contains a statute of frauds section applicable to sales-of-goods contracts, with $500 as the operative amount. A contract for the sale of goods costing less than $500 is enforceable whether proved by written evidence or by uncorroborated oral testimony, but a contract involving a sale of goods for the price of $500 or more requires some sort of corroboration to be enforceable. Under the modern view which the Code follows, any of several different types of corroboration will suffice. The most obvious type of corroboration consists of a written memorandum signed by the alleged promisor (that is, the person against whom an attempt is being made to enforce the alleged contract promise). Under certain conditions a written memorandum signed by the alleged promisee (the party who is attempting to enforce the alleged contract promise) will be sufficient. Other circumstances which show sufficient corroboration in the absence of a written memorandum are: (1) special manufacture, (2) admission in a lawsuit, and (3) payment for or acceptance of goods.

a. Written Corroboration

Signed by the Promisor. For the usual type of written corroboration to be adequate, the Code requires:

. . . some writing sufficient to indicate that a contract for sale has been made between the parties and signed by the party against whom enforcement is sought or by his authorized agent or broker. A writing is not insufficient because it omits or incorrectly states a term agreed upon but the contract is not enforceable under this paragraph beyond the quantity of goods shown in such writing.[9]

As the authors of the Code explain:

Only three definite and invariable requirements as to the memorandum are made by this subsection. First, it must evidence a contract for the sale of goods; second, it must be "signed," a word which includes any authentication which identifies the party to be charged; and third, it must specify a quantity.[10]

Thus the written memorandum need not state other terms of the alleged contract, such as the amount to be paid, method of payment, time and place of delivery, quality of goods, etc. Oral testimony is adequate to prove these terms.

Signed by the Promisee. Recall the well-known adage that a person cannot pull himself up by his own bootstraps. Likewise a person who writes and signs a memorandum usually cannot expect his own signature to prove anything at all against someone else. However, if the nonsigning person sees the memorandum at a time when he could be expected to object if it were not true, his failure to object tends to corroborate the truth of the writing. Under the Code, if a written memorandum is signed by the party who is attempting to enforce an alleged contract, the memorandum is usable against the other party and is sufficient corroboration to satisfy the statute of frauds if *all* of the following conditions are present:

---

9. U.C.C. Sec. 2–201.
10. Comment to U.C.C. Sec. 2-201.

1. Both parties are businessmen acting in their mercantile capacity.
2. The writing was sent to the other party in confirmation of the alleged contract and would constitute sufficient corroboration to satisfy the statute of frauds if the sender were being sued on the alleged contract.
3. The writing was received by the party to whom sent within a reasonable time after formation of the contract (if a letter correctly addressed and stamped is properly mailed, it is presumed to be received by the addressee in due course of time; if the addressee denies receipt, a jury may nevertheless conclude that the letter was received, especially if the envelope bore a return address and was never returned).
4. Within ten days the recipient did not send written objection to the contents of the writing.

It should be emphasized that failure to object under the above conditions merely indicates that *probably* a contract was formed between the parties. It is sufficient corroboration to open the statute-of-frauds gate and permit the plaintiff (the sender of the written memorandum) to enter the courtroom. As the authors of the Code point out:

> The only effect . . . is to take away from the party who fails to answer the defense of the Statute of Frauds; the burden of persuading the trier of fact [the jury or the judge if the trial is held without a jury] that a contract was in fact made orally prior to the written confirmation is unaffected.[11]

b. Corroboration Without Written Memorandum

Special Manufacture. Generally a manufacturer will not undertake the expense of producing something which will be of value to only one particular buyer unless the latter has

actually contracted to buy it. Admittedly this is not conclusive proof that a contract has been formed, but the special manufacture of unique goods tends to indicate that a contract exists. It is sufficient to enable the manufacturer to unlock the statute-of-frauds gate and gain entrance to the court, where he then has the chance to enforce the contract, if he can satisfy the court by oral testimony that such a contract was actually formed. The operative facts for this situation are stated by the Code as follows:

> A contract which does not satisfy the requirements of subsection (1) [which pertains to written memoranda] but which is valid in other respects is enforceable . . . if the goods are to be specially manufactured for the buyer and are not suitable for sale to others in the ordinary course of the seller's business and the seller, before notice of repudiation is received and under circumstances which reasonably indicate that the goods are for the buyer, has made either a substantial beginning of their manufacture or commitments for their procurement....

Note that the Code (like the prior Uniform Sales Act in this respect)[12] does not prescribe a percentage of unsuitability. All that is required is that the goods be "not suitable for sale to others in the ordinary course of the seller's business" with no express reference concerning how much (or little) it might cost to make the goods suitable for others after the buyer repudiates the contract.

Admission in Lawsuit. As the authors of the Code explain:

> If the making of a contract is admitted in court, either in a written pleading, by stipulation or by oral statement before the court, no additional writing is necessary for protection against fraud. Under this section it is no longer possible to admit the contract in court and still treat the Statute [statute of frauds] as a defense. However, the contract is

---

11. Comment to U.C.C. Sec. 2-201.

12. Uniform Sales Act, Sec. 4.

TABLE 9.1 APPLICABILITY OF STATUTE OF FRAUDS REQUIREMENTS

Type of Contract	Requirements	
	Applicable (to)	**Not Applicable (to)**
A. Guarantee of another's debt	1. Agreements of surety or guaranty.	1. Agreements of indemnity. 2. If for primary benefit of guarantor.
B. Consideration of marriage	1. Property agreement as part of consent to marry.	1. Agreement of marriage.
C. Real estate contracts	1. Land, buildings, real property interests. 2. Vegetation and minerals transferred in place. 3. Leases beyond one year.*	1. Severed minerals and vegetation, and cultivated crops. 2. Leases of one year or less.*
D. Contracts to be performed beyond one year from their making	1. Agreements not performable within one year of date made.	1. Agreements possibly performable within one year.
E. Sale of goods contracts	1. Agreements where price is $500 or more.	1. Agreements where price is less than $500. 2. Sec. 2-201 (1) where party to be charged has not signed. 3. Sec. 2-201 (3) (a) special manufacturer. 4. Sec. 2-201(3)(b) admission. 5. Sec. 2-201(3)(e) payment.

* A few states use a longer period.

not thus conclusively established. The admission so made by a party is itself evidential against him of the truth of the facts so admitted and of nothing more....[13]

The plaintiff can go ahead and prove by oral testimony the details of the actual contract between the parties and enforce it, but only for the quantity of goods admitted. Payment for

or Acceptance of Goods. The Code states that a contract is enforceable,

. . . with respect to goods for which payment has been made and accepted or which have been received and accepted. [Goods are "accepted" when they are retained by the buyer in a manner which indicates that he considers them as belonging to him].[14]

13. Comment to U.C.C. Sec. 2-201.

14. U.C.C.Sec. 2-606.

In other words, such conduct of the parties is sufficient indication that a contract exists so that oral testimony can be safely relied upon. Note that the contract is enforceable only as to the portion of goods paid for or accepted. If the subject matter of the contract cannot be apportioned, a part performance is not corroboration and will not make an oral contract enforceable for any quantity.

A summary of the applicability of the statute of frauds requirements is presented in Table 9.1.

D. Contract Modifications

After a contract has been formed, one of the parties will sometimes assert that the parties entered into a later agreement modifying or canceling the original contract. The mere fact that the original agreement was in writing ordinarily will not prevent a later oral change or cancellation, and the later agreement can be proved by oral testimony without any need for corroboration. However, if the original agreement was one to which a statute of frauds applied, the question can be raised as to whether a modification of such a contract need be in writing. The rule is that if an agreement to modification of an existing contract causes the contract as modified to be within the scope of the statute of frauds then the modification must be in writing. On the other hand, if the modification causes a contract previously covered by the statute of frauds to be outside the coverage of the statute after the modification, then the modification need not be in writing. It should be noted that the doctrine of estoppel may be involved where an oral modification is acted upon even though it should have been in writing.

II. Written Contracts not Involving the Statute of Frauds

Although not required by the statute of frauds to be in writing, any contract may be reduced to writing if the parties so desire. There are many practical and legal reasons for wanting to reduce an agreement to writing. Later disputes over what was actually agreed to can be avoided or settled by reference to the written document or, if a lawsuit does develop, proof of the agreement and its terms is easily accomplished. Furthermore, because of legal rules which prevent testimonial proof of contracts by a surviving party against a deceased party, reduction to writing may provide the only means of proving a contract.

A. Agreement as to Effect of Writing

If nothing is said about a written agreement at the time an oral contract is made, no obligation to sign a written agreement devolves upon the parties. Accordingly, even though one party may later try to insist upon the signing of a written document one party's refusal will not affect the validity of the original oral contract. However, if circumstances show that it was intended by the parties that the oral agreement would not be binding until a written contract was signed, the oral agreement will not have a legally binding effect.

B. Death of One Contracting Party

The fact that no statute of frauds applies for many types of contracts reflects the decision of the legislature that, as a matter of policy, the risk of perjured and honestly mistaken testimony is not so great as to justify a general rule declaring such contracts unenforceable unless corroborated. In such situations the only protection a person has against perjured and honestly mistaken testimony is his own

Example. A and B were partners operating a business, A agreeing that all control and management be in B's hands. For the business, B orally contracted for and received labor and materials from S, in the amount of $3,000. B died several months later. A few months after B's death, S presented his claim for $3,000. This was the first that A knew of any contract made with S, and the partnership records did not refer to the contract. S sued A.

S would not be competent to testify to any dealings with B, the decedent. If S could prove his claim by some written memorandum or by the testimony of an impartial witness, S could collect, otherwise not.☐

testimony in rebuttal. If the person has died, the representative of his estate may often be at a disadvantage; the representative may know nothing about an alleged transaction and the decedent of course is no longer available to deny claim made against him. In almost all states the legislatures feel that even in situations not otherwise coming under a statute of frauds, if one contracting party had died, the risk of false claims is sufficiently great to require relief. In most states the relief consists of a rule barring the surviving party from testifying. The typical statute can be summarized as follows:

> Where any party to an agreement or contract is dead (or has been adjudged a lunatic), any surviving or remaining party to such an agreement or contract, or any other person whose interest shall be adverse to the right of the decedent (or lunatic) party, shall not be a competent witness to any matter occurring before the death of said party (or the adjudication of his lunacy). [Usually such statutes do not apply to litigation involving the rights of partners among themselves.]

The effect of such a statutory provision, sometimes referred to as a *deadman's statute*, is that if death has closed the mouth of one party, the law will close the mouth of the other party. If, without using his own testimony or the testimony of any other person with an interest adverse to the decedent's, the surviving party can prove the existence and terms of a contract, he can enforce it against the decedent's estate, otherwise not. One

method of proof allowable would be presentation of a written contract signed by the decedent.

C. "Written Modifications" Provisions

If a contract or its modification does not involve the statute of frauds the general rule exists that the contract, even though written, can always be modified by oral agreement. In order to prevent such oral modifications, people sometimes insert provisions in written contracts which, by their wording, purport to require that all modifications must be in writing. This situation is treated one way under common law principles and another way by the Code.

After a contract has been formed, one of the parties will sometimes assert that the parties entered into a later agreement modifying or canceling the original contract. The mere fact that the original agreement was in writing ordinarily will not prevent a later oral change or cancellation and the later agreement can be proved by oral testimony without any need for corroboration. However, if the modified agreement is one to which a statute of frauds applies, the statute would have to be satisfied for the alleged later agreement to be enforceable.

The reasoning in Part 2 of the preceding example is indisputably sound legal theory. However, businesses frequently include restrictive provisions in their contracts (to the

Example. A landlord and tenant signed a written agreement, leasing certain described premises to the tenant for six months, at a monthly rental of $100 payable in advance on the first of each month. Four months later, they orally agreed to shorten the total duration of the lease to five months, and at the end of the fifth month the tenant moved out. The landlord thereupon changed his mind about the modification and sued the tenant for the sixth month's rent.

Part 1. Society believes that persons should be fairly free to make whatever contracts they wish, even several contracts which, in succession, cancel or modify their previous contracts. Therefore, if the original six-month lease had been oral, certainly no rule of law would prevent the parties from later orally changing it to a five-month lease. (Note that the duration of the lease is too short for the ordinary type of statute of frauds to apply and require a written memorandum.) Merely because the original six-month lease was in writing would be no reason to deny to the parties the same freedom of contract. Therefore so long as they actually agreed, the change from a six-month lease to a five-month lease would be effective, whether oral or in writing

Part 2. Suppose that the original written lease also contained the following provision: "This lease agreement cannot be added to, altered, or rescinded except by written agreement signed by both parties hereto."

As pointed out in Part 1 above, the mere fact that an agreement is put in writing is no reason to prohibit its later oral modification. If therefore parties have both the power and the right to orally modify their previous written agreement, then their oral modification agreement will automatically modify or rescind that portion of their written agreement which states that it cannot be orally modified. For this reason the rule developed at common law that the quoted restrictive provision is ineffective; the parties could still validly change the lease to a five-month lease by their later *oral* agreement.☐

effect that no changes can be made except by written memoranda), and do so in order to avoid the risk of litigation and possible loss, should one party later dishonestly allege that an oral modification was made. A policy question is thus raised—should the law continue to recognize full freedom of contract, including the freedom to change as well as to make contracts, or instead should the law give effect to the assumption of businesses that a restriction on oral modifications means something? For sales-of-goods contracts the authors of the Code feel that the latter choice is the better policy. In effect, therefore, the Code permits parties to add to the ordinary statute-of-frauds situations by writing their own statute of frauds in regard to any future modifica-

tion of a written sales-of-goods contract. To accomplish this, the Code states:

> A signed agreement which excludes modification or rescission except by a signed writing cannot be otherwise modified or rescinded, but except as between merchants such a requirement on a form supplied by the merchant must be separately signed by the other party. [15]

Thus for sales-of-goods contracts, if the original agreement is in writing and expressly states that it cannot be amended or canceled except by a signed writing, any later attempt to change the original contract by oral agreement will not be effective, even if the price is less than $500.

---

15. U.C.C. Sec. 2-209.

TABLE 9.2 ADMISSIBILITY OF EVIDENCE UNDER PAROL EVIDENCE RULE

Timing of Statement Offered in Relation to Written Contract	Evidence	
	Oral	Written
Prior	Not admissible	Not admissible
Contemporaneous	Not admissible	Admissible
Subsequent	Admissible	Admissible

D. "Written Contracts" Statutes

A few states specifically provide, by statute, that any written contract can only be modified by another written statement or a fully performed oral agreement. These statutes abrogate the general common law rule allowing oral modifications of written contracts.

III. Parol Evidence Rule

During the course of negotiating a written contract, parties frequently propose and discuss various possible provisions before they agree on final terms and enter into a contract. Later if one of the parties is disappointed with the contract, he may dishonestly assert that the parties actually agreed on additional or different terms than those stated in the writing. Or a person may honestly believe that the agreement included other than the written terms. One of the chief reasons for putting an agreement in writing is to minimize disputes and to protect both parties from the need for (and uncertainty of) future litigation to determine the actual terms of their agreement. Also if a writing purports to be a statement of the entire agreement, it seems reasonable to expect that a person will refuse to sign until the writing completely states the agreement.

Based both upon the diligence expected of a reasonable person (to have his written contract completely and accurately state his agreement), and upon the known inclination of a person to try to escape from what has later proven to be a bad bargain, the law considers it to be sound policy to say that if persons put their agreement in writing, regardless of whether required to do so or not, and the writing appears to be a complete expression of the agreement, then the writing actually is the entire agreement up to that point.

No oral or *written* evidence of understandings, negotiations or agreements which occurred prior to the acceptance of a written contract can be admitted to prove that the expressed or implied terms of the written contract are not the final terms agreed upon. Furthermore, contemporaneous oral statements are also inadmissible; however, contemporaneous written statements may be proven as an integral part of the agreement. The parol evidence rule does not apply to nor affect the validity of oral or written modifications. Modifications are governed by the rules stated in the previous section. The applicability of the parol evidence rule is summarized in Table 9.2.

A number of exceptions to the rule exist which are designed to prevent injustice. Accordingly, parol evidence can be used to

Example. A seller resided in a town some distance from a tract of vacant farmland which he owned. The owner of an adjoining tract of farmland went to the seller's home with an offer to buy the seller's land for $400. When the seller confessed ignorance of land values in the area, the buyer said that he was familiar with the values of such lands, that the seller's tract was poor pasture land worth about $400, and that the buyer desired the land only because it would give him more convenient access to some of his own farmland. The seller gave the buyer a deed transferring the land to the buyer for $400. The deed said nothing concerning value or the buyer's intended use. Several months later the seller learned that at the time of the transfer the buyer knew of a valuable granite deposit under the seller's land, that the buyer desired the seller's land for the purpose of opening and operating a quarry, and that because of the granite the value of the land when transferred was $15,000 rather than $400. When the buyer refused to return the land upon the seller's tender of $400, the seller sued to rescind the transfer.

Land contracts and deeds usually do not contain any provision concerning value or intended use. Although the writing was a complete expression of the agreement, proof of the fraud would not change or qualify any term of the deed and therefore the seller could have the transfer canceled. Note that the buyer was guilty of an express lie rather than mere nondisclosure.

Suppose that an agent for the buyer made the fraudulent statement without the buyer's knowledge or consent. Since the seller wished rescission rather than damages, the seller could rescind even under the narrower rule.

show that a contract was never in fact made, that the writing produced is actually only part, not all, of an agreement, that the contract resulted from fraud, duress or mistake, that the contract is voidable because of incapacity, that it was illegal or that a special interpretation was intended. The difficulty with these exceptions can be seen below.

Suppose that after a written agreement has been signed, one of the parties claims that his consent was obtained through fraudulent misrepresentations of certain facts. Although he may not directly claim that any terms different from those expressed in the writing were actually agreed upon, his assertion will sometimes indirectly involve the parol evidence rule. The most common fact situations can be classified in the following way:

1. Assume that proving the alleged fraud will not change or qualify in any way what is stated in the written contract.

(a) Assume further that the other contracting party made or authorized the fraudulent mis-

representation. If these assumptions can be proved, the defrauded party should certainly be entitled to relief from the contract. He can either rescind the contract or affirm the contract and recover damages.

(b) Assume that the fraudulent misrepresentation was made by the agent of one of the parties and was neither authorized by nor participated in by the agent's employer or principal. If the defrauded party wishes to rescind, he should be permitted to do so, in order to prevent the other party from enjoying the benefits obtained by his agent's fraud. If, however, the defrauded party wishes to affirm and recover damages instead of rescinding, the courts are not agreed. In most states if the misrepresentation concerns a matter about which an agent might be expected to give information, the principal, although himself innocent, will be held responsible for his agent's conduct and liable for the damages sustained by the defrauded party. A few states apply a narrower rule (as further explained in

Example. A company in the business of furnishing advertising services, supplied its agents with printed order forms to be signed by dealers wishing to subscribe for the service. Signed forms would then be sent to the company for acceptance.The forms contained the following waiver provision: "Neither party will be held responsible for any provision or representation not embodied in writing herein." One of the company s salesmen contacted a dealer who operated a heating and plumbing supply business, and induced him to subscribe for the advertising service. To obtain the dealer's agreement, the salesman fraudulently stated that the company had a business connection with a cooperative buying association, that if the dealer subscribed for the advertising service he would become a member of the buying association, that through the association he could buy heating and plumbing fixtures at 12 1/2 percent below jobbers' prices, and that he could become a member of the association only through subscribing for the advertising service. As the dealer could see from reading the printed order form, it contained no reference to any buying association. The dealer signed the order form agreeing to pay $260 for certain described advertising materials, and shortly afterwards received notice of the company's acceptance of the order. Later the dealer learned that there was no such buying association as the agent had described, and refused to accept any of the contracted advertising materials from the company. The company had had no previous notice of the salesman's fraudulent tactics, and sued the dealer for $260.

Although the dealer's consent was obtained by means of the agent's fraud, the principal was innocent of the fraud. Therefore in some states the dealer could not rescind. Under the facts in this example, the Pennsylvania Superior Court held[16] that the advertising company could fully enforce the contract. □

16. *Lloyd & Elliot, Inc. v. Lang,* 118 Pa. Super. 190, 180 A. 74(1935).

Chapter 18), holding that a defrauded party cannot recover damages from the other party when the latter neither authorized nor participated in his agent's fraudulent statement.

2. Assume that proving the alleged fraud will change or qualify some provision in the written contract. Most such cases involve the effect which should be accorded to an oral-representation-waiver provision such as the following:

> This writing contains the entire agreement of the parties. No statements, representations, or promises, not included herein, shall be binding, valid, or of any effect between the parties.

Should such a provision immunize the contract from the effects of an oral fraudulent misrepresentation? If the fraud was practiced by the other contracting party, either person-ally or through his authorized agent, the oral-representation-waiver provision will usually not be effective to shield the defrauding party. The innocent party will be entitled to relief from the contract, either through rescission or through affirmance and recovery of damages. On the other hand, if the oral fraudulent misrepresentation was entirely the idea of the other party's agent and was neither authorized nor participated in by the agent's principal, the case is not so clear cut. On one side it can be argued that even though the principal is innocent of his agent's fraud, it is not fair to permit him to retain any benefit (including the contract) obtained by means of the fraud. On the other side is the argument that if a person gives clear notice that his agent lacks authority to make any representations, he is justified in assuming that no person will enter into a contract in reliance on any representations of the agent, and that therefore a contract negotiated through the agent should be binding and enforceable according to its terms. Of the usual remedies for fraud (rescission or affirmance with recovery of damages) courts in some states say that the defrauded party is entitled to either remedy, courts in a second group of states say that because of the oral-representationwaiver provision, the defrauded party has only the first but not the second remedy, and courts in a third group of states say that he has neither remedy, that the contract is valid and binding—unless in addition to making the fraudulent misrepresentation the agent also, by a dishonest trick, prevented the representation from being included in the written contract. For example, if the innocent party explains that he is unable to read the contract form (because of eye, language, or literary deficiency) and the agent misreads or misstates what the written contract says, the agent is fraudulently preventing inclusion of the misrepresentation in the written contract, and the defrauded party may rescind the contract even in a state falling into the third group (assuming that the defrauded party can prove these facts).

* * *

Problems

1. By oral agreement a landlord leased a certain described house and lot to a tenant at an annual rental of $1,200, payable monthly in advance, and the tenant began occupancy on the effective date of the lease. No mention was made as to any right to cancel. (Assume that the statute of frauds of the state involved prescribed a three-year period for real estate leases.)

(a) The agreement was entered into on February 1 of a certain year, for three years starting the same day. (1) On June 20 of that year, the landlord decided he wished to terminate the arrangement. What was the earliest date the landlord could end the tenant's legal right to occupy? Explain. (2) On June 20 of the following year, the landlord decided he wished to terminate the arrangement. What was the earliest date the landlord could end the tenant's legal right to occupy? Explain.

(b) The agreement was entered into on February 1 of a certain year, for four years starting the same day. (1) Same additional fact as in Part (1) above. Answer the same question (2) Same additional fact as in Part (2) above. Answer the same question.

(c) The agreement was entered into on January 21 of a certain year for three years starting February 1 of that year. (1) Same additional fact as in Part (1) above. Answer the same question. (2) Same additional fact as in Part (2) above. Answer the same question.

2. S owned a vacant lot which adjoined his house at 459 West 28th Street. On the other side of the lot was a house numbered 463 West 28th Street. S orally agreed to sell the lot to B for the price stated below.

(a) At the time of their oral agreement, B signed and gave S a check on a local bank made out to S for the full price, and S said that he would give B possession and a deed in two weeks. On the check B wrote the following: "In full payment for vacant lot between 459 and 463 West 28th Street, this city." A few days later S returned the check to B and refused to go ahead with the sale. S had not yet indorsed the check in any way. B sued S for specific performance of the contract and offered the check in evidence. (1) The price upon which S and B orally agreed and for which the check was made out was $400. Briefly explain (a) the reasoning upon which S might attempt to defend, (b) the reasoning upon which B might attempt to win, and (c) whether the court should decree specific performance of the agreement. (2) The price upon which S and B orally agreed and for which the check was made out was $600. Would your answers be the same as in Part (1) above? (3) Explain whether your answers in Parts (1) or (2) above would be affected by assuming the following additional fact: W, an impartial person with no interest in the agreement, was present when S and B reached their oral agreement; W recalls and is available to testify to what S and B said and did.

(b) The price upon which S and B orally agreed was $1,000. Upon reaching their agreement B paid S $100 in cash as a down payment and S gave B the following receipt, after writing the date and name of their city on the receipt: "Received from B. Brown $100 to apply on purchase of lot between 459 and 463 W. 28 Street, this city. (signed) S Smith." (1) A few days later B changed his mind about purchasing and so notified S. S insisted that B go through with the agreement, tendered a deed to B and demanded $900, and upon B's refusal, S sued B for $900. Explain (a) the reasoning upon which B might attempt to defend, (b) the reasoning upon which S might attempt to collect, and (c) which party should be given judgment. (2) A few days later S changed his mind about selling and so notified B, offering to return the $100 to B. B refused to accept return of the money and sued S for specific performance of the contract, offering S's receipt in evidence. Explain (a) the reasoning upon which S might attempt to defend, (b) the reasoning upon which B might attempt to win, and (c) whether the court should decree specific performance of the agreement.

3. B wished to buy goods on credit from S. S refused to sell except for cash, whereupon G who was favorably known to S called S on the telephone and said, "If you sell goods to B on 30 days' credit and B fails to pay, I'll pay up to the amount of $300." S thereupon sold $200 worth of goods to B on 30 days' credit and notified G of the sale. B failed to pay when due and S sued and obtained judgment against B. Because of B's insolvency, S could not collect. S then sued G.

(a) G denied liability on the ground that he received nothing for his promise. Explain whether this defense would be good.

(b) Explain what other defense G might attempt to raise.

(c) Explain whether S could collect from G.

4. B was 17 years old, had a full-time job, and although he still lived with his parents, he was permitted to retain all of his earnings except for an agreed amount which he paid for room and board. B with his father, F, went to S's store where B looked at two new suits priced at $100 apiece. Although the additional suits were not necessary, B said he would like to buy them and requested 30 days' credit. S apologetically refused credit because of B's age. F then made the proposal quoted below. S agreed and delivered the suits to B. When B failed to pay within 30 days, S sued F.

(a) In inducing S to deliver the suits to B, F said: "Let my son have the suits on 30 days' credit and if he fails to pay, I'll pay." Explain whether S could recover in his lawsuit against F.

(b) In inducing S to deliver the suits to B, F said, "Let my son have the suits and charge them to me." Explain whether S could recover in his lawsuit against F.

5. B. Berg owned and operated a retail clothing store under the name "Berg's Men's Shop." B stocked suits manufactured by several different manufacturers. The labels in the suits read, "Tailored Especially for Berg's Men's Shop, Centertown, Illinois, by [name of manufacturer]." His stock of suits manufactured by S being low, B called S on the phone and placed an order for fifty suits of specified styles, sizes, and colors, as stated in S's catalog, at a stated price totaling over $500. Each suit was to have the label quoted above sewn in the usual place on the inside lining of each suitcoat. S orally accepted the order. Three weeks later S had the suits ready for shipment when B canceled the order. S sued B for damages for breach of contract.

(a) Assume that S manufactured the fifty suits after receiving B's order. Explain (a) the reasoning upon which S might attempt to collect, (2) the reasoning upon which B might attempt to defend, and (3) which party should be given judgment.

(b) Assume that S had in stock sufficient suits to fill B's order and all that S did to prepare them for shipment was to attach the proper labels. Answer the same three questions asked in Part (a) above.

6. (a) B. Brown, a university professor of history, went to the store of S. Smith, a dealer, and orally ordered a television set of a particular make and model for the total price of $600, to be delivered to B's home within two weeks and installed in B's living room. S orally accepted the order and B made a down payment of $100 in cash. S made out and gave to B the following receipt: "[Date] Received from B. Brown $100 to apply on TV set. (signed) S. Smith." (1) When S tendered delivery of the set according to the oral agreement, B refused to accept delivery, saying that he had changed his mind about making the purchase. S sued B for damages for breach of contract. Would S be entitled to obtain judgment? Explain. (2) S refused to deliver at the agreed time and B sued S for damages for breach of contract. Would B be entitled to obtain judgment? Explain.

(b) Assume the same facts as in Part (a, 1) except for the following change: When S sued B for damages for breach of contract, B filed a counterclaim in the same lawsuit to recover the $100 he had paid, alleging the facts of his oral order, payment, and refusal to receive delivery. What would be the outcome of the lawsuit? Explain.

(c) B. Brown, a university professor of history, orally ordered a television set of a stated make and model from S. Smith, a dealer, for $400, to be delivered to B's home in two weeks and installed in his living room. B made no down payment. S orally accepted the order and later sent to B a signed written confirmation, entitled "Purchase Memorandum No. 1208," containing all of the terms of the order. A duplicate of the purchase memorandum was enclosed with a request that B sign and return it to S. B kept both copies without signing either. When S tendered delivery of the set according to the oral agreement, B refused to accept delivery, saying that he had changed his mind about making the purchase. S sued B for damages

for breach of contract. Would S be entitled to obtain judgment? Explain.

(d) Assume the same facts as in Part (c) except for the following change: The total price was $600. Answer the same question as is asked in Part (c).

(e) Assume the same facts as in Part (c) except for the following changes: The total price was $600. Two days after receiving the "Purchase Memorandum No. 1208," B dated and sent the following note to S: "To S. Smith: Referring to your Purchase Memorandum No. 1208, please be advised that I am canceling this order. (signed) B. Brown." What would be the result of S's lawsuit against B? Explain.

(f) Assume the same facts as in Part (c), except for the following changes: The total price was $600. S refused to deliver at the agreed time and B sued S for damages for breach of contract. Would B be entitled to obtain judgment? Explain.

(g) B. Brown, owner and operator of a hotel, orally ordered a television set of a stated make and model from S. Smith, a dealer, for $1,000, to be delivered in two weeks, and installed in the hotel lounge. B made no down payment. S orally accepted the order and later sent B a written confirmation, entitled "Purchase Memorandum," containing all of the terms of the order. A duplicate copy of the purchase memorandum was enclosed with a request that B sign and return it to S. B kept both copies without signing either. When S tendered delivery of the set according to the oral agreement, B refused to accept delivery, saying that he had changed his mind about making the purchase. S sued B for damages for breach of contract. Was S entitled to obtain judgment? Explain. (Modified from A.I.C.P.A., Nov.50- 10.)

7.0n May 14 L and T signed a written lease agreement under which L leased to T for one year beginning June 1, of the same year, the business premises known as 17 East 10th Street in a specified city, and T agreed to pay a total rent of $3,600, payable monthly in $300 installments at the beginning of each month. The lease contained the following provision: "This lease agreement cannot be added to, altered, or rescinded except by written agreement signed by both parties hereto." T took possession on June 1 and was making payments as agreed when on September 15, T told L that business conditions were poor and that he would be unable to continue using the premises at the agreed rental. L asked if $200 per month would be satisfactory. When T replied "Yes," L said, "All right, I'll agree that beginning this October 1, and for the balance of the lease period, the total monthly rent will be $200." T agreed to this proposal, thanked L, and paid $200 to L on October 1. T made this payment by his own check which was drawn on a local bank, named L as payee, and contained no notation concerning its purpose. L promptly indorsed the check (by signing his name on the back) and cashed it. On October 27 L phoned T that he had changed his mind, that he wanted another $100 for October, and that T would have to pay $300 on November 1. T objected, and on November 1 tendered to L a check for $200, marked "Payment of rent in full to November 30, this year, for 17 East 10th Street, this city." L refused the check and sued T.

(a) What result? Explain.

(b) Other facts remaining the same, assume that T marked on his October 1 check, "The October rent in full for 17 East 10th Street, this city." Would this additional fact affect the result in L's lawsuit against T? Explain.

8. B. Brown, shopping for a living room suite, visited S. Smith's retail store and looked at a display. On the sofa of the display was a tag reading "Smith Furniture Store. Living room suite. Manufactured by Martin Company, Model 220. Price $600." B stated that he wished to buy the suite and S slipped a red "sold" tag on the same string that held the price tag. Printed on the red tag were the words, "Sold. Smith Furniture Store," and written on the tag by S was the name, "B. Brown." B said he would return in about an hour and make a partial payment of $200 and would pay the balance within thirty days. To this S agreed. Before B returned, P, a friend of S's, came into the store and said he would like to buy the living room suite. S

expected another shipment soon and thought B would not mind waiting, and so drew a line through B's name on the red tag and wrote P's name. When B returned he insisted upon receiving this particular living room suite and when S refused, B sued for damages. Explain (1) the reasoning upon which S might attempt to defend, (2) the reasoning upon which B might attempt to recover, and (3) which party should be given judgment.

9. (a) A printer contacted a milk dealer to interest him in ordering calendars to give to his customers. The printer showed the dealer a certain type of calendar with a sample of the advertising statement which could be printed on the calendars along with the dealer's name, and quoted the price for 1,000 calendars as $200, payable thirty days after delivery. The following day the dealer phoned the printer and ordered 1,000 calendars of the type which the printer had showed to the dealer, and with the printing on them that the printer had described. The printer accepted the order during the phone conversation. Within a reasonable time the printer had the calendars ready for delivery, but the dealer died from a sudden heart attack. The dealer's will appointed his son as executor and left all of his property to his son. The dealer's business records contained no reference to the transaction with the printer. The dealer's son assumed operation of the business but refused to accept the calendars. The printer sued the son as executor for damages for breach of contract. Explain (1) the reasoning upon which the printer could attempt to collect, (2) the reasoning upon which the son could attempt to defend, and (3) which party should be given judgment.

(b) Other facts being the same, assume the following additional facts: The calendars were delivered to the dealer, but no receipt was given for them. The dealer distributed the calendars among his customers, and had about 100 left over in his office when he suffered the heart attack and died without making any payment for the calendars. When the son as executor refused to pay, the printer sued for the agreed price for the calendars.

Explain whether your answers would be different than in Part (a) above.

10. In December, the owner of a nightclub was solicited for advertising by an agent who represented the publisher of a weekly magazine known as Nightlife. When the owner expressed reluctance to obligate himself for a year's advertising, the agent said that the contract form permitted an advertiser to cancel at will. Relying upon the agent's statement, and without reading the agent's printed order form, the owner signed a subscription for advertising in 52 weekly issues at $6 per issue. The printed order form stated, "Oral agreements will not be recognized," and contained no provision regarding cancellation. The publisher accepted the subscription and the advertising began in the January 1 issue. In February the owner told the publisher that he wished to cancel the advertising. When the publisher objected, the owner told the publisher of what the agent had said. This was the first that the publisher knew of the agent's statement. The publisher explained that the agent had no authority to say that advertising contracts could be canceled, but offered that if the owner would continue to advertise, the publisher would release him from the written contract if the owner was still dissatisfied, and the owner could then terminate the advertising at will. The owner agreed and continued to pay for advertising until April, when he notified the publisher to cancel his advertising for the remainder of the year. The publisher refused to permit cancellation, and sued the owner for damages. The owner raised two defenses: (1) that he was induced to sign the December contract through the agent's fraud, and (2) that the December contract was superseded by the February agreement under which the publisher had said that the owner could cancel at will. Explain (1) the reasoning upon which the publisher could attempt to answer the first defense, (2) the reasoning upon which the publisher could attempt to answer the second defense, and (3) which party should be given judgment in the lawsuit.

10 Excuses for Nonperformance and Illegality

Excuses for Nonperformance and Illegality

JUST AS IT IS ESSENTIAL in modern society that most contracts be legally enforced, so also is it considered necessary social policy that, if certain unexpected events occur, persons should be excused from their contractual obligations—sometimes completely excused, sometimes partially. The discussion of Mistakes Concerning Extrinsic Facts in Chapter 8 concerns fact situations in which, unknown to the parties, certain circumstances were in existence at the time they entered into their contract. Excuse in the present chapter will concentrate on circumstances or events occurring *after* the parties enter into their contract. The two types of fact situations are closely related and sometimes overlap, so that the applicable policy factors will often be the same.

Two types of excuse from contract obligations are widely accepted as being wise and desirable public policy—namely (1) excuse resulting from the expiration of the period of a statute of limitations, and (2) excuse resulting from a discharge in bankruptcy. Other situations in which questions of excuse frequently arise are much less clear cut. The most important of these situations involve (1) performance more burdensome or impossible—new circumstances (or newly discovered circumstances) adversely affect the expense of performance or the ability of the party claiming excuse to perform at all, and (2) disappointment in exchange performance—new circumstances (or newly discovered circumstances) adversely affect the item

which the party claiming excuse is to receive in exchange for his agreed performance.

I. Obligations No Longer Enforceable

A. Statutes of Limitations

Various statutes fix periods of time within which any type of lawsuit, tort as well as contract, must be brought. A defendant may have a good defense to a plaintiff's claim, but after a time his evidence may be lost and his witnesses may forget or die. The purpose of the various statutes of limitations is to prevent the unfair enforcement of stale claims after the expiration of such a period of time as could adversely affect the proof of a defense. The period of time is designated by the legislature of the state concerned, and, being a policy determination, can be expected to vary in different states and with different types of lawsuits. The Uniform Commercial Code prescribes a limitation period for contracts involving the sales of goods, stating:

1. An action for breach of any contract for sale must be commenced within four years after the cause of action has accrued. By the original agreement the parties may reduce the period of limitation to not less than one year but may not extend it.

2. A cause of action accrues when the breach occurs, regardless of the aggrieved party's lack of knowledge of the breach. A

Example.   On June 1, S and B entered into a contract for the sale and purchase of a certain quantity of cotton owned by S and stored in an independent warehouse in another city, the parties agreeing on a stated price and specifying June 10 as the delivery date. The cotton was destroyed in a fire and a question arose concerning what effect the destruction of the cotton should have on the contract between S and B.

If the fire occurred on May 31, the question would be whether the casualty was sufficient to prevent an enforceable contract from being formed on June 1. This type of question is discussed in Chapter 6.

If the fire occurred on June 2, it would of course not affect the *formation* on June 1 of a valid and enforceable contract between the parties. The question instead would be whether the casualty should cancel or excuse performance of the contract already formed. □

* * *

Example. A builder entered into a contract with a landowner in which, for a stated price, the builder agreed to excavate for a cellar of certain stated dimensions on the landowner's land. Unexpectedly the builder soon encountered solid rock which would increase his costs far beyond the original contract price for the job.

Some would classify this case as involving a mutual mistake concerning a condition in existence at the time the contract was formed, some others would classify the case as concerning a circumstance (discovery of the rock condition) arising after formation of the contract. Clearly whichever way the case is classified, the same policy factors will apply in determining whether the builder should be bound by his contract or excused from it. □

breach of warranty occurs when tender of delivery is made, except that where a warranty explicitly extends to future performance of the goods and discovery of the breach must await the time of such performance the cause of action accrues when the breach is or should have been discovered.[1]

The limitation periods for other types of contracts (involving services, loans, and sales of land) vary among the different states. Some states prescribe a shorter period for unwritten contracts than for written contracts, other states make no such distinction. For other than sales-of-goods contracts, most of the statutory periods in the various states fall between two and six years for unwritten contracts and between three and twenty years for written contracts. Some statutes distinguish between sealed and unsealed prom-

ises, some allowing a longer time for a sealed promise, and a few not providing any statute of limitations at all for a sealed promise. In the latter type of state, usually the expiration of a substantial period of time (for example, twenty years) gives rise to a presumption that a sealed obligation has been paid. The presumption is not conclusive and, if evidence affirmatively shows that a sealed promise has not been performed, it can be enforced even after expiration of the twenty-year period. Statutes in most states make no distinction in regard to sealed promises. The Uniform Commercial Code follows this view by providing in regard to sales-of-goods contracts:

The affixing of a seal to a writing evidencing a contract for sale or an offer to buy or sell goods does not constitute the writing a sealed instrument and the law with respect to

1. U.C.C. Sec. 2-725.

sealed instruments does not apply to such a contract or offer.[2]

After expiration of the prescribed limitation period, an obligation is considered stale and cannot be enforced without the obligor's consent. The statutory period usually begins to run on a particular promise from the time a lawsuit could be brought to enforce the promise. Starting at that time, the claim begins to grow stale. Should the obligor later admit that there is an enforceable obligation, he is admitting, as of that date, that he has no defense and that there is no longer any reason for the time which has already passed to prevent enforcement of his obligation. The claim becomes as fresh and enforceable as it was when originally contracted. With the further passage of time after such an admission, the claim again begins to grow stale. Such an admission, therefore, whether made before or after the expiration of the limitation period, has the effect of starting the limitation period running again.

An admission which is sufficient to renew the running of the limitation period can be made in various ways, including: (1) a clear, unequivocal promise to pay, or an acknowledgment of the obligation in such a manner as to imply a promise to pay, or (2) a part payment of the particular obligation in question.

If a debtor owes his creditor two separate obligations arising from two separate and distinct extensions of credit, and the debtor makes a payment smaller than the amount of either debt, and fails to specify the debt upon which he is making a payment, the creditor is usually permitted to apply the payment to the oldest debt—even though the collection of that debt is barred by the statute of limitations. Such an application by the *creditor*, however, certainly cannot be construed as an admission by the *debtor* as to the continued validity and enforceability of any particular debt, and, therefore, would not start the lim-

itations period running anew on the older debt. On the other hand, if a debtor opens a charge account and makes a series of purchases, even though each purchase is a separate contract, the charge account obligation is a running account, a single extension of credit, which is understood by the parties to be a single obligation. Any payment by the debtor, therefore, would be an admission as to the entire account.

If, when a debtor is sued on an obligation, he fails to claim promptly the defense of the statute of limitations, it seems fair to construe his conduct as an admission that the obligation is enforceable, just as if he had expressly acknowledged the existence and enforceability of the obligation, and with the same effect.

Occasionally a contract includes an express provision that the contract promise will remain enforceable no matter how much time passes. In most states in which the question has arisen, such a provision is considered against public policy and not effective at all. Cases in some states consider such a waiver effective for a limited time. In one case, for example,[3] the court accorded limited effect to an unlimited waiver. In this case an obligor stated in his promissory note, "I also disclaim all limitations of whatever kind." The court said that this provision extended the obligation for an additional statute of limitations period, and that after the expiration of double the statutory period, the obligation could not be enforced.

B. Bankruptcy

The affairs of a person or business in financial difficulty may be settled in one of two ways: (1) through a liquidation of assets, which of course terminates the business enterprise, or (2) through financial rehabilitation, which enables the business to continue. Either of these two can be accomplished without court action (by agreement between the insolvent

---

2. U.C.C. Sec.. 2-203.

3. *Hoffman v. Fisher*, 2 W.N.C. (Pa.) 17 (1875).

debtor and his creditors), or by court action, either through a state court insolvency proceeding or though a Federal court bankruptcy proceeding. Whichever is the objective—liquidation or rehabilitation—all debts will very rarely be paid in full. Participants in such a proceeding are well aware of this and therefore usually expect that any obligations remaining after available assets are exhausted will be canceled. Such a cancellation can be accomplished in one of two ways: (1) by each creditor voluntarily entering into an agreement discharging all unpaid claims, or (2) through a discharge decreed upon completion of a bankruptcy proceeding. After a bankruptcy discharge, the unpaid portion of most (but not all) debts cannot be collected. The debtor is, in effect, excused from the balance of such obligations. A state court insolvency proceeding cannot discharge the claim of any creditor who refuses to agree to a discharge, the United States Constitution and Congress having reserved that power exclusively for Federal bankruptcy proceedings.

A bankruptcy proceeding has two important objectives: (1) to assure a fair distribution of the insolvent debtor's available assets among all his creditors, and (2) to free the debtor from his debts. The first objective is obviously fair, the second may be challenged. Some will argue that if a person incurs a just debt, he ought to be held to his obligation until it is paid. More persuasive, however (as evidenced by the fact that since an early date Congress has been so persuaded), is the argument (1) that a debtor's insolvency is not necessarily the result of his poor judgment, but may instead be the result of economic conditions against which he is powerless, and (2) regardless of who is at fault in a debtor's becoming insolvent, if he remains saddled with an overwhelming burden of debt, his incentive and ability are stifled and he ceases to be a producing member of society. A method by which an honest debtor may be freed from oppressive indebtedness and re-

stored as a contributing party in the economy is sound policy from which all of society benefits.

C. Statutory Right of Rescission

In recent years numerous federal and state statutes have been passed which are designed to protect the general public, especially consumers, from the consequences of certain kinds of contracts. These contracts can generally be classified as ones where there is a special disparity of bargaining power or where an improvident decision could have significant adverse consequences.

The basic approach to these statutorily defined contract situations is to allow a "Cooling Off" period after formation of the contract is made during which an individual might reconsider the agreement and, if desired, cancel the contract. From a theoretical viewpoint this concept might be viewed as a right of rescission implicitly made part of the agreement by the operation of law or the waiting period might simply be considered as a required element of the creation of the contract itself.

For example, the Federal Trade Commission has issued regulations applicable to door-to-door sales of goods and services of $25 or more which gives a consumer three days after the signing of a contract to rescind the agreement. Several states have adopted similar statutes.

A Pennsylvania law provides:

> Where merchandise having a sale price of twenty-five dollars or more is sold or contracted to be sold to a consumer, as a result of, or in connection with, a direct contact with or call on the consumer at his residence, that consumer may avoid the contract or sale by notifying, in writing, the seller within three full business days following the day on which the contract or sale was made and by returning or holding available for return to the seller, in its original condition, any mer-

chandise received under the contract or sale....[4]

It should be remembered though that these are exceptions to the general rule that once a contract is agreed upon a person is legally obligated, then and there.

II. Performance More Burdensome or Impossible

Many contracts include "excuse" or "escape" provisions which state that the occurrence of certain specified events will excuse the parties from their contractual commitments. For example, sales-of-goods contracts frequently contain strike-escape provisions. Suppose, however, that some event not covered by an express escape provision unexpectedly occurs and renders a promisor's performance considerably more burdensome or even impossible. If the strict letter of the contract is all that matters, the promisor must nevertheless perform in spite of the unexpected occurrence—or pay damages for nonperformance. Before the present century the courts were inclined to hold persons rigidly to their contracts. The chief mission of the courts in contract disputes was limited to defining the terms of agreements, interpreting their meaning, and enforcing them. Present-day society, on the other hand, has broadened the role of the courts. In the words of Professor Morris Cohen,

> The roots of the law of contract are many rather than one.... The law must also go beyond the original intention of the parties, to settle controversies as to the distribution of gains and losses that the parties did not anticipate in the same way....[5]

In other words, it is considered sound, overall policy to permit persons *sometimes* to escape from burdensome contracts. Explaining in greater detail, Professor Cohen writes:

> Now the human power to foresee all the consequences of an agreement is limited, even if we suppose that the two parties understand each other's meaning to begin with. Disputes or disagreements are therefore bound to come up; and the law of contract may thus be viewed as an attempt to determine the rights and duties of the two parties under circumstances that were not anticipated exactly in the same way by the two contracting parties, or at any rate were not expressly provided for in an unambiguous way. One can therefore say that the court's adjudication *supplements* the original contract as a *method of distributing gains and losses*.
>
> From this point of view we may look upon the law of contract as a number of rules according to which courts distribute gains and losses according to the equities of such cases; and the pretense that the result follows exclusively from the agreement of the two parties is fictional. Just as the process of interpreting a statute is really a process of subsidiary legislation, so is the interpretation of a contract really a method of supplementing the original agreement by such provisions as are necessary to determine the point at issue.
>
> If we view the law of contract as directed to strengthening the security of transactions by enabling men to rely more fully on promises, we see only one phase of its actual workings. The other phase is the determination of the rights of the contracting parties as to contingencies that they have not foreseen, and for which they have not provided. In this latter respect the law of contract is a way of enforcing some kind of *distributive justice* within the legal system. And technical doctrines of contract may thus be viewed as a set of rules that will systematize decisions in this field and thus give lawyers and their clients some guidance in the problem of anticipating future decisions.... In any case, the essential problem of the law of contract is the problem of distribution of risks. The other phase, namely, the assurance that what the parties

---

4. 73 P.S. Sec. 201-7.
5. Morris Cohen, LAW AND THE SOCIAL ORDER (New York: Harcourt, 1933), p. 110

have actually agreed on will be fulfilled, is a limiting principle. [Emphasis added.] [6]

Some theorists suggest that when a court is determining the circumstances under which a contract duty should be considered excused, the court is merely interpreting what the parties would have intended if they had thought of the unexpected event. In the passage just quoted, Professor Cohen rejects this view. So also does Professor Roscoe Pound. who has written:

> Often the words finally written in a contract after a long negotiation are the result of hard-fought compromises. They are not ideal provisions from the standpoint of either side, but are what each is willing to concede in order to reach agreement. After some frustrating event has happened, and a party who has suffered damage from nonperformance is suing for it, to say that he intended and would have consented to insert a condition which the court conjures up to relieve the promisor is to make a new contract under the fiction of interpretation. This sort of interpretation, which has much vogue in the service state, is said by a judge of one of our courts to be a process of distillation. We are told that the meaning is distilled from the words. It might be suggested that distilling is often illicit and the product moonshine. [7]

To avoid "distilling moonshine" and to achieve Professor Cohen's "distributive justice," the courts recognize that society is a necessary third party in every contract. The courts represent the interests of society in determining and allocating risks in a socially desirable way. This function imposes a difficult task on the courts. Weighing heavily on one side is the strong economic and social necessity for contractual commitments to be stable and not easily avoided. Woven into this is the fact that the obligation from which a

promisor is seeking to be excused is one which he voluntarily assumed without any express agreement for an escape provision covering the event in question. Against this the courts must weigh the nature and degree of the unexpected burden resulting from the particular event which has occurred.

A. Classification of Burdens

In balancing the stability against flexibility, events are sometimes classified according to their effect. Accordingly, they can be classified as rendering performance more burdensome (but not impossible) personally impossible, or completely impossible.

1. INCREASED BURDEN

When used in distinction to the term "impossibility," the term "increased burden" means that although performance has become more difficult or expensive, the burden is not so extreme or unreasonable as to make performance prohibitive.

2. PERSONAL IMPOSSIBILITY

Sometimes also called "subjective impossibility," the term "personal impossibility" refers to a situation in which, while it is impossible (or extremely unreasonable) for the promisor himself to perform his contractual commitment, performance exactly according to the contract is possible by someone else.

3. COMPLETE IMPOSSIBILITY

Sometimes also called "objective impossibility," the term "complete impossibility" is used to describe a situation in which it has become impossible (or extremely unreasonable) for the promisor or anyone else to perform the commitment according to the contract.

The general tendency of the courts is frequently (but not always) to favor excusing a promisor in the case of complete impossibility, but usually not in cases of personal impossibility or increased burden. This general

---

6. *Op. cit.*, pp. 101-102.
7. Roscoe Pound, AN INTRODUCTION TO THE PHILOSOPHY OF LAW (New Haven: Yale U.P., 1954), Yale paperback ed., 1959, p. 167.

Example. A sales contract involves standardized goods. Before the seller can make delivery, the goods which he intends to deliver are destroyed through no fault oft his own.

Since the goods are standardized, other persons have goods which exactly meet the description in the contract. However, if the seller has insufficient funds or credit to procure additional goods, performance will be impossible for he seller personally, although the contract is capable of being performed exactly according to its terms by some other person. ☐

* * *

Example. A sales contract involves a rare, original painting which, through no fault of the seller, is destroyed before the seller can deliver it to the buyer.

Inasmuch as the contract involves unique goods, the casualty renders performance of the contract completely impossible. Nobody can perform it, neither the seller nor anyone else. ☐

tendency can be further discussed and illustrated by briefly examining work and service contracts and contracts for sales of goods—two types of contracts in which questions involving the effect of impossibility or increased burden frequently arise.

B. Work or Services Contracts

If a promisor's contractual commitment is to perform work or services of the type which cannot be delegated to another (as discussed in Chapter 11), and the promisor becomes incapable of performing, performance can be classified as completely impossible. The duty of the promisor to perform such a personal contract is excused if the promisor dies or is prevented by illness from performing (unless the evidence clearly shows that the promisor's incapacity is self-induced to avoid the contract). On the other hand, if the contracted work or services are such that performance could be delegated to some other person, the promisor's death or other incapacity would render his performance personally impossible rather than completely impossible. Although the dead or incapacitated promisor cannot personally perform, another person can render performance exactly in accordance with the contract. Generally the duty of a promisor to perform an impersonal contract is not excused and the

promisor (or if he is dead, his estate) will be held liable if the contractual commitment is not performed.

C. Sales of Goods Contracts

When a question of possible excuse arises in a contract for the future sale and delivery of goods, one important factor to consider is the status of the goods at the time the contract is formed, whether the goods are (1) identified, or (2) merely described but not yet identified. Goods are identified when certain particular goods are segregated or designated for delivery under the contract. On the other hand, a contract for delivery of described but unidentified goods states the quantity and kind of goods involved, but the particular item, lot, or batch which fits the description and is to be delivered under the contract is not yet segregated or designated.

I. GOODS IDENTIFIED WHEN CONTRACT FORMED

The Uniform Commercial Code provides:

> Where the contract requires for its performance goods identified when the contract is made, and the goods suffer casualty without fault of either party before the risk of loss passes to the buyer . . . then
>
> (a) if the loss is total the contract is avoided; and

Example (*involving identified goods*). A seller, a college student, owner of a new copy of a book entitled INTRODUCTION TO BASIC LEGAL PRINCIPLES showed the book to a buyer, after which the seller entered into a contract with the buyer, the seller agreeing to sell and deliver "this book" to the buyer one week later and the buyer to pay $5 upon delivery. That night the seller's book was destroyed through no fault of the seller.

It seems a fair interpretation of the intent of the parties that their contract presupposed the continued existence of the very book which both had in mind when they reached their agreement. While other copies of the same title might be readily available, the seller's contract was to deliver the specified or identified book. not just any copy of the book. ▢

* * *

Example (*involving unidentified goods*). A buyer phoned a book dealer and ordered one copy of a book entitled INTRODUCTION TO BASIC LEGAL PRINCIPLES, for $5 to be delivered one week later and paid for on delivery. The dealer accepted the order. That night through no fault of the dealer, his one remaining copy of the book was destroyed.

Since the parties were not dealing with one particular copy of the book but rather with any copy of the described book, the continued existence of the dealer's copy would not seem to be an implied term of the contract nor important for enforcement of the contract. ▢

(b) if the loss is partial or the goods have so deteriorated as no longer to conform to the contract the buyer may nevertheless demand inspection and at his option either treat the contract as avoided or accept the goods with due allowance from the contract price for the deterioration or the deficiency in quantity but without further right against the seller. [8]

The "risk of loss" referred to in the above quotation usually (but not always) remains with the seller until he ships the goods, or if transportation of the goods is not contemplated, until he turns the goods over to the buyer (see Chapter 21). Notice that the casualty referred to in the above-quoted rule is treated as rendering performance completely impossible, thus fully excusing both parties from their contract.

---

8. U.C.C. Sec. 2-613.

2. GOODS NOT IDENTIFIED WHEN CONTRACT FORMED

The Uniform Commercial Code provides:

Except so far as a seller may have assumed a greater obligation . . . :

(a) Delay in delivery or nondelivery in whole or in part by a seller who complies with paragraphs (b) and (c) is not a breach of his duty under a contract for sale *if performance as agreed has been made impracticable by the occurrence of a contingency the nonoccurrence of which was a basic assumption on which the contract was made* or by compliance in good faith with any applicable foreign or domestic governmental regulation or order. . . .

(b) Where the causes mentioned in paragraph (a) affect only a part of the seller's capacity to perform, he must allocate production and deliveries among his customers but may, at his option, include regular customers not then under contract as well as his own requirements for further manufacture. He may so allocate in any manner which is fair and reasonable.

(c) The seller must notify the buyer seasonably that there will be delay or non–delivery and, when allocation is required under paragraph (b), of the estimated quota thus made available for the buyer. [Emphasis added.] [9]

In other words, excuse depends upon the risks which parties assume, or which as a matter of policy they should be considered to assume when entering into contracts. If the event which renders performance unreasonably burdensome or impossible concerns a matter totally unexpected, a matter assumed by the parties to be stable and not subject to variation, it is a matter concerning which they are not assuming the risk of some casualty or change. In such a case it seems fair, reasonable, and practical to hold that the occurrence of the unexpected event excuses performance. Notice that the key factor—risk—is the same as applied to *Mistakes Concerning Extrinsic Facts*, discussed in Chapter 8. Notice also that any attempt to formulate a statement of this principle is so inexact that it leaves considerable latitude to courts to differ in particular situations concerning the risks which contracting parties should be considered to assume, and concerning the policy conclusions which should be reached in balancing (on the one side) fairness, reasonableness, and practicality against (on the other side) the need for stability of contracts. In view of this vagueness and indefiniteness, a careful businessman should attempt to look ahead to unexpected but possible occurrences, and consult his lawyer in regard to escape provisions which it would be wise for him to include in his future business contracts.

The most common casualties which may occur in connection with described but uni-

dentified goods concern either (1) the seller's possession (that is, his procuring and preparing the goods for shipment) or (2) the seller's ability to make shipment.

a. Occurrences Affecting Seller's Possession

Such occurrences may be further subdivided according to whether or not the seller is the producer of the goods which he has contracted to sell.

1. **Seller is to produce the contract goods**. If a seller agrees to manufacture the contract goods at his factory or to grow them on his farm, accidental destruction of the seller's factory or failure of his crop causes, to some extent at least, complete impossibility. Even though the described goods are standardized, similar goods procured elsewhere do not exactly fit the contract description, since the contract specifies the particular source. Although from the standpoint of assignment and delegation discussed in Chapter 11, the contract may be nonpersonal, so that the seller could validly delegate performance and the buyer be required to accept goods from another source, still, in allocating losses resulting from a destruction of the seller's production facilities, many courts feel that since the seller has lost the facilities specified in the contract, the buyer should bear the loss of his bargain under the contract—with the result that the buyer cannot enforce the contract against the seller. Although the cases tend in this direction, court decisions in the various states are not uniform.

If a contract makes no reference to the seller's factory or farm, it is arguable that such a reference is implied if the parties contemplate that the seller is to produce what he has agreed to sell.

If a seller is unable to manufacture and deliver because his factory is closed by strike, the seller is usually not excused. A labor dispute is considered as a moderate, foreseeable increase of burden. When the seller's factory

---

9. U.C.C. Sec. 2-615.

is destroyed, his loss is great (even though the physical plant is insured), and there is strong urge to allocate losses between the parties by excusing the seller from his contract. There is not nearly as great a loss or the same urge when a labor dispute prevents the seller from performing.

2. Seller is not to produce the contract goods. If the seller is not expected to produce the goods he has contracted to sell, any casualty to his expected source or to his inventory usually will not excuse the seller.

b. Occurrences Affecting Seller's Ability to Ship

Sometimes (as for example when a general railroad strike occurs) a seller's contemplated means of transportation suddenly becomes unavailable to him. An old Pennsylvania case[10] excused a seller when a flood destroyed the navigation facilities which the seller had intended to use, and it is arguable that this would also be the correct view under the Uniform Commercial Code. However, most court decisions have, in the past, taken the opposite view, holding that if a disruption of transportation is not highly extraordinary, it is a risk which a seller assumes and, therefore, is not an excuse.

III. Disappointment in Other Party's Performance

Suppose that A and B enter into a contract under which A agrees to pay a specified sum, or to perform in some other way, in exchange for certain performance by B. Suppose further that, after formation of the contract, an event occurs which depreciates the value of what B does or is to do, or otherwise disappoints A in what he is to receive in exchange for his own performance. A might thereupon argue that he should no longer be obliged to

pay or otherwise perform his own part of the contract. The principal events which might thus cause A to be disappointed in B's performance and consequently claim to be excused, can be classified as follows:

1. Solvency reasonably doubtful: A learns that B is insolvent, and therefore A fears that he will not be paid for his performance.
2. Defective performance: B fails to perform fully or properly according to the agreement, and A is unwilling to pay anything at all for B's partial or defective performance.
3. Frustration of purpose: Although B performs in full accordance with the agreement, B's performance is of less value to A than when the contract was formed and for this reason A is unwilling to pay.

A. Solvency Reasonably in Doubt

Suppose that a builder contracts with a landowner for construction of a certain building for $50,000 payable at stated times as the work progresses, and suppose further that after formation of the contract, the landowner becomes insolvent. Even though the time for payment may not yet have arrived so that technically the landowner cannot be said to have breached his contract, there is a strong likelihood that he will breach the contract. Under such circumstances it would be quite unreasonable to require the builder to continue his performance. Therefore when one party to a contract is insolvent, the other party is excused from performing unless and until he receives adequate assurance that he will be fully paid.

Actual proof of insolvency may be difficult. Therefore (as discussed in Chapter 18) in phrasing this rule for sales-of-goods contracts, the Uniform Commercial Code[11] extends the excuse to cases in which the seller has reasonable grounds to be worried about

---

10. *Lovering v. Buck Mt. Coal Co.*, 54 Pa. 291 (1867).

11. U.C.C. Sec. 2-609.

the buyer's solvency, even though evidence subsequently produced shows that the buyer was not actually insolvent.

B. Defective Performance

If the performance of a contract obligation is somewhat defective in certain respects, a question frequently arises as to whether the party who performed is entitled to partial payment for the portion of his performance which does conform to the contract. The party who performs defectively, the recipient of the performance, and society in general all have interests in such a question. If the performing party is unable to recover for the portion of his performance which is properly done, to that extent he is penalized or punished for what may be an inadvertent and unimportant breach of contract. On the other hand, if the recipient of the performance is required to make a partial payment for defective performance, to that extent he is forced to pay for something which he did not agree to buy. Society, of course, has an interest in encouraging proper and complete performance of contract obligations and in not unduly weakening the stability of contracts. Upon weighing the various conflicting interests, the courts have decided that *in some cases* it is sound policy (fair, reasonable, and practical) to permit partial recovery for slightly defective performance. In formulating and applying this principle, the courts weigh the following interrelated factors:

1. The amount of deviation or defect (extent and value) in proportion to the entire contract.

2. The reason for the deviation—that is, whether it results from a deliberate and intentional disregard of the contract or only from an inadvertent and careless oversight.

3. The benefits received by the party for whom the performance is rendered.

4. The forfeiture threatened to the performer if recovery is denied.

5. The adequacy of money damages to fully protect or compensate the party for whom the performance is rendered.

6. The time when the deviation is discovered in relation to the time for performance of the entire contract.

7. The feasibility of the performer correcting the defects so that his performance will exactly comply with the contract.

The question of whether or not recovery should be allowed for substantial but incomplete performance most often arises in connection with land contracts (either sale or construction contracts); recovery for defective performance is seldom permitted in sales-of-goods contracts.

1. CONSTRUCTION AND SALE-OF-LAND CONTRACTS

Partial recovery for incomplete performance is most often permitted in connection with the construction of a building on land already owned by the other party to the contract, the party for whom the building is being constructed. While the landowner has a right to receive a building constructed according to the contract and completed on time, if the owner is permitted to reject a building completely because of minor defects or a minor delay the builder will lose much of his labor and material. Taking back a building as a unit is a limited remedy; taking back the materials usually leaves the builder with a pile of rubble. It seems fair, therefore, to say that if the owner can be fully compensated by money damages, the builder should recover for his substantial performance less any damages the owner sustains.

No exact definition or formula can be stated for determining when a certain building will be considered as substantially complying with a construction contract. The degree of correct compliance is a major factor. Thus, defective performance is not substantial unless the defects can be corrected for a cost which is low in comparison with the entire contract price. Also, for performance to be substantial, the defects must concern unimportant details which do not affect the general plan and purpose of the building. However, while the percentage of compliance is quite important, the other factors which have been previously listed are also important.

If a builder's performance is not substantial, he is not entitled to be paid the contracted compensation. However, if a landowner derives a benefit from accepting and using what the builder has done, some courts argue that since the purpose of the civil law (as distinguished from the criminal law) is not to punish or to penalize the builder, he should be able to recover for the value of the benefit which the owner actually receives. Other courts however argue that since an owner cannot be expected to give up the use of his land, he really has no opportunity to reject a building or work done to a building on his land. These courts have held, therefore, that the benefit to the owner does not entitle the builder to collect anything at all unless his performance is sufficient to be classed as substantial.

A building construction contract will often contain a provision specifying the amount of damages which the builder must pay to the owner for each day of delay after a certain date. Such a provision is called an agreed or liquidated damage provision. If reasonably related to actual loss, the liquidated damage provision is enforceable. If, on the other hand, no reasonable relationship appears between the agreed damage provision and the actual losses which might possibly result, the provision really amounts to a penalty which the civil courts will not enforce.

In a contract for the sale and purchase of land, it is common for the parties to agree on a certain settlement time, a date when the seller is to deliver the deed for the property and the buyer is to pay the agreed price. Many such contracts expressly state, "Time is of the essence of this contract." Such a provision will be enforced; for even a slight delay by one party, the other may cancel the entire contract. On the other hand, if time is not made vitally important (or of the essence) either expressly or by circumstances, a delay will justify cancellation only if it is a material delay. A "time is of the essence" provision is uncommon in building construction contracts. However, if such a provision is included, it will be enforced; the builder cannot collect under the contract even though his delay is slight. Even so, if the work which the builder has done is on the owner's land and the owner makes use of it, some will argue that the owner should be obliged to pay for the value of the benefit which he receives.

2. SALES-OF-GOODS CONTRACTS

Society's permitting a building contractor to recover a partial payment when his performance is slightly defective, is based mainly on the builder's inability to remove an already completed building from the owner's land, and the consequent severe loss or penalty the builder would sustain. A seller of goods on the other hand can take the rejected goods back. Generally, therefore, in sales-of-goods contracts (unless delivery in installments is involved, as discussed later) a buyer is permitted to reject for any deviation at all.

Some earlier court decisions excepted from this general rule cases in which goods had been specially manufactured for the particular buyer in question and were not suitable for others (for example, a machine specially designed for the buyer and useless to anyone else except as scrap metal). Permitting the buyer to reject for minor defects would penalize the seller, forfeiting much of his labor. However, such a case still differs from the case of a building erected on an owner's land,

Example. A builder and a landowner entered into a contract under which the builder agreed to construct a building on the owner's land according to certain plans and specifications, and the owner agreed to pay $77,000, payable in installments at stated times as the work progressed, with the final payment of $3,500 to be made after completion of construction. The specifications provided that the pipe used for plumbing should be "wrought-iron pipe, galvanized, lap welded, standard grade, manufactured by the Reading Company." The pipe used met these specifications exactly except that inadvertently about one-half of the pipe used was made by manufacturers other than the Reading Company. The deviation was not discovered until the architect was going over the invoices, which was after all of the plastering was completed. The owner refused to make the final payment until the pipe manufactured by others was replaced by Reading Company pipe. The builder refused to tear out the walls in order to change the pipe, and sued the owner for the amount of the final payment.

Admittedly, there was nothing in the circumstances sufficient to excuse the builder from performing his commitment. He, therefore, would be liable for any damages which might result from his defective performance.

However, in the case upon which this example is based, the court (the New York Court of Appeals)[12] decided that under the circumstances (substantial performance, inadvertent deviation, penalty to builder and gratuitous gift to owner if recovery denied) the builder was entitled to recover under the contract, less damages for the deviation. Since under the Particular circumstances the owner could prove no actual damages, the builder recovered the entire final payment for which he had sued.

The decision was a close one, four to three. The three minority judges felt that the builder should not recover because, through his neglect, he failed to give the owner the pipe for which the owner had contracted, regardless of the reason why the owner wanted pipe from a certain company and even though designating that certain company might have been only a whim of the owner's. ☐

* * *

Example. A builder contracted to build a certain type of roof on an owner's building for $325. Upon completion of the work, the owner wrote to the builder that the roof was not satisfactory, that it was leaking in several places, was not smooth, not saturated between layers, and not adequately covered, and that the owner would not pay unless the builder would take off the unsatisfactory roof and put on one that conformed to the contract. The builder denied that the roof was defective. Although the owner used the building without having the new roof fixed, he persisted in his refusal to pay. The builder sued the owner for the agreed price. From the evidence the jury concluded (1) that the roof was defective and would cost $80 to repair in order to conform to the contract, and (2) that because of leakage through the defective roof, the walls of the owner's building were damaged to the extent of $75. The trial court entered a judgment for the builder for $170, the contract price, ($325) less the cost of remedying the defects, ($80) and less the amount of damages caused by the defects ($75).

---

12. *Jacob & Young, Inc. v. Kent*, 230 N.Y. 239, 129 N.E. 889, 23 A.L.R. 1429 (1921).

Example (*continued*)

In the case upon which this example is based, the Wisconsin Supreme Court[13] reversed the judgment and directed the trial court to enter judgment against the builder for the owner's $75 damages. The court said that the builder could recover nothing under the contract because his performance was not substantial, and that since the owner had no reasonable alternative but to continue to use his building, his use of the roof which the builder had constructed would not give rise to any obligation to pay anything for the roof.

Some courts would be in complete agreement with this conclusion, while other courts would agree only partially. The latter courts would agree that since the builder's performance was not substantial, he would not be entitled to any recovery measured by the contract price. However, these courts nevertheless would say that since the owner derived a benefit from the builder's work, he should be required to pay the builder whatever was determined to be he money value of that benefit. ☐

13. *Nees v. Weaver*, 222 Wis. 492, 269 N.W. 266, 107 A.L.R. 1405 (1936).

because when the buyer rejects the machine, he does not retain or enjoy any benefit from the seller's work. Other early court cases, therefore, declared as a matter of policy that there should be no distinction between specially manufactured goods and standardized goods. The Uniform Sales Act (which was formerly in effect in about two-thirds of the states) and the Uniform Commercial Code[14] which supersedes the Sales Act, both follow this latter view. Even goods specially manufactured for a buyer and not reasonably useful to others, can be rejected if they do not *exactly* conform to the contract in all respects—quality, quantity, time and place of delivery, etc. (except in installment delivery contracts). Note, however, that it is possible for a particular shipment actually to conform to a contract even though it is somewhat defective. This is so when a certain percentage of defects are considered as commercially acceptable, by virtue of a usage or custom of the particular trade involved. For example, in one case involving a contract for a quantity of goat skins, the evidence showed that dealers of such goods could expect from 1 1/2 to 3 percent of the skins in a sizable shipment to be defective. If the quantity of defective skins in a shipment did not exceed this percentage,

the shipment would be considered as fully conforming to the contract. The Uniform Commercial Code states this rule as follows:

> A course of dealing between parties and any usage of trade in the vocation or trade in which they are engaged or of which they are or should be aware give particular meaning to and supplement or qualify terms of an agreement.[15]

Goods are supposed to be delivered in a single lot unless installment delivery is agreed upon or understood. In a contract for delivery in installments, any one installment is only a fraction of the entire contract, even though it may be a sizable fraction.[16] If a defect in a shipment is minor and the shipment is only a portion of the total contract, the defect, already minor, shrinks to insignificance from the standpoint of the entire contract. The authors of the Uniform Commercial Code therefore feel (following a similar view in the Uniform Sales Act) that it is sound policy to deny to a buyer a right to reject for such an insignificant defect. The Code provides:

> The buyer may reject any installment which is non-conforming *if* the non-conformity sub-

14. U.C.C. Sec. 2-601.

15. U.C.C. Sec. 1-205.
16. U.C.C. Secs. 2-307, 2-612.

stantially impairs the value of that installment and cannot be cured.... [Emphasis added.]

However, the authors of the Code further suggest[17] that if, for a commercially sound reason, a contract expressly requires exact compliance, then even under the Code a court could decide that *any* noncompliance in an installment would amount to a substantial breach and justify rejection.

C. Frustration of Purpose

Several English cases, generically referred to as the "Coronation Cases"[18] are probably the most famous lawsuits involving the question of excuse on the ground of frustration of purpose. When Edward VII ascended to the English throne after the death of Queen Victoria, an elaborate coronation ceremony was planned for a certain date, to include a parade over a specified route and a naval review. Numerous contracts were entered into by persons seeking to obtain facilities for viewing the pageantry. One defendant contracted to pay a certain sum for use, on the stated date, of the window space in the plaintiff's apartment which overlooked the line of the parade. Another defendant, intending to take paying passengers to watch the naval review, contracted to hire a ship for the stated date. When the King became ill the coronation plans were indefinitely postponed, and the defendants sought to avoid their contract obligations, while the plaintiffs tendered the contracted window space and ship and sued to collect the agreed payments. Notice the similarity of such cases to mistake in value cases discussed in Chapter 8, where disappointment arises from some extrinsic fact in existence but unknown at the time a contract is formed. The only difference is that in the

Coronation Cases the event occurred *after* the formation of the contracts. The plaintiffs were able to tender the exact physical items they had contracted to give, a seat by a certain window on the contract date, the use of a certain ship on the contract date. The postponement of the coronation made no change at all in the window or the ship, it merely changed their expected use and value to the defendants. Since the window or the ship, it merely changed their expected use and value to the defendants. Since value is constantly fluctuating as innumerable conditions constantly change, the law feels that it is usually not sound policy to excuse a person from his contract to buy a described item merely because later events have decreased its value. Sometimes, however, the courts soften this rule by attempting to spread losses which result from totally unexpected occurrences. In the Coronation Cases the court somewhat arbitrarily (as the court admitted) ruled that the defendants would be required to pay all that became due and payable under their contracts up to the time the coronation plans were changed—even if this was the entire contract price—but that any amounts due and payable after the change was announced could not be collected. Some legal scholars argue that a party should be discharged from a promise on the theory of frustration of purpose if the following conditions are *all* present:[19]

1. A later event completely changes or eliminates a certain fact situation which both parties, at the time of contracting, assumed would exist in the future.
2. The assumed fact situation was the motive for both parties entering into the contract.
3. The assumed fact situation concerned a matter reasonably believed by both parties to be stable and not subject to variation, and a matter as to which persons

---

17. Comment to Sec. 2-612.
18. Chiefly the following: *Herne Bay S.S. Co. v. Hutton*, 2K.B. 683 (1903); *Krell v. Henry*, 2K.B. 740 (1903); *Civil Serv. Co-op Soc. v. Gen. Steam Nav. Co.*, 2K.B. 756 (1903); *Chandler v. Webster*, 1K.B. 493 (1904).

19. See Restatement. Contracts. Sec. 288.

Example. A landlord leased to a tenant a described piece of land and the building erected thereon for a period of five years, beginning on June 1 of a certain year, for an annual rental of $1,200, payable in monthly installments in advance. The tenant enjoyed occupancy and use of the building until August 25 of the first year, when a fire completely destroyed the building. When the tenant abandoned the premises after the fire and refused to pay any further rent, the landlord sued the tenant. Nothing in the lease covered such an eventuality.

At common law, and in many states, the tenant would remain obligated to pay rent for the entire leasehold period. In any discussion of the rights and duties of landlords and tenants, two legal principles predominate: (1) for a person to become a tenant of certain premises, he must have an agreement or contract with the landlord, and (2) such an agreement grants to the tenant a real estate interest in the rented premises. Since a tenant has a real estate interest, he is actually a limited owner of the rented premises for the duration of the lease. If an entire building is leased to a tenant, his interest includes not only the building but also the land upon which it stands. As a limited owner of a property interest, the tenant enjoys the advantages and bears the burdens of ownership—he gains if the property increases in value, he loses if value declines or the property becomes worthless. If the tenant is conducting a business on the premises and is only half as successful as he had hoped, his disappointment does not mitigate his obligation to pay rent. If he is not excused when he is 50 percent disappointed, it is arguable that he should not be excused when he is 100 percent disappointed. He is still the limited owner of the property interest for which he agreed to pay a stated rent.

Other factors are also involved in the case of total destruction of a rented building, including the following:

Sharing of Losses. Since the landlord loses the total value of his building, losses are somewhat shared if the tenant loses the value of his leasehold use. In other words, if the tenant has paid the full amount of the rent in advance, he should not recover it; if he still owes rent, his obligation continues. (Of course if the landlord has fire insurance, that fact and the amount of insurance becloud but do not necessarily negate this factor.)

Inducing Carefulness. In cases involving the destruction of a leased building, the facts often state that the tenant was not at fault. Frequently, however, this is a conclusion resulting from the absence of evidence to prove otherwise. Since the tenant is in exclusive occupancy, a valid argument can be made that if the law requires the tenant to bear the risk of loss as a limited property owner, he will be induced to use greater care. Therefore it is considered sound policy under the common law of many states to hold that a casualty to the premises will usually not excuse a tenant from his obligation to pay rent. That the landlord is reimbursed under his fire insurance policy and refuses to repair or rebuild is usually immaterial; usually it is also immaterial that the casualty may have resulted from a concealed defect in the building (for example, defective wiring, unless the defect was actually known to the landlord at the time of leasing.

On the other hand, if only a portion of a building (an apartment or an office) is leased to a tenant, the tenant has a real estate interest in that portion of the building but no interest in the land. It would be impractical to consider that occupants of different portions of a building have interests in sections or slices of the land upon which the building stands, or interests in portions of the air space over the surface of the land. Therefore it seems fair, reasonable, and practical to say that a casualty sufficient to prevent the tenant's beneficial use of the portion leased to him destroys the *entire* interest of the tenant and frees him from further payment of rent. ☐

entering into such contracts could not reasonably be expected to assume the risk of change.

Under this suggested theory it is arguable that the defendants in the Coronation Cases would be considered excused from paying for the contracted window space or ship.

The field of real estate leasing has provided many frustration-of-purpose cases, with the general tendency being that a tenant who obtains the interest contemplated by the lease is not excused from paying rent when a later occurrence lessens the value of his leasehold interest or renders it entirely worthless. If the use specified in the lease has become totally illegal (as in liquor prohibition cases), some courts have recognized an exception and considered a tenant excused.

IV. Illegality

An agreement is illegal if either its formation or its performance involves a crime or a tort, or is otherwise opposed to public policy. The principal fact situations which may involve illegal transactions include the following: (1) ordinary kinds of crimes, (2) torts, (3) businesses or professions requiring licenses, (4) excessive interest for loans of money (usury), (5) gambling or wagering, (6) Sunday laws, and (7) other conduct contrary to public policy.

Since it would be absurd for a court, which is supposed to uphold the law, to help a person in breaking the law, a court should not aid a person to collect benefits from his own illegal conduct or to protect him from a burden or loss resulting from his illegal conduct. Therefore, if a lawsuit between two persons concerns an illegal transaction they have entered into, the court will usually leave the parties in the same position they were in when they came into court. This will often result in a ruling actually favorable to one or the other party. However, the court is not by

design preferring one over the other. This is merely the result of the court's refusal to assist *either* party.

Accordingly, the general rule is that an illegal contract cannot be enforced by either party to it, nor can such a contract be rescinded or the consideration given be recovered. However, if the legal and illegal part can be separated, the part which is lawful will often be enforced. Sometimes a change in the law will occur between the time the contract was made and the desire to enforce it arises.

If the contract was *illegal* when it was made, but a change in the law makes this type of contract legal, it will not be enforced. A common example involves prohibition. Two persons make a contract to sell and buy alcoholic drink when it is prohibited by law; then, prior to performance, prohibition is ended. The contract illegal at its start remains illegal.

On the other hand, a contract may be perfectly legal when made but becomes illegal by subsequent events. Such a contract will not be enforced either, but in order to ameliorate the harshness this might have on a party who rendered all or part of his performance before the illegality, such a party will be allowed to recover for the performance he rendered before the contract became illegal.

A. Types of Illegality

I. CRIMES

The term "ordinary crimes" includes murder, robbery, assault, buying goods known to be stolen, and the other common crimes. An agreement to suppress evidence of a crime is itself a crime called *compounding a felony* (if the suppressed crime is serious or *compounding a misdemeanor* (if the suppressed crime is minor). Obviously the courts should not aid parties in connection with agreements involving any of these crimes.

Example. A distributor of liquefied petroleum gas contracted to buy all of his requirements from a gas company at stated prices for the next five years. A year later an oil company, knowing of this contract, offered the distributor a better price and thereby induced him to disregard his prior contract and enter into a contract to buy all of his requirements from the oil company. Afterwards the oil company itself defaulted on its contract and the distributor sued the oil company.

Since to the knowledge of both the distributor and the oil company, the second contract involved a breach of the previous contract (between the distributor ,and the gas company), the general view is that the second contract would be illegal and unenforceable. Under this view, neither party to the second contract could enforce it against the other. ⬚

2. TORTS

Torts are discussed in Chapter 4. Since a tort is a wrongful act, the courts will refuse to lend their aid to parties in connection with agreements which involve the commission of torts. Since it is usually a tort to interfere intentionally with the contract relations of others, a contract involving such interference is illegal and unenforceable.

3. LICENSING STATUTES

Numerous statutes require licenses for persons engaging in various businesses and professions. Some of these are taxing statutes, intended merely to raise revenue, while others are competency statutes, designed to prescribe and enforce qualifications for persons to engage in certain businesses or professions (such as law, medicine, engineering, real estate brokering, and many others).

If the statute requiring a license is a tax measure, the courts in the various states are not agreed as to the result the lack of a license will have on contracts. On the other hand, if the statute is intended to assure the qualifications of persons carrying on specified businesses or professions, any contracts made by an unlicensed person who is engaging in one of these occupations will usually be considered illegal and unenforceable. Although the unlicensed person performs the agreed services

completely and competently, he cannot recover any compensation.

4. USURIOUS INTEREST

The expression "legal rate of interest" has two different connotations. It may be referring to the maximum rate of interest which can lawfully be charged, or instead it may refer to the rate of interest which parties are presumed to intend when they agree that interest will accrue but fail to specify the exact rate of interest. In some states the maximum rate and the presumed rate are not the same. For example, the presumed rate in some states is 6 percent while the maximum rate permitted by law for the same type of obligation is 18 percent. In some other states the two rates are the same. In such states, for obligations which do not come under some special statute, both the presumed rate of interest and the maximum which can lawfully be charged are the same.

Many states have statutes authorizing higher than the usual maximum rate of interest for certain situations, particularly for loans by licensed small loan companies. Rates of 1, 2, or 3 percent per month are commonly permitted, varying with the amount and duration of the loan. These statutes recognize and meet the social need of persons without property or steady employment to be able to borrow small sums of money. Loans to such persons involve greater risks and thus justify higher than the ordinary rates of interest.

With the great increase in inflationary pressures in recent years, interest rates have fluctuated considerably, especially on the high side. Many states have taken action to increase traditional rate ceilings or have tied the interest rate maximum to some governmental index. For example, in Pennsylvania, the maximum home mortgage rate is raised or lowered by the state government, administratively, in accordance with a legislative formula based upon the rate applicable to federal government obligations.

A rate of interest exceeding the maximum which can lawfully be charged is called *usurious interest*. The states differ as a matter of policy on the validity and effect of contracts involving usurious interest. In some states a lender who tries to charge a usurious rate of interest cannot collect even the principal amount of the loan, in some other states he can collect the principal but no interest, while in still other states he has the right to collect the principal amount of the debt together with interest calculated at the lawful rate.

A sale on credit is not treated as a loan of money. Usually the *carrying* or *finance charge* which a seller adds to the amount the buyer is to pay is not considered the same as interest on a loan of money, and therefore is not automatically regulated by the usury statutes. Unless a state also has a statute expressly applying to sales on credit, a seller is unrestricted in the amount he may charge for permitting deferred payments. Some states have no limiting statutes, other states regulate the carrying charges for all credit sales, while still other states prescribe a maximum carrying or finance charge for sales of certain items only.

5. GAMBLING

In most states generalized gambling is prohibited. Agreements involving prohibited gambling activities are unenforceable. Care must be taken to verify what type of gambling is prohibited in a given state because in recent years a number of states have authorized specialized types of gambling. Nevada allows generalized gambling, hence casinos abound, and even supermarkets and other stores may have an aisle or two of slot machines. A large share of the receipts are taken by the state government as a tax. It is this aspect of gambling which has encouraged other states to allow limited types of gambling. Accordingly, a number of states allow track betting on horse racing, harness racing, and dog racing. Once such betting is allowed, authorization for off-track betting may be considered and authorized. Additionally, state lotteries have been authorized in many states, again as a revenue measure, which permit this specialized type of gambling. And, in the 1970's New Jersey authorized casino gambling in the seaside resort of Atlantic City, competing with Nevada's monopoly.

A contest in which a prize is awarded on the basis of merit does not involve gambling, but it is gambling if an award or payment is to be made on the basis of a fortuitous happening. Unless special statutory exception is made, the definition of gambling will include bingo games run by churches and other charitable organizations as well as raffles or other gambling types of fund-raising devices.

In the case of insurance, the possibility of a loss, called an insurable interest, distinguishes an enforceable insurance contract from an unenforceable gambling contract. For insurance on another's life, the one buying the policy must have an insurable interest at the time he buys the policy; it is immaterial that such interest may cease before the death of the insured person. On the other hand, for fire and similar insurance, the insurable interest must exist not only at the time the policy is taken out but also at the time the insured loss occurs.

6. SUNDAY AND HOLIDAY CLOSING LAWS

At common law no prohibition existed as to the day upon which a contract could be made or performed. However, most states have statutes prohibiting most types of business on Sunday. Such statutes have frequently been challenged as violating the First and Fourteenth Amendments of the United States Constitution; when these two Amendments are read together, the resulting rule pertaining to religion can be paraphrased as follows:

> Neither Congress nor a State shall make a law respecting an establishment of religion, or prohibiting the free exercise thereof.

Sunday statutes have been uniformly upheld as welfare rather than religious laws. In a recent challenge before the United States Supreme Court, Chief Justice Warren, writing for a majority of the court, said:

> Throughout this century and longer both the federal and state governments have oriented their activities very largely toward the improvement of the health, safety, recreation and general well-being of our citizens.... Sunday Closing Laws like those before us have become part and parcel of this great governmental concern wholly apart from their original purposes or connotations. The present purpose and effect of most of them is to provide a uniform day of rest for all citizens; the fact that this day is Sunday, a day of particular significance for the dominant Christian sects, does not bar the State from achieving its secular goals....
>
> It is true that if the State's interest were simply to provide for its citizens a periodic respite from work, a regulation demanding that everyone rest one day in seven, leaving the choice of the day to the individual, would suffice.
>
> However, the State's purpose is not merely to provide a one-day-in-seven work stoppage. In addition to this, the States seek to set one day apart from all others as a day of rest, repose, recreation and tranquility a day which all members of the family and community have the opportunity to spend and enjoy together, a day on which there exists relative quiet and dissociation from the everyday intensity of commercial activities, a day on which people may visit friends and relatives who are not available during work days.
>
> Obviously, a state is empowered to determine that a rest-one-day-in-seven statute would not accomplish its purpose.... Furthermore, it seems plain that the problems involved in enforcing such a provision would be exceedingly more difficult than those in enforcing a common-day-of-rest provision.
>
> Moreover, it is common knowledge that the first day of the week has come to have special significance as a rest day in this country. People of all religions and people with no religion regard Sunday as a time for family activity, for visiting friends and relatives, for late sleeping, for passive and active entertainments, for dining out, and the like. . . .. Sunday is a day apart from all others. The cause is irrelevant; the fact exists. It would seem unrealistic for enforcement purposes and perhaps detrimental to the general welfare to require a State to choose a common day of rest other than that which most persons would select of their own accord.[20]

Some statutes prohibit the making of contracts on Sunday, others prohibit secular work and labor, still others are phrased as "business" or "labor" or "work of a man's ordinary business." Works of charity or necessity are generally excepted from the statutes. *Necessity* is usually considered to be a thing which needs to be done in order to preserve life, health or property. Specific exceptions of one kind or another exist in various states.

Violations of Sunday statutes are common. The extent of criminal enforcement varies in different communities, depending upon local policy.[21] However, regardless of what may be the enforcement wishes and policy of any particular community, the effect of Sun-

---

20. *McGowan v. Maryland,* 366 U.S. 420, 81 S. Ct. 1101, 6 L. Ed. 2d 393 (1961).

21. It is poor government and a dangerous practice to enact criminal statutes phrased so broadly that exact, complete enforcement is obviously not intended, and

Example.   On August 1, a Sunday, a seller and buyer entered into an agreement for the sale and purchase of a home freezer for $200. In entering into the agreement the buyer relied upon the seller's stating, "This freezer is in A-1 condition and will maintain a uniform temperature of 15 degrees. "

1. The seller delivered the freezer to the buyer on August 1 (Sunday).

(a) The buyer's agreement was to pay $200 within 10 days. When the buyer failed to pay, the seller sued. The seller could not recover, since the court would not enforce the buyer's Sunday promise. Neither could the seller recover possession of the freezer. Title was transferred upon delivery to the buyer and the court would not cancel the transfer merely because it occurred on a Sunday. If the court were to undo what had been completed on Sunday, the court would to that extent be helping the seller to avoid a loss incurred through his engaging in illegal conduct. The court would leave the parties in the position they were in when they came into court, with the buyer in possession of both the freezer and his money.

(b) The buyer paid $200 on delivery August 1. Upon putting the freezer into use, the buyer found that contrary to the seller's statement, the device would not maintain a temperature lower than 30 degrees. Evidence showed that the seller was fully aware of the freezer's defective condition when he made the above-quoted statement. The buyer would have no right to recover damages, either for breach of warranty or for fraud. The buyer's loss resulted from his joining in an illegal agreement, and the court would not help him either to enforce the contract or to avoid the resulting loss.

2. The Sunday agreement provided that the seller deliver the freezer to the buyer on Monday and that the buyer pay $200 within one week. Accordingly the Seller delivered and the buyer accepted e freezer on Monday. When the buyer failed to pay as agreed, the seller sued. The seller could recover. Delivery and acceptance of the freezer on Monday was conduct showing continued agreement between the parties, and 3made the agreement as an enforceable Monday agreement. The court would look to what was said on Sunday for the terms s to price and time for payment. ☐

day statutes on contracts is uniform throughout each state. If a contract involves a violation of the Sunday law, a court will not lend its aid to either party to the contract. The court will leave the parties exactly as they were when they came into court; any acts performed on Sunday will not be disregarded or canceled, but any portion of the agreement not yet performed will not be enforced.

Dating an agreement as of some day other than Sunday does not change the effect of the agreement between the parties, if it can be proved that the parties actually entered into the agreement on a Sunday. If an agreement formed on a weekday expressly requires performance in violation of the Sunday law, the agreement is illegal and unenforceable. However, an agreement formed on a day other than Sunday is not made illegal and unenforceable by the fact that some of the negotiations took place on Sunday. Also, even though an agreement is formed on Sunday, if the parties afterwards, on a weekday, mani-

---

21. (cont'd) then to leave to enforcement officials the discretion to enforce or not to enforce the statutes as they see fit, or as they feel the community desires. The practice is clearly inconsistent with one of the requirements of good government, as recognized and stated so clearly by the founders of the American system of government, "that this shall be a government of laws and not of men."

Example. The proprietor of a parking lot whostored cars for the general public used claim checks which provided that the proprietor of the lot would have no liability for loss of cars through fire or theft. A car stored in the lot was stolen as a result of negligence in operation of the lot, and the owner of the car sued the lot proprietor.

The proprietor would be liable. On the grounds of public policy, a business which stores goods for hire for the general public is not permitted to contract away its liability for negligence. Even if actually agreed to by the car owner, the exemption provision in the claim check would be invalid and unenforceable. ▢

* * *

Example. Five persons organize a corporation to operate a small business. Each person owns 200 shares of stock, a 1/5 interest in the business. They want to keep it a "closed" corporation. However they realize that in years to come, one or some of the original five might becomedissatisfied and want to sell stock to an outsider, or might die and the stock of the decendent be inherited by his heirs.

1. They agree and make it a part of the corporation rules that none of the stock will be transferable, except to thecorporation or another shareholder. This "absolute" restraint on a person's freedom to sell what he owns is against public policy and not enforceable.

2. They agree and make it a part of the corporation rules that before any stock can be sold or transferred, it must first be offered to the other shareholders at the he then book value of the stock. This gives the other shareholders "first option" to buy. Any stock not bought by the shareholders when so offered to them will be transferable to outsiders. This partial restraint, to accomplish a reasonable and proper purpose, is not against public policy and is enforceable. ▢

fest their continued mutual agreement, the courts will usually consider the agreement by implication remade on the weekday and enforce it as such; what was done and said on Sunday can be used to show the terms of the weekday agreement.

If the day an agreement is formed is a legal holiday, this is usually immaterial. Many holiday statutes do not prohibit the transaction of business; unless the holiday statute expressly states otherwise, the observance of holidays is permissive rather than compulsory. Thus under a typical holiday statute, a contract made on July 4, for example, would be fully enforceable.

B. Public Policy Questions

Agreements which are contrary to public policy are illegal and unenforceable. What is considered necessary or desirable for the general public is determined by the legislatures, and for situations not covered by statutes, by the courts. Public policy is involved in a wide variety of situations.

1. BRIBERY AND UNDUE INFLUENCE

Most situations of bribery or the use of undue influences of public officers, business personnel, agents and the like are covered by criminal statutes. Even in the absence of statutes, an agreement will be contrary to public policy if it has the tendency to tempt an agent to disregard his duty to his principal, whether or not the principal is thereby injured. (For a further discussion, see Chapter 18.)

2. EXEMPTIONS FROM LIABILITY

Exemption from liability for future acts of negligence in types of transactions which involve businesses catering to the general

Example. The owner of an established neighborhood grocery store learned that a newcomer planned to build and operate a grocery store across the street. The established owner paid the newcomer $1,000 for the newcomer's agreement that he would not open a grocery store within a radius of one mile of the established store. The newcomer afterwards decided to follow his original plan and build across the street from the established store, and the established owner sued to enforce the agreement.

Not being a part of an employment or sale of business contract, the restraint was against public policy, and would be unenforceable. ☐

* * *

Example. The owner of a grocery store in Collegeville, Illinois, (assume a population of 5,000 people) sold the store, equipment, merchandise, and goodwill to a buyer. As part of the contract, the seller agreed that he would not own, operate, work in, or have an interest in a grocery store anywhere in the area described below. A year later the seller planned to build and operate a grocery store across the street from his previous location. The buyer sued for an injunction to restrain the seller from proceeding with his plan.

1. The area described in the agreement was: "Anywhere in Illinois." The restraint extended much further than the area affected by the store. The injunction would be refused.

2. The area described in the agreement was "Anywhere in Collegeville, Illinois." The restraint was reasonably related to the area affected by the store. The injunction would be granted.

3. The area described in the agreement was: "Anywhere in Collegeville, Illinois, or elsewhere." The court would usually slice off the invalid "or elsewhere" and grant an injunction restraining the seller from associating himself with a grocery store in Collegeville, Illinois. ☐

public or which involve an unreasonable risk of bodily injury to the general public are frequently considered against public policy and unenforceable. Thus if an agreement otherwise valid contains an invalid exemption from liability provision, the provision will be declared unenforceable while the balance of the agreement remains enforceable. (For a further discussion, see Chapter 26.)

3. RESTRAINT OF TRADE

In the absence of statute, the decision as to when restraints are unreasonable must be made by the courts. In general, it is considered in the public interest that owners be free to use and dispose of their property as they wish and that persons be free to engage in whatever businesses they wish, wherever they wish.

a. Restraint on Use or Transfer of Property

In general, an absolute, complete restraint on alienability is not valid or enforceable, but a partial restraint, to accomplish a reasonable and proper purpose, is not contrary to public policy and is enforceable.

b. Restraints on Trade or Competition

Generally such a restraint is not against public policy and therefore is enforceable if the restraint meets all of the following conditions:

1. It does not tend to harmfully affect the general public.

2. It is part of an employment contract or a contract for the sale or leasing of a business or property interest.

3. The restraint is limited to what is appropriate for proper protection of the contracting parties. If the restraint is too broad in scope, the court will try to separate the invalid from the valid part of the restraint. If the restraint is not so divisible, the court will not attempt to rewrite the agreement for the parties but instead will declare the entire restraint invalid.

* * *

Problems

1. On his thirteenth birthday, B purchased a bicycle from S, an adult, for $95, payable $10 down and the balance to be paid at the rate of $5 per month. After making two monthly payments, B made no further payments. S did nothing concerning the bicycle until three months after B came of age. Two months after B came of age he sold the bicycle to P. One month thereafter S sued B to recover the unpaid balance of the purchase price of the bicycle. (Assume minority ends at age 18 and that the applicable statute of limitations is 5 years.)

(a) Explain (1) the reasoning upon which B might attempt to defend, (2) the reasoning upon which S might attempt to collect, and (3) which party should be given judgment.

(b) Other facts remaining the same, assume that B never sold the bicycle, but that two months after coming of age, he orally promised S that within one month he would pay the full amount of the balance due on the bicycle. When B defaulted on this promise, S sued. Answer the same questions asked in Part (a). (Modified from A.I.C.P.A., Nov. 51-6.)

2. On February 1, C loaned his good friend D $500 to be repaid within six months. By the middle of the year D was in financial difficulty and C did not press for repayment. Although D and C saw each other frequently, nothing further was said about the loan until March, ten years later, when D, during a conversation with C, said that in going over some old records he had been re-

minded of the $500 loan. D added, "I can't pay right now but don't worry, I'll pay you as soon as I can." C replied, "Oh, forget it—I have." However, the following June, when D unexpectedly inherited a large sum of money, C reminded D of the $500 obligation When D failed to pay by September 1, C sued.

(a) Assume that the statute of limitations on such debts was five years. Explain (1) the reasoning upon which D might attempt to defend, (2) the reasoning upon which C might attempt to collect, and (3) which party should be given judgment.

(b) Assume that the statute of limitations on such debts was ten years. Answer the same questions as are asked in Part (a).

3. On thirty different occasions between January 1 and November 1, a supplier sold and delivered to a contractor, on open account, various building materials in the aggregate amount of $4,550. Assume that open-account purchases were payable by the tenth of the month following the month of purchase. Most of the supplies were purchased before June 1. From June 2 until November 1 the total sales aggregated only $500, after which the contractor made no further purchases from the supplier. From time to time the contractor made nine payments on the account, in varying amounts totaling altogether $2,500. The last two payments were of $100 each and were made on June 20 and July 10 respectively. On July 6, four years later, the supplier started a lawsuit against the contractor for the $2,050 balance due. Explain (1) the reasoning upon which the contractor might attempt a complete or partial defense, (2) the reasoning upon which the supplier might attempt to collect the entire amount claimed, and (3) how much if anything the supplier was entitled to recover in his lawsuit.

4. R who owned and operated a small manufacturing business employed E as purchasing agent on a five-year contract at a salary of $8,000 per year. Three years later, business reversals not at all the fault of R rendered R's business hopelessly insolvent. In an action initiated by R's credi-

tors and vigorously opposed by R, the state court appointed a receiver for R's assets and ordered the sale of all assets, thus forcing the termination of R's business. E filed a claim with the receiver for (1) $1,000 wages due and unpaid at the time of the court adjudication, and (2) $500 damages sustained by E as a result of the termination of R's business and consequently of E's job. Should E's claims be allowed?

5. For some years T had successfully operated various dance pavilions. Knowing this, O, the owner of a newly constructed dance hall leased the hall to T for two years at a stated rental. One year later T died. T's executor considered the lease terminated and so notified O. No provision in the lease covered this eventuality. O refused to agree to termination of the lease and when the executor refused to pay any rent accruing after T's death, O sued T's estate. Explain (1) the reasoning upon which T's executor might attempt to defend, (2) the reasoning upon which O might attempt to collect, and (3) which party should be given judgment.

6. An engineering company employed E as a beginning draftsman for a six-month period, at $250 per month, $175 of which was to be paid to E at the end of each month, with the balance payable to E upon the satisfactory completion of his six-month's service. During the next four months E's work was satisfactory. At the end of the fourth month, E, while driving carefully on a weekend fishing trip, was killed in an auto accident by a car carelessly driven by D. The company sustained $400 damages through being suddenly deprived of E's services.

(a) E's administrator requested payment of the withheld portion of E's salary and when the company refused to pay, the administrator sued the company. What result? Explain.

(b) The company sued D for damages sustained through being deprived of E's services. What result? Explain.

7. E was a bookkeeper for the R Mills, receiving his salary monthly under a contract which pro-

vided that if E left without giving a two-week notice, he would receive nothing for wages accrued during the current month. On May 31 E was arrested for manslaughter following an auto accident. Unable to pay bail, E was kept in the county jail until trial. Upon trial E was convicted and sentenced to state prison. R Mills refused to pay E any salary for the month of May. The damages with R Mills sustained through being deprived of E's services without two-week's advance notice, exceeded the amount of E's May Salary.

(a) Would E be entitled to any salary for May? Explain.

(b) Other facts being the same, assume that E's trial was held early in June, and that E was acquitted of the crime charged and released. Would E be entitled to any salary for May? Explain. (Modified from A.I.C.P.A., Nov. 30-9.)

8. The owner of a plot of land entered into a written contract with a contractor under which the contractor agreed to excavate for a cellar of stated size at a certain location on the owner's land, for which the owner agreed to pay a stated amount upon completion of the work. Soon after the contractor commenced work he encountered considerable solid rock. Neither the contractor nor the owner had suspected the presence of the rock. The contractor met with the owner and they orally agreed that the contractor would complete the excavation described in the written contract, and that the owner would thereupon pay a specified unit price for all rock excavated. The agreed price for excavating rock was about nine times greater than the price for excavating earth; the parties had used the latter figure in calculating the original contract price for the entire job. After the parties reached their second agreement, the contractor completed the excavation. Rock constituted about two-thirds of the entire material excavated. Upon completion of the job, the owner paid the contractor only the original contract price, and the contractor sued for the additional compensation promised. Explain (1) the reasoning upon which the owner might attempt to defend, (2) the reasoning upon which the contractor might attempt

to collect, and (3) which party should be given judgment.

9. A landlord and a tenant entered into a ten-year lease agreement for a warehouse building at a described location in a certain city. The warehouse was constructed of wood and the lease included a provision, that if during the leasehold term the building should be damaged or destroyed by a fire not the fault of the tenant, the landlord would with all possible diligence repair or rebuild the building for the tenant's continued use. After about three years the building was completely destroyed by fire through no fault of the tenant. Meanwhile the city had amended its earlier zoning laws. Under the amended ordinance, new erection of wooden commercial buildings in that area was prohibited. When the landlord refused to rebuild the destroyed building, the tenant sued the landlord for damages. Explain (1) the reasoning upon which the landlord might attempt to defend, (2) the reasoning upon which the tenant might attempt to win, and (3) which party should be given judgment. (Modified from A.I.C.P.A., Nov. 22-5.)

10. S, owner of a large apple orchard, entered into a written contract under which S was to sell and deliver to B by a certain date 1,000 bushels of apples to be picked from S's orchard, and B was to pay $2 per bushel upon delivery.

(a) Before the apples were ripe enough to be picked, a windstorm destroyed the entire crop. When S failed to deliver any apples to B, B sued for damages. What result?

(b) Assume that the windstorm destroyed half of the crop. On the agreed delivery date, S tendered to B 500 bushels. What were the rights of the parties? (Modified from A.I.C.P.A., May 59-10.)

11. In January, S Company entered into a contract with B Company under which S Company agreed to sell and deliver to B Company and B Company to buy at 4 3/4 cents per gallon, 1,500,000 wine gallons of refined blackstrap molasses of the usual run, from the M Company refinery, to test about 60 percent sugars, delivery to be in stated installments over most of the year. In February, because of rising sugar prices, the operators of M Company refinery decided to decrease output, a decision over which S Company had no control. During that year, the refinery's output totaled only 485,000 gallons, of which 344,083 gallons were allotted by M Company to S Company and by S Company to B Company. The market price for such molasses went up and in June was 7 1/2 cents per gallon and by October 8 1/4 cents per gallon. The above-mentioned 344,083 gallons was all the molasses S Company shipped to B Company during the contract period. Upon expiration of the contract period, B Company sued S Company for damages for failure to deliver the contracted quantity of molasses.

(a) Assume that at the time of the January contract, S Company had a contract with M Company to buy during the year a quantity of molasses greater than that specified in the S Company-B Company contract. When B Company sued S Company, explain (1) the reasoning upon which S Company could attempt to defend, (2) the reasoning upon which B Company could attempt to win, and (3) which party should be given judgment.

(b) Assume that over the prior several years, without any advance contract with M Company, S Company had regularly ordered and received from M Company a greater quantity of molasses than was specified in the S Company-B Company contract, and that therefore S Company, reasonably believing it to be unnecessary, had no advance contract with M Company for deliveries during the year of the S Company-B Company contract. Answer the same questions asked in Part (a).

12. S entered into a written contract with B agreeing to manufacture and deliver to B, at a stated price, 5,000 ladies' sweaters of specified types, deliveries to be made in equal quantities over a five-month period. Before any deliveries could be made, S's employees went on strike which remained unsettled for three months beyond the last delivery date.

(a) B sued S for damages for breach of contract. What result? Explain.

(b) If you were S, and were negotiating the above contract with B, what would you have done and why, in order to avoid such a dispute as described above. (Modified from A.I.C.P.A., May 29-3.)

13. On June 1, a seller, desiring to sell a certain house and lot, listed the property with a real estate broker. On June 15 the broker negotiated a written contract between the seller and a buyer for the sale and purchase of the premises for $20,000, conditioned upon the buyer being able to obtain a first mortgage loan in the amount of $15,000. The contract specified that closing was to be on or before July 15. On June 15 the buyer applied to a building and loan association for a loan which was approved on June 24. The mortgage loan funds were made available on July 20, and the broker notified the seller to appear in the office of the loan association attorney on that date or at any time thereafter to close the transaction. The seller refused, saying that there had been too long a delay, whereupon the buyer sued the seller for breach of contract, the damages claimed being $100 for expenses and $1,000 for loss of the bargain. Explain (1) the reasoning upon which the seller might attempt to defend, (2) the reasoning upon which the buyer might attempt to win, and (3) which party should be given judgment.

14. The owner of a real estate lot entered into a contract with a builder for the construction of a small house on the owner's lot, according to certain plans and specifications, for $12,000, payable $8,000 at stated intervals during construction, and $4,000 upon completion of the house. The agreed plans and specifications called for building paper to be placed between the inner siding and outer sheeting boards of the house. About half of the outer sheeting boards had been attached when the owner noticed that the builder's workmen, through oversight, had not tacked building paper over the siding boards before nailing on the sheeting boards. When the owner called this to the attention of the builder, the builder had building pa-

per tacked over the remainder of the exposed siding but refused to remove the sheeting boards already in place in order to insert building paper. By this time the owner had paid the builder $7,000. When the building was completed, the owner moved in but refused to make any further payments until the builder installed the omitted building paper. The builder sued for the remaining $5,000. Evidence in the lawsuit showed that removal of the portion of sheeting boards involved, attaching the omitted building paper, and replacing the sheeting boards would cost about $1,000. The evidence also showed that the fair value of the building at the time of the lawsuit was $10,000.

(a) Did the builder substantially perform the contract?

(b) Assume that the court would decide that the builder's performance was substantial, explain (1) the reasoning upon which the owner could attempt to defend in the builder's lawsuit for $5,000, (2) the reasoning upon which the builder could attempt to recover, and (3) which party should be given judgment.

(c) Assume that the court would decide that the builder's performance was not substantial. Answer the same questions asked in Part (b).

15. Near a small town with a total population of about 300 people, a large manufacturing company decided to construct extensive research and fabrication facilities, which, after completion, would employ about 5,000 people. Large numbers of homes were built by various contractors, and when the company's buildings were completed and in full operation, the population in and near the town grew to over 3,000 families. For a number of years, T had owned and operated the largest retail store in the town, using a building rented from the owner, O. When manufacturing began, T's lease, providing for a monthly rental of $75, had one year yet to run. During this year T's store operations and profits multiplied tremendously. Upon expiration of the lease, O and T entered into a new five-year lease for the store building at a rental of $300 per month. One year later, the man-

agement of the company was changed and the new board of directors unexpectedly decided to completely abandon the new plant. A year and a half after the start of T's five-year lease, the plant was closed down and the population of the area shrank to less than 1,000 people. With the drastic decrease in the volume of his business, T could no longer profitably pay $300 per month rent. O refused to renegotiate the lease and a few months after the plant closed, T moved his store to another location, still owing rent for the past three months. O thereupon sued T for all unpaid rent to date. Explain (1) the reasoning upon which T might attempt to defend, (2) the reasoning upon which O might attempt to claim, and (3) which party should be given judgment.

16. The owner of a plot of land entered into a contract with a builder for the construction of a summer resort hotel building on the owner's land, according to certain plans and specifications. The agreed price was $80,000, of which $75,000 was to be paid at stated intervals during the construction and the remaining $5,000 upon final completion, which was to be three months after the date the parties formed the contract. The contract provided that for each day's delay in final completion beyond the contracted completion date, the builder would be liable to the owner for damages in the amount of $50 per day. Each of the following is a separate fact situation; for each, assume that the contract contained no provision expressly referring to such a situation.

(a) One month after formation of the owner-builder contract, when the work was about one-third completed, the builder, through no fault of his own, was seriously injured in an auto accident. He was in a coma for two weeks, unable to conduct any business for another two weeks, and confined in his hospital bed for six weeks longer. Explain the effect of this on the builder's contract obligation.

(b) Two months after formation of the owner-builder contract, when the work was about two-thirds completed, a hurricane occurred of unprecedented ferocity for that part of the country.

(1) The resulting flooding conditions made it impossible for any work to be done on the job for the next three weeks. Explain the effect of this on the builder's contract obligation. (2) The force of the wind and flooding totally destroyed the two-month's construction work. Explain the effect of this on the builder's contract obligation.

(c) One week after formation of the owner-builder contract, and before any steel had been delivered to the job, there was a steel strike coupled with a tense international situation, as a result of which the government issued an order freezing all steel supplies except for certain essential purposes—which did not include summer resort hotels. The freeze order continued in effect for the next six months. Explain the effect of this on the builder's contract obligation .

(d) One week after formation of the owner-builder contract, the owner was adjudged bankrupt in a Federal court bankruptcy proceeding. Explain the effect of this on the builder's contract.

(e) One week after formation of the owner-builder contract, when the builder began to excavate, he discovered quicksand at various points. The condition had been unknown to either party, had not been disclosed by the test borings, and would increase the cost of construction several thousand dollars. When the owner refused to agree to any increase in the contract price, the builder refused to proceed with construction. Explain the effect of this on the builder's contract obligation. (Modified from A.I.C.P.A., Nov. 52-7.)

17. By use of a skeleton key, a college student named Sly wrongfully gained entrance to the college stenciling room where final examinations had been prepared and stole from a shelf two ink-stained but legible copies of the final exam prepared for a certain course. He sold one copy to a student for $25 cash, and the other copy to a student who did not have the immediate cash but who promised to pay $35 within five days. Sly assured each buyer that this was the exam to be used

for the coming final exam in that particular course. Sly reasonably believed that this was true.

(a) On the sixth day and before the date set for the exam, the student who purchased on credit refused to pay for his copy and Sly sued for the agreed $35. Explain whether Sly could recover.

(b) The instructor learned what had been done and used another exam as the final exam. The student who had paid for his copy sued Sly to recover the $25 paid. Explain whether he could recover.

18. In January, R. Roger, owner of the Roger Hotel and holder of a liquor license for the premises, hired E. Edwards as manager at a salary of $500 per month to begin March 1, and to continue from month to month until terminated by either party giving the other one week's notice. E assumed his duties on the agreed date and continued for six months when, after a quarrel with R, E gave the proper notice and quit. Never having received any payment for his services, E sued R for $3,000. The facts in the case showed that from the previous December to June 1, E was also the owner and operator of Edward's Restaurant and held a liquor license issued for the restaurant. Also during this same period (ending June 1) E was manager of the local Sportsmen's Club which also had a liquor license. E's connection with the tavern and the club did not in any way detract from the competency with which E performed his job for R, and R had no grounds to complain concerning E's work. In the latter part of May, E decided to reduce his activities and therefore effective June 1, resigned as manager of the club and also sold his tavern and transferred his liquor license. E continued as manager of the Roger Hotel until September 1. The State Liquor Statute provides: "It shall be unlawful for any hotel, restaurant, or club liquor licensee to be, at the same time, employed directly or indirectly by any other person engaged in the sale of liquor, malt, or brewed beverages or alcohol." Explain (1) the reasoning upon which E might attempt to recover in his lawsuit against R, (2) the reasoning upon which R might attempt to defend, and (3) how much if anything E should recover.

19. The promoter of a championship boxing bout sold to the A television network the exclusive rights for television coverage of the bout. The plaintiff, who designed and made a television camera which was battery-operated and small enough to conceal in a press photographer's camera, approached the D television network with a proposal. The parties agreed that the plaintiff would attend the bout and surreptitiously transmit to D network's mobile pickup unit satisfactory television coverage of the bout, for which D network agreed to pay the plaintiff $5,000. The plaintiff performed his part of the agreement with remarkable success but after the bout the A network filed a lawsuit against the D network. Fearing adverse publicity, D network refused to pay the plaintiff the agreed $5,000 and the plaintiff sued. Explain (1) the reasoning upon which the plaintiff could attempt to recover, (2) the reasoning upon which the D network could attempt to defend, and (3) which party should be given judgment.

20. A homeowner approached a builder to inquire about putting asbestos shingles on the owner's house. When he learned the price, the owner said he did not care to have the job done since he expected to sell his house soon. The builder explained that the new siding would increase the value and resale price of the house. The builder also said that he had considerable contact with people looking for homes and would be willing to assist the owner in selling his house, and, since he was not a licensed real estate broker, he would charge the owner only 2 percent commission if successful in negotiating a sale, rather than the standard 5 percent charged by licensed real estate brokers in the area. The owner had the builder put new siding on the house and completely paid for the job. Three months later the owner notified the builder that he wished to sell for $17,000. The builder said he thought the house could be sold for $20,000 and the owner in writing agreed to pay the builder a 2 percent commission if he negotiated a sale. The builder posted in his office a picture of the owner's house with a notation of its availability for $20,000, and during the next few weeks showed several people

through the house. Soon the builder secured and brought around to the owner a buyer to whom the owner sold for $20,000. The owner failed to pay the builder the agreed commission and the builder sued the owner. Explain (1) the reasoning upon which the builder might attempt to recover, (2) the reasoning upon which the owner might attempt to defend, and (3) which party should be given judgment.

21. While making an audit for a businessman, an accountant found among the accounts payable an indebtedness of $2,500 arising from the businessman's purchase of a light motor truck for business purposes. The record showed that the businessman bought the truck from a certain dealer for $3,000, paying $500 down and agreeing to pay the $2,500 balance in three months. The accountant also learned that the dealer's selling price for that type of vehicle was $2,400 if payment was made in cash. In the state where the credit purchase took place, the maximum contract rate of interest permitted by law was 10 percent per year. The accountant wondered whether the transaction as usurious. Explain whether or not it was. (Modified from A.I.C.P.A., May 59-8.)

22. A builder advertised construction of a certain type of dwelling for $7,625, of which the builder would finance $7,125 to be paid off in monthly payments over a period of ten years. A buyer entered into a contract with the builder for construction of such a dwelling on a lot owned by the owner. Upon completion of the building, the buyer paid the builder $500 in cash and gave the builder a mortgage on the house and lot for $11,400 ($7,125 plus ten years' interest on that amount at the rate of 6 percent per year), payable in 120 monthly installments of $95 each. The maximum interest rate permitted by law was 6 percent per year. The buyer paid monthly installments for eight years and then ceased his payments. The builder brought a lawsuit to collect the balance claimed due or to foreclose the mortgage. Explain (1) the reasoning upon which the buyer might attempt to defend, (2) the reasoning upon which

the builder might attempt to collect, and (3) what should be the result of the lawsuit.

23. In a state where gambling was and always had been unlawful, a debtor owed a creditor a gambling debt. The creditor engaged an agent to collect the debt, agreeing that the agent could retain 25 percent of what he collected as his compensation. The agent collected the entire amount of the debt from the debtor but refused to pay any part of it to the creditor. The creditor sued the agent. Explain whether the creditor could recover. (Modified from A.I.C.P.A., Nov. 34-10.)

24. Each of the large number of participants in a bridge tournament paid an entrance fee of $5, most of which, as was announced in the advance publicity, was used to purchase a costly prize for the top scorer. During the playing the disagreeable personality of the player who accumulated the highest score alienated almost everybody, and the ones in charge of the tournament thereupon refused to turn over to him the first prize award. The winner sued. What result?

25. A manufacturer purchased a quantity of raw material. Under the manufacturer's usual production and marketing schedule, the finished article made from this raw material would be sold six months later. To protect himself from loss in case of a drop in the price of the raw material during that six-month period, the manufacturer, at the time that he purchased the raw material, entered into a hedging contract to sell a like quantity of raw material six months later. It was the intent of the manufacturer and the plaintiff with whom he made the hedging contract that no materials would be delivered under the contract; rather, after expiration of the six months, the parties would settle at the then market price. The market price of such raw materials rose and at the end of the six-month period was double the price six months earlier. The manufacturer refused to perform his hedging contract and the plaintiff sued. Explain (1) the reasoning upon which the manufacturer might attempt to defend, (2) the reasoning upon which the plaintiff might attempt to enforce the

hedging contract, and (3) which party should be given judgment.

26. On the night of Sunday, March 19, a buyer met a seller at a small hotel in a farming community. Upon learning that the buyer wished to purchase some mules for the government the seller said that he had 15 mules for sale, and the parties went to the hotel yard where 13 of the seller's mules were corralled and looked at them by the light of a lantern. The seller said that his remaining two mules were just like those in the yard and could be turned over to the buyer the next day. The price of $180 apiece was discussed, with the seller assuming the risk of the mules not passing government inspection, but finally the parties agreed on $160 apiece with the buyer to assume that risk. The parties returned to the hotel and the buyer gave the seller a thirty-day note for $2,400, dating it March 20. The parties then told the hotel keeper that the seller's 13 mules had been sold to the buyer and directed that their keep be charged to the buyer for that night. The next day the seller obtained his two additional mules and added them to the ones in the yard and the buyer thereupon took away the 15 mules purchased from the seller. When the buyer failed to pay the note upon its due date, the seller sued. What result? Explain.

27. Immediately after termination of World War II, as civilian production of automobiles returned to normal, demand greatly exceeded supply. Many used-car dealers acquired new or almost new cars and sold them at prices considerably in excess of the list prices for new cars. New-car dealers wished to curb the operation of such a "gray market." Smith, a new-car dealer operating under the name Smith Agency, adopted the practice of having a buyer to whom he sold and delivered a new car sign the agreement quoted below. B. Brown purchased a new car from S and signed such an agreement. One week later B resold the car to a used-car dealer for more than the price B had paid for the car. A few days later, when S learned of B's resale, S sued B for $500.

(a) The agreement signed by B read as follows: "[Date] in consideration of the sale and delivery to B. Brown of the following described new car [then followed a description of the car by make, model, and serial number] and with an intent to be legally bound, B. Brown hereby agrees with the Smith Agency that B. Brown will not sell the above described car nor any interest in said car during the period of six months from the above date. In case of B. Brown's violation of this agreement B. Brown promises to pay to the Smith Agency the sum of $500 as liquidated damages, which sum the Smith Agency will then pay to the local chapter of the American Red Cross. (signed) B. Brown." In S's lawsuit against B, explain (1) the reasoning upon which B might attempt to defend, (2) the reasoning upon which S might attempt to collect, and (3) which party should be given judgment.

(b) The agreement signed by B read as follows: "[Date] in consideration of the sale and delivery to B. Brown of the following described new car [then followed a description of the car by make, model, and serial number] and with an intent to be legally bound, B. Brown hereby agrees with the Smith Agency that for the period of six months from the above date B. Brown will not sell the above described car nor any interest in said car without first offering to sell the said car to the Smith Agency for a price equal to the price B. Brown hereby pays for the car less 3 percent per month depreciation. In case of B. Brown's violation of this agreement, B. Brown promises to pay the Smith Agency the sum of $500 as liquidated damages, which sum the Smith Agency will then pay to the local chapter of the American Red Cross. (signed) B. Brown." Answer the same questions asked in Part (a) of this problem.

28. For 10 years O owned and operated a restaurant in Centerville, Illinois (assume a population of about 5,000 people). Learning that N intended to open a restaurant in the same town, O entered into a written agreement with N under which O paid N $5,000 and N agreed not to operate a restaurant in the area stated below for the next 5 years. A year later N opened a restaurant in Centerville and O sued to enforce the agreement and restrain N from operating his restaurant.

(a) In the written agreement, N agreed not to operate a restaurant any place in Illinois. Explain whether O was entitled to win the lawsuit.

(b) In the written agreement, N agreed not to operate a restaurant any place in Centerville, Illinois. Explain whether O was entitled to win the lawsuit. (Modified from A.I.C.P.A., May 52-6.)

29. P. Porter, operating a dancing school in Philadelphia, hired D Davis for a period of one year, at a stated compensation, as a dancing instructor, supervisor, and interviewer, and at the start of the contract period gave D a course of training in dance instructing. The written employment agreement signed by both parties contained the following provision:

"For a period of two years after termination of Miss Davis' employment, she will not, without the written consent of P. Porter, directly or indirectly engage in teaching dancing to any person within a radius of 25 miles from P. Porter's Philadelphia studio."

To obtain the job, D told P that she was 22 years old, although she was actually only 17 years old. At the expiration of the one-year period, D quit P's employment and the following week, opened and started operating a dancing studio in a small town less than 25 miles from P's studio. P sued D for an injunction to restrain her from operating her dancing studio. D raised the defenses of minority and illegality. Explain (1) the reasoning in support of D's defenses, (2) the reasoning in support of P's lawsuit, and (3) the result of the lawsuit.

30. S, a CPA operating a public accounting office, entered into a contract with M Company to perform certain specified accounting services monthly for M Company for one year, for a stated fee. Six months later S sold his office, his practice, and all outstanding contracts to B, another CPA, and agreed in writing with B that S would not perform any accounting services in that city for the next five years. M Company did not wish B to perform the accounting services specified in the contract with S, and demanded that S perform the specified services. S was willing, but B brought a lawsuit against S for an injunction to prevent S from doing so. Explain (1) the reasoning upon which B might attempt to obtain such an injunction, (2) the reasoning upon which S might attempt to defend and prevent issuance of the injunction, and (3) whether the court should grant the injunction.

11 Third Party Rights and Duties

Third Party Rights and Duties

A. Definition and Introduction

When the term "remote party" is used in connection with a contract, it refers to a person who is not a party to the particular contract in question. While a remote party must respect other persons' contracts and is guilty of a tort if he maliciously interferes with the contract rights of another (see Chapter 10), it is obvious that a duty to perform a particular contract cannot be cast upon someone without his consent. And just as he has no obligations, so also a remote party ordinarily has no right to meddle or interfere by attempting to enforce a contract to which he is not a party and in which he has no legally recognized interest. Society maintains the civil court system for the purpose of defining and enforcing individual rights usually by requiring a defendant who wrongfully violates a plaintiffs rights to compensate the plaintiff for the money loss thereby sustained. Society will not permit this purpose to be perverted or misused by speculators. Suppose, for example, that immediately after a pedestrian has been grazed in an encounter with a car, a spectator dashes up, helps the bruised and shaken pedestrian to his feet, and pays him $100 cash for an assignment of all of his rights against the driver of the car; then the spectator as the assignee of the pedestrian's claim sues the driver for damages. As Sir Frederick Pollack has written:[1]

It is not thought good for justice, peace, or fair dealing that hostile rights of action, claims for the redress of personal injuries as distinct from claims which are in substance for damage to property, should be marketable. This principle is found, I believe, in all civilized laws; it is at the bottom of the rules of the Common Law against "maintenance" and "champerty," rules which at first sight look technical and even capricious, but which were called forth by real dangers and abuses.[2]

Certainly the right to recover for physical injuries should be considered personal to the injured person (or to his estate if he has died) and not transferable to another. In the early days of the common law, claims for breach of contract were also considered personal. To quote again from Sir Fredrick:

. . . most archaic laws, including those of Rome, gave a creditor enormous powers of self-redress, even to imprisoning and practically enslaving the debtor in default of payment. Under such a system the personal character and temper of the creditor might

1. Sir Frederick Pollack, A FIRST BOOK OF JURISPRUDENCE (New York: St. Martin's Press, paperback ed., 1961), p. 122.
2. The crimes of "maintenance" and "champerty," offenses against public justice, are committed when a person with no legitimate interest pays for another's lawsuit or bargains to share in his recovery. Blackstone has called such persons "pests of society, who officiously interfere in other men's quarrels." (BLACKSTONE'S COMMENTARIES OF THE LAW, Washington Law Book Company, 1941, pp. 806-807.)

obviously be no less important to the debtor than the debtor's honesty or means of payment to the creditor. [3]

Gradually punishment as a remedy for non-payment of a debt disappeared from the law, and the law began to recognize that, while physical injury claims and some contracts are quite personal, most contracts are fairly impersonal. With physical injuries, the extent of injury caused by a defendant's wrongful act, and the money loss resulting, may vary considerably with the health, strength, economic status, etc., of the injured person, while the extent of damages resulting from a breach of contract is usually impersonally controlled by the scope of the contract itself. Remedies for breach of contract are accorded to the owner of the contract, and it is essential in modern society for the law to recognize that contract rights are also property rights, usually just as marketable as any other items of property. Therefore, while it is a sound and necessary rule that a remote party cannot officiously interfere by suing to enforce a contract to which he is not a party, nevertheless a person who has purchased contract rights or to whom contract rights have otherwise been transferred should usually have a right to sue.

The topic of remote parties also contains another facet. Some contracts are expressly made for the benefit of certain remote parties. Suppose, for example, that A and B enter into a contract under which for a consideration paid by A to B, B agrees to perform in a certain way for another person, C. While C is not a party to the contract he is the person who is intended to receive a benefit from performance of the contract, and as a matter of fairness should not be ignored when damages for breach of the contract are being calculated. As the New York Court of Appeals has said:

Contracts for the benefit of third persons have been the prolific source of judicial and academic discussion.... The general rule, both in law and equity ... was that privity between a plaintiff and a defendant is necessary to the maintenance of an action on the contract.... On the other hand, the right of the beneficiary to sue on a contract made expressly for his benefit has been fully recognized in many American jurisdictions, either by judicial decision or by legislation, and is said to be "the prevailing rule in this country." . . . It has been said that "the establishment of this doctrine has been gradual, and is a victory of practical utility over theory, of equity over technical subtlety." . . . The reasons for this view are that it is just and practical to permit the person for whose benefit the contract is made to enforce it against one whose duty it is to pay.[4]

To recapitulate, while a remote party cannot officiously intermeddle in someone else's contract, he can (in many but not in all cases) purchase the contract and, as the assignee of the assignor's rights, sue to enforce the contract; or the remote party can sue if he is a third-party beneficiary.

B. Assignment of Contracts

I. RIGHTS AND DUTIES IN GENERAL

Because a person who is the complete owner of something of value is usually free to do what he wants with it—either utilizing it himself or transferring it to another—there is no reason to deny such freedom of action to a creditor who owns a contract right to collect money from an obligor. It should make no difference to the obligor to whom he makes his contract payment so long as the payment will adequately discharge his obligations.

---

3. *Op.cit.* p. 114, fn.1.

---

4. *Seaver v. Ransom,* 224 N.Y. 233, 120 N.E. 639 (1918). The expression "privity of contract" is briefly defined and illustrated on page 265, footnote number 19.

Example. A seller sells and delivers certain goods to a buyer in exchange for the buyer's note promising to pay the seller $1,000 in 60 days. The seller is free either to hold the promissory note until maturity and collecton it himself, or instead to transfer the note to a third person who will then have the right to collect from the buyer when the note matures. ☐

* * *

Example. A buyer orders certain goods from a seller for $1,000, the terms for payment being stated as "net 60 days." The seller ships pursuant to the order and records in his accounting books that he is to receive $1,000 from the buyer in 60 days. Since not evidenced by a promissory note or a similar document, the buyer's obligation is usually referred to as an "open account," "book account," or "account receivable." As with the promissory note in the preceding example, the seller is free to assign or transfer the account receivable to a third person who will thus obtain the right to collect when the obligation matures. ☐

Suppose that a sales contract is bilateral, both parties agreeing to perform at stated future dates; for example, the seller to deliver certain goods 30 days after the date of the contract and the buyer to pay the $1,000 purchase price 60 days after receiving the goods. Under this bilateral contract the seller has not only a right to receive money but also a duty to deliver the described goods. If before the time for delivery the seller wishes to make a complete transfer of the contract, he will not only pass along to the transferee the right to receive money, but will also arrange with the transferee for the latter to deliver the described goods to the buyer. The buyer might argue that the contract calls for goods to be delivered by the original seller, not by the transferee. However, as pointed out in Chapter 5 most contracts do not require personal performance. It seems sound policy to say that if goods which conform to the contract are tendered to the buyer, he is obtaining all that he is entitled to under the contract, and he has no ground to object regarding the source of the goods. However, even though the seller has transferred the contract, if the buyer fails to receive satisfactory performance, he should still be able to enforce the contract against the seller. The buyer's willingness to enter into a contract with a certain seller is based at least partly on the seller's reputation for good faith and on his financial ability to perform contract obligations which he assumes. Having contracted with a particular seller, the buyer should not, without his consent, be deprived of his right to enforce the contract against that seller. Therefore, even though the seller arranges for the goods to be delivered by his transferee, the seller remains liable if the transferee should fail to satisfactorily perform the contract. In other words, while the seller can transfer his *right,* and thus completely divest himself of the right, he cannot completely divest himself of this *duty* without the consent of the other contracting party.[5] To distinguish between the effects of transferring rights as compared with transferring duties, the law usually speaks of the transfer of a right as an "assignment" and the transfer of a duty as only a "delegation." Of course not every contract right can be assigned nor contract duty delegated. A contract can be transferred (right assigned and/or duty delegated) only if the transfer will not change what the other con-

---

5. A three-party agreement between a seller, buyer, and third person, in which the buyer consents to the substitution of the third person in place of the seller is commonly called a contract of *novation.*

tracting party is to do or to receive under the contract. If a transfer will make a material change in the performance of the contract, the consent of the other contracting party is necessary for the transfer to be valid.

The general rules which result from the foregoing policy considerations can be summarized as follows:

1. Unless a contract prohibits assignment, a right arising under the contract can be assigned without the consent of the other contracting party, so long as the assignment does not materially change the obligation of the other contracting party.

2. Unless the contract provides otherwise, the performance of a duty can be delegated, without the consent of the other contracting party, so long as performance by the one to whom delegated will conform to the original contract.

3. Delegating performance of a contract duty does not free the original obligor from his contract obligation.

4. A valid assignment gives the assignee or delegate a right to enforce the contract against the other contracting party.

2. APPLICATION OF GENERAL RULES

To illustrate the application of these basic principles, assignments of various of the common types of contracts will be briefly considered.

Work and Service Contracts

A person may contract to perform services for another and, nevertheless, not be an employee. For example, a physician is usually not considered to be an employee of his patient. Only if the one for whom work or service is being done has the right to supervise and control the details of performance, does the one who contracts to do the work become an employee. If the one being served has the right to direct only the end result and no right to control the details involved in reaching that result, the one performing the service is called an independent contractor. Suppose that a landowner engages a builder to construct a home according to certain plans and specifications. While the owner can dictate the end of result—a building conforming to the agreed plans—he has no right to direct how the builder's business is run, what employees he hires, the amount of their wages, etc. The builder is an independent contractor who contracts to perform services for the landowner.

Employer and Employee. An employer's right to control the details of his employee's performance necessarily makes the contract personal to both parties. An employee might be willing to dig a certain ditch for his original employer, but not for some third person; the employer might be willing to hire his original employee, but not some equally competent third person. Although the general nature of the work would remain the same, the actual performance could vary materially from one employer to another or from one employee to another. Therefore, an employer's contract right to his employee's services cannot be assigned unless the employee consents, and the employee cannot delegate to a substitute the duty of performance unless the employer consents.

Hirer and Independent Contractor. If the service to be rendered by an independent contractor is of such a nature that the quality of performance may vary materially from one person to another, then it is obvious that the hirer engages a certain contractor because of his personal skills and qualifications. Clearly such a contractor cannot delegate the duty of performance to a substitute without the hirer's consent. Likewise, if the performance of services involves a personal relationship between the contractor and the hirer, the latter cannot assign his rights to such services without the contractor's consent. However if

Example. A driller contracted in writing with a landowner to drill a gas well to a specified depth on the owner's property. Under the contract, the driller was to furnish all lumber, tools, cables, and the like, and the landowner was to furnish machinery and water and to pay $3 per foot for drilling. On the same day that he made the contract, the driller orally assigned all of his rights and duties to an assignee for $500. The assignee was also an experienced driller.

Work of this type necessarily requires the labor and attention of a number of men. Therefore, in the absence of circumstances showing reliance on some special knowledge, experience, or pecuniary ability of the driller, there was nothing of a personal nature in the contract. Personal performance by the driller not being required, the driller could validly delegate to the assignee the duty to drill the well. The landowner would be obliged to accept the assignee's tender of performance or become liable for damages for breach of contract. Upon completion of the work the assignee would be entitled to recover the agreed compensation from the landowner. ▢

special skills and personal trust and confidence are not involved, a contract right to the services of an independent contractor can be assigned, and a contract duty to perform the services can be delegated.

Real Estate Leases

Even though a rented apartment or building is not subjected to intentional or negligent damage, the ordinary wear and tear on the premises may be much greater with one tenant than with another. For other reasons also, a certain tenant may be either more or less desirable than another tenant. Nevertheless, the law usually considers that a landlord's main interest in a lease contract is his right to receive the specified rent money. Therefore, *unless a lease expressly prohibits assignment,* a tenant's right to occupy for the leasehold period is assignable, and the tenant's assignment is valid and effective without the necessity of the landlord's consent. Because the law takes this view, most standard-form leases expressly provide that a tenant cannot assign or sublet without the written consent of the landlord.

If a tenant is not hindered in his occupancy and enjoyment of rented premises, it is usually immaterial to the tenant who actually owns the property. Therefore, a landlord who sells his property can transfer the lease,

thus validly assigning to the buyer the landlord's lights under the lease and delegating performance of any duties the lease imposes on the landlord.

Contracts for Cash Transfers of Real Estate

Assignment and Delegation by the Buyer. Unless the contract prohibits assignment, a buyer who contracts to purchase real estate for cash may assign his right without the consent of the seller. Upon tendering the stated purchase price, the assignee would be entitled to enforce the contract and receive a deed from the seller.

Assignment and Delegation by the Seller. Usually in a contract to transfer real estate, a seller agrees to give a deed in which he will warrant the title to be free and clear of all mortgages or other encumbrances. For several policy reasons, what might be called a "rule of integration or merger" applies to transfers of real estate. If after a buyer enters into a land-purchase contract, he accepts a particular deed as satisfactory performance of the contract, the provisions of the contract are usually considered as merged into or superceded by the deed. In other words, unless clearly stated otherwise by the parties, any provisions of the contract which are not

Example. S, owner of a large tract of land, had the land surveyed and divided into numbered building lots. He then contracted in writing to sell Lot Number 1 to B for a stated price. The contract specified one month later as the settlement date—the day on which the buyer was to pay the stated price and the seller was to deliver to the buyer a warranty deed for the property. Two weeks after entering into the S-B contract, S sold and, using a nonwarranty deed, transferred the entire tract to T, subject to the S-B contract which T in writing agreed to perform. On the date specified in the S-B contract for settlement, T signed and tendered to B a warranty deed for Lot Number 1.

If B should accept T's deed, B would obtain title and T's warranty of title, but B would have no warranty which he could enforce against S. Thus, if B should desire to hold S to a warranty of title, B would have a right to refuse T's tender unless accompanied by an enforceable written warranty of title signed by S. ☐

included or repeated in the deed are considered as waived and no longer enforceable. One result of this is that a seller's contract duty to give a warranty deed (a deed in which the seller guarantees title) cannot be delegated to another without the consent of the buyer.

Contracts for Credit Transfers of Real Estate

Often a contract for the transfer of real estate will provide that when the seller transfers a deed to the buyer, the buyer is to make a partial payment and sign a mortgage promising to pay the balance of the price at stated future times. Suppose that the buyer then assigns the contract to a third person. Under the expanded parol evidence rule or rule of merger described in the preceding paragraph, the seller is not required to deliver a deed to the buyer's assignee solely on the assignee's mortgage. Thus the buyer's obligation under a credit real estate contract cannot be delegated to another person without the seller's consent.

Contracts for Sales of Goods[6]

In connection with contracts for sales of goods, the Uniform Commercial Code provides:

> Unless otherwise agreed all rights of either seller or buyer can be assigned except where the assignment would materially change the duty of the other party, or increase materially the burden of risk imposed on him by his contract, or impair materially his chance of obtaining return performance.

The Code also provides:

> A party may perform his duty through a delegate unless otherwise agreed or unless the other party has a substantial interest in having his original promisor perform or control the acts required by the contract. No delegation of performance relieves the party delegating of any duty to perform or any liability for breach.

Note that the above-quoted Code provisions merely reiterate the usual common law rules

----

6. U.C.C. Sec. 2-210.

Example. By written contract S agreed to sell and B to buy a described tract of land for $15,000, payable as follows: $500 on signing of the contract, $2,500 on the settlement date one month later, and a three-year mortgage for the $12,000 balance with interest at 6 percent per year. A few days after signing the contract and paying the first $500, B in writing assigned the contract to T for$ 1,200 which T paid to B. T notified S of the assignment, and on the settlement date T tendered $14,500 in cash to S and requested a deed for the property. When S refused, sayinq that he wanted the agreed mortgage, T sued S for specific performance.

S would not be required to transfer the land to T either on a mortgage signed by T or on tender of the entire price in cash. Payment of the entire price on the settlement date would deprive S of the $2,160 interest (6 percent of $12,000 for three years) to which he had a contract right. Only if T tendered performance exactly in accordance with the contract ($2,500 in cash, a $12,000, three-year, 6 percent mortgage plus an enforceable guaranty of the mortgage debt signed by B) could S be obliged to deliver a deed to T. ☐

which apply to all contracts. The last sentence of the latter quotation emphasizes two points:

1. A buyer can assign his right to receive goods and delegate his duty to pay, even though the contract is a credit contract which provides for payment at a specified time after delivery. Some courts have held that a contract for delivery of goods on credit cannot be assigned, saying that a seller cannot be required to accept the credit of the assignee in place of the buyer's credit. Such holdings overlook the fact that while the buyer assigns his right to receive goods, he only delegates to the assignee the duty to pay, and that such a delegation cannot (without the seller's consent) relieve the buyer from his obligation to pay. The rule of merger discussed in connection with land contracts does not apply to sales-of-goods contracts. The seller can deliver to the assignee without worrying about the assignee's credit; if the assignee fails to pay, the seller can collect, either from the assignee or from the buyer.

2. A seller can delegate his duty to deliver even though the contract contains an express warranty. Unlike a land transaction with the rule of merger, the seller remains liable on the express warranty contained in his contract, even after the buyer accepts goods from the seller's delegate.

Rights to Receive Money

The right to receive money is one of the most impersonal of all contract rights and in almost all cases is fully assignable. When a businessman makes an assignment of a money claim, his purpose is usually to raise funds for the regular operation of his business. Such assignments can be called financing assignments. The method of making a financing assignment and the relative rights of the obligor, the assignor, and the assignee are prescribed by Article 9 of the Uniform Commercial Code which covers financing and secured transactions (see Chapter 7). Assignments which are not associated with the day-to-day conduct of the assignor's business are nonfinancing assignments, and are expressly excluded from the Code. The principal *nonfinancing assignments* include, (1) an assignment made to expedite the collection of an overdue account, (2) a transfer of accounts receivable in connection with the sale of the assignor's business, (3) an isolated assignment involving an insignificant amount, (4) an assignment of wages or sal-

Example. On June 1, a manufacturer borrowed a substantial sum of money from a bank to finance his manufacturing operations, promising to repay the loan one year later. As collateral security, the manufacturer signed a paper assigning to the bank "all of the accounts receivable now held by the manufacturer or hereafter to be acquired by him." On the following December 1, the manufacturer sold and delivered $1,000 worth of goods to a dealer who had never previously made a purchase from the manufacturer. Because the dealer had a good credit rating, the manufacturer did not hesitate extending 60 days' credit. When the manufacturer delivered the goods on December 1, an account receivable arose, consisting of the right to collect $1,000 from the dealer 60 days later.

As soon as the account receivable arose on December 1, the prior June 1 assignment served to validly assign the account to the bank. ☐

ary, and (5) an assignment of an entire unperformed contract, that is (in the language of the Code), "a transfer of a contract right to an assignee who is also to do the performance under the contract."

Assignment of Wages or Salary. Wages to be earned under a contract not yet made or a job not yet obtained (that is, the mere prospect of earning wages from some future job) is a future right which, as discussed in the next paragraph, cannot be assigned. On the other hand, a wage or salary due or to become due under a contract already in existence is at common law as freely assignable as any other money claim. In some states, however, statutes prohibit or restrict the assignment of wages or salary. Such statutes are based on the public's interest in protecting an employee and his family from an imprudent disposal of their means of livelihood.

Future Rights. If at the time a money obligation is assigned, the obligation is not yet collectible, it is frequently referred to as a future right. Future rights are of two general types, those which are to arise from contracts already in existence, and those which are expected to arise from contracts not yet entered into (as for example future accounts receivable). In the case of nonfinancing assignments (which do not come under the Uniform Commercial Code) the law takes a

conservative view. Traditionally, society has considered it unwise and contrary to the general good to permit a person to be able to dispose not only of all that he has but also of everything he hopes to acquire anytime in the future. In general, a line is drawn between a right already created by an existing contract and a right to arise under a possible future contract not yet formed. A right created by a contract already in existence can be assigned, even though the right is unmatured and contingent. However, if the contract which is expected to create the right is not yet formed, usually no valid assignment can be made. On the other hand, the less conservative, commercial view is followed for financing assignments. Over the years as business increased in volume and complexity, it gradually appeared desirable from a commercial standpoint that a person sometimes should be able to make a binding contract to dispose of interests which he had not yet acquired. The law responded to the needs of business and developed various ways to accomplish this. In consolidating the devices available for raising money, the authors of the Uniform Commercial Code continue this trend. Under the Code therefore, it is possible to make a valid financing assignment of rights to arise under contracts to be entered into in the future. The assignment automatically becomes operative and effective when the assignor later enters into a contract which brings the assigned right into existence.

Partial Assignments. Suppose that after entering into a certain transaction as a result of which an obligor incurred a $600 obligation to his creditor, the creditor attempted to assign $200 of this claim to one assignee and $300 to another assignee. If the law were to sanction splitting the assigned claim between two assignees, could the law find a reason to prevent splitting the claim among two hundred assignees? Drawing two hundred separate checks would be a substantial burden which the obligor had not foreseen when he incurred the $600 obligation to the single creditor. Similarly, an obligor's burden would be materially increased if he could be subjected to two or more separate lawsuits as a result of the partial assignment of a single obligation. In determining as a matter of policy whether partial assignees should have any rights against an obligor, the starting point is the general rule that the assignment cannot be made if it will materially change what the obligor is to do. In applying this rule, courts in some states flatly deny any validity to partial assignments. Some other states limit the enforcement of partial assignments to equity lawsuits in which all claimants join together in one lawsuit and the obligor can make one payment which the court will distribute among the various claimants. Some states give at least some effect to partial assignments. In view of this diversity of opinion, it is unwise for an obligor to completely ignore a partial assignment and to go ahead and pay the full amount of his obligation to his original creditor. Such an obligor is risking a lawsuit and should consult his lawyer before making any payment.

3. CONTRACTS EXPRESSLY PROHIBITING ASSIGNMENT

Persons who enter into an impersonal contract and do not specify otherwise are presumed not to care who performs or receives performance under the contract. In such a contract, therefore, the rights can be assigned and the duties delegated. Sometimes, however, parties include in their contract a provision expressly prohibiting any transfer of the contract. Since it is considered socially desirable to accord to parties considerable freedom in making contracts, the law will enforce their restriction—until it clearly appears to be harmful to the overall good of society. When weighed against public policy, the effect of such a restrictive provision can be summarized in the following way:

1. **Restriction on Delegation of Duties.** Suppose that a contract for the sale and delivery of certain standardized goods contains a provision stating that the duty of delivery cannot be delegated. Without such a restriction, the duty unquestionably could be delegated. However, the restriction is perfectly valid. Because of the restriction the buyer cannot be required to accept goods from any person other than the seller.

2. **Restriction on Assignment of Rights.**

   (a) *Restriction on right to receive performance other than money.* Usually a contract may validly restrict performance to the contracting parties only. For example, if a real estate lease expressly prohibits assignment, the landlord cannot be required, without his consent, to permit the tenant's assignee to occupy the leased premises.

   (b) *Restriction on right to receive money.* Courts in the various states disagree as to the effect which should be given to a contract provision expressly prohibiting the assignment of a money claim. While some courts give full effect to the provision, other courts hold that in spite of such a provision, a creditor can nevertheless assign the claim. Under the latter view, as soon as the obligor learns of the assignment, he is bound by it, and when the obligation comes due, the obligor can be required to pay the amount of the obligation to the assignee. The courts holding this view consider that the right to receive money is so impersonal that it is similar to the ownership of tangible property, and, apply the rule discussed in Chapter 10, that an absolute restraint on the alienation of property is against public policy and unenforceable. The Uniform Commercial Code adopts this view;[7] for a financing assignment and for assignment of a right to receive payment for goods delivered by the assignor, any contract provision which prohibits assignment is ineffective and the money claim can be assigned despite the express stipulation otherwise.

4. RIGHTS OF ASSIGNEES AGAINST OBLIGORS

Suppose that a seller sold and delivered certain goods to a buyer for $1,000 payable in one month, and then made an assignment of the $1,000 account receivable. As the courts frequently say, an assignee "stands in the shoes" of the assignor, with the same rights the assignor would have had to collect from the obligor. Suppose, however, that the seller was guilty of fraud in inducing the obligor to make his purchase, and that upon discovering the fraud, the obligor gave proper notice of his desire to cancel the contract. If the account had not been assigned, the obligor's defense of fraud would certainly be effective to prevent enforcement of the obligor's promise to pay $1,000. Should the defense also be effective against the assignee who was completely innocent of any fraud?

---

7. U.C.C. Secs. 2-210. 9-318.

In answering such a question, courts frequently say that an assignee's rights are like water, which cannot rise higher than its source. At first glance, an assignee's rights appear to be exactly comparable to water in this respect; it would seem to be an impossibility for a person to transfer better rights than he himself owns. And the law so holds in respect to *ordinary* property and contract rights. However, various policy factors compel a different view with certain extraordinary types of property and contract rights. Suppose, for example, that a thief stole a rare book and sold and delivered it to a buyer who paid full value, honestly and reasonably believing that the thief owned the book and had the right to sell it. If the owner succeeded in tracing his book to the buyer's possession, the owner would have the right to recover the book. No matter how innocent the buyer was, he would obtain no better rights than the thief had. Now suppose that the owner had hidden $2,000 in the book, that the thief used the money to purchase a car, and that somehow the owner was able to trace the money and prove that the $2,000 in the innocent car-dealer's possession was the identical currency that had been stolen from the owner. The owner could not recover the money. Of course the thief himself would have no better right to the money than to the book. Nevertheless, while the innocent transferee of the *book* would obtain no better right than was held by his transferor (the thief), the innocent transferee who gave value for the *money* could obtain a better right than his transferor had and would become the absolute owner of the money. In thus distinguishing between such items as books and money, the law calls the former *nonnegotiable* and the latter *negotiable*. A book is, of course, transferable—but nevertheless nonnegotiable. Hence it is clear that the word "negotiable" is not synonymous with "transferable." Rather, the term "negotiable" is a tag which the law applies to any of several types of property interests, as to which it is possible for an innocent transferee for value to obtain a better right than was held by his transferor. Money has this attribute, and at an early date, it was recognized as essential in the conduct of business and commerce for certain other property and contract rights to be accorded the same attribute. Thus, while an account receivable not evidenced by a note is not negotiable—although it is assignable—a promissory note will be negotiable, if it complies with certain formal requirements. For example, the following note is negotiable in form:

> Centerville, Ill [Date]
> One month after date I promise to pay to the order of Sam Smith One Thousand ($1,000) Dollars.
> *(signed)* Bert Brown

Notice that the quoted note is payable to the "order of" the named payee. For a note to be negotiable it must be payable either to the order of the payee or to the bearer. In addition there are other formal requirements with which a note must comply to be negotiable. Notes which are in common use frequently contain more provisions than the preceding example. Some additional provisions will not interfere with negotiability, whereas some others will render a note nonnegotiable. The requirements for negotiability and its effects are more fully explained and illustrated in Chapter 23. The purpose of the present discussion is to point out that a note payable to "order" or to "bearer" may possibly be a negotiable note, and especially to emphasize that the discussion of assignments in this chapter relates solely to *nonnegotiable* rights.

If a nonnegotiable note or an account receivable is assigned, the assignee will obtain no better rights than his assignor had. Furthermore, until notice of the assignment is given to the obligor, if anything further occurs between the obligor and the assignor which would affect the assignor's right to recover if the account had not been assigned, the assignee's right to recover will likewise be affected. The most obvious example of this is the case of an obligor who, not knowing of the assignment of his account, makes a payment to his original creditor. The assignee will be bound by this payment. On the other hand, after an obligor is notified of an assignment, he is thereafter aware of the assignee's interest in the assigned account and can do nothing from then on to decrease its value. To recapitulate:

1. Until receiving notice of assignment, an obligor is justified in making payment according to his original contract. If the contract does not provide otherwise, the obligor is justified in paying his original creditor (the assignor) and such a payment will discharge the obligor's debt. *After* receiving notice of an assignment, the obligor should pay strictly in accordance with the notice.

2. The right of the assignee to collect from the obligor (1) will be subject to any defenses which the obligor has against the assignor arising from the original contract,[8] and also (2) will not only be subject to the defense of prior payment but also will be subject to any other defenses or claims which the obligor has or acquires against the assignor up to the time the assignee notifies the obligor of the assignment.

On the other hand, if an assigned claim is evidenced by a *negotiable* note, then:

1. The obligor should refuse to pay without seeing the note. Even though the obligor is not notified of a transfer, his contract obligation is to pay the actual owner of the note, whoever that may be. If the obligor pays his original creditor, and the latter dishonestly accepts the payment without disclosing that he no longer holds the note, the obligor can

---

8. Recent authority indicates the assignee is also subject to the defenses which the obligor could assert against the assignor. See *Thomas v. Ford Motor Credit Company,* Md. App. 429 A. 2d 277(1981).

Example. A manufacturer sold and delivered $1,000 worth of goods to a dealer on 60 days' open account. (Each of the following numbered parts is a separate fact situation.)

1. A supplier to whom the manufacturer owed an overdue claim of $2,000 obtained a judgment against the manufacturer, and knowing of the $1,000 account which the dealer owed to the manufacturer, had the sheriff levy on this obligation. The sheriff handed the dealer a formal attachment paper notifying him that the obligation which he owed to the manufacturer was attached by the supplier. Through his attachment the supplier obtained a claim or lien against the $1,000 account owed by the dealer to the manufacturer, and thereby became a lien creditor as to that account.

2. Some of the manufacturer's creditors initiated a proceeding in which the court adjudged the manufacturer to be insolvent and appointed a receiver to take over all of the manufacturer's assets for the benefit of his creditors. Included among the assets which the receiver obtained was the $1,000 account payable by the dealer. The receiver promptly gave the dealer formal notice of the insolvency adjudication together with an instruction that when due, the account should be paid to the receiver. The receiver would hereby become a lien creditor as to the hereby become a lien creditor as to the $1,000 account. ☐

be required to pay again to the proper person. While the obligor will, of course, have the right to recover this mistaken payment from the original creditor, the right is worth no more than the assets which are available for a sheriff's levy.

2. The obligor may be obliged to pay the note even though he has not fully received the item which he was supposed to obtain in exchange for the note. As is explained in Chapter 23, many defenses (including failure of consideration and fraud) are cut off when a negotiable note is properly transferred to an innocent purchaser for value.

5. RIGHTS OF ASSIGNEES AS TO THIRD PERSONS

When a debtor defaults and refuses or fails to pay his creditor, the creditors remedy is the usual collection remedy which applies to any unsecured obligation, namely:

1. The creditor will obtain a judgment against the debtor for the amount of the past-due obligation.

2. After obtaining a judgment, the creditor will have the sheriff levy on (that is, attach or seize) some property interest belonging to the debtor.

3. The creditor will then attempt to realize the amount of his judgment from the attached property interest usually through a public-auction, sheriff's sale.

Property interests which belong to the debtor and which the creditor can have attached include not only tangible property in the possession of the debtor (such as the debtor's house or car), but also intangible rights which the debtor owns, including any right which the debtor has to collect money from someone else.

In the above example, suppose that immediately after delivering the $1,000 worth of goods to the dealer, the manufacturer had assigned the $1,000 account to a bank, and that after this assignment but without knowledge of it (1) the supplier attached the account, or (2) the receiver was appointed and took over all of the manufacturer's assets. This would raise a question of priority between the assignee (the bank) and the lien creditor (either the supplier or receiver). In other words, as between the lien creditor and the assignee, which party would have a better claim to the assigned account and therefore a better right to collect from the dealer? Another possible claimant could be a second assignee. Suppose that (in the above example) after assigning the $1,000 account to the bank, the manufacturer wrongfully made a second assignment of the same account to a finance company, which had no knowledge of the first assignment. Again a question of priority would arise: between the first assignee (the bank) and the second assignee (the finance company), which would have a better right to collect the $1,000 account? Questions such as these, concerning relative priorities of equally innocent parties, are policy questions. The overall problem is, what should an assignee be required to do, as a matter of public policy, to protect his interest in an assigned account against subsequent lien creditors or subsequent assignees? Such situations are subdivided according to whether the first assignment is a financing assignment (and thus ruled by the Uniform Commercial Code) or a nonfinancing assignment. If the assignment of an account receivable is a financing assignment, then to protect his interest against a later party (lien creditor or assignee), the first assignee should file in the proper public office a statement which gives notice of the assignment (as is more fully discussed in Chapter 27). The assignee should consult his lawyer to accomplish the necessary filing. If the assignment of an account receivable is a nonfinancing assignment, then in many states the claimant who first gives notice to the obligor who owes the account, will have the better right to collect the account. Thus to protect his interest in a nonfinancing assignment the assignee must notify the obligor of the assignment before

the obligor learns of the interest of a later lien creditor or second assignee.

C. Third-Party Beneficiaries

I. NATURE OF THE RELATIONSHIP

Generally when a person enters into a contract and gives consideration for the promise of the other contracting party, the promisee intends that he himself will be the recipient of the promised performance. However, sometimes the promise for which the promisee contracts is by its terms to be performed for a specified third party. In such a contact, since the one intended to receive the promisor's performance is not a party to the contract, he is commonly referred to as the third-party beneficiary of the contract. The following example first reviews the effect of an assignment of rights and delegation of duties and then fits the third-party beneficiary contract into the picture. The interrelationship of the parties as a result of the two contracts described in the example is illustrated by the diagram on p. 326.

The persons involved in a third-party beneficiary contract are usually referred to as the *promisor* (the one who makes the promise in question—Edwards in the above example), the *promisee* (the one to whom the promisor makes his contract promise—Brown in the above example), and the *beneficiary* (the person intended by the promisor and promisee to receive performance or to be primarily benefited by the performance of the promise—Smith in the above example).

2. THE ELEMENT OF INTENT

In order for a third-party beneficiary to have any rights under the promisor-promisee contract, the promisee must have intended to confer some benefit on the third party.

Often the performance of a contract may incidentally or collaterally, be beneficial to persons other than the contracting parties. For example, the construction of a beautiful

Example. On June 1 Smith and Brown entered into a written assignment contract under which Smith agreed that he would sell and deliver certain described goods to Brown on July 1, for $1,000 payable on delivery. The contract said nothing concerning assignments. On June 5 Brown entered into a written contract with Edwards, under which Brown assigned to Edwards all of Brown's rights under the Smith-Brown contract, and Edwards agreed that he would accept the described goods on July 1 and pay Smith $1,000 on delivery. Smith was given prompt notice of the Brown-Edwards assignment contract. (Each of the following numbered and lettered parts is a separate fact situation.)

1. Edwards tendered $1,000 to Smith on July 1, demanded the goods described in the Smith-Brown contract, and when Smith refused to deliver, Edwards sued Smith for damages for breach of contract.

Edwards could recover. Under the Smith-Brown contract, Brown had a right to receive the described goods on July 1. By the Brown-Edwards contract, Brown assigned his right to Edwards. Since the Smith-Brown contract did not prohibit assignment, and since such a contract would be classified as an impersonal contract, Brown's right was assignable. As Brown's assignee, Edwards would be entitled to receive the goods and could enforce Smith's contract obligation to deliver.

2. On July 1, Smith tendered delivery of the goods to Edwards, and when Edwards refused to accept or pay for the goods, Smith notified Brown and tendered the goods to Brown, who also refused to accept them or pay for them.

(a) Smith sued Brown for damages for breach of contract.

Smith could recover damages from Brown. Under the Smith-Brown contract, Brown had a duty to accept the goods and pay $1,000 for them. Brown's delegation of this duty to Edwards could not, without Smith's consent, free Brown from his contract obligation.

After Smith recovered damages from Brown, Brown could in turn sue Edwards and recover damages. Under the Brown-Edwards contract, in exchange for the assignment of Brown's right under the Smith-Brown contract, Edwards promised that he would take over Brown's duty under that contract, namely that he would accept the goods and pay Smith $1,000.

As the promisee of Edwards' promise, Brown would certainly have a right to enforce it.

(b) Smith sued Edwards for damages. Although Edwards promised in the Brown-Edwards contract to accept the goods and to pay Smith, Smith was not a party to that contract. However, although Edwards made his promise to Brown, the promise was to accept goods from Smith and to pay Smith for them. Smith was the third-party beneficiary of the Edwards-Brown contract, and in most states could sue Edwards directly and enforce Edwards' promise. 🗀

home in a residential area will increase the value of the surrounding land. Suppose a lot owner enters into a contract with a builder for construction of a home on his lot. The purpose of the contract is to benefit the lot owner; he is the intended recipient of the performance of the contract. Any benefit to the neighbors is only incidental. Such *incidental beneficiaries* are not third-party beneficiaries and have no rights to enforce con-tracts which they have not personally entered into and which have not been assigned to them.

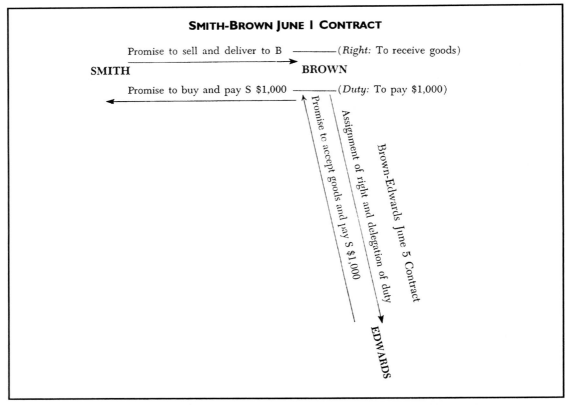

SMITH-BROWN JUNE 1 CONTRACT

Promise to sell and deliver to B ———(*Right:* To receive goods)

SMITH   **BROWN**

Promise to buy and pay S $1,000 ———(*Duty:* To pay $1,000)

Promise to accept goods and pay S $1,000

Assignment of right and delegation of duty

Brown-Edwards June 5 Contract

EDWARDS

3. CLASSIFICATION OF THIRD-PARTY BENEFICIARIES

There are two main types of third-party beneficiaries—*creditor beneficiaries* and *donee beneficiaries*. Which type a particular third-party beneficiary is depends upon the relationship existing between the promisee and the beneficiary at the time the third-party beneficiary contract is made. If a debtor-creditor or obligor-obligee relationship exists, that is if the promisee owes an obligation to the beneficiary and contracts for the promisor's promise in order to perform that obligation, the beneficiary is a creditor beneficiary. If the promisee owes no obligation to the beneficiary but instead contracts for the promise as a favor or gift to the beneficiary, the beneficiary, is a donee beneficiary.

4. ENFORCEMENT OF THIRD-PARTY BENEFICIARY CONTRACTS

Obviously, since the promisee is a party to the promisor-promisee contract, he can enforce it. In most states, regardless of whether a third-party beneficiary is a donee beneficiary or a creditor beneficiary, he has a right to enforce the promisor-promisee contract. The Uniform Commercial Code adopts this view for creditor beneficiaries of sales–of–goods contracts, stating:

> An assignment of "the contract" or of "all my rights under the contract" or an assignment in similar general terms is an assignment of rights and unless the language or the circumstances (as in an assignment for security) indicate the contrary, it is a delegation of performance of the duties of the assignor and

Example. A debtor owes a creditor $1,000 payable on a stated date. The debtor enters into a contract with a promisor under which, for a consideration moving from the debtor to the promisor, the promisor promises that he will pay $1,000 to the creditor on the stated due date.

The creditor, the third-party beneficiary of the debtor-promisor contract, is a creditor beneficiary. The debtor enters into the contract with the promisor as a way to satisfy the obligation which the debtor owes to his own creditor. □

* * *

Example. An uncle enters into a contract with a promisor under which for a consideration moving from the uncle to the promisor, the promisor promises that he will pay $1,000 to the uncle's nephew at a stated future date.

The nephew is the third-party beneficiary of the uncle-promisor contract. If the uncle owes no obligation to his nephew, the uncle is entering into the contract as a way of making a gift to his nephew, and the nephew is a donee beneficiary. □

its acceptance by the assignee constitutes a promise by him to perform those duties. This promise is enforceable by either the assignor *or the other party to the original contract.* [Emphasis added][9]

5. RESCISSION OF THIRD-PARTY BENEFICIARY CONTRACTS

Donee Beneficiary Contracts

Suppose that intending to make an unconditional gift, a donor gives a donee $1,000 in cash. If the donor should happen to change his mind the following day, he cannot recover the money. Once an unconditional gift is made, ownership of the given item passes to and vests in the donee, and the donor no longer has any right to that item or control over it—unless he expressly reserved some control at the time he transferred it. For the same reason the right of a donee beneficiary to enforce a third-party beneficiary contract is considered irrevocable. After a right to enforce the promisor's promise vests in the donee beneficiary, the promisor and promisee cannot change or cancel their contract without the donee beneficiary's consent, unless they have reserved such a power

when first forming their contract. As to when a right vests in a donee beneficiary, the various courts follow one of two theories. Courts in some states say that no right vests until the beneficiary is given notice of or learns of the promisor-promisee contract. On the other hand, courts in some other states assume that the beneficiary will be agreeable to the third-party beneficiary contract and willing to accept its benefits, therefore consider obtaining his actual consent a needless formality, and hold that an irrevocable right vests in the donee beneficiary as soon as the promisor-promisee contract is made.

Creditor Beneficiary Contracts

If a third-party beneficiary is a creditor beneficiary, there is no intent to make a gift to him and therefore in theory no irrevocable right immediately vests in him. Unless injustice would result, the promisor and promisee can amend or cancel their contract without the consent of the beneficiary, and thus change or cancel the beneficiary's right to collect under the contract.

Usually such a change or cancellation is not unfair to the beneficiary. He still has his right as a creditor to collect from his debtor (the promisee of the third-party beneficiary con-

---

9. U.C.C. Sec. 2-210.

tract). However, if the beneficiary has materially changed his position in reliance on the contract (for example, by starting a lawsuit against the promisor) it would be unfair and unjust for the contract afterwards to be changed or canceled; the creditor beneficiary's material action under the contract would therefore make his right to collect from the promisor irrevocable.

* * *

Problems

1. A manufacturing company from another state planned erection of a plant in a small town. The company enlisted the aid of a lawyer to assist in procuring land desired by the company, without inflating the land values. On March 20 the lawyer entered into a contract with the owner of a 9-acre tract of land, under which the owner agreed to sell and the lawyer to buy the described land for $14,000, payment and transfer of the deed to be made the following July 1. At the time the agreement was signed, the lawyer knew that the new manufacturing plant was to be located in close proximity to the owner's land, knew that the owner was ignorant of that fact, and during negotiations refrained from mentioning anything as to the purpose for which the lawyer wanted the land. On April 2 the plans for the company were made public and within 60 days, the value of owner's land increased 100 percent. The lawyer assigned the contract to the company and the owner was notified. On July 1, when the company tendered $14,000, the owner refused to transfer the land. The Company sued the owner for specific performance. The Owner's defense was (a) that he had not agreed to sell to the company, and (b) that he had been defrauded. What result?

2. A lumber-mill operator, who also was a logging contractor, entered into an agreement with a lumber dealer in which the lumberman agreed to sell and the dealer to buy the quantity of lumber described below, cut in specified sizes, the dealer to pay specified prices thirty days after delivery f.o.b. the mill. One month later the lumberman sold his logging and mill business to a buyer and assigned to the buyer the lumberman's contract with the dealer. The dealer refused to accept lumber from the assignee, and the assignee sued the dealer for damages for breach of contract.

(a) The contract was for all of the merchantable lumber for certain specified tracts of land, to be delivered six months after the formation of the contract. Explain whether the assignee could recover from the dealer.

(b) The contract was for the entire output from the lumberman's mill for the period of one year after the formation of the contract. Explain whether the assignee could recover from the dealer.

3. Under a written contract S agreed to sell and B to buy 200 drums of a stated kind of acid, meeting stated specifications as to purity. Delivery was to be at the rate of two drums per day, title to pass upon delivery. After each delivery, the acid was to be sampled and tested, and if found satisfactory to B, was to be paid for within one week after delivery, the amount paid to be the market price prevailing in New York City on the delivery date. One week after formation of the contract B sold his business, including the contract with S, to E. S refused to make deliveries to E, who thereupon sued S for damages. Explain (1) the reasoning upon which S could attempt to defend, (2) the reasoning upon which E could attempt to recover, and (3) which party should be given judgment. (Modified from A.I.C.P.A., 27-6.)

4. S. entered into a contract with B for sale and delivery to B of certain described, standardized goods at a stated price, to be delivered at a stated time.

(a) Before the time for delivery or payment under the contract, B assigned to E the entire contract, E agreed with B to perform the contract, and S was notified of the assignment. (1) The contract between S and B contained no provision pertaining to assignment; under the contract, payment was to be made upon delivery. When the time came for delivery, E tendered to S the proper price but S refused to deliver to E. E sued S for damages. Explain whether E was entitled to recover. (2) Other facts remaining the same, suppose that the contract provided for payment 30 days after delivery. Explain whether this would change your answer to Part (1) above. (3) The contract between S and B contained a provision stating that neither party could assign his rights or delegate his duties under the contract, and that payment was to be made upon delivery. When the time came for delivery, E tendered to S the proper price but S refused to deliver to E. E sued S for damages. Explain whether E was entitled to recover.

(b) Under the contract, payment was to be made 30 days after delivery. S made delivery to B according to contract, and then assigned to F the right to receive payment. F notified B of the assignment. The contract contained a provision stating that neither party could assign his rights or delegate his duties under the contract. B refused to pay F but instead made payment to S. Before F could obtain the money from S, S became insolvent and a receiver was appointed who took over all of S's assets. F sued B for the purchase price of the goods. Explain whether F could recover.

5. A manufacturer sold and delivered certain machinery to an oil refiner on open account for $2,000, payable in 60 days. A few days later the manufacturer sold and assigned this account to a bank which paid the manufacturer full value less the usual discount fee. A month later the refiner sold and delivered to the manufacturer a quantity of oil on open account for $800, payable in 30 days. The manufacturer defaulted on the $800 obligation owed to the refiner, whereupon the refiner refused to pay the manufacturer anything on the past-due $2,000 obligation. At this point the bank claimed $2,000 from the refiner. This was the first that the refiner knew of the manufacturer's assigning the account. When the refiner refused to pay, the bank sued the refiner. What result?

6. Smith and Brown entered into a written contract under which Smith agreed to sell and deliver to Brown 500 units of certain described, standardized goods, in monthly installments of 100 units

on the first of the next month, and 100 units on the first of each month thereafter, for which Brown agreed to pay $5 per unit, payable 10 days after each delivery. The day after formation of the contract, Smith and Edwards entered into a written agreement under which Smith sold and assigned the Smith-Brown contract to Edwards, and Edwards agreed to make the contract deliveries to Brown. When Brown was notified of Smith's transfer of the contract, Brown did not express any objection. Thereafter Brown received from Edwards the first two installments, which conformed with the Smith-Brown contract in every respect (except for being delivered by Edwards instead of Smith), and Brown paid Edwards for the goods. At the time for delivery of the third installment, the market price for such goods had advanced and Edwards refused to deliver any more goods to Brown. Brown promptly notified Smith who refused to take any action. Brown sued Smith for damages for breach of contract.

(a) Smith argued that Brown could recover damages from Edwards, and that therefore Smith was no longer liable on the contract. Could Brown recover damages from Edwards? If so, would this be a good defense in Brown's lawsuit against Smith? Explain.

(b) Smith argued that since Brown had accepted two shipments from Edwards, Smith was no longer liable on the contract. Would this be a good defense? Explain.

7. Effective January 1, a manufacturer and a labor union entered into a contract upon which the manufacturer agreed that thereafter he would pay wages at a specified rate to employees who were members of the union. E, a member of the union, had been employed by the manufacturer for many years at a lesser rate. E continued working at the old rate for six months after the date of the union contract before he learned of the terms of the union contract. E sued the manufacturer for the difference between the wages he received and the wages specified in the union contract, for the six-month period. The manufacturer denied liability on the ground that E was not a party to the Jan-

uary 1 contract. What result? (Modified from A.I.C.P.A. May 49-3.)

8. At a time when D owed C $100 due in one month, R sought to borrow $100 from D. D lent $100 to R upon R's oral promise to D to pay C in one month the $100 which D owed to C. When R failed to pay, C sued R.

(a) R claimed the statute of frauds as a defense. Explain whether this would be a good defense.

(b) What other defense might R attempt to raise? Would it be a valid defense? (Modified from A.I.C.P.A., Nov. 41-8.)

9. The owner of a business employed a general manager under a three-year contract at a salary of $800 per month. The manager's duties required skill and sound judgment. The owner also employed a file clerk under a one-year contract at a salary of $200 a month. The assigned duties of the file clerk were such as could be done by any mediocre clerk. Six months after making the above mentioned employment contracts, the owner entered into a written agreement with a buyer under which the owner sold his business to the buyer and assigned to the buyer all outstanding customer and employment contracts, and the buyer agreed to perform satisfactorily all of the owner's outstanding contracts.

(a) When the buyer took over the business, the manager and the clerk both decided to quit. In separate lawsuits the buyer sued the manager and the clerk for damages for breach of contract. What result?

(b) When the buyer took over the business, he decided to dispense with the services of the manager and the file clerk and fired them. In separate lawsuits the manager and the clerk sued the buyer for damages for breach of contract. What result?

10. An owner of certain land planned the construction and leasing of a number of store buildings to form a shopping center. The owner entered into contracts with various persons for various phases of construction and outfitting of the stores. The owner made one such written con-

tract with a dealer who handled General Electric products only. Under the contract the owner agreed to buy from the dealer and the dealer agreed to sell at stated prices all the refrigeration equipment required by the plans and specifications referred to in the contract. The dealer, in turn, informed the General Electric Company of the contract and sent a copy of the specifications. The dealer made the contract in his own name, not in the name of the General Electric Company. The dealer was not an employee or agent of the General Electric Company; he was an independent retail dealer with a contract arrangement to handle GE refrigeration products for the area. Later the owner obtained a better price on some Westinghouse refrigeration equipment and had this equipment installed in various of the store buildings, instead of GE equipment. The General Electric Company sued the owner for damages. Explain (1) the reasoning upon which the General Electric Company might attempt to recover, (2) the reasoning upon which the owner might attempt to defend, and (3) which party should be given judgment.

11. An elderly woman who was being cared for by her niece wished to reward the latter, but, at the same time, did not want to ignore her nephew. On February 1, the aunt signed and delivered to the niece a deed transferring a certain house and lot to the niece, in exchange for which the niece dated, signed, and gave to her aunt the following writing: "In consideration of the transfer to me of the house and lot at [describing the property], I hereby agree with the grantor of the premises that I will pay the sum of $8,000 to the grantor's nephew [naming him] within six months after the grantor's death." A few months later the aunt changed her mind about providing for her nephew and, on April 15, dated and signed with her niece the following writing: "In consideration of the promise herein made by my niece [naming her] to care for me for the remainder of my life, I hereby release my niece from her obligation to pay $8,000 to my nephew [naming him] as previously provided in the agreement signed by my niece on February 1 of this year." The niece properly cared

for her aunt until the latter died in December. When the nephew demanded $8,000 six months later, the niece refused to pay, and the nephew sued the niece.

(a) Assume that the aunt told her nephew of the February 1 agreement immediately after it was signed. In the lawsuit of the nephew against the niece, explain (1) the reasoning upon which the nephew might attempt to collect, (2) the reasoning upon which the niece might attempt to defend, and (3) which party should be given judgment.

(b) Assume that the nephew first learned of the February agreement shortly after his aunt's death. Answer the same questions asked in Part (a).

12. In connection with extensive remodeling of an owner's house, a builder agreed with the owner not only that the builder would do a certain described portion of the work for $5,000, but also that the builder would loan the owner a total of $7,000 to finance the remodeling. The owner signed and gave to the builder a written promise to repay the $7,000 loan within five years with interest at 10 percent, and, as security, gave the builder a mortgage on the premises. The parties orally agreed that the builder would disburse the $7,000 as follows: (1) the builder would retain $5,000 as payment in full for labor and materials in connection with his part of the remodeling, (2) the builder would pay a plumber selected by the owner the amount of the plumber's charges (but not exceeding the balance of the loan fund) for plumbing work in connection with the remodeling, and (3) the builder would then pay to the owner any balance that remained. The owner engaged a certain plumber who agreed to do the described work for $1,000, if this amount was agreeable to the builder. When the owner told the builder of the plumber's proposition, the builder agreed and said to the owner that he would pay $1,000 to the plumber. Upon learning of this, the plumber began work. When the remodeling including the plumbing was finished, the owner requested that the builder pay the entire $2,000 balance of the loan ($7,000 minus the builder's

$5,000) to the owner. The builder did so. When the owner thereafter failed to pay the plumber, the plumber sued the builder who argued in defense that his promise was oral and that it was changed by the later arrangement between the builder and the owner. Explain (1) the reasoning upon which the plumber might attempt to collect from the builder, (2) the reasoning upon which the builder might attempt to defend, and (3) which party should be given judgment.

13. A entered into a valid contract with B, a builder, whereby A agreed not only to pay B for the cost of building A's new house, but also agreed to pay B's laborers and materialmen in the event B was unable to pay them. Soon after B began construction, he purchased $5,000 worth of lumber from the XYZ Lumber Co. Just before the house was complete, B ran out of funds and therefore did not pay XYZ Lumber Co., whereupon XYZ sued A for $5,000. Would XYZ's suit be successful?

CHAPTER OUTLINE

Products Liability

I. Historical Background

Before the era of mass production and sophisticated advertising techniques, the manufacturer and retailer were generally one and the same person. Therefore, if the product sold was defective, the purchaser could directly contact his seller in seeking legal redress. Now, however, the retailer merely serves as a conduit between the manufacturer and the ultimate consumer. The question that soon developed was the extent of the manufacturer's liability for products he manufactured but did not sell to the consumer. This question has resulted in a relatively new, important, and rapidly developing field of law, known as *products liability*. The field of products liability illustrates excellently how the law continues to evolve to meet changing social needs. As with almost all legal liability, products liability has traditionally been based on some sort of fault on the part of a seller either tort (usually negligence) or breach of contract (that is, breach of warranty). Well into the present century, liability existed only between persons who were in "privity of contract" (that is, persons who contracted directly with each other). For example, if A were to sell certain goods to B who in turn sold them to C, A and B would be in privity of contract as also would B and C, but A and C would not be in privity of contract.

For products liability cases based on a manufacturer's negligence, the 1842 English case of *Winterbottom v. Wright*[1] firmly implanted the privity-of-contract requirement into both English and American law. The courts feared that manufacturers would be swamped with ruinous lawsuits unless recovery was limited to parties who had contracted directly with each other. Only gradually, and largely under the impetus of Justice Cardozo's celebrated decision in the 1916 New York case of *MacPherson v. Buick Motor Co.*,[2] has privity of contract been almost eliminated as a requirement for holding a negligent manufacturer liable. In addition, the Uniform Commercial Code has helped to modify and in some cases eliminate the need for privity.

II. Bases for Recovery

As the law has developed, the liability of manufacturers and sellers (or any person in the chain of transfer from the manufacturer to the consumer) for defective products is based primarily upon one or a combination of the following bases: (1) warranties—express and implied; (2) negligence; (3) strict liability; and (4) misrepresentation—fraudulent and nonfraudulent.

A. Warranties

As has been previously discussed in Chapter 8, a person who enters into a contract in reliance on an express misrepresentation (1) may recover damages if the misrepresen-

---

1. 10 M. & W. 109, 152 Eng. Rep. 402 (1842).
2. 217 N.Y. 382, 111 N.E. 1050 (1916).

tation is dishonest, and sometimes if the misrepresentation is negligent; or (2) may rescind the contract and recover what he has given or paid under the contract, whether the misrepresentation is tortious or innocent. For various historical and policy reasons, the law concerning the effect of misrepresentations developed along divergent lines for different types of contracts. In connection with contracts involving the sale of goods, rules of law gradually developed which permit a misled person to recover damages even for an honest and reasonable misrepresentation, and even if the misrepresentation is made by implication through conduct rather than expressly in words. Such obligations are called *warranties*.

The warranties discussed here are those pertaining to sales of goods. Principles pertaining to land warranties differ in many respects from sales-of-goods warranties, for various reasons including: (1) different historical developments, land warranties having developed from landholding under feudal tenure; (2) the requirement that all land transfers must be in writing (Chapter 9); and (3) the principle that when a land transfer deed is accepted by a buyer, it constitutes the entire agreement between the parties, any provisions in their preceding agreement being considered as waived or superseded if omitted from the deed. Warranties accompanying sales of land are usually studied as a part of the law of real estate and will be discussed in Chapter 30.

I. EXPRESS WARRANTIES

A person is free to make any contract he wishes—so long as it is not against the law or otherwise opposed to public policy. If he so desires, he may make a contract that a certain thing will happen or exist in the future, and the contract obligation will be fully enforceable against him, even though the contracted event is dependent on factors over which he has only partial control or no control at all.

When a person enters into a contract that is dependent on a future event which he cannot fully control, he is in reality agreeing that he will pay for any damages or losses sustained if the contracted future event does not occur. Thus if a paint manufacturer enters into a contract that his paint will never fade or peel, he is not promising to do something after he makes a sale to prevent the paint from fading or peeling. Rather he is agreeing that if the paint does fade or peel, he will pay money damages for any loss that could reasonably be expected to result. The manufacturer's contractual promise or assertion concerning the condition or quality of the paint is called a "warranty" or guarantee. If what is promised or asserted is not true or does not occur, the warranty is considered as breached.

The formation of a legally enforceable warranty agreement does not require any particular formula of words. Suppose that in inducing a buyer to buy paint, the manufacturer as the seller makes one of the following three statements:

1. "I agree that if this paint fades or peels, I will pay whatever damages you sustain.
2. "I agree (or promise or warrant) that this paint will not fade or peel."
3. "This paint will not fade or peel."

Reasonably interpreted, the manufacturer undertakes the same contractual obligation, whichever one of the three statements he makes.

Warranty liability is not restricted to manufacturers or producers who know or should know the quality of the goods they sell. Any person who sells goods, whether he is a producer, a wholesaler, a retailer, or a nonmerchant, may undertake a binding warranty liability. Compare for a moment the relative bases of tort liability and contract liability. Modern tort liability is almost always based on some sort of wrongdoing or fault—usually the defendant's intentional misconduct or unreasonably careless misconduct. On the other hand, contract liability arises if a defendant voluntarily agrees to perform in a certain way or agrees that a certain event will occur, and then fails to perform as agreed or the event fails to occur, whether the failure is the defendant's fault or not (so long as performance is not prevented by the other party to the contract). Thus, as discussed in Chapter 10, increased costs, shortages, and even the impossibility of obtaining the goods in question ordinarily will not relieve or excuse a seller from his contract obligation to deliver as agreed. In modern theory a warranty is usually considered as a part of a contract, so that warranty liability is a type of contract liability. Therefore when a seller warrants goods in certain respects he will be liable for breach of warranty if the goods are not as warranted (in other words, because the contract agreement is not fully performed), even though the seller honestly and reasonably believes in the truth of what he asserts in his warranty. Suppose that a retailer enters into a contract to sell a quantity of paint of a certain type, grade, and color. If he unexpectedly cannot obtain from his distributor the paint he intended to deliver in fulfillment of the contract, he is not relieved from the contract obligation which he voluntarily assumed. He must obtain the described paint elsewhere, paying a higher price if necessary, or be liable for damages for failure to deliver. Likewise with quality; a retailer may honestly and reasonably believe that the paint is colorfast and will not peel, perhaps because the manufacturer has said so. Nevertheless, if the retailer asserts colorfastness, and after delivery to the buyer the color fades, the seller is liable for breach of this term of his contract—that is, for breach of warranty.

The basic principles applicable to express warranties are stated in the Uniform Commercial Code as follows:

1. Express warranties by the seller are created as follows:

(a) Any affirmation of fact or promise made by the seller to the buyer which relates to the goods and becomes part of the basis of the bargain creates an express warranty that the goods shall conform to the affirmation or promise.

(b) Any description of the goods which is made part of the basis of the bargain creates an express warranty that the goods shall conform to the description.

(c) Any sample or model which is made part of the basis of the bargain creates an express warranty that the whole of the goods shall conform to the sample or model.

2. It is not necessary to the creation of an express warranty that the seller use formal words such as "warrant" or "guarantee" or that he have a specific intention to make a warranty, but an affirmation merely of the value of the goods or a statement purporting to be merely the seller's opinion or commendation of the goods does not create a warranty. [3]

2. IMPLIED WARRANTIES

Frequently the parties to a contract do not expressly state all of their contractual provisions, but rather leave some details to custom or understanding. Suppose that an agreement between strangers for the sale and purchase of goods says nothing about the time and manner of payment. It is certainly safe to assume that if they mean to extend credit, they will say so. The purchase price therefore is to be paid on delivery of the goods. Cash on delivery is an implied term of the contract, "implied" because not expressly stated, but a very real term of the contract because payment with delivery appears to be the intent of the parties.

Consider another example. A homeowner is approached by a boy, a stranger, who solicits a lawnmowing job. They agree that if the boy will "mow the lawn," the owner will pay him $2. The boy tries to cut 16-inch swaths with a 14-inch lawnmower, leaving ridges of uncut

---

3. U.C.C. Sec. 2-313.

grass in regular rows over the entire lawn. Although it was not expressly stated that the grass should be cut uniformly and without ridges, no one (with the possible exception of the boy himself) will seriously contend that the $2 has been earned. Before he is entitled to the $2, the boy must "mow the lawn." Since the parties do not specifically define the word "mow," they are attributing to the word its common or usual meaning. The boy might argue that this is the way he always mows lawns, and therefore that this is what he means by the word "mow" in the agreement with the owner. But the boy is bound by what he reasonably leads the owner to understand is meant. Not having stated otherwise he is taken to mean the usual or customary lawn-mowing job. In other words, it is an implied term of their understanding that the usual or customary job be done. Whether it includes trimming would be a matter for more serious argument.

Implied Warranty of Merchantability

Suppose that a buyer wishes to secure from a dealer, not himself a publisher, a new copy of a certain book. Besides stating author and title, the buyer's order might specify that the pages be bound, and that there be no reverse, double, or smeared printing. When the dealer accepts the order, a contract is formed. If the dealer ships a book which contains defective printing, the dealer breaches his contract; he fails to ship the quality of book which he *expressly* agreed to ship. The book may be in the original wrapper in which it came from the publisher and the defects may be unknown to the dealer. Nevertheless, since the dealer fails to perform the contract obligation which he expressly and voluntarily assumed, he will be liable for damages. On the other hand, suppose that the buyer merely orders a copy of the specified book without expressly mentioning the quality of printing. It is clear that he means "book" as the term is usually or customarily used—just

as the homeowner in the preceding paragraph meant "mow the lawn" as that term is customarily used. Books usually do not have reverse, double, or smeared printing and are usually bound. Therefore, one free of these defects and bound is what the buyer actually (by implication) orders, and what the dealer agrees to sell when he accepts the order. It is *implied* that the book be of standard, usual, or marketable quality—that is, merchantable. In other words, from the normal meaning of the words used in the contract, the law finds that the dealer has impliedly agreed to a warranty of merchantability.

The basic principles applicable to implied warranties of merchantability are stated in the Code as follows:

1. Unless excluded or modified . . . , a warranty that the goods shall be merchantable is implied in a contract for their sale if the seller is a merchant with respect to goods of that kind....

2. Goods to be merchantable must at least be such as

(a) pass without objection in the trade under the contract description;

(b) in the case of fungible goods are of fair average quality within the description;

(c) are fit for the ordinary purposes for which such goods are used;

(d) run, within the variation permitted by the agreement, of even kind, quality and quantity within each unit and among all units involved;

(e) are adequately contained, packaged, and labeled as the agreement may require; and

(f) conform to the promises or affirmations of fact made on the container or label if any.[4]

---

4. U.C.C. Sec. 2-314

Example. A customer went into a grocery store for a loaf of Star brand bread. The grocer sold to the customer the bread he requested, wrapped in a sealed package as it had come from the Star Baking Company, the baker. The grocer made no statements concerning the quality or fitness of the bread. Unknown to the parties, a pin had accidentally fallen into the dough during its preparation and this particular loaf had been baked with the pin concealed within the bread. The pin seriously injured the customer's mouth while he was eating the bread, and an infection resulted requiring the removal of two teeth. The customer sued the grocer for the damages sustained.

The customer could recover. When the customer requested a loaf of bread, he meant what usually comes in the market under that name—in other words merchantable bread. By selling the bread to the customer the grocer asserted that it was bread of the usual quality. Bread does not usually come with pins baked in it. Therefore the grocer did not perform his contract with the customer and for his breach of contract (that is, for his breach of the implied warranty of merchantability) the grocer would be liable for any loss or injury resulting to the customer. ☐

Implied Warranty of Fitness for Particular Purpose

As part of his sales contract, a seller may agree that the goods he sells are appropriate or fit for some particular purpose. He may expressly so state and there will be no question as to his contractual liability. Or he may through his conduct impliedly assert the fitness of the goods for a particular purpose—and such an implied term will be just as real a part of the contract and as binding as if expressly stated. Suppose that a buyer, not by trade a painter, enters a seller's paint store, says that he intends to repaint his baby's crib and requests some nonpoisonous paint. The seller states as to a particular type of paint that it contains no poisonous substances and sells a can to the buyer. Clearly the seller's assertion is a part of his contract, and there is no difference whether the seller says, "I warrant that this paint contains no poisonous substances," or merely, "This paint contains no poisonous substances." If the paint actually contains substances poisonous to a baby chewing on it, the seller has not delivered to the buyer the kind of paint he has contracted to deliver and will be liable for any resulting damages. And as previously discussed, it is immaterial that the seller may honestly and

reasonably believe that the paint is safe. He has made a contract and his nonperformance is a breach of contract, even though the nonperformance may be the result of circumstances unknown to him and beyond his control.

Suppose, however, that the seller makes no express statement about the ingredients in the paint, but sells a can of paint to the buyer in response to his request for a nonpoisonous paint to repaint his baby's crib. By the act of selling, the seller accepts and agrees to the terms stated by the buyer; in other words, the seller contracts that the paint is nonpoisonous paint.

Now suppose that all the buyer says when he enters the seller's paint store is that he wants some white paint to repaint his baby's crib. Although the buyer does not add that he wants a nonpoisonous paint, the inclination of babies to chew on cribs is well known. The buyer is relying on the seller as a dealer to select paint suitable for the announced purpose. By the mere act of selling, the seller asserts that the paint is suitable for the buyer's purpose. Although not expressly stated, the implied assertion is a real part of the seller's contract. When the law holds the seller liable if the paint is poisonous and the baby becomes ill from chewing on it, the law is enforcing the agreement which the parties by their conduct show that they intend to make. That this is the actual intent of the parties can be easily verified. Suppose that in response to the buyer's request for paint to repaint his baby's crib, the seller presents a can, states the price, and adds "I don't guarantee this is nonpoisonous." Of course the buyer will immediately refuse to buy. The buyer states his purpose because he wishes to buy paint suitable for that purpose.

Note that the bases for this implied warranty of fitness for a particular purpose are two-fold: (1) that the seller knows the buyer's purpose and (2) that the buyer relies on the seller to select something suitable. If the seller is a dealer in goods of that type and the buyer is unskilled, it is usually clear that the buyer is relying on the seller's superior knowledge. The Uniform Commercial Code states these basic principles as follows:

> Where the seller at the time of contracting has reason to know any particular purpose for which the goods are required and that the buyer is relying on the seller's skill or judgment to select or furnish suitable goods, there is unless excluded or modified . . . an implied warranty that the goods shall be fit for such purpose. [5]

Implied Warranty of Title

Generally, by his conduct of selling certain goods and not saying otherwise, a seller is impliedly asserting that he owns the goods, and has the right to sell them and to transfer good title, free from any outstanding claims. This assertion or implied warranty of title becomes an enforceable part of the sales contract.

There is no such implied assertion or warranty if circumstances clearly show that the seller is not claiming title or is selling only whatever limited title exists. Suppose that a

sheriff levies on the property of a debtor and sells the property at a sheriff's auction sale. Clearly he is only selling whatever title the debtor has; the sheriff is not, through his conduct of selling, asserting that there is good title.

These basic principles are stated in the Code as follows:

> 1. Subject to subsection (2) there is in a contract for sale a warranty by the seller that
>
> (a) the title conveyed shall be good, and its transfer rightful; and
>
> (b) the goods shall be delivered free from any security interest or other lien or encumbrance of which the buyer at the time of contracting has no knowledge.
>
> 2. A warranty under subsection (1) will be excluded or modified only by specific language or by circumstances which give the buyer reason to know that the person selling does not claim title in himself or that he is purporting to sell only such right or title as he or a third person may have. [6]

B. Exclusion of Warranties

I. EXPRESS WARRANTIES

By definition, an express warranty is based upon some statement made by the seller. Obviously then, a seller can avoid an express warranty by not making or agreeing to any express promise or assertion of fact. In this connection, oral sales are a frequent source of disputes. A buyer may assert that the seller made certain oral statements of fact while the seller denies having made any such statements. If the parties cannot agree as to exactly what was said and done, a jury (or a judge if the case is tried without a jury) must determine the correct facts. It is wise for the parties to eliminate this source of dispute by putting their agreement in writing and having the writing state that it is the complete agreement of the parties. Then under the parol evidence

---

5. U.C.C. Sec. 2-315.

6. U.C.C. Sec. 2-312.

rule, no express warranty accompanies the sale unless stated in the agreement. (This applies to express warranties. As explained under the next heading, the parol evidence rule does *not* exclude implied warranties.)

2. IMPLIED WARRANTIES

The entire field of limitations of warranties and exclusions of warranties has been considerably complicated by the growing use of standardized, form contracts. Admittedly such contracts play a vital role in the present-day mass distribution of goods; problems arise from the fact that usually the forms are drafted and printed by sellers, who can be expected to slant the contract provisions in their own favor. When form contracts become shockingly unfair, the courts will refuse to enforce them. To this effect, the Uniform Commercial Code provides for sales-of-goods contracts:

> If the court as a matter of law finds the contract or any clause of the contract to have been unconscionable at the time it was made the court may refuse to enforce the contract, or it may enforce the remainder of the contract without the unconscionable clause, or it may so limit the application of any unconscionable clause as to avoid any unconscionable result.[7]

Explaining this provision, the authors of the Code have written:

> This section is intended to allow the court to pass directly on the unconscionability of the contract or particular clause therein and to make a conclusion of law as to its unconscionability. The basic test is whether, in the light of the general commercial background and the commercial needs of the particular trade or case, the clauses involved are so one-sided as to be unconscionable under the circumstances existing at the time of the making of the contract.... The principle is one of the prevention of oppression and unfair

surprise . . . and not of disturbance of allocation of risks because of superior bargaining power.[8]

Some "rugged individualists" might argue that a basic dogma of the free-enterprise system is freedom of contract, that if persons have agreed to a certain proposition, it should be enforceable whether the contract is individually negotiated or filled in on a printed form, and that if a person signs a written contract, he is bound by its terms, whether or not he has read and understands the contract—including small-print provisions which cannot be read without a strong magnifying glass. A quick answer is that society has never been willing to enforce all agreements. Agreements obtained by duress or fraud certainly should not be enforced, and likewise oppressive agreements which are clearly against the best interests of society should not be enforced. As Professor Morris Cohen has written:

> To put no restrictions on the freedom to contract would logically lead not to a maximum of individual liberty but to contracts of slavery, into which, experience shows, men will "voluntarily" enter under economic pressure—a pressure that is largely conditioned by the laws of property. Regulations, therefore, involving some restrictions on the freedom to contract are as necessary to real liberty as traffic restrictions are necessary to assure real freedom in the general use of our highways.[9]

And as Chief Justice Hughes has written:

> We have had frequent occasion to consider the limitations on liberty of contract. While it is highly important to preserve that liberty from arbitrary and capricious interference, it is also necessary to prevent its abuse, as otherwise it could be used to override all public interests and thus in the end destroy the very

7. U.C.C. Sec. 2-302.

8. Comment to U.C.C. Sec. 2-302.
9. LAW AND THE SOCIAL ORDER (New York: Harcourt, 1933), p. 105.

freedom of opportunity which it is designed to safeguard.[10]

In a landmark case decided in 1960,[11] the New Jersey Supreme Court wrestled skillfully and at length with two very formidable questions: (1) should a contract provision amounting to an almost complete disclaimer of liability[12] be effective to exclude an implied warranty of merchantability in connection with the sale of a complex and potentially dangerous machine such as an automobile, and (2) should a manufacturer be considered as impliedly warranting to the ultimate consumer that an automobile is safe. The court's views as to this second question will be noted later in this chapter. In answering the first question. the court said, in part:

> The traditional contract is the result of free bargaining of parties who are brought together by the play of the market, and who meet each other on a footing of approximate economic equality. In such a society there is no danger that freedom of contract will be a threat to the social order as a whole. But in present-day commercial life the standardized mass contract has appeared. It is used primarily by enterprises with strong bargaining power and position. "The weaker party, in need of the goods or services, is frequently not in a position to shop around for better terms, either because the author of the standard contract has a monopoly (natural or artificial) or because all competitors use the same clauses. His contractual intention is but a subjection more or less voluntary to terms dictated by the stronger party, terms whose consequences are often understood in a vague way, if at all.". . .

> "In recent times the marketing process has been getting more highly organized than ever before. The standardized contract with its broad disclaimer clauses is drawn by legal advisers of sellers widely organized in trade associations. It is encountered on every hand. Extreme inequality of bargaining between buyer and seller in this respect is now often conspicuous. Many buyers no longer have any real choice in the matter. They must often accept what they can get though accompanied by broad disclaimers. The terms of these disclaimers deprive them of all substantial protection with regard to the quality of the goods. In effect, this is by force of contract between very unequal parties. It throws the risk of defective articles on the most dependent party. He has the least individual power to avoid the presence of defects. He also has the least individual ability to bear their disastrous consequences."

> The warranty before us is a standardized form designed for mass use. It is imposed upon the automobile consumer. He takes it or leaves it, and he must take it to buy an automobile. No bargaining is engaged in with respect to it. The form warranty . . . is the uniform warranty of the Automobile Manufacturers Association. Members of the Association are: General Motors, Inc., Ford, Chrysler, Studebaker-Packard, American Motors, (Rambler), Willys Motors, Checker Motors Corporation, and International Harvester Company. . . .

> The gross inequality of bargaining position occupied by the consumer in the automobile industry is thus apparent. There is no competition among the car makers in the area of the express warranty. Where can the buyer go to negotiate for better protection? Such control and limitation of his remedies are inimical to the public welfare, and, at the

---

10. Dissenting opinion in *Morehead v. New York,* 298 U.S. 587, 56 S. Ct. 918, 80 1 . Ed. 1347 (1938).

11. Henningsen v. Bloomfield Motors, 32 N.J. 358, 161 A 2d 69, 75 A.L.R. 2d 1 (1960)

12. The printed contract form contained the uniform warranty of the Automobile Manufacturers Association which stated that the seller "warrants each new motor vehicle . . . to be free from defects in material or workmanship under normal use and service. It's [the seller's] obligation under this warranty being limited to making good . . . any part or parts thereof which shall, within ninety (90) days after delivery . . . or before such vehicle has been driven 4,000 miles, whichever event shall first occur, be returned . . . and which its examination shall disclose to its satisfaction to have been thus defective; this warranty being expressly in lieu of all other warranties expressed or implied, and all other obligations or liabilities on its part, and it neither assumes nor authorizes any other person to assume for it any other liability in connection with the sale of its vehicles...."

very least, call for great care by the courts to avoid injustice through application of strict common-law principles of freedom of contract....

Courts keep in mind the principle that the best interests of society demand that persons should not be unnecessarily restricted in their freedom of contract. But they do not hesitate to declare void as against public policy contractual provisions which clearly tend to the injury of the public in some way....

Public policy at a given time finds expression in the Constitution, the statutory law and in judicial decisions. In the area of sale of goods, the legislative will has imposed an implied warranty of merchantability as a general incident of sale of an automobile by description. The warranty does not depend upon the affirmative intention of the parties. It is a child of the law; it annexes itself to the contract because of the very nature of the transaction. . . . The disclaimer of the implied warranty and exclusion of all obligations except those specifically assumed by the express warranty signify a studied effort to frustrate that protection. True, the Sales Act authorized agreements between buyer and seller qualifying the warranty obligations. But quite obviously the Legislature contemplated lawful stipulations (which are determined by the circumstances of a particular case) arrived at freely by parties of relatively equal bargaining strength. The lawmakers did not authorize the automobile manufacturer to use its grossly disproportionate bargaining power to relieve itself from liability and to impose on the ordinary buyer, who in effect has no real freedom of voice, the grave danger of injury to himself and others that attends the sale of such a dangerous instrumentality as a defectively made automobile. In the framework of this case, illuminated as it is by the facts and the many decisions noted, we are of the opinion that . . . [the] attempted disclaimer of an implied warranty of merchantability and of the obligations arising therefrom is so inimical to the public good as to compel an adjudication of its invalidity.

The Uniform Commercial Code draws some basic guidelines which must be followed in order for provisions which exclude the various types of implied warranties to be effective. Note that all exclusionary provisions are also controlled by the provision (previously quoted) declaring unenforceable any terms which the courts find to be "unconscionable."

Exclusion of Implied Warranty of Title.[13] There is no implied warranty of title if either the seller's words or the circumstances of the transaction lead the buyer to understand that the seller does not claim title in himself, or that the seller is selling only whatever limited title he has the power or authority to transfer.

Exclusion of Implied Warranties of Quality.[14] An implied warranty which would otherwise arise under the circumstances of a particular transaction can usually be excluded by any of the following:

1. Express exclusion.

(a) *Merchantability*. An effective exclusion of an implied warranty of merchantability may be either oral or in writing; the exclusionary provision however must include the word "merchantability," and if in writing, the exclusionary provision must be conspicuous.

(b) *Fitness for Purpose*. An effective exclusion of an implied warranty of fitness for purpose must be in writing and conspicuous, but need not state directly that it refers to this type of implied warranty. As the Code states:

Language to exclude all implied warranties of fitness is sufficient if it states, for example, that "There are no warranties which extend beyond the description on the face hereof."

2. Language that the sale is made "as is," "with all faults," or the like will exclude implied warranties of quality.

3. To the extent that a buyer inspects, he is not relying on any implied assertion or understanding concerning the goods. Likewise, a

---

13. U.C.C. Sec. 2-312.
14. U.C.C. Sec. 2-316.

seller's demand that the buyer fully inspect the goods, gives the buyer notice that the seller is not undertaking any implied obligation concerning the quality of the goods. Therefore a buyer's inspection before buying will exclude any implied warranty regarding defects which, under the circumstances, such an inspection ought to reveal, and a buyer's refusal to inspect after the seller demands that the buyer make a full inspection will exclude any implied warranty concerning defects discoverable by such an inspection.

4. A prior course of dealing between the parties or a custom in their type of business can show that the parties do *not* intend implied warranties.

Under the Uniform Commercial Code, the parol evidence rule does not exclude implied warranties of quality. Suppose that parties enter into a written agreement which shows that it is their complete agreement; suppose further that the agreement contains an express warranty but does not expressly exclude an implied warranty. If the circumstances are such as to give rise to an implied warranty of quality, such a warranty is also a part of the contract—unless inconsistent with the express warranty. If the express and implied warranties would be inconsistent with each other, the Code provides:

> Express warranties displace inconsistent implied warranties other than an implied warranty of fitness for a particular purpose.[15]

In other words, if an express warranty is inconsistent with an implied warranty of merchantability, the implied warranty is considered as excluded. On the other hand, if the circumstances are such that an implied warranty of fitness for particular purpose arises, and such a warranty is not expressly excluded, the implied warranty will remain even in the face of an inconsistent express warranty.

---

15. U.C.C. Sec. 2-317.

C. Warranties and Remote Parties

Present-day marketing of most any mass-produced goods involves a succession of sales through which goods are transferred from producers or manufacturers to wholesalers, then to retailers, and finally to the ultimate consumers. Since the manufacturer and the ultimate consumer do not deal directly with each other, their relationship in the channels of commerce is classed as remote; to each other they are remote parties. Many marketing practices are designed to speed goods through commercial channels on their way to ultimate consumers. Thus it is quite common for packers, manufacturers, or wholesalers, (1) to package and label goods in such a way that they can be sold and delivered to the ultimate consumers without further packaging or labeling, (2) to advertise in order to induce consumers to buy from independent retailers, and (3) to supply retailers with descriptive circulars for them to distribute in order to promote sales. If the statements which a manufacturer makes in his advertisements or circulars are inaccurate, incomplete, or misleading, or if goods are defective, either or both of two questions will frequently arise:

1. To what extent is an independent retail dealer liable to his customers for the accuracy of a manufacturer's (or wholesaler's) statements?

2. To what extent is a manufacturer or wholesaler liable to a remote consumer for inaccurate statements or for defective goods?

1. BUYER'S RIGHTS AGAINST IMMEDIATE SELLER

At the present state of legal evolution, the soundest basis for warranty liability is believed to be the intent of the parties, an intent which is either expressly stated or implied from conduct. In other words, warranty liability rests upon the express or implied assumptions which become a part of the bargain between the seller and buyer in question. Thus not only a dealer's express statements but also statements appearing on the goods or on their containers or labels would seem logically to become a part of a dealer-customer contract. This thought is expressed in the previously quoted Code definitions of express warranties and of merchantability.

A more difficult question is presented when a statement made in a manufacturer's advertisement or descriptive circular is not repeated in a dealer's sales talk or stated on the labels or containers. In appraising the legal effect of advertisements and circulars, a starting point is to note that a buyer's decision to purchase a certain item may be motivated by a wide variety of considerations, even including, for example, advertisements published by manufacturers of competitive products or the location of the selling dealer's showroom and service facilities. Certainly *all* of the factors that may bring about a purchase should not be considered as becoming a part of a dealer-buyer contract. In the absence of an express agreement, no one would contend that a dealer is bound by statements made in advertisements of competitive products, or that a dealer is obligated to continue operating his establishment in a certain locality. But what about statements which are made in advertisements sponsored by the manufacturer of the very items being handled by a dealer? Since the dealer has no control over the manufacturer's advertisements, it would not seem fair, in the absence of the dealer's express agreement, to impose on him a contract obligation as to the accuracy of the advertised statements. The question becomes more debatable when the dealer's own voluntary act brings the manufacturer's statements to the customer's attention, as when the dealer displays and distributes circulars supplied to him by the manufacturer. Certainly a strong argument can be made that the dealer should be held liable for statements contained in a circular which he displays with the products he is selling. The argument against

holding the dealer liable is not quite so obvious, but in the eyes of many courts it is an even stronger argument. First, the dealer is not the author of the circular and has no control over what it says. Also, and more important, the dealer in question may not be the source of the particular copy of the circular upon which a customer is relying. Although the dealer has such circulars on display, this particular customer may have obtained his copy of the circular directly from the manufacturer, from another dealer, or even from his next-door neighbor. Or the customer may have obtained the circular several months before the time of his purchase. Can a circular obtained otherwise than directly from the selling dealer, or obtained at a remote time, logically be said to become automatically a part of the selling dealer's *contract*? It would seem not. Therefore if the dealer is to be held liable for circular statements, his liability would seem to depend upon when and where a particular customer obtained his copy of the circular. However, from the standpoint of the customer, what induces him to buy is the circular itself and not when or where he obtained it. Holding the dealer liable therefore would present an anomalous situation: the chief legal basis for the dealer's liability to the customer would be a fact (the dealer's supplying the circular in connection with the sale in question) which to the customer would be unimportant and fortuitous. He would be relying on the circular; where he obtained it would be entirely immaterial to him. The business community and society as a whole are not yet ready to recognize as sound policy a rule which would hold a dealer liable for *all* statements or claims made by manufacturers. Until legal evolution reaches this point, if it ever does, the fairest policy rule would seem to be to limit a seller's contractual obligation to statements or conditions which reasonably appear intended by the parties to be part of their bargain. The courts usually hold therefore that even though a dealer displays a manufacturer's circulars and sells his goods, these two facts alone do not mean that the dealer is adopting the manufacturer's statements and making them a part of the dealer's contract with his customer. Unless the dealer himself in some way actually repeats the circular or advertising statements when he induces a customer to buy, the statements are usually not a part of the dealer-customer contract.

2. BUYER'S RIGHTS AGAINST REMOTE SELLER

Suppose that after buying goods from a seller, the buyer in turn resells the goods to a second buyer or subpurchaser. As to the first seller, the subpurchaser is a remote party, there being no direct contract relationship between them. If the goods are not discovered to be defective until after the resale to the subpurchaser, the question arises whether the subpurchaser can hold the original seller liable for damages for breach of warranty.

Warranty to Subpurchaser Expressed

In most sales-of-goods contracts, a seller does not express any intent to give a warranty in favor of a subpurchaser. In the case when a seller wishes to undertake such a warranty liability, he may do so through a third-party beneficiary agreement or (more commonly) through an agency arrangement.

Third-Party Beneficiary Agreement. A third-party beneficiary agreement involves a provision in the buyer-seller contract under which the seller agrees to be liable to a subpurchaser for some specified breach of warranty. Generally such a subpurchaser can enforce a contract provision which is thus made for his benefit, even though he is not a party to the contract. Since third-party beneficiary contracts are not often encountered in connection with warranties, further discussion of such contracts were discussed in Chapter 11.

Agency Arrangement. Quite often in sales of certain types of goods, such as automobiles and their accessories, a manufacturer intends to undertake an express warranty liability to ultimate consumers. In order to do so the manufacturer supplies the dealer with warranty forms bearing the manufacturer's name; this appoints the dealer as the manufacturer's agent for the limited purpose of making a warranty contract in the manufacturer's name whenever the dealer makes a sale to a consumer. Clearly the consumer can hold the manufacturer liable for breach of such a warranty. However, the scope of such express warranties is frequently limited, for example, to replacement of defective parts only, which would not cover personal injuries or business losses.

Warranty to Subpurchaser Not Expressed

In most sales transactions, sellers do not expressly undertake warranty liability in favor of subpurchasers. In most cases, therefore, a subpurchaser will have no warranty rights against a remote seller unless (1) the intermediate buyer (who does have warranty rights arising from his direct contract with the seller) makes a valid assignment of such rights to the subpurchaser, or (2) a fact situation exists from which the law implies a warranty in favor of a subpurchaser.

Assignment of Warranty Rights. A general discussion concerning the assignment of contract rights was discussed in Chapter 11. In regard to sales-of-goods contracts, the Uniform Commercial Code provides[16] that a buyer may assign all of his contract rights, unless the assignment would materially increase the burden or risk undertaken by the seller. Two points stand out:

1. The buyer must expressly show an intent to assign his warranty rights to his subpurchaser. Usually upon making a resale to a sub-

16. U.C.C. Sec. 2-210.

purchaser, the buyer will himself be warranting that the goods are merchantable. If the subpurchaser should thereafter recover from the buyer for breach of this warranty, the buyer would in turn want to be able to recover from his seller. However, if the buyer had assigned his rights he would have thereby relinquished any right to recover from the seller. Certainly in the absence of an express statement the buyer should not be presumed, every time he makes a resale, to intend an assignment and consequent relinquishment of his own rights. Therefore there is an assignment only if it is expressly stated; the buyer's act of reselling goods does not automatically or impliedly assign the buyer's warranty rights.

2. The buyer's warranty right must be capable of assignment. Because of the rarity of such an assignment, relatively few cases have arisen. The cases indicate that warranties of title and of quantity can be assigned, but raise some doubt as to whether a warranty of quality can be validly assigned. Some hold the view that a warranty of quality is, like indemnity insurance, personal to the recipient of the right and not assignable without the consent of the one granting the right.

Implied Warranty to Subpurchaser. When subpurchasers who are injured by defective goods attempt to collect from remote sellers, the theories which are most often attempted are (1) negligence and (2) implied warranty. Negligence liability is well settled. If goods are defective because of a manufacturer's negligence, he is liable for the foreseeable injuries which result to a remote consumer or to anyone else. On the other hand, warranty liability is quite doubtful. In fact, whether or not an implied warranty extends to a subpurchaser is one of the most controversial questions in commercial law.

Under the traditional contract theory of warranties, an implied warranty is thought of as resting upon an assumed consent or understanding of the parties. The existence and scope of this assumed consent is largely a matter of social policy. When parties enter into a transaction (and do not expressly provide otherwise), they are assumed to agree to the usual terms and provisions which society feels will best conform both to common business understanding and to the overall welfare of society. The policy view which most courts take at the present time with respect to implied warranties in sales-of-goods transactions can be summarized as follows:

1. There is no warranty in the absence of a sales contract.

2. Unless the seller expressly assumes a greater liability, the only person to whom the warranty obligation is owed, and who therefore can recover from the seller for breach of warranty, is the one who (either directly or through an agent) buys from the seller. The buyer can of course recover for all of his damages, both personal and property. In addition, the Uniform Commercial Code provides:

> A seller's warranty whether express or implied extends to any natural person who is in the family or household of his buyer or who is a guest in his home if it is reasonable to expect that such person may use, consume or be affected by the goods and who is injured in person by breach of the warranty.[17]

Some courts believe that the class of persons who are covered by implied warranties should be extended further than this. The law is still developing in connection with the warranties to remote parties, and the authors of the Code are careful to point out, in their Comment to the section just quoted, that:

> This section expressly includes as beneficiaries within its provisions the family, house hold, and guests of the purchaser. Beyond this, the section is neutral and is not intended to enlarge or restrict the developing case law on whether the seller's warran-

---

17. U.C.C. Sec. 2-318.

Check Case. A depositor drew a check for $100 on his account in a New York City bank, naming P as payee. While visiting his uncle in Chicago, P needed money and indorsed and transferred the check to his uncle who paid P $100. Not finding it convenient to go to his bank, the uncle indorsed and transferred the check to his neighbor for $100. The neighbor indorsed and cashed the check at a grocery store. The grocer in turn indorsed and deposited the check in his account in a Chicago bank. After being promptly forwarded to New York City, the check was returned to the Chicago bank with a notation that the balance in the depositor's account was insufficient for payment of the check. The Chicago bank therefore charged the amount of the check back against the grocer.

The grocer could in turn sue and collect from the neighbor for whom the grocer cashed the check, or instead could skip the neighbor and collect from the uncle. As discussed in Chapter 24, when a person endorses a check and does not expressly limit his liability, the indorser *impliedly* promises that if the check is dishonored, he will pay its amount to *any holder* who acts diligently. This implied promise is enforceable not only by the immediate transferee but also by any later transferee of the check. ☐

* * *

Sales Case. A California manufacturer sold a shipment of ladders to a Chicago wholesaler. The wholesaler sold some of the ladders to a Chicago retailer who in turn sold one of the ladders to a customer. Unknown to any of the parties (manufacturer, wholesaler, retailer, or customer) there was a hidden defect in the wood, so that the first time the ladder was used the top broke off, throwing the customer to the ground and injuring him severely. The retailer having become insolvent and the manufacturer being nearly two thousand miles away, the injured customer sued the wholesaler.

Unless the wholesaler-retailer contract provided otherwise, the wholesaler impliedly warranted to the retailer that the ladders were merchantable. However, the wholesaler's liability for breach of this warranty would be *limited* to the retailer (and to members and guests of his household). Since the customer had no direct contract relationship with the wholesaler, the customer could *not* recover from the wholesaler. ☐

ties, given to his buyer who resells, extend to other persons in the distributive chain.[18]

When it is considered desirable policy, the law readily agrees that an implied promise or warranty liability can extend beyond the parties to a particular contract. Commercial paper (note, draft, or check) provides one of the most common examples. Compare a typical check case with a sales of goods case.

A comparison of the amount of liability and the causal basis of liability in these two types

of cases will show the chief policy differences. In a check case:

1. As to the amount of liability: at the time an endorser endorses and transfers a check, the amount of his possible liability is definite and certain—namely, the face amount of the check.

2. As to the causal basis of liability: in general, an indorser becomes liable when the bank upon which a check is drawn dishonors the check by refusing to pay it. In any lawsuit that follows, all parties have equally ready access to impartial evidence which will prove

---

Comment to U.C.C. Sec. 2-318.

conclusively whether or not the check was actually dishonored.

In a check case, therefore, the fact that the plaintiff and defendant are remote parties does not at all affect either the amount of liability or the causal basis of the defendant's liability, nor otherwise complicate reaching a fair adjustment of the rights of the parties. In addition (as discussed in Chapter 24) sound policy reasons exist for recognizing remote party liability on checks and other commercial paper. It is both feasible and desirable therefore for the law to conclude, as it does, that unless expressly agreed otherwise, the promise or warranty of an indorser goes along with the check and can be enforced by any later holder. On the other hand, in a sales-of-goods case the following considerations apply:

1. As to the amount of liability: the extent of personal and property injuries which may result from defective goods will vary considerably from one owner or user of goods to another. In view of this, it can be strongly argued in the ladder case that it would be unfair to consider the wholesaler liable to any person who happens to buy from the dealer, for damages which might be practically unlimited in amount. This argument is not conclusive since it is often possible for a wholesaler to be indirectly liable for the full amount of the remote customer's damages. If the customer recovers from the retailer for breach of warranty, the retailer can in turn sue the wholesaler on any warranty which was a part of the retailer-wholesaler contract. Unless limited by that contract, the damages recoverable by the retailer would be measured by the amount of the retailer's legal liability to his customer. However, although not conclusive, the fact that the extent of damages is variable within very wide limits is a significant factor in determining whether it is sound policy to recognize an implied warranty in favor of a sub-purchaser.

2. As to the causal basis of liability: liability for breach of a sales-of-goods warranty rests upon proof of the following facts: (1) that the goods were actually defective when they were sold by the defendant, and (2) that such defects caused the injuries suffered by the plaintiff. Compare the simplicity of determining whether or not a check was actually dishonored, with the very complex fact questions of whether goods were actually defective, exactly when the defect arose, and what damages actually and unavoidably resulted. How can a remote seller prove with any certainty what might have happened to goods after they left his hands and passed further along the channels of commerce? The evidence in many goods-warranty cases is quite uncertain, is subject to varying opinions, is not equally available to both plaintiff and defendant, and is frequently impossible to corroborate (or disprove) by impartial evidence. When evidence is uncertain and not equally available, allegations are difficult to disprove and the risk of collusive and faked claims increases. And the more hands the goods have passed through, the more uncertain the evidence and the greater the risk of faked claims. Also juries are often inclined to be quite sympathetic, sometimes even gullible, in a lawsuit involving physical injuries when the defendant is a "big, bad corporation."

Because of these uncertainties in amount and causal basis of liability, the courts (with some exceptions) formerly denied recovery even for negligent (that is, tortious) processing or manufacturing, unless the injured plaintiff had purchased directly from the negligent processor. Over the past fifty years the courts have changed in their view of what is the best policy to follow; now an injured sub-purchaser is usually able to recover from a negligent processor without the necessity of a contract relationship between the parties. The important factors responsible for this change of policy include the following:

1. Under modern manufacturing and marketing processes, goods almost invariably pass through a number of hands before reaching the intended user.

2. The intended user is the one primarily jeopardized when goods are defective.

3. Negligence which causes defects in goods is wrongful and blameworthy conduct, and should be discouraged.

The first two of these numbered factors are also present in a breach of warranty lawsuit brought by an ultimate consumer against a remote seller. Generally these two factors are not sufficient to justify recognizing an implied warranty liability in the absence of a direct contract relationship between the plaintiff and defendant. However, if an additional circumstance is also present, as significant as the third numbered factor above, many courts will recognize that an implied warranty runs in favor of a subpurchaser. The two most important of these special fact situations involve:

1. **Goods for Human Consumption.** If through the fault of a packer or manufacturer, goods intended for human consumption are unwholesome, the packer or manufacturer is held liable to the ultimate consumer. Many such cases are tort actions, in which the injured plaintiff takes advantage of the presumption that the presence of a harmful substance in food is of itself evidence of negligence in preparation. However, even if a packer uses proper care and thereby avoids tort liability, the risk to society is sufficiently great, when products intended for human consumption are unwholesome, that most states also recognize a contract obligation based on an implied warranty running from the packer or manufacturer to the ultimate consumer, to the effect that the goods as packed or processed are merchantable.

2. **Misrepresentations in Advertising**. If a manufacturer intentionally misstates facts in his advertising, he is liable to the ultimate consumer for the tort of fraudulent misrepresentation. To prove false advertising to be fraudulent, however, requires proof of the advertiser's guilty knowledge, and clear-cut proof of this is frequently quite difficult to obtain. Therefore, some courts say that a manufacturer by implication warrants to ultimate consumers that his advertising statements are true.

To return now to the hypothetical case of the purchaser of the defective ladder who sued the wholesaler: courts in the majority of states would hold that, at the present state of legal evolution, business understanding does not contemplate a warranty running from the wholesaler to the remote customer, and social policy does not require such a warranty.

In the landmark case of *Henningsen v. Bloomfield Motors* (previously referred to on page 341) the New Jersey Supreme Court found little difference between goods intended for human consumption and other potentially dangerous goods, and therefore held that a manufacturer should be considered as implying a warranty to an ultimate consumer, the safety of a complex and potentially dangerous machine such as an automobile. The court, however, admitted that only a minority of states would reach the same conclusion. In the course of its opinion the court said:

> There is no doubt that under early common-law concepts of contractual liability only those persons who were parties to the bargain could sue for breach of it. In more recent times a noticeable disposition has appeared in a number of jurisdictions to break through the narrow barrier of privity[19] when dealing with sales of goods in order to give realistic recognition to a universally accepted

---

19. The term "privity" is commonly used in the law to signify a *direct* contractual relationship between two persons. Thus if A sells certain goods to B who in turn sells them to C, A and B are in privity of contract, as also are B and C, but A and C are not in privity of contract.

fact.... The limitations of privity in contracts for the sale of goods developed their place in the law when marketing conditions were simple, when maker and buyer frequently met face to face on an equal bargaining plane and when many of the products were relatively uncomplicated and conducive to inspection by a buyer competent to evaluate their quality.... With the advent of mass marketing, the manufacturer became remote from the purchaser, sales were accomplished through intermediaries and the demand for the product was created by advertising media. In such an economy it became obvious that the consumer was the person being cultivated.... Thus where the commodities sold are such that if defectively manufactured they will be dangerous to life or limb, then society's interests can only be protected by eliminating the requirement of privity between the maker and his dealers and the reasonably expected consumer. In that way the burden of loss consequent upon use of defective articles is borne by those who are in a position to either control the danger or make an equitable distribution of the losses when they do occur....

The concept was expressed in a practical way by the Supreme Court of Texas in . . . [a case involving defective food]:

"In fact the manufacturer's interest in the product is not terminated when he has sold it to the wholesaler. He must get it off the wholesaler's shelves before the wholesaler will buy a new supply. The same is not only true of the retailer, but of the housewife, for the housewife will not buy more until the family has consumed that which she has in her pantry. Thus the manufacturer or other vendor intends that this appearance of suitability of the article for human consumption should continue and be effective until someone is induced thereby to consume the goods. It would be but to acknowledge a weakness in the law to say that he could thus create a demand for his products by inducing a belief that they are suitable for human consumption, when, as a matter of fact, they are not, and reap the benefits of the public confidence thus created, and then avoid liability for the injuries caused thereby merely because there was no privity of contract between him and the one whom he induced to consume the food...."

Although only a minority of jurisdictions have thus far departed from the requirement of privity, the movement in that direction is most certainly gathering momentum. Liability to the ultimate consumer in the absence of direct contractual connection has been predicted upon a variety of theories. Some courts hold that the warranty runs with the article like a covenant running with land; others recognize a third-party beneficiary thesis; still others rest their decision on the ground that public policy requires recognition of a warranty made directly to the consumer....

Most of the cases where lack of privity has not been permitted to interfere with recovery have involved food and drugs.... In fact, the rule as to such products has been characterized as an exception to the general doctrine. But more recently courts, sensing the inequity of such limitation, have moved into broader fields: home permanent wave set ... soap detergent ... inflammable cowboy suit ... exploding bottle ... defective emery wheel ... defective wire rope ... defective cinder blocks....

Under modern conditions the ordinary layman, on responding to the importuning of colorful advertising, has neither the opportunity nor the capacity to inspect or to determine the fitness of an automobile for use; he must rely on the manufacturer who has control of its construction, and to some degree on the dealer who, to the limited extent called for by the manufacturer's instructions, inspects and services it before delivery. In such a marketing milieu his remedies and those of persons who properly claim through him should not depend "upon the intricacies of the law of sales. The obligation of the manufacturer should not be based alone on privity of contract. It should rest, as was once said, upon 'the demands of social justice.' " "If privity of contract is required" then, under the circumstances of modern merchandising, "privity of contract exists in the consciousness and understanding of all right-thinking persons.". . .

Accordingly we hold that under modern marketing conditions, when a manufacturer puts a new automobile in the stream of trade and promotes its purchase by the public, an implied warranty that it is reasonably suitable for use as such accompanies it into the hands of the ultimate purchaser.

The New Jersey court thus argues that in the case of potentially dangerous goods, the legal concept of implied warranty should be extended to run from manufacturers to sub-purchasers. It is interesting to compare the court's argument and conclusion with the following view expressed by Dean Prosser, an eminent legal scholar:

> No one doubts that, unless there is privity, liability to the consumer must be in tort and not in contract. There is no need to borrow a concept from the contract law of sales; and it is "only by some violent pounding and twisting" that "warranty" can be made to serve the purpose at all. Why talk of it? If there is to be strict liability in tort, let there be strict liability in tort, declared outright, without an illusory contract mask. Such strict liability is familiar enough in the law of animals, abnormally dangerous activities, nuisance, workmen's compensation, and respondeat superior [that is, a principal's liability for his agent's torts]. There is nothing so shocking about it today that cannot be accepted and stand on its own feet in this new and additional field, provided always that public sentiment, public demand, and "public policy" have reached the point where the change is called for. There are not lacking indications that some of the courts are about ready to throw away the crutch, and to admit what they are really doing, when they say that the warranty is not the one made on the original sale, and does not run with the goods, but is a new and independent one made directly to the consumer; and that it does not arise out of or depend upon any contract, but is imposed by the law, in tort, as a matter of policy.[20]

---

20. "Strict Liability to the Consumer," 69 *Yale L J.* 1099, p. 1134 (1960).

D. Remedies for Breach of Warranty

If a contract includes an express warranty, frequently there is also included a provision stating what shall be the remedy or remedies for breach of warranty. For example, a buyer's remedy may be limited to return of goods and refund of price, or to repair and replacement of defective goods or parts. If no implied warranty would arise under the circumstances, or if one which would have arisen is properly excluded, the express agreement iS the limit of the seller's warranty liability. On the other hand, if parties have not agreed on any limitation of remedies, then when a warranty is breached the buyer usually has the right to select whichever one of two remedies he wishes. He may (1) retain the goods and recover for the damages resulting from the breach of warranty, or (2) rescind the contract and recover anything already paid plus any damages resulting from the breach of warranty. Some of the details of these remedies are discussed in Chapter 22. Two points can be emphasized here:

1. Since a breach of warranty action is a type of action for breach of contract, the contract rule of waiver applies. If performance falls short of what is required under a contract, but the other party nevertheless shows himself to be fully satisfied with the defective performance, this satisfaction constitutes a waiver or excuse of any defect, and usually the satisfied party cannot afterwards change his mind. He thus gives up any right he may have to cancel the contract or even to collect damages.

2. After a buyer has used goods for more than merely testing them, he usually cannot return them (that is, he cannot cancel the contract) even though the goods are defective. Instead, the buyer's only remedy is to recover damages.

The Uniform Commercial Code expresses these two points as follows:

Where a tender [of goods] has been accepted . . . the buyer must within a reasonable time after he discovers or should have discovered any breach notify the seller of breach *or be barred from any remedy....* [Emphasis added.]

Revocation of acceptance [which can be accomplished, for example, by the buyer giving notice that he desires to return defective goods] must occur within a reasonable time after the buyer discovers or should have discovered the ground for it and before any substantial change in condition of the goods which is not caused by their own defects.[21] [Emphasis added.]

E. Federal Warranty Law

I. PURPOSE

In response to increasing consumer complaints of deceptive manufacturer and retailer practices, including the disclaimer of implied warranties under the Uniform Commercial Code, Congress passed the Magnuson-Moss Warranty Act (Act)[22] which grants to the Federal Trade Commission (FTC), an administrative agency, new and unprecedented authority in the field of consumer warranty protection. The Act specifically states that:

In order to improve the adequacy of information available to consumers, prevent deception, and improve competition in the marketing of consumer products any warrantor warranting a consumer product to a consumer by means of a written warranty shall, to the extent required by rules of the Commission, fully and conspicuously disclose in simple and readily understood language the terms and conditions of such warranty.[23]

21. U.C.C. Secs. 2-607, 2-608.
22. 15 U.S.C. Secs. 2301-2312.
23. 15 U.S.C. Sec. 2302(a).

2. Application and Designation of Warranties

The Act applies only to written warranties of consumer products and to *written* service contracts where the services relate to the maintenance and/or repair of a consumer product. It does not invalidate or restrict any right or remedy of any consumer under state law; therefore, the warranty provisions under the U.C.C., as previously discussed, are still in effect. The application of both state U.C.C. warranty law and federal warranty law under the Act poses an interesting dilemma for the seller. If he is silent, thereby not imposing warranty responsibility on himself under the Act, he would, of course, subject himself at least to an implied warranty of merchantability under the U.C.C. The only way the seller could protect himself is to give an oral exclusion which might be difficult to prove at a later date. On the other hand, if the seller excludes all implied warranties in writing, he might subject himself to the provisions of the Act.

It should be emphasized that the Act does not require the issuance of a warranty. But if a warrantor wishes to warrant any consumer product costing more than $5, the terms of the written warranty must be made available to the consumer prior to the sale. Rules proposed by the FTC, in addition, require each warrantor to fully and conspicuously disclose, in simple and understandable language, the general nature of the warranty including dispute settlement procedures. The intent of the proposed rule is to facilitate comparative shopping and to insure the availability of a remedy if the product is faulty.

Written warranties on consumer products actually costing the consumer more than $10 must be designated as either "full" or "limited" in accordance with federal standards. The minimum standards for a "full warranty" are set forth in Section 104 of the Act as follows:

1. A warrantor will remedy a consumer product within a reasonable time and without charge in event of a defect, malfunction, or failure to conform with such written warranty;

2. A warrantor may not impose a limitation on the duration of any implied warranty;

3. A warrantor may not exclude or limit consequential damages unless such exclusion is printed conspicuously on the face of the warranty;

4. If the product contains a defect or malfunction after a reasonable number of repair attempts, the warrantor must permit the consumer to elect either a refund for or replacement of the product;

5. Generally, a warrantor may not impose any duty on the consumer except notification, unless it can demonstrate the duty is reasonable;

6. The FTC may, by rule, define the duties referred to in 5 above;

7. These duties extend to anyone who is entitled to enforce the warranties applicable to the product, i.e., transferees and third party beneficiaries during the duration of the warranty; and

8. The warrantor does not have to perform if the problem was caused by damage or unreasonable use on the part of the consumer.

If the minimum standards for a "full warranty" are not met, the warranty would be classified as a "limited warranty." Therefore, as consumers become more familiar with the "full" and "limited" warranty designations, they will know exactly what to expect from a seller-warrantor.

3. REMEDIES

In order to obtain a remedy for breach of warranty under the U.C.C., the dissatisfied consumer would have to pursue his claim through the complexities of the court system just as he would with any contract or tort case.

The consumer may conclude that the cost of litigation, including attorney's fees, far exceeds the cost of the defective product; hence, there would seem to be little justification in pursuing a warranty claim. (Even if the matter was successfully pursued in a small claims court without the assistance of an attorney, collecting on a judgment presents still another problem which would tend to discourage the potential litigant.) Recognizing these problems, the drafters of the Act have provided for, and encouraged, warrantors to establish informal procedures for the settlement of consumer disputes. In fact, warrantors may require consumers to comply with their informal settlement procedures, if approved by the FTC, before pursuing any other legal remedy. Where informal settlement procedures have not been established, a consumer may start his warranty suit in any state court of competent jurisdiction, or in a federal district court if three requirements are met: (1) each individual claim exceeds $25; (2) the aggregate amount in controversy exceeds $50,000; and (3) if brought as a class action, the number of named plaintiffs exceeds one hundred. It is interesting to note that if a consumer prevails, he may, in some cases, be allowed by the court to recover his expenses, including attorney's fees.

Although it remains to be seen just how effective the Act will be, it clearly demonstrates a positive legislative response to changing social conditions. The twentieth century is far removed from the day of barter and exchange when the doctrine of *caveat emptor* (let the buyer beware) was king. Under U.C.C. and Magnuson-Moss warranty law, the seller has been forced into the position of assuming some social responsibility for the product he sells. Some practitioners feel that the Act has ushered in a new era of consumer protection and a greater sense of social responsibility.

In addition to the Magnuson-Moss Warranty Act, Congress has enacted a number of regulatory provisions that are designed to protect consumers from physical harm caused by unsafe products. One example is the Consumer Product Safety Act which created an administrative agency called the Consumer Product Safety Commission. Its function is to create rules and regulations dealing with product safety. It also has the power to ban unsafe products and impose civil and criminal penalties for violation of the Act.

E. Negligence

If an injured party cannot proceed against a manufacturer or seller on a contract warranty theory (perhaps warranties had been effectively excluded or there was lack of privity), the injured plaintiff can always proceed on the tort of negligence. As previously noted in this chapter, beginning with the *MacPherson* case, a cause of action based upon negligence does not require privity of contract between the parties. Proceeding on a warranty theory presents less problems for the injured party because all he has to show is that the product malfunctioned. However, proceeding on a negligence theory presents a more difficult problem. Now, not only must the injured party show that the product malfunctioned, but he must also prove why it malfunctioned. In short, he must show that the manufacturer or retailer breached his duty of due care in the manufacture or distribution of the product and that such breach was the proximate cause of the injury.

1. MANUFACTURERS

The Restatement of the Law of Torts, Second, §395, sets forth the duty of the manufacturer to exercise reasonable care and the consequences if he does not as follows:

A manufacturer who fails to exercise reasonable care in the manufacture of a chattel, which, unless carefully made, he should recognize as involving an unreasonable risk of causing substantial bodily harm to those who lawfully use it for a purpose for which it is manufactured and to those whom the sup-

plier should expect to be in the vicinity of its probable use, is subject to liability for bodily harm caused to them by its lawful use in a manner and for a purpose for which it is manufactured.

The duty to exercise reasonable care extends from the initial product design, selection of materials and fabrication of component parts to final inspection and testing of the product. In addition to exercising care in design and production, a manufacturer must also be sure to give adequate warnings and instructions for the safe use of his product. His warnings must cover not only the dangers which are known to him but also possible dangers which, in the opinion of society, he *should* be aware of. In other words, he is required to scrutinize his product through the eyes of experts and with pessimistic imagination as to potential dangers.

2. RETAILERS

Since a retailer acts only as an intermediary to get the product from the manufacturer to the consumer, his duty of care is obviously less than that of the manufacturer. Therefore, the majority rule as set forth in The Restatement of the Law of Torts, Second, §402, is as follows:

A seller of a chattel manufactured by a third person, who neither knows nor has reason to know that it is, or is likely to be, dangerous, is not liable in an action for negligence for harm caused by the dangerous character or condition of the chattel because of his failure to discover the danger by an inspection or test of the chattel before selling it.

On the other hand, the minority view is to the effect that the retailer owes a duty to the consumer to discover and disclose defects which could be ascertained by a normal inspection. But the retailer owes no duty to discover and disclose concealed defects. A new car dealer, for example, would not be required to disassemble a car before it is sold,

Example. M manufactured power rotary lawn mowers. C purchased one of M's rotary mowers from a retailer who delivered it to C in its original box. Upon opening the box, C did not find any instructions on the mower's use, so he simply put gas in the tank and started it. A short time later, the blade came off and severely cut C's right foot. It was discovered that the manufacturer had failed to secure the blade with a lock washer and that the injury might not have occurred if a protective device had been properly adjusted. M, the manufacturer, was clearly negligent in two respects: first, he failed to fabricate and inspect the product properly; and second, he failed to provide adequate instructions about how the protective device should be adjusted to provide maximum safety. ☐

but he would have a duty to inspect its safety features and roadability and discover any defects which would normally result from such an inspection.

Sometimes the duty imposed upon the manufacturer or retailer is established by statute. If, for example, a contractor fails to use the wire specified in a local building code, and as a result the structure burns down, the contractor is negligent *per se*, that is, without the necessity of proving each of the elements of negligence.

G. Strict Liability

Apart from the Magnuson-Moss Warranty Act, strict liability is the most recent and significant development in the area of products liability. In effect, strict liability is a tort theory of recovery; however, unlike the traditional tort of negligence just discussed, the injured plaintiff is not required to prove how or why the product became defective. The plaintiff needs only to show (1) that he was injured by the product, (2) that the defective condition of the product is unreasonably dangerous (this element is not required in some jurisdictions), (3) that the seller is engaged in the business of selling the product, and (4) that at the time he was injured the condition of the product was not substantially changed from what it was at the time it was sold by the manufacturer or other seller. Under the strict liability theory, therefore, the difficulties of

proving the elements of negligence do not exist. Strict liability is more akin to warranty than any other products liability theory, and is often a theory which is used interchangeably with warranty theory by the courts.

The American Law Institute approved a strict liability theory in 1965 which was published as §402A of The Restatement of the Law of Torts, Second, as follows:

1. One who sells any product in a defective condition unreasonably dangerous to the user or consumer or to his property is subject to liability for physical harm thereby caused to the ultimate user or consumer, or to his property, if (a) the seller is engaged in the business of selling such a product, and (b) it is expected to and does reach the user or consumer without substantial change in the condition in which it is sold.

2. The rule stated in Subsection (1) applies although (a) the seller has exercised all possible care in the preparation and sale of his product, and (b) the user or consumer has not bought the product from or entered into any contractual relation with the seller.

The import and meaning, in both a historical and contemporary sense, is more fully set forth in the official comments to §402A some of which are set forth below:

a. This Section states a special rule applicable to sellers of products. The rule is one of strict liability, making the seller subject to liability to the user or consumer even though he has exercised all possible care in the preparation and sale of the product. The Section is inserted in . . . [this] Chapter [of the Restatement] dealing with the negligence liability of suppliers of chattels, for convenience of reference and comparison with other Sections dealing with negligence. The rule stated here is not exclusive, and does not preclude liability based upon the alternative ground of negligence of the seller, where such negligence can be proved.

b. *History.* Since the early days of the common law those engaged in the business of selling food intended for human consumption have been held to a high degree of responsibility for their products. As long ago as 1266 there were enacted special criminal statutes imposing penalties upon victualers, vintners, brewers, butchers, cooks, and other persons who supplied "corrupt" food and drink. In the earlier part of this century this ancient attitude was reflected in a series of decisions in which the courts of a number of states sought to find some method of holding the seller of food liable to the ultimate consumer even though there was no showing of negligence on the part of the seller. These decisions represented a departure from, and an exception to, the general rule that a supplier of chattels was not liable to third persons in the absence of negligence or privity of contract. In the beginning, these decisions displayed considerable ingenuity in evolving more or less fictitious theories of liability to fit the case. The various devices included an agency of the intermediate dealer or another to purchase for the consumer, or to sell for the seller; a theoretical assignment of the seller's warranty to the intermediate dealer; a third party beneficiary contract; and an implied representation that the food was fit for consumption because it was placed on the market, as well as numerous others. In later years the courts have become more or less agreed upon the theory of a "warranty" from the seller to the consumer, either "running with the goods" by analogy to a covenant running with the land, or made directly to the consumer. Other decisions have indicated that the basis is merely one of strict liability in tort, which is not dependent upon either contract or negligence.

Recent decisions, since 1950, have extended this special rule of strict liability beyond the seller of food for human consumption. The first extension was into the closely analogous cases of other products intended for intimate bodily use, where, for example, as in the case of cosmetics, the application to the body of the consumer is external rather than internal. Beginning in 1958 with a Michigan case involving cinder building blocks [in which three of the eight Judges dissented], a number of recent decisions have discarded any limitation to intimate association with the body, and have extended the rule of strict liability to cover the sale of any product which, if it should prove to be defective, may be expected to cause physical harm to the consumer or his property.

c. On whatever theory, the justification for the strict liability has been said to be that the seller, by marketing his product for use and consumption, has undertaken and assumed a special responsibility toward any member of the consuming public who may be injured by it; that the public has the right to and does expect, in the case of products which it needs and for which it is forced to rely upon the seller, that reputable sellers will stand behind their goods; that public policy demands that the burden of accidental injuries caused by products intended for consumption be placed upon those who market them, and be treated as a cost of production against which liability insurance can be obtained; and that the consumer of such products is entitled to the maximum of protection at the hands of someone, and the proper persons to afford it are those who market the products.

d. The rule stated in this Section is not limited to the sale of food for human consumption, or other products for intimate bodily use, although it will obviously include them. It extends to any product sold in the condition, or substantially the same condition, in which it is expected to reach the ultimate user or consumer. Thus the rule stated applies to an automobile, a tire, an airplane, a grinding wheel, a water heater, a gas stove, a power tool, a riveting machine, a chair, and an insecticide. It applies also to products which, if they are defective, may be expected to and do cause only "physical harm" in the form of damage to the user's land or chattels, as in the case of animal food or a herbicide.

e. Normally the rule stated in this Section will be applied to articles which already have undergone some processing before sale, since there is today little in the way of consumer products which will reach the consumer without such processing. The rule is not, however, so limited, and the supplier of poisonous mushrooms which are neither cooked, canned, packaged, nor otherwise treated is subject to the liability here stated.

f. *Business of selling.* The rule stated in this Section applies to any person engaged in the business of selling products for use or consumption. It therefore applies to any manufacturer of such a product, to any wholesale or retail dealer or distributor and to the operator of a restaurant. It is not necessary that the seller be engaged solely in the business of selling such products. Thus the rule applies to the owner of a motion picture theatre who sells popcorn or ice cream, either for consumption on the premises or in packages to be taken home.

The rule does not, however, apply to the occasional seller of food or other such products who is not engaged in that activity as a part of his business.... The basis for the rule is the ancient one of the special responsibility for the safety of the public undertaken by one who enters into the business of supplying human beings with products which may endanger the safety of their persons and property, and the forced reliance upon that undertaking on the part of those who purchase such goods. This basis is lacking in the case of the ordinary individual who makes the isolated sale, and he is not liable to a third person, or even to his buyer, in the absence of negligence.

g. *Defective condition.* The rule stated in this Section applies only where the product is, at the time it leaves the seller's hand, in a condition not contemplated by the ultimate consumer, which will be unreasonably dangerous to him. The seller is not liable when he delivers the product in a safe condition, and subsequent mishandling or other causes make it harmful by the time it is consumed. The burden of proof that the product was in a defective condition at the time that it left the hands of the particular seller is upon the injured plaintiff; and unless evidence can be produced which will support the conclusion that it was then defective, the burden is not sustained.

* * *

i. *Unreasonably dangerous.* The rule stated in this Section applies only where the defective condition of the product makes it unreasonably dangerous to the user or consumer. Many products cannot possibly be made entirely safe for all consumption, and any food or drug necessarily involves some risk of harm, if only from overconsumption. Ordinary sugar is a deadly poison to diabetics, and castor oil found use under Mussolini as an instrument of torture. That is not what is meant by "unreasonably dangerous" in this Section. The article sold must be dangerous to an extent beyond that which would be contemplated by the ordinary consumer who purchases it, with the ordinary knowledge common to the community as to its characteristics. Good whiskey is not unreasonably dangerous merely because it will make some people drunk, and is especially dangerous to alcoholics; but bad whiskey, containing a dangerous amount of fusel oil, is unreasonably dangerous. Good tobacco is not unreasonably dangerous merely because the effects of smoking may be harmful; but tobacco containing something like marijuana may be unreasonably dangerous. Good butter is not unreasonably dangerous merely because, if such be the case, it deposits cholesterol in the arteries and leads to heart attacks; but bad butter, contaminated with poisonous fish oil, is unreasonably dangerous.

j. *Directions or warning.* In order to prevent the product from being unreasonably dangerous, the seller may be required to give directions or warnings, on the container, as to its use....

* * *

Where warning is given, the seller may reasonably assume that it will be read and heeded; and a product bearing such a warning, which is safe for use if it is followed, is not in defective condition, nor is it unreasonably dangerous.

k. *Unavoidably unsafe products.* There are some products which, in the present state of human knowledge, are quite incapable of being made safe for their intended and ordinary use. These are especially common in the field of drugs. An outstanding example is the vaccine for the Pasteur treatment of rabies, which not uncommonly leads to very serious and damaging consequences when it is injected. Since the disease itself invariably leads to a dreadful death, both the marketing and the use of the vaccine are fully justified, notwithstanding the unavoidable high degree of risk which they involve. Such a product, properly prepared, and accompanied by proper directions and warning, is not defective, nor is it unreasonably dangerous....

* * *

Illustration

1. M manufactures and packs a can of beans, which he sells to B, a wholesaler. B sells the beans to C, a jobber, who resells it to D, a retail grocer. E buys the can of beans from D, and gives it to F. F serves the beans at lunch to G, his guest. While eating the beans, G breaks a tooth, on a pebble the size, shape, and color of a bean, which no reasonable inspection could possibly have discovered. There is satisfactory evidence that the pebble was in the can of beans when it was opened. Although there is no negligence on the part of M[24], B, C, or D, each of them is subject to liability to G. On the other hand, E and F, who have not sold the beans, are not liable to G in the absence of some negligence on their part.

m. *"Warranty."* The liability stated in this Section does not rest upon negligence. It is strict liability, . . . The basis of liability is purely one of tort.

---

24. Why wouldn't the mere presence of the pebble in the can of beans be *prima facie* evidence of negligence on the part of the packer, M? [Footnote added.]

A number of courts, seeking a theoretical basis for the liability, have resorted to a "warranty," either running with the goods sold, by analogy to covenants running with the land, or made directly to the consumer without contract. In some instances this theory has proved to be an unfortunate one. Although warranty was in its origin a matter of tort liability, and it is generally agreed that a tort action will still lie for its breach, it has become so identified in practice with a contract of sale between the plaintiff and the defendant that the warranty theory has become something of an obstacle to the recognition of the strict liability where there is no such contract. There is nothing in this Section which would prevent any court from treating the rule stated as a matter of "warranty" to the user or consumer. But if this is done, it should be recognized and understood that the "warranty" is a very different kind of warranty from those usually found in the sale of goods, and that it is not subject to the various contract rules which have grown up to surround such sales.

The rule stated in this Section does not require any reliance on the part of the consumer upon the reputation, skill, or judgment of the seller who is to be held liable, nor any representation or undertaking on the part of that seller. The seller is strictly liable although, as is frequently the case, the consumer does not even know who he is at the time of consumption.... The consumer's cause of action...is not affected by any disclaimer or other agreement whether it be between the seller and his immediate buyer, or attached to and accompanying the product into the consumer's hands. In short, "warranty" must be given a new and different meaning if it is used in connection with this Section. It is much simpler to regard the liability here stated as merely one of strict liability in tort.

n. *Contributory negligence.* Since the liability with which this Section deals is not based upon negligence of the seller, but is strict liability, the rule applied to strict liability cases . . . applies. Contributory negligence of the plaintiff is not a defense when such negligence consists merely in a failure to discover the defect in the product, or to guard against the possibility of its existence. On the other hand the form of contributory negligence which consists in voluntarily and unreasonably proceeding to encounter a known danger and commonly passes under the name of assumption of risk, is a defense under this Section as in other cases of strict liability....

Strict tort liability has become the prevailing remedy in products liability cases in this country. Four reasons are generally given for the emergence of strict tort liability as the dominant products liability theory even though warranty, negligence, and misrepresentation continue to be widely used. First, strict liability has its theoretical basis in tort, not contract. Second, the concept of strict liability was viewed as an extension of the common law food warranty. As noted earlier in this chapter, food warranty is implied. It was presumed that the manufacturer of foodstuffs had vouched for its wholesomeness and fitness for human consumption. Third, as previously suggested, sales warranty law was viewed as inadequate to deal with exploding product lines and expanding public needs. Warranty in most cases requires privity, notice, disclaimer and compliance with applicable statutes of limitation which were increasingly viewed by the public as technical legal traps for the unwary. And fourth, the consuming public expressed a need for greater protection from manufacturers. This is accomplished under strict liability by shifting the burden of proof from the plaintiff to the defendant and eliminating privity.

H. Misrepresentation— Fraudulent and Nonfraudulent

Fraudulent misrepresentation (see Chapter 8) is another remedy available to the injured consumer. The fraud may consist of an intentional misrepresentation, where, for example, the product is falsely advertised or its container is purposely mislabeled, or defects are concealed. In either case, the misrepresentation made it very similar to an express or implied warranty and often has been used as an alternate or simultaneous theory on which to base a claim. However, The Restatement of Torts, Second, §402B, provides that even though the statements made are not fraudulent or negligent and privity of contract does not exist, an injured consumer still can recover damages from the one engaged in the business of selling the product. Specifically, §402B provides that:

> One engaged in the business of selling chattels who, by advertising, labels, or otherwise, makes to the public a misrepresentation of a material fact concerning the character or quality of a chattel sold by him is subject to liability for physical harm to a consumer of the chattel caused by justifiable reliance upon the misrepresentation, even though
>
> (a) it is not made fraudulently or negligently, and
>
> (b) the consumer has not bought the chattel from or entered into any contractual relation with the seller.

Some of the official comments to this Section are useful in explaining its meaning and placing it in context with the other product liability theories just discussed.

> a. The rule stated in this Section is one of strict liability for physical harm to the consumer, resulting from a misrepresentation of the character or quality of the chattel sold, even though the misrepresentation is an innocent one, and not made fraudulently or negligently. . . .
>
> b. The rule stated in this Section differs from the rule of strict liability stated in §402A, which is a special rule applicable only to sellers of products for consumption and does not depend upon misrepresentation. The rule here stated applies to one engaged in the business of selling any type of chattel, and is limited to misrepresentations of their character or quality.
>
> c. *History*. The early rule was that a seller of chattels incurred no liability for physical

harm resulting from the use of the chattel to anyone other than his immediate buyer, unless there was privity of contract between them.

Shortly after 1930, a number of the American courts began, more or less independently, to work out a further extension of liability for physical harm to the consumer of the chattel, in cases where the seller made misrepresentations to the public concerning its character or quality, and the consumer, as a member of the public, purchased the chattel in reliance upon the misrepresentation and suffered physical harm because of the fact misrepresented. In such cases the seller was held to strict liability for the misrepresentation, even though it was not made fraudulently or negligently. The leading case is *Baxter v. Ford Motor Co.* [a 1932 Washington case], in which the manufacturer of an automobile advertised to the public that the windshield glass was "shatterproof," and the purchaser was injured when a stone struck the glass and it shattered....

d. *"Warranty.*" The theory finally adopted by most of the decisions, however, has been that of a noncontractual "express warranty" made to the consumer in the form of the representation to the public upon which he relies.... The liability stated in this Section is liability in tort, and not in contract; and if it is to be called one of "warranty," it is at least a different kind of warranty from that involved in the ordinary sale of goods from the immediate seller to the immediate buyer, and is subject to different rules.

e. *Sellers included.* The rule stated in this Section applies to any person engaged in the business of selling any type of chattel.... It is not limited to manufacturers of the chattel, and it includes wholesalers, retailers, and other distributors who sell it.

The rule stated applies, however, only to those who are engaged in the business of selling such chattels. It has no application to anyone who is not so engaged in business. It does not apply, for example, to a newspaper advertisement published by a private owner of a single automobile who offers it for sale.

f. *Misrepresentation of character or quality.* The rule stated applies to any misrepre-sentation of a material fact concerning the character or quality of the chattel sold which is made to the public by one so engaged in the business of selling such chattels. The fact misrepresented must be a material one, upon which the consumer may be expected to rely in making his purchase, and he must justifiably rely upon it.

Illustration

1. M manufactures automobiles. He advertises in newspapers and magazines that the glass in his cars is "shatterproof." B reads this advertising, and in reliance upon it purchases from a retail dealer an automobile manufactured by M. While B is driving the car, a stone thrown up by a passing truck strikes the windshield and shatters it, injuring B. M is subject to strict liability to B.

g. *Material fact.* The rule stated in this Section applies only to misrepresentations of material facts concerning the character or quality of the chattel in question. It does not apply to statements of opinion, and in particular it does not apply to the kind of loose general praise of wares sold which, on the part of the seller, is considered to be "sales talk," and is commonly called "puffing"—as, for example, a statement that an automobile is the best on the market for the price.... In addition, the fact misrepresented must be a material one, of importance to the normal purchaser, by which the ultimate buyer may justifiably be expected to be influenced in buying the chattel.

h. *"To the public."* The rule stated in this Section is limited to misrepresentations which are made by the seller to the public at large, in order to induce purchase of the chattels sold, or are intended by the seller to, and do, reach the public. The form of the representation is not important. It may be made by public advertising in newspapers or television, by literature distributed to the public through dealers, by labels on the product sold, or leaflets accompanying it, or in any other manner, whether it be oral or written.

Table 12.1 Products Liability

	Warranty	Negligence	Strict Liability	Misrepresentation
Recovery based upon Privity required	Contract Yes, except where a) Plaintiff is third party beneficiary b) Plaintiff is an assignee under a valid assignment c) The goods are for human consumption d) The goods have been falsely advertised	Tort No	Tort No	Tort No
Proof why product malfunctioned required	No	Yes	No	No
Seller is	A merchant with respect to goods sold	Any seller in the chain	One engaged in the business of selling the product	One engaged in the business of selling the product
Notice of defect required	Yes, within a reasonable time	No	No	NO
Liability can be excluded	Yes	No	No	No

Table 12.1 highlights the similarities and differences among the four products liability theories.

Illustrations

2. R manufactures wire rope. He issues a manual containing statements concerning its strength, which he distributes through dealers to buyers, and to members of the public who may be expected to buy. In reliance upon the statements made in the manual, B buys a quantity of the wire rope from a dealer, and makes use of it to hoist a weight of 1,000 pounds. The strength of the rope is not as great as is represented in the manual, and as a result the rope breaks and the weight falls on B and injures him. R is subject to strict liability to B.

3. J manufactures a product for use by women at home in giving "permanent waves" to their hair. He places on the bottles labels which state that the product may safely be used in a particular manner, and will not be injurious to the hair. B reads such a label, and in reliance upon it purchases a bottle of the product from a retail dealer. She uses it as directed, and as a result her hair is destroyed. J is subject to strict liability to B.

i. *Consumers.* The rule stated in this Section is limited to strict liability for physical harm to consumers of the chattel. The Caveat leaves open the question whether the rule may not also apply to one who is not a consumer, but who suffers physical harm through his justifiable reliance upon the misrepresentation.

"Consumer" is to be understood in the broad sense of one who makes use of the chattel in the manner which a purchaser may be expected to use it. Thus an employee of the ultimate purchaser to whom the chattel is turned over, and who is directed to make use of it in his work, is a consumer, and so is the wife of the purchaser of an automobile who is permitted by him to drive it.

The foregoing discussion of product liability leads to the conclusion that one or any combination of theories—warranty, negligence, strict liability, or misrepresentation—may be appropriately used by an injured plaintiff. Certainly strict liability from the proof standpoint, would be the simplest theory to pursue. However, under modern pleading practices, all four may be pleaded simultaneously. Given all the possible consumer remedies, an interesting question to consider is whether or not the pendulum has swung too far to the side of consumer interests. After all, it is the consumer who must ultimately bear the expense of compliance by the manufacturers and other sellers.

* * *

Problems

1. S, a manufacturer of certain types of refrigerator equipment, bought a welding unit from its manufacturer, M, for $500. In inducing S to purchase the unit, M orally and also in a descriptive circular which he gave S, asserted to S that the welding unit was well made and would do certain specified welding jobs. Before S made any use of the unit, he changed his manufacturing processes and had no need for such a unit. About six months later S sold and delivered the unit for $300 to B another manufacturer. In inducing B to buy the unit, S said that he had never used the unit and also said and did what is described below. When B attempted to use it, he discovered that it was so defective in design that it was unable to do any of the welding jobs specified in M's circular. B demanded that S take back the unit and return B's $300 and when S refused, B sued S. S conclusively proved that he had honestly and reasonably believed that the unit would perform as described in M's circular.

(a) In inducing B to buy, S showed B the circular received from M, and said that he himself had had no experience with the unit. Was B entitled to return the welding unit to S and recover $300? Explain.

(b) S was unable to find M's circular. However S remembered what the circular had said and so told B: "This unit is well made and will do welding jobs such as [and then S mentioned the jobs]." Was B entitled to return the unit to S and recover $300? Explain.

2. B lived in a small town, a short distance from one large city and a greater distance from another large city. Both cities were in the same direction from B and each city had an FM radio station. Adjacent channels were assigned to the two stations and in B's location, an ordinary FM receiver could not separate the signals from the two stations and could not receive for satisfactory listening the weaker signal from the more distant city. B went to S's radio store to look at a new model of FM receiver. S showed B a descriptive circular from the manufacturer, stating in part: "This receiver can tune with pinpoint sharpness, and because of a newly designed circuit, can separate a weak signal from a stronger signal even on adjacent channels in the same direction." B bought the set, paying $50 down and promising to pay the balance of $250 in one month. In B's location, the set functioned no better (nor worse) than other FM receivers. B still could not separate the weaker signal from the stronger one. B wanted to cancel the contract and made no further use of the receiver. S re-

fused to accept return of the receiver and when the one month expired, sued B for the balance due.

(a) Explain (1) the reasoning upon which B could attempt to defend, (2) the reasoning upon which S could attempt to collect, and (3) which party should be given judgment.

(b) In addition to the above facts, assume that when S was showing the receiver and circular to B, S said, "This receiver is guaranteed, the company stands behind it." Explain whether your answer would be different than that in Part (a) of this problem.

3. A customer in a small grocery store (not a self-service store) requested a can of food (the customer's request is quoted below), and bought what he requested for 90 cents. The can received by the customer had been sold by the Star Packing Company to a wholesaler and by the wholesaler to the grocer. While eating the food in his home, the customer broke his dental plate on a small stone which had been in the can with the contents. A new plate cost the customer $700. The customer sued the grocer.

(a) In stating what he wanted, the customer said, "I want a medium size can of pork and beans. Any brand will do." Explain whether the customer could recover from the grocer and if so how much.

(b) In stating what he wanted, the customer said, "I want a can of Star Brand pork and beans. I've been looking all over town for that, and I see you handle it." Explain whether the customer could recover from the grocer and if so how much.

(c) In stating what he wanted, the customer said, "I want a can of pitted cherries. Any brand will do." The stone on which the customer broke his plate was a cherry pit, still inside one of the cherries. Explain whether the customer could recover from the grocer and if so how much.

(d) Other facts being the same assume that the grocer operated a self-service store. The customer selected a can of peas from the shelf and paid the cashier 30 cents. The small stone on which the cus-

tomer broke his plate had been in the can with the contents. Explain whether the customer could recover from the grocer and if so how much?

4. A heating dealer sold an oil conversion unit to B, a homeowner, and installed it in B's furnace. Neither the conversation nor the written contract between the dealer and the buyer contained any reference to quality or warranty. When he installed the unit, the dealer took it from the original box as it had come from the manufacturer. One week later a defect in the unit, of which the dealer had been unaware, caused a costly fire in B's house. The defect resulted from faulty manufacture and was such that a dealer using reasonable care would not discover it during his inspection and installation of the unit. The dealer offered to take back the defective unit in exchange for a new one but denied any liability for the fire damages.

(a) B sued the dealer for the full amount of the fire damages. What result?

(b) Other facts being the same, assume that the written contract between the dealer and B stated: "The dealer warrants the described unit to be free from defects in workmanship and materials for thirty days. Liability under this warranty is limited to replacement of any unit shown to be defective within that period. This is in lieu of all other warranties express or implied." B sued the dealer for the full amount of the fire damages. What result?

5. B, a baker, decided to air-condition his small bakery shop. He measured floor space and ceiling height, calculated volume, and consulted a chart recommending the proper size air-conditioning unit necessary to cool the calculated area to 72 degrees Fahrenheit. B ordered and bought from S, a dealer in heating and ventilating equipment, an air-conditioning unit the size indicated by the chart, paying a portion of the price down and agreeing to pay the balance in certain monthly installments. S installed the unit in B's shop and, at his request, set the controls for 72 degrees. Although installed and functioning properly, the unit failed to lower the temperature in the shop below 82 degrees. B consulted S who measured

and verified B's calculation of area. It then occurred to S that in calculating for the size of unit to buy, B had failed to take into account the output of heat from his baking ovens. The size of unit B had selected was proper for an ordinary shop of that area but was not adequate for the baking shop because of the heat from the ovens. B then proposed to S that either they cancel the contract, or reduce the price so that B could purchase an additional unit. S refused cancellation or reduction. B had the unit disconnected, no longer used it, and told S that he was holding the unit for S. When B failed to make the contract payments, S sued B.

(a) Explain (1) the reasoning upon which B could attempt to defend, (2) the reasoning upon which S could attempt to collect, and (3) which party should be given judgment.

(b) Other facts being the same, assume the following: B took the shop dimensions to S and told S that he wanted an air-conditioning system that would maintain a temperature of 72 degrees Fahrenheit in his bakery shop. S visited B's shop to verify the measurements, determined from a chart the size of unit to use to maintain the desired temperature for that area, and installed such a unit in B's shop. The contract between the parties contained no express warranty. The unit was the same size as in the preceding part of this problem, with the same result. S had overlooked the heat-producing ovens. When B disconnected the unit, offered to return it, and made no further payments, S sued. Explain whether the changed facts would change any of the answers given for Part (a).

(c) Other facts being the same as in Part (b), assume that the written contract between S and B contains the following provision: "S warrants the described equipment to be free from defects of material and workmanship, for the period of six months. This warranty is in lieu of all other warranties express or implied." Would this additional fact change any of the answers given for Part (b)? Explain.

6. Paying $30.00, B, a housewife, purchased from a retail dealer a cotton dress which B had se-

lected from a rack bearing a sign reading as stated below. The dress had been purchased by the dealer from the manufacturer and bore the manufacturer's label. Shortly after the first time B wore the dress she became afflicted with a severe skin irritation. B sued the dealer to recover damages for her injuries. In the lawsuit, it was proved by B's doctor that B had a skin sensitivity or allergy and that the dress dye contained a substance extremely irritating to B. The dealer proved that he had no previous knowledge of the presence of an irritating substance in the dress, that he had sold thousands of this type of dress without any complaint, and that analysis of this type of dress showed it to contain nothing irritating to ordinary persons.

(a) The sign on the rack read: "Sale $30.00." Explain whether B was entitled to recover from the dealer.

(b) The sign on the rack read: "Sale $30.00. Guaranteed." Explain whether B was entitled to recover from the dealer.

7. A thief stole an adding machine from the office of its owner. About a month later the thief sold the adding machine to a dealer who handled both new and used office equipment. The dealer honestly and reasonably thought that the thief owned the machine and paid the thief $140, a fair price. The dealer cleaned and adjusted the machine and put it on display. About a month later the dealer sold and delivered the machine to an accountant for $175, a fair price. Nothing was stated by the dealer or the accountant as to title or ownership; both honestly and reasonably assumed that the dealer owned the machine which he was selling. A year later a part in the machine broke. The accountant returned the machine to the manufacturer for repair. The manufacturer noticed from the serial number that the machine was one reported as having been stolen. The manufacturer notified the owner who proved his ownership and obtained a court order that the machine should be given to him. The accountant then sued the dealer for the value of the machine. Explain whether the accountant could recover.

(b) Other facts being the same as above, assume the following: About six months after the accountant bought the machine, he retired from active practice and sold the machine to a lawyer. Nothing was stated by the accountant or the lawyer as to title or ownership, both honestly and reasonably assuming that the accountant owned the machine he was selling. When the machine broke down six months later, the lawyer returned it to the manufacturer. When the court awarded the machine to the owner, the lawyer sued the accountant. Explain whether the lawyer could recover from the accountant.

8. With the baked goods he was handling in his self-service store, a retailer had cakes which had been baked by a certain baker, sold by the baker to a wholesale food distributor, and sold and delivered by the food wholesaler to a retailer. Unknown to any of the parties (baker, wholesaler, or retailer) a pin accidentally fell into the cake batter during its preparation. The cakes on the retailer's shelf were baked from this batter and one of the cakes had the pin baked inside the cake. To stimulate purchase, the retailer had an employee cut one of the cakes into small pieces and walk up and down the aisles offering samples of the cake to customers. One customer who was shopping in the store, took one of the pieces of cake being passed out by the retailer's employee, and started to eat the piece of cake as he pushed his cart up and down the aisles in the store. This piece contained the concealed pin. As the customer, using proper care, bit into the piece of cake, the pin was jammed into his gums, causing a serious infection. The failure of the retailer or any of his employees to discover the pin was not negligence. Explain whether the customer could recover (a) from the retailer, (b) from the wholesaler, or (c) from the baker.

9. A thief stole an auto from its owner, forged the necessary papers, and sold the car to a dealer who bought for value and without knowledge that he was buying from a thief. The dealer sold the car to a buyer for $775 which the buyer paid, without knowledge that it was a stolen car. The buyer used the car continuously for two years before the car was traced and returned to the owner. The car had depreciated and had a value of $400 when taken from the buyer. When informed of the facts, the dealer offered to pay the buyer $400 in full settlement of the buyer's claims against the dealer. The buyer refused the settlement and sued for $775. Explain (1) the reasoning upon which the buyer might attempt to collect $775, (2) the reasoning upon which the dealer might attempt to defend, and (3) how much, if anything, the buyer could recover.

10. Discuss the circumstance under which you would choose warranty, negligence, strict liability, or misrepresentation as the basis or theory on which an injured consumer might rely in a products liability case.

11. In late May 1985, Bob purchased a travel-trailer from Sam. The trailer was manufactured by Smith Industries and was heated by a propane heater manufactured by Heat Corporation. The heater was installed by Smith Industries.

Bob used the trailer only twice for long trips from May to October of 1985. The heater was not used prior to October of the year. However, because only summer months had intervened since the purchase of the trailer, in October, Bob entered the trailer for the purpose of "winterizing" the vehicle. He turned the heater on in uniformity with his understanding of the instructions riveted to the heater. An explosion resulted, seriously injuring Bob. Whom could Bob sue to recover for his injuries and on what theory or theories? Do you think the lawsuit would be successful?

12. Marvin purchased a new 1975 automobile from Excellent Auto Sales. The car was fully warranted by the manufacturer, Specific Motors, for one year or 20,000 miles whichever occurred sooner. There was no warranty disclaimer by either the manufacturer or the retailer. The car contained a hidden defect insofar as the retailer was concerned, i.e., one that could not be discovered with reasonable care except during manufacture. The defect caused Marvin to have a serious acci-

dent which damaged the car and injured him. From whom could Marvin recover and on what theories? (Modified from A.I.C.P.A., May 75-40.)

13. Ace Auto Sales, Inc., sold Williams a secondhand car for $9,000. One day later Williams parked the car in a shopping center parking lot. When Williams returned to the car, Montrose and several policemen were waiting. It turned out that the car had been stolen from Montrose who was rightfully claiming ownership. Subsequently the car was returned by Williams to Montrose. Williams seeks recourse against Ace Auto Sales who had sold him the car with the usual disclaimer of warranty. Will he be successful? (Modified from A.I.C.P.A., 81-16.)

14. H, a housewife, purchased an electric sweeper from S, a merchant-dealer in electric sweepers. Before she left S's store, S asked H to "Try the sweeper out." H was in a hurry and told S to deliver it to her house where she would try it later. H then paid S $300 by signed check for the sweeper and left the store. Several days later, after S made delivery, H tried the sweeper for the first time. It worked fine. However, the next day, the motor burned out through no fault of H's and H returned the sweeper to S and demanded her money back. On what specific legal theory or theories would H's demand be based and with what success?

15. Why has strict liability become the prevailing remedy in products liability cases in the United States?

13 | Labor Management Relations

CHAPTER OUTLINE

Labor Management Relations

I. Introduction

The employment relationship is governed by several laws: the law of Agency, the federal labor laws regarding labor-management relations and unionization, the federal and state laws regulating compensation, the federal laws directed at work place safety, and the federal equal opportunity laws. This chapter addresses the problems of unionization and employment-at-will.

II. Background Of Labor Relations

A. Employment–at–Will

Before the twentieth century American labor movement introduced union contracts into the employment relationship, all employment contracts were based on the laissez-faire economic theory of freedom of contract. This permitted both employers and employees to terminate employment relationship anytime and without any justification. The freedom of contract concept is known as the *employment-at-will* doctrine. As one court has stated:

> "Individuals must be left, without interference to buy and sell as they please and to discharge or retain employees at will for good cause or for no cause, or even for bad cause without thereby being guilty of an unlawful act per se. It is a right which an employee

may exercise in the same way, to the same extent, for the same cause or want of cause as the employer."

Without the freedom to terminate an employment contract, an employee forced to work involuntarily for a particular employer would effectively be subjected to slavery. The mutuality concept of contract law is used to extend this doctrine to employers providing them a symmetrical right. Employers should be permitted to terminate an employee-at-will because it's unfair to require the employer to accept substandard services or retain an untrustworthy employee. The vast majority of employees in the United States are covered by the employment-at-will doctrine permitting either party to terminate the employment-at will.

1. EXCEPTIONS TO EMPLOYMENT–AT–WILL

Although the laissez-faire, free market ideals are deeply rooted in the American law heritage, there are numerous exceptions to the employment-at-will doctrine. First, there are several federal statutes that prohibit an employer from terminating an employee on the basis of: (1) unlawful discrimination, (2) garnishment of the employees' wages, (3) reporting unsafe or unhealthful working conditions to regulators or (4) the employee's involvement in union organization activities. These subjects are discussed in greater detail later in this chapter and again in Chapter 13 on Employment Law. Second, the majority of

Example. Charles was a middle manager at the BC Insurance Company for five years. He was assured by supervisors that his employment would be continued as long as he was "doing the job." When Charles inquired about job security he was given the BC Company personnel manual which stated terminations occur only for "just cause." Charles sued the BC Insurance Company claiming his discharge after five years of good performance was in bad faith .

An indefinite term employment contract can legally provide for job security. The employer may establish a policy of firing only for good cause which presumably enhances the employment relationship.

The employer secures an orderly, cooperative and loyal work force and the employee is assured with peace of mind about job security and fair treatment. This employment security need not be part of preemployment negotiations but can be inferred from the employer's policies and practices. In such cases, the discharge of an employee for allegedly unsatisfactory work subjects employer's acts to judicial review. This requires the employer to have documented the employee's poor performance. Sudden changes in an employee's performance evaluation draw into question the employer's good faith in assessing performance. Employees may not selectively enforce rules or policies without being exposed to judicial review.

the states have created remedies in tort or in contract to protect employees from arbitrary dismissal.

Many states prohibit an employer from dismissing an employee who refuses to violate the law if ordered to by a supervisor. This is known as an *abusive discharge* where an employer attempts to violate public policy and uses the threat or actual termination of employment to coerce employees. For example, whistle blowers are protected in many states when they report to authorities that the employer is committing crimes. Similarly, employees may not be fired for their required participation in the justice system by serving on a jury.

Employment at will may be based on an implied contractual term in which the employer expressly or impliedly guarantees continued employment. The written personnel policy manuals or guidelines of many employers directly state or clearly imply that employees will be discharged only for "good cause" or "just cause." These policy manuals become part of the employment contract and thereby prevent employers from discharging employees without good cause. Many employers have reacted by removing the just cause language from their personnel manuals or by requiring employees to "sign off" on a separate document that acknowledges the employee manual is not part of the employment contract.

In a few states, the courts imply a *covenant of good faith and fair dealing* into employment contracts effectively exposing the employer's intent in an employment termination decision to judicial scrutiny. For example, one court required reinstatement of a salesman who was terminated just before becoming qualified for retirement benefits. The employer acted in bad faith with a view to depriving the salesman of his employment benefits. Before the Federal Equal Opportunity Laws defined sexual harassment as an illegal activity, the covenant of good faith and fair dealing was interpreted to protect employees from arbitrary termination based on sexual harassment. The growth in the employment-at-will exceptions has slowed in recent years. Fewer courts permit employees to sue for punitive damages and some states have codified the abusive discharge suit limiting the employees remedies to compensatory damages.

2. TERMINATING FOREIGN SALES AGENTS

Many foreign nations provide protection from termination for local agents representing firms based in other nations. Often these are in the form of *dealer protection laws* that require the payment of money damages for unjust termination of sales agents, distributors, and/or dealers. These laws presume that local agents contribute to the goodwill and success of the foreign firm doing business in the host nation. These laws in most European nations are limited to the protection of agents. Such laws in the Middle East and Latin America provide broader protection to both agents and distributors.

The laws protecting agents generally require their registration and sometimes require the filing of the agency contract. Where these statutes are effective, terminations are not impossible but the foreign firm must prove *just cause* for a termination, otherwise the firm becomes liable for money damages to the agent terminated. The types of events constituting just cause are often specified in the statute. Written advance notice of all terminations is usually required (three to six months). Generally, the foreign firm may not require the agent to surrender the statutory right to be given notice or receive money damages. Some nations have additional provisions: suspension of the foreign firm's right to appoint a substitute agent, continued liability for employment taxes, and post-termination obligations to honor warranties on goods and provide replacement parts. Although the dealer protection laws in foreign nations may be unconstitutional or violate bilateral treaties, it is generally difficult to challenge their validity.

B. Early Labor Conflicts

The employment-at-will contract does not protect job security sufficiently for many employees. The industrial empires which grew up after the Civil War consolidated employment power into the hands of a few powerful men. As workers became dissatisfied with their arbitrary treatment under the employment-at-will doctrine prevailing at that time, they began to ban together for mutual aid and comfort.

In the early 19th Century, the state courts impeded the evolution of unions from craft societies or guilds into the bargaining representative status they have for workers today. Concerted union activities were considered criminal conspiracies that were "inimical to the public welfare." Many states' courts prohibited strikes and the Sherman Antitrust Act was interpreted to prohibit labor organizations as a restraint of trade. By 1914, however, the Clayton Act specifically exempted unions' concerted activities from antitrust enforcement.

The famous Pullman Palace Car Strike in 1893 became a focal point for unionization. Violence broke out after the employer refused to negotiate with the American Railway Union. This began a 30-year period of tumultuous conflict between labor and employers in which union power increased and employers used spies, threats, and blacklisting to impede the growth of unions.

C. The Federal Labor Statutes

Public attention on the strength of the forces underlying this labor conflict and the potential it raised for harmful violence led to several steps by the federal government to placate this strife. Unionization first advanced during World War I as President Wilson's National War Labor Board permitted unions to bargain collectively and prohibited violence that might have disrupted war production. However, after the war ended, these procedures were abandoned as employers adopted "scientific management" defining a fair day's pay for a fair day's work.

TABLE 13.1 FEDERAL LABOR LAWS

Law	Purpose and Requirements
Railway Labor Act (1926)	Promote comprehensive collective bargaining between air or rail carriers and unions that represent employees.
Norris-La Guardia Act (1932)	Prohibits the federal courts from halting employees' collective activities such as union meetings, picketing, or strikes. Federal courts may enjoin unlawful acts such as violence or strikes in violation of a valid "no-strike" clause.
National Labor Relations Act [NLRA, also called Wagner Act](1935)	Promotes comprehensive collective bargaining between all employers and employees not already covered under the Railway Labor Act.
Labor-Management Relations Act [LMRA, also called Taft-Hartley Act] (1947)	Subjects unions to unfair labor practice charges if employees exercising self-organization rights are intimidated by union or otherwise interfered with.
Labor-Management Reporting and Disclosure Act [LMRDA, also called Landrum-Griffin Act] (1959)	Prohibits unfair or undemocratic union election procedures. Union officials must disclose certain information about their conflicts of interest, union finances, and union operations.
Worker Adjustment and Retraining Notification Act [WARN, also known as the Plant Closing Law] (1988)	Requires employers to notify employees, unions, and surrounding communities of mass layoffs or plant closings.
Employee Polygraph Protection Act [Federal Lie Detector Act] (1988)	Prohibits employers from requiring employees to submit to lie detector tests and prohibits retaliation for employee refusals to submit to tests.

Eventually the labor strife arose again leading Congress to pass it's first permanent federal labor law in 1926. The Railway Labor Act (RLA) gave railroad workers and, today, airline workers the right to organize into labor unions and conduct concerted activities. The RLA requires railroad and airline employers to bargain collectively with unions. Two federal regulatory agencies were created under the RLA: The National Mediation Board and the National Railroad Adjustment Board. These agencies act much like the National Labor Relations Board by providing arbitration and mediation services in labor disputes.

The first comprehensive federal labor statute applying to unions in other industries was passed in 1932, the Norris-LaGuardia Act. This law only prevents the federal courts from issuing injunctions against unions' collective activities (e.g., union meetings, picketing, strikes). Norris-LaGuardia essentially permits unionization activities, but it does not require employers to bargain collectively with unions. Norris-LaGuardia outlaws *yellow-dog contracts* in which an employer requires the employees to refrain from union activities at the risk of losing their jobs.

The most comprehensive federal labor statute was passed in 1935. It is known as the Wagner Act or the National Labor Relations Act (NLRA). The NLRA extends the collective bargaining requirement, first given to the railroads under the RLA, comprehensively to all employees. The NLRA also created the National Labor Relations Board (NLRB), the primary regulatory body responsible for administering the NLRA.

These federal labor laws gave great strength to the labor movement throughout the 1930s and 1940s. However, eventually the public became dissatisfied with the growth of union power. This was fueled by reports of union corruption and Communist influence. As a result, two further laws were passed in the 1940s and 1950s to restrain the growth of unions. First, the Taft-Hartley Act was passed in 1947 defining certain unfair labor practices of unions. Second, allegations of corruption by union officials was addressed by the Landrum-Griffin Act in 1959. This law prohibits embezzlement by union officials and requires extensive financial disclosures of union transactions.

III. The NLRB

The NLRA establishes a comprehensive and uniform national policy for labor negotiations. However, before collective bargaining between a union representing employees and their employer may begin, employees must ban together into logical groups and select a bargaining representative. Congress intended the NLRB to provide federal regulatory guidance in this selection process.

The NLRB is a five-member board appointed by the President with the advice and consent of the Senate. The members serve 5-year staggered terms and can be removed by the President only for "malfeasance in office or neglect of duty." The Board has a separate Division of General Counsel headed by an independent person appointed by the President for a 4-year term and requires Senate confirmation. The General Counsel investigates charges, issues complaints, and prosecutes violations before the NLRB. Cases usually begin in trial like hearings before an administrative law judge (ALJ) who sits in one of the various regional NLRB offices. The NLRB is responsible for defining appropriate bargaining units and must resolve charges of unfair labor practices. Most cases are resolved through informal settlement proceedings although many receive the full administrative process and may be appealed through the Federal Courts of Appeals.

IV. Union Certification

Unions are usually selected as the bargaining representative for a grouping of employees after a representation election. The NLRB regional directors are responsible to oversee these elections by certifying elections, determining the appropriate bargaining unit, certifying election results, and deciding other representation questions.

An *appropriate bargaining unit* is a rational group of employees with similar interests in employment conditions. Designation as an appropriate bargaining unit entitles employees to vote together as a unit and be represented by a single bargaining representative. Any employee on the payroll during the preceding payroll period is an eligible voter. Representation elections are initiated by the filing of a petition with the NLRB. After an NLRB hearing the election may be conducted. There must be at least some support among employees for voting on a particular union. An election may be ordered when at least 30 percent of the employees in the bargaining unit support the particular union.

A. Elections

The most common method for employees in an appropriate bargaining unit to select a bargaining representative is through the union election. A certification election is called when employee support is demonstrated through authorization or membership cards, membership applications, dues receipts, or employees' signed petitions. A union certified in an election is given at least one year of exclusive representation before another union may attempt to organize employees in that appropriate bargaining unit.

Where the employer and the proposed union agree which workers belong in the appropriate bargaining unit, a *consent election* may be held. By contrast, disagreement over the bargaining unit may result in a *contested election*. While employees typically empower unions in an election, a union may also lose power in an election. For example, a *decertification election* removes the union's power to represent workers in the appropriate bargaining unit. A certified union may be retained but will lose some of its bargaining powers after a *de-authorization election*. *Runoff elections* become necessary where there are several unions competing on the same ballot to represent workers in the bargaining unit. The union must be certified by a majority vote so a mere plurality is insufficient to certify the union.

B. Appropriate Bargaining Unit

Each group of workers may be represented by only a single union as their certified bargaining representative. Large employers in complex industries often have numerous separate groups of employees with distinct interests. Employees are often classified according to the type of work they perform. For example, a firm might have delivery drivers, maintenance workers, production workers, and workers subjected to unique hazards such as mine workers. A large employer may be

required to bargain with several unions each representing employee groups with different economic interests, job classifications, and bargaining power. The appropriateness of including any particular group of workers into a bargaining unit depends on factors such as the worker's similarity of economic interests, job classifications, and their bargaining power.

The NLRB is empowered to determine the appropriateness of a particular grouping of employees into a bargaining unit. Typically the NLRB evaluates the employee's similarity of interests, their skills, wages, hours and working conditions, employees' desires, any existing employee group, and the employees' collective bargaining history. The NLRB also considers the similarity of employer, craft units, plant units, and recognized subdivisions within the employer's organization. Applying these standards it would be inappropriate to include professional employees with nonprofessionals without the professional's consent. Plant guards clearly have interests different from other employees because they must protect the employer's property during intense labor disputes.

C. EMPLOYER RECOGNITION AND AUTHORIZATION

There are alternative union selection process to the certification election. These have developed in the courts as time saving and efficient alternatives to the potential divisiveness of an election. An employer may simply recognize a particular union's support by employee groups if a majority of employees show this support. Unions may poll employees or receive authorization through membership cards, authorization cards, petitions, or employee applications for union membership. When a majority of employees show support in this manner, an election is unnecessary if the employer willingly recognizes this union. Of course, an employer may refuse to recognize a union without an election hop-

---

TABLE 13.2
UNFAIR LABOR PRACTICES

EMPLOYER'S UNFAIR LABOR PRACTICES

Interference with employees' self-organization rights
Interference with employees' legitimate concerted activities
Domination or support of a union
Discrimination on the basis of union membership in hiring, firing, benefits, or conditions of employment
Discrimination against employee exercising rights given by labor laws
Refusal to bargain with certified union in good faith
Conspiracy with union to conduct secondary boycott

UNION'S UNFAIR LABOR PRACTICES

Interference with employee's self-organization rights
Coercion of employer into discrimination against nonunion employees
Refusal to bargain in good faith
Conduct of concerted activities in illegal manner: strikes, picketing, secondary boycotts
Pressuring employer with picketing to recognize a noncertified union
Conspiracy with employer to conduct secondary boycott
Pressuring employer to accept "featherbedding" (payment for work not performed)
Discrimination or excesses in union fees and dues if in a union shop

---

ing to electioneer with employees and convince them to reject certification of the particular union.

Unions without a foothold in an employer may have difficulty conducting an effective campaign. Nonunion employers often impede unionization by restricting union officials access to employees while at work and by refusing to provide an accurate list of employees names. Courts have responded by requiring employers to give unions an employee list at least seven days before an election. However, seven days is seldom sufficient time for successful electioneering. Therefore, some unions cease electioneering immediately after receiving this *Excelsior List* to take more time for electioneering. The union is prohibited from beginning another election campaign for six months after an election is called off.

V. Employer Unfair Labor Practices

The NLRA prohibits employers from interfering with, restraining, or coercing employees involved in their self-organization rights. Many employers perceive unions as harmful to their business so there is a natural incentive to disrupt a union's organization activities. As a result, the NLRA defines several specific employer acts as unfair labor practices (ULP) where the employer inhibits the employees' free choice to unionize. Coercive conduct by the union is also possible so ULP's by unions are prohibited. The NLRA is designed to maintain "laboratory conditions" without coercive election campaign tactics such as threats of economic reprisals, promises of benefits, misrepresentations, deception, or anything creating a confusing and fearful atmosphere.

Employers are prohibited from intimidating workers because this would upset ideal elec-

Example. Employees of the E Company attempted to distribute a union newsletter that urged support for the union and supported other employee concerns including opposition to a right to work bill and criticism of a presidential veto of a federal minimum wage bill. The union alleged E Company's management committed an unfair labor practice when it prohibited distribution of the newsletter. E Company was ordered by the NLRB to cease and desist from interfering with the employee's concerted activities.

The NLRA permits employees to engage in concerted activities for their mutual aid and protection. This permits the distribution of union newsletters among a unionized work force. The fact that employees may seek to improve terms and conditions of their employment through legislative channels outside the employment relationship is valid. Mutual aid or protection includes activities beyond self-organization and collective bargaining. The NLRB is in the best position to determine when concerted activities are too tenuously related to employees' mutual aid or protection so that an employer may prohibit the activities on the employer's premises. ☐

tion conditions. For example, employers may not use intimidating interrogation tactics on employees inquiring about their unionization sympathies. Employers may legitimately poll employees about the union's organization progress. However, any use of this information to retaliate against employees is an unfair labor practice. The use of secret ballots to protect employee's identity is the most legitimate polling method. An employer's use of spies, informers, and coercive interrogation or surveillance is an unfair labor practice.

A. Federal Lie Detector Prohibitions

Employers are prohibited from using lie detectors on employees unless a reasonable suspicion of losses can be attributed to those employees. The Employee Polygraph Protection Act prohibits lie detector use unless the employee is given a written statement showing a reasonable suspicion the employee was involved in misappropriating or damaging the employer's property. Questions asked may relate only to the allegations of misconduct. The interrogation cannot form the only basis for dismissing the employee. An employer may not retaliate against employees refusing the polygraph test. Employers are

subject to punitive damages, civil fines, and attorney's fees for violations of the Federal Lie Detector Act. However, there are liberal exemptions for governments, government defense contractors, drug producers, and companies providing security protection services.

B. Employers Interference with Union Solicitation of Employees

Unions typically begin campaigning with the efforts of union representatives from the national headquarters or local union chapter. These union personnel visit directly with employees and distribute their literature in an effort to create support for unionization and support for that particular union. Because of the difficulty in identifying all employees effectively, unions usually must electioneer nearby the employer's plant. However, employers have a property right to prevent outsiders from interfering with their business activities on the employer's property. The union official's presence is often considered a trespass. The NLRA balances this tension by requiring employers to tolerate at least some inconvenience while unions are electioneering. Employers may validly restrict non-employee union officials from trespassing in

Example. A union obtained authorization cards from a majority of employees of the G Packing Company. However, G Packing refused to bargain with the union claiming that authorization cards are inherently unreliable. Thereafter, G Packing Company vigorously campaigned against unions. The NLRB cited G Packing Company for unfair labor practices and required it to bargain with the union based on certification through the authorization cards.

Certified board elections are not the exclusive method to certify a union as the collective bargaining representative for the bargaining unit. The union need only demonstrate convincing evidence of majority employee approval. The antiunion campaign conducted by G Packing Company was reasonably intended and understood by employees as a threat to dismiss employees. Where the employer has no basis for assumptions that the union will cause damage to the employer, the NLRB may designate this electioneering as coercive and prohibited as an unfair labor practice. ☐

work areas to prevent interference with work or safety hazards. To counteract these difficulties, most unions enlist a few sympathetic employees who contact their fellow workers during free time, breaks, meals, and before and after work. Solicitations made offsite can be made by anyone and at any time.

Employers have the right to restrict distribution of union literature and authorization cards to nonworking areas, exits, parking lots, lunchrooms, and restroom areas. Off-duty employees may be restricted from soliciting on company premises. However, an employer may not discriminate against unions with these restrictions, so all solicitations, such as charity fund raising and club membership drives, must be treated equally with unionization activities.

C. Employer Electioneering

Employer's share the same first amendment rights to speak to employees as does the union. However, the employer has strong powers of intimidation over employees giving them an undue level of influence over their voting. Therefore, coercive antiunion employer's statements are unfair labor practices and are unprotected by the First Amendment. Threats of reprisal or force directed toward employees is prohibited. Employers have a captive audience while employees are on work time permitting employers to give speeches at the worksite. Employers are not required to give unions equal time. Both the union and the employer are prohibited from requiring employees to attend speeches during the 24-hour period before a representation election. However, both parties may use less coercive communications such as distributing literature or issuing noncoercive radio messages right up to the time of the election.

Employer's speeches must be carefully worded to avoid coercion. For example, predictions of future consequences after a union is certified are coercive unless they are merely forecasts based on objective facts outside the employers control. For example, statements such as "I intend to deal hard with the union" or "striking workers may be replaced" are not automatically coercive unless the employer has the power to implement these predictions unilaterally. Simple observations about labor strife at other union plants is usually not coercive and therefore not prohibited. However, threatening promises to shut a plant down if the union is certified is coercive. Both the union and the employer must refrain from making misrepresentations or threatening statements to employees involved in a certification election.

Employers are also prohibited from bribing employees with promises to confer economic benefits just before an election. It is a coercive ULP to promise additional benefits such as paid holidays, vacation time, or overtime pay that act as reminders that the employer controls employees' economic future. These promises are referred to as "the iron fist in the velvet glove." Employers must maintain business as usual in its personnel policies just before an election.

D. Employer Domination and Support of a Union

It is an unfair labor practice for an employer to sponsor a union. This is an inherent conflict of interest because an independent union is necessary for affective arm's length bargaining with the employer. Therefore, an unfair labor practice arises where an employer provides financial support to a particular union. For example, an unfair labor practice arises where the employer's management solicits workers to join a particular union or provides undue assistance by drafting the union's bylaws or opposing a competing union. It is unfair to provide financial support or other services such as legal counsel, office space, secretarial services, printing services to one union while denying such assistance to a competing union. It is an unfair labor practice for union bylaws to give the employer a voice or vote in union governance. Employers must maintain neutrality among competing unions and avoid favoritism or domination.

1. CODETERMINATION

In Germany the government requires a labor practice that could arguably constitute an employer's domination and therefore could constitute an unfair labor practice. Under *codetermination* or "mitbestimmung," labor unions are permitted representation on the employer's corporate boards. German corpo-

rations have two boards: first, the *supervisory board* that intermediates between shareholders and management and oversees the managing board, and second, the *managing board* which actually determines and executes corporate policy. The supervisory board has three members, one represents labor, one represents sales, and one represents production. The managing board has five labor members, stockholders elect five members, and the whole board selects an eleventh director to represent the public interest, cast tie-breaking votes, and mediate disputes on the managing board.

Codetermination implements the German ideal of harmonious labor relations through increasing employee participation in decisionmaking and enhancing the challenge and interest of labor's job designs. The practice has generally resulted in peaceful industrial relations, reduction of worktime due to strikes, better morale, and improved working conditions. However, its application to the U.S. could be problematic. The NLRA is premised on adversarial confrontation focused through collective bargaining and union concerted activity all to overcome labor's inherent inequality in bargaining power. Codetermination reduces employee's independence from the employer and would diminish the importance of collective bargaining. Without full union support, codetermination, or some of the weaker variants (e.g., quality circles) could not be easily attained in the U.S. However, there is great promise of better understanding and enhanced productivity with the adoption of these more cooperative employment relations.

E. Employer Discrimination

It is an unfair labor practice for a employers to impede unionization by discriminating in employment practices such as hiring, firing, or job tenure. Employers are prohibited from denying employment or promotions to union sympathizers or granting them to employees

Example. The DM Company owns several textile companies, one of which was successfully organized by the Textile Workers Union. DM dissolved and liquidated the unionized subsidiary and sold it's equipment. The union charged the plant closing with an unfair labor practice.

While it is illegal to destroy a union with a discriminatory lockout, the DM Company's actions here do not constitute a runaway shop. An employer is permitted to close the entire business even if motivated by vindictiveness towards unionization. An unfair labor practice may be proved where a discriminatory motive underlies a partial plant closing. The NLRB is empowered to make findings on the issue of the purpose and effect of a partial plant closing. ☐

who promise not to join. Of course, an employer intent on punishing employees sympathetic with the union could simply claim there was some other reason to make the particular hiring, firing, or promotion decision. However, if a pattern of antiunion employment practices are shown and there is no strong independent evidence documenting the employee's poor performance, then an antiunion bias may be inferred. For example, a string of good work records that suddenly changes after an employee becomes involved in unionization, suggest the inference of an unfair labor practice.

The employer's discrimination in hiring and firing decisions based on the employee's union affiliation is prohibited. Changes in working conditions such as layoffs, demotions, transfers or work change assignments are illegal if based on the employers antiunion bias. In one case, the employer's offer of twenty years of seniority to employees who crossed striking picket lines was an unfair labor practice.

I. PLANT CLOSINGS

Both the employer and employee may cease doing work to bring economic pressure on the other side. Employees' strongest economic weapon is the strike. Employers symmetrical weapon is to close down the plant if negotiations come to an impasse and there are valid justifications for the plant closing. The economic pressure of a strike or plant closing can induce the other side into settlement.

Some employers find it economically viable to close a whole facility down permanently and either discontinue that work or move it to another locality. A large employer with numerous facilities might close one plant as a signal to employees at other plants to discourage unionization. This practice is called the runaway shop and it is unlawful if the primary motive is antiunion bias. Of course, employers may terminate their entire business for any reason they desire. Where sound economic consideration support moving a plant, no unfair labor practice arises.

2. PLANT CLOSING LAW

Congress has restricted plant closings under the Worker Adjustment and Retraining Notification Act of 1988 (WARN). Under the federal plant closing law, employers must give notice to employees at least 60 days prior to closing a plant. The law is designed to provide employees an opportunity to adjust to their loss of employment and income. This 60 day notice requirement applies to employers with 100 or more employees. Employers must give employees notice in two instances:

(1) **Mass Layoffs**. Where a third of the full-time work force or at least 500 employees working at a single site will be laid off, or

(2) **Plant Closings**. Which temporarily or permanently discontinue operations effecting 50 or more full time employees for at least 30 days.

Employers must notify individual nonunion employees, all unions representing unionized employees, and local governments. Notification to local governments is necessary to permit them to plan for the adverse impact from mass layoffs and plant closings on the surrounding community.

The WARN Act includes several exemptions permitting employers to avoid or relax the notification requirements. The first exemption recognizes that giving notice may make it difficult for the employer to raise capital or negotiate new business contracts. If the employer can show it is actively seeking capital or new business and this would be necessary to continue the plants in operation, the employer may reduce the amount of notice given.

The second exception includes plant closings or mass layoffs triggered by unforeseeable business circumstances. In such instances the 60 day notification period may be reduced. The third exemption reduces the 60 day notice period where natural disasters, flood, earthquakes or drought make it impossible to give the full 60 day notice. The fourth exemption dispenses with notice when a temporary facility is closed or a project is completed and employees knew their employment was limited. For example, no notice is required when a construction project is completed. The fifth exception dispenses with notice where a plant closing or layoff occurs during a strike or plant lockout held legally under the National Labor Relations Act.

There are penalties for employers that violate the plant closing law. First, employers are liable for back pay and benefits to each employee terminated. Employers must pay a fine of $500 per day for each day that notice is not given to the local government if employees are not paid within the three week period following the closing or lay off. The federal courts have discretion to reduce these damages and penalties if the employer is found to have acted in good faith. Additionally, courts may award attorney's fees to the parties prevailing.

The plant closing law calls for the controller general to conduct a cost benefit analysis of the law by 1991. However, since the Act's passage, it appears that most notifications have been given with little negative impact on the employers. Controversial issues remain concerning what constitutes a facility for firms with widely dispersed operations and how flexibly the courts will apply the exceptions.

VI. Union Interference, Restraint and Coercion

Both unions and employers are prohibited from coercing employees as they exercise their rights of organization and concerted action. Unions may be guilty of unfair labor practices during the organization process but usually to a lesser extent than employers. For example, it would be an unfair labor practice for a union to make statements during unionization campaigns such as "those who do not join the union will eventually loose their jobs," or "we have ways of handling people that argue against the union." Union representatives and employees sympathetic to the union are entitled to express their opinions but they may not act in a coercive manner.

Inflammatory, racial, or ethnic slurs made during unionization activities are prohibited. Unions may not threaten violence against employees perceived as uncooperative to the union's efforts. Even union violence directed against company property may provide the basis for a reasonable inference that violence is also threatened against employees unsympathetic to the union. While it seems less likely a union will confer economic benefits or make promises to members, such actions have happened in the past and are prohib-

377

ited. For example, it is an unfair labor practice for a union to threaten termination of payments from a union operated health fund for employees opposing the union. A union's promise to reduce or waive membership fees or dues to sympathetic employees is also unlawful. It is unlawful for unions to pressure the employer to discriminate among employees on the basis of their union membership. Finally, it is an unfair labor practice for unions to sponsor coercive and intimidating activities directed at nonunion employees.

A. Good Faith Bargaining

Good Faith Bargaining is the ultimate objective of the union election and certification process. The NLRA requires both the employer and the certified union to engage in an interactive process of negotiation with a view to reach agreement over wages, hours, and other terms and conditions of employment. A collective bargaining agreement (i.e. the union contract) results from this negotiation process. The contract establishes work rules, defines the form and mix of compensation, prioritizes elements of the work environment between management and labor, standardizes these terms among competitors in the same product market, and provides for flexibility in the labor markets as economic necessity evolves. Economic equilibrium is attained in the labor markets as terms and conditions are negotiated through labor contracts.

B. Collective Bargaining

Labor negotiations are focused through an interactive process called *collective bargaining*. The parties involved usually have opposite goals resulting in a zero-sum game: one party's gain results in a loss for the other party. As a result, one party usually assembles a proposal made up of terms highly favorable to that party and communicates this as a first offer. Typically, the other party then responds

with a counter proposal containing terms that are most favorable to the counter proposal. In most instances these two proposals are far apart on many issues, particularly those involving compensation. Thereafter, a series of counter proposals is usually made where each party gradually moves towards other party's proposal until some common ground is reached and a compromise is agreed upon.

Both the union and management elect a team of representatives, their respective bargaining committees, who are authorized to make or receive offers regarding wages, hours, and other terms and conditions of employment. The proposals, counter proposals, and final agreement usually include specifications of the compensation for each classification of employees, the definition of work hours and overtime contingencies, the types and amounts of fringe benefits, and a classification scheme defining the job class of all covered employees. The management team must usually be authorized to make or accept proposals from the union. However, the union representatives traditionally have no authority to conclude a contract and must receive approval by ratification vote from the rank and file union members in the bargaining unit. The resulting agreement usually reflects the parties' relative strengths and weaknesses.

There are numerous factors which may affect the strength of bargaining positions on both sides in a labor negotiation. A neutral site is usually selected for the negotiations to avoid either parties' "home court advantage." The parties often agree to considerable confidentiality to avoid the damage resulting from an inflammatory public exposure or adverse publicity. Experienced negotiators come well prepared to the meetings with financial statements, cost projections, and other economic data. Often the noneconomic items are negotiated first: grievance procedures, no-strike clauses, seniority, and work assignments.

In recent years, some labor negotiators have made offsetting concessions between work rules and compensation issues. For example, the traditional work rules usually permitted workers to perform only certain work. However, this can negatively effect the employer's flexibility to use all workers for various types of work. Therefore, concessions on job classifications given by the union can be offset by higher compensation given by the employer.

Negotiators typically ask for more than their side hopes to get out of the negotiation. Each side gives up something to the opposition and assumes a fallback position making lesser but acceptable demands. Thereby, it appears that each party has made concessions to obtain a compromise. This process can be facilitated by third party intermediaries, mediators, who tend to diffuse adversarial relations, reduce irrational feelings, point out unreasonable demands, and generate alternatives for graceful retreats that permit negotiators to save face. Federal law provides for mediators to assist in labor negotiations in some industries. Mediators help both parties remain focused on reaching an agreement. Individual employees may not negotiate separately where there is a certified union with exclusive authority to represent all the employees in that bargaining unit.

C. Duty to Bargain in Good Faith

Both the union and the employer have an obligation under the federal labor law to bargain in good faith: meet at reasonable times and confer in good faith. Either party may be guilty of an unfair labor practice for refusing to bargain collectively. This requires making a sincere good faith effort to participate in negotiations, avoid fictitious or surface bargaining, and do more than just "go through the motions" of collective bargaining.

Good faith bargaining is usually defined negatively in terms of what constitutes bad faith. The refusal to meet at reasonable times, reduce the agreement to writing, confer with the opposition, or bargain on mandatory bargaining subjects is considered *bad faith*. Mandatory subjects of bargaining include wages, hours, and other terms and conditions of the employment. The NLRB and the courts typically examine the total conduct of each party to determine bad faith.

Bad faith may be inferred from the harassing or confusing behavior of one party. For example, it is bad faith to offer and quickly withdraw a proposal before the opposition can evaluate or accept it. The parties must furnish information necessary to support its claims. For example, when an employer claims it cannot pay the higher wages desired by the union it must provide financial statements to support this claim. However, this disclosure requirement is balanced against the employer's right to confidentiality so the employer may often withhold confidential trade secrets from the union.

Bad faith is also inferred from a party's bargaining conduct. For example, it would be bad faith bargaining to refuse to offer meaningful counter proposals, to refuse discussing certain terms until other terms are resolved, to use delaying tactics, to withdraw concessions made in earlier counter proposals, or to undertake an adverse publicity campaign against the opposition. None of the factors mentioned are conclusive of bad faith bargaining, so the NLRB and the courts must make subjective evaluations of the bargaining environment on an ad hoc basis.

As a result of the court's attitude about Boulwareism in the example above, the adversarial model of contract negotiations by self-interested negotiators will continue. This means that parties are likely to enter negotiations by beginning with unrealistic offers and make counter that only eventually approach realistic demands. Therefore, labor negotiations will probably take much longer than necessary and occur in an adversary atmosphere that is divisive in many instances.

Example. Following a crippling strike in 1940's the G Company adopted new bargaining tactics in its negotiations with its unions. The G Company vice president, Mr. Boul, approached labor negotiations as if he was marketing a product. First, Mr. Boul collected employees comments revealing their expectations for compensation and benefits. Mr. Boul then researched the effectiveness of such benefits to formulate a "product" which became the G Company's only proposal. Thereafter, Mr. Boul aggressively sold a proposed union contract with an avalanche of publicity to employees and to the public. Mr. Boul hoped to avoid union pressure, strikes, and the traditional negotiation process by assembling the company's only proposal into a "middle-ground" proposal. This take or leave it approach became known as "Boulwareism".

During the 1960 negotiations between the G Company and its unions this Boulwareism approach was used. The G Company broadly publicized its opinion that the union's proposals were unreasonable, and refused to provide cost estimates to union negotiators. The G Company ignored the negotiations and unilaterally gave nonunion employees a 3% wage increase and gave all employees an insurance and pension plan. This caused the union to strike and the G Company intensified its negative publicity campaign with personal attacks on the union's negotiators and with threats of termination for strikers. After the union gave in to the G Company's proposals, the NLRB sued the G Company for bad faith bargaining.

The G Company was guilty of unfair labor practices in failing to provide the union with information. Further, the G Company's bad faith bargaining position was inferred from its patronization of union negotiators and its pursuance of the take it or leave it strategy. The G Company's tactics were inherently divisive making negotiations difficult and uncertain and subverting the cooperation necessary to obtain a union contract. ▢

There is a trend to better align the financial interests of both employees and employers in hopes of transforming labor negotiations into a positive sum game. When the parties are able to expand the number of bargaining points and thereby give both sides a chance to win something, labor negotiations may evolve away from the confrontational model. The N LRB has power to order either party to bargain in good faith or to cease and desist from bad faith bargaining. In unusual cases, the NLRB has ordered the payment of compensatory damages where one party's refusal to bargain is flagrant. However, nothing in the labor law forces either party to accept a particular contract provision or to make concessions.

I. SUBJECTS OF BARGAINING

There are three basic categories of contract terms over which management and unions are required to bargain. First, *mandatory collective bargaining subjects* include "wages, hours, and other terms of conditions of employment or the negotiation of agreement, or any questions arising thereunder." Neither party may refuse to bargain over mandatory subjects because they always directly affect the contract terms. Second, *permissive collective bargaining subjects* include company or union policies within an indirect impact on the employment relationship. For example, new negotiations to modify an existing labor contract before expiration, the employers' contributions to charitable institutions, the employer's corporate form, supervision, the employer's general business practices, the location of the employer's facilities are permissive subjects. The parties need not bargain on these subjects but may not refuse to bargain on mandatory subjects to coerce bargaining over permissive subjects.

The third type of bargaining subjects are illegal and *prohibited collective bargaining subjects*. Neither party may insist on bargaining and may not bargain over these topics. It is illegal to bargain over or make part of a collective bargaining agreement any term which would inhibit employees from distributing union literature, would require employees to become union members before hiring, or would require the union to renounce its status as the exclusive bargaining representative for the appropriate bargaining unit.

D. Impasse

For the parties to maintain good faith in their bargaining process, they must make a good faith attempt to reconcile their floundering negotiations and continue bargaining until they reach impasse. An *impasse* in collective bargaining occurs when neither party can make a counter proposal more favorable to the opposing party. The parties must continue to bargain in good faith even during concerted activities such as picketing, a strike, a shutdown, an employer lockout, or layoff. When a legitimate impasse is reached, the deadlock in bargaining permits the employer to solicit striking employees to return to work on the terms stated in the old contract. However, the employer may not unilaterally increase wages above the prior contract level. This is an unfair labor practice because it undermines the union's bargaining strength.

Before Congress amended the bankruptcy law in 1984, an employer could file for voluntary reorganization under Chapter 11 of the federal bankruptcy law. During reorganization, all contractors and creditors of the reorganizing corporation must renegotiate their contracts. This tactic could permit management to renounce the collective bargaining agreement and force the union to renegotiate for lower compensation. However, after the much publicized *NLRB vs. Bildisco* case, Congress amended the bankruptcy law to make it difficult for companies to force an impasse by reorganization. The federal bankruptcy judge must approve any rejection and renegotiation of an existing labor contract. The judge must find that modification of the labor contract is necessary to the survival of the bankrupt firm. Collective bargaining agreements may be rejected and renegotiated only where: (1) creditors are all treated equitably, (2) the union was without good cause in rejecting the bankrupt corporations proposal to modify the contract, and (3) on balance it is equitable to reject the union contract.

E. Union Security Agreements

Unions have a natural incentive to become strong. This gives employees' concerted activities a greater impact on the collective bargaining process. The union's bargaining position is strengthened where the employees' skills are unique, the employees are not easily replaced, all employees enthusiastically support the union, and the union is financially sound. To gather such strength, unions typically attempt to employ *union security devices* that may require union membership or require the payment of dues.

The *closed shop* agreement is the strongest union security device because it requires union membership before employment eligibility. A closed shop clause in the collective bargaining agreement requires the employer to verify union membership before hiring a new worker. This gives the union tremendous control over the workers available to become employees and assures employers are enthusiastic about the union. However, a closed shop agreement coerces employees to blindly accept the policy decisions of union leaders

Example. The U.S. Postal Service fired Mr. B after he was engaged in an altercation with another employee. Mr. B's union declined to arbitrate his grievance even though the local union chapter had recommended arbitration. B sued the Postal Office and his union charging that his dismissal was made without good cause and the union breached its duty of fair representation by not arbitrating his grievance.

A union may be held liable for part of an employee's lost wages if it fails to fairly represent that employee. Employment controlled by a collective bargaining agreement is not terminable at will but must be processed according to the termination provisions of the contract. An employee has the right to receive damages caused by the employer's arbitrary action or the union's failure to protect the employee's rights. The union may not waive the employee's right to arbitration, otherwise it must pay damages for the employee's lost wages. □

and represses dissent. As a result of the coercive effect of close shop agreements, they are now outlawed since the 1947 Taft-Hartley Act. Today, union are permitted to operate a *hiring hall* or system of *job referrals*. These devices are not equivalent to a closed shop but simply provide employers with a list of qualified union members but do not require the employer to hire exclusively from that list.

Today, the *union shop* agreement is the strongest union security agreement permissible. A union shop agreement requires all employees to join the union after working for a probationary period of at least 30 days. In the construction industry this period is only 7 days because construction work is short term and seasonal. Employees who have bona fide religious objections to giving financial support to a union may not be required to join the union or pay dues. Instead, the employee may be required to pay an amount equivalent to the initiation fee and periodic dues to some other non-religious, nonlabor, tax exempt charitable organization. Union shop agreements often include a *check-off* provision requiring the employer to deduct union dues periodically from the employees' paycheck.

A slightly weaker form of union security device is the *agency shop*. In this arrangement union membership is not required but a service fee or bargaining assessment must be paid to the union by employees. Union members may renounce their membership under a *maintenance of membership* agreement. This permits them to stand outside the reach of union discipline. A certified union must represent all members in the appropriate bargaining unit equally without reference to their membership, payment of dues, or pro-union support.

I. RIGHT TO WORK LAWS

The Taft-Hartley Act of 1947 opened one area of labor law to the state legislatures. Any state may enact a *right to work law* that restricts or prohibits union or agency shops. Over twenty states, largely in the South and in the West have some form of a right to work law that permits employees to choose not to join the union and refrain from paying dues. The unionization process is probably slowed in these states which may enable them to attract new businesses more readily. However, even in the Midwest and industrial Northeast where most states do not have right to work laws, a union may choose not to seek a union security device. Where the union has no security device, employees need not join the union nor pay fees. The union must nevertheless fully represent each employee in the collective bargaining with the employer. This is known as the union's *duty of fair representation* that prohibits the union from discriminating against nonunion members or against members of minority groups.

VII. Union Concerted Activities

Employees have been given the right to engage in "concerted activities for the purpose of collective bargaining or other mutual aid or protection" by the Norris-LaGuardia Act and the NLRA. Unorganized employees not represented by a certified union may also engage in concerted activity. For example, it was an unfair labor practice for the employer to fire nonunion employees who walked off the job protesting extremely cold working conditions. However, after a particular union is certified as bargaining representative, all grievance activities must be focused through the union.

Not all employee or union concerted activities are protected by the labor laws. Concerted activities that are unlawful, in bad faith, or are actions without an objective are unlawful. For example, concerted activity must be conducted in a nonviolent manner, may not breach the existing union contract, and must be at least minimally related to a work matter. The employees' right to conduct concerted activities must be balanced against the loyalty they must show to their employer. Where employees publicly discouraged customers from doing business with their employer but this boycott campaign was unrelated to any grievance, the union's actions were disloyal and therefore unprotected by the labor law.

A. Regulation of Strikes

Both the employer and employees have a strong economic weapon to pressure the other side into accepting its demands. The employer may *lockout* employees depriving them of their livelihood and pressuring them into a collective bargaining agreement. The employees acting through their union, have a symmetrical right of striking which terminates the employer's economic activity. Of course,

employees may seek replacement jobs during the lockout and an employer may hire replacement workers during a strike. However, the viability of these options is limited where there are insufficient nonworking trained employees in the work force or equivalent jobs are hard to find.

The right to strike has never been precisely defined or nor directly permitted under the law. Instead, the right to strike is inferred from a number of diverse laws. First, the Norris-LaGuardia Act prohibited federal courts from issuing injunctions against strikes. Second, the NLRA permits employees to "engage in concerted activity." Third, the First Amendment to the United States Constitution assures freedom of speech, press, and assembly. Fourth, the Fifth Amendment due process clause prohibits the deprivation of life, liberty, or property. Fifth, the Thirteenth Amendment prohibits slavery and involuntary servitude. When these various rights are combined, a protected zone is created around the right to strike.

Employees' right to strike is not unlimited and may be declared illegal if: (1) a strike causes or occurs during a national emergency, (2) a strike occurs in breach of a valid no-strike clause, or (3) a strike occurs against a health care institution. Strikes against health care institutions and hospitals or by air traffic controllers are prohibited because they jeopardize the health of patients and passengers.

I. TYPES OF STRIKES

Strikes are classified according to their legality: *illegal strikes* are those involving violence or discrimination, are made during a valid cooling-off period, are made to compel featherbedding or hot cargo provisions, or are made to advocate recognition of a noncertified union when another union is already certified. *Sit-down* strikes are also illegal where employees suddenly refuse to work while on the job. This also includes disruptive or sporadic shutdowns or partial work stoppages.

Example. The B Market Company, a grocer, and its retail clerks union had a collective bargaining agreement with a no strike clause. The agreement required that labor disputes be resolved by arbitration and it prohibited work stoppages, lock outs, picketing, and boycotts. However the union began striking after a dispute arose and a federal court enjoined the strike.

When a union enters into a collective bargaining agreement that includes a no strike clause it effectively gives up the right to strike. The Norris-LaGuardia Act was passed to prevent employers from using the court ordered injunction to frustrate union concerted activities. The Norris-LaGuardia Act should not be used to permit unions to breach no strike provisions if they freely and willingly negotiate them. If the courts could not enjoin illegal strikes in violation of a no strike clause, employers would have little incentive to agree to binding arbitration of disputes. The law encourages alternative dispute resolution methods such as binding arbitration, so the Norris-LaGuardia Act does not bar federal injunctions against illegal strikes. ☐

The striking union must give the employer notice of the strike in advance. Therefore, an unnotified strike is an illegal wildcat strike. Strikes designed to protest an outstanding unfair labor practice by the employer are known as unfair labor practice strikes. Although temporary replacements may be hired during an *unfair labor practice strike,* the employer may not fire strikers. Unfair labor practice strikers are entitled to reinstatement even if temporary replacements must be fired. Additionally, unfair labor practice strikers must be paid back wages.

Most of the better publicized strikes involve economic matters. Typically, employees intend the strike to bring economic pressure on the employer to give in to the union's demands for increased compensation and other contract terms. These are known as *economic strikes* and strikers have no right to reinstatement if replacements are hired. Economic strikers are only entitled to nondiscriminatory review of their reapplication. However, the employer may abolish their positions if economic conditions have deteriorated during the strike. For example, a strike might cause the employer to breach a key contract with a customer or supplier preventing the employer's return to normal business operations.

In most instances, an economic strike ultimately leads to settlement of the contract negotiations. Unions commonly insist that the new contract include a term that requires the employer to reinstate all strikers replaced by temporary workers. This happened in the 1987 National Football League strike where the striking players were reinstated and only a very few of the replacement "scab" players were retained by the National Football League teams. A recent Supreme Court decision has raised controversy over whether strikers must be rehired to displace strike breaking workers. Congress may pass legislation limiting the employer's right to hire temporary replacements in the early weeks of an economic strike.

2. NO STRIKE CLAUSES

Some employers insist on including a term in the collective bargaining agreement that prohibits strikes: the *no strike clause*. Unions may be held liable for breach of contract and damages for conducting unauthorized strikes in violation of a no strike clause. When a collective bargaining agreement contains a no strike clause, it typically also includes a parallel right for the employer, the *arbitration clause*, which requires the employer to arbitrate grievances. These provisions work in tandem to prohibit strikes and reduce their probability while requiring grievances to be arbitrated. The Norris-LaGuardia Act does not prohibit the federal courts from issuing injunctions against strikes that violate a valid no strike provision.

3. NATIONAL EMERGENCY STRIKES

The Taft-Hartley Act includes an important provision to prevent strike activities from impairing the nation's health or safety. The Taft-Hartley Act empowers the President of the United States to order a *cooling-off period* during which the threatened strike is temporarily halted. The President first appoints a board of inquiry which investigates the causes and circumstances underlying the labor dispute. The President considers the board's report and may thereafter direct the attorney general to seek an injunction in federal court halting the threatened strike. The federal court may issue an injunction prohibiting a strike for 80 days if it determines that the strike will impair the national health or safety. The 80 day cooling-off period is designed to facilitate negotiations between the parties which is often enhanced by mediators from the Federal Mediation and Conciliation Service. If the strike resumes after the 80 day cooling-off period, Congress must take responsibility to change the underlying national emergency or its causes. The President used this power in 1963 to prevent a national transportation disaster when the railroad unions threatened a strike.

B. Picketing

Picketing is a process separate from striking. Although striking workers often picket the employer's premises during a strike, the term *picketing* generally refers to the gathering and patrolling on an employer's premises by employees with the intention of informing or disrupting others. Picketing commonly occurs near the employer's premises where confrontations between picketers and other employees or customers may occur. Picketing is unlawful and may be enjoined if it: (1) violates federal law (2) constitutes an unfair labor practice, or (3) violates state law. For example, violent picketing conducted in a non-peaceful manner is unlawful. Where verbal exchanges or threatening gestures are likely, the picketing may also be enjoined.

Picketing is generally classified according to how close the relationship is between the picketers and the employer whose premises are picketed. *Primary picketing* is the most justifiable where an employee of the employer is involved in the picketing. *Stranger picketing*, by non-employees, may be regulated under state law and must be done only for a lawful purpose. However, an uncertified union may picket as part of a campaign to organize the bargaining unit.

When employees picket at a business site other than the employer's own premises, the picketing is considered *secondary picketing*. Most secondary picketing and other forms of secondary pressure are illegal or may be enjoined. Consider the example of a grocery chain that begins construction of a new store at a new site. If the construction contractor uses non-union employees, the local construction union might seek to protest the use of non-union workers by picketing another site where the grocery store is already operating. Such picketing is usually intended to pressure the grocery store owner to bring pressure on the construction contractor to use union employees. However, this is illegal secondary picketing.

C. Secondary Pressure

The term secondary in relation to other union activities refers to the connection between the employees involved in the action and the target of their secondary pressure. *Primary pressure* is directed by employees against their own employer with whom they may have a dispute. The labor law provides little protection for *secondary pressure* where the employees of a primary employer pressure another employer with whom they have no direct dispute in an attempt to enlist the secondary employer to aid them resolving in their dispute. As just discussed, secondary picketing is often prohibited and secondary strikes or boycotts also receive very little legal protection.

An illegal *secondary boycott* involves pressure brought on a secondary employer where a union strikes or refuses to handle the goods of the secondary employer. Where this secondary boycott pressure is intended to coerce the secondary employer to enter into a hot cargo agreement, the pressure is illegal. A *hot cargo agreement* is one which the secondary employer ceases doing business with the primary often nonunion employer. Secondary boycotts are generally permissible under the Railway Labor Act.

Secondary picketing is particularly problematic where there are several employers working at a common site. For example, at a construction project there are numerous subcontractors, each with its own separate set of employees. If employees of a single subcontractor were permitted to picket the entire site and other unions respected the picket line, the one small union could halt all construction by all unions serving all the employers working at that site. Although the subcontractors employees must be permitted to picket the site, the law permits a single construction site to be served by several separate entrance gates for customers, the various subcontractors, and others. Picketing may be relegated to one gate so that the business or construction at the entire site is not halted by a single picketing union. For example, the union representing the store clerks at one shop in a large shopping center began picketing inside the mall. The picketing activity intimidated customers of the primary employer and of all other shop owners. Traditionally, the employees of the other shop owners, and suppliers of all shop owners might either respect the picket line by not making deliveries or could be intimidated by the picketing activity. Therefore, secondary picketing may be regulated to avoid this "secondary" effect on other employers with whom the union has no direct grievance.

The union's free speech rights prevail over those of the shopping center owner or the other shop owners with whom the employees have no direct dispute. This tangential secondary pressure must be tolerated by secondary employers because shopping centers are "dedicated to a public use and their public access areas must be kept open for public use." However, where a large hardware store was held open to the public but was the only tenant of the large building, the premises were not equivalent to a shopping center. If alternative communications methods exist for picketing workers there is no constitutional right to trespass on private property.

VIII. Labor Arbitration and Grievance Settlement

Collective bargaining agreements that include arbitration clauses to settle work disputes require both the employer and employees to use the process. *Labor arbitration* involves the use of a neutral, independent third party(s) to hear and settle grievances in a trial-like hearing procedure. Grievances typically begin with a hearing by lower-level management persons. The collective bargaining agreement may require several levels of appeal usually through management and ultimately to an arbitrator selected by the parties or by the collective bargaining agreement. Unions must usually assist in processing employee grievances. Arbitrators are often selected from neutral agencies such as the American Arbitrator's Association or the Federal Mediation and Conciliation Service.

Labor arbitrators are usually persons familiar with labor policies, labor disputes, and labor law. However, they need not be labor lawyers nor members of any particular association. The American Arbitration Association has become so well experienced at the informal arbitration process and in establishing low cost arbitration procedures that many collective bargaining agreements select this association. The collective bargaining agreement may control the arbitrator's authority to settle disputes or make interpretations or applications of the labor contract's provisions. Arbitrators typically decide the facts of the events involved in the dispute. Arbitrators are not bound by precedents although the more experienced labor arbitrators follow general patterns derived from their own experience. An arbitrator's award may be appealed to the NLRB only if it was conducted in an unfair or irregular manner, the arbitrator went beyond mere factual findings, the arbitrator was biased, or there were intentional delays in the arbitration process.

A. Union Democracy

The Taft-Hartley Act of 1947 and the Landrum-Griffin Act of 1959 limit the powers of union officials. News of coercive activities by union leaders led to a Congressional backlash to regulate union democratic principles. Unions are permitted to discipline members for interfering with union activities, working below union scale, or spying for the employer. However, unions are prohibited from punishing employees for their political or civic activities including testimony given about the union's law violations.

B. Labor's Bill of Rights

Unions may not restrict their members' rights of free speech, assembly, or participation in union elections. Financial assessments (e.g., initiation fees, dues, other fees) may be levied or changed only upon approval by union membership after a secret ballot. Unions must provide impartial hearings before rendering discipline on its members for alleged

violation of union rules or nonpayment of dues.

The courts may intercede where fair union elections are not held. The Landrum-Griffin Act requires that all union members be given the right to vote. Local union officials elections must be held every three years and elections for officers of the national or international union must be held every five years. Secret ballots are required in local elections although delegates to national and international conventions may cast their votes openly. All members must be given the opportunity to nominate candidates and qualifications for eligibility must be reasonable. In one case, a union eligibility rule required attendance at so many union meetings during the years prior to an election that over 97% of the union's membership was effectively ineligible to run for union office. This eligibility requirement was unfair and judged unreasonable.

C. Trusteeship

When a local union chapter becomes corrupt, union officials misappropriate union assets or frustrate union democracy, the national union may oust these corrupt officials. In this process, the local union chapter looses control over its own affairs under a process known as *trusteeship*. The process is regulated under the Landrum-Griffin Act because some national union leaders used the process to intimidate local chapters into quieting their dissention or the national plundered the local chapter's treasury. Trustees must file semi-annual reports with the Secretary of Labor to permit their oversight of local chapters. National unions are prohibited from imposing excessive assessments upon local chapters if it might deplete their financial resources.

* * *

Problems

1. Henry sued his employer for wrongful discharge claiming that he was fired because he refused a direct order to pump toxic chemicals into a river alongside the employer's premises. An environmental regulator had told Henry that the disposal of toxic wastes into waterways was illegal. Henry's employer claimed it discharged Henry for insubordination and poor quality work. On what basis might Henry recover a tort damage claim for wrongful discharge? What evidence might be relevant to prove the employer's case?

2. How does a union become the certified collective bargaining agent for a grouping of employees working for a particular employer?

3. The clerical workers of ABC Company petitioned the NRLB for a representation election. ABC and the candidate union agreed that the clerical workers at ABC's Company headquarters would constitute an appropriate bargaining unit. The union lost by only one vote and challenged the election because the spouses of the owner's of ABC were included in the appropriate bargaining unit. These spouses worked as accounting clerks and receptionists at the firm. On what basis might the union successfully challenge the election? On what basis might ABC argue that the election was conducted properly and the union lost fair and square?

4. The International Brotherhood of Tireworkers is attempting to organize the employees of the XYZ Tire and Rubber Company. XYZ has a tall electrified fence around its entire premises and employees' parked vehicles are within XYZ's grounds. The union's officials are routinely barred from entering the premises. Union organizers have spent many hours following workers home after they leave the plant premises and have successfully solicited petitions from almost 35% of the employees at XYZ. However, the union has been unsuccessful in tracking down any other employees. What tactic might the union use to improve its chances of contacting the other XYZ employees?

5. Consider the facts and the question above. XYZ uniformly prohibits union sympathizers or organizers from entry onto its property. However, XYZ has commonly permitted local charities and other clubs and organizations to come on its property and solicit XYZ employees. On what basis might the union claim that XYZ has violated the labor law? What arguments might XYZ make about its restrictions of labor electioneering on its property?

6. The Computer Equip. Co. has adopted a new management quality control technique called quality circles. This involves assigning employees to committees of 15 to 20 workers in groupings along the assembly line. These groups meet to discuss improving quality and productivity through the identification of problem areas and eliminating defects. These groups are also generally required to handle grievances among employees and their supervisors. Each quality circle has a supervisor heading the committee who generally questions employees at the end of the fiscal year about compensation and other terms and conditions of employment. Computer Equip. Co. is a nonunion plant. What argument might the NLRB make about Computer Equip. Co. quality circle program? How might Computer Equip. Co. modify its quality circle program to avoid a legal challenge?

7. Employees of the M Company signed a sufficient number of authorization and membership cards to constitute a majority in support of the union. The union presented M Company with legitimate evidence of these signed authorization and membership cards and demanded M Company bargain with the union. Managers of the M Company believed that they could convince workers to reject the union as unnecessary and ill advised, so they refused to bargain with the union. Thereafter the union filed an unfair labor practice charge with the NLRB charging M Company with refusal to bargain. On what basis might M Company justify its refusal to bargain with the union at this time? If the employees showed overwhelming support for the union and M Company's manage-

ment recognized the futility of fighting the union, what might M Company do?

8. The F Motor Company operated an in-plant cafeteria and food vending service. Prices charged were generally lower than at other similar cafeteria and vending outlets. The F Company chose to raise prices to market levels and turn the food service into a profit center. After F Company notified the union of its plans to increase prices. The union representing F Company's employees requested that F Company bargain over the food service price changes. After F Company refused to bargain, the union charged F Company with an unfair labor practice of failing to bargain over terms and conditions of employment. On what basis might the union prevail in this suit? What arguments might F Company make that it need not bargain over these prices?

9. The Keystoner Company has been struck by its employees. Bargaining continued for several weeks in which the union demanded a $5 an hour increase in wages but Keystoner claimed it could offer only $2 an hour. Contract negotiators had exhausted their creativity and could not find a compromise so Keystoner attempted to restart its operations by hiring replacement workers. Under what conditions would striking workers be entitled to reinstatement? Under what conditions would striking workers not be entitled to reinstatement?

10. The M Drydock Company operated a ship repair facility on the Pacific Coast. Typically the crew of a ship would sail into the M Drydock facility while their ship was being refitted. The M Drydock operated as a prime contractor that subcontracted work to many separate and independent subcontractors: electrical companies, welding companies, structural steel contractors, and others. The sailors of one ship had a dispute with their ship's owner. The sailors struck and picketed while their ship was under repairs at the M Drydock Company. The M Drydock Company charged the sailors with trespassing at the M Drydock facility and the local sheriff arrested the sailors. What kind of picketing activity is involved in this case?

Are the sailors or employees of subcontractors working at the M Drydock Company permitted to picket at this site at all?

14

Employment Law

CHAPTER OUTLINE

Employment Law

MANY YEARS BEFORE the law sanctioned unions' collective bargaining with employers as the primary definition of the employment relationship, there were pressures to regulate the compensation, safety, and employment discrimination. Still today, it is often argued that with less than 20% of the U.S. labor force covered by union collective bargaining agreements, most employment relationships are defined by contract, federal law, and state law. This chapter discusses how these employment regulation matters are defined for nearly all U.S. workers, whether they are unionized or not.

I. Occupational Safety and Health

Many labor economists and other employment specialists recognize that employees should be compensated for the health and safety risks they must endure on the job site. In an efficient employment market, both employers and employees would negotiate adjustments to employment compensation and conditions to reflect these risks. However, industrial health and safety hazards are not always evident to either employers or employees. Without this information the parties are unable to effectively negotiate higher compensation. These employment market imperfections have burdened society with externalized costs of providing medical and employment compensation, mostly through higher insurance premiums.

By the 1950's and 1960's the complexity of industrial processes made the workplace increasingly risky. Public pressures on Congress resulted in the passage of the Occupational Safety and Health Act (OSHA). This law is designed to reduce the risks inherent in using high technology manufacturing techniques such as microwaves, lasers, toxic chemicals, high-speed processing machinery, atomic energy, and other unknown dangers. Congress intended OSHA to "insure so far as possible every working man and woman in the nation, safety and healthful working conditions to preserve our human resources." OSHA applies to all employers which have at least one employee and are engaged in business affecting interstate commerce. A few industries are exempt from OSHA where other laws provide significant regulatory safety programs: the Coal Mine Safety Act, Railway Safety Act, and Nuclear Regulatory Act. OSHA is inapplicable to domestic household employees and the religious activities of religious organizations.

A. The OSHA Administration

Congress created three new federal agencies with the passage of the OSHA law in 1970. First, the Occupational Safety and Health Administration (OSHA Administration) passes regulations that set safety standards for the workplace. The OSHA administration is part of the Department of Labor, a cabinet level agency controlled by the President. The OSHA administration is responsible for inspecting employers' premises to ensure compliance with OSHA regulations.

The second agency created by OSHA is the National Institute for Occupational Safety and Health (NIOSH). This agency conducts research into health and safety hazards. NIOSH produces recommendations made to the OSHA Administration for new regulations to define health or safety standards. NIOSH conducts education and training programs for both employers and employees. NIOSH is an agency responsible to a different department, the Department of Health and Human Services, which is also controlled by the President.

The third agency created by OSHA is an independent commission that processes appeals from determinations made by the OSHA Administration. The Occupational Safety and Health Review Commission (OSHRC) is an independent regulatory commission that is not directly responsible to any cabinet level department or to the President. The OSHA law made the OSHRC into a quasiindepen-dent agency to limit the political influence that might be exerted on the health and safety regulation process by employers or employee groups. OSHRC commissioners are appointed by the President for staggered six year terms and their appointments must be confirmed by the Senate. These three agencies work together to increase workplace safety although both employers and employees involvement in record-keeping and safety efforts are critical.

B. Employer's Duty of Safety

Employers are required under OSHA to maintain a safe work environment to prevent unreasonably hazardous conditions. The employers' duty of safety arises only in situations where the employment relationship creates an unsafe environment. In most cases, the employer's duty arises from a general recognition among all employers in the industry that serious health or safety hazards exist. This duty generally requires employers to remove or safeguard against safety and health hazards where feasible under modern technology.

The general duty of safety requires the employer to identify and remedy unsafe or unhealthful conditions in the workplace. In addition, there are separate, more specific duties of safety derived from the specific health and safety standards set by the OSHA administration. OSHA regulations require employers to modify particular conditions of the employers' workplace that create safety or health hazards. Specific duties are often derived from research conducted by NIOSH which recommends promulgation of "legally enforceable regulations governing conditions, practices, or operations to ensure safe and healthful workplace." The OSHA Administration is not required to accept NIOSH recommendations. Many OSHA regulations have been initiated after NIOSH research while some is the result of rulemaking the OSHA Administration commenced on its own initiative.

1. DESIGN VS. PERFORMANCE STANDARDS

When Congress created the OSHA Administration the agency was immediately required to adopt over 4,000 "consensus standards." These were assembled from various existing federal regulations and from voluntary industry codes already in existence at that time. Today, many of these original consensus standards are obsolete so the OSHA Administration often comes under pressure from the political system to establish more modern and often more stringent standards.

In the early years, the OSHA administration mainly used *design standards* that specify minimum specifications for the construction of protective equipment. For example, an OSHA design standard regulation for a hard hat might require its construction from particular materials (e.g., fiberglass) and specify a minimum thickness. Design standards permit only one method to achieve the desired level of protection. Therefore, design standards seldom provide flexibility to utilize alternative construction materials for a hardhat, and this stifles innovation.

As a result of the inflexibility of design standards, the President now requires OSHA Administration to pass only cost effective regulations. The President's guidelines has shifted OSHA regulations from design to performance standards by encouraging more effective and less costly designs to achieve the same level of protection. *Performance standards* regulations specify a level of protection rather than a particular device that will achieve the same level of protection. OSHA standards rewritten as performance specifications permit the use of hard hats made of different substances or thicknesses if they provide the same level of head protection as the design standard.

During the early years of the OSHA Administration, the agency mostly analyzed workplace safety problems and predominantly specified safety regulations. Safety problems are usually more obvious because a safety related accident results in the worker's sudden and immediate disability. However, over the years, the vast majority of unsafe workplace conditions have been addressed. Therefore, the focus of OSHA Administration regulations has shifted to health concerns. Unhealthful working conditions are far less obvious because they seldom become widely known through an accident. Instead, long term workplace exposures to low levels of toxic substances eventually lead to disease. The manifestation of work related diseases are often delayed after many years of exposure. Workers have great difficulty pinpointing the precise cause of a work-related disease. The OSHA Administration has increased performance standards to reduce

workers' exposure to environmental and toxic health hazards in the workplace.

2. HEALTH AND SAFETY RULEMAKING PROCESS

The OSHA Administration follows the same basic informal rulemaking process discussed in Chapter 2 on Administrative Law. This process may begin with a research study conducted by NIOSH that reveals a hazardous working condition. The OSHA Administration begins a rulemaking process either after a NIOSH recommendation or after the OSHA Administration discovers a risk either through its own research or after inspecting various workplaces. The OSHA Administration then drafts a regulation proposal that is published in the Federal Register. Interested parties, including the effected industry and labor groups, may submit their views about the adequacy, feasibility, or propriety of the rule proposed. Sometimes a rule proposal will be revised by the OSHA Administration until the effected parties are somewhat satisfied.

The OSHA Administration, as a dependent federal regulatory agency within the Department of Labor, must comply with the policies set by the Presidential administration. During the 1970's and 1980's the Carter and Reagan administrations established a cost-benefit/analysis process to require that OSHA regulations produce more benefits than their costs. This process, also discussed in Chapter 2, empowers the President's Office of Management and Budget to interact with most federal agencies to assure that when new regulations are promulgated, the benefits outweigh the costs.

C. Variances

Employers must comply with OSHA regulations during the "phase-in time" imposed by the regulation. However, exceptions are usually granted by the OSHA Administration if an employer is unable to immediately comply. Variances are granted where the employer

Example.   Pressures from labor groups on the OSHA Administration led to a recognition that benzene, a well known cancer causing chemical (carcinogen) was at unsafe levels in many workplaces. Medical studies existed showing that workers exposed to benzene suffer much higher levels of blood disorders, leukemia and other cancers. These studies indicate that benzene exposures above 10 parts per million (ppm) were factors causing these cancers and diseases. However, there were no studies nor reliable evidence that reducing benzene exposures below 10 ppm significantly improved workers health. Nevertheless, the OSHA Administration promulgated a very strict benzene exposure standard outlawing workplace exposures above 1 ppm.

The OSHA Administration may not arbitrarily set workplace exposure standards at artificially low levels, particularly if there is no recognized or accepted technology to feasibly reduce these exposures to the levels suggested. The OSHA Administration must have credible evidence that hazardous exposure levels pose a "significant risk" of material health impairment. The OSHA Administration must conduct a cost-benefit/analysis and a feasibility study before imposing any specific limit on workplace exposure to protect from a suspected carcinogen. ☐

has installed all available and feasible safety measures and can promise to meet a reasonable schedule to fully comply with the OSHA standard. Variances may be granted on a permanent basis if the employer has installed satisfactory alternatives to protect safety or health and provide equal or greater worker protection. The OSHA Administration does not consider compliance cost in granting variances. Employees may challenge a variance if it will increase hazards or risks in the workplace.

Health or safety equipment that interferes with production may also be excused under certain conditions. Where employees intentionally defeat or refuse to use safety or health equipment, the employer's strict compliance may be excused temporarily.

For example, some employees refuse to wear heavy protective clothing or masks during hot weather. However, if the employer is generally aware that employees regularly defeat safety procedures, the employer may still be held liable for failing to enforce the safety rules among employees. However, isolated employee noncompliance may be excused. This situation clearly illustrates why the standard setting process should involve both

employers and employee groups to assure that the health and safety equipment used is acceptable and effective. It also strongly suggests that employers should repeatedly educate employees and reinforce the importance of health and safety regulations.

D. OSHA Enforcement Procedures

The OSHA law and OSHA regulations are enforced by the OSHA Administration. Information is routinely collected by OSHA Administration regulators from employers, employees, and from on-site inspections of the employer's premises. When the OSHA Administration discovers violations, it often issues citations for violations and it may assess penalties. The OSHA law prohibits employers from retaliating against employees who report workplace safety or health violations.

1.   RECORDKEEPING AND REPORTING REQUIREMENTS

Employers are required to report unsafe incidents, accidents, fatalities, lost work days, job transfers, terminations, medical treatments, or work restrictions resulting from unsafe or unhealthful workplace conditions. OSHA *incident reports* are filed with the Secretary of

Labor and detailed logs must be kept by the employer. Recordkeeping requirements are relaxed for employers with fewer than 11 employees. An employer must notify the OSHA Administration within 2 days following any accident that results in a single fatality or in hospitalization of more than 4 employees. Employers must also provide employees with information regarding their rights under the OSHA law.

2. OSHA ADMINISTRATION INSPECTIONS

Another important source of information about health and safety violations comes from the OSHA Administration's conduct of on-site inspections. The OSHA Administration has no right to conduct surprise on-site inspections without a warrant. As discussed in Chapter 2 on Administrative Law, warrantless inspections violate the 4th Amendment of the Constitution which protects private citizens and businesses against unreasonable searches and seizures. Therefore, an employer may refuse access to its business premises when an OSHA Administration inspector requests access for an inspection. An OSHA Administration inspector must secure a search warrant from a federal magistrate based on administrative probable cause. This is usually permitted when there has been a previous accident, employees have complained about unsafe conditions, or the industry has a history of dangerous and hazardous conditions.

When the OSHA Administration inspector has a search warrant or the employer consents to the inspection, a representative of the employer usually accompanies the inspector during the visit. OSHA inspectors are permitted to question employees directly unless an employee representative also accompanies the inspection team. For example, the inspector must question an elected union shop steward rather than employees performing work. The inspection should not disrupt production.

3. OSHA VIOLATIONS

The OSHA Administration uses several remedies in its enforcement process. Written citations are given to employers after the agency discovers violations of safety or health standards. The OSHA Administration may assess penalties that vary with the size of the employer's business, the employer's record of safety, the severity of the violation, and the employer's good faith. Citations must be posted prominently near to where the violation was discovered to adequately notify employees.

OSHA violations fall into several levels of seriousness permitting the OSHA Administration to impose various penalties for noncompliance. First, *de minimis* violations do not directly relate to safety so penalties are seldom imposed. For example, non-private toilet facilities, a lack of waste containers, and a lack of new clean papercups were all considered de minimis OSHA violations. The next higher category of violations are considered *non-serious violations*. These are violations that are unlikely to cause death or serious physical harm but which at the OSHA Administration's discretion, monetary penalties are often levied. For example, a non-serious violation might arise where poor housekeeping could lead to an employee tripping. If an employer fails to provide employees with instruction for the safe use of machinery a nonserious violation could be penalized.

Serious violations are those which pose a substantial probability of death or serious physical harm to employees. The OSHA Administration often levies monetary penalties for serious violations. Employers that repeatedly violate safety or health standards and thereby create repeated serious violations may be penalized with fine or imprisonment. A serious violation is one that might lead to imminent danger of an employee's likely death or serious physical harm. Larger fines and longer imprisonment penalties may be levied against employers who willfully repeat serious violations

E. State Occupational Safety Laws

A number of states have enacted additional workplace safety and health laws. Many of these are "right to know" laws that require the employer to disclose the any toxic, carcinogenic, or potentially harmful chemicals used in the workplace. The OSHA Administration now requires uniformity in these disclosures. Notices must be posted by all employers of the chemicals used in each facility or building. Employees must be educated on methods to safely handle these chemicals. There is question whether the OSHA Administration's regulations pre-empt state laws of homicide, assault, or reckless endangerment. Some zealous local prosecutors have charged employers and company officials for work-related injuries and death. Employers' advocates have argued the OSHA law displaces all state laws in this regard. However, the issue remains unsettled.

II. Workers' Compensation

The system of Workers' Compensation laws preceded the more comprehensive occupational safety and health regulation. Workers' compensation provides at least minimal compensation to workers injured on the job site. The common law system of negligent torts seldom provided just compensation for worker injuries or adequate incentives for employers to modify the workplace for safety. Employers may defend suits brought by an injured employee under the *fellow servant doctrine* if the injury is partially caused by another employee's negligence. Additionally, the plaintiff peril defenses of contributory negligence and assumption of risk are interposed to defend a negligence suit brought by an injured employee. The workers' compensation system developed in most states because the fault system provided insufficient compensation.

All states have workers' compensation laws that create a form of compulsory insurance to make payments to workers injured at the workplace. Workers' compensation systems vary by state, some states permit employers to self-insure, other states permit the purchase of private insurance, while many states require employers to participate in a state managed workers' compensation insurance fund. Employers with good safety records often pay reduced workers' compensation premiums under the *merit rating system.* This provides an incentive for employers to identify workplace dangers and thereby prevent injuries.

A. Workers' Compensation Administration

Workers' compensation systems are typically administered by separate state regulatory agency. Although the title of the agencies vary, they are typically called the state industrial commission or workers' compensation bureau. These agencies often perform many different governmental tasks including: (1) legislative duties such as promulgating workers' compensation regulations, (2) executive functions such as setting policy, investigating workers' compensation claims, and management of the workers' compensation insurance fund, and (3) judicial functions such as holding hearings to adjudicate payment of workers compensation claims.

The processing of workers' compensation claims usually commences after a worker is injured. The injured worker typically applies for benefits through the state workers' compensation agency which assigns a claims examiner to verify the extent of the workers' injury. Claims may be certified and paid after this procedure. However, the agency may disallow a claim in novel cases or when the facts are in dispute. Thereafter, the injured worker must usually proceed through an appeal process that may go through several levels including an informal proceeding before a hearing officer, review by the agency's appeal board, review before the agency's commissioner, and perhaps appeal through the state's court system. Claims involving novel questions of the coverage of occupational diseases must usually be appealed through this process. The state workers' compensation law usually requires payment of benefits once an injured worker's claim is proved.

B. Benefits

Injured workers are entitled to benefits from the workers' compensation insurance fund to pay for medical expenses, disability, and death benefits. Many benefits are precisely specified as scheduled benefits where established dollar amounts are paid for the loss of certain bodily functions. *Scheduled benefits* are often classified according to the injured employee's level of disability. *Temporary total disability* is a condition where the employee cannot work for a short time. *Temporary partial disability* is a condition where the employee is unable to perform all work activities for a short time. *Permanent partial disability* exists when the employee has limited work capabilities for the remainder of the employee's work life. A *permanent total disability* is a condition where the employee cannot work for the remainder of the work life, usually from such losses as eyesight, limbs, or paralysis. *Death benefits* are usually limited to a few thousand dollars, merely to cover burial expenses. While most state workers' compensation plans offer far less compensation than would be awarded under the tort system or other disability insurance, only a few states pay substantial benefits to replace the worker's lost income.

C. Compensable Injuries

There are two important questions in a workers' compensation claim that the worker must answer satisfactorily before an injury award is made. First, the worker must have been injured while on the job. Second, the injuries suffered must be identifiable and generally recognized by medical science. While it might seem these are rather clear cut questions, most of the workers' compensation litigation has involved novel questions of on-the-job status and what constitutes a compensable injury.

The first inquiry into whether the worker has been injured on the job is a similar question as addressed in the tort law analysis of respondeat superior. Workers' injuries are compensable only when they are incurred on the job because the employer has the right to control the employee's activities and therefore has responsibility for employee safety. Independent contractors' injuries are not compensable by the employer. Instead, the independent contractor who employs an independent worker is responsible for these injuries.

Injuries are compensable if they arise "in the course and arising out of employment." Injuries sustained while an employee is *going and coming* to or from work are not compensable. Only while the employee is located at a fixed and limited place on the employers' worksite do workers' compensation benefits accrue. Usually an employee is covered after arriving at the employers' parking lot and remains covered until leaving at the end of the work day. Employees are usually covered by workers' compensation while working on the employer's premises, during preparation for work, while dressing into safety gear, while being shuttled to the job site by the employer, and even off the premises during lunch if there are no dining facilities on the employers' premises. Employees are also covered while traveling away from the employers' premises to a remote job site. There is disagreement over whether workers' compensation covers injuries sustained during co-worker misconduct. For example, if a worker is injured by a coworker's horseplay, the injury

Example. Mr. J, a foreman at the A Steel Company had worked there for twenty years. The A Steel Company eliminated overtime work and pay after its shop was unionized. The A Steel Company directed J to "go out into the shop and prod the men to expedite the work." This made Mr. J a rather unpopular figure among employees and caused considerable friction. Mr. J was instructed to fire an employee after a heated discussion over the employee's overtime pay. Mr. J "became distressed, developed chest pains, and nausea" after which Mr. J ceased to work at the A Steel Company. Mr. J had numerous symptoms of "a chronic anxiety state mixed with depression and comatized reaction neurocirculatory asthenia" diagnosed from symptoms such as continual pain, sweatiness, shortness of breath, headaches and depression.

Mr. J applied for worker's compensation benefits from the Massachusetts Workers' Compensation Commission but these benefits were reversed and denied by the Worker's Compensation Review Board. In an appeal to the Massachusetts Superior Court, Mr. J's worker's compensation benefits were reinstated. The worker's compensation insurer admitted that Mr. J suffered mental and emotional disability. However, the insurer argued Mr. J's condition resulted from gradual wear and tear and should not be a compensable personal injury.

Personal injuries are compensable even if they involve mental disorders or disabilities that are connected to mental trauma or shock arising out of the employment. There is no valid reason to distinguish between physical and emotional or mental injuries for the purposes of compensation. Of course, the lack of a sudden episode makes it more difficult to be certain that workplace exposure is the primary cause of an employee's injury. Here, there was no evidence of shock or stress in Mr. J's off-the-job life. It is within the power of the Worker's Compensation Board to identify a series of particular stressful episodes as the causal factor for a workers injury. Mr. J's injury was not the result of everyday wear and tear but is related to a series of identifiable stressful work related incidents for Mr. J. is entitled to worker's compensation for this disability. ⬚

will be compensable if the conduct should have been prohibited by the employer.

Many of the same difficulties encountered by the OSHA Administration in defining dangerous conditions also confronts workers' compensation regulators in the definition of compensable injuries. Sudden and obvious physical injuries causing the loss of limb or other bodily functions are clearly compensable. However, occupational diseases that are contracted only on the jobsite are often difficult to connect to a jobsite exposure. Workers' compensation does not apply to ordinary diseases that are contracted off the jobsite or are communicated by coworkers. For example, occupational exposure to cancer or allergic reaction to a job related chemical exposure is difficult to pinpoint precisely. Addi-

tionally, it is difficult to prove that mental injuries are caused by worksite exposures. Today, courts increasingly provide benefits to workers subjected to job stress which results in anxiety, depression, high blood pressure, vertigo, or other aspects of work strain.

III. Equal Employment Opportunities

There are numerous Constitutional provisions and federal laws that make discrimination unlawful. The 13th, 14th, and 15th Amendments and the Civil Rights Act of 1866 were passed during the reconstruction period that followed the Civil War. These laws were the first major legislation to correct the discriminatory abuses existing prior to the

Civil War. By the 1960's, social pressures mounted for the establishment of more effective anti-discrimination laws and the 25th Amendment. These laws are designed to create equal opportunities and end discriminatory practices in voting, housing, employment, promotions, working conditions, and compensation systems. This section addresses the equal employment laws because they constrain managers' decisions on the hiring, firing, promotion, and working condition decisions made by most employers.

A. Equal Pay Act

Congress passed the Equal Pay Act of 1963 to prohibit discrimination in the rate of pay given for work requiring "equal skill, effort, and responsibility" if based on the employee's sex. The Equal Pay Act amends the Fair Labor Standards Act by requiring employers to cease giving unequal pay for equal work according to sex. The Act requires that when two substantially similar jobs are held by a male and a female, the employer is generally prohibited from paying these employees at different rates. This requires employers to specify a *job description* for all jobs so it is possible to compare the two jobs for their substantial similarity.

Employers may validly pay different amounts to two employees in similar jobs if the differential is based on factors other than sex. Employers may base the differentials on the time of a work shift, the *shift differential*. However, shift rotation must be open equally to persons of both sexes. Pay differentials are also valid between two workers when one is a new employee involved in a rotational job training program. However, valid job training programs must be open equally to persons of both sexes.

I. COMPARABLE WORTH

The *comparable worth* theory was originally developed during World War II, and has experienced a resurgence from time to time. This theory expands the equal pay requirement beyond two substantially similar jobs to those requiring similar skill, effort, and responsibility performed under similar working conditions. A male and female employee holding different jobs may be required to receive equal pay if the two jobs have roughly equal levels of responsibility and difficulty. For example, a female administrative assistant to a top manager might perform different tasks but have equal responsibility and skill to a male middle manager. If the comparable worth theory applies, both employees must receive equal pay. The theory is justified as the only effective way to equalize the injustice of sexual discrimination in pay and employment.

The comparable worth theory is alleged to directly limit the operation of the free market to set prices for labor services. By ignoring the supply and demand for particular job skills, the comparable worth system tends to reward employees equally who have unequally desired skills. Although comparable worth is not applicable to most employment relations in the United States, the theory is applicable to some civil service employees in some states and local governments, and is applicable to all employees in some Canadian provinces. The U.S. Supreme Court has suggested that the comparable worth theory may be derived from the Equal Pay Act, the Civil Rights Act of 1964, and may apply to suspect classifications other than sex.

B. Civil Rights Act of 1964

The anti-discrimination law with the most profound effect on business and its employment practices is found in Title VII of the Civil Rights Act of 1964. The Civil Rights Act prohibits discrimination by employers who have fifteen or more employees, by unions representing appropriate bargaining units with fifteen or more employees, by union hiring halls, and by employment agencies. Title VII prohibits discrimination in hiring, firing, compensation, or in setting the terms, conditions, or privileges of employment. Discrimination may not be based on race, color, religion, national origin or sex. These classifications of the employees are referred to as *protected classes*. Employers may be held liable for depriving persons in a protected class of employment opportunities when the discrimination is based on: (1) disparate treatment, (2) disparate impact, (3) or a pattern or practice of discrimination.

Title VII does not require hiring quotas for the hiring or promotion of any particular person. However, where employment decisions are based on an employee's membership in one of the protected classes, the employer's employment decision is illegally biased. The term anti-discrimination does not mean that an employer may not discriminate on the basis of an applicant's ability to perform in a particular job or on the employee's prospects for success after promotion. Instead, outlawed discrimination is based on the employee or prospective employee's race, sex, religion, color, national origin, disability, or age.

I. THEORIES OF DISCRIMINATION

Under Title VII, employers are prohibited from using discriminatory policies that result in a *disparate treatment* on an employee or applicant in the hiring, promotion, or firing process. Disparate treatment is an announced policy or the actual use of an intentionally discriminatory employment practice that is more favorable to one protected class than to another protected class. For example, an employer's statement such as "blacks need not apply" or "this is a man's job" are clearly overt practices that result in a disparate treatment of persons in a protected class.

Soon after Title VII was passed in the mid 1960's, most employers removed and actively discouraged the use of any disparate treatment language from their employment practices and literature. As direct or circumstantial evidence of disparate treatment became unavailable, the courts developed another useful theory to eliminate subtle discriminatory policies. Most discrimination today is hidden in the job qualifications or the evaluation process employers use. Therefore, discrimination may be proved where these discriminatorY policies result in a *disparate impact* on a suspect class.

Employment policies that appear neutral on the surface but nevertheless result in a disparate impact on an employee in a protected class may be proved by inference from statistical evidence. For example, on first examination a height requirement for employees in certain job classifications appears unbiased. However, it would clearly have a disparate impact on some protected classes. Females and orientals are often excluded by height restrictions. Aptitude or general intelligence and achievement tests are allegedly biased in favor of the background of certain individuals. For example, in recent years the scholastic aptitude tests (SAT) has been alleged to discriminate against blacks and women because the matters tested are most often within the experience and background of white males. Job requirements must be directly related to the necessary job qualifications and the expected use of those skills on the job site.

In both disparate impact and pattern or practice of discrimination cases the plaintiffs often use statistical evidence showing the demographic makeup of the employer's workforce for comparison with the population at large. However, this may be an invalid comparison as suggested above. For example, if the employer has fewer females in managerial positions than are represented in the population at large the comparison may be faulty. The employer's profile of employees should be compared with the number of qualified female applicants. If the number of qualified applicants is insufficient, then it is irrelevant that the employer has fewer female managers than the total proportion of females in the

Example. The WCP Company operated salmon fish canneries in Alaska. WCP employees were divided into two basic groups: (1) unskilled "cannery jobs" predominately held by nonwhites paid at a lower scale and (2) higher skilled "noncannery jobs" generally held by whites at higher pay scales. Some cannery employees charged WCP with discriminatory acts in violation of Title VII of the Civil Rights Act of 1964: nepotism, rehire preferences, a lack of objective practices in hiring, establishment of two separate hiring channels, and the failure to promote from within. Once the plaintiffs had established a prima facie case, the lower courts shifted the burden of proof to WCP Company requiring them to establish that no discrimination occurred from these practices.

Plaintiffs in a Title VII disparate impact case must establish more than a mere prima facie case. For example, if statistical proof exists that the employer's employment practices have a disparate impact on persons within a protected class, the methodology used must be sound. Particularly where the lack of minorities holding skilled positions is caused by the lack of qualified minority applicants, the plaintiff is not permitted to infer the employer's employment practices and selection methods are discriminatory to nonwhites. Plaintiffs in a disparate impact discrimination case must prove specific and particular employment practices are at fault in the disparate impact proved. ▢

outer population. The comparison should be made between the employer's profile of employees and the qualified applicant pool. Therefore, sex discrimination is proved by statistical comparison only when the employer has failed to hire females in proportion to the number of qualified females available in the outer population. To do otherwise would establish a quota system that would require employers to hire less qualified minorities to achieve racial or equality balance. From time to time, Congress has attempted to pass legislation that would establish such quotas but has been unsuccessful in this attempt thus far.

Another theory of discrimination is based on the employers pattern or practice of discrimination. The *pattern* or *practice* theory extends the analysis of an employer's disparate impact on a particular person to the whole protected class. Where qualified persons in a protected class perceive the employer's discriminatory reputation is a deterrence effectively preventing them from applying for employment, it can be inferred the employer has established a pattern or practice of discrimination affecting all individuals in that class.

The evidence used in pattern or practice theory cases comes from similar statistical inference as used in the example above. Statistical comparisons are used to show the employer has under utilized applicants from a protected class. In a pattern or practice case, the circumstantial evidence derived from statistical inference is used to show a broad systematic discrimination against all persons in that protected class. For example, where qualified minorities are available yet the employer has utilized few of them or there is evidence of disparate pay for minorities and women in comparable jobs, a pattern or practice emerges. Pattern or practice discrimination may become so widespread in an entire industry that other employers mimic the discriminatory activity.

2. PROTECTED CLASSES

The key to establishing employment discrimination is the definition of benchmarks for comparison and defining the variables of comparison. Discrimination is prohibited in

Example.   Mr. H, a T Airline Company Maintenance employee, commonly used his seniority to opt out of Saturday work, his Sabbath Day. However, after Mr. H was transferred to another department, his seniority was reduced and the T Airline Company required him to work on his Sabbath. Mr. H sued the T Airline Company under Title VII seeking an injunction to permit his observance of the Saturday Sabbath.

The T Airline Company had made reasonable accommodations for Mr. H's religious practices. However, some employers operate round-the-clock fulltime operations. The T Airline Company chose not to arbitrarily assign work over weekends but left these decisions to the non- discriminatory collective bargaining with the union representing Mr. H. The employer is not required to undertake the additional cost of hiring a replacement worker. An employer satisfies the equal opportunity obligations imposed by the anti-discrimination laws if reasonable accommodation is made in the establishing the work week and a valid non-discriminatory seniority system is established through collective bargaining. ▢

employment practices when based on a person's membership in a protected class, the variable of comparison. *Protected classes* are demographic variables that permit the classifications of persons and thereby test for historical discrimination in hiring, firing, and other employment practices. Protected classes under the various antidiscrimination laws include. race, religion, national origin, sex, age, and disability.

Many constitutional and statutory provisions prohibit discrimination based on race. The original focus during the post-Civil War period was to correct the pervasive discrimination against blacks. However, because all persons are members of a particular race, sex, religion, national origin, or age, the discrimination laws apply to all persons. It has also been held that *reverse discrimination* may be illegal where preference is given to minorities of a protected class over others not in that class.

A major reason the early European colonists traveled to the new world and established the United States was to eliminate discrimination based on religious intolerance. The separation of church and state and many First Amendment freedoms create a protected zone for the religious beliefs of all persons. While the term religion clearly refers to standard denominations, it also applies to a person's ethical or moral-based beliefs that are sincerely held. Because there is such a broad array of religions beliefs, it could become difficult for employers to accommodate all their various rituals and holidays. Therefore, the discrimination laws draw a balance between the hardships imposed on the employer and hardships imposed on the employee's religious observance.

All persons have forebears who come from some nation. Discrimination based on a person's national origin is illegal. This type of discrimination is usually proved with evidence of disparate impact or pattern or practice discrimination. For example, hiring persons with surnames typical of a particular national origin or requiring fluency in speaking English is discriminatory against persons on the basis of national origin. An English fluency requirement is permitted only if communication with customers, suppliers, or fellow employees is a business necessity. For example, college level teaching assistants are increasingly required to demonstrate English fluency in U.S. universities.

Discrimination based on sex is clearly prohibited in an effort to correct the stereotypical roles of the sexes in society. Historically, this has resulted in discrimination against females. For example, women were granted the right to vote the Nineteenth Amendment only by 1919. Before the passage of the Pregnancy Discrimination Act in 1978 employers could discriminate against pregnant females. Today, with over 40% of the workforce is populated by females and there is a clear trend to enlarge and equalize the economic activity of women.

Although Title VII does not prohibit discrimination on the basis of an employee's age, the Age Discrimination in Employment Act of 1957 as amended in 1978, protects persons between the ages of 40 and 70 years. Despite the preference of some employers for younger workers because of a perception of strength, appearance, and lower average compensation, it is illegal to specify age as a job selection criteria where the impact would be adverse on the persons between 40 and 70 years. There are exceptions for jobs requiring physical fitness, visual ability, or quick reactions so long as measurable standards are used to identify the qualified applicants. For example, jobs with a public safety impact such as bus driver, pilots, firefighters, or police officers, may have physical fitness or performance job qualifications even if this results in an adverse impact on older workers. A federal statute, effective in 1991, prohibits forced retirements after certain ages except for employees in policy-making positions that have extensive employer financed-pensions.

Although Title VII does not clearly protect handicapped workers, at least two additional laws have extended protected class status to handicapped workers. The Vocational Rehabilitation Act of 1973 requires federal contractors to consider using handicapped workers if reasonable accommodations can be made. Congress passed the Americans with Disabilities Act in 1990 requiring all employers to make reasonable accommodations for handicapped workers. Handicaps include both physical and mental impairments that substantially limit a person's major life activity. For example, handicaps result from diabetes, heart disease, retardation, blindness, paraplegia, quadriplegia, alcoholism or drug abuse. Employers may not consider this handicap in a hiring, firing, or job condition decision. Many handicaps raise significant controversy because of the costs they impose on society. For example, discrimination against AIDS victims and genetic testing of job applicants may become the major anti-discrimination questions during the 1990s.

3. STATUTORY EXCEPTIONS

Title VII establishes three major statutory exceptions that permit discrimination based on sex, age, national origin, and religion, and sometimes race where the employer can establish that there is: (1) a bona fide occupational qualification, (2) the results of a professionally developed aptitude test, or (3) a validly established nondiscriminatory seniority system.

The *bona fide occupational qualifications* (BOFQ) is a discrimination permitted against a person in a protected class if required by a business necessity. The employer has the burden of proving that hiring persons outside the BOFQ class would undermine the success of the employer's business. For example, religious institutions may validly require certain religious characteristics for some job candidates. Churches may require that only ordained ministers be hired within their denomination, Jewish butchers may be required for a Kosher butchery, language fluency may be required for tour guides, and females required to model women's fashions. Employers are not justified in establishing a BFOQ if hiring outside the class would merely inconvenience the business. For example, even though female flight attendants are considered superior to males in provide better

Example. The collective bargaining agreement between the T union and various trucking companies established a seniority system permitting the most desirable driving jobs to go to the more senior employees. The U.S. Attorney General brought suit against the T union alleging the seniority system constituted a pattern or practice against blacks and Hispanics who had lower seniority because they were hired into lower paying and less desirable jobs. The lower courts required the T union to remake its seniority system and establish a complex sub-sectioning of the T union membership to reduce this discrimination.

When Congress established the National Labor Relations Act and Title VII of the Civil Rights Act it intended to permit the continued use of seniority lists. Of course, seniority systems may have a discriminatory effect by freezing the effects of past discrimination. However, to outlaw valid and nondiscriminatorily established seniority systems is contrary to Congressional purpose in these two laws. Of course, if it could be shown that a seniority system had a discriminatory objective, the system could be invalidated under Title VII. ⬜

reassurance to anxious passengers this is not a BFOQ. Similar preference by customers of gourmet restaurants for male waiters does not justify a BFOQ. At this writing there is still controversy over admitting persons of the opposite sex into locker rooms. It has been held a valid BFOQ to require female locker room attendants at female exercise clubs. However, the exclusion of female sportswriters from the locker room of male professional sports teams is discriminatory. Despite this difference, incidents of discrimination and reaction to this rule will probably continue.

Employers may validly use *professionally developed aptitude tests* where they accurately discriminate on the applicant's skill and abilities needed on the job. However, it is difficult to design tests that always precisely measure only those characteristics needed on the job. Tests often measure other characteristics unrelated to job requirements. In order for an employer to use a professionally developed aptitude test to measure the qualifications of job applicants, the tests must be validated as accurate and reliable predictors for job performance. For example, one company required janitorial workers to pass the Wonderlick Aptitude Test and possess a high school diploma. Neither job qualifications

had a bearing on success in janitorial services. This case established the precedent that when tests disqualify members in a protected class based on measures unrelated to the job tests, the test is invalid and its use is discriminatory.

Aptitude tests and all job qualifications must have a valid probability of predicting the applicant's job success. Validity may be established as *criterion validity* where the test indicates that an applicant will perform the job tasks successfully or unsuccessfully. Another measure of validity, *content validity* will permit the use of a test that contains a representative sample of job tasks that are part of the job specified description. *Construct validity* exists where the test measures characteristics considered useful for the job. For example, a psychological test demonstrating a trial lawyer's ability to withstand the stresses of litigation would demonstrate construct validity. Before job qualifications or ability tests are used, the employer must establish and publish a job description that accurately reflects the catalog of tasks required for each job. Qualifications and tests may examine applicants only for the presence or quality of these characteristics.

Title VII permits discrimination when a bona fide seniority system has been established that is not designed to further discrimination. Employers may legitimately discriminate in favor of the more senior employees in decisions to fire, hire, promote or give merit raises. Seniority systems are legitimized because they can eliminate favoritism and the employer can retain its more experienced workers. However, the use of seniority systems tends to reinforce discriminatory practices used in the past. During an economic downturn, the most recent hires may be terminated first under a seniority system. This action tends to perpetuate discriminations made in the past. This problem pits the anti-discrimination goals of Title VII against the collective bargaining ideal embodied in the National Labor Relations Act.

C. Sexual Harassment

Although Title VII has no specific provisions prohibiting sexual harassment, both the courts and the Equal Employment Opportunity Commission (EEOC) have established a prohibition against sexual harassment. *Sexual harassment* exists where an employee is forced to submit to the employer or a supervisor's sexual harassment as a term or condition of employment. This is discriminatory conduct and prohibited separately under EEOC guidelines on sexual harassment. Sexual harassment arises where an employee experiences unwelcome sexual advances, requests for sexual favors, or even where there are verbal or physical contacts of a sexual nature. Employees not granted a promotion or pay raise for refusing to submit to sexual harassment or those passed over when favoritism is given to another employee who granted sexual favors, have a right of action under Title VII or under the EEOC sexual harassment guidelines.

As with other forms of discrimination, sexual harassment is not as overt and obvious today as it was once. Indeed, a hostile working environment can arise from sexual innuendoes because they create an intimidating and offen-

sive environment. Employers are required to provide a work environment free of sexual hostility. In one example, a female employee repeatedly submitted to her supervisor's sexual advances because she feared her noncompliance would lead to her job termination. Despite the employer's sexual harassment policy and grievance procedure, the employer's failure to stop this conduct constituted a hostile working environment. Employers are required to take appropriate corrective action if they know or should know about sexual harassing behaviors by other employees.

A sexual harassing or hostile working environment may arise in situations where it is difficult to distinguish between non-offensive social gestures and unlawful sexual harassment. Many persons of both sexes have difficulty judging behavior in this area. As a result, EEOC regards prevention as the best approach to elimination of sexual harassment. Many firms now provide guidance to employees with seminars and discussion groups. These groups permit employees the opportunity to discuss employee conduct and communicate the groups' assessments of the harassing character of hypothetical behaviors to all workers. This process is enhanced with video enactments of sexual harassing behavior in both categories of overt actions and subtle innuendoes. The following EEOC guidelines define sexual harassment rather broadly:

"Unwelcome sexual advances, or request for sexual favors other verbal or physical conduct of a sexual nature constitutes sexual harassment when:

1. Submission to such conduct is made either explicitly or implicitly a term or condition of an individual's employment,

2. Submission to or a rejection of such conduct by an individual is used as the basis for employment decisions affecting such individual, or

3. Such conduct has the purpose or effect of reasonably interfering with an individual's work performance or creating an intimidating, hostile, or offensive work requirement."

D. Equal Employment Opportunity Commission

Congress created the Equal Employment Opportunity Commission (EEOC) to enforce the various anti-discrimination laws in 1972. The EEOC is federal administrative agency that may investigate, mediate and conciliate, and prosecute grievances against employers and other employees where an applicant or employee claims a violation of the discrimination laws. The EEOC has rulemaking authority to implement the antidiscrimination laws.

EEOC regulations require employers to keep records that assist discriminated applicants and employees in proving a pattern or practice or disparate impact suit. Biographical and demographic records must be kept concerning all new applicants, employees changing positions, and in decisions concerning promotions, demotions, transfers, layoffs, and compensation changes.

The EEOC is empowered to investigate, review, and remedy discrimination claims when a complaint is levied by an employee or job applicant. Discrimination suits are commenced when an aggrieved employee or applicant receives an unlawful discrimination. Initially, the employee must file with the state's anti-discrimination agency before pursuing the claim through the federal EEOC. If the state agency is unresponsive for 60 days, the claim may be forwarded to the EEOC within 180 days after the alleged discriminatory act or within 300 days if there is no state law. The EEOC must notify the employer of the claim and may investigate by using subpoena power. Most claims are settled through conciliation, a form of mediated settlement where the EEOC persuades the employer to provide a remedy when there is clear evidence of a discrimination violation. If the EEOC fails to proceed with conciliation, it issues a right to sue letter and thereafter the employee is permitted to file suit within the next 90 days in a federal district court.

E. Affirmative Action

Some courts have implied rights in addition to those established in the Civil Rights Act of 1964. Remedies requiring the establishment of *affirmative action* programs are designed to eliminate the underlying discriminatory conditions in the employer future workforce. Affirmative Action usually establishes a goal, quota, or timetable requiring the employer to hire more persons from classes which have historically suffered discrimination by the employer. Of course, affirmative action programs suggest reverse discrimination. Qualified white males have often argued that quotas require the hiring of less qualified minorities and this distorts the labor markets. Underlying this argument is the deep rooted resentment toward placing the entire burden of achieving racial equality on those qualified individuals who claim reverse discrimination.

F. Executive Order Program

Several U.S. Presidents have issued executive orders, the equivalent of a federal statute, to further eliminate discrimination in the federal government or by private companies that contract with the federal government. All contracts between the federal government and private contractors must include a provision prohibiting discrimination. Additionally, non-discriminatory hiring practices by federal contractors must be used or the federal contract may be canceled or suspended. Another executive order created the Office of Federal Contract Compliance Programs to oversee the affirmative action programs required for federal contractors. This office requires federal contractors to develop affirmative action programs to achieve balance among the pro-

Example. The BK Restaurant Company assigns managerial, supervisory, and production responsibilities to all assistant managers. During peak service hours at meal time, assistant managers participate equally with other production workers in the preparation and service of food. Assistant managers often work over forty hours per week but the BK Restaurant Company does not pay overtime for these extra hours. BK insists that assistant managers are exempt from the overtime pay and record keeping provisions of the FLSA because they are "executives." The Department of Labor challenged the BK Restaurant Company's activities.

Assistant managers at fast food restaurants may be classified as executives so long as they do not spend a majority of their time on production work for which the FLSA overtime standards are applicable. The BK Restaurant Company's plan to avoid hiring additional production workers during high demand time by diverting assistant managers' time is a creative and flexible plan that does not violate the FLSA. In determining whether a particular worker is covered by the FLSA or should be considered a salaried executive, the Secretary of Labor should consider the time, relative importance of duties, frequency of discretionary power, freedom from supervision, and payment of salary in determining whether a particular job class is covered or exempt. Because assistant managers at the BK Restaurant Company are solely in charge of the restaurant for much of the time and are the ultimate supervisors both in fact and title, they are exempt from the FLSA overtime supervisions. ▢

tected classes in their work forces. Federal contractors must analyze their work forces and compare them with the population at large to implement affirmative action programs through goals and quotas.

IV. Employment Compensation

There are numerous state and federal laws covering employment standards and other employment compensation issues. The Fair Labor Standards Act, as amended, sets the standard for working hours during the work week and it regulates minimum wages and child labor. State laws establish the unemployment compensation system, an insurance fund administered much like worker's compensation. Additionally, federal laws establish the parameters and operations of pension benefits, particularly the social security system and private pension plans. These matters are of vital importance to employers not only

because of employers have a duty to comply but also proper design of these plans helps an attract and retain a competent workforce.

A. Minimum Wage

The Fair Labor Standards Act (FLSA) applies to all employers engaged in interstate commerce with gross annual sales above $250,000. Separate federal statutes apply to federal government employees and government contractors. Numerous exemptions from the FLSA apply to *white collar* workers "executive, administrative, and professional" employees. Additionally, some employees are exempt in industries such as agriculture, commercial fishing, household domestic service, and the retail trade where a salary is paid.

The *minimum wage* is actually a set of standards and methods to compute each employee's wage rate, overtime, and compensable time. The FLSA sets the standard work week at forty hours per week. All hours worked in excess of forty per week must be paid at an overtime rate, generally time and half. The minimum wage of $4.25 per hour (effective after April 1991) may be adjusted by the reasonable cost of food, lodging, and other facilities which the employer furnishes, tips or gratuities in excess of $20 per month, and other regularly owed bonuses and incentive pay. Employees must generally be paid for all "compensable time" which generally includes *preliminary activities* and *postliminary activities* such as preparing for or cleaning up after the work performed.

The FLSA is administered by the wage and hour provision of the Employment Standards Administration a subdivision of the U.S. Department of Labor. The division is supervised by an administrator appointed by the President with Senate confirmation. The Division's staff is responsible for promulgating regulations, investigating FLSA violations, and enforcing the FLSA. The Division is also responsible for the FLSA child labor provisions which are designed to encourage school attendance. Today these regulations generally prohibit the employment of children under thirteen and restrict employment for children between thirteen and seventeen years. Additionally, children sixteen or seventeen years old may not be employed in hazardous industries (explosives, logging, excavation) and the division designates approved jobs for children fourteen or fifteen years of age (e.g. retail sales clerks, food service establishments, service stations). Exemptions exist for child workers in the agricultural and entertainment industries.

B. Unemployment Compensation

After the U.S. experienced the tremendous hardships imposed by unemployment during the Great Depression, the states enacted unemployment compensation laws to reduce the serious impact. Congress reinforced this system by reducing the social security withholding tax (FICA) in every state that enacts an unemployment compensation system by taxing employers' payrolls. Employers are en-

couraged to support state legislation establishing unemployment compensation because employers' FICA payments are reduced by 3%. Employees covered by unemployment compensation are entitled to receive benefits if they become unemployed. Employers generally pay at least 3.4% in unemployment taxes for the first $6,000 paid to each employee in annual wages. These payments are collected by a state operated insurance fund that distributes unemployment compensation benefits to unemployed workers.

Employees qualify for unemployment compensation only after they have worked consistently for a minimum time period. This time period and the benefits payable are established by the state unemployment compensation statute and regulations of the state's unemployment compensation agency. The minimum earnings and work periods are a prerequisite to an employee's eligibility to prevent misuse of the unemployment compensation system. Additionally, unemployed claimants must be actively seeking alternative employment to qualify for benefits. Benefits are usually unavailable to fired striking workers. Employers with a track record of low employee turnover may be permitted to pay lower unemployment compensation premiums than employers with high turnover rates.

C. Retirement Income

Before the Great Depression most workers had no retirement benefits. Workers either had no retirement at all because they worked until death or disability or workers were required to save or live with family after retirement. Congress passed the Social Security Act in 1935 to cushion this economic hardship on retirees and their families. Social security benefits supplement the income and other pension benefits typically paid to retirees. Today, the more significant portion of most retirees' income comes from private pension plans which make payments from the investment proceeds of the contributions made for each plan participant.

I. THE FEDERAL INSURANCE CONTRIBUTIONS ACT

The Federal Insurance Contributions Act (FICA) created the social security trust fund to accumulate the tax withholdings from nearly all employees in the United States. The Internal Revenue Service (IRS) collects these taxes along with other federal income tax payments made by both employers and withheld directly from employees' paychecks.

The social security trust fund differs from private pension plans in that employees' tax contributions are not invested in the same way that pension payments are invested by the pension plan trustee. Social security is a cash flow rather than an accumulation system. It is based on a "pay as you go" scheme. The FICA taxes withheld from current employees do not accumulate for their retirement but instead go almost immediately to pay benefits to currently retired persons. It is a widely held myth that contributions made by employees who worked throughout the 1940's, 1950's, 1970's and 1980's accumulated in some static fund to make benefit payments to these workers' during their retirement. As a result of this widespread misconception, there are tremendous economic pressures on the social security system particularly as the number of retirees grows much larger and the number of currently contributing employees remains static or decreases.

Social security taxes are paid by nearly all employees and by their employers. The FICA tax is levied on an employee's wages up to the maximum wage base. The FICA tax rate, a percentage applied to the employee's actual wages up to the maximum wage base, results in determination of the actual FICA taxes withheld. In 1990, the FICA tax rate was 7.51% paid by each employee with an equal amount paid by the employer. Self-employed employees pay at a higher rate, 13.02%, reflecting the lack of an employer's contribution.

The retirement income benefits of the social security system are paid to eligible retirees who worked for minimum vesting periods during their work lives. Employees qualify when they have worked a minimum number of calendar quarters (three month periods) equaling or exceeding the number of years of service after reaching the age of 21. Employees who have worked less may still qualify, but for reduced benefits. Benefits are paid monthly to retired persons after reaching age 62. The amount of benefits is based on each employee's base pay during their work lives. The children and spouses of deceased workers may be paid benefits even if the worker had not yet qualified for retirement benefits. Some of social security benefits are taxable and proposals arise from time to time to fully tax social security benefits or reduce the tax exclusion for high income retirees.

In 1965 Congress extended the social security benefits to include a form of mandatory health insurance for the aged and disabled. *Medicare* provides hospital insurance covering most hospital expenses for persons over 65 years of age. However, Medicare benefits are insufficient to cover all medical expenses so an active private insurance market has arisen to fill the gap with the so-called *medigap insurance*. Congress repealed the Medicare Catastrophic Coverage Act originally passed in 1988 to fill this gap because it was unpopular.

2. PRIVATE PENSION PLANS

A growing portion of pension benefits for most retirees are paid from privately administered pension plans. In 1974 Congress passed the Employee Retirement Income Security Act (ERISA) which standardized private pension plans because many employers operated them in a discriminatory manner. ERISA entitles employees to make tax free contributions to a qualified pension plan and income taxes are paid on these earnings only after retirement as the funds are withdrawn.

Pension plans qualified under ERISA must be administered by a pension trustee who acts as a fiduciary towards all pension beneficiaries. This requires the trustee to act skillfully and carefully as a reasonably prudent person in carefully investing pension contributions and administering payouts. The ERISA law splits the regulatory power over pension plans between the Internal Revenue Service and the Department of Labor. ERISA requires all plans to publish annual financial statements and provide each beneficiary with an annual summary of their financial interests.

The ERISA law changed the prior practice of many unfair pension plans that denied retirement benefits to employees based on technicalities. For example, an employee might work for thirty-nine and one half years before disability and be denied pension benefits because the employee failed to work the minimum forty years to qualify for benefits. ERISA establishes the concept of *pension vesting* which makes the employers' contributions to each beneficiaries pension account irrevocable after a minimum employment period. This minimum vesting period is set by the pension plan's creator, usually the employer or in a collective bargaining agreement made with the union. Vesting may be set between zero and ten years but after ten years the employer's contribution becomes irrevocable and these pension benefits vest. Designers of a pension plan have flexibility to permit vesting at any time during that ten years or even in partial amounts according to a sliding scale during that time period. Of course, any contributions made by the beneficiary become vested immediately.

Pension plans may be created as *defined benefit plans* where a specific payment amount is defined in a formula or other schedule that depends on the employee's age at retirement, length of service, and/or base salary during employment. Another type of plan, the defined contribution plan, requires the employer and/or employee to make specified contributions determined by formulas based on the employee's compensation level and job classification. The amount of benefits paid after retirement from a *defined contribution plan* may vary according to the investment successes of the plan's administrator while the employee's funds are in the trustee's custody.

From time to time Congress has established additional types of retirement plans and has given employees a variable level of pension tax breaks. For example, Keogh Plans may be established for some small businesses. Individual retirement accounts (IRA) may be maintained by nearly all individuals but they receive varying tax breaks according to the contributor's current income. Deferred payment annuities and the so called 401K plans are also available to supplement a retiree's income.

* * *

Problems

1. An employee of ABC Co., operated a punch press on the assembly line. Such machines typically place thousands of pounds of pressure on a work piece placed in a work area. The punch press operated by George punched four half inch holes into each work piece that George processed through it. OSHA requires that all punch presses be fitted with a safety device to prevent the employee from operating the machine until the operator's hand is removed from the dangerous work area. The safety gate and interlock protection device on George's punch press malfunctioned. George complained to his supervisor about the failure of the safety feature but was told to continue using the machine anyway. George refused and was immediately fired. What argument might George make that his dismissal was wrongful? What counter-argument might ABC Co. make to justify its termination of George?

2. The OSHA system requires comprehensive safety and health maintenance procedures and devices in the workplace. By contrast, the workers' compensation system in each state provides for compensation for workers injured at the jobsite. While the OSHA system appears to be preventative and the workers' compensation curative, is there a more fundamental relationship between the two?

3. Both the OSHA and workers' compensation systems developed as a result of inadequacies in the tort compensation systems and from a general impression that workplaces were unsafe. Describe the major barriers to an employee's maintenance of a damage action for a workplace injury.

4. Joe and Sue are co-workers at the ABC Company each performing nearly identical tasks. However, Joe is paid nearly 20% more than Sue for this substantially similar work. On what basis might Sue argue that this comparative compensation violates the Equal Pay Act? On what basis might the employer respond that Joe is entitled to higher compensation?

5. The State Retirement Plan requires contributions from both the state and each employee into the state pension system. Both contributions and benefits are computed based on actuarial and mortality tables of life expectancy. Females typically live seven to eight years longer than males and will therefore be able to collect considerably higher retirement benefits. As a result, the pension plan administrator requires females to make considerably higher contributions than male employees. On what basis might females covered under this state retirement plan complain that the contribution levels constitute unlawful sex discrimination? On what basis might the plant administrator argue that equal contributions constitute unlawful sex discrimination?

6. The Alabama statute establishing its prison and rehabilitation system prohibited females from appointment as rehabilitation counselors for prisons holding all males under maximum security conditions. The rule prohibited women employees wherever there was "contact" requiring close physical interaction with male inmates. On what basis might a female applicant for a counselor's position argue this rule violated Title VII of the Civil Rights Act? On what basis might the state justify its use of the "contact" rule?

7. The G Company, a large integrated automobile manufacturer, operated a subsidiary, the GF Company, that financed the purchase of the G Company's automobiles. GF employed many persons from each of its district offices to collect overdue accounts and repossess automobiles after the owners defaulted. GF employees averaged over 50 hours of work each week usually without direct supervision because they were busy collecting or repossessing in the field. Although the G Company had a policy of accurate reporting of all hours worked, lower level supervisors at the GF subsidiary generally intimidated these employees into reporting only forty hours per week. Is this activity a violation of the overtime provisions of the FLSA?

15

Antitrust Law

Antitrust Law

$\mathbf{T}$HE **ANTITRUST LAWS** are designed to maintain competition among businesses and prevent the natural tendency to collude. The Antitrust Laws create legal rights and a regulatory environment encouraging business to act consistently with the assumptions underlying the perfect competition model. This chapter discusses the predominant antitrust restrictions on monopolies, mergers, restraints of trade, price fixing, resale price maintenance, division of markets, price discrimination, tying, exclusive dealerships, and other unfair trade practices. Additionally, the challenges of regulating competition in international trade are discussed.

I. Federal Antitrust Laws

During the post-Civil War period of the industrial expansion, businesses grew to enormous size with fewer firms competing for larger market shares. This concentration of wealth and power triggered a populist reaction against the anticompetitive practices of some large businesses. For example, the railroads had a monopoly over transportation and allegedly charged discriminatory prices favoring some large customers. Monopolies were created in the oil and steel industries that exerted unfair pressure on customers and suppliers. Congress enacted antitrust laws in reaction to these and other allegations that true competition did not exist because large companies routinely set arbitrary prices and reduced their production below socially optimal levels. Pressure from the populists resulted in passage of several regulatory laws in addition to the federal antitrust statutes.

A. Sherman Act

Congress passed the Sherman Act in 1890 to prohibit anticompetitive practices and prevent restraints of trade where monopolists erect barriers to free competition. Section 1 of the Sherman Act outlaws any contract, combination, or conspiracy in restraint of trade. Section 2 makes it a criminal act to monopolize or attempt to monopolize or for combinations or conspiracies to monopolize any part of the trade or commerce among the several states or with foreign nations. Although the Act originally made monopolization a misdemeanor, today it is a felony.

B. Clayton Act

Criticism over the government's lackluster enforcement of the Sherman Act during its first twenty years resulted in Congress passing the Clayton Act in 1914. While the Sherman Act was written in rather general terms, the Clayton Act is more specific about which acts are outlawed. The Sherman Act requires proof of completed anticompetitive effects before the Act is violated. By contrast, the Clayton Act is violated if an anticompetitive tendency arises from the defendant's conduct. Section 3 of the Clayton Act specifically prohibits tie-in sales, exclusive dealing arrangements, and requirements contracts that substantially lessen competition or tend to create a monopoly. Section 7 of the Clayton Act prohibits interlocking directorates and merger activity that results in a substantial lessening of competition. The Clayton Act's greater specificity, its more sensitive standards for violation, and its treble damage provisions have made it the stronger antitrust law.

C. Federal Trade Commission Act

Another part of the legislative package Congress passed in 1914 included the Federal Trade Commission Act (FTC Act). This Act created the Federal Trade Commission (FTC) and gave it broad enforcement powers over unfair methods of competition, unfair deceptive acts or practices, and responsibility to enforce the Sherman and Clayton Acts.

Congress has passed additional antitrust laws in later years that strengthen the FTC's power and the pro-competitive antitrust law scheme. The Robinson-Patman Act was passed in 1936 outlawing price discrimination. The Celler-Kefauver Act amended the Clayton Act by extending the merger prohibition to corporate combinations affected through the sale of assets. The Hart-Scott-Rodino Antitrust Improvements Act was passed in 1976 expanding the Justice Department's powers to investigate antitrust violations. This Act requires public notice of mergers prior to actual completion. It also empowers the various states' Attorneys General to prosecute antitrust violations that damage the state's citizens.

II. Non-Competitive Market Structures

The Antitrust Laws are designed to maintain atomized economic power and avoid its concentration into the hands of fewer persons. Such enforcement allegedly prevents the buildup of economic power that can be used to fix artificially high prices or reduce production below socially optimal amounts. The Antitrust Laws favor the classic perfect competition market model. When markets have a sufficient number of informed buyers and sellers there will be sufficient quantities produced to satisfy demand at prices that provide a fair but not excessive return to producers.

The antitrust laws draw their name from a business organization form used in the late 19th century to create a monopolies. *Trusts* are contractual arrangements in which the owners of property convey legal title to a trustee who manages that property. The owners of several competing firms would transfer their ownership to a single trustee who would vote the shares to elect directors who willingly colluded to fix prices and set production output. The antitrust laws were originally designed to break up this type of monopoly. Today, of course, a monopoly could be secured through merger or by collusion among distinct and separate competitors. The Sherman Act was used to break up the members of the Standard Oil Trust into the familiar present day constituents: Standard Oil of California (Chevron), Standard Oil of Indiana (Amoco), Standard Oil of New York (Mobil), Standard Oil of New Jersey (Exxon), and Standard Oil of Ohio (Sohio, BP Oil), and others.

A. Industrial Organization

The theoretical underpinnings of antitrust law is derived from traditional economic analysis. This defines five basic market structures used to predict the behavior of consumers and producers. These structures include: perfect competition, monopoly, oligopoly, monopolistic competition, and monopsony. Few markets actually exhibit all the characteristics of any of these basic market structures. However, they are useful analytical tools to predict purchasing behaviors of consumers and production and pricing behaviors of sellers.

1. PERFECT COMPETITION

Perfect competition, the goal of the antitrust laws, is a market structure where a large number of buyers and sellers exist. No individual producer or consumer has enough market power to influence prices or production quantities. Perfectly competitive markets have low barriers to entry, rather uniform products and buyers and sellers are well informed about market conditions and the characteristics of all producers' products. While perfect competition probably does not exist in the real world, it is possible to modify some of the model's assumptions and implications. The retail markets for securities, gasoline, and groceries in larger markets often come close to this perfect competition model.

2. MONOPOLY

A *monopoly* is a market dominated by one large seller. The seller's product has no close substitutes. It is difficult for other seller's to enter the market due to high *barriers to entry*. These may come from legal sources such as a patent, copyright, or franchise. Barriers may also arise naturally by virtue of the large number of assets needed to produce a complex product. The producers of patented goods and most utilities are the best contemporary examples of monopolies.

3. OLIGOPOLY

An *oligopoly* is a market structure where there are a small number of sellers; each has some market power to influence prices or the amount of available supply. Typically there are high barriers to entry for new or substitute products and the potential for collusion is great. Oligopolistic markets tend to have higher prices and lower quantities produced than under perfect competition but are somewhat less restrictive markets than under monopoly conditions. The domestic U.S. steel market was regarded as an oligopoly in the early 20th century.

4. MONOPOLISTIC COMPETITION

Monopolistic competition is a hybrid market form in which there are few sellers with products that are slightly differentiated from each other but are somewhat substitutable. For example, the automobile market is allegedly a monopolistic competitive market. The various models produced by each auto maker can be distinguished in the minds of consumers yet most automobiles are interchangeable for the general purpose of basic transportation. Monopolistic competitive markets are not perfectively competitive.

5. MONOPSONY

Monopoly powers may be held by buyers. This market structure is often referred to as a *monopsony*. Where a single buyer possesses monopoly buying power, a monopsony exists. This gives the buyer great control over the prices charged or amount purchased. *Oligopsony* conditions exists where there are a few buyers each possessing some market power. A single employer in a company town is an example of the monopsony buyer's market power over labor in that town. These forms of industrial organization are summarized in figure 15-1.

B. Approaches to Antitrust Enforcement

The strength of antitrust enforcement efforts over the past century have varied quite widely. The court initially reacted to the Sherman Act by ignore it and continue to applying the *laissez-faire* economic theory restraining government from intervening in the markets. Populist reaction to this lack of enforcement led to passage of the Clayton and FTC Acts and it triggered a swing towards more active enforcement. From time to time, depending on the economic and political theories of the presidential administration, antitrust enforcement has varied between laissez-faire and strict enforcement.

FIGURE 15.1 FORMS OF INDUSTRIAL ORGANIZATION

Competitive Market Structure	Characteristics and Effects
Perfect Competition	Marketplace consists of many sellers and buyers all with perfect information. There are low barriers to a new seller entering the market. Numerous other products may be substituted for the product in question. Results: efficient market
Monopoly	Marketplace consists of one seller with the market power to set prices, and lower production / output. There are high barriers to entry and few substitutes. Results: abnormal monopoly profits to the monopolist and little innovation..
Oligopoly	Marketplace consists of few sellers with at least some market power to set prices. There are high barriers to entry and few adequate substitutes. Results: some abnormal monopoly profits to oligopolists and slow innovation
Monopolistic Competition	Marketplace consists of few sellers with some market power and high barriers to entry. Substitutes exist but "appear" inadequate in consumers' minds. Results: some abnormal monopoly profits to monopolistic competitors and slow innovation.
Monopsony	Marketplace consists of single buyer with market power to set low prices and require flexible amount of production. There are high barriers to entry by other buyers. Results: buyer uses market power to transfer seller's profits to buyer.

1. STRUCTURALISTS

There are three general approaches to anti-trust enforcement derived from two schools of thought that have become the ideological homes for anti-trust enforcement theorists. *Structuralists* examine the existing organization of each industry with a view to identify noncompetitive market structures. They examine the existing buyers and sellers and infer the degree of industry concentration. Structuralists quantify the size of the market, the number of sellers, the degree of differentiation among competing products, and the barriers to entry. They often recommend strict antitrust enforcement to eliminate anti-competitive effects in their incipiency.

2. CONDUCT APPROACH

A middle ground is represented by the *conduct approach* that examines the actual business practices and behaviors of firms and the resulting inefficiencies and breakdowns in competition. The pricing and production policies of existing firms are examined for illegal acts. Conduct analysts suggest antitrust enforcement when there is anticompetitive conduct in production, pricing, advertising, research, and innovation.

3. PERFORMANCE APPROACH

A third school of thought focuses on the actual performance of the market in question.

Rather than inhibiting firms behavior based on inferences about their potential or actual conduct, *performance analysts* look to how well the market actually performs. They use measures of economic efficiency, technical innovation, the reasonability of profits and pricing performance, and the barriers to entry resulting in the marketplace. Performance analysts would urge the most lenient antitrust enforcement of the three approaches.

4. HARVARD SCHOOL VS. CHICAGO SCHOOL

The three approaches just discussed are the subject of a continuing debate between the two ideological homes of antitrust enforcement. The Harvard or traditional school advocates vigorous antitrust enforcement. The Harvard School presumes that concentration of economic power leads to monopolistic behavior. The Chicago School take the opposite approach insisting on a carefully structured economic analysis of a challenged market before initiating antitrust enforcement. Chicago School theorists tolerate some monopolistic activities if their effects are short term. Chicago School theorists prefer nonintervention by government into the markets relying on the natural tendency of markets to correct anticompetitive behavior.

C. International Antitrust Enforcement Problems

The trade laws of most nations are designed to favor each nation's domestic industry at the expense of foreign firms. Tariffs and controls over export and imports are often inherently anticompetitive because they erect barriers to competition from foreign firms. However, proponents of these laws claim they actually encourage competition from their emerging national industries because it is difficult to enter an established marketplace already dominated by large foreign corporations from well developed countries. Subtle anticompetitive trade barriers are also erected by foreign nations' regulatory programs that impose excessive taxes, inspection delays, or costs to adapt products for foreign markets. While most industrialized nations have adopted antitrust laws, they vary greatly. Few foreign antitrust laws are as well developed as U.S. law. Some nations still resist any vigorous antitrust enforcement, presumably to favor their home industries for nationalistic and political reasons.

The competition laws of the European Economic Community (EEC) are among the most specific and of great potential interest to U.S. competitors. The Treaty of Rome that established the EEC, generally prohibits agreements and concerted anticompetitive practices that fix prices, control production, limit development of markets or technologies, allocate markets, impose discriminatory supply contract terms, require tying relations, or are monopolistic. These matters are generally illegal under U.S. antitrust laws and are discussed in greater detail later in this chapter.

I. EXTRATERRITORIALITY OF U.S. ANTITRUST LAWS

The U.S. antitrust laws are written broadly enough to apply to the anticompetitive acts of non-U.S. corporations when they impact U.S. imports, exports, or competition in the U.S. At one time, U.S. antitrust enforcement authorities and some U.S. private plaintiffs urged broad application of the U.S. antitrust laws to the alleged anticompetitive acts of foreign corporations. At that time, few nations had monopoly laws as well developed as U.S. laws; many nations had no antitrust laws at all.

Foreign courts can refuse to enforce a U.S. antitrust judgment against the foreign nation's home corporation if the nation has no antitrust law similar to U.S. law. However, judgments are still effective against the foreign corporation's assets held in the U.S. or held by its U.S. subsidiary. U.S. courts also restrict the U.S. antitrust laws from applying to

Example. A U.S. union, the International Association of Machinists and Aerospace Workers, charged the Organization of Petroleum Exporting Countries (OPEC) with violating the Sherman Act through its price fixing of world petroleum prices. The union sought an injunction against OPEC's implementation of its price fixing scheme. Under this scheme, OPEC member nations colluded to set "fair" world oil prices to permit OPEC members to achieve economic and political independence.

Each nation is an independent sovereign with control over its economic activities. U.S. courts will not decide politically sensitive issues involving the legality of a foreign sovereign government's act. Political assessments of a foreign nation's acts are best left to negotiation by the U.S. Executive branch, not the U.S. courts. Court action might insult foreign nations and frustrate foreign policy-making. This is an exclusive responsibility of the executive branch requiring the advice and consent of the U.S. Senate. The OPEC suit was dismissed as an excessive incursion into the other nations' sovereign rights. ☐

the anticompetitive acts of foreign corporations or foreign governments. The U.S. courts may exercise jurisdiction: (1) when the foreign action affects international commerce with the U.S., (2) the U.S. antitrust law does not conflict with the foreign nation's law, (3) compliance is likely, and (4) the right of foreign governments to act independently to protect their home industries are considered. U.S. courts' consideration of these factors is now required under the Foreign Trade Antitrust Improvements Act of 1982.

2. BLOCKING LAWS

Many foreign nations have attempted to thwart enforcement of the U.S. antitrust laws with the passage of *blocking laws*. These laws make it illegal in the foreign nation to provide documents requested in a pre-trial discovery request by a U.S. plaintiff or regulator. Some blocking laws require notification of the foreign government before compliance giving foreign regulators an opportunity to block compliance.

Blocking laws make it difficult to prove collusive activity by non-U.S. corporations. U.S. courts must tolerate a foreign defendant's position when blocking laws or foreign government action compels them to refrain from cooperating with U.S. antitrust litigation. For example, the U.S. courts are more lenient when a foreign government compels an antitrust defendant to take some anticompetitive action or the foreign government prohibits the defendant from testifying or supplying information in pre-trial discovery.

III. Antitrust Exemptions

The Antitrust Laws and several other regulatory programs provide exemption for some business activities. Some industries or activities may freely use restraints of trade to insure their survival or encourage their development. For example, public utilities are granted a limited monopoly within a specified geographic service area because the cost of competition would burden society too greatly. The anti-competitive pricing tendencies of monopolies are generally controlled through public utility rate regulation. Patent holders are given a government granted monopoly for 17 years to encourage innovation and development of new ideas and processes. Society permits this limited monopoly for a short time in exchange for the eventual revelation of the invention into the public domain. In addition to these regulatory programs, some other industries have gained specific antitrust exemption.

A. Agricultural Cooperatives

Nonprofit agricultural cooperatives are specifically exempt from the Clayton Act. Cooperatives provide mutual assistance to farmers and others engaged in agricultural production. The exemption extends to fisherman's cooperatives but not to packing houses or associations involved in both production and distribution.

B. Labor Unions

The concerted activities of labor unions are inherently noncompetitive. Labor unions provide a forum for employees to collude and effectively fix prices through their concerted bargaining power in negotiating with employers. This is considered justifiable because employers exert monopsonistic market power in their purchase of employment services. The National Labor Relations Act is a comprehensive federal regulatory program for labor union activities. It is considered a substitute regulatory program for the competitive practices of labor-management relations. However, the antitrust laws are still applicable to labor union activities that result in a conspiracy to restrain trade. Labor union activities that create monopolies or control marketing are not exempt. A union's insistence that the employer not deal with a particular supplier or customer is an anticompetitive act.

C. State Action

Sometimes governmental actions result in restraints of trade or monopolization. This is usually considered a valid exercise of state action and is exempt from the Sherman Act. For example, states license the sale of liquor and firearms which often results in fewer sellers of these products. The states may validly exercise their police powers to protect the public from dangerous substances or activities. Therefore, state action that creates the restraint of trade may be exempt from the antitrust laws.

The state action exemption applies where there is a clearly defined state policy regarding the regulated activity. However, where a government is involved in nongovernmental functions there is no state action exemption and the antitrust laws may apply. For example, in one case a conspiracy by municipally owned utilities was subject to antitrust enforcement. In another case, a conspiracy between a city's sports stadium and it's airport authority was designed to exclude a particular brand of beer from sale at either facility. In another case, the state action exemption was held inapplicable to a city's restriction of the local cable television operator's expansion into a new service territory.

D. Regulated Industries

There are several industries that are regulated comprehensively by state or federal regulatory schemes. Many of these of these industries activities are exempt from the antitrust laws. For example, the insurance industry collects actuarial information from all insurance companies, to better understand insurance risks. This activity would probably be illegal as price fixing. The McCarren-Ferguson Act of 1945 gave a special exemption for insurance companies. However, if insurance companies become involved in boycotts, or intimidation of competitors, these activities would probably not be exempt. Stock exchanges also share a limited form of antitrust exemption. Banks and other financial institutions are often merged together without regard to the antitrust laws.

E. Professions

The learned professions have often been held exempt from the antitrust laws. The professional codes of conduct applicable to lawyers, doctors, and engineers have often had an anti-competitive effect. For example, local bar associations routinely set minimum prices for legal services in a "minimum fee schedule."

These fee structures were justified as a method of assuring minimum quality of legal services. A similar provision in the Ethical Code for Engineers prohibited them from bidding competitively for engineering engagements. However, this provision was also invalidated as a restraint on competition. Most of the activities of professional sports are subject to the antitrust laws. However, only professional baseball is entitled to an antitrust exemption, other sports remain subject to the antitrust laws: professional football, boxing, hockey, and basketball. Pressures to make sports more competitive have resulted in the rules of "free agency."

IV. Monopolies

The Sherman Act originally targeted monopolies as the basic form of anticompetitive industrial organization. Monopolists have the power to fix prices, reduce output, and exclude competitors. The Sherman Act's prohibition against intentional acts of monopolization is analyzed through a focus on the exercise of monopoly power within a relevant market. This requires the court to determine the geographic and product markets and then examine the alleged monopolist's market share and predatory acts.

Monopoly power is usually determined by examining the elasticity of demand in the challenged product market. Highly elastic markets seldom permit the exercise of monopoly power because there are numerous producers but none of them has market power. Therefore, if one producer raises its price, consumers can quickly and easily switch to make their purchases from other producers. Small changes in price result in large changes in the amount of a product purchased from any single particular producer.

Markets with monopoly power are generally *inelastic*. Purchasers are less able to switch and make their purchases from other producers or purchase substitute products if one

seller changes its price significantly. In an inelastic market one seller could raise it's price without loosing many customers because other sellers do not produce sufficient quantities to make up for the lost supply. For example, the manufacture of a key microprocessor is usually able to raise its price without loosing most of its customers. Electronic chips are proprietary so other firms usually do not make identical chips and so other firm's chips are often functionally incompatible. By contrast, when a single gas station raises it's price there are usually many other competing gas stations with sufficient inventories of gas. If they stay at the lower price then purchasers can quickly and easily switch to other sellers. Such markets are elastic and not susceptible to monopolization. The determination of monopoly power requires definition of the relevant market.

A. Determination of Relevant Market

The concept of a monopoly is meaningful only when it is defined by boundaries of the alleged monopolist's relevant market. This requires an identification of the geographic market and the product market over which the monopolist allegedly exercises market power. Relevant market analysis is used in monopoly cases as well as in cases of mergers and illegal restraints of trade. The basic inquiry is to determine the size of the product or service market, then, identify all other competitors, their respective market shares, and all other products or services that are functionally interchangeable and available to the same pool of potential consumers.

I. GEOGRAPHIC MARKET

The predominant factor in determining the geographic market is the cost of transporting goods or the ease with which consumer's can gain access to various sellers. A monopolist has market power only within a specific re-

421

Example.   DP Corp. produced 3/4 of the cellophane (plastic food wrap) in the United States. However, cellophane represented only about 20 percent of all flexible packaging materials sold in the U.S. The Justice Department charged DP Corp. monopolized the cellophane market. DP responded that the relevant market constituted all flexible packaging material including wax paper, aluminum foil, and plastic bags.

In determining the relevant market, analysis must focus on all those products that are reasonable interchangeable for the defendant's products. The cross-elasticities of demand for all reasonably substitutable products must be considered. Despite DP Corp's monopoly power over the cellophane market, their small market share of the broader, flexible packaging material market was too small to constitute a monopoly. ☐

gion. Where consumers can easily change to make their purchases from among different nearby sellers, this defines a geographic region. The litigants in a monopoly case must usually present evidence about buyers' commuting patterns.

Geographic markets may be considered local (neighborhood, metropolitan), regional (single state, few states), national, or multinational. For example, the geographic market for grocery shopping could be within a neighborhood in a large city like New York City where many consumers use public transport or walk to the grocery store. By contrast in most suburban areas, consumers use their automobiles exclusively and the geographic boundary of a retail grocery market might be expanded to an entire county within a metropolitan area.

2. PRODUCT MARKET

A monopoly can exist over several products or services that consumers use for the same basic purpose. In determining the relevant product market, there is usually a comparison of physically dissimilar products that are perceived by consumers as reasonably interchangeable or substitutable. The price, use, and quality of somewhat different but similar products are analyzed to determine whether they should be combined together to comprise a single market. For example, while butter and margarine are chemically different products, many consumers view them as reasonably substitutable for the same purposes.

Economists have developed the concept of *cross-elasticity of demand* to determine the relationship between two potentially substitutable products. In an antitrust suit the plaintiff typically alleges that the defendant's products are not substitutable with other products. If the plaintiff is successful, the size of the product market is diminished and this tends to make the defendant's portion of that market appear larger, more like a monopoly. Defendant's have an opposite incentive, they attempt to show there are numerous substitute products to the defendant's product. When defendants are successful in proving this, the market is enlarged, making the defendant's portion appear much smaller and less likely to constitute a monopoly. This creates a tension between plaintiffs and defendants and their expert witnesses in monopolization cases. One side seeks to expand the market by proving numerous products are substitutable while the other side hopes to restrict substitutes by alleging low cross-elasticities of demand.

The product market analysis used in the example above needs refinement to better capture specific consumer preferences and buying patterns. For example, in the flexible packaging market, some of the substitute

Example.   After its patent expired, the A Company of America remained the only producer of virgin aluminum ingot in the U.S. A Company had successfully deterred two attempts by competitors to enter the aluminum industry. Whenever it appeared that demand would rise for aluminum, the A Company built new production capacity and brought it on line just in time to satisfy all the new demand.

The preemptive acts of A Company constituted exclusionary acts purposely conducted to prevent competitors from entering the market. This is not a case of a producer passively having the market thrust upon it. Nothing compelled it to double and redouble its capacity before others could enter the field. Therefore, the intentional exclusionary acts of the A Company can be inferred from it's conscious addition of capacity, which preempted the entry of other competitors into the field.

products used to expand the relevant market are clearly not substitutable for some consumer's uses. It was inappropriate to include all aluminum foil sales within the flexible packaging market because aluminum foil has some unique uses for which plastic is unsuitable (barbecue grilling). Likewise, plastic and paper flexible packaging materials are suitable for some uses for which aluminum is unsuitable (in microwave ovens). Therefore, it is inappropriate to include all the production of both types of flexible packaging material in the total market. By doing so the analysis makes the impossible assumption that all users of either product could switch to the other product for any use. A more accurate analysis would reduce a portion of total sales from the substitute products for which they are unsuitable. Such a refinement tends to narrow the relevant market and the defendant comes closer to monopolization.

Another problem with the cross-elasticity analysis of substitutes involves how perfectly these other products actually substitute for the purpose of the product in question. For example, most consumers consider resealable plastic bags superior to cellophane for wrapping sandwiches and other foods. However, if the price of plastic bags increased significantly over the price of cellophane many more persons would probably substitute cellophane for plastic bags. It is hard to imagine

any two different products that are perfectly substitutable for each other without adjusting for their difference in price. Cross-elasticity analysis is also used to restrict markets that may first appear to be larger. For example, professional championship boxing matches are considered a market distinct from all boxing generally, major and minor league baseball are distinct markets, and gospel music is a market distinct from popular music.

3.   MARKET SHARE

Relevant market determination is the first step in judging whether a monopoly is unlawful. The next step is to measure the defendant's market share, the percentage or fraction of the total market the defendant controls. The fraction is computed by inserting the defendant's sales as the numerator and the total sales of all competitors and all manufacturers of substitutes as the denominator. While there are no magic formulas to test this market share for the presence of a monopoly, it is obvious that higher percentages suggest monopoly while lower percentages do not represent a monopoly.

B. Monopolization

It is not illegal to possess monopoly power, the Sherman Act makes it illegal to intentionally use monopoly power to gain a monopoly. *Monopolization* is the intentional misuse of a monopoly power through undertaking purposeful acts to harm competitors, consumers, and deter potential competitors from entering the market. Proof of monopolistic intent is essential to the prohibition of a monopoly.

Purposeful acts of monopolization may be inferred from other acts. For example, a lease only policy was considered exclusionary and unlawful by the major computer manufacturer because it never sold the product. Another exclusionary activity is *predatory pricing*, pricing below the producer's marginal cost. A manufacturer's marginal cost is the additional expense necessary to produce one more unit. When a producer prices below *marginal* cost, it is taking losses on all those units sold. The manufacturer may attempt to subsidize these losses by making profits on sales made in other regions that are not part of this geographic market or by making profits on sales on the first few units sold at higher prices. Predatory pricing is designed to undercut a competitor with unprofitable sales to drive them out of business. After competitors are eliminated, the seller can raise prices and recoup losses from the units sold below marginal cost.

C. Attempted Monopolization

In cases where a seller has no clear monopoly power, the Sherman Act still prohibits any attempt to monopolize. Where the seller uses methods, means, and practices that might accomplish a monopolization or come close to monopolization, then an illegal attempt to violate the Sherman Act is also prohibited. In attempted monopolization cases the law requires a more stringent burden of proof, the prosecutor must prove specific intent to monopolize. Intent to monopolize can be inferred from the circumstances such as the use of discriminatory pricing, the refusal to deal with particular customers, or inducing the boycott of a competitor's product.

V. Mergers

Merger activity is regulated under several regulatory schemes. First, the actual merger process is governed by the corporation law of the state of the corporation. Second, battles for the control of publicly-traded corporations usually involve the proxy solicitation process or a tender offer, these have an impact on the national securities markets. Regulations of the Securities and Exchange Commission and enforcement powers created in the Williams Act apply to this part of the merger process. The anti-trust laws are fundamental to the regulation of mergers because the industrial organization of producers is altered in that market. Anti-trust law prohibits mergers or acquisitions which tend to create an illegal monopoly.

A. Types of Mergers

Mergers are business combinations that bring together two previously independent firms, one firm survives and the other is dissolved after transferring its assets and liabilities to the survivor. The same economic affect is accomplished with a *consolidation* which arises after the merging firms both dissolve and a new third entity is created to inherit the merging firms' assets and liabilities. When one firm purchases the assets of another firm the transaction also resembles a merger. An *acquisition* involves the purchase of one firm's stock by another firm. The anti-trust analysis discussed here treats all these transactions as mergers. They are all judged by whether the business combination will result in an monopoly. Generally the Clayton Act is used to oppose mergers even though the broader Sherman Act could be adapted to challenge mergers that result in a monopolization.

Section 7 of the Clayton Act generally provides that no person engaged in commerce shall acquire directly or indirectly the whole or any part of the stock or assets of another company where the combination would tend

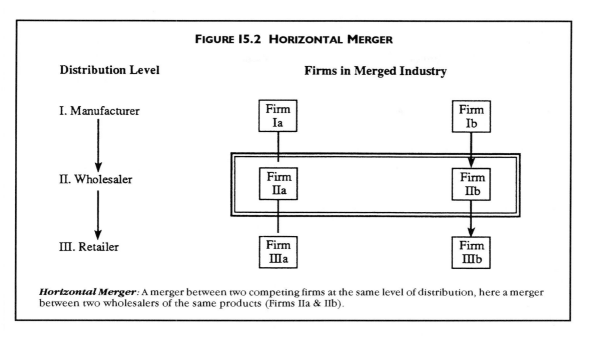

FIGURE 15.2 HORIZONTAL MERGER

Distribution Level

Firms in Merged Industry

I. Manufacturer

II. Wholesaler

III. Retailer

Firm Ia   Firm Ib

Firm IIa   Firm IIb

Firm IIIa   Firm IIIb

Horizontal Merger: A merger between two competing firms at the same level of distribution, here a merger between two wholesalers of the same products (Firms IIa & IIb).

to create a monopoly in any line of commerce or activity affecting commerce. *Horizontal mergers* are the least justifiable under the anti-trust laws because they involve combinations between competitors. Such mergers often result in acquisition of excessive market power facilitating monopolization.

Mergers between firms that stand in a supplier/customer relationship are called *vertical mergers*, a form of vertical integration along the same chain of distribution such as when manufacturers acquire their sales outlets or their suppliers. Mergers that cannot be classified as either horizontal or vertical are generally considered conglomerate mergers. These typically involve numerous acquisitions of firms in other industries, in other product lines, and at any level of production.

B. Analyses of a Horizontal Merger

The regulation of horizontal mergers is the least controversial because a combination of competitors is most likely to lead to monopolization. A variation of monopoly analysis is used in merger cases. This requires a determination of the relevant market and market shares controlled by the two firms before and after the merger. Therefore, it is essential to determine the relevant geographic market and product markets as discussed in the previous section. Figure 15.2 depicts a horizontal merger.

I. HERFINDAHL INDEX

The U.S. Justice Department is the primary enforcement agency that challenges allegedly illegal mergers. The Justice Department has developed guidelines to determine the extent of market concentration that will result from a proposed merger and therefore whether it will lead to a monopoly. Concentrated markets have fewer firms each with greater market power. Atomized or unconcentrated markets have many selling firms and therefore

425

Example. A proposed merger between V Grocery Store Company and the SB Food Stores, both operating in the Los Angeles area, were challenged by the Justice Department. The V Grocery Store Chain ranked third in market share and SB ranked six. After the merger, the combined company would have only 7.5% of the Los Angeles retail grocery trade. Both companies had experienced tremendous growth in recent years while at the same time this growth displaced small independent grocers at a rapid rate.

The obvious trend in the market towards concentration and the elimination of small competitors is a decisive factor in blocking this merger even though it results in a combined market share of less than 10%. The immediate impact of the merger as well as predictions of the future impact of the merged enterprise upon competitive conditions permit blocking this merger. The Clayton Act may be used to stop anti-competitive tendencies in their beginning. In this case a continuous decline in the number of small businesses and rapid concentration of the industry to a few large sellers is sufficient evidence to block this merger. ☐

approach the perfect competition ideal so little harmful monopoly power is held by any particular firm.

The Justice Department uses the *Herfindahl Index* as an indicator of the degree of market concentration. This index is computed by summing the squares of each individual competitors' market share. As the Herfindahl Index number grows higher the market becomes dominated by a few sellers with market power. For example, where a market has one firm with 50% market share and five firms each with 10% market share, the Herfindahl Index would be computed as $50^2 + 10^2 + 10^2 + 10^2 + 10^2 + 10^2 = 3,000$. Herfindahl Index numbers can range from a high of 10,000 where a single firm with a pure monopoly has a 100% market share ($100^2 = 10,000$) to less than I for a perfectly competitive market with hundreds of sellers.

The Justice Department challenges mergers where the change in Herfindahl Index number rises significantly from before the merger to afterwards. For example, where the Herfindahl Index is 1800 before the merger and rises by more than 50 points afterwards, the merger will be challenged. If the index lies between 1,000 and 1,800, a merger is challenged if the Herfindahl Index number increases by 100 or more. The Justice Department is unlikely to challenger mergers where the Herfindahl Index number lies below 1,000. While the Herfindahl Index number is quite influential in determining whether a merger will be challenged by the Justice Department, it is not binding on the courts. However, as a practical matter, most mergers are not attempted if a Justice Department challenge is probable.

The courts are empowered to block a challenged merger if it will result in a substantial lessening of competition. The Clayton Act does not require proof of attempts at predatory conduct or monopolistic acts. While complex quantitative economic analysis or projections of the merger's effect are not required in merger litigation, both the Justice Department and the FTC use such measures in their merger analysis.

C. Analysis of Vertical Mergers

Mergers between suppliers and customers are analyzed by the same method used for horizontal merger analysis. The relevant geographic and product markets of the potential merger partners are first determined. Next, the expected effect the proposed merger will

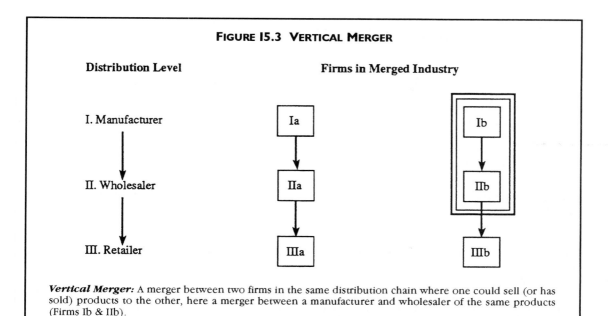

FIGURE 15.3 VERTICAL MERGER

Distribution Level   Firms in Merged Industry

I. Manufacturer

II. Wholesaler

III. Retailer

Vertical Merger: A merger between two firms in the same distribution chain where one could sell (or has sold) products to the other, here a merger between a manufacturer and wholesaler of the same products (Firms Ib & IIb).

have on competition is analyzed. This requires consideration of historical trends towards concentration, the nature and purpose of the merger, and barriers to entry resulting from the merger are considered. However, because vertical mergers do not immediately result in more concentrated markets, the merger's impact on competition may be unclear. The focus of analysis is on the potential foreclosure on competition and the resulting barriers to new firms entering the market. For example, a vertical merger could be anti-competitive if other competitors were required to integrate vertically in order to compete more effectively against the merged firm. Figure 15.3 depicts a vertical merger.

Vertical mergers may facilitate collusion in a highly concentrated upstream market (among the suppliers). If manufacturers own their retail outlets competing manufacturers' prices become more visible. Competing manufacturers must reveal their prices to sell to

retail outlets owned by a vertically integrated manufacturer. By contrast, when numerous competing retail outlets maintain their independence, manufacturers are forced to compete for the retail outlets' business. Vertical mergers are challenged when the resulting market would have less competitive discipline permitting price fixing or the loss of competitive pressure on pricing and innovation.

D. Analysis of Conglomerate Mergers

The regulation of conglomerate mergers is the most controversial because ostensibly there appears to be no anti-competitive effect. Opponents of conglomerate mergers point out they tend to reinforce oligopoly conditions. This arguably weakening independent firms ultimately leading to an elimination of competition. When large firms enter new

Example. The merger between the B Shoe Company and the K Shoe Company was challenged as an illegal vertical merger. Both companies manufactured and retailed shoes. The merger was blocked because it was likely to substantially lessen competition as a result of its vertical effects.

When a retail customer is tied to a particular supplier, competition by other suppliers to gain shelf space at that retailer is substantially lessened. The retailer will either carry the manufacturers' products exclusively or give them preference with more competitive prices, adequate inventories supplies, and promotional activity. The size of these two shoe companies was so great that a substantial portion of the shoe market would be foreclosed and this would lessen competition. □

markets by acquiring smaller firms, the large firm brings financial resources and the goodwill of popular name brands to the merged firm. These resources make it more difficult for independent firms to compete in the acquired firm's market. A large conglomerate can use discriminatory and exclusionary practices to intimidate and discipline smaller competitors resulting in a substantial lessening of competition. Figure 15.4 depicts a conglomerate merger.

I. POTENTIAL ENTRANT

One basis for challenging conglomerate mergers is the *potential entrant* or *potential competitor* effect. This theory suggests that competitors will remain efficient, price their products competitively and strive toward innovation only while they perceive that an outside firm may come into the market. These outside firms, known as potential entrants, are perceived to be waiting in the wings so their presence imposes discipline on existing competitors. This *edge effect* is lost if the potential entrant simply merges within an existing firm thereby eliminating the competitive discipline from the potential competitor. A conglomerate merger may eliminate any future pro-competitive deconcentration of the industry. Under this theory, it is preferable for the potential entrant to enter the market on its own and thereby increase the number of competitors.

Those challenging a conglomerate merger must prove that the existing competitors in the market perceived that an outside firm was likely to enter the market soon. Without this perception, there is no competitive discipline that could be lost by market competitors in response to the merger so the merger should probably not be prohibited. The second factor to be proved is that the acquiring firm had a reasonable means to enter the market without a merger. Such a firm should not merge with an existing competitor because it would reduce competitive discipline. Instead, competition would be enhanced if the potential entrant joined the market *de novo.* The third factor requires that only a few potential entrants exist. If there are numerous potential entrants the elimination of only one would probably not be harmful to the competitive discipline exerted by the edge effect.

E. Defenses to Merger Challenges

When merging firms are challenged by regulators they may be able to justify the transaction with a merger defense. First, the merging firms may claim the merger will result in greater efficiency. For example, if the merged firm might eliminate jobs and unnecessary facilities without reducing production, then the lowered cost could be passed on to consumers through lower price. The second defense is the failing firm defense. Merging firms might allege that one of the merger partners

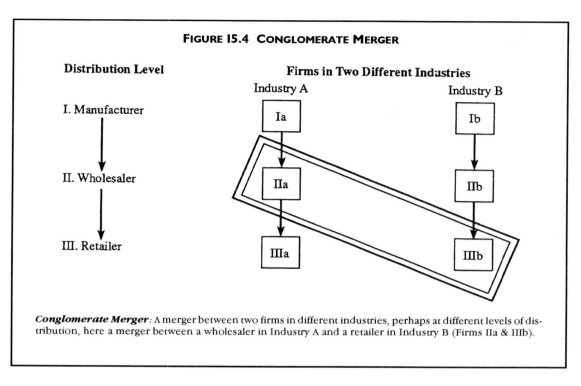

FIGURE 15.4 CONGLOMERATE MERGER

Distribution Level

I. Manufacturer

II. Wholesaler

III. Retailer

Firms in Two Different Industries

Industry A

Industry B

Ia

Ib

IIa

IIb

IIIa

IIIb

Conglomerate Merger: A merger between two firms in different industries, perhaps at different levels of distribution, here a merger between a wholesaler in Industry A and a retailer in Industry B (Firms IIa & IIIb).

will go bankrupt unless it is saved by the merger. However, the courts have been receptive to this argument only where the failing firm is unable to successfully reorganize under Chapter 11 of the bankruptcy laws. Additionally, the failing firm must have attempted to find reasonable alternate merger partners that would not pose as drastic a reduction in competition as the proposed merger before the courts will accept the failing firm defense.

VI. Horizontal Combinations and Restraints of Trade

Horizontal restraints of trade include a wide range of collaborations among competitors in the same industry. The famous economist, Adam Smith, observed that: "People in the same trade seldom meet together, even for merriment and diversion, but that the conversation ends in a conspiracy against the public or in some contrivance to raise prices." The Sherman Act has been interpreted to prohibit restraints of trade under two categories: the per se rule of illegality and the rule of reason.

A. Per Se Violations

Certain business agreements are designated illegal per se which means they are considered unreasonable and therefore always prohibited. There is no justification for competitors involved in a per se violation. For example, price fixing among competitors is never justifiable.

The designation of a particular activity as per se illegal provides judicial efficiency by shortening trials and preventing unnecessary at-

429

Example. The PG Company, a large consumer products firm, acquired the largest manufacturer of fabric bleach, the C Company. PG was a predominant producer of cleaners, soaps, and detergents with the largest advertising budget of any firm in the world. The FTC challenged this merger claiming that PG was a potential entrant into the bleach market. The FTC claimed that PG's acquisition of C Company would deter new competitors from entering the bleach market, discourage active competition among existing bleach companies, and eliminate the edge effect because the PG Company was the most likely potential entrant.

This conglomerate merger had a potential to substantially lessen competition from its likely future impact. The bleach market was highly concentrated. PG was the most likely potential entrant but the merger eliminated much of the market discipline that PG's presence on the edge exerted. Barriers to entry created by the PG's size, advertising budget, and trademark goodwill would deter other firms from entering the market. ▢

tempts to justify the restraint. The courts have had continued experience with certain types of restraints of trade that almost always produce unjustifiable and substantial restraints of trade. Therefore, judicial efficiency is enhanced after proof of the unreasonable act. Per se violations include price fixing, group boycotts, concerted refusals to deal, tie-in relationships, and the division of markets. The greatest challenge in cases involving per se violations is determining whether the act in question actually falls within a per se category. Challenged actions that are not clearly within a per se illegal category might be justified if there is evidence the conduct is not harmful to the competitive environment.

B. Rule of Reason

The Sherman Act's prohibition of every contract, combination or conspiracy in restraint of trade is tempered by the court's application of reasonableness. Every contract restrains trade in at least some small way so the plain meaning of the Sherman Act should not be used to invalidate all contracts. Clearly it was not Congress' intent to invalidate economically useful contracts, so the courts have added the rule of reason to make the Sherman Act more realistic.

Under the rule of reason contracts that restrict competition are held illegal only when they suppress or destroy competition. This requires an ad hoc examination of the facts peculiar to the business to which the restraint applies. This business must be examined before and after the restraint to determine its effect. Relevant evidence includes the history of the restraint, the evil believed to exist, the reason the restraint was adopted, and the purpose or end sought to be obtained. The rule of reason permits a simple economic analysis but has evolved into complex and quantitative economic analysis of the direct and indirect effects.

C. Price Fixing

Contracts by which two or more competitors set the resale prices for their goods are illegal per se as price fixing. Price fixing eliminates competition and permits an inefficient oligopoly to pass on its costs to consumers. There is no justification for price fixing. For example, an agreement to fix minimum prices is illegal as well as an agreement to set maximum prices because low prices can drive out competitors, reduce nonprice competition for optional features, and tends to illegally stabilize prices at the maximum.

Example. Several oil companies organized a program to monitor the amounts of surplus gasoline available on the spot market in an attempt to stabilize and slowly raise the wholesale prices of gasoline. These companies purchased excess supplies in an effort to prevent competitive bidding from forcing down the price of gasoline. The oil companies claimed that the presence of "distress" or "excess gasoline" on the market would result in ruinous competition and financial disaster for the oil industry.

Combinations that tamper with the structure of the market's pricing system are a per se illegal activity. Any scheme that raises, depresses, fixes, pegs, or stabilizes the price of a commodity in commerce is illegal per se. Even if the members of the price fixing group do not have monopoly control, their impact on prices produces an anti-competitive effect. The program to remove excess supplies of gasoline off the spot market was an illegal form of price fixing. □

Price fixing may be accomplished through indirect means. If sellers limit their production, the resulting constricted supply forces buyers to bid up the price of the goods still available. This is an illegal form of price fixing. For example, the Organization of Petroleum Exporting Countries (OPEC) set production quotas for all member nations to assure that there will not be an excess supply of oil on world markets that might permit the price of oil to fall. If OPEC was subject to the American anti-trust laws, their production fixing activities would be considered illegal.

Credit terms and freight charges may also become terms susceptible to price fixing. Where credit is an inseparable part of a product's price and all purchases rely on the sellers' extension of credit, an agreement to eliminate credit would be illegal price fixing. Agreements among competitors to fix freight rates charged (phantom freight) is also a disguised form of price fixing.

I. TRADE ASSOCIATION ACTIVITIES

Price fixing can be performed through many types of interaction among competitors. The price fixing prohibition is so strong that even the mutually beneficial activities of competitors in their trade associations are suspect. When competitors exchange their own pricing information with other competitors price

fixing allegedly becomes easier. Some observers allege that trade associations form a convenient clearinghouse for the exchange of price information. As a result of the tendency for competitors to join together with trade associations and the anti-competitive potential of their price fixing, great care must be taken to avoid illegitimate exchange of pricing information.

Trade associations have many legitimate objectives. For example, for certain industries to maintain world competitiveness, they must exchange information about business practices. An industry's tendency to network and promote its collective success may be critical particularly where product quality is improved and efficiencies result. The tension between the potential for illegal price fixing and the justifiable activities of trade associations have caused close scrutiny by regulators.

Trade association activities are illegal if they tend to lessen competition or reinforce the oligopoly strength of the participants. While many trade associations have good intentions for the participants' legitimate self-improvement, some trade associations have simply distributed price fixing information among competitors.

It is clear that when a trade association exchanges information identifying its customers and other competitors' pricing this is an illegal price fixing scheme. This is contrasted

Example. The hardwood manufacturers trade association required its members to report details of the individual sales made, the total production of each participant, inventory levels, and each members current price lists. The trade association facilitated distribution of this information to all participants. At national meetings of the trade association, industry analysts constantly warned the members of the association to avoid overproduction.

The hardwood trade association's activities resulted in sharp hardwood price increases. The activities were held illegal when the government challenged the practice. A similar plan by the paper box industry was also held illegal. The paper box trade association distributed price quotes identifying customers so the plan was held illegal as it tended to stabilize prices. □

with the less harmful activities of some trade associations which exchange less specific information. For example, the maple flooring industry trade association circulated information among its members concerning average costs, freight rates, and past transactions without identifying individual buyers and sellers. Such a plan is not illegal because this information has less effect on the future pricing behavior. Exchanges of information of about customers that fail to timely pay their bills is also justifiable. For example, the cement manufacturers association distributed lists identifying contractors that abused the free delivery of cement. Since this information protected members from fraud by its customers it was considered justifiable.

Care must be taken by contractors to avoid the allegation their trade association activities might amount to an illegal bidding ring. A bidding ring involves a pre-selected winner for each of several different construction projects. Eventually all participants end up with some work but prices are not set through true competition. The pre-selected winners price is lower than the other bidders but generally higher than a genuine competitive bidding process would produce.

Some trade associations attempt price fixing through self-regulation. Many trade associations have industry codes that in reality fix prices. For example, a rule among professional engineers prohibited them from bidding competitively on construction projects. The engineers alleged that this self-disciplinary rule was intended to maintain high quality in engineering services. However, in reality the prohibition on competitive bidding tended to raise prices. In another example, the local bar associations representing lawyers had traditionally published and enforced minimum fee schedules that fixed the minimum price lawyers may charge for particular legal services. Although the bar association attempted to justify this practice as a quality control measure, it constituted price fixing.

D. Division of Markets

Monopoly power is easy to exercise when there are fewer competitors in a particular geographic region. Competitors could achieve this monopoly power by agreeing to allocate or divide markets among each other. This would require certain producers to serve particular regions or specified customers and it thereby discourages other competitors from servicing these customers. The primary seller servicing these customers is usually free to raise prices, limit production, or be slow to innovate and become efficient. As a result, a division of markets or territorial allocation is illegal per se.

Some competitors have attempted to hide their division of markets by permitting other producers to occasionally sell within the primary sellers' market area. However, the pre-

Example.   One of the newswire services is a joint venture among thousands of members among the media, newspapers, radio, and television broadcasters. A competitor was denied access to the newswire. This group boycott placed it at a considerable competitive disadvantage. The by-laws of one newswire service permitted any member to blackball a new member. Therefore, the joint venture posed a substantial barrier to entry for new media firms. Under the rule of reason this joint venture activity tended to substantially lessen competition. ☐

ferred firm still maintains some market power and can exercise discipline over other competitors. Therefore, this practice is also illegal. Consider the example of an independent grocer's buying network. The agreement had two major parts: 1. An agreement to purchase groceries on the wholesale market together to obtain volume discounts, 2. Territorial restrictions assuring that no two competitors would compete in the same neighborhood market. While the group buying plan was justifiable, the territorial allocation constituted an illegal division of markets. The independent grocers' intent to strengthen themselves in an effort to compete more effectively against chain stores did not justify the practice.

E. Group Boycotts

Another activity considered illegal per se is the group boycott. Although sellers usually may individually deal with whom they please, any agreement among them to boycott a certain individual or group is illegal per se. Boycotts tend to discipline buyers into accepting prices and features that the selling group dictates. For example, there was an illegal group boycott when an apparel manufacturer's trade association suggested its members boycott retailers who sold pirated designs (fake designer clothes). Another illegal group boycott was found when the national football league attempted to enforce its rule requiring a team that hires a free agent to compensate the players' former team. Another illegal group boycott by the American Medical Asso-

ciation resulted from its rule prohibiting doctors from participation in prepaid medical plans if they received a salary for practicing medicine. These examples illustrate that group boycotts are illegal even if they are written as a professional ethical code or code of conduct.

F. Joint Ventures

Joint ventures may be illegal if they form an unreasonable restraint of trade. A *joint venture* is a partnership-like arrangement in which two or more entities, usually corporations, conduct a limited business activity together. Joint ventures are legally justified if they obtain economic efficiencies and do not restrain trade. Most courts judge joint ventures by the rule of reason permitting a balancing between the alleged potential anticompetitive effect and the participants' allegations that the arrangement will create economic efficiencies. However, a few courts have threatened application of the per se rule creating considerable uncertainty for joint ventures.

Joint ventures, particularly among international competitors, are arising with much greater frequency. Typically a foreign firm is unwilling or unable to make the rather substantial investment necessary to establish a new production facility or to produce a new product without the assistance of a domestic firm as partner. Such arrangements are usually not illegal particularly where the joint venture is intended to last for a limited time. For example, General Motors and Toyota formed the NUMMI joint venture to produce compact cars. Reports indicated that General Motors was interested in learning Toyota's production techniques and Toyota was interested in the viability of producing cars in the United States. The NUMMI project has a fixed term after which Toyota will withdraw. However, some joint ventures have been found illegal. The joint ownership of local theaters by movie making companies was held an illegal joint venture because new releases from the participants were not made available to non-member theaters. This restriction on sales of movies tended to substantially lessen competition. Congress reinforced applicability of the rule of reason to research and development joint ventures in passing the National Cooperative Research Act of 1984 and is considering extending the rule of reason to production joint ventures.

G. Proof of a Horizontal Restraint

Regulators often find it difficult to find direct proof of an illegal agreement or combination. If the participants are sophisticated and intend to hide their illegal activities, they will not leave a clear trail of evidence. Their contracts in restraint of trade would be made off-the-record or they can become involved in clandestine tactics, secret meetings, and communicate in code. The Sherman Act requires proof of criminal guilt beyond a reasonable doubt so prosecutors often have a difficult task. As a result, indirect and circumstantial evidence can be used permitting the fact finder to infer illegal concerted activity from the circumstances.

I. CONSCIOUS PARALLELISM

It is possible to prove illegal price fixing through conscious parallelism in which competitors intentionally mimic the pricing behaviors of their industry leader. The Supreme Court has condoned the proof of price fixing through conscious parallelism under the so-called *Interstate formula*: "It is enough that,

knowing that concerted action was contemplated and invited, the distributors of feature films gave their adherence to the scheme and participated in it." The crucial question is whether the competitors' pricing stems from independent decisions or from an agreement, tacit or expressed. Parallel behavior is not illegal. However, intentional mimicry of a competitors' price to prevent competition is illegal. Of course, in many volatile markets sellers are justified in quickly changing prices to avoid loosing market share.

2. INTERLOCKING DIRECTORATES

Interlocking directorates may be illegal under the Clayton Act. It provides: "no person shall at the same time be a director in two or more corporations which are competitors if an agreement between them would eliminate competition in violation of the anti-trust laws." Interlocking directorates exist when the same person sits on the board of two different competitors. It is presumed that the common director will perform a convenient conduit for collusive exchange of information.

Several exceptions have developed because of the difficulties in recruiting sufficient and competent directors. For example, interlocking doctorates are not illegal between suppliers and customers who are in a vertical relationship or between firms in different industries. Indeed, in Japan the practice of Keritsu involves interlocking directorates and cross-share ownership among suppliers, manufacturers, and retail outlets which allegedly strengthens their relationships.

Indirect interlocks are permissible. For example, an employee of a financial institution, bank, or investment banker may sit on the boards of two competing industrial firms. Additionally, there is no illegal interlocking directorate where a nondirector employee of one competitor sits on the board of another competitor. There has never been vigorous enforcement of the interlocking directorate

Example.   Wine producers in California were required by state law to file price schedules with the state. Under the regulatory program, wines were required to be sold at specific prices. Although the state could not directly control wine prices, if wines were sold below posted prices, wine wholesalers could be fined or have their liquor licenses suspended. A wine wholesaler challenged the law as an illegal vertical resale price maintenance with an anticompetitive effect.

The wine pricing system constituted illegal resale price maintenance. The state's requirement for the pricing notification process provided no antitrust immunity under the state action exemption. This program had no clearly articulated state policy nor active state supervision necessary for an exemption from the antitrust laws. This was not a statutory scheme designed to permit state's power to regulate the traffic in intoxicating liquor but instead represented a violation of the Sherman Act. □

provision, the FTC has usually permitted the challenged director to simply resign one of the two positions.

H. Vertical Price Restraint: Resale Price Maintenance

Manufacturers may exercise direct control over their distributors through resale price maintenance. This is a vertical price restraint in which the seller specifies a minimum or maximum resale price that the retailer must charge consumers. Resale price maintenance is considered a per se violation of the Sherman Act because it may be used by retailers as an indirect price fixing scheme. For example, retailers might pressure their supplier to require all retailers to charge uniform prices, a hidden method to fix prices horizontally between the retailers. Artificial minimum resale prices are clearly anticompetitive because they preclude price competition below the minimum price. Additionally, a specified maximum resale price is also illegal because it can become an unspoken minimum price.

I. FAIR TRADE

Resale price maintenance was legalized between 1937 and 1975 by the Miller-Tydings Act. Congress passed this statute under pressure from small retailers who argued that if they could maintain high resale prices, they

could prevent destructive competition. This system was intended permit small businesses to survive with an assured profit level. Chain stores were growing in number during the Great Depression forcing many small retailers and wholesalers out of business. They argued that products should be sold at "fair prices" that permitted a fair rate of return for all retailers, regardless of their size. The Miller-Tydings Act permitted resale price maintenance if the state passed a separate statute legalizing the practice.

Resale price maintenance was strongest during the 1950's, by then 45 states had passed fair trade laws and over 1,500 manufacturers enforced resale price maintenance provisions in their distribution contracts with wholesalers and retailers. Retailers were prohibited from selling goods below "list price" even if the retailer did not sign the resale price maintenance contract. Resale price maintenance prevented discounting of many consumer goods until the proliferation of mail order houses in the1960s. Eventually resale price maintenance eroded and became unpopular and the Miller-Tydings Act was repealed in 1975. The Reagan and Bush Administrations have generally permitted resale price maintenance. Recent decisions do not invalidate resale price maintenance unless the manufacturer and retailer(s) intentionally set a specified price. Pressure is mounting in Con-

Example. PD and Company manufactured drugs and vitamins sold over-the-counter through drug stores. PD included a resale price maintenance policy in the wholesale catalogs distributed to retail drug stores. Vitamins were to be marked up by nearly 50% over wholesale cost. Some retailers began advertising and selling PD vitamins at prices discounted from this price mark-up. PD threatened to discontinue selling PD vitamins to these retailers but they ignored the warnings. PD urged its wholesalers to refuse to fill vitamin orders for these retailers. Sales were resumed only after the retailers agreed to discontinue advertising their discount prices.

The active policing and harassment activities of PD constituted an illegal resale price maintenance scheme. Manufacturers may simply refuse to deal with a retailer that ignores published pricing policies but the efforts of PD and its wholesalers to enforce retail prices here amounted to a combination or conspiracy in restraint of trade illegal under the Sherman Act. Here the manufacturer organized a price maintenance combination with an effect to fix prices among all resellers. ▢

gress to invalidate the practice dubbing it as "vertical price fixing."

2. REFUSALS TO DEAL

Although direct resale price maintenance is illegal, manufacturers may discipline their retailers in other ways into observing minimum prices in some instances. Manufacturers are permitted to refuse to deal with retailers who do not sell at or above specified prices. The Colgate Doctrine was developed by the Supreme Court legitimizing the supplier's refusal to deal even though there is no contract obligation requiring the retailer to sell at specific prices. Instead, the manufacturer may simply announce its refusal to deal with distributors who sell below the fixed minimum prices.

Refusals to deal may be illegal and coercive if the manufacturer actively harasses or monitors the retailer's pricing activities. Any effort by the manufacturer to suspend or reinstate retailers who fail to comply with the announced pricing policy is illegal.

3. CONSIGNMENT SALES

Consignment sales may constitute a form of resale price maintenance. A *consignment* is a contingent transaction where the manufacturer holds ownership of the goods (title) until the retailer sells the goods to the consumer. In a true consignment the retailer acts only as an agent for the manufacturer or supplier and is therefore obligated to sell at the manufacturer's prescribed price. Although consignments are generally justifiable, when used to legalize price maintenance the consignment is illegal. Consignment sales are legitimate where the supplier seeks to retain title to goods because the retailer is in financial trouble. The consignment permits the supplier to retain adequate collateral to assure payment. GE patented the light bulb and sold them through retailers exclusively on consignment. This permitted GE to set the retail price for all light bulb sales and compensate retailers with a commission. GE's consignment system was eventually found illegal as resale price maintenance after it's patents expired. Consignment arrangements are illegal without a legitimate purpose such as to provide security for inventory shipped but not yet paid for.

I. Vertical Non-Price Restraints

With the demise of fair trade laws and the courts' unwillingness to accept policing of resale price maintenance, manufacturers have

Example.   The GTE Company sold its television sets through a limited number·of retail franchisees. Its marketing strategy was to limit the number of retailers selling its products within a given region so the each retailer would a have sufficient profit incentive to adequately promote the GTE television. GTE reasoned that this would increase interbrand competition with other brands of television. The CTV Company in San Francisco complained to GTE that another retailer received a franchise in the San Francisco area. This embittered the CTV retailer who cancelled its large order with GTE and began to sell its TVs through a new store in Sacramento. GTE refused to give CTV a Sacramento franchise and punished CTV by cutting its credit line.

Vertical nonprice restraints are subjected to rule of reason analysis. The action taken by GTE here was not a per se violation. Where there is substantial interbrand competition, a vertical restriction such as this may be procompetitive. Even though vertical restrictions reduce intrabrand competition by promoting interbrand competition, the vertical restraint may have a procompetitive effect.

sought to develop alternative vertical restraints. Agreements between suppliers and resellers which do not specify price yet restrain the reseller's freedom of action to compete may be considered vertical nonprice restraints. For example, a manufacturer might prohibit a retailer from reselling goods to discount stores. Vertical non-price constraints sometimes have legitimate purposes so they are increasingly judged by the rule of reason.

I. EXCLUSIVE DEALING

An *exclusive distributorship* is a contract awarded to a retailer giving it the exclusive rights to sell the manufacturer's products within a given region. Although manufacturer's generally have freedom to pick the retailers or wholesalers they will use, an exclusive distributorship may be illegal if it excludes all dealers from selling the manufacturer's products in that region. Exclusive distributorships are an unjustifiable restraint of trade and illegal per se if one distributor pressures the manufacturer to halt sales to a competing distributor.

A *exclusive dealing* relationship arises from a supplier's contract that prohibits the retailer from selling the products of competing manufacturers. The Clayton Acts specifics prohibits exclusive dealing which tends to create a

monopoly or substantially lessens competition. It is illegal for a supplier to precondition sales on the reseller's promise not to sell a competitor's products. These contracts are generally tested by the quantitative substantiality test designating the contract illegal if a substantial dollar volume of business is involved.

Manufacturers can get around the prohibition on exclusive dealing by including *adequate representation* clauses in their supply contracts. Manufacturers generally have a legitimate interest to assure retailers spend sufficient resources in expert sales personnel, advertising, maintenance of inventory, provision of customer service, and other sales efforts. Supply contract terms that require the retailer to make a substantial effort to sell the manufacturer's products are generally considered legal.

2. RESTRICTIONS ON CUSTOMERS OR TERRITORY

It is illegal for a manufacturer to restrict its retailers from selling to particular customers or in specific geographic regions. This prevents competition between two retailers of the same brand of manufactured goods.

Customer and territorial restraints are judged by the rule of reason. This analysis focuses on whether the challenged vertical restriction tends to limit competition and whether there are legitimate economic or business objectives for the restriction. Some vertical restrictions actually tend to enhance *interbrand competition*, competition between different brands of the same product. Where interbrand competition is limited, a manufacturer's vertical restraint is unreasonable. By contrast, supporters of vertical restraints argue that intrabrand competition can be harmful. *Intrabrand competition* arises between different retailers of the same product brand. Intrabrand competition involves differences in price, service, and other features of the two retailers which sell the same brand of product.

3. TYING

Tying relationships are prohibited under the Clayton Act. In a tying or tie-in supply arrangement, a customer is required to purchase certain goods to qualify to sell other goods. The seller refuses to sell the *tying* or desirable product unless a customer also agrees to purchase the *tied* or less desirable product. For example, an electronics manufacturer might refuse to sell its desirable 27" big screen TVs to retailers unless they also purchase a minimum number of smaller TVs and VCRs. Tying arrangements are anti-competitive because buyers are coerced to purchase less desirable products if they want to purchase the more desirable products. The tying arrangement ties the desirable purchases to sales of other, supplementary, and less desirable purchases. Tying relationships permit the seller to exercise market power in the less desirable tied product market. Tying is illegal when one good is tied to another. It is inapplicable when services or land sales are tied to good sales.

Tying is undesirable because buyers are forced to purchase tied products at higher prices, in larger quantities, or at lower quality than if the tying relationship did not exist. If the customer was unrestrained by a tying agreement, alternate substitutes could be purchased from other sellers, perhaps at higher quality or lower prices. Customers forced to purchase undesirable goods from the manufacturer pay higher prices or receive lower quality than if a free market existed in the tied product. Tying tends to make it difficult for competitors to enter into the market for the tied product. This reinforces the seller's monopoly in both the tying and tied product. Tying is similar to economic duress because it eliminates the customer's free choice.

Some tying relationships involve products that are used in fixed proportions with each other. For example, the sale of nuts and bolts or tires on automobiles may be necessary for the successful use of these products. In other instances, there is no fixed proportion between the tying and tied products. For example, computer disks may be purchased in large or small numbers depending on the purchasers intended use.

Tying relationships occur more often now for two reasons. First, the courts tend to judge tying relationships by the rule of reason and have stopped applying the per se analysis as previously done in tying cases. Second, some sellers have successfully argued that there is only one product and not two separate products tied together. The sale of a single product cannot involve tying. For example, an automobile and it's built in radio may be viewed as separate products. Similarly a television set and it's picture tube could be viewed as two separate products. If the manufacturer insists on selling cars with built in radios or televisions with built in picture tubes, it could be argued that this was a tying relationship. However, the analysis should focus on whether there is a substantial market for the installation of picture tubes in television sets or radios into automobiles. Television picture tubes are installed in televisions only when first manufactured and for replacement and

▼ **Example.** P operated two McD restaurants but was denied a third franchise because the McD Company believed P could not effectively operate three restaurants. P attacked the McD Company alleging that it was imposing an illegal tying relationships. The McD Company required all its franchisees to pay royalties for use of the franchise and to rent the McD store premises from the McD Company. Franchisees may not select the location for their own store and must accept only the lease terms provided by the McD Company.

Franchise relationships may make greater use of vertical restraints than in nonfranchise distribution relationships. A franchise system is successful only when the franchiser exercises control over the quality of all franchisees. Therefore, the right to sell under the McD name and the requirement to lease the store premises from the McD Company are not two separate products but instead only one product. The unique attraction of a franchise system to customers involves a complete and integrated package of business and product. ☐

repair. By contrast, there is a healthy installation after-market for car stereos and radios. Additionally, it would be economically inefficient to sell televisions without an installed picture tube.

Some manufacturers justify tying relationships where the quality of the tied product sold by that manufacturer is higher than those of competitors. The manufacturer typically claims that if tied products from competitors are substandard and should not be used with the manufacturer's tying product. For example, at one time IBM required the use of IBM brand computer punch cards with its computers. Similarly, the Bell System once required the use of Western Electric brand telephones and switching equipment with it's telephone service. In each case, the seller argued that the quality of it's computer cards or telephones was higher than those produced by competitors.

The quality control problem could be resolved by simply specifying the design and minimum performance standards. For example, the size, shape, and resilience of computer punch cards could be specified so that other manufacturer's punch cards could be produced to prevent damage to the IBM computer. Similarly, the electronic characteristics of telephone instruments can be specified so that stray electronic signals are not emitted

into the telephone lines that could possibly damage the Bell System's equipment. Although both of these companies successfully tied the sales of their tied products for many years, today they are permitted only to specify the required characteristics for the tied products. Telephones sold in the United States must carry an FCC specification that indicates the telephone will perform without damaging the Bell System's switching equipment.

VII. Price Discrimination

Price discrimination was one of the first anticompetitive acts regulated under federal law. *Price discrimination* is the seller's practice of charging different prices to various buyers for goods of like grade and quality. The Interstate Commerce Commission was established in the late 19th Century to prevent the railroads from discriminating in prices charged to different shippers. However, the practice did not become illegal for sellers of goods until passage of the Robinson-Patman Act in 1936.

Under the perfect competition model, price discrimination is believed impossible because buyers are presumed to have perfect information of the prices charged by all sellers. Any buyer confronting a higher price than offered by other sellers would simply buy from an alternate seller charging a lower price. However, as the restrictive assumptions of the perfect competition model are relaxed to reflect how real world markets actually operate, it becomes clear that some buyers or sellers have market power. Not all buyers have perfect information about prices nor about the relative quality of goods from different sellers. Therefore, price discrimination may occur in practice but it is illegal where it tends to create a monopoly or lessens competition.

Price discrimination cannot occur where buyers and sellers have perfect information and there is excess supply capacity. Market conditions lead to price discrimination if buyers are ignorant of prices paid by other buyers. Even where prices and other terms of sale are rather visible, price discrimination may occur if some buyers are given secret price concessions or kickbacks. Information about prices is one of the strange conflicts and inherent ironies of the Antitrust laws. Price fixing is often presumed where sellers exchange pricing information. However, in markets where buyers are ignorant of the various sellers' pricing policies, price discrimination is encouraged.

Three general situations lead to price discrimination. First, prices charged to some customers may be higher than those charged to others if some are willing to pay higher prices. The early buyers of new and innovative products are usually willing to pay more than later buyers. For example, the first hand-held calculators cost hundreds of dollars yet better products today typically cost less than $10. Second, price discrimination can occur between geographic regions if competition is vigorous in some regions while some sellers have market power in other regions. The third situation conducive to price discrimination is where the products of various producers are somewhat different, are sold under different brand names, or are sold at different types of retail establishments. This permits higher prices to be charged for goods

of perceived higher value but which actually are substantially identical to more generic brands.

A private plaintiff or government enforcement agency may bring an action alleging price discrimination under the Robinson-Patman Act. The plaintiff must prove there were two different purchasers and at least one of the sales transactions crossed a state line (the interstate commerce requirement). If the two purchases are not fairly close in time (contemporaneous) then market conditions may explain the price differential. Nonprice terms such as preferential credit or promotional expenses (advertising rebates) may constitute part of a price discrimination. To establish a price discrimination, the following elements must be proved.

Proof of Price Discrimination
1. Discrimination in price
2. Between two different purchasers
3. Effect on interstate commerce
4. Purchases involve commodities of like grade and quality
5. The price discrimination causes a substantial lessening of competition or a tendency to create a monopoly.
6. Injury is caused to competitors of the seller or to the buyer or to the buyer's customers.

A. Commodities of Like Grade and Quality

The Robinson-Patman Act prohibits any two sales from a single seller involving commodities of like grade and quality. Because only commodities are involved, the Act is inapplicable to intangible property, services, and mixed sales of services with goods. However, like with tying, the Sherman Act may apply if the price discrimination or tying relationship amounts to an illegal restraint of trade or attempt to monopolize. Additionally the FTC Act could apply to price discriminations involving services or mixed contracts (goods

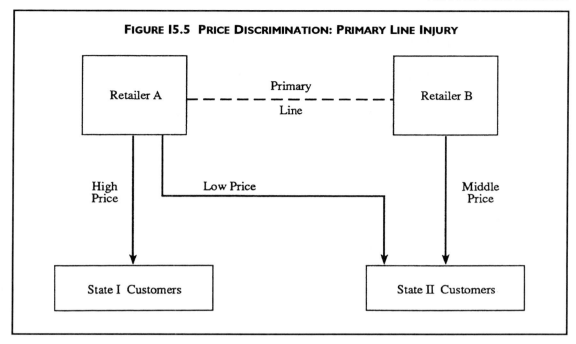

FIGURE 15.5 PRICE DISCRIMINATION: PRIMARY LINE INJURY

Retailer A — — — Primary Line — — — Retailer B

High Price | Low Price | Middle Price

State I Customers | State II Customers

and services) if they constituted an unfair method of competition.

Goods of like grade and quality share nearly identical physical and chemical composition. Two seemingly different products may be interchangeable and of like grade and quality if consumers accept them for the same use. For example, small differences between two brands of goods may be insufficient to separate them as different commodities. However, it may be justifiable to sell generic goods at lower prices if there is more advertising or promotional expense, and higher marketing costs associated with promoting and selling the name brand.

B. Primary Line Injury

Price discrimination is illegal if it substantially lessens competition or tends to create a monopoly or it injuries, destroys, or prevents competition. The plaintiff must prove actual injury to competition in order to win a price

discrimination case. Both the price discriminating seller or a buyer who knowingly benefits from a price discrimination may be held liable. Plaintiffs often seek to prove lost profits or diverted business opportunities as a measure of their injury. In contrast, regulators may allege injuries on competition in the whole market. Price discrimination injuries are often categorized according to the point where injury occurs along the chain of distribution. An injury may occur at the seller's level (primary line injury), at the buyer's level (secondary line injury), at the level of the customer's buyer (tertiary line injury), or at any lower level where a customer of a customer suffers injury (fourth line injury).

Primary line injuries are suffered by sellers who compete with the price discriminating seller. For example, if seller A operates in two distinct geographic markets and seller B operates in only I of these markets, seller A could charge a low price in seller B's market and make up the losses with higher prices charged

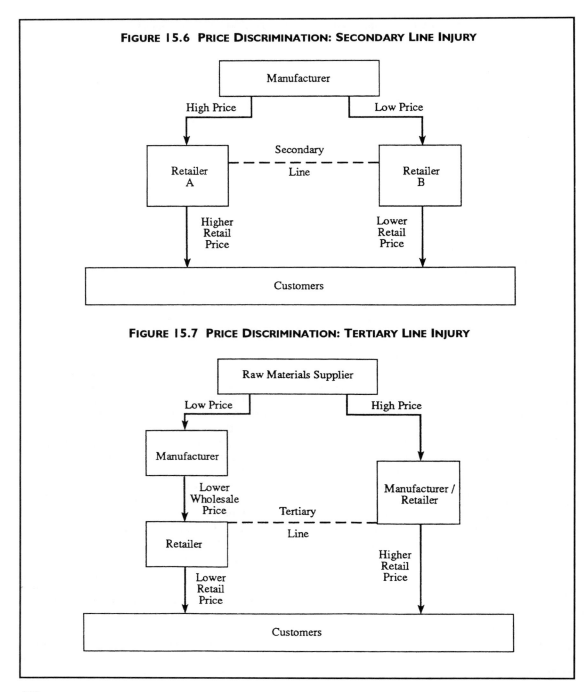

FIGURE 15.6 PRICE DISCRIMINATION: SECONDARY LINE INJURY

Manufacturer

High Price   Low Price

Retailer A — Secondary Line — Retailer B

Higher Retail Price   Lower Retail Price

Customers

FIGURE 15.7 PRICE DISCRIMINATION: TERTIARY LINE INJURY

Raw Materials Supplier

Low Price   High Price

Manufacturer   Manufacturer / Retailer

Lower Wholesale Price   Tertiary Line

Retailer

Lower Retail Price   Higher Retail Price

Customers

Example. The U Pie Company sold frozen pies in the Salt Lake City market from its local plant. Occasionally outside national brands were sold in the Salt Lake City market at prices well below those sold outside the Salt Lake City market. The local pie producer charged these outside manufacturers with price discrimination by selling their pies in the Salt Lake City market at prices lower than they sold elsewhere.

When an outside producer subsidizes losses made on sales in one geographic market with higher profits made in another region, it is reasonable to infer an intent to drive the local seller out of business. After the local producer is eliminated the outside producer may raise its prices above competitive levels to obtain additional subsidies for these temporary destructive competition losses. The existence of this predatory intent reinforces the anticompetitive effect of an interregional price discrimination. ⌐

in seller A's other market. This cross-subsidization results in higher prices to purchasers in one market and it may well drive the competing seller out of business. Figure 15.5 illustrates primary line injury.

C. Secondary Line Injury

A price discrimination injury may be suffered by one of two buyers in a single market. Where one buyer has a lower cost for the same goods as another buyer, the higher paying buyer suffers a competitive injury. For example, if one buyer pays a high price and another buyer pays a lower price, the customers of these two buyers will likely prefer to purchase from the buyer paying the lower wholesale price. The buyer forced to pay a higher wholesale price suffers the damage. The wholesale cost advantage of the buyer paying a lower price can either be passed on to its customers or retained as abnormally high profits. Figure 15.6 illustrates secondary line injury.

D. Tertiary Line Injury

A few cases have been brought concerning injuries suffered by the buyer of the buyer. In theory, a competitive injury from price discrimination may occur at any level along the chain of distribution. The tertiary line injury is identified as one suffered by customers of the

buyers. For example, if a raw materials supplier sells to one manufacturer at a lower price than charged to another manufacturer that owns its retail stores, injury may be suffered by the integrated manufacturer retailer and its customers. Customers will prefer to shop at the retailers who can pass on the competitive cost advantage. Figure 15.7 illustrates tertiary line injury.

Price discrimination injury may occur along any chain of distribution even those with several intermediate purchasers, wholesalers, and resellers. A fourth line injury is possible where a manufacturer sells through two wholesale levels, through a retailer, and then to the ultimate customers.

E. Price Discrimination Defenses

Occasionally the price discrimination behaviors of a seller may be justified with an affirmative defense. Sales to governments or nonprofit institutions are usually exempt from the Robinson-Patman Act if they are not resold into the retail market. Export sales are also exempt because the Act applies only to goods sold for resale within the United States. Three additional defenses are found in the Robinson-Patman Act.

A price discrimination may be justified if conditions in the market have changed so drastically that the price charged to the last few customers become unrealistic. The Act permits price changes from time to time in response to *changing conditions* affecting the marketability of goods. These conditions include problems such as the imminent deterioration of perishable goods, the obsolescence of seasonal goods, distress sales under court process, or sales in good faith if a business is liquidated and discontinued. The changed conditions defense is generally unsuccessful for price discriminators unless the physical nature of the goods require an immediate sale at whatever price can be secured. For example, low price sales of the leftover inventory remaining at the end of the automobile model year is a classic example justifying the changing conditions defense. However, businesses that regularly fabricate "going out of business" sales are not exempt.

Another defense includes legitimate *cost differentials* where the seller has different costs associated with different sales. Sellers may make due allowance for differences in the cost of manufacturer, sale, or delivery resulting from differing methods or quantities sold. The cost differential defense is most useful in justifying quantity discounts where the seller actually saves costs by selling in bulk. However, the determination of cost is a rather controversial subject due to different interpretations of the proper allocation of indirect costs (overhead). A seller is most justified in asserting the defense where there are measurable savings in packaging, handling, and transportation costs.

A price discrimination is also permitted where the seller discriminates in good faith to meet a competitor's equally low price. This is the *meeting the competition in good faith* defense. It is available when the seller reasonably believes that lowering the price is necessary to win the sale. The seller must exactly meet the competitor's price but not sell below it. How can the seller effectively learn the competitor's price without exchanging price information which might lead to an allegation

of price fixing? The courts must examine whether the discriminating seller is acting in good faith when it investigates the buyer's claim that a competitor is charging a lower price. For example, the seller might require such buyers to bring in a competitor's ad or written price estimate to prove the lower price.

VIII. Unfair Trade Practices

There are numerous loopholes in the Sherman and Clayton Antitrust Laws coverage of anticompetitive practices. Congress sought to fill in these gaps and address a wide range of unfair trade practices by passing the Federal Trade Commission Act of 1914 (FTC Act). This law created the Federal Trade Commission, a quasi-independent federal regulatory agency empowered to enforce some of the antitrust laws and other prohibitions against unfair trade practices as contained in the FTC Act.

A. Federal Trade Commission Enforcement Powers

The FTC is empowered to investigate and prosecute complaints of unfair trade practices. The FTC may issue cease and desist orders, a strong form of injunction that carries the stigma of the repeat offender. The FTC may pursue claims in federal district courts but often settles these charges with a consent decree. This permits the defendant to settle charges but without admitting or denying the FTC's allegations. Most defendants consent to refrain from engaging in the unfair trade practice in the future.

The FTC conducts internal proceedings concerning alleged violations that are heard by an administrative law judge. Defendants who are dissatisfied with the outcome of internal FTC proceedings may appeal directly to the Federal Trade Commissioners and then on through the federal court system in appeals to the U.S. Court of Appeals and ultimately the U.S. Supreme Court. The FTC's administrative remedies are enforceable with contempt citations, fines and imprisonment.

B. FTC Policymaking and Rulemaking Powers

The FTC attempts to provide guidance to business on what is considered fair and unfair trade practices. Advisory opinions of the FTC are issued from time to time providing the Commission's opinion of the legality of specific proposed conduct. The FTC often provides comprehensive industry guidelines intended to create a "safe harbor" legitimizing business in conformance with the guidelines and avoiding prosecution. Administrative opinions and guidelines do not have the force of law and may be reinterpreted by the courts.

The FTC has extensive regulatory power to prohibit "unfair methods of competition and unfair or deceptive acts or practices in or affecting commerce." This gap filling power permits the FTC to prosecute unfair trade practices that violate the spirit of the Sherman and Clayton Acts but not the letter of these Acts. This permits the FTC to prohibit acts that are not clearly illegal under other antitrust laws. Additionally, the FTC may issue specific trade regulation rules which are interpreted like any other federal regulation. For example, the requirement that octane numbers must appear on gasoline pumps at filling stations is the result of such an FTC requirement. Finally, the FTC may control deceptive advertising.

* * *

Problems

1. Describe the four forms of market structure: perfect competition, monopoly, oligopoly, and monopolistic competition.

2. The General Motors Corporation had almost 50% of the domestic United States automobile market. General Motors attained this position through aggressive acquisitions of small companies and through aggressive cost reduction programs and the large economies of scale of its huge factory operations that reduce its cost per unit. Analyze GM's actions as a potential monopolization of the automobile market.

3. Not all activities are regulated by the antitrust laws. Describe and exemplify the business activities that are exempt from the Sherman and Clayton Antitrust laws.

4. A new soft drink company begins to produce a line of caffeinated and decaffeinated, artificially and naturally sweetened colas. After it obtained 75% of the cola market, regulators charge the company with monopolization. Regulators define the relevant market as the U.S. market for cola products making the new cola company's market share seem very high. How might the cola company response to this allegation in an effort to avoid charges of monopolization?

5. Describe the three major forms of merger and provide examples for each: horizontal merger, vertical merger, and conglomerate merger.

6. Both horizontal and vertical restraints of trade are analyzed under two different standards under the antitrust laws. Identify these two standards, explain their differences, and provide examples of restraints of trade that fall within each category.

7. Mr. and Mrs. G signed a home purchase contract and the finance company required an examination of the title. Mr. and Mrs. G called numerous attorneys, the only professionals legally permitted to perform title examinations, to find the lowest price for a title examination. Eventually it became obvious that all attorney's charged at least a minimum fee required by the local bar association. What arguments might Mr. and Mrs. G make against this practice? How might the attorneys and the bar association defend their practice?

8. The Big Steel Company had a 40% market share in the production of raw ingot steel. Four other major producers controlled another 50% of the steel market. Big Steel commonly initiated price changes in the per ton rate it charged for the steel. If Big Steel initiated a price increase or a price decrease, the other four steel producers usually followed within a few days by exactly matching Big Steel's price. What arguments might be offered by regulators attacking this steel pricing policy? How might the steel producers justify their pricing behaviors?

9. Retail computer discounters in the mail order business traditionally advertised prices for national brands of microcomputers and their peripherals (monitors, printers, disk drives, modems). Suddenly, nearly all discounters stopped advertising in the major microcomputer magazines. What argument might be made by a regulator that this practice constituted an illegal restraint of trade? How might the computer manufacturers or magazine publishers respond to these allegations?

10. The F Car Company is organized into a franchise system where the manufacturer produces or procures automobiles manufactured overseas and sells them through an independent dealer network each of whom is franchised to sell the F brand cars. After oil prices sky rocketed in 1990 F Company continued to produce large cars and trucks that generally get poor gas mileage. This increased the demand for F Company's domestic and foreign made high mileage small cars. One dealer ordered only high mileage small cars and none of the large trucks or cars that were selling poorly. The F Company indicated that this dealer must purchase at least some large cars and trucks in order to get the number of small cars the dealer wanted. On what basis might regulators charge that the F Company practice is an illegal restraint of trade? How might the F Company defend against these allegations?

11. The RL Clothing Company is perceived by consumers as a high priced and exclusive line of fashionable casual clothing. RL has sold through numerous large department stores at premium prices. RL management decides to move into markets in smaller cities through smaller department stores. In order to gain a foothold in the smaller city markets RL charges 30% less at the wholesale level to the small department stores than is currently charged to its big city retailers. This lower wholesale pricing makes it possible for the RL Clothing line to compete much more effectively against middle market competitors such as the L Jeans Company and The G Store. What illegal activity is described here and describe the competitive injury and its level in the chain of distribution?

16 Securities Regulations

CHAPTER OUTLINE

Securities Regulations

I. Introduction

The following chapter provides an overview of the securities laws and their effect on business and its ability to raise capital. The securities laws require businesses to proceed carefully, both in capital raising on the securities markets and thereafter as those securities trade on the stock exchanges.

Before the Great Depression of the 1930's the laissez-faire market philosophy prevailed. There was little government intervention in the capital markets, only the state common law of contracts and torts provided remedies for disputes arising between investors, brokers, and the corporate issuers of securities. Although a few states had experimented with securities laws as early as 1919, the stock market crash of 1929 provided the impetus to abandon some free market ideals by replacing them with the federal securities laws.

Many observers today attribute the efficiency and liquidity of the American securities markets to the federal securities laws. They suggest the stock market crash of the late 1980's and the widespread scandals involving insider trading and securities fraud hurt the U.S. securities markets. Confidence has eroded due to the free wheeling attitudes of speculators in securities and commodities. However the Congress and the Securities and Exchange Commission (SEC) continue to refine the American securities laws. This evolution should permit the capital markets to be maintained as relatively safe havens for investments by individuals.

This chapter first reviews the primary federal securities statutes. Next, there is a discussion of initial public offerings of new securities made through investment banking syndicates that must register these securities. To understand when the federal securities laws apply, it is necessary to define what a security is and discover which new securities offerings may be exempt from registration as private placements. The insider trading and securities fraud controversies are examined next. This discussion is followed by an examination of the federal regulation of the proxy solicitation process and tender offers. Finally, the Racketeer Influenced and Corrupt Organization law (RICO) and the Foreign Corrupt Practices Act are examined.

II. The Federal Securities Statutes

The Federal Securities Laws are composed of nine major statutes and numerous amendments passed by Congress since 1933. These laws and the accompanying regulations passed by the SEC have had a direct effect on the securities markets. These statutes include: the Securities Act of 1933, the Securities Exchange Act of 1934, the Public Utility Holding Act of 1935, the Trust Indenture Act of 1939, the Investment Company Act of 1940, the Investment Advisors Act of 1940, the Securities

Investors Protection Act, the Foreign Corrupt Practices Act, and the Racketeer Influenced and Corrupt Organizations Provisions of the Organized Crime Control Act. There have been efforts to consolidate these several laws into a single federal securities code. However, its passage is uncertain at this writing and new pressures are underway to consolidate the securities laws into a single integrated financial code also regulating the commodities, banking, and financial services industry.

A. Securities Act of 1933

After the stock market crash, in the midst of the Great Depression, Congress enacted the first securities law which became effective during Franklin D. Roosevelt's first administration. The Securities Act of 1933 (1933 Act) requires the issuers of new securities to provide investors with sufficient financial information to make reasoned investment decisions. All new issues of new securities must be registered with the SEC. This includes stock, bonds, limited partnerships interests, stock options, and other investment contracts commonly known as securities. Issuers, usually a corporation obligated by the securities, files a registration statement on the new securities it intends to sell to the public for the first time. This is known as an initial public offering (IPO). The 1933 Act provides for penalties for false statements or misleading information given to potential investors. The sales tactics and devices used during an IPO are also regulated.

B. Securities Exchange Act of 1934

Soon after passage of the 1933 Act, Congress created the SEC in the Securities and Exchange Act of 1934 (1934 Act). This law is intended to protect investors trading securities on exchanges. These are previously issued securities such as the outstanding stock trading on the New York Stock Exchange. The 1934 Act extends the disclosure duties created by the 1933 Act to all later years in which issuers have their securities traded. This requires dissemination of periodic financial information to all security holders in quarterly reports, annual reports, and other occasional reports. The 1934 Act also outlaws securities fraud, prohibits insider trading, and regulates some aspects of corporate democracy through the regulation of proxies, proxy contests, and tender offers. Additionally, it requires registration of securities market professionals: brokers, dealers, investment advisors, stock issuers, and security exchanges. The 1934 Act gives the SEC power over most of these regulatory matters.

C. Public Utility Holding Company Act of 1935

Congress extended the securities regulation framework to the public utility industry in 1935, with passage of the Public Utility Holding Company Act of 1935. This Act required restructuring of the parent and subsidiary relationships of most public utilities. The Act broke up a pyramid scheme in which numerous layer upon layer of holding companies existed. These families of corporations operated most of the public utilities across America. After its passage most utilities became more responsive to their shareholders and customers. The Act resulted in creation of many smaller sub-units. The original subsidiaries of the holding companies were required to confine their business within small regions managed by local management. This arguably made them operate more efficiently. This Act forever changed the capital structure of public utilities. Today it prevents a reversion to the complex pyramid capital structure existing before 1935.

D. Trust Indenture Act of 1939

Before 1939 corporate bondholders held a weak position in the corporate capital structure. Although bonds typically have priority over equity in the payment of current interests or in bankruptcy liquidation, their position may be at risk from management's actions. Corporations are controlled by shareholders through their voting in directors' elections and on various resolutions. Over the years, bondholders have strengthened this weak position somewhat by designating a third party intermediary, the indenture trustee, to protect bondholders' interests.

The SEC discovered that many indenture trustees were not safeguarding bondholders' interests sufficiently. Some trustees yielded to conflicts of interests that arose because they had other contractual obligations to the corporation's managers. Congress responded to the potential for bondholders poor representation with passage of the Trust Indenture Act of 1939. This Act requires all indenture trustees to maintain independence from the corporations that issue the debt.

Indenture trustees have a fiduciary duty to bondholders and may not give special treatment to the corporate issuer. The trustee must monitor the issuers performance of the bond indenture contract. This includes monitoring the issuers' prompt payment of periodic interest to all bondholders, assurances that prompt and sufficient payments are made into sinking funds intended to eventually repay the bond principal, and assure adequate maintenance of the value of collateral. This Act requires the trustee to monitor compliance with the bond indenture contract. The Act also permits bondholders to communicate among themselves to further their mutual self-interest.

E. Investment Company Act of 1940

The Investment Company Act of 1940 regulates investment companies. These are commonly known as mutual funds, bond funds, and money market funds. Investment companies are separate corporations whose primary business is the investing, reinvesting, and trading in securities of other firms. Investors who purchase investment companies shares are able to get a small chunk of a large and diversified investment portfolio. The investment company passes on its profits to its own shareholders. The Act requires registration of investment companies with the SEC and mandates disclosures of their financial condition, investment policies, and listings of their investments. Underwriters, investment bankers, and brokers are prohibited from owning excessive amounts of investment company shares. Investment companies may not issue debt or have a pyramid capital structures. The consulting and service contracts that investment companies have with brokers, dealers, and investment advisors must be fair, arms-length transactions.

F. Investment Advisors Act of 1940

Congress gave the SEC power to regulate investment advisors, persons who charge a fee to advise investors about their securities transactions. The Act requires registration of investment advisors with the SEC and mandates disclosure about their backgrounds, business affiliations, and methods of compensation. Investment advisors must keep good records. The Act provides for criminal and other penalties for fraudulent activities.

G. Securities Investors Protection Act of 1970

The stock market became quite popular in the late 1960's with an ever increasing volume of securities transactions conducted through stock brokerages. Eventually several of the smaller and less efficient brokerage houses were unable to keep up with the increased paperwork load of this increased trading activity. Investors suffered large losses when some brokerages became bankrupt because their securities and funds are often held in the brokerage firm's name (street name) for custody and safekeeping.

Congress passed the Securities Investors Protection Act in 1970 to create a nonprofit insurance fund, the Securities Investors Protection Corporation (SIPC), which insures investor's funds if a brokerage company goes bankrupt. The SIPC collects flat fee insurance premiums from all broker/dealers based on their trading volume. These premiums accumulate into a fund for the protection of investors' accounts. The Act permits the SIPC to assist in liquidating insolvent brokers and guarantee customers accounts with the proceeds of the insurance fund.

III. Securities Market Structure

The markets for corporate securities originally began as informal and unorganized groups of stock traders who met along the street curbs in New York City. As they met more frequently this eventually developed into the organized marketplaces known as stock exchanges. Today, the stock exchanges are liquid markets in that they generally provide sufficient buyers and sellers to facilitate trades. The exchanges form the secondary or trading markets for securities that are already issued and outstanding. When stocks or bonds are first issued, they are sold through broker/dealers into the primary or initial issuance market and trade among investors on the exchanges thereafter.

A. Stock Exchanges

There are numerous securities exchanges throughout the United States and around the world. The predominant market in the United States include the New York Exchange (NYE), the American Stock Exchange (AMEX) and the over the counter market (OTC) that trades over the telephone and computer screen system known as the National Association of Securities Dealers automated quotation service (NASDAQ). Important stock exchanges

around the world include the Toronto and Montreal Stock Exchanges in Canada, the Tokyo Exchange in Japan, the Exchange in Hong Kong and in Sydney, Australia. Important European markets include the London Stock Exchange, the Frankfurt Stock Exchange, and other exchanges in Brussels, Belgium; Milan, Italy; Paris, France; Stockholm, Sweden; Zurich, Switzerland; and Amsterdam in the Netherlands. Smaller but emerging markets exist in Madrid, Spain; Seoul, South Korea; Singapore; Taiwan; Indonesia; and in Mexico City.

There are two other major markets in the United States that trade commodities or "derivative instruments" that can affect the stock markets. These include the Chicago Board Options (CBOT), and the Chicago Mercantile Exchange (MERC). Telephone and computer links between the world's markets and the harmonization of international securities laws promise to bring together these diverse markets into a single and unified capital market. The U.S. securities laws provide a model for other nations' security regulations and the European Economic Community (EEC) efforts to harmonize European laws should work together to form a uniform securities regulatory scheme worldwide. However, the unique features of several nations laws may obstruct the harmonization of diverse institutional structures in the near term.

Securities exchanges are physical facilities organized to support an auction-like atmosphere for purchase and sale of securities between members who hold a "seat" on the exchange. These members trade securities for the benefit of their customers, the investors who patronize brokerages. Thereby, when an investor seeks to purchase or sell a security, the investor's local broker transmits the buy or sell order to an affiliate on the floor of the stock exchange. The affiliate signals a floor broker to execute the trade who makes a record of the transaction on small slips of paper. In the future, floor brokers may use small hand-held terminals to record the time, date, amount, price, and identity of the other party.

There are other trading methods that bypass the trading floor of the exchange. For example, two brokerages can make trades over the telephone or on computer terminals. A broker can also fill its customer's orders from the broker's inventory of securities. Very large trades can be processed through a master computer at the exchanges (e.g., NYSE's Super-DOT). This is how much of the so-called "program trading" occurs.

I. THE SPECIALIST SYSTEM

The trading methods mentioned above may seem somewhat unreliable if there are no ready and willing buyers to fill a seller's trade or insufficient sellers to sell to a ready buyer. Another market structure has developed to create a more dependable supply of buyers and sellers: the specialist system. *Specialists*, known as *market makers* in the OTC market, are well-known persons who primarily buy and sell the stock of only one or a few companies. All other floor traders can locate specialists because they are positioned at well-known physical locations on the exchange floor. Market makers in the OTC market are usually available by telephone.

Specialists maintain an inventory of the securities they specialize in to fill the buy orders of other traders' customers. Specialists also purchase excess supply of securities when there are more sellers than buyers. Specialists make a profit on the "spread," the difference between the price bid by buyers and the price asked by sellers which is usually slightly higher. Some specialists also receive a portion of the customer's commission paid by the broker. Specialists record the purchase and sell·orders of other brokers' customers in a journal, the "specialists' book." An analyses of the specialists book can reveal inside information about the supply and demand for a security. This information enables specialists to make additional profits justified because they

are obligated to maintain an orderly market. The specialists book must be kept confidential except when subpoenaed by regulators.

As transactions are completed by specialists, exchange brokers, or on the OTC market, the prices and number of shares (volume) in each trade are reported through ticker tape and other data reporting services. These are usually made available to investors and brokerage companies over computer data retrieval services and on some financial news networks. Price quotes between OTC brokers and dealers are communicated by NASDAQ computer terminals. This system most closely resembles the "national market system" that Congress mandated in its effort to consolidate all securities markets. Additionally there are computer links among those who deal in private placement securities and between several major stock exchanges in the world: NYSE-London Stock Exchange. Brokers representing foreign clients may be required to register in the United States or use a correspondent American brokers to purchase or sell U.S. securities for their foreign clients.

IV. The Securities and Exchange Commission

Congress established the Securities and Exchange Commission (SEC) in the 1934 Act. The SEC administers the securities laws as an independent bipartisan agency of the United States Government. The SEC is composed of five commissioners who must represent a political balance, only three commissioners may represent any one political party at any one time. SEC commissioners are appointed by the President and confirmed by the Senate, serving for staggered five year terms. The SEC has substantial staff in its Washington home office and its nine regional and branch offices in major financial centers. SEC staff includes accountants, lawyers, engineers, economists, and securities analysts who provide advice and research for the commissioners.

A. SEC Divisions

The SEC is divided into five major divisions and several other offices. Each is charged with separate regulatory duties. The Division of Corporate Finance establishes financial reporting disclosure standards after studying the economic impact that particular financial information has on investors. Disclosures in IPO's, annual reports, quarterly reports, prospectuses, registration statements, and proxy statements must conform to SEC rules developed by this division.

The SEC Division of Market Regulation is responsible for licensing brokers, dealers, and exchanges. This division inspects these securities markets professional and advises the commission on new regulations in that area. The SEC Enforcement Division is responsible for investigations and bringing enforcement action against all potential wrongdoers. The division is the prosecutorial arm of the SEC responsible for bringing suits in the federal courts, pursuing administrative actions within the SEC, and referring cases to the Justice Department for criminal prosecution.

The Division of Investment Management Regulation is responsible to investigate and inspect mutual funds and investment advisors. This division provides policy advice to the SEC, often resulting in new regulations of mutual funds and investment advisors. The SEC Division of Corporate Regulation administers the Public Utility Holding Company Act of 1935. From time to time, the division has provided advice to bankruptcy courts on the impact of corporate reorganization on the securities of firms emerging from Chapter 11 bankruptcy proceedings.

There are several additional offices within the SEC that provide specialized services to the commissioners. For example, the Office of the Chief Accountant provides expert advice on auditing and standards matters. This office is largely responsible for the studies and advice leading to changing accounting standards the SEC imposes. The office of the General Counsel is the prosecutorial arm of the Commission in judicial proceedings. The Directorate of Economic and Policy Analysis provides empirical market study information and recommendations for new regulation proposals. The Office of International Affairs negotiates memoranda of understanding (MOU) with the securities regulators in many foreign nations. It is also responsible for international enforcement. For example, insider traders in the United States might attempt to use secret numbered Swiss bank accounts to execute their trades in an effort to hide from detection. The Office of International Affairs is responsible for negotiating general and specific agreements to receive information from foreign banking regulators about who actually owns these accounts.

B. Investigations by the SEC

The SEC has investigatory powers, similar to criminal prosecutors, to discover violations of the securities laws. The SEC and its various divisions may interview witnesses, examine brokerage records and collect trading data from the stock exchanges. SEC investigations are triggered by investors' complaints, surprise inspections, or through observation of unusual trading activity that may be correlated with known events such as a takeover. When the SEC staff has gathered sufficient information during this informal investigation stage to suggest wrong doing, the SEC votes to issue a formal order of investigation (FOI).

Once the FOI is granted, the SEC enforcement staff may issue subpoenas to examine witnesses under oath and secure documents. However, witnesses and the custodians of documents may refuse to comply with an SEC subpoena until it is enforced by a federal district court. The suspected wrongdoer, or target of an investigation, is not legally entitled to receive notice that the SEC is seeking documents for testimony from other persons. Unless the SEC is acting in bad faith or with-

Example. The SEC began an investigation of Harry and several firms he dealt with. The SEC authorized a formal investigation with an FOI and subpoenas of financial records of Harry's broker were issued. Harry's broker sued to prevent the SEC from enforcing its subpoenas for information about Harry's trading activities. The broker argued that an investigation made without giving notice to the target would deprive the target (Harry) of due process.

Targets of investigations have no right to receive notice that subpoenas are issued to other parties nor can they stop the investigation. Investigations do not involve any constitutional right to confront witnesses and there is no compelled self-incrimination because the documents held in the hands of other persons, like those held by Harry's broker, do not require a person to testify against himself. There is no illegal search or seizure because information communicated to another party (e.g., consultant, broker dealer, accountant), even if in confidence, is not objectionable if that information is conveyed to law enforcement authorities.

The practical effect of a notice requirement for regulators like the SEC would impose highly burdensome compliance procedures. Notice might permit the target to impede the legitimate investigation. For example, the target might discourage the third party recipients of the subpoena from complying, intimidate witnesses, alter or destroy documents, or transfer its funds out of the reach of government enforcers. Therefore the SEC may pursue its investigations without notifying investigatory targets when documents or witnesses are subpoenaed.

out statutory authority, the courts usually enforce these subpoenas.

C. Enforcement Powers of the SEC

The SEC has a wide range of actions and remedies it may bring against potential violators of the securities laws. After an investigation, the SEC may hold an in-house hearing and order particular remedies against certain offenders: (1) suspend traders from their activity on securities exchanges, (2) deny, suspend, or revoke the dealer registrations, (3) issue cease and desist orders, (4) censure violators, or (5) assess civil damage penalties against willful violators of the antifraud provisions of the securities laws. The Enforcement Remedies and Penny Stock Reform Act of 1990 also gives the SEC power to regulate the coercive aspects of the penny stock market, regulate program trading, or close down the securities markets unless the President vetos the action.

When stronger action is needed, the SEC may bring suit in the federal district courts.

The SEC usually seeks an injunction and other ancillary equitable remedies. The new enforcement law permits the SEC to ask courts to bar securities professionals from serving as officers or directors of public companies if they violate the securities laws. In very serious cases, the SEC may refer the evidence it has gathered to the Justice Department which may prosecute criminal actions brought by the local United States Attorney.

The SEC's powers to secure ancillary relief may take several forms. Illegal trading profits may be disgorged and remitted to the court for repayment to the victims of insider trading. In some cases the SEC has been successful in getting a receiver appointed to operate a grossly mismanaged company. Some companies have been forced to accept SEC approved directors. In addition, there have been changes in accounting practices, changes in the board of directors, changes in business practices, and special corrective disclosures ordered as part of court approved settlement (consent decree).

Example. The SEC required D Indus. to disclose several illegal payments it made to foreign purchasers. After D Indus. made several additional clarifications, the SEC provided these documents to the Justice Department. D Indus. sued to prevent the transfer of information from the SEC to the Justice Department. D Indus. claimed that because the SEC's civil investigations powers are broader than the Justice Department's criminal investigations power the referral would impermissibly expand the scope of criminal discovery.

The SEC may freely share investigative information with other agencies such as the Justice Department. Although Congress restricts the amount of information the Internal Revenue Service may refer to the Justice Department, the SEC has no similar restriction. Parallel investigations by more than one regulatory agency are quite common and do not deprive the regulated entities of their constitutional rights. While there may be a small probability of inconsistent results from two agencies' investigations, the SEC's market protection function is more important. Therefore, one agency need not wait for the outcome of a protracted investigation by another agency before initiating enforcement. ☐

The SEC's regulatory powers overlaps somewhat with other agencies' powers permitting parallel investigations. However, if the SEC or any other regulatory agency assesses punitive penalties, rather than remedial remedies like disgorgement, the penalty is considered punishment under the double jeopardy clause of the U.S. Constitution. Thereafter, a defendant cannot be convicted and punished criminally for the same violations. The SEC's custom of referring its investigatory files to the Justice Department does not impermissibly expand the scope of criminal discovery.

D. Rulemaking by the SEC

Periodically the SEC proposes, revises, promulgates, rescinds, and enforces rules and regulations to further the purposes of the securities laws. SEC rulemaking is a quasi-legislative power to interpret and extend the existing securities laws. The SEC's rules are quite significant in the areas of securities fraud, insider trading, corporate financial disclosure, proxy contests, tender offers, and regulation of securities professionals. In most instances, the SEC must follow the notice and comment (informal) rulemaking process discussed previously in the chapter on Administrative Law.

V. Registration of Securities for Initial Offering

Traditionally, securities are first offered to the public in an initial public offering (IPO). For companies that were previously closely held this process is know as "going public." Few companies can sell their securities successfully to the public without the assistance of an underwriter. The underwriter is any person who has purchased securities from an issuer with a view to distributing the security and who offers and sells any security for an issuer in connection with an IPO. Underwriters typically assemble a syndicate or group of other underwriters each of which will purchase a portion of the issuer's securities. Underwriters are like wholesalers who resell through members of the underwriting syndicate and eventually to ultimate investors. The underwriting process also involves the professional services of securities law firms and independent auditors all of whom verify information or assist in the process of registering the new issue of securities with the SEC.

A. Registration Process

The 1933 Act requires the issuers of new securities to provide financial and other information for investors to evaluate the new securities offered. These disclosures must be made in two documents: (1) a registration statement filed with the SEC and (2) a prospectus. The *prospectus* is any notice circular, advertisement, letter or communication written or by radio or television offering any security for sale. Both documents must include audited financial statements, 5 years of financial comparative information, and management's discussion and analysis of the issuers financial condition, information about the issuers' management, a description of the security being offered, and an explanation of the proposed use of the proceeds from the IPO sale. The prospectus must be delivered to all potential investors to whom an offer is made (*offerees*).

The registration process begins with a prefiling period during which the issuer is prohibited from selling securities or making public announcements that tend to condition the market. *Preconditioning* occurs if the issuer or the underwriter distributes press releases or makes any other public announcements that predict success for the issuing company or the offering of new securities. Preconditioning tends to stimulate investor demand before the prospectus information is publicly known inducing investors to purchase without assessing the quality of the securities. This was precisely the problem that occurred during the Roaring 20s that Congress intended to prohibit by passing the 1933 Act. During the prefiling period issuers are permitted to contact their investment bankers for advice and negotiate with underwriters who might participate in the syndicate. The registration statement and prospectus must be prepared for filing with the SEC. Issuers must maintain

business as usual by continuing communications with its current security holders, customers, suppliers, the press and securities analysis.

After filing of the registration statement with the SEC, a waiting period of approximately 20 days or so begins. During this time no contracts may be made to sell the new securities. The waiting period provides time for SEC review and clearance of the registration statement. However, the SEC does not make judgments of the firm's investment value.

During the waiting period, the issuer and underwriter may distribute statutory offers to buy or sell securities but may not complete these contracts with an acceptance to buy or sell. Four types of statutory offers may be made during the waiting period. First, the issuer may make *tombstone ads* in the financial press which announce the offering, identify the security, the underwriters and dealers, and mention a probable price range. Tombstones are notices often seen in the business press with a distinctive boarder and the name of the firm in the middle with names of the underwriting syndicate at the bottom. The second communication permitted is the *red herring prospectus*, actually a draft copy of the prospectus with red ink in the margins clearly disclaiming that any offer is made by it. This is a highly detailed document, it must omit stating the price. The third type of permissible communication is an oral offer including those made over the telephone. It is permitted so long as there is no acceptance. The fourth permitted communication is a summary prospectus providing information condensed from the preliminary prospectus.

The *post effective* period begins after the waiting period is over or it begins when the SEC accelerates the effective date of the registration statement. This period lasts 40 days or until all the securities are sold out to investors. After the registration statement becomes effective the preliminary, red herring prospectus may not be used. All persons who re-

FIGURE 16.1 REGISTRATION PROCESS: INITIAL PUBLIC OFFERINGS OF SECURITIES

	Registration Statement Filed with S.E.C		*Registration Statement Becomes Effective*
	Pre-Filing Period	**Waiting Period**	**Post-Effective Period**
Time Period	All the time before an issuer files a registration statement with the SEC. Filing is the 1st public disclosure of the issuer's intent to sell new securities to the public. Preparation for going public typically takes several months.	This period begins with the issuer's filing of the registration statement at the SEC. This period ends after 20 days passes or SEC clearance is given for sale of the new securities. Period may be extended if SEC suggests revision to registration.	The period begins with the SEC clearance or with the passage of 20 days. This period lasts until all securities are sold to investors..
Prohibitions	No offers, contracts for sale, or sales of securities. No pre-conditioning the market to stimulate investor demand.	No contracts to sell or sales of securities.	No "Red Herring" prospectus may be distributed.
Permissible/ Necessary Activities	Issuer must negotiate with an investment banker which assembles an underwriting syndicate of other participating investment bankers and dealers. The registration statement and drafts of the prospectus are prepared for filing and ultimate distribution. Issuer must maintain its "business as usual" in all communications with existing security holders, suppliers, customers, press, and securities analysts.	Issuer can make certain offers to sell securities: – Oral offers – Tombstone ads – "Red Herring" or preliminary prospectus SEC Clearance Final prospectus prepared	Securities registered may be sold to investors. Formal/Final prospectus must be delivered before or with the securities sold and memos confirming sales. Must attempt to sell all securities registered unless made in a shelf offering.

Example. Florida vacationers staying at a resort were often driven through orange groves owned by the resort operator. Many vacationers were offered and some purchased portions of producing orange groves in a land sale contract. Most of these purchasers also contracted for the cultivation and marketing services of another company related to the land seller. These service contracts gave the service company complete and exclusive possession of the acreage. All investor's land was contiguous, there were no fences or markers dividing their parcels. The harvested crop was pooled and purchasers shared profits in the proportion their land stood to the total land owned by all investors. Most investors were nonresident professionals with no citrus growing expertise.

These investments were considered securities under the investment contract definition. Clearly there was an investment of money made by these investors. Because all the land was treated as a single producing farm the investment was a common enterprise. The orange groves were marketed with promises of profits which came primarily from the efforts of the affiliated cultivation service company. This common management and pooling of profits is the most important factor in finding this arrangement constituted a security. ☐

ceive securities or confirmations of sale must be given a formal, definitive, final prospectus. Additionally, the issuer must attempt to sell all the newly registered securities out quickly. The registration process is summarized in figure 16.1.

I. SHELF REGISTRATION

The issuer is usually responsible to sell all securities in the issue as quickly as possible after the post-effective period begins. However, there is an important exception under the shelf registration rule. The issuer may go through all the steps of the registration process previously discussed but delay making the actual sales until the proceeds are needed or until market conditions are optimal. The registered securities are placed in the issuer's inventory, "on the shelf," for later sale. Shelf issuers may avoid the use of underwriters altogether and arguably avoid the additional costs.

B. What is a Security?

There is a fundamental question that determines whether the securities laws are applicable to a plan of financing: "What is a security?"

There are many forms of investment but the securities laws are not intended to apply to purely commercial or consumptional transactions, to commodities transactions, or to foreign currency transactions. The 1933 Act generally defines the term security in precise terms but leaves the definition flexible with the catch-all term investment contract.

Definition of a "Security"

A security is any note, stock, treasury stock, bond, debenture, evidence of indebtedness, transferable share, *investment contract,* voting trust certificate, certificates of deposit for a security, or fractional undivided interest in oil, gas, or other mineral rights, any put, call, straddle, stock option or warrant.

Most of the traditional securities trading on the public exchanges clearly falls within this definition. Congress intended for this list to be nonexclusive so that any new investment devices that involve the raising of capital and have the similar characteristics is designated as a security. The list quoted above includes the catchall provision, investment contract which permits application of the securities laws to new and innovative transactions. An *investment contract* involves the investment

Example. L sold his family lumber business by selling all the stock in the closely held corporation that operated the business. The purchasers had trouble making their new business successful. They sued L for fraud under the securities laws. L claimed that the transaction involved the sale of a whole business and should therefore be exempt from the securities laws. Additionally, the buyer was primarily responsible for the success of the business so allegedly the fourth element of the investment contract definition was not satisfied.

The investment contract catchall applies only when the investment is not one enumerated on the list in the 1933 Act definition. The seller here sold stock with all the traditional characteristics of stock. Most persons realize that sales of traditional stock are governed by the securities laws. There is no "sale of business doctrine" exception to the definition of a security. This sale of a business was governed by the securities laws because the parties chose to make their transaction through a sale of all the corporation's stock rather than through a sale of the corporation's assets.

of money into a common enterprise or scheme where the investor is lead to expect profits derived from the promoter's efforts.

Investment Contract

1. investment of money
2. common enterprise or scheme
3. expectation of profits
4. efforts of promoter

This broader definition has been applied to designate the following investment schemes as securities: limited partnership interests, equipment trusts certificates, certain franchises, and pyramid selling schemes. Securities tend to be speculative and sold in a public manner to investors who need the greater legal protections of the securities law than is provided by the law of contracts or torts.

Land sales are seldom considered securities as in the example above. However, where the investor/purchasers are promised some profit from the efforts of others, a land sale resembles a security. For example, condominiums and time share arrangements are often marketed primarily as investments because they are attractive to renters. Therefore, under such circumstances land sales are considered securities. A similar analysis was applied to the distiller of Scotch whiskey. The distiller sold warehouse receipts representing Scotch while it was aging in the barrel. The purchase

contracts obligated each investor to resell the Scotch back to the distiller for later bottling and sale. Because the investor is separated from the promoter's efforts that produce income, a security is involved.

C. Registration Exemptions

Compliance with the SEC's securities registration process may sometimes be inapplicable and other times is modified in certain transactions. Exempt securities include all securities issued by governments (e.g., federal, state, industrial revenue), those securities issued by banks, religious and charitable institutions, savings and loans, as well as most insurance policies and annuities, and securities issued in a bankruptcy reorganization. Additionally, short term commercial paper issued by corporations for a commercial purpose with a maturity of nine months or less is exempt.

In addition to these exempt securities there are exempt transactions that permit a reduced registration requirement due to the size, scope, or extent of the distribution. For example, registration is not required if an issuer exchanges a new security for a previously outstanding security so long as no commission is paid. This exception is intended to cover recapitalizations, reorganizations, and mergers. No new money may be solicited from investors as part of an exempt exchange transaction.

I. INTRASTATE OFFERINGS

The securities laws require no registration for intrastate sales made wholly within one state. This exemption is based on the federalism principle permitting the states to regulate matters with no substantial impact on interstate commerce; only the state's blue sky securities laws apply.

The SEC has clarified this exemption with the *safe harbor* of Rule 147. Intrastate sales of unregistered securities are permitted if they meet three requirements. First, all the purchasers of the security must be residents of the state. Second, the issuer must be domiciled and doing business within that state. Third, the majority of the economic activity involved must be located largely in that state as judged by the three 80% rules: (1) 80% or more of the issuers' gross revenues comes from that state, (2) 80% or more of the issuer's assets are located within the state, and (3) 80% of the proceeds raised in the offering must be spent in that state. Securities sold in an interstate offering must include a restriction printed directly on the certificates (legend) warning about the intrastate restriction. For example, consider the hypothetical Keystone Corp. domiciled in Pennsylvania which quarries limestone from mines in Pennsylvania for use primarily in Pennsylvania state government buildings. Keystone may avoid the 1933 Act registration process if it issues stock only to Pennsylvania residents and the 80% rules stated above are satisfied.

2. SMALL ISSUES

Small firms may offer up to $1.5 million worth of securities with reduced registration requirements. An *offering statement* must be filed with the SEC including unaudited financial statements and a description of the issuer. These small issues are offered under Regula-tion A. The offering statement must be given to all potential buyers who are solicited. Use of the small issue exemption has declined in recent years due to the expansion of the private placement exemption under Regulation D.

3. PRIVATE PLACEMENTS

The biggest growth in exempt transactions is in private placements made under section 4(2) of the 1933 Act or under the SEC's Regulation D. Private placements are made by many types of issuers: small and risky companies, big blue chip corporations, and they are used for many leveraged buy out transactions. In the future, many foreign companies may issue securities in the United States under the private placement exemption. Issuers need only file Form D with the SEC showing minimal information.

Most of the investors in private placements are big institutional investors: insurance companies, pension funds, or other accredited investors. *Accredited investors* are those considered financially sophisticated with sufficient net worth, experience, and knowledge of the securities markets to fend for themselves. Rule 504 under Regulation D permits sales of up to $1 million worth of securities during any 12 month period. There are no limits on the number or qualifications of investors but no public solicitation may be made. Under Rule 505, $5 million of securities may be sold within any 12 month period to 35 nonaccredited investors and an unlimited number of accredited investors. Under Rule 506, an unlimited amount of proceeds may be raised from 35 nonaccredited investors and an unlimited number of accredited investors. Under Rules 505 or 506, if sales are made to nonaccredited investors, then certain disclosures must be made.

Issuers are entitled to this private placement exemption only if there are assurances that the shares will not trade widely among the public. To prevent the limited number of un-

Example. BC Corp was involved in the construction of bowling alleys during that industry's big building boom. BC went public at about the same time the bowling industry became over-built. BC's registration statement reflected various false statements including an omission that bowling alley operators had begun to default on payments to BC. Investors sued the officers, directors, underwriters, and auditors, for misrepresentation. The defendants responded that they acted with due diligence and should not be liable.

The officers and directors attended director's meetings and were intimately familiar with the firm's financial condition. If they truly misunderstood the firm's financial condition, they were negligent in their duties under the securities laws. The auditing firm made little inquiry into the accounts as recorded by management. Auditors must proceed with greater diligence when errors are discovered and important financial records are found missing. Underwriters are required to do more than superficial analysis of an issuers current financial condition and future prospects. There is no hard and fast rule of what constitutes due diligence rather it is determined by the circumstances as in any other instance of professional malpractice. □

accredited and accredited investors from reselling these restricted securities more broadly to the public, the SEC has imposed *resale restrictions*. Securities sold under a Regulation D exemption are restricted from resale for 2 years except to Qualified Institutional Buyers (QIB). A QIB generally includes any institutional investor with securities investments of over $100 million. Financial institutions such as savings and loans, must satisfy more stringent net worth requirements to participate in this market. This private placement resale market was created by Rule 144A. It provides access for foreign corporate issuers to the U.S. capital markets.

D. Securities Act Liabilities

Issuers guilty of misstatements, omissions or fraud in the sale of new securities are liable for damages caused to investors. The issuer may be ordered to repurchase the securities from a defrauded investor or pay damages equal to the difference between the initial offering price and the security's actual value at the time of suit. All persons involved in an IPO are subject to liability including: the issuer, underwriters, control persons, and any person signing the registration statement (e.g.,

officer, director, auditor, law firm). Those involved with the IPO may escape liability if they are not negligent. The *due diligence* defense shields these responsible parties from liability if they reasonably believe the registration statement contained no errors. Some parties may be required to reasonably investigate the true facts.

VI. Insider Trading

Insider trading is prohibited by state law, the federal securities laws, and is illegal by inference under laws prohibiting fraud. While the term insider trading is still not well defined, it generally includes trading in a firm's securities by persons who have access to confidential, non-public information that gives them an advantage over outsiders. This is a form of fraud by omission because unsuspecting investors trade with insiders who have abused their position of trust to the corporation.

Some theorists argue that insider trading is harmless. First, they claim that it is a victimless crime. Next, they claim it has no negative effects because if it did the firm's shareholders would certainly prohibit it. Third, some opponents of restricting insider trading argue that corporate managers should be permitted insider trading privileges as part of their compensation package. Finally, some theorists argue that the market becomes more efficient when insiders trade. Insiders' trades signal other investors about the secret information insiders possess by inferring positive or negative information from the direction of price movements.

Despite the arguments in favor of insider trading, the practice is considered unfair and illegal. Insiders possess an informational advantage that outsiders cannot overcome no matter how hard they work. If insider trading becomes rampant, the investing public may lose its trust in the markets leading to a loss in public confidence. This will impede businesses ability to raise capital. Opponents of insider trading also point out that most firms today prohibit insider trading. If managers expected insider trading profits could supplement their income, they would be motivated to manipulate the release of information to investors. As a result, most market professionals, the Congress, the SEC and the courts have made insider trading illegal. Nevertheless, insider trading opportunities still exist because detection and enforcement is often difficult.

A. Short Swing Profits

The first Congressional prohibition of insider trading was made part of the 1934 Act in Section 16(b). Short swing profits made by officers, directors, or 10% shareholders must be repaid to the corporation. Insiders also include all those persons performing officer-like duties or who are deputized to act as directors by another corporation. Any person owning 10% or more of any class of equity security is a 10% shareholder. These big block shareholders are presumed to have sufficient influence on management to regularly receive inside information. If several related family members beneficially own 10% or more of a security, they will be considered an insider as a group.

I. PURCHASE AND SALE REQUIREMENT

Section 16 (a) requires that the insiders defined by section 16 must report every purchase or sale they make in the issuer's equity securities. This provision is intended to deter short swing profits because short swing profits are easy to detect. Profits made on a purchase followed by a sale within any six month period belong to the corporation. This is a sliding six month scale that captures any two transactions made within any six month period. Although profits are usually made on purchase that precede sales in a rising market, if a sale precedes the purchase in a falling market, the insider is nevertheless liable for the loss foregone.

2. DAMAGES FOR SHORT SWING PROFITS

Short swing profits may be recovered either by the corporation or any shareholder acting on its behalf. Short swing profits are computed as the difference between the purchase and sale price, or the sale and purchase price. These damages are paid directly into the corporate treasury and do not belong to any shareholder individually.

The law permits the courts to match purchase against sales irrespective of the actual stock certificates bought or sold in order to maximize the apparent profit and thereby maximize the penalty. Therefore, the FIFO (first in, first out) method of matching stock certificates is not used. This means the prices of the securities first purchased are not compared with the prices of those first sold to determine damages unless that would maximize the damage result. Rather, the lowest purchase price and the highest sale price within any six monthly period are compared to maximize the measure of illegal trading profits. For example, if a statutory insider purchases shares at $20 in January and sells shares for $25 in April, a $5 illegal trading profit occurs. However, if another purchase is made in July at $ 15 then the illegal trading profit is $10—this is the July purchase compared with the

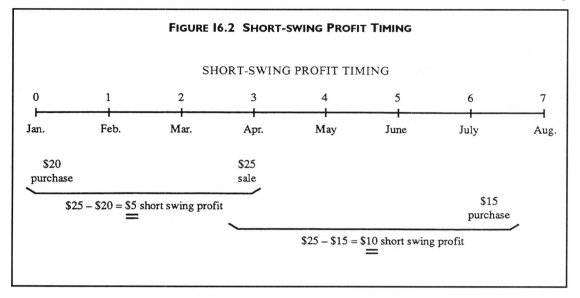

FIGURE 16.2 SHORT-SWING PROFIT TIMING

April sale. Figure 16.2 illustrates this matching process. Short swing profit damages are maximized to create a strong deterrent to insiders' short swing profits. Section 16 presumes that insiders have access to inside information so it is unnecessary to prove any use of inside information in a suit to recover short swing profits.

B. Insider Trading Under Rule 10b-5

The more familiar basis for the insider trader prohibition is derived from the common law of fraud (deceit) and the antifraud provisions of the securities laws. Under this theory, it is unlawful for insiders who owe a fiduciary duty to their shareholders to omit disclosing important insider information when they trade with shareholders. This duty originated in the early twentieth century when special circumstances dictated that insiders should act fairly with their shareholders.

I. RULE 10B-5

The 1934 Act prohibits deception with Rule 10b-5. This rule is the basic insider trading provision used in prosecutions today. The SEC passed Rule 10b-5 to implement the anti-fraud objectives inherent in the 1934 Act.

Rule 10b-5

It shall be unlawful for any person, directly or indirectly by the use of any means or instrumentality of interstate commerce, or of the mails, or of any facility of any national securities exchange,

(1) to employ any device, scheme, or artifice to defraud,

(2) to make any untrue statement of a material fact or to omit to state a material fact that is necessary in order to make the statements made, in the light of the circumstances for which they were made, not misleading, or

(3) to engage in any act, practice or course of business which operates or would operate as a fraud or deceit upon any person, in connection with the purchase or sale of any security.

Example. The controlling stockholder of a firm approached many shareholders to purchase their shares. The controlling shareholder omitted to disclose that he was involved in negotiations to sell the firm's assets for an amount that would yield a value per share that far exceeded what he paid them for their shares. The minority shareholders sued claiming his insider knowledge created special circumstances and a duty to disclose those facts before purchasing their shares.

Insiders have a fiduciary duty and occupy a trusteeship like status when they have special inside information that affects the value of other shareholder's interests. The misuse of this information for personal gain effectively misappropriates a corporate secret for the personal benefit of the misappropriator. Insider trading is illegal under state corporate law and under the tort of deceit. □

Insiders at all levels within the corporation are prohibited from insider trading under the "disclose or abstain" rule. This rule effectively requires insiders to disclose their inside information before trading. Of course, if the information is truly valuable, the market will react quickly and any insider trading opportunities will be lost. However, an insider who discloses confidential data or other information may damage the corporation and thereby violate the insider's fiduciary duty.

Factors in Rule 10b-5 Insider Trading

1. Identity of insider
2. Tippee's liable for trading on stock tips
3. Fiduciary duty of insider
4. Materiality of misstatements or omissions
5. Victim's reliance on misrepresentations or omissions
6. Identity of persons entitled to sue
7. Measure of damage or penalties

2. IDENTIFICATION OF INSIDERS

The insiders subject to Rule 10b-5 liability are somewhat broader than the statutory insiders defined under Section 10(b). Officers and directors are nearly always insiders restricted under Rule 10b-5. However, there are instances when 10% shareholders such as hostile takeover bidders do not have access to inside information. In some instances lower level employees have access to inside infor-

mation. As a result, a person's status as an insider is determined on an ad hoc, subjective basis. The SEC uses the following factors to determine when a person has insider trading responsibilities: 1. a relationship gives access to confidential information, 2. the information is intended only for corporate purposes, and 3. the person uses the information unfairly and for other personal benefit.

This insider definition creates an ambiguity for many market participants. It is clear that illegal activities such as eavesdropping, bribery, or wiretapping gives illegal access to inside information. Numerous persons outside the firm may occasionally have access to confidential information. There should be an objective rule so persons can easily understand when their trading is illegal. This raises questions of insider trading liability for a number of outsiders including corporate consultants and tippees.

3. OUTSIDER LIABILITY

Under certain circumstances, non-employees of the firm whose shares are traded may be held liable for insider trading. Anyone aiding and abetting an insider trader may be held liable. For example, brokers and investment advisers who tip inside information to customers are liable. However, there has been some difficulty in determining when the information given to a tippee is tainted trigger-

Example. TG Company was involved in mineral exploration in Canada. TG drilled core samples that revealed remarkably rich copper, zinc and silver deposits. Rumors leaked to the market of the discovery, but TG Corp denied any discovery was made to permit TG to lease adjoining mineral lands. Several TG corporate executives purchased TG stock and call options before TG disclosed the mineral discovery to the public. The SEC sued claiming legal insider trading and fraudulent corporate disclosure in falsely denying the rumors.

TG Corp was not obligated to inform adjacent land owners of its mineral find in negotiating mineral leases with them. However, its denial of the mineral find was fraudulent to investors. The insiders trading without first disclosing their knowledge amounted to illegal insider trading. These insiders had an unfair informational advantage over outside investors. ☐

* * *

Example. The CW Corp directors voted to reduce its dividend below the existing level. One director worked for a brokerage company and called his office before CW Corp had issued a press release about the dividend cut. Several of the director's personal customers sold their stock in CW Corp before the news of the dividend cut was made public causing its price to fall. The SEC claimed that the director and the brokerage company were liable for insider trading.

The brokerage company gained access to confidential inside information indirectly through its employee who served as director for CW Corp. Both the director and the brokerage had an affirmative duty to disclose all material information before trading with others in the market. The director's special relationship gave access to information that was intended only for corporate purposes until publicly disclosed. The director's misuse of the information for his clients' purposes was an improper act of insider trading. ☐

ing the disclose or abstain duty. Someone in mere possession of insider information cannot be held liable for insider trading unless they breach a duty to someone. Tippees are restricted from insider trading if they have reason to know they received information from an insider who breached a fiduciary duty by transferring the information (tipping). This rule generally means there is no insider trading liability for tippees who receive information via public rumor or that is announced in a public place.

It would be harmful to the markets to impose a duty to disclose or abstain simply if a person receives material nonpublic information from an insider. The tippee's knowledge of the tipper's breach of fiduciary duty and improper receipt of consideration are essential to distinguish between improper, illegal tips and the legal product of legitimate investigation

like that done by D in the example above. It is common for analysts to ferret out and analyze information from inside sources, this information helps make the market more efficient.

Another category of insiders includes the consultants who work for the corporation. Underwriters, accountants, lawyers, financial printers, and other outside consultants may be considered *temporary insiders* during the time they are employed by the corporation. Temporary insiders have a fiduciary duty to the issuer and therefore must abide by the disclose or abstain duty. Consultants are often exposed to confidential information that they or their employees could misappropriate for personal profit. Outside consultants and their employees are considered temporary insiders who must refrain from insider trading.

Example. Because of D's position as a security analyst for a New York broker dealer he received information from S, a former officer of the EF Corporation. EF had vastly overstated its assets as a result of numerous fraudulent corporate practices. After D's visit with corporate officers and other employees, he confirmed the fraud and openly discussed these findings with his clients and with other brokers at the brokerage. Before he notified the SEC, his clients sold nearly $16,000,000 worth of EF Corp.'s stock. During this time EF Corp.'s stock price plunged from $26 per share to $15. EF eventually became insolvent. The SEC censured D for transmitting this inside information to clients.

D had no general duty under Rule 10b-5 to disclose the information publicly or abstain from disclosing to clients and trading. A tippee does not inherit the disclose or abstain duty unless the information is received improperly. This improper receipt arises when a tippee knows or should know the tipper breached a fiduciary duty to the corporation by tipping the information. Additionally, the tipper must gain some benefit directly or indirectly from making the tip. This benefit provides the basis for the improper conduct which breaches the fiduciary duty. The benefit that generally flows from tippee to tipper can include the payment of money or even the unspoken expectation that the tippee will return the favor with inside information in the future. □

4. MISAPPROPRIATION THEORY

Another basis for identifying insiders and restricting their trading activities is based on the misappropriation of confidential information. The misappropriation theory restricts both traditional insiders, outside consultants, and outside tippees from trading in the shares of the corporation if the information was stolen or misappropriated from the corporation. Once the corporation's information is wrongfully misappropriated, all later uses of that information are illegal. This provides the basis for holding a tippee liable that had reason to know of the misappropriation and gave a personal benefit to the tipper. The misappropriation theory forms the basis for insider trading prosecutions of employees of one corporation that intends to make a takeover bid for another corporation.

It is a common misconception that inside information always originates from inside the issuer whose shares are traded. However, takeovers provide outsiders with significant nonpublic information about a potential takeover. Once the public learns a target corporation may be subject to a takeover, its stock price usually rises. Insiders and tippees of the takeover bidder who know of the impending takeover might purchase shares in the target just before the takeover is announced in the hopes they will benefit from the price rise after the takeover is announced. The restriction on insider trading applies to insiders of a takeover bidder and to its consultants including: underwriters, investment bankers, law firms, financial printers, accountants, and others. Therefore, the disclose or abstain duty applies to all the participants in a takeover if information is misappropriated from some participant before it becomes known publicly.

C. Insider Trading Sanctions Act

Congress has reinforced the illegality of insider trading through passage of the Insider Trading Sanctions Act of 1984 (ITSA). The ITSA permits the SEC to seek a civil triple penalty in insider trading cases. ITSA cases are tried by a judge, not a jury. The SEC may seek a penalty of up to 3 times the victim's damages which is payable upon conviction into the

Example.   C and A worked together at the MSN and Co. investment banking firm during which time they exchanged information about potential takeovers rather freely. Clients of C and A were given this information and purchased shares of takeover targets before the public announcement of the takeovers. Additionally, C, A, and their friends used secret Swiss bank accounts to purchase shares in the takeover targets and shared their profits among the elicit group. The Justice Department charged them with a pattern of criminal securities fraud and illegal trading under Rule 10b-5.

A, C, and their cohorts were guilty of criminal fraud perpetrated on purchasers or sellers of securities in the market. A and C have misappropriated information from their employers and the tippees clearly knew this. A and C harmed the reputations of their employing underwriters because it became widely known that these companies were no longer safe repositories for the confidential information of their clients. ▢

U.S. Treasury. The ITSA's penalties may exist in addition to other remedies available under the short-swing profit Rule 16b, under Rule 10b-5, or under the tender offer insider trading rule (Rule 14e-3). Often a portion of the treble damages are set aside for the payment of victims' damages and to pay income tax on the undeclared illegal income made by inside traders.

D. Insider Trading and Securities Fraud Enforcement Act

After further revelations of insider trading abuses during the mid 1980's, Congress passed an additional statute, the Insider Trading and Securities Fraud Enforcement Act of 1988. This law raises the maximum jail sentences insider trading convictions from 5 to 10 years. Maximum criminal fines are also increased for individual defendants from $100,000 to $1,000,000. For law firms, brokerages, financial printers, investment bankers, exchanges the maximum fine is raised from $500,000 to $2,500,000. Additionally, the SEC is given discretion to award bounty payments to persons providing information about insider trading, up to ten percent of the penalty imposed or settlement reached with the SEC. Any investor trading contemporaneously, near in time with the inside traders,

may sue for damages. This law also expands the SEC's powers to solicit and assist foreign securities enforcement authorities in cases involving foreign, domestic, and international insider trading cases.

VII. Proxies

The 1934 Act regulates participants in the market for corporate control. This includes transactions initiated by individual financiers, other corporations, takeover specialists, and dissident shareholder groups who solicit the votes or the sale of shares to gain control over corporations. The traditional method of taking corporate control involves the proxy solicitation. This is an electioneering process designed to persuade other shareholders to vote for the solicitor, the solicitor's candidates for directors, or the solicitor's particular proposals when brought before a shareholder meeting.

A. Proxy Solicitation

The process by which management or dissident shareholders secure other shareholders' votes it through the proxy solicitation process. Proxy solicitations in closely held corporations are regulated by state corporation law. The 1934 Act regulates the proxy solicitation

FIGURE 16.3 COMPARISON OF INSIDER TRADING THEORIES

	Rule 10b-5	Section 16
Plaintiffs	SEC Justice Department Shareholder trading contemporaneously	Issuer Shareholder in derivative suit
Defendants/ Insider	Any employee of issuer, temporary insider, misappropriator, and some tippees	Statutory Insiders: – Officers – Directors – 10% Shareholders Nominees, Assistants
Covered Securities	Any security whether or not registered	Any registered equity security
Access to Inside Information	Misappropriation necessary	Presumed; so no proof required
Disclosure	Disclose inside information or abstain from trading	Statutory Insiders must file Form 3 or Form 4, 10 days after month of purchase or sale
Tippees	Liable if tippee knows or has reason to know insider tipper breached fiduciary duty in tipping, tip transferred for improper purpose, tippee trades	None
Damages	Disgorgement ITSA treble penalty Civil and criminal fines	Highest sale matched to lowest purchase

process for publicly traded corporations. State law supplements the federal securities laws on matters not directly addressed by the federal securities laws. The 1934 Act is intended to maintain a level playing field for fair electioneering by requiring full disclosure, the prohibition of fraud, and the facilitation of shareholder proposals. A *proxy* is the agency or power of attorney that a shareholder grants to another person to vote their shares. Under the 1934 Act a proxy includes any proxy, consent, or authorization to vote shares. The term proxy usually refers to the actual written ballot and the accompanying electioneering materials.

Proxy solicitations are always conducted by corporate management every year to assure they can elect their slate of directors at the annual shareholders' meeting. The proxy solicitation is an electioneering process designed to convince other shareholders to permit the solicitor to vote their shares or asking shareholders to vote in a particular manner. The 1934 Act regulates proxy solicitations whenever one of a wide variety of communications is made, including: any request to give or revoke the proxy, the furnishing of a proxy form, advertising in the media, and solicitations made directly by mail to shareholders.

Example. N Industries acquired a third of TSC's voting shares and placed five of its nominees on the TSC board. With control of the TSC by N Industries, TSC proposed to sell all of its assets to N Industries and buy out the remaining TSC shareholders. Both N Industries and TSC issued a joint proxy statement to shareholders of both corporations who approved the transaction. After TSC was liquidated, dissolved, and its assets transferred to N Industries, a former TSC shareholder sued claiming the proxy statement was false and misleading. The proxy statement admitted that N Industries' president was on TSC's board and that N Industries was probably a parent corporation of TSC under SEC's rules. A shareholder further alleged that if this and other disclosures were made it would be apparent to other TSC shareholders that there was a conspiracy and TSC shareholders would not have granted their proxies.

Proxy solicitors need disclose only those matters that are material. Materiality is a threshold of importance that requires truthful disclosure of matters that would have an actual significance in the deliberations of a reasonable shareholder deciding whether to vote or grant proxy. The omissions in the proxy statements here were not material because there was disclosure of N Industries substantial control over TSC.

The 1934 Act requires that any person who solicits proxies from shareholders of a publicly traded company must file a proxy statement. Proxy statements are all the various communication devices used by the proxy solicitor to request or advocate a particular vote on issues or to support particular director candidates. The proxy statements must be filed with the SEC prior to their use and they must include the following information: the solicitor's identity, the legal terms of the proxy, information about the directors to be elected, details of any extraordinary corporate transactions voted on at the meeting (e.g., merger, sale of assets, recapitalization), and the financial statements of the issuer.

When management solicits proxies for the election of directors it must always include the company's latest annual report. Even if management does not solicit proxies it must distribute an *information statement* containing substantially identical information. The proxy consent form itself looks much like a standard ballot with blank date lines and boxes identifying each proposition to be voted.

I. SHARES HELD IN STREET NAME

Many investors either hold their shares for only a short time (short term speculators) or have borrowed funds on margin loan from the broker dealer to make their investment. In most of these cases the broker dealer does not register the stock in the name of this investor. Although the shareholder has a beneficial interest in shares held in *street name*, the shares are registered in the name of the broker dealer or its nominee. Beneficial shareholders are still entitled to the right to vote by proxy so the broker dealer must forward proxy materials to them.

B. Proxy Contests

In battles between corporate management and an outside dissident shareholder or takeover bidder shareholders are best served with accurate information from all solicitors. The SEC requires all proxy solicitors to file preliminary drafts of their proxy solicitation materials. Management has easy access to the names and addresses of all voting shareholders and the number of shares each holds. Management may use the corporation's funds to pay for its own proxy solicitation expenses. Outside dissident shareholders must usually finance their own proxy solicitation. The corporation's management has the option of providing the dissident a shareholder list or directly mailing the dissident's proxy solicitation materials. Dissidents have some trouble making follow-up contacts to shareholders if management refuses to share the shareholder list. The shareholdings of many large institutional investors are publicly known permitting dissidents to contact them in some instances.

C. Mandatory Shareholder Proposals

The cost of proxy solicitations in large publicly traded corporations often run into six or seven figures. SEC regulations permit small shareholders an alternate solicitation procedure that must be financed by the corporation. SEC regulations require management to include qualified shareholder proposals along with management's own proxy mailing. This procedure gives small shareholders at least a minimum level of participation in corporate elections. However, the SEC has tightened this process because it was abused by small shareholders during the 1960's to air political and social views unconnected with the issuers operations. Dissident shareholders must have a meaningful investment in the corporation so they must have held their shares for at least one year and own at least one percent or $1,000 in market value of the securities before submitting a proposal. These shareholders are limited to one proposal per year and the corporation may limit the proposal to 500 words.

Management may also omit certain proposals under SEC guidelines if the proposal is improper, illegal, or not a proper subject for voting as illustrated by the following listed factors.

Management Exclusion of Shareholder Proposals

1. Proposal is illegal.
2. Proposal violates SEC rules.
3. Proposal involves a personal grievance.
4. Proposal is unrelated to corporation business.
5. Proposal addresses corporation's ordinary business operations.
6. Proposal duplicates another proposal.
7. Proposal is moot.
8. Proposal would censure a particular director.
9. Proposal requires declaration of a dividend.

D. Proxy Enforcement

The theory underlying the proxy liability rules is that anyone who solicits another's vote must be completely honest and not mislead them. The proxy liability rules prohibit all intentionally inaccurate statements and those which are misleading. The proxy antifraud rule applies to preliminary communications, the definitive proxy solicitation package, and any post-solicitation communications. A proxy solicitor must correct any previous statements that have become false or misleading after subsequent events. Proxy solicitors must refrain from predicting future security prices if the solicitor is successful. It is unlawful to make defamatory attacks on the personal character or integrity of board candidates, to create the impression that one solicitor's materials are part of another solicitor's campaign, or to make unsubstantiated claims of the success of a proxy's solicitation.

Proxy solicitation stand on a different footing than other antifraud contexts within the securities laws, usually it is necessary to prove the misrepresenter intended to defraud others. However, because a proxy solicitation implies a trust relationship, any misstatements or omissions made negligently trigger proxy fraud liability.

Example. S Corp. owned over 50% of GOA's stock. The boards of both corporations approved a statutory merger between them and a proxy solicitation was mailed to shareholders. The solicitation stated that other prospective purchasers had expressed interest but none had made arrangements to purchase GOA's assets or stock. Shareholders approved the merger by proxy and GOA's assets were sold to S Corp. Some minority shareholders of GOA sued claiming the proxy solicitation was false and misleading.

Statements in a proxy solicitation are a form of trust from the proxy solicitor to the shareholders solicited. A more sensitive standard of culpability reinforces this high degree of care solicitors owe to shareholders. Therefore, shareholders suing for proxy fraud need not prove evil motive or a reckless disregard for the facts. The negligence standard applies. ▢

E. Contemporary Proxy Problems

As it became more difficult to conduct hostile takeovers in the late 1980's, proxy contests have regained importance. Dissident shareholder groups have proposed proxy contests that have a real chance of passage. Management has often agreed to settle such proxy contests by adopting the essence of the dissident proxy proposal. This process can be more efficient than the expenditure of millions of dollars on proxy solicitations. For example, several negotiated settlements were made in the late 1980's resulting in the corporation involved adopting the secret balloting processes for shareholder elections, electing compromise candidates to the board, creating shareholder advisory committees, and similar shareholder democracy concerns. However, some proxy contest settlements can result in the payment of greenmail to the dissident shareholder solicitor, subverting the entire process.

Proxy contests activists have pursued several corporate governance matters directly in shareholder votes in recent years. For example, social responsibility concerns have arisen such as termination of business in South Africa, animal rights activism, and limitations on political action committee (PAC) activities. Corporate governance matters have also been popular proxy contests subjects including: eliminating director staggered terms, return-

ing to cumulative voting, and the adoption or dismantling of anti-takeover defense matters such as poison pills and golden parachutes. The SEC now permits proxy proposals concerning top management compensation. Pennsylvania's new anti-takeover law severely restricts the proxy contest process. The proxy process will probably retain its importance during the 1990's.

VIII. Tender Offers

The British practice of using the takeover bid in the acquisition of a new businesses has been a popular method to participate in the market for corporate control since the 1960s. The American takeover bid is called a *tender offer*. Usually the bidder makes a public announcement offering to purchase some or all of the outstanding shares of the target corporation. The takeover is often financed with junk bonds or with funds derived from the borrowing capacity of the target firm. After a successful tender offer, the bidder may merge the target firm into the bidding firm or restructure the target by selling off certain assets.

Tender offers often occur very quickly giving little time for shareholder evaluation of the transaction. Congress passed the Williams Act in 1968 amending the 1934 Act with provisions to regulate tender offers. These regula-

Example. R acquired more than 5% of M Corp.'s outstanding shares but failed to file a Schedule 13D. R immediately stopped purchasing M Corp.'s stock after M Corp's chairman informed R these purchases were in violation of the Williams Act. Thereafter R filed a satisfactory Schedule 13D. M Corp. sought to prevent R from voting or pledging his stock, acquiring additional shares, and to force him to sell the stock he already owned.

The Williams Act's is intended to insure public disclosure of an impending takeover and thereby prevent the level of hysteria observed during the quick tender offers of the 1960s. Management should be given an opportunity to respond to shareholders about the takeover bidder and comment on bidder's ability to run the company or finance the takeover. Because R had not attempted to gain control of M Corp. and eventually filed a proper Schedule 13D, the danger of hysteria was minimized. Minor violations not made in bad faith do not trigger remedies or sanctions under the Williams Act. ☐

tions tend to slow the takeover process so that shareholders receive fuller disclosure and can thereby make better reasoned decisions.

A. Williams Act Notification

The Williams Act requires potential tender offer bidders to publicly disclose their shareholdings after they accumulate more than 5% ownership of any equity security of a publicly traded issuer. The Schedule 13D Report must be filed by anyone who acquires 2% or more of any registered equity security within 12 months and the purchase results in combined ownership of 5% or more. Schedule 13D must include information about the purchasers' identity and background, the source of the funds used for the purchase, the number of shares then own, any contracts they have concerning the issuers' securities (e.g., options), and their present and future plans for controlling the target corporation.

Many of the "stock parking" violations of the late 1980's were intended to avoid revealing the size of the bidder's ownership in a Schedule 13D. Typically, a bidder persuades business associates to acquire large blocks of the target's shares with the expectation they would sell their holdings to the bidder. Because no single individual personally owns

more than 5%, no one is required to personally file a Schedule 13D. Therefore, the group illegally keeps its holdings secret. However, this technical violation is an intentional attempt to defraud shareholders by hiding the fact that a takeover is eminent, frustrating the notification protections envisioned in the Williams Act.

B. Definition of a Tender Offer

The term tender offer is not defined in the Williams Act although SEC interpretations provide some guidance. *Tender offers* typically involve wide-spread public solicitation of shareholders with a view to induce them to tender (send in) their shares to the offeror. Privately negotiated stock purchases do not constitute a tender offer. The tender offeror bids at a premium price usually made significantly higher than the prevailing market price. This is intended to encourage shareholders to tender their shares, but it can induce hysteria and a stampede pressuring others to sell when the offer is open for only a short time or is made to less than all shareholders. Tender offerors usually make their offer contingent on receiving a minimum portion of shares they seek. The tender offeror

Example. H Corp. became frustrated with its unsuccessful attempt to takeover SCM so it terminated its tender offer and returned all shares tendered back to the shareholders. Within the following two hours H Corp. made five privately negotiated cash purchases from arbitrageurs and speculators who held large blocks. These 5 purchases resulted in H Corp.'s acquisition of 25% of SCM's stock. SCM sued claiming H Corp. had conducted a second tender offer by making the privately negotiated purchases but without complying with the Williams Act.

The characteristics of the H Corp. "street sweep" purchases do not come within the SEC tender offer guidelines. Private negotiations with 5 of the nearly 23,000 SCM shareholders was clearly not a widespread or public solicitation of shareholders. These five shareholders were highly sophisticated professionals who were clearly not pressured by the imminence of any tender offer. The prices of the sales were hardly at premium prices because they were less than a dollar over the current market price. Finally, there was no contingency on H Corp.'s acquisitions to designate the street sweep as a tender offer. ☐

can refuse to purchase the shares tendered if insufficient shares are tendered.

SEC Criteria Characterizing a Tender Offer

1. Wide spread solicitation of shareholders (more than 10 shareholders)
2. Substantial percentage of target shares sought (more than 5%)
3. Premium offered over prevailing market price (5% or $2)
4. Terms nonnegotiable
5. Offer contingent on tender of minimum number of shares
6. Offer open for short duration (45 days)
7. Pressure on shareholders to sell
8. Public announcement of offer

The SEC has sought to control the street sweeps mentioned in the example above but has not yet passed any definitive rulings.

C. Tender Offer Mechanics

The Williams Act has adapted the proxy solicitation rules to the tender offer context. It requires the target management to send the bidder's tender offer documents to shareholders. Alternatively, the target's management may give the bidder access to a shareholder list. Of course, the bidder must pay all reasonable expenses of the tender offer solicitation and mailing.

Tender offers must be held open for at least twenty days to allow shareholders time to analyze the offer. The bidder is not obligated to purchase or bid any minimum percentage of shares. However, if more shares are tendered than the bidder plans to purchase they must be purchased on a pro rata basis. This prevents any shareholders tendering early from gaining an advantage over those tendering later. This stampede is one of the problems the Williams Act sought to cure. Tendering shareholders have the right to withdraw their shares for the fifteen days following their tender. It is illegal for shareholders to tender shares they don't already own, a *short tender*, in hopes they may purchase the shares later and pocket the profit.

D. Tender Offer Disclosures

The tender offeror must file a Schedule 14B-I Tender Offer Statement with the SEC, the target corporation, and the stock exchange. Schedule 14B-I includes all the same information required in 13D. In addition, it must include a description of any negotiations between the tender offeror and issuer, the purpose of tender offer, the bidder's plans for the target (e.g., merger, restructuring), financial statement of the bidders, and exhibits of the documents used in the tender offer.

Disclosures are also required from the management of the tender offer target. Within ten days after the bid is made, management must file Schedule 14B-9 to inform shareholders of management's recommendation to accept or reject the tender offer or of their neutrality. Additional management filings are necessary if management makes a competing tender offer or plans to go private to avoid the tender offerors' takeover.

E. Tender Offer Liability

There is liability for violation of the tender offer rules. The Williams Act prohibits fraud or other manipulative acts during or leading up to a tender offer. The failure to file the required schedules and reports can result in the tender offer process being delayed.

F. State Tender Offer Laws

Most states have some form of tender offer legislation largely designed to prevent hostile takeovers and retain the business activity that target companies do within the state. State laws may not interfere with the Williams Act but may regulate shareholder democracy. Many state anti-takeover laws include *control share acquisition provisions*. Generally, these permit the shareholders remaining after a tender offer to take a vote that either grants or prohibits the tender offeror from voting the shares purchased. Some acts permit the corporation to redeem the shares purchased by the tender offeror, that is force the tender offer or to sell back the tender shares to the corporation at fair market value.

Several states anti-takeover laws include shareholder protection provisions such as a *merger moratorium*. Typically this prohibits a merger of the tender offeror and the target until approved by the target corporation's management. This effectively prevents hostile-type takeovers requiring the bidder to negotiate with the target management. The Pennsylvania anti-takeover law prohibits greenmail and permits corporations to consider interests of other corporate stakeholders aside from shareholders including: customers, suppliers, employees, and the communities surrounding the corporation's facilities.

IX. Miscellaneous Securities Laws

There are several additional state laws with an impact on the securities markets and corporations generally. These include state blue sky laws for the registration of securities, issuers, and broker dealers; the Racketeering Influenced and Corrupt Organization provisions of the Organized Crime Control Act; and the Foreign Corrupt Practices Act of 1977 empowering the SEC and the Justice Department to prohibit foreign bribery and require certain accounting practices to prevent bribery.

All the U.S. states have securities laws generally referred to as "Blue Sky Laws." This terminology was probably adopted because the state legislators who originally passed the Blue Sky Laws sought to prevent fraudulent stock sale practices. Stock promoters during the "Roaring Twenties" were known to make extravagant claims of the investment's expected performance. This practice was referred to as selling "building lots in the blue sky" an expression that illustrates why anti-fraud provisions predominate in the Blue Sky Laws. The Uniform Securities Act has been adopted in whole or in part by most states. However, the New York state blue sky law is significantly different than other states and generally must be complied with separately.

Blue Sky Laws typically follow a similar pattern as the federal securities laws in the prohibition of fraud, licensing of broker/dealers and the registration of new securities issues.

Example. I Corp. was a foreign company with a contract to supply S Corp. with electronic components produced in the United States. I Corp. and S Corp. were to split the profits but S. Corp believed I Corp. had inflated bills and charged S Corp. for nonexistent expenses. S Corp sued for treble damages under RICO. I Corp. countered that a civil RICO action could not be brought until there was a previous criminal conviction of the predicate acts underlying the racketeering claim.

The RICO statute does not use the term conviction anywhere. The underlying or predicate offenses need only be chargeable or indictable and punishable under the various criminal laws. This means that a RICO plaintiff may be successful even if the defendant has never been convicted of the underlying predicate offense. Since the burden of proof is lower in civil actions, preponderance of the evidence, RICO defendants may be held liable to civil plaintiffs for acts that prosecutors might have difficulty proving beyond a reasonable doubt. ☐

State blue sky laws provide penalties for violators of their provisions. Most blue sky laws permit a coordination procedure to comply with nearly all states provisions simultaneously. Blue sky laws are the only applicable securities regulations to the intrastate and private placement offerings that are generally exempt from the federal securities laws.

A. Racketeer Influenced Corrupt and Organizations

The Organized Crime Control Act in 1970 included provisions to outlaw racketeering activities, the Racketeer Influenced Corrupt and Organizations (RICO) provisions. RICO gives powerful civil and criminal powers to regulators and to private citizens when a pattern of racketeering activity is involved. Securities fraud is a predicate offense under the RICO provisions so a RICO violation is often alleged in both civil and criminal securities suits.

The civil RICO provisions permit a private plaintiff to sue for treble damages. The triple penalty is so substantial that it actually represents a form of punitive damages. Federal prosecutors using the RICO provisions in criminal actions can seize the assets of a RICO defendant before the trial. Most financial professionals need their financial assets to effectively conduct their business. The pretrial seizure of substantial capital can effectively shut their business down giving federal prosecutors great clout to settle disputes.

The plaintiff or prosecutor in a RICO action must prove the defendant: (1) committed at least two prohibited (predicate) acts, (2) that constitutes a pattern, (3) of racketeering activity, (4) by which the defendant invested in and maintained an interest in or participated in, (5) an enterprise, (6) affecting interstate or foreign commerce. Although the RICO provisions were originally directed at organized crime, the provisions have been used successfully against a wide range of legitimate businesses that become involved in a series of illegal acts.

The RICO treble damage and pre-trial seizure provisions have been severely criticized in recent years. The Supreme Court has approved the use of RICO provisions against securities violations and other courts continue to expand the reach of RICO. However, some courts have slowed the expansion of RICO. Most states have a separate RICO type law but their provisions vary significantly regarding multiple damages and pre-trial seizures.

There have been several efforts to limit the applicability of RICO in securities-fraud situations. Some industries have sought exemption from RICO in proposed legislation before Congress. However, at this writing it

475

Example. The W.W. Corp., a registered publicly traded firm, was engaged in wholesale and retail coin business but had no inventory control or security over its coin vaults and other precious metal assets. Employees were generally unsupervised and would singlehandedly appraise, purchase, and sell coins. Particular coins were not identified by serial number and employees would take them off the premises without signing receipts. Employees could draw checks on the firm's bank accounts without consultation from the treasurer or another officer. Almost $2 million worth of checks were written by the president and his associates that could not be accounted for.

The SEC charged W. W. with keeping inadequate books and records and an inadequate internal accounting control system all in violation of the FCPA. The FCPA accounting standards provisions are designed to prevent misappropriation of corporate assets for use as foreign bribes. Books and records must reflect transactions under general accepted accounting principles and prevent misrepresentation, concealment, and falsification. Transactions must be property reflected on the corporate's books and records. The particular accounting controls necessary for any firm depend on the circumstances. Here, certain employees should have been bonded, presigned checks should not have been available to all employees, inventory should have been identified and properly recorded, and accounting records periodically reconciled with a physical inventory. Because these accounting systems were insufficient, W. W. was in violation of the accounting standards provisions of the FCPA. ☐

does not appear that RICO will be substantially changed any time soon.

B. Foreign Corrupt Practices Act

After the Watergate scandal public inquiry was focused on corporate misuse of its funds for unethical and illegal purposes. The SEC had investigated numerous questionable payments made by domestic U.S. firms to foreign officials and campaign contributions that arguably led to the grant of business to U.S. firms. In 1977 Congress passed the Foreign Corrupt Practices Act (FCPA) to outlaw foreign bribery and establish accounting standards that could help prevent bribery. The FCPA prohibits bribery because it is considered an unethical activity and investors may lose confidence in corporations and the securities markets.

Foreign bribery is prohibited by all *domestic concerns* which includes any individual who is a citizen, national, or resident of the United States and any corporation, partnership, association, joint stock company, business trust, unincorporated association, or sole proprietorship with its principal place of business in the U.S. It is illegal to pay, offer, or give anything of value to foreign officials to influence their decisions. Under the FCPA, foreign officials include persons with discretionary powers in business or government who might be influenced to grant business to the domestic concern involved in the bribe.

Congress clarified the FCPA with the Foreign Corrupt Practices Act Amendments of 1988. The Act clarifies permissible *facilitating payments*, often called grease payments, that are made to lower echelon foreign agents without discretionary powers, these are not illegal bribes. In many foreign countries, customs officials and other government agents routinely expect a gratuity to expedite the clearance of incoming goods or the processing of business orders. Grease payments do not constitute bribes and are not illegal under FCPA. How-

Example. The SEC charged P. Enterprises with misuse of the firm's mansion, limousine service, personal tax and legal consulting services, insurance policies, flights on the P. Enterprise jet plane, automobile use, hotel and club charges, and loan guarantees. Although the firm's president paid for some of these expenses, many of the benefits were given out freely to business associates and his family members.

The SEC charged that P. Enterprises had failed to adhere to the FCPA accounting standards provisions requiring accountability for the use of corporate assets. P Enterprises claimed that these extensive personal expenses were necessary for its president to maintain his high profile lifestyle because it created visibility and a casanova image contributing to the firm's profits. However, hundreds of thousands of dollars of firm's assets were given to its president, his friends, his family, and other business associates without any approval by the board. P. Enterprises agreed to change it's auditors and install and maintain a system of internal accounting controls to account for the use of all assets in the future .

ever, if such payments are illegal in the foreign country involved they are illegal in the United States as well. The FCPA amendments permit bona fide promotional expenses and contract performance expenses including free lodging given to foreign officials.

I. ACCOUNTING STANDARDS PROVISIONS

The FCPA gives the SEC power to oversee the prevention of bribes in publicly traded firms. The FCPA requires publicly traded firms to maintain accurate books and records and to install and maintain a system of internal accounting controls. These controls are the various accounting procedures necessary to reconcile and oversee corporate books and assets. An adequate accounting system with internal accounting controls helps to adequately safeguard assets from misappropriation. It also prevents the accumulation of assets and other funds for use as foreign bribes. SEC rules make if unlawful to falsify accounting records or make misrepresentations to any accountant.

2. FCPA ENFORCEMENT

Both the SEC and the Justice Department have enforcement powers under the FCPA. The Justice Department is responsible for criminal investigations and criminal bribery prosecutions of all types of firms. The SEC has civil enforcement powers over publicly traded firms and enforces the accounting standards provisions. The U.S. Attorney General may issue guidelines to assist firms in complying with the FCPA. This is important when particular payments or actions are taken abroad so the domestic concern can be assured this activity does not constitute a bribe. The SEC may assess civil penalties up to $ 10,000 for each individual. Fines of up to $2 million may be levied against publicly traded corporations and individual violators can be subjected to fines of up to $100,000 and/or imprisonment of up to 5 years. Much of the FCPA enforcement history has not involved actual prosecutions or suits. Instead, consent decrees between the defendant and either the SEC or Justice Department have been the most typical remedy.

The accounting standards provisions are applicable to publicly traded corporations whether or not they are involved in international business. The FCPA has been used in certain contexts involving ethical considerations such as excessive perquisites (perks). Perks are profits or benefits an employee receives in addition to regular compensation.

While perks may help to "perk up" an employee's performance, excessive perks may actually be a hidden way for executives to misappropriate the firm's assets. Publicly traded firms must maintain accountability for the use of its corporate assets by executives and all other employees. All payments must be made for a legitimate corporate purpose.

* * *

Problems

1. A Wall Street underwriting firm distributed thousands of copies of an information brochure describing the investment prospects of the scientific discovery of superconductivity. This new technology permits the efficient transmission of electricity with almost no loss. Within a few months, the underwriter took on a new client that sought to sell a new issue of securities in an IPO. This client had developed the superconductivity technology in magnets to make certain electric motors operate at higher powers with less electricity. Explain the basis on which the SEC might challenge the underwriters information distribution or the relationship between the issuer and the underwriter.

2. Co-op City is a large complex of middle income subsidized housing in a large U.S. city. In order to qualify for an apartment in Co-op City a potential tenant must purchase "stock" entitling them to rent an apartment. Although the certificate is labelled as stock, it provides for no voting power and no distribution of dividends or profits from the operation of Co-op City. It represented no ownership interest in this government owned subsidized housing complex, and when tenants move out of Co-op City the tenant must sell back the stock to Coop City at the original purchase price. What argument might the SEC make that the stock should be registered? What arguments might the Co-op City officials make that this so-called stock was not really a security under the 1933 Act?

3. The A Corp. offered shares that were not registered with the SEC. A Corp. is a Pennsylvania corporation with offices only in the state of Pennsylvania. A Corp.'s shares were sold only to Pennsylvania residents. The funds from stock offering were used for A Corp.'s expansion into real estate development in Maryland and New Jersey. None of the funds were used within the state of Pennsylvania. Comment on the likely arguments the SEC would probably make in an enforcement action against A Corp. How is A Corp. likely to respond to the SEC's allegations and what basis might it claim exists for selling these as unregistered securities?

4. What are the various arguments for restricting or permitting insider trading?

5. An officer of X Corp. purchased 1,000 shares of the corporation in January at $10. In February he learned that earnings for the year would be less than expected so he sold his shares for $13. In March a new internal report indicated that earnings would be better than previously expected so the director purchased more shares at $9. When the public learned of the earnings projections in May, the price rose to $15 so the director immediately sold all his remaining shares. On what basis might the corporation recover profits made by this director? How would profits be determined in this situation?

6. An employee of a major auditing firm discovers during the course of an audit of the ABC Corp. that it's officers and directors have been misappropriating the firm's assets for several years. Before the employee reports this finding to the partner in charge of the audit, the employee tips his spouse and other relatives about this information. His relatives sell all their stock in ABC Corp. before the audit report becomes public. On what basis would the auditor be found guilty of insider trading? On what basis would the auditor's family members be found guilty of insider trading?

7. What penalties exist in a SEC enforcement action against the insider traders mentioned in the question above? What inducements does the SEC

have to encourage informants to come forward with information about insider traders like in the question above?

8. A dissident shareholder group of XYZ Corp seeks to include it's shareholder resolutions in management proxies solicitation package at the corporation's expense. On what basis might the management justifiably refuse to include the following proxy solicitations:

a. dissident shareholders own 50 shares together with a market value of approximately $500 and have held these shares for 3 months.

b. a resolution will oppose apartheid in South Africa and require the company to cease doing business with that government.

c. a proposal directing the marketing staff to discontinue advertising to children.

d. a proposal to raise the regular quarterly dividend from $.50 to $1.00 per share.

9. A famous takeover arbitrageur has acquired 4% of the stock of XYZ Corp. In an effort to hide his ownership from the public the arbitrageur has contacted business associates asking them to each secretly purchase up to 4% of XYZ stock and hold it for the benefit of the arbitrageur. The arbitrageur plans to make a tender offer for 50% of XYZ stock and his business associates promise to tender their stock to him. None of these individuals has tiled a Schedule 13D indicating their amount of their ownership in XYZ stock. Does this scheme violate the Securities Laws?

17

Environmental Law

Environmental Law

IN THE LAST TWO DECADES, environmental law has become a significant portion of the legal environment for owners and managers of business enterprises. While traditional tort theory permits parties to sue wrongdoers for personal injuries or property damage, injuries caused by long term exposure to pollutants are often difficult to prove. In addition, property damage is often difficult to trace to a particular source.

During the 1960's, numerous citizens and special interest groups concerned with environmental issues requested that Congress enact laws responding to the deterioration of the environment. The proponents of environmental legislation cited the poor air quality in a number of major cities as well as the polluted lakes and streams throughout America as examples of environmental damage resulting from an industrialized society not placing a high enough value upon products and production methods that would reduce the discharge of toxic emissions. This Chapter will provide an overview of the major environmental laws and regulations affecting the operation of a business enterprise.

I. The Environmental Protection Agency

By executive order, President Nixon created the Environmental Protection Agency (EPA) to centralize federal environmental regulation. The EPA is now one of the largest federal agencies. Most environmental legislation directs the EPA to develop regulations and standards to implement the overall policy set forth in the statute. Congress may determine that a substance is harmful, but it will delegate the authority to establish safe exposure limits to the EPA. In turn, those standards will be published in the Code of Federal Regulations and will be enforced pursuant to the dictates of the statute.

Industry and the EPA are often at odds with respect to the standards established by the EPA. At times, businesses or industries may challenge the standards established by the EPA as being beyond cost competitiveness. Complying with standards beyond those that can be economical applied could arguably result in the closing of an assembly line, laying off workers, or closing a plant.

II. The National Environmental Policy Act and the EPA

The National Environmental Policy Act (NEPA) was primarily the result of the environmental movement of the 1960's. NEPA went into effect in January 1970, creating the Council of Environmental Quality within the executive branch of the federal government. It requires preparation of an environmental impact statement for every recommendation or report on legislation and for every major federal action significantly affecting the quality of the environment. NEPA requires a fed-

✎ **Example.** The buyers of automobiles desire to breathe clean air, while the inherent nature of the internal combustion engine results in air pollution. Banning the internal combustion engine would all but ban the automobile from the roads. This would not be acceptable to the American consumer. If the standards became too stringent, automobile production would cease. This would cost the U.S. tens of thousands of jobs. Consumers must ultimately determine the price they are willing to pay for clean air with respect to their automobiles. Under current technology, emission controls on automobiles increase the price of each unit. This too represents a cost-benefit relationship. □

eral agency to consider the environment impact of a project before the project is undertaken.

NEPA requires that each environmental impact statement contain the following:

1. A description of the environmental impact of the proposed action.
2. A discussion of those impacts that cannot be avoided.
3. An analysis of the differences between the short-term impacts and the long-term impacts.
4. A discussion of the alternatives to the proposed action.
5. A detailed listing of any commitment of resources that would be irreversible.

Individual citizens have the power to go to court to force federal agencies to comply with the terms of NEPA, requiring an environmental impact statement for a project prior to its undertaking.

III. Air Quality

A. Clean Air Legislation

Congress enacted the first major piece of air quality legislation in 1963 by passing the Clean Air Act. The Act has been amended and updated numerous times with changes in attitudes and technology. Under the Clean Air Act, the EPA has the power to set forth rules to control the emissions of the various types of air pollutants. Some of these air pollutants are visible, such as smog, while others cannot be seen, but are dangerous when breathed. The EPA is charged with the responsibility of setting both the primary air quality standards which are designed to protect the public's health, as well as the secondary air quality standards which are designed to protect vegetation, minerals, climate, visibility and economic values.

The Clean Air Act further requires the EPA to regulate the emission of toxic air pollutants. Pursuant to this authority, the EPA has set toxicity standards for asbestos, mercury, vinyl chloride, radionuclides, as well as a host of other toxic materials.

The EPA has the power to control the contents of automobile fuel and fuel additives. The most significant change in this area directed by the EPA has been the elimination of lead from automobile gasoline.

The Clean Air Act also controls those sources of air pollution that are stationary, such as manufacturing plants and public utilities. The EPA has established maximum levels of pollutants that may be permitted in the air. The Act further charges state governments with the responsibility of establishing emission controls on particular sources of pollutants to reduce emissions levels. A number of major U.S. cities are having difficulty reducing their overall air pollution levels so that they fall within the maximum ambient standard. In these cities, new factories or other generators of air pollution are generally not permitted to open or expand while the city is above the maximum ambient standard. In addition, the Clean Air Act requires newly built facilities that are sources of air pollution to use the best available technology to reduce air pollution emissions.

The primary responsibility for enforcing these air quality standards lies with each state. But, the federal government has the right to enforce the standards if the states fail to do so. In addition, the Clean Air Act also permits citizen's suits to force an industry or the government to fully comply with the provisions of the Clean Air Act.

In 1990, the Clean Air Act was significantly amended. The law was changed in five major areas. First, the air standards for ozone, the main ingredient of smog, were adjusted to require reductions in cities of moderate pollution or worse by 15% within six years. Almost 100 major cities were not in compliance with the federal standards at the time of the 1990 amendments. Following the six year period, those cites must make 9% reductions every three years until they meet all EPA standards.

Second, industrial polluters that emit as little as 10 tons per year [1] of smog forming chemicals may have to reduce their emissions, depending on their locations. The scope of the law was vastly expanded with respect to industrial polluters.

Third, the amended law requires the reformulation of gasoline that is cleaner burning. Tougher automobile pollution standards include requiring manufacturers to build cars that maintain their tailpipe standards for 10 years or 100,000 miles.

Fourth, the majority of plants emitting toxic substances will be required employ the best available technology to reduce their emissions of 189 toxic chemicals by 90% within 10 years.

Fifth, the 111 dirtiest power plants in 21 states must significantly cut their sulfur diox-

ide emissions by 1995 to reduce acid rain. More than 200 additional plants must make large cuts by the year 2000.

B. Indoor Air Quality

As a result of the energy conservation efforts of the 1970's to the present, buildings and other living spaces have been made as air tight as possible in order to preserve the temperature controlled air. As a result, there are fewer changes of fresh air inside a climate temperature controlled building. This has become a problem in facilities containing asbestos and other toxic materials. The EPA has already established guidelines regarding asbestos within buildings. This has lead to the closing of a number of buildings and the gutting the remodeling of many others, including schools.

The EPA has recently established what it considers to be the threshold level of safety for exposure to radon gas which naturally occurs in the environment and seeps through foundation cracks in buildings. Due to the lack of air changes, radon gas accumulates in buildings in those parts of the nation containing greater concentrations of radon in the earth. In addition, the EPA has established safety levels and other regulations pertaining to wood stoves, coal stoves, cleaning products and insulation compounds containing formaldehyde. As different dangers are identified, one should expect the EPA to promulgate regulations and enforce them.

IV. Water Quality

The majority of water pollution is caused by the discharge of waste substances into oceans, rivers and lakes. Municipal and industrial waste accounts for most water pollution. In addition, the chemical fertilizers used by agricultural operations combined with the animal wastes generated within those operations add to the water pollution problem.

The various forms of water pollution have different effects upon human, animal and

---

1. The previous standard was 100 tons per year.

plant life. Some forms of pollution cause water to be unfit for drinking. Other forms of pollution interfere with biological growth. Even the heated water from electric power plants can interfere with the reproduction of some types of fish.

In 1948, Congress passed the Federal Water Pollution Act. This law has been significantly amended a number of times and today is commonly known as the Clean Water Act. The Clean Water Act is as comprehensive a law with respect to the regulation of water pollution as the Clean Air Act is to air pollution.

Under the Clean Water Act, each state has the primary responsibility for preventing, reducing and eliminating the pollution of water. This is accomplished through a national framework with the EPA empowered to step in if a state does not fulfill its obligation. The Act requires industrial sites discharging waste water into a waterway to install and operate the best available water pollution control technology. New industry sites must employ the "best available demonstrated control technology."

As in the case of air quality, the EPA is responsible for setting the guidelines regarding the best available technologies. The EPA designates the uses of specific bodies of water for recreation, public water supply, propagation of fish and wildlife, and agricultural and industrial water supply. Following the designation, the EPA establishes maximum daily loads of various pollutants with regard to the designated use of the water. The Act further requires all municipal and industrial waste dischargers to obtain permits that set out the amounts and specific pollutants that the permit holder may discharge and the steps that the permit holder must take to reduce its present or anticipated discharge of pollutants. In order to enforce these regulations, dischargers are required to install and maintain monitoring equipment and to take and record discharge samples.

Violations of the Clean Water Act can result in a minimum fine of $2,500 for the first offense and up to $50,000 per day and two years in prison for subsequent violations. Anyone knowingly violating this law is subject to more severe criminal penalties, including fines between $5,000 and $50,000 per day and imprisonment of up to 3 years, or both. The maximum penalties may be doubled for subsequent knowing violations. In addition, a person committing a violation with knowledge that it placed another person in imminent danger of serious bodily injury faces penalties of up to 15 years imprisonment and a fine of up to $250,000. An organization committing such a violation is subject to a criminal fine of up to $1 million.

Citizens or groups of citizens adversely affected by water pollution have the power to bring a citizen's suit against the EPA and the violators to see that the provisions of the law are enforced.

V. Hazardous Wastes and Toxic Substances

A land's past can be disguised. Between 1942 and 1953, the Hooker Electro-Chemical Company placed almost 22,000 tons of chemical waste in a canal in New York that a visionary by the name of William Love had hoped would provide cheap hydroelectric power for his model city. Love Canal was abandoned when alternating current was invented, thus eliminating the need for industrial plants to be located at power sites. This sleepy community in New York used this canal for many years as a neighborhood swimming hole.

In a title deed that warned that the land had been filled with waste products, the Hooker Electro-Chemical Company sold the property for $1 in 1953 to the Niagara Falls Board of Education. The Board of Education later built a brick elementary school on the site. A neighborhood grew up in the area.

In the 1970's, the children of Love Canal evidenced a disproportionate number of birth defects, cleft palates, deformed ears and teeth, and mental retardation. Experts may never determine the extent of the link between the chemicals and the health disorders in the community. But, the furor over the existence of the toxins, the months of living in hotels and military housing and the years of political battles prompted an extraordinary transformation of what was believed to be an average American neighborhood into the focal point of national environmental safety awareness.

Today, the school is buried beneath a 22 acre clay cap intended to prevent human contact with the toxins, to reduce the amount of water infiltrating the canal and to curtail airborne emissions. Laboratory analyses and sediment samples taken from Love Canal demonstrated the presence of more than 200 chemicals, including dioxin, considered to be one of the more toxic chemicals ever manufactured; benzine which has been linked to leukemia; and other substances that have been linked to nervous system disorders, liver problems, respiratory distresses, deafness and cardiac arrest.

A. CERCLA

By 1980, in addition to Love Canal, thousands of hazardous waste sites were identified throughout the United States as being responsible for significant surface and groundwater contamination. In response to these problems, Congress enacted the Comprehensive Response, Compensation, and Liability Act (CERCLA). This law is commonly referred to as the Superfund Law. CERCLA was adopted to facilitate the cleanup of hazardous waste sites threatening human health or the environment. These sites include landfills, industrious properties where spills or dumping occurred, sites where illegal dumping occurred and a variety of other waste locations.

CERCLA established the Hazardous Substance Response Trust Fund, which is the Superfund itself. This fund finances the cleanup of hazardous waste sites. The Superfund is financed by excise taxes on oil, certain chemicals and motor fuel as well as by special taxes included in the corporate alternative minimum income tax and other government revenues. The EPA has the power to use the Superfund to finance the cleanup of hazard waste sites. If the EPA targets a site for cleanup, it may withdraw money from the Superfund to have the cleanup performed. The EPA may then sue the "potentially responsible parties" for the cost incurred and paid by the Superfund. A "potentially responsible party" includes the current owner and operator of a facility and any person who at the time of the disposal of any hazardous substance owned or operated the facility. Transporters of hazardous wastes can also fall within the scope of CERCLA.

One of the unexpected results of CERCLA was to lead to the liability of lenders who foreclosed upon properties securing loans that turned out to be hazardous waste sites. Courts reached this conclusion by the plain reading of the statute which stated that the owner of a facility could be a potentially responsible party. After a mortgage foreclosure or a trustee's sale, the lender does in fact become the owner of the property. But, the lender in most cases was not aware that toxic substances or other hazardous wastes had been dumped, buried or spilled on the property.

B. SARA

In response to this lender liability problem as well as to extend the life of CERCLA, the Superfund Law was amended in 1986. These changes were combined in a bill known as the Superfund Amendments and Reauthorization Act (SARA). The drastic impact of CERCLA against certain parties, such as lenders, was reduced somewhat by creating "an innocent landowner" defense.

To understand how the innocent landowner defenses works, one must examine CERCLA's liability framework. As a general rule, CERCLA targets liability on four categories of persons:

1. Current owners or operators of hazardous waste facilities.
2. Past owners or operators of hazardous waste facilities at the times wastes were disposed.
3. Persons who arranged for treatment or disposal of wastes at a facility.
4. Persons who transported hazardous substances for treatment or disposal at the facility.

To establish an innocent landowner defense, it is necessary for a party to prove that it did not know or that it did not have any reason to know that a hazardous substance had been disposed of in the facility. It must also prove that once it discovered the presence of the hazardous substance, it exercised due care with respect to the hazardous substance and that it took precautions against foreseeable acts or omissions of any such third party and the consequences that could foreseeably result from such acts or omissions .

In establishing that it had no reason to know that any hazardous substances had been released or disposed of at the facility, an owner will likely be required to show that it made an appropriate inquiry into the previous ownership and uses of the property consistent with good commercial or customary practices. A court will take into account the specialized knowledge or experience of the owner as well as the relationship of the purchase price to the value of the property if uncontaminated. Also, any information regarding the land which is commonly known within the community or reasonably ascertainable from the public records will be charged to the knowledge of the owner.

The innocent landowner defense is not available to any party who was involved in the management or operation of the facility in any fashion.

Through SARA, Congress enacted a series of requirements for public notification of spills and accidents involving hazardous materials. Anyone releasing certain listed chemicals into the environment, even through an accidental spill, must notify a designated government office if the discharge exceeded listed permissible levels.

C. Manufacturing and Distributing Hazardous Materials

In 1976, Congress passed both the Toxic Substances Control Act (TSCA) and the Resource, Conservation and Recovery Act (RCRA). The TSCA was designed to control the manufacturer, distribution and sale of hazardous chemicals. RCRA was established to regulate the transportation and disposal of hazardous wastes.

I. TSCA

TSCA requires chemicals be tested by manufacturers or processors to determine their effects on human health or the environment before the chemicals are introduced into the marketplace. The EPA has the power under this Act to regulate chemical substances or mixtures that present an unreasonable risk of injury to health or the environment. The EPA may take action against the sale or distribution of any such material that poses an imminent hazard.

This law was enacted in response to public concern that thousands of new substances were being released into the environment each year, sometimes without adequate testing for potential harm to the environment or humans. It is the intent of the legislation to provide for greater public safety while at the same time not unduly impeding or creating unnecessary economic barriers to technological advances.

2. RCRA

The Resource Conservation and Recovery Act requires generators of hazardous waste material to maintain records on the quantity and composition of their waste products. It further requires these parties to comply with EPA standards for labelling, storing, and transporting the waste. Any generator disposing of hazardous wastes off-site must comply with a transportation procedure established under the RCRA. This requires written document describing the hazardous waste and designating the facility to which the material will be transported. This manifest must accompany all shipments of hazardous materials to disposal sites. The manifest must be returned to the generator after the hazardous waste has been delivered to the site. If the manifest does not return to the generator of the hazardous waste within 30 days, the EPA must be notified.

RCRA also regulates those generators of hazardous wastes who dispose of materials on-site. On-site disposal requires a permit from the EPA. The EPA requires that a generator of the hazardous wastes train its employees for handling hazardous materials, establish monitoring and safety procedures, and erect proper fencing and warning signs.

RCRA requires that generators of hazardous materials meet a certain financial responsibility standard, usually through the purchase of insurance policies. Violations of RCRA can lead to fines of $50,000 per day and imprisonment of up to two years. Violations of the record keeping provisions are punishable by fines of $25,000 per day and imprisonment up to a year for the first conviction and $50,000 per day and imprisonment up to two years for subsequent convictions.

3. FIFRA

Agricultural chemicals are regulated by the EPA through the Federal Insecticide, Fungicide and Rodenticide Act (FIFRA). Under this act, the EPA has the authority to register pesticides before they can be sold. The EPA also can restrict pesticides to certain designated uses and to set limits of pesticide residue permitted on crops that provide food for animals and humans.

The Administrator of the EPA has power to suspend registration of a material and to remove it from the marketplace if there is evidence to support that its continued use would pose an imminent hazard. In addition, the Administrator has the power to commence a "cancellation of registration" proceeding against any substance within the scope of the Act that the Administrator believes yields environmental risks that outweigh the benefits of its use. If such a proceeding is initiated, all interested parties, including manufacturers, distributors, users, scientists and environmentalists may present evidence at the hearing. The registration of the material will be canceled if the evidence supports that the substance causes an unreasonable adverse effect on the environment. It was under this procedure that the insecticide DDT was banned for most uses in the United States.

VI. Citizen's Suits

In 1970, Congress included in the Clean Air Act a provision allowing concerned citizens to bring suits against both the EPA and the air polluters for violations of the Act. This provision permitted citizens to sue polluters who violated certain requirements of the Act and to sue the EPA if it failed to carry out a nondiscretionary duty established by the Act.

This was the first time that Congress had empowered individual citizens to act as "private attorneys general" to enforce environmental laws. Congress decided to grant citizens this

Example. Airborne residue or other gases from a manufacturing facility drifting onto the property of others is an actionable nuisance. But, in some situations, a court will not order a manufacturing facility to completely cease operations even if a nuisance is established. Courts will generally order a reduction in the release of the offending material in a scheme of economic feasibility unless the material poses an imminent danger to the public. If that is the case, the activity can be stopped under a number of theories at common law as well as under state and federal statute. □

right for two primary reasons. First, it was recognized that the resources of the federal government could be insufficient to achieve complete compliance. Second, Congress perceived that it was necessary to hold the EPA accountable for undertaking the many nondiscretionary statutory duties that Congress required the agency to fulfill.

A citizen's suit provision has been included in each of the following federal environmental statutes: The Clean Water Act, The Resource Conservation and Recovery Act, The Toxic Substance and Control Act, the Noise Control Act, the Endangered Species Act, the Comprehensive Environmental Response, Compensation, and Liability Act, and the Safe Drinking Water Act.

Under these statutes, Congress has granted citizens the power to initiate an enforcement action in federal court to insure that the EPA carries out the mandates of each environmental statute listed. Therefore, owners and managers of business enterprises must be aware that enforcement actions cannot only be initiated by the EPA and state regulatory agencies, but also by individual citizens having a good faith belief that environmental statutes or regulations are being violated.

VII. Liability Under Common Law

In spite of a myriad of federal and state environmental statutes and regulations, actions under common law tort may still be pursued by persons seeking to recover for damages caused by pollution. If one negligently causes toxic material to be released on or over the property of another, he can be held liable for the damage. The same would hold true for personal injuries suffered by individuals as the result of the negligent release of a toxic substance. An entity may also be found liable for negligently failing to warn residents of an area of a potential risk resulting from the release of a toxic material.

If the release of a toxic material is deemed to constitute an ultrahazardous condition, the offending party may be liable under a strict liability theory. This would relieve the plaintiff from having to prove that the defendant was negligent.

Nuisance is another common law cause of action available to aggrieved parties. A nuisance action can be established if the plaintiff can prove that the defendant is unreasonably interfering with the plaintiff's use or enjoyment of her real property or is otherwise endangering the public welfare.

The presence of a common law cause of action alone is seldom seen. Actions by private citizens against a commercial defendant generally employ both common law causes of action coupled with allegations that state and federal environmental laws have been violated. Many times, common law actions alone are not effective unless coupled with state and federal causes of action or unless a personal injury can be proven. This is because local courts are at times reluctant to enjoin the activities of an industrial facility within the area, which is often the major employer for that community.

* * *

Problems

1. Identify the major features of the National Environmental Policy Act.

2. What is the Environmental Protection Agency's responsibility with respect to environmental legislation?

3. How does the Clean Air Act affect manufacturing, automobiles and electric power generation?

4. Explain who has the primary responsibility for preventing, reducing and eliminating the pollution of water? Who establishes clean water guidelines and under what authority?

5. Identify environmental violations that can lead to criminal liability.

6. A resident of a small community near an oil refinery began noticing an offending odor coming from the facility. The resident also observed what appeared to be paint stripping from cars and the corrosion of aluminum siding as a result of the refinery's fumes. If the resident's observations are correct, does she have a cause of action against the refinery at common law? Explain.

7. What steps may the EPA take in the event it identifies a hazardous waste site endangering public heath and safety?

8. Identify the major laws affecting the manufacture and distribution of hazardous materials. What are the enforcement vehicles in each?

9. Explain the purpose of "Citizen's Suits" in the framework of environmental law.

10. Compare and contrast statutory liability and common law liability for injuries and property damage arising from improper handling, transportation, storage or use of hazardous materials.

11. A paint company is in default to its primary lender. The bank has a mortgage on the paint company's buildings and surrounding land. One member of the bank's senior management wants to foreclose on the land and buildings. Another member wants to work with the company to save it so long as the paint company will permit the bank to become active in the management of the company. What advise would you give to the bank? Include in your answer all information that would you need to provide an informed opinion?

18

Agency

Agency

IN MODERN SOCIETY all people, businessmen and nonbusinessmen alike, are affected by the rules of law which have developed in connection with agency relationships. In the broadest sense, an *agent* is a person who has agreed (1) to act on behalf of someone else (called the principal), and (2) either to be under the close supervision of the principal, or at least to have an obligation to advance the principal's best interests.

When the term "agent" is used in this broad sense, two types of persons are included, servants and independent contractors. The relationship between an employer and his employee is commonly termed by the law a master-servant relationship. In general, if a principal has the right to control the physical conduct of his agent, the latter is classified as a servant. On the other hand, if the principal has only a right of general control—for example, a right to give directions as to the desired result to be accomplished or the general method of performance, but no right to control the detailed physical acts of the agent—the agent is classified as an independent contractor.

I. Creating Agency Relationships

Usually an agency is created by a contact in which the principal hires the agent and agrees to pay him for his services. An employment contract, however, is not essential. For exam-

ple, if a buyer who has a charge account at a department store requests as a favor that his neighbor purchase a specified item and charge it to the buyer, the neighbor has no expectation of being compensated; nevertheless the neighbor is the buyer's authorized agent.

An agency relationship can arise from an express authorization or it may arise by implication, either (1) from prior conduct of the parties, (2) from one person having a right to control the physical acts of another, or (3) to some extent from the parties being married. A person can also obtain the rights and liabilities of a principal through approving or ratifying a contract which has been made for him, but without his prior authorization.

A. Agency Implied from Prior Conduct

Just as contract rights and obligations can arise from the conduct of parties without any expressly stated agreement, so also an agency relationship can arise or be found to exist through the conduct of the parties.

B. Agency Implied from Right to Control Another's Acts

Sometimes even though no agency relationship is expressly undertaken, one person will have a legal right to control the physical conduct of another person while the latter is performing certain acts. To that extent, the one with the right of control is the master, and the

Example. A buyer purchased and received a car from a dealer, paying part of the price in cash and giving a one-month negotiable promissory note for the $500 balance. On the following day the dealer sold, indorsed, and transferred the note to a finance company. When the note matured, the buyer not knowing of the transfer of the note, paid $500 to the dealer. Before the dealer turned the money over to the finance company, he was adjudged insolvent and a court-appointed receiver took over the dealer's assets (including this $500) for the benefit of all of the dealer's creditors. When the finance company was unable to collect the $500 from the dealer, the company sued the buyer for $500.

According to the law concerning negotiable notes (discussed in Chapter 15), even though an obligor is given notice of the transfer of a note, he is obligated to pay the actual owner of the note, whoever that may be; if the obligor pays his original creditor, the obligor will have to pay again to the proper person, if the recipient of the first payment fails to give the money to the owner of the note. Therefore in this example the buyer's payment to the dealer would be binding on the finance company only if the dealer was an agent with authority to collect for the finance company.

Although the finance company had never expressly appointed the dealer as its collecting agent, the evidence showed that during the three-year period before this dispute arose, the dealer transferred a large number of similar notes to the finance company, and that on an average of ten or fifteen times a week the dealer received payments on the transferred notes, periodically remitting to the finance company the money so collected. Each time the dealer received a payment he made out a receipt in triplicate. One copy of the receipt was given to the party making payment. Then when next remitting to the finance company, the dealer presented with the money the other two copies of each receipt. The finance company retained one copy of each receipt so as to know to whose account each payment should be credited, and initialed and returned to the dealer the third copy of each receipt as evidence that the dealer had turned over to the finance company the money described in the receipt.

The conduct of the parties over the three-year period showed that the dealer was actually an agent to collect for the finance company. The buyer's payment to an authorized agent of the finance company was a sufficient payment, and therefore the finance company was unable to require the buyer to pay a second time. ☐

other person, when performing those certain acts, assumes the status of a servant. One of the most common instances in which this implied master-servant relationship arises is when the owner of a car permits another to drive while the owner rides as a passenger. Generally, by virtue of his presence and ownership, the owner has the right to control the manner in which his car is being driven and thus the owner is the master and the driver is his servant. The owner's *right* to control make

him the master; whether he is exercising control or is asleep in the back seat is immaterial. It is, likewise, immaterial whether the particular journey is benefiting the owner or the driver. If the owner-passenger has no legal right to control the driver, as for example when the driver is the husband of the owner (in the eyes of the law the husband being the head of the family and not subject to his wife's control), a master-servant relationship does not arise.

Agency

C. Agency Implied from Marital Relationship

Ordinarily no agency relationship arises solely from the fact that persons are married; husbands and wives are not automatically agents in the conduct of their spouses' business affairs. However, unless a different arrangement is shown to exist, a wife usually serves as the manager of her husband's household, and as such is by implication an agent to purchase in her husband's name items for the ordinary day-to-day care and maintenance of the household.

D. Ratification

Suppose that an agent purporting to act for a certain principal enters into a contract with a third person, that in doing so the agent exceeds his authority so that the principal is not bound by the contract, and that when the principal later learns of what the agent had done, the principal expresses (either to the agent or to the third person) his approval and willingness to be bound by the contract. Since the contract was originally made in the principal's name, the third person certainly intends that the principal be bound by the contract and have rights under it. It is usually considered sound policy, therefore, to permit the principal, by his postcontract ratification, to obtain rights under the contract and to assume its obligations. On the other hand, if an agent does not purport to be acting for a principal when he enters into a contract with a third person, then the latter does not manifest any intent to form a contract with anyone other than the agent. If the contract is assignable, the principal can obtain rights through receiving an assignment from the agent, but the theory of ratification will not apply. An undisclosed principal who attempts to ratify the unauthorized contract of an agent obtains nothing through his attempted ratification.

Any conduct that evidences the fact that a purported principal approves of a contract and is willing to be bound by it is sufficient to constitute a ratification. A person's accepting or retaining benefits under a contract, with full knowledge of the facts, generally shows such approval. A purported principal's failure to repudiate a contract upon learning of it may show approval if, under the circumstances, a reasonable person would be expected to express objection if he disapproved of the contract. If the one making an unauthorized contract is actually the principal's agent and merely exceeds his authority (as contrasted with a person who is not an agent and has no authority whatsoever to act for the purported principal), the principal is usually expected to notify promptly the third person of his disapproval of the unauthorized contract. In such a case the principal's failure to repudiate the unauthorized contract would indicate approval and constitute ratification.

E. Capacity to Act as Agent

If pursuant to his principal's instructions, an agent enters into a contract with a third person in the principal's name, the parties who are legally bound by the contract are the principal and the third person. The agent's legal capacity to bind himself by contracts is immaterial. Therefore, a minor can be as effective an agent as an adult can be.

II. Rights and Obligations Between Principals and Agents

A. Duties of Agents to Principals

When an agent is entrusted with his principal's affairs, the agent has the power to cause considerable loss to his principal. It is sound policy, therefore, for the law to hold agents to a high standard of conduct—to require them to obey their principals' instructions, to use proper care in performing services or transacting business for their principals, and to be

Example. P authorized A to make certain purchases in foreign countries and to ship the purchased goods to P by certain specified carrier systems. After making one such purchase, which according to instructions was to be shipped by a carrier passing through Country X, A was reliably informed that a revolution in Country X was imminent. Since a revolution would jeopardize the shipment, A attempted to communicate with P. Unable to contact P before the time for shipment, A made a reasonable decision to have the goods shipped by a different carrier through Country Y. Although no revolution occurred in Country X, an unexpected revolutionary uprising in Country Y resulted in destruction of the entire shipment. P sued A for the value of the destroyed goods.

The three conditions under which an agent is permitted to deviate reasonably from his instructions having been present, the agent would not be liable to his principal for loss of the shipment.

loyal to their principals' best interests. If an agent fails to meet these standards, he is liable for any loss which the principal thereby sustains, and, of course, an agent is not entitled to any compensation for services which are defectively or improperly performed.

I. DUTY OF OBEDIENCE

In performing services for his principal, an agent is obliged to comply with his principal's instructions; if the agent disobeys his instructions without justification, he is liable to the principal for any damages which result. Usually the agent is liable even though his deviation from instructions is in good faith and reasonable. However, in the rare case in which all of the following three conditions are present, the agent will be considered as justified in deviating from his instructions to the extent that seems reasonably necessary to prevent loss to the principal; the three conditions are: (1) after creation of the agency an unforeseen event occurs; (2) this event threatens a substantial loss to the principal if the agent acts as instructed; and (3) it is impracticable for the agent to communicate with his principal in time to prevent the loss.

2. DUTY OF CARE

An agent is obliged to use the care of a reasonable person having the skill which the agent professes. For failure to use such care the agent is guilty of negligence and is liable to his principal for any loss that results.

3. DUTY OF LOYALTY

An agent with power over another's property interests is always subject to temptations to misuse his power for his own benefit. The law attempts to reduce temptation to a minimum by prohibiting any exercise of the agency powers for the agent's own personal benefit, unless the principal consents. In attempting to assure that an agent will act solely for the benefit of his principal, the law prohibits all acts for the agent's personal benefit, even though a particular act does not actually harm the principal. The chief situations to which this prohibition applies include the following:

1. An agent has a personal interest in a contract negotiated for his principal.
2. An agent derives a gain from business transacted for his principal.
3. An agent acts for both sides in a contract negotiation.
4. An agent misuses confidential information.

a. Personal Interest

Unless the principal consents, an agent is not permitted to have a personal interest in any business he transacts for his principal.

Example. P engaged A, a stockbroker, to act as P's agent in purchasing for P fifty shares of the stock of the Carter Corporation at not over $60 per share. A was unable to locate on the market a block of fifty shares which he could purchase. However, A himself owned one hundred shares in that corporation and arranged a transfer of fifty of these shares to P for $50 per share. After P paid for the transfer, the corporation was adjudged insolvent, to the complete surprise of many people, including A who had honestly and reasonably believed that the stock was worth $50 per share. After the collapse of the corporation, P for the first time learned that A had previously owned the stock for which P had paid. P sued A to recover the $2,500 P paid for the stock.

P would recover. In a similar case, the Pennsylvania Supreme Court said that the rule "forbids that anyone intrusted with the interests of others shall in any manner make the business an object of personal interest to himself, because, from a frailty of nature, one who has the power will be too readily seized with the inclination to use the opportunity for serving his own interests at the expense of his principal.... It matters not that no fraud was meditated, and no injury done. The rule is not intended to be remedial of actual wrong, but preventive of the possibility of it.[1]

1. *Haines v. Biddle*, 325 Pa. 441, 188 A. 843 (1937).

Usually an agent will be considered as violating his duty to his principal if he so mingles his principal's money or property with his own that all separate identity is lost. Such conduct is improper because not only does the agent appear to acquire a personal interest in his principal's funds, but also he improperly subjects his principal's funds to the claims of the agent's creditors.

b. Outside Benefit

An agent's compensation is supposed to be limited to the amount agreed upon by his principal. Thus unless the principal consents an agent is not permitted to obtain any additional gain or benefit for performing services or transacting business for his principal, and anything an agent receives in violation of this duty must be surrendered to the principal. Some states have implemented this rule by statute. For example, one such statute provides, in effect:

> Whoever offers or gives to any agent, to a member of his family, or to anyone for his use or benefit, directly or indirectly, any commission, money, property, or other valuable thing, without the knowledge and consent of the principal, and in relation to the affairs of business of the principal, or whoever accepts or takes the same, is guilty of a misdemeanor, and subject to a fine not exceeding $500 or imprisonment not exceeding one year, or both. That the making of such gifts is customary in any business shall not be a defense in any prosecution under this section. This section does not apply to the practice commonly known as "tipping."

c. Double Agency

An agent who is negotiating a contract between two parties is not permitted to act as agent for both parties unless, before the contract is negotiated, both parties consent to the double agency. If a contract is negotiated by a double agent without the consent of both parties, it can be canceled by either party, and the agent is not entitled to compensation from either party for his services.

d. Confidential Information

If through his agency an agent acquires information concerning his principal's business affairs, he owes to the principal a duty not to

Example. The co-owners of certain land listed the property with A, a real estate broker, for $60,000, and agreed to pay A $1,200 for negotiating a sale at that price. A buyer desiring to purchase the property engaged A to negotiate a purchase, agreeing to pay A a 2 percent commission for his services. Neither the owners nor the buyer knew of A's commission arrangement with the other until after A had negotiated the transfer of the property for $60,000. When the owners learned of A's arrangement with the buyer, they refused to pay A the agreed $1,200, and A sued the owners.

A's argument: He was engaged merely as a middleman or intermediary to bring the owners and buyer together, and held a neutral position between them. Because no discretionary authority was vested in A and he had no obligation or opportunity to exercise his judgment, there was no possibility that he could injure either side by preferring one over the other. Therefore, he was not subject to any temptation to show preference and could properly represent both sides.

In a similar case, the Pennsylvania Superior Court held that A could not recover, saying: "He placed himself in the doubtful position of being active for each and claims that he was the immediate and efficient cause in effecting the sale or at least in bringing the two parties together.... The defendants had a right to repose special trust and confidence in him as their agent, and . . . he owned to them the utmost good faith, which required him to keep them fully apprised of every fact and circumstance relating to the business or to their interest. No broker, agent or middleman can recover for services which uncover double dealing and a secret agreement with one of the persons." [2]

2. *Linderman v. McKenna*, 20 Pa. Super. 409 (1902).

use the information in a way that will benefit the agent at the expense of the principal.

Many employment contracts provide that for a stated period after termination of the employment the employee will not engage in a business which competes with his former employer. Even in the absence of such a restrictive provision, a former agent owes to his former principal a duty not to make use of or to disclose confidential information or trade secrets. What information should be classed as confidential or secret is a matter of public policy. Any definition of these terms must be both fair and realistic or practical, taking into account the exact nature of the information and the expressed or assumed intent of the principal. For example, if a deliveryman quits his job with the Old Bakery and goes to work for the New Bakery, it would be neither fair nor realistic to say that the deliveryman should forget the names of the customers with whom he became acquainted while working for the Old Bakery. Therefore, in the absence of a restrictive provision in his employment contract, the deliveryman has a right to contact his old customers and to urge them to switch their patronage to the New Bakery. However, it would not be fair for the deliveryman while working for the Old Bakery to copy from the office records a list of customers served by the other drivers, and then after starting for New Bakery to contact all of these customers. The court would restrain the deliveryman from using his "stolen" list. Determining when information concerning trade and production techniques should be treated as confidential is especially difficult. Through associating with a certain business a man gains general experience and knowledge which is properly valuable to himself and to

Example. P, the owner of a certain real estate, engaged A, a real estate broker, to negotiate a sale of the property within the next three months for $20,000 and agreed to pay A a 5 percent commission in the event of sale.

1. As a result of A's efforts, B decided to purchase the property. A obtained B's signature on a written contract from which A then took to P who also signed. The written contract stated that P agreed to sell and B to buy the described property for $20,000, title to be transferred and purchase price to be paid one month later. Upon expiration of the month, B said that he had changed his mind and refused to accept a deed or to pay any money for the property. A nevertheless demanded a commission from P.

The expression "in the event of sale" is usually interpreted as pertaining to the rate of commission and not as stating a condition or time for payment. Therefore, the quoted words do not require consummation of the transfer as a condition for payment of the commission. Such expressions as "at settlement" or "for bringing about a sale" have been similarly interpreted. Thus, since B committed himself to a contract which P could enforce against B, and since A's commission was not expressly made dependent on consummation of the transfer, A earned his commission by negotiating the contract.

2. As a result of A's efforts, B, a responsible person, decided to purchase the property for the listed price and signed a written contract form to that effect. However, P refused to sign the contract. A sued P for the agreed commission.

When A produced B ready, willing, and able to buy at the listed price, A earned his commission.

3. B, attracted by the "For Sale" sign A erected on the property, contacted P directly. After some negotiation directly between B and P, P transferred the property to B for $19,500 which B paid to P. A sued P for a 5 percent commission on $19,500.

A was an effective cause of the sale in that something he did was material in bringing about the sale. Therefore, A would be entitled to collect the claimed commission .

4. Two months after the listing, B, a resident of another town, learned directly from P of the latter's desire to sell his property. B bought the property from P for $20,000 which B paid directly to P. Nothing A did was an effective or procuring cause of the sale. A sued P for his commission.

Just as in Part 1 of this Example, the expression "in the event of sale" would not be construed as a statement of a condition or of a time for payment. P did not agree to pay A a commission regardless of who effected a sale. Since the sale was not produced by A, A would not be entitled to any commission on the sale.⬚

some new employer, and which it is neither fair nor possible to completely erase. Thus a man can continue to use the general skill and knowledge which he acquired while working for a former employer, but at the same time he should refrain from using or disclosing unique production processes which his former employer was keeping secret.

B. Duties of Principals to Agents

The chief obligations of a principal to his agent are to reimburse the agent for any personal expense he incurs at the principal's request and to pay the agent the compensation agreed upon in the agency contract. Sometimes a principal and an agent disagree as to

Example. P. Porter, the owner of certain real estate, entered into the following written contract with A. Adams, a real estate broker: "[Date] I hereby list exclusively with you for the non-withdrawal period of three months from date the following real estate [describing the property] for $20,000, and in the event of a sale, agree to pay you a commission of 5 percent of the purchase price. (signed) P. Porter. Accepted, I hereby agree to use my best efforts to negotiate a sale of the above described premises. (signed) A. Adams." Two months later P sold and transferred the property to B for $20,000 which B paid directly to P, and P promptly notified A of the sale. The transfer was made entirely through P's efforts, and not brought about by anything done by A or by any other broker. Up to the time P notified A of the sale, A had not found a buyer for the property. A sued P for the amount of commission he would have earned if he had negotiated the sale.

P did not expressly agree to pay A a commission regardless of who effected the sale. Therefore in many states the agreement would be construed as creating an exclusive-agency rather than an exclusive-sale relationship. If P had sold the property through the efforts of another broker, P would have breached his exclusive-agency agreement with A; for breach of the agreement, A would have been entitled to damages in the amount of the agreed commission. In making a sale not procured through any broker, P did not breach the exclusive part of the agreement. However, in selling during the three-month period, P breached his agreement to leave the property with A for three months. For breach of this agreement, A would be entitled to recover the costs and expenses he incurred in attempting to sell the property up to the time P notified A of the sale. ☐

whether the agent's performance is sufficient to entitle him to the compensation specified in the contract. Useful examples can be found in disputes between property owners and real estate brokers engaged to negotiate sales of properties. The rules that apply to such cases may be classified as follows:

1. The parties may expressly agree that the broker will be entitled to a commission only when a transfer at the listed price is consummated.

2. The parties may expressly agree that the broker will be entitled to a commission if a transfer is consummated during the contract period even though the transfer is not brought about by anything the broker does. In many states such agreements are further classified into types:

(a) **Exclusive Agency Agreement**. The owner expressly agrees that during the contract period he will not sell through another broker. If the owner violates this agreement, the broker is entitled to recover as damages the amount of the agreed commission, but a sale of property solely through the owner's own efforts does not violate an exclusive agency arrangement.

(b) **Exclusive Sale**. The owner expressly agrees that if the listed property is sold during the contract period, no matter who brings about the sale, the broker will be entitled to the stated commission.

3. In the absence of any special agreement to the contrary, a broker is entitled to an agreed commission if any *one* of the following three events occurs:

(a) The broker procures a buyer with whom the owner makes a contract.

(b) The broker procures a buyer ready, willing, and able to buy at the listed price.

(c) The broker is an effective or procuring cause of a sale which is actually completed.

499

III. Rights and Obligations Between Principals and Third Persons

Sometimes a person who enters into a contract may, unknown to the other contracting party, actually be acting as an agent for another person. If a party is unaware that he is dealing with an agent, the principal for whom the agent is actually acting is said to be "undisclosed." If a party is aware that he is dealing with an agent but does not know whom the agent represents, the principal is said to be "partially disclosed." A principal is classified as "fully disclosed" if, at the time his agent enters into a contract, the other contracting party (1) knows that he is dealing with an agent, and (2) knows the identity of the person for whom the agent is acting.

A. Contract Liability of Fully Disclosed Principals

The courts frequently reiterate that a person deals with an agent at his own risk. This means that if a principal denies liability for a contract made in his name by a particular agent, the other party to the contract has the burden of proving the agent's authority. The principal is not bound unless the agent acts either within his actual or his apparent authority.

1. ACTUAL AUTHORITY

Actual authority may be express or implied:

1. Express authority is that authority which the principal has expressly granted to his agent.
2. Implied authority is that authority which, although not expressly mentioned by the principal, is implied or understood, either from what the principal has expressly authorized the agent to do or from some other conduct of the principal and agent. Suppose that the general manager of a retail food store is expressly authorized to make sales to customers and to collect the purchase prices, to hire and fire employees and fix their wages, to purchase a stated quantity and kind of produce locally, and to maintain a checking account in the name of the store. Even though he may not be expressly authorized to purchase fuel for heating that store building, it is fair to conclude that the manager has the implied (and therefore actual) authority to do so if no other arrangement has been made by the principal. The finance company example on page 345 is a situation in which actual authority was implied from the conduct of the parties.

What is sometimes called an agency or authority "by necessity" is one type of implied authority. While the conductor on a freight train ordinarily has no authority to make contracts in the name of the employer railroad, if a crewman is injured in the middle of the night at some remote location and needs immediate medical attention, the conductor as the highest person in authority present is authorized to engage a physician in the name of the railroad.

2. APPARENT AUTHORITY

Although the act of an agent in a principal's name is outside any actual authority (either express or implied) granted to the agent, the principal will nevertheless be bound by the agent's act if the following three conditions are all present: (1) A certain situation or appearance exists, (2) for which the principal is responsible, and (3) from which the third person is justified in assuming that the agent has the authority he presumes to exercise. If these conditions are all present, the agent is said to have the appearance of authority to bind his principal. When a principal denies liability for an agent's act and a third person is unable to prove that the agent actually had the authority he was presuming to exercise, the third person will usually attempt to prove that the agent was acting within his apparent authority, thereby obligating the principal. In such a case the chief issue usually is the third condition listed above—namely, justification for assuming that the agent had the authority in question. In business transactions this issue arises most often in cases involving agents having actual authority to sell or negotiate sales of goods, and with agents having actual authority to manage any of their principals' business affairs.

a. Goods Salespeople

Salesmen of goods can be classified into two types, (1) those who have actual authority to make contracts in their principals' names, and (2) those whose authority is merely to solicit orders for goods. The latter type of salesman, the order taker, has no authority to make a contract binding on his principal; he merely solicits orders (offers to buy) which he forwards to his principal. The principal then decides whether or not to sell the ordered goods, and no contract arises until the principal accepts the offer. If a principal authorizes his salesmen to make binding contracts, he runs the risk of being overcontracted. Several of his salesmen might unexpectedly have phenomenal success and contract to sell more goods than the principal can deliver. For this reason the most common type of salesman is merely an order taker.

A salesman, whether a contracting salesman or merely an order taker, has the apparent authority to do what is usual or customary for the type of transaction which he is actually authorized to negotiate. A salesman authorized to sell and deliver goods or to make a contract for sale has the apparent authority to sell at the usual price and to make such warranties as are usual in such transactions. Generally his apparent authority is limited to contracting for cash payable on delivery rather than for sales on credit. Therefore a salesman (contract maker or order taker) generally has the apparent authority to collect a portion or all of the purchase price only if and when he delivers goods to the buyer. If the principal delivers to the buyer directly and not through the salesman, the latter usually has no apparent authority to collect for the goods.

Whether knowledge acquired by a salesman, but not reported to his principal, is nevertheless binding on the principal depends on several factors, including the type of information and the time it is acquired by the salesman. Generally a salesman has the apparent authority to receive notices (1) at the time he is dealing with a third person, and (2) which come under the actual authority of the agent in regard to the contract he is making or the order he is soliciting.

An agents having authority to enter into a contract does not of itself give him the appearance of authority *at a later date* to modify the contract or to receive a notice affecting rights under the contract. For example (as discussed in chapters 12 and 22), if a warranty accompanies the sale of goods, a buyer may lose his right to collect for breach of warranty unless he gives prompt notice to the seller that the goods are defective. It may seem quite reasonable for the buyer to give such a notice to the salesman through whom he ordered the goods, but to adequately protect his rights the buyer should also give a notice directly to the seller.

Partnership dissolution cases provide an excellent illustration. It is a rule of partnership law (as discussed in Chapter 19) that if a business is continued after the withdrawal of one partner, a creditor who had previously extended credit to the partnership can hold the withdrawing partner liable for obligations incurred by the business after that partner withdrew, unless the creditor had personal knowledge of the partner's withdrawal. A number of courts have held that if a salesman's only authority is to take orders, he has no apparent authority to receive partnership withdrawal notices. On the other hand, if in addition to taking orders the duties of a salesman include reporting on the credit standing of customers or making collections, the salesman has ap-

Example. On March 9 a salesman employed by a Chicago meatpacker visited a wholesaler in a distant community and solicited an order for 50 cases of pigs' feet placed in cans of a specified size, at $2.30 per case, payable on delivery. The order blank signed by the wholesaler stated: "All orders are subject to approval by the packer at the Chicago office. All merchandise is guaranteed first quality. No claims for defective merchandise shall be entertained unless made within 30 days after receipt of merchandise." After the salesman sent the order to Chicago, the packer shipped the ordered goods to the wholesaler who received and paid for the shipment on March 21. On April 1 the wholesaler received a complaint from a retailer to whom two cases had been sold that the contents of some of the cans were spoiled. The wholesaler immediately discontinued making any further sales from the shipment. The following day, when the packer's salesman again called on the wholesaler, the latter told the salesman of the complaint and together they opened several cans, finding the contents of most of them spoiled. Admittedly the cans were not first quality. The salesman said he would notify the packer and ask for instructions as to return or other adjustment. When the wholesaler heard nothing further by May 15, he wrote to the packer offering to return the merchandise. The packer refused to make any adjustment and the wholesaler sued the packer for damages. The salesman testified that he had forgotten to report the defective cans to the packer.

Under somewhat similar facts, the Pennsylvania Superior Court held[3] that the wholesaler failed to give proper notice to the packer and could not recover. Generally a salesman who solicits orders has no apparent authority to receive a notice that the goods shipped in response to the order are defective. The April 2 notice to the salesman, was not notice to the packer, and the May 15 notice to the packer was not within the thirty-day period specified in the contract. □

3. *Foell Packing Co. v. Harris*, 127 Pa. Super. 494, 193 A. 152(1937).

parent authority to receive notices pertaining to credit matters. In such a case, if notice that a partner has withdrawn is given to the salesman along with an order, it will be binding on the salesman's principal even though the salesman neglects to pass the information along.

b. Buying Agents

An agent with authority to buy is usually expected to make cash purchases; usually he has no appearance of authority to buy on his principal's credit. An implied authority (as distinguished from apparent authority) to buy on credit can arise from the prior conduct of the parties or from the fact that the principal neglects to give the agent funds with which to make the authorized purchases.

c. Loaning Agents

In many cases the courts have pointed out that an agent authorized to negotiate a loan of his principal's money is not necessarily the proper party to whom the debt should be repaid when it matures. Suppose that an agent (1) negotiates a loan, (2) has actual authority to collect interest on the loan as it periodically comes due, and (3) is in possession of the document which evidences the loan. These three facts taken together do not necessarily clothe the agent with the appearance of authority to collect a payment on the principal amount of the loan when it comes due especially if the agent's possession of the loan document is appropriate or convenient for his collecting and noting the periodic interest payments.

If a debtor is making a loan repayment to an agent, the debtor should verify the agent's actual authority to collect—or as is frequently simpler, should pay by check made out to the principal himself and thereby avoid any question of the agent's authority to collect money. The debtor thus shifts to his bank the question of the agent's authority if the agent should ignore his principal's name and attempt to cash the check. The bank will usually ask to see the agent's written, express authorization to indorse his principal's checks, because an agent generally has no authority to indorse his principal's name to commercial paper (notes, checks, and drafts) unless the principal *expressly* authorizes the agent to do so. Only very rarely is an agent considered as having implied or apparent authority to indorse.

d. Subagents

An agent of the type classified as a servant generally has no apparent authority to delegate performance of his duties to an assistant or subagent. An independent contractor may also be likewise limited. However, with many types of independent contractors, it may clearly appear that the principal expects the agent to engage one or more assistants to help. An example is a broker or factor who receives from a number of different owners goods to sell on commission. Such an agent will usually be expected to work through a staff of employees and the act of one of the agent's authorized subagents may therefore be binding on the principal.

e. Managing Agents

A servant with authority to manage his principal's business affairs over a period of time, or to manage a continuing segment of his principal's affairs has fairly broad implied and apparent authority to do what is usual in such cases. A retail store manager commonly has the authority to hire necessary employees, as well as the authority of a selling and buying agent as previously discussed.

Although a managing agent will frequently have implied or apparent authority to purchase on his principal's credit, he generally will have no authority to borrow money in his principal's name unless such authority is *expressly* granted to him. Only very rarely is an agent considered as having implied or apparent authority to borrow money.

3. RATIFICATION

If a principal receives an actual benefit from the performance of a contract made by someone acting as the principal's purported agent, it is not fair for the principal to retain the benefit and at the same time repudiate the contract as being outside the agent's actual and apparent authority. When fully apprised of the facts, the principal must return or account for such actual benefit, or be assumed to ratify and thus become bound by his agent's contract.

B. Undisclosed and Partially Disclosed Principals

Suppose that pursuant to instructions from P, A enters into a contract with T for P's benefit, but that either by design or inadvertence, A fails to disclose that he is acting for P. Since P directs A to make the contract and intends the contract for his own benefit, it is only fair that P should be bound by the contract. For these reasons it seems equally fair that P should have rights under the contract. When P claims contract rights, T might protest that he had no intention of making a contract with P; T might further object that he would have refused to enter into the contract had he known it was being made for P. T's protest is fully met, however, by the same reasoning that supports assignments of contracts (discussed in Chapter 11). If an assignment does not materially change the obligation of the other contracting party, then unless the contract prohibits as-

Example. Pauline Porter, an elderly widow residing in a southern state, appointed Albert Adams as her agent to manage her extensive real estate holdings and investments in a distant community, signing and giving to A a form power of attorney, authorizing A as follows:

> To take charge of, care for, manage, control, and sell any and all real estate now or hereafter owned by me; to sign and deliver any and all deeds or other instruments in writing which may be at any time necessary or advisable to convey the title thereof; to collect the interest and principal of any mortgage now or hereafter held by me and in case of default to foreclose the same by sale or otherwise; to effect any insurance necessary or proper to protect any property belonging to me; to pay all taxes and other assessments; and in general to do every act and thing concerning the premises, which I might myself do if personally present. It is understood the foregoing enumeration of specific powers does not in any way limit or cut down the general powers herein granted, or which should have been granted in order to carry out the purposes hereinbefore expressed. Hereby granting unto my said agent full power and authority to act in and concerning the premises as fully and effectually as I might do if personally present. This authority is to continue until expressly revoked by me.

1. A year later, A decided to redecorate some of the properties. The funds on hand being insufficient to pay for the redecoration, A went to a local bank, showed his written power of attorney to the bank, explained the purpose of the loan, and borrowed $1,500, signing a three-month note, "Pauline Porter by Albert Adams, her agent." A used the $1,500 for the stated purpose. Upon maturity of the note and demand for payment, P learned for the first time of the loan and the redecorations. Claiming, as was true, that the properties did not need redecorating and that she had never authorized A to undertake any redecorating, P refused to pay and the bank sued P.

Since P did not expressly grant A authority to borrow money, he had no such authority, actual or apparent. However, whether P would have desired the redecorating or not, her property obtained an actual net benefit or gain from the borrowed money. To disaffirm the loan, P would therefore have to return to the bank the borrowed $1,500. If P failed to repay the borrowed money to the bank, P would in effect be ratifying the loan and would be bound by the note signed by A.

2. Soon A began speculating in his own name with funds collected through his management. Within a year, A had lost through speculations about $7,000 of P's money. The funds were so depleted that there was not sufficient to pay some of the current taxes on the various properties. Believing that some of his speculations would permit recoupment of past losses, A applied to a local bank for a three-month loan of $1,500. A showed his written power of attorney to the bank, explained that the money was to pay real estate taxes on the various properties, and falsely said that the temporary shortage of funds was due to expenses of redecorating various of the properties. The bank made the loan and A signed a three-month note, "Pauline Porter by Albert Adams, her agent." A used the $1,500 to pay the taxes. Thereafter A's investments further depreciated and A disappeared. Upon maturity of the note and demand for payment P learned for the first time of A's dishonesty. P refused to pay and the bank sued P.

As stated in the answer to Part 1 of this Example, A had no authority to borrow. Furthermore although the loan was used to pay taxes on P's property, P received no net benefit from the loan, the money merely making up for sums A had previously embezzled. The bank could not recover from P. ☐

signment, a right arising under the contract can be assigned without the consent of the other party. If an assignment by A to P would not be unfair to T, it is not unfair to accord to P a contract right by virtue of his responsibility for the contract. If the identity of the person who may obtain contract rights is so important to a contracting party, he can specify in the contract that it is not assignable and that no undisclosed principal will have any rights under it. If an agent lies about the existence or identity of a principal, the agent would be guilty of fraud, which would enable the third person to cancel the contract. However if the third person neglects to ask whether the other party is acting as an agent, the latter's failure to volunteer the information is not fraud.

C. Tort Liability of Principals

Suppose that an employer hires an employee to drive a delivery truck, uses proper care in selecting a competent driver, and instructs the driver to operate the truck carefully and never in excess of 35 miles per hour; later while driving his route the employee drives carelessly, at 50 miles per hour, and runs into a third person's carefully driven car, injuring the third person. While the driver would, of course, be liable for his own tort, employee drivers are frequently financially unable to pay for damages they cause. Usually therefore injured third persons will seek to collect from employers. It seems fair that as between the two equally innocent parties—the third person and the employer—the employer should bear the expense or burden resulting from the accident if (1) as the employment relationship implies, the employer has the right to control the physical conduct of the employee, *and* (2) at the time of the accident the employee is advancing the employer's general interests, or, in other words, is acting within the general scope of his authorized services. If either of these two numbered elements is missing, it is usually not considered

fair to hold a principal liable for his agent's tort. As previously discussed, a principal has no right to control the physical conduct of an agent who is an independent contractor as distinguished from a servant. Lacking the right of control, the principal is usually not liable for the torts of such an agent—with the possible exception of misrepresentations, discussed later. If the agent is a servant, but the tort which he commits occurs while he is acting outside the general scope of his authorized services, the principal is not liable.

Even though a servant is disobeying certain specific instructions of his master, the servant's conduct can nevertheless be within the general scope of his service. Usually a servant is acting within the general scope of his authorized services if his conduct, (1) is of the same general nature as the service he is authorized to perform, or (2) is incidental to such authorized conduct, or (3) is not a highly unusual or totally unexpected way to perform the authorized services. For example, if a short-order cook at a lunch counter, although instructed to be considerate of the welfare of customers, is carelessly wielding his spatula in exaggerated flourishes while he is cooking, and strikes and injures a customer, the cook is acting within the general scope of his services; but if the cook becomes irritated at a remark made by one of the customers and strikes out with the spatula, hitting and injuring the customer, the cook's conduct would be outside the general scope of his service.

A servant's wrongful act may be done while he is performing authorized services and nevertheless be outside the *scope* of his services. An employee carelessly smoking on the job provides a good illustration of this. The employer is liable only if the employee's smoking is done at such a time and under such circumstances that his carelessness in smoking makes him careless in the manner in which he performs authorized services.

If an agent is guilty of making a fraudulent misrepresentation in negotiating a contract

Example. An owner listed his house with a real estate broker to negotiate a sale for $20,000. As the owner knew, the broker had in his employ a salesman who assisted the broker in negotiating sales. While a prospective buyer was being taken by auto to examine the owner's house, the driver of the auto was negligent and injured the buyer.

1. The driver was the broker and the injured buyer sued the owner. Since the owner had no right to control the physical conduct of the broker, the broker was an independent contractor type of agent, and the owner would not be liable for the broker's tort.

2. The driver was the broker's salesman and the injured buyer sued the broker. Since the broker had the right to control the physical conduct of his salesman, the latter was a servant of the broker, and the broker would be liable for the salesman's negligence. ▢

* * *

Example. A father, needing medicine for his sick child and not wishing to leave the child for the time required to go to the drugstore ten miles away, requested his neighbor to drive to the drugstore and procure the medicine. While performing the errand, the neighbor drove negligently and injured a third person. The third person sued the father.

1. At the father's request, the neighbor used the father's car for the errand. When ownership of the instrumentality being used and sole benefit from its use are combined in the same person, the owner usually has the right to control the physical conduct of the user. Under these circumstances, therefore, the neighbor could be considered the servant of the father, thus rendering the father liable for the neighbor's negligence.

2. The neighbor used his own car for the errand. The fact that the errand was the sole benefit of the father's family, would not, standing alone, give the father any right to control the manner in which the neighbor drove his own car. Therefore, a master-servant relationship would not exist and the father would not be liable for the neighbor's negligence. ▢

between his principal and a third person, the agent is of course liable to the third person for damages. Also, unless the contract limits the agent's power concerning making statements, the third person has a right to cancel the contract dishonestly negotiated by the agent and to recover from the principal anything paid under the contract. However, whether the defrauded third person can hold the principal liable for damages is a point upon which the courts do not entirely agree. In most states, the question of a principal's liability for his agent's fraudulent misrepresentation is decided on the basis of the actual or apparent authority of the agent to make representations. If a representation involves a matter concerning which an agent might be expected to make statements in dealing with third persons, the agent has the apparent authority to make such a statement. If the agent makes a misstatement in regard to such a matter, his principal has a contract obligation to the third person for the misstatement, and (in most states) likewise a tort liability for a misstatement fraudulently made. A few states, however, do not impose tort liability on a principal unless he actually participates in his agent's fraud.

Example. An ice-cream manufacturer employed a truck driver and helper to deliver ice cream to various stores. The driver was instructed to collect the purchase price on delivery but to use no force in making collections, and in cases of dispute to call the manufacturer's office. On one occasion when the driver tendered boxes of ice cream to a retailer, the latter refused to accept delivery, claiming that the ice cream had been permitted to thaw and had become too soft. When the driver insisted on leaving the ice cream, the retailer refused to pay and locked his cash register to prevent the driver from taking the payment. The driver and his helper then attempted to carry the cash register away. This resulted in a struggle for possession of the cash register, during the course of which the retailer was kicked and severely beaten by the driver and his helper. The retailer sued the manufacturer for the damages sustained.

In a similar case, the Connecticut Supreme Court held that the manufacturer was liable because the driver was acting within the general scope of his services. In the course of its opinion, the court said, "When the servant is doing or attempting to do the very thing which he was directed to do, the master is liable, though the servant's method of doing it be wholly unauthorized or forbidden."[4]

The quoted statement should be limited to the facts of the case. If the driver has pulled a gun, shot and wounded the retailer, and then stepping over the unconscious retailer, had taken the ice-cream money from the cash register, the court would probably have held that although the servant's act was a means of accomplishing the authorized result, it was done in so outrageous a manner and with force so totally out-of-line with performance of the authorized acts that the servant would be acting outside the general scope of his services—with the result that the manufacturer would not be liable for the driver's violence. ☐

4. *Son v. Hartford Ice Cream Co.*, 102 Conn. 696, 129 A 778 (1925).

IV. Rights and Obligations Between Agents and Third Persons

A. Contract Obligations of Agents To Third Persons

I. AGENTS WITH AUTHORITY

An agent who enters into a contract for his principal usually has no contract liability himself, even though the principal breaches the contract, if the agent (1) identifies the principal for whom he Is acting, (2) has authority (either actual or apparent) to bind the principal by the particular contract, and (3) does not expressly guarantee the principal's performance or otherwise make himself a party to the contract.

a. Fully Disclosed Principal

Even though a principal is fully disclosed and a contract is authorized, if the Contract is in writing the agent may sometimes be held liable as a co-party or a guarantor because of the manner in which he signs. The most common forms in which agent's signatures have been made are as follows (assume P. Porter is the principal and A. Adams, the agent):

Form 1. "P. Porter by A. Adams, his agent."

Form 2. "P. Porter hereby agrees as follows . . . (signed) A. Adams, his agent."

Example. An oil refiner employed a driver to deliver gasoline in the refiner's tank truck. While delivering gasoline to a manufacturer's plant, the driver unavoidably spilled some gasoline. While still in the process of delivering the gasoline, the driver lighted a cigarette and carelessly tossed the match into some of the spilled gasoline. The resulting conflagration destroyed part of the manufacturing plant and the manufacturer sued the refiner.

The driver's careless smoking would make him a careless deliveryman; for negligence within the scope of the driver's authorized services, the employer would be liable.

Suppose that while driving the gasoline tank truck toward the manufacturing plant, the driver lighted a cigarette and carelessly tossed the lighted match out the window, starting a costly grass fire. The driver's careless smoking would not make him a careless truck driver, and therefore the employer would not be liable for the grass-fire damages. ▢

Form 3. "P. Porter A. Adams"

Form 4. "P. Porter Corporation
A. Adams, President"

Form 5. "A. Adams, President
P. Porter Corporation"

Form 6. "A. Adams, agent for
P. Porter" or "A. Adams,
agent for P. Porter
Corporation."

Form 7. "A. Adams, agent."

The first form, of course, is the best for an agent to use. In Form 1, and (under the better-reasoned decisions) in Form 2, the agent clearly shows that he is making the contract for his principal and in his principal's name, and that he does not intend to obligate himself personally. The other numbered forms leave the agent's intended status open to some argument. The better view is that if the intention of the parties (of both the agent and the other contracting party) is not made clear by the writing or is ambiguous from the name in which the agent signs; oral evidence may be heard to prove what the parties intended. In the absence of such oral evidence, the agent would be liable if he signs as in Forms 3 and 7, and some courts would hold him liable if he signs as in Forms 4, 5, and 6.

b. Partially Disclosed or Undisclosed Principal

If at the time a contract is entered into by A and T, T is unaware that A is acting as an agent, clearly A is a party to the contract and is bound by it. If T is aware that A is an agent, but does not know who A represents, then usually T is to some extent relying on A's good faith and solvency, and unless the parties clearly state otherwise, A is a party to the contract and is bound by it.

2. PURPORTED AGENTS

Through his conduct of entering into a contract in the name of another person, a purported agent is asserting as a fact that he has the authority he is presuming to exercise. If he lacks such authority, either actual or apparent, the other contracting party can hold the purported agent liable for damages for breach of this implied assertion or warranty of authority.

B. Tort Liability of Agents

Whether a person who commits a tort is acting for himself or as an agent for another, he is personally liable for the damages resulting from his tort. If a principal instructs an agent to do an act which constitutes a tort, the agent is not relieved from liability by that fact that he was merely carrying out his principal's in-

Example. In a small community in which all houses were not yet concerned with the recently expanded sewer system, an owner listed his house with a real estate broker to negotiate a sale for $15,000, the broker to receive a 3 percent commission. The owner instructed the broker to tell prospective buyers that the house still used a septic tank, not yet having been connected to the new sewer line. Falsely saying that he had investigated and found that the house was connected with the sewer line, the broker interested a buyer in buying the premises. The buyer signed a contract form and paid $500 down. The broker then took the contract form to the owner who also signed it. By the contract the owner agreed to sell and the buyer to buy the described house and lot for $15,000, $500 of which was stated as having been paid, with the balance to be paid upon delivery of the deed thirty days later. No reference to any sewer connection was made in the contract. Of the $500 paid by the buyer, the broker turned over to the owner $50, retaining $450 as his commission. At the time for settlement the buyer learned the truth concerning the sewerage system of the house and the owner for the first time learned of the broker's fraudulent misrepresentation. To excavate through underground rock and connect the house with the new sewer line would cost $1,500.

1. The buyer subtracted the sewer connection cost from the balance due under his contract, tendered $13,000 to the owner, and demanded a deed for the property. When the owner refused to give a deed for less than $14,500 the buyer sued for a decree of specific performance to require the owner to deliver the deed for $13,000.

In many states the buyer could recover. In a few states the buyer would not be entitled to a deed unless he would pay the owner the full $14,500, inasmuch as the owner did not authorize or participate in the broker's fraud.

2. The buyer demanded that the $1,500 cost of connecting to the sewer line be deducted from the purchase price. When the owner refused, the buyer thereupon said that the deal was off and demanded return of his $500 down payment. When the owner refused this, the buyer sued the owner for $500. The owner in turn tendered a deed to the buyer and filed a counterclaim against the buyer for the $14,500 purchase price due under the contract.

The owner would not be permitted to retain the benefit (the contract) obtained through his agent's fraud. This would be true even in the few states which would refuse to hold the owner liable for tort damages. Therefore, the owner would recover nothing from the buyer on the counterclaim, while the buyer would have a right to recover from the owner the amount of the $500 down payment. ☐

structions. If an agent is unaware that carrying out his principal's instructions will constitute a tort, the agent is nevertheless liable for any tort for which guilty knowledge is not a requisite—such as a tort involving an unjustified interference with another's person or property.

As discussed in Chapter 4, liability for negligence is not unlimited. If the plaintiff who is suing for damages sustained as a result of the defendant's carelessness is not of the class unduly jeopardized by the defendant's act, the plaintiff cannot recover. In other words, as to this particular plaintiff, the defendant's careless act is not considered a tort. One of the common applications of this policy rule in agency situations arises when an agent carelessly gives his principal erroneous information upon which some third person relies to this detriment. As is more fully discussed in

Example. On a printed order form supplied by a sign manufacturer, two signs were ordered to be constructed and erected for $795. The signs were to advertise a soft-drink product called "Osce-Y-Ola." The order form read as follows (the portions printed on the form are italicized):

> *Enter our order for* two signs [stating specifications and price] at Osce-Y-Ola C., Steeplechase Pier, Atlantic City, N.J. (signed) Arthur Adams by Sec. & Treas. Osce-Y-Ola.

When the price was not paid, the sign manufacturer sued Arthur Adams who denied personal liability and asserted that he was contracting as an agent for the Osce-Y-Ola Sales Company. Since no oral evidence was offered by either party, the case turned entirely on the meaning and effect of the written order.

The Pennsylvania Superior Court held that, in the absence of further evidence, Adams was personally liable on the contract. The court pointed out that Adams had not disclosed the full name of the corporation for which he claimed to be acting, and also said:

> ... the individual signature imports a personal liability.... The addition of a corporate name *in connection with other evidence* might tend to contradict this import of personal liability; but here no other evidence was offered. We must conclude that the mere addition of the words "Sec. & Treas. Osce-Y-Ola" were insufficient, standing alone, to indicate that the defendant did not sign in his individual capacity[5] [Emphasis added.] ☐

5. *Flexume Corp. v. Norris*, 98 Pa. Super. 530 (1929).

Chapter 8, unless bodily injury and not merely property damage is threatened by a negligent misrepresentation, the courts are reluctant to extend liability beyond the parties to the information-supplying contract. Thus an agent who makes a negligent misrepresentation to his principal is usually not committing a tort to a third person—unless bodily injury to such a person is a foreseeable result of the erroneous information.

C. Liability of Third Persons to Agents

Generally, unless an agent is a party to a contract, he has no right to enforce the contract.

V. Termination of Agency

Usually a principal appoints an agent and grants him power to act in order to obtain for himself the benefit of the agent's perfor-mance. However, sometimes a person will grant an agency power over certain of his property in order to assure that an obligation owed to the recipient of the power will be paid, or perhaps as a way of paying or performing the obligation. A common example is a pledge transaction in which an obligor who owns corporate stock borrows a sum of money from a bank signs a note promising to repay the loan at a stated time, and, as collateral security, delivers to the bank his stock certificate together with an authorization to sell the stock should the obligor default in repaying the loan. This power—to sell the stock in the obligor's name—is an agency power which is held and exercised for the primary benefit of the holder of the power (the obligee bank) rather than for the grantor of the power (the obligor). Such an agency power is frequently termed an agency given as security, or a power coupled with a creditor's obligee's interest. It would be contrary to the parties'

Example. The owner of a plot of land engaged a real estate broker to negotiate a sale of the land for not less than $20,000. The broker was to receive as compensation a commission of 3 percent but only if and when an actual transfer of the property and full payment of the price were completed. The broker interested a buyer in buying the property and obtained the buyer's signature on a contract form. The broker then took the contract form to the owner who also signed it. In the contract the owner agreed to sell and the buyer to buy the described real estate for $20,000;performance (payment of the price and delivery of the deed) was to take place one month later. On the settlement date the buyer announced that he had changed his mind and refused to go through with the contract. When the owner decided not to undertake the expense and inconvenience of attempting to enforce the contract against the buyer, the broker himself sued the buyer for damages for breach of contract, claiming a right to recover the amount of the commission the broker would have earned if the buyer had not defaulted on the contract.

Not being a party to the contract, the broker would have no right to enforce the contract and could not collect damages from the buyer for breach of the contract. (Whether the owner would be liable to the broker for not attempting to enforce the contract against the buyer, is a point upon which court decisions conflict.) □

* * *

Example. P, a resident of New York City, inherited a tract of land in Colorado. The tract consisted partly of pasture land and partly of rocky wasteland. After receiving from A, a Colorado real estate broker, an appraisal of the land, P in writing authorized A to sell the land for $5,000, the appraised price. Shortly afterwards A learned that uranium had been discovered on adjoining land.

Obviously A's authority to sell for $5,000 would be terminated or at least suspended until A could tell P of the new development . □

intent and quite unfair to the obligee to permit this agency power to be revoked or terminated before the obligation is satisfied. Therefore, the rules for termination of ordinary agency powers do not apply in situations involving agency powers coupled with an obligee's interest.

A. Ordinary Agency Powers

An agency relationship or power can end in any of a variety of ways. Since an agency relationship involves the consent of both the principal and the agent, the relationship can be terminated as they provide in their original agreement or in any later agreement. Other ways in which the relationship can end or be suspended include: (1) revocation or renunciation, (2) occurrence of an event reasonably leading the agent to doubt that he should proceed, and (3) death of the principal.

1. REVOCATION OR RENUNCIATION

Since an agency relationship involves personal trust and confidence, the law will not compel parties to continue such a relationship if either wishes to repudiate it. If a repudiation breaks a contract between the principal and agent, the repudiating party is liable to the other for damages for breach of contract—but the agency is terminated. Thus it is frequently said that either party has the *power* even though he may not have the *right* to terminate the agency.

Example. P of Chicago owned a store in Harrisburg, Pennsylvania, known as the Elite Clothing Store, and employed M as the local manager. As authorized by P, store funds were handled through a checking account in a Harrisburg bank, the account being in the name of "Elite Clothing Store, by M. Martin." P authorized M to purchase merchandise in the name of the store from various manufacturers, including S Shirt Company of New York City and T Tie Company of Boston. All such orders were signed, "Elite Clothing Store by M. Martin." Both S Company and T Company knew that P owned the store. Purchases from T Company were c.o.d., paid by M out of store funds; purchases from S Company were on thirty days' credit, paid by M with checks drawn on the Harrisburg account. Every month M sent P a report of all income and disbursements, and remitted the net profits by check drawn on the Harrisburg account. After operating in this way for several years, P sold the store to M and inserted in a Harrisburg newspaper a classified advertisement telling of the transfer, and consequent termination of M's authority to act as P's agent. Later, by orders signed in the same way previous orders had been signed, M ordered shirts from S Company and ties from T Company. Both conformed to quantities previously ordered and both orders were for thirty days' credit. The goods were delivered to the store, and when payment was not made when due, both companies investigated and learned for the first time of the transfer of the business. Both companies sued P for the unpaid goods sold after transfer of the store to M.

The usual credit-reporting services watch for and file termination of authority notices. Since a seller who is asked to extend credit for the first time is expected to make a credit investigation, P's advertisement was all that should be expected of him in order to give notice to the public generally (including businesses like T Company), and P would have no liability to T Company.

A seller who has already been extending credit will not make a new credit investigation every time a new order is received. Therefore, P should have given S Company a personal notice of the sale of the store and the consequent termination of M's authority. A personal notice not having been given, M had the apparent authority to bind P, and S Company could recover from P. ☐

2. CHANGE OF CIRCUMSTANCES

The purpose of an ordinary agency is the performance of services for the principal. Since the agent is obligated to act for the best interests of his principal, it is reasonable to assume that an agent's authority will be terminated, or at least suspended, if the agent learns facts which should reasonably lead him to doubt that the principal still wishes the agency carried out.

3. DEATH OF PRINCIPAL

Since an agent is to act for the benefit of his principal and subject to the principal's direction and control—and also subject to the principal's power to terminate the agency at any time—it is reasonable to say that the death of the principal will terminate the agent's authority or power.

The common-law rule which is followed in most states holds that the principal's death will immediately terminate the agent's authority, even though neither the agent nor a third party with whom the agent is dealing knows of the principal's death. However, the courts in some states feel that what is sometimes called the civil-law rule is more fair and more closely attuned to business practices. These courts hold that although the death of the principal revokes the agency, the revocation becomes effective only when the agent learns of the principal's death. The legislatures in some states, convinced of the fairness

Example. T owes D $1,000, payable $100 per month over the next ten months. D borrows $500 from C and gives C a written authorization to collect T's payment of $100 per month until D's $500 debt to C is fully paid. Since D's $500 debt is smaller than T's $1,000 debt. D does not assign to C all of D's claim against T but merely authorizes C to collect for the next five months. C therefore acquires no property interest in T's obligation.

Some courts would hold that although D cannot withdraw the authorization he has given to C, D's death will terminate C's authorization.

Other courts would hold (and this appears to be the modern trend) that even though C acquires no property interest in D's claim against T, an agency power such as this is not revocable either by D's act or death, since the power is given at the time D's obligation to C arises, and also is given either to secure D's debt or as a method for paying the debt. ☐

of the civil-law rule, have adopted it by statute, some statutes covering all agencies and some being limited to certain special agents, such as agents representing members of the armed services or agents authorized to sell land.

4. APPARENT AUTHORITY AFTER TERMINATION

As previously discussed, a principal may be bound not only by what his agent is actually authorized to do, but also by an act within the agent's apparent authority. An agent authorized to enter into only a single, isolated transaction has no apparent authority outside that transaction; on the other hand, a continuing or general agent, engaged to enter into a series of transactions, has a much broader apparent authority. If a continuing agency is terminated, a third person who is unaware of the termination is justified in assuming that the agency still exists until the principal takes reasonable steps to give notice of its termination. What the principal should do to give notice to a particular third person depends on the prior experience of that third person with the agent. If the third person previously extended credit to the principal through the agent, or if to the knowledge of the principal the agent has commenced negotiating with the third person for a particular contract, the agent's authority will reasonably appear to continue until the principal gives the third person personal notice of termination. On the other hand, the principal's inserting a classified advertisement in a newspaper published in the town where the agency is carried on is sufficient notice to third persons who have not so completely relied on the agency.

B. Agency Coupled with Obligee's Interest

An agency power given to an obligee as security for an obligation or as a way to collect the obligation cannot be revoked without the obligee's consent and is not terminated by the obligor's death.

Some courts distinguish between two types of agencies coupled with obligees' interests:

1. An agency in which the obligee has an actual property interest in, or possession of, the item concerning which he holds the agency interest—for example an obligee bank in possession of a stock certificate pledged by the obligor as collateral security for his obligation. The bank's agency cannot be withdrawn by the obligor and is not terminated by the obligor's death.

2. An agency in which the grant of agency power to the obligee does not give him an actual property interest in or possession of the

item over which the power is to be exercised. The status of this type of agency is summarized in the following example.

* * *

Problems

1. A traveling salesman, authorized to contract to sell certain securities at par, reported to his principal that he had contracted in the principal's name to sell a large quantity at 1 percent below par. The principal withheld action upon the report for one month and then notified the buyer that the contract was repudiated. Was the principal bound by the contract? (Modified from A.I.C.P.A., Nov. 47-89.)

2. O. Osborn, the owner of a building and the land on which erected, listed the premises with A. Adams, a real estate broker, to find a purchaser at not less than $50,000, for which O agreed to pay A a 3 percent commission in case he effected a sale. Shortly afterwards, A told O that three parties were dickering for the property. A had O sign a contract form in which O agreed to sell the described premises for $50,000. The name of the purchaser was to be filled in by A. The agreement also stated: "O. Osborn is to pay A. Adams a 3 percent commission on the amount of this sale. Deed is to be delivered to purchaser and price paid one month from date hereof." A few weeks later, A filled in his wife's name as the buyer and notified O. O replied that he would not pay the commission. On the closing date specified in the signed agreement, O transferred the property to A's wife, receiving her check for $50,000, but O still refused to pay any commission. A sued O for $1,500. Explain whether A was entitled to recover.

3. M Company, a manufacturer of farm machinery, employed A at a fixed monthly salary as factory representative for a territory covering the western half of North Dakota. A's duties included making sales, writing contracts, helping local dealers, and making collections. D who held the dealer-franchise to sell M Company's products in three specified counties in the western half of North Dakota, proposed to A an arrangement under which if A would help D to establish subdealers in D's territory, the subdealers to receive one-half of the commissions on their sales D and A would split the remaining one-half. A agreed to the arrangement and established subdealers, made sales, took secondhand machinery in trade, accepted payments, and made collections on behalf of D. D failed to pay, and A sued for $4,500, his share of the commissions earned through the subdealers' sales. Was A entitled to judgment against D? Explain.

4. Most of the real estate brokers in a certain community formed an association, one of the chief features of which was an arrangement for sharing listings. Under the arrangement, whenever a member of the association received an exclusive listing and failed to sell the listed property within one month, he would report the property to the association office which would then send a description of the property to all members. If a sale of the property were later negotiated by a broker other than the one with whom it was originally listed, the commission earned on the transfer would be equally split between the two brokers. Each included in his advertising a statement that he was a member of the association and that a listing with him would be a listing with all the association brokers.

A and B were both members of the association. O, the owner of certain property, signed an exclusive sale agreement with A, listing the property with A for $80,000 and agreeing to pay A a 5 percent commission in the event of sale within the next six months, no matter by whom the sale was negotiated. After one month, descriptions of the property were sent to all association members. A few weeks later P consulted B and inquired concerning a certain type of property. B showed P a list containing descriptions of various properties, including that belonging to O. P expressed an interest in O's property and engaged B to negotiate a purchase, agreeing to pay B a 4 percent commission. B agreed to use his best efforts to negotiate a purchase agreeable to P. B then called A who notified O that B had a prospective buyer. After B and P inspected O's property, B negotiated a transfer from O to P for $70,000. O paid A a 5 percent commission on the transfer, but B returned to A the check for 2 1/2 percent which A sent to B. However, P then refused to pay B the agreed 4 percent and B sued P. What result? Explain.

5. R owned several retail shops selling women's clothing. At one of the shops, which was operated on rented premises, he employed his sister and brother as salesclerks. About six months before expiration of the lease, R commenced negotiations with the landlord for a five-year renewal. The negotiations were still pending when R left the city for two weeks on a business trip. Unknown to R, his sister and brother were planning to form a partnership to operate a women's clothing store. During R's absence from the city his sister and brother told the landlord of their business plans and successfully negotiated a five-year lease of the store premises to themselves, the lease period to begin upon expiration of R's lease two months later. When R returned to the city his sister and brother gave him a one-month notice that they were leaving his employment. When R learned of the new lease, R sued his sister and brother and requested the court to decree that they assign the new lease to him. What result? Explain.

6. (a) A was a salesman employed by P to travel a certain territory and to solicit orders from hardware dealers. A received an order for 10 garden plows from T, a hardware dealer. A sent the order to P who then shipped the plows to T. At the end of the month A collected the purchase price of the plows from T, but failed to turn the money over to P. P had given A no express authority to collect. Could P require T to pay again? Explain.

(b) Assume that A promised to have the plows shipped promptly to T and that in gratitude and without ulterior motive or agreement T gave A a radio as a gift. Assume further that there was no custom or agreement between P and A permitting the latter to accept a gift in such circumstances. P learned of the gift and demanded the radio. Would

A be required to give the radio to P. Explain. (Modified from A.I.C.P.A., May 54-4a,c.)

7. P engaged A as a traveling salesman to sell certain goods and instructed A not to deliver to any buyer unless payment was made by certified check naming P as the payee. On his first trip A sold and delivered certain of these goods to T. T paid the price to A in cash, without knowledge of A's instructions and without any investigation of A's authority to collect. A disappeared with the money, and P sued T to recover either the purchase price or the goods. Was P entitled to recover? Explain.

8. Wishing to acquire a site for his factory without provoking a rise in the price of land, P, in writing, engaged A, a real estate broker, to secure certain specified pieces of land without disclosing that he was acting for P. Following this plan, A entered into a written contract in his own name with S to buy S's lot for a stated price, transfer to be made on the following June 1. Believing that B, another real estate broker would succeed better with T for T's lot, A engaged B for that purpose, and B signed a contract with T to buy T's lot for a stated price, transfer to be made on the following June 1. Actually T's lot was not contiguous with the other lots P was acquiring and, therefore, not within the actual authority given by P to A. However, when P learned of the contract, he decided that he wished to acquire T's lot also. One week prior to the time for transfer of title under the two contracts, P notified S and T to have deeds made out to P. P's plans having by that time been publicized, the value of all real estate in the area advanced sharply. On the contract settlement date, S and T refused to transfer to P. In separate lawsuits P sued S and T to enforce the contracts made by A and B.

(a) Could P enforce the contract entered into by A and S? Explain.

(b) Could P enforce the contract entered into by B and T? Explain.

(c) Other facts remaining the same, assume that after P gave the above-described notices to S and T, P gave them each a second notice stating that he had changed his mind, and on the settlement day, P refused to accept deeds from either S or T or to pay anything for their lands. (1) Could S enforce against P the contract entered into by A and S? Explain. (2) Could T enforce against P the contract entered into by B and T? Explain. (Modified from A.I.C.P.A., Nov. 48-12.)

9. A plaintiff began a lawsuit against a defendant who was an elderly widow. The widow thereupon made an appointment with her lawyer. The widow's sister who lived about a mile from the widow's house owned a car. Having no car herself, the widow asked her sister to take her to the lawyer's office to keep the appointment. On the way to the office, the widow was busy looking over various documents she was going to give the lawyer and was paying no attention to her sister's driving. The sister negligently failed to stop at a stop sign and collided with a car being carelessly driven by X. The widow suffered severe personal injuries as a result of the accident. In agreeing to drive the widow to the lawyer's office, the sister was doing a favor with no expectation or right of compensation.

(a) Assume that the widow sued her sister for damages. Could the widow recover? Explain.

(b) Assume that the widow sued X for damages. Could the widow recover? Explain.

10. P, a dealer in household furnishings sold a piano to B on a title-retaining installment contract. B fell behind on his payments and P sent A to B's house. A was employed by P to collect unpaid installments and to repossess from defaulting buyers. P instructed A to repossess the piano but only if he could take it without trouble. P particularly instructed A not to commit assault and battery or otherwise break the law. With two other of P's employees, A went to B's house and when B refused to permit removal of the piano, A and his men threatened B, pushed him around, and removed the piano. B sued P for damages of assault and battery. Was B entitled to judgment against P. Explain.

11. T Convoy Company was in the business of trucking new automobiles, and had interstate and state carrier permits for that purpose. Forty trucks were used in the business, fifteen owned by T Company and twenty-five owned by the individual drivers. The drivers of the company-owned trucks received a specified fixed compensation, the amount depending on the haul made and the number of autos delivered. For each haul made by an owner-driver, T Company paid him 77 percent of the freight rate charged for the haul; this payment was compensation for use of the truck and compensation to the driver. Except for the method of calculating pay, both classes of drivers were treated alike. The practice was for both classes of drivers, after completion of a run, to report to the company terminal and receive: (1) a load of autos and the freight bill which stated the name and address of the consignee, the description of the cargo, and the trucking charges; (2) instructions as to the route to be taken; and (3) oil, gas, and necessary cash for traveling expenses. All drivers were instructed to drive carefully. For some consignees T Company instructed the drivers to collect the trucking charges upon delivery; for others T Company extended credit and billed the consignees after delivery.

While returning to the terminal over the route prescribed by T Company after delivering a load of autos, D was driving negligently and collided with P, causing considerable injury to P's person and property. D's carelessness was the sole cause of the accident. P sued T Company.

(a) T Company owned the truck which D was driving. Explain (1) the reasoning upon which P might attempt to base his claim, (2) the reasoning upon which T Company might attempt to base its defense, and (3) which party should be given judgment.

(b) D owned the truck which he was driving. Explain whether this would change any of the answers given in Part (a).

12. A map of the Eastwood Acres Subdivision was on file in the county courthouse, showing the location of the subdivision and the location and size of numbered lots in the subdivision. S, owner of Lot No. 40, engaged a surveyor to survey the property and place stakes showing the boundaries. Through the negligence of one of the surveyor's linemen, the stakes that were placed included one-half of Lot 39 and omitted half of Lot 40. B, considering purchasing S's lot, went with S to view the lot. B inquired as to the location of the boundaries. S indicated the stakes that his surveyor had placed and said, "These stakes are on the boundary lines." Satisfied with the property, B purchased the lot, paying S $2,000 and receiving from S a deed for "Lot Number 40 of the Eastwood Acres Subdivision, as shown on a plat recorded in the Recorder of Deeds office in this county in Map Book, Volume 4 at Page 300." B engaged a contractor to fill and grade his new lot, pointing out the stakes to the contractor as the boundaries of the lot. Later when B engaged an architect to draw plans for a building, the erroneous placement of the stakes was discovered. Of the $1,000 B paid for filling and grading, one-half was spent on Lot 39. Would B have a right to recover $500 (a) from N, the owner of Lot 39, (b) from the surveyor, (c) from S? Explain.

13. A wholesaler employed an agent to sell and deliver certain goods, and instructed him not to sell below $1.50 for 25-pound sacks, and not to give any warranties of quality. The agent sold some of the goods in the wholesaler's name at $1 for 25-pound sacks, the then market price, and with a warranty of quality similar to that given by other sellers of such goods. The agent honestly believed that the goods were of the quality warranted. The goods were delivered to the buyer by the agent, and the buyer paid the agent the agreed $1 per sack.

(a) Assume that the goods were of the proper quality. (1) Briefly explain if the wholesaler would have a right against the buyer either to recover the goods or to collect an additional $0.50 per sack.

(2) Briefly explain the wholesaler's rights, if any, against the agent.

(b) Assume that the goods were not of the quality warranted. Briefly explain if the buyer would have a right to collect (1) from the wholesaler for breach of warranty; (2) from the agent for breach of warranty. (Modified from A.I.C.P.A., May 42-2.)

14. P, a seventeen-year-old orphan, gave A, an adult stock and bond broker, a sum of money and instructed A to purchase certain bonds for P. A purchased the bonds from T and paid for them with P's money. When A purchased the bonds, he disclosed that he was buying for P. Although A knew P's age and knew that P was a stranger to T, it did not occur to A to say anything to T about P's age. By the time P reached eighteen years of age, the bonds had depreciated in value. On his eighteenth birthday, P returned the bonds to T, who under protest repaid P the amount A had paid for the bonds. T then sued A. On what theory and with what result? Explain. (Modified from A.I.C.P.A., Nov. 36-7.)

15. On June 20, an agent, in the name of his principal, mailed to a merchant an order for certain goods. As authorized by his principal, the agent had an arrangement with the merchant for goods to be shipped to the principal's place of business on the agent's periodic orders. The principal died June 21, and the agent sent a notice of this to the merchant. Before he received the notice, the merchant shipped the goods to the principal's place of business. The principal's executor refused to accept or pay for the goods. From whom, if anyone, could the merchant recover damages? Explain. (Modified from A.I.C.P.A., Nov.47-8f.)

16. For a number of years F. Martin, as sole proprietor, owned and operated a business engaged in quarrying and burning limestone under the name "Martin Lime Company." F employed his two sons, A and B, in the production part of the business; F himself did all the buying for the business. From time to time, S, a coal dealer, at-

tempted to sell coal to F, but F never made any purchases from him. F then sold his entire business and plant to the two sons, A and B, for a substantial sum, payable to F in stated installments. A and B thereafter conducted the business under the same name and F withdrew from any participation in it. A and B purchased quantities of coal from S, the purchases being made on credit in the name of "Martin Lime Company." After several months S for the first time learned of the transfer of the business, S as well as the general public having had no prior knowledge of the sale, although there had been an attempt to keep the transfer secret and F, A, and B had all talked of it to their friends and acquaintances. When the company failed to pay S for $3,000 worth of coal, S sued F. Upon what grounds and with what result? Explain.

17. In addition to the facts in Problem 16, assume the following: All of the purchases A and B made from S were on orders obtained by S's salesman. The first time A and B gave the salesman an order, they told him of the change of the ownership, but the salesman neglected to pass the information on to S. How, if at all, would this additional fact affect the lawsuit of S against F? Explain.

18. D borrowed money from C and gave C, as security, a power of attorney to collect future rents from D's tenants.

(a) Would this power of attorney be canceled by D's death prior to the repayment of the loan? Explain.

(b) Could a tenant knowing of D's death discharge his obligation for rent accrued prior to D's death by paying C? Explain. (Modified from A.I.C.P.A., Nov. 34-5.)

Partnerships

CHAPTER OUTLINE

Partnerships

I. Forms of Business Organization

Most business organizations are either sole proprietorships, partnerships, or corporations. In a *sole proprietorship*, the business is owned and operated by one individual. He may employ hundreds of assistants and delegate to certain of them most of the decision making in the business, but the ultimate control and the right to change or countermand any employee's decision rests exclusively in the sole proprietor.

A *partnership* can be termed a co-owned proprietorship as distinguished from a sole proprietorship. Instead of having a single owner, a partnership is owned and operated by two or more co-owners.

In legal theory a *corporation* can be termed a sole proprietorship in which the business is owned and operated by an artificial person created by the law rather than by a natural person. In other words, a corporation is considered as having a legal personality separate and distinct from the persons who own and operate the business. This concept is frequently referred to as the "separate entity theory." A similar theory is associated with the legal and philosophical concept of a sovereign state. Suppose that the United States entered into a treaty with England in 1830, and that since then the treaty has never been expressly nor impliedly canceled. Although none of the actual persons who negotiated the 1830

treaty is still alive (in fact no person who was a citizen of either country at that time is alive today), the treaty would still be considered as a binding undertaking between the nations. It is a binding undertaking today because the United States and England, today, are the same legal entities which entered into the treaty in 1830. People come and go, but the nation as an entity exists and continues to exist separate and distinct from the individual citizens who are its inhabitants at any particular time. Each individual nation also finds it highly convenient, essential, in fact, to treat the political subdivisions within the nation as separate legal entities. Thus, if New York City entered into an obligation in 1830, the obligation is just as binding today, because the city today is the same legal personality that existed and assumed the obligation in 1830.

Although a nation or a city is a separate legal personality, it is an artificial rather than a natural legal person; it cannot act for itself but must necessarily act through natural persons as its agents. A tiny baby is in a somewhat analogous position. In the eyes of the law the baby is a separate legal personality with legally protected rights. A premeditated, unjustified killing of the baby would be murder, a wrongful injury of the baby would be a tort, even though the baby cannot act for himself but is entirely dependent on his parents for support. The separate-entity theory was recognized as a needful legal tool and adapted to business operations in the early days of business growth and expansion. A New York

Example. An owner of real estate in Virginia had his property divided into building lots which he began selling to various persons including S. Every deed by which the subdivider transferred title included the following restrictive provisions: "Title to this land is never to vest in a person or persons of African descent." Shortly after buying one lot, S contracted to sell the property to a corporation known as "People's Pleasure Park Company, Inc." This corporation was formed, owned, and operated by Negroes who intended to establish and operate on this lot an amusement park for Negroes. The subdivider sued S and the corporation to have the contract canceled and to have S restrained from selling the property in violation of the restrictive provision. The Supreme Court of Appeals of Virginia decided that the transfer did not violate the restrictive provision and refused to restrain the transfer. In the course of its opinion the court said:

> Such a conveyance, by no rule of construction, vests title to the property conveyed in "a person or persons of African descent" . . .
>
> "A corporation is an artificial person, like the state. It is a distinct existence—an existence separate from that of its stockholders and directors." . . .
>
> Professor Rudolph Sohm, in his Institutes of Roman Law, pp. 104-106, says: "In Roman law the property of the corporation is the sole property of the collective whole; and the debts of a corporation are the sole debts of the collective whole.... It represents a kind of ideal private person, an independent subject capable of holding property, totally distinct from all previously existing persons, including its own members. It possesses, as such, rights and liabilities of its own. It leads its own life, as it were, quite unaffected by any change of members. It stands apart as a separate subject or proprietary capacity, and, in contemplation of law, as a stranger to its own members. The collective whole, as such, can hold property. Its property, therefore, is, as far as its members are concerned, another's property, its debts another's debts.... Roman law contrived to accomplish a veritable masterpiece of juristic ingenuity in discovering the notion of a collective person; in clearly grasping and distinguishing from its members the collective whole as the ideal unity of the members bound together by the corporate constitution; in raising this whole to the rank of a person (a juristic person, namely); and in securing it a place in private law as an independent subject of proprietary capacity standing on the same footing as other private persons.[1] ☐

---

1. *People's Pleasure Park Co., Inc., v. Rohleder,* 109 Va. 439, 61 S.E. 794 (1908). This case is used here as a corporate theory case, on which point the decision of the court is as true today as it was when it was decided in 1908. In the field of constitutional rights, as interpreted in more recent decisions of the United States Supreme Court, a restrictive provision such as the one in this case would be unenforceable even if S were selling to one of African descent rather than to a corporation.

judge has written in a frequently quoted opinion:

The vast growth of corporate organizations in this country and the extension of the rights and powers granted to them by the legislatures of the several states during the past three-quarters of a century are facts familiar to every student of the law. The corporate conception, however, long antedated this period. The reason for its vastly extended use in this later period lay in the need for greater aggregations of capital to develop the tremendous potential resources of the country than were reasonably available to any single individual or small group of individuals. Furthermore, many of the projects confronting the pioneers of business, whereas offering great probabilities of profit presented corresponding possibilities of loss, and whereas the inherent natural willingness of the pioneering spirit furnished an incentive to gamble for the rich reward which would crown success in the enterprise, the substratum of caution interposed an inhibition to the act of placing the total resources of the individual at the hazard of the event. Finally, many of the most promising projects of construction and development were of such considerable magnitude that their completion might well postdate the lives of the individuals who initiated them. The need for a method of organization which would eliminate these three difficulties was met by the conception of the modern business corporation, and it is the presence of these three characteristics which furnishes the essential points distinguishing a corporation from every other variety of business organization.

To meet this need, the several Legislatures provided from time to time that one or more individuals might devote specified portions of their capital to the promotion of a clearly stated business object without personal financial liability for any sums beyond those voluntarily dedicated thereto, and that the sums thus contributed should remain dedicated to the object, irrespective of the deaths of the contributors unless or until a specified percentage of their number should signify the desire to terminate the enterprise....[2]

The basic legal distinction between a partnership and a corporation is that a partnership is not considered to be a separate legal entity, while the corporation is a legal entity separate and distinct from the person or persons who form, own, and operate the corporation. From this distinction in legal theory flow the following chief differences between partnerships and corporations.

1. **Manner of creating the business unit**. A partnership is formed by the agreement of the parties while a corporation cannot exist unless the state creates it or breathes legal life into it.

2. **Activities in which the business unit is permitted to engage**. Persons combined as partners are permitted to engage in any activity which they could engage in as individuals. On the other hand, since the corporation is a separate legal personality, it has only the powers granted to it by the state which has created it.

3. **Authority to act for the business**. Since there is really no separation between the partnership and the partners, each partner is necessarily a representative of the partnership; a corporation with a legal personality separate from its stockholders is not necessarily represented by any one of its shareholders nor bound by his act.

4. **Liability for business debts**. The debts of a partnership business are the debts of the individual partners, while, if a creditor extends credit to a corporation, the debt is owed by the corporation rather than by the ones who own stock in the corporation.

5. **Transfer by an owner or death of an owner.** Since a partnership is an aggregate of co-owners, any change in the identity of the co-owners is a change in the partnership itself. In a corporation, a shareholder's transfer of his stock, or the shareholder's death, has no effect on the separate legal life being enjoyed by the corporation.

6. **Citizenship**. Since a partnership is not a separate legal entity, the partnership firm is not considered as having citizenship separate from the citizenship of its members, while a corporation is a citizen of the state in which it is created or incorporated, regardless of the citizenship of its shareholders. Thus a corporation incorporated in Delaware is a citizen of that state, even though all of its shareholders may be citizens of California.

The law applicable to partnerships and corporations is largely statutory. Most states have adopted the Uniform Partnership Act, and all states have statutes pertaining to the formation and operation of corporations.

---

2. *In re Steinberg's Estate*, 153 Misc. 339, 274 N.Y.S. 914 (1934)

II. Formation of Partnerships

The Uniform Partnership Act definition of a partnership may be summarized as follows:

A partnership is an unincorporated association of two or more persons to carry on as co-owners a business for profit. [3]

A partnership is formed by a contract. Any person who has the capacity to enter into a contract may become a partner. Since a minor is not prohibited from making contracts, he can become a partner; however, he can disaffirm his partnership contract and thus avoid future liability.

Usually, when persons form a partnership, they enter into an express contract to that effect—preferably in writing. However, since contracts may be made by implication, it is possible for persons to actually form a partnership even though they do not expressly state an intent to do so. It is possible that even though persons expressly state that they are not partners, their conduct may amount to forming a partnership agreement. In determining whether or not a partnership exists, the principal question is whether the parties have undertaken an association which, as a matter of policy, the courts feel should carry with it the rights and obligations of a partnership. This question most often arises when a creditor, unable to collect from his business debtor seeks to hold liable a person who was associated with the debtor in the business operation. Partners are co-owners of a business, but all co-owners of property are not necessarily partners. The Partnership Act states:

Joint tenancy, tenancy in common, tenancy by the entireties, joint property, common property, or part ownership does not of itself establish a partnership, whether such coowners do or do not share any profits made by the use of the property. [4]

If co-ownership of property is an isolated or temporary arrangement, the co-owners' working together to handle their property usually does not show an implied agreement to become partners. But if their co-ownership and co-management are to extend over a substantial period of time and to involve a major part of their attention, the parties would seem to be actually carrying on a business and to be partners.

A partnership almost invariably involves a sharing of profits, but the fact that persons are sharing profits from a business operation does not of itself necessarily make them partners. The Partnership Act states:

The sharing of gross returns does not of itself establish a partnership, whether or not the persons sharing them have a joint or common right or interest in any property from which the returns are derived....

The receipt by a person of a share of the profits of a business is prima facie evidence [sufficient without any other proof] that he is a partner in the business, but no such inference shall be drawn if such profits were received in payment:

(a) As a debt by installment or otherwise,

(b) As wages of an employee or rent to a landlord,

(c) As an annuity to a widow or representative of a deceased partner,

(d) As interest on a loan, though the amount of payment vary with the profits of the business,

(e) As the consideration for the sale of a good-will of a business or other property by installments or otherwise. [5]

If parties share profits *and* management in a substantial undertaking, they are usually considered partners.

Sometimes although a person is not actually a partner with the owner of a particular business, he will indicate that he is a partner in order to help the owner borrow money or pur-

---

3. Uniform Partnership Act (U.P.A.), Sec. 6.
4. U.P.A. Sec. 7.

5. *Ibid.*

Example. A food distributor entered into an agreement with X and Y who were partners in the ownership and operation of a cannery business. The agreement provided that, for the one-year duration of the contract:

1. The distributor would, if requested, supply all cans, cases, and labels, and provide sufficient money to pay employees and purchase produce.

2. The distributor would have the exclusive right to sell the entire output of the cannery. For his services as sole distributor, the distributor would receive 5 percent of gross sales.

3. At the expiration of the contract year, the distributor would be repaid for all money and supplies advanced for operation of the cannery. As interest for such advances, the distributor would be entitled to 50 percent of the net profits of the year's operations.

4. X and Y would retain full ownership and control of the cannery and would be liable for all losses. The distributor would have no liability for any losses.

5. The distributor would have the right to determine salaries and wages paid by the cannery during the contract year.

During the contract year, a supplier sold certain goods to X and Y for operation of the cannery. When X and Y failed to pay for these goods, the supplier sued the distributor.

Under similar facts, the Maryland Court of Appeals decided[6] that in addition to sharing in profits, the distributor held substantial power to participate in management of the cannery, and therefore had actually become a partner in the business and was liable for its debts. ☐

6. *Southern Can Co. v. Sayler,* 152 Md. 303, 136 A. 624 (1927)

chase on credit. Calling such a person a "partner by estoppel," the Partnership Act, as a matter of fairness, provides that if by words or conduct a defendant represents himself as a partner in a business, or consents to being represented as a partner, a creditor who extends credit to the business relying on the representation can hold the defendant liable as if he were actually a partner. If such a representation is made to the general public, it is presumed that subsequent creditors rely on the representation, and proof of actual reliance by a particular creditor is unnecessary.

III. Rights and Obligations Between Partners

The proprietary interest of a partner in a partnership business usually includes the following rights: (1) a right to participate in management, (2) a monetary interest in the part-nership, and (3) an ownership interest in specific partnership property.

A. Partners' Rights as to Management

Unless a partnership agreement expressly provides otherwise, the partners' rights as to management are as follows:

1. Each partner has an equal voice in the management and conduct of the partnership business, regardless of the ratio in which the partners contribute to the partnership capital or the ratio in which they agree to distribute profits and losses.

2. If partners cannot agree, the decision of a majority controls in matters involving the ordinary day-to-day operation of the business; when there is no majority, no action can be taken. On the other hand, unanimous consent of all partners is required in matters which go further than the ordinary conduct of

the partnership business (for example a decision involving a change in the nature or location of the business or a change in the partnership agreement).

A partner can, if he wishes, agree with his co-partners to relinquish some or all of his right to participate in management. Thus, a partnership agreement can validly specify that all management decisions shall be made by certain designated members of the partners, or even by one specified partner—who would then be called the managing partner.

B. Partners' Monetary Interests

Unless the partnership agreement provides otherwise, the partners' monetary interests are as follows:

1. Each partner is entitled to an equal share in profits, and must contribute toward losses in the same ratio in which he is to share profits.

2. Upon liquidation of the partnership business, each partner is entitled to share equally in the surplus remaining after payment of all debts and repayment to each partner of the amount of the contribution, advances, and loans which he made to the partnership.

3. No partner is entitled to remuneration for acting in the partnership business—except for a surviving partner who is winding up the partnership business.

4. The partnership must indemnify each partner for payments made and liabilities incurred by him in the ordinary and proper conduct of the partnership business.

C. Partners' Ownership Interests In Partnership Property

Whether property used in a partnership is partnership property or is individual property owned personally by one or more of the partners is determined by the intent of the parties. If, upon formation of a partnership, property was brought into the partnership by one of the partners, a question may arise whether the ownership or merely the use of the property was contributed to the partnership. It is wise for the parties to settle this question in their partnership agreement. If, after formation of a partnership, the parties purchase property with partnership funds, they are presumed to intend that the property become partnership property unless they express a different intent.

The three chief types of property co-ownership which developed under the common law are tenancy in common, joint tenancy, and tenancy by entireties. None of these being entirely suited to the co-ownership of partnership property, the Partnership Act creates a fourth type of co-ownership, called "tenancy in partnership." The chief characteristics of this form of co-ownership are:

1. Unless agreed otherwise, the partners have co-equal rights to possess partnership property for partnership purposes. A partner has no right of possession for any other purpose without the consent of his co-partners.

2. A partner cannot make an assignment or transfer his co-ownership interest separate from the interests of the other partners.

3. A partner's individual creditors cannot levy on partnership property.

4. Upon the death of a partner, his heirs will not inherit any ownership interest in specific partnership property.

D. Transfers of Partners' Interests

Since a partnership can arise only from the agreement of all parties, a right to participate (or to interfere) in the management of a partnership cannot vest in outsiders without the consent of all the partners. Therefore a partner's monetary interest is the only interest, (1) which a partner can assign without the consent of his co-partners, (2) which a partner's individual creditors can levy on, or (3) which a deceased partner's heirs can inherit.

The individual creditor of a partner can obtain what is called a "charging order" order of court requiring that when profits (and upon liquidation, advances and surplus) are being distributed, the share due the debtor partner shall be paid to his attaching creditor up to the amount of the creditor's claim.

A partner who assigns to an outsider his interest in a partnership may intend merely to pledge his interest as collateral security for a personal obligation, and have no intent to separate himself from the partnership business. Therefore, the Partnership Act expressly provides that a partnership is not automatically dissolved either when a partner assigns his interest or when an individual creditor of a partner levies on his interest.

E. Obligations of Partners to Each Other

The chief obligations of a partner to his co-partners include the following:

1. Each partner must contribute toward losses in the same ratio in which he is to share profits, unless the partnership agreement provides a different loss-sharing ratio.

2. A partner must on demand give his co-partners true and full information concerning all things affecting the partnership.

3. Each partner must account to the partnership for any benefit derived without his co-partners' consent from any transaction connected with the conduct of the partnership or the use of its property. As the United States Supreme Court has said, it is well settled:

> . . . that one partner cannot, directly or indirectly, use partnership assets for his own benefit; that he cannot, in conducting the business of a partnership, take any profit clandestinely for himself; that he cannot carry on another business in competition or rivalry with that of the firm, thereby depriving it of the benefit of his time, skill, and fidelity, without being accountable to his co-partners for any profit that may accrue to him therefrom; that he cannot be permitted to secure for himself that which it is his duty to obtain,

if at all, for the firm of which he is a member; nor can he avail himself of knowledge or information which may be properly regarded as the property of the partnership, in the sense that it is available or useful to the firm for any purpose within the scope of the partnership business.[7]

4. If any loss results from a partner's wrongful conduct, he is obliged to indemnify the partnership or his co-partners.

IV. Obligations of Partners to Third Persons

Each partner is personally liable for all of the debts and liabilities of the partnership business. In determining whether an obligation is a partnership liability, the law recognizes that each partner has the apparent authority of a general agent in the conduct of the partnership business. Although partners usually cooperate in the day-to-day operation of their business, they can agree among themselves that certain functions (for example the buying of goods for the business) shall be handled exclusively by a certain partner; they can even agree that all management powers shall be vested in one partner. However, third persons who are not advised otherwise are justified in assuming that the partnership business is being operated in the customary way—through the equal cooperation of all partners. The Partnership Act states:

> (1) Every partner is an agent of the partnership for the purpose of its business, and the act of every partner, including the execution in the partnership name of any instrument, for apparently carrying on in the usual way the business of the partnership of which he is a member binds the partnership, unless the partner so acting has in fact no authority to

7. *Latta v. Kilbourn*, 150 U.S. 524, 14 S Ct. 201, 37 L. Ed. 1169 (1893).

act for the partnership in the particular matter, and the person with whom he is dealing has knowledge of the fact that he has no such authority.

(2) An act of a partner which is not apparently for the carrying on of the business of the partnership in the usual way does not bind the partnership unless authorized by the other partners.

(3) Unless authorized by the other partners or unless they have abandoned the business, one or more but less than all the partners have no authority to:

(a) Assign the partnership property in trust for creditors or on the assignee's promise to pay the debts of the partnership,

(b) Dispose of the goodwill of the business,

(c) Do any other act which would make it impossible to carry on the ordinary business of a partnership,

(d) Confess a judgment,

(e) Submit a partnership claim or liability to arbitration or reference.

(4) No act of a partner in contravention of a restriction on authority shall bind the partnership to persons having knowledge of the restriction.[8]

Since each partner is an agent of the partnership, the liability of the partnership (and of every partner) for torts committed by a partner is the same as the liability of a principal for his agent's torts. Accordingly, the Partnership Act states:

Where, by any wrongful act or omission of any partner acting in the ordinary course of the business of the partnership or with the authority of his co-partners, loss or injury is caused to any person, not being a partner in the partnership, or any penalty is incurred, the partnership is liable therefore to the same extent as the partner so acting or omitting to act.[9]

---

8. U.P.A. Sec. 9.
9. U.P.A. Sec. 13.

A. Limited Partnerships

Many states believe that permitting what might be called an investment partner accomplishes a useful economic purpose, and have adopted statutes accordingly. The chief statute in effect in a number of states is the Uniform Limited Partnership Act. Under this act:

1. A limited partnership may be formed but must include at least one general partner who is individually liable for all partnership obligations.

2. The name of the business must not include the name of any limited partner.

3. A signed statement identifying the co-partners and designating them as general and limited (and also giving some other details) must be filed in a specified public office.

4. If the business becomes insolvent, the limited partner can lose his investment but will have no personal liability for obligations of the partnership.

5. A limited partner becomes liable as a general partner if he takes part in the control of the business.

B. Silent and Secret Partnerships

Sometimes a person's connection with a partnership business is not publicly known, perhaps not known by anyone outside of the business itself. Such a person is frequently called a secret partner. Some partners have no duties or obligations in regard to management or conduct of the partnership business, and are commonly called silent or dormant partners. A partner may achieve limited liability only as provided by a statute, such as the Limited Partnership Act. Therefore (assuming a limited partnership has not been properly formed) a secret partner, once his membership in a firm is discovered, or a silent partner, or one who is both secret and silent, is a general partner with full liability for partnership obligations.

C. Partnerships Providing for Immunity from Debt

Suppose that when A, B, and C form a partnership, they expressly agree that A shall have no liability for debts. If A is not a limited partner in a limited partnership formed according to statute, then he is a general partner with full liability to third persons for partnership obligations. The immunity agreement is merely an arrangement among the partners, and means that whatever A is forced to pay to creditors, he can recover from B and C. Since this is merely an arrangement among the partners for sharing losses, a creditor who extends credit to the partnership with knowledge of the immunity agreement is not thereby agreeing to release A from personal liability.

D. Obligations after Change of Membership

Suppose that a business is owned and operated by a partnership consisting of A, B, and C; A retires and sells his interest to D who, with the consent of B and C, takes A's place in the firm. As a matter of law, the partnership of A, B, and C is dissolved and a new partnership is formed consisting of D, B, and C. Since such a change in membership is not unusual, the law attempts to give effect to the intent and understanding of businessmen (without, however, actually changing the law as to the dissolution of the old partnership and the formation of a new one) by speaking in terms of an incoming or new partner, a withdrawing partner, and the continuation of a partnership business after a change in membership. Thus the Partnership Act provides, in effect:

1. If a change occurs in the membership of a partnership and the business is continued without liquidation of the partnership affairs, the creditors of the first or dissolved partnership are also creditors of the new partnership (or of the sole proprietor or corporation) so continuing the business.

2. A person admitted as a partner into an existing partnership is not personally liable to creditors for debts incurred before he joined the partnership unless the incoming partner expressly assumes such a liability. An incoming partner, however, is obliged to contribute towards losses of the partnership of which he is a member. In view of Item I above, therefore, the contribution of an incoming partner can be used to pay old debts (that is, debts incurred before the incoming partner joined the partnership), and the incoming partner is liable to his co-partners for all losses—including the portion of losses resulting from the old debts.

3. If a partner withdraws from a partnership and terminates his association with the business, he (or his estate in the case of a deceased partner) remains liable for debts incurred before his withdrawal—except, of course, there would be no liability to any creditor who enters into an enforceable agreement releasing the withdrawing partner.

4. If a partner withdraws from a partnership, he (or his estate in the case of a deceased partner) is liable for a debt incurred by the business *after* he ceases to be a partner, if the creditor with whom the debt is incurred (1) knew of the former partner's membership in the firm, (2) is unaware of the dissolution of the former partnership, and (3) did not receive proper notice of the dissolution. For a creditor who extended credit to the firm before the withdrawal or dissolution, personal notice is required; for a creditor who had not so extended credit, public notice is sufficient. A public notice is properly given if notice of the withdrawal is published in a newspaper of general circulation in the place where the dissolved partnership business was operating at the time of its dissolution.

V. Termination of Partnerships

A. Causes of Termination

Since a partnership is formed by the agreement of all partners, it can be terminated as they provide in their original agreement or in any later agreement. Other ways in which a partnership can be ended include (1) renunciation, (2) death or bankruptcy of any partner, and (3) decree of court.

I. RENUNCIATION

Since a partnership involves mutual confidence in the personal competence, goodwill, and loyalty of the partners, the law will not compel a party to remain a partner against his will. However, if a partner who repudiates and, thus, terminates a partnership, breaks a contract with his co-partners, the repudiating partner is liable to the others for damages resulting from the breach of contract. Thus, as with agency, a partner has the *power* even though he may not have the *right* to terminate a partnership.

2. DEATH OR BANKRUPTCY

Under the Partnership Act, a partnership is automatically dissolved by the death or bankruptcy of any partner. The surviving or solvent partner or partners may, if they wish, continue to operate the business, but unless agreed otherwise, the survivors must pay to the estate of the deceased partner (or of the bankrupt partner) the net value of his interest at the time of the partnership dissolution. As a practical matter paying off the deceased or bankrupt partner's interest may be impossible without liquidation of the business. A well-planned partnership agreement therefore, will often attempt to avoid such a forced liquidation of the business, by providing that each partner's life be insured for the benefit of the partnership in an amount equal to each partner's interest in the business; the agreement should also provide a formula for calculating each partner's interest at any particular time. A partnership agreement may also provide that upon dissolution of the partnership by death or bankruptcy of any partner, his investment shall remain in the partnership business for a stated period of time. Such a contract provision is binding upon the heirs of a deceased partner, and upon the creditors or receiver of an insolvent partner.

3. DECREE OF COURT

Upon petition by any partner, a court is empowered to decree dissolution of a partnership for various reasons, including the following:

1. A partner is adjudged mentally incompetent.

2. A partner persistently breaches the partnership agreement, or otherwise so conducts himself in matters relating to the partnership-business that it is not reasonably practical to carry on the business in association with him.

3. The business of the partnership can only be carried on at a loss.

Note that bickering or disagreement among partners, even bitter animosity between partners, is not grounds for a court to decree dissolution, unless the disagreement prevents successful operation of the business.

B. Distribution upon Liquidation

The Partnership Act provides:

In settling accounts between the partners after dissolution, the following rules shall be observed, subject to any agreement' lo the contrary:

(a) The assets of the partnership ate:

(I) The partnership property,

(II) The contributions of the partners necessary for the payment of all the liabilities specified in clause (b) of this paragraph.

(b) The liabilities of the partnership shall rank in order of payment, as follows:

(I) Those owing to creditors other than partners,

(II) Those owing to partners other than for capital and profits,

(III) Those owing to partners in respect of capital,

(IV) Those owing to partners in respect of profits,

(c) The assets shall be applied in the order of their declaration in clause (a) of this paragraph to the satisfaction of the liabilities.

(d) The partners shall contribute . . . the amount necessary to satisfy the liabilities; but if any, but not all, of the partners are insolvent, or, not being subject to process, refuse to contribute, the other partners shall contribute their share of the liabilities, and, in the relative proportions in which they share the profits, the additional amount necessary to pay the liabilities.

*****

(f) Any partner or his legal representative shall have the right to enforce the contributions specified in clauses (d) of this paragraph.

*****

(h) When partnership property and the individual properties of partners are in possession of a court for distribution, partnership creditors shall have priority (m partnership property and separate creditors on individual property, saving the rights of lien or secured creditors as heretofore.[10]

The Partnership Act provision pertaining to a partner's obligation to contribute toward losses must be kept in mind in connection with the above rules for distribution. If a partner's share of losses exceeds his capital contribution, any loan he made to the partnership should not be repaid to him unless his obligation to contribute toward losses is fully-satisfied.

---

10. U.P.A. Sec. 40.

Problems

1. O was the sole proprietor of a picture frame manufacturing business which he operated in a building rented from L. Deciding to sell the business, O entered into a written agreement with a business broker, engaging the services of the broker to negotiate a sale of the business for a stated price. One paragraph of the agreement stated: "If the described business shall be sold or exchanged during the term of this contract, whether the sale or exchange shall be effected by the above-named broker, by the owner, or by any other person, the owner shall pay the broker a commission of 5 percent of the selling price." Within the term of the contract, O's lease expired and L refused to renew it. O so informed the broker and moved his materials and equipment into another building where P was already conducting a similar business. O and P pooled their respective assets and formed a partnership to trade under the name, "Artistic Products Company," the name O had previously used. Neither partner put any cash into the business, but O was credited on the books with a capital contribution of $9,400, the fair value of the assets of his sole proprietorship business. When the broker learned of the formation of the partnership, he sued O for a 5 percent commission on $9,400. What result? Explain.

2. A, B, and C, partners engaged in the real estate and stock and bond brokerage business, were in financial difficulty and being pressed by their creditors. Much of their capital was tied up in investments which, if held for a longer time, might be profitable, but if disposed of quickly, would result in considerable loss. They entered into an agreement with X which provided: (1) X loaned to the firm two million dollars, to be repaid in five years; as collateral security various stocks and bonds owned by the firm were pledged with X; (2) As compensation for the loan, X was to receive 40 percent of the net profits of the firm, but not over $500,000 nor less than $100,000 per year, payable at stated times; (3) During the term of the agreement, management of the firm was to be in A's hands; (4) X was to have the right to inspect the

firm's books at any time; (5) X was to have the right to veto any business transaction X seemed inadvisable. During the next three years, the firm of A, B, and C incurred certain obligations to T. T, not having been paid, sued X. What result? Explain.

3. O owned a completely equipped summer resort hotel. On March 1, O entered into an agreement with M the main provisions of which can be summarized as follows: (1) O leased to M the described premises together with all equipment, for a term of 3 months from June 15, to be used exclusively as a summer hotel; (2) M would give his undivided attention and best efforts to promotion and operation of the business; (3) O or his authorized representative would have the right of unlimited access to the premises to make inspections at any time; (4) As rent, M would pay O for a total of $20,000 in four equal installments at times specified in the agreement; (5) Upon termination of the lease, in addition to the $20,000, O would receive 80 percent of the net profits; (6) A person to be designated by O would keep the books, act as cashier, receive all money coming into the business, deposit the money in his own name, and make all payments for expenses incurred by M in operation of the business; (7) Upon termination of the lease, M would receive 20 percent of the net profits; (8) O could terminate the lease upon twenty-four hour's notice to M and at once resume possession of the premises; (9) Upon expiration of the lease or its prior termination by O, M would receive $1,000 from O; (10) M would have absolute control and management of the business during the continuance of the lease and O would not be liable for any debts or obligations incurred by M in the operation of the business.

During the summer, a supplier sold a large quantity of goods to thehotel on which $1,800 remained unpaid. The supplier sued O for payment. Explain (1) the reasoning upon which the supplier might attempt to collect, (2) the reasoning upon which O might attempt to defend, and (3) which party should be given judgment.

4. Frank and Sam Andrew, father and son, were engaged in business under the name "Andrew Paper Works." Becoming insolvent, they entered into a written agreement with B Brown and C Carter, two of their many creditors. The agreement was in the nature of a deed of trust, by which the Andrews transferred the business to B and C as trustees; B and C were to carry on the business under the name "Andrew Paper Company," were to divide the profits among the creditors pro rata, and when all were paid, were to retransfer the business to the original proprietors. During the subsequent operation of the business, B and C borrowed $1,000 from P, signed a note "Andrew Paper Company by B. Brown and C. Carter, Trustees," and used the money in the business. The note was not paid when due, and P sued B, C, and also D who was another of the original creditors of the Paper Works. What should be the decision? Explain. (Modified from A.I.C.P.A., Nov. 29-2).

5. After managing the grain and hay business of Carter Corporation for a number of years, A. Adams retired and was replaced by B. Brown. After several years, B resigned from Carter Corporation to start his own business. Shortly after B's resignation, the following news item appeared in a newspaper published in that community: "B. Brown, who managed the grain and hay business of Carter Corporation since the retirement of A. Adams, has concluded to embark in the same business on his own account, having formed a co-partnership with A. Adams for that purpose. Mr. Brown is a gentleman of experience and ability and will undoubtedly meet with the full measure of success." Actually A and B had not formed a partnership, and A did not authorize or see the article. When A was informed of the news item, he asked B to have the statement denied. There was no further publication in the paper, but B distributed a circular to the trade announcing that he was embarking on the grain and hay business under the name of B. Brown 8 Company. S, a grain dealer who had seen the newspaper item, sold a carload of rye to B. Brown & Co., and when it was not paid for, S sued A and B. What result? Explain.

6. On May 1 the three partners in the firm of A, B, and C signed a dissolution agreement whereby

the firm's affairs were to be liquidated as of the following June 30. On May 15, B, without the knowledge of A or C, procured for himself a five-year lease on the premises occupied by the firm, to run from the following July 1, and on July 1, B sold the lease at a profit. Did A and C have a legal right to share in B's profit? (Modified from A.I.C.P.A., Nov. 4 1-6b).

7. A, B, and C, as equal partners, operated a small luggage manufacturing plant under the trade name "C & Company." In August, after several years successful operation, the partners discussed expanding to include the manufacture of table model TV receivers. C opposed any such expansion. During September, while C was away on a one-month vacation, A and B began laying plans for manufacture of TV receivers, sure that C would agree when he learned the details of their plan. On September 21, in the firm name and with concurrence of B, A ordered from a manufacturer for thirty-day delivery, a quantity of speakers suitable for the type of receiver A and B were planning. On September 25, the manufacturer in writing accepted the order and agreed to ship. Upon delivery according to order, C for the first time learned of the order. C's opposition continued and, to avoid further dispute, A and B moved the speakers to different premises, started a TV manufacturing business, and notified the manufacturer that they had taken over the speakers from C & Company. The manufacturer replied that he was not agreeable to releasing C & Company and the partners from liability. The speakers not being paid for, the manufacturer sued A, B, and C. How much could the manufacturer recover from C? Explain.

8. Adams and Brown were partners in a refrigerator manufacturing business, operating under the name "Brown & Company." A borrowed $500 from a bank, made out a note to the bank promising repayment in one month, and signed the note "Brown & Company by A. Adams, Partner." The note was not paid when due, and the bank sued A and B as partners for recovery of the $500. B proved in defense that he had never authorized or received any benefit from the loan, and had no knowledge of it until the bank demanded payment, the money, unknown to the bank, having been used by A for personal purposes. Was the bank entitled to judgment against B as well as against A? Explain.

9. A, B, and C were partners operating a saw mill. C had contributed three-fourths of the firm capital, A and B together one-fourth. By the terms of the partnership agreement, C was to receive one-half of the profits and A and B were to share the balanced equally. From time to time the firm had purchased supplies from S. C thought it inadvisable to deal further with S, but when he expressed this view to his partners, they did not agree. C then notified S that he, C, would not be liable for goods furnished the mill. Following this, A and B ordered and received from S further supplies necessary for carrying on the mill, giving S a note signed in the name of the partnership by A. Subsequently the mill and A and B became insolvent, and S sued C on the unpaid note. Was S entitled to judgment against C? Explain.

10. A, B, and C as partners carried on a business as real estate brokers. A and B, older and more experienced than C, instructed C to be scrupulously honest and truthful in all dealings. O, owner of a lot in a suburban section, listed his lot with the realty firm to negotiate a sale. While showing the lot to P, fully aware that he was ignorant of true conditions, C fraudulently said to P that there was a water supply in the street on which the lot fronted. Relying on this, P purchased the lot, paying his money to and receiving a deed from O. O had no knowledge of the statement made by C to P, and the deed said nothing about the water main. According to the agreement, the real estate firm received from O a commission of $50 for negotiating the sale. About a year later P began construction of a house and discovered that there was no water supply in the street. To connect with the nearest water main cost P $600. P demanded this sum from the real estate firm of A, B, and C, and A and B for the first time learned of the statement C had made concerning the water line. A and B offered to pay P the $50 the firm had received as real estate

commission, but P refused to settle for $50 and sued A for $600 damages. What result? Explain.

11. The partnership articles of A and B stipulated that A should furnish all the capital, and that B should manage the business, but without any liability on B for firm debts. S, knowing of these provisions, sold goods on credit to the firm.

(a) If the firm failed to pay for the goods, from whom could S recover? Explain.

(b) Other facts remaining the same, assume further that the partnership articles also stipulated that B was a limited partner, and assume further that the proper certificate of limited partnership was duly filed. If the firm failed to pay for the goods, from whom could S recover? Explain. (Modified from A.I.C.P.A., May 45-8d).

12. F. Smith and S. Smith, father and son, as partners, operated a hardware store in a small town in Georgia, under the name "Smith Hardware Store." They purchased from various sources including a Chicago manufacturer. An agent, as the sole Georgia salesman for the manufacturer, solicited orders subject to acceptance by the manufacturer, reported to the manufacturer references given by new credit customers, and in a general way reported on the business conditions of the manufacturer's customers. For almost a year, about every thirty days, this agent visited the Smith store soliciting and receiving orders for items of hardware which were shipped and paid for on delivery. On September 1, the partnership was dissolved, the father withdrawing from the business and selling his interest to the son who took over entire ownership, and management and retained the same name for the store. Notice of the partnership dissolution was published in a local paper, but no written notices were sent to any businesses. On September 17 the agent again visited the store and took an order for a quantity of hardware, to be shipped on thirty days' credit. The order was signed "Smith Hardware Store by S. Smith," and was forwarded by the agent to the manufacturer.

(a) The father instructed his son to inform the agent of the father's withdrawal. However, the son

forgot to do this. On September 27, the manufacturer shipped the ordered goods. When payment was not made when due, the agent and the manufacturer learned for the first time of dissolution of the partnership. The manufacturer sued both father and son. Could the manufacturer collect from the father? Explain.

(b) When signing the order, the son told the agent his father had withdrawn from the business. This information was not written on the order and the agent neglected to tell the manufacturer of the change. On September 27, the manufacturer shipped the ordered goods. When payment was not made when due, the manufacturer learned for the first time of dissolution of the partnership. The manufacturer sued both father and son. Could the manufacturer collect from the father? Explain.

13. A, B, C, and D were general partners. According to their agreement, A contributed $5,000 to the firm capital, B $10,000, C nothing, and D $25,000. A devoted one-half of his time to the business, B one-third, C all of his time, and D no time. The agreement said nothing as to the ratio of sharing profits or losses or as to salaries. After commencement of the business, A made a loan of $5,000 to the firm without interest. Several years later the partners decided to liquidate the business.

(a) $55,000 was realized on liquidation of assets, liabilities to outside creditors totaled $20,000. How much would each party receive or be required to pay? Explain.

(b) $80,000 was realized on liquidation of assets, liabilities to outside creditors totaled $20,000. How much would each party receive or be required to pay? Explain.

14. A and B formed a partnership, each contributing $20,000. Several years later C joined the firm and paid $20,000 as his capital contribution. When C joined the business, he did not expressly assume liability for existing debts. A few years later the partnership business became insolvent and was dissolved. The partnership agreement did not specify the ratio for sharing profits or losses. Upon

liquidation, the partnership assets realized $25,000. Debts owed by the business to outside creditors totaled $40,000. Of this total obligation, $ 15,000 was incurred before C joined the firm, $25,000 after C joined the firm. On final settlement and distribution, how much would each partner receive or be required to pay.

(a) If A, B, and C were fully solvent? Explain.

(b) If A and B were insolvent and unable to contribute anything but C was fully solvent? Explain.

15. A, B, and C formed a partnership, A contributing $10,000, B, $4,000, and C, $1,000. The agreement did not specify any ratio for sharing of profits or losses. A year after the partnership was formed, C, at the request of A and B, loaned $5,000 to the partnership, without interest, and A and B signed a note promising in the partnership name to repay the loan to C in one year. A year later the partnership was insolvent and dissolved. Upon liquidation, the partnership assets realized $30,000, debts owed to outside creditors totaled $19,000. C was personally insolvent, One of C's creditors with a judgment against C for $8,000 had the sheriff serve attachment papers on all the partners, attaching the $5,000 which the partnership owed to C. On final settlement and distribution, who would get how much? Explain.

Corporations

CHAPTER OUTLINE

Corporations

I. Entity Concept

The chief characteristic of a corporation arises from the separate entity theory; a corporation is considered as having a legal personality separate and distinct from its members. However, the law does not permit this entity theory to be perverted and misused to the detriment of the public welfare. As an outstanding Federal judge has written:

> If any general rule can be laid down, in the present state of authority, it is that a corporation will be looked upon as a legal entity as a general rule, and until sufficient reason to the contrary appears; but, when the notion of legal entity is used to defeat public convenience, justify wrong, protect fraud, or defend crime, the law will regard the corporation as an association of persons. This much may be expressed without approving the theory that the legal entity is a fiction, or a mere mental creation; or that the idea of invisibility or intangibility is a sophism. A corporation, as expressive of legal rights and powers, is no more fictitious or intangible than a man's rights to his own home or his own liberty.[1]

It is not fraudulent or improper for a businessman to use the corporate device for the primary purpose or even for the sole purpose of avoiding personal liability for the debts of his business; limited liability is one of the chief incidents and advantages of the corporate form of business. But if a businessman attempts to hide behind the corporate's separate entity to accomplish a dishonest or illegal purpose, the courts will disregard the separate entity. The fact that one corporation owns all the stock of another (such corporations commonly being called parent and subsidiary corporations), and the fact that the parent corporation carries on part of its functions through the subsidiary are not reason for legal theory to merge the two corporations. Unless the separate entity theory is being misused, it will be observed even though the same persons serve as officers and directors of both the parent and the subsidiary corporations.

If the owner and operator of a corporate business completely ignores the separate legal personality of the corporation, the courts will also be inclined to ignore the separate legal entity. A person (or group of persons or parent corporation) who wishes to use the corporate device to secure from the debts of a business, must not only have the business organized as a corporation, but should also use proper corporate formalities in the operation of the business.

II. Formation of Corporations

Corporations are usually formed under the authority of the general corporation statute of some state. The Model Business Corporation

---

1. *U.S. v. Milwaukee Refrigerator Transit Co.*, 142 F.247 (1905)

Example. O owned and operated a small manufacturing business. The business premises included two buildings, one smaller and older than the other and usable only as a warehouse. Both buildings were insured for their fair replacement value. O was in financial difficulty and having no further need for the small building, secretly set fire to the building and destroyed it. The insurance investigator, however, found evidence sufficient to prove O's wrongful act.

1. Assume that the business and its assets were owned and operated by O as a sole proprietor. O sued the insurance company to collect for the destroyed building. O would not be permitted to recover. The law will not permit a person to profit from his own wrongful act.

2. Assume that the business and its assets were owned and operated by a corporation in which O held all of the stock. The corporation sued the insurance company to collect for the destroyed building. Ordinarily the corporation would be considered as a separate legal entity distinct from O. However, to permit the corporation to recover would be permitting O to accomplish indirectly the illegal purpose which he clearly could not accomplish directly. Therefore, in such a case the court would disregard the separate entity and consider the corporation as identical with the sole shareholder. ☐

* * *

Example. If a railroad could carry on a wholesale or retail business and transport its goods to market on its own lines, the railroad would be hauling at cost and have a rate preference over noncarriers in the same line of business. To prevent such rate preference, a Federal statute provides in effect that it is unlawful for any railroad to transport in interstate commerce any article or commodity owned by the railroad, except such articles as are necessary and intended for use in the conduct of its business as a common carrier.

A railroad corporation which owned a coal mine organized a subsidiary corporation to own and operate the coal mine and to engage in the wholesale and retail selling of the coal. The railroad then entered into a contract with the mining corporation to haul the coal to market, and claimed that since the coal was not owned by the railroad, but instead by the mining corporation, the railroad was not violating the above statute.

Since the separate entity of the mining corporation was being used to accomplish an illegal purpose, the railroad doing indirectly what it was prohibited from doing directly, the court would disregard the separate entity of the mining corporation and rule that the railroad was violating the above statue. ☐

Act, which is typical of many such statutes, says:

> One or more persons, or a domestic or foreign corporation, may act as incorporator or incorporators of a corporation....

The usual procedure involves the organizers (or incorporators as they are usually called) applying to the proper state government office for a charter. Statutes usually term this application the "articles of incorporation." Various facts concerning the proposed corporation are stated in the application or articles, such as the type of business the corporation is to operate, the name it will use, its principal place of business, the amount of capital stock it will be authorized to issue, and the rights which stockholders are to have. Then, as a typical statute provides:

> If the Department of State [office to which the articles are submitted] finds that the articles conform to law, it shall forthwith en-

dorse its approval thereon, and when all . . . charges have been paid, as required by law, shall issue to the incorporators . . . a certificate of incorporation, to which shall be attached the approved articles.... The articles, upon being approved by the Department of State, shall constitute the charter of the corporation. . .

Upon the approval of the articles of incorporation by the Department of State, the corporate existence shall begin . . .

Some statutes require each incorporator to subscribe for at least one share of stock. However he is not required to retain the stock. He can transfer his stock as he wishes, and even before the corporation is formed, can validly contract that he will transfer his stock when it is later issued to him. Therefore, under the statutes in most states, it is both possible and proper to have a corporation in which all the stock is held by one person or by one corporation.

If in forming a corporation the incorporators inadvertently overlook some formal requirement specified by the state corporation statute, it cannot be said that the corporation has come into existence strictly in accordance with law. Third persons who deal with the purported corporation may later discover the oversight, claim that no corporation was ever formed, and assert therefore that those who are associated together in carrying on the business are partners and are personally liable as such. However, if the third person believed he was dealing with a corporation and was not injured by the oversight of the corporators, there is no reason as between the parties to consider the business unit as anything other than a corporation in fact. This reasoning is known as the "corporation de facto" theory. In most jurisdictions, a corporation de facto will be declared to exist if:

1. There is a statute under which such a corporation could have been organized.
2. The incorporators in good faith

attempted to organize a corporation under such statute.
3. The business unit has been operated as a corporation.

Statutes frequently adopt and simplify the corporation de facto theory and at the same time reserve a right to the state to insist upon exact compliance with the statute in material matters. For example, one typical statute provides:

The certificate of incorporation shall be conclusive evidence of the fact that the corporation has been incorporated, but proceedings may be instituted by the state to dissolve, wind up and terminate a corporation which should not have been formed under this act, or which has been formed without a substantial compliance with the conditions prescribed by this act as precedent to incorporation.

III. Operating a Corporate Business

The rules for operating a corporate business are found in statutes, in the corporate charter, and in the corporate bylaws. For example, a typical statute provides:

The by-laws may contain any provisions for the regulation and management of the affairs of the corporation not inconsistent with law or the articles....

The shareholders shall have the power to make, alter, amend, and repeal the by-laws of a business corporation, but the authority . . . may be vested by the articles or the by-laws in the board of directors, subject always to the power of the shareholders to change such action.

The corporate method of operation is quite similar to the operation of representative government in a state or nation. The shareholders as contractual owners of the business enterprise elect representatives—the directors. The directors determine business policy which is then carried out by the executive officers and other employees who are usually chosen by the directors.

A. Shareholders' Roles

The role of shareholders in corporate management under a typical corporation statute may be summarized as follows:

1. At least one meeting of the shareholders is held each year for the election of directors, at such time and place as provided in the bylaws.

2. At a shareholders' meeting, each shareholder has the right of one vote for every share of voting stock standing in his name on the books of the corporation.

3. A shareholder may vote either in person or by proxy, but he cannot sell his vote or proxy. Unless coupled with a creditor's interest, a proxy is revocable at will. Even if unrevoked, a proxy is not valid for longer than eleven months unless a longer time is expressly stated. If a longer time is expressly stated, a proxy (unless coupled with a creditor's interest) may still be revoked at will, and if not revoked, will not be valid for longer than three years.

4. In electing directors, cumulative voting is permitted. In cumulative voting, a shareholder multiplies the number of shares which he is entitled to vote by the number of directors to be elected. The shareholder can then cast this total number of votes for one candidate or distribute his votes among any two or more candidates. For example, if three directors are to be elected, a shareholder owning 100 shares of stock has a total of 300 votes; he can cast all 300 votes for one candidate or distribute his votes as he wishes among two or three candidates.

5. A shareholder who pledges his shares (for example by delivering his share certificate to a bank as collateral security for a loan) can vote the pledged shares unless and until a transfer to the pledgees is noted on the books of the corporation. After a pledge is noted on the

corporate stock records, the pledgee will vote the stock.

6. Unless a record date is fixed by the bylaws or by the board of directors, shares transferred on the books of the corporation within the ten-day period preceding a shareholders' meeting are not entitled to vote. The bylaws may specify a record date; if they do not, the board of directors may specify a record date not more than fifty days prior to the date of the shareholders' meeting. If a record date is thus specified, only persons who are on the corporate records as shareholders on that date are entitled to vote.

7. Being a part owner of the corporate business, a shareholder is entitled to information concerning the affairs of the business, and has the right to inspect corporate records for this purpose. In addition, an annual report must be rendered to each shareholder.

8. As to minority shareholders: a person who invests money in a corporation should realize that he is entrusting his investment to the will of the majority. So long as the majority act lawfully and in good faith, a minority shareholder has no legal right to "take his marbles and go home." However, if the majority makes a major change in the corporation, a minority shareholder who dissents is entitled to withdraw his capital from the business enterprise. Changes which would be classed as major and therefore not binding on a dissenting shareholder include (1) a merger or consolidation, (2) a disposal of substantially all of the corporate assets other than in the ordinary course of the operation or relocation of the corporate business, and (3) a major change in the corporate purpose or in the stock rights of shareholders.

B. Directors' Roles

The chief provisions of a typical corporation statute, may be summarized as follows:

1. The affairs of a business corporation are managed by a board of directors.

2. A director must be a natural person (that is, not another corporation) and of full age. A director need not be a resident of the state nor a shareholder in the corporation, unless the articles or bylaws so require. A director may be a salaried officer of the corporation.

3. Unless the bylaws provide otherwise, a majority of the directors is necessary to constitute a quorum for the transaction of business; if a quorum is present at a director's meeting, the action of a majority of the directors present at that meeting is binding on the corporation.

4. Each director must be loyal to the best interests of the corporation and use the same care which an ordinarily prudent man would use in his personal business affairs. If a director acting in his personal capacity contracts with the corporation of which he is a director, the contract is not valid unless (1) it is fair and reasonable to the corporation, *and* (2) it is approved by an impartial, disinterested majority of the board of directors.

5. Directors will not be compensated unless compensation in a stated amount is authorized by the articles or by a majority vote of the shareholders.

C. Officers' Roles

A typical corporation statute will usually provide as follows:

1. Every business corporation must have at least a president, a secretary, and a treasurer, and may have additional officers. The treasurer may be another corporation (for example, a bank or trust company) or may be a natural person of full age. The president and secretary must be natural persons of full age. If the bylaws so provide, any two of the required offices may be held by the same person except that the same person cannot be both president and secretary.

2. Officers may (but do not have to be) directors.

3. The officers owe to the corporation the same duties of loyalty and care that a director owes to the corporation.

4. Compensation for any particular officer must be authorized by an impartial majority of the board of directors.

D. Promoters' Contracts

While the incorporators are the persons who apply to the state for a charter, one person, called a promoter (or a couple of such persons), may be doing the work of organizing the corporation and laying the groundwork for it to begin operations. Sometimes such a promoter believes it advisable to enter into contracts for goods, lands, or buildings, even before the corporation is formed. If the promoter enters into such a contract in the name of the proposed corporation, an unusual agency question arises, because the promoter is purporting to act in the name of a principal (the corporation) which does not yet exist. For this reason the promoter is personally liable on such a contact and remains liable unless expressly released by the other contracting party or adopted by the corporation. A release may be written into the original contract or agreed to later. Adoption can be made either expressly (for example, by a resolution of the board of directors) or by implication (for example, by accepting benefits under the contract).

E. Corporate Powers

A typical corporation statute provides:

> A business corporation shall have the capacity of natural persons to act, but shall have authority to perform only such acts as are necessary or proper to accomplish the purpose or purposes for which it is organized, and which are not repugnant to law.

If a corporation engages in activities which are beyond its power, such activities are commonly referred to by the Latin term *ultra vires*. At common law, until an *ultra vires* contract is performed either by the corporation or by the other contracting party, the contract is completely unenforceable, but after either party performs his part of the contract, he is entitled to collect for his performance. Recognizing that if a corporation exceeds its powers, the only ones really concerned with that fact are the shareholders and the state, most modern corporation statutes have liberalized the common-law rule. For example, one such statute provides, in effect:

> No limitation upon the business, purpose, or powers of a corporation shall be asserted in order to defend any action between the corporation and a third person involving any contract to which the corporation is a party.

> A shareholder may sue a corporation to enjoin its performance of an unauthorized contract. If the court deems such action equitable, it may set aside and enjoin the performance of the contract. In doing so, the court shall allow to the corporation or to the other contracting party, as the case may be, compensation for the loss or damage sustained by either of them, as a result of the court's setting aside the contract but anticipated profits shall not be a factor in calculating the amount of recoverable damages.

> The state may sue a corporation to enjoin the transaction of unauthorized or unlawful business.

F. Foreign Corporations

The term "foreign corporation" applies to a corporation outside the state of its incorporation. Thus a business incorporated in Kansas is a foreign corporation in Ohio. The status of out-of-state business under the American constitutional system is a synthesis of two concepts, (1) interstate commerce, and (2) interstate citizenship.

1. INTERSTATE COMMERCE

Under the American constitutional system, no state can unreasonably interfere with interstate commerce.

2. INTERSTATE CITIZENSHIP

In assuring the formation of a unified nation rather than a loose federation of independent states, the drafters of the United States Constitution included what is frequently referred to as the "privileges and immunities" or "interstate citizenship" provision, which reads as follows:

> The citizens of each State shall be entitled to all privileges and immunities of citizens in the several States.

As used in this provision, the term "citizen" is limited to a natural person—a political citizen—and does *not* extend to a corporate citizen.

Under these two concepts therefore, a corporation does not have the right of mobility possessed by a natural person. While a state cannot interfere with a foreign corporation carrying on interstate commerce, a state can completely exclude foreign corporations from carrying on local business, and therefore can admit them subject to conditions and regulations. For example, a typical statute provides as follows:

> A foreign business corporation, before doing any business in this state, shall procure a certificate of authority to do so from the Department of State, in the manner hereinafter provided in this statute, unless the entire business operations of the corporation within this state are within the protection of the Commerce Clause of the Federal Constitution, in which event the corporation may engage in such business operations without procuring a certificate of authority.

To obtain a certificate for carrying on a local business or (in the language of the statutes of some states) to register for carrying on a local business, a foreign corporation must file an application which (among other things) must state the corporation name and business and describe its share structure.

What constitutes carrying on a local business is not always clear. The Model Business Corporation Act prepared under the auspices of the Commissioners on Uniform State Laws contains the following definition, which is a useful summary of the majority of the court decisions:

Without excluding other activities which may not constitute transacting business in this state, a foreign corporation shall not be considered to be transacting business in this state, for the purpose of this Act, by reason of carrying on in this state any one or more of the following activities:

(a) Maintaining or defending any action or any administrative or arbitration proceeding, or effecting the settlement thereof or the settlement of claims or disputes.

(b) Holding meetings of its directors or shareholders or carrying on other activities concerning its internal affairs;

(c) Maintaining bank accounts.

(d) Maintaining offices or agencies for the transfer, exchange, and registration of its securities, or appointing and maintaining trustees or depositaries with relation to its securities.

(e) Effecting sales through independent contractors.

(f) Soliciting or procuring orders, whether by mail or through employees or agents or otherwise, where such orders require acceptance without this state before becoming binding contracts.

(g) Creating evidences of debt, mortgages, or liens on real or personal property.

(h) Securing or collecting debts or enforcing any rights in property securing the same.

(i) Transacting any business in interstate commerce.

(j) Conducting an isolated transaction completed within a period of thirty days and not in the course of a number of repeated transactions of like nature.[2]

If an interstate sale of goods involves local installation by the seller, the usual view is that a highly technical installation of intricate mechanism, which is to be completed in a fairly

short time, is considered a part of the interstate sale, and the seller is not required to register in the buyer's state. Any other installation, whether done by workmen brought in from outside the state or by local workmen, is considered local business.

3. FAILURE TO REGISTER

The penalty imposed upon a foreign corporation for transacting local business without registering varies in different states. Most statutes include some variation of the following penalties:

a. Criminal Punishment

The following is a typical statutory provision:

Any foreign business corporation which is required by the provisions of this act to procure a certificate of authority, but has not done so, or any person, agent, officer or employee who shall transact any business within this state for any foreign business corporation, which is required by the provisions of this act to procure a certificate of authority, but has not done so, or any person, agent, officer or employee who shall transact any business within this state for any foreign business corporation, which has failed to procure a certificate of authority . . . shall be guilty of a misdemeanor, and, upon conviction thereof, shall be punished by imprisonment not exceeding thirty days, or by a fine not exceeding one thousand dollars ($1,000), or both....

b. Limitation on Contract Enforcement

In most states if a foreign corporation has not registered to carry on a local business in that particular state, it Is not permitted to sue on any contracts made while transacting such business. In some states if the corporation registers later and pays a fine, it can then enforce contracts made before the corporation registered. In some other states, the corporation's registration enables it to enforce subsequent contracts only; local contracts made

---

Model Business Corporation Act, Sec.99.

Example. The articles of a particular corporation describe the share structure as follows: "The corporation shall be authorized to issue 1,000 shares of $100 par value, 6 percent, cumulative, participating preferred stock, and 2,000 shares of $100 par value common stock." All of the authorized stock is issued and outstanding. After paying no dividends last year, the directors decide at the end of the present year to payout $3,000 in dividends.

The division of the money is calculated as follows:

	Preferred Stock	Common Stock
For last year	$6,000	Nothing
For the present year	$6,000	$12,000
Additional profit-sharing	$2,000	$4,000
Total	$14,000	$16,000

Each preferred shareholder receives $14 per share and each common shareholder $8 per share. The reasons can be summarized as follows:

1. The preferred stock is 6 percent preferred. This means that each preferred shareholder is entitled to a dividend of 6 percent of the $100 par value of the stock (that is, $6 per share) before any dividend is paid to a common shareholder.

2. The preferred stock is cumulative. This means that for any year in which a 6 percent dividend is not paid, the right to receive that amount accumulates and must be paid before any other distribution of profits is made. In many states preferred stock is presumed to be cumulative unless the articles expressly state otherwise. On the other hand since common stock is not assured any particular dividend at all, it would not have any cumulative rights.

3. The preferred stock is participating. This means that after there is allocated to the common shareholders a dividend at the same rate paid to the preferred shareholders for the current year, the preferred shareholders have the right to share proportionately with the common shareholders in any further distribution of profits. In many states preferred stock is presumed to be fully participating unless the articles expressly state otherwise. Common stock is always fully participating. □

prior to the late registration remain unenforceable by the corporation.

IV. Corporate Stock

Two of the principal results from a corporation being a separate legal entity are (1) that the ownership interest can be divided among a large number of people (called shareholders or stockholders), and (2) that such owners have no liability, or only a limited liability, for the debts of the corporate business.

A. Shares of Stock

An ownership interest in a corporation is referred to as a "share" or sometimes as a "share of stock."

The rights of a shareholder, as an owner of a business enterprise, usually include at least some of the following:

1. A right to share in management, through voting at shareholders' meetings (unless the stock is expressly stated to have limited or no voting rights).

2. A right to share in distribution of profits, through dividends, and in the distribution of surplus upon liquidation of the corporation.

3. A first option to buy a certain percentage of newly issued stock, usually called a preemptive right.

Frequently it is advantageous for the organizers of a corporation to provide for various classes of stock with differing rights. The following is a typical statutory provision which makes this possible:

> Every business corporation shall have power to create and issue one or more classes or kinds of shares, any or all of which classes or kinds may consist of shares with par value or shares without par value, with full, limited, or no voting rights, and with such designations, preferences, qualifications, privileges, limitations, options, conversion rights, and other special rights as shall be stated or authorized in the articles.

If two classes of shares are issued with different rights, usually one will have some preferences or priorities over the other and, therefore, will be termed "preferred."

If the certificate which the corporation issues to evidence share ownership (share or stock certificate) states on its face the amount of consideration received by the corporation in exchange for the certificate, the stock is called "par value stock." If the certificate merely evidences a stated ownership interest in the corporation without stating the consideration received upon issuance of the certificate, the stock is called "no par value stock."

B. Immunity from Business Debts

I. OBLIGATION TO PAY FOR STOCK

After a share of stock is issued and paid for, the owner can sell it for any price he wishes; he can even give it away. However, when a share is first issued by a corporation, the laws of most states require that (1) if the share has a par value, at least that amount must be paid to the corporation, in money or other property, and (2) if the share has no par value, the board of directors determines the amount of consideration which must be paid to the corporation. Unless this amount (par value, or the consideration fixed by the directors for no par stock) is paid to the corporation, the stock cannot be considered fully paid for. If stock is not fully paid for, either the corporation or, in case of insolvency, its creditors, can require the person to whom the stock was issued to make up the shortage in payment. In most states, innocent transferees of such stock are not liable, but the person to whom the stock was first issued remains liable even after he has disposed of the stock.

2. STOCK SUBSCRIPTIONS

A subscriber may be defined as a person who agrees either before or after formation of a corporation, to buy from the corporation a stated number of previously unissued shares. The agreement may provide either for a lump-sum payment or for payment by installments. When payments are deferred, a question sometimes arises whether a subscriber is a shareholder, or instead is a contract buyer intended to become a shareholder at some future time, usually upon his making certain payments. If a subscriber is a shareholder, he has a right to vote and to receive dividends. Also, if the corporation should become insolvent, the subscriber-shareholder can be required, for the benefit of creditors, to pay the balance due on his subscription. On the other hand, if a subscriber is a contract buyer and not yet a shareholder, he has no stock rights, and cannot be required to pay the balance due on his subscription unless the corporation tenders to him the stock and stock rights for which he agreed to pay. A corporation which is adjudged insolvent is for all practical purposes dead and its stock lifeless. After a corporation is adjudged insolvent, the stock rights for which the buyer agreed to pay can no longer be tendered to him, and therefore he cannot be required to pay anything more on his subscription agreement. The chief rules for determining the status of a subscriber may be summarized as follows:

a. Preincorporation Subscriptions

1. A person who subscribes for stock in a corporation not yet organized can cancel his agreement at any time before the corporation comes into existence. If he so notifies the organizers, he never becomes a shareholder and has no further liability. However, some statutes and courts prohibit recovery of payments made before cancellation or revocation of the subscription for 6 months.

2. Under some corporation statutes, all subscribers who have not previously given notice canceling their subscriptions, immediately and automatically become shareholders when a charter is issued to the corporation. (Notice that such statutes recognize that a person can be a shareholder before he pays anything for his stock and before a stock certificate is issued to him.)

b. Postincorporation Subscriptions

If a person makes an offer to an existing corporation to buy a certain number of previously unissued stock, and the corporation accepts the offer, a contract is formed. The status of a subscriber before completing his agreed payment is determined by the manifested intent of both parties. When not expressly stated, the intent of the parties is implied from their conduct. Thus, if a corporation extends to a subscriber a right usually exercised only by shareholders, and the subscriber exercises the right, he is a shareholder; otherwise he is only a contract buyer and not yet a shareholder.

3. LIABILITY OF HOLDERS OF FULLY PAID SHARES

If stock is classed as assessable, this means that the holder has agreed that the directors can assess him and require him to pay some specified additional amount to the corporation. Assessable stock is fairly rare.

In most states, if stock is fully paid for and nonassessable, the shareholder has no liability for any debts of the business. However, a few states feel that it is sound policy to impose a limited liability upon shareholders. For example some statutes have provided, in effect:

> A shareholder of fully paid, nonassessable stock shall not be personally liable for any debt or liability of the corporation, except for salaries and wages due and owing to its employees. To this extent, every shareholder shall be personally liable in an amount equal to the value of his shares, but no shareholder shall be so liable unless suit for the collection of such salaries and wages shall be brought against him within six months after the same shall become due. The term value, as used here, means the aggregate par value of the shares or in the case of shares without par value, the consideration received by the corporation on the original issuance of such shares.

> In any lawsuit brought to enforce this liability, the plaintiff employee may sue the corporation and any one or more shareholders as defendants. If the plaintiff wins his lawsuit, judgment shall be entered against the corporation and the defendant shareholder or shareholders. Execution upon such judgment shall be first levied on property of the corporation located within Pennsylvania; if sufficient property cannot be found, then execution shall be levied on the property of the defendant shareholder or shareholders for the amount of his or their liability. The defendant shareholder or shareholders shall, for the amount so collected, have a right to collect from the corporation, and if contribution from the corporation is unobtainable, then the defendant shareholder or shareholders shall have a right to collect pro rata from other solvent shareholders to the extent of their original liability for the claims on which the plaintiff obtained judgment.

Example. To evidence O's stock ownership in a particular corporation, the corporation issued to O a stock certificate for 100 shares, made out to O. O sold the stock to B, indorsed the certificate by merely signing his name on the reverse side, and delivered the certificate to B. B, who was purchasing other shares in the same corporation, wished to wait and submit all of his purchased shares together for transfer on the corporation records, and therefore locked in his safe the certificate obtained from O. That night a thief broke into B's safe, stealing various items including this stock certificate. The thief sold and delivered the certificate to P who purchased for value, in good faith, and with no knowledge that the certificate had been stolen. When P had the certificate submitted to the corporation for transfer, the corporation notified B who had previously advised the corporation of the theft. B sued P and requested the court to order return of the certificate to B.

The thief never became the owner of the certificate. However, since the certificate was negotiable, P, the innocent purchaser for value, took the certificate free from all adverse claims; he obtained better rights than the thief had and became the owner of the certificate and the share interest which it evidenced. Therefore, the court would refuse B's request. ☐

C. Transfer of Stock

Stock certificates are usually transferred by delivery of the certificate to the transferee, together with any one of the following: (1) the registered owner's indorsement on the stock certificate, (2) an assignment of the stock certificate, signed by the registered owner, or (3) a power of attorney authorizing assignment of the stock certificate, signed by the registered owner. To facilitate transfer, stock certificate forms are frequently prepared with assignment or power of attorney forms printed on the reverse side.

The transferee becomes the owner of the certificate and the rights it evidences as soon as it is transferred to him by the transferor with the latter's appropriate signature. Usually the transferee then has the certificate sent to the issuing corporation which notes the transfer on its records and issues a new certificate to the transferee. Until the transfer is noted on the corporation records, the corporation is permitted to treat the registered owner as the person entitled to vote and to receive notices and dividends. Stock certificates are negotiable, just like negotiable commercial paper, order bills of lading, and order warehouse receipts. Thus, a bona fide purchaser who receives a stock certificate together with a transfer signed by the registered owner, acquires not only the rights of his transferor, but also acquires the certificate free from the adverse claims of any other person. The legal concept of negotiability is discussed in Chapter 23.

D. Preemptive Rights

Suppose that in a corporation which has 1,000 shares authorized and issued, O owns 100 shares. O therefore owns a 100/1,000 or a 1/10 interest in the corporation. His voting strength and his right to share in dividends is 1/10. Suppose further that in order to raise additional capital, a majority of the directors and shareholders approve increasing the authorized stock to 1,500 shares, and that the charter of the corporation is amended accordingly. If when the 500 additional shares are issued, O is given no opportunity to purchase any, then while O still retains his 100 shares, his interest in the corporation will shrink from 1/10 to 100/1,500 or 1/15.

If, on the other hand, O is given a right (called a "preemptive right") to purchase 1/10 of the newly authorized shares, and does so, O will then own 150 shares or a 150/1,500 interest, and will thus maintain intact his 1/10 interest in the corporation. When presented in this simple situation, it seems only fair that O should be accorded a preemptive right. However, the stock structure of most corporations is not this simple, and various complex questions can arise, including:

1. Should the holder of common stock have a preemptive right to purchase a new authorization of preferred stock—and vice versa?

2. If the corporation previously issued only a specified portion of its originally authorized stock, should a shareholder have a preemptive right when the directors decide to issue the remainder of the stock?

3. If the corporation share structure already consists of common stock Class A and common stock Class B, each with voting powers but having slightly different stock rights, and the new authorization is also voting stock but with still different stock rights in respect to dividends or liquidation, so that it is called common stock Class C, should a shareholder of A or B stock have a preemptive right to purchase C stock?

4. If because of the corporation's favorable prospects a new issuance of stock can be marketed at more than par value, should a shareholder's preemptive right be to purchase at par or at the higher price the corporation can obtain elsewhere?

Instead of attempting to write a rule which could fit these and other complex situations, the drafters of some of the modern corporation statutes have decided that whatever preemptive right a shareholder is to have should be written by the corporate managers for their particular situation. Thus, for example, the Pennsylvania statute provides in effect:

> Unless otherwise provided in its articles, a corporation may issue shares, option rights, or other securities without first offering them to shareholders of any class.

E. Dividends

In most states, a corporation cannot lawfully pay a money dividend which will exceed the amount of the corporation's earned surplus. If there is sufficient earned surplus so that this basic requirement is met, then the decision as to whether or not to declare a dividend, or as to the amount of the dividend, is pretty much left to the discretion of the board of directors. Thus if the directors decide to retain profits for some valid business purpose, a court will not attempt to substitute its judgment for that of the directors. Only in the rare case when the directors' refusal to declare a dividend (or to declare a higher dividend) is for a dishonest or otherwise improper motive will the courts interfere.

If a money dividend which unlawfully exceeds a corporation's earned surplus is declared and paid, the corporation will sometimes attempt at a later date to obtain reimbursement from the directors or shareholders. Any director who approves of an unlawful dividend is personally liable to the corporation for the amount paid out. Some states relieve a director from this liability if he relied in good faith on a misleading financial statement which had been certified as correct by the corporate officers or an independent accountant. In most states a shareholder need not return an illegal dividend if at the time he received it (1) he was unaware that it was an illegal dividend, and (2) the corporation was a solvent, going concern.

As soon as the directors declare a lawful dividend, a contract right to receive the amount of the dividend attaches to and becomes a part of the stock ownership. For the amount of the declared dividend, the shareholders are creditors of the corporation, with the same rights as any other corporate creditors. More specifically:

1. Neither a resolution of the directors canceling a dividend nor a vote of the majority of shareholders to that effect will cancel the debt.

2. Should the corporation become insolvent and be liquidated before paying the dividend (assuming, of course, that there was sufficient surplus when the dividend was declared), then:

(a) For the amount of the dividend debt, shareholders are entitled to share equally (that is, proportionately) with outside creditors in the distribution of available assets.

(b) If while still solvent, the corporation set aside a fund for the purpose of paying the dividend (for example by opening a dividend checking account), this fund must be applied exclusively to the dividend debt and cannot be reached by other creditors of the corporation.

3. If the resolution declaring a dividend does not specify a record date, the actual owner of stock on the resolution date is the owner of the dividend claim. If the resolution specifies a record date (for example, a resolution of June 1, declaring a dividend payable December 1 to all shareholders of record on July 1), the actual owner of shares on the record date is the owner of the dividend claim. In either case the corporation is permitted to send the dividend to the person registered on its books as the shareholder. If another person was the actual owner of the stock on the resolution date (or the record date, if specified), the registered owner holds the dividend money for the benefit of that person, unless the parties have agreed otherwise.

4. If a stockholder, as a debtor, pledges and delivers his stock to a creditor who holds it as collateral security for an obligation, the corporation may, nevertheless, send to the debtor any dividend that is declared unless a transfer to the pledgee is noted on the books of the corporation. However, any stock dividend which the debtor receives he should turn over to the pledgee to be held as additional collateral; any money dividend the debtor receives he should turn over to the pledgee if the latter wishes to apply the money immediately to the debtor's obligation.[3]

* * *

Problems

1. To separate their mercantile operations from realty holdings, the operators of the Roger Mercantile Corporation had another corporation formed, entitled the Roger Realty Corporation. The entire stock of the Realty Corporation was owned by the Mercantile Corporation, and although separate books and records were kept, the officers and directors of the two corporations were the same. The owner of certain property leased it to the Realty Corporation for a term of ninety years, at a rental of $300,000 per year, plus taxes and assessments, and with a provision binding the Realty Corporation to erect, within one year, a building costing $1,500,000. The Realty Corporation in turn leased the premises to the Mercantile Corporation for a term of ten years. Within the time stipulated, a building costing the specified amount was erected. Before expiration of the ten-year lease, the Mercantile Corporation moved to a new location but continued to pay rent until the expiration of the ten-year term. When that term expired, the Realty Corporation was unable to procure a new tenant and, having no assets but this lease, defaulted in its payment of rent to L. L sued the Mercantile Corporation to recover the unpaid rent. What result? Explain.

2. A. Adams was the sole proprietor of a business operating under the name, "Adams Manufacturing Company." Through sound business policies, A increased both his individual and business wealth; whereupon A decided to form a corporation to operate the business so that he would no longer be risking all of his personal assets in the

---

3. U.C.C. Sec.9-207.

business. With A and two of his employees acting as incorporators, a charter was obtained, forming a business corporation under the name, "Adams Manufacturing Company," with a capitalization of 1,000 shares of $100 par value common stock. The two employees as incorporators each subscribed for one share of stock. After formation of the corporation each transferred to A the right to receive the one share of stock. A transferred to the corporation all of the assets of the business, reasonably worth $100,000, and made out to himself a certificate for 1,000 shares of stock. A signed the certificate as president and had his chief bookkeeper sign as secretary and treasurer. A gave proper advertised and personal notice of the formation of the corporation. For the next two years, A continued operating the business in the same manner and following the same policies as he had before formation of the corporation. However, because of a depression of business conditions and not at all the fault of A, the business became insolvent. C who had extended considerable credit to the business with knowledge that it was a corporation, sued to hold A individually liable for the debt. At the trial, A produced the corporation share register and minute book, showed the charter of the corporation, and showed in the minute book the description of the transfer of the business assets to the corporation in exchange for its stock. This was the only notation in the minute book. C proved that A's purpose in forming the corporation was to avoid personal liability for its debts. In C's lawsuit against A individually, explain (1) the reasoning upon which A might attempt to defend, (2) the reasoning upon which C might attempt to recover, and (3) which party should be given judgment.

3. A, B, and C obtained a charter for a business corporation to conduct a small manufacturing business. They were the sole shareholders, directors, and officers, and their stock was fully paid and nonassessable. Admittedly, the only reason they formed the corporation was to avoid personal liability for business debts. A few years later, after the corporate business sustained net losses and was close to insolvency, C, driving the corporate truck on corporate business, failed to see a stop

sign and collided with a car being carefully driven by T. T sustained serious personal and property injuries in the amount of $25,000. It was then discovered that B, treasurer of the corporation, had overlooked renewing the corporate liability insurance on the truck, and the insurance had expired. T sued A, B, and C personally for tort damages, arguing that the corporate device could properly be used to shield the owners and operators from liability for contracts of their business, but that it is improper to use the corporate separate entity to shield persons from tort liability. What result? Explain.

4. A, B, and C were the incorporators, shareholders, directors, and officers of the Adams Corporation, a small manufacturing concern. The total authorized stock (300 shares of $20 par value stock) was issued equally to A, B, and C, in exchange for which each paid the corporation $2,000. In addition each party loaned $5,000 to the corporation, without interest, for which each received a note signed in the corporate name by themselves as officers. After the parties operated the business for several years, using proper corporate formalities, the corporation was adjudged insolvent, and a receiver was appointed by court to liquidate the corporate assets. The receiver realized $15,000, the fair value of the assets, and outside creditors filed claims against the corporate business totaling $30,000. In addition A, B, and C filed claims on their notes.

(a) The outside creditors argued that A, B, and C had no right to collect on their notes until after outside debts were paid in full. Was this contention correct? Explain.

(b) The outside creditors argued that A, B, and C were personally liable for the unpaid debts of the corporation. On what theory and with what result? Explain.

5. After operating a retail hardware store for a number of years under the name, "Economy Hardware," S, the sole proprietor, sold the store premises, equipment, stock in trade, and goodwill to B. The written transfer agreement contained the

following provision: "S. Smith agrees that he will not operate a retail hardware store within a radius of one mile of [describing the location of the Economy Hardware], for the period of five years from date hereof . "

(a) One year later S entered into a partnership with P and the partnership began operating a retail hardware store within the proscribed area, under the name "Thrifty Hardware." B sued for an injunction. What result? Explain.

(b) One year later S and P formed a corporation which began operating a retail store within the proscribed area, under the name "Thrifty Hardware Company." B sued for an injunction. What would be the result (1) if S and P each owned 50 percent of the corporate stock; (2) if S owned 75 percent of the corporate stock and P 25 percent? Explain.

6. A and M owned all the stock of a business corporation, each owning the number of shares stated below. At a shareholders' meeting held for the election of five directors, M cast all his votes equally for five candidates, namely, M, N, O, P, and Q. A voted as stated below.

(A) Assume that there was no provision in the corporation charter or bylaws specifically covering the matter in dispute.

(1) A owned 400 shares, M 600 shares.

(a) A cast all the votes he lawfully could for A. Was A elected as a director? Explain.

(b) A cast all the votes he lawfully could, equally, for A and B. Were A and B elected as directors? Explain.

(c) A cast all the votes he lawfully could, equally, for A, B, and C. Were A, B, and C elected as directors? Explain.

(2) A owned 200 shares, M 800 shares.

(a), (b), (c). Assume the same additional facts and answer the same questions as in (1) above.

(3) A owned 150 shares, M 850 shares.

(a), (b), (c). Assume the same additional facts and answer the same questions as in (1) above.

(B) Assume that a bylaw adopted when the corporation was organized, provided: "Every shareholder shall have the right to one vote for each share held by him for as many persons as there are directors to be elected. No cumulative voting for directors shall be permitted." A knew of this bylaw at the time he acquired his stock.

(1) (a), (b), (c). Assume the same additional facts and answer the same questions as in (1) above.

(2) (a), (b), (c). Assume the same additional facts and answer the same questions as in (2) above.

7. The directors of a corporation passed a resolution directing that $5,000 worth of the corporate stock be issued to each director after the directors successfully procured subscriptions for $1,000,000 of unissued corporate stock, the money being necessary for success of the corporation. The directors procured such subscriptions, but a shareholder filed a bill in equity to restrain the directors from issuing any stock to themselves. What result? Explain. (Modified from A.I.C.P.A., Nov. 47-9e.)

8. A business corporation needed an additional plot of land for its business operations. The board of directors was comprised of five members, A, B, C, D, and E. A owned a plot of land and offered to sell it to the corporation for $5,000. The directors adopted a resolution accepting the offer, the vote being as stated below. Several months later before any use had been made of the land, the membership of the board changed. The new directors, D, F, M, N, and O decided to build elsewhere, offered to return the land to A, and upon his refusal, brought an action in the name of the corporation to cancel the prior transaction. In the lawsuit it was proved that at all times the reasonable value of the land to the corporation was $5,000.

(a) The vote on the resolution approving the purchase was A, B, and C in favor, D and E against. Should the court decree cancellation of the land purchase transaction? Explain.

(b) The vote on the resolution approving the purchase was A, B, C, and D in favor, E against. Should the court decree cancellation of the land purchase transaction? Explain.

(c) Other facts remaining the same, suppose that in the lawsuit it was proved that at all times the reasonable value of the land to the corporation was $2,500. The evidence also showed that, without doubt, A and the other directors who had approved the purchase had acted honestly, in good faith believing the land was reasonably worth $5,000. Would this additional fact change the answers in Parts (a) or (b) above? Explain.

9. A and B were the only shareholders and respectively president and secretary of the Adams Building Supply Corporation, a successful corporation, organized for the purpose, as stated in its charter, "to sell at wholesale and retail lumber and other building supplies." Together with C and D, A and B formed another corporation under the name "Brown Construction Corporation," to acquire land and construct and sell a large number of homes. The Construction Corporation wished to engage a certain contractor to excavate for a row of homes and lay water and sewer lines, payment to be made upon completion of the entire work. The contractor was unwilling to accept the job on the credit of the Construction Corporation alone. Thereupon A and B, as officers acting in the name of the Supply Corporation, gave the contractor a written guaranty that the Construction Corporation would pay for the contractor's work. Several months later the Construction Corporation project was abandoned, hopelessly insolvent, and the Supply Corporation went into bankruptcy. The contractor filed a claim against the Supply Corporation for the value of the work done. Other creditors of the Supply Corporation objected to allowance of the claim. On what ground and with what result? Explain.

10. S Company, a Delaware corporation, was registered to carry on local business in Illinois and had its principal place of business in Chicago. S Company entered into a written contract with B who was building a hotel building in a town in South Dakota. Under the contract, S Company agreed to furnish and install specified furnishings and equipment for the hotel (including kitchen equipment, all bedroom, lounge, and dining room furniture, wall and floor coverings, dishes, silverware, glassware, etc.) for the agreed price of $36,000, payable $1,000 when the contract was signed, $7,000 when installation was completed, and the balance in stated installments. When construction of the building was completed, shipments of the equipment and furnishings began to arrive, some from S Company's Chicago warehouse but most directly from various manufacturers outside South Dakota, from whom S Company was purchasing, and S Company sent a crew of its employees to install the equipment and furnishings. S Company completely performed its contract within two months, which was a reasonable time, but B who had made the initial $5,000 payment, failed to make any further payments under the contract. Explaining that it was only an extra precautionary measure, S Company's lawyer had S Company thereupon register with South Dakota as a foreign corporation to carry on a local business in South Dakota, and sued B in the Federal District Court for South Dakota for the unpaid price. South Dakota statute required foreign corporations carrying on local business in South Dakota, as distinguished from interstate commerce, to register with the state. The statute further provided, in effect: "Every contract made by a foreign corporation before it shall have complied with the provisions of this statute shall be wholly void on its behalf but shall be enforceable against it." What would be the result of S Company's lawsuit against B? Explain.

11. M Company, a Michigan corporation, manufactured articles and merchandise used all over the United States. Its business in Massachusetts was handled by S who operated a large jobbing house, purchasing from various manufacturers, in-

cluding M Company, and reselling to retailers in Massachusetts. M Company did not own or control S's business nor have any voice in S's management. M Company maintained no office in Massachusetts, was never licensed to do business in Massachusetts, and paid no taxes to that state. Four times a year salesmen from the home office of M Company canvassed the retail trade in Massachusetts, instructing customers in the most efficient use of M Company's products, and taking orders. Such orders were immediately turned over to S by the salesmen, and S filled the orders from his own warehouse with merchandise previously purchased by S from M Company. The state of Massachusetts levied taxes against M Company on the business thus done and added heavy penalties on the ground that M Company was doing business in Massachusetts without having obtained the necessary license. Was the state correct? Explain. (Modified from A.I.C.P.A., May 24- 11).

12. Together with a number of other persons, some signing the same paper before and some after B, B signed a paper agreeing to subscribe and pay for 15 shares of $50 par value common stock to be issued by a proposed business corporation, the money payable on call of the promoters, balance payable upon formation of the corporation. The paper stated that the subscription was irrevocable. At various times thereafter, meetings of the subscribers were held, with B attending, for arrangement of some of the preliminary details. Expenses incurred were paid out of a fund raised through each subscriber paying a proportionate amount on his subscription. In this way B paid in $187.50. Some time thereafter, B notified the promoters of withdrawal of his subscription and of his determination to go no further in the enterprise. The promoters replied that they refused to release him and would hold him liable on his original agreement. The remaining parties proceeded with their preparations, procured a charter, and organized the corporation. The corporation sued B for the balance due on his subscription. B counterclaimed for return of the $187.50 he had paid. What result? Explain.

13. An accountant rendered services connected with the reorganization of a corporation. His services were fairly and reasonably worth $5,000 and the accountant rendered a bill to the reorganized corporation for that amount. Instead of paying the accountant in cash, the directors authorized the issuance to him of 100 shares of fully paid, nonassessable, $100 par stock of the corporation. The accountant accepted the stock as payment in full for his services. Later the corporation was adjudged insolvent. Could the accountant be held liable for the benefit of outside creditors? Explain. (Modified from A.I.C.P.A., Nov. 21-10).

14. A business corporation had issued an outstanding 1,500 shares. One hundred shares were issued to D, and were pledged by him with the corporation as collateral security for an obligation of $9,000 owed by him to the corporation. Fifteen years later, this obligation together with a considerable accumulation of unpaid interest had been in default for several years, whereupon the five directors unanimously voted to foreclose the pledged stock and transfer it to the corporation, as permitted by the terms of the pledge. At the same meeting, the five directors unanimously authorized the sale of the one hundred shares to P at $80 per share. P was the president of the corporation, one of the directors, and owned 656 shares. No prior notice of the sale was given and the company had no need for additional capital. M, an owner of 16 shares had at various times expressed dissatisfaction with the volume of business done by the corporation and the profits it was making, but had never previously objected to any particular decision of the directors. However, after the August meeting M brought an equity action against the corporation and the directors to have the sale to P declared void. The evidence indicated that the small block oS shares could not have been sold for more than $8 per share. What should be the result of M's lawsuit? Explain.

15. A business corporation was organized for the purpose of constructing and operating a radio broadcasting station. The incorporators, A, B, and C subscribed equally for the entire stock, fully paid

for their shares in cash and other property, and as sole shareholders, elected themselves as directors and officers. Fifteen years later, the corporation engaged an appraisal firm which appraised all assets at their current valuation, and reported to the directors that the assets were worth $20,000 more than the value shown on the books of the corporation. The directors, therefore, had the book value increased by $20,000 and balanced that with a like increase in the surplus account. The balance sheet of the corporation five years after this, showed a surplus of $5,000. At the end of the following year, net profits totaled $12,000 whereupon the directors declared and paid out a dividend totaling $6,000. Two months later, the three shareholders sold their stock to other persons, who, as the new shareholders, directors, and officers, instituted an action in the name of the corporation against A and B to recover the dividend payment of $6,000. What result? Explain.

16. From 1903 to 1916 the Ford Motor Company was phenomenally profitable. Starting in 1911, a regular dividend of 5 percent per month was paid, and in addition special dividends were declared and paid from time to time. In 1916, the board of directors decided to continue the regular dividend (5 percent per month) but to discontinue declaring and paying special dividends. Dodge, a minority shareholder, sued for a court decree to force the Ford Company to pay a larger dividend. Admitted facts included the following: (1) The corporation had a surplus of $112 million and yearly net profits of $60 million; (2) After completion of expansion plans approved by the board of directors and payment of the regular 5 percent dividend, there would remain a surplus of $20 million; (3) It had been the policy of the company for a considerable time to reduce the selling price annually while keeping up or improving its quality; (4) The 1916 plans called for a reduction in price of $80 per car, although the total plant output could have been sold at the previous price; (5) Henry Ford stated . . . "My ambition is to employ still more men, to spread the benefits of this industrial system to the greatest possible number, to help them build up their lives and their homes. To do this we are putting the greatest share of our profits back in the business." What should be the result of Dodge's lawsuit? Explain.

17. The stock structure of a corporation consisted of both preferred stock and common stock, both having a par value of $100. The charter of the corporation provided:

The holders of the preferred stock shall be entitled to receive when and as declared and the corporation shall be bound to pay a yearly cumulative dividend of 6 percent before any dividend shall be set apart on the common stock.

No dividend was declared on either preferred or common stock until, at the end of the fourth year, a dividend of $24 per share was declared on the preferred stock, covering the current year and all arrearages, and at the same time a dividend of $12 per share was declared on the common stock. There was sufficient surplus for payment of the declared dividends.

(a) Would a common shareholder be able to restrain payment of the declared dividend to the preferred shareholders? Explain.

(b) Would a preferred shareholder be able to restrain payment of the declared dividend to the common shareholders? Explain.

18. On December 2 the board of directors of a business corporation passed a resolution declaring a lawful 12 percent dividend. By the terms of the resolution the dividend was divided into four equal installments of 3 percent each, payable on February 15, May 15, August 15, and November 15 of the following year. The first installment was duly paid. On May 6, however, the directors decided to purchase additional property and equipment for expansion of the business of the corporation, and also decided to increase reserves for losses. Both decisions were reasonable. To carry them out, the directors unanimously adopted a resolution amending the December 2 resolution to read that the total rate of the dividend by 3 percent payable February 15. The resolution, as amended, conformed to what had been done up

to May 5, inasmuch as 3 percent had already been paid on February 15. On May 15, X, who had been a registered shareholder of the corporation for over 2 years, protested the action of the directors in amending the December 2 resolution, and demanded that he be paid a 3 percent dividend for the May installment. X made similar demands on August 15 and November 15. The directors disregarded each demand and refused to pay anything further. On November 21, X sued the corporation to recover the amount of a 9 percent dividend on his shares. What result? Explain.

19. On February 1, D, a registered shareholder in a business corporation, indorsed his share certificate for 50 shares ($100 par value), by merely signing his name, and delivered it to C as security for an eight-month loan of $1,000 from C to D. No attempt was made to transfer the shares on the books of the corporation at any time, by any person, although the corporation had knowledge of the pledge.

(a) At the annual shareholders meeting held May 15, who was entitled to vote the 50 shares?

(b) On June 1, the board of directors declared a legally valid dividend of $6 per share, payable on July 1. (1) Immediately after declaration of the dividend, C requested that the corporation treasurer send the dividend check to C to apply on D's debt. The corporation treasurer refused and on July 1, before any checks had been sent out, C sued the corporation to recover the amount of the dividend due on D's stock. Was C entitled to recover? Explain. (2) On July 1, C not having demanded from the corporation that it send the dividend check to him, the corporation sent the dividend check to D who immediately cashed it. C demanded from D the money so received to apply on the debt and, upon D's refusal to pay, C sued D on July 3. D proved that no part of the debt was due until October 1. Was C entitled to recover from D in the July 3 lawsuit? Explain.

(c) On September 5, without permission from D, C sold, indorsed and delivered to B the certificate for 50 shares. On October 1, when D came to repay the loan to C, D learned for the first time of C's wrongful sale of the stock. B was able to prove that he bought the stock honestly, thinking C was the owner, paid C $5,000, its fair value, and knew nothing of the transaction between D and C. B still had the certificate he had obtained from C, B not having registered the transfer. Stock in the corporation being closely held, D was unable to purchase any of the stock anywhere. (1) D offered B $1,000, the amount of the loan for which the stock had been pledged, and demanded return of the certificate. When B refused, D sued B to recover the certificate. Was D entitled to recover from B upon paying $1,000 into court for B? Explain. (2) D offered B what the latter had paid for the stock and demanded return of the certificate. When B refused, D sued B to recover the certificate. Was D entitled to recover from B upon paying $5,000 into court for B? Explain.

The Sale and Lease of Goods: Contract Formation

The Sale and Lease of Goods: Contract Formation

I. Introduction to Uniform Commercial Code

A. Historical Development

The Uniform Commercial Code is a compilation of rules and standards drafted to govern business transactions. It evolved from early English contract law. As England evolved from an agricultural economy to a trading economy, traditional contract law was not sufficient to resolve trading disputes or to provide certainty of meaning of legal concepts important to parties attempting to draft binding business agreements. As a result of this inadequacy, merchants developed an entirely separate and distinct body of commercial law known as the "Law Merchant." It established a separate system for hearing disputes between merchants who voluntarily submitted to the merchants' court's jurisdiction. Its success resulted in its adoption by the common law courts of England.

In 1853, the English principles of commercial sales were codified as the Sales of Goods Act. This Act lead the way for the drafting and enactment of the Uniform Sales Act by the National Conference of Commissioners for Uniform State Laws ("NCCUSL") and The American Law Institute ("ALI"). In 1951, NCCUSL and the ALI modernized the Uniform Sales Act and incorporated it into the first draft of the Uniform Commercial Code ("UCC"). The Uniform Sales Act became Article 2 of the UCC.

B. The Scope of the UCC

The UCC consists of ten substantive articles, each covering a significant portion of commercial law. A separate article governs construction and application of the Code as a whole. The Uniform Commercial Code has been adopted in all or part by all 50 states. The Uniform Commercial Code is not a federal law. It is a proposal to each state suggesting that the commerce of each state would be served if each state adopted a uniform approach to governing certain types of commercial transactions. Many states have made minor changes to various Code sections in response to local concerns.

The articles of the Uniform Commercial Code cover the following material:

Article 1	Construction, application, general definitions and principals of interpretation.
Article 2	Sales
Article 2A	Leases
Article 3	Commercial Paper
Article 4	Bank Deposits and Collections
Article 4A	Funds Transfers
Article 5	Letters of Credit
Article 6	Bulk Transfers
Article 7	Warehouse Receipts, Bills of Lading and other Documents of Title
Article 8	Investment Securities
Article 9	Secured Transactions, Sales of Accounts, Contract Rights and Chattel Paper

C. Judicial Interpretation of the Code

Courts traditionally interpret and apply law narrowly. The UCC significantly changes this by commanding that the Code shall be liberally construed and applied to promote the underlying purposes and policies of the Code.[1]

The underlying purposes and policies of the Code are to simplify, clarify and modernize the law governing commercial transactions; to permit the continued expansion of commercial practices through custom, usage and agreement of the parties; and to make uniform law among the various jurisdictions.[2]

The Code further retains all principles of law and equity, including the law merchant and the law relative to capacity contract, principle and agent, estoppel, fraud, misrepresentation, duress, coercion, mistake, and bankruptcy unless displaced by a particular provision of the UCC. This means that when studying the legal environment, one must take into account the provisions of common law and equity as well as the terms and provisions of the Code.

In short, the underlying goal of the UCC is to promote commerce. The ends of commerce are served when the parties are confident in the rules governing commerce as well as in their consistent application.

II. Article 2— Sales of Goods

A. The Scope of Article 2

Article 2 of the UCC governs sales of goods. The most common type of business transaction is a sale of personal property. A sale under Article 2 is the passing of title of goods from a buyer to a seller for a price. Passing title is the transfer of a seller's right to own and possess the goods to the buyer.

It is very important to be mindful of the Article 2 definition of goods. This is important because it determines whether or not Article 2 of the Code governs the transaction. Under Article 2 of the Code, goods are defined as all things that are movable at the time of identification of the goods to the contract for sale.

By definition, goods also include the unborn young of animals, growing crops and other identified things attached to realty that are to be severed from realty subject to certain provisions in Article 2.

Goods must both be existing and identified to the contract before any interest in them can pass. Goods which are not both existing and identified are deemed "future" goods. Certain goods associated with real property will be considered goods even though they are fixed to real property. Oil, gas and other minerals that are to be severed by the seller will be considered goods.

In addition, things attached to realty which can be severed without material harm to the real property can fall into the definition of goods.

Investment securities (which are governed by Article 8 of the Code) and the money in which the price for the subject matter of the contract are specifically excluded from the definition of goods.

It is important to distinguish the sale of goods from the sale of services. While there is no clear cut rule, one must look to the totality of the circumstances to determine whether or not a transaction was substantially a sale of goods. A meal at a restaurant would fall within the definition of goods under Article 2 even though the buyer is also purchasing the services of the restaurant staff and the temporary enjoyment of the atmosphere of the location.

Article 2 does not govern gifts, leases, or bailments because those transactions do not involve the transfer of title to goods in return for a price. Moreover, the Code specifically states

---

1. UCC Sec. 1-102(1).
2. UCC Sec. 1-102(2).

Example. An automobile dealership is a merchant with respect to automobiles. But, if the dealer were to sell used furniture from its showroom, the dealership would not be a merchant with respect to the furniture. On the other hand, variety stores are merchants with respect to a myriad of items, ranging from clothes to lawn equipment. ☐

that a sale of an investment security is governed by Article 8 of the UCC, rather than Article 2. In addition, any transaction intended to operate only as a security transaction is specifically excluded from the coverage of Article 2. This excludes from Article 2 all sales of mortgages on personal property. But, this does not exempt from Article 2 conditional sales contracts so long as title to the good passes to the buyer even if the seller retains a security interest under Article 9. The key is to focus on whether the buyer received title to a "good" in exchange for a price.

Article 2 does not supersede other state statutes regulating the sales of goods to special classes of buyers such as farmers or consumers. For example, many states have adopted the Uniform Consumer Credit Code which regulates financial transactions involving extensions of credit to individuals for personal, family or household purposes.

The price to be paid by the buyer to the seller may be in money, goods, real property, personal property or services.

B. The Significance of Merchant Status

Article 2 employs special provisions when a sale involves a merchant. Merchant status can be acquired in one of three ways. First, one can be a merchant by dealing in the kind of goods that are the subject of the sale. Second, one is deemed a merchant if she holds herself out as having knowledge or skill peculiar to the practices or goods involved in the transaction. Third, one will acquire merchant status by hiring a merchant to act on one's behalf.

C. Formation of a Sales Contract

I. THE REQUIREMENT OF GOOD FAITH

Unless the Code has a provision to the contrary, the standard law of contracts applies to contracts for sales of goods. The Code requires that all parties to these contracts exercise good faith. Good faith is defined as "honesty in fact in the conduct or transaction concerned."[3] A duty of good faith is imposed on every transaction arising under the UCC. While the Code's definition of good faith does not identify specific boundaries of conduct, it does permit courts to examine all facts of circumstances of a given transaction to determine if the parties conducted themselves fairly and honestly. This standard further requires parties to behave in a fair and honest manner when the general circumstances would lead a reasonably prudent and honest person to question the propriety of a transaction. Article 2 further requires that merchants observe "reasonable standards of fair dealing in the trade."[4]

2. OFFER

Consistent with contracts falling outside the scope of Article 2, a contract for the sale of goods requires both an offer and an acceptance. But under the UCC, mere discussions and correspondence may lead to the existence of an offer. A contract for the sale of goods may be formed in any manner sufficient to show the existence of an agreement.[5]

---

3. UCC Sec. 1-201(19).
4. UCC Sec. 2-103(1)(b).
5. UCC Sec. 2-204(1)

Example.   Sam agrees to sell his 5 horses to Mary. They do not discuss price. If a reasonable person could conclude from the circumstances that the parties intended to form a contract, the missing price term will not prevent the formation of the contract because this is a contract for the sale of goods. A court would determine a reasonable price. ☐

This includes proving the existence of a contract through conduct of the parties demonstrating the existence of an agreement.5 The Code does not require that the parties be able to identify the exact moment that a contract was made.[6]

a.   Filling Open Terms

In keeping with the Code's underlying the purpose to promote commerce, Article 2 liberalizes certain contract formalities. For instance, a contract will not fail for indefiniteness if the parties have demonstrated an intent to make a contract and there is a reasonably certain basis for awarding an appropriate remedy for breach.[7]   The Code implements this process through what have become known as "gap fillers." The concept behind gap fillers is to prevent agreements from failing for the lack of a technical requirement. The interests of commerce will be promoted if a binding agreement can be found when two parties intend to enter into a binding agreement and there is any reasonably certain basis for granting a remedy in the event of a breach.

Using "gap fillers," the Code will supply certain missing terms relating to, among other things, price, delivery, passage of title, risk of loss, remedies and warranties.

The Code does not infringe on the parties' freedom of contract, but merely supplies terms that the parties may fail to include. Freedom of contract is expressly recognized and preserved in the UCC by permitting parties to vary Code provisions by agreement unless the Code specifically prohibits such a variation. An example of one of the few prohibitions would be parties attempting to opt out of the Code's provisions requiring good faith, diligence and reasonableness.

I.   OPEN PRICE TERMS

The material terms in every contract include the identification of the parties, an adequate description of the subject matter of the agreement, and the price to be paid by the purchaser. While price is a material term, the Code permits the parties to the contract to leave the price term open to be agreed upon later.[8] For instance, parties may agree to have the price fixed by a market standard or to be determined by a third party. Market fluctuations represent the most common reason why the parties will leave a price term open.

If the parties intended to form a contract for sale even though the price was not settled, the Code mechanism will determine the price.[9] The price will be a "reasonable price" at the time of delivery if:

(a) nothing is said as to the price; or

(b) the price is left to be agreed by the parties and they fail to agree; or

(c) the price is to be fixed in terms of some agreed market or other standard as set or recorded by a third person or agency not so set or recorded.

6. UCC Sec. 2-204(2).
7. UCC Sec. 2-204(3).
8. UCC Sec. 2-305.
9. UCC Sec. 2-305(1).

If the agreement permits one of the parties to set a price and that party fails to do so or the price is not fixed through the fault of one of the parties, the other party may, at its option, treat the contract as canceled or that party itself may fix a reasonable price. [10]

But, if the parties do not intend to be bound to a contract unless a price can be fixed or agreed upon and the price is not fixed or agreed upon, then there is no contract. If that happens, the buyer must return any goods already received. If the goods are not available for return, the buyer must pay the reasonable value for those goods at the time of delivery and the seller must return any portion of the price paid on account.

2. OPEN QUANTITY TERMS

As with an open price term, the parties may form a contract without fixing a specific quantity. The most common forms of open quantity contracts are requirements and output contracts. A requirements contract is one in which the buyer promises to purchase all of its requirements of a given commodity from a specific seller. An output contract is one in which a seller agrees to sell its entire output to a particular buyer. A requirements or output contract protects the promisor against uncertainties in demand or production. Therefore, the promisor is not obligated to buy or sell a fixed quantity but rather all that it may be able to use or to produce.[11]

In order to curb abuses, the Code requires that the parties conduct themselves in good faith which includes refraining from unreasonable deviation from any stated estimate of an output or requirement. In absence of such an estimate, there must not be any unreasonable or disproportionate variation from comparable prior output or requirements.

---

10. UCC Sec.2-305(3).
11. UCC Sec. 2-306.

3. OPEN DELIVERY TERMS[12]

Unless the parties agree otherwise, the place for delivery of goods is the seller's place of business. If the seller has no place of business, then the place of delivery is the seller's residence. There is a different rule if a contract for the sale of identified goods involves an item located at a specific place known by both the buyer and seller at the time they entered into the contract. If the buyer and the seller both have the knowledge that the subject of the contract is at a different location, then that location will be deemed the place for delivery. If the contract does not state an exact time the goods are to be shipped, the Code requires that shipment or delivery must take place within a reasonable time.[13]

Unless otherwise agreed, all goods subject to a sales contract must be tendered in a single delivery unless the circumstances give either party the right to make or demand delivery in lots. Payment is due only upon a proper tender of delivery. If the tender of delivery is in lots, payments may be apportioned accordingly.[14]

4. OPEN TIME OF PAYMENT TERMS[15]

Unless the parties otherwise agree, payment is due at the time and place at which the buyer is to receive the goods. This is the rule even if the place of shipment is the place of delivery. Payment must be made in cash or a commercially reasonable substitute, including checks. But, if the seller demands cash, the buyer must be given a reasonable amount of time to obtain legal tender.

5. OPEN DURATION TERMS[16]

If the parties have developed a continuing relationship without a stated time of termi-

---

12. UCC Sec. 2-308.
13. UCC Sec. 2-309(1).
14. UCC Sec. 2-307.
15. UCC Sec. 2-310.
16. UCC Sec. 2-309.

Example. Pat, the owner of Pat's Stereo Hut, offers to sell a Magna Wheel compact disk player to Vanna for $499. Pat promises in writing to keep the offer open for 1 week. During that period, Pat may not revoke the offer. If Pat failed to state a time period in the written offer, the court could insert one so long as it did not exceed 3 months. ▢

nation, the party desiring to terminate such a continuing contractual relationship must give reasonable notice in good faith prior to terminating the relationship. Any agreement dispensing with notification of a party is invalid if its operation would be unconscionable.

6. OPEN SHIPMENT TERMS

If the contract requires the seller to ship the goods, but no shipping details are set forth in the contract, the seller must ship the goods using good faith and commercial reasonableness appropriate for those goods and the buyer's known circumstances.

Unless otherwise agreed, specifications relating to assortments of goods are at the buyer's option. The buyer is subject to the Code's requirement of good faith and commercial reasonableness in selecting the assortment.

Merchant's Firm Offer

Oftentimes, a potential buyer will discuss the purchase of a good from a merchant but will not desire to enter into a contract at that time. The buyer may wish to compare the price and quality features of similar products offered by different merchants. A buyer may yet to have established the financing or other resources needed to fund the purchase. Recall that under traditional contract law, an offer may be withdrawn any time prior to acceptance. Holding an offer open for a specified period time under traditional contract law requires the payment of consideration. This forms an option contract.

In order to provide buyers and sellers a vehicle to keep offers open for a specified period of time without the payment of considera-

tion, the Code provides what is known as "merchants firm offer." [17] An offer by a merchant to buy or sell goods can be irrevocably held open for a period not to exceed 3 months if the offer is in writing and it is signed by the merchant.

If the merchant is a seller and the buyer provides a form containing firm offer language for the seller's signature, the "firm offer" form must be signed separately by the seller. During the period of the firm offer, the offer cannot be revoked by the party against whom it is being used, usually a merchant-seller. Under the Code, "signed" includes any symbol executed or adopted by a party with the present intent to authenticate the writing. This means that any mark made by someone intending for it to be his signature, will have it serve as his signature. This will include initials, rubber stamps, and the like. The signature issue must be considered when one evaluates a merchant's firm offer for validity.

3. ACCEPTANCE OF OFFERS

a. In General

Article 2 departs from traditional contract law regarding methods of acceptance of contract offers in a number of ways. Under the Code, unless the offeror indicates otherwise in an unambiguous fashion, an offer to make a contract shall be construed as inviting acceptance in any manner and by any medium reasonable under the circumstances. [18] As a general rule, this makes acceptance effective upon dis-

17. UCC Sec. 2-205.
18. UCC Sec. 2-206(1).

Example. Mary's exotic pet shop orders 500 pounds of Acme monkey chow for prompt shipment from National Pet Foods (NPF). NPF is out of the Acme brand, but instead ships 500 pounds of a more expensive brand of dry monkey food at a lower price. NPF's prompt shipment in response to the order was an acceptance of the offer. Shipping the wrong product was a breach of the contract that was just formed by its acceptance of the offer. NPF could have prevented this breach by seasonally notifying Mary that the shipment was merely an accommodation. Accommodation shipments do not form contracts. They represent offers to potential purchasers. □

patch of the acceptance rather than upon its arrival. Under common law contracts, an offeree could bind the offeror immediately upon sending her acceptance only if she transmitted her acceptance by a means expressly authorized by the offeror or if the offeror was silent as to the means to be used, by using the same means employed by the offeror to communicate the offer.

Under the Code, one may accept an offer by telephone even though the offer itself was sent by mail. In addition, the Code permits an order or other offer to buy goods for prompt or current shipment to be accepted by a prompt promise to ship the requested goods or by the prompt or current shipment of conforming or nonconforming goods, but such a shipment of nonconforming goods does not constitute an acceptance if the seller seasonably notifies the buyer that the shipment is offered only as an accommodation to the buyer.

A seller must be careful when shipping goods in response to an order. A shipment of nonconforming goods represents an acceptance of a contract and an immediate breach of the contract unless the seller seasonably notifies the buyer that the nonconforming shipment was made as an accommodation to the buyer. An accommodation shipment serves as a counter offer to the buyer that can be rejected by the buyer.[19]

What is the value of permitting a seller to ship nonconforming goods as an accommodation

to a buyer? This permits a seller who is out of a particular good to choose a reasonable substitute for the buyer's approval. If the buyer needs the good promptly and agrees to the substitution, such a shipment benefits the buyer and the seller. If the buyer is not happy with the substituted goods, the buyer may reject the entire shipment.

If the seller chooses to accept the contract by shipping conforming or nonconforming goods, the seller must notify the buyer of the shipment within a reasonable period of time. Otherwise the buyer may treat the offer as lapsed, although the buyer may not do so until a reasonable time has passed. The seller's act of shipping goods in response to an offer is sufficient proof that the seller intended to accept the offer.

b. Battle of the Forms

With its relaxed provisions regarding contract formalities, contract formation is much easier under the Code. This is consistent with its purpose of promoting commerce. Such flexibility makes it easier for buyers and sellers to do business.

Recall that the common law mirror image rule governing acceptance of offers requires that an acceptance of an offer must reflect that offer exactly. Under this rule, different or additional terms of acceptance are deemed a rejection of the original offer and a counter offer.

The Code alters the mirror image rule with respect to additional terms to a contract offer.

19. UCC Sec. 2-206(1)(b).

Example. Burton's Manufacturing sends a purchase order to Simpson Supply for 1,000 feet of wire. The form is silent regarding private arbitration of disputes. Simpson responds with a sales acknowledgment form that contains an arbitration clause. The arbitration clause would not be considered to be a material change to the original offer. Simpson ships the wire. Burton's receives the wire and pays for it. A dispute develops.

First, there is a contract between the parties. Second, because Burton failed to object to the addition of the arbitration clause within a reasonable time, it became part of the contract. Therefore, it will govern the dispute. ▢

* * *

Example. Referring to the previous example, assume Burton is a non-merchant. In this case, Burton is free to ignore the additional terms as suggestions. The additional terms will not become part of the contract unless Burton specifically agrees to them. ▢

Under the Code, a definite and seasonable expression of acceptance or a written confirmation which is sent within a reasonable time will operate as an acceptance even though it states additional or different terms from those offered or agreed upon unless the acceptance is expressly made conditional to the other party's approval to such different or additional terms.[20] So, what is done with the conflicting or additional terms stated in the acceptance?

The Code's solution requires the placement of the parties to the contract into one of two categories.

Category 1. When both parties are merchants; or

Category 2. When one or both of the parties is a non-merchant.

In Category 1, a merchant seller and a merchant buyer are attempting to form a contract. In this situation, the offeree makes an unequivocal statement that the offer is accepted, but in doing so, inserts additional or different terms to the original offer. This often occurs when merchants respond to each other on their own pre-printed order forms. Seldom do these forms contain identical terms. When an offeree responds to a pre-printed offer form with an acceptance presented in a pre-printed form of its own, a conflict exists as to the final terms of the contract. This situation is often called "the battle of the forms."

To resolve this problem between merchants, additional or different terms contained in the acceptance of the offeree shall become a part of the contract unless:

1. The offer expressly limits acceptance to the terms of the offer;
2. They materially alter the original offer (A material alteration means the result would cause unreasonable surprise or work an undue hardship on the other party.); or
3. The offeror fails to notify the offeree of its objection to the additional of different terms within a reasonable time after notice of them is received.

In Category 2, neither of the parties or only one of the parties to the contract is a merchant. Remember that the offeree has already communicated an unequivocal statement of acceptance of the original offer. In this case, additional or different terms contained in the acceptance shall be construed as proposals for changes to the contract. The offeror is under no obligation to accept or comply with the proposal for additional or different terms.

20. UCC Sec. 2-207(1).

Example. Hardy Company orally agrees to buy 1,000 muffler bearings from Crawford Inc. for $1.00 each. Crawford confirms in writing the order for 1,000 units at $1.00 each. Hardy received the confirmation on January 5. On January 30, Hardy refuses the shipment, claiming that the order was not enforceable because it was not in writing. Crawford will prevail because Hardy did not object to the confirmation within 10 days of its receipt. □

The most expedient way to prevent additional and different terms from becoming a part of the original offer is to make the original offer subject to an acceptance only upon the terms of the original offer. By the same token, an offeree may state that its acceptance is conditioned upon the offeror's acceptance the different or additional terms.

The advantages of this section of the Code are speed and convenience in forming contracts for the sale of goods. Merchants may form contracts quickly without many of the problems caused by common law technicalities. Minor terms, such as shipping arrangements, may be resolved in the period following contract formation, rather than being stumbling blocks to contract formation.

4. FORMALITIES

a. Consideration and Contract Modification

The UCC modifies the traditional contract law rules requiring the presence of "bargained for" consideration. Under traditional contract law, consideration must flow between the parties to the contract for a contract modification to be valid. The UCC makes contract modification more flexible by permitting a contract for the sale of goods to be modified without consideration. All parties still must agree to the terms of the contract modification. Once a contract is formed, neither party has an obligation to agree to a modification. Also, keep in mind that all modifications must be sought in good faith.[21]

b. Statute of Frauds

The UCC has retained the traditional contract law Statute of Frauds. This requires certain contracts to be evidenced by a signed writing or memorandum identifying the parties, nature of goods, price and quantity, unless covered by open term provisions.[22]

With respect to the sale of goods, the Statute of Frauds provision in the Code requires that any contract for the sale of goods of $500 or more be evidenced by a writing or memorandum. It also requires that a contract modification resulting in a contract for the sale of goods for $500 or more be evidenced by a writing or memorandum signed by the party against whom it will be enforced.

For sales between merchants, if one party sends a written confirmation of an oral agreement within a reasonable time and the other party does not object within 10 days, both parties are bound as if each had signed the memorandum.[23]

There are exceptions to the Statute of Frauds defense. Some contracts for goods equal to or exceeding $500 in amount can be enforced even though they are not evidenced by a writing. They are as follows:

1. An oral contract for specially manufactured goods. These goods must not be suitable for resale in the ordinary course of business and the seller must have substantially started to manufacturer the goods or has

---

21. UCC Sec. 2-209.
22. UCC Sec. 2-201.
23. UCC Sec. 2-201.

Example.   Michael orders a special pair of custom made, glow in the dark dancing shoes with the letters "M J" on them. No statute of fraud defense would be available to Michael once the manufacturing process commenced. ☐

* * *

Example.   Scheer Ltd. orally agrees to buy 200 turkeys from Nick's Turkey Farm for $6.00 each. Scheer takes delivery of a shipment of 100 turkeys. Scheer then refuses to pay the $600 due Nick for the first part of the order. Scheer will not be able to use the statute of frauds defense due to its acceptance of the partial shipment. But, it will have a valid defense as to the rest of the order.

made commitments with others so that the manufacturer may commence.

2. Admitting in court documents or in a court of law that a contract existed.

3. Accepting or receiving all or part of the goods to a purported contract will result in an enforceable contract to the extent the goods are accepted or received.

4. A buyer making part payment for goods makes a purported contract enforceable to the extent payment has been made for the goods.

C.   THE PAROLE EVIDENCE RULE

If a contract has been reduced to writing, the Parole Evidence Rule as adopted in the Code prevents one from introducing into evidence prior or contemporaneous oral statements for the purpose of changing the meaning of the writing. But, in some circumstances, such evidence or statements may be introduced to explain vague terms or inconsistencies within a written contract.

For instance, the parties' prior course of dealing may be introduced as well as trade usage to explain the agreement. But if specific language in the contract is contrary to trade usage or prior dealing, the contract terms will prevail.[24]

Courts will examine the parties' course of performance in searching for the meaning of vague terms in a contract. Course of perfor-

mance is the conduct of the parties during the term of the contract. The UCC strives for consistency in the behavior of the parties.

It is also important to be mindful of the prior course of dealing and trade usage when entering into contracts. Course of dealing refers to conduct of the parties in previous transactions between them. A court may interpret a contract in light of prior conduct of the parties when it appears to have formed the basis for an understanding between the parties.

Trade usage is a practice commonly observed in a place, vocation, or trade. An applicable usage of trade in the place where any part of performance is to occur shall be used in interpreting the agreement as to that part of performance.[25] Trade usage or customs may catch new enterprises off guard. For instance, some industries sell on the basis of estimates by trade custom. This could result in a shortfall for an industry novice. Such a result could be prevented by inserting language clearly stating that the terms of the contract govern over trade usage or custom.

When there are problems in interpreting contracts, the courts apply these rules in the following order:

1.   The express terms of the contract.
2.   Course of performance.
3.   Course of dealing.
4.   Usage of the trade or customs.

---

24. UCC Sec. 2-205, 2-208.

25. UCC Sec. 1-205(5).

5. UNCONSCIONABILITY

Unconscionability is a doctrine that originated at common law. It describes a contract or a contract provision that is so one-sided that is shocks the conscience of the court. The drafters of the UCC chose to adopt this doctrine for interpreting contracts under Article 2.[26]

The code permits a court to examine each clause of a contract for unconscionability. The court will examine each questionable term of a contract to see if it was unconscionable at the time it was made. Subsequent events and misfortunes experienced by any of the parties are not relevant in determining unconscionability. The key is to examine the contract at the time it was made. If any part of the contract was unconscionable, the court has three options:

1. The court can refuse to enforce the entire contract.

2. The court can refuse to enforce the unconscionable clause of the contract but enforce the rest of the contract.

3. The court can limit application of the unconscionable clause to avoid any undesirable result.

With society's interest in consumer protection rising to a higher level in recent years, courts have become increasingly active in application of this doctrine. The existence of an uneven bargaining position will increase a court's likelihood that it will grant a remedy under this theory.

6. AUCTIONS

A sale by auction presents many of the same problems and issues as other transactions in goods, but also involves issues peculiar to auctions. All bids at auctions are offers to buy made by those who attend the auction. The auctioneer is the offeree or the agent for the offeree. The auctioneer is generally at liberty to accept or reject any and all offers.

At an auction, an offer is accepted and a sale is completed by the fall of the hammer or in any other customary manner.[27] The auctioneer must manifest a willingness to accept the offer thus forming a contract with the highest bidder. If a new bid is made while the hammer is falling, the auctioneer is entitled to reopen the bidding at the auctioneer's discretion. Because the auctioneer is an offeree and has the power either to accept or reject bids, she will be under no duty as a general rule to sell any item, even if it has been placed on the auction block and the bidding has begun.

As a general rule, an auctioneer may withdraw an item at any time. A bidder may retract a bid at any time prior to acceptance. But, if the auction was advertised or the auctioneer stated explicitly that the auction was to be "without reserve," once an item has been placed on the block and at least one bid has been received on it, the item must be sold. An item can be removed from the block only if no bid is received after a reasonable time. This prevents the auctioneer from placing an item on the block and immediately removing it in order to end-run the without reserve rule.

Bidding at an auction by, on behalf of, or at the request of the seller is forbidden unless the seller gives notice that this right has been reserved by the seller. If an auctioneer knowingly receives a bid in violation of this rule, the buyer of any item has the option to avoid the sale or to take the goods at the last good faith bid before the seller began bidding. This is intended to prevent a seller from inflating bids artificially or from circumventing the rule concerning auctions without reserve. Keep in mind that this limitation does not apply to court ordered sales.

---

26. UCC Sec. 2-302.

27. UCC Sec. 2-328.

III. Leasing Goods under Article 2A

In recent years, both consumers and businesses increasingly have opted to lease goods rather than buy them. Examples include the lease of automobiles, computers, furniture and construction equipment. Changes in the tax laws as well as financing alternatives are partially responsible for the growth in the leasing sector. Despite the dramatic growth of the lease as a substitute for purchase, a comprehensive body of law governing personal property leasing transactions did not exist until recently.

Each lease involves a lease agreement. A lease agreement is the understanding of the parties regarding the transfer of the right to possession and use of the goods that are the subject of the lease. Each lease involves a lessor, the person who sells the right of possession and use of the goods under a lease agreement, and the lease, the person who acquires the right to possession and use of the goods.

It is important to distinguish leasing of goods from leasing real property. The Uniform Commercial Code does not govern transactions in real property unless they fit within the minor exceptions involving certain goods attached to real property. While Article 2 of the UCC governs "Transactions in Goods," the thrust of Article 2 is sales rather than lease transactions. In addition, Article 9 of the UCC, which governs security interests in personal property, governs only those personal property leases intended as collateral security.

In response to a need for a uniform law governing transactions involving the lease of personal property, the ALI and the NCCUSL drafted and approved Article 2A of the UCC entitled "Leases" in 1987.

Article 2A applies to "any transaction, regardless of form, which creates a lease."[28] The Code defines a lease as "a transfer of the right to possession and use of goods for a term in return for consideration."[29]

Article 2A tracks Article 2 of the Code closely in many respects. It employs the more liberal contract formation and performance principles of Article 2. It contains a Statute of Frauds, a Parole Evidence Rule, a firm offer rule, warranty provisions and risk of loss provisions. In addition, Article 2A includes rules governing the assignability of leases, subsequent leases, sale or sublease of the goods by the lessee, and the consequences of the leased goods becoming fixtures.

Article 2A recognizes the performance principles of anticipatory repudiation and adequate assurance in the same fashion as Article 2. The default provisions were drawn from Article 2. They include the concepts of acceptance, revocation of acceptance, rejection of goods, cure and buyer's and seller's remedies, including the lessee's right to cover and the lessor's right to dispose of goods by a substitute lease.

Several states have adopted Article 2A. It is being considered by a number of others.

IV. Transferring Goods from Seller to Buyer

A contract for the sale of goods requires the transfer of ownership to the goods from a seller to a buyer. In order for a sale to be consummated, the specific goods to be sold must be identified at some point. This is known as identification of goods to the contract.

A. Identification of Goods to the Contract

Identification of goods to the contract requires two things. First, the goods must be in existence. Second, the specific goods to be transferred from the seller to the buyer must

28. UCC Sec. 2A-102.

29. UCC Sec. 2A-103(1)(j).

be singled out.[30] Therefore, identification of goods is the designation of goods as the subject matter of the sales contract.

This designation may be accomplished in a number of different ways. For instance, one may record the serial number of an item, record the specific description of the item or merely separate it from the other items. Identification of the goods to the contract is important because it determines when the buyer has a right to obtain insurance on the goods, to recover from a third person who damages the goods and in some cases, to obtain possession of the goods from a seller who refuses to release them.

The Code also recognizes as "future goods" those goods not currently both existing and identified. Goods scheduled to be manufactured but yet not existing are deemed future goods.

I.   TIME AND MANNER OF IDENTIFICATION

As demonstrated by much of Article 2, if the parties fail to specifically designate a time and manner of identification of the goods to the contract, the Code will fill in the gaps.[31] In absence of an agreement by the parties, the following rules apply.

a. If the goods are already existing and identified, identification occurs when the contract is made.

b. If the goods are future goods, identification occurs when the goods are shipped, marked or otherwise designated by the seller as goods to which the contract refers.

c. Unborn young of animals are identified to the contract when they are conceived if the young are to be born within twelve months after contracting.

d. Growing crops are identified when they are planted if the plants are to be har-

vested within twelve months or the next normal harvesting season after contracting whichever is later.

2.   FUNGIBLE GOODS

How would one specifically identify 1,000 barrels of oil in an oil storage tank? How would one specifically identify the sale of 1,000 bushels of wheat in a grain storage silo? The Code responds to this dilemma by defining certain items as fungible goods. Fungible goods are goods in which every unit is exactly like the other units. Both stored oil and wheat represent fungible goods. Under Article 2, fungible goods may be identified as a specific portion, weight or quantity of an identified bulk or larger mass. To properly identify fungible goods, one must provide a specific location of the storage facility, including a tank number or storage unit number, and identify the quantity portion of the goods to be sold.

B. Passage of Title

The term title refers to a person's ownership rights in property. When title to a good passes from seller to buyer, the buyer is the owner of that property. In absence of an agreement, the Code will determine when title passes. Most cases involving the question of title fall into one of four situations: (1) transfer by shipment of goods, (2) transfer by delivery of goods, (3) transfer by delivery of documents of title, and (4) transfer without moving goods or delivering documents of title. The key question is at what point did the seller manifest an intent to transfer title to the buyer.

I.   TRANSFER BY SHIPMENT

Buyers often orders goods without stipulating the method of delivery. In these cases, the Code provides that title passes to the buyer upon shipment by the seller.[32]

---

30. UCC Sec. 2-105(2).
31. UCC Sec. 2-501.

---

32. UCC Sec. 4-201(2)(a).

2. TRANSFER BY DELIVERY

If the goods are to be moved from their location at the time of the contract and the contract specifies either the time or the place of delivery, or that delivery must be made by the seller, title will pass at the time and place of delivery.

3. TRANSFER BY DELIVERY OF DOCUMENTS OF TITLE

The term "documents of title" refers to documents that evidence ownership to goods that are in the possession of some third party, such as a warehouse operator or a common carrier. This third party is holding the goods for delivery to a person holding the documents. In some instances, the parties provide neither for shipment nor delivery of the subject goods, designating only delivery of documents of title. The parties may intend for the buyer to pick up the goods, or that the goods will be used or resold from that location at the time of the contract. In these instances, the Code provides that title passes at the time and place of delivery of the documents.[33]

4. TRANSFER WITHOUT MOVING THE GOODS OR DELIVERING DOCUMENTS OF TITLE

If the goods are not to be moved and documents of title are not to be delivered, title passes at the time and place the contract was formed.[34] If the parties are in different locations at that time, the place of contracting is generally considered to be the location of acceptance of contract.

5. PASSAGE OF TITLE TO FUTURE GOODS

With respect to future goods, the title passes to the buyer when the seller completes the duty of physically delivering the goods. But, if

the contract provides for shipment to the buyer pursuant to a "free on board–point of shipment" arrangement, title will pass at the time and place the goods are delivered to the carrier. If a "free on board–point of destination" arrangement has been made by the parties, title will pass at the time and place the goods are tendered at the specified destination.

6. PASSAGE OF TITLE FOR GOODS SOLD ON A TRIAL BASIS

a. Sale on Approval

A sale on approval permits the buyer to take items from a seller on a trial basis. So, it is not technically a sale until the buyer has decided to accept the goods. It is basically an offer to sell goods with a bailment created while the buyer has possession of the goods. Under the terms of a sale on approval, the buyer can return the goods within a specified period. If the buyer does so, the buyer must notify the seller. Title to the goods only passes to the buyer upon final acceptance of the goods. Prior to that, the buyer's creditors have no rights with respect to the goods because the buyer does not have an ownership interest in the goods.

The approval period can ripen into a sale. This can occur if the buyer acts in a fashion inconsistent with the seller's ownership rights, such as selling the goods during the trial period. In addition, the approval period can ripen into a sale if the buyer does not return the goods at the end of the trial period.

b. Sale or Return

Under a sale or return transaction, the seller delivers goods to the buyer with an understanding that the buyer may retain any portion of the goods and send back any portion of the goods during a specified term. But, any items retained are deemed sold to the buyer and the buyer must pay accordingly.

---

33. UCC Sec. 2-401(3)(a).
34. Id.

Unlike sale on approval, the buyer in a sale or return arrangement has title to the goods at the moment that the goods arrive. A sale or return is therefore deemed a sale from the outset, but the buyer has a chance to rescind the sale within a certain period of time.[35]

Unless the parties agree otherwise, if goods are intended for the buyer's use, the Code deems it a sale on approval. If the goods are intended for the buyer's resale, the Code deems it a sale or return transaction.[36]

c. Consignment

A consignment transaction is treated as a sale or return. Consignment transactions involve the seller taking her goods to another person to sell. Title is transferred to the consignee (the person who is trying to sell the items). Because title is in the consignee, creditors of the consignee can seize the assets being held for sale on consignment. But, there is relief for the consignor. The consignor may protect her property by doing any one of the following three things:

1. If local law permits, the consignor may protect her interest by putting up a sign in the store giving the public notice of the identity of the true owner.
2. The consignor may introduce proof in court that the consignee is generally known by its creditors as one substantially engaged in selling goods owned by others.
3. The consignor may file a public notice pursuant to Article 9 of the UCC.

C. Insurable Interest

Identification of goods to the contract gives the buyer an insurable interest in the goods.[37] As a general rule, a person has insurable in-

---

35. UCC Sec. 2-326.
36. UCC Sec. 2-326.
37. UCC Sec. 2-501.

terest if she will be exposed to monetary damage in the event of loss, damage, destruction or theft of property. During the period the seller is the owner of the subject goods, he has an insurable interest in them. The Code designates the time of identification of goods to the contract as the point in which the buyer has an insurable interest. Therefore, it is possible for both the buyer and the seller to each have an insurable interest in the goods to be sold. The buyer's insurable interest continues from the point of identification through the time she acquires title to the goods. The seller retains an insurable interest as long as he either has title to the goods or retains a security interest in the goods.

With respect to future goods, the buyer has an insurable interest when the goods come into existence and are identified to the contract.

D. Shipping Terms

It is common for sellers to engage carriers to transport the purchased goods to the buyer. A number of alternatives exist, each providing variations in the type of transportation, liability for expense of shipment and risk of loss in the event the goods are lost, damaged or destroyed. The terms commonly used are as follows.

I. F.O.B. (Free On Board)

When the term F.O.B. is used in conjunction with the shipping point, the seller is only responsible for getting the goods to the shipping point. The seller is responsible for any loading or loading expenses at the point of shipment. The seller will bear the risk of loss up to the point of shipment.

If F.O.B. is used with respect to a point of destination, it is the seller's responsibility and risk of loss to see that the goods arrive at the point of destination. If a common carrier is engaged, the seller will be responsible for the risk of loss up to the point the carrier makes the goods available to the buyer at the point of destination.[38]

Contracts that only require the seller to bear the expense and risk of loss up to the point of shipment are known as "shipment contracts." Contracts that require the seller to bear the expense and risk of loss in seeing that the goods arrive at a point of destination are designated "destination contracts."

2. F.A.S. (FREE ALONGSIDE SHIP)

This is the maritime equivalent of F.O.B. shipment contract. This requires the seller to bear the expense and risk of loss up to the point the goods are delivered alongside the vessel in the manner usual in the designated port or dock.[39]

3. DELIVERY EX-SHIP (FROM THE SHIP OR CARRIER)

The term "delivery ex-ship" requires delivery from a ship that has reached the named port of destination. The expense of shipment and risk of loss do not pass to the buyer under this term until the goods leave the ship's tackle or are otherwise unloaded.[40]

4. C.L.F. AND C. & F. (COST, INSURANCE AND FREIGHT)[41]

These contracts are also used for maritime goods transportation. The term C.I.F. means that the buyer promises to pay a price for the goods that includes the cost of the goods as well as the insurance and freight charges to the named destination. The terms C.& F. or C.F. mean that the price includes the cost of the goods and the freight to the named destination.

A C.I.F. contract requires the seller to obtain negotiable bills of lading to cover transportation of the goods to the named destination. It is the seller's responsibility to have the goods loaded, pay the cost of loading, obtain a receipt from the carrier showing that the freight has been paid, obtain an appropriate certification of insurance to the benefit of the buyer, prepare an invoice and obtain any other necessary documentation. The seller must then forward the documents to the buyer. Risk of loss will pass to the buyer on delivery of the goods to the carrier.

A C.& F. contract imposes the same obligations and risks on the parties as a C.I.F. term except that the seller is not required to purchase insurance for the goods.

Full performance by the seller requires the seller to tender all necessary documents. Once all of the proper documents, including the negotiable bill of lading have been tendered to the buyer, the buyer is obligated to pay the full purchase price for the goods even if the goods have yet to arrive.

5. NO ARRIVAL, NO SALE

Under a "no arrival, no sale" delivery agreement, the seller promises to ship conforming goods but assumes no obligation with respect to the goods arrival other than an obligation not to interfere or otherwise cause non-arrival of the goods. If the goods arrive by any means, they must be tendered to the buyer on arrival.[42] The seller pays the expense of shipping. If the goods are lost, destroyed, or have deteriorated so completely that their entire value is compromised, there is no further obligation on the part of either party. The transaction is deemed canceled. If the deterioration is partial, resulting in goods that have value but do not conform to the contract, the buyer has the right to inspect the goods and either treat the loss as a total loss or to take the goods at a reasonably adjusted price. This term is particularly useful during times of civil unrest or when the transaction involves

---

38. UCC Sec. 2-319.
39. UCC Sec. 2-319.
40. UCC Sec. 3-222.
41. UCC Sec. 3-320.

---

42. UCC Sec. 2-324.

goods which are highly susceptible to deterioration, such as agricultural products.

E. Risk of Loss

It is an inherent risk in sales that goods may be lost, damaged or destroyed prior to the seller's receipt of them. Under the Code, the parties are free to agree in advance when this risk of loss will pass from the seller to the buyer.[43] The Code provides a system of rules in the event the parties do not specify when risk of loss passes. These rules are incorporated in a number of the shipping terms just discussed. Because the Code provides a set of distinct rules with respect to risk of loss in common shipping terms, most shipping arrangements do not mention risk of loss specifically. The parties, aware of the Code's rules, often select a shipping term that incorporates agreeable risk of loss provisions.

1. BREACH OF CONTRACT AND RISK OF LOSS

Under section 2-510 of the Code, risk of loss will be affected by a breach of contract in the following situations:

   a. In the event a tender of delivery of goods fails to conform to the contract, resulting in a buyer's right to reject the goods, the risk of loss remains on the seller until the seller cures the breach or the buyer accepts the goods.

   b. In the event a buyer rightfully revokes acceptance, the buyer may treat the risk of loss as having rested on the seller from the beginning to the extent of any deficiency in the buyer's insurance coverage.

   c. Where goods have already been identified to the contract and the buyer has repudiated the contract or otherwise breached before the risk of loss passed to the buyer, the seller may treat the risk of loss as resting on the buyer for

a commercially reasonable time to the extent of any deficiency in the seller's insurance coverage.

2. WHEN THE LOSS IS CAUSED BY ONE OF THE PARTIES

In the event one of the parties causes loss or damage to the identified goods, the party at fault bears the risk of loss. Negligence is included in the Code's concept of "fault."

3. LOSS, DAMAGE OR DESTRUCTION OF THE GOODS THROUGH NO FAULT OF THE PARTIES AFTER RISK OF LOSS HAS PASSED

Once the risk of loss has passed to the buyer, the buyer will bear any loss even if the buyer was not at fault. The buyer may pursue an action against the party who caused the loss. In addition, the buyer may have an opportunity in certain circumstances to recover from a common carrier for damages under a strict liability theory.

4. THE POINT RISK OF LOSS SHIFTS FROM SELLER TO BUYER

a. Agreement by the Parties

The buyer and seller may agree upon specific terms governing the exact moment and circumstances that risk of loss will pass from the seller to the buyer.[44]

b. Shipment of Goods by Common Carrier

If the seller is required or authorized to ship the goods to the buyer, the point at which the risk of loss passes to the buyer depends upon whether the parties have chosen a "shipment" or "destination" contract. If the seller is merely required to tender the goods to a carrier (a shipment contract), such as a F.O.B. shipping point contract or a C.I.F. contract, the risk of loss passes to the buyer when the goods are delivered to the carrier.[45] As a re-

---

43. UCC Sec. 2-319, 2-509

44. UCC Sec. 2-509.
45. UCC Sec. 2-509(1)(a).

Example. John, who lives in Denver, orders a personal computer from Bitworld, located in Kansas City. The parties agreed to shipment terms of "F.O.B. Kansas City." Bitworld properly tendered the computer to a carrier. The computer was damaged in shipment. Because this was a "shipment contract," Bitworld is in no way liable to pay for the damage to the goods because the risk of loss had passed to the buyer prior to the damage. ☐

* * *

Example. If the parties in the previous example had agreed to a destination contract (F.O.B. Denver), Bitworld would be liable to compensate John for the in-transit damages because they occurred prior to the risk of loss shifting to John. ☐

sult, if the goods are lost, damaged or destroyed during shipment, the buyer will experience the loss.

If the seller is required to deliver the goods to a point of destination, (a destination contract), such as a F.O.B. destination point contract, the risk of loss passes to the buyer when the goods are made available by the carrier to the buyer at the destination point.[46] So, if the goods are destroyed in transit, the seller will experience the loss.

Under the Code, a shipment contract is presumed.[47] Therefore, if the parties do not use language indicating an F.O.B. destination contract, risk of loss will pass to the buyer at the point the seller tenders the goods to the carrier.

F.A.S. agreements follow shipment contract and destination contract rules. C.I.F. and C.& F. agreements place risk of loss on the buyer from the time the seller tenders the goods to a common carrier. The named city or port has no bearing on the risk of loss.

c. "Sale on Approval" and "Sale or Return"

As previously discussed, a sale on approval agreement requires the seller to deliver goods to a buyer for a stated period of time, or a reasonable period of time if no time is stated.

---

46. UCC Sec. 2-509(1)(b).
47. UCC Sec. 2-504.

During that term, the buyer may use the goods. Ownership and risk of loss will remains with the seller until the buyer accepts the goods. If the goods are lost or destroyed in transit while they are being returned to the seller following the buyer's refusal to "approve" the sale, the seller will bear the loss.

In a sale or return transaction, risk of loss shifts to the buyer pursuant to the other rules governing risk of loss under the Code as if the transaction were a regular sale of goods. Unless parties agree otherwise, the buyer will bear the risk of loss and expense in returning the goods to the seller.

d. When Goods Are in the Possession of a Bailee or Are Delivered Without Moving the Goods

Goods stored with a bailee, such as those stored at a warehouse, may be sold and deemed delivered to the buyer without moving the goods. Under the Code, a bailee is a person or entity who hold goods under a contract to deliver them to a stated person. If goods are in the possession of a warehouse operator who has issued a receipt or some other document of title, that document of title must be presented to receive the goods from the warehouse.

In bailee situations, risk of loss passes to the buyer when:

1. The buyer receives a negotiable document title;

Example. Mary buys a television from a dealer. She informs the dealer that she cannot pick it up from the dealer until the following day. If the television is destroyed in a fire that night, the loss will be suffered by the seller. ▢

* * *

Example. Joe purchases a sofa from a furniture store that agrees to deliver the sofa to him in two days. During the delivery, the furniture store truck is destroyed in an accident. Risk of loss had yet to shift to Joe. Therefore, the store will suffer the loss. The same would be true if the store left its delivery in front of the buyer's house after finding the buyer not at home. If the furniture would be stolen or damaged, the merchant would bear the loss because the buyer had yet to take physical possession of the purchase. ▢

* * *

Example. Jane agreed to purchase Lauren's car. Lauren exchanged the keys and the car title for the purchase price and informed Jane that the car would remain in front of Lauren's house to be picked up by Jane any time. If the car was damaged or stolen, it would be Jane's loss. The same would be true even if Lauren had later agreed to drive the car to Jane's house using a spare set of keys and the car was destroyed in an accident that was not Lauren's fault. Keep in mind that Jane would not be left without a remedy. Jane could pursue an action against the party who caused the damage to her property. ▢

2. When the bailee acknowledges that the buyer has the right to pick up the goods; or
3. When the buyer receives a non-negotiable document of title and has had a reasonable time to present the document to the bailee and demand the goods.[48]

e. When No Carrier or Other Bailee is Involved

This is another situation when it is important to distinguish a merchant seller from a non-merchant seller because the risk of loss rules are different for each. If the transaction involves a merchant seller, the risk of loss shifts to the buyer when the buyer takes possession of the goods.

The rule is different if the seller is not a merchant. The risk of loss is on the non-merchant seller until the seller tenders delivery to the buyer. This means that once the non-mer-

chant seller has made the goods available to the buyer, the risk of loss shifts to the buyer.

F. Sales By Non-Owners

Sometimes an unsuspecting buyer will purchase goods from a seller and not be aware that the seller did not have full title to the goods. This is the case when a seller, in possession of stolen goods or goods obtained by fraud, sells such goods to a buyer.

The general rule is that a seller can transfer only that interest owned by the seller. When a buyer receives goods from a seller in which the seller did not possess full ownership rights, the buyer obtains imperfect title. Imperfect title falls into two categories, either **void title or voidable title**.

I. Void Title

A thief has no title to the goods he has stolen. Therefore, the thief has void title. Anyone who purchases a stolen item from the thief receives only the title that the thief possesses,

---

48. UCC Sec. 2-505.

Example. Joe takes his wrist watch to a jewelry store to have it repaired. The store sells wrist watches. Under the doctrine of entrustment, the jeweler has the power to sell Joe's wrist watch to a good faith purchaser in the ordinary course of business. Joe's remedy is to sue the jewelry store for damages resulting from the loss of the watch. ☐

void title. Stolen goods will always be subject to being reclaimed by the rightful owner.

2. VOIDABLE TITLE

Voidable title falls in between void title and good or perfect title. One who purchases goods from a minor obtains voidable title because the minor may avoid or disaffirm a contract. One who obtains goods through fraud, such as purchasing goods with a check that is returned unpaid for insufficient funds, receives voidable title.

The purchaser is vested with voidable title as opposed to void title because the seller intended to transfer the ownership interest to the buyer. As long as the goods are in the buyer's possession, they may be reclaimed by the seller. But here is where the distinction between void and voidable title is important. If the initial buyer transfers all of her ownership interest to a good faith purchaser in exchange for something of value, the third party purchaser will be vested with full and complete title. If the third party purchaser was aware that the initial buyer was vested with only voidable title, then the transaction will be deemed as one lacking good faith and full and complete title will not vest in the third party purchaser. The original seller may reclaim goods sold to a buyer who was not a purchaser in good faith.[49]

G. Entrustment

When one entrusts goods to a merchant who deals in goods of that kind, the merchant has the power to transfer all rights of the entrustor to a buyer in the ordinary course of business.[50] Entrusting includes any delivery and any acquiescence in the merchant's possession of the entrusted goods by the owner. The UCC adopted the common law doctrine of "market overt." This is based upon the concept that at some point the rights of a good faith purchaser should outweigh those of the real owner of the goods. The purpose is to encourage confidence in commercial transactions by protecting the good faith purchaser. Confidence in the system results in stability in ordinary buy and sell agreements.

The buyer cannot have personal knowledge that the sale would be a violation of the owner's rights. Such knowledge would prevent a buyer from being a buyer in good faith. In addition, if a thief entrusts stolen goods, then the true owner still has superior title, even superior to that of an innocent good faith purchaser. This is because the act of entrustment only passes title that the entrustee received from the entrustor. A thief has void

---

49. UCC Sec. 2-403(1).
50. UCC Sec. 2-403(2).

title. Therefore, the entrustee could only receive and pass void title.

V. International Sales Contracts

A. The Convention on Contracts for the International Sale of Goods

Throughout history, merchants have desired to participate in the largest marketplace possible. Unfortunately, differing political ideologies have made it difficult for merchants among the many nations to freely trade with each other. Commerce flourishes in an environment of stability and predictability. Even among friendly nations, conflicts in the interpretation of agreements can yield disastrous results.

Merchants have no incentive to enter into commercial agreements if there is a chance that the agreement will not be interpreted consistent with the laws of their home nations. Often, domestic lawyers are ill equipped to assimilate judicial systems and legal traditions of other nations. Merchants must be able to understand the legal environment of a business market prior to making legal commitments. In response to the desire of many nations to establish better trading practices and to create a better environment for the international trade of their merchants, the United Nations introduced The Convention on Contracts for the International Sale of Goods ("the Convention" or "CISG").

The United States ratified the CISG on December 11, 1986. The CISG went into force on January 1, 1988, between the United States and 10 other ratifying countries. The original 10 countries to the Convention were: Argentina, China, Egypt, France, Hungary, Italy, Lesotho, Syria, the United States, Yugoslavia, and Zambia.

The CISG sets out substantive law to govern the formation of most international sales contracts and the rights and obligations of buyers and sellers. However, the parties to such contracts may provide for other laws to apply, in which case the CISG yields to the expressed wishes of the parties. If the parties to the contract are each in a different country that has become a party to the Convention, the CISG will be applied to the contract unless the agreement states otherwise. This means a contract between a merchant in the United States and a merchant in Italy would be governed by the CISG. The CISG would supersede all laws, including Article 2 of the UCC, unless the parties agreed otherwise. It is therefore important for international merchants to become aware of the CISG and its provisions.

The general effect of the CISG will be to give an adopting nation two sales laws: a domestic sales law and the CISG. Both the Uniform Commercial Code and the CISG are enforceable in the United States.

I. CONTRACTING STATES

As of May 30, 1990 the following countries are contracting states: Argentina, Australia, Austria, Byelorussian S.S.R., Chili, China, Czechoslovakia, Denmark, Egypt, Germany, Finland, France, Hungary, Iraq, Italy, Lesotho, Mexico, Norway, Sweden, Switzerland, Syria, Ukrainian S.S.R., United States, Yugoslavia, and Zambia.

The Canadian provinces of Nova Scotia, Ontario and Prince Edward Island have passed legislation for the eventual implementation of the Convention, but Canada has not yet acceded.

2. CONTRACTS GOVERNED BY THE CISG

The Convention applies to contracts for the sale of goods between parties whose places of business are in different states (nations) when those states are contracting states (the states have ratified or acceded to the Convention)

Example. Assume that the seller has its place of business in California while the buyer has its place of business in Austria. If the parties have not excluded the CISG from their contract and a dispute is brought before a California court, the CISG will govern the contract. But, if the seller has its place of business in California while the buyer has its place of business in Brazil, the CISG will not be applied to the dispute even if the applicable choice of law rules would direct the court to use the CISG. This is because Brazil has not ratified and the U.S. has exercised its right to opt-out of the CISG when a party is from a non-ratifying nation. ☐

* * *

Example. Assume that the manufacturer of a digital audio tape machine (DAT) has its place of business in Germany. If the manufacturer sells one of the machines to a visiting tourist from Memphis, Tennessee who purchases the unit for his own enjoyment. This sale would not be governed by the CISG. But, if the manufacturer sold 50 DAT machines to a wholesaler who has its principal place of business in Memphis, Tennessee the Convention would govern the sale unless the parties agreed otherwise. ☐

or when the rules of private international law call for the application of the law of a contracting state.

3. WHAT IS AN INTERNATIONAL CONTRACT?

The CISG classifies a contract as international when the seller and the buyer have their places of business in different states without regard to whether the goods move from one country to another. Both parties must be on notice that their businesses are in different countries. When a party has more than one place of business, the place of business is that which has the closest relationship to the contract and its performance. If a party does not have a place of business, reference is to be made to the party's habitual place of residence.

The United States will only enforce the CISG if both the buyer and the seller have their places of business in contracting states. The United States has opted-out of the provision which can make the CISG applicable if the choice of law rules of a particular country would direct resolution of a dispute under the CISG. This opt-out provision is authorized by the CISG.[51] Therefore, a U.S. court is required to apply the CISG only if the parties to

the dispute have their places of business in different contracting states.

4. EXCLUDED TRANSACTIONS

The CISG excludes certain transactions from its coverage. The most important of these exclusions are consumer and service transactions.

a. Consumer Transactions

The CISG expressly excludes sales to persons who buy goods for personal, family or household use. This is similar to the UCC definition of a consumer transaction.

b. Service Transactions

The CISG excludes contracts by which the "preponderant part" of the seller's obligations is to supply services.[52] The CISG also excludes contracts by which the buyer supplies a "substantial part" of the materials necessary for production of the items sold. The CISG does not define "substantial" or "preponderant."

---

51. CISG Art. 95.
52. CISG Art. 3(2).

Example.   A seller in France delivers a piece of road grading equipment to a buyer in New York. A defect in the electrical system causes a severe shock to an employee of the buyer as well as resulting in an electrical fire which destroys the equipment. The CISG would not govern the liability for the injury to the employee but would govern damages to the equipment and other personal property of the buyer. ▢

* * *

Example.   Assume that a seller has a place of business in Mexico and the buyer has a place of business in New Hampshire. Under the contract, the parties agree that if the seller fails to perform as agreed it will pay as damages the amount of $50,000. Under U.S. law, the UCC would not necessarily enforce a large liquidated damage clause if it was unreasonably large in light of the anticipated or actual harm. Assume that Mexican law would uphold this term. Whether this term is enforceable or not is resolved by the CISG, which leaves the issue to the traditional conflict of law analysis between the two nations. ▢

* * *

Example.   Assume the seller is a company in Indiana and the buyer is located in Norway. In the sales agreement, the seller chooses to reserve title to the goods sold as security for payment of the purchase price. If the enforceability of this term is called into question, the CISG will not resolve the issue. It will be resolved under the domestic law made applicable under through the conflict of law analysis between the two nations. ▢

c.   Other Sales Excluded from the CISG

The following types of goods have also been excluded from coverage of the Convention. They are:

1. Goods bought at auction.
2. Stocks, securities, negotiable instruments and money.
3. Ships, vessels or aircraft.
4. Electricity

5.   ISSUES EXCLUDED FROM THE CISG

The CISG excludes from its coverage most product's liability issues, issues of validity, and questions of what effect the contract for sale has on property claims to the goods sold.

a.   Products Liabilities Claims

The CISG governs only the rights and obligations of the seller and the buyer to the sales contract. By implication, the CISG does not cover claims against other parties in the manufacturing or distribution chain. Further-more, the Convention expressly excludes claims for death or personal injury caused by the defects in goods sold.

b.   Issues of Contract Validity

Issues of contract validity are excluded from CISG coverage. These issues are to be resolved by the domestic laws of the parties. These issues include questions of fraud, duress, illegality and unconscionability. There are problems in defining issues of validity because a broad reading by a court would result in undermining the uniformity of international sales law that the CISG is designed to promote.

The CISG is considered equally authentic in each of the 6 United Nations languages. (Arabic, Chinese, English, French, Russian, and Spanish). It is advisable to resolve the language issue during contract negotiations. The contract should state what language will be used in the contract and all other communications or agreements associated with it.

Example. Assume that a purchaser has a place of business in Florida and the seller has its place of business in Denmark. Assume the parties have a written contract stating: "The terms of this agreement shall be governed by the law of the State of Florida." It is not clear whether or not the CISG has been effectively excluded from governing this provision. The United States Constitution requires the courts of the state of Florida to enforce the CISG pursuant to Article 6 of the U.S. Constitution. Therefore, reference to the law of the State of Florida is ambiguous.

c. The Effect of Sale on Property Claims

The CISG is not concerned with the effect the contract may have on the property claims to the goods sold. Therefore, domestic law will govern these issues.

B. Comparing the CISG with the UCC

I. FREEDOM OF CONTRACT

The parties to any contract may exclude application of the CISG or vary the effect of any provision subject to minor exceptions.

Parties desiring to exclude application of the CISG should do so explicitly. There is some doubt as to whether the CISG may be excluded from a contract by implication. If the parties desire to exclude the CISG from controlling the contract, the contract should state what law is applicable.

2. THE STATUTE OF FRAUDS

Recall that the UCC has a statute of frauds provision which requires that certain agreements be in writing, namely agreements for the sale of goods priced at $500 or more. The CISG has no statute of frauds. Under the CISG, a contract "need not be concluded in or evidenced by writing and is not subject to any other requirements as to form. It may be proved by any means, including witnesses."[53] The parties may reduce the risk of disagreements regarding unwritten terms by requir-

ing that the agreement be in writing. In accordance with this, the CISG further provides that a contract may be modified or terminated by mere agreement of the parties. The CISG requires that a modification or termination of a contract shall be in writing if the parties have so agreed.

The CISG gives each nation the opportunity to opt-out of the effectiveness of Article 11 (that a contract need not be in writing) and Article 29 (permitting modification or termination of a contract without a writing). The United States has not opted-out of these provisions. Argentina, China and Hungary have opted-out. When doing business with a nation that has chosen to opt-out, one must determine which country's law will govern the issue by the application of the conflict of laws rules. In any event, the prudent route is to get all contracts in writing. In addition, a written contract should state that it may only be modified or terminated by a written instrument signed by both parties.

3. THE PAROLE EVIDENCE RULE

The Uniform Commercial Code recognizes the Parole Evidence Rule by prohibiting the introduction of oral statements or previous negotiations to interpret the meaning of a written contract. The CISG does not incorporate the Parole Evidence Rule. The CISG states that in "determining the intent of a party or the understanding a reasonable person would have had, due consideration is to be given to all relevant circumstances of the case including the negotiations, any practices

---

53. CISG Art. 11.

which the parties have established between themselves, usages and any subsequent conduct of the parties."[54]

It is easy to see the drastic difference between the treatment of parole evidence by the UCC and the CISG. A party to a contract should consider whether or not there should be language in a contract to exclude prior negotiations, especially when one is not sure what representations were made by agents with that express authority. Trade usage should also be explicitly excluded from the contract when the scope and application of those rules are uncertain.

4. FIRM OFFER

The UCC permits the buyer to obtain the firm offer of a seller who signs a writing agreeing to keep an offer open for a period not longer than three months. A firm offer under the UCC does not need to be supported by consideration.

Under the CISG, an offer cannot be revoked if it indicates that it is irrevocable, whether by stating a fixed time for acceptance or otherwise.[55] The key is determining whether or not the language of the offer establishes that the offer is revocable or irrevocable. This will be determined by the intent of the parties, which involves severe proof problems. An offer under the CISG should clearly state whether or not it is revocable or irrevocable during a certain time.

5. THE BATTLE OF THE FORMS

The Uniform Commercial Code permits an offeree to accept an offer with additional terms to become part of the contract under certain conditions so long as the changes are not material. The CISG provides a stricter "mirror-image" rule. Under the CISG, a reply to an offer that alters the original offer will be deemed a rejection and counter offer under the CISG.

6. TRADE USAGE AND COURSE OF DEALING

Parties to contracts governed by the CISG are bound to trade usages to which they agree and by their course of dealing. The parties are considered to have impliedly agreed to be bound by trade usage which the parties "knew or ought to have known and which in international trade is widely known to, and regularly observed by, parties to contracts of the type involved in the particular trade concerned."[56] This is a much narrower interpretation of the trade usage provisions contained in the Uniform Commercial Code.

7. OFFER AND ACCEPTANCE

The CISG considers a communication between the parties an offer when it is "sufficiently definite and indicates the intention of the offeror to be bound."[57] Quantity or price could be implicitly specified in an advertising brochure or catalog not otherwise a part of the contract between the parties. The CISG establishes a presumption that an advertisement or a circular is not an offer unless the contrary is clearly indicated by the person making the proposal.

8. OPEN PRICE TERMS

Under the UCC, if a price is not specified in an offer or acceptance, a reasonable price will be fixed. CISG states that where price is not established, the price will be that price charged "for goods sold under comparable circumstances in the trade concerned."[58] Therefore, if the buyer and seller fail to specify the price for the goods, a court will be able to look to the marketplace to make its own determination of the appropriate price.

---

54. CISG Art. 8(3).
55. CISG Art. 16.

56. CISG Art. 9(2).
57. CISG Art. 14.
58. CISG Art. 55.

9. ACCEPTANCE AND THE TIME OF CONTRACT FORMATION

Under the UCC, an offer may be accepted by any means reasonable under the circumstances. Once an offer has been accepted, a contract is formed at that moment.

Under the CISG, the dispatch of an acceptance to an offer cuts off the offeror's right to revoke the offer, just as it does under the UCC. But, the acceptance of an offer does not become effective until the moment the indication of assent reaches the offeror.[59] An acceptance may be withdrawn if the withdrawal notification reaches the offeror before or at the same time the acceptance would have become effective.[60] This demonstrates that the CISG provides greater rights to the offeree who would otherwise be bound to a contract once it dispatches acceptance or engages in any conduct consistent with acceptance of the contract.

* * *

Problems

1. B. Brown, a wholesaler, entered into the following written agreement with S. Smith, a miller:

S. Smith hereby agrees to sell and B. Brown to buy the following commodities, f.o.b. car of initial carrier at shipping point, freight allowed to Chicago, Ill.

Time of Shipment: December 1 of this year, unless ordered out sooner. Destination: Track, Chicago, Ill.

Terms of payment: 2/10 net 30 from date of each shipment. quantity: 630 barrels

Shipping dates: to follow

Brand of flour	Price per barrel
Confidence	6.65
Harvester	6.45
De Luxe Pastry	6.40
Sierra Pastry	5.90

[**Date**] (*signed*) S. Smith
(*signed*) B. Brown

In accordance with the contract and at B's direction, S milled and delivered to B 210 barrels of Confidence brand flour on April 15, for which B paid according to contract. B refused to order any more flour and after December 1, S sued B for damages. Explain (1) the reasoning upon which B might attempt to defend, (2) the reasoning upon which S might attempt to collect, and (3) which party should be given judgment.

2. In writing S agreed to sell and B to buy 10,000 bushels of a specified kind and type of grain, to be delivered in installments of 2,000 bushels by the tenth of each month for five successive months, beginning on a specified month. The only provision as to price read: "The price B is to pay for each installment shall be the Chicago market price on the date of shipment f.o.b. Chicago, payable within ten days after delivery. "When S tendered delivery of the first installment according to contract, B refused to accept. S sued B for damages. Explain (1) the reasoning upon which B might attempt to defend, (2) the reasoning upon which S might attempt to collect, and (3) which party should be given judgment.

3. B. Brown received the following typewritten letter, dated February 2, from S. Smith: "Dear Mr. Brown: We have Mason green jars of one quart capacity complete with caps that we can offer you at this time for immediate acceptance at $8 per gross, delivered in your city. Terms 60 days or less, 2 percent for cash in 10 days. Awaiting your orders we are yours truly, (signed) S. Smith." B promptly replied by telegraph as follows: "Your February 2 letter just arrived. Enter order for 500 gross complete goods." The February 2 letter had not been in response to any inquiry from B. Five hundred gross was a reasonable quantity for B to order and not in

---

59. CISG Art. 18.
60. CISG Art. 22.

excess of what S, from his knowledge of the business of B, might reasonably expect B to order. S answered the telegraph: "We can enter order for only 250 gross." B sued for breach of contract for S's refusal to ship 500 gross of jars.

(a) Was B entitled to judgment? Explain.

(b) Explain how, if at all, S could have avoided the possibility of this dispute arising, without further limiting his freedom of action.

(c) Other facts remaining the same, assume the February 2 letter was printed and the salutation read: "Dear Customer." Was B entitled to judgment against S for refusing to ship 500 gross? Explain.

4. On March 10, Brown Seed Company received the following letter from S. Smith, a farmer residing at Lowell, Nebraska: "Brown Seed Co., Omaha, Nebraska. Gentlemen: I have for sale about 1800 bu. of millet seed of which I am mailing you a sample enclosed with this letter. This millet is recleaned and was grown on sod and is good seed. I want $2.25 per hundredweight for this seed, f.o.b. Lowell. (signed) S. Smith." The same day B Company sent S the following telegram: "S. Smith, Lowell, Nebraska. Sample and letter received. Accept your offer. Millet like sample two twenty-five per hundred. (signed) Brown Seed Co." S received the telegram the same day it was sent. S refused to sell, having found another buyer and B Company sued S for damages.

(a) Explain (1) the reasoning upon which B Company could attempt to collect, (2) the reasoning upon which S could attempt to defend, and (3) which party should be given judgment .

(b) Explain how, if at all, S could have avoided the possibility of this dispute arising, without limiting his freedom of action.

5. B was in the business of exporting crude petroleum to France, his trade amounting to about 100,000 barrels a year. S, an oil refiner, contacted B, suggesting that B purchase his requirements of oil from S and further suggesting that B attempt, by a visit to Pairs, to increase his export trade. To assist B on his trip, S on March 1 signed and gave B a letter reading in part: "In accordance with our interview, I am willing to enter into a contract with you for the furnishment of Pennsylvania crude oil for a term of two years in the amount of 400,000 barrels of 42 gallons each, per year, at the following price . . . [specifying a price and details of transportation and handling charges]. I extend to you a refusal of making the contract on the above basis for the term of four months from this date. Should it not be accepted in writing on or before that time the above is to become null and void and without effect between us." B traveled to Paris at his own expense and after some negotiations succeeded in entering into contracts with various French refiners to supply them with crude petroleum totaling 400,000 barrels a year.

(a) Thereafter, S sent B the following: "May 23. I wish to advise you that I withdraw my offer of March 1. You will therefore consider the same canceled." To this B replied: "May 24. I hereby notify you that I accept and will fully carry out the option and contract you gave me by your letter of March 1. I hereby repudiate your attempted withdrawal of said option." Each letter was received by the respective addressee the day following the date of mailing. Upon S's refusal to deliver oil to B, B sued for damages for breach of contract. Was B entitled to judgment against S? Explain.

(b) Assume facts the same as in Part (a) of this problem, except that the date of S's letter to B was June 23 and the date of B's answering letter to S was June 24. Was B entitled to judgment against S? Explain.

6. On December 8, in reply to an inquiry S telegraphed to B: "Will sell you 2,000-5,000 tons of 50 pound iron rails for $54 per gross ton, cash, f.o.b. cars our mill, March delivery. If offer accepted, expect to be notified of same prior to December 20." Assume that under the particular circumstances this constituted an offer. On December 16 B telegraphed S: "Enter order 1,200 tons rails as per your wire of December 8." On December 18 S telegraphed B: "Cannot book your order of 16th at that price." On December 19 B telegraphed S: "En-

ter order 2,000 tons as per your wire of December 8." S received this telegraph on December 19 but did not reply until January 19 when, after repeated inquiries from B, S stated that he would not ship the rails. B sued S for damages for breach of contract. Explain (1) the reasoning upon which B might attempt to collect, (2) the reasoning upon which S might attempt to defend, and (3) which party should be given judgment.

7. On February 1, B, a manufacturer of refrigerator cases, sent to S, a supplier, a written order for 300 latches of a certain style called "spring lock" at $2 per latch, f.o.b. shipping point, 2/10 net 30. This was S's first order from B, and S desired to obtain B as a customer. However, S had no spring lock latches on hand and could procure them only at a price which, with S's normal markup, would make S's selling price $3 per latch. S had on hand a quantity of "roll-lock" latches on which S's normal selling price was $2.15 per latch. As S knew, many manufacturers had found the roll-lock latch as satisfactory as or superior to the spring lock latch. In response to B's order and without any further communication, S, on February 3, shipped to B 300 roll-lock latches invoiced to B at $2 apiece. On tender of delivery B noticed that the latches were roll-lock latches and refused to receive delivery. The railroad returned them to S on S's payment of the freight charges. B demanded but S refused to ship any other latches.

(a) If S sued B for the loss resulting from B's refusal to receive delivery, could S recover? Explain.

(b) If B sued S for the loss resulting from S's refusal to ship other latches, could B recover? Explain.

(c) How if at all could S have shown that he desired to serve B promptly and still have avoided the dispute and lawsuit? Explain.

8. Brown ordered 100 cases of Delicious Brand peas at list price from Smith Wholesaler. Immediately upon receipt of Brown's order, Smith sent Brown an acceptance which was received by Brown. The acceptance indicated that shipment would be made within ten days. On the tenth day,

Smith discovered that all of its supply of Delicious Brand peas had been sold. Instead Smith shipped 100 cases of Lovely Brand peas, stating clearly on the invoice that the shipment was sent as an accommodation only. Was a contract formed between Brown and Smith? (Modified from A.I.C.P.A May 81-15.)

9. B Company sent to S Company a signed printed purchase order form reading in part: "Please enter our order for the following described goods," followed by a typewritten description of the goods ordered and prices. The form contained no reference to strikes. In reply S Company sent to B Company a signed printed form titled "Purchase Memo," the pertinent part of the printed form reading: "This acknowledges receipt of your order for the following described goods, which we accept, subject to the terms and conditions on the reverse side hereof." The description of goods and prices were typewritten on the S Company form, as copied from the B Company's purchase order. On the reverse side of S Company's purchase memo form, among other things, was printed: "S Company will not be liable for any delay in delivery or failure to deliver, resulting from labor trouble or strike." B Company did not reply.

(a) Before S Company could ship the ordered goods, its plant was closed by a strike. B Company sued S Company for damages for nondelivery. Assume that the ordinary rule concerning strikes (see Chapter 12) would apply, that is, that a seller's labor trouble will not excuse him from his contract obligation to deliver unless his contract expressly contains a strike excuse or escape provision. Explain (1) the reasoning upon which B Company might attempt to win the lawsuit, (2) the reasoning upon which S Company might attempt to defend, and (3) which party should be given judgment.

(b) Receiving no reply from B Company, S Company shipped the ordered goods with reasonable promptness. B Company had decided not to purchase (without informing S Company of this fact), and refused the shipment. S Company sued

B Company for damages for breach of contract. What result? Explain.

10. On November 9 B wrote to S, a manufacturer, ordering certain described packing materials, at a stated price, one-tenth of the total quantity ordered to be shipped as soon as possible, and the remainder to be retained by S until requested by B, since B had no storage space; the goods were to be billed only when and as shipped on B's instructions and B was to give shipping instructions for all the ordered goods within the next four months. On November 12 S replied that he could not store and ship in that way without charging an extra 5 percent for the accommodation. On November 15 B wrote S refusing to pay an extra 5 percent, stating that B had dealt under those terms with other manufacturers, and hoping that S would reconsider and enter B's November 9 order. Without further correspondence, S began to manufacture the described material and on December 15 shipped the one-tenth portion requested in B's November 9 letter, billed "as per your November 9 order," at the price in the original order. Assume that under the circumstances this shipment was "as soon as possible," within the meaning of B's November 9 order.

(a) B refused the shipment and S sued B for damages for breach of contract. Explain (1) the reasoning upon which S might attempt to recover, (2) the reasoning upon which B might attempt to defend, and (3) which party should be given judgment.

(b) B accepted delivery and paid as billed. Shortly afterwards B wrote to S that no further shipments would be accepted. By that time the manufacture of all of the packing material was completed. After repeated vain attempts during the next four months to induce B to accept more of the packing materials, S sued B for breach of contract. Answer the same questions as are asked in Part (a).

11. On April 7 S mailed a letter to B, offering to sell two carloads of specified goods for a stated price, and saying nothing as to the method of re-

plying to the offer. The letter containing the offer was delivered to B in due course at 10 AM., April 9. B replied as described in (a) or (b) below. At 9:30 AM. on April 9, S dispatched a telegram to B reading "Disregard my letter of April 7. Have sold goods elsewhere." B received this telegram at 10:55 A.M., April 9. B maintained that there was a contract. S denied this and refused to deliver. The market price for such goods having gone up, B sued S for damages for breach of contract.

(a) Assume that at 10:30 A.M., April 9, B mailed to S a letter of acceptance. The letter was postmarked 11 A.M., April 9 and delivered to S, 10 AM., April 11. Was B entitled to judgment in his lawsuit against S? Explain.

(b) Assume that at 10:30 A.M., April 9, B dispatched to S a telegram of acceptance. The telegram was delivered to S, 11:30 A.M., April 9. Was B entitled to judgment in his lawsuit against S? Explain. Would your answer be different if through the sole fault of the telegraph company, the telegram was delayed and not delivered to S until 5 P.M., April 12? Explain.

(c) Explain how, if at all, S could have phrased his letter to avoid the possibility of such a dispute as arose here.

12. At 10 A.M., March 10, S of Philadelphia sent an air-mail letter to B of Portland, Oregon. Under the circumstances, the letter constituted an offer to sell certain described goods to B at a stated price f.o.b. Philadelphia. The letter concluded by saying: "You have three days in which to accept." B received the letter in due course at 10 A.M., March 12. At 4 P.M. March 14, B mailed by regular mail a letter accepting S's offer. S received the accepting letter in due course of mail at 10 A.M., March 17. Learning of a chance to sell to someone else at a higher price, S refused to ship to B and B sued S for damages. Explain (1) the reasoning upon which S might attempt to defend, (2) the reasoning upon which B might attempt to collect, and (3) which party should be given judgment.

13. S decided to replace a machine in his factory with one of more modern design. Recalling

interest in the machine previously expressed by his friend B, owner of a small machine shop, S, on a Wednesday, dictated a letter to his secretary offering to sell the described machine to B for $400. After the letter was typed, S sent his secretary out to deliver a folder in another building, and before she returned S had to leave for a business conference. He signed the letter containing the offer to B and left it on his secretary's desk, together with a separate note that he would be out the remainder of the day. After the secretary returned, she began working on some files in an adjoining room. A few minutes later B came into the office to see S. Noticing that the letter on the secretary's desk was addressed to him, B read it. Also seeing the note that S would not be back, B left without seeing S's secretary.

(a) Before leaving, B wrote on the bottom of S's letter, "Accepted. Thanks a lot" and signed it. Was a contract formed and if so, when? Explain.

(b) Assume that although B read S's letter, he wrote nothing on it. At 5 P.M. S's secretary mailed the letter and it was delivered to B the following morning (Thursday) at 10 A.M. Late Wednesday afternoon B wrote a letter to S accepting the offer made in the letter B had seen in S's office. B mailed his accepting letter at 6 P.M. and it was delivered to S Thursday morning at 11 A.M. By this time S had changed his mind and at 11 :30 A.M. Thursday he phoned B that the deal was off. B sued S for breach of contract. Was a contract formed, and if so, when? Explain.

14. After exchanging telegrams not constituting offers, relative to the price of Puerto Rico potatoes for prompt shipment, B, on Friday, February 2, sent to S, an importer, a telegram reading "Ship 150 barrels Puerto Ricos today at your quoted price. Wire car number." S replied by telegram the same day, "Will ship Monday." The potatoes were not shipped on Monday, and B wired S on Wednesday, February 7, "When are you going to ship potatoes? Booked shipment. Answer quick." By "booked shipment" B meant that he had in turn already entered into a contract to sell the potatoes to someone else. Upon receiving this wire on February 7, S did not reply, inasmuch as he had written and mailed a letter to B on February 6, explaining that he was unable to ship on account of weather conditions. Assume that this reason would not excuse a person from performing any contract he may have entered into. S shipped the potatoes on February 10 and wired B at the time of shipment, giving the car number. On February 14, when the potatoes arrived in due course, B refused to accept them. S sued for damages for breach of contract. Was S entitled to judgment against B? Explain.

15. On July 1 B, a doctor, signed in duplicate a printed order furnished by S. Smith, a car dealer, reading in part: "To S. Smith: I hereby order you to equip and deliver to me at Scranton, Pennsylvania, as soon as reasonably possible, the following described motor vehicle which I agree to accept at the price and according to the terms set forth below and on the reverse side hereof." Appropriate spaces on the front of the order form were filled in with the make, model, and price of the car B wanted. On the reverse side was printed: "It is agreed that the seller will not be held liable for any delay or failure to make delivery through any cause whatsoever." On the same day, S dated and signed both copies of the form after the printed word, "Accepted," and delivered one copy to B. On July 10, before S had tendered any car to B, B notified S to cancel the order. On July 15, which was a reasonable time for delivery of a car ordered on July 1, S tendered to B a car exactly complying with the description in the order form. When B refused to accept delivery, S sue B for damages for breach of contract. Explain (1) the reasoning upon which B might attempt to defend, (2) the reasoning upon which S might attempt to collect, and (3) which party should be given judgment.

16. (a) A trucker who owned and operated several trucks for short distance hauling was negotiating with a distributor of petroleum products. On January 28 the distributor wrote to the trucker the following, which under the circumstances legally constituted an offer: "I hereby offer to sell you Star Brand Motor Oil, SAE 20 at 60 cents a gallon and

Star Brand Regular Gasoline at 15 cents a gallon, in such quantities as you may order, delivery to be made within 5 days after order, payment within 30 days after delivery, 2 percent off for ten days. Upon acceptance by you of this offer, the agreement will continue in effect for six months from February 1." Receiving two copies, the trucker wrote on the bottom of one copy, "Accepted, January 30," signed it, and returned it to the distributor. During February, March, and the first part of April the trucker ordered, received, and paid for various quantities of gas and oil from the distributor. On April 15 the trucker sent an order, received by the distributor April 16, for 5,000 gallons of gasoline. On April 17 the distributor wrote a letter received by the trucker April 18, saying: "I regret I will be unable to deliver your April 15 order or any further orders at the previous prices. Our costs have advanced sharply and I'm sure you will understand my position. I shall be happy to fill your April 15 order and any further orders in any quantities you wish, at my current prices of $1 a gallon for oil and 25 cents a gallon for gasoline of the grades you have previously been buying." The trucker protested but the distributor remained firm and refused to deliver at the January prices. On April 22 the trucker sent an order received by the distributor April 23 for 1,000 gallons of oil, the trucker specifying that he was ordering under the January agreement. The distributor refused to deliver. On May 6 the trucker sent an order, received by the distributor on May 9, for 3,000 gallons of gasoline, the trucker specifying that he was ordering under the January agreement. The distributor refused to deliver. These three orders conformed in quantity and frequency with the trucker's orders during the previous two and a half months. Each time the distributor refused to deliver, the trucker purchased the same grade elsewhere at the lowest obtainable prices of 80 cents a gallon for oil and 20 cents a gallon for gasoline. The trucker sued the distributor for damages consisting of the amounts the trucker had to pay over the prices in the January agreement, namely (1) $250 on the April 15 order, (2) $200 on the April 22 order, and (3) $150 on the May 6 order. Disregard-

ing court costs and interest, state how much, if anything. the trucker was entitled to recover. Explain.

(b) Other facts being the same, assume that the three orders were dated May 15, May 22 and June 6 and that the distributor's letter first giving notice of the price increase was dated May 17, received May 18. Disregarding court costs and interest, state how much, if anything, the trucker was entitled to recover. Explain.

17. On May 16 a salesman for a manufacturer of farm machinery solicited an order from a farmer for a certain type of farm machine at a stated price. The order form signed in duplicate by the farmer concluded by stating: "This order is not subject to countermand. No verbal understanding of the agent is to affect this order, all conditions under which this order is given are specified herein. All orders are subject to approval of the manufacturer." The order form contained no warranty of any kind. The salesman sent the signed copies of the order form to the manufacturer. On May 23, before anything further had been done about the order, the farmer notified the manufacturer canceling the order and stating that he would not accept the machine. On May 26 the manufacturer wrote on both copies of the order form: "Accepted, will ship today, May 26," signed both copies, and mailed one copy to the farmer. Assume that under the circumstances this was within a reasonable time. The manufacturer shipped the machine to the farmer on May 26, but the farmer refused to receive it from the carrier. The carrier returned the machine to the manufacturer, who again reshipped it back to the farmer. The salesman then on June 30 induced the farmer to receive delivery and permit the machine to be installed, the salesman expressly warranting in the manufacturer's name that the machine would operate in a certain way. The machine did not perform as warranted and the farmer demanded that the manufacturer remove it. The manufacturer refused and sued the farmer for the purchase price.

(a) Was an enforceable contract between the manufacturer and farmer formed on May 26? Explain.

(b) Was an enforceable contract between the manufacturer and farmer formed on June 30? Explain.

(c) Was the manufacturer entitled to recover the purchase price from the farmer? Explain.

18. On June 22 a retailer orally ordered from a manufacturer 60 dozen shirts of stated sizes, colors, and styles at $4.75 per dozen, and the manufacturer orally accepted the order. On August 11 the manufacturer wrote to the retailer: "Due to labor increases as effected by a new contract signed by the garment industry with the clothing workers' union, we are compelled to add a surcharge of $2.50 per dozen on existing shirt orders now in the process of manufacture, among which yours is included. We ask your permission to add the surcharge as listed above to existing orders, and will await billing any additional merchandise for your account until we receive your permission to do so. If you are unwilling to pay this additional charge which is right and proper from every angle, we will be willing to accept cancellation on that portion of your order to which the surcharge would be applicable. In view of the replacement costs which are much higher than our price plus surcharges, we would strongly advise that you accept the merchandise under these conditions." On August 14 the retailer replied by letter: "In answer to your letter of August 11, we ask that you please rush the shirts on back order, and add the $2.50 surcharge." On August 18 the manufacturer shipped the 60 dozen shirts which the retailer had ordered. The retailer paid $285 (the price of 60 dozen at $4.75 per dozen). When the retailer refused to pay any more, the manufacturer sued for $150 as balance due. Assume that under the circumstances a shipment on August 18 was reasonably prompt for the June 22 order.

(a) Explain (1) the reasoning upon which the manufacturer might attempt to recover, (2) the reasoning upon which the retailer might attempt

to defend, and (3) which party should be given judgment.

(b) Would your answer be different if the retailer's reply of August 14 had been made orally by long-distance phone? Explain.

19. On June 6 a New York City importer and seller of souvenir postal cards sent a letter to a Washington, D.C., dealer, enclosing a sample of a new card showing various Washington views. The letter stated that the regular price of the cards was $15 per thousand but that the seller was making a price to jobbers of $10 per thousand. This letter was typed by the seller's stenographer from a circular letter which stated a price of $10 per thousand. She erroneously typed "$1" instead of "$10." The dealer replied by letter: "This is in reply to your letter of the 7th. Your sample card sent us is very good and owing to the price you quote us, the stock must be faulty in some way or your stenographer made a mistake in the price. If the stock is good and the price correct as quoted, we will take several thousand." The seller looked up a copy of the circular letter from which the letter sent to the dealer had been typed (no carbon copy of the letter sent having been retained) and replied by letter that the cards were first class in every respect, that they were being sold at cost, and that the seller would guarantee them in every respect. On receipt of this letter, the dealer wrote ordering "25,000 cards as per sample at price quoted in your letter of the 7th." The seller shipped the ordered cards and mailed a bill to the dealer, billing the cards at $10 per thousand. The dealer received the cards the following day, unpacked them and placed them on his shelves. Later the same day the dealer received the bill and immediately wrote: "We have just received your bill for postal cards and return it for correction. The price of these cards is $1 instead of $10 as you bill them. We refer to your letter of the 7th when you sent us sample and price." The seller replied: "There is evidently an error some place. The price of the cards as quoted you was $10 per thousand and not $1. The import duty alone on these cards costs us $2.25 per thousand, and you can readily understand that it would be

impossible for us to sell them at any such price as $1 per thousand. If the price of $10 per thousand is not satisfactory, we request that you send us the cards immediately. Kindly return to us the letter in which you state that you are quoted $1 per thousand." The dealer refused to return the cards and tendered $25 plus shipping charges as payment in full. The seller refused and sued for $250. Explain (1) the reasoning upon which the seller might attempt to collect, (2) the reasoning upon which the dealer might attempt to defend, and (3) which party should be given judgment.

20. On June 13 R. Roger, a retailer in Chicago, telegraphed M. Martin, a manufacturer in New York City, "I can use one hundred children's and juniors' dresses at close-out price." The same day M gave to the telegraph office in New York for transmission to R, the following telegram, "To R. Roger, Chicago. Can ship two hundred junior dresses in linen, silkette, dotted plain and fancy voile at $2.75 net, also six dozen children's dresses, cotton shantungs, voile, poplins, and linens at $16.50 net dozen, advise all close-out prices wonderful opportunity for a big sale. (signed) M. Martin." Because of negligence in transmission, the telegram delivered to R read as to the first price "twenty seventy-five net" instead of $2.75. R assumed that this meant $20.75 per dozen, and on the same day wired M, "Send entire lot of dresses as per your telegram." On the next day M shipped the described dresses to R and mailed an invoice calculated at $2.75 for each junior dress. Two days later R wired M, "Invoice received does not agree with your telegram of the 13th, will not accept merchandise unless billed as bought wire answer."

(a) Explain the legal effect of each telegram.

(b) Was there a contract between the parties, and if so what were the terms? Explain.

21. On October 3, S. Smith of New York City sent to B. Brown of Chicago a letter which, under the circumstances, constituted an offer to sell to B certain described goods at a stated price. Receiving the letter on October 5, B immediately dispatched a telegram accepting the offer. The message B gave to the telegraph office in Chicago was addressed to S and read: "Your offer of October 3 accepted. (signed) B. Brown." Through negligence of the telegraph company, the message was garbled in transmission so that the telegram delivered to S in New York on October 5 read: "Your offer of October 3 rejected. (signed) B. Brown." After S sold the goods to another purchaser, the above facts were discovered, and B sued S for damages for breach of contract. Explain (1) the reasoning upon which B might attempt to collect, (2) the reasoning upon which S might attempt to defend, and (3) which party should be given judgment.

22. B wished to buy goods on credit from S. S refused to sell except for cash, whereupon G who was favorably known to S called S on the telephone and said, "If you sell goods to B on 30 days' credit and B fails to pay, I'll pay up to the amount of $300." S thereupon sold $200 worth of goods to B on 30 days' credit and notified G of the sale. B failed to pay when due and S sued and obtained judgment against B. Because of B's insolvency, S could not collect. S then sued G.

(a) G denied liability on the ground that he received nothing for his promise. Explain whether this defense would be good.

(b) Explain what other defense G might attempt to raise.

(c) Explain whether S could collect from G.

23. B. Berg owned and operated a retail clothing store under the name "Berg's Men's Shop." B stocked suits manufactured by several different manufacturers. The labels in the suits read, "Tailored Especially for Berg's Men's Shop, Centertown, Illinois, by [name of manufacturer]." Hisstock of suits manufactured by S being low, B called S on the phone and placed an order for fifty suits of specified styles, sizes, and colors, as stated in S's catalog, at a stated price totaling over $500. Each suit was to have the label quoted above sewn in the usual place on the inside lining of each suitcoat. S orally accepted the order. Three weeks later S had the suits ready for shipment when B

canceled the order. S sued B for damages for breach of contract.

(a) Assume that S manufactured the fifty suits after receiving B's order. Explain (a) the reasoning upon which S might attempt to collect, (2) the reasoning upon which B might attempt to defend, and (3) which party should be given judgment.

(b) Assume that S had in stock sufficient suits to fill B's order and all that S did to prepare them for shipment was to attach the proper labels. Answer the same three questions asked in Part (a) above.

24. (a) B. Brown, a university professor of history, went to the store of S. Smith, a dealer, and orally ordered a television set of a particular make and model for the total price of $600, to be delivered to B's home within two weeks and installed in B's living room. S orally accepted the order and B made a down payment of $100 in cash. S made out and gave to B the following receipt: "[Date] Received from B. Brown $100 to apply on TV set. (signed) S. Smith." (1) When S tendered delivery of the set according to the oral agreement, B refused to accept delivery, saying that he had changed his mind about making the purchase. S sued B for damages for breach of contract. Would S be entitled to obtain judgment? Explain. (2) S refused to deliver at the agreed time and B sued S for damages for breach of contract. Would B be entitled to obtain judgment? Explain.

(b) Assume the same facts as in Part (a, 1) except for the following change: When S sued B for damages for breach of contract, B filed a counterclaim in the same lawsuit to recover the $100 he had paid, alleging the facts of his oral order, payment, and refusal to receive delivery. What would be the outcome of the lawsuit? Explain.

(c) B. Brown, a university professor of history, orally ordered a television set of a stated make and model from S. Smith, a dealer, for $400, to be delivered to B's home in two weeks and installed in his living room. B made no down payment. S orally accepted the order and later sent to B a signed written confirmation, entitled "Purchase

Memorandum No. 1208," containing all of the terms of the order. A duplicate of the purchase memorandum was enclosed with a request that B sign and return it to S. B kept both copies without signing either. When S tendered delivery of the set according to the oral agreement, B refused to accept delivery, saying that he had changed his mind about making the purchase. S sued B for damages for breach of contract. Would S be entitled to obtain judgment? Explain.

(d) Assume the same facts as in Part (c) except for the following change: The total price was $600. Answer the same question as is asked in Part (c).

(e) Assume the same facts as in Part (c) except for the following changes: The total price was $600. Two days after receiving the "Purchase Memorandum No. 1208," B dated and sent the following note to S: "To S. Smith: Referring to your Purchase Memorandum No. 1208, please be advised that I am cancelling this order. (signed) B. Brown." What would be the result of S's lawsuit against B? Explain.

(f) Assume the same facts as in Part (c), except for the following changes: The total price was $600. S refused to deliver at the agreed time and B sued S for damages for breach of contract. Would B be entitled to obtain judgment? Explain.

(g) B. Brown, owner and operator of a hotel, orally ordered a television set of a stated make and model from S. Smith, a dealer, for $1,000, to be delivered in two weeks, and installed in the hotel lounge. B made no down payment. S orally accepted the order and later sent B a written confirmation, entitled "Purchase Memorandum," containing all of the terms of the order. A duplicate copy of the purchase memorandum was enclosed with a request that B sign and return it to S. B kept both copies without signing either. When S tendered delivery of the set according to the oral agreement, B refused to accept delivery, saying that he had changed his mind about making the purchase. S sued B for damages for breach of contract. Was S entitled to obtain judgment? Explain. (Modified from A.I.C.P.A., Nov. 5010.)

25. (a) A printer contacted a milk dealer to interest him in ordering calendars to give to his customers. The printer showed the dealer a certain type of calendar with a sample of the advertising statement which could be printed on the calendars along with the dealer's name, and quoted the price for 1,000 calendars as $200, payable thirty days after delivery. The following day the dealer phoned the printer and ordered 1,000 calendars of the type which the printer had showed to the dealer, and with the printing on them that the printer had described. The printer accepted the order during the phone conversation. Within a reasonable time the printer had the calendars ready for delivery, but the dealer died from a sudden heart attack. The dealer's will appointed his son as executor and left all of his property to his son. The dealer's business records contained no reference to the transaction with the printer. The dealer's son assumed operation of the business but refused to accept the calendars. The printer sued the son as executor for damages for breach of contract. Explain (1) the reasoning upon which the printer could attempt to collect, (2) the reasoning upon which the son could attempt to defend, and (3) which party should be given judgment.

(b) Other facts being the same, assume the following additional facts: The calendars were delivered to the dealer, but no receipt was given for them. The dealer distributed the calendars among his customers, and had about 100 left over in his office when he suffered the heart attack and died without making any payment for the calendars. When the son as executor refused to pay, the printer sued for the agreed price for the calendars. Explain whether your answers would be different then in Part (a) above.

26. B looked at and expressed satisfaction with a particular commercial refrigerator in S's showroom. The parties then entered into a written contract under which S unconditionally sold the refrigerator to B, and B signed a thirty-day promissory note for the purchase price. B's store, in which the refrigerator was to be installed, was under construction and scheduled to be finished in about two weeks, and S agreed to keep the refrigerator for B, without any charge for storage, until it was wanted and picked up by B. Thereafter completion of the store was delayed, and S agreed to store the refrigerator for a longer time. Upon maturity of the note, B did not pay it and has not since paid it. Now about six weeks after the sale B has run into some unexpected, temporary financial difficulty. C, one of B's creditors, has obtained a judgment against B and has had the sheriff levy on the refrigerator still in S's stock room. Although B is temporarily financially embarrassed, he is fully solvent and has been so at all times.

(a) (1) In whom is legal title to the refrigerator? Explain. (2) Must S turn the refrigerator over to the sheriff? Explain.

(b) Other facts remaining the same, assume that C obtained his judgment and had the levy made two weeks after the date of the S-B contract. Would this change in fact affect either of the answers given in Part (a)? Explain.

27. Calling his establishment the S Stables, S carried on the business of boarding and training horses for various owners, and also buying and selling horses. X, the owner of a valuable racehorse, delivered the horse to S for training. Y was another owner of a valuable racehorse. A thief who carried on business as a horse dealer stole Y's horse and sold it in the ordinary course of business to P who bought innocently and for value. P delivered this horse to S for training. Although S had no authority or right to sell either of the horses left with him by X and P, S wrongfully sold and delivered both horses to B who bought in the ordinary course of S's business and paid fair value, honestly and reasonably thinking that S owned both horses and had every right to sell them. After considerable difficulty, X and Y succeeded in tracing the two horses and conclusively proved the above facts. As between B, P, X, and Y, respectively, who had the better right to the horses? Explain.

28. B, a retail appliance dealer, ordered from S, a wholesaler, five refrigerators of a certain specified make and model. The agreed terms for the transaction included the following: the refrigerators were shipped to B on consignment; B was to place them in stock in his store and sell them at the list price of $195.50 apiece; after sixty days B was to remit $125 to S for each refrigerator sold and return at S's expense the unsold refrigerators; ownership was to remain in S until sale by B. One week after B received the refrigerators, a creditor with a judgment against B and ignorant of B's agreement with S, had the sheriff levy on various items in B's store, including these five refrigerators. Between S and the attaching creditor, who would have the superior interest in the refrigerators? Explain.

29. Morgan Electric Products Inc. manufactures a wide variety of electrical appliances. Morgan uses the consignment as an integral part of its marketing plan. The consignments are "true" consignments rather than consignments intended as security interests. Unsold goods may be returned to the owner-consignor. Morgan contracted with Wilson Distributors Inc. an electrical appliance wholesaler, to market its products under this consignment arrangement. Subsequently Wilson became insolvent and made a general assignment for the benefit of its creditors. Edwards, the assignee, took possession of all of Wilson's inventory, including all the Morgan electrical products. Morgan has demanded return of its appliances asserting that the relationship created by the consignment between itself and Wilson was one of agency and that Wilson never owned the appliances. Furthermore, Morgan argues that under the consignment arrangement there is no obligation owing to Morgan at any time, thus there is nothing to secure under the secured transactions provisions of the Uniform Commercial Code. Edwards has denied the validity of these assertions claiming that the consignment is subject to the Code's filing provisions unless the Code has otherwise been satisfied. Morgan sues to repossess the goods.

a. What are the requirements, if any, to perfect a true consignment such as discussed above?

b. Will Morgan prevail? (Modified from A.I.C.P.A, May 81-3a)

30. A claim has been made by Oliver to certain goods in Brown's possession. Oliver will be entitled to the goods if it can be shown that Smith, the party from whom Brown purchased the goods, obtained them by

a. Deceiving Oliver as to his identity at the time of the purchase.

b. Giving Oliver his check which was later dishonored.

c. Obtaining the goods from Oliver by fraud, punishable as larceny under criminal law.

d. Purchasing goods which had been previously stolen from Oliver. (Modified from A.I.C.P.A. May 82-1(47).)

The Sale and Lease of Goods: Contract Performance and Remedies

The Sale and Lease of Goods: Contract Performance and Remedies

CONTRACTS FOR THE SALE OF GOODS involve performance concepts that are very similar to contracts for the sale of other types of property. Many of the common law rules have been adopted in Article 2 while others have been materially changed. One must keep in mind that Article 2 was designed to promote commerce as well as to promote fairness in circumstances in which the common law rules were deemed too formal. This chapter will examine the performance obligations of both the buyer and the seller under Article 2 as well as those acts or omissions constituting breaches of those agreements. Finally, this chapter will evaluate various remedies belonging to sellers and buyers upon breaches of contracts involving sales of goods.

I. The Duty of Good Faith and Commercial Reasonableness

The Code imposes an obligation of good faith and commercial reasonableness upon all parties to contracts for sales and leases of goods. Commercial reasonableness requires each party to act reasonably in light of the specific circumstances. Open terms to a contract for the sale of goods must be satisfied by each party in good faith and commercial reasonableness.[1] Good faith applies to all parties at all times. It can never be disclaimed orally or

in writing. The Code's requirement of good faith means that all parties must deal fairly with each other and with honesty in fact.[2] In addition, every merchant must observe the reasonable commercial standards of fair dealing in the trade.[3] Merchants are held to a higher standard of conduct than non-merchants under the Code.

II. Performance of a Contract for the Sale of Goods

In concise terms, each seller has an obligation under a contract for the sale of goods to transfer and deliver goods that conform to the contract. The buyer has an obligation to accept conforming goods and to pay the agreed upon price for them.[4]

A. Performance— Concurrent Conditions

Under the Code, if the parties have not otherwise agreed when each obligation to perform will arise, the obligations of the seller and the buyer to perform will be deemed concurrent conditions. This means that the party must go forward with performance before it can bring an action against another party for not performing or refuse to perform. This require-

---

1. UCC Sec. 2-311(1).

2. UCC Sec. 1-203(1)(b).
3. UCC Sec. 2-103(b).
4. UCC Sec. 2-301.

ment may be satisfied in any one of three ways:

1. By performing according to the contract.
2. By tendering performance according to the contract. This means offering to perform in such a way that nothing further remains to be done.
3. By becoming excused from tendering performance.

B. The Seller's Obligations

Each seller is obligated to have and hold conforming goods for the buyer's disposal and to give the buyer notice of the same to enable the buyer to take delivery of the goods.[5]

Tender of delivery does not mean actual delivery in all circumstances. In some cases, tender of delivery occurs upon the seller's notifying the buyer that the goods are available for the buyer's retrieval. But in all cases, tender of delivery must occur at a reasonable hour and manner. This requires a seller to be aware of the particular circumstances of the buyer. For instance, a seller should not generally attempt to make a delivery after regular business hours. In addition, a buyer in the restaurant business with a regular lunch crowd would be justified in refusing to accept a delivery during the lunch rush.

Delivery of the purchased goods must be tendered in a single delivery unless otherwise agreed, unless circumstances are such that either party might rightfully require the delivery in lots.[6]

I. PLACE OF DELIVERY

a. Common Carriers—
Shipment Contracts

If the contract is a shipment contract, the seller must:

---

5. UCC Sec. 2-503(1).
6. UCC Sec. 2-612, 2-307.

1. Tender goods to the carrier.
2. Make a contract for transportation that is reasonable under the circumstances. The seller should take steps to preserve perishable items.
3. Obtain and deliver to the buyer any necessary documents of title permitting the buyer to obtain the goods at the point of destination.
4. Promptly notify the buyer that the shipment has been made.

If the seller fails to meet any of the above requirements and a material loss or delay results from such a failure, the buyer will be entitled to reject the shipment. Parties may agree to lower the standard determining what constitutes a material loss so that even a minor loss can justify rejection of the shipment.[7]

b. Common Carriers—
Destination Contracts[8]

Under destination contracts, the seller must:

1. Ensure that the goods arrive at the point of destination.
2. Tender the goods to the buyer at a reasonable hour. (This does not necessarily mean that the goods will be delivered to the doorstep of the buyer, but could mean making the goods available at the carrier's unloading dock at the city of destination).
3. Hold the goods for the buyer's disposal for a reasonable length of time.
4. Give appropriate notice to the buyer that the goods are available.
5. Provide any necessary documents of title for the buyer to obtain the goods.

---

7. UCC Sec. 2-319–2-322.
8. UCC Sec. 2-503.

Remedies

c. Transportation Contracts Not Involving Common Carriers

If not designated by contract, the buyer must obtain the goods at the seller's place of business, or the seller's residence if the seller has no place of business.[9] If the goods identified to the contract are stored at another location, such as a warehouse, and both parties are aware of that location, then delivery is made there.

2. DELIVERY OF CONFORMING GOODS

Traditional contract law employs what is known as "the perfect tender rule." This rule requires the seller to deliver goods in exact conformity with the contract. The slightest variation will be considered a breach of contract. The Code adopted this rule which provides that if the goods tendered fail in any respect to conform to the terms of the contract, the buyer may:

1. Reject the entire shipment.
2. Accept the entire shipment.
3. Accept any commercial unit or units and reject the rest.[10]

In order to reconcile the inflexibility of the perfect tender rule with the Code's purpose of bringing simplification and flexibility to modern commercial transactions, certain exceptions to the perfect tender rule have been provided. They include: agreement of the parties, cure and certain provisions affecting installment contracts.

a. Agreement of the Parties

The parties are free to enter into a contract altering the rigid effect of the perfect tender rule. Consider the problems that are regularly experienced by those shipping perishable goods. Under the perfect tender rule, one rotten apple could cause the entire shipment to be rejected. In most cases, parties buying and

selling perishable commodities will agree to modify the perfect tender rule in order to permit a reduction in the purchase price according to the arrival condition of the goods. This also opens the door for parties shipping nonperishable goods to permit the seller to repair or replace damaged items. Employing this exception can prevent the waste of time and money resulting from the "all or nothing" impact of the perfect tender rule.

b. Cure

While not defined in the Code, the concept of seller's "cure" is employed by implication.[11] Cure is the seller's right to repair, replace and adjust nonconforming goods prior to the seller's deadline for tendering performance. It works this way: When a buyer rejects a tender of delivery on the basis that the goods were nonconforming, and the time for performance has yet to expire, the seller can notify the buyer promptly of its intention to cure the breach. Upon doing so, the seller may attempt to cure the breach within the contractual time to perform. Once the time for performance has expired, the seller can still exercise the right to cure if the seller had reasonable grounds to believe that the nonconforming tender would have been acceptable to the buyer. This is to protect a seller from unfair surprise by a buyer who has repeatedly accepted reasonable substitutes from that seller.

If a buyer rejects goods on the basis of nonconformity, but fails to disclose the nature of the nonconformity, the buyer cannot later assert the existence of a specific defect as a defense to nonpayment if the defect was one that the seller could have cured.[12] Recall that a buyer must act in good faith in rejecting goods.

9. UCC Sec. 2-308.
10. UCC Sec. 2-601.

11. UCC Sec. 2-508.
12. UCC Sec. 2-605.

c. Installment Contracts

Parties may agree to the delivery of goods in two or more separate shipments or lots. These shipments are often called installments. Each installment or lot is accepted and paid for separately. The buyer can reject an installment only if the nonconformity substantially impairs the value of that installment.[13] Unless the nonconformity substantially impairs the value of the whole contract, the buyer cannot reject an installment if the seller gives adequate assurance of its cure.

A nonconforming installment that substantially impairs the value of the whole contract entitles the buyer to all of its remedies under the Code, including cancellation of the contract. But, the buyer reinstates the contract by accepting another installment without having seasonably notified the seller of its intent to cancel, or by bringing a law suit against the seller with respect to only past installments or demands performance of future installments.[14]

d. The CISG and Conforming Goods

Under the CISG, the buyer must examine the goods promptly. The buyer loses the right to rely on a lack of conformity of the goods as a defense if the buyer does not give notice to the seller specifying the nature of the lack of conformity within a reasonable time after it has been discovered or should have been discovered.[15]

Unless the time is extended by contract, the buyer will loose the right to rely upon a lack of conformity as a defense if it does not give the seller notice within two years after the date upon which the goods were actually received by the buyer.

3. SUBSTITUTION OF CARRIERS

In the event the agreed manner of delivery becomes unavailable or impracticable through no fault of either party, but a commercially reasonable substitute is available, the substitute method is sufficient to tender the goods to the buyer.[16] This flexibility is especially useful in the event that the specified shipper goes on strike. But, any extra costs involved in substituting a carrier will be borne by the seller.

4. DAMAGE TO OR DESTRUCTION OF THE IDENTIFIED GOODS

If the goods identified to the contract are destroyed prior to the risk of loss passing to the buyer, through no fault of either party, both parties will be excused from further performance.[17]

If the loss is partial or if the goods have deteriorated to the point that they no longer conform to the contract, the buyer may either avoid the contract or accept the goods with a price adjustment for the deterioration or deficiency in quality. If the buyer chooses either of these options, he will not have any additional rights or remedies against the seller.[18]

5. COMMERCIAL IMPRACTICABILITY

When something occurs to hinder or to prevent performance by either party or such performance has been made commercially impracticable by the occurrence or non-occurrence of a contingency which was the basic assumption on which the contract was entered into, the perfect tender rule will be set aside.[19] Delay or nondelivery under such circumstances will not be considered a breach of contract. But, the seller must notify the buyer of this occurrence as soon as reasonably possible. It is important that the commercial impracticability be caused by an unforeseen su-

---

13. UCC Sec. 2-612(2).
14. UCC Sec. 2-612.
15. CISG Art. 39.

16. UCC Sec. 2-614(1).
17. UCC Sec. 2-613(a).
18. UCC Sec. 2-613.
19. UCC Sec. 2-615.

Example. The U.S. Department of Agriculture places a ban on the sale of apples treated with a particular pesticide. As a result, one half of the seller's inventory must be destroyed. The seller is unable to locate apples from other suppliers. The seller must notify its buyers of this and offer to fairly allocate among them. ▢

pervening occurrence that was not contemplated by the parties at the time of the contract. This should not be confused with the business risks that buyers and sellers must take every day with respect to problems such as, but not limited to, inflation, drastic changes in interest rates and rapid price increases.

If a seller can partially fill orders under these adverse circumstances, the seller must notify the buyers of its inability to fill orders in full and offer to allocate fairly among them. A buyer may reject a partial shipment as nonconforming.

C. The Buyer's Obligations

Each buyer has an obligation to accept delivery of conforming goods and to pay the agreed price for those goods. In absence of further agreement, the buyer must also furnish facilities reasonably suited for receiving the goods.[20] In addition, the buyer must pay the contract price for the goods at the time and place the buyer receives the goods.[21]

I. PAYMENT

If the parties do not agree otherwise, payment must be made at the time and place the goods are received by the buyer.[22] If credit arrangements have been made, the buyer must pay according to the terms of the credit agreement. The credit period will begin on the date of shipment.[23] The buyer may pay in cash or

in any other commercially acceptable medium.[24]

a. Buyer's Right to Inspect

Unless the parties have agreed otherwise or the shipping arrangement is C.O.D. (Collect On Delivery), the buyer has an absolute right to inspect the goods prior to acceptance. This gives the buyer a chance to determine if the goods are in conformity with the contract. There is no duty to pay for nonconforming goods. The opportunity to inspect the goods is a condition precedent to the seller's right to enforce payment.[25] The buyer will not have a right to inspect the goods before paying if the buyer has agreed to pay upon presentment of a document of title, such as a bill of lading.[26] The time, place and manner of the inspection must be reasonable.

A buyer can rightfully reject a C.O.D. shipment unless the contract specifically called for a C.O.D. shipment. This is because the right to inspect before paying for the goods could be denied to the buyer by using a C.O.D. shipment. If the buyer agrees to accept a C.O.D. shipment, the buyer has waived the right to inspect the goods prior to payment.[27]

b. Payment on Documents of Title

On C.I.F. and C.& F. contracts, payment is due on receipt the bill of lading or other documents even if the goods have yet to arrive at the appointed destination unless the buyers

---

20. UCC Sec. 2-S03(1)(b).
21. UCC Sec. 2-310(a).
22. UCC Sec. 2-511.
23. UCC Sec. 2-310(d).

24. UCC Sec. 2-511.
25. UCC Sec. 2-513(1).
26. UCC Sec. 2-513.
27. UCC Sec. 2-513(3).

knows that the goods are nonconforming or the parties have specifically agreed otherwise.[28] This represents another exception to the buyer's right to inspect the goods prior to payment.

2. ACCEPTING CONFORMING GOODS

a. Manifesting Acceptance

The buyer may manifest her acceptance of conforming goods as follows:

1. By words or conduct.[29]
2. By failing to reject the goods within a reasonable time after having had a reasonable opportunity to inspect.[30]
3. By acting in a fashion inconsistent with the seller's ownership interest in the goods. For instance, if the buyer resells the goods, they will be deemed accepted by the original buyer. But, the buyer's limited use for testing and inspecting does not constitute an acceptance of the goods.[31]

b. Revocation of Acceptance

As a general rule, once a buyer accepts the goods, they cannot later be rejected. But, this does not foreclose all of the buyer's opportunities to return nonconforming goods. A buyer who has accepted goods may revoke its acceptance as to a lot or a commercial unit if it is so nonconforming that its value is impaired substantially.[32] Revocation of acceptance is permitted if:

1. The buyer accepted the goods under a reasonable belief that the seller would cure any defect seasonably; or
2. The buyer accepted the goods without discovering the nonconformity

and the acceptance was induced either by the difficulty of reasonable discovery of the defect prior to acceptance or by the seller's assurances that the goods were conforming to the contract.

In order to revoke acceptance, the buyer must notify the seller within a reasonable time following the time the buyer discovered or should have discovered the nonconformity. This must occur prior to any substantial change in the goods caused by something other than the defect. If the buyer properly revokes, the buyer has the same rights as it would have had it originally rejected the goods. If the buyer has the right to revoke acceptance, it may revoke acceptance of less than all of the goods under the contract but not less than a commercial unit.

III. Anticipatory Repudiation

If a party engages in business for a substantial length of time, it will likely encounter another party who is unwilling or unable to perform following formation of a contract. It is especially difficult to wait for performance when one has evidence that the other party will not be performing. If prior to the time for performance, a party clearly communicates an intent not to perform, this constitutes a breach of contract under the doctrine of anticipatory repudiation.[33] It is important to keep in mind that this is a breach that takes place prior to the time to perform under the contract.

If this happens, the aggrieved party may:

1. Await performance by the repudiating party for a commercially reasonable time; or
2. Resort to any remedy for breach of contract even if the aggrieved party has notified the repudiating party that he is awaiting performance and

---

28. UCC Sec. 2-310(b), 2-513(3).
29. UCC Sec. 2-606(1)(a).
30. UCC Sec. 2-602(1). 2-606(1)(b).
31. UCC Sec. 2-606(1)(c).
32. UCC Sec. 2-608.

---

33. UCC Sec. 2-610.

has urged retraction of the repudiation.

In either event, the aggrieved party may suspend performance of his duties under the contract. In addition, a seller has the right to identify goods to the contract in spite of the breach and may salvage unfinished goods.

In concise terms, the non-breaching party may pursue two routes. First, the non-breaching party may treat the breach as a final breach and pursue any remedy pursuant to Article 2. Second, it may wait for the other party to perform.

If the aggrieved party delays taking action, the breaching party has a limited ability to retract the anticipatory repudiation. This can occur if the performance by the breaching party has yet to come due and the aggrieved party has not materially changed its position. Under these circumstances, the repudiation may be retracted by any method which would clearly indicate an intent to perform. It must include any assurance of performance justifiably demanded under Article 2.[34] Once the retraction has been effected, the rights of the repudiating party are reinstated.[35]

IV. Demands for Adequate Assurance of Performance

If a party has reasonable grounds to believe that the agreed performance will not take place, the aggrieved party may demand written assurance of due performance. Until such assurance is received, further performance may be suspended by the aggrieved party without liability. If this situation arises between merchants, the grounds for suspension of performance are determined by commercial standards governing their particular type of business.[36]

---

34. UCC Sec. 2-609.
35. UCC Sec. 2-611.
36. UCC Sec. 2-609.

If the demanded assurances are not made within a reasonable time, not to exceed 30 days, the non-response may be treated as a repudiation. In addition, the Code requires parties to cooperate with each other. If a party fails to reasonably cooperate during the performance of a contract, the other party may suspend performance without liability and hold the other party in breach.[37]

V. Resolving Disputes Under the CISG

A. Exemptions from Contract Liability

The CISG provides the parties a number of exemptions from contract liability.

A party will not be liable to perform any obligation if it can establish that its failure to perform was due to a cause beyond its control and that it could not have been expected to have taken the impediment into account at the time of the conclusion of the contract or to have avoided or overcome the impediment or its consequences.

If a party's failure to perform was due to the failure of a third party whom the party engaged to perform the whole or a part of the contract, that party will be exempt from liability only if:

1. The party would be exempt as described above; and
2. The person to whom the party has en-gaged would be exempt if the provisions of the paragraph were applied to him.

The exemption provided by this Article only applies to the period during which the impediment exists.

The party who fails to perform must give notice to the other party of the impediment and

---

37. UCC Sec. 2-3 11(3).

its effect on the party's ability to perform. If the notice is not received by the other party within a reasonable time after the party who fails to perform knew or should have known of the impediment, liability will be found for damages resulting from such nonreceipt.[38]

B. Extensions of Time for Performance

The CISG provides parties with much more latitude in resolving their disputes privately than does the UCC. For instance, the CISG permits either party to grant additional time for the other to perform. Unless the party granting the extension of time has received notice from the other party that it will not perform as agreed within the fixed period, the granting party may not resort to any remedy for breach of contract during that period. The granting party retains the power to recover for damages resulting from the delay in performance.[39]

In addition, a seller may, even after the date for delivery, remedy at its own expense any failure to perform its obligation if this can be done without an unreasonable delay and without causing the buyer unreasonable inconvenience. This must be done without any uncertainty of the seller's reimbursement of expenses advanced by the buyer. The buyer retains the right to recover for damages as set forth in the Convention. This is subject to a party's right to avoidance the contract.

If the seller requests that the buyer make known whether the buyer will accept performance and the buyer does not comply with the request within a reasonable time, the seller may perform within the time indicated in the seller's request. If this occurs, the buyer may not resort to any remedy which is inconsistent with performance by the seller during the stated period. Any notice by the seller that it will perform within a specified period of time is assumed to include such a request that the buyer make its decision known. Notice of the request must be received by the buyer to be effective.[40]

VI. Remedies for the Breach of a Sales Contract

The Code provides both buyers and sellers with a number of remedies to seek in response to a breach of contract. The remedies available under the Code are not exclusive. This means that an injured party may resort to any combination of available remedies. The goal of the system of remedies is to place the non-breaching party in as good a position as if the other party had fully performed. This end may be achieved through one or a combination of available remedies under the Code.

The Code permits parties to provide for their own remedies in their contracts. The parties may specify that their remedies are in substitution of the remedies available under the Code or in addition to those set forth in the Code. The parties have the power to limit or alter the measure of damages available under the Code, within limits. It is not uncommon to see an agreement limit a buyer's remedies to returning or replacing nonconforming goods or to refund of the purchase price.

The Code limits the parties' ability to modify or limit the Code's available remedies. Any agreement must leave each party with an adequate remedy. If circumstances result in an exclusive or limited remedy that "fails its essential purpose" or deprives either party of the substantial benefit of the bargain, the remedies under the Code are reinstated.[41] If contract provisions overwhelmingly favor one

---

38. CISG Art. 79.
39. CISG Arts. 47 & 63.

40. CISG Art. 48.
41. UCC Sec. 2-719(2).

side, as often found in adhesion contracts,[42] a court may declare that such an unfair limitation of available remedies is unconscionable.[43] The parties also have the power to limit or exclude consequential damages so long as such an exclusion or limitation is not unconscionable. Unless the parties agree otherwise, contractually provided remedies are optional and not exclusive.

A. Seller's Remedies

A buyer may breach a contract in a number of ways. It may repudiate before the seller's performance is due. It may fail to pay the purchase price of the goods delivered. It may wrongfully reject conforming goods. A buyer may wrongfully revoke a previous acceptance of conforming goods. A seller has a wide variety of remedies available to respond to these breaches. These remedies vary according to the circumstances, including the existence and location of the goods. Keep in mind that remedies may be combined if appropriate under the circumstances.

I. If the Goods are not Under the Buyer's Control

a. Withholding Delivery

In general, a seller can withhold delivery of the goods identified to the contract upon the buyer's breach. A seller can withhold the entire undelivered balance of goods if the buyer's breach is a material breach.[44]

If the breach results from the buyer's insolvency, the seller can refuse to deliver the goods until the buyer pays the full amount in cash.[45] The buyer is insolvent under the Code

when one ceases to pay her debts in the ordinary course of business, cannot pay debts as they come due or if she is insolvent within the meaning of the federal Bankruptcy Code.[46] If the buyer files for bankruptcy, or is forced into involuntary bankruptcy, the seller has no obligation to ship the goods to the buyer or the bankruptcy trustee unless cash payment is tendered.

b. Stopping a Carrier or Bailee from Delivering the Goods

If the seller delivers goods to a bailee such as a warehouse person or a carrier and the buyer has not received them, the goods are considered "in transit." If the seller learns of the buyer's insolvency while the goods are in transit, the seller may stop delivery.

If the buyer is not insolvent, but otherwise breaches the contract, the seller can only stop goods in transit if the quantity shipped is at least a carload, truck load, plane load or a larger shipment.[47] This is due to the enormous burden that stoppage of goods in transit represents to carriers.

In order to stop delivery, the seller must timely notify the carrier or other bailee. If a carrier has sufficient time to stop the goods, the goods must be held and delivered according to the seller's orders. The seller must pay all additional costs involved. The carrier will be liable to the seller if the carrier fails to act properly.[48] The seller will lose its right to stop delivery under the following circumstances:

1. The buyer obtains possession of the goods.

2. The carrier acknowledges the buyer's right to the goods by reshipping or storing the goods upon the instructions of the buyer.

---

42. An adhesion contract is one in which one of the parties drafts the entire agreement without negotiation and presents to the other party in a "take it or leave it" scenario.
43. UCC Sec. 2-302.
44. UCC Sec. 2-703.
45. UCC Sec. 2-702(1).

46. UCC Sec. 1-201(23).
47. UCC Sec. 2-705(1).
48. UCC Sec. 2-705(3).

3. A bailee other than a carrier acknowledges that the goods are being held. for the benefit of the buyer.
4. Negotiating a negotiable document of title covering the identified goods to the buyer.

2. IF THE GOODS ARE UNDER THE BUYER'S CONTROL

a. Recovering the Purchase Price (and incidental damages in certain circumstances)

A seller can sue the buyer for the purchase price of the goods and incidental damages under any one of the following circumstances:

1. The buyer has accepted the goods and has not revoked the acceptance, thus giving the buyer title to the goods.
2. Conforming goods have been lost or damaged after the risk of loss has passed to the buyer.
3. The buyer has breached the contract after the goods have been identified to the contract and the seller has been unable to sell the goods.[49] If this happens, the goods must be held for the benefit of the buyer. In the event they are eventually sold by the seller prior to full collection of the purchase price and any other damages awarded to the seller and against the buyer, the sale of proceeds must be credited to the buyer's balance.

These are the only situations in which an action for payment of the contract price will be allowed.

Incidental damages include any commercially reasonable charges, expenses or commissions incurred for the stoppage of delivery and the transportation, care and custody of

goods after the buyer's breach. The seller will be entitled to incidental damages relating to the return or the resale of the goods or otherwise caused by the buyer's breach.[50]

b. The Limited Right to Reclaim Goods

If the seller discovers that the buyer received goods on credit while insolvent and the buyer has had possession of the goods for ten days or less, the seller has the right to demand and reclaim the goods. The ten day limit does not apply if the buyer misrepresented it's solvency in writing within three months prior to delivery of the goods.[51]

The right to reclaim goods is subject to the rights of a good faith purchaser for value or other buyer in the ordinary course of business who purchases the goods before the seller reclaims them.

The seller's right of reclamation gives the seller an advantage over other creditors of the buyer with respect to the goods reclaimed. Because of this, the Code bars the seller from pursuing other remedies against the buyer with respect to any other damages suffered in connection with the reclaimed goods.[52] The seller's right of reclamation is very important if the buyer files for bankruptcy protection or is forced into involuntary bankruptcy. This is because section 546(c) of the Bankruptcy Code limits a bankruptcy trustee's rights with respect to a seller's statutory and common law rights if the debtor received goods while insolvent. In that situation, the seller need only demand the return of the goods.

c. Identifying, Reselling or Salvaging Goods

If the goods have not left the seller's possession, the seller can identify conforming goods to the contract even if they had not been identified at the time of the breach. After identify-

---

49. UCC Sec. 2-709(1).

50. UCC Sec. 2-710.
51. UCC Sec. 2-702(2).
52. UCC Sec. 2-702(3).

ing goods to the contract, the seller can resell the goods and sue the buyer for damages resulting from any loss incurred.

If the goods were unfinished at the time of the breach, the seller has two options:

1. Discontinue work on the goods and sell them for scrap or salvage value.
2. Finish the goods, identify them to the contract, and resell them. If the seller chooses this alternative, the seller must be reasonable and exercise good faith in attempting to resell the goods under the circumstances. The seller has a duty to mitigate damages.[53]

In either event, the resale must be in a commercially reasonable manner and in good faith. The seller can recover any deficiency between the original contract price and the price actually received from the resale. The seller may also recover incidental damages, such as the costs of transporting, protecting, storing, and reselling the goods.[54] The seller will not be liable for any profit it might realize in the event of a resale.[55] Requiring a seller to pay the buyer for any profit realized under such circumstances would reward the buyer for its breach.

Resale of the goods may be public or private. The sale may be in a single unit or in parcels. The seller must give reasonable notice to the buyer of the time and place of the sale, unless the goods are perishable or will otherwise rapidly decline in value. In such an event, the seller must attempt to dispose of the goods in a commercially reasonable manner attempting to mitigate further losses.[56]

A bona fide purchaser of resold goods take title to the goods free of all claims of the original buyer, even if the seller did not comply with all the provisions of the Code in the resale.

---

53. UCC Sec. 2-704(2).
54. UCC Sec. 2-706(1), 2-710.
55. UCC Sec. 2-706(6).
56. UCC Sec. 2-706(2) and (3).

d. Recovering Damages after Wrongful Repudiation or Non-acceptance of Conforming Goods

In the event the buyer refuses to accept conforming goods or repudiates, the seller is entitled to damages for the breach. Usually, the basic measure of damage for the buyer's breach is the difference in the market price of the goods at the time and place of tender and the unpaid contract price, together with any incidental damages, but less any expenses saved as a consequence of the breach.[57]

If the seller's action for damages is brought as the result of an anticipatory repudiation, the damage calculation is based upon the market price at the time the seller learned of the repudiation rather the market price at the time of the tender.

If the general measure of damage is inadequate to put the seller in as good a position as the seller would have been had the contract been fully performed, the seller is entitled to an alternative measure. In this event, the measure of damage is the profit that the seller would have made from the transaction (including reasonable overhead), together with incidental damages and an allowance for costs reasonably incurred, reduced by any payments by the buyer and any proceeds of resale.[58] This section assists the "lost-volume seller." The Code recognizes that the lost volume seller in fact has lost profit even though the seller can resale the goods for the contract price.

e. Cancellation of the Contract

If the buyer wrongfully rejects conforming goods, wrongfully revokes acceptance of conforming goods, fails to pay, or repudiates the contract in whole or in part, the seller can cancel the contract with respect to the goods in-

---

57. UCC Sec. 2-708(1).
58. UCC Sec. 2-708(2).

volved.[59] If the breach is material, the entire contract can be canceled.

If the seller chooses to cancel the contract, the seller must give the buyer notice of cancellation. From that point on, the seller is discharged. The buyer's obligation is not discharged, but rather, the buyer remains in breach of contract and may be sued for damages.[60] If the seller's cancellation is not justified, the seller is in breach of contract and may be sued for damages.

B. Buyer's Remedies

The buyer's basic remedies are set forth in Section 2–711 of the Code. The buyer has various rights upon the seller's breach that vary with the circumstances as set forth below.

I. PRIOR TO TENDER OF DELIVERY OF THE GOODS

a. The Right to Reject Nonconforming or Improperly Delivered Goods

If the seller tenders goods that fail to conform to the contract in any respect, the buyer may reject them. The buyer has the option of keeping those goods that conform to the contract and rejecting those that do not.[61] The rejection must be effected within a reasonable time and the seller must be seasonably notified.[62] After the buyer rejects the goods, the buyer cannot exercise any ownership interest in them. Any acts inconsistent with rejection will be deemed an acceptance of the goods by the buyer.[63] The buyer should identify particular defects to justify the rejection and to establish whether or not the seller could have cured the breach.

If the seller has no agent or place of business at the place of rejection, the buyer must follow any reasonable instruction from the seller with respect to taking care of the rejected goods. The Code requires the seller to reimburse the buyer for the cost of caring for the goods and following the seller's instructions.[64] The same is true if the buyer has rightfully revoked acceptance.[65] If no instructions are received and the goods are perishable, the buyer may resell the goods in good faith and retain an appropriate reimbursement for its expenses from the proceeds.[66] Otherwise the buyer may store them for the seller's account or reship them to the seller.[67]

b. The Right to Recover Identified Goods from an Insolvent Seller

If a seller goes into bankruptcy or becomes insolvent while in possession of the goods that the buyer has paid all or part of the purchase price, the buyer may recover the goods if the seller became insolvent within 10 days after receiving the first payment if the goods have been identified with the contract. But, the buyer must pay any unpaid balance due on the goods. If the buyer does not exercise[68] this right, the buyer will stand in line with all other creditors hoping for a distribution from the bankruptcy proceeding. History has proven convincingly that the buyer should attempt to recover identified goods as opposed to hoping for a miracle in the bankruptcy court and to receive a distribution.

c. The Right to Retain Goods and Enforce a Security Interest

A buyer who rightfully rejects goods or who justifiably revokes acceptance of goods has a security interest in those goods for the purpose of enforcing the buyer's right to recover expenses relating to holding those goods for the seller's benefit. The security interest covers payments made on the goods as well as ex-

---

59. UCC Sec. 2-703(f).
60. UCC Sec. 2-703, 2-106(4).
61. UCC Sec. 2-601.
62. UCC Sec. 2-602.
63. UCC Sec. 2-606.

64. UCC Sec. 2-603.
65. UCC Sec. 2-608(3).
66. UCC Sec. 2-603(1).
67. UCC Sec. 2-604.
68. UCC Sec. 2-502.

penses for inspection, transportation, care and custody.[69] The buyer may enforce this security interest to recover expenses resulting from resale of the goods, withholding delivery and stoppage of delivery. If the goods are resold, the buyer must account for the proceeds and remit all remaining funds to the seller.[70]

d. Cover

A buyer who has rightfully rejected or revoked acceptance may exercise the remedy of cover. Cover is the purchase of substitute goods from another source. This is also available when the seller repudiates or otherwise fails to deliver conforming goods. The buyer must act in good faith and without unreasonable delay in obtaining cover.[71]

The buyer is entitled to an award of damages equal to the difference in the cost of cover and the contract price plus consequential damages, less any costs that were saved.

The buyer's consequential damages may include any loss suffered that the seller could have foreseen at the time of the contract and any injury to the buyer's person or property resulting from a breach of warranty.[72] Product warranties will be discussed in the next chapter.

Buyers are not required to exercise the remedy of cover. Buyers may still attempt to exercise other remedies.[73] But, if the buyer does not cover when it was reasonably possible to do so, the buyer will not be entitled to consequential damages that could have been avoided by purchasing substitute goods.[74] This policy was designed to encourage mitigation of damages.

---

69. UCC Sec. 2-711 (3).
70. UCC Sec. 2-711(3), 2-706(6).
71. UCC Sec. 2-712.
72. UCC Sec. 2-715(2).
73. UCC Sec. 2-712(2)(a).
74. UCC Sec. 2-715(2)(a).

e. Specific Performance

The buyer can sue for specific performance when the goods are unique.[75] Works of art, patents, copyrights and collectable items fall into this category. Monetary damages are deemed inadequate under the circumstances.

f. Replevin

Replevin is an action to recover goods from someone who is wrongfully withholding property from its rightful possessor. The buyer has a right of replevin with respect to goods identified to the contract if the seller has repudiated or otherwise breached. But, the buyer must demonstrate that it was unable to effect "cover" for such goods or that the circumstances reasonably indicated that such a course of action was unavailable.[76]

g. Cancellation of the Contract

The buyer can cancel or rescind the contract when the seller repudiates or otherwise fails to make proper delivery. In addition, the buyer can cancel or rescind the contract upon rightful rejection or revocation of acceptance with respect to any part of the contract directly involved in the breach. If the breach is substantial and materially impairs the value of the whole contract, the buyer may cancel or rescind the whole contract.

Upon the buyer giving notice of cancellation to the seller, the buyer is relieved from all further obligations. The buyer retains its right to pursue any and all available remedies against the seller.

h. Recovery of Damages for Nondelivery or Repudiation

The measure of damages under these circumstances is the difference between the contract price and the market price at the time the buyer learned of the seller's breach. The market price is determined at the place where the

---

75. UCC Sec. 2-716(1).
76. UCC Sec. 2-716(3).

seller was to deliver the goods. The buyer may, in some cases, get incidental and consequential damages less expenses saved.[77] The damages here are based upon the time and place the buyer would have obtained cover.

2. AFTER TENDER OF THE GOODS

A buyer has a reasonable time to notify the seller that the accepted goods did not conform to the contract. The reasonableness of the amount of time that elapsed will be measured form the time the buyer discovered or should have discovered the nonconformity.[78]

When the buyer accepts nonconforming goods, the buyer is entitled to recover from the seller any loss resulting in the ordinary course of events as determined by any manner which is reasonable. This is available for both breach of contract and breach of warranty.[79]

The buyer may, upon notice to the seller, deduct all or any part of the damages suffered by the buyer from any part of the sales price still due in payable.[80]

In the event there has been a breach of a seller's warranty, damages will be calculated by taking the difference between the value of the goods as accepted and the value of the goods had they conformed to the warranty.

A buyer's customer can bring an action for a breach of seller's warranty. When the buyer is sued by its customer for problems with goods warranted by the seller, the buyer has two options:

1. The buyer may give the seller written notice of the litigation. Unless the seller enters the lawsuit and defends after a seasonable receipt of such notice, the seller will be bound by any factual determination in any subsequent legal action.

2. The buyer can defend the action and later bring an action against the original seller.

C. Remedies under the CISG

While the CISG contains numerous provisions to promote resolution of disputes between parties, there will be times when the aggrieved party will desire to resort to formal remedies. The CISG provides for a wide array remedies for breach of contract. With the exception of an unusual damage formula, the CISG's remedies are similar to those of the American common law. Unlike American common law, the CISG establishes specific performance as the primary remedy. The contracting parties may agree to vary the remedy provisions to suit their mutual desires. The Convention permits the parties to limit remedies to repair or replacement of nonconforming goods. Remedies under the CISG include money damages, avoidance of the contract and specific performance.

1. MONEY DAMAGES

It is common for an aggrieved party to desire relief in the form of monetary damages. The aggrieved party may desire compensation based upon the difference in the contract price and the market price. In addition, parties often claim relief in the form of lost profits resulting from reasonably foreseeable consequences of a breach of contract.

The CISG permits a party to recover damages for breach of contract equal to the sum of the loss, including lost profit resulting from the consequence of the breach. The party in breach will not be held liable for damages that could not have been foreseen at the time of the conclusion of the contract.[81]

A party who relies upon a breach of contract must take such measures as are reasonable under the circumstances to mitigate the loss,

77. UCC Sec. 2-713.
78. UCC Sec. 2-607(3)(a).
79. UCC Sec. 2-714(1).
80. UCC Sec. 2-717.

81. CISG Art. 74.

including loss of profit. Failing to take steps to mitigate the loss can result in a reduction of damages to the aggrieved party.[82]

2. AVOIDANCE OF THE CONTRACT

The CISG contains provisions permitting parties to refuse deliveries of nonconforming goods or returning nonconforming goods under certain circumstances once defects are discovered. While the UCC refers to these remedies as "rejection" and "revocation of acceptance," the CISG refers to this concept as avoidance of the contract.[83]

The right of either party to avoid a contract is triggered by a fundamental breach. A fundamental breach is a breach resulting in a detriment to the other party that substantially deprives it of what it would be entitled to expect under the contract, unless the party in breach did not foresee, and a reasonable person in the same circumstances would not have foreseen such a result.[84] This means that minor problems such as shipping problems will not be deemed fundamental breaches and therefore will not trigger a party's power to avoid the contract.

a. Avoidance by the Buyer

A buyer has the power to avoid a contract under the following circumstances:[85]

1. If the failure by the seller to perform any of its obligations under the contract amounts to a fundamental breach of contract; or
2. In case of nondelivery of the goods, if the seller does not deliver the goods within the additional period of time fixed by the buyer or declares that it will not deliver goods within the period so fixed. Keep in mind that the buyer does not have a duty to fix

an additional time period for performance by the seller.

The buyer does not have the duty to accept or pay for nonconforming goods. The buyer is not required to sue for damages in a court of law. The CISG permits the buyer to notify the seller that it is avoiding the contract and returning the goods for a full refund. This may work out well for a buyer who would prefer to avoid a contract in a market where the price of goods is rapidly declining. If the buyer sought money damages in a court of law, the difference between the market price and the contract price would yield very little monetary relief for the buyer. The opportunity to avoid the contract frees the buyer of the legal entanglements so that it may enter into another arrangement with a different seller.

b. Avoidance by the Seller

The seller can declare a contract avoided under either of the following two conditions:[86]

1. The buyer fails to perform any of its obligations resulting in a fundamental breach of contract; or
2. If the buyer does not, within the additional period of time fixed by the seller, perform its obligations to pay the price or take delivery of the goods, or declares that it will not do the same within the period so fixed. The seller cannot be compelled to extend the time for performance.

If the contract is avoided, the seller has no further obligation to the buyer. It is relieved from the obligation to deliver the goods. If the goods have been delivered, the seller has the right to reclaim the goods.

3. SPECIFIC PERFORMANCE

Specific performance is an equitable remedy generally reserved for extraordinary situa-

---

82. CISG Art. 77.
83. CISG Arts. 49 & 64.
84. CISG Art. 25.
85. CISG Art. 49.

---

86. CISG Art. 25.

Example. A buyer purchases snow removal equipment from a seller during the summer season. The limitation period with respect to the warranty will not begin to run until the winter season begins because both parties understand that is when the product will be in operation. ☐

* * *

Example. If a seller is sued for both a breach of warranty and on a strict liability theory for injuries resulting from a defective machine, the UCC statute of limitation period will govern only the breach of warranty suit. The state law limitation period will govern the strict liability portion of the lawsuit. ☐

tions. U.S. courts will not enforce specific performance as a contract remedy when money damages will adequately compensate the aggrieved party. One of the few circumstances in which a contract for the sale of goods would justify the court ordering specific performance would be a contract for the sale of an unique item. Items that are one of a kind and that cannot be reproduced, such as works of art or other collectable items, fall within the scope of the proper use of specific performance as a remedy. A party can demand the performance of any obligation by another party within limits. The CISG permits specific performance only in those circumstances in which a court would do so under its domestic law.[87]

In the United States, a court hearing a plea for specific performance against a party would look to the domestic law of the United States, the Uniform Commercial Code, to determine whether or not specific performance would be appropriate in that particular case. Therefore, the CISG will function very much like the UCC when a dispute is heard in a United States Court. But, if the matter is heard in the court of another nation that has approved the CISG, the result could be much different. Other nations are much more likely to require a seller to deliver subject matter of a contract even if monetary damages could suffice. It is very important for a seller to re-

view the laws and customs of its buyers' nations to determine the legal impact of such a breach.

VII. The Statute of Limitations

Under the Code, an action for breach of a sales contract must commence within 4 years after the cause of action arises.[88] The Code permits parties to reduce the limitation period by agreement to a period of not less than one year. The Code does not permit the parties to extend the period beyond the four year term. By adopting a uniform statute of limitations, the Code attempts to avoid possible conflicting limitation periods applicable to interstate transactions and goods. In addition, because most business retain records for at least four years, the Code's statute of limitations increases the likelihood that important documents and other relevant evidence will be available to resolve disputes between the parties.

The limitation period begins to run once a breach of contract occurs, even if the other party is unaware of its occurrence. In general, a warranty period will begin upon the seller's tender of delivery of the goods unless the warranty explicitly extends to future performance of the goods and discovery of any breach must await the time of that performance. To avoid an unfair result for buyers

---

87. CISG Art. 28.

88. UCC Sec. 2-725.

purchasing goods for future use, the Code provides that when a warranty explicitly extends to future performance, discovery of the breach of warranty must await the time of performance.[89]

In the event a lawsuit is brought on a theory not covered by the Code, the limitation period stated by the Code will not apply. The state law statute of limitation period for that particular cause of action will be applied.

VIII. Liquidated Damages

The parties can agree in advance to a specific monetary remedy in the event either party breaches. These damages are called liquidated damages. They must be reasonable within view of the anticipated or actual loss caused by the breach. If enforceable, the aggrieved party is limited to recovery of only those damages set forth. If the amount of unreasonably large, it will be declared void as a penalty and the court will determine the damages. This determination is made by examining what the usual remedy would have been in that situation.[90]

* * *

Problems

1. S, owner of a large apple orchard, entered into a written contract under which S was to sell and deliver to B by a certain date 1,000 bushels of apples to be picked from S's orchard, and B was to pay $2 per bushel upon delivery.

(a) Before the apples were ripe enough to be picked, a windstorm destroyed the entire crop. When S failed to deliver any apples to B, B sued for damages. What result?

(b) Assume that the windstorm destroyed half of the crop. On the agreed delivery date, S tendered to B 500 bushels. What were the rights of the parties? (Modified from A.I.C.P.A., May 59-10.)

2. In January, S Company entered into a contract with B Company under which S Company agreed to sell and deliver to B Company and B Company to buy 4 3/4 cents per gallon, 1,500,000 wine gallons of refined blackstrap molasses of the usual run, from the M Company refinery, to test about 60 percent sugars, delivery to be in stated installments over most of the year. In February, because of rising sugar prices, the operators of M Company refinery decided to decrease output, a decision over which S Company had no control. During that year, the refinery's output totaled only 485,000 gallons, of which 344,083 gallons were allotted by M Company to S Company and by S Company to B Company. The market price for such molasses went up and in June was 7 1/2 cents per gallon and by October 8 1/4 cents per gallon. The above-mentioned 344,083 gallons was all the molasses S Company shipped to B Company during the contract period. Upon expiration of the contract period, B Company sued S Company for damages for failure to deliver the contracted quantity of molasses.

(a) Assume that at the time of the January contract, S Company had a contract with M Company to buy during the year a quantity of molasses greater than that specified in the S Company-B Company contract. When B Company sued S Company, explain (1) the reasoning upon which S Company could attempt to defend, (2) the reasoning upon which B Company could attempt to win, and (3) which party should be given judgment.

(b) Assume that over the prior several years, without any advance contract with M Company, S Company had regularly ordered and received from M Company a greater quantity of molasses than was specified in the S Company-B Company contract, and that therefore S Company, reasonably believing it to be unnecessary, had no advance contract with M Company for deliveries during the year of the S Company-B Company contract. Answer the same questions asked in Part (a).

---

89. UCC Sec. 2-725(2).
90. UCC Sec. 2-718.

3. S entered into a written contract with B agreeing to manufacture and deliver to B, at a stated price, 5,000 ladies' sweaters of specified types, deliveries to be made in equal quantities over a five-month period. Before any deliveries could be made, S's employees went on strike which remained unsettled for three months beyond the last delivery date.

(a) B sued S for damages for breach of contract. What result? Explain.

(b) If you were S, and were negotiating the above contract with B, what would you have done and why, in order to avoid such a dispute as described above. (Modified from A.I.C.P.A., May 29-3.)

4. B, in Buffalo, contracted to buy 20 cases of a specified brand and size of canned corn from S, of Chicago, for a contract price of $600 payable in thirty days. Pursuant to the contract, S selected and set aside 20 cases meeting the contract description and tagged them with B's name. The contract required S to ship the corn to B via the Norfolk & Western Railway Company, f.o.b. Chicago. Before S delivered the corn to the railroad, the 20 cases were stolen from S's warehouse.

(a) Between S and B, who would stand the loss of the corn? Explain.

(b) Suppose S had delivered the corn to the railroad. After the corn had been loaded on a freight car, but before the train left the yard, the car was broken open and its contents, including the corn, stolen. Between S and B, who would stand the loss? Explain.

(c) Other facts remaining the same, would the answer in Part (b) be the same if: (1) The terms were $600 c.o.d.? (2) The terms were $600 sight draft, bill of lading attached, cash against documents? (3) The terms were $600, sight draft, bill of lading attached, inspection allowed? (4) The terms were $600, c.i.f., Buffalo, New York? (Modified from A.I.C.P.A., Nov. 50-8.)

5. Bob purchased a typewriter from Sam. Sam is not in the business of selling typewriters. Sam tendered delivery of the typewriter after receiving payment in full from Bob. Bob informed Sam that he was unable to take possession of the typewriter at that time, but would return later that day. Before Bob returned, the typewriter was destroyed by a fire. The risk of loss

(a) Passed to Bob upon Sam's tender of delivery.

(b) Remained with Sam, since Bob had not yet received the typewriter.

(c) Passed to Bob at the time the contract was formed and payment was made.

(d) Remained with Sam, since title had not yet passed to Bob. (Modified from A.I.C.P.A. May 84-1(48).)

6. Smith Co. owned 100 tires which it deposited in a public warehouse on April 25, receiving a negotiable warehouse receipt in its name. Smith sold the tires to Brown Co. On which of the following dates did the risk of loss transfer from Smith to Brown?

(a) May—Brown signed a contract to buy the tires from Smith for $15,000. Delivery was to be at the warehouse.

(b) May 2—Brown paid for the tires.

(c) May 3—Smith negotiated the warehouse receipt to Brown.

(d) May 4—Brown received delivery of the tires at the warehouse. (Modified from A.I.C.P.A. Nov. 83-1(46).)

7. S, the owner of a retail furniture store, entered into an agreement with B under which S delivered a chair to B's home. B was to use the chair for one week, and then either return it to the store or pay S the purchase price of $75. Before B communicated with S or did anything further in regard to the chair, B's home and its contents (including the chair) were destroyed by fire, through no fault of B.

(a) Assume that the fire occurred five days after B received the chair. As between S and B, upon whom would the loss of the chair fall? Explain.

(b) Assume that the fire occurred ten days after B received the chair. Upon whom would the loss of the chair fall, S or B? Explain. (Modified from A.I.C.P.A., Nov. 52-8b.)

8. B, a retail appliance dealer in Chicago, ordered from S of Philadelphia 25 refrigerators of a specified make, model, and price. The terms were as stated below. Although B used proper care, the refrigerators were destroyed in an accidental fire one week after they were delivered to B.

(a) The agreed terms between S and B were f.o.b. Chicago, price payable within sixty days, but B was to have the right to return at his own expense within the sixty-day period any one or more of the refrigerators (if still unused), and thereby cancel his obligation to pay for the returned refrigerators. Nothing was stated between S and B as to ownership or risk, and there were no further communications between them from the time B received the goods until after their destruction. Had risk of loss passed to B, and if so, when? Explain.

(b) The agreed terms between S and B were: goods on consignment to B, B to place them in stock in his store and sell at the list price of $195.50 apiece; after sixty days B was to remit $125 to S for each refrigerator sold, and return at S's expense the unsold refrigerators; ownership was to remain in S until sale by B. Nothing was stated as to risk, and there were no further communications between S and B from the time B received the goods until after their destruction. Had risk of loss passed to B, and if so, when? Explain.

9. On April 3, S entered into a written contract with a railway, under which S agreed to sell and the railway to buy, within thirty days, 40 white oak poles of a specified size, at a stated price, f.o.b. cars at a designated station along the railway's line. By April 28, S accumulated poles of the required size and number at the designated station and notified the railway to send cars. In spite of S's repeated requests, the railway failed to bring the necessary cars to that station, and two weeks later, although S had piled the poles properly, an unusually heavy rainstorm washed the poles into the river, and they were lost. S sued the railway for the value of the poles. Was S entitled to recover? Explain.

10. On April 1, B. Brown, a grocery wholesaler in Pittsburgh, gave the following order to A. Adams, a salesman for S. Smith, a sign manufacturer:

Chicago, Illinois   Order No. 1321
                                       [Date]

Sold to: B. Brown,
                Pittsburgh, Pennsylvania
Ship: via U.P.S.
When: At once.
Terms: 2/10 net 30 f.o.b. Chicago

As it is impossible to make the exact quantity, it is agreed that an overage or shortage, not to exceed 10 percent shall be accepted as filing this contract. All contracts are taken contingent upon strikes and accidents beyond S. Smith's control. Not subject to countermand.

Quantity	Price
75 window signs reading "Teas & Coffees" $1.35 per sign [as per sketch enclosed]	$1.35 per sign

(*signed*) A. Adams, Salesman
(*signed*) B. Brown

On April 3 S wrote to B accepting the order. On April 20 S delivered to the Chicago office of the carrier company for transportation to B 117 window signs reading "Teas & Coffees," made according to the sketch which had accompanied B's order. The signs were lost in transit by the carrier company. S demanded that B pay. B refused but did not claim that there had been an undue delay in filling the order. S sued B. Was S entitled to judgment against B, and if so, for how much? Explain.

11. B sent to S an order for 3,000 gears to be shipped by rail f.o.b. S's place of business. The goods were received by B, but inspection revealed that the gears were badly pitted and did not conform to the contract specifications. B promptly no-

tified S that he refused to accept the shipment and was holding the gears for S's disposal. The day after S received notification of the refusal, a fire in B's warehouse further damaged the gears. S notified B that B must pay the agreed contract price for the gears, or at least pay for the damage caused by the fire. Neither party had insurance on the gears damaged by the fire. Did B have any liability to S? (Modified from A.I.C.P.A. Nov. 75-5d.)

12. By letter addressed to S's place of business (stated below) B, a dealer in Boston, Massachusetts, ordered certain goods at a specified price. The terms for payment were stated as "2/ 10 net 30." On February 1, S properly shipped the goods to B in accordance with the contract, and on the same day, dated and mailed the invoice.

(a) B received the goods within the usual transportation time. (1) S's place of business was in New York City. B received the invoice on February 3 and the goods on February 5. By what date would B have to pay in order to obtain the 2 percent discount? Explain. (2) S's place of business was in Los Angeles, California. B received the invoice on February 4 and the goods on February 16. By what date would B have to pay in order to obtain the contracted 2 percent discount? Explain.

(b) S's place of business was in New York City. B received the invoice on February 3 and should have received the goods on February 5, but did not actually receive them until February 10, the delay in transit being solely the fault of the carrier. By what date would B have to pay in order to obtain the 2 percent discount? Explain.

13. On June 1, B, of Cleveland, sent an order to S, of New York City, for a specified standardized machine for $1,000, f.o.b. New York City, to be shipped on August 1 and paid for by October 1. S promptly sent B a written acceptance. On July 26, B telegraphed S canceling the order. Since the contract gave B no right to cancel S replied by telegraph that he intended to hold B to the contract, and shipped the machine. When the machine arrived in Cleveland, B refused to receive delivery. There being no market for the machine in Cleve-

land or any place closer than New York City, S had the machine returned to New York. The freight charges for the round trip to Cleveland and back to New York totaled $600, which S had to pay to the carrier before the carrier would redeliver the machine to S. S then resold the machine to another purchaser for $800, the best price that S, through reasonable effort, could obtain. S thereupon sued B for damages. How much, if anything, could S recover form B? Explain.

14. A shoe manufacturing company received from a retailer an order for 2,000 boys' and men's canvas play shoes of stated sizes at a stated price. The shoe company accepted the order, set up its machines to fill the order, and was approximately two-thirds finished with the manufacture of the shoes when it received a letter from the retailer cancelling the order. Since the remaining work only involved completion of the stitching and cutting the eyelets, the shoe company disregarded the cancellation letter and completed the shoes. The retailer claimed that he was only liable for the cost at the time of the receipt of the cancellation letter, plus the profit which the shoe company would have obtained under the terms of the contract. The shoe company sought to hold the retailer liable for the difference between the proceeds from the sale of the goods at the prevailing market price and the amount the retailer was obligated to pay under the terms of the contract. Could the shoe company recover the full amount it claimed? (Modified from A.I.C.P.A. Nov. 73-6b.)

15. B sent S a written order for 100 scales of a certain type at $45 apiece, to be shipped in three weeks, f.o.b. shipping point. The stated terms for payment were $1,500 down, the balance payable in two equal installments, one installment three months after shipment, the other six months. B accompanied the order with his check for $1,500. S promptly wrote to B acknowledging receipt of the order and agreeing to ship as ordered. However, a few days later S's bank returned B's check to S marked, "payment refused because of insufficient funds." When S notified B that his check had bounced, B explained that he had inadvertently

overdrawn his account and was depositing further funds, and requested that S redeposit the check. S did so and was paid the $1,500. S then had a credit investigation made and learned that over the past three years ten judgments had been entered against B, totaling $700, all still unsatisfied, S wrote to B refusing to ship the scales unless B would pay the balance on delivery. B refused and bought the same type of scale from another supplier on the same credit terms, paying $65 per scale, the lowest price B could reasonably find. B then sued S for damages for breach of contract. The evidence showed that although slow in paying some of his accounts, B was solvent at all times.

(a) What would be the result of B's lawsuit against S? Explain.

(b) Other facts remaining the same, assume that S had already shipped the goods and they were still in transit when B's check bounced and S's investigation gave S reasonable grounds to doubt B's solvency. What could S do? Explain.

16. On April 16, B, of Chicago, sent a letter to S, of New York City, ordering 15 refrigerators of a specified standard make and model, at a stated price, terms 2/10 net 30, f.o.b. New York City. B had never made any specific statement as to solvency, but he had made frequent prior credit purchases. Therefore, without further investigation of B's credit, S, on April 18 shipped the goods by railway freight on a straight bill of lading naming B as consignee, and mailed the bill of lading to B, together with an invoice for the goods. Nothing was stated as to title, security interest, or risk of loss. On April 19, B suffered financial reverses and became insolvent, and thereafter remained insolvent. On April 23, S learned of B's insolvency, immediately investigated as to the location of the 15 refrigerators, and discovered the facts stated below.

(a) On April 23, the goods had left New York City and not yet arrived in Chicago. Assuming S would pay any railroad charges due, would S have the legal right to obtain possession of the goods from the railroad, (1) If the 15 refrigerators consti-

tuted a full carload shipment? (2) If the refrigerators constituted about one-half of a carload? Explain.

(b) Assume that the goods constituted a full carload shipment. On April 23, the goods were in the Chicago railroad freight station, and B had been notified of arrival. Because of B's failure to pay or tender freight charges, the goods could not be delivered to B. The free time provided in the bill of lading had expired so that the railroad's liability had become that of a warehouseman and storage charges were accruing. Assuming that S would pay any freight and storage charges due, would S have the legal right to obtain possession of the goods from the railroad? Explain.

(c) B had entered into a contract in the ordinary course of his business to sell to T, of St. Louis, 15 refrigerators of this same make and model, f.o.b. St. Louis, at a specified price, payable in ten days. Upon receiving notice from the railroad of the arrival of the shipment in Chicago, B directed the railroad to ship the goods to T in St. Louis. The railroad issued to B a straight bill of lading naming T as consignee, and B forwarded the bill of lading to T. Assume that the goods constituted a full carload shipment. On April 23 the goods were in the Chicago freight station, not yet having been loaded for shipment to St. Louis. Assuming that S would pay any railroad charges due, would S have the legal right to obtain possession of the goods from the railroad? Explain.

17. On January 3, B, an appliance retailer, sent to S, a manufacturer, a written order for 10 TV sets of a specified model at a stated price to be paid 3 months later. The order stated nothing as to title, security interest, or risk. B had never made to S any specific statement of solvency but had made frequent prior purchases on the same credit terms. On January 6, S shipped the ordered goods consigned to B. The sets were of contract quality and current models for which S had a ready market for sale.

(a) On January 12, when the sets arrived at their destination, B wrote S that he had changed his mind and did not wish to purchase the sets. When B refused delivery, the carrier returned the goods to S. Upon receiving the sets, S notified B that the goods would be held for B, and on April 25 S, still holding the goods for B, sued B for the purchase price. What result? Explain.

(b) On January 12, when the sets were delivered, B wrote S that he had changed his mind and did not wish to purchase the sets, and was holding the sets for S. S replied refusing to accept return of the goods. Nothing further was done as to the goods and on April 25 S sued B for the purchase price. What result? Explain.

(c) On January 12, when the sets were delivered, B put them in his stockroom. There were no further communications between the parties until April 15 when S wrote requesting payment. (1) B offered to return the sets. S refused and on April 25 sued B for the purchase price. What result? Explain. (2) When B failed to reply or pay, S on April 25 sent an agent to B's store to reclaim the sets. B refused to surrender possession but still failed to make any payment. Did S have a right to obtain possession of the sets? Explain.

18. On March 15, a wholesaler of greeting cards sent to a manufacturer a written order for 500,000 Christmas cards of a certain style number as listed in the manufacturer's catalog. The order specified that the cards were to be shipped by August 1 and that the price of $3,000 was to be paid by September 1. The manufacturer accepted the order in writing. On July 16, the wholesaler wrote to the manufacturer canceling the order. The manufacturer's method of operating was to produce cards when ordered rather than to maintain large quantities in stock. Since production of the cards ordered by the wholesaler was already completed by July 16, the manufacturer refused to accept the cancellation and notified the wholesaler that the cards would be held for him. The wholesaler persisted in his refusal to receive the cards, and on September 2, the manufacturer sued the wholesaler for $3,000. The evidence in the case showed that wholesalers usually placed orders for Christmas cards by April 1, that after July 1 no

wholesale market existed for Christmas cards, and that retail orders were placed with wholesalers in the fall. What would be the result of the lawsuit of the manufacturer against the wholesaler? Explain.

19. S contracted to sell to B 1,000 cases of first-quality blue roofing shingles which were to be exactly one-fourth of an inch thick. The contract required that delivery be made by November 1. S made delivery on October 15, and was notified on October 20 that 100 cases contained shingles which were less than one-fourth of an inch thick and that 50 additional cases contained shingles which were off-color. These cases had inadvertently been included in the shipment as the result of a new employee's selecting some cases from an area which contained seconds. S immediately notified B that he would ship 150 replacement cases. The cases were delivered on October 30, but B refused to accept them. B insisted that the contract had been breached and that B was no longer obligated to perform. B also indicated that all cases would be returned to S. Assuming that B returned all the cases of shingles, would B have any liability as a result of his action? (Modified from A.I.C.P.A. Nov. 69-6b.)

20. B ordered 1,000 units of merchandise from a wholesaler at a unit price of $50 each, with delivery to be made at B's warehouse after April 11 but in no event later than April 15, with payment to be made 30 days after delivery. The wholesaler accepted B's offer. If the wholesaler notifies B on April 10 that he will not be able to deliver the merchandise until May 2 (select one of the following responses):

(a) B may notify the wholesaler that he is treating the contract as terminated immediately, but if he does so he waives any right to damages for breach of contract.

(b) If B elects to do nothing, he will be bound if the wholesaler subsequently tenders the goods on April 15.

(c) The wholesaler's notification is without legal effect until actual breach occurs.

(d) The wholesaler's action gives B no right of recovery if the wholesaler can show that a sudden rise in the market occurred and the wholesaler would have suffered a greater loss if the contract had been performed. (Modified from A.I.C.P.A. May 74-2(22).)

21. Smith contracted to sell to Brown 75 Wonder model typewriters. The terms were $600 per typewriter, delivery and payment to be made one month from the date of the execution of the contract. Two weeks after the contract was executed Smith notified Brown that the obligation would not be fulfilled because prior commitments had entirely depleted Smith's supply of Wonder typewriters. Brown immediately purchased 75 Wonder typewriters elsewhere at the prevailing market price of $625 per typewriter. Prior to the expiration of the one month delivery date contained in the original contract between Smith and Brown, New Corporation introduced a revolutionary new typewriter. This depressed the market price for Wonder typewriters to $550, which was the prevailing market price at the scheduled delivery date to Brown. What were the rights of the parties? (Modified from A.I.C.P.A. Nov. 69-2c.)

22. On March 5, B, a metal products manufacturer, ordered by telegram from S, a copper producer, a stated quantity of copper of specified purity and size, at 70 cents per pound, f.o.b. shipping point, the copper to be shipped April 1 and paid for by May 2. S accepted by telegram the same day. On March 21, S had copper conforming to the contract ready for shipment and marked with B's name. However, on March 21, without any legal justification, S telegraphed B canceling the contract. S did not thereafter reply to the answering telegram received the same day from B demanding that S retract his cancellation. The market prices for this type of copper were as follows: from March 21 through March 27, 75 cents; March 28 through April 4, 72 cents; April 5 through April 12, 75 cents; April 13 through April 20, 77 cents; from April 21 to the time of trial of the lawsuit described below, 85 cents. From March 21 on, B had ample opportunity to purchase from other sellers at current market prices the quantity of copper described in the S-B contract.

(a) On the date specified below, B purchased copper conforming to the contract from another supplier. The purchase price was the market price current on the date of purchase, and B paid that amount on May 2. On May 5 B sued S for damages. Ignoring costs and interest, how much per pound (if anything) could B recover if the date of B's repurchase was: (1) March 25; (2) April 1, (3) May 2? Explain.

(b) Making no attempt to purchase copper elsewhere, B, on April 1, demanded that S ship according to the contract. S refused. (1) The copper S had set aside for the contract and marked with B's name was still so set aside and marked when, on April 2, B sued S to obtain possession of the copper. Was B entitled to win the lawsuit? Explain. (2) S had sold elsewhere the copper that had been set aside for shipment to B but was in possession of copper of the same type and quantity. On April 2, B sued S to obtain possession of copper sufficient to fill the contract. Was B entitled to win the lawsuit? Explain. (3) After S's April 1 refusal to ship, B made no attempt to obtain copper from S or to purchase elsewhere. On May 5, B sued S for damages. Ignoring interest and costs, how much per pound (if anything) was B entitled to recover? Explain.

23. Brown Wholesalers Inc. ordered 1,000 scissors at $2.50 a pair from Smith Inc. on February 1. Delivery was to be made not later than March 10. Smith accepted the order in writing on February 4. The terms were 2/10 net 30, F.O.B. seller's loading platform in Baltimore. Due to unexpected additional orders and a miscalculation of the backlog of orders, Smith subsequently determined that it could not perform by March 10. On February 15, Smith notified Brown that it would not be able to perform, and cancelled the contract. Smith pleaded a reasonable mistake and impossibility of performance as its justification for cancelling. At the time the notice of cancellation was received, identical scissors were available from other manufacturers at $2.70. Brown chose not to purchase

the 1,000 scissors elsewhere, but instead notified Smith that it rejected the purported cancellation and would await delivery as agreed. Smith did not deliver on March 10, by which time the price of the scissors had risen to $3.00 per pair. Brown is seeking to recover damages from Smith for breach of contract.

(a) Will Brown prevail and, if so, how much will it recover?

(b) Would Brown be entitled to specific performance under the circumstances?

(c) Assuming that Smith discovers that Brown was insolvent, will this excuse performance? (Modified from A.I.C.P.A. May 82-5b)

24. In writing, B ordered from S 1,000 units of certain described first quality goods for $5 apiece, f.o.b. destination, terms 2/10 net 30. "First," "second," and "third" quality were recognized commercial standards for the kind of goods involved. The goods were not perishable, and the market price was stable. S in writing accepted the order, but then S shipped to B 1,000 units of the described kind of goods which were actually of "third" quality and reasonably worth to B only $3 apiece. Three weeks later B had not yet paid for the goods.

(a) B inspected with proper promptness and thoroughness, but the defect in the quality being difficult to discover, B did not detect it. After three weeks B discovered the lower quality. Assume that this was proper diligence. B immediately notified S of the nonconformity and of what B wished to do. The goods were still in the same condition as when received by B. Would B have a legal right to: 1) reject the goods; 2) keep the goods with an obligation to pay S only $3 apiece; 3) keep half the goods, paying the proper price for them and reject the remainder of the goods? Explain.

(b) On reasonably prompt inspection B discovered the defect in quality and immediately notified S that although the goods did not conform, B was accepting and would use the goods, but would expect an adjustment in the price. After a reasonable attempt to use the goods for three weeks, which

was a reasonable time, B found that because of the lower quality the goods were wholly unusable by him and immediately notified S to that effect and of what B then wished to do. The goods were still in the same condition as when received by B. Would B have a legal right to 1) reject the goods; 2) keep the goods with an obligation to pay S only $3 apiece; 3) keep half the goods, paying the proper price for them and reject the remainder of the goods? Explain.

25. Smith Manufacturing shipped 300 designer navy blue blazers to Brown Clothiers. The blazers arrived on Friday, earlier than Brown had anticipated and on an exceptionally busy day for its receiving department. They were perfunctorily examined and sent to a nearby warehouse for storage until needed. On Monday of the following week, upon closer examination, it was discovered that the quality of the linings of the blazers was inferior to that specified in the sales contract. Smith argues that Brown must retain the blazers since it had an opportunity to inspect them upon delivery and had accepted them. What are the rights of the parties? (Modified from A.l.C.P.A. Nov. 80-1(12).)

26. On May 30 Brown ordered 1,000 spools of nylon yarn from Smith of Norfolk, Va. The shipping terms were "f.o.b. Norfolk & Western RR at Norfolk." The transaction was to be a cash sale with payment to be simultaneously exchanged for the negotiable bill of lading covering the goods. Title to the goods was expressly reserved in Smith. The yarn ordered by Brown was delivered to the railroad and loaded in a boxcar on June 1. Smith obtained a negotiable bill of lading made out to its own order. The boxcar was destroyed the next day while the goods were in transit. Brown refused to pay for the yarn and Smith sued Brown for the purchase price. What result? (Modified from A.I.C.P.A. Nov. 78-5c.)

27. Buyer ordered goods from Seller. The contract required Seller to deliver them f.o.b. Buyer's place of business. Buyer inspected the goods, discovered they failed to conform to the contract, and rightfully rejected them, notifying Seller to come

and get them. In the event of loss of the goods, which of the following is a correct statement?

(a) Seller initially had the risk of loss and it remains with him after delivery.

(b) Risk of loss passes to Buyer upon tender of the goods f.o.b. 8uyer's place of business, but it is shifted to Seller upon rightful rejection.

(c) Buyer had the risk of loss, but it is shifted to Seller upon rightful rejection.

(d) If Seller had used a public carrier to transport the goods to Buyer, risk of loss is on Buyer during transit. (Modified from A.I.C.P.A. May 80-1(33).)

28. Brown by telegram to Smith Corp. ordered 10,000 yards of fabric, first quality, 50% wool and 50% cotton. The shipping terms were F.O.B. Brown's factory in Akron, Ohio. Smith accepted the order and packed the fabric for shipment. In the process it discovered that one half of the fabric packed had been commingled with fabric which was 30% wool and 70% cotton. Since Smith did not have any additional 50% wool fabric, it decided to send the shipment to Brown as an accommodation. The goods were shipped and later the same day Smith wired Brown its apology informing Brown of the facts and indicating that the 5,000 yards of 30% wool would be priced at $2 a yard less. The carrier delivering the goods was destroyed on the way to Akron. Under the circumstances, who bears the risk of loss? (Modified from A.I.C.P.A. May 84-1(49) and Nov 82-1(48).)

29. Smith Corp. received an order for $11,000 of assorted pottery from Brown Inc. The shipping terms were F.O.B Lime Ship Lines, seller's place of business, 2/ 10 net 30. Smith packed and crated the pottery for shipment and it was loaded upon Lime's ship. While the goods were in transit to Brown, Smith learned that Brown was insolvent in the equity sense (unable to pay its debts in the ordinary course of business). Smith promptly wired Lime's office in Galveston, Texas, and instructed them to stop shipment of the goods to Brown and to store them until further instructions. Lime com-

plied with these instructions. Regarding the rights, duties, and liabilities of the parties, which of the following is correct?

(a) Brown is entitled to the pottery if it pays cash.

(b) Smith's stoppage in transit was improper if Brown's assets exceeded its liabilities.

(c) The fact that Brown became insolvent in no way affects the rights, duties, and obligations of the parties.

(d) Once Smith correctly learned of Brown's insolvency, it had no further duty of obligation to Brown. (Modified from A.I.C.P.A. May 84-1(51) and Nov 82-1(50).)

Commercial Paper: Negotiability

Commercial Paper: Negotiability

ARTICLE 3 of the Uniform Commercial Code, entitled "Commercial Paper," is concerned with notes, drafts, checks, and certificates of deposit. Most such instruments are negotiable in form. Other types of negotiable property interests which are not considered commercial paper (e.g., stock and bond certificates, order or bearer bills of lading and warehouse receipts) are covered by other articles of the Code.

During the early days of the England trading companies, the traders and merchants developed their own customs and practices pertaining to commercial paper. As these customs and practices evolved, a body of rules gradually emerged. These rules were referred to as the law of the merchants (or as it was frequently termed, the law merchant). Gradually with the expansion of common law courts and formal legal systems, disputes involving merchants began to appear in courts on a regular basis. In deciding the increasing number of such disputes, the courts gradually adopted much of the law merchant. Eventually, these rules were systematized and codified by legislation. The Uniform Negotiable Instruments Law (frequently abbreviated NIL) was the first of the uniform business statutes drafted and presented to the states. The NIL was adopted by the legislatures of all the states and provided the basic pattern for Article 3 of the Uniform Commercial Code, which supersedes the NIL.

I. Commercial Paper Defined

Commercial paper represents a written promise or order to pay a specific sum of money. The Code defines a promise as "an undertaking to pay and must be more than an acknowledgment of an obligation."[1] The Code defines an order as "a direction to pay and must be more than an authorization or request. It must identify the person to pay with reasonable certainty. It may be addressed to one or more such persons jointly or in the alternative but not in succession."[2] Any reference in Article 3 to an instrument means that the reference is to a negotiable instrument.[3]

II. The Uses of Commercial Paper

Commercial paper serves two purposes in the economy. It serves as a substitute for money as well as a credit device. A common example of commercial paper serving as a substitute for money is the writing of a check. Checks did not originate as a modern tool of commerce. Merchants in the Middle Ages began storing their gold and silver with intermediaries so that they would not have to bear the burden of transporting it from place to place. Moreover, transporting significant quantities

1. UCC Sec. 3-102(c).
2. UCC Sec. 3-102(b).
3. UCC Sec. 3-102(e).

of gold and silver created security risks. To solve the problem, merchants would issue instructions to the intermediaries holding their gold and silver to pay a certain amount to the person named on the order. The order would be taken to the intermediary for collection. These orders became known as bills of exchange. Checks serve the same function in our present economy.

Commercial paper may also represent an extension of credit. Purchasing an item with a piece of paper representing a promise to pay a specific sum in the future is in effect a loan from the seller for that period of time. The advantage of commercial paper payable in the future is that the payee may negotiate the instrument to a third party for immediate cash. The ease of transferability also demonstrates that the paper represents a reasonable cash substitute. The rules governing commercial paper permit those instruments meeting certain standards to be transferred with little difficulty and with less risk to the transferee than a normal assignee of a contract would face. Instruments meeting this standard are identified as negotiable instruments.

III. Types of Commercial Paper

The Code sets forth four categories of commercial paper or negotiable instruments. They are drafts, checks, certificates of deposit and notes.[4]

A. Drafts

Drafts are sometimes also referred to as bills of exchange. A draft is an unconditional written order by one party to a second party to pay a specific sum of money to a third party. There are always three parties to a draft, although one person may assume two roles with respect to a draft. The parties to a draft are:

---

4. UCC Sec. 3-104(2).

The Drawer: this is the party giving the order.

The Drawee: this is the party receiving the order and must carry out the instructions.

The Payee: this is the party to be paid.

A common type of draft employed for the purchase of goods and materials is known as a *trade acceptance*. This is a draft drawn by a seller of goods against the credit of a buyer. A trade acceptance is a substitute for selling goods on open account. This type of draft orders the buyer to pay a specific sum of money to the seller at a specific time in the future. The seller plays the roles of both the drawer and payee. The buyer is in the role of the drawee, the party receiving the order. The buyer's role is similar to that of a bank with respect to checks. The seller creates a draft which orders the buyer to pay the seller at some point in the future. In order to complete the deal, the buyer must "accept it."

The buyer accepts it by indicating this on the face which requires the buyer's signature. Once that occurs, it is an enforceable obligation of the buyer. On the date the instrument is due, the seller or any indorsee of the seller can present it to the drawee-buyer for payment. The advantage of this type of instrument is that the buyer is getting an extension of credit because the instrument is payable in the future. The seller may negotiate the trade acceptance to a third party prior to the due date so that the seller of the goods or services can convert the instrument to immediate cash.

An example of a trade acceptance is presented in figure 23.1. In this example, Big Ed's Security (BES) desires to purchase material for his alarm business from Palmer Electronics, Inc. BES does not have sufficient cash for the purchase. Palmer does not want to extend credit to BES. To solve this problem, Palmer creates a trade acceptance. Palmer, as drawer, draws a draft upon BES as drawee. It is made payable to Palmer in the amount of the purchase. It is a "time draft" payable one

Trade Acceptance

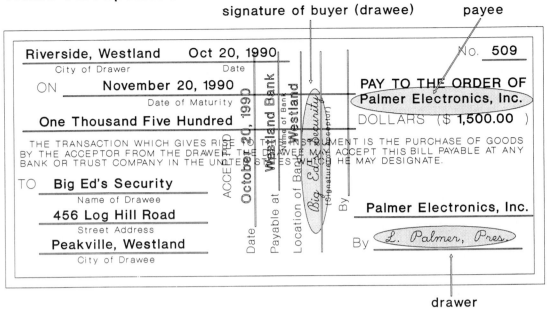

signature of buyer (drawee)　　　　payee

Riverside, Westland　　Oct 20, 1990　　No. 509

City of Drawer　　　　Date

ON　　November 20, 1990

Date of Maturity

One Thousand Five Hundred

THE TRANSACTION WHICH GIVES RISE TO THIS INSTRUMENT IS THE PURCHASE OF GOODS BY THE ACCEPTOR FROM THE DRAWER. THE DRAWER MAY ACCEPT THIS BILL PAYABLE AT ANY BANK OR TRUST COMPANY IN THE UNITED STATES WHICH HE MAY DESIGNATE.

TO　　Big Ed's Security

Name of Drawee

456 Log Hill Road

Street Address

Peakville, Westland

City of Drawee

ACCEPTED October 20, 1990

Date

Payable at Westland Bank

Name of Bank

Location of Bank Westland

Big Ed's Security

(Signature of Acceptor)

By

PAY TO THE ORDER OF

Palmer Electronics, Inc.

DOLLARS ($ 1,500.00)

Palmer Electronics, Inc.

By　L. Palmer, Pres.

drawer

month from the date the instrument was drawn. BES then "accepts" the instrument by signing it on its face. This makes BES primarily liable for payment of the instrument when it matures in one month. Palmer may negotiate the trade acceptance to a third party at a discounted price in exchange for cash. The third party may then present it at maturity to BES for payment.

B. Checks

Checks are drafts that are drawn on banks and payable on demand. They are a subset of drafts in that drafts may be drawn upon any drawee, but checks must be drawn on a bank. In addition, drafts may be payable in the future, such as trade acceptances. But, checks may only be payable on demand. The drawee-bank will be clearly indicated on the check. The bank must carry out its customer's order to pay the sum specified on a properly presented check if sufficient funds are available. An example of a check is presented in figure 23.2.

A check issued by a bank from a checking account established for itself in which it is both the drawer and the drawee is known as a *cashier's check*. Banks may pay their obligations to other parties with cashier's checks. In addition, banks can issue these checks on behalf of their customers. Under those circumstances, a bank's customer is known as the *remitter* of the check.

C. Certificates of Deposit

A certificate of deposit is a bank's acknowledgment that it has received money from a party and that it has promised to pay it to the bearer or a specified party at a certain date. Larger certificates of deposit are generally negotiable by their terms. Negotiable certificates of deposit are commonly bought and sold by investors and are often pledged to secure repayment of loans. An example of a certificate of deposit is presented in figure 23.3.

D. Promissory Notes

A promissory note involves only two parties, as opposed to drafts which involve three par-

Check

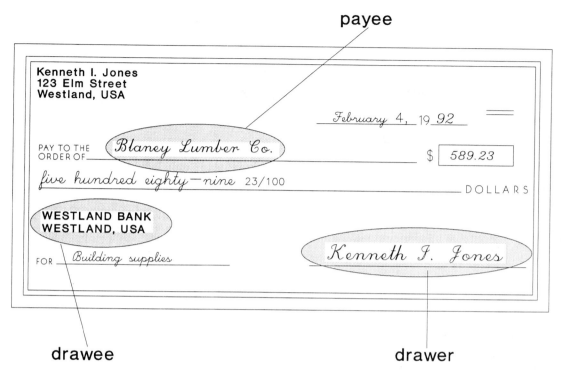

payee

Kenneth I. Jones
123 Elm Street
Westland, USA

February 4, 19 92

PAY TO THE
ORDER OF _Blaney Lumber Co._

$ 589.23

five hundred eighty—nine 23/100 ____ DOLLARS

WESTLAND BANK
WESTLAND, USA

FOR _Building supplies_

Kenneth I. Jones

drawee

drawer

Certificate of Deposit

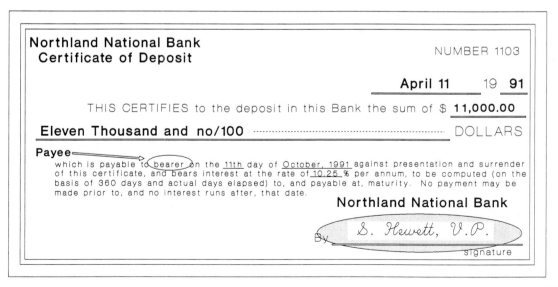

Northland National Bank
Certificate of Deposit

NUMBER 1103

April 11   19 91

THIS CERTIFIES to the deposit in this Bank the sum of $ 11,000.00

Eleven Thousand and no/100 ·· DOLLARS

Payee
which is payable to bearer on the 11th day of October, 1991 against presentation and surrender of this certificate, and bears interest at the rate of 10.25 % per annum, to be computed (on the basis of 360 days and actual days elapsed) to, and payable at, maturity. No payment may be made prior to, and no interest runs after, that date.

Northland National Bank

By S. Hewett, V.P.

signature

PROMISSORY NOTE - COMMERCIAL

DEBTOR'S NAME AND ADDRESS	CUSTOMER NO.	NOTE NO.	DATE OF NOTE	MATURITY DATE	PRINCIPAL

INTEREST RATE, PAYABLE AT A FLUCTUATING RATE PER ANNUM				
INTEREST PAYABLE	PRINCIPAL PAYABLE	FIRST INSTALLMENT DUE	INSTALLMENT AMOUNT

	RENEWAL OF #	OFFICER	
	NEW LOAN		

COLLATERAL

PURPOSE OF LOAN IF EXCESS OF $5,000:

For value received, the undersigned (the "Makers") agree to all the terms of this Note and promise to pay to the the order of the Lender named below the Principal Amount, together with interest, all as set forth above. Installments of Principal and Interest are payable on the same day of the month as the First Installment. The unpaid balance of the Principal and Interest shall become payable on the Maturity Date, and any amount not paid when due shall bear interest at a rate of 5% greater than the per annum interest rate set forth above.

Changes in the rate charged on this Note are effective without notice to Makers on the same day as the effective change in the base or prime rate as established from time to time by the Lender named below unless a different rate is written or typed herein; provided, however, that in no event shall the interest charged hereunder exceed the maximum allowed by law.

This note and all other obligations of Makers to holder, and all renewals and extensions thereof are secured by the collateral described herein, together with all other collateral heretofore or hereafter given Lender.

At the options of the holder, the unpaid balance of this Note, and all other obligations of Makers to the holder, whether direct or indirect, absolute or contingent, now existing or hereafter arising, shall become immediately due and payable without notice or demand upon the occurrence or existence of any of the following events or conditions: (a) Any payment required by this or any other note or obligation of Makers to holder or to others is not made when due; (b) Any default occurs in the performance of any covenant, obligation, warranty, or provision contained in any loan agreement or in any instrument or document securing or relating to this or any other note or obligation of Makers to holder or to others; (c) Any warranty, representation, financial information, or statement made or furnished to Lender by or in behalf of Makers proves to have been false in any material respect when made or furnished; (d) Any time Lender in its sole discretion believes that the prospect of payment of this Note is impaired.

All parties hereto shall each be regarded as a principal and each party agrees that any party hereto with the approval of the holder and without notice to the other parties may from time to time renew this Note or consent to one or more extensions or deferrals of the Maturity Date hereof for any term or terms, and all parties shall be liable in the same manner as on the original note; and all parties hereto hereby waive presentment, notice of dishonor and protest, and consent to partial payments, substitutions or release of collateral and the addition or release of any party or guarantor.

It is specifically agreed that the sum of all the advances under this Note may exceed the Principal Amount as shown above, but the unpaid balance shall never exceed said Principal Amount. Advances and payments shall be recorded on the records of the Lender, and such records shall be prima facie evidence of said advances, payments and unpaid principal balance of this Note. Subsequent advances shall be at the Lender's option, and the procedure described herein shall not be construed or interpreted as granting a continuing line of credit for the Principal Amount.

No waiver of any payment or other right under this Note or any related agreement shall operate as a waiver of any other payment or right. All parties agree to pay reasonable costs of collection, including an attorney's fee of   % of all sums due upon default.

Any indebtedness due from the holder hereof to any party hereto including, without limitation, any deposits or credit balances or any other indebtedness due from holder is pledged to secure the payment hereof and any other indebtedness to holder of any other party hereto and may at any time while the whole or any part of such indebtedness remains unpaid, whether before or after maturity hereof, be appropriated, held or applied toward the payment of this Note or any other indebtedness to holder of any party hereto.

This note is to be construed according to the laws of the State of Pennsylvania.

NORTHLAND NATIONAL BANK
NORTHLAND, U.S.A.

ties. A promissory note is a written promise by the *maker* to pay a certain sum of money to the *payee*. Promissory notes can be payable on demand or at a specific time. A promissory note may name the bearer as payee. This means that the party holding the instrument may present it for payment. An example of a promissory note is presented in figure 23.4.

Promissory notes may be further classified by the type of collateral supporting their repayment. Promissory notes that are supported by real property mortgages are often referred to as more mortgage notes. Promissory notes supported by collateral consisting of personal property are often called collateral notes or chattel notes. In addition, promissory notes requiring repayment in installments are often referred to as installment notes.

IV. Other Classifications of Commercial Paper

A. Demand vs. Time

Instruments may be payable on demand. They include those payable at site or upon presentation. Instruments in which no time for payment is stated will also be deemed payable on demand.[5] Time instruments include those with the following payment terms: Payable on or before a stated date, payable at a fixed period after a stated date, payable at a fixed period after site, payable at a definite time subject to any acceleration, payable at a definite time subject to the extension at the option of the holder, payable subject to extension to a further definite time upon the option of the maker or acceptor, or payable automatically upon or after a specified event.[6] An instrument by which its terms is otherwise payable only upon an act or an event that is uncertain as to the time of its occurrence will

---

5. UCC Sec. 3-108.
6. UCC Sec. 3-109.

not be deemed payable at a definite time even if that act or event has occurred.

Drafts can be classified as time drafts or site drafts. Time drafts are payable on or after a stated time in the future. Site drafts are payable upon presentation to the drawee. These arc also known as demand drafts.

B. Orders to Pay vs. Promises to Pay

Commercial paper involving the payment of money must contain a promise to pay or an order to pay. Checks and drafts represent orders to pay. Certificates of deposit and promissory notes represent promises to pay.

C. Negotiable Instruments vs. Non-negotiable Instruments

A negotiable instrument represents a right to payment. This right can be transferred with great ease and therefore represents a substitute for money. Instruments of limited transferability are said to be non-negotiable. One must carefully examine a document's form and content to determine if it is negotiable. The elements of negotiability are set forth in Section 3-104 of the Code. If an instrument is negotiable, its transfer is governed by Article 3 of the Code. If the item does not meet the standards of negotiability set forth in Article 3, its transfer as well as the rights and liabilities of the party holding il will be governed by contract law and not by Article 3 of the Code.

D. Other Important Terms Regarding Negotiable Instruments

Indorser. A person may transfer a note or draft by indorsing it. For one to become an indorser, she must sign the back of the instrument at the appropriate place and deliver the instrument to another person with intent to transfer. Both elements are required for an effective indorsement.

Indorsee. This is a party receiving an indorsed instrument. An indorsee has the power to present an instrument to the maker or drawee for payment at the appropriate time or may indorse the instrument and deliver it to another party.

Bearer. This party has physical possession of an instrument that is payable to bearer, or cash, or was payable to a specific person who indorsed the instrument in blank. Any instrument with such a payee designation or indorsement is payable to anyone holding it.

Holder. A person in possession of an instrument drawn, issued or indorsed to him, to his order, to bearer or in blank will be deemed a holder. It is possible that the holder of an instrument and the owner may not be the same person. This is because a thief who is in possession of a bearer instrument will be deemed a holder under the Code. But, a thief certainly is not the owner of the instrument. But, under the Code, a thief may legally negotiate a bearer instrument to a third party who then becomes the new holder of the instrument. A thief cannot negotiate order paper because any attempt to indorse the instrument by the thief will be a forgery.

Acceptor. A drawee of a check or a draft who has, by signing the instrument on its face engages to pay the check or draft when it comes due, is an acceptor. Acceptors are commonly found in transactions involving trade acceptances. In addition, when a bank certifies a check of one of its customers, the bank is said to have accepted it.

Accommodation Party. This is a party who signs an instrument in a special capacity for the purpose of lending his name to another party to the instrument. In effect, this party is lending her credit to the party to whom the accommodation is made.[7] An accommodation party becomes liable in the same capacity as the party being accommodated. Thus, an accommodation party may be an accommodation maker, an accommodation drawee or an accommodation indorser. An accommodation party is never liable to the party she is assisting. But, if the accommodation party has to pay the obligation of the party she is assisting, the accommodation party has a right of recourse to seek full repayment from the accommodated party.

V. The Concept of Negotiability

One of the main goals of the Code is to promote commerce. The commercial paper concepts set forth in the Code promote commerce through making negotiable instruments freely transferable and thus functioning as a substitute for money. The usefulness of negotiable instruments is further enhanced through their ability to function as a credit device.

It is important to be able to distinguish negotiable instruments from non-negotiable instruments because separate bodies of law govern them. Recall that negotiable instruments are governed by Article 3 of the UCC while non-negotiable instruments are governed by traditional contract law.

A. Advantages of Negotiability under Article 3

Under contract law, one can only transfer to a third party the actual rights she possesses under a contract. If a defense to enforcement exists, it may be raised against any and all transferees of the contract. Even if the transferee purchased the contract rights in total ignorance of the existence of defenses to enforcement, those rights will be burdened by that defense. A contract representing the right to receive a payment of money may have value, but that value will significantly decline if prospective buyers will be subject to unknown defenses that could prevent payment of the money under the contract.

---

7. UCC Sec. 3-415

Under the Code, most defenses to enforcement of negotiable instruments cannot be raised against a holder in due course. This too demonstrates that commercial paper can function as a close substitute for money. The concept of "holder in due course" and the defenses to enforcement of commercial paper will be discussed in the next chapter.

B. The Requirements for Negotiability

Section 3-104 (1) of the Code sets forth the requirements for the form of a negotiable instrument. They are:

I. IT MUST BE IN WRITING

A negotiable instrument must be in written form. The Code defines a writing as including printing, typewriting or any other intentional reduction to tangible form.[8] This means that the item must be in a form that lends itself to permanence. In addition, to meet the Code's underlying purpose of having commercial paper operate as a substitute for money, the writing must have some element of portability in order to be freely transferable.

Instruments need not be written in ink or on special paper. They may be written in pencil or any other type of marking that would not disappear quickly. A writing could be created on a tablecloth or a paper napkin. The Code does not prescribe a set visual form for a writing.

2. IT MUST BE SIGNED BY THE MAKER OR THE DRAWER

Recall that the Code provides great latitude in what constitutes a signature. A signature includes any symbol executed or adopted by a party with the present intent to authenticate a writing.[9] This permits the use of trade names, assumed names or any mark substituting for a written signature so long as the party making such a mark intends that it serve as his signature.[10] Valid signatures may also include initials, a rubber stamp, thumb prints and even false names. A court will permit introduction of parole evidence to determine the correct identity of the signer. In addition, there is no specific requirement that a signature must be placed at the bottom of an instrument. The signature may appear anywhere on the face of the instrument, even in the body of the instrument.

The Code presumes that all signatures on instruments are valid. The burden of proving that a signature is a forgery is initially on the party attempting to escape paying or honoring the instrument.

The signatures of authorized agents are valid for purposes of negotiability. Authorizing an agent to sign on one's behalf requires no formal appointment, court order or public filing. It merely requires proof that the principal gave the agent the authority to sign on his behalf.[11] A principal will be liable on an instrument signed by his agent as if the principal himself had signed. If the agent had no authority to sign, only the agent will be liable on the instrument.

3. IT MUST STATE AN UNCONDITIONAL PROMISE OR ORDER TO PAY

In this context, unconditional means that the obligation must be absolutely determinable from the language of the instrument. The fact that an instrument is subject to implied or constructive conditions does not violate this requirement because certain implied conditions will always exist. For instance, every check implies that there are sufficient funds in the bank to cover the check. Moreover, the Code itself implies a condition of good faith on the parties to the instrument. But, if the instrument sets forth particular circumstances

8. UCC Sec. 1-201(46).
9. UCC Sec. 1-201(39).

10. UCC Sec. 3-401(2).
11. UCC Sec. 3-403.

or conditions which must occur prior to payment, the negotiability is destroyed.

Any instrument stating that it *must* be paid out of a particular fund or from a particular source also fails to meet this test.

Checks, drafts and trade acceptances all set forth unconditional orders to pay. Examination of such instruments that meet this requirement of negotiability will always set forth "pay to the order of...." Requests such as "I wish you would pay" or "I hope you will pay" are conditional and do not represent unconditional orders to pay.

Consider that if the order or promise on an instrument were subject to other conditions, it would not serve as a very good substitute for money. Prospective transferees would not want to take any instrument that required continued investigation to see if a condition existed.

a. References to Consideration

It is acceptable for an instrument to refer to its underlying transaction. References indicating that a promissory note or draft is being exchanged for tangible or intangible goods will not destroy negotiability.

b. References to Separate Agreements

It is acceptable for the instrument to state that it was a part of a group of transactions or that other agreements exist such as security agreements providing collateral support. Such references to the existence of security agreements and other liens are common. But, negotiability will be destroyed if the instrument states that it is "subject to" or "governed by" any other agreement. For instance, if a note or draft states that it is subject to the terms and conditions of a separate mortgage or security agreement, the instrument will be non-negotiable.

c. References to Particular Funds or Accounts

It is acceptable for an instrument to make a reference to a particular account or fund for the purpose of assisting the internal accounting or management of the maker or drawer of the instrument. But, if the instrument clearly states that its payment must come from the resources of a particular fund or account, negotiability will not exist.

There is a slight exception to this rule. Government agencies are permitted to issue instruments that are paid out of particular funds without losing their status as negotiable instruments. In addition, it is permissible for an instrument to limit its payment to the entire assets of a trust, estate, partnership or unincorporated association without destroying negotiability.

4. IT MUST REFLECT A SUM CERTAIN IN MONEY

Anyone examining the face of the instrument must be able to determine the exact amount of money to be paid. In addition, the instrument must designate payment in money, not in goods or services. The key issue is whether or not a specific amount of money can be determined. The "sum certain" requirement is not destroyed even though the instrument provides for a different interest rate if the instrument goes into default. It is permissible to set forth certain discounts or penalties to be paid on or after fixed dates of payment. None of these will destroy negotiability.

In response to the widely fluctuating interest rates of the late 1970's and early 1980's, many commercial promissory notes are now tied to a variable interest rate, such as prime or base rates established by major banks, government rates, or foreign bank rates. The problem with variable rates is that the exact amount to be paid under the instrument cannot be calculated on its face because a record of past interest rates is not affixed to it. It is a cardinal rule that if one must look beyond the face of an instrument to determine if it is negotiable, it is non-negotiable. Several states have modified their versions of Article 3 to deem instruments expressing repayment with variable rates of interest will be negotiable notwithstanding the fact that such notes do not reflect a "sum certain."

The Code declares that an instrument is payable in money if the medium of exchange in which it is payable is money at the time the instrument is made. An instrument payable in currency or current funds is payable in money.[12] A promise or order to pay a sum certain stated in a foreign currency is considered to be a sum certain in money that can be satisfied by payment in that currency unless a different medium is specified in the instrument.

As a general rule, negotiability will not be affected by statements within instruments providing for the collection of costs and attorneys fees upon default if necessary to enforce payments.[13] A few states have prohibited these provisions, causing the presence of them to destroy an instrument's negotiable status.

5. IT MUST BE PAYABLE ON DEMAND OR AT A DEFINITE TIME

This requirement provides the holder an assurance of a time that she will be paid just as the sum certain requirement sets forth a specific amount to be paid.

a. Demand Instruments

A demand instrument is payable at the time the holder chooses to present it for payment. Demand instruments include those which state that they are payable on demand, payable on presentation, payable on site, or those in which no time for payment is stated.[14] In addition, an instrument that is undated is still negotiable so long as it meets the other standards of negotiability.[15] Such an in-

strument will be deemed a demand instrument.

Postdating or antedating will not affect an instrument's negotiability. Any dated instrument not explicitly stating another time for payment is deemed a demand instrument. But, a postdated demand instrument cannot be properly presented for payment until the stated date.

b. Time Instruments

Recall that commercial paper is often used as a credit device to facilitate the purchase of goods and services as well as the loan of money. Time instruments must be payable at a definite time in the future.

If the face of the instrument states that it is payable at a certain time in the future, then there is no obligation to pay the instrument until that time. The instrument may state that it is payable at a fixed time after sight (presented for payment or acceptance); or following a fixed period after a stated date; or upon a specified and certain act or event that is readily determinable. But, if the instrument is only payable upon the act or event of an uncertain time of occurrence, then no definite time has been stated which renders the instrument non-negotiable. Negotiability will not be affected if the instrument states that it is payable on or before a certain date. Additionally, acceleration clauses do not destroy negotiability because the instrument still has a date certain for payment. Acceleration is a means to demand full payment of all sums due and owing under an instrument following an event of default.

Extension clauses extend the maturity date into the future. To be negotiable, the instrument must state a definite period of extension if the maker has the choice to extend. Negotiability will not be affected if the holder is given a choice to extend payment under the instrument to some future date to be declared

12. UCC Sec. 3-107(1).
13. UCC Sec. 3-106(1)(e).
14. UCC Sec. 3-108.

15. UCC Sec. 3-114(1).

by the holder. This is because the holder is in effect altering a rule that is designed to protect the holder by seeing that she receives payment on or before a certain time. A holder cannot be heard to complain about an extension of time if it was her choice.

6. IT MUST BE PAYABLE TO ORDER OR TO BEARER

The requirements that an instrument contain the words "pay to the order of" or "pay to bearer" must be met without any variance. It is a strict rule that contains no margin for error. These terms are often referred to as "magic words" when it comes to determining the negotiability of an instrument. If the magic words are not present, the instrument is not negotiable.

a. Order Instruments

An instrument is called an order instrument when it is payable to the order of a person specified with reasonable certainty. Such an instrument is payable only to a certain person or persons or entities.[16] The person named in the instrument must be named with certainty because that person will have to indorse the instrument in order to further negotiate it. Statements on the face of an instrument such as "pay only to John Smith" or "payable to John Smith" do not meet the standard of negotiability. In addition, a reference such as "pay to the order of my doctor" does not involve the requisite certainty to meet the standard of an order instrument.

b. Bearer Instruments

Bearer instruments do not designate specific payees.[17] Bearer instruments are made payable to the bearer, cash or are order instruments indorsed in blank.[18] Notations such as "pay to bearer," "payable to the order of bearer," "payable to Jane Smith or bearer," "payable to bearer," "pay cash," "pay to the order of cash" or any other indication which does not purport to designate a specific payee creates bearer paper. Notice that the word "order" is not necessary for creating bearer paper.[19]

Instruments payable to the bearer or payable to the order of bearer are commonly found when one writes in the word "bearer" on a preprinted form such as a check. Negotiability is not destroyed by such a reference. Bearer paper is created as a result.

An instrument promises to pay "John Smith or Bearer" creates bearer paper. If an instrument states "pay the order of John Smith and Bearer," the instrument is payable to order unless the bearer words are handwritten or typewritten.[20] The Code requires examination of the bearer language if the maker or drawer inserts order language and the name of a specific payee. The Code deems this an indication of an intent that the instrument be payable to order. But a handwritten insertion of the word "bearer" will be deemed an intention to make the instrument a bearer instrument.

VI. Rules of Construction

Under Article 3, there are certain rules of construction that as a general rule may not be altered or varied by the parties. These rules include:[21]

1. If there is doubt as to whether an instrument is a draft or a note, the holder may treat it as either. A draft drawn on the drawer is effective as a note. This means that a bank issuing a check on itself, such as a cashier's check, may be treated by the holder as a promissory note.

---

16. UCC Sec. 3-110(1).
17. UCC Sec. 3-111.
18. UCC Sec. 1-201(5).

19. UCC Sec. 3-111.
20. UCC Sec. 3-110(3).
21. UCC Sec. 3-118.

2. Handwritten terms control over type-written and printed terms. Typewritten terms control over printed terms.

3. Words control over figures except if the words are ambiguous, then the figures control. This should be kept in mind when examining checks.

VII. Certain Terms or Omissions will not Affect Negotiability

While the Code sets forth distinct requirements regarding an instrument's qualification for negotiable status, Code Section 3-112 identifies potential problems that by definition will not destroy the negotiable status of an instrument. These include:

1. The omission of a statement regarding consideration exchanged or the place where the instrument was drawn or made payable.

2. A statement that collateral has been given to secure repayment of the obligation .

3. A promise or power to maintain or protect collateral or to give additional collateral .

4. A term authorizing a confession of judgment on the instrument if it is not paid when due.

5. A term purporting to wave the benefit of any law intended for the advantage or protection of any obligor.

6. A term in a draft providing that the payee by indorsing or cashing the instrument acknowledges full satisfaction of an obligation of the drawer.

VIII. Negotiation of Commercial Paper

It is important to remember that the rules set forth in Article 3 govern only those writings meeting the negotiable instrument standard. Unless the holder can ascertain all of the essential terms from the face of the instrument, the instrument will not be negotiable.[22]

One of the primary purposes of Article 3 is to create instruments that can be transferred freely from party to party. Under contract law, this process of transfer is called assignment. Although commercial paper can be assigned rather than negotiated, the benefits of Article 3 will not be transferred to a mere assignee. The value of commercial paper is its negotiability which leads to certain advantages for a transferee.

A. Comparing Assignment and Negotiation

The processes of assignment and negotiation have similar qualities. In either case, certain contractual rights are transferred. But, assignment is governed by contract law while negotiation is governed by Article 3 of the Code. Under assignment, the assignee has only those rights possessed by the assignor at the time of the assignment. The assignee may be subject to a large array of defenses to enforcement of the instrument.

A negotiation is the transfer of a negotiable instrument in such a manner that the transferee becomes a *holder*.[23] At the very least, the transferee takes all of the rights possessed by the transferor of the instrument.[24] But, transfer by negotiation makes it possible for the transferee to receive more rights than the prior possessor.[25] A holder of these superior rights is identified under the Code as a

---

22. UCC Sec. 3-105 Official Comment 8.
23. UCC Sec. 3-202(1).
24. UCC Sec. 3-201(1).
25. UCC Sec. 3-305.

"*holder in due course.*" A holder in due course will be subject to fewer defenses than would an assignee of a contract under the same circumstances. The rights of a holder in due course will be discussed in the next chapter.

Recall that a holder is a person who is possession of an instrument drawn, issued or indorsed to her, her order, to bearer or in blank.[26] In concise terms, a holder is anyone in possession of an instrument with the right to demand payment.

B. Negotiating Order Paper and Bearer Paper

An instrument payable to the order of a specific party is negotiated by completing two steps. First, the necessary indorsement must be placed on the instrument. Second, the holder must deliver the paper to the desired party with an intent to transfer his rights.[27]

Bearer paper can be negotiated through delivery only. No indorsement is required.[28] In either event, delivery must be intentional. A thief stealing an instrument from a holder is not a proper delivery. Therefore, a thief's acquisition of an instrument is not a negotiation. But, if a thief delivers a bearer instrument to a third party, the Code deems the transfer a negotiation. This demonstrates the danger inherent in bearer paper.

C. Indorsements

An indorsement is a signature by or on behalf of the holder on an instrument or on separate piece of paper firmly attached to an instrument. The attached paper is identified as an allonge.[29] An indorsement customarily appears on the reverse side of an instrument, but it may appear anywhere on the instrument subject to bank regulations requiring indorsements on checks to be in a specific loca-

tion to expedite the collection and clearing process. Failure to place an indorsement at the proper place designated on a check may delay or halt the collection process.

D. Indorsement Classifications

Order instruments require indorsements for negotiation. Bearer instruments may be indorsed but it is not necessary for negotiation. An indorsement may be a signature alone or it may include additional words or instructions. Indorsements generally fall into the following classifications: (1) blank or special, (2) qualified or unqualified and (3) restrictive or non-restrictive. An indorsement will have one of the characteristics from each of the three classifications. An example of each classification is presented in figure 23.5.

I. BLANK OR SPECIAL

A blank indorsement may consist of a mere signature. It specifies no particular indorsee.[30] A special indorsement indicates a specific person to whom the instrument is payable. This party is known as the indorsee.[31] No special words or terms are required to effect a special indorsement so long as it is clear from the terms employed that the indorser intended a special indorsement. Terms such as "pay to the order of John Smith" or "pay to Jane Smith" are permissible.

Blank indorsements create bearer paper. Special indorsements create order paper even if the word order is not used in the special indorsement. This is because it is clear from the terms of the special indorsement that the instrument must be paid to a specific individual. An order instrument can be converted to a bearer instrument through a blank indorsement.[32] By the same token, a bearer instrument can be converted into an order instrument through the use of a special indorse-

26. UCC Sec. 1-201(20).
27. UCC Sec. 3-202(1).
28. *Id.*
29. UCC Sec. 3-202(2).

30. UCC Sec. 3-204(2).
31. UCC Sec. 3-204(1).
32. UCC Sec. 3-204(3)

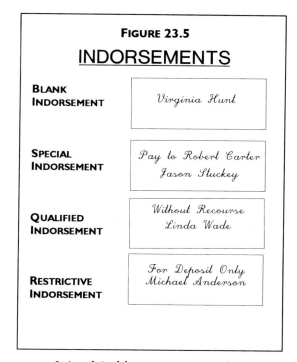

FIGURE 23.5

INDORSEMENTS

BLANK INDORSEMENT	*Virginia Hunt*
SPECIAL INDORSEMENT	*Pay to Robert Carter* *Jason Stuckey*
QUALIFIED INDORSEMENT	*Without Recourse* *Linda Wade*
RESTRICTIVE INDORSEMENT	*For Deposit Only* *Michael Anderson*

ment. It is advisable to use a special indorsement whenever possible as opposed to using a blank indorsement which creates bearer paper. Remember that bearer paper may be intercepted by a thief and negotiated to an innocent third party who may qualify as a holder in due course.

2. QUALIFIED OR UNQUALIFIED

The second classification in which each indorsement must fall is qualified or unqualified. Unless an indorsement specifically provides that it is qualified, the indorsement will be considered unqualified. Unless an indorsement is qualified, an indorser will be secondarily liable on the instrument. An indorser's signature has the effect of guaranteeing payment to those later parties.[33]

---

33. UCC Sec. 3-414(1).

If a party does not want to make such a promise to the subsequent holders of the instrument, it will be necessary to make sure that the indorsement is a qualified indorsement. A qualified indorsement is commonly created with the words "without recourse." This negates the secondary contract liability.

The Code prevents widespread use of unqualified indorsements through Section 3-201(3) which holds that unless the parties have otherwise agreed, any transfer for value of an instrument which is not a bearer instrument gives the transferee the specifically enforceable right to have the *unqualified* indorsement of the transferor. This means that any party taking an order instrument may refuse to give value for that instrument until the current holder places an unqualified indorsement on the instrument. Holders of bearer paper cannot be compelled to indorse instruments.

3. RESTRICTIVE OR NON-RESTRICTIVE INDORSEMENTS

An indorsement may be either restrictive or non-restrictive. A restrictive indorsement is one that places a condition on the transfer of the instrument or appears to prohibit further negotiation of the instrument. If the indorsement does not fall within these two categories, it will be deemed a non-restrictive indorsement.

The restrictive or non-restrictive classification requires an examination of the indorsement for any limitations on the payment of the instrument to the indorsee. The subsequent transferee from a holder who received an instrument under a restrictive indorsement must see that any value paid to that holder is paid consistent with the restriction, or must be without notice that the money will be used for improper purposes. While restrictive indorsements purport to prohibit further negotiation of an instrument, they do not have that effect.[34] Section 3-205 of the Code classifies restrictive indorsements as follows:

1. Conditional indorsements.
2. Indorsements purporting to prohibit further transfer of the instrument.
3. Indorsements containing the words "for collection," "for deposit," "pay any bank" or like terms signifying a purpose of deposit or collection.
4. Indorsements for the benefit or use of the indorser or another person.

a. Conditional Indorsements

An indorsement such as "pay to Acme Corporation if it delivers the rock crusher by November 3," (signed) Joseph, represents a conditional indorsement. Although such an indorsement may impose a condition to payment, this does not make the promise or order to pay conditional. Do not confuse a conditional indorsement with the unconditional payment requirement that is necessary on the face of an instrument for negotiability.

Non-bank transferees of an instrument bearing a conditional indorsement as well as depositary banks must ascertain whether or not the stated condition occurred in order to be in compliance with the indorsement.[35] If the transferee pays the instrument without verifying that the condition occurred, the transferee may be required to pay the instrument a second time to the person imposing the condition. In modern commerce, one seldom sees conditional indorsements because parties do not want to be burdened with verifying the conditions.

b. Indorsements Purporting to Restrict Further Transfer

If an indorsement contains such terms as "pay Jane Jones only," the word "only" may be disregarded in the context of prohibiting further

negotiation. The indorsee may indorse the instrument and further negotiate it without restriction.

c. Indorsements for Deposit or Collection

These indorsements are the most common within the restrictive indorsement classification. This form is widely used in banking. Indorsements such as "for deposit only," "for deposit and collection only" or similar terms indicate that the instrument can be negotiated solely for the purposes of deposit or collection. The legal effect is the same as if the indorsement were a conditional indorsement. Other than the depositary bank, any other bank in the collection process will not be held liable for violations of this type of restrictive indorsement.[36] These indorsements are often used to protect a person depositing a check for collection from payment to an unauthorized person. These indorsements lock an instrument into the bank collection process. Such an indorsement puts a depositary bank on notice that the instrument is being negotiated for the specific purpose of collection. Once a bank has indorsed such an instrument in the collection process, only a bank may acquire the rights of a holder until the check has either been returned to the party making the deposit or has been specially indorsed by a bank to a non-bank.

d. Trust or Other Beneficial Indorsements

These indorsements are commonly used when trusts are involved. Indorsements such as "pay to Mary in trust for James" or "pay to Linda for the benefit of Kenny" are examples of such indorsements.[37] Under these circumstances, the indorsee has the legal power to further negotiate the instrument but must apply the proceeds consistent with the indorsement. The right of subsequent holders of the

---

34. UCC Sec. 3-206(1).
35. UCC Sec. 3-206(3)
36. *Id.*
37. UCC Sec. 3-206(4).

instrument will not be affected even if the trustee does not follow the order in the indorsement unless the indorsee has actual knowledge that the trustee has violated his fiduciary duty.

E. Other Indorsement Issues

I. INDORSEMENTS DIFFICULT TO CLASSIFY

Words of assignment, condition, waiver, guaranty, limitation or disclaimer of liability accompanying an indorsement will not affect its character as an indorsement. An indorsement such as "I assign all of my rights to Larry Fein" would be treated as special indorsement.

2. WRONG OR MISSPELLED NAMES

An instrument made payable to a person under a misspelled name or one other than her own name may be indorsed in that name, in her own name or both. A person paying or giving value for such an instrument can compel the signature of both names.[38]

3. UNINDORSED ORDER PAPER

Receiving an assignment of unindorsed order paper does not create holder status. But, if the transfer was for value, the transferee can compel the appropriate indorsement.[39]

4. INSTRUMENTS PAYABLE TO TWO OR MORE PERSONS

If the instrument is payable to two or more persons in the alternative, usually by using the word "or," any one payee or indorsee may effectively indorse and negotiate the instrument. If the instrument is not payable to the order of two or more persons in the alternative, but rather to all of them jointly, it may only be negotiated following the indorsements of all.[40]

---

38. UCC Sec. 3-203.
39. UCC Sec. 3-201(3).
40. UCC Sec. 3-116.

5. BANK'S POWER TO SUPPLY MISSING INDORSEMENTS

A bank has the power to supply the indorsement of its customer unless the instrument strictly prohibits it.[41] Be mindful that government checks often state "the payee's indorsement is required."

IX. Holder In Due Course

Whether or not a party is entitled to payment for an instrument may be determined by the defenses available to the maker, drawer, and/or indorsers. Obtaining holder in due course status provides special protection for the holder against many of the defenses that could be raised against an ordinary holder or assignee. This is why holder in due course status is critical to the issue of an instrument's enforceability.

A. Holder vs. Holder in Due Course

A holder is a person who is in possession of a negotiable instrument drawn, issued, or indorsed to that person's order, or to bearer, or in blank. This means that it must be free of forgeries of those names necessary to the chain of title. If a holder is not a holder in due course, the holder only obtains those rights that his transferor had in the instrument.

B. Elements of Holder in Due Course Status

A holder in due course is a special type of holder. A holder in due course takes an instrument free from most defenses to enforcement. Section 3-302 of the Code sets forth the requirements for holder in due course status. A holder must meet all three requirements, taking the instrument:

1. For value
2. In good faith

---

41. UCC Sec. 2-205(1).

635

3. Without notice it is overdue, has been dishonored, or that any person has a claim or defense to it.

I. Taking the Instrument for Value

To obtain holder in due course status, the holder must give value for the instrument. Obtaining an instrument by gift or inheritance is not sufficient.[42] For holder in due course status, a holder gives value in one of three ways:

a. A holder gives value to the extent the agreed upon consideration has been paid. In contract law, a promise to perform is sufficient consideration to support a contract. But, under the Code, mere promises are not sufficient to serve as value for holder in due course status. One must have completed the agreed upon performance for value to be established. If performance has been partially completed, value has been given only to the extent of the value of the partial performance. If an instrument was given as collateral for a loan, value has been given to the extent funds have been advanced under the loan.

b. A holder gives value if the instrument is used for payment or security for a prior claim. In contract law, a prior or antecedent claim could not qualify as consideration to support a present contract. Under the Code, a discharge of a prior claim can be considered value for the payment of an existing debt or claim. So, issuing a check to a party to whom one owes money would be an example of exchanging value for an instrument.

c. A holder gives value for an instrument by exchanging it for a negotiable instrument or for an irrevocable commitment to a third person. Therefore, exchanging a negotiable instrument for another negotiable instrument is considered an exchange for value under the Code.

d. Exceptions. Under certain circumstances, one can exchange value for an instrument and still not obtain holder in due course status. Such circumstances include purchasing an instrument at a judicial or bankruptcy sale; taking an instrument in the capacity of an estate administrator; and purchasing an instrument as part of a bulk transfer (such as buying the commercial paper portfolio of another company).[43]

2. Taking the Instrument in Good Faith

Taking an instrument in good faith means that the purchaser-holder must have acted honestly. Recall that good faith is defined by the Code as "honesty in fact in the conduct of the transaction concerned."[44] The key issue in examining an instrument to test it against the good faith standard is whether or not the purchaser honestly believed that the instrument was without defect. Disproportionate exchanges, such as purchasing a promissory note with a face value of $1,000 in exchange for $100 should put the purchaser on notice that the instrument may have been stolen or that the transferor may be attempting to act outside of the scope of her authority.

3. Taking the Instrument Without Notice of Defect

One cannot obtain holder in due course status if that person knew or should have known that the instrument was defective in any of the following ways:

a. That is was overdue
b. That is had been dishonored
c. That there was a defense against it or that there was a claim to it in addition to the purchaser's claim to it.

This test is linked to the holder's notice at the time the instrument was acquired. One can obtain notice of defects directly from another

---

42. UCC Sec. 3-303.

43. UCC Sec. 3-302(3).
44. UCC Sec. 1-201 (19).

party. Notice may be derived from the circumstances.

a. No Notice that the Instrument was Overdue

A time instrument is overdue the day after the due date stated on the instrument. If the due date falls on a holiday or weekend, the next business day is the due date. Missing a principle installment payment is notice that the instrument is overdue. But, missing an interest payment alone is not considered notice that the instrument is overdue.

Knowledge that demand for payment has been made on a demand instrument is knowledge that it is overdue. In addition, the passage of an unreasonable length of time after a demand instrument's issue date is knowledge it is overdue. A check payable within the United States is presumed to be overdue if it has been longer than 30 days after its issue.[45] This does not mean that the check is no longer valid, but represents a rebuttable presumption against holder in due course status. Otherwise, determining whether an instrument is overdue or not will vary with the circumstances.

b. No Notice that the Instrument has been Dishonored

To be a holder in due course, the purchaser must have taken the instrument without notice that it has been dishonored. As a general rule, dishonor occurs when a draft is presented to the drawee for acceptance or payment and the drawee refuses to accept or pay it. Dishonor of a note occurs when it is presented to the maker who refuses to pay it.[46] Dishonor is often indicated on the face of the instrument. Receipt of notice dishonor will be impossible to deny if it appears on the face of the instrument.

---

45. UCC Sec. 3-304(3)(c).
46. UCC Sec. 3-507.

c. No Notice that the Instrument is Subject to a Claim or Defense

A holder who takes an instrument aware that it is subject to a claim or defense cannot obtain holder in due course status. A holder may obtain notice of a defense by observing the appearance of the instrument. If an instrument appears to be incomplete, bears visible evidence of forgery or alteration, or is otherwise so irregular that its ownership, validity, meaning, or the party to be paid is placed into doubt, the holder will be considered to have notice of a defense.

A purchaser also has notice of a claim or defense to the instrument if the purchaser takes it with notice that the obligation of any party is voidable in whole or in part, subject to other defenses or that all of the parties to the instrument have been discharged. If the purchaser is aware that the instrument was issued or transferred as a result of fraud or material misrepresentation or that there has been a breach of warranty or failure of consideration, the purchaser cannot qualify for holder in due course status.

In addition, a purchaser has notice of a claim or defense against the instrument if she has knowledge that a fiduciary, such as a trustee, has breached his duty with respect to the instrument. But, mere knowledge that a prior holder is or was a fiduciary does not by itself put a party on notice of a claim or defense.

d. Factors that do not Represent Notice of Defects

While certain facts may be suspicious, the Code has deemed that certain factors will not be considered "notice of a defect" on the part of the holder.[47] These factors include:

a. The antedating or postdating of an instrument.

b. The holder knew that the instrument was issued in return for an executory

---

47. UCC Sec. 3-304(4).

promise, unless the purchaser had knowledge of an offense or claim arising from that promise.

c. A party signed the instrument as an accommodation party.

d. That the instrument was an incomplete instrument that had been completed by another party, unless the holder has specific knowledge that the instrument had been completed improperly.

e. That any party negotiating the instrument was acting in a fiduciary capacity.

f. There has been a default with respect to the interest payments. But, knowledge that there has been a default with respect to principle payments is knowledge of a defect.

g. Nonpayment of another instrument by the same maker or drawer, unless it was an instrument of the same series as the instrument in question.

X. The Shelter Doctrine

The shelter doctrine greatly expands the scope of holder in due course status by providing that the transfer of an instrument by a holder in due course vests in her transferee the same rights as a holder in due course. This is true even though the transferee may not qualify as a holder in due course on her own merits.[48] The Code's mechanism for the transfer of rights causes a transferee to take all of the rights of a transferor. Thus, if the transferor was a holder in due course, the transferee takes all of the rights of her transferor. Whether or not the transferee can qualify as a holder in due course on her own merits is not an issue.

The shelter doctrine may be viewed as a logical application of the rules of contract assignment. Each party takes the rights of the previous party. To employ the shelter doctrine, a holder need only be able to find a holder in due course somewhere in the chain of title prior to his obtaining the instrument.

But, the shelter doctrine has certain limitations. In order to prevent unscrupulous individuals from employing the shelter doctrine to obtain holder in due course status by laundering instruments through innocent third parties, the rule prohibits reacquisition of an instrument for the purpose of using the shelter doctrine. Any transferee who has been a party to fraud or illegality affecting the instrument or who, as a prior holder, had notice of a claim or defense against the instrument, cannot improve her position by reacquiring the instrument from a holder in due course. Without such a provision, the shelter doctrine could be used as a tool by dishonest parties to easily defraud unsuspecting victims, leaving them with few defenses to protect themselves.

XI. International Finance— Letters of Credit

A letter of credit is an agreement by one party (the issuer) to substitute its financial strength for another (the account party), with that undertaking to be triggered by the presentment of a draft, demand for payment or other documents. A letter of credit may be employed in a number of situations, but generally the account party seeks the strength of the issuer's financial integrity or reputation so that a third party (the beneficiary of the credit) will give value to the account party. The letter of credit's beneficiary extends credit by selling goods or services to the account party on credit, by taking the account party's negotiable paper, or by lending the money to the account party.[49]

---

48. UCC Sec. 3-201(1).

49. UCC Sec. 5-103(1).

While many courts refer to a letter of credit undertaking as a contract, the law does not treat the undertaking in the same fashion as most contracts. The law of contracts merely supplements Article 5 of the Code, the body of law governing letter of credit transactions in most states. The legal principles governing letter of credit transactions are unique. For instance, letters of credit need no consideration.[50] Letters of credit must be in writing.[51]

Letters of credit are transferable only in limited circumstances.[52] There are unique provisions for damages in the event of breach.[53]

Existence of a letter of credit is dependent upon an undertaking by an issuer to honor drafts or other demands for payment. Without such an engagement, there is no letter of credit. For instance, if a bank engages to issue a letter of credit, the bank is agreeing to honor demands for payment out of its own funds, not out of the funds of its customer.

A letter of credit is an importance device for both financing and collateralizing transactions. Letters of credit are widely used in both domestic and international trade. A number of countries, including the United States, have bodies of the law governing letters of credit. Those commonly engaged in letter of credit usage often agree among themselves as to which body of law will govern the transaction. The parties can agree to be bound by Article 5 of the UCC, or they may decide to be governed by the Uniform Customs and Practice for Commercial Documentary Credits (UCP), a private Code devised by the Congress of the International Chamber of Commerce.

Letters of credit fall within two basic categories, the commercial (or documentary) letter of credit and the standby letter of credit.

---

50. UCC Sec. 5-105.
51. UCC Sec. 5-104.
52. UCC Sec. 5-116.
53. UCC Sec. 5-115.

A. Commercial (or Documentary) Letters of Credit

Commercial letters of credit are commonly used for international sales between parties who are not comfortable enough to extend credit to each other. Buying and selling between foreign countries can be facilitated through the use of commercial letters of credit and documents of title. They are often called documentary letters of credit when presentment of documents of title or other documents necessary to claim the goods are required in order to obtain payment. By using these devices, parties reduce the risk of the seller's nondelivery of the goods and the buyer's nonpayment of the price.

Such a transaction would commonly involve a bank in each country to handle the letters of credit and the documents of title. The buyer would typically enter into a contract with the bank in its home country who would issue a letter of credit directed to the seller or the seller's bank that states that the buyer's bank will honor a draft drawn against it for the purchase price, so long as the draft is accompanied by certain documents relating to the goods. These documents commonly include a bill of lading, an invoice, and an insurance policy covering the goods. If the seller complies with the terms of the letter of credit, it will be assured of payment by the buyer's bank. If the bank has to honor the demand for payment, the buyer will be required to reimburse the bank and pay a commission. Often, the buyer will be required to pay the issuer in advance for the letter of credit.

The seller may engage a bank in its own country to act as confirming bank. The advantage is that the confirming bank will be more experienced in handling letters of credit and documents of title as well as often having more information regarding the bank in the buyer's country. By using a confirming bank, the seller obtains an engagement from a bank with which it is more familiar to pay the agreed sum. The confirming bank will charge

AN INTERNATIONAL SALES TRANSACTION FINANCED BY A LETTER OF CREDIT

Assume: An automobile import dealership desires to purchase one German Motor Works (GMW) model 325 L.

Seller: German Motor Works, Germany.

Buyer: Mike Anderson Automobile Imports, Inc., Southland, USA.

Price: $42,000.00 U.S.

Payment
Terms: Presentation of a letter of credit in the amount of $42,000.00 issued by National Giant Bank, New York, N.Y., naming German Motor Works as beneficiary with payment to be made upon presentment of the letter of credit, a bill of lading and GMW's statement of the vehicle's origin.

The Mechanics of the Transaction

1. Anderson arranges for a letter of credit with the designated bank, National Giant Bank, in the amount of $42,000.00. Anderson may purchase the letter of credit for cash or the bank may agree to finance the letter of credit in whole or part. GMW is named as the beneficiary of the letter of credit. The terms of the letter of credit will require GMW to present it for payment along with a bill of lading establishing that the vehicle has been placed in the possession of a reputable carrier and GMW's statement of the vehicles origin. A manufacturer's statement of origin is necessary for an automobile buyer to meet import requirements and to obtain a certificate of title from a governmental unit. The bank will charge Anderson a fee for the letter of credit and related services.

2. Anderson sends the letter of credit to GMW with his order for the vehicle.

3. GMW verifies the authenticity of the letter of credit. Upon verification, it delivers the vehicle to a reputable carrier and enters into a contract for the shipment of the vehicle to the designated U.S. port. GMW receives a bill of lading from the carrier.

4. GMW has its local bank or a courier present the letter of credit, the bill of lading and the manufacturer's statement of origin to National Giant Bank.

5. National Giant Bank examines the documents for authenticity and compliance with the terms of the letter of credit.

6. Upon verification, National Giant Bank wires or otherwise tenders $42,000.00 to GMW or its designated representative.

7. National Giant Bank delivers the bill of lading and the manufacturer's statement of origin to Anderson.

8. Anderson presents the bill of lading to the carrier at port designated on the bill of lading and receives the vehicle.

a fee for its services. An example of an international sale facilitated by a documentary letter of credit is presented in figure 23.6.

B. Standby Letters of Credit

A standby letter of credit, which is used widely both internationally and domestically, does not involve the sale of goods. A standby letter of credit is an engagement by the issuer, usually a bank, to pay a sum to the beneficiary upon the account party's default in the performance of an obligation, usually a financial obligation. Standby letters of credit are often used as financial backup behind large credit arrangements. A large real estate developer may be required by a lender to obtain a standby letter of credit from another bank as security that it will not default on the loan. If the developer defaults on the loan, the beneficiary of the standby letter of credit, (the primary lender) will be entitled to payment from the issuer of the letter of credit upon presentation of evidence that the borrower defaulted on the original obligation. The real estate developer will then be obligated to repay the bank issuing the letter.

Keep in mind that the obligation of the issuer of a letter of credit is a primary obligation to pay that is independent of other contracts or relationships. The issuer may not assert suretyship defenses as a guarantor or surety to avoid repaying the obligation. In addition, letters of credit require presentation of specific evidence before the obligation to pay arises.

While the uses of standby letters of credit are limited only by the imagination, the following demonstrate the most common uses:

1. Real estate development. A lender may condition a loan commitment upon some contribution to the project by the developer in the form of a letter of credit. In other words, the lender wants to see that the developers have some of their own money at risk. In other cases, a lender may desire to see a standby letter of credit to support a liquidated damage clause, to cover costs in connection with the closing of the long term "take-out" loan, to cover working capital for the completed project or to serve in lieu of the lender's loan commitment fee.

2. Obligations under municipal regulations. Developers often face requirements from municipalities to furnish security for obligations owed to the municipality. The developer will often be required to supply security when it seeks approval for a project to provide improvements, such as roads, utility services and other additions. To secure these obligations, municipalities customarily require surety company bonds or bonds supported by cash or government securities. An advantage for a developer using a standby letter of credit is that it is much less expensive than engaging a surety bonding company.

3. Obligations evidenced by promissory notes. A lender or credit seller will often ask its obligor to secure the balance due represented by promissory notes with a standby letter of credit. This significantly reduces the credit risk faced by the holder of a promissory note.

4. Performance bonds. Standby letters of credit have been used to guarantee a party's performance or payment as well as for appeal bonds and bid bonds.

5. Leases. A standby letter of credit may secure the balance due on a real estate lease or an equipment lease and the requirement that the lessee return the goods upon the expiration of the lease.

6. Securities. Standby letters of credit have assisted those attempting to privately place securities to guarantee obligations in connection with such placements. Standby letters of credit have also been helpful in assisting companies in marketing their short term promissory notes in the commercial paper market. Industry ratings of commercial paper will be higher thus yielding a lower rate of interest, if a commercial bank standby letter of credit is securing the commercial paper in the event of default.

Problems

1. Determine whether or not each of the following quoted or described instruments is negotiable.

(a) "I.O.U or bearer due on demand $500. (signed) M. Martin."

(b) "Philadelphia, Pa., [Date]. Three months after date, we promise to pay P. Porter or order $300 for the privilege of one framed advertising sign, size____X____, in one end of each of 159 street-cars of the North Philadelphia City Railway Company, for a term of six months from date hereof. (signed) M. Martin Company."

(c) "Philadelphia, Pa., [date]. I hereby certify that P. Porter had deposited with me $500 which I promise to pay to his order on demand with interest from date, on the return to me of this instrument and of my guarantee for the note of $500 dated this date made by said P. Porter to A. Adams. (signed) M. Martin." (Modified from A.I.C.P.A., Nov. 22-1.)

(d)

Mr. C. Carter   [Date]

Cashier of the First National Bank, Centerville, Ill. Pay to the order of P. Porter the sum of $500 and charge the same against the $1,000 insurance draft issued by the Hartford Insurance Company in my favor, the same being the balance of my account with him.

Respectfully,

(signed) R. Roger

(e)

First National Bank of Centerville, Ill.   [Date]

Pay to the Order of P. Porter $500.00

Five hundred and 00/100 ....Dollars

Preferred Stock Dividend Account

(signed) R. Roger Corp.

by T. Thomas, Treas.

(f)

New York, N.Y.   [Date]
Sixty days after date pay to the order of ourselves $500. The obligation of the acceptor hereof arises out of the purchase of goods from the drawer, maturity being in accordance with the original terms of purchase.
To E. Edward
Chicago, Ill.   (*signed*) R. Roger Co.

(g)

First National Bank of Centerville, Ill.   [Date]
Pay to the order of Porter Realty Co. $500.00
Five hundred and 00/ 100.......................Dollars
For earnest money on 123 Main St., Centerville, check must be returned if deal not consummated

(signed) R. Roger

(h) [Date] I, Mary Miller, hereby promise to pay to the order of Porter Motors five thousand dollars ($5,000) upon the receipt of the final distribution from the estate of my deceased uncle, Carleton Miller. This negotiable instrument is given by me as the down payment on my purchase of a 1981 Lincoln Continental to be delivered in two weeks. (signed) Mary Miller. (Modified from A.I.C.P.A., Nov. 81-1(40).)

(i) "Philadelphia, Pa., [Date]. Five years after date I promise to pay to P. Porter or order $3,000 with interest at the rate of 4 percent per year, payable annually from date until paid: provided however that if any of the principal or interest due on this note is not paid on or before maturity, it shall bear interest at 6 percent (signed) M. Martin."

(j) "London, England, [date]. One month after date I promise to pay to the order of P. Porter One thousand Pounds. Payable at the First National Bank of Centerville, Ill., USA. (signed) M. Martin."

(k) "Chicago, Ill., [date]. One year after date, for value received, we promise to pay to the order of P. Porter $3,000 with interest at the office of the Martin Corp., Chicago, Ill., or at the option of the holder hereof upon the surrender of this note, to issue to the holder hereof in lieu thereof thirty shares of the preferred stock of the Martin Corp. and to pay to the holder hereof in cash the interest then due upon said sum. (signed) Martin Corp. By M. Martin, President" (Modified from A.I.C.P.A., Nov. 20-1).

(l) "Centerville, Ill., [date]. One year from date, for value received, I promise to pay to the order of the First National Bank of Centerville, the sum of $216, there having been deposited herewith as collateral security Pass Book No. 15043 issued by your savings department in my name and I agree to deposit in said savings account the sum of $18 on the fifteenth of every month hereafter until a total of the face amount of this note shall have been deposited. (signed) M. Martin." (Modified from A.I.C.P.A., Nov. 38-7.)

(m) On April 1, induced by P's fraudulent misrepresentations, M bought and received certain goods from P for $500. M signed and gave P a one-month note for that amount, made out on the standard judgment note form of the Pennsylvania National Bank and Trust Company (as reproduced on page 439). On April 2, P sold, indorsed, and transferred the note to H who received it for value, without knowledge of the fraud. On April 3, M discovered that he had been defrauded. M offered to return the goods to P and demanded back his note. Upon P's refusal, M set the goods aside and made no further use of them. When the note came due, M refused to pay, and H sued M. M contended that the note was nonnegotiable. If M's contention was correct, H could not recover from M. Was M's contention correct?

(n) In the preceding problem, suppose that there was no fraud but that M signed the described note intending a gift to P. Would M have a good defense against H?

(o) "Chicago, Ill. [date]. One year after date I promise to pay to the order of P. Porter $1,000. As security for this note, I have this day executed and delivered to the payee a security agreement on the chattels described therein, and agree that upon default in the performance of any of the covenants in said security agreement, the balance then owing on this note, as enlarged by the amount of all advances and expenses that may have been paid by the secured party for taxes, levies, assessments, and other impositions levied upon the goods and chattels, as well as for insurance premiums and the cost of repairs to or maintenance of the said goods and chattels, shall, at the option of the holder, at once become due and payable. (signed) M. Martin."

(p) "I promise to pay bearer $500. (signed) M. Martin."

(q) "Chicago, Ill., [date]. One year after date or on demand, I promise to pay to the order of P. Porter $500. (signed) M. Martin."

(r) Centerville, Ill.   [Date]
Six months after date for value received I promise to pay to the order of the First National Bank of Centerville, Ill., $4,500 with interest from maturity until paid at the rate of 6 percent per year. To secure the payment of this note and of any and all other indebtedness which I owe to the holder hereof, or may owe him at any time before the payment of this note I have hereto attached as collateral security the following:

Stock certificate No. 137 of the Porter Refrigerating Company of Centerville for 50 shares of the stock of said company, par value $5,000.

The above collateral has a present market value of $6,250. If, in the judgment of the holder of this note, said collateral depreciates in value, the undersigned agrees to deliver when demanded additional security to the satisfaction of said holder; otherwise this note shall mature at once. And I hereby authorize the holder hereof on default of this note, or any part thereof, according to the terms hereof to sell said collateral or any part thereof, at public or private sale and with or without notice.

(signed)
M. Martin

(s) Desiring to make a gift to P, M signed and gave P the following instrument: "Centerville, Ill., [date]. One month after date I promise to pay P.

643

Porter $1,000 at the First National Bank of Centerville, Ill. (signed) M. Martin." Two weeks later P indorsed the note, "Pay to the order of H. Howard" and sold and transferred the note to H who paid fair value without knowledge of the purpose for which the note was given. On maturity, M refused to pay and H sued M. H could recover if the note was negotiable. Was it negotiable?

(t)

First National Bank of Centerville. Ill.   [Date]
This is to certify that P. Porter has deposited in this bank $500, payable six months from date with interest at the rate of 2 percent per year, upon return of this certificate properly indorsed. No payment before, and no interest after, maturity
                                                (signed) C. Carter, Cashier

(u)

First National Bank of Centerville, Ill.   [Date]
Pay to the order of Bills Payable $50.00
Fifty and 00/100...Dollars
                                        (signed) Roger Corp.
                                        by T. Thomas, Treas.

2. R drew and delivered to P. Porter a negotiable check for $500, naming P. Porter as payee. P. Porter indorsed the check in blank and delivered it to H. Howard in payment of a debt. H wanted to keep the check for a few weeks, but did not want to restrict himself to eventually depositing it in a bank. What risk, if any, would H be assuming if he merely put the check into his billfold? What should H do?

3. H. Howard, owner and operator of a grocery store, regularly takes in a number of checks drawn on various banks. H's regular practice is to send one of his clerks, each morning, to deposit the previous day's checks in H's account in the Centerville, Ill., First National Bank. H wishes to assure maximum protection to himself from loss of the money represented by the checks, should the checks be lost or stolen while his clerk is on the way to the bank. What should H do?

4. M signed and delivered to P. Porter a six-month negotiable promissory note for $500, naming Porter as payee. T stole the note from Por-

ter, without authority indorsed the note "(signed) P. Porter," and sold and transferred the note for value to A. A sold, indorsed, and transferred the note to B who paid value and had no knowledge of the prior circumstances. Upon maturity, B presented the note to M for payment. M having been advised of theft of the note, refused to pay. B asserted that he was a holder in due course. Was he?

5. On August 1, S sold goods to B, to be delivered the following day, and B agreed to pay $200 in 30 days, signing and giving S a negotiable promissory note to that effect. On August 3, S sold and indorsed the note to H, an innocent party, for $190.

(a) H paid S $190 on August 3. Upon maturity of the note H demanded payment from B. Since S had never delivered the agreed goods B refused to pay H. H asserted that he was a holder in due course. Was he?

(b) H paid S $50 on August 3 and agreed to pay the balance on August 15. By August 10, S still had not delivered the goods and B so informed H. On August 15, H paid S the agreed balance, and upon maturity of the note, demanded payment from B. The goods were still undelivered and B refused to pay. H asserted that he was a holder in due course. Was he? (Modified from A.I.C.P.A., May 48-1a and Nov 77-3(36).)

6. S sold a refrigerator to B's Restaurant and accepted B's negotiable promissory note for $600 as payment. The note was payable to S's order one year after the date of issue. Thirty days after receiving the note, S indorsed the note with a blank indorsement and sold it to National Bank for $550. National credited S's checking account with $550, which brought S's balance to $725. S drew checks for a total of $675 which National honored. National then learned that the refrigerator had not been delivered by S. The note is now due and unpaid. When National brings suit, B pleads lack of consideration on the note. Was National a holder in due course? (Modified from A.I.C.P.A. Nov. 77-3(37).)

7. On January 10, S and B entered into a written contract under which: (1) S sold to B for use in B's restaurant a certain air-conditioning unit for $350; (2) B paid $50 down and agreed to pay $30 a month for ten months, as evidenced by B's note; (3) title was to remain in S until completion of the payments; (4) S guaranteed satisfactory operation of the machine for one year. On the contract form, underneath the signatures of the parties was a row of perforations across the paper, below which was printed a promissory note form. This was filled in for $300 payable in monthly installments of $30, S was named as payee, B was the signer, and the note, otherwise negotiable in form, stated: "This note is given to cover deferred installments under a contract of this date. Upon default in payment of any installments, the entire balance shall immediately become due and payable at the election of the holder."

On January 12, S assigned the contract and indorsed the note (the two still being fastened together) to H Bank for $270 paid to S, and B was notified to make payments to the bank. S's indorsement on the note read, "Pay to Howard Bank without recourse. (signed) S. Smith."

After paying two monthly installments, B notified S and the bank that the machine was not operating satisfactorily, which was true. Upon their refusal to repair or replace the machine, B requested either or both of them to remove the machine and return his $110. They refused, and B made no further payments and no further use of the machine.

(a) On April 15, the bank sued B for $240. What result?

(b) On April 15, the bank sued S for $240. What result?

8. Intending to make a gift, M gave his son, P, an unsealed, negotiable promissory note for $1,000, payable in two months, signed by M and naming P as payee. By the time the note came due, M had died and his administrator refused to pay the note, still held by P. P sued M's estate. Was P entitled to judgment?

9. Paul Porter, the payee of a negotiable note, sold and transferred the note to A. He, in turn, indorsed the note "Pay to Harry Howard without recourse (signed) Albert Adams," and sold and transferred the note to H. The maker was financially unable to pay the note when H duly presented it at maturity H immediately notified P and A. This was the first they knew of the maker's insolvency. H sued to collect the amount of the note. State whether H could collect from P or from A.

(a) if when P transferred the note he wrote on the back of it "(signed) Paul Porter."

(b) if when P transferred the note he wrote on the back of it, "I hereby assign to Albert Adams all my right, title, and interest in this note (signed) Paul Porter." (Modified from A.I.C.P.A., May 33-2.)

10. On January 25, R. Roger as drawer signed a negotiable check for $1,000 naming P. Porter as payee and delivered the check to P. R postdated the check one week, dating it February 1. Upon receiving the check P transferred it to A. Adams, indorsing the check, "Pay to A. Adams only." A immediately took the check to the drawee bank and had it certified. A then endorsed the check in blank and transferred it to H. Howard in payment for materials purchased and received by A from H. On February 1, when H presented the check to the drawee bank, the bank refused to pay H.

a. Did the indorsement to A stop the negotiability of the check and limit the drawee bank's payment of the check to A only?

b. Can H qualify as a valid holder of the check with all the rights of a holder in due course? (Modified from A.I.C.P.A., May 75-7c.)

11. Martin Miller purchased a large order of business supplies from Porter & Company by paying 10% in cash and giving Porter & Company the following instrument to cover the balance due:

Centerville, Ill., [date]
One year after date for value received, I, Martin Miller, hereby promise to pay my debt of One thousand thirty and 26 / 100 dollars ($1,030.26) to Porter & Company or to their order. The maker

may at his option pay within one month of the date of this instrument and receive a 1% discount.

(signed) Martin Miller

Which of the following is true with respect to this instrument?

(a) The instrument is a trade draft.

(b) Since Miller can pay earlier than the due date, the instrument is thereby rendered nonnegotiable.

(c) The language "for value received" is necessary in order to satisfy the requirements for negotiability.

(d) The instrument is negotiable. (Modified from A.I.C.P.A., May 77-2(19).)

Holder in Due Course and Commercial Paper Rights and Liabilities

Holder in Due Course and Commercial Paper Rights

I. Defenses to Repayment

Makers, drawers and indorser of commercial paper may have legal reasons to avoid paying instruments they have issued or negotiated. Certain defenses may permit parties to escape liability. Other defenses will be valid against all parties except holders in due course. It is important to be able to distinguish the various defenses from each other and to understand the effectiveness of each. Defenses may be classified as either personal defenses or as real (universal) defenses. A real defense may be effective against any holder, including a holder in due course. A personal defense may be effective against an ordinary holder but not against a holder in due course.

II. Real Defenses

Section 3-305(2) of the Code sets forth the real or universal defenses that may be raised to prevent a holder in due course from obtaining payment on an instrument. They are identified and explained individually as follows:

A. Infancy (also known as Minority)

If the party who signed the instrument did not have legal capacity to enter into a contract as a result of her age, she will have a real defense to liability on the instrument. Infancy may be asserted as a defense even if state law renders the contract merely voidable and not void.

B. Incapacity

Persons who have been declared mentally incompetent by a court of law are deemed not to have the capacity to enter into a contract. In addition, corporations that have not been properly incorporated or that have had their charters suspended do not have legal capacity to enter into contracts. One must be careful to examine whether or not state law would deem such contracts void from their inception and not merely voidable. If state law would deem the contract void, the defense is a real defense. Otherwise, it is only a personal defense which could be defeated by a holder in due course.

C. Illegality

If the law of the subject state would consider a transaction void due to its illegality, this would serve as a real defense even if the holder in due course was not a party to the illegality. But, if the law of the state would deem such a contract voidable, it would only be a personal defense.

D. Duress

Duress occurs in varying levels. The type of duress that results in a real defense occurs when the duress is so severe that it causes a party to act against her will. One must examine the law of the subject's state to determine at what point duress moves from being merely pressure to becoming a force taking

Example. Fraud in the execution would include a situation in which a person deceived a celebrity into signing a promissory note by making it appear she was merely signing an autograph for a fan at a crowded public appearance. Deceiving a person who cannot read written English into signing an instrument written in English is another example of fraud in the execution. ☐

away a party's ability to act voluntarily. Signing an instrument at gunpoint is certainly enough duress to constitute a real defense. But, signing an instrument in response to threats to prosecute one's daughter may not be sufficient to constitute a real defense depending upon whether or not state law would deem the conduct sufficient to render the contract void and not merely voidable.

E. Fraud in the Execution (also known as Real Fraud and Fraud in the Factum)

There are two types of fraud, real and personal. Real fraud results from a party being tricked or otherwise misled into signing something that he did not know was an instrument. Fraud in the execution results from a misrepresentation which induces a party to sign an instrument "with neither knowledge nor a reasonable opportunity to obtain knowledge of its character or essential terms."[1]

A person will not be able to raise this defense if he had an opportunity to read or otherwise examine the instrument. The signer must prove both lack of knowledge and lack of reasonable opportunity to obtain knowledge. The court may consider the signer's inability to read, mental capacity, lack of education and inability to effectively understand the English language.

F. Discharge in Bankruptcy or Insolvency Proceedings

Obligations arising from negotiable instruments may be discharged by a bankruptcy court or in other insolvency proceedings. This excuses the subject debtor from honoring the instrument. This is a real defense in favor of that party thereby preventing enforcement of the instrument against the bankruptcy debtor.

G. Material Alteration

Any alteration of an instrument is considered a material alteration if it changes the contract of any party to the instrument in any respect.[2]

Material alterations include the following:

1. Changes in the number or relations of the parties.
2. An unauthorized completion of an incomplete instrument.
3. Adding to an instrument or removing part of the instrument (such as cutting off part of the paper containing an undesirable paragraph and changing the numbers or rates set forth on the instrument). But, correcting a mathematical error will not be considered a material alteration.

If a material alteration is readily apparent on the face of an instrument, a holder cannot qualify for holder in due course status because the holder should have observed the potential defect at the time he acquired it.

---

1. UCC Sec. 3-305(2)(c).

2. UCC Sec. 3-407(1).

Example. Leaving spaces in the body of the instrument, thereby making it easy to insert words or numbers is a negligent act. Completing an instrument in pencil is another example of this type of negligence. □

But, if an agent disobeys the instructions of her principle in completing an instrument, a holder in due course may enforce the instrument according to its completed terms so long as the holder was not aware of the agent's disobedience.[3] Knowledge of the agent's disobedience would destroy holder in due course status because the holder would have knowledge of a defense against the instrument.

While a material alteration is a real defense, it is only a partial defense with respect to subsequent holders in due course. The Code permits subsequent holders in due course to enforce the instrument according to its original tenor. This means that the holder in due course can demand enforcement of the instrument pursuant to its original terms.

Negligence of the Maker or Drawer

If the maker or drawer was negligent in issuing or completing an instrument, thereby contributing to a material alteration, the negligent party cannot raise this as a defense against a subsequent holder in due course.

H. Forgery

A forgery is an unauthorized signature. This includes both straight forgeries and signatures by agents acting without authority. An unauthorized signature is wholly ineffective as the signature of the person whose name was signed.

Failure to have all valid signatures necessary an instrument's chain of title, including the signatures of the payee of an order instru-

ment and all special indorsees, prevents any subsequent party from obtaining holder in due course status. This results from lack of holder status. One must be a holder before one can obtain holder in due course status. Forgery of a name necessary to the chain of title prevents any subsequent party from having the instrument properly negotiated to her.

The defense of forgery is limited if negligence contributed to the occurrence of an unauthorized signature.[4] Any party who by his negligence substantially contributed to the entry of an unauthorized signature shall be precluded from asserting that defense against a holder in due course, the drawee or other payor who pays the instrument in good faith and in accordance with reasonable commercial standards. Such conduct reduces the forgery from that of a real defense to that of a personal defense. This concept will be discussed in greater depth later in this chapter with respect to signature liability.

III. Defenses Raised by a Party with Whom the Holder has Dealt

Section 3-305 (2) of the Code states that a holder in due course takes the instrument free from all defenses of any party to the instrument with whom the holder has not dealt except for those real defenses enumerated. This means that any party who has dealt directly with one claiming holder in due course status may still raise all defenses, including

---

3. UCC Sec. 3-407(3)

4. UCC Sec. 3-406.

real defenses. It is difficult for a party to claim obtain holder in due course status against a party with whom it has dealt because the holder will generally have notice of any claims or defenses between them.

IV. Personal Defenses

While these defenses are not valid to prevent enforcement of payment to a holder in due course, these defenses may be raised against all other parties. Personal defenses basically consist of those defenses that are not real defenses. Examples and explanations of certain personal defenses are set forth below.

A. Breach of Contract

A party will have an action for breach of contract any time an instrument is transferred to another party who fails to perform under the contract. A party may attempt to refuse to pay an instrument as a result of the breach of contract. But, a holder in due course may enforce payment of the instrument notwithstanding the breach of contract. In that event, the only recourse for the party issuing the instrument is to bring an action against the breaching party.

B. Lack or Failure of Consideration

Negotiating an instrument in exchange for goods that never arrived or for work that was not completed represents a lack or failure of consideration.

C. Fraud in the Inducement

Fraud in the inducement describes a situation where a party exchanges an instrument for items or services represented to have certain qualities or characteristics, but prove not to live up to the described standards. The fraudulent representations induced the party to negotiate the instrument.

D. Illegality not Resulting in a Void Transaction

If the appropriate state law would define the transaction as merely voidable as opposed to void from its inception, the illegality would constitute only a personal defense and not a real defense.

E. Mental Incapacity Resulting in a Voidable Transaction

If under state law, the transaction would be deemed voidable, as opposed to void, the defense would only be a personal defense. Intoxication usually falls into this category. A person negotiating an instrument in an intoxicated condition may raise this defense against all holders except holders in due course.

F. Voidable Duress

The duress must be evaluated against the law of the subject's state. If the state law would not deem the duress in question as rendering the transaction void from the outset, but rather voidable at the option of the victim, the defense would be a personal defense.

G. Discharge by Payment or Cancellation

If a party desires to pay an instrument prior to its maturity, it is important for that party to obtain possession of the instrument or to write "Paid" on the face of the instrument. Otherwise the instrument could continue circulating in the stream of commerce. Because payment or cancellation is merely a personal defense, a holder in due course could obtain the instrument and rightfully obtain payment from that party a second time.

In the event that the party is required to pay an instrument twice, it has a right of recourse against the party who wrongfully placed the instrument back into circulation.

Example. In the past, consumers were often victimized by unscrupulous sales persons offering goods of inferior quality for home improvements or substandard workmanship in exchange for promissory notes issued by the consumer. These sellers soon learned that they could enter into arrangements with third party finance companies to purchase the promissory notes from them at a discount. The finance companies became holders in due course of the promissory notes executed by the consumers. The sales persons received money from the finance company and would continue to operate in the same fashion until they either were sued in civil court or pursued by the police for fraud. Unfortunately for the consumer, the finance company was able to employ the doctrine of holder in due course to require the consumers to pay the promissory notes according to their terms even though the consumers received very little in exchange. The consumer's only recourse, to pursue the wrongdoers, usually resulted in little recovery because the culprits fled the jurisdiction or often escaped liability in the bankruptcy courts. ☐

H. Unauthorized Completion of an Incomplete Instrument

In the event an agent completes an instrument against the instructions of his principle, the unauthorized completion serves as a personal defense against an ordinary holder. But, a holder in due course who has no knowledge that the agent failed to follow the principle's instructions may enforce the instrument. Therefore, because the defense is only a personal defense, a holder in due course could enforce the instrument as completed.

I. Nondelivery

Delivery means voluntary transfer of possession.[5] A maker or drawer who loses or who has stolen from her a bearer instrument has the defense nondelivery. While this defense will defeat an ordinary holder, it may not be raised against a holder in due course.

---

5. UCC Sec. 1-201(14).

V. Consumer Protection and the Holder in Due Course Doctrine

With the rapid increase of consumer protection laws and regulations during the last three decades, many parties sought changes in the holder in due course doctrine as it was applied to instruments issued by consumers. Various activists urge a complete repeal of the holder in due course doctrine as it applies to consumers. The proponents of change argue that the doctrine unjustly deprives consumers of the ability to protect themselves because they cannot raise the defenses of lack of consideration and fraud in the inducement against holders in due course.

A. The Federal Trade Commission Rule

As a result of these abuses, many states enacted laws imposing some type of restriction on the holder in due course doctrine with respect to consumer transactions. The Federal

Trade Commission established rules and regulations in 1976 having the effect of abolishing the holder in due course doctrine in credit sales of goods or services to consumers.[6] Under these regulations, the seller must include the following notice (in at least a 10-point typeface) in any contract evidencing a sale or lease of goods or services to a consumer on credit:

NOTICE

Any holder of this consumer credit contract is subject to all claims and defenses which the debtor could assert against the seller of goods or services obtained pursuant hereto or with the proceeds hereof. Recovery hereunder by the debtor shall not exceed amounts paid by the debtor hereunder.

Failure to include this notice is deemed an unfair and deceptive trade practice, violating Section 5 of the Federal Trade Commission Act.

This notice has the effect of destroying the holder in due course status of any party holding the instrument because it will be subject to all defenses. Keep in mind that this rule applies only to consumer transactions and not to commercial transactions. Consumer transactions are primarily for personal, family or household purposes.

Those opposing the FTC rule argue that it is contrary to the goals of the system permitting the negotiation of commercial paper: to encourage the free negotiation of instruments in the marketplace as both substitutes for money and as credit instruments. Without the protection afforded by holder in due course status, the pool of potential purchasers of consumer paper has been greatly reduced.

---

6. 16 C.F.R. Secs. 433.1-433.3.

B. State Laws and the Uniform Consumer Credit Code

The Uniform Consumer Credit Code (UCCC), which has not been widely adopted by the various states, virtually eliminates the benefits of negotiable instruments in the area of consumer transactions. The UCCC prohibits a seller from deriving the benefits of Article 3, including holder in due course status, other than by accepting a check. This was intended to have a significant effect on the use of promissory notes in the consumer setting.

The current trend appears to be against further limits on the holder in due course doctrine.

VI. Liability of the Parties

There are two types of liability with respect to negotiable instruments. The first type of liability is contract liability on the instrument. This arises when a party signs an instrument. The second type of liability is warranty liability. This occurs when one transfers an instrument or presents it for payment. The transferor's signature on the instrument is not necessary to create warranty liability.

VII. Contract Liability on the Instrument

One becomes contractually liable to pay an instrument upon signing it. This can be done in the capacity of maker, drawer or indorser. Keep in mind that the Code liberally defines signature to mean any mark or symbol placed on an instrument with the intent to authenticate it. But, there are exceptions to the creation of contract liability.

A. Unauthorized Signature

A party will not be liable if his signature was forged on the instrument. Forged signatures are deemed inoperative. But, if a person whose name was signed without authorization ratified the signature or is precluded from denying it, the signature operates as if it had been authorized.[7] A party who accepted the benefits of a transaction financed by an instrument he purportedly signed cannot later refuse to pay the instrument by claiming that his signature was unauthorized.

In addition, a party will not be able to escape signature liability if his negligence substantially contributed to the situation resulting in an unauthorized signature. But, the signature will also operate as the signature of the unauthorized signer in favor of any person who in good faith pays the instrument or takes it for value. So, if the unauthorized signer can be located, the instrument may be enforced against her.

The loss usually falls on the first party to take the forged instrument. The taker of a forged instrument cannot be a holder because it was not properly negotiated to her. For purposes of negotiation, a forged indorsement is no indorsement at all. But, in two situations in which improper signatures are involved, the loss will still fall upon the maker or the drawer. The situations are described as "the imposter rule" and "the fictitious payee rule."

I. THE IMPOSTER RULE

This situation occurs when someone induces a maker or drawer to issue an instrument to someone impersonating the payee. The maker or drawer believes the imposter is really the person named as the payee. Because the maker or drawer intended to issue the instrument to the person who received it, the indorsement will not be deemed unauthorized when it is negotiated to an innocent party.[8] Therefore, the indorsement is not a forgery. As a result, the maker or drawer will not be able to claim that the indorsement was a forgery in an attempt to escape liability.

---

7. UCC Sec. 3-404(1).
8. UCC Sec. 3-405.

This rule was established to place the loss on the party in the best position to prevent it. In this case, the maker or drawer would be in the best position to prevent the loss by attempting to ascertain the identity of the person to whom the instrument would be issued.

2. THE FICTITIOUS PAYEE RULE

This involves a person signing as or on behalf of a maker or a drawer intending that the payee have no interest in the instrument.[9] The instrument may be issued in the name of a real person, or it may be issued in the name of a person who does not exist. This usually occurs when a company has a dishonest employee who either has the power to sign checks or convinces his employer to sign checks that are issued in the name of a person who has no right to receive a payment. The issuer will bear the loss because the issuer was in the best position to prevent the loss.[10]

B. Signatures by Agents

A signature can be generated by an agent or other representative of a principle to legally bind the principle to the instrument. A valid agent's signature has the same force and effect as if the principle itself had signed it. The agent's signature must have been made in accordance with the principle's authority. The signature should reflect that the agent was signing on behalf of the principle, clearly reflecting the identity of the principle. The Code does not require a particular form of appointment to establish an agent's authority to sign on behalf of her principle.[11]

An authorized agent who signs his own name on the instrument will not be personally obligated if he identifies his principle as a part of his indorsement and indicates his representative capacity.

---

9. UCC Sec. 3-405(b), (c)
10. UCC Sec. 3-405.
11. UCC Sec. 3-403(1).

Example. Assume that W. E. Coyote is the President of the Acme Corporation and has authority to execute instruments on behalf of the corporation. Acme will be bound by any of the following signatures:

1. *Acme Corporation*
W.E. Coyote, *President*

2. *Acme Corporation,* W.E. Coyote

3. *Acme Corporation*

* * *

An agent should clearly disclose his agency capacity to avoid being liable on the instrument. Identifying oneself as an agent or an officer of a corporation will be sufficient to put subsequent holders on notice.

In the situation where Coyote signed the corporation's name followed by his name without disclosing a corporate office or agency relationship, both the corporation and Coyote will be liable. But, the Code will permit parol evidence to be introduced to settle any liability dispute between them.

If an agent, following instructions of a principle, signs an instrument with her own name forgetting to disclose the identity of the principle and the fact that she is an agent, there the agent alone will be bound. Parol evidence will not be admissible because no ambiguity exists on the instrument.

But, if the agent signed her name, "Amanda Anderson, Agent," parol evidence will be admissible to settle any liability dispute between her and her principle.

While a principle will not be bound by an unauthorized signature, recall that makers and drawers can be held liable on instruments if they contributed to a situation resulting in an unauthorized signature. A common problem involves companies who terminate agents but do not inform their regular clients of the termination.

Principles may ratify unauthorized signatures by accepting the benefits of the unauthorized act.[12]

VIII. Contract Liability— Primary and Secondary

When a party signs an instrument, it becomes either primarily or secondarily liable. The only exception is for those signing as qualified indorsers who disclaim any contract liability. Qualified indorsers are those who indorse "without recourse."

A. Primary Contractual Liability

When a party makes a promise to pay an instrument in all events, the party is deemed primarily liable. Primary liability is most often associated with makers of promissory notes. A person signing a promissory note makes an absolute promise to pay the instrument according to its terms at the time of its signing or according to its terms as completed if signed while it was incomplete.[13]

A primarily liable party must pay the instrument when due unless he can establish a real defense.[14] This liability becomes effective as soon as the instrument becomes due and pay-

12. UCC Sec. 3-404(1).
13. UCC Sec. 3-413(1).
14. UCC Sec. 3-305.

able. The holder of an instrument is not required to take any special action against the maker of an instrument to establish primarily liability.

Primary liability may also be created by accepting drafts. Drawee banks that certify checks are "accepting" those checks. The process of accepting the draft is in effect a promise by the bank to pay the instrument just as a maker promises to pay a promissory note.

B. Secondary Contractual Liability

This is contingent liability. Something must occur before secondary liability is triggered. A person may be secondarily liable on a promissory note by indorsing it. A party may be secondarily liable on a check or draft by being the drawer or an indorser.

To establish secondary liability on a promissory note, the maker has to default upon his obligation. On a draft, the drawee must first fail to pay or accept the instrument, whichever is required, prior to secondary liability being established. Each drawer represents that she will pay the amount of the draft to the holder if the check or draft is dishonored.

C. Conditions Precedent to Secondary Contractual Liability

In order to establish the secondary liability of parties to an instrument, the following events must occur:

1. The instrument must be timely presented to the appropriate party.
2. The instrument must be dishonored.
3. Notice of dishonor must be timely given to the secondarily liable parties.

Beware that an instrument can be written to provide for the waiver of the requirements of presentment, dishonor, and notice of dishonor. Depending upon how such waivers are placed on the instrument, it may be binding upon all parties or just one party. For the purposes of examining this material, it will be assumed that the instruments discussed do not contain such waivers.

If the above three requirements are not met, indorsers will be discharged unless there is an excuse for a late presentment or notice of dishonor.[15] Any drawer, acceptor or maker will not be discharged unless the instrument was drawn "without recourse" or the drawer or acceptor of a draft payable at a bank or the maker of a note payable at a bank was deprived of her funds as a result of the bank's insolvency during an unexcused period of delay in presentment or giving notice of dishonor. In such a case, drawee may be excused from his obligation by assigning his claim against a failed bank to the holder of the check.[16]

Observe that the drawee, usually a bank (because most drafts in today's market are checks), is neither primarily nor secondarily liable. This is because the bank has not promised pay the check. The bank has been ordered to pay the check if sufficient funds are present. Therefore, there is no party with primary liability with respect to the average check. The only time a bank is primarily liable on a draft or check is when it certifies (accepts) it.

A bank is not secondarily liable on an instrument because the order to pay does not operate as an assignment of any funds owned by the bank. It is merely an order to the bank to pay the instrument according to its terms so long as sufficient funds exist to carry out the order.

On the other hand, indorsers, excluding qualified indorsers, promise to pay instruments in the event of presentment, dishonor, and notice of dishonor. The difference between indorsers and drawers is that indorsers are usually relieved from liability if there is an improper presentment (such as a late pre-

15. UCC Sec. 3-502(1)
16. UCC Sec. 3-502(1)(b).

sentment), late notice of dishonor or failure to receive notice of dishonor.

1. PRESENTMENT

Presentment is a demand for acceptance or payment made upon the maker, acceptor, drawee or other payor by or on behalf of the holder of an instrument.[17] Presentment must be made to the proper party, in the proper method and in a timely manner. A promissory note and a certificate of deposit must be presented to the maker. A draft, including a check, must be presented to the drawee for payment or acceptance, whichever is required. One may present an instrument in the following ways:

1. By mail, although the presentment will not be effective until the instrument is received.
2. Through a clearinghouse system (this would be depositing a check with a bank other than the drawee bank).
3. At a place specified on the instrument. If the instrument does not specify a place for presentment, the instrument must be presented at the place of business or the residence of the person required to pay or accept the draft. Instruments must be presented at a reasonable hour of the day. If a person is presenting an instrument to a bank, the presentment must be made during regular banking hours.

a. Timely Presentment of a Demand Instrument

Most problems in establishing secondary liability occur through failure to timely present an instrument for payment. Presentment of a demand instrument, including a check, must occur within a reasonable time after the

---

17. UCC Sec. 3-504(1).

drawer or indorser signs the instrument. What is reasonable will vary depending upon the type of instrument and the circumstances. The Code sets forth time periods under which it is presumed checks drawn and payable within the United States should be presented. With respect to the liability of the drawer, it is presumed that the check should be presented for payment within 30 days after the date on the check or the date of issue, whichever is later. With respect to the liability of any indorser, it is presumed that the instrument should be presented for payment within seven days after the date of that indorsement.

Any presentment due on a day which is not a full business day for either the person making the presentment or the party to pay or accept the instrument, shall be due on the following full business day for both parties.[18]

b. Timely Presentment of Time Instruments

Time instruments payable at or following a stated period after any presentment for acceptance must made on or before the date the instrument is payable.[19] An instrument that shows the date on which it is payable requires presentment on that date.[20]

2. DISHONOR OF AN INSTRUMENT

Dishonor occurs when the instrument is properly presented for payment or acceptance and the drawee or maker refuses to pay or accept the instrument according to its terms. Examples of dishonor include checks returned for insufficient funds, account closed or payment stopped. An instrument is not deemed dishonored by a bank if the check was returned because a signature was missing, a signature had been forged, the instrument was presented to the wrong bank for payment or the instrument had been altered.

---

18. UCC Sec. 3-503(2)7 (3).
19. UCC Sec. 3-503(1)(a).
20. UCC Sec. 3-503(1)(c).

Payment of an instrument may be deferred without dishonor pending a reasonable examination of the instrument to determine whether it is properly payable. But, payment must be made in any event before the close of the business on the day of presentment. If an item has been presented for acceptance, the decision may be deferred without dishonor until the close of the next business day following presentment.[21] In addition, the holder may also take an additional business day if acting in good faith to determine whether or not to accept an instrument. This extension is not considered a dishonor of the instrument. Therefore, it does not discharge the parties that are secondarily liable.

3. NOTICE OF DISHONOR

The final element required to establish secondary liability on an instrument is transmitting notice of dishonor. Unless a party has been legally excused from giving notice of dishonor, failure to do so will discharge all indorsers and could possibly discharge the drawer if the bank were to fail during the period delay.[22]

Notice that the instrument has been dishonored may be given by or on behalf of the holder, any party who has received notice of dishonor or any other party who can be forced to pay the instrument. In addition, an agent or a bank in whose hands the instrument was dishonored may give notice to his principle or customer or to another agent or bank from which the instrument was received.[23]

Notice may be given in any reasonable manner. It may be oral or written and in any terms which identify the instrument and state that it has been dishonored. If the notice involves a misdescription of the instrument, notice of dishonor will still be effective so long as the

misdescription did not mislead the party notified. Sending the instrument bearing a stamp, ticket or writing stating that acceptance or payment has been refused or sending a notice of debit with respect to the instrument is sufficient to constitute notice of dishonor. If notice of dishonor is given in writing, the notice is effective when sent, even if it is not received.[24]

Notice to one partner is notice to all members of a partnership, even if the partnership has been dissolved. If a party is involved in a bankruptcy or insolvency proceeding after thc issuance of the instrument, notice may be given either to the party or the trustee of the estate. In the event a party dies or is declared mentally incompetent, notice may be sent to the last known address or given to the personal representative.

Notice of dishonor operates for the benefit of all parties who have rights against the party notified. Therefore, once a party receives notice, the remaining individuals who would normally give notice of dishonor do not have to each give notice to that party.

4. TIME OF NOTICE

If a bank must give notice of dishonor, it must do so before its midnight deadline. The midnight deadline is defined as midnight of the next banking day following its receipt of the instrument. In all other situations, notice of dishonor must be given prior to midnight of the third business day after dishonor or receipt of notice of dishonor.

5. PROTEST

While informal notice of dishonor is usually adequate, there are times when a formal "protest" is required. A protest is a certificate of dishonor made under the hand and seal of a United States consul, vice consul, notary public or any other person authorized to certify dishonor by the law of the place where the

21. UCC Sec. 3-506.
22. UCC Sec. 3-502(1)(b). 23.
23. UCC Sec. 3-508(1).

24. UCC Sec. 3-508.

dishonor occurs. It may be made upon information satisfactory to such person.[25] The protest must identify the instrument and certify either that due presentment has been made or the reason why it was excused and that the instrument has been dishonored by nonacceptance or nonpayment. The protest may also certify that notice of dishonor has been given to all parties or to specified parties.

Protest is only necessary for dishonor of drafts drawn or payable outside the United States. The protest serves as proof that the instrument has been dishonored in the event there is litigation regarding liability on the instrument. A party has the option to formally protest presentment of an instrument drawn within the United States.[26]

D. Order of Secondary Liability

Unless a party indorses an instrument "without recourse," she engages that upon dishonor and any necessary notice of dishonor or protest, she will pay the holder (or any subsequent indorser) for the instrument according to its terms at the time of her indorsement. Unless indorsers agree otherwise, they are liable to one another in the order in which they indorse, which is presumed to be the order in which their signatures appear on the instrument.[27]

E. Liability of Guarantors and Accommodation Parties

Guarantors and accommodation parties sign instruments in special capacities. When a party adds to its signature "payment guaranteed" or equivalent words, the signer engages that if the instrument is not paid when due, it will pay the instrument according to its terms without the holder having to look to any other party for payment.[28] An indorser who guar-

antees payment waives not only presentment, notice of dishonor and protest, but also waives the need for any demand upon the maker or drawee.

"Collection guaranteed" or equivalent words added to a signature mean that the signer will pay the instrument according to its tenor if it is not paid, but only after the holder has reduced his claim against the maker or acceptor to judgement and execution has been returned unsatisfied, or after the maker or acceptor has become insolvent or it is otherwise apparent that it is useless to proceed against the maker or acceptor. A guarantee of collection also waives formal presentment and notice of dishonor and protest. Words of guarantee added to a signature of a sole maker or acceptor will not affect the liability of the maker or acceptor. Any guarantee written on an instrument is enforceable notwithstanding any statute of frauds.

An accommodation party is one who signs an instrument in any capacity for the purpose of lending her name (and credit capacity) to a party on the instrument. An accommodation party will be liable in the capacity in which she signed the instrument. An accommodation maker or acceptor is bound on the instrument without any resort to the principle, while an accommodation indorser may be liable only after presentment and notice of dishonor or protest. If the accommodation party signs as a maker or acceptor, the accommodation party is primarily liable on the instrument. If the accommodation party signs as an accommodation indorser, the accommodation party is secondarily liable.

If an accommodation party is required to pay, she may pursue the party she accommodated for full recovery. An accommodation party has no liability to the party she accommodated.[29] Any indorsement on an instrument which does not appear to be in

25. UCC Sec. 3-509(1).
26. UCC Sec. 5-301 (3).
27. UCC Sec. 3-314.
28. UCC Sec. 3-416(1).

29. UCC Sec. 3-415.

the chain of title is notice that it was an accommodation indorsement.

IX. Warranty Liability

In addition to contract liability, a party negotiating an instrument faces warranty liability. Each party presenting an instrument for payment or acceptance, or transferring an instrument for consideration, makes certain warranties. While contract liability requires a party's signature on the instrument, warranty liability requires no signature. Certain warranties are made even when one negotiates bearer paper by delivery alone. But, signing an instrument can affect the scope of warranty liability. There are two types of warranties: presentment warranties and transfer warranties.

A. Presentment Warranties

Any person who seeks payment or acceptance of a negotiable instrument warrants to any person who pays or accepts the instrument in good faith that:

1. The party presenting the instrument has good title (ownership) or is authorized by the owner to obtain payment or acceptance of the instrument.
2. The party presenting the instrument has no knowledge that the signature of the maker or drawer was not authorized (a forgery).
3. The instrument has not been materially altered.

There is an important exception to keep in mind with respect to holders in due course. The presentment warranties numbered 2 and 3 are not given by a holder in due course acting in good faith to a maker, drawer or acceptor. The reason behind this exception is that the party to whom the instrument has been presented should be in a better position than the holder to verify the accuracy of the information regarding the note or draft.[30]

B. Transfer Warranties

While presentment warranties run to the party paying or accepting the instrument, transfer warranties may be made to all subsequent transferees and holders who take an instrument in good faith. When a party transfers an instrument, whether by delivery alone, or by indorsement and delivery, she warrants that:

1. She has good title (ownership) or is authorized to obtain payment or acceptance of the instrument.
2. All signatures are genuine or authorized.
3. The instrument has not been materially altered.
4. No defense of any party is good against the transferor (but a qualified indorser, one who indorses "without recourse," limits this warranty to one of "no knowledge" that a defense is good against the transferor).
5. She has no knowledge of any insolvency proceeding (such as bankruptcy) against the maker, acceptor or drawer of an unaccepted instrument.

If the instrument was transferred by indorsement, the transfer warranties extend to all subsequent holders of the instrument. But, if the instrument was transferred by delivery alone, such as the negotiation of a bearer instrument, the transfer warranties extend only to her immediate transferee.

X. Discharge of Liability

A party's exposure to primary or secondary liability must eventually come to an end. The

---

30. UCC Sec. 3-417.

Example. John issued a promissory note to the order of "cash" and delivered it to Mary. Mary placed the instrument on her coffee table. John's friend, Linda, visited Mary's home and stole it. Linda presented it to John for payment, admitting her theft. John paid it. This payment was in bad faith. This will not discharge John's liability. ☐

point the liability is discharged varies with the circumstances. Under some circumstances, liability initially may be partially discharged followed by complete discharge at a later date. The following describes the various types and times of discharge as set forth in Section 3-601 of the Code.

A. Discharge by Payment

Paying the instrument is one of the most common ways to discharge liability. The liability of any party is discharged to the extent of his payment or satisfaction to the holder. This is true even if the payment was made with knowledge that another party was claiming the instrument unless, prior to such payment or satisfaction, the person making the claim either supplied an indemnification bond or obtained an injunction preventing the payment or satisfaction.

The Code also permits discharge of liability by satisfaction of the parties. This means that a payment of money in exchange for the discharge of liability is not required so long as the parties can agree upon the type and extent of consideration.[31] But, payment or satisfaction will not discharge liability if a party pays or satisfies an instrument in bad faith.

Payment or satisfaction will not discharge liability of a party who pays or satisfies the holder of an instrument which has been restrictively indorsed in a manner not consistent with the terms of the indorsement. An intermediary bank or a payor bank which is not the depositary bank is not subject to liability for violations of restrictive indorsements that lock the instrument into the bank collection process.

Remember that payment or satisfaction is a personal defense. Upon paying an instrument, one should indicate this fact on the face of the instrument or retain possession of it. There is risk if the instrument falls into the hands of a holder in due course who demands payment. Because payment is only a personal defense, a holder in due course will prevail, requiring the issuer to pay the instrument a second time.

Once the party with primary liability pays the holder of an instrument in full, all parties will be discharged. The same is true if a drawee pays a check or draft in full and in good faith to a holder.

But, if an indorser pays, it will discharge only those subsequent parties on the instrument. This is because the subsequent parties have lost a source of payment on the instrument. The indorser who pays may seek payment from any previous party on the instrument.

B. Discharge by Tender of Payment [32]

If a party tender's payment to the holder of an instrument and the holder refuses to accept the payment, the party tendering the payment will be discharged of liability for any subsequent interest, costs, or attorney's fees. In addition, anyone who would have a right of recourse against the party making tender will be wholly discharged under the obligation.

---

31. UCC Sec. 3-603

32. UCC Sec. 3-604.

C. Discharge by Cancellation or Renunciation[33]

The holder of an instrument may discharge any party on the instrument in any manner apparent on the face of the instrument or the indorsement. This may be done by intentionally canceling the instrument, canceling a party's signature, destroying the instrument, mutilating the instrument or striking out a party's signature. Any destruction of the instrument must be done with the intent to cancel the instrument. Accidental destruction of an instrument will not constitute a discharge. Courts will permit parole evidence to establish that the instrument existed.

A party may indicate an intent to cancel the instrument by writing "paid" or "canceled" across the instrument. If a party discharges an indorser by striking that indorser's signature, all indorsers following the stricken indorsement will be discharged. But, indorsements prior to the canceled indorsement will remain valid.

D. Discharge By Reacquisition[34]

If a party to an instrument reacquires an instrument, that party may cancel any indorsement which is not necessary to her title and reissue or further negotiate it. Any intervening party will be discharged as against the reacquiring party and subsequent holders not in due course. If a party's indorsement has been canceled, his liability will be discharged as against subsequent holders in due course as well.

So, if one reacquires an instrument, the intervening indorsers are discharged except against the claims of holders in due course. Intervening indorsers will still be subject to the claims of holders in due course unless their indorsement was specifically canceled.

The holder of an instrument may, without consideration, discharge any party by renouncing his rights in a signed writing or by surrendering the instrument to the party to be discharged.[35] But, no discharge of any party is effective against a subsequent holder in due course unless that holder had notice of the renunciation at the time the he acquired the instrument.[36]

E. Discharge by Impairment of Recourse or of Collateral [37]

A holder discharges any party to an instrument to the extent the holder, without consent or an express reservation of rights, agrees not to sue, releases or otherwise discharges a party who otherwise would have been liable on the instrument.

A holder discharges any party to an instrument to the extent the holder without consent unjustifiably impairs any collateral given to secure repayment of the instrument given by or on behalf of any party against whom the holder had a right of recourse. Because a party could look to existing collateral for payment of the instrument, the loss of that collateral destroys a source of payment. Therefore, any party prejudiced by such a loss or destruction of collateral will be discharged.

F. Discharge by any Act that Would Discharge a Contract [38]

Any party will be discharged from her liability on an instrument by any act or agreement which would discharge her simple contract for the payment of money. This would include successful negotiations resulting in an accord and satisfaction, a composition agreement, a novation, rescission or other mutual agreements.

---

33. UCC Sec. 3-605.
34. UCC Sec. 3-208.

35. UCC Sec. 3-605(1)(b).
36. UCC Sec. 3-602.
37. UCC Sec. 3-606(1).
38. UCC Sec. 3-601(2).

G. Discharge by Fraudulent and Material Alteration

As against any person other than a holder in due course, an alteration of an instrument will result in the discharge of any person whose contract is changed if (1) the alteration was made by the holder; (2) the alteration was fraudulent and (3) the alteration was material.[39] A holder in due course may still enforce the instrument according to its original tenor.

If the party asserting the discharge has, through his own negligence, contributed to the alteration, there is no discharge. A holder in due course or other good faith payor can enforce the instrument as altered.

Incomplete instruments may be enforced according to the authority given. But, a subsequent holder in due course may enforce an incomplete instruments as completed.

H. Discharge by Certification of a Check

Recall that when a bank certifies a check, the bank becomes primarily liable on the instrument by engaging to pay the check according to its tenor at the time of presentment. Upon certification, the drawer and all indorsers prior to the certification are discharged.

* * *

Problems

1. A. Adams falsely stated that he represented P. Porter, head of the Porter Health Center, a charitable tuberculosis camp, and that he was soliciting funds for the camp. R signed and gave A a negotiable check for $100, naming P. Porter as payee, as a contribution to the camp fund. A indorsed the check with P's name and transferred it for cash to B who indorsed and transferred the check to H. Both B and H received the check for value, in good faith, and with no knowledge of the prior circum-

---

39. UCC Sec. 3-407.

stances. A few days later R learned that there was no such person as P. Porter and no such camp as the Porter Health Center, and notified his bank not to pay the check. The bank accordingly refused payment when H made prompt presentment. H asserted that he was a holder in due course. Was he?

2. R who had a checking account in a Philadelphia bank frequently signed checks with a rubber-stamp facsimile of his handwritten signature. R always kept the stamp in a compartment inside his safe. This compartment was locked and the key was kept in a drawer in the safe, behind some papers. This drawer was locked and the key was kept in another, unlocked drawer in the safe. The safe had a key lock rather than a combination lock. The safe key was kept in a small wooden box which was kept in a larger wooden box, on top of another safe. The signature stamp was removed, apparently by an employee who R had no previous reason to distrust, and applied to several check forms. The drawee bank paid these checks. When the bank refused to comply with R's demand that the bank restore to R's account the amount paid on the forged checks, R sued the bank. What result?

3. Smith Company of Chicago, Ill., carried on a mail-order business and distributed with its catalog the following printed order form:

Smith Company Order Form

To Smith Company Chicago, Ill.

Please enter the following order for the described goods at the prices stated, f.o.b. Chicago, Ill.:

[A space was left here on the order form for a buyer to insert a description of the goods he was ordering and the prices.]

Smith Company Warranty: Any buyer who is not perfectly satisfied with any item purchased from Smith Company may, within ten days after receipt, return the item at Smith Company's expense; Smith Company will thereupon refund any payment made for such item and cancel any unpaid charges.

Terms for Payment: In payment for the above described goods and subject to the Smith Company warranty (as stated in the immediately preceding paragraph) I hereby promise to pay to Smith Company or order the sum of _____Dollars, within two months after date, less 2 percent discount if payment is made within ten days after date.

Date_____   Buyers signature_____
                Buyer's Address_____

On February 1, B completely filled in such an order form for good totaling $500. Not having in stock the items ordered by B, S Company sent substitute goods together with a letter explaining the circumstances and assuring that if the substitute goods were not satisfactory, B could return them. Finding the substitute goods unsatisfactory for his purposes, B returned them and thought nothing more about the transaction until April 1, when a local bank presented a note to B and demanded payment. The note consisted of the lower portion of the above form, cut between the second and third lines in the "Terms of Payment" paragraph. Without knowledge or notice of the note's being cut from an order form, or of the transaction between S Company and B, a Chicago bank had, on February 11, discounted the note for S Company, paying S Company the face amount less its usual discount fee. On March 25, S Company was adjudged bankrupt. On March 30, the Chicago bank indorsed and mailed the note to B's local bank for collection. When B refused to pay, the Chicago bank sued B. What result?

4. R, owner and operator of a business, maintained a checking account in his own name. While away on business trips, it was R's practice to leave some signed blank checks in the safe for use by his trusted employees. On night while R was away on a business trip the safe was broken open and among other things some signed checks were stolen. The thief completed one of the checks, inserting $250 as the amount, and naming P. Porter, an assumed name, as payee, and in that name cashed

the check at the drawee bank. Upon being advised of the facts, the bank refused to restore to R's account the amount paid. R sued the bank. What result?

5. R was about to leave his office for a luncheon engagement, to be followed by an afternoon conference which would keep him away from the office for the remainder of the day. The bookkeeper stopped R at the office door and explained that they needed $50 for petty cash that afternoon. R had the bookkeeper fill in a standard check form, making it payable to "cash" and inserting the amount of $50 in figures. R signed the check and gave it to the bookkeeper, instructing him to run the check through the check writing machine (which would impress the amount in words) and then obtain the needed petty cash from the bank. After R left the office, the bookkeeper added another zero to the "$50" and impressed "Five Hundred Dollars" on the check with the check writing machine. The bookkeeper cashed the check and absconded. R had no previous reason to doubt the bookkeeper's honesty. Discovering what had happened, R demanded that the bank restore $450 to his account and upon the bank's refusal, R sued the bank. What result? (Modified from A.I.C.P.A., May 24-4).

6. M. Martin purchased some securities form P. Porter. In exchange for the securities M executed and delivered the following instrument to P: "Chicago, Ill., [Date]. For value received I promise to pay to the order of P. Porter six months after date $900. If at any time the holder of this note shall so desire he may declare the note due immediately. (signed) M. Martin." M's signature was placed by him at the bottom of the instrument with a rubber stamp. With a blank indorsement P negotiated the instrument to A for value. A had no knowledge of the securities transaction, and on the due date presented the instrument to the maker for payment. M refused to pay the note alleging a failure to consideration, and claimed that the securities were absolutely worthless. A sued M.

(a) What was the effect of the signature having been made by rubber stamp?

(b) What was the effect of the holder having a right to declare the note due immediately? (c) If the securities were worthless, would M be justified in refusing to pay the note? (Modified from A.I.C.P.A., Nov. 56-8 and Nov. 77-3(35).)

7. Desiring to make a gift to P, M dated, signed and gave P a negotiable demand note, naming P as payee, and made out for $1,000 with interest at the rate of 6 percent per year. Ten days later P sold, indorsed, and transferred the note to A for $1,000 which A paid to P, without knowledge of the prior circumstances. Two years later A sold, indorsed, and transferred the note to H for $1,000, which H paid to A without knowledge of the prior circumstances. Two weeks after purchasing the note, H demanded payment from M and upon M's refusal to pay, H sued M. Was H entitled to recover from M and if so, how much?

8. H was the holder of the following note:

[Date]

Seven months after date I promise to pay to the order of P. Porter $500.

(signed) M. Martin

On the reverse side, reading downward from the top were written: "Without recourse (signed) P. Porter; (signed) A. Adams"; "Without recourse (signed) B. Brown"; "Payment guaranteed (signed) C. Carter." These were four separate indorsements, each signed at a different time. C sold and delivered the instrument to D. Davis who in turn sold and delivered it to E. Edwards. On the fourth month after the date on the note, E told H of obtaining the instrument from D and delivered it to H. A, B, C, D, E, and H were each in turn holders in due course of the note. Neither D nor E indorsed the note.

(a) Through sudden business reverses, M became insolvent during the fifth month after the date on the note, and remained insolvent thereafter. When H presented the instrument to M and demanded payment, on the date stated below, M was unable to pay because of his insolvency, and H immediately gave notice of the dishonor to P, A, B,

C, D, and E and made no further attempt to collect form M. (1) H presented the note, demanded payment, and gave the notices mentioned above, all on the day the note came due, which was a full business day for all parties. Could H collect from P? From A? From B? From C? From D? From E? (2) With one month after the due date as the date of presentment, dishonor, and notice of dishonor, answer the same questions as in (1) above.

(b) The note was given for M's losses in an all-night poker game with P and others. When H presented the note to M and demanded payment, M refused to pay on the ground that it was a gambling note. H immediately gave notice of the dishonor to P, A, B, C, D, and E. (1) Same additional facts as in Part (a1) above. Could H collect from M? From any of the other parties named above? (2) Same additional facts as in Part (a2) above. Could H collect from M? From any of the other parties named above?

9. Paul Porter, the payee of a negotiable note, sold and transferred the note to A. He, in turn, indorsed the note "Pay to Harry Howard without recourse (signed) Albert Adams," and sold and transferred the note to H. The maker was financially unable to pay the note when H duly presented it at maturity. H immediately notified P and A. This was the first they knew of the maker's insolvency. H sued to collect the amount of the note. State whether H could collect from P or from A:

(a) if when P transferred the note he wrote on the back of it "(signed) Paul Porter."

(b) if when P transferred the note he wrote on the back of it, "I hereby assign to Albert Adams all my right, title, and interest in this note (signed) Paul Porter." (Modified from A.I.C.P.A., May 33-2.)

10. In payment for goods purchased from P. Porter, R signed and gave P a negotiable check for $1,000 drawn on the E Bank, naming P as payee. The next day P indorsed the check "(signed) P. Porter" and transferred it to A. Adams who, the same day, transferred the check to H. Both A and H were holders in due course. Upon H's due presentment of the check, E Bank refused to pay and H

promptly notified R, A, and P of the nonpayment. The evidence showed that: (1) the balance in R's account was $1,500; (2) R was in financial difficulty; (3) a prominent businessman in the community had requested the bank to hold the balance in R's account pending a lawsuit the businessman was going to initiate against R; (4) it was for the latter reason that the bank refused to pay H. H sued for the amount of the check.

(a) If H sued E Bank, could H recover?

(b) If H sued R, could H recover?

(c) If H sued P, could H recover?

(d) If H sued A, could H recover, assuming that A had: (1) indorsed "(signed) A. Adams"? (2) Indorsed "Without recourse (signed) A. Adams"? (3) Not indorsed at all?

11. Through fraudulent misrepresentations P induced R to purchase certain goods. In payment for the goods R signed and gave P a negotiable check, drawn on the E Bank, in the amount of $400, naming P as payee. The next day, P indorsed "Without recourse (signed) P. Porter" and transferred the check to A who, the next day, transferred the check to H. Both A and H were holders in due course. Discovering the fraud, R stopped payment on his check, and E Bank accordingly refused to pay when H made due presentment. H promptly notified R, P, and A, and sued for $400.

(a), (b), (c), (d) Answer the same questions as are asked in Problem 19.

12. For this problem, assume that April 1 was a Monday. On April 7, R signed and delivered to P a negotiable check so dated, naming P as payee and drawn for $150. On the date stated below, H cashed the check for P, giving P $145. When the check was returned to H marked "Payment stopped," H immediately notified R. R refused to pay H, and proved that he originally gave the check to P as a gift, a fact previously unknown to H. H sued R. How much could H recover from R, if H cashed the check for P (a) on May 9, (b) on April 29?

13. On September 21, a thief stole a car belonging to P. Porter, and also stole the certificate of title for the car, and various identifying papers belonging to P. On September 23, the thief took the car to R, a reputable car dealer, introduced himself as P, and showed P's identifying papers. R agreed to buy the care for $1,200 and signed and gave to the thief a negotiable check for that amount. The check named P as the payee and was dated September 25. The entire check, including the date, was written in broad, rounded words and figures. R dated the check ahead to give himself time to verify the title to the car. On September 24, R learned of the theft and immediately stopped payment on his check. On September 29, the thief bought a car from H, another car dealer. The thief offered to pay the price of $764 with R's $1,200 check, the thief indorsing the check with the payee's name and using P's identifying papers again to deceive H into thinking that the thief was P. H in good faith believed that he was dealing with P and took the check, paying the thief the difference of $436 in cash. Shortly after H deposited the check in his own bank, the check was returned marked, "Payment stopped." H sued R.

(a) Was H entitled to recover from R?

(b) In addition to the above facts, assume that when H received the check, it was dated September 28 instead of September 25, the "5," unknown to H, having been changed to an "8" by a straight narrow, diagonal line in a type of ink different from that used in making the "5." Would H be entitled to recover from R?

14. In payment of an obligation, R, without negligence, signed and gave P a negotiable check drawn on E Bank in the amount of $9, naming P as payee. The next day P transferred the check to A. Adams with an unqualified indorsement. The same day A dishonestly raised the check to $190, so skillfully that the alteration was not noticeable on ordinary inspection, indorsed the check "Without recourse (signed) A. Adams," and transferred it to B. Brown, who, the following day, transferred the check to C who on the following day and with-

out further indorsing the check, transferred it to H. H, C, and B were holders in due course.

(a) Upon presentment of the check, E Bank paid H $190. Upon receiving his statement and canceled checks, R promptly notified E Bank of the alteration. (1) Could E Bank properly charge the $190 payment against R's account? (2) Could E Bank recover from P? (3) Could E Bank recover from A? (4) Could E Bank recover from B, assuming that he had: (a) Indorsed "(signed) B. Brown"? (b) Indorsed "Without recourse (signed) B. Brown"? (c) Not indorsed at all? (5) Could E Bank recover from H?

(b) Pursuant to R's stop payment order, E Bank refused to pay the check when H duly presented it and H promptly notified all prior parties. (1) Could H recover from R? (2) Could H recover from P? (3) Could H recover from A? (4) Could H recover from B, assuming the additional facts stated in (a), (b), and (c) in part (a4) of this problem?

15. On May 1, P. Porter made out a negotiable check on the E bank, in the amount of $500, naming himself as payee, and without authority signed R's name as drawer. On May 2, P indorsed the check "Without recourse (signed) P. Porter," and transferred the check to A. Adams, who transferred it to H. Both A and H were holders in due course. On May 5, unaware of the forgery, E Bank paid $500 on the check. Upon receiving his statement and canceled checks, R promptly notified E Bank of the forgery.

(a) Could E Bank charge the $500 payment against R's account?

(b) Could E Bank recover from H?

(c) Could E Bank recover from A, assuming that he had (1) Indorsed "(signed) A. Adams"? (2) Indorsed "Without recourse (signed) A. Adams"? (3) Not indorsed at all?

(d) Could E Bank recover from P?

16. Other facts remaining the same as in the preceding problem, assume that the bank refused to pay the check. H sued A. Assume the same facts

as in (1), (2), and (3) of Part (c) above. Could H recover from A?

17. R signed and gave P. Porter a negotiable check drawn on the E Bank in the amount of $500, dated May 1 and naming P as payee. A thief stole the check from P, without authority indorsed the check, "(signed) P. Porter," and on May 2 transferred the check to A. Adams, who transferred the check to H on May 4. Both A and H gave value for the check, without knowledge of the prior circumstances. In good faith and without carelessness, E Bank paid H $500 on the check on May 5. Upon receiving his statement and canceled checks, R promptly notified E Bank of the forged indorsement.

(a) Answer the same questions asked in Parts (a), (b), (c), and (d) in Problem 24.

(b) Other facts remaining the same, assume that R, advised of theft of the check, stopped payment. Accordingly, E Bank refused payment when H presented the check on May 5. H promptly notified all prior parties. (1) H sued A. Assume that the same facts as in (1), (2), and (3) of Part (c) of Problem 24. Could H recover from A? (2) Could H recover from P?

18. P, an appliance dealer, made a practice of discounting with H Bank the security agreements with notes attached that arose from his sale of appliances. The procedure was that when a sale was in prospect, P would report to H Bank the name of the prospective customer. If the bank found the credit rating of the prospective customer satisfactory, P would make the sale and have the customer sign a contract form and a negotiable note form. Both forms were on the same sheet of paper, with the paper perforated between them. P would then take the paper to the bank where, after the proper amounts were inserted, P would transfer the paper to the bank. On May 1 M bought and received a TV set from P and signed both the contract and a note form. The following day P took the paper to the bank, where the paper was correctly filled in for a total of $291.92, payable in stated monthly installments. For value received from the bank, P then as-

signed the contract and indorsed the note to H Bank "without recourse."

(a) Thereafter M discovered that he had been defrauded by P into making the purchase, returned the TV set to P, and repudiated the agreement. Upon maturity of the note, the bank sued. Could the bank recover (1) from M? (2) from P?

(b) Thereafter the TV set was destroyed through M's carelessness. M proved that he was a minor, which fact neither P nor the bank had previously known, and stated that he was disaffirming his contract. Upon maturity of the note, the bank made due presentment, gave prompt notice to P of nonpayment, and sued. Could the bank recover (1) from M? (2) from P?

(c) Thereafter through no fault of M the picture tube burned out. Although the picture tube was still covered by P's warranty, P refused to replace the tube. Consequently M refused to make any payments. Assume that the note contained an acceleration provision under which the bank properly declared the entire $291.92 immediately due, and demanded payment from M. When M refused to pay, the bank gave prompt notice to P and sued P. Could the bank recover from P?"

19. In payment for goods purchased, R drew a negotiable check on the E Bank naming P as payee. P indorsed, sold, and delivered the check to H, a holder in due course, who held the check more than three months before presenting it for payment. During that time E Bank failed. R had withdrawn all of his money and closed his account before the failure. H sued R for the amount of the check. What result? (Modified from A.I.C.P.A., May 23-2.)

20. R was a seller of goods with whom E. Edwards had frequent dealings. Knowing of this, P. Porter forged an order bill of lading purporting to evidence goods shipped by R to E, and drew a sixty-day negotiable draft on E, naming P as payee. P signed R's name to the draft as drawer, attached the forged draft to the forged bill of lading and sent them to a bank in E's town. Believing that the draft covered goods which R was shipping to E, E ac-

cepted the draft by writing "Accepted (signed) E. Edwards" across the face of the instrument. The bank delivered the bill of lading to E and returned the draft to P. P transferred the draft to H. Howard by indorsing "Pay to H. Howard (signed) P. Porter." H was a holder in due course. When the draft came due, H presented it to E for payment. E had learned of the forgery and refused to pay. H sued E. What result?

21. To pay a debt R signed and sent P a negotiable check for $ 180. The check was drawn on E Bank and named P as payee. An employee of P stole the check from P's office, without authority indorsed P's name, and delivered the check to a grocer for $30 in groceries and $150 in cash, with which the employee absconded. The grocer indorsed the check "for deposit" and deposited it in his account with C Bank, which collected it from E Bank and credited the $180 to the grocer's account. E Bank charged R's account. When P complained to R that he had not received the check, the parties discovered what happened to it. What are the rights and liabilities of each of the following with respect to the check: R, E Bank, C Bank, the grocer, P? (Modified from A.I.C.P.A., May 72-4c.)

22. Induced by P's fraudulent misrepresentation, R purchased and received certain goods from P, paying for them by negotiable check drawn by R on the E Bank, in the amount of $500, naming P as payee. Discovering the fraud through due diligence, R stopped payment on the check and returned the goods to P. Accordingly, the bank refused to pay when the holder, identified below, duly presented the check. The holder sued for the amount of the check.

(a) At the request of R, E Bank had certified the check before it was delivered to P. (1) P was the holder suing. Could P collect (a) from R? (b) from E Bank? (2) H, a holder in due course, was suing. Could H collect (a) from R? (b) from E Bank?

(b) At the request of P, E Bank certified the check after it was delivered to P but before R stopped payment. (1), (2) same additional facts and questions as above.

23. (a) On May 1, in payment of an obligation, R, without negligence, signed and gave P a negotiable check drawn on E Bank in the amount of $9, naming P as payee. On May 2, P transferred the check to A with an unqualified indorsement. The same day, A dishonestly raised the check to $190, so skillfully that the alteration was not noticeable on ordinary inspection. On May 4, E Bank certified the check at the request of A. Adams who then indorsed "Without recourse (signed) A. Adams" and transferred the check to B. Brown who the following day transferred the check to H. Both H and B were holders in due course. H did not immediately cash the check and still had it in his possession when, on June 3, in a conversation with R, H learned that the check had been raised. Before R could notify the bank, H presented the check and received $190 from E Bank. With due diligence R notified E Bank of the alteration. Could E Bank recover? (1) from H? (2) from A?

(b) Other facts remaining the same, assume that E Bank refused to pay the check when H presented it. Could H recover from B, assuming that B had: (1) Indorsed "(signed) B. Brown"? (2) Indorsed "Without recourse (signed) B. Brown"? (3) Not indorsed at all?

24. On April 1, P. Porter induced R. Roger by fraudulent misrepresentation to purchase certain goods for which R paid with his negotiable check drawn on the E Bank of Philadelphia in the amount of $500, naming P as payee. On April 2, R discovered that he had been defrauded, returned the goods to P, and in the manner described below, requested E Bank not to pay the check. On April 4, through an oversight of one of the bank's employees, E Bank inadvertently paid the check to P.

(a) On April 2, R went to E Bank and told the cashier that he wished to stop payment on a check. The cashier gave R a printed card, which, when filled in, signed, and returned to the cashier, read as follows:

Stop-payment Request

To E Bank Philadelphia, Pa.

I hereby request that, as a favor to me, you do not pay my check number 1234, dated April 1 of this year, drawn in favor of P. Porter in the amount of $500.

I expressly agree, with an intent to be legally bound hereby, that should you unintentionally pay the above-described check in the ordinary course of your business, you will not be in any way liable for the payment. This request will expire in 30 days from date unless renewed in writing.

[Date]   (signed) R. Roger

Could E Bank charge the payment against R's account?

(b) On April 2, R phone E Bank and told the cashier he wished to stop payment on his check, describing the check as above. The cashier asked R to stop in the bank at his earliest convenience and sign a written stop-payment request. R went to the bank on April 5 to sign such a request. (1) Could E Bank charge the payment against R's account (a) if the payment was made to P? (b) if the payment was made to H, a holder in due course? (2) Could E Bank recover from the person to whom it inadvertently paid the check, (a) if that person was P? (b) if that person was H, a holder in due course?

25. (a) Without receiving any consideration, and to enable P to borrow $500, M signed a negotiable promissory note in that amount, naming P as payee. P indorsed and transferred the note to H for value. When H took the note, he knew that M had received no consideration for it. When the note matured, P was in financial difficulty and H sued M. Could H recover from M? (Modified from A.I.C.P.A., Nov. 45-3a.)

(b) Other facts being the same, assume that to avoid a lawsuit M paid H. Could M obtain a judgment against P?

26. On February 1, M dated, signed, and delivered to P. Porter the following: "[Date] For value received I promise to pay to the order of P. Porter the principal sum of $600, said principal sum to be

payable as follows: $100 on the first of next month, and $100 on the same day of each and every month thereafter until the entire amount has been paid. In the event of my failure to pay any of such installments at the time specified herein, all of the remaining principal shall at the option of the holder become immediately due and payable. (signed) M. Martin." On February 9, P indorsed the note, "(signed) P. Porter" and sold it to H for value. H immediately notified M of the transfer, but made no presentment until July 2. M paid H $100 on March 1, $50 on April 1, $25 on April 15, $25 on May 2, $50 on June 1, and nothing further. On July 2, H presented the note to M and demanded payment of the entire unpaid balance. Upon M's failure to pay, H promptly notified P, who had previously been aware of any default. H sued P. How much if anything was H entitled to recover?

27. R drew a negotiable sight draft on E. Edwards, naming P as payee. P promptly presented the draft to E who wrote on it, "Accepted, payable in 10 days (signed) E. Edwards." At the expiration of the ten-day period, P demanded payment from E and upon E's failure to pay, promptly notified R. This was the first R knew of any difficulty concerning the draft, P sued R. What result? (Modified from A.I.C.P.A., Nov. 53-4b.)

28. Arthur Adams, together with several other members of an incorporated club, indorsed the club's negotiable note with named P as payee. The club defaulted on the note, and P procured from the president of the club a typed list stating the names and addresses of the indorsers. When P attempted to verify the addresses by comparing with the current telephone directory, he found an Arthur Adams listed at an address different from the one on the typed list. Within proper time, P sent a notice of dishonor of the note, by certified mail, addressed to Arthur Adams at the address stated on the typed list. Four days later the post office returned the letter to P with a notation, "Moved, left no address." P then promptly contacted Arthur Adams at the telephone directory address, found that it was the same Arthur Adams who had indorsed the note, and gave him notice of

dishonor. This was the first time Arthur Adams knew of nonpayment of the note. Could P hold Arthur Adams liable as an indorser? (Modified from A.I.C.P.A., May 35-6.)

29. Donald Davis cashed a check for Charles Carter which was made to the order of Paul Porter by Roger Investments & Securities. The check had the following indorsements on the back: (1) "(signed) Paul Porter"; (2) "Without recourse (signed) Albert Adams"; (3) "Pay to the order of Charles Carter (signed) Ben Baker"; (4) "Pay to the order of Donald Davis." Carter neglected to sign his indorsement when he gave the check to Davis, and Davis did not notice this until the following day. Before Davis could locate Carter and obtain his signature, Davis learned that Porter had fraudulently obtained the check from Roger (the drawer). Davis finally located Carter and obtained his signature. Davis promptly indorsed the check in blank and cashed it at Howard Bank. Through normal banking channels Howard Bank caused the check to be presented to the drawee bank for payment. Pursuant to a valid stop order the drawee bank refused to pay. Howard Bank contacted Davis and informed him of the situation. Davis repaid the amount and the check was returned to him with Howard Bank's blank indorsement on the back. Davis sued Roger on the check. What result? (Modified from A.I.C.P.A., May 27-2b.)

30. Thomas bore a remarkable physical resemblance to Porter, one of the town's most prominent citizens. He presented himself one day at the Roger Finance Company, represented himself as Porter, and requested a loan of $500. The manager mistakenly, but honestly, believed that Thomas was Porter. Accordingly, being anxious to please so prominent a citizen, the manager required no collateral and promptly delivered to Thomas $500 check payable to the order of Porter. Thomas took the check and signed Porter's name to it on the back and transferred it to Howard, who took in the ordinary course of business (in good faith and for value). Upon learning the real facts, Roger stopped payment on the check. Howard now seeks recov-

ery against Roger. Under these circumstances, which of the following statements is correct?

a. Roger could not validly stop payment on the check.

b. Thomas' signature of Porter's name on the check constitutes forgery and is a real defense which is valid against Howard.

c. Since both Roger and Howard were mistaken as to Thomas' real identity, they will share the loss equally.

d. Thomas' signature of Porter's name on the check is effective and Howard will prevail against Roger. (Modified from A.I.C.P.A., Nov. 78-1(47).)

31. Tanner had an $80 check payable to the order of Parker that Parker had indorsed in blank. The check was drawn by Roger on State Bank. Tanner deftly raised the amount to $800 and cashed it at Friendly Check Cashing Company. Friendly promptly presented it at State Bank where it was dishonored as an overdraft. Tanner has been apprehended by the police and is awaiting trial. He has no known assets. Friendly is seeking collection on the instrument against any or all of the other parties involved. Will Friendly recover against Roger, State Bank, or Parker? (Modified from A.I.C.P.A., Nov. 79-3b.)

32. T stole one of R's negotiable checks. The check was already signed by R as drawer and made payable to P. The check was drawn on E Bank. T forged P's signature on the back of the check and cashed the check at the H Check Cashing Company which in turn deposited it with its bank, C Bank. C Bank proceeded to collect on the check form E Bank. None of the parties mentioned was negligent. Who will bear the loss assuming the amount cannot be recovered from T? (Modified from A.I.C.P.A., May 80-1(15).)

33. P stole one of R's blank negotiable check forms, made it payable to himself, and forged R's signature to it as drawer. The check was drawn on E Bank. P cashed the check at H Check Cashing Company which in turn deposited it with its bank, C Bank. C Bank proceeded to collect on the check

from E Bank. The theft and forgery were quickly discovered by R who promptly notified E Bank. None of the parties mentioned was negligent. Who will bear the loss, assuming the amount cannot be recovered from P? (Modified from A.I.C.P.A., May 80-1(30).)

34. Marshall Miller purchased $1,050 worth of inventory for his business from Parker Enterprises. Parker insisted on the signature of Miller's former partner, Adams, before credit would be extended. Adams reluctantly signed. Miller delivered the following instrument to Parker:

[Date]

We, the undersigned, do hereby promise to pay to the order of Parker Enterprises Inc. One Thousand and Fifty Dollars ($1,050) three months from date.

Memo: *A Adams signed as an accommodation for Miller*	*(signed)* Marshall Miller *(signed)* Arthur Adams

Miller defaulted on the due date. Which of the following is correct?

a. The instrument is nonnegotiable.

b. Adams is liable on the instrument but only for $525.

c. Since it was known to Parker that Adams signed as an accommodation party, Parker must first proceed against Miller.

d. Adams is liable on the instrument for the full amount and is obligated to satisfy it immediately upon default. (Modified from A.I.C.P.A., Nov. 80-1(6).)

35. Morton gave Porter his 90-day negotiable promissory note for $10,000 as a partial payment for the purchase of Porter's business. Porter had submitted materially false unaudited financial statements to Morton in the course of establishing the purchase price of the business. Porter also made various false statements about the business' value. For example, he materially misstated the size of the backlog of orders. Porter promptly negotiated the note to Harrison who purchased it in

good faith for $9,500, giving Porter $5,000 in cash, a check for $3,500 payable to him which he indorsed in blank and an oral promise to pay the balance within 5 days. Before making the final payment to Porter, Harrison learned of the fraudulent circumstances under which the negotiable promissory note for $10,000 had been obtained. Porter has disappeared and the balance due him was never paid. Morton refuses to pay the note. In the subsequent suit brought by Harrison against Morton, who will prevail? (Modified from A.I.C.P.A., May 81-2a.)

36. Howard, a holder in due course, presented a check to the First Bank, the drawee bank named on the face of the instrument. The signature of the drawer, Roger, was forged by Thomas who took the check from the bottom of Roger's checkbook along with a cancelled check in the course of burglarizing Roger's apartment. The bank examined the signature of the drawer carefully, but the signature was such an artful forgery of the drawer's signature that only a handwriting expert could have detected a difference. The bank therefore paid the check. The check was promptly returned to Roger but he did not discover the forgery until thirteen months after the check was returned to him.

a. Roger seeks to compel the bank to credit his account for the loss. Who will prevail?

b. The facts are the same as above, but you are to assume that the bank discovered the forgery before returning the check to Roger and credited his account. Can the bank in turn collect from Howard the $1,000 paid to Howard?

c. Would your answers to (a) and (b) above be modified if the forged signature was that of the payee rather than the signature of the drawer? (Modified from A.l.C.P.A., May 812b .)

37. Porter sold her grain business to Roger for $150,000 and received a check drawn on Edward Bank for that amount naming Porter as payee. In addition she entered into a contract for the purchase of a ranch for the same amount. The closing on the ranch is to take place in five days. The sales contract regarding the ranch requires payment by cash, by buyer's certified check payable to the buyer's order and indorsed to the seller. Porter intends to have Roger's check certified by Edward Bank and use it as payment. Which of the following is correct?

a. If the bank refuses to certify the check is has been dishonored.

b. If Roger's account has sufficient funds to honor the check, Porter has the right to have it certified.

c. Certification by the bank will discharge Roger from liability as the drawer.

d. Only Roger can obtain certification of the check. (Modified from A.I.C.P.A., May 821 (39) .)

38. Roger & Company was encountering financial difficulties. Howard, a persistent creditor whose account was overdue, demanded a check for the amount owed to him. Roger's president said that this was impossible since the checking account was already overdrawn. However, he indicated he would be willing to draw on funds owed by one of the company's customers. He drafted and presented to Howard the following instrument. "[Date] To Edward Fabrications Inc. Pay Roger & Co. $1,000 30 days after acceptance, for value received in connection with our shipment of August 11 of this year. (signed) Roger & Co. by R Roger President." Roger indorsed the instrument on the back as follows: "Pay to the order of H Howard (signed) Roger & Co. by R Roger, President." Howard asserts that he is a holder in due course.

(a) Is the instrument negotiable?

(b) Assume that the instrument is negotiable and accepted by Edwards, but prior to payment, Edwards discovers the goods are defective. May Edwards successfully assert this defense against Howard to avoid payment of the instrument? (Modified from A.I.C.P.A., Nov. 83-2b .)

Banks, Checks and Electronic Funds Transfers

Banks, Checks and Electronic Funds Transfers

THE MOST FREQUENTLY used form of commercial paper is the check. It is a demand draft which is drawn on a financial institution. A check is a form of commercial paper. And previously discussed, commercial paper is governed by Article 3 of the Code. Article 4 governs bank deposits and collections. It governs banks as they deal with each other in the collection process for payments of checks. It also governs checking account relationships between banks and their customers. When there are conflicts between Articles 3 and 4 of the Code, Article 4 will control.

In addition, banks and their customers may modify these rules within certain limits. For instance, the parties may not contract to relieve the bank of its duty to act in good faith or to exercise ordinary care. In addition, a bank cannot limit its liability for damages arising from a failure to meet its responsibilities.[1]

A check is a draft drawn on a bank and payable on demand.[2] The payee of a check, as its holder, has the right to transfer or negotiate the check, or demand payment of the check. Any subsequent holder of a check has these same rights.

A check is an order to pay arising out of an agreement between the drawee-bank and its customer. A check is not an assignment of funds. The drawee-bank is not liable to the payee or any holder for not paying the check upon presentment. This is true even if there

are sufficient funds to cover the check. Upon nonpayment, it is the holder's burden to recover payment from a liable party.

If a bank wrongfully dishonors a properly presented check, its customer (the drawer) may sue the bank for damages arising out of the wrongful dishonor.

1. Special Types of Checks

A. Certified Checks

A certified check is a check that has been accepted by a bank. When a bank accepts a check, it has agreed to become primarily liable on it. When a bank certifies a check for its customer, the amount of the certification is collected by the bank through either the collection of cash, by debiting the customer's account for that amount, or by extending a loan to the customer.

The certification requires a date, the exact amount of the certification and the signature and title of the bank's representative certifying the check. These requirements establish the bank's primary obligation. An example of a certified check is presented in figure 25-1.

A drawee-bank is not obligated to certify any check unless it has specifically promised to do so. A bank's failure to certify a check upon presentment does not constitute a dishonor. If the drawer has her own check certified, she remains secondarily liable. If the holder has the check certified by the drawee bank, the

---

1. UCC Sec. 4-103.
2. UCC Sec. 3-104(2)(b).

674

Certified Check

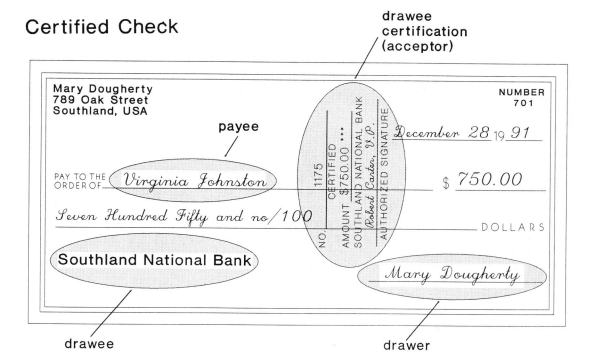

drawee certification (acceptor)

payee

drawer

drawee

Mary Dougherty
789 Oak Street
Southland, USA

NUMBER 701

PAY TO THE ORDER OF _Virginia Johnston_

Seven Hundred Fifty and no/100

Southland National Bank

NO. 1175 CERTIFIED AMOUNT $750.00 *** SOUTHLAND NATIONAL BANK _Robert Carter, V.P._ AUTHORIZED SIGNATURE

December 28 19 _91_

$ _750.00_

DOLLARS

Mary Dougherty

drawer and any prior indorsers are completely discharged.[3]

The bank has an extremely limited ability to revoke its certification. It cannot revoke a certification if a good faith holder has changed his position in reliance upon the certification. In addition, the certification constitutes an acceptance under the UCC, thereby preventing a bank from revoking its acceptance against a holder in due course whether or not the holder in due course has changed her position.

If a certified check is altered after the certification, the bank is still obligated to pay the check according to its original tenor.

B. Cashier's Checks

This is a check that a bank draws upon itself. The bank is both the drawer and drawee of a cashier's check. The public perceives cashier's checks as more reliable than a check from a

---

3. UCC Sec. 3-411(1).

stranger because bank's almost always honor their own checks. A bank has the power to stop one of its cashier's checks, but should carefully consider the consequences of doing so. If it became known in the community that a bank may not honor its cashier's checks, depositors would lose confidence in the institution and remove their funds. Without a steady deposit base, a bank cannot survive.

C. Traveler's Checks

A traveler's check is ordinarily a type of a cashier's check, distinguished by the fact that it can be sold in varying face amounts and quantities. When one is drawn on an institution other than bank, it is often designated as "Traveler's Cheque," as in the case of American Express, which draws its instruments on itself. In spite of this, the rights and obligations of the parties are the same as for any cashier's check. The issuing institution is obligated to pay the instrument. The purchaser must sign it when issued and countersign it when exchanged for money, goods or services.

II. The Relationship Between a Bank and Its Customer

The relationship between a bank and its customer has a number of characteristics. First, it is a contractual relationship. The parties enter into a deposit agreement. This governs the checking account relationship. The customer agrees to deposit money in an account with the bank and to write checks according with the rules of the bank and the regulatory bodies. The bank in turn promises to carry out the orders issued by the customer in the form of checks.

The parties also have a debtor-creditor relationship. When a customer deposits money in a checking account, it is a creditor of the bank. By the same token, the bank is indebted to the depositor.

In addition, the relationship between a bank and its customer can be viewed as that of a principal-agent relationship. This occurs in the check collection process. When a bank customer deposits a check drawn upon another bank, the depository bank will, on behalf of its customer, put the check into the collection system in an attempt to reduce the instrument to cash on behalf of its customer (principal).

III. The Obligations of a Bank to its Customer

Banks have two basic duties with respect to its customer's checking accounts. First, the bank has the duty to accept deposits of U.S. currency and to collect checks payable or indorsed to its customers. Second, a bank has the duty to honor its customer's checks for the withdrawal of funds on deposit.

A. The Duty to Accept Deposits and to Collect Checks

A bank has the duty to accept its customer's deposits in the forms of U.S. currency or checks. Checks are accepted subject to collection of U.S. currency. A bank will give its customer a provisional credit for each check deposited. The provisional credit will become a final credit when the check is honored by the payor bank (the drawee). If a deposited check is dishonored, it will be returned through the check collection system to the bank where it was deposited. The amount of the check will be charged back to the depositing customer's account.

B. The Check Collecting System

The check collecting system consists of the banks throughout the United States as well as the Federal Reserve Banks in each region. It is important to be able to distinguish between the various roles and identities of the banks within the system. They are:

The Depositary Bank

This is the bank where a check is deposited.

The Payor Bank

This is the drawee bank. If the check is honored, this will be the check's last stop in the system.

Collecting Banks

A collecting bank is any bank except the payor bank that handles the check during the collection process.

Intermediary Banks

An intermediary bank is any bank except the payor bank and the depositary bank to which the item is transferred in the course of the collection process.

Example.   Hardy deposits an item to his bank account at 3:15 PM. on Monday. The bank has a posted notice that its banking day ends at 3 P.M. Therefore, the deposit will be posted to Tuesday's business. This means the bank's midnight deadline is Wednesday midnight because Wednesday is the next banking day after the official date of deposit, Tuesday. Remember that banking holidays often fall on a Monday. This means that an item deposited after the close of business on Friday will have a midnight deadline of Wednesday midnight if Monday was a holiday. Even if a bank operates its facilities on Saturday, it will not be deemed a banking day under the collection rules. □

The Presenting Bank

The presenting bank is the bank that presents the check to the payor (drawee) bank. This is often a Federal Reserve Bank.

Observe that the presenting bank is also an intermediary bank and a collecting bank.[4]

The Federal Reserve banks located in major cities across the nation serve as the major intermediary banks in a nationwide check collection and clearing system. If both the depositary bank and payor banks are located in the same city or region, a local or regional clearinghouse may be used to present the check. A clearinghouse is an association of banks or other payors regularly clearing checks within a region.

Occasionally, a customer will deposit a check in her account that is drawn upon that same bank. Such an item is called an "on-us" item. If a bank does not dishonor an onus item by the opening of the second day following its receipt, it is deemed paid. This will entitle the customer to withdraw the funds represented by the deposit.[5] When a bank receives an item not drawn on itself, it puts it in the clearing process. The bank may present the item directly to the payor bank or it may present it through intermediary banks.

Each bank in the collection process must decide to honor or dishonor the check on or before midnight of the next banking day follow-

ing its receipt. This is known as the midnight deadline. If a bank does not honor or dishonor the check by its midnight deadline, it becomes responsible to pay the item.[6]

Banks are permitted to engage in what is known as deferred posting. This assists a bank in meeting its midnight deadline. Deferred posting means that a bank is allowed to set the end of its banking day to a period earlier than the traditional end of the business day, such as 2 P.M. It is common to see such a notice in a bank announcing that items deposited after 2 P.M. will be reflected on the next day's business.

C. Restrictive Indorsements

The bank will not be bound by any restrictive indorsement of any person except the that of the holder who transfers or presents the instrument for payment. Therefore, only the first bank to which the item is presented for payment or collection must act in a manner consistent with the restrictive indorsement. This means that the depositary bank must follow instructions such as "For Deposit Only." If the depositary bank does not follow these instructions, it will be the only bank in the collection process facing liability for this violation. The rational behind this rule is obvious. Millions of checks are processed through the check collection system each day. It would be

4. UCC Sec. 4-105.
5. UCC Sec. 4-213(4)(b).

6. UCC Sec. 4-202(2).

impossible for every collecting bank to verify compliance with each restrictive indorsement of each check handled.

D. A Bank's Obligation to Honor Its Depositors' Checks

A bank has the duty to honor properly presented checks written by its customers so long as sufficient funds exist in the account. If a bank does not honor a properly presented check on an account containing sufficient funds, its customer may sue the bank for wrongful dishonor. There is no bank liability if the dishonor of the check was proper, such as a check being dishonored for insufficient funds.

A bank is permitted to pay a check even if sufficient funds do not exist to cover the check. The amount of the check will be charged to the account resulting in a negative balance. It is the burden of the bank to collect this difference from its customer. The bank may enter into a contract with the customer to honor checks, even on insufficient funds. These arrangements are either tied to authorizations to transfer funds from savings accounts or to existing loan agreements. If such an arrangement exists, a bank may not dishonor a check drawn upon insufficient funds in the checking account so long as the terms of the other agreements have not been violated by its customer.

When a bank dishonors a check, either properly or improperly, the bank's customer (the drawer) will be liable to the payee or holder for the amount of the check. In addition, depending upon the circumstances, the customer may face criminal charges if intent to defraud can be established.

I. STALE CHECKS

The bank is under no obligation to pay a check, other than a certified check, presented more than six months after the check's date. These checks are referred to as stale checks.[7]

The bank may honor the check if it can do so in good faith. It is advisable for a bank to contact its customer prior paying a check presented more than six months after its date.

2. APPLYING MISSING INDORSEMENTS

A depositary bank that has taken an item for collection may supply any missing indorsement of its customer which is necessary for negotiation unless the item states "Payee's Indorsement Required" or similar words. In the absence of such a requirement, a statement placed on an item by the depositary bank to the effect that it was deposited by the customer or credited to the customer's account will be sufficient to serve as the customer's indorsement.[8]

3. DEPOSITOR'S ORDER TO STOP PAYMENT

Only the bank's customer has the power to order a stop payment on her checks. An order for stop payment must be received in time to afford the bank a reasonable opportunity to act upon the order.[9] Once a check has been accepted or certified, the check cannot be stopped because the bank has become primarily liable on the instrument.

While stop payment orders are often made in writing, most states permit stop payment orders to be made orally. But, oral stop payment orders are valid for only 14 calendar days unless the customer confirms the stop payment order in writing within that period. A written order is effective for six months unless the customer renews it in writing.[10]

If a bank makes a mistake and pays a check that has been ordered stopped, the bank will only be liable for the actual loss suffered by the drawer. This means that if a customer stops the check because he only received part of his order, the customer will not be entitled

7. UCC Sec. 4-404.
8. UCC Sec. 4-205(1).
9. UCC Sec. 4-403(1).
10. UCC Sec. 4-403(2).

to the full amount of check. But rather, the customer will be entitled to recover from the bank an amount equal to the value of the goods that the customer did not receive.

Keep in mind that even if a customer stops payment on a check, a holder may still bring a legal action to enforce the instrument. If the holder is a holder in due course, he will prevail unless the customer has a real defense to enforcement.

4. DRAWER'S FORGED SIGNATURE

A forged signature of the drawer has no legal effect. Each bank is responsible for knowing the signatures of its customers. This is the reason banks have their customers complete signature cards upon the opening of accounts. This provides evidence of each customer's signature.

A drawee-bank has no right to recover from a holder who, without knowledge that the drawer's signature was forged, obtains payment from the bank on a check. Therefore, unless the bank can prove that the party presenting the check had knowledge of the forgery, the bank's only recourse is to find the forger. Keep in mind that this is a special situation involving the forging of the drawer's signature only. This is because the bank is in the best position to tell if the drawer's signature was forged. Under these circumstances, a bank will not be permitted to disrupt the transaction and recover payment from the holder who presented it.

5. DEPOSITOR NEGLIGENCE

If the depositor's negligence contributed to the forgery of its signature on an issued check, the bank will not be required to recredit the negligent party's account if the check was honored upon presentment. This situation is often caused by a business's failure to control access to its checkbook or check writing equipment. Individuals not exercising reasonable control over access to their checkbooks will also be subject to this rule.

6. ALTERED CHECKS

A bank has the duty to examine a check before making a final payment. If a bank fails to detect an alteration, it will be liable for the loss resulting from the alteration. The loss is defined as the actual loss. This means the difference between the original amount and the altered amount. The bank may still charge its customer's account for the original amount of the check. The bank may pursue the party who presented the item for payment (unless he was a holder in due course) for a breach of the presentment warranty that the instrument had not been altered. Holders in due course do not make the present warranty that the instrument had not been materially altered.

If the bank were the drawer of the check, such as in the case of a cashier's check, it could not recover from the presenting party if the party was a holder in due course acting in good faith. The rational behind this rule is that the bank was In a much better position than the holder in due course to recognize when one of its own instruments has been altered. In addition, a holder in due course acting in good faith does not warrant to the bank that a certified check has not been altered either before or after the certification.[11]

A loss caused by an alteration may be shifted to the customer if the customer was negligent in writing the check. An example would be a check written with large gaps that could be used for inserting increased dollars sums or additional payees.

7. PAYMENT ON FORGED INDORSEMENTS

The bank must recredit a customer's account if it pays an item containing a forgery. When a bank pays a forged check on a customer's account, it has failed to carry out the customer's order to pay the designated party. It becomes the bank's problem to locate and recover under breach of warranty principles from the

---

11. UCC Sec. 4-207(c).

party who presented the item for payment or its indorsers.

8. THE DEPOSITOR'S DUTY TO TIMELY EXAMINE STATEMENTS AND CHECKS

A depositor has a duty to report alterations and forgeries to his bank promptly. If a customer fails to do so, or is careless in the examination of his bank statement or checks, the customer will bear the loss.[12]

If there is a series of forgeries or alterations by the same wrongdoer, the customer must discover and report it within a reasonable period, not to exceed 14 calendar days after the receipt of the statement (or having the statement and items available for examination) evidencing or containing the first forged or altered item.[13] If the customer fails to do so, the bank will not be liable for the loss caused by any subsequent altered or forged checks by the same wrongdoer unless the customer can establish that the bank failed to exercise ordinary care in paying the items.

Without regard to the lack of care exercised by either party, the customer will be precluded from recovery from his bank on his own forged signature or any alteration on the front or back of an instrument one year from the date she received the statement containing the item or had the items made available to her. The same holds true for discovery of forged indorsements except that the time limit will be three years.[14]

9. DEATH OR INCOMPETENCE OF A DEPOSITOR

If a bank did not know of the adjudication of incompetence or death of its depositor at the time a check was issued (or at the time a check's collection had been undertaken), the bank may pay the check without any liability. A bank may pay items of a depositor who has died or been declared incompetent until it has learned of the situation and has had a reasonable time to respond.[15]

Even with knowledge of its customer's death, a bank may pay or certify checks drawn on or prior to the date of death for a period not to exceed ten days after the date of death unless ordered to stop payment by a person claiming an interest in the account. Observe that this extension only applies to a customer's death and not to a customer who has been declared mentally incompetent.[16]

IV. The Expedited Funds Availability Act

For many years banks have faced problems with customers who deposited checks for collection while writing checks on the uncollected funds. The primary risk facing banks in this situation is that a deposited check will be returned unpaid resulting in a negative balance in the customer's account. In response to this, many depositary banks began placing "holds" on checks deposited by their customers'. Under this policy, a bank would refuse to permit a customer to withdraw funds represented by a deposited check until sufficient time had passed to determine whether or not the payor bank would honor the check.

Unfortunately, many banks abused this technique by placing unreasonably lengthy holds on deposited checks. In effect, a depositary bank could obtain an interest free loan from its customers on these deposits from the period following the collection of funds to time the bank would make the funds available to its depositors.

Responding to complaints, Congress passed the Expedited Funds Availability Act.[17] This Act requires banks to make funds available to its depositors within specific time periods and

---

12. UCC Sec. 4-406(1).
13. UCC Sec. 4-406(2).
14. UCC Sec. 4-406(4).

15. UCC Sec. 4-405(1).
16. UCC Sec. 4-405.
17. 12 USC 4001-4010.

to disclose their funds availability policies in writing. The Federal Reserve Board has implemented the provisions of this act through its Regulation CC.[18]

With regard to interest bearing accounts, the Act requires that banks begin crediting interest to these accounts no later than the day the bank receives credit for the deposit. This means interest must start accruing on the deposit in most cases one or two days after the deposit of a check.

Under Regulation CC, funds availability depends on the type of the deposit. For deposits in the forms of cash; electronic payments; checks drawn on the United States Treasury; a Federal Reserve Bank or a home loan bank; checks drawn by a state or a unit of a local government; U.S. Postal Service money orders; cashier's or certified checks; "on-us" checks (so long as the branches of the same bank are located in the same check processing region); will be available to the customer on the first business day following the banking day of deposit.

In addition, the first $100 of any amount deposited by checks that are not subject to next day availability may be withdrawn by cash or check on the first business day following the banking day of deposit.

The availability schedule of the remainder of deposits depends upon their classification as either local or non-local checks. A local check is a check deposited in a bank located in the same Federal Reserve processing region as the drawee-payor bank. A non-local check is a check deposited in a bank located in a different check processing region.

Under Regulation CC, local checks must be available for withdrawal by the second business day following the banking day of deposit. Non-local checks must be available for withdrawal by the fifth business day following the banking day of deposit.

Banks in Alaska, Hawaii, Puerto Rico and the US Virgin Islands are permitted to extend these holding periods by one business day. In addition, the regulations recognize certain exceptions for new accounts. New accounts are defined under Regulation CC as accounts established for 30 days or less. A new account established by a customer who has an account that has been in existence for greater than 30 days at the same bank will not be deemed a new account under these rules.

Deposits of $5,000 or less on any one banking day in the forms of cash, certain electronic deposits, checks drawn on the United States Treasury, cashier's checks, certified checks and similar forms will be subject to the same rules as existing accounts. But, deposits in other forms, and amounts over $5000 can be held up to eight business days, being made available no later than the ninth business day.

V. Electronic Fund Transfers

The rapid growth of computer technology has made it possible for banks to effectuate transactions for their customers at remote sites and with third parties without the necessity of presenting documents. Paperless transactions now represent a significant portion of the total. Consumer electronic fund transfers are governed by the Electronic Fund Transfer Act.[19] This 1978 law was enacted to provide a basic framework for establishing the rights, liabilities and responsibilities of participants in electronic fund transfer systems. The Act was primarily designed to protect individual consumer rights. The Act permits states to pass stricter rules to achieve this end.

With respect to commercial fund transfers, The National Conference of Commissioners on Uniform State Laws and the American Law Institute approved the addition of Article 4A, entitled "Funds Transfers," to the Uniform Commercial Code. It has been adopted by a

---

18. 12 C.F.R. part 29.

19. 15 U.S.C. 1693 et seq.

number of states. It is anticipated that most states will eventually adopt this new addition to the Code. Article 4A specifically states that any transaction covered by the Electronic Fund Transfer Act will be covered by that Act and are excluded from coverage from Article 4A.

Consumer transactions under the Electronic Fund Transfer Act will be discussed first, followed by a discussion of commercial fund transfers under Article 4A of the Code.

A. Consumer Electronic Fund Transfers

The Electronic Fund Transfer Act defines an electronic fund transfer (EFT) as any transfer of funds (other than one initiated by check, draft, or similar paper instrument) that is initiated through electronic terminal, telephone, computer, or magnetic tape ordering, authorizing or instructing a financial institution to debit or credit an account. No physical transfer of a check or other negotiable instrument is involved or required. The Act governs only consumer transfers, meaning only those involving individuals for personal, family or household purposes.

B. Types of Consumer Electronic Transfers

I. AUTOMATIC TELLER MACHINES (ATM)

This is the most common type of electronic fund transfer. If a bank offers this product, a customer may enter into a contract with her bank so that a card and a personal identification number (PIN) will be issued making it possible for her to access an ATM. An ATM has the capability to receive deposits, dispense money, transfer funds between accounts, make credit card loan advances and receive loan payments.

2. POINT OF SALE SYSTEMS (POS)

Point of sale systems involve the presentation of a card to a merchant making it possible for the amount of the purchase to be immediately debited from the customer's account. These are often called debit systems.

3. DIRECT DEPOSITS OR WITHDRAWALS

Direct deposits or withdrawals are accomplished through the exchange of computer records between banks and clearinghouses. Examples of direct deposit transactions include regular electronic deposits of governmental benefits and payroll deposits. In addition, regular payments, such as loan payments or insurance premium payments, can be made through an automatic debit to a customer's account.

4. PAY BY TELEPHONE SYSTEMS

Some banks offer a service to their customers permitting them to pay bills and transfer funds by making a telephone call to a bank computer. Some bank systems now accommodate home computer users.

C. The Scope of the Electronic Fund Transfer Act

The Electronic Fund Transfer Act is basically a disclosure law. It requires institutions to make certain disclosures to those consumers desiring these services. The Act is administered by the Board of Governors of the Federal Reserve System. The set of regulations issued to implement the EFT Act is known as Regulation E.

The EFT Act governs financial institutions offering EFT services to consumers. The Act defines financial institutions as banks, savings and loans, credit unions and other entities holding accounts for customers, such as securities brokerage firms.

For a transfer to be covered under the Act, it must be a part of a prearranged plan under which periodic or recurring transfers are contemplated. The Act requires that the financial institution disclose to the customer his liability for unauthorized transfers, how to report a loss or theft, how much it will cost to use the system, how to correct errors and the customer's right to see written evidence of transactions.

Each financial institution is required to provide a receipt for each transaction at a terminal at the time of each transfer. But, this is not required for telephone transfers. In addition, customers must be provided with periodic statements fully describing each transaction made, including dates, amounts, and locations. It must also show an address and phone number for inquiries and error notification. A customer must also be notified promptly if an automatic deposit was not made as scheduled.

D. Stopping Transactions and Reversibility

For a customer to stop a preauthorized EFT, she must notify the financial institution orally or in writing any time up to three days before the scheduled date of the transfer. The customer may be required to provide written confirmation within 14 days of an oral notification. But, once an electronic transfer has been made, the customer cannot reverse it.

E. Error Correction

Each customer has a duty to examine her periodic statement for errors. A customer has 60 days after the statement has been mailed or delivered by the financial institution to notify the institution of errors that appear on the statement. The financial institution is required to investigate and report to the customer within 10 business days following the customer's notification of an error. If the financial institution needs more time, it may take up to 45 days to complete its investigation. But if it chooses this route, the financial institution must recredit the customer's ac-

count for the amount in dispute during this period.

If the financial institution determines that it made a mistake, it has one business day to adjust it. If no mistake has been made, the financial institution must give a full, written report with conclusions to the customer. If it can be established that the financial institution failed to investigate the alleged error in good faith, the institution will be liable for treble damages. This means the institution will be required to pay a customer three times the amount of the provable damages.

F. Customer Liability for Unauthorized Transfers

For a financial institution's customer to be held liable for an unauthorized transfer, the EFT Act requires proof that the transfer resulted from the use of an accepted means of access to the system and that the customer had been provided with a means of security from unauthorized transfers, such as a PIN number. Therefore, if a customer gives the card and PIN number to a family member or friend, the customer cannot seek recovery from the financial institution if that person withdraws more money than agreed.

Customer liability will be limited if the access card or other device is lost, misplaced or stolen. Liability for unauthorized transfers will be limited to $50 if the customer notifies the financial institution within 2 business days after learning of the loss or theft. If notification occurs more than 2 days after loss of the card but not later than 60 days, the customer's liability will be limited to $500. After 60 days, the customer's liability will be unlimited.

G. Financial Institution Liability

A financial institution will be liable to a customer for all damages proximately caused by the institution's failure to make a transfer according to the agreed terms and conditions. This includes an institution's failure to execute a transaction in an accurate and timely manner. A financial institution will not be liable for failure to execute a transaction if the customer did not have sufficient funds in his account, or the customer's funds had been seized pursuant to a court order or by the Internal Revenue Service. The financial institution will also be excused if a terminal was broken or if it did not contain sufficient cash.

If a financial institution violates the EFT Act, its customer may recover actual damages plus punitive damages from $100 to $1,000. In addition, it is a federal misdemeanor to violate the EFT Act.

Anyone attempting to use an EFT device to obtain funds fraudulently faces a federal criminal conviction subject to a fine of up to $10,000 and 10 years in prison.

VI. Article 4A: Funds Transfers

Each day, almost $1 trillion is transferred through wholesale funds networks. These transfers serve many purposes, including funding commercial acquisitions, paying commercial loan obligations and settling commercial accounts. Funds transfers occur within banks, between banks, and throughout the United States via two main systems. These systems are the Fedwire, operated by the Federal Reserve System, and CHIPS, operated by the New York Clearing House Interbank Payments Systems.

Arrangements between the participating banks on the Fedwire are covered by Federal Regulation J.[20] Arrangements between participating banks in CHIPS are covered by the New York Clearing House rules. In addition, transfers by automatic clearing houses are governed by uniform rules adopted by various associations of banks, Federal Reserve rules or operating circulars.

---

20. 12 CFR 210, subpart B.

Until recently, no comprehensive set of rules or laws governed transactions between corporate clients and banks. Major corporate clients and their banks often had difficulty in reaching agreeable terms regarding the handling of transfers and resolving disputes. As a result, in dollar volume, most transfers were made with no provision for the assignment of liabilities should problems occur. Unfortunately, problems occurred.

In response to these problems, the National Conference of Commissioners on Uniform State Laws and the American Law Institute completed Article 4A to the Uniform Commercial Code and submitted it to the various states for adoption. A number of states have adopted Article 4A with most states expected to adopt it in the near future.

Both the banking industry and corporate users of commercial funds transfers were permitted extensive input and commentary into the drafting of Article 4A. Neither group obtained all that it wanted, but both groups agreed to certain provisions insisted upon by the Federal Reserve for the benefit of the overall payments system.

The major objectives of Article 4A are:

1. Preserving a fast, efficient, reliable system to transfer large volumes of funds rapidly at a low cost.

2. Providing certainty as to responsibilities, obligations and liabilities to safeguard the integrity of funds transfers.

3. Establishing the basic rights and responsibilities of the participants except as varied by the agreement of the parties or system rules.

A. The Scope Of Article 4A

A payment order can be oral, in writing, or electronic. A payment order is an unconditional (except as to timing) instruction to pay a fixed or determinable amount of money to a beneficiary.[21] In that context, it is similar to a check. But, a check is not a payment order because a payment order must be transmitted by the sender (not the payee) directly to the receiving bank or to an agent, funds transfer system, or communication system for transmittal to the receiving bank. For the same reason, the concept of payment order excludes payment by credit card.

Because payment orders must involve banks, funds transfers made by Western Union and the like are excluded from Article 4A coverage. Credit transfers through Automated Clearing Houses (ACH) are included under Article 4A. But, debit transfers, including those by an ACH, are excluded because they involve sufficiently different considerations.[22] Finally, a funds transfer that in any way is governed by the Electronic Fund Transfer Act and its implementing Regulation E, is excluded from Article 4A to avoid conflicting rules. [23] However, a consumer purpose transfer over the Fedwire outside the scope of the EFT Act could be subject to Article 4A.

B. Important Features of Article 4A

1. UNAUTHORIZED AND ERRONEOUS ORDERS

An authorized payment order may be properly executed by the receiving bank, binding the party identified as the sender. The order may be expressly or impliedly authorized, or the sender may be bound by apparent authority.

If the order was not authorized, the bank will be deemed to have acted improperly if the order was executed. But, if a commercially reasonable security procedure was in place, the payment order cleared it, and the bank complied with any instructions of the customer as to a proper account to debit, even an unau-

thorized order will be effective.[24] The one exception to this rule is that the customer will not bear the loss if the customer proves that the order was not caused by any operation of the customer or anyone entrusted with the payment order or security system.[25] The customer may lose interest owed on any refundable amounts if it does not use ordinary care to detect any unauthorized orders and it does not notify the bank.[26]

2. IMPROPERLY EXECUTED ORDERS

The reasons for using a funds transfer as opposed to a cashier's or similar check are speed and economy. However, because of the large dollar sums involved, there is considerable risk if something goes wrong. If the banks transmitting the orders had to bear the risk of improper or late execution, funds transfers would take much more time and would cost much more.

Accordingly, absent a contrary agreement, Article 4A generally relieves a bank from potential liability for consequential damages resulting from an improper or late execution or the failure to execute a payment order. But, a bank will be liable for interest, losses and applicable expenses in the event of delay, noncompletion or failure to follow instructions. Reasonable attorney's fees are also recoverable if a justified demand for compensation is made and refused.[27]

3. FINALITY OF PAYMENT

Acceptance of a payment order by the beneficiary's bank generally obligates it to pay the amount of the order to the beneficiary.[28] However, in some cases, the bank itself may not receive settlement for the order. In such an event, the obligation of payment and pay-

21. UCC Sec. 4A-103(a)(1).
22. UCC Sec. 4A-103(a)(2).
23. UCC Sec. 4A-108.

24. UCC Sec. 4A-202(b).
25. UCC Sec. 4A-203.
26. UCC Sec. 4A-204.
27. UCC Sec. 4A-305.
28. UCC Sec. 4A-404(a).

ment itself are still final as to the beneficiary. Any attempt to make it conditional by agreement is ineffective, unless (1) a rule of the funds transfer system used in the transfer provides for provisional payment and this rule has been accepted by the affected parties after notice but before initiation of the transfer, or (2) the order was transmitted over a funds transfer system that has a loss-sharing agreement among participants and the system fails to complete the settlement under its rules with respect to any payment order in the funds transfer.[29]

C. Advantages For Corporate Users

Article 4A provides the following benefits for corporate users over the terms traditionally offered by banks and the uncertainties of existing common law:

1. **Finality of payment**. Funds transferred under Article 4A are essentially equivalent to cash.
2. **Protection from improper execution**. If there is an improper execution, the bank must generally see that the customer receives a full recovery.
3. **Discharge of the underlying obligation**. A statutory discharge of the underlying obligation occurs upon acceptance by the beneficiary's bank.
4. **Commercially reasonable security procedures**. Substantial incentives exist under Article 4A for a bank to provide reasonable security procedures or otherwise the bank will absorb the loss for an unauthorized order.
5. **Error reporting and loss limitations**. All users have the duty to report errors and unauthorized orders. A failure to do so within a reasonable time results only in the

loss of interest or responsibility for loss to the bank up to the amount of the order. No other damages will be imposed.

6. **Loss apportionment**. If a loss results from an authorized order, tested against the security procedures agreed upon, the receiving bank suffers the loss unless the bank can prove the security procedure was commercially reasonable, the bank followed the procedure, the bank acted in good faith, and the bank compiled with the customer's written agreement or instructions restricting acceptance of payment orders. Even if the bank proves all of the above, the loss will fall upon the bank if the customer proves it has made no mistake.

7. **Damages for dishonor**. If the beneficiary's bank has accepted the order and the beneficiary demands payment, the bank may be liable for damages, including consequential damages, for failure to pay the beneficiary.

D. Advantages For Banks

The advantages that Article 4A provides banks over their traditional agreements with corporate users and over the common law are as follows:

1. **Certainty**. Article 4A provides certainty as to the liability and responsibility of each party. This promotes sound credit policy and financial management. Because Article 4A largely adopts current operating practices, the efficiency of the present system is preserved.
2. **Limitation of liability**. Generally, Article 4A limits bank liability for failure to carry-out a payment order to the loss of interest and any loss of

---

29. UCC Sec.4A-405

principle. In particular cases, incidental costs and attorneys fees may be recovered. Consequential damages are recoverable only in the event of an intentional dishonor with specific notice of particular circumstances and foreseeable damages.

3. **Statute of limitations**. Article 4A employs a one year limitation period for objecting to an order from the time the customer receives notice of order execution .

4. **Creditor processes**. Under Section 502 of Article 4A, banks are protected from attempts by creditors to enforce remedies against the funds represented by an order unless the bank receives sufficient advance notice to have an opportunity to respond.

5. **Choice of law**. Section 507 of Article 4A provides a system of rules which remove much of the uncertainty regarding the applicable law.

6. **Netting of obligations**. Article 4A permits authorization for bilateral and unilateral netting of payment obligations thereby reducing the risk of non-bank parties in the event of bank insolvency.

7. **Reliance on numbers**. If the bank discloses to the customer that the bank will rely on numbers, Article 4A authorizes banks to rely upon numbers in making payment. Because processing is electronic and rapid, reliance upon numbers facilitates funds transfers.

8. **Reliance on a test message**. Article 4A permits reliance upon a message that tests the security procedure unless the customer proves that the payment order was unauthorized and the breach of confidential security information did not result from a source controlled by the customer.

A bank must have offered a commercially reasonable security procedure, followed the procedure and followed any customer written agreement or instructions. The bank must have acted in good faith with respect to all actions. What constitutes a commercially reasonable security procedure depends upon the circumstances.

E. The Mechanics of a Commercial Electronic Fund Transfer

Article 4A creates a set of rules to govern dispute resolution. The effect of these rules may be varied by the agreement and the operating rules of a funds transfer system (with some specific exceptions to protect fundamental policy choices relating to uneven bargaining position or the unfortunate circumstances of one party).[30] The ability to vary the effect of the statutory rules allows for flexibility and the development of new methods. The statutory rules stand as a "safety net" to resolve matters upon which parties either did not agree or anticipate.

A funds transfer is defined as the series of transactions, beginning with the originator's payment order, made for the purpose of making payment to the beneficiary of the order. The term includes any payment order issued by the originator's bank or by an intermediary bank intended to carry-out the originator's payment order. A funds transfer is completed by acceptance of a payment order for the benefit of the beneficiary by the beneficiary's bank.[31]

A funds transfer can be a simple transaction in which a corporate originator orders its bank to debit one of its accounts and credit an account of another party at the same bank. It becomes more complicated if the originator instructs its bank to pay a beneficiary that is a customer of another bank. This requires the originator of the order to instruct its bank to

---

30. UCC Sec. 4A-501.
31. UCC Sec. 4A-104(a).

issue the payment order to the beneficiary's bank. This may involve a funds transfer system such as the Fedwire or CHIPS, or perhaps an intermediary bank who will issue another order to the beneficiary's bank.

Payment orders do not embody independent rights and liabilities for the payment of money. Rather, the rights and liabilities of the parties to a payment order arise out of the contract formed. A receiving bank, other than the beneficiary's bank, accepts a payment order if it executes it. It need not reject those orders it does not accept, unless otherwise provided by agreement of the receiving bank and the receiving bank had sufficient funds of the sender on hand to cover the order.

A receiving bank that accepts a payment order and that is not the beneficiary's bank is obligated to issue a payment order. This includes complying with the sender's orders and generally following any instructions as to routing and method. If the resulting payment order does not comply, the sender is not responsible for the error and need not pay the bank other than to the extent of proper execution. Upon learning of an improper execution, the sender has a duty to notify its bank. If a funds transfer is not completed by acceptance by the beneficiary's bank (of a payment order instructing payment to the beneficiary in accordance with the sender's order), the sender is not obligated to pay for its order or is entitled to its money back.[32]

A beneficiary's bank may accept a payment in a variety of ways, such as by paying or notifying the beneficiary. It also accepts a payment by passage of time after receiving the order if the amount of the sender's order is fully covered by a withdrawable credit balance.

Acceptance of an order entitles the bank to payment by the sender. This obligates the bank to pay the amount of the order to the beneficiary. Failure to do so or to give notice of the receipt of the order subjects the bank to liability for damages. If the beneficiary's bank accepts the order, the underlying debt of the originator is discharged to the extent of the amount of the order.[33]

* * *

Problems

1. Explain the rights and obligations of a bank to its customers.

2. Explain:

(a) The process involved in a bank's certification of a check.

(b) How the rights of a drawee bank are affected when it certifies a check.

(c) How the rights of a holder in due course are affected when a check is certified.

3. Compare and contrast the following:

(a) a certified check.

(b) a cashier's check.

(c) a traveler's check.

4. Identify the various relationships that exist between a bank and its customers.

5. Distinguish the various parties involved the check collecting process.

6. What effect does a restrictive indorsement have on the various parties in the check collection process?

7. With respect to stop payment orders:

(a) Who has the power to order one?

(b) What is required to effectuate one?

(c) How long is such an order valid?

(d) If the order is not followed, who is liable and what is the measure of damages?

---

32. UCC Sec. 4A-402.

33. UCC Sec. 4A-406.

8. What are the rights belonging to a customer who discovers that her bank paid one of her checks that was presented with a forged signature or indorsement? Under what circumstances would her rights be limited?

9. Charles, an employee of Big Red productions, forged 10 checks on Big Red's account at the Lindsay National Bank. Charles wrongfully obtained $15,000 from the bank through these forgeries. Is Big Red entitled to have the bank credit its account for the $15,000 Charles wrongfully obtained? In your answer, explain what additional information you will need to reach a proper conclusion.

10. Assume you have moved to a new community. You go to the First National Bank of Jenkins to open a new account. You have for deposit a social security check for $500, a check for $250 from your sister who banks in another state and a certified check from your previous bank in the amount of $1,500. Explain how the Expedited Funds Availability Act will affect your immediate access to each item for deposit.

11. To what type of transactions does the EFT Act apply?

12. Explain the error resolution process of the EFT Act.

13. To what type of transactions does Article 4A of the UCC apply?

14. What are the major objectives of Article 4A?

15. What are the advantages for corporate users of commercial electronic funds transfers? What are the advantages to banks?

Bailments, Documents of Title and Investment Securities

CHAPTER OUTLINE

Bailments, Documents of Title and Investment Securities

IN ADDITION TO the Uniform Commercial Code's treatment of negotiable instruments, including bank deposits and collections, it also governs transactions involving documents of title and investment securities. Documents of title and investment securities are unique types of documents under the Code.

A document of title properly in the hands of a person gives her the power to receive, hold and dispose of that document and the goods it covers. Investment securities are instruments representing a share or interest in property or an enterprise; or otherwise evidence an obligation of the party issuing the instrument.

In order to understand transactions involving documents of title, the concept of "bailment" must be introduced. Following an analysis of bailments and documents of title, transactions concerning investment securities will be examined.

I. Bailments

In order to lay the groundwork for analyzing documents of title, it is necessary to understand bailments. Whether one realizes it or not, people regularly engage in bailment transactions. Loaning a jacket to a friend, renting a car, and storing goods at a warehouse all create bailments.

A bailment is created by delivering personal property, without transferring title (ownership), to another party for a particular purpose, usually pursuant to an agreement.

The party who delivers the property is the bailor. The party receiving the property is the bailee. Once the purpose of the bailment has been completed, the bailee has a duty to return the property to the bailor or to a party designated by the bailor. Subject to certain exceptions, the property should be returned to the bailor in the same condition as when delivered to the bailee.

A bailment can be created without the existence of a contract. Loaning property out of the kindness of one's heart, expecting nothing in return, creates a bailment. Loaning a compact disc to a friend would be an example of a gratuitous bailment. Bailments can be based upon a contractual relationship. Leaving your car at a dealership for repairs creates a bailment arising out of a contract.

It is very important to remember that a bailment is not a sale or a gift. A sale or gift involves an intent to transfer ownership. A bailment reserves ownership in the bailor. Therefore, a bailment is not a sale or a gift.

A. How are Bailments Created?

First, a bailment must affect personal property. Land and its improvements cannot be the subject of the bailment. Second, a bailment requires delivery of property without the passage of title. The delivery element is the key portion of this requirement. With respect to delivery, there are three key factors to keep in mind:

Example. One cannot create a bailment by tossing his coat on an unattended coatroom counter at a restaurant. The coat must be delivered to a person with the power to act on behalf of the restaurant. If an attendant received the coat, a bailment would be created.

What if a person had a wristwatch in the pocket of a coat and failed to inform the coatroom attendant of its presence? Because the bailee did not knowingly accept the wristwatch, only the coat would be considered properly bailed. ☐

1. The bailee must be given exclusive possession and control of the property.
2. The bailee must knowingly accept possession of the property.
3. If the bailor delivers property to the bailee, but restricts or otherwise interferes with the bailee's exclusive possession and control of the property, a bailment will not exist.

Moreover, if the bailee does not know that she is in possession of the subject's property, a bailment cannot exist.

But, courts are becoming more sympathetic to the losses experienced by persons in certain situations. For example, when one delivers a car to the parking lot attendant who retains possession and control of the car, it is not necessary to inform the attendant that there is a spare tire in the trunk. It is reasonably anticipated that such an item will be present within the bailed property. This rule may also be applied to the presence of gloves within coats bailed to coat-check rooms because it is reasonable to expect the presence of gloves within coat pockets.

Using self service coat racks does not create a bailment. There is no actual delivery of personal property to the owner of the coat rack. Moreover, there is no exclusive control. Anyone within the building has access to the coat rack.

Consider the different types of parking lots. There are some parking lots in which the owner of the car delivers possession and control of the car to an attendant by leaving the keys. A claim check is issued to the owner of the car who presents it upon her return. The attendant then retrieves the car and delivers it back to the owner. This creates a bailment. Compare and contrast this with a parking lot that operates upon self service. These lots in effect rent a parking space to a person for a short period of time. This does not create a bailment because exclusive possession and control of the vehicle were not delivered to another party.

Certain situations create involuntary bailments. When a person finds the property of another person or accidently receives the property of another person, the law often deems the possessor an involuntary bailee. While the technical elements of a bailment may not exist, public policy dictates that there are certain responsibilities upon a person who comes into the possession of property not belonging to her. The involuntary bailee has a duty to seek the rightful owner and to contact the appropriate authority if the owner cannot be located.

The final element in the creation of a bailment requires an agreement that the property be returned to the bailor or otherwise be disposed of according to the bailor's directions. The existence of this element further demonstrates that this is a temporary relationship between the bailor and the bailee. The ultimate power still rests with the bailor, who is the owner of the property.

Example. Assume an oil producer stored its product at a tank facility. When the producer requests the return of its stored property, the exact oil it tendered need not be returned. The law requires only that oil of the same type, grade and quality be returned. ☐

B. The Bailment Agreement

A bailment agreement may be express or implied. The agreement need not be in writing unless required under the Statute of Frauds. For instance, a bailment contract that cannot be performed within a year would fall within the Statute of Frauds.

A bailment agreement requires that the subject property be returned to the bailor or to another party at the direction of the bailor. Even if this requirement is not expressed in the contract, return of the property will be implied. In the event that fungible goods are the subject of a bailment agreement, the law requires that fungible goods of the same type, grade and quality, be returned.

A bailment with an option or offer to purchase the property permits the bailee to use the property during an agreed period. At the end of this period, the bailee must return the property or purchase it. The bailment is terminated upon the return or purchase of the property. A standard example of such a bailment is a "sale on approval." Recall that under a sale on approval arrangement, title remains with the seller and will not shift to the buyer until the buyer agrees to purchase it. During the interim period, a bailment exists between the potential seller and buyer.

C. Ordinary Bailments

Bailments can be classified into three categories. It is important to distinguish bailments within these classifications because it will ultimately affect the standard of care that the bailee must exercise. The three classifications are:

1. BAILMENT FOR THE SOLE BENEFIT OF THE BAILOR

This is a gratuitous bailment. In this situation, the bailor requests that the bailee hold property for him without compensation. An example of this would be asking someone to hold your coat for you until you return. Having someone agree to take care of your dog while you are on a trip would be another example. There is no compensation involved.

The standard of care the bailee must exercise is slight. The bailee will only be liable for damage to the bailed property if the bailee's conduct constitutes gross negligence.

2. BAILMENT FOR THE SOLE BENEFIT OF THE BAILEE

This too is a gratuitous bailment. There is no compensation involved. An example of this type of bailment would be loaning property to someone so that she can use it. Loaning a car to a person who needs to drive to a store to pick up an item is an example of such a bailment. Loaning a jacket to someone who wants to wear it is another example.

The standard of care owed by the bailee toward the subject property is very high. In these situations, a bailee will be liable for even slight negligence.

3. BAILMENT FOR THE MUTUAL BENEFIT OF THE PARTIES

This is the most common kind of bailment. It involves a party holding or using the property of another in exchange for compensation. It is a contractual bailment. An attended coat room at a restaurant would fall within this classification because there is a mutual benefit arising out of a business relationship. Another example is renting goods, such as renting a car. Paying a warehouse to store property is another type of mutual benefit bailment.

The standard of care owed by a bailee of a mutual benefit bailment falls between the standards of the two previous categories. The bailee will be liable for his ordinary negligence or failure to observe the ordinary care of a reasonably prudent person under the same circumstances.

D. The Rights and the Duties of a Bailor

In any bailment, a bailor has a right to expect that his property will be handled, managed or stored in an appropriate manner. With these rights, certain duties attach. The following is a summary of these rights and duties.

I. RIGHTS OF A BAILOR

a. To expect that his property will be protected with the proper standard of care.

b. To expect the bailee to utilize, or not to utilize the property, whichever is applicable, pursuant to the agreement.

c. To expect the bailee to return or otherwise relinquish the property at the end of bailment pursuant to the bailor's instructions.

d. To expect that the bailee will not convert, modify or otherwise alter the goods except as agreed.

e. To be free from any limitation on the bailee's liability unless the bailor was aware of such a limitation or the limitation remains otherwise enforceable by law.

f. To expect that repairs or service on the bailed property will be completed without defective workmanship.

2. THE DUTIES OF A BAILOR

A bailor has the duty to provide goods to the bailee that are free from hidden defects that could result in injury. With respect to a mutual benefit bailment, the bailor must give notice of all known defects and any hidden defects, as well as any defects the bailor could have discovered with any reasonable diligence and proper inspection.

In a bailment for the sole benefit of the bailee, the bailor must give notice to the bailor of all known defects. The bailor does not have a duty to test the property for defects beyond those that are easily discoverable.

Consider these two different standards with respect to providing a car to a bailee. In a mutual benefit bailment, a car rental company would have the duty to give the bailor notice of all known defects, as well as any defects that could have been discovered with reasonable diligence and inspection. There is a duty upon car rental companies to test and inspect their vehicles prior to placing them in the hands of the bailee. On the other hand, loaning a car to a friend who desires transportation would relieve the bailor of the duty to test and inspect the vehicle prior to placing in the hands of the bailee.

A bailor may also offer a warranty with respect to the quality of the goods. If the warranty is breached, the injured party may also pursue a breach of warranty action. Consider also that Article 2A of the Code, which covers the lease of goods, extends the UCC's implied warranties of merchantability and fitness for a particular purpose to leased goods. One associated with equipment renting or leasing should keep these principles in mind.

E. The Rights and Duties of a Bailee

In each bailment, a bailee has the right to expect certain conduct from the bailor and to accept certain responsibilities. Here is a summary of those rights and responsibilities.

Example. If a bailee had agreed to take care of the bailor's cat while the bailor was on vacation, the bailee has the right to be reimbursed for any medical expenses incurred in the event the cat had to be taken to a veterinarian. ☐

I. THE BAILEE'S RIGHTS

a. The Right to Possession of the Bailed Property

The bailee has the right to utilize the property in such a fashion to accomplish the purpose of the bailment. In order to determine if the bailee is being afforded that right, one must examine the purpose of the bailment. If the bailee is renting a car, the bailee has the right to drive the car. This is opposed to a bailee who is being paid to store a car in an automobile warehouse. In that situation, a bailee may not operate the car except the purposes of moving it into a storage area or moving it out of danger.

b. Compensation in Some Cases

If the bailment is for the mutual benefit of the parties, the bailee has the right to expect that the bailor will pay compensation or convey some benefit upon the bailee pursuant to the agreement.

c. To Sue for Damage to the Property

The bailee has the right to recover from a third party who damages the property during the course of the bailment. The bailee has standing to bring an action in any court with proper jurisdiction.

d. Reimbursement

The bailee has the right to reimbursement for expenses incurred under the bailment agreement. This includes expenses incurred pursuant to gratuitous bailments for the benefit of the bailor.

The bailee may enforce this right of compensation by retaining possession the property

and claiming a possessory lien. Should the bailor refuse to pay the amount due and owning under such a possessory lien, the property may be sold to satisfy the lien.

e. To Limit Liability in Some Cases

An ordinary bailee has the right to limit her liability in advance so long as two requirements are met. First, the limitation of liability must be called to the attention of the bailor. Second, the limitation cannot be contrary to public policy.

While the bailee is not required to read any limitation to the bailor, it is essential that the bailor be made aware of the limitation. Large signs making announcements such that "This business will not be liable for losses due to fire, theft, or vandalism" may or may not be held to be proper notice to the bailor. The issue of whether or not the limitation has been called to the attention of the bailor is an issue for the finder of fact at a trial. In a jury trial, the jury would make determination. In a nonjury trial, the judge would decide whether or not the limitation had been properly called to the bailor. The majority of courts have ruled that messages in fine print on the back of receipts or ticket stubs are not sufficient to put a party on notice of limitations of liability.

Assuming that a bailor received proper notice of an attempted limitation of liability, the disclaimer may still be deemed void as against public policy. Courts view with displeasure disclaimers that relieve a party from liability for its own negligence or other wrongs. If a parking receipt states that the car owner assumes all risks and agrees to relieve the parking lot owner from all liability relating to any loss or damage to the car, a court may permit the car owner to bring a negligence action against the lot operator if it appears that an employee of the lot was negligent. The courts will not permit parties to disclaim liability for their own wrongs.

2. THE BAILEE'S DUTIES

The bailee has a duty of care with respect to the bailed property. These varying standards have been discussed previously with respect to each type of bailment.

The bailee has a duty to surrender possession of the property at the end of the bailment. Failure to return the property to the bailor or to otherwise follow the bailor's instructions can constitute the tort of conversion. It may also lead to the bailee being found liable for breach of contract.

Liability may also arise from delivery of the subject property to the wrong person. This is referred to as misdelivery. Therefore, it is very important for a bailee to be sure it knows to whom it is delivering the bailed property.

The bailee may also be liable for negligence if the property is not returned to the bailor or is returned in a damaged condition. The law of governing bailments presumes that the bailee was negligent if the property was lost or damaged. This is very similar to the tort doctrine of res ipsa loquitur. This is not automatic liability. A bailee has the right to introduce evidence to rebut the negligence presumption. The bailee may be able to demonstrate that an unforeseen intervening act was responsible for the damage which could relieve the bailee of liability.

F. Termination of the Bailment

Bailments do not last indefinitely. Termination may occur in a number of ways. In many circumstances, the parties have entered into an agreement which specifically has set forth the date or events which will cause the bailment relationship to conclude. But, if the parties have not reached such a mutual agree-

ment, a bailment will come to an end upon the occurrence of any of the following:

1. By demand of either party.
2. The completion of the purpose of the bailment.
3. An act of the bailee inconsistent with the terms of the bailment.
4. By operation of law.

II. Documents of Title under Article 7

In modern commerce, goods are regularly transported by seller to buyer via common carriers. Many times, goods are stored by commercial warehouses. Bailments exist while these goods are in the hands of common carriers and warehouse operators. The concept of bailment interacts with the Code through the documents of title that are issued to represent rights to possess such goods. Article 7 governs documents of title.

Documents of title are special instruments utilized by carriers and warehouse operators. The Code describes documents of title as including bills of lading, dock warrants and receipts, warehouse receipts, orders for delivery of goods as well as any other document which in the regular course of business or financing is treated as adequately evidencing that the person in possession of the document is entitled to receive, hold, and dispose of the document and the goods it covers. In order to qualify as a document of title, a document must purport to be issued by or addressed to a bailee and purport to cover goods in the bailee's possession.[1]

For instance, a person who desires to store goods for a period of time may deliver those goods to a commercial warehouse. The operator will issue a document entitled a "warehouse receipt" in return. The warehouse functions as the bailee and the party desiring

---

1. UCC Sec. 1-201(15).

FIGURE 26.1

Uniform Straight Bill Of Lading—Not Negotiable
The Roger Railroad Company

Received, subject to the classifications and tariffs in effect on the date of issue of this Bill of Lading, the property described below, in apparent good order, except as noted (contents and condition of contents of packages unknown), marked, consigned, and destined as indicated below, which the carrier agrees to carry to its usual place of delivery at said destination, if on its own road or water line, otherwise to deliver to another carrier on the route to said destination. It is mutually agreed that every service to be performed hereunder shall be subject to all the conditions herein contained, including the conditions on back hereof, which are hereby agreed to by the shipper.

Date _____ [date] _____ At _____ Philadelphia, PA _____ From _____ S. Smith _____
Consigned to _____ B. Brown _____
Destination _____ Centerville _____ State of _____ Illinois _____

No. Pkgs.	Description of Articles	Weight
5	Television Sets	240 lbs.

The carrier shall not make delivery of this shipment without payment of freight and all other lawful charges.

The agreed or declared value of the property is hereby specifically stated by the shipper to be $1,000

Shipper __ (signed) S. Smith __ Freight Agent __ (signed) A. Adams __

---

to have her goods stored is the bailor. A person who wants to ship goods to another party may take them to a carrier who will in turn issue a document known as a "bill of lading." The carrier is the bailee and the person desiring the shipping service is the bailor.

In some circumstances, the document of title can be issued by the bailor. For instance, a "delivery order" is a written order to deliver goods which is directed to a warehouse person, carrier, or other person who in the ordinary course of business issues warehouse receipts or bills of lading.[2]

A. The Various Types of Documents of Title

I. BILLS OF LADING

A *bill of lading* is a document evidencing the receipt of goods for shipment issued by a person who is in the business of transporting or forwarding goods. This also includes air bills and freight receipts.[3] An air bill is a document of title utilized exclusively by the air transportation industry.

A person named in a bill of lading to whom the goods are to be delivered or to whose or-

---

2. UCC Sec. 7-102(1)(d).

3. UCC Sec. 1-201(6).

der the goods are to be delivered is known as the consignee. The person named in the bill of lading from whom the goods have been received for shipment is identified as the consignor.

There is no particular format required for a bill of lading, but it must be in writing and it must adequately record the fact that it was issued in receipt for goods to be shipped. An example of a non-negotiable bill of lading is presented in figure 26.1.

There are three types of bills of lading. They are:

a. Destination Bills of Lading

In most circumstances, the bill of lading is issued by the carrier at the point of shipment. Sometimes, the goods will arrive at the destination before the document of title reaches the consignee. If that happens, the goods must remain in storage until the document of title reaches the consignee. This problem can be avoided by the carrier issuing a "destination bill." This bill would be issued by a carrier at the request of the consignor at the point of destination or any other point designated in the consignor's request. Presentment of this bill entitles the consignee to receive the goods when they arrive.

The issuer of the bill of lading may procure a substitute bill of lading to be issued at any place designated in the request of anyone entitled to control the goods while in transit. The outstanding bill of lading or other receipt must be surrendered as a part of the substitution.[4]

b. Through Bills of Lading

This type of bill of lading is issued by a carrier who accepts liability for the transportation of the goods from the point of shipment to the point of destination, using other connecting carriers. Connecting carriers are those carriers who are involved with the shipment of the

goods after the initial carrier. Connecting carriers act as agents for the through bill carrier and are liable for any loss while the goods are in their possession.[5] In using a through bill of lading, it is presumed that the last carrier received the items in good condition.

c. Freight Forwarder Bills of Lading

This type of bill of lading is issued by a middle person who marshals less than carload amounts of goods into carload quantities. The purpose of such a bill is to provide continuous title documentation while the goods are in transit.

2. WAREHOUSE RECEIPTS

Warehouse receipts are issued by a person engaged in the business of storing goods for hire.[6] A warehouse operator is required to keep the goods covered by each warehouse receipt separate to permit identification and delivery of the particular goods stored. There is an exception made for fungible goods, such as grains or oil. These goods may be commingled. Because this is a bailment, goods of the same type, grade and quality must be returned to the bailor upon termination of the bailment.

The Code does not require a particular form for a warehouse receipt. But, it must be in writing and it must contain certain terms in order for the warehouse operator to avoid liability for damages caused by the omission of the terms.[7] These terms are:

1. The location of the warehouse.
2. The date of the issue.
3. The consecutive number of the receipt.
4. A statement whether the goods received will be delivered to the bearer, to a specified person, or to a specified person or his order.

---

4. UCC Sec. 7-305.

5. UCC Sec. 7-302.
6. UCC Sec. 1-201(45).
7. UCC Sec. 7-202.

5. The rate of storage and handling charges, except that where the goods are stored under a field warehousing arrangement, a statement of that fact is sufficient on a non-negotiable receipt.
6. A description of the goods or of the packages containing them.
7. The signature of the warehouse operator, which may be made by her authorized agent.
8. If the receipt is issued for goods of which the warehouse operator is the owner, either solely or jointly or in common with others, the fact of such ownership.
9. A statement of the amount of advances made and of liabilities incurred for which the warehouse operator claims a lien or security interest.

B. Negotiability and Documents of Title

Documents of title may be negotiable or non-negotiable. A warehouse receipt, bill of lading, or other document of title is negotiable if:[8]

1. By its terms the goods are to be delivered to bearer or to the order of a named person; or
2. Where recognized in overseas trade, the document runs to a named person or assigns.

An example of a negotiable bill of lading is presented in figure 26.2.

Any document not meeting the standard set forth above renders it a non-negotiable document of title.[9] The Interstate Commerce Commission requires that negotiable bills of lading appear on yellow paper. Non-negotiable or "straight bills of lading" must be printed on

white paper. Air-bills issued by air express companies as well as interstate shipments made by railroad carriers are commonly negotiable in form.

I. THE SIGNIFICANCE OF NEGOTIABILITY

The holder of a negotiable document of title may acquire more rights than her transferor had in the document. This is similar to the special status granted to certain holders of negotiable instruments under Article 3. It is important to remember that a document of title represents a right to the underlying goods whereas a negotiable instrument represents a right to money. A holder to whom a negotiable document of title has been duly negotiated acquires title to the document and the underlying goods.[10] But, a transferee of a negotiable or non-negotiable document of title to whom the document has been transferred but not negotiated, acquires only those rights to the document and the underlying goods which her transferor had the power and authority to transfer.[11]

Therefore, the applicability of the provisions permitting a holder of a negotiable document of title to obtain superior rights turns on whether or not the document of title was duly negotiated. This is similar to the holder in due course concept discussed in Article 3 of the Code.

2. DUE NEGOTIATION

Due negotiation is a unique form of transfer of a negotiable document of title which makes the transferee a holder. A holder to whom a document has been duly negotiated acquires title to the document, title to the goods, and the right to obtain possession of the goods (in the event the goods are in possession of a bailee). In addition, the issuer of a duly negotiated document of title has an obligation to hold or deliver goods to the holder according

---

8. UCC Sec. 7-104(1).
9. UCC Sec. 7-104(2).

10. UCC Sec. 7-502.
11. UCC Sec. 7-504(1).

FIGURE 26. 2

Uniform Order Bill Of Lading
The Roger Railroad Company

Received, subject to the classifications and tariffs in effect on the date of issue of this Bill of Lading, the property described below, in apparent good order, except as noted (contents and condition of contents of packages unknown), marked, consigned, and destined as indicated below, which the carrier agrees to carry to its usual place of delivery at said destination, if on its own road or water line, otherwise to deliver to another carrier on the route to said destination. It is mutually agreed that every service to be performed hereunder shall be subject to all the conditions herein contained, including the conditions on back hereof, which are hereby agreed to by the shipper.
The surrender of this original ORDER Bill of Lading properly indorsed shall be required before the delivery of the property. Inspection of property covered by this bill of lading will not be permitted unless provided by law or unless permission is indorsed on this original bill of lading or given in writing by the shipper

Date _____[date]_____ At _____Philadelphia, PA_____ From _____S. Smith_____
Consigned to the ORDER of _____S. Smith_____
Destination _____Centerville_____ State of _____Illinois_____
Notify _____B. Brown_____ At _____Centerville_____ State of _____Illinois_____

No. Pkgs.	Description of Articles	Weight
5	Television Sets	240 lbs.

The carrier shall not make delivery of this shipment without payment of freight and all other lawful charges.
The agreed or declared value of the property is hereby specifically stated by the shipper to be $1,000

Shipper __(signed) S. Smith__ Freight Agent __(signed) A. Adams__

to the terms of the document of title, free of any claim or defense. These rights accrue to the holder of the document of title even though the negotiation or any prior negotiation constituted a breach of duty, or the document was obtained from a prior possessor by misrepresentation, fraud, accident, mistake, duress and similar misdeeds.[12]

Section 7-501(4) of the Code establishes that "due negotiation" is effected by negotiating the document to a holder:

1. Who purchases the document in good faith and without notice of any defense against or claim to it on the part of any person,
2. For value,
3. In the regular course of business or financing; and
4. In a transaction not involving mere settlement or payment of a money obligation.

There are a number of similarities between an Article 3 holder in due course and a holder under Article 7. But, there are differences. A

---

12. UCC Sec. 7-502.

holder under Article 7 must take the negotiable instrument in the ordinary course of business of the transferor while a holder in due course under Article 3 is not subject to this requirement. So, there can be no "due negotiation" of an order document running to a person who is not regularly engaged in holding this class of documents for commercial purposes. For instance, there would be no due negotiation of a document running to the order of a full time rock musician .

Not all third party claims are cut off by good faith purchasers of negotiable documents. If any necessary indorsement on the document is forged, the transferee cannot become a holder and therefore does not defeat the claim of a person whose name is forged. In addition, a good faith purchaser will not be protected if the original bailor was a thief. A thief cannot acquire the power to transfer good title simply by storing or shipping stolen goods.

3. THE SHELTER DOCTRINE

A transferee of a negotiable or non-negotiable document to whom the document has been delivered, but not duly negotiated, still acquires the title and rights which her transferor had or had the actual authority to convey.[13]

So, in the same way that the shelter doctrine assists certain holders of negotiable instruments under Article 3, it too exists under Article 7.

4. INDORSEMENTS AND WARRANTIES

Indorsement of a document of title issued by a bailee does not expose the indorser to liability for a default by the bailee or by previous indorsers.[14] This is not the case under Article 3, under which an indorser or transferee can be held liable by those subsequent transferees. The only recourse for a transferee under

Article 7 would be an action directly against the nonperforming bailee.

There are certain warranties made by a person who negotiates or transfers a document of title. Unless otherwise agreed, the party negotiating or transferring the document warrants to her immediate transferee only, in addition to any warranty made in selling the goods:

a. That the document is genuine;
b. That she has no knowledge of any fact that would impair the document's validity or worth; and
c. That her negotiation or transfer is rightful and fully effective with respect to the title to the document and the goods it represents.[15]

5. DEFEATING THE RIGHTS OF A HOLDER OR TRANSFEREE

Recall that the rights of a holder in due course under Article 3 of the Code are not superior in all circumstances. Real defenses are the most common examples of situations causing the rights of holders in due course to yield to the rights of others. Article 7 also recognizes certain situations where the rights of holders or transferees will be subject to certain defenses.

First, a document of title will convey no rights to the underlying goods if the goods have been stolen and stored by a thief who subsequently obtained a negotiable warehouse receipt.[16]

Second, a buyer in the ordinary course of business of fungible goods sold and delivered by a warehouse person who is in the business of buying and selling such goods, takes them free of any claim under a warehouse receipt, even though it has been duly negotiated.[17] This is often represented by the case of a warehouse person who is also a grain dealer who becomes insolvent. The holders of nego-

13. UCC Sec. 7-504(1).
14. UCC Sec. 7-505.

15. UCC Sec. 7-507.
16. UCC Sec. 7-503.
17. UCC Sec. 7-205

tiable warehouse receipts from that warehouse desire to be able to trace and recover fungible goods, such as grain shipped to purchasers from that grain elevator. Under this section, they cannot attempt to recover grain sold to a buyer in the ordinary course of business.

Third, mirroring the real defense of forgery against a holder in due course under Article 3, a holder who takes an "order" negotiable of title with a forged indorsement has no rights in either the document or the underlying goods.

C. Liability for Damage to or Loss of the Bailed Goods

I. WAREHOUSING

A warehouse person is held to the standard of care of a reasonable person under the same circumstances. Liability for damages for loss to goods will be imposed for failure to act in accordance with this standard.[18] The Code further permits warehouse persons to limit their liability by written agreement. A warehouse person will be held liable for any loss caused by commingling of nonfungible goods.[19]

2. COMMON CARRIERS

Common carriers, under common law definition, are persons or entities holding themselves out to perform carriage of goods for hire to all of those who apply. Today, common carriers are licensed by the government to provide transportation services to the general public. While private carriers can pick and choose their clients, a common carrier cannot turn away business unless it is contrary to its license or other governmental regulations.

---

18. UCC Sec. 7-204(1).
19. UCC Sec. 7-207.

The distinction between a common carrier and a private carrier (or special carrier) is important because it affects the carrier's liability for loss or destruction of the goods. A private carrier will be liable to the same standard as most bailees, that is, the negligence standard. Whereas a common carrier is a qualified insurer of goods entrusted to it by the person shipping the goods. While a contract with the common carrier is a mutual benefit bailment, the standard of care is higher. As a general rule, common carriers are strictly liable for loss, damage or destruction of the bailed property. This means if the sender's property is lost or damaged, it will not be necessary to prove that the carrier was negligent or engaged in any other wrongdoing. The liability will be established as a matter of law.

A carrier's strict liability begins when the goods are delivered into the carrier's possession and accepted for immediate shipment. But, if a carrier comes into possession of the goods but has to wait for shipping instructions from the shipper, the carrier is in effect a warehouse person during that period. If loss damage or destruction occurs to the bailed goods during such a waiting period, the carrier will be liable for its negligence only, the standard of care applied to a warehouse person. The same principles hold true upon the goods reaching their destination.

A carrier's strict liability will come to an end when a carrier tenders delivery of the goods to the consignee at a suitable time and place, giving the consignee a reasonable opportunity to receive the goods. If the consignee has yet to take possession of the goods after having had a reasonable opportunity to do so, the carrier is again a warehouse person. The standard of care again falls to that of negligence, instead of strict liability.

There are five generally recognized exceptions to a common carrier's strict liability for loss, damage or destruction of the bailed goods. It should be noted that even if a carrier can establish one of the recognized exceptions, the carrier remains liable unless it also establishes that it used reasonable care to prevent the loss. The five exceptions are:

1. An act of God

In general terms, an act of God results from an event of solely natural forces without human intervention. Earthquakes, high winds, tornadoes, hurricanes, lightning and other violent storms are considered acts of God.

2. An act of a public enemy

Destruction caused by an active militarized force while the country is at war will fall within this exception. This exception will not cover acts of thieves, robbers, hijackers, or other persons engaged in civil disturbances.

3. An act of public authority

The carrier will be excused from liability if goods have been taken by a valid legal process, such as through a writ of replevin, execution or attachment to satisfy an unpaid money judgment against the owner. This also applies to the government's power to seize goods, such as stolen goods or contraband. If goods are taken by a public authority, the carrier is under a duty to notify the sender promptly so that the it may have an opportunity to defend its property rights.

4. An act of the shipper

If a shipper (the party sending the goods) improperly packs or loads the goods, the carrier will not be liable for damages arising from such causes. The carrier will not be permitted to raise this defense if the packing or loading problems were apparent or the carrier otherwise was aware of defective packing or loading.

5. The inherent nature of the goods

Perishable items, such as meats, fresh fruits and vegetables, represent a spoilage risk for both the shipper and the carrier. While the carrier may raise this as a defense in the event the goods were spoiled upon delivery, the carrier bears the burden of showing that the loss was due solely to the inherent nature of the goods and that the carrier's negligence did not contribute to the loss. If the carrier was negligent in delaying transportation of the goods, the carrier will remain liable if the goods spoiled as a result of the delay.

3. LIMITING LIABILITY BY AGREEMENT

A warehouse operator may limit liability for loss or destruction stored goods by disclosing such terms in the warehouse receipt or storage agreement. But, the bailor is not always required to accept the warehouse persons's liability limitation. At the time the bailor signs the storage agreement or within a reasonable time after receiving the warehouse receipt, the bailor may request that the warehouse person increase its liability on all or part of the stored goods. If this occurs, the warehouse operator must assume the added liability but can charge an increased rate unless it would violate its tariff or other governmental restrictions. A warehouse operator cannot wholly exclude or disclaim liability for negligence because the law permits only a limitation of liability.[20]

Similar to the cases of a warehouse operator and an ordinary bailee, a common carrier is permitted to limit its liability for loss damage or destruction in a written contract with the shipper. Article 7 of the Code as well as the Interstate Commerce Act employ rules consistent with those applied to warehouse receipts, allowing rates to be increased depending on the value of the goods shipped. In addition, carriers may disclaim responsibility for undeclared articles of extraordinary value that are hidden from view. Although a common carrier's liability at common law is nearly absolute, liability is often limited by contract between the carrier and the shipper

---

20. UCC Sec. 7-204(2).

by exchanging a reduced rate for a decreased liability limit.

D. The Obligation to Deliver

A warehouse operator or carrier must deliver the goods to a person entitled under a document unless a valid excuse can be established.[21]

A person entitled under a document means a holder in the case of a negotiable document, or the person to whom delivery is to be made by terms of or pursuant to written instructions under a non-negotiable document. While a carrier is responsible for unexcused nondelivery or misdelivery, a carrier who merely delays delivery will be liable only if the carrier's negligence caused the delay.

III. Investment Securities under Article 8

Article 8 of the UCC, entitled "Investment Securities," has been significantly modified since its introduction in the 1962 official text of the Code. In 1977, a new text was introduced. Its coverage was expanded to include both securities which are represented by certificates or other instruments and those which are not. Article 8 now identifies securities which are represented by certificates or other instruments as "certificated securities." These constituted the entire scope and coverage of the 1962 official text. Uncertificated securities were not covered under the 1962 official text. Revisions were introduced and adopted in the 1977 official text to cover the rights and duties of issuers and parties dealing with both certificated and uncertificated securities.

The purposes of Article 8 are to set forth certain rights and duties of issuers and the parties that deal with investment securities, both certificated and uncertificated. But, unlike a corporation code, it does not set forth general

---

21. UCC Sec. 7-403(1).

rules defining property rights that accrue to holders of securities. Moreover, it does not set forth specific requirements for disclosing to the public the nature of the property interest represented by the security, as would a "blue sky" statute. Article 8 sets forth rules relative to the transfer of the rights in securities and establishes those rights that may exist against the issuer and other parties.

As is true with respect to all other articles of the Code, parties may vary their rights and duties between themselves by contract. But, the Code limits the prejudice of the rights to those who are not a party to the agreement. In addition, general legal principles are permitted to supplement those areas specifically not covered by Article 8.

A. What is an Investment Security under Article 8?

Section 8-102(1)(a) defines a "certificated security" as a share, participation or other interest in property or an enterprise of the issuer or an obligation of an issuer which is:

(1) represented by an instrument issued in bearer or registered form;
(2) of a type commonly dealt in on securities exchanges or markets or commonly recognized in any area in which it is issued or dealt in as a medium for investment; and
(3) either one of a class or series or by its terms divisible into a class or series of shares, participations, interests, or obligations.

An "uncertificated security" is a share, participation or other interest in property or an enterprise of the issuer or an obligation of an issuer which is:

(1) not represented by an instrument and the transfer of which is registered upon the books maintained for that purpose by or on behalf of the issuer;

705

(2) of a type commonly dealt in on security exchanges or markets; and

(3) either one of a class or series or by its terms divisible into a class or series of shares, participations, interests or obligations.[22]

It is important to note that a certificated security is governed by Article 8 of the Code and not by Article 3, even though it meets the requirements of Article 3. For instance, a corporate bond can meet every element of negotiability under Article 3. But by definition, such an instrument will be dealt with under Article 8 of the Code. One of the key factors to watch will be whether or not the instrument is commonly dealt in on securities exchanges or markets or commonly recognized as a medium for investment.[23]

Article 8 does not apply to money. If a certificated security has been retained by or surrendered to the issuer or its transfer agent for reasons other than registration of transfer, other temporary purpose, payment, exchange, or acquisition by the issuer, that security shall be treated as an uncertificated security for the purposes of Article 8. [24]

I. REGISTERED FORM

A certificated security is in registered form if:

(1) It specifies a person entitled to the security or the rights it represents; and

(2) Its transfer may be registered upon the books maintained for that purpose by or on behalf of the issuer, or the security so states that it is registered.[25]

---

22. UCC Sec. 8-101(1)(b).
23. UCC Sec. 8-102(1)(c).
24. Id.
25. UCC Sec. 8-102(1)(d).

2. BEARER FORM

A certificated security is in bearer form if it runs to bearer according to its terms and not by reason of any indorsement.[26]

B. The Issuer

An issuer of an investment security includes one who:

(1) Places its name on a security to evidence that it represents a share, participation, or other interest in its property; or

(2) Directly or indirectly creates fractional interests in its property.[27]

I. THE RESPONSIBILITIES OF AN ISSUER

The issuer of a security will be bound by the terms stated upon a certificated security and those contained in the initial transaction statement into the purchaser of an uncertificated security and those terms that are made a part of the security by reference to another instrument.[28]

When a security is issued in registered form and has not been indorsed, the person in whose name it was issued is generally deemed to be the owner.

A security, other than one issued by a governmental unit, is valid in the hands of the purchaser for value without notice of a particular defect even if that defect goes to the validity of the security.[29] But, according to Section 8-203 of the Code, staleness of the instrument may be sufficient to put purchasers on notice of potential defects in the instrument. Staleness may be evidenced by a missed payment or exchange dates that are over a year old.

---

26. UCC Sec. 8-102(1)(e).
27. UCC Sec. 8-201.
28. UCC Sec. 8-102(1).
29. UCC Sec. 8-202(2).

2. THE RIGHTS OF AN ISSUER

Each issuer has a complete defense to honoring a nongenuine security.[30] This defense is valid even against a purchaser in good faith for value with notice of defects. This is the only real defense available to the issuer.[31]

An issuer will not be able to raise the defense of nongenuine signature if the security was signed by an employee or agent of the issuer.

In the event a security has been improperly altered, it remains enforceable according to its original terms.[32]

C. Loss, Destruction or Theft of Securities

Any person against whom the transfer of a security is wrong, (except as against a bona fide purchaser for value and in good faith), may reclaim possession of a certificated security wrongfully transferred; obtain possession of a new certificate representing all or part of the same rights; compel the origination of an instruction to transfer to him or a person designated by him an uncertificated security consisting of all the same rights; or be entitled to damages.

If the transfer is wrongful due to an unauthorized or otherwise forged indorsement of a certificated security, the owner may reclaim or retain possession of the security or a new certificated security even from a bona fide purchaser for value who was acting in good faith.[33]

In the event the owner of a certificated security loses or has the security stolen from her, it is advisable for her to notify the issuer as soon as possible. Doing this will put her in a better position to protect her rights. If she notifies the issuer within a reasonable time of the loss and before a subsequent good faith purchaser presents the security for registration in the purchaser's name, the original owner will be entitled to the issue of a new security to replace the lost security so long as the original owner files an indemnity bond with the issuer and satisfies any other reasonable requirement imposed by the issuer.[34]

But, the original owner will not be permitted to take advantage of an unreasonable delay to the detriment of the issuer.

Otherwise, a good faith purchaser for value will be entitled to having the security issued in his name and the true owner's right to reclaim the original or new security will be cut off.[35]

If, after the issue of a new certificated or uncertificated security, a bona fide purchaser of the original certificated security presents it for registration or transfer, the issuer must register the transfer (subject to problems of overissued securities which are governed by Section 8-104). In addition to any rights on the indemnity bond, the issuer may recover the new certificated security from the person to whom it was issued or any person taking under him except a bona fide purchaser or may cancel the uncertificated security unless a bona fide purchaser or any person taking under a bona fide purchaser is then the registered owner or registered pledgee.[36]

An overissue of a security means that it has been issued in an amount in excess of the amount the issuer has the corporate power to issue. In the event the Code compels the issue of a security, and it would result in an overissue, the issuer is not required to comply with the rule. But in the alternative, must issue an identical security which does not constitute an overissue if one is reasonably available for purchase. If one is not available, the person entitled to the issue or validation may recover from the issuer the price she or the last purchaser for value paid for it with interest from the date of her demand.[37]

---

30. UCC Sec. 8-202(3).
31. UCC Sec. 8-205.
32. UCC Sec. 8-206.
33. UCC Sec. 8-315(2).

34. UCC Sec. 8-405.
35. UCC Sec. 8-405(1).
36. UCC Sec. 8-405(3).
37. UCC Sec. 8-104.

D. Purchase and Transfer of Investment Securities

Purchase and transfer of investment securities under Article 8 include the receipt of the security from its original issuance as well as all subsequent transfers in registered or bearer form. A restriction on the transfer of securities imposed by the issuer, even if it is otherwise lawful, will not be effective against any person without actual knowledge of the restriction unless the security is certificated and the restriction is conspicuously noted on the face of the security. In the case of an uncertificated security, there must be a notation of the restriction in the initial transaction statement sent to the original person to whom it was issued or to the registered owner or the registered pledgee in order to restrict its transfer.[38]

A purchaser of a security acquires the rights that her transferor had or had actual authority to convey.[39] But, any transferee of a certificated security who has been a party to any fraud or illegality affecting the security, or who has been a prior holder of that security and had notice of an adverse claim, cannot improve her position by taking the security from a bona fide purchaser.[40] This is similar to the restrictions placed upon the shelter doctrine in Article 3. A transferee who has been a party to a wrong cannot attempt to cleanse her position by attempting to wash the instrument through a good faith purchaser for value.

In addition to acquiring the rights of a purchaser, a bona fide purchaser also acquires his interest free of any adverse claim.[41]

A purchaser of a security will be charged with notice of an adverse claim if the security has been indorsed "for collection" or "for surrender" or for some other purpose not involving a transfer. The same is true if the security is in bearer form containing an ambiguous statement that the security is the property of a person other than the transferor.[42] Also remember that any evidence on the face of the security that the instrument is stale (beyond any date set out for presentment, surrender, redemption or exchange or six months from any date set for payment of money against presentment or surrender) will constitute notice of an adverse claim.[43]

A person who presents a certificated security for registration of transfer or for payment or exchange makes certain warranties. In presenting the security, the person warrants to the issuer that he is entitled to the registration, payment or exchange of the security as requested.[44] But, a purchaser for value who is without notice of an adverse claim who receives a new, reissued or re-registered security, warrants only that he has no knowledge of any unauthorized signature in a necessary indorsement.[45]

In addition, a person transferring a certificated security to a purchaser for value warrants only that:

1. Her transfer is effective and rightful;
2. The security is genuine and has not been materially altered; and
3. She knows of no fact which might impair the validity of the security.[46]

E. The Effect of an Unauthorized Indorsement or Instruction

Unless the owner or pledgee has ratified an unauthorized indorsement or instruction, or is precluded from asserting its ineffectiveness:

1. He may assert its ineffectiveness against the issuer or any purchaser other than a purchaser for value

---

38. UCC Sec. 8-204.
39. UCC Sec. 8-301 (1).
40. UCC Sec. 8-302(4).
41. UCC Sec. 8-302(3).

42. UCC Sec. 8-304(1).
43. UCC Sec. 8-305
44. UCC Sec. 8-306(1)
45. *Id.*
46. UCC Sec. 8-306(2).

without notice of adverse claims who has in good faith received a new, reissued, or re-registered security; and

2. An issuer who registers the transfer of a security upon the unauthorized indorsement is subject to liability for improper registration.[47]

* * *

Problems

1. As a favor and without consideration, O loaned his car to D of St. Louis, Missouri, for avowed purpose of driving from St. Louis to Memphis and return in order to make an audit in Memphis. Without O's knowledge of consent, D also drove this car to Kansas City and return, and on the return trip, although D was driving with proper care, the car was damaged as a result of a highway defect. This trip to Kansas City was occasioned by an unexpected request that D make an audit there. O was not in any way associated with D and had no interest in or connection with either of these audits. Could O hold D financially responsible for the damage to the car? Explain. (Modified from A.I.C.P.A., Nov. 40-5.)

2. D hired an automobile from the Drive-Yur-Self Auto Company at $1 an hour. Through no fault of D's the car was damaged in a collision with a truck carelessly driven by T.

(a) The renting corporation sued D to recover for the damages to the car. What result? Explain.

(b) The renting corporation sued T to recover for the damages for the car. What result? Explain. (Modified from A.I.C.P.A., Nov. 27-5.)

3. P, making an automobile trip from New York City to Boston, agreed to take a valuable parcel belonging to his friend O and to deliver it to O's son in Providence. When P stopped in Bridgeport for dinner, he took his own property out of the car but

---

47. UCC Sec. 8-311.

left O's parcel in the car. The parcel was stolen from the car while P was eating dinner. What are the principles involved? (Modified from A.I.C.P.A., Nov. 29-6.)

4. O took his best suit to a dry-cleaning company to have the suit altered, cleaned, and pressed. He delivered the suit to the manager and received a receipt in which the suit was described, the work to be performed indicated, and the charge shown. A week later, O returned to the store, presented his receipt and asked for his suit. The manager searched the racks but was unable to find the suit. He asked O to return in a few days as he thought the suit had not yet been returned or had been misplaced. The manager then contacted the cleaning plant; the suit could not be located there, and the records indicated that the suit had been returned to the store with other garments. The manager diligently searched through all the clothing in the store and questioned all of his employees, but to no avail. O returned five days later, presented the receipt, tendered the amount due, and demanded the suit. The manager explained that the suit had just disappeared, that neither he nor any of his employees had taken it or knew what had happened to it. O sued the company for the value of his suit.

(a) Explain who would prevail in the lawsuit if both parties proved only the facts stated.

(b) Suppose that the suit had been destroyed by an accidental fire in the store, and the company could prove that the fire had started through no fault of its own. Explain who would prevail in O's lawsuit against the company. (Modified from A.I.C.P.A., May 61-6.)

5. When the owner of a valuable fur coat delivered the coat to a fur dealer for storage over the summer months, the parties signed the following written agreement: "[Date]. Fur storage agreement for the following described coat: [then followed a brief description of the coat]. In consideration of $25 charges to be paid upon return of the above-described fur coat to the undersigned owner on October 1 of this year, the undersigned

dealer agrees to keep the said coat free from damage by moths and return the said coat to the owner on October 1, in the same condition as when received by the dealer." On October 1 the coat could not be found. Investigation disclosed that without fault or negligence on the part of the dealer, the coat had been stolen and disposed of by one of the dealer's employees who previously had been wholly trustworthy. The owner sued the dealer for the value of the stolen coat. What result? Explain.

6. When O delivered 20 shirts to a launderer, O was given a duplicate laundry slip upon which was printed, "The liability of the laundry for loss or damage regardless of nature or cause, shall be limited to an amount not exceeding ten times the charge for laundering the items described hereon." Through the launderer's carelessness, all 20 shirts were lost. The total value of the shirts was $125, the charge for laundering 20 shirts was $3. How much, if anything, would O have a right to collect from the launderer? Explain.

7. A common carrier accepted a shipment of goods at Chicago for delivery to a buyer in Boston, Massachusetts. The goods were in transit between the two cities when they were destroyed by the incident described below. For each of the following, explain what would be the carrier's liability:

(a) The goods were destroyed by a fire caused by a bolt of lightning.

(b) The goods were destroyed by a riot of 100 people.

(c) A discharged employee, holding a grudge against the carrier, caused a wreck which destroyed the goods.

(d) The goods were destroyed by in a fire caused by the negligence of a third party.

(e) The goods were destroyed because of improper packing by the shipper of the goods.

(f) The goods were destroyed in a fire resulting from train robbers derailing the train in order to steal a shipment of gold bullion carried on the train. (Modified from A.I.C.P.A., Nov. 49 -7.)

8. O, of New York City, planned to move to Chicago and delivered his office furniture to the Porter Warehouse and Transit Company. The company was to transport the furniture as soon as it had available van space. Before the company had shipped the furniture, O telephoned that he had decided not to move to Chicago, and that therefore he desired the company to hold the furniture for further instructions. The day after this phone call, the company's warehouse and contents, including O's furniture, were destroyed by fire, through no fault of the company. One week later O, ignorant of the fire, wrote instructing the company to ship the furniture to St. Louis. In what capacity and to what extent, if at all, was the company liable for the loss of O's furniture? Explain. (Modified from A.I.C.P.A., May 53-10.)

9. Declaring a value of $1,000, O shipped a package by United Parcel from New York City to be delivered to O at 123 Main Street, Centerville, Ill. When the package arrived in Centerville, it was loaded on a delivery truck which at 2 o'clock Wednesday afternoon, started for the Main Street address. While driving with proper care, the truck driver was involved in a collision with a carelessly driven auto. The collision started a fire and the truck driver was unable to save the package from being destroyed. Since the driver of the auto was insolvent and uninsured, O sued United Parcel Service for $1,000.

(a) The collision and fire occurred while the truck was on the way to the Main Street address. What would be the result of O's lawsuit? Explain.

(b) The collision and fire occurred while the truck was on the way from the Main Street address back to the United Parcel office. The package was still on the truck because nobody had answered when the driver had rung the doorbell at the Main Street address. Could O recover from the carrier? Explain.

10. A railroad company transported goods to their destination and notified the consignee that the goods were ready for delivery. The consignee did not call for the goods until a week later. The

day before he called for the goods they were destroyed by fire without negligence on the part of the carrier. Was the railroad company liable for the loss of the goods? Explain. (Modified from A.I.C.P.A., Nov. 45-9.)

11. P owned a panel truck which he used to operate a parcel delivery service for several women's and children's low-price specialty shops. One day while he was making a delivery to an apartment house in the suburbs, a number of packages were stolen from the truck.

(a) P had left the truck unlocked. Would P bear the loss? Explain.

(b) P had carefully placed a strong padlock on the truck, which the thief had been obliged to break in order to steal the packages. Would P bear the loss? Explain.

(c) Would the answer to Part (b) be different if, other facts remaining the same, P had been engaged by a few exclusive jewelry stores rather than by a group of specialty shops? Explain. (Modified from A.I.C.P.A., May 60-7b.)

12. R was a retailer who occasionally purchased goods from M, a local manufacturer. A thief phoned M, pretended to be speaking for R, and ordered certain small goods worth $500 to be delivered to R's store on thirty-days' credit. Immediately after the goods had been delivered to R's receiving room, the thief phoned R, pretended to be speaking for M, and said some goods had been delivered to R by mistake and would be called for by M's office assistant. The thief then went to R's store, introduced himself as M's office assistant, received the goods which had been delivered by M, and disappeared. When the parties discovered the fraudulent trick, M sued R for $500. What result? Explain.

13. One evening O and two other young women attended a session at a dancing school operated by P. The fee for the class was 90 cents with an additional charge of 10 cents for checking wraps. O paid $1 at the ticket booth and received a ticket to be presented at the checking window with the items checked. O was wearing a topcoat worth $50, and a separate fur neckpiece worth $300. Knowing that checked items were placed in bins rather than hung on hangers, O folded her topcoat with the neckpiece inside and gave the bundle to the checkroom attendant together with the checking ticket. The attendant put the bundle in a numbered bin and gave O a claim check bearing the same number. When the class was finished, O presented the claim check at the check window and received back her topcoat folded in the same manner as O had folded it. However, the fur neckpiece was not inside the bundle and could not be found anyplace. O sued P for $300. What result? Explain.

14. P planned to attend a dance at a dancing pavilion known as the Lakeside Park. P borrowed $50 from O, promising to repay the money within one week, and also borrowed O's car for the dance, promising to return the car the following day. When P drove into the parking lot at the Lakeside Park, he paid 10 cents to an attendant at the entrance, and parked in the space indicated by another attendant. When P paid the 10 cents he received a cardboard tag upon which was printed:

In consideration of the charge made upon issuing this tag, the Lakeside Park leases to the holder hereof, space on its premises sufficient for the purpose of parking his auto. It is expressly stipulated that the lessee of such space assumes all risk of fire, theft, or other damages while on the premises, and that Lakeside Park at no time assumes the custody of said auto or any of its contents. No attendant has any authority to vary, modify, alter, or enlarge any of the foregoing conditions.

P read the tag and then pocketed it together with the car key, after locking the car. About an hour later, P returned to the parking lot to get his girl's purse which she had left in the car. As P was unlocking the car door, someone came from behind an adjoining car and struck P on the head, knocking him unconscious. The assailant took P's wallet which contained the $50 P had borrowed from O, took the car key, and drove away in O's car. In rifling P's pockets, the thief missed the

Lakeside Parking tag in P's coat pocket. At the time of the theft, an attendant was still on duty at the entrance to the parking lot, but he did not see or hear the assault, and he made no attempt to stop the car as the thief was driving away.

(a) Would P be liable to O (1) for the stolen money? (2) for the stolen car? Explain.

(b) Would the Lakeside Park be liable (1) for the money? (2) for the car? Explain.

15. A merchant who subscribed for use of a bank's night deposit facility said that on the evening of June 16 he put $6,549 in a proper container and dropped it in the bank's night deposit chute. Five days later, not receiving confirmation of his deposit, the merchant phoned the bank and was told that the bank had no record of the deposit ever having been made and no explanation of what might have happened to it. The night deposit agreement between the merchant and the bank provided that the bank would have no liability for such deposit until counted and recorded by the bank and that the bank's report of contents of the night deposit safe would be binding on the merchant. The merchant sued the bank. What result?

16. The proprietor of a parking lot in the theater district of a city displayed a large sign reading, "Evening Parking 50C. Lot closes at 1 A.M.," and operated the lot in the following manner: A driver would stop his car at the entrance to the lot, get out, and pay 50 cents to the proprietor. The proprietor would give the driver a ticket stub with an identifying number, place the remainder of the ticket bearing the same number under the windshield wiper of the car, and drive the car into the lot and park it. All keys were left in the cars. If a person returned before 1 A.M., he would surrender his ticket stub to the proprietor who would secure the car from the lot and bring it to the exit, for the owner to drive away. At 1 A.M. the proprietor would make sure that no car remaining in the lot was blocked in by another car and would then depart. Any person returning to the lot after 1 A.M. would locate his car in the lot and drive it away.

O used the lot a number of times and knew the manner in which it was operated. One evening O returned to the lot about 2 A.M., later than his usual time. A few cars were still in the lot, but O's car was missing. It had been stolen, and O sued the parking lot proprietor for the value of the car. What result? Explain.

17. A man and his wife stopped for dinner at a restaurant in Philadelphia. The headwaiter escorted them to a table and summoned the waiter. The waiter assisted the woman in removing her fur coat and, after holding her chair while she sat down at the table, hung the coat on the nearest empty hook, about 25 feet from the table. The man removed his overcoat and hung it on the empty hook beside his wife's coat. Finishing the meal, the man paid the waiter, received his change, and gave the usual tip to the waiter. The waiter drew back the woman's chair while she arose from the table, and then the waiter and the man went to the hooks where the coats had been hung. Both coats were missing and diligent search and investigation by the restaurant staff and by the police failed to disclose the whereabouts of the coats. Both the man and the woman sued the restaurant owner for the value of their respective coats, $300 for the man's coat and $700 for the woman's. What result? Explain.

18. For some years, a manufacturing jeweler made periodic business trips to various towns in Illinois. While in Centerville, the jeweler always stopped at the Howard Hotel. A woman, a resident of Centerville, had a ring (a large sapphire surrounded by diamonds, in a platinum setting) which had been made by this jeweler. Losing one of the diamonds, she wrote to the jeweler concerning its replacement. In his answering letter, the jeweler told the woman that he would be in Centerville the week of October 21, staying at the Howard Hotel, and that she could give her ring to him then. On October 23, the woman taped her ring between two pieces of cardboard, sealed the envelope, and wrote the jeweler's name on the front of the envelope. She took the envelope to the Howard Hotel and asked the desk clerk if the

jeweler was in. The desk clerk replied that the jeweler was registered at the hotel but was out at the time. The woman asked the clerk if he would give the envelope to the jeweler when he came in, and the clerk replied that he would. The woman gave the envelope to the clerk and left the hotel. At that moment several other persons came into the hotel to register and the clerk laid the envelope down on the counter while he was waiting on the newcomers. When he looked for the envelope, it was gone. Diligent search and investigation by the hotel staff and by the police failed to disclose the whereabouts of the ring. The woman sued the hotel for $2,000, the reasonable value of the ring. What result? Explain .

19. O, a retail jeweler from Newark, bought various items of jewelry in New York City for a total of $2,800, put the jewelry in a briefcase, and returned to the railroad station. Learning that the next train to Newark would leave in forty-five minutes, O put his briefcase in a coin-operated locker, inserted 10 cents, and removed the key, locking the locker. After finishing lunch, O returned for his briefcase, unlocked the locker, and found it empty. When O reported the loss, an agent from the locker company came with a master key and opened and looked in vain in all of the lockers in that particular area. Under the rules of the locker company (as printed on a tag on each locker) the company would remove the contents of a locker after twenty-four hours. However, O's briefcase had been in the locker for only a half an hour. The locker company denied having removed the briefcase or having any knowledge at all concerning its whereabouts. O sued the locker company for $2,800. What result? Explain.

20. M operated a factory in which he manufactured sport shirts. His usual method of business was to have customers furnish the cloth and patterns, while M would furnish buttons, thread, linings, and other minor materials, in addition to performing all of the labor and machine work to make the completed garments. O delivered a quantity of cloth, described below, to M to be made into shirts. While the shirts were in process, a fire occurred in the building adjoining M's factory. The material was severely damaged by smoke and water, and there was no practical means of recovering damages from the persons at fault in causing the fire.

(a) The cloth O delivered to M was sufficient rare imported wool gabardine material to make up 1,000 dozen shirts for an exclusive trade. Would M or O bear the burden of damage done to the material? Explain.

(b) The cloth O delivered to M was sufficient standard broadcloth material for 10,000 dozen shirts. At the time of the fire M was using part of this material to complete a rush order for another customer, knowing that there would be no difficulty in replacing the broadcloth in time to complete the order for O. Would M or O bear the burden of the damage done to the material? Explain. (Modified from A.I.C.P.A., May 60-7a.)

21. S owed $1,000 to a common carrier of goods for the carrier's transportation of S's automobile. Subsequently S delivered a truck to the carrier for transportation, receiving from the carrier a negotiable bill of lading naming S as consignee. S indorsed, sold, and delivered the bill of lading to B who paid S $5,000 for it. The transportation charges on the truck were $200.

(a) For how much would the carrier have a lien on the truck? Explain.

(b) If B tendered the bill of lading and $200 to the carrier, which the carrier refused to accept, could B compel the carrier to deliver the truck to him? Explain.

(c) If the bill of lading were nonnegotiable, and the carrier, ignorant of S's transfer of the bill of lading to B, delivered the truck to S without obtaining the bill of lading, would B have any rights against the carrier? Explain. (Modified from A.I.C.P.A., Nov. 52-2.)

22. By letter, B, a dealer in Erie, Pennsylvania, ordered from S, a wholesaler in Philadelphia, 100 units of certain described goods at a stated price, f.o.b. Philadelphia. Terms were sight draft, bill of

lading attached, cash against documents. S promptly accepted the order by return mail and shipped goods to Erie, receiving from the carrier a bill of lading stating that it covered, "ten boxes marked as each containing ten units of [the described goods]." S drew a sight draft on B and sent it, together with the bill of lading. However, for the reason stated below, the carrier refused to deliver to B the ten boxes described in the bill of lading. Three weeks after B's payment, S became insolvent and all of his assets were taken over by a court-appointed receiver.

(a) The goods S delivered to the carrier for shipment to Erie conformed to B's order and to the description on the bill of lading. While the goods were in transit toward Erie, S received from P, a customer in Buffalo, a rush order for the same kind and quantity of goods. The shipment to Erie had exhausted S's supply, but S expected within a week to obtain a new supply from the manufacturer. Accordingly, S requested the carrier to divert the Erie shipment and deliver the goods to P in Buffalo. The carrier did so. Neither S nor his receiver made any additional shipment to B. B, not receiving any of the boxes described in the bill of lading, sued the carrier for the value of the goods. (1) The bill of lading was an order bill of lading, naming S as consignee, indorsed in blank by S. Was B entitled to judgment in his lawsuit against the carrier? Explain. (2) The bill of lading was a straight bill of lading, naming B as consignee. Was B entitled to judgment in his lawsuit against the carrier? Explain.

(b) Although the carrier gave S a bill of lading for ten boxes marked as each containing ten units of the described goods, S delivered to the carrier only nine boxes, assuring the freight agent that he would bring in the tenth box the following day. S failed to bring in the tenth box, and his receiver refused to do so. The carrier delivered the nine boxes to B, and B sued the carrier for the value of the tenth box. (1) Same additional fact and question as in (1) above. (2) Same additional fact and question as in (2) above. (3) If the railroad had stamped on the bill of lading, "Shipper's weight,

load, and count," would this additional fact change any of your answers? Explain.

(c) The goods S delivered to the carrier for shipment to Erie conformed to B's order and to the description on the bill of lading. However, S had stolen the goods from their owner, O. O located the goods when they arrived in Erie, and both O and B claimed them from the carrier. (1) The bill of lading was an order bill of lading, naming S as consignee, indorsed in blank by S. As between O and B, who had the better title to the goods? Explain. (2) The bill of lading was a straight bill of lading, naming B as consignee. As between O and B, who had the better title to the goods? Explain.

23. By letter, B, a dealer in Chicago, ordered from S, a manufacturer in Philadelphia, certain described goods for $400, f.o.b. Chicago, terms sixty-day trade acceptance, bill of lading attached. S shipped the goods by railway freight, requesting and receiving from the carrier an order bill of lading naming S as consignee. S indorsed the bill of lading in blank, drew a sixty-day draft on B, and mailed the documents to a bank in Chicago. T, a dealer in such goods, stole the documents from the mail, threw away the draft, and sold and indorsed the bill of lading to P who paid fair value to T in the regular course of business, without knowledge of the preceding details involving the bill of lading. T then disappeared. The parties learned of the theft, and when the goods arrived in Chicago, B and P both claimed them.

(a) Assume that S will be paid whatever is legally owed to him. As between P and B, who would have the better right to obtain the goods from the carrier? Explain.

(b) Would the winner in Part (a) above have an obligation to S, and if so, what obligation? Explain.

(c) Would the loser in Part (a) have an obligation to S, and if so, what obligation? Explain.

24. B, of Louisville, Kentucky, ordered ten tractors of a specified make and model from S in Philadelphia, Pennsylvania, making a cash deposit of

25 percent of the purchase price at the time the order was placed and agreeing to pay the balance on a sight draft with the bill of lading attached. At S's request the railroad placed an empty car on S's siding. Shortly afterwards S notified the freight agent that the shipment was being loaded and would be completely loaded before the end of the day, and requested and received a straight bill of lading for 10 tractors. S drew a sight draft on B, attached the bill of lading, and sent the documents to a Louisville bank. B paid the draft and received the bill of lading. Shortly afterwards S was adjudged bankrupt, without ever having loaded and shipped the ten tractors. B sued the railroad company for the price paid. What result? Explain.

25. S. Smith owned 10 cases of canned fish and stored them in a public warehouse. S asked for and received from the bailee a negotiable warehouse receipt according to which the goods were deliverable to bearer. S sold the document in the ordinary course of business for cash to B. Brown. S delivered the document and indorsed it "Deliver to the order of B. Brown (signed) S. Smith." A thief stole the document from B and forged the signature of B. Brown. The thief then sold and delivered the document to H. Howard who bought it for cash in good faith and in the ordinary course of business. Who has better right (1) to the document, (2) to the goods. (Modified from A.I.C.P.A., Nov. 81-1(47).)

26. Thieves broke into the warehouse of Airways Co. and stole a shipment of computer parts belonging to Owner Co. Owner had in its possession a negotiable bill of lading covering the shipment. The thieves transported the stolen parts to another state and placed the parts in a bonded warehouse. The thieves received a negotiable warehouse receipt which they used to secure a loan of $20,000 from Finance Co. These facts were revealed upon apprehension of the thieves. Regarding the rights of the parties which of the following is correct:

a. Finance is entitled to a $20,000 payment before relinquishment of the parts.

b. Airways will be the ultimate loser of the $20,000.

c. Owner is entitled to recover the parts free of Finance's $20,000 claim.

d. Owner is not entitled to the parts but may obtain damages from Airways. (Modified from A.I.C.P.A. Nov. 83-1(47).)

Secured Transactions

Secured Transactions

ALMOST **ALL BUSINESSES** employ debt to fund their asset structures. Billions of dollars are borrowed and repaid each year to assist business entities in acquiring inventory, equipment and working capital. Often, enterprises seeking to borrow money do not have the size or a history of sufficient cash flow to justify borrowing money supported only by a naked promise to repay.

Lending money is very risky. In order to reduce the credit risk to a level that would make a lender more comfortable, it will agree to take collateral as security for repayment of the loan. In the event of default, this gives the lender something of value to sell or apply to the outstanding loan balance.

The first part of this chapter will discuss Article 9 of the Uniform Commercial Code which governs secured transactions. The remaining of this portion of this chapter will discuss the principles of suretyship. Suretyship is not governed by the UCC. Suretyship is a concept involving a party providing its credit strength to a principle borrower resulting in the surety becoming primarily liable on the debt along principle.

Closely related to suretyship is the concept of guaranty. A guaranty agreement arises when a guarantor agrees to make himself secondarily liable under a separate contract of guaranty. Lenders look more favorably upon loans to individuals with less than stellar borrowing capacity who manage to find a creditworthy person or entity to serve as a surety or

a guarantor. Again, this reduces the lender's risk of loss in the event of loan default.

I. Secured Transactions— Article 9

A secured transaction requires the presence of a buyer and seller or a borrower and a lender. In both circumstances, the buyer or borrower gives a security interest in personal property or fixtures to secure performance of an obligation. The interest created in the property is known as a security interest.[1]

It is important to remember that secured transactions involve only personal property or fixtures as collateral. A mortgage granted to secure a real estate loan does not fall within the scope of Article 9. Security interests created under Article 9 could cover, for instance, accounts receivable, documents, equipment, computers, vehicles, bank accounts, instruments, chattel paper, stocks, bonds, general intangibles and certificates of deposit.

A. Transactions excluded from Article 9 Coverage

Article 9 was designed primarily with commercial financing in mind. But, section 9-104 specifically excludes certain transactions. Those transactions include:

---

1. UCC Sec. 1-201(37).

1. Liens arising under statute or common law by virtue of status, not by consent or agreement of the parties, such as mechanic's and materialman's liens as well as governmental liens.
2. Any interest in or lien upon real estate, including a lease or landlord's lien.
3. Transfers of claims for wages, salary or other compensation of an employee.
4. The sale of accounts or chattel paper as a part of a sale of a business out of which they arose.
5. An assignment of accounts or chattel paper for the purpose of collection only.
6. Rights under life insurance policies and deposit accounts, except where said policies or accounts were obtained with the proceeds of collateral.
7. Court claims and judgements. (Other than judgements taken on a right to payment which was collateral).

B. Key Terms

Security Interest. A security interest is an interest in personal property or fixtures which secures payment or performance of an obligation under Article 9.[2]

Goods. Goods include all things which are movable at the time security interest attaches or which are fixtures. This does not include money, documents, instruments, accounts, chattel paper, general intangibles or minerals or the like (including oil and gas) before extraction. Goods also includes standing timber which is to be cut and removed under a conveyance or contract for sale, the unborn young of animals and growing crops.[3]

Fixtures. Goods become fixtures when they become so related to a particular parcel of real estate that an interest in them arises under real estate law.[4] This means that the goods have been permanently affixed to the real property thereby becoming recognized as part of the real property under the law.

Secured Party. A secured party is either a lender, seller or other person in whose favor there is a security interest, including a person to whom accounts and chattel paper have been sold.[5]

Debtor. A debtor is a person or entity who owes payment or other performance of an obligation secured by collateral. Under Article 9, when the debtor and the owner of the collateral are not the same person, the term debtor also means the owner of the collateral.[6] So, debtor may be used to describe both the person who owes the money or performance as well as the true owner of the collateral, even if that true owner does not owe any money or performance to the secured party.

Security Agreement. The security agreement is the agreement which creates or provides for the security interest.[7]

Collateral. The collateral is the property subject to the security interest.[8]

11. Analyzing Secured Transactions

In analyzing a secured transaction, one must ask two key questions.

1. Does the creditor have an enforceable security interest in specific property of the debtor?
2. Assuming the creditor has an enforceable security interest, will the creditor take priority over the claims of other

---

2. *Id.*
3. UCC Sec. 9-105(h).

4. UCC Sec. 9-313.
5. UCC Sec. 9-105(m).
6. UCC Sec. 9-105(d).
7. UCC Sec. 9-105(1).
8. UCC Sec. 9-105(c).

creditors in the event the debtor defaults on the underlying obligation?

To reach the answer to these questions, one must determine if and when the creditor's security interest attached. If the security interest has attached, one must also determine if and when the secured party's security interest was perfected.

III. Attachment of the Security Interest

A creditor must have a security interest in the debtor's collateral before it can become a secured party. So, what does it take for a creditor to have an enforceable security interest? Three things must happen for the creation of a security interest.

1. There must be an agreement between the debtor and the creditor (a security agreement).
2. The creditor must have given something of value to the debtor.
3. The debtor must have rights in the collateral.

It takes all three elements for the creation of an enforceable security interest. When all three elements are present, the security interest is said to have "attached" at that moment. Once the security interest has attached to the collateral, the creditor has enforceable rights in the collateral. Until the point of attachment, the creditor has no rights in the collateral.

A. The Security Agreement

The debtor and creditor must agree to the terms by which the collateral is to be pledged in support of the underlying obligation. Unless the collateral is in possession of the secured party pursuant to the agreement, the Code requires that the debtor must have

signed a security agreement containing a description of the collateral. A specimen of a security agreement is presented in figure 27.1. In addition, when the security interest covers crops growing or to be grown or timber to be cut, the written security agreement must contain a description of the land concerned.[9]

The formalities of a written and signed security agreement provide reliable evidence concerning the existence of the terms of the security agreement, including the property serving a collateral. Keep in mind that a written agreement is not required when collateral is in possession of the secured party. It is logical to conclude that the presence of the collateral in the hands of the secured party is reliable evidence of the debtor's consent.

The security agreement must contain a description of the property. The description does not need to be exact but need only reasonably identify the pledged property. With respect to security agreements, a serial number or similar strict test of identification is rejected.

B. Value Given to the Debtor

The secured party must give value to the debtor in order for the security interest to attach.[10] Unlike traditional contract law, the value may be represented by a preexisting obligation. In addition, value may also be represented by an obligation to lend money. But, the obligation to lend money cannot be revocable at the will of the secured party. The obligation must be firm.

C. The Debtor Must Have Rights in the Collateral[11]

Often, the property pledged is owned or controlled by the person obligated to repay the borrowed money or otherwise perform. Col-

9. UCC Sec. 9-203(1)(a).
10. UCC Sec. 9-203(1)(b).
11. UCC Sec. 9-203(1)(c).

SECURITY AGREEMENT

Date _____ , 19 _____

(Name)	(Street Address)

(City)	(County)	(State)

hereinafter called "Debtor," hereby assigns and grants to NORTHLAND NATIONAL BANK, Northland, USA, hereinafter called "Bank," a security interest in the following described property, hereinafter called "Collateral":

(a) All inventory of Debtor, now owned or hereafter acquired;

(b) All contract rights of Debtor, now existing or hereafter arising;

(c) All accounts receivable of Debtor, now existing or hereafter arising;

(d) All instruments, documents of title, policies and certificates of insurance, securities, chattel paper, deposits, cash or other property owned by Debtor or in which it has an interest which are now or may hereafter be in possession of Bank;

(e) Proceeds and products of the foregoing.

Bank will from time to time lend Debtor on the foregoing Collateral such amounts as Bank may determine and on such terms as Bank may specify, but the aggregate unpaid principal of all of such loans outstanding at any one time shall not exceed _____% of the lower of cost or market of all inventory owned by Debtor, plus _____% of the unpaid face amount of qualified accounts receivable, together with such amount on Debtor's contract rights as Bank may from time to time determine.

The security interest granted is given to secure an advance of $_____ evidenced by a promissory note executed and delivered by Debtor to Bank dated, _____, 19_____, together with all liailities of all kinds of Debtor to Bank whether created directly or acquired by Bank by assignment or otherwise, and whether now existing or hereafter arising, absolute or contingent, joint or several, due or to become due.

DEBTOR EXPRESSLY WARRANTS AND COVENANTS:

1. Debtor will not agree to any material modification of any of the terms of any of his or its accounts receivable or contracts without the written consent of Bank. Debtor will not sell, encumber or otherwise dispose of inventory except in the ordinary course of business without the written consent of Bank.

2. Bank shall have the right to notify account and contract debtors obligated on any or all of the Collateral to make payment thereof directly to Bank and Bank may take control of all proceeds of any of the Collateral, which rights Bank may exercise at any time whether or not Debtor is then in default. Until such time as Bank elects to exercise such rights. Debtor is authorized, as agent of Bank, to collect and enforce all such contracts and accounts. The cost of such collection and enforcement, including attorney fees and expenses shall be borne by Debtor whether the same is incurred by Bank or Debtor.

3. Debtor will upon receipt of checks, drafts, cash, and other remittances in payment or on account of Debtor's accounts receivable or contract rights or received as proceeds of inventory, deposit all of the same in a special bank account maintained with Bank over which Bank alone has power of withdrawal. The funds in said account shall be held by Bank as security for all loans made hereunder and all other indebtedness of Debtor to Bank. Said proceeds shall be deposited in precisely the form received, except for the endorsement of Debtor where necessary to permit collection of items, which endorsement Debtor agrees to make, and which Bank is also authorized to make on Debtor's behalf.

4. Except for the security interest granted hereby, Debtor is, and as to inventory to be hereafter acquired, shall be, the owner of the inventory free from any lien, security interest or encumbrance, and Debtor shall defend the inventory and proceeds and products thereof against all claims and demands of all persons at any time claiming the same or any interest therein adverse to Bank.

Secured Transactions

5. Debtor will insure all inventory with companies acceptable to Bank against such account of Debtor's accounts receivable or contract rights insurance policies shall be written for the benefit of Debtor and Bank as their interests may appear, and such policies or certificates evidencing the same shall be furnished to Bank. All policies or insurance shall provide at least ten (10) days prior written notice of cancellation to Bank.

EVENTS OF DEFAULT. Debtor shall be in default under this agreement upon the happening of the following events or conditions:

1. Default in the payment of performance of any obligation, covenant or liability contained or referred to herein;
2. Any warranty, representation, or statement made or furnished to Bank by or in behalf of Debtor proves to have been false in any material respect when made or furnished;
3. Any event which results in the acceleration of the maturity of the indebtedness of Debtor to others under any indenture, agreement or undertaking;
4. Any time the Bank believes that the prospect of payment of any indebtedness secured hereby or the performance of this agreement is impaired; or
5. Death, dissolution, termination of existence, insolvency, business failure, appointment of a receiver over any substantial part of Debtor's property or any part of the Collateral. assignment for the benefit of creditors or the commencement of any proceeding under any bankruptcy or insolvency law by or against Debtor or any guarantor or surety for Debtor.

REMEDIES. Upon such default and at any time, thereafter, Bank may declare all obligations secured hereby immediately due and payable, and may proceed to enforce payment of the same and exercise any and all of the rights and remedies provided by the Uniform Commercial Code as well as other rights and remedies possessed by Bank. Bank shall be entitled to the immediate possession of all books and records evidencing the accounts and contract rights covered by this agreement and shall have authority to enter upon any premises on which the same may be situated and remove the same therefrom. Bank will give Debtor reasonable notice of the time and place of any public sale of the Collateral or of the time after which any private sale or any intended disposition thereof is to be made. The requirement of reasonable notice shall be met if notice is mailed, postage prepaid to the address of Debtor shown at the beginning of this agreement, at least 10 days before the time of sale or disposition.

EXPENSES. Debtor shall be liable for and agrees to pay to Bank any and all expenses incurred or paid by Bank in protecting or enforcing its rights under this agreement including reasonable attorneys' fees and legal expenses.

WAIVERS. No waiver by Bank of any default shall operate as a waiver or any other default and the terms of this agreement shall be binding upon the heirs, executors, administrators, successors and assigns of the parties hereto.

Signed and delivered the day and year first above written.

SECURED PARTY;   DEBTOR:

NORTHLAND NATIONAL BANK   _____
Northland, USA   (Name)

                                                           _____
By_____   (Name)
     (Name)   (Title)   _____
                                                           (Corporate or partnership name)
722   _____
                                                           (Name)   (Title)

Example. The description "my computer" is sufficient if the debtor has only one computer. If the debtor has more than one, such a description is not sufficient. ☐

* * *

Example. A hardware store may desire to borrow money from a bank to purchase new display fixtures. Once the debtor has the right to gain possession of those fixtures, even prior to actual possession, this element of the attachment test has been met. ☐

* * *

Example. Mary seeks to borrow $10,000 to buy new equipment for her new accounting practice. The bank has informed Mary that it will not make the loan unless additional collateral is pledged. Mary receives the assistance of her Aunt Margaret, who agrees to pledge her Porsche automobile as collateral. Under Article 9, both Mary and her Aunt are considered debtors, even though Mary's Aunt Margaret is not obligated on the loan. Because Aunt Margaret owns the automobile, she has rights in the collateral, meeting the third requirement for attachment. ☐

lateral may also come from a third party, such as a friend, family member, or business associate who is motivated to assist the completion of the transaction by pledging collateral. This employs the Code's duel use of the word "debtor," meaning the person obligated on the debt as well as a person pledging property as collateral. In either event, debtor must have rights in the collateral to meet this requirement.

D. Purchase Money Security Interest

A purchase money security interest (PMSI) is a special type of security interest. A purchase money security interest arises when someone borrows money to buy goods or fixtures that will also serve as the collateral to support the loan. A bank loan to purchase inventory that will be pledged as collateral represents a purchase money security interest. Buying goods from a manufacturer on credit with the manufacturer retaining a security interest in the goods represents a purchase money security interest.

E. After Acquired Property as Collateral

As a general rule, a valid security agreement may create an interest in property to be acquired in the future. The interest will attach to the property as soon as the debtor acquires an interest in the collateral. This collateral includes proceeds from the sale of existing collateral and "floating liens" which cover aggregations of specific items that are continually changing.

Examples of collateral subject to floating liens include inventory and accounts receivable. This technique is commonly employed in inventory financing. A manufacturer or merchant may borrow money from a lender who in turn receives a security interest in all of the debtor's inventory and/or accounts receivable. The size of the lien floats with the increases and decreases in inventory and receivables. Security interests creating floating liens contain "after-acquired property clauses." This type of clause states that the debtor is pledging, for example, all of its inventory "presently owned and hereafter acquired."

There is an exception with respect to after acquired property clauses. After acquired property clauses are ineffective with regard to consumer goods (other than accessions) when given as additional collateral, unless the debtor acquires rights in the goods within 10 days after the creditor gives value.

A security interest can cover future advances of credit and cash by the secured party. Commercial debtors often arrange for continuing lines of credit with lenders. These lines of credit permit debtors to borrow up to certain limits, with full repayment due upon a certain date. Future advances clauses are often used in conjunction with after acquired property clauses to provide debtors with flexibility in borrowing within a predetermined range, while giving the secured party more collateral coverage as the debt increases.

F. Classification of Collateral

Collateral under Article 9 can be classified into tangible versus intangible collateral. In addition, some collateral falls into a special class identified as "proceeds."

1. TANGIBLE COLLATERAL

Tangible collateral includes all things that are moveable at the time the security interest attaches. This also includes fixtures that are subsequently attached to real property. There are four types of tangible collateral:[12]

a. **Consumer goods**. These are good used primarily for personal, family or household purposes.
b. **Farm products**. This category includes crops, livestock, or supplies used or produced in farming operations.
c. **Inventory.** Goods held for sale or lease or to be furnished under a contract are deemed inventory.
d. **Equipment.** These are goods used or purchased for use primarily in business. This is a catch-all category. If tangible collateral does not fit within the

---

12. UCC Sec. 9-109.

other three categories, it is usually considered equipment. At times, equipment will be divided into farm and nonfarm equipment.

2. INTANGIBLE COLLATERAL

There are five types of intangible collateral. They are:

a. **Instruments**. This category includes promissory notes, bills of exchange, stocks, bonds, and similar items.
b. **Documents of Title**. Bills of lading, warehouse receipts and other papers evidencing a right to possess or control goods falls into this classification.
c. **Accounts**. Any right to payment not evidenced by an instrument, whether or not it has been earned by performance, will be deemed an account.
d. **Chattel Paper.** Chattel paper is a writing (or package of writings) evidencing both a monetary obligation and a security interest in specific goods, excluding the charter of vessels.
e. **General Intangibles**. This is the catch-all category of intangible collateral. Any intangible collateral not falling within the scope of the other classifications will be deemed a general intangible. General intangibles include patents, trademark rights and copyrights.

3. PROCEEDS

Proceeds differ from other types of collateral in that proceeds constitute any collateral that has changed in form from a previous category. If a merchant has pledged her inventory as collateral, the money received in exchange for that collateral will be considered proceeds of the pledged inventory. When the debtor disposes of collateral and receives something in return, the property received will be deemed proceeds.

Example. If an automobile dealership has a pickup truck for sale on its lot, it will be considered inventory to that dealer. But, if it is purchased by an individual for personal driving purposes, it will be considered a consumer good. If a hardware store purchases a pickup truck from the dealer for the purpose of making deliveries, the pickup truck will be classified as equipment. If a farmer purchases a pickup truck for use on a farm it will be considered farm equipment.

Insurance payable resulting from loss or damage to the collateral will be considered proceeds, except when it is payable to third persons and not to the secured party.[13]

4. CLASSIFICATION OF COLLATERAL MAY DEPEND UPON ITS USE

In determining the type of collateral, one must examine the relationship of the debtor to the collateral. What is inventory to a merchant may be a consumer good to an individual and equipment to an enterprise.

IV. Perfecting a Security Interest

A creditor's goal in obtaining a security interest is to provide security to support the loan in the event that the debtor defaults. But, the secured party may have to compete for its interest in the collateral with a number of adverse parties, including purchasers of the collateral from the debtor, other creditors of the debtor (secured and unsecured, and possibly the debtor's trustee in bankruptcy), and other priority creditors, such as common law and statutory lien holders, as well as federal, state and local lien holders.

It would not serve the interests of a lender to obtain a security interest in collateral that could be taken by competing parties to satisfy their claims first. To bring order to the marketplace, a system of rules exists under Article 9 for determining which party will have ulti-

mate priority to satisfy its claim against the collateral. This system determines the order that the remaining parties may rightfully assert claims against the collateral, should any value exist after the claim of the first party is satisfied.

This system of priorities is based upon a concept known as "perfection" of a security interest. Perfection of a security interest is the key to a secured party being able to satisfy its claim against the collateral in the event the debtor defaults. While attachment deals with enforceability, perfection determines priority. If a secured party does not take steps to perfect its security interest as soon as possible, another secured party may be entitled to possession and disposal of the collateral upon the debtor's default.

There are a few circumstances when a perfected, nonpossessory security interest will be subordinated to the claim of another party. These will be examined later in this chapter. In some cases, perfection is automatic, needing no further action on the part of the secured party. However, in most cases, perfection requires either filing a financing statement with the proper public authority or taking possession of the collateral.

A. Methods of Perfection

Perfection may be accomplished a number of different ways. In some circumstances, perfection may be completed by more than one method. In other circumstances, perfection must be accomplished by a single specified method. Each method and its appropriate application are discussed below.

---

13. UCC Sec. 9-306(1).

Example. The description of real property standard would be met with a description such as "The air conditioning system affixed to the building located at 900 E. College Ave., Norman, Ok."

I. PERFECTION BY FILING

A security interest in any type of collateral, except negotiable instruments and other writings which normally require delivery in order to transfer the obligation (such as stock certificates and checks), may be perfected by filing a public notice of the security interest.[14]

a. Filing the Financing Statement

The Code requires "notice" filing. It does not require that a copy or abstract of the actual security agreement be filed. Notice is given to the world by filing a "financing statement" having certain specified elements.[15] A financing statement is also referred to as a "UCC–1" or a "UCC form 1." A specimen is presented in figure 27.2.

The required elements of a financing statement are:

1. The signature of the debtor.
2. The address of the secured party from whom information concerning the collateral may be obtained.
3. The mailing address of the debtor.
4. A description of the types of or the items of collateral.

It is very important that the secured party carefully describe the collateral in the financing statement. While an exact description is not required, the description must be sufficient to adequately inform inquiring parties of the collateral encumbered. If the collateral is crops or fixtures, the financing statement must also contain a description of the loca-

tion of the real estate where the crops or fixtures are located. But, the real estate description need not be the exact legal description one would find on a title deed. The description need only contain enough detail to sufficiently identify the land.

It is acceptable for the security agreement itself to be filed as the financing statement. If the secured party chooses to file the security agreement, it must examine it to be sure that all of the required elements are met. In a similar fashion, a purported real estate mortgage listing fixtures and containing all of the elements of a financing statement will be effective as a financing statement for perfecting a security interest in fixtures.

b. The Place of Filing

The Code is specific with respect to where financing statements shall be filed. The place of filing for each state is designated by each state's legislature in its adoption of Article 9 of the Code. The version of Article 9 for each state designates the office of a certain public official as the proper place for "central filing" as well as the office of a public official in each county or parish to accomplish "local" filing. It is important to classify the collateral with respect to its place of filing, either central or local. Many states designate their Secretaries of State as the proper officials to receive financing statements that must be centrally filed. Locally filed financing statements vary according to state, including the Clerk of the county court, the county Registrar of Deeds or the county recorder's office.

To accommodate the wide variety of state notice systems involving the various types of col-

---

14. UCC Sec. 9-302, 9-304.
15. UCC Sec. 9-402.

PARTIES

Debtor name (last name first if individual) and mailing address:

1

Debtor name (last name first if individual) and mailing address:

1a

Debtor name (last name first if individual) and mailing address:

1b

Secured Party(ies) name(s) (last name first if individual) and address for security interest information:

2

Assignee(s) of Secured Party name(s) (last name first if individual) and address for security interest information:

2a

Special Types of Parties (check if applicable):

☐ The terms 'Debtor' and 'Secured Party' mean 'Lessee' and 'Lessor', respectively.

☐ The terms 'Debtor' and 'Secured Party' mean 'Consignee' and 'Consignor' respectively.

☐ Debtor is a Transmitting Utility.

3

SECURED PARTY SIGNATURE(S)

This statement is filed with only the **Secured Party's signature** to perfect a security interest in collateral (check applicable box(es))-

a. ☐ acquired after a **change of name, identity, or corporate structure** of the Debtor.

b. ☐ as to which the **filing has lapsed.**

c. already subject to a security interest in **another county** in Pennsylvania -

☐ when the collateral was moved to this country.

☐ when the Debtor's residence or place of business was moved to this county

d. already subject to a security interest in **another jurisdiction** -

☐ when the **collateral was moved** to Pennsylvania

☐ when the **Debtor's location was moved** to Pennsylvania

e. which is **proceeds** of the collateral described in block 9, in which a security interest was previously perfected (also described proceeds in block 9, if purchased with cash proceeds and not adequately described on the original financing statement.)

Secured Party Signature(s)
(required only if box(es) us checked above):

_____

_____

_____

4

STANDARD FORM - FORM UCC-1
Approved by Secretary of Commonwealth of Pennsylvania

FINANCING STATEMENT
FINANCING STATEMENT
Uniform Commercial Code Form UCC-1

Filing No. (stamped by filing officer):   Date, Time, Filing Office (stamped by filing officer):

5

This **Financing Statement** is presented for filing pursuant to the Uniform Commercial Code, and is to be filed with the (check applicable box):

☐ Secretary of the Commonwealth.

☐ Prothonotary of _____ County.

☐ real estate records of _____ County.

6

Number of Additional Sheets (if any):

7

Optional Special Identification (Max. 10 characters):

8

COLLATERAL

Identify collateral by item and/or type:

(check only if desired) Products of the collateral are also covered.

9

Identify related real estate, if applicable: The collateral is or includes (check appropriate box(es)) -

a. ☐ **crops** growing or to be grown on -

b. ☐ **goods** which are or are to become **fixtures** on -

c. ☐ **minerals** or the like (including oil and gas) as extracted on -

d. ☐ **accounts resulting from the sale of minerals** or the like (including oil and gas) at the wellhead or minehead on -

the following real estate:

Street Address:

Described at: Book ___ of (check one) ☐ Deeds ☐ Mortgages,
at Page(s)_____

for _____ County. Uniform Parcel Identifier _____

☐ Described on Additional Sheet.

Name of record owner (required only if no Debtor has an interest of record):

10

DEBTOR SIGNATURE(S)

Debtor Signature(s):

1 _____

1a _____

1b _____

11

RETURN RECEIPT TO:

12

727

lateral, the drafters of Article 9 provided three different alternatives for the states to adopt.[16]

Each student is encouraged to examine Section 9-401 of the Code to compare and contrast these three systems. Most states follow this system of classification:

1. **Consumer goods or farm related collateral**. If the collateral is consumer goods, farm equipment, farm products, farm accounts or general intangibles related to a sale of farm products by a farmer, the filing is accomplished locally in the county where the goods are located.

2. **Fixtures**. If the collateral is or will become a fixture, filing must occur in the office where a lien on real estate would be filed. In some cases, the secured party may not be certain whether or not the particular collateral will qualify as a fixture. In those cases, it is prudent to file the financing statement in the real estate records and at the place designated for fixtures under Article 9.

3. **All Other Cases**. In all other cases, including all business collateral (except fixtures), the filing must take place at the central location designated by the state.

4. **Filing at the Improper Place**. Should the secured party file the financing statement at the wrong office, it will be deemed ineffective except as to those persons who have actual knowledge of the contents of the financing statement. Therefore, if a competing creditor obtains information regarding the existence of an improperly filed financing statement, it will be charged with the same notice it would have received had the financing statement been properly filed.

---

16. UCC Sec. 9-401(1).

c. How Long is the Filing Effective?

The original filing of a financing statement is effective for five years.[17] There is an exception for real estate mortgages that are filed for perfecting security interests in fixtures. This type of filing remains effective until the mortgage is released or satisfied.

d. Continuation Statements

A continuation statement may be filed during the last six months of the effective period of a prior filing. This will continue the effectiveness of the filing for five more years from the original date of filing. The signature of the debtor is not required. The secured party may sign it alone. There is no limit as to how many times a financing statement's effectiveness may be continued, so long as the underlying obligation remains valid.

e. Cancellation of Financing Statements

Once the debtor has repaid the debt and the secured party has no obligation to make further advances, the secured party must, upon demand of the debtor, provide the debtor with a termination statement within ten days. In the case of consumer goods, the secured party must file the termination statement within one month of the satisfaction of the debt, or within ten days if the debtor demands it in writing.

2. MOTOR VEHICLES AND CERTIFICATES OF TITLE

Most states issue certificates of title to evidence ownership of motor vehicles, such as automobiles and motorcycles. The Code recognizes the existence of these state laws. It provides those states with an option of requiring perfection through a certificate of title lien entry system. This involves the secured party taking possession of the certificate of title and transmitting it with the appropriate documentation to the motor vehicle regulatory

---

17. UCC Sec. 9-403.

body of that state. The state official will enter the existence of the lien on the face of the certificate of title.

Under a lien entry system, a potential purchaser of a vehicle will need only to examine the face of the certificate of title to see if it is encumbered by a lien. In a state is using a lien entry system under a certificate of title law, filing a financing statement under Article 9 is neither required nor effective for any person or entity using a motor vehicle.

But, security interests created by dealers in motor vehicles held as inventory for sale are still perfected under ordinary Article 9 rules even though a certificate of title covering each vehicle may exist.

Security interests in domestic aircraft and rolling stock are perfected according to federal law with the appropriate federal agencies.

3. PERFECTION BY TAKING POSSESSION OF THE COLLATERAL

It is not necessary for a secured party, or a bailee for a secured party, to file a financing statement if the secured party or her bailee has possession of the collateral, including goods, negotiable instruments, documents of title or chattel paper.[18]

If this method is employed, the time of perfection will depend upon whether the secured party is actually in possession of the collateral or whether the collateral is in the hands of a bailee.

If the secured party takes actual possession of the collateral, perfection occurs from the moment of possession and continues as long as possession is retained. If the collateral is in the hands of a bailee, a secured party is deemed perfected at the moment the bailee receives notice of the secured party's interest.

A security interest in money or instruments (other than certificated securities or instruments which constitute part of chattel paper)

can be perfected only by taking possession of the collateral, subject to temporary perfection exceptions.[19] This section of Article 9 was amended to coordinate with a change made to Article 8 of the Code which governs investment securities. Perfection of an interest in an investment security, whether or not a certificate has been issued to evidence of its existence, is governed by Section 8-321 of the Code. This section holds that perfection of a security interest requires transfer of the security to the secured creditor or the secured creditor's nominee. Once the transfer is made, the security interest attaches. Once the secured creditor has given value, it has a perfected security interest. Because it is impossible to have a security interest attach without having given value, attachment and perfection under this section of Article 8 take place at the same time.

The transfer of a security to the secured party or the nominee requires either possession of the certificate or its functional equivalent. The transfer of an certificated security to a secured party occurs upon the registration of the security in the name of that party by the issuer; or at the time a financial intermediary, not a clearing corporation, enters the transfer on its books and sends confirmation of the transfer to the secured party. For uncertificated securities, this is the functional equivalent of the secured party's possession.

For those jurisdictions not recognizing the 1977 amendments to Article 8 with respect to certificated and uncertificated securities, perfection of a security represented by a certificate requires the secured party to obtain possession of the certificate.

4. AUTOMATIC PERFECTION

Under certain circumstances, neither filing a financing statement nor possession of the collateral is required for the secured party to have a perfected security interest. Automatic

---

18. UCC Sec. 9-305.

19. UCC Sec. 9-304.

perfection takes place in situations where possession of the collateral is not feasible and public filing of notice would impose an undue burden on the recording system. Automatic perfection was created to address those instances when the benefits of public notice are outweighed by the undue burden that would be placed upon the recording system. The automatic perfection rules are limited in that they apply to only certain types of collateral; they are often limited in duration; and they sometimes fail to protect the secured party against all third party claimants.

a. Purchase Money Security Interests in Consumer Goods

A purchase money security interest in consumer goods is perfected as soon as it attaches. Filing a financing statement or taking possession of the collateral is not required for perfection. A seller has a purchase money security interest when the security interest was taken to secure repayment of the purchase price. A person other than the seller has a purchase money security interest when the security interest was taken to secure a loan of money (or other value) to the debtor to enable the debtor to purchase the collateral, provided that the debtor uses the money to acquire the collateral.

There are exceptions to this rule. Filing a financing statement is always required with respect to fixtures. Those states using lien entry systems for motor vehicles requiring certificates of title do not fall within this rule of automatic perfection.[20]

By allowing automatic perfection with respect to consumer goods, a costly burden is lifted from sellers of consumer goods. Merchants often sell items on credit that cost very little in comparison to the cost burden that would be placed upon the filing system if those interests had to be filed for perfection.

Secured creditors relying upon automatic perfection of purchase money security interests in consumer goods run some risks. For instance, a third party who purchases the collateral from the debtor, intending to use the item for personal, family or household purposes, not knowing that the security interest exists, will take the item free of the security interest unless a financing statement was filed prior to the purchase.[21] Most credit sellers, such as the nation's major department store chains, find the cost of the documentation and filing such interests too costly to justify perfection by filing. These enterprises assume the risk that a certain percentage of the collateral perfected by automatic possession will be lost in a number of ways, including to third party purchasers.

b. Small Scale Assignments of Accounts

A security interest is automatically perfected in an assignment of accounts which do not alone, or in conjunction with other assignments to the same assignee, transfer a significant part of the outstanding accounts of the assignor.[22] This section is designed to exempt from filing casual or isolated assignments of a single account or a small group of accounts under circumstances not related to business financing. This is a very limited exception to the filing requirement.

c. Proceeds

Perfection of an interest in proceeds of the original collateral remains valid in most situations involving a proper perfection of the original interest by filing. This includes identifiable cash proceeds.[23] But, in certain situations, a filing does not automatically cover proceeds:[24]

---

20. UCC Sec. 9-302.

21. UCC Sec. 9-307(2).
22. UCC Sec. 9-302(1)(e).
23. UCC Sec. 9-306(3)(b).
24. UCC Sec. 9-306(3).

First, if the proceeds are collateral of the type requiring perfection by filing in a different office than the original place of filing, then a proper filing in that office is required to continue the perfection.

Second, if cash proceeds are used to acquire collateral of a different description than those described in the original filing, then a new filing is necessary.

In the event the perfection in the proceeds does not continue automatically, the interest will remain perfected for 10 days following the debtor's receipt of the proceeds. If the debtor properly perfects the interest (by any manner permissible under the Code) prior to expiration of the 10 day period, the original interest remains perfected. If not, the interest becomes unperfected.

5. TEMPORARY PERFECTION

a. Special Cases Involving Instruments or Documents

There are two situations involving security interests in instruments (not including certificated securities which are controlled by 8-321) or documents of title in which the secured party will be temporarily perfected for a 21 day grace period.

First, a security interest in instruments (other than certificated securities) or negotiable documents of title will be perfected automatically for a 21 day period following attachment of the interest so long as it arose (1) in exchange for new value and (2) pursuant to a written security agreement.[25]

Second, a party with a perfected interest in instruments or documents of title through possession will retain that interest for a 21 day period following the relinquishment of possession so long as the delivery of the collateral was to permit the debtor (1) to sell or exchange the goods covered by the documents; or to store, load, unload, ship, process or oth-

erwise deal with the goods in a manner preliminary to their sale or exchange; or (2) to sell, exchange, present or collect the instrument.[26] This rule recognizes that there are times when instruments or documents of title need to be released to the debtor for a very short period of time to complete matters necessary to their purpose.

Unless the secured party gains possession of the instrument or document or otherwise properly perfects its interest prior to the expiration of the 21 day period, the interest will be unperfected. In addition, if an instrument or document of title is negotiated to a holder in due course during the 21 day period, the rights of the secured party are cut off in favor of the holder.[27]

b. Moving Collateral to Another State

Where collateral is taken from one state to another, perfection in the first state remains valid for four months after the collateral was taken to the second state. Remember that collateral subject to lien entry on a certificate of title remains perfected so long as the evidence of the lien appears on the face of the title.

While the four month rule may appear unfair, imagine the burden that would be placed upon the business community if the records of each county of all fifty states had to be checked to ensure that the collateral was not subject to any other liens was true. The system places responsibility upon the secured creditor for monitoring the location of the collateral. While this places some burden and risk upon the existing secured creditors, the chilling effect that would result from the lack of such a rule would far outweigh the benefit in the domestic lending market.

25. UCC Sec. 9-304(4).

26. UCC Sec. 9-304(5).
27. UCC Sec. 9-309.

Example. On March 2, the Hardy Corporation borrows money from the First National Bank giving a security interest in its automated welding machine. On March 3, Hardy Corporation makes a contract to sell the equipment to Mann Manufacturing, who pays the contract price. Mann is unaware of the security interest granted to First National Bank. On March 4, the First National Bank properly files a financing statement, perfecting the security interest. On March 5, Mann Manufacturing takes delivery of the equipment. In this case, the First National Bank will prevail over Mann Manufacturing because even though the purchaser paid for the item prior to the bank perfecting its security interest by filing, it did not take possession prior to that date.

If Mann Manufacturing had both paid for the item and received delivery prior to perfection, the bank would be without recourse to recover its collateral. [28]

28. UCC Sec. 9-301(1)(c).

B. Priorities Between Conflicting Interests

The overriding purpose of Article 9 is to provide a system for allocating rights and priorities between conflicting interests. Conflicts may arise between a secured party and the purchaser of the collateral, a lien creditor (often a bankruptcy trustee) or another secured party. Article 9 provides a framework for resolving these disputes. This provides lenders and other creditors a basis for structuring secured transactions to protect their collateral rights while avoiding these conflicts.

C. The Danger of not Perfecting the Security Interest

As a general rule, a buyer will prevail against an unperfected security interest if the buyer is without knowledge of the interest, gives value and receives delivery of the collateral prior to its perfection.

With respect to general intangibles and the sale of accounts (not treated as creating a security interest), a buyer in good faith and without knowledge of an unperfected security interest is protected against an unperfected interest. There is no requirement that the purchaser take delivery prior to perfection.

A bankruptcy trustee and other lien creditors will prevail over an unsecured security interest in collateral if the bankruptcy petition was filed or the rights of the lien creditor came into existence prior to the perfection of the security interest.

It is important to note that a purchase money security interest will be given 10 days from the date the collateral, other than inventory, comes into possession of the debtor to perfect the security interest. If the interest is perfected, it will prevail over a bankruptcy trustee, other lien creditor, or other perfected security interests. Some states have adopted grace periods of greater than 10 days for the perfection of purchase money security interests.

If two or more secured creditors are competing for the same collateral and none have perfected their security interests, the priority of payment will be established according to the date each security interest attached.[29]

29. UCC Sec. 9-312(5)(b).

Example. Harold's Inc., a men's and women's clothing store, has given the Second National Bank a security interest in its inventory of sweaters to secure its loan. Harold's sells one of these sweaters to Lauren. Lauren knows that the bank has a security interest in Harold's inventory of sweaters. Even so, Lauren takes free of the bank's security interest because she is entitled to assume that the agreement between the bank and Harold's permits such sales.

In the unlikely event that the bank had an agreement with Harold's that permission must be obtained for the release each sweater, Lauren would take her purchased item subject to the bank's security interest if she was aware that her purchase was a violation of the agreement. When collateral is expensive per item and the volume of sales is small, lenders will often require financially weak borrowers to obtain permission prior to releasing the collateral to a buyer. A buyer in the ordinary course of business, acting in good faith, will only take the collateral subject to a perfected security interest if that buyer had specific knowledge that the seller was violating a security agreement with respect to that particular sale. ▢

D. Conflicts Between Perfected Security Interests

1. PERFECTED SECURITY INTERESTS VERSUS BUYERS

As a general rule, a perfected security interest in goods (not including nonpossessory interests in negotiable instruments or chattel paper) will prevail against subsequent buyers.[30] But, in a few instances, a buyer will defeat even the rights of a perfected secured party.

The first exception relates to buyers in the ordinary course of business. A buyer who purchases goods from a seller who is engaged in the business of selling goods of that kind (except a person buying farm products from a farmer) takes the goods free of the perfected security interest, even if the buyer is aware of the perfected security interest, unless he also knows that the sale is in violation of the terms of the security agreement.

A second exception applies to consumer goods. Recall that purchase money security interests in consumer goods are perfected automatically. However, an individual who purchases an item for personal, family or household purposes takes it free from security interests if the purchase was made without knowledge of the security interest and before the filing of a financing statement. Therefore, while a holder of a purchase money security interest in goods is perfected against lien creditors and other security interests without filing a financing statement, the security interest is not enforceable against a consumer purchaser unless a financing statement had been filed.[31]

2. SPECIAL RULES FOR FARM PRODUCTS

In 1985, Congress passed the Food Security Act of 1985[32] which provides protection for the purchasers of farm products. This federal law supervenes the Code's treatment of this subject matter in each state. Under this law, one who, in the ordinary course of business, buys farm products from a seller engaged in farming operations takes them free of any security interest created by the seller, even if the security interest had been perfected under Article 9 and the buyer was aware of it.

A similar rule protects commission merchants and selling agents who sell farm products for others in the ordinary course of busi-

---

30. UCC Sec. 9-301, 9-307.

31. UCC Sec. 9-307.
32. 7 USC 1631.

ness. Under the Food Security Act, a secured party can protect itself by giving advance notice of the security interests to the purchasers, commission merchants, or selling agents. Notice may be given directly by the secured party. In addition, the statute permits states to establish an optional central filing system, which generates statewide lists of security interests that are furnished to prospective purchasers, commission merchants, or selling agents. A number of states have adopted these central filing systems which are separate sets of records apart from other UCC filings.

3. PERFECTED SECURITY INTERESTS VERSUS LIEN CREDITORS

A person who becomes a lien creditor while a security interest is perfected, takes the collateral subject to the security interest to the extent that it secures advances made before the competing party became a lien creditor, or within 45 days thereafter, or to the extent advances were made without the knowledge of the lien or pursuant to a commitment entered into without knowledge of the lien.[33]

4. PRIORITY CONFLICTS BETWEEN PERFECTED INTERESTS

Competing perfected security interests are ranked according to their time of perfection. The collateral will be applied to satisfy the first security interest perfected. If proceeds remain after satisfaction of a prior perfected interest, the remaining value will be applied to the next interest in line.

Priority dates from the earlier of the time the financing statement was filed[34] or the time the security interest was first perfected, provided that there was no intervening period during which the interest was unperfected, either

through a lapse in the filing or loss of possession of the collateral.[35]

5. SPECIAL PRIORITY RULES

a. Purchase Money Security Interests

A purchase money security interest in inventory has priority over a conflicting security interest in the same collateral if:

1. It was perfected at the time the debtor obtained possession of the collateral; and

2. Any secured party who had a previously perfected security interest in the same collateral received written notification of the purchase money security interest before the debtor received possession of the inventory. This notification must state that the purchase money party has or expects to take a purchase money security interest in inventory of the debtor described by kind or type.

b. Purchase Money Security Interests Not Involving Inventory

A purchase money security interest in non-inventory collateral has priority over conflicting security interests in the same collateral or its proceeds if the interest was perfected prior to or within ten days following the debtor receiving possession of the collateral. There is no requirement that the secured party notify other holders of security interests. Some states have extended the ten day period to as much as thirty days for the perfection of purchase money security interests.[36]

---

33. UCC Sec. 9-301(4).
34. A secured party may file a financing statement prior to the attachment of the security interest. It will not be valid until attachment.

---

35. UCC Sec. 9-312(5)(a).
36. UCC Sec. 9-312(4).

Example. On November 1, the Second National Bank made a loan to Ozzy's Record Store and took a security interest in Ozzy's existing inventory and all after acquired inventory. A financing Statement was filed, perfecting the interest. On December 1, the Third National Bank promised to loan Ozzy $10,000 to purchase a special lot of compact disks. The Third National Bank immediately filed a financing statement and notified the Second National Bank of the impending loan and its purchase money interest. The loan was made to Ozzy, who endorsed the Third National Bank loan proceeds check over to the compact disk distributor in exchange for the compact disks. The Third National Bank's purchase money security interest has priority over the Second National Bank's after acquired property interests in the inventory purchased with the loan proceeds. ☐

E. Conflicting Interests in Fixtures and Accessions

Article 9 provides special rules concerning the priority of a security interest in fixtures over a security interest in the real estate to which the fixtures were attached; and the priority of a security interest and in an accession over a security interest in the personal property to which it was attached.

1. Fixtures

A party with a prior perfected interest in a fixture will prevail over a subsequent real estate interest. This means a fixture filing is good against a subsequent real estate mortgage or deed of trust. Mortgages, deeds of trust or other real estate interests appearing in the land records prior to a fixture filing will prevail over the interest in the fixture. But, there are exceptions:

a. A purchase money security interest perfected within the ten day grace period will prevail over all real estate interests, even prior filed real estate interests.
b. A construction mortgage has priority over a security interest in fixtures to be installed during construction, even purchase money security interests, so long as the construction mortgage was recorded before the goods

became fixtures if the goods became fixtures before the completion of the construction.[37]

A fixture filing, as opposed to a regular UCC filing under Article 9, is not required for the perfection of an interest in fixtures under any of the following circumstances:

(a) The collateral is a readily moveable office or factory machine. A regular UCC filing is sufficient under the circumstances.

(b) The collateral is a readily removable replacement of a domestic appliance that constitutes consumer goods.

(c) The owner of the real property and the real estate mortgagee agree in writing to permit the holder of the security interest in the fixture to retain a superior claim.

(d) If the debtor has the right to move the fixtures over the objection of the real estate owner, the attached security interest has priority. For instance, a debtor has a right to remove her trade fixtures. Therefore, an attached security interest in the trade fixtures will have priority over the real estate mortgage holder and the building's owner.

---

37. UCC Sec. 9-313(6).

2. ACCESSIONS

An accession is something attached to an item of personal property that was not originally a part of the collateral. A security interest in an item before it was attached to another article of personal property takes priority over a security interest in the item to which it was affixed or included. This priority exists even if the security interest is unperfected. All that is necessary to maintain the priority is that the security interest attached before the collateral was affixed to other chattel.

There are exceptions to this general rule. First, a subsequent advance made by the holder of a prior security interest in the main chattel will take priority over a security interest in the accession if the subsequent advance was made or contracted for without knowledge of the security interest in the accession and prior to any perfection of the security interest in the accession.

Second, an unperfected prior interest can be cut off by lien creditors, buyers, or takers of the security interest who acquire their interests without knowledge of the security interest in the accession and before it was perfected.

V. The Secured Party's Rights upon the Debtor's Default

Article 9 does not define default. In the context of Article 9, the plain meaning of the word default is that the debtor has failed to live up to its obligations respecting the borrowing agreement or the security agreement.

Parties are free to specifically define events of default in both the promissory note and the security agreement. In either event, failure to make scheduled payments constitutes an event of default. Parties may agree that the debtor's bankruptcy will be an event of default. The secured party may seek language of default that includes discovery of fraudulent misrepresentations on the debtor's loan ap-

plication and supporting documents as well as the debtor's failure to properly maintain the collateral.

A. To Take Possession and Dispose of the Collateral

1. POSSESSION

The secured party may take possession of the collateral upon default by self help or with the assistance of the courts. If the secured party attempts to take possession of the collateral by self help, it must do so without breaching the peace.

If the secured party desires to gain possession of the collateral with the use of the courts, it must petition a court for an order directing the debtor to turn the collateral over to the secured party. The order is often issued in the form of a writ of replevin. Prior to the debtor being required to relinquish possession of the collateral, a court must give the debtor notice and an opportunity for a hearing to dispute the secured creditor's claim.

2. SELLING THE COLLATERAL

Disposal of the collateral may be either by public sale (often at auction) or private sale, and by one or more contracts.

The general test as to the validity of the sale is commercial reasonableness at to method, manner, time, place and terms.[38] The mere fact that a better price could have been obtained from a sale at a different time or in a different manner is not sufficient to establish that the sale was not commercially reasonable. A sale will be deemed to have been conducted in a commercially reasonable manner if it was in the usual manner in a recognized market or at the market price in such a market at the time of the sale.

The sale was commercially reasonable if it conformed with reasonable commercial stan-

---

38. UCC Sec. 9-504(3).

dards among dealers in the kind of goods sold. Some courts have required the secured party to clean or perform minor maintenance on the collateral prior to sale, in the same manner as would a dealer in that kind of good.

3. NOTICE OF SALE

Unless the collateral is perishable or threatens to decline rapidly in value, or is of a kind ordinarily sold in a recognized market (such as commodities or stock traded on an exchange), reasonable notice must be given to the debtor regarding the time and the place of a public sale or the time after which a private sale will be made. But, after default, the debtor may waive in writing his right to notice the sale. Except for consumer goods, the same notice must be given to all secured parties who have notified the possessing secured party of their interests.

4. APPLICATION OF THE PROCEEDS

Upon sale of the collateral, the proceeds are first applied to the expenses of repossessing and selling the collateral. The remaining balance is then used to satisfy the claim of the secured party with first priority. If any proceeds remain, they are applied to the debts of any remaining secured creditors in the order of priority as established by Article 9. Any surplus after the payment of all claims goes to the debtor. If the collateral does not bring a sales price sufficient to pay the expenses of the sale and to satisfy all secured parties, each unsatisfied secured creditor is entitled to a deficiency judgment against the debtor.

5. RETAINING THE COLLATERAL IN SATISFACTION OF THE DEBT

In cases involving consumer goods as collateral, and the debtor has paid at least 60% of the cash price or repaid at least 60% of a purchase money loan, the secured party must sell the collateral within ninety days after repos-

session, unless the secured party gets a signed waiver from the debtor after default.

In all other cases, the secured party may propose to the debtor in writing and to all other secured parties from whom the secured party has received notice of a claim that the foreclosing secured party will keep the collateral in satisfaction of the debt. The debtor may provide a written waiver of his right to notice after default. Unless the debtor or any other party entitled to notice objects within twenty-one days after notice was dispatched, the secured party may keep the collateral in satisfaction of the debt. But, if the secured party chooses this route, it cannot seek a deficiency judgment against the debtor.[39]

B. Debtor's Right of Redemption

Until the secured party has sold the collateral or has discharged the debt by retention of the collateral, the debtor may redeem the collateral by paying all of the obligations secured by the collateral plus the reasonable expenses incurred by the secured party in relation to the repossession, including reasonable attorney's fees. After default, the debtor may agree in writing to waive this right.[40]

C. Termination of the Security Interest

When the debt has been paid in full, the secured party has the duty to file a termination statement with the proper officer informing the public that the secured party no longer has an interest in the collateral. Failure to do so can subject the secured party to liability for damages arising out of failure to perform this obligation.

---

39. UCC Sec. 9-505.
40. UCC Sec. 9-506.

D. Other Rights of the Secured Party upon Default

The secured party has the option to forgo taking possession and selling the collateral and instead, to bring an action for the amount due and owing under the obligation. Once the creditor obtains the judgment against the debtor, it may pursue any lawful collection technique, including a judicial action to seize all nonexempt property of the debtor to be sold in satisfaction of the judgment. The disadvantage of this method is it takes longer to obtain lawful possession of any of the debtor's assets. In addition, the debtor may relocate or dispose of his assets. Also, the debtor could declare bankruptcy with the bankruptcy trustee owning all of the debtor's nonexempt assets. In some cases, this method is the only route that a secured creditor may take. If there would be insufficient proceeds from a sale to satisfy creditors with prior perfected rights, a junior secured party should forego any action against the collateral and pursue the debtor directly for repayment of the obligation.

VI. Suretyship

In the first part of this chapter, the secured party's right to satisfy its claim against specific property pledged by the debtor was discussed. There are times when the debtor's creditworthiness is not sufficient to cause a seller or lender to extend credit to the debtor, even with the existence of collateral. In these circumstances, it may be possible to convince a creditor with a promise by a third party to perform the debtor's obligation in the event the debtor does not. This third party serves as a surety with respect to the debtor's obligation.

A. Suretyship and Guaranty

The principle of suretyship governs both suretyship contracts as well as guaranty contracts.

Suretyship describes situations in which one agrees to answer for the debts or financial obligations of another with a right of reimbursement against the debtor in the event the surety has to pay the obligation.

Suretyship is basically a three party relationship. All suretyship contracts involve a principle debtor, a creditor and a surety or guarantor.

The principle debtor is the party bearing the ultimate burden of performing obligation. The principle owes a duty to both the creditor and the surety. The creditor is the party to whom the obligation is owed and to whom the surety is bound. The surety is the party who agrees to be liable for the obligation on behalf of the debtor. It is important to recognize that the surety is primarily liable on the obligation. The surety's duty is not strictly conditioned upon the default of the principle debtor. The surety is liable if the debtor fails to perform for any reason.

B. Suretyship Versus Guaranty

While these terms are often used interchangeably in both business and the law, they are technically different contractual relationships resulting in different rights and liabilities among the parties.

1. SURETYSHIP CONTRACTS

This is a contract generally created at the same time as the primary contract. It is considered a part of the same transaction that created the obligation. Therefore, there is no need for separate consideration to support the suretyship contract. The surety is primarily liable to perform the primary obligation of the debtor to the same extent as the debtor.

2. GUARANTY CONTRACTS

This type of contract is created separately from the contract establishing the debtor's obligation. Therefore, there must be separate consideration supporting a guaranty contract. In addition, a guarantor's liability is secondary. It is conditioned upon the default of the promisor of the primary contract.

Guaranty contracts fall within a number of different categories. Guarantee of collection (sometimes known as a conditional guaranty) is a special type of guaranty agreement requiring the creditor to establish that the debtor is in default and to exhaust all legal remedies against the debtor prior to attempting to collect the debt from the guarantor. Ordinary or absolute guaranty contracts entitle the creditor to bring an action against the guarantor immediately following the debtor's default.

Guaranties may also be classified as limited or unlimited. A limited guaranty will state some type of limitation, including the maximum liability that the guarantor may face. The agreement may also establish a date upon which the guarantor will no longer guarantee new obligations of the debtor. Guaranty agreements are usually limited by the transaction described in the agreement, but if the guarantor agrees to a "continuing guaranty agreement," the guarantor will be liable to the creditor for all obligations of the debtor from the time of the agreement up to the point that the debtor has no further obligation to the creditor.

Because the legal results are usually the same under modern suretyship and guaranty contracts, the following discussion of suretyship is intended to apply to both suretyship and guaranty relationships unless otherwise indicated.

C. Formation of a Suretyship Contract

As a general rule, a suretyship contract is governed by the contract law of the state in which it was formed. It requires a valid offer and acceptance. It does not need consideration separate from the existence of the primary contract. And because suretyship and guaranty contracts are agreements to answer for the debt of another, they fall within the scope of the Statute of Frauds. This means that suretyship and guaranty contracts must be in writing to be enforceable. There is an exception to this rule. Contracts that are entered into primarily for the benefit of the surety, rather than for the benefit of the debtor, fall outside the coverage of the Statute of Frauds. This is referred to as the "main purpose doctrine."

D. The Rights of a Creditor under a Suretyship Contract

1. RIGHTS AGAINST THE PRINCIPLE DEBTOR

Unless the parties have agreed otherwise, the creditor may proceed immediately against the debtor upon default. There is no requirement that the creditor must first allow the surety to pay the debt. In situations where the debtor owes more than one debt, the creditor may apply any payment received to the debt of its choice unless the debtor has specified otherwise. Under this rule, if two debts are owed, and only one is guaranteed, the creditor is free to apply funds solely toward satisfaction of the unsecured debt. By applying proceeds in this fashion, the debt supported by the surety remains unpaid, thereby preserving the opportunity for the creditor to pursue the surety if necessary.

2. RIGHTS AGAINST THE SURETY

A creditor may proceed immediately against the surety upon default unless the parties have agreed otherwise. A creditor has no duty to attempt collection of the obligation from the debtor or to notify the surety of the debtor's default.

3. RIGHTS AGAINST THE COLLATERAL

Upon default, the creditor is not bound to resort existing collateral for repayment before enforcing a surety or guaranty agreement. If the creditor chooses to proceed against the collateral first, any amount realized from its disposition in excess of the amount due must be returned to the debtor. But, if the collateral is insufficient to satisfy the debt, the creditor has the right to proceed against both the debtor and the surety for the balance due. If the creditor holds collateral pledged by both the debtor and the surety, the creditor must first proceed against the debtor's collateral for satisfaction of the debt.

If the creditor releases the collateral or causes the collateral to lose value, the surety's obligation will be reduced by the extent of the loss.

E. The Rights of the Surety

1. RIGHTS BEFORE THE DEBT IS PAID

The creditor is not normally bound to pursue the debtor for payment prior to enforcing the surety's obligation. The creditor's failure to first try to enforce the obligation against the debtor will not discharge the surety's obligation. If a surety desires to be bound only after all of the creditor's remedies against the principle are exhausted, the surety should enter into a contract as a "guarantor of collection" as opposed to a pure suretyship contract. A number of states have enacted statutes that allow a surety to compel the creditor to sue the principle upon request. In these states, if the creditor receives written notice but fails or refuses to attempt collection of the debt from the principle debtor, the surety will be discharged to the extent of the loss caused by the creditor's failure to proceed.

A surety may request that the creditor resort first to any collateral securing the debt if that collateral is rapidly depreciating in value or the surety can demonstrate that an undue hardship would result otherwise.

A surety may also seek exoneration. This is the surety's right before paying the creditor, to compel the principle to perform upon its obligation. Exoneration is a remedy in equity based upon the premise that the principle debtor owes the surety a duty to perform the principle obligation, thereby exonerating the

surety from liability. It would not be equitable to subject the surety to the inconvenience and possible loss if the principle were able to do so. An action for exoneration requests a court order the principle debtor to pay the creditor according to the terms of the arrangement.

2. RIGHTS AFTER PAYMENT OF THE PRINCIPAL DEBT

a. Right of Reimbursement or Indemnity

This is the surety's right to recover from the debtor for the obligation performed by the surety. The surety's rights vary according to the circumstances. They are as follows:

1. In the event the debtor consented to the retention of a surety, the surety may recover from the debtor in the amount the surety actually paid.
2. Where the surety was retained without the consent of the debtor, the surety is entitled to recover from the debtor only to the extent that the debtor has been unjustly enriched.
3. If the surety's payment was voluntary, the surety is not entitled to reimbursement. The situation may arise where both the surety and the debtor have a legal defense, such as the statute of limitations, and the surety voluntarily pays the debt out of a sense of moral obligation.

b. Subrogation

Once the surety has paid the debt or otherwise performed the debtor's obligation, the surety succeeds to the rights of the creditor. So, the surety has the right to enforce any lien, pledge, or mortgage securing the underlying debt to the extent that an excess value existed after satisfying the creditor's claim.

F. Co-Suretyship

In the event two or more sureties are liable on the same obligation to the same creditor, the obligation is shared by each surety. As a general rule, the rights and duties between co-sureties are fixed by the contract. If the rights between the co-sureties are not established by contract, common law rules apply. The common law rules establish that the co-sureties are jointly and severally liable. But, as between co-sureties, each is individually liable only in the amount personally guaranteed. Co-sureties may exist even if they don't know of each other's existence.

1. RIGHT OF CONTRIBUTION BETWEEN CO-SURETIES

Co-suretyship has a proportionate loss sharing mechanism known as contribution. There are times when a co-surety will be forced to pay more than her proportionate share. It would be unfair to place this burden upon a co-surety. Therefore, the law recognizes the right of contribution for any co-surety to recover the excess amount she was required to pay from the other co-sureties.

Once a party has fully performed her suretyship obligation, whether to a creditor or to co-sureties, no further obligation on the part of that surety exists. Therefore, if a surety has limited her liability by contract, when she has paid that amount, she is free from the obligation. This is true even if the result would leave the creditor unpaid due to the insolvency of another surety.

Any co-surety paying more than his proportionate share on behalf of another cosurety succeeds to the rights of that co-surety under the doctrine of subrogation. This can occur in the event of the bankruptcy of a co-surety. In the event a co-surety bears a larger loss as a result of the bankruptcy of another co-surety, the solvent co-surety may file a claim against the bankruptcy estate of the insolvent co-surety.

Each co-surety has a right of exoneration against any other co-surety to the extent such a co-surety is paid more than his proportion-

ate share, limited to the amount of the other co-surety would have to pay as contribution.

2. RELEASE OF A CO-SURETY

When a creditor releases one of several co-sureties, the obligation of the remaining co-sureties is reduced by the amount the released co-surety would have been compelled to pay under the doctrine of contribution. So, the liability of each remaining co-surety is computed as if the released surety had contributed her full share.

In addition, in the event a co-surety retains possession of collateral that was supporting the underlying obligation, that co-surety must share the value of that collateral proportionately with the other co-sureties. Each co-surety is entitled to an interest in the collateral in proportion to his liability on the principles debt. Each co-surety has a duty to account to the other for any such benefits received.

G. Defenses Available to a Surety

If a surety is being sued on the underlying obligation, certain defenses may exist. These include payment by the principle debtor, acts of the creditor harming the surety, and certain personal defenses. A surety may raise a suretyship defense even if it would result in only partial relief from the obligation.

1. PAYMENT OF THE DEBT BY THE PRINCIPLE

A surety will be discharged to the extent that the principle pays the debt. If the principle partially pays the debt, the surety is entitled to credit for that payment. A surety is completely discharged in the event the principle pays the debt in full.

2. REJECTION OF TENDER

If the creditor rejects payment of the debt when tendered, the principle and the surety are both discharged from the obligation of immediate performance. In addition, the refusal of a valid tender has the effect of stopping the accumulation of interest. Keep in mind that the debt itself is not discharged, but the obligation of the surety is discharged. It would not be equitable for the creditor to increase the surety's risk by refusing immediate payment. The principle is obligated only to make payments available to the creditor in a reasonable manner.

3. ALTERATION OF THE ORIGINAL OBLIGATION

Any change in the terms of the original contract between the creditor and the debtor without the permission of the surety will discharge the surety to the extent that the surety was adversely affected. Because the surety made an agreement based upon the original contract, changes adversely affecting the surety unilaterally are not permitted.

4. RELEASE OF THE PRINCIPLE

The surety's purpose in a debtor/creditor transaction is to protect the creditor from nonperformance by the debtor. If a creditor releases the debtor, it is certain that the debtor will not be performing. It follows then that the creditor should have no right to recover against the surety. So, as a general rule, when the creditor releases the debtor, the surety is discharged.

But, there are two important exceptions to this rule. First, the surety will not be discharged if the creditor has reserved her rights against the surety in the instrument containing the release of the debtor. A release with the reservation of the rights against the surety is regarded as preserving the surety's rights of both reimbursement and subrogation. It does not serve as a discharge of the underlying debt. This type of release is treated as a promise by the creditor not to sue, as opposed to a complete release of the debtor which would destroy the debt and automatically release the surety. The surety's method of protection under this scenario is to immediately demand

payment from the debtor on the grounds of subrogation or reimbursement. A reservation of rights against the surety puts the debtor on notice that the surety may be coming after him.

The second exception arises if the surety consents to remain bound despite the release of the debtor. In effect, the surety agrees to assume the obligations of the debtor.

5. DEFENSES OF THE PRINCIPLE

A surety may raise many of the same defenses that the debtor could raise in the event the debtor were sued. Defenses arising out of the transaction between the debtor and the creditor, such as misrepresentation, illegality, fraud, duress, and undue influence may be raised. A surety cannot raise defenses that are entirely personal to the debtor, such as bankruptcy, insanity, or the principle's minority.

6. THE SURETY'S PERSONAL DEFENSES

Personal defenses not arising out of the transaction are available to the surety if they are personal to the surety and not to the debtor. So, if the surety did not have complete legal capacity to enter into a contract, such as being mentally impaired or not of legal age to enter into a contract, the agreement is voidable to the same extent as any other contract. In addition, surety may defend a claim for payment on the grounds of the running of the statute of limitations and noncompliance with the Statute of Frauds.

7. FRAUD IN THE INDUCEMENT OF SURETYSHIP

If a creditor fraudulently induces someone to become a surety, the suretyship contract will be voidable at the option of the surety. Most jurisdictions require a creditor to inform a prospective surety of all known financial risks regarding the principle unless the creditor reasonable believes the prospective surety is aware of them.

8. IMPAIRMENT OF COLLATERAL

In the event there is collateral supporting repayment of the debt as well as the obligation of a surety, the creditor is not permitted to release the collateral or unreasonably permit it to diminish in value without the consent of the surety. If the creditor violates this obligation, the surety will be discharged to the extent of the impairment. If the collateral has been released, the reduction of liability will be equal to the fair market value of the collateral. If the collateral is damaged or otherwise has decreased in value as a result of the creditor's action or inaction, it follows that the surety will be released to the extent of the reduction in value. This rule applies only to collateral existing at time of the making of the suretyship contract. The surety has no right to rely upon collateral pledged by the debtor after the suretyship obligation was created.

* * *

Problems

1. (a) Carter loaned Davis $1,000, and Davis signed the following note and gave it to Carter, together with the stock certificate described in the note:

New York, N.Y.   [Date]

One year after date I promise to pay to the order of C. Carter $1,000 with interest. To secure payment of this note I have hereto attached as collateral security a certificate for 15 shares of $100 par value common stock of the Porter Manufacturing Company of Chicago, Ill., and hereby authorize the holder hereof, on default of this note, to sell said collateral.

(signed) D. Davis

The market value of the 15 shares of stock was $2,000 when the note was signed, $1,500 two months before the due date, $1,100 on the due date, and $500 four months after the due date. At all times there was a ready market for Porter Company stock at the market price. D failed to pay the note when it came due and four months later C sold the stock for its then market value and sued D for the balance of the obligation. What result?

(b) Same facts as in Part (a) plus the following: Two months before the due date, D requested C to sell the stock immediately since the market price was declining. C agreed to do so but did not make the sale until four months after the due date. Would this additional fact affect the outcome of the lawsuit of C against D? Explain.

(c) Same facts as in Part (b) except that the due date was the date of D's request and C's agreement. Answer the same question asked in Part (b).

(d) Same facts as in Part (c) plus the following: Before D signed the note, C orally agreed that he would sell the stock at any time upon D's request if the proceeds would be sufficient to pay the debt. Answer the same questions asked in Part (c).

2. On June 1, B, an appliance dealer, ordered 20 refrigerators of a specified model from S, to be shipped by motor truck, f.o.b. shipping point, the purchase price of $2,000 to be paid within 60 days. On June 3, S shipped the described refrigerators by the T Truck Company, receiving a straight bill of lading naming B as consignee, which S mailed to B. On June 4, B borrowed $1,600 from the First Bank, delivered the T Company bill of lading to the bank, and signed and gave the Bank an agreement promising to repay the loan on demand and giving the First Bank a security interest in the described 20 refrigerators until the loan was repaid. On June 5, when T Company notified B of arrival of the refrigerators, B directed that they be stored in the T Company warehouse and received from T Company a nonnegotiable warehouse receipt. On June 6, B borrowed $1,500 from the Second Bank, delivered the T Company warehouse receipt to the Second Bank, and signed and gave the bank an agreement promising to repay the loan on demand and giving the Second Bank a security interest in the described 20 refrigerators until the loan was repaid. On June 7, B applied to the Third Bank for a $1,400 loan, offering to give a security interest in the stored 20 refrigerators as collateral secu-

rity for the loan. After verifying that the refrigerators were stored in the warehouse, the Third Bank made the loan to B, and B signed and gave to Third Bank an agreement promising to repay the loan to Third Bank on demand and giving Third Bank a security interest in the described 20 refrigerators. Third Bank promptly notified T Company of the security transaction which as the first T Company knew of B's transactions with any bank concerning the 20 refrigerators. On June 10, upon petition by some of B's creditors, the court adjudged B insolvent and appointed a receiver to take over all of B's assets. B absconded, and, on June 12, B's receiver and the three banks for the first time learned of B's transactions with the others. The receiver, the three banks, and S, each claimed the 20 refrigerators still in the T Company's warehouse. What result?

3. On October 1, an obligor borrowed $1,500 from a bank and signed and gave the bank a written agreement promising to repay the bank in three months with 6 percent interest, and giving the bank security interests in a described TV set and a described freezer. On December 26, the obligor sold and delivered the TV set to a buyer who paid the obligor fair value in full. The buyer's purpose in buying and his knowledge of the bank's interest were as stated below. On December 26, a creditor with a $1,000 judgment against the obligor had the sheriff levy on the freezer in the obligor's possession. In the questions below, assume that a sheriff's sale under the levy had not yet been held, that at the time of the levy, the creditor had no actual knowledge of the bank's security interest, and that the obligor paid nothing on his obligation to the bank. On December 27, the bank first learned of the obligor's selling the TV set and of the creditor's attaching the freezer.

(a) As he told the bank he would, the obligor used the money the same day it was borrowed to buy and pay for in full the TV set and freezer described in the agreement. (a) Assume that from October 1 to December 26, as the bank knew, the two units were installed in the obligor's home and used by the obligor and his family, (a) The bank did not file a financing statement pertaining to its transaction with the obligor. Answer the following questions: (1) Assume that the buyer bought and used the TV set for his own personal home enjoyment, without having knowledge of the bank's interest. Between the bank and the buyer, which had the superior interest in the TV set? Explain. (2) Assume that the buyer bought and installed the TV set in his barber shop, for business use, without having knowledge of the bank's interest. Between the bank and the buyer, which had a superior interest in the TV set? Explain. (3) As between the bank and the attaching creditor, which had a superior interest in the freezer? Explain. (b) On October 1, the bank filed a financing statement pertaining to its transaction with the obligor. Answer the following questions: (1) Assume that the buyer who bought from the obligor, bought and used the TV set for his own personal home enjoyment, without having knowledge of the bank's interest. Between the bank and the buyer, which had a superior interest in the TV set? Explain. (2) Between the bank and the attaching creditor, which had a superior interest in the freezer? Explain. (2) Assume that from October 1 to December 26, as the bank knew, the two units were new, unused merchandise, displayed in the obligor's retail appliance store for sale to customers. (a) The bank did not file a financing statement pertaining to its transaction with the obligor. Between the bank and the attaching creditor, which had a superior interest in the freezer? Explain. (b) On October 1 the bank filed a financing statement pertaining to its transaction with the obligor. Answer the following questions: (1) Assume that the buyer who bought from the obligor bought and installed the TV set in his barber shop, for business use, without having knowledge of the bank's interest. Between the bank and the buyer, which had a superior interest in the TV set? Explain. (2) Assume that the buyer bought from the obligor and installed the TV set in his barber shop, for business use, with knowledge of the bank's interest at the time he bought. As between the bank and the buyer, which had a superior interest in the TV set? Explain. (3) Between the bank and the attaching creditor, which had a superior interest in the freezer? Explain. (3) Assume that from October 1 to December 26, as the bank knew, the two units were installed in and used in the operation of the obligor's restaurant. The bank did not file a financing statement pertaining to its transaction with the obligor. Answer the following questions: (a) Assume that the buyer bought from the obligor and installed the TV set in his barber shop, for business use, without having knowledge of the bank's interest. Between the bank and the buyer, which had a superior interest in the TV set? Explain. (b) Between the bank and the attaching creditor, which had a superior interest in the freezer? Explain.

(b) As he told the bank he would, the obligor used the borrowed money for a vacation trip. Before giving security interests to the bank, the obligor owned clear title to the TV set and the freezer described in the agreement. From October 1 to December 26, as the bank knew, the two units were installed in the obligor's home and used by the obligor and his family. Answer the following questions: (1) The bank did not file a financing statement pertaining to its transaction with the obligor. Between the bank and the attaching creditor, which had a superior interest in the freezer? Explain. (2) On October 1, the bank filed a financing statement pertaining to its transaction to with the obligor. Between the bank and the attaching creditor, which had a superior interest in the freezer? Explain.

4. On June 1, S. Smith, a manufacturer sold and delivered a freezer case to a retailer, B. Brown. When installed in B's store, the case did not become a part of the real estate. Nothing was said between the parties as to title or security interest. Of the $450 purchase price, B paid $50 down and orally agreed to pay the balance by July 15. On June 1, S assigned the obligation to a bank by the writing quoted below, which was delivered to the bank.

(a) The assignment read as follows: "[Date]. For $395 paid me, receipt of which is hereby acknowledged, I hereby sell, assign, and transfer to the Centerville National Bank all my right and interest to the $400 obligation owed to me by B. Brown, which is payable July 15 of this year. (signed) S. Smith." On June 1, the bank notified B of the assignment and directed him to pay the bank. By July 20 B had not paid any portion of the $400. (1) On July 20, did the bank have the legal right to repossess the freezer case? Explain. (2) On July 20, did the bank have the legal right to collect money from B, and if so, how much? Explain. (3) On July 20, did the bank have a legal right to collect money from S, and if so, how much? Explain.

(b) The assignment read as follows: "[Date]. On July 15 of this year, for value received, I hereby promise to pay to the Centerville National Bank $400. As collateral security for this note, I hereby assign and transfer to the bank all my right and interest to the $400 obligation owed to me by B. Brown, which is payable July 15 of this year. (signed) S. Smith." By July 20, neither B nor S had paid any portion of the obligations, and the bank notified B of the assignment and directed him to pay the bank. (1) On July 20, did the bank have a legal right to repossess the freezer case? Explain. (2) On July 20, did the bank have a legal right to collect money from S, and if so, how much? Explain.

(c) The assignment read as follows: "[Date]. For $395 paid to me receipt of which is hereby acknowledged, I hereby sell, assign, and transfer to the Centerville National Bank, all my right and interest to the $400 obligation owed to me by B. Brown, which is payable July 15 of this year, and guaranty payment thereof. (signed) S. Smith." On June 1 the bank notified B of the assignment and directed him to pay the bank. By July 20, B had not paid any portion of the $400. Answer the same questions asked in Part (b) above.

5. A manufacturer of clocks shipped $100,000 in merchandise to various customers on credit with payment due in 60 days. As soon as the goods were shipped, the manufacturer sold and assigned the accounts to Factors, Inc., which purchased them for $95,000 pursuant to a written agreement. Factors, Inc., paid the manufacturer and took possession of the duplicate invoices covering the

goods shipped. The original of each invoice was stamped: "This invoice has been assigned to Factors, Inc." Factors, Inc., did not file a financing statement. A month later a judgment creditor of the manufacturer levied on the accounts. As between the attaching creditor and Factors, Inc., which would have the better right to collect the accounts from the customers? (Modified from A.I.C.P.A. May 71-3c.)

6. Retailer Corp was in need of financing. To secure a loan, it made an oral assignment of its accounts receivable to C Creditor, a local investor, under which Creditor loaned Retailer on a continuing basis, 90% of the face value of the assigned accounts receivable. Retailer collected from the account debtors and remitted to Creditor at intervals. Before the debt was paid, Retailer filed a petition in bankruptcy. Which of the following is correct?

(a) As between the account debtors and Creditor, the assignment is not an enforceable security interest.

(b) Creditor is secured creditor to the extent of the unpaid debt.

(c) Other unpaid creditors of Retailer Corp who knew of the assignment are bound by its terms.

(d) An assignment of accounts, to be valid, requires the debtors owing the accounts to be notified. (Modified from A.I.C.P.A. Nov. 80-1(36).)

7. By written contract a dealer agreed to sell to a customer a large refrigerator for $ 1,200, which amount the customer agreed to pay in stated installments, title to remain in the dealer until the full price was paid. After the customer paid a total of $700, he failed to make further contract payments and, after giving proper notice, the dealer resold the refrigerator elsewhere, realizing the amount stated below, exclusive of costs.

(a) Assume that when the customer defaulted, the dealer, as provided by the agreement, was still in possession of the refrigerator. What would be the rights of the parties if the reseal netted (1) $800; (2) $300? Explain.

(b) Assume that the customer had possession of the refrigerator when he defaulted and that the dealer repossessed the refrigerator. What would be the rights of the parties if the resale netted (1) $800; (2) $300? Explain.

8. Two Uniform Commercial Code concepts relating to secured transactions are "attachment" and "perfection." Which of the following is correct in connection with the similarities and differences between these two concepts?

(a) They are mutually exclusive and wholly independent of each other.

(b) Satisfaction of one automatically satisfies the other.

(c) Attachment relates primarily to the rights against the debtor and perfection relates primarily to the rights against third parties.

(d) It is not possible to have a simultaneous attachment and perfection. (A.I.C.P.A. Nov. 82-1(54) and Nov. 79-1(23).)

9. Harris Hardware, Inc., a wholesaler distributor of hardware products, needed $100,000 of additional working capital. It made arrangements to borrow this amount from a bank. The parties signed a loan agreement which provided that the bank would lend Harris $100,000 secured by a security interest in "Harris's present and future inventory and accounts receivable and the proceeds thereof." The parties also signed a financing statement containing the same description of the collateral. The bank then filed the financing statement containing the same description of the collateral. The bank then filed the financing statement in the appropriate public office. One week later the bank loaned Harris $ 100,000. One year later Harris defaulted in the repayment of the loan and the bank attempted to enforce its security interest. Harris contended that the security agreement was unenforceable because (1) the loan was not made on the day that the security agreement was signed; (2) the bank could not acquire a secu-

rity interest in future inventory and future accounts receivable; and (3) the description of the collateral in the security agreement and the financing statement was legally insufficient. What result? (Modified from A.I.C.P.A. Nov. 71-7a.)

10. On October 1 an obligor obtained a loan commitment of $250,000 from a bank. The bank filed a financing statement on October 2. On October 5 the $250,000 loan was consummated and the obligor signed a security agreement granting the bank a security interest in inventory, accounts receivable, and proceeds from the sale of the inventory and collection of the accounts receivable. The bank's security interest was perfected (a) on October 1, (b) on October 2, (c) on October 5, (d) by attachment. (Modified from A.I.C.P.A., Nov. 821(56).)

11. A loan company (lender) made secured loans to a householder, a collector, and a clothier. The householder gave the lender a security interest in his household furniture. The collector delivered to the lender his rare-coin collection as a pledge. The clothier's loan was evidenced by his promissory note, payable over three years in monthly payments and secured by a security interest in the inventory of the clothier's clothing store, a sole proprietorship owned by the clothier. Proper security agreements were made and financing statements were duly signed and filed with respect to all of these transactions on the dates of the transactions. Answer "true" or "false" to the following statements.

(a) A filing of a financial statement was not required to perfect the security interest in the householder's household furniture.

(b) The lender's security interest in the collector's coin collection was perfected before a financing statement was filed.

(c) On filing a financing statement covering the clothier's inventory, the lender's security interest therein was perfected for a maximum period of one year.

(d) The financing statement for the clothier's inventory must include an itemization and valuation of the inventory for the financing statement to be valid. (Modified from A.I.C.P.A. Nov. 73-1(9).)

12. Wonder Television Manufacturing, Inc., manufactures television sets under its brand name, Wonder TV, and sells the sets directly to retail stores. To increase sales, Wonder incorporated WOMAC Financial Corporation to provide credit to customers who purchased Wonder TV sets from the retail stores. Wonder's arrangement with the retailers stipulates that WOMAC will provide the financing for the purchase of Wonder TV sets to any customer who meets WOMAC's financial requirements. These financial requirements are based on standard credit practices. The financing is put in motion by the retailers telling their customers that financing is available through WOMAC if they wish to purchase a set on time. After a recent analysis of its experience, WOMAC has found that it would be cheaper not to file a financing statement covering each individual set purchased by the retailers' customers. As a result, WOMAC is considering an alternative plan whereby WOMAC will take a negotiable promissory note and a security agreement signed by the borrower-purchaser. These papers will be retained by WOMAC, and monthly collections will be made on the notes. The retailers will receive immediate payment on a discounted basis for each sale financed. Assuming WOMAC implements its alternative plan, discuss its rights against each of the following:

(a) A retailer upon the default by one of its customers who purchased a Wonder TV financed by WOMAC.

(b) The creditors or the trustee in bankruptcy of a purchaser of Wonder TV financed by WOMAC in the event of a default by the purchaser.

(c) A subsequent bona fide purchaser who bought a used set from an original retail customer who had financed his original purchase through WOMAC. (Modified from A.I.C.P.A. Nov. 74-4c.)

13. A radio dealer borrowed $15,000 from First Bank and entered into a written agreement which

gave the bank a security interest in all of the radios that the dealer had in inventory plus any that were acquired later. On the date of the loan the bank filed a proper financing statement. Subsequently, the dealer borrowed $2,000 from Second Bank to purchase 100 new radios. Second Banks immediately filed a proper financing statement covering its security interest in the new radios before allowing the dealer to take possession of them. When the dealer defaulted on both loans, Second Bank attempted to seize the 100 new radios but First Bank claimed that its security interest prevailed. Between First Bank and Second Bank, which had the superior interest in 100 radios? (Modified from A.I.C.P.A. May 72-2d.)

14. A lender loaned $600 to an obligor to purchase a television set for his home. The security agreement between the parties provided that, pending payment of the loan, the lender was to have a security interest in the television set as well as in all other consumer goods thereafter owned by the obligor. Three months later the obligor bought a refrigerator for cash for his home. Thereafter the obligor defaulted on the loan and the lender sought to seize the refrigerator which he claimed was subject to his security agreement. Answer "true" or "false" as to each of the following statements.

(a) The lender had no security interest in the refrigerator.

(b) If the obligor acquired the refrigerator 30 days after the lender made the loan, the lender's security interest would attach to the refrigerator.

(c) The clause in the security agreement which provided for a security interest in the refrigerator is called an after-acquired property clause.

(d) The lender had a purchase-money security interest in the television set.

(e) A financing statement would have to be filed by the lender to perfect his security interest in the television set. (Modified from A.I.C.P.A. May 72-2b.)

15. An obligor owned 30 sewing machines which he used in his business of manufacturing fancy tablecloths. The obligor borrowed $3,000 for a bank under a security agreement dated December 1 which provided that the obligor give the bank a security interest in the 30 machines and all other machines thereafter acquired. The bank filed a financing statement on December 2 in the proper office. Later, on January 21, the obligor bought 20 additional sewing machines from a seller under a written agreement to pay for the machines in monthly installments and to give the seller a security interest in the 20 sewing machines until the purchase price was paid. The machines were delivered to the obligor on January 28. On January 30, the obligor defaulted on his indebtedness to the bank and the bank immediately seized all 50 sewing machines. On February 2, the seller properly filed a financing statement covering the 20 machines. Between the seller and the bank, which had the superior interest in the 20 sewing machines? (Modified from A.I.C.P.A. May 71-3f.)

16. A buyer, owner, and operator of a machine shop, purchased a power lathe and took immediate delivery on June 10 from an equipment company. The buyer agreed to pay the full price in cash within 60 days. The buyer purchased a second lathe from the equipment company on the same terms on July 7. The buyer, although solvent, was experiencing cash difficulties and failed to pay the equipment company for the lathes at the times agreed upon. The price of the two lathes still had not been paid in December when the buyer ordered two more lathes form the equipment company, agreeing to pay cash on delivery and also agreeing to pay for the first two lathes on delivery of the last two. In order to raise the cash necessary for this purpose, the buyer negotiated a loan with a bank. The loan was closed on December 6. At the closing the buyer executed a security agreement giving the bank a security interest in the four lathes and also executed and delivered a financing statement to the bank in connection with the transaction. The buyer then paid the loan proceeds to the equipment company on December 6 and took de-

livery of the two new lathes. The bank filed the financing statement on December 10.

Although the bank did not know it at the time of the loan, the buyer had given a security interest on June 1 in all of his machinery and equipment, including any machinery and equipment thereafter acquired, to a steel company, a major steel supplier. The buyer's objective was to secure credit purchases of steel from the steel company. On December 8, the steel company filed the financing statement furnished by the buyer concerning the transaction.

Six months have now elapsed and the buyer's financial condition has not improved. The bank is concerned about its security, having now learned of the steel company's security interest. What are the relative rights of the bank and the steel company in the buyer's lathes? (Modified from A.I.C.P.A. May 73-5.)

17. National Finance Company engages in a wide variety of secured transactions which may be broken down into three categories.

I. Consumer loans in connection with the purchase of automobiles, appliances, and furniture. National makes these loans in two ways. First, it makes direct loans to the consumer-borrower who then makes the purchase with the proceeds. Second, it is contacted by the seller and provides the financing for the purchase by the customer. In either case National takes a security interest in the property purchased.

II. Collateralized loans to borrowers who deliver possession of property, such as diamonds, to National secure repayment of their loans.

III. Loans to merchants to finance their inventory purchase. National takes a security interest in the inventory and proceeds.

Except for category III, National does not file a financing statement.

(a) When does National's security interest in the various types of property attach?

(b) As a secured creditor, against what parties must National protect itself?

(c) Does National have a perfected security interest in any of the above property? If so, against whom?

(d) If the facts indicate that National does not have a perfected security interest against all parties, what should it do?

(e) Can National fully protect itself against all subsequent parties who might claim superior rights to the property involved? (A.I.C.P.A. Nov. 78-2a.)

18. Debtor Furniture Inc. found that its credit rating was such that it was unable to obtain a line of unsecured credit. Creditor Bank indicated that it would be willing to supply funds based upon a "pledge" of Debtor's furniture inventory which was located in two warehouses. The bank would receive notes and bearer negotiable warehouse receipts covering the merchandise securing the loans. An independent warehouseman was to have complete control over the areas in the warehouse set aside as field warehousing facilities. The Warehousing Corporation was selected to serve as the independent warehouseman. It was to retain keys to the posted area in which the inventory was contained. Negotiable bearer warehouse receipts were issued to Debtor when it delivered the merchandise to Warehousing. The receipts were then delivered by Debtor to Creditor to secure the loans which were made at 80% of the market value of the furniture indicated on the receipts. Upon occasion, Debtor would take temporary possession of the furniture for the purpose of packaging it, Creditor surrendering the warehouse receipt for this limited purpose. As orders were filled out in the field warehouse inventory, the requisite receipt would be relinquished by Creditor, the merchandise obtained by Debtor, and other items substituted with a new receipt issued.

(a) Based upon the facts given, is the field warehousing arrangement valid?

(b) When does a security interest in the negotiable warehouse receipts attach?

(c) What, if anything, is necessary to perfect a security interest in goods covered by negotiable warehouse receipts?

(d) What are the dangers, if any, that Creditor faces by relinquishing the warehouse receipts to Debtor? (Modified from A.I.C.P.A. May 80-4b)

19. The Martin Manufacturing Company manufactures various types of lathes. It sold on credit 25 general-use lathes to Hardware City, a large retail outlet. Hardware City sold one of the lathes to Brown for use in his home repair business, reserving a security interest for the unpaid balance. However, Hardware City did not file a financing statement. Brown's creditors are asserting rights against the lathe. Which of the following statements is correct?

(a) The lathe is a consumer good in Brown's hands.

(b) No filing was necessary to perfect a security interest in the lathe against Brown's creditors.

(c) Martin Manufacturing could assert rights against the lathe sold to Brown in the event Hardware City defaults in its payments.

(d) The lathe was inventory in both Martin and Hardware's hands and is equipment in Brown's, and both Martin and Hardware City must file to perfect their interests. (Modified from A.I.C.P.A. Nov. 80-1(33).)

20. F Financial loans money on the strength of negotiable warehouse receipts. Its policy is always to obtain a perfected security interest in the receipts and to maintain it until the loan has been satisfied. Insofar as this policy is concerned, which of the following is correct?

(a) F can not perfect a security interest by filing.

(b) Relinquishment of the receipts is not permitted under any circumstances without the loss of the perfected security interest in them.

(c) F has a perfected security interest in goods which the receipts represent.

(d) If the receipts are wrongfully but duly negotiated to a holder, F's perfected security interest will not be prejudiced. (Modified from A.I.C.P.A. Nov. 81-1(44).)

21. The Finance Company is a diverse, full-line lending institution. Its "Problems & Potential Litigation" file revealed the following disputes involving loans extended during the year of examination.

Finance loaned Brown $4,500 to purchase a $5,000 video recording system for his personal use. A note, security agreement, and financing statement, which was promptly filed, were all executed by Brown. Unknown to Finance, Brown had already purchased the system from Smith Stores the previous day for $5,000. The terms were 10% down, the balance monthly, payable in three years, and a written security interest granted to Smith. Smith did not file a financial statement until default.

Finance loaned the Furniture Co. $13,000 to purchase certain woodworking equipment. Furniture did so. A note, security agreement, and financing statement were executed by Furniture. AS a result of an oversight the financing statement was not filed until 30 days after the loan-purchase by Furniture. In the interim Furniture borrowed $11,000 from the Bank using the newly purchased machinery as collateral for the loan. A financing statement was filed by Bank five days prior to Finance's filing.

What are the priorities among the conflicting security interests in the same collateral claimed by Finance and the other lenders? (Modified from A.I.C.P.A. Nov. 83-2a).

22. On January 5, Brown purchased and received delivery of new machinery from the Manufacturer Corp. for $50,000. The machinery was to be used in Brown's production process. Brown paid 304b down and executed a security agreement for the balance. On January 9, Brown ob-

tained a $150,000 loan from the Bank. Brown signed a security agreement which gave Bank a security interest in Brown's existing and after-acquired machinery. The security agreement was duly filed by Bank that same day. On January 10, Manufacturer properly filed its security agreement. If Brown defaults on both loans and there are insufficient funds to pay both Manufacturer and Bank, which party will have a superior security interest in the machinery purchased from Manufacturer? (Modified from A.I.C.P.A. May 84-1(58).)

23. A manufacturer sells baseball equipment to distributors, who in turn sell the equipment to various retailers throughout the U.S. The retailers then sell the equipment to consumers who use the equipment for their own personal use. In all cases, the equipment is sold on credit with a security interest taken in the equipment by each of the respective sellers. Which of the following is correct?

(a) The security interests of all of the sellers remain valid and will take priority even against goods faith purchasers for value, despite the fact that resales were contemplated.

(b) The baseball equipment is inventory in the hands of all parties concerned.

(c) The manufacturer's security interest is automatically perfected since the manufacturer qualifies as a purchase money secured party.

(d) The manufacturer and the distributors must file a financing statement or take possession of the baseball equipment in order to perfect their security interests.

(e) The only parties who qualify as purchase money secured parties are the retailers. (Modified from A.I.C.P.A. Nov.84-1(58) and Nov.82-1(58).)

24. A buyer purchased from the Retailer Co. a new saw for his home workshop for cash. One week later, the buyer was called by the Finance Co. Finance explained to the buyer that it had been financing Retailer's purchases from the manufacturers and that to protect its interest it had obtained a perfected security interest in Retailer's entire inventory of hardware and power tools, including the saw which the buyer bought. Finance further explained that Retailer had defaulted on a payment due to Finance, and Finance intended to assert its security interest in the saw and repossess it unless the buyer was willing to make payment of $100 for a release of Finance's security interest. If the buyer refuses to make the payment, which of the following statements is correct?

(a) Even if the buyer had both actual notice and constructive notice via recordation of Finance's interest, he will prevail if Finance seeks to repossess the saw.

(b) Finance's security interest in the saw in question is invalid against all parties unless its filing specifically described and designated the particular saw the buyer purchased.

(c) The buyer must pay the $100 or the saw can be validly repossessed and sold to satisfy the amount Retailer owes Finance and any excess paid to the buyer.

(d) The buyer will not take free of Finance's security interest if he was aware of said interest at the time he purchased the saw. (Modified from A.I.C.P.A. Nov.84-1(59) and Nov.82-1(53).

25. A buyer purchased a computer and a stereo from Sounds Inc. for personal use. With regard to the computer, the buyer signed an installment purchase note and a security agreement. Under the terms of the note the buyer was to pay $100 down and $50 a month for 20 months. The security agreement included a description of the computer. However Sounds did not file a financing statement. The buyer paid $800 cash, the full price, for the stereo.

Two months later, the buyer sold the computer to a purchaser for $600 cash. The purchaser purchased the computer for personal use without knowledge of the Sounds' security interest.

Three months later, the buyer brought the stereo back to Sounds for repair. Inadvertently, one of Sounds' sales persons sold the stereo in ordinary course of Sounds' business to a restaurant for use in its restaurant business.

(a) Did Sounds fulfill the requirements necessary for attachment and perfection of its security interest in the computer?

(b) Will the purchaser take the computer free of Sounds' security interest?

(c) As between the buyer and the restaurant, who has title to the stereo? (Modified from A.I.C.P.A. Nov.84-4).

26. On June 3, Finance loaned Trucker $20,000 to purchase four computers for use in Trucker's trucking business. Trucker contemporaneously executed a promissory note and security agreement. On June 7, Trucker purchased the computers with the $20,000, obtaining possession that same day. On June 10, a judgment creditor of Trucker levied on the computers.

(a) When if at all did Finance's security interest attach?

(b) If Finance files a financing statement on June 11, which of the parties will have a superior interest in the computers? (Modified from A.I.C.P.A. May 85-1(44 & 45).)

27. Buyer purchased a stereo for personal use form Audio, a retail seller of appliances. Buyer paid 30% of the $600 sales price and agreed to pay the balance in 12 equal principal payments plus interest. Buyer executed a security agreement giving Audio a security interest in the stereo. Audio properly filed a financing statement immediately.

(a) After making six payments Buyer defaulted and Audio repossessed the stereo. What should Audio do?

(b) If after making the third installment payment, Buyer sold the stereo to a purchaser for personal use, who would have a superior interest in the stereo assuming the purchaser lacked knowledge of Audio's security interest? (Modified from A.I.C.P.A. May 85-1 (47 & 48).)

28. A manufacturer sold and delivered a piece of kitchen equipment to a householder for $5,000. The householder paid $2,000 and promised to pay the balance in monthly installments of $500. The contract contained an acceleration provision under which, if the householder failed to pay any installment when due, the entire balance could be declared due immediately. In the contract the manufacturer warranted the equipment to be free from defects for five years, and retained a security interest until full price was paid. The contract form also contained the required FTC claims and defense notice. The manufacturer promptly sold and delivered the chattel paper contract to a bank which notified the householder of the assignment. Before the first installment came due a defect in the equipment caused a fire completely destroying the equipment but fortunately not damaging the householder's kitchen. The householder demanded that the manufacturer refund the $2,000 the householder had paid but the manufacturer was insolvent and unable to pay.

(a) When the householder refused to make any further payment the bank sued the householder for the unpaid balance of the purchase price. What result?

(b) When the manufacturer failed to refund the householder's payment, the householder sued the bank. What result?

Debtor–Creditor Relations

Debtor–Creditor Relations

EACH DAY, MILLIONS of dollars of credit purchases and other credit transactions are consummated. For instance, individuals often purchase automobiles on credit. Credit cards are employed both by individuals and business representatives to obtain goods and services without immediate payment.

In each situation, there is a debtor, the party who has incurred an obligation or debt, and a creditor, the party to whom the obligation is owed. Most debtor-creditor relationships arise through an agreement. But, the law can impose debtor creditor status upon parties under certain circumstances.

Example. If an individual is injured by a corporations's product and wins a money judgment against that corporation in court, the injured party becomes a judgment creditor and the corporation becomes a judgment debtor. 🗀

With respect to the marketplace, keep in mind that there are two types of credit arrangements, each depending upon the parties and the type of transaction. A transaction involving an individual borrowing money or obtaining goods or services on credit for personal, family or household purposes is deemed a consumer credit transaction. Commercial transactions are those for business, profit or institutional oriented purposes. For some purposes, farm credit will be segregated from commercial credit.

I. Laws Assisting Creditors

Recall that creditors can either be secured or unsecured. A secured creditor is a creditor who has rights in a debtor's property (collateral) for the purpose of repaying the debt in the event of a default. As discussed in the chapter on secured transactions, a secured creditor is entitled to receive payment from the proceeds of the disposal of collateral before unsecured creditors and the debtor.

Creditors who have no collateral to pursue for repayment are identified as unsecured creditors. The only recourse for an unsecured creditor is to pursue the nonexempt assets of the debtor.

A. Consensual and Nonconsensual Liens

A lien is a claim encumbering a piece of real or personal property. A lien may be enforced by selling the property and applying the proceeds to the unpaid debt. The holder of the lien will have priority of payment from the proceeds of the sale of the lien unless the property is subject to a mortgage filed or a security interest perfected prior to the attachment of the lien.

Liens can be classified as either consensual or nonconsensual. A consensual lien is created when a debtor agrees to pledge an interest in his property to the creditor. A security interest created under Article 9 is a common example of a consensual lien. In addition, mortgages of real property are considered consensual liens.

Nonconsensual liens are created by statute, common law or judicial decree.

1. STATUTORY LIENS

Statutory liens are imposed or authorized by a statute and arise upon specific circumstances or conditions. An example of a statutory lien is a "mechanic's and materialman's lien." A mechanic's and materialman's lien affects only real property. When a person or entity supplies skilled labor or building materials to repair or improve real property, a lien may be filed with the appropriate government authority in the event the owner of the real property does not pay for the services or goods. In order for the lien to be enforceable, the supplier of the labor or materials must file its lien at the appropriate public office. The lien claim is made for an amount equal to value of the services or goods rendered to the property. There is a time limit in which the lien must be filed. Each state has its own laws in this area. Compliance rules vary from state to state.

Another type of lien created by statute is the tax lien. Tax liens are filed by local, state or federal government tax collection agencies. If the tax lien arises from unpaid real property taxes, that specific parcel of real property will be the only property subject to the lien. Federal tax liens may attach to both real and personal property of the taxpayer.

2. COMMON LAW LIENS

A number of common law liens are discussed below. These were liens developed by legal tradition and adopted by the courts through the years to assist artisans, innkeepers, landlords and others in the collection of payment for services rendered. Many states have adopted these liens as statutory liens.

a. Artisan's Liens

An artisan's lien may only attach to personal property. It is usually a lien for the repair or improvement of personal property.

Example. Assume an individual had his television repaired at a local electronics shop. If the owner does not pay the bill, the repair shop will be deemed a creditor for the value of the work and parts. The repair shop may retain possession of the television until the bill is paid.

An important thing to keep in mind with respect to artisan's liens is that they are only effective so long as the artisan retains possession of the property. That is why this type of lien is called a possessory lien. The lien will be lost if the creditor loses possession of the item unless he records notice of the lien under the state recording statutes. This is not a UCC filing system lien, but rather a separate filing system. If the debtor does not pay for the repairs or other work, the creditor may satisfy the lien by selling the property and applying the proceeds to pay the debt. If any balance remains, it must be paid to the debtor.

b. Innkeeper's Liens

An innkeeper's lien can be applied by an innkeeper against the property of a guest of the inn who has not paid her obligation as agreed. This too is a possessory lien requiring that the innkeeper retain possession of the debtor's property. In modern commerce, one seldom sees innkeepers revert to this common law remedy. Innkeepers usually protect themselves by requiring a guest pay in advance or register by presentment of a credit card.

c. Bailee's Liens

A bailee's lien is granted to carriers and warehousepersons permitting them to retain possession of goods entrusted to them pending payment for the charges incurred for shipment or storage.

3. JUDICIAL LIENS

Judicial or judgment liens are created when a judgment creditor registers her lien with the appropriate governmental officer. In most states, the filing of a judgment in the county where real property is owned by the debtor will create a judgment lien against that property as of the time of filing. With respect to personal property, laws of most states generally require that a writ of execution be issued by a court against specific property of the debtor.

Remember that a judgment is merely a piece of paper. A judgment gives the creditor the right to call upon the state's police power to execute upon the debtor's nonexempt assets. Once a judgment is obtained, the process calls for the creditor to seek a writ of execution from a court clerk. This is served upon the debtor by a local sheriff or police official. The writ of execution directs the sheriff or local police official to seize the property identified in the writ. The debtor will get an opportunity to come before the court and raise valid defenses to the sale of the property, such as, the property is not owned by the debtor or that the property is exempt from execution by statute.

B. Prejudgment Remedies

In certain circumstances, a creditor may have the right to satisfy a claim from the debtor's assets prior to judgment. Article 9 of the UCC permits security agreements to contain language entitling a secured creditor to repossess the collateral without judicial authorization. Other than secured transactions under Article 9, prejudgment remedies are considered extraordinary and provisional because the creditor's ultimate right to satisfy the debt depends upon the creditor's success in obtaining a judgment. There are also constitutional issues regarding the debtor's right to

due process prior to being deprived of his property by a state official.

1. REPLEVIN AND SELF-HELP

Replevin is a statutory remedy enabling the creditor to recover possession of specific goods wrongfully taken or detained. Replevin is only available to a creditor who has a lien upon property or a right to possess specific property of the debtor. Replevin is used widely by secured creditors to repossess collateral after default.

Repossession of automobiles occurs hundreds of times each day. Sometimes a creditor will engage the services of a private contractor who can recover an automobile pledged as collateral without incident. But, other times, the creditor must petition the court for a writ of replevin. This entails filing an affidavit setting forth the creditor's right to the property as well as posting a bond that will be used to pay damages in the event the creditor was not entitled to the property. The court will order the clerk to issue a writ of replevin directing the sheriff or other police official to seize or replevy the identified property pending resolution of the rest of the lawsuit.

A creditor may use self-help repossession to recover collateral held by the debtor. Self-help is specifically authorized by Article 9 of the UCC. It is faster and cheaper than obtaining the collateral with the assistance of the court. But, it is very important that the person attempting to recover the property not breach the peace or otherwise violate the debtor's property rights, such as forcibly taking the property or breaking and entering into the debtor's residence.

2. PREJUDGMENT ATTACHMENT

Prejudgment attachment is available to a creditor who is concerned that the debtor may squander, hide, or fraudulently transfer property that could be used to satisfy the claim. Some states authorize the use of a prejudgment writ of attachment to assure that assets

Example. Assume an automobile dealership is in default to its major lender. The lender is concerned that the management of the company no longer has an incentive to properly maintain the going concern value of the company or is squandering the assets of the company. In order to preserve the value of the assets, the lender petitions the court to have a receiver appointed. If appointed, the receiver will serve as the temporary owner and manager of the entity until the judicial action is resolved. ▢

are available to pay a judgment if and when it is obtained. The prejudgment writ of attachment directs the sheriff to take possession of the debtor's property and hold it pending the outcome of the trial. A creditor seeking to use this remedy must post bond that will be used to reimburse the debtor for the impairment of his property should the debtor prevail. The debtor will be able to recover damages from a creditor for wrongful attachment.

3. PREJUDGMENT GARNISHMENT

Garnishment is a collection remedy directed to a third party who is holding property of the debtor. A typical garnishment summons is directed toward the bank holding deposits of the debtor. But, it may also be directed to an employer, insurance company, or any other third party who owes money or other property of the debtor. Prejudgment garnishment is similar to prejudgment attachment in that the goal is to preserve assets for satisfaction of the judgment. Courts will not freeze financial assets of a debtor without a hearing demonstrating that the creditor will more likely than not prevail upon its legal action and that the asset will likely be unavailable for postjudgment satisfaction of the claim.

4. RECEIVERSHIPS

Another extraordinary remedy available to creditors is an action for a receivership. In this situation, a creditor requests that the court appoint a receiver to take possession of and administer, preserve and manage certain property of the debtor.

A receivership action can benefit all creditors in that the action itself does not establish a better position for one creditor over another. The property is preserved while various creditor priorities are resolved.

5. CONSTITUTIONAL ISSUES AFFECTING PREJUDGMENT REMEDIES

The 14th Amendment to the United States Constitution prohibits any state from taking property from a person without due process of law. Prejudgment remedies of attachment, garnishment and replevin deprive the debtor of her property. In order to meet the constitutional standard, it is necessary for a debtor to receive notice of a hearing and to have an opportunity to be heard prior to the government assisting a creditor in taking the debtor's property. This constitutional protection does not require that a hearing actually take place. The debtor may choose to ignore the summons informing the debtor of her opportunity to be heard. The key is that notice of the opportunity to be heard must be served upon the debtor prior to the governmental action, thus giving the debtor an opportunity to come to court and raise any valid defense to the action.

C. Post–judgment Remedies

It can be very difficult for a creditor to collect money or other property from the debtor after a judgment has been entered. The majority of legal actions brought against debtors are resolved with very little conflict. Debtors often have no assets to satisfy judgments. Some debtors make it very difficult to find attachable assets. The following are the procedural resources available to creditors in collecting judgments.

1. POST-JUDGMENT EXECUTION

After the creditor obtains a judgment against the debtor, a creditor requests the clerk of the court to issue a writ of execution directing the sheriff or other appropriate police official to seize or take control of the debtor's personal or real property for the purpose of selling it at a public sale. Notice must be given to the debtor as well as to the public of the date of the sheriff's sale in order to comply with statutory requirements.

2. POST-JUDGMENT GARNISHMENT

The process of post-judgment garnishment is similar to prejudgment garnishment. A creditor has a garnishment summons issued by a court clerk which is served upon a party holding property of the debtor, known as the garnishee. The garnishee will have a limited period of time to file an answer to the garnishment summons stating what property, if any, it holds or owes to the debtor. If the garnishee is holding property of the debtor or otherwise owes money to the debtor, the garnishee is required to turn the property over to the court for disposition to the judgment creditor.

With respect to garnishing the wages of a debtor, federal law prohibits the garnishment of more than 25 percent of the debtor's disposable earnings for that pay period. Some states prohibit garnishment of wages except for spousal or child support following a divorce.

3. MORTGAGE FORECLOSURES AND TRUSTEE'S SALES

A secured real property loan transaction involves two documents. It involves the signing of a promissory note and the execution of a mortgage or deed of trust. In the case of the mortgage, the debtor is the mortgagor and the lender is the mortgagee. In those states employing deeds of trust as the documents evidencing pledges of real property as collateral, the debtor is required to sign a trust deed placing legal title to the property into the name of a trustee, usually an officer of the bank. This trust represents only a restriction on the legal title of the property. The original property owner still has the exclusive right to possess and enjoy the property.

Upon missing a mortgage payment or other default, the creditor may take steps to obtain control of the property and dispose of it. The two most common methods are judicial mortgage foreclosure sales and sales under a power of sale clause.

A mortgage foreclosure action begins by the creditor filing suit against the debtor, claiming default on the promissory note and requesting that the court foreclose the debtor's rights in the property through a judicial sale. If the court finds that the debtor has defaulted and the mortgage is valid, the court will order a sheriff to hold a public sale of the property. The party buying the property at the sale will become the new owner. The proceeds of the sale are applied first to cover the costs of the sale. The remainder is applied to satisfy the mortgage or mortgages in the order of priority. If any proceeds remain, they are remitted to the debtor.

The other system of enforcing a creditor's collateral rights against real property pledged is selling a property pursuant to a power of sale clause. This is a nonjudicial sale. The mortgage or deed of trust involved in this situation will have language granting the lender the right to sell the property without judicial intervention. In order to employ this system, the secured creditor must give notice both to the debtor and to the public that the property will be sold at a certain time and place to the highest bidder. The power of sale language permits the mortgagee or trustee to execute a new deed in the name of the highest bidder.

These two systems may be distinguished by the amount of time each procedure involves. With respect to a judicial foreclosure, depending upon the court's schedule and the cooperation of the parties, the action could take from several months to a year from the time the action commenced. A power of sale procedure requires much less time. In those states permitting power of sale actions, there will usually be a minimum time that must pass between the public notice of the sale and the actual sale of the property. This time period is usually 45 days or less.

A power of sale procedure is usually less expensive than a judicial mortgage foreclosure. A judicial mortgage foreclosure involves hiring legal counsel, paying court fees and sheriff's fees. On the other hand, a power of sale action can be handled by the mortgagee or trustee, although it is usually done with the supervision of legal counsel. Even with the assistance of counsel, attorney's fees involved in a power of sale action are a fraction of those required to complete a judicial mortgage foreclosure.

So why would one ever desire to dispose of property through judicial sale as opposed to a power of sale system? First, a number of states have yet to enact the power of sale statutes. Second, if there is a major dispute regarding title to the property or the debtor has threatened legal action against the lender with respect to the handling of the debt, a power of sale procedure may conclude with a questionable title. These matters often end up in court anyway. Therefore, the lender, in anticipation of such a dispute, may want to take the initiative and resolve all matters in court. Finally, if the real property sold does not bring a price sufficient to satisfy the debt, a deficiency will exist. Under a mortgage foreclosure action, a court may enter a deficiency judgment as a part of the lawsuit. In a power of sale action, a creditor will have to file a lawsuit in order to obtain a deficiency judgment. A creditor should consider these factors in choosing

whether or not to initiate the action in court with a judicial foreclosure to resolve all disputes in one action.

4. THE DEBTOR'S RIGHT OF REDEMPTION

Many states recognize a debtor's right to redeem both real and personal property prior to the time it is sold. In order for a debtor to redeem property, she must pay all of the debt due and owing as well as all expenses incurred up to the time of the sale, including attorney's fees. Once the sale has been completed, the debtor's right of redemption expires. In a few jurisdictions, there is a very short period of time after the time of the sale but prior to the buyer taking possession of the property in which the debtor has the opportunity to redeem the property. A number of states do not grant debtors the right of redemption.

D. Bulk Transfers and Article 6

Until recently, the National Conference of Commissioners on Uniform State Laws and the American Law Institute included Article 6, "Bulk Transfers," as a part of the Uniform Commercial Code. But, in 1988, those two bodies jointly recommended repeal of Article 6 to each state government that had previously adopted it. In the alternative, a revised version was recommended. These two professional bodies observed that changes in both modern business practices and commercial law have made regulation of bulk sales virtually unnecessary.

Article 6 was designed to protect creditors from a debtor who attempted to defraud them by selling substantially all of its business to a third party. Such a debtor would often flee the jurisdiction with the proceeds or otherwise squander them. Article 6 required that a bulk seller provide the purchaser with a sworn list of creditors. The purchaser had to give notice to those creditors of the pending sale at least ten days prior to payment or the date the purchaser was to take possession of the property.

If a creditor did not complain after getting such notice, the creditor's rights would be cut off. But, if a creditor did not get notice under old Article 6, the creditor was able to bring an action against the property of the debtor that had been transferred into the hands of the new purchaser. There was a window of six months following the date of transfer for such injured creditors to operate and pursue this remedy.

Creditors may still protect themselves from such injuries by using other laws, including the laws of each state prohibiting fraudulent transfers. With the buying and selling of entire businesses commonplace in today's business environment, compliance with the terms and provisions of Article 6 proved more burdensome than beneficial. A number of states have already repealed their versions of Article 6 with the trend expected to continue.

E. Fraudulent Conveyances

Oftentimes debtors will attempt to hinder the collection efforts of a creditor. One common tactic of debtors is to transfer assets to friends, relatives or business associates. With the assets titled to a party other than in the name of the judgment debtor, the creditor cannot obtain court assistance directly against that asset. A transfer of assets by a debtor with the intent to delay, hinder or defraud creditors is known as a fraudulent conveyance.

The common law of most states has continually recognized the power of the court to reverse certain fraudulent transfers by debtors. Many states enacted their own fraudulent conveyance acts. The National Conference of Commissioners on Uniform State Laws drafted the Uniform Fraudulent Conveyance Act (UFCA) in 1918. In 1984, the Conference adopted a revision of the UFCA and titled it the Uniform Fraudulent Transfer Act (UFTA). This Act was designed to integrate fraudulent conveyance law with the Uniform Commer-

cial Code and the Bankruptcy Code. The majority of the states have adopted either the UFCA or the UFTA.

Under common law as well as both the UFCA and UFTA, any transfer made or obligation incurred with actual intent to hinder, delay, or defraud any creditor is deemed fraudulent against both present creditors and future creditors. In addition, both the UFCA and the UFTA deem that a transfer made or obligation incurred by a person receiving less than the reasonably equivalent value in exchange is fraudulent without regard to the debtor's actual intent in any of the following three situations:

1. If the transfer or obligation leaves the debtor with assets that are unreasonably small to conduct the business or transactions in which the debtor is engaged.
2. If the debtor intended to incur, or believed that he would incur debts beyond his ability to repay them as they mature.
3. If the debtor was insolvent at the time or as a result of the transfer. But, this situation applies only to present creditors, not to future creditors.

What can the creditor do in the event of a fraudulent transfer? As a general rule, creditors may take either one of two courses. Under the first track, a creditor may request that the court set aside the conveyance. Then the creditor can levy upon the asset now titled in the debtor.

Under the other track, a creditor may levy execution directly upon the conveyed property in the hands of the transferee. A transferee usually cannot claim innocence because the circumstances of a fraudulent transfer should put a reasonable person on notice that the transfer was not in good faith.

A creditor may have other remedies available, including requesting that the court enjoin the debtor from making further transfers of the property. In severe situations, a court may appoint a receiver to take charge of the debtor's property.

There are a number of warning signs indicating the existence of a possible fraudulent conveyance. These are known as "badges of fraud" which have been used to distinguish fraudulent transfers from nonfraudulent transfers. Badges of fraud include the following types of transfers:

1. A transfer involving all or substantially all of the debtors assets.
2. The debtor selling the property but retaining possession or beneficial use of the property after the transfer.
3. A transfer made in secret.
4. A transfer made to a family member, such as to her spouse or to her child.
5. A transfer made without consideration or for less than full or adequate consideration.
6. A transfer made in anticipation of or during litigation, or in anticipation of financial difficulty.

Not all fraudulent conveyances will justify a creditor's remedy. Under both the UFCA and the UFTA, a creditor may not recover a transfer from a good faith purchaser for value. This means that someone who pays a reasonable equivalent of the fair market value for the property and has no knowledge of the fraud at the time of the purchase will be free from having the property attached by creditors or otherwise taken away by a court.

II. Laws Protecting Debtors

Commercial and consumer debt levels have steadily increased each year from the post World War II period to the present. In recent years, debt levels have risen to the point that defaults on credit obligations by overextended borrowers are common. Often, creditors have superior bargaining power through both size and expertise. In an attempt to provide an equal footing for debtors, a number of federal and state statutes have been passed to assist debtors in obtaining credit on fair terms and to protect debtors from unfair or oppressive collection techniques. Much of the legislation has been enacted to assist debtors in making informed decisions regarding credit choices. Other laws, including those prohibiting unfair or oppressive credit collection techniques, are designed to bring order to the marketplace as well as rid the credit market of unscrupulous operators.

Other statutes are intended to keep debtors from being deprived of basic human necessities as well as providing fresh starts for those overwhelmed with obligations that cannot be met. The Bankruptcy Code, a federal statutory law, will be discussed in the next chapter. Bankruptcy relief is an attempt to give a debtor a fresh start by permitting the debtor to discharge or otherwise reorganize certain debts. In terms of protecting debtors from having creditors seize even those assets necessary for ordinary human existence, exemption or homestead statutes were enacted.

A. Exemption Laws

Most states have enacted laws which exempt certain types of property from attachment or levy of execution. The most common type of exemption is the homestead exemption. Many states have laws which permit a debtor to retain the family home, either in its entirety or up to a specific dollar amount, free from the claims of unsecured creditors. Remember that if the residence is pledged as collateral in support of the debt, the holder of the mortgage or deed of trust will be permitted to foreclose or otherwise proceed to take possession of the collateral in the event of default. Some western states prohibit unsecured creditors from levying or otherwise attaching homesteads within city limits without regard to the property's value, so long as the lot does not exceed a certain size. This means that a debtor owning a home valued at two million dollars might be able to prevent her creditors from levying execution or otherwise attaching the house or its value for the collection of an unsecured debt.

State exemption statutes usually exempt personal property essential for daily living from satisfaction of judgment or other debts. These categories include:

1. Household furniture up to a specific dollar amount.

2. Clothing and certain personal possessions, such as family bibles and pictures.

3. A vehicle used by the debtor for transportation (this is usually limited by a specific dollar value).

4. Pets and certain farm animals, subject to limits.

5. Tools of the debtor's trade or equipment used in the debtor's profession, up to a specific dollar value.

Exemption statutes vary from state to state. Exemption statutes in western states are very debtor oriented. Many of these statutes were enacted during the populist political movement of the early 1900's when large businesses and banks were viewed as public enemies by members of that political movement.

B. The Federal Regulation of Credit

In order to prevent creditors from arbitrarily denying credit to deserving consumers and from misrepresenting contractual terms, Congress enacted the Consumer Credit Protection Act. The Consumer Credit Protection Act includes three major laws relating to the extension of consumer credit. Those laws are known as the Equal Credit Opportunity Act, the Fair Credit Reporting Act, and the Truth-in-Lending Act. Each of these laws is supplemented by federal regulations setting forth the details of implementation.

I. THE EQUAL CREDIT OPPORTUNITY ACT

The Equal Credit Opportunity Act (ECOA) prohibits discrimination in credit transactions on the basis of sex, marital status, religion, race, color, national origin or age. The ECOA also prohibits discrimination on account of all or part of the applicant's income is derived from a public assistance program or because the applicant in good faith exercised any right under the Consumer Credit Protection Act. Creditors under the ECOA include financial institutions, retail stores and credit card issuers. An applicant under the ECOA is any individual (including some small business organizations) requesting or receiving an extension of credit. An application for an extension of credit may be an oral or a written request made in accordance with the procedures established by the creditor for the type of credit requested.

The ECOA permits suits for money damages by victims of credit discrimination. Individual victims may recover actual damages, which can include recovery for public humiliation and mental distress. In addition to actual damages, victims may be able to recover their attorney's fees and other legal costs plus punitive damages up to $10,000. In addition to the existence of private remedies, the government may bring a suit to enjoin any violation of the ECOA and to assess civil penalties against creditors in violation.

The Act further prohibits discriminatory advertising. Advertising must be directed to the entire community in a nondiscriminatory manner. Creditors found guilty of discriminatory advertising may be ordered to conduct an affirmative advertising campaign directly aimed at the group suffering from past discrimination.

The ECOA restricts the type of information that a creditor may request from the applicant and limits the use of that information. A credit application cannot request the applicant's race, color, religion, or national origin. While a creditor may be permitted under certain circumstances to ask the applicant's sex, marital status or age, the use of this information must be limited to lawful purposes. A creditor may not request data concerning an applicant's spouse unless both spouses are applying for the credit, such as co-makers of a promissory note or a joint credit card.

Creditors may request some types of information only if they advise the applicant that the information is optional. For example, the application may request the applicant's title if the application states that the information is optional. (Mr., Miss, Mrs., Ms.) The applicant is not required to disclose the receipt of alimony, maintenance or child support unless the applicant will be relying upon those payments as a source of income for credit purposes.

The ECOA requires that a creditor notify the applicant of the decision to extend or not to extend credit within 30 days after receiving the application. Any creditor who takes adverse action against an applicant must state specific reasons for the adverse action. Notification to the applicant is required in the event the creditor denies or revokes the credit of the applicant, changes the terms of an existing credit arrangement, or refuses to extend in the amount or terms requested.

2. THE FAIR CREDIT REPORTING ACT

The Fair Credit Reporting Act (FCRA) was enacted to prevent abuses in credit reporting systems. In addition, Congress desired to protect an individual's privacy and to ensure that the information within the report was accurate.

The FCRA defines a consumer credit reporting agency as a person or organization that, for a fee or on a cooperative nonprofit basis, regularly assembles or evaluates credit or other information on consumers for use by third parties. Consumer reporting agencies do not include creditors that provide information to third parties concerning only the creditor's own experience with the consumer.

a. The Scope of the FCRA

The FCRA regulates use of two types of reports prepared by consumer reporting agencies. It regulates both consumer reports and investigative consumer reports. Consumer reports are defined as oral or written reports from a consumer reporting agency that concern a consumer's creditworthiness, credit standing and credit capacity. As a general rule, consumer reports contain information collected by the agency from public records and the consumer's other creditors.

Investigative consumer reports contain information concerning the subject's character, general reputation, personal characteristics, or mode of living. This information is usually collected by personal interviews with the consumer's neighbors, friends, or acquaintances. A creditor may not request an investigative consumer report without disclosing to the consumer that such a report will be obtained as a part of the credit decision.

A consumer reporting agency may only provide consumer reports to parties that the agency has reason to believe will use the information in connection with a legitimate extension of credit, review of a credit account, evaluation of an employment application or for insurance purposes. In addition, an agency may release a consumer report to a court of law or to the subject applicant.

b. Accuracy of the Report

The FCRA prohibits consumer reporting agencies from disclosing obsolete adverse credit information in a consumer report. This would include bankruptcies that are 10 years older than the report and other adverse information that antedates the report by more than 7 years, such as judgments and lawsuits (unless the statute of limitations period has not expired on the judgment), as well as paid tax liens, accounts placed for collection, and criminal records of arrest, indictment or conviction. Furthermore, before releasing information from an investigative consumer report, the agency must verify any adverse information that was obtained more than three months prior to the date of the report.

The FCRA permits consumers to examine their credit reports and to verify the accuracy of the information. A creditor who denies consumer credit because of a consumer report must notify the credit applicant of the name and address of the consumer reporting agency that provided the report. In response, the consumer may request that the agency disclose the nature and substance of the information in the agency's file as well as the sources of information and receipts of reports during the preceding six months. If the consumer contests the accuracy of any information, the consumer reporting agency must reinvestigate the information and delete any incorrect information. If the agency decides that the information is accurate, the consumer is entitled to file a statement explaining the dispute. If the consumer requests, the reporting agency must provide notice of a decision or the consumer statement explaining a dispute to a creditor who received the report during previous six months. In all subsequent reports the agency must include the consumer statement explaining the dispute or a summary of the statement.

c. Remedies for Violations

The FCRA is administratively enforced by the Federal Trade Commission and other federal agencies. There are both civil and criminal penalties for violations of any provision. In addition, a consumer may sue a credit reporting agency for actual damages and punitive damages as well as a reasonable attorney's fee in a successful action. Any party obtaining information under false pretenses on a consumer from a credit reporting agency is subject to I year in prison and a fine of up to $5,000 or both. Any employee or officer of a consumer credit reporting agency who knowingly or willfully provides information to an unauthorized person is subject to the same penalties.

3. THE TRUTH-IN-LENDING ACT

The Truth-In-Lending Act (TILA) applies to any individual or organization in the business of offering or extending credit. The Act is regulated and enforced by the Federal Reserve Board pursuant to the Board's set of rules collectively identified as "Regulation Z."

The express purpose of TILA is to assure the meaningful disclosure of credit terms so that a consumer will be able to compare more readily the various credit terms available to her. This is to avoid the uninformed use of credit and to protect the consumer against inaccurate and unfair credit billing and credit card practices.

Three elements must be present for TILA and Reg Z to govern a transaction. They are:

1. The applicant for credit is a consumer with respect to the credit requested. This means the proceeds of the loan must be used for personal, family or household purposes as opposed to business purposes.
2. The creditor must offer or extend consumer credit on a regular basis, meaning 25 or more times during the previous calendar year or at least 5 times during the previous calendar year if the credit was secured by the applicant's dwelling.
3. The repayment of the credit extended is subject to a finance charge or is evidenced by a written agreement that allows for more than 4 installment payments.

Extensions of credit exceeding $25,000 are exempted from the Act. It is presumed that consumer debtors borrowing over $25,000 have sufficient business sophistication to protect themselves. This may be true except for extensions of credit relating to a purchase of a personal residence. Therefore, mortgage transactions involving personal residences are not exempted from the Act's requirements regardless of the dollar amount involved.

a. The Requirement of Certain Disclosures

The overriding purpose of TILA is to encourage consumer debtors to shop and compare credit terms prior to entering into a transaction. In order to make this possible, the Act requires creditors to disclose certain information with respect to a potential credit transaction. The Act has many technical requirements relating to disclosures. Creditors must be very careful to comply with all of the terms and provisions. The most significant disclosures required under TILA are:

1. *The Amount Financed.* The amount financed is determined by taking the loan principal and adding any other amounts financed by the creditor that are not a part of the finance charge, and subtracting any prepaid finance charge. The Act requires that the amount must be stated as a dollar figure and clearly marked as "Amount Financed."

   Regulation Z requires that the credit terms of the transaction be disclosed clearly and conspicuously in a written form that the consumer may keep.

   The two most important credit terms are the "finance charge" and the "annual percentage rate," which must be disclosed more conspicuously than other information provided to the creditor except the creditor's identity.

2. *Finance Charge.* The finance charge must be disclosed in the form of a dollar figure. The finance charge demonstrates to the applicant what the credit transaction will cost over the term. It includes all charges paid by the applicant when securing the extension of credit. It is more than just the total of all interest payments. It includes all fees charged by the creditor as a cost of extending credit. These fees include service or carrying charges, loan fees, finder's fees, fees for appraisals and credit reports, charges for insurance paid by the debtor to protect the creditor if the debtor defaults, and certain other insurance premiums.

3. *The Annual Percentage Rate.* The Annual Percentage Rate (APR) can be used by applicants to compare the cost of obtaining credit. By setting a standard based upon an annual rate, a cost comparison is made very easy for consumer applicants. The TILA and Regulation Z provide a detailed explanation of the method of calculating the APR with Regulation Z including tables to assist the creditor.

b. Enforcing the Truth-in-Lending Act

Violations of TILA expose the violator to both criminal and civil sanctions. An individual may recover money damages equal to two times the finance charge subject to a minimum of $100 and a maximum of $1,000. In a class action lawsuit for improper disclosures, there is no limit on an individual's claim, but the class can recover only the lessor of $500,000 or 1 percent of the creditor's net worth.

But, creditors will not automatically be subject to liability in the event a bona fide error is made in a disclosure. Bona fide errors include inaccurate disclosures due to clerical, printing, or computer mistakes. Technical violations, if not material, do not create grounds to hold a creditor liable for money damages.

The justice department has the power to bring criminal actions against creditors violating TILA. To be criminally liable, a creditor must knowingly and willfully fail to make adequate and accurate disclosures. Criminal violations are punishable up to a $5,000 fine or up to one year in prison, or a combination of both.

c. Open-end Credit versus Closed-end Credit

An open-end credit is a consumer credit under a plan in which:

1. The creditor reasonably contemplates repeated transactions;
2. The creditor may impose a finance charge from time to time on an outstanding unpaid balance; and
3. The amount of credit that may be extended to the consumer during the term of the plan (up to any limit set by the creditor) is generally made available to the extent any outstanding balance is repaid.

A typical open-end credit is a bank credit card arrangement. The consumer has a line of credit upon which she may make purchases or draw cash advances against. The card issuer reasonably contemplates the card holder use the card repeatedly. The issuer imposes a finance charge, usually monthly, on the unpaid balance.

A closed-end credit is defined as a consumer credit other than an open-end credit. A typical closed-end credit would be a car loan from a bank to be repaid in monthly installments for a term of three years. The lease of an automobile would also be a closed-end credit.

The TILA requires different disclosures for open-end credit plans and closed-end credit plans. A creditor entering into an open-end credit plan must make certain disclosures in writing in a statement issued at the time the account is opened and in statements issued on a periodic basis according to the creditor's billing cycle in which the account has a credit or debit balance or in which a finance charge is imposed. The opening statement must include the conditions under which a finance charge is made, the method of determining the finance charge, the method of determining the balance upon which the finance charge is based, the periodic interest rate, and the APR.

The periodic statement provides similar information applied to specific transactions that occur during the billing period: the previous balance, identification of each transaction, credits and payments, the balance subject to the finance charge, the finance charge, the periodic interest rate, and the APR. A creditor is also required to make other disclosures to the consumer when changes in the credit terms occur.

Prior to commencing a closed-end credit transaction, the creditor must provide a written disclosure statement that includes the identity of the creditor, the finance charge, the APR, the amount financed, the total of payments (the sum of the finance charge and the amount financed) and the number, amount, due dates of payments as well as the fees to be imposed upon late payments. If a creditor is taking a security interest in the debtor's property, the security interest must be disclosed. If the creditor is also the seller of the property for which the credit transaction was arranged, the disclosure statement must also show the "total sales price," indicating the cash price plus the additional charges plus the finance charge.

d. The Right of Rescission

Another important feature of the TILA is the consumer's limited right to rescind certain credit transactions in which the creditor will acquire a security interest in the principal residence of a consumer. The property need not be the principal dwelling of the borrower. A third party may provide her home as security for an obligation of another.

Each consumer whose ownership interest is subject to a security interest will have the right to rescind the transaction. The right of rescission may be exercised until midnight of the third business day after the latest of the following:

1. Consummation of the transaction.
2. Delivery of the notice of the right of rescission; or
3. The delivery of all "material disclosures" which must be given to the debtor under TILA.

Note that all three of these elements must be met before the three day clock starts running. This means if the creditor forgets or neglects to deliver the notice of the right of rescission to the party pledging the residence as collateral, the transaction may be rescinded if all other requirements of rescission are met by the debtor. But, even if the required notices or material disclosures are not delivered, the right to rescind expires three years following consummation of the transaction, upon transfer of all of the consumer's interest in the property, or upon the sale of the property, whichever occurs first.

If the consumer has received the loan proceeds, and the property owner notifies the creditor that the transaction will be rescinded, the loan proceeds must be returned. There are transactions that are exempt from the right of rescission. They include residential mortgage transactions. A residential mortgage transaction is one in which a lien is taken on the consumer's principal dwelling to finance the acquisition or initial construction of that dwelling. In addition, a refinancing by the same creditor if the existing credit is already secured by a consumer's principal dwelling is exempt from the right of rescission unless the new amount financed exceeds the unpaid principal balance plus any earned but unpaid finance charge on the existing debt.

4. THE FAIR CREDIT BILLING ACT

The TILA also encompasses the Fair Credit Billing Act, which regulates the billing practices and the dispute resolution process for open-end credit accounts. The Fair Credit Billing Act includes procedures that the debtor and creditor must follow when billing errors occur. Creditors must annually furnish the debtor with statements outlining the debtor's rights and the creditor's responsibilities under the Act.

5. THE FAIR DEBT COLLECTION PRACTICES ACT

The Fair Debt Collection Practices Act (FDCPA) was designed to prevent abusive, deceptive and unfair debt collection practices by overly aggressive debt collectors. The FDCPA is directed toward those in the business of collecting debts owed to someone else. Creditors attempting to collect their own debts are exempt from the law under the rationale that a creditor would not engage in an unfair debt collection practice with an existing customer, thereby damaging goodwill and public relations with that debtor and the community. Creditors will be subject to the FDCPA's provisions if they attempt to collect the debt by using a name that does not reveal the creditor's identity.

This law is applicable only to the collection of consumer debts. It is assumed that business debtors are sophisticated enough to protect themselves from unfair practices.

The Act limits contact between bill collectors and neighbors or employers of the debtor, but does not totally prohibit it. Third parties contacted may not be informed that the consumer owes a debt. When the debtor is represented by an attorney and the bill collector is aware of it, the collector may not contact anyone else except the attorney unless the attorney fails to respond to the collector's attempts to communicate.

The Act prohibits collectors from physically threatening the debtor, using obscene language, pretending to be an attorney, threatening the debtor with garnishment unless the creditor or collector is legally entitled to resort to such action and intends to take it, or telephoning the debtor repeatedly with the intent to annoy. The Act requires a collector using the telephone to make a meaningful disclosure of his identity. A collector is prohibited from telephoning the debtor from before 8 a.m. local time and after 9 p.m. local time.

If a debtor desires to stop repeated contacts, he need only notify the collector in writing of this desire. Any further contact by the collector following such notification violates the Act. This leaves the collector with the sole remedy of suing the debtor and reducing the debt to a judgment.

Violations of the FDCPA entitle the debtor to sue the collector for money damages, including damages for invasion of privacy and infliction of mental distress as well as for court costs and attorney's fees. The debtor must demonstrate the existence of actual damages. But, in the event actual damages are not proven, the court may still order the collector to pay the debtor up to $1,000 for violations of the Act.

6. THE REAL ESTATE SETTLEMENT PROCEDURES ACT

The Real Estate Settlement Procedures Act (RESPA) requires the disclosure of all costs to buyers and borrowers prior to the consummation of a real estate transaction. This is another attempt by lawmakers to provide debtors with an opportunity to shop for credit and to reduce settlement costs.

The law requires the use of a standard form for advanced disclosure of closing costs and for the actual charges that will be incurred at settlement. The form covers both the costs typically paid by the sellers as well as those paid by the buyer. This would include disclosing the amount and who will pay for loan origination fees, loan discount points, appraisal fees, attorney's fees, inspection fees, title charges, and the cost of surveys.

RESPA also prohibits giving kickbacks to parties for referring a borrower to a lender, charging or accepting a fee for something other than services actually performed and requiring that a home seller purchase title insurance from any particular title company. If the title insurance provision is violated, the violator will be liable for an amount equal to three times the cost of the title insurance.

RESPA prevents a lender from requiring that an unreasonable amount be paid in advance for the purposes of paying real property taxes and insurance when they are due. The lender can require the borrower to pay at closing, as escrow, an amount equal to the number of months between the closing date and the last time the bills for taxes and insurance were paid. In addition, the lender can collect at closing a cushion of 2 months of the total estimated costs of taxes and insurance for the next year.

7. OTHER FTC REGULATIONS

In addition to restricting holder in due course rights with respect to negotiable instruments involved in consumer credit transactions, as discussed in the material explaining Article 3 of the UCC, the Federal Trade Commission has been given the authority by Congress to prevent a number of unfair business practices. The FTC has established rules preventing unfair and deceptive business practices with respect to home solicitation and advertising.

The FTC rules with respect to home solicitation cover any sale, lease or rental of consumer goods with the purchase price of $25 or more, at places of business other than the normal place of business of the seller. The FTC rules do not cover mail order or telephone sales or sales in which the buyer has requested that the seller visit her home.

The law requires that the seller furnish the buyer a copy of the contract in the language that was used in the oral presentation. This may require the contract to be in a language other than English. The contract cannot be in type smaller than 10 point type. It must notify the buyer that the transaction may be canceled at any time prior to midnight of the third business day after the date of the contract. Furthermore, the seller must furnish the buyer with a form to be used to cancel the contract, so that all the buyer would be required to do is sign the form and mail it to the seller. The seller must orally inform the buyer of the existence of the right to cancel.

The seller must honor the notice of cancellation within ten days. This requires the seller to refund all payments made and all property traded in, and return any instruments signed by the buyer. Cancellation of the contract cancels all security or other collateral arrangements. If the goods have been delivered to the buyer prior to cancellation, the seller must notify the buyer within 10 days whether the seller will repossess the goods or abandon the goods.

8. STATE LAWS PROTECTING DEBTORS

Many states have enacted statutes supplementing the provisions of federal legislation protecting debtors. Some state statutes and regulations place stricter requirements on creditors and impose more severe penalties for violations.

a. The Uniform Consumer Credit Code

A number of states have adopted the Uniform Consumer Credit Code (UCCC). Its purpose was to replace fragmented state consumer credit laws with a single comprehensive code. The UCCC regulates interest rates, garnishment, home solicitation and referral sales, credit insurance, contract terms and disclosures, and creditors' remedies.

b. Usury

Every state has enacted some form of usury statute that establishes a maximum rate of interest that may be charged for borrowing or credit purchases. Usury means charging an in-

terest rate higher than the highest rate allowed by law.

In many states, the usury law establishes two maximum interest rates. The first rate, known as the "legal rate," applies to transactions in which parties did not agree on an interest rate. This would apply in situations involving a person or business purchasing goods or services on open account and failing to pay. A creditor may charge the legal rate of interest on the outstanding balance if state law so permits.

The second maximum rate of interest is known as the "contract rate." This rate applies to transactions which the parties have agreed to a specified rate of interest. In almost all situations, the maximum contract rate is higher than the maximum legal rate. In many states, if a transaction involves commercial credit, the usury law does not apply. The rational behind the exemption is that business persons are sophisticated in negotiating interest rates and therefore do not need protection from the state.

Violations of state usury laws can lead to a creditor forfeiting all interest collected, even the interest below the maximum allowable rate. In some states, a usury violation will cause the entire contract to be deemed void.

* * *

Problems

1. Identify by category function those laws assisting creditors in the collection of debts.

2. What are the various types of liens? How is each perfected or otherwise enforced against the debtor and competing creditors?

3. Lou hires Golden Dome heating and plumbing to install a football-shaped hot tub in his house. Ten days after the job was completed, Lou informs Golden Dome that he will not pay the bill. Advise Golden Dome of its rights. Include in your advise the steps that should be taken to protect its

rights as well as any enforcement procedures that exist.

4. Explain the potential liability a creditor faces with respect to the various types of prejudgment remedies.

5. What are the post-judgment remedies available to creditors?

6. Compare and contrast a mortgage foreclosure and a trustee's sale under a deed of trust .

7. What is the debtor's right of redemption? How long is it available?

8. Jack sells his Mercedes-Benz automobile to his brother at 1/10 of the fair market value because he knows a judgment creditor is on the verge of attaching all of his nonexempt assets to satisfy its claim against him. Does the judgment creditor have any recourse? Explain your response, including the elements that must be satisfied.

9. What are exemption laws and who may benefit from them?

10. Explain the scope of coverage and purpose of the following federal laws regulating credit: (a) The Equal Credit Opportunity Act. (b) The Fair Credit Reporting Act. (c) The Truth-in-Lending Act. (d) The Fair Credit Billing Act. (e) The Real Estate Settlement Procedures Act.

11. What is the "right of rescission" under the Truth-in-Lending Act and who is entitled to exercise this right?

12. Explain how states have regulated credit to protect debtors.

Bankruptcy

CHAPTER OUTLINE

Bankruptcy

INDIVIDUALS who are hopelessly in debt have little chance of making any contribution to the economy. This nation was founded by individuals who were concerned with the hopelessness experienced by individuals who, through lack of education, unfortunate circumstances or their own devices, were in debt to a point that no matter how hard they worked, they would never recover financial solvency. In an attempt to bring order and finality to such situations, the drafters of the United States Constitution directed Congress to establish uniform laws on bankruptcy.[1] Therefore, bankruptcy is a federal law. Bankruptcy courts are special federal courts presided over by federally appointed bankruptcy judges.

There are two main goals in bankruptcy law. The first is to provide relief and protection to debtors who are burdened with a level of debt from which they cannot recover. The second goal is to provide a fair means of distributing a debtor's assets among all of his creditors. So, the bankruptcy law affects and protects the rights of both debtors and creditors.

The current bankruptcy law is known as the Bankruptcy Reform Act of 1978. The bankruptcy law is collectively referred to as the "Bankruptcy Code." While the Code has been amended and fine tuned by Congress, the 1978 Code retains its basic form and structure. The most significant change since 1978 has been the creation of a special chapter pro-

viding special relief to family farmers which will be discussed at the end of this chapter.

I. Avoiding Bankruptcy

Before we discuss the provisions and application of the Bankruptcy Code, it is appropriate to examine the negotiations between debtors and creditors prior to this drastic remedy.

Bankruptcy proceedings are extremely expensive. Courts have approved requests for attorney's fees in excess of $1 million in a number of corporate reorganizations. In addition, bankruptcy proceedings can be very time consuming. If a debtor intends to reorganize its business affairs by restructuring its debts, doing it under the jurisdiction of the bankruptcy court will leave a cloud of doubt in the eyes of the debtor's customers, lenders, dealers and suppliers. The longer the period of doubt lasts, the likelihood of a successful reorganization decreases. Therefore, there is an incentive for both debtors and creditors to avoid bankruptcy.

Debtors will usually entertain an alternative that is faster and less expensive than bankruptcy. Creditors have an incentive to avoid bankruptcy because their chances of recovery are greater outside the realm of a bankruptcy action.

---

1. Article 1, section 8.

II. Debt Workout Agreements

Many financial institutions have a department known as "Special Assets" or the "Workout Department." Most nonperforming loans are assigned to the experts in this department. These individuals are skilled financial analysts and negotiators charged with the task of maximizing the lender's recovery on a nonperforming loan. Maximization of recovery may be through pursuing all legal remedies in an attempt to recover as much as possible against the debtor in the shortest period of time. This strategy often forces the debtor into bankruptcy. Lenders are mindful of the bankruptcy alternative, and often will consider a "workout" arrangement with the debtor. Debt workouts can be classified more precisely as composition agreements and extension agreements.

A composition agreement is a contract between a debtor and two or more creditors under which the creditors agree to accept a partial payment in full satisfaction of the claim. When a lender is one of many creditors attempting to collect money from a failing company, a composition agreement may be more beneficial to each creditor than having the company go into bankruptcy. The problem with attempting a composition agreement is getting all of the creditors to agree to the same terms. Objecting creditors may force the debtor into bankruptcy, destroying the purpose.

An extension agreement extends the time of payment of the debt. An extension agreement may involve lowering the principal payments, forgiving interest, extending the maturity date, or any other terms on which the parties can agree. If a debtor has a legitimate chance of reorganizing an enterprise into a viable business, a composition agreement will preserve the going concern value of the company which, in turn, will maximize each creditor's recovery.

III. Assignments for the Benefit of Creditors

Another alternative to bankruptcy is known as an assignment for the benefit of creditors. In this situation, a financially burdened debtor transfers all non-exempt assets to a trustee who liquidates the assets and distributes the proceeds to the creditors. This is a common law or state statutory remedy that functions somewhat similar to a liquidation under the Bankruptcy Code.

Unanimous creditor consent is not required for an assignment for the benefit of the creditors. But, a creditor may challenge the assignment as a fraudulent conveyance unless the assignment conveys all of the debtor's property without restriction to the trustee. A significant difference from a bankruptcy liquidation is that a debtor is not discharged from any debts remaining unpaid after its property is sold and the money is distributed to the creditors. Therefore, any creditor with a deficiency after receiving payment from the sale of the property may pursue the debtor for the unpaid balance. Because of this, this tool is used mainly by corporate debtors. Once a corporation's assets are exhausted, a creditor has no one left to pursue for a deficiency unless there is a surety or guarantor.

Assignments for the benefits of creditors are seldom successful in modern times. This is because the Bankruptcy Code permits creditors, under certain circumstances, to force a debtor into bankruptcy by filing an "involuntary petition." Creditors dissatisfied with the assignment terms or the pattern of distribution can be expected to upset the transaction by initiating an involuntary bankruptcy petition.

IV. The Bankruptcy Code

The Bankruptcy Code is a federal law. It preempts any state law on the subject. Therefore, states cannot enact bankruptcy laws or grant discharges from debt. But, the Bankruptcy Code does incorporate state laws under certain circumstances.

The concept of bankruptcy law in this country originated in England. It was designed to ensure a fair distribution of the debtor's assets to his creditors. The debtor benefitted from the proceeding by being discharged from his obligations. While the United States bankruptcy policy has involved a primary goal of an orderly and fair distribution of the debtor's assets, providing the debtor with relief and a fresh start from an overwhelming debt burden is also considered a significant policy goal.

The Bankruptcy Reform Act of 1978, and its amendments, are located in Title 11 of the United States Code. The Bankruptcy Code is divided into the following Chapters:

Chapter 1   General Provisions
Chapter 3   Case Administration
Chapter 5   Creditors, the Debtor and the Estate
Chapter 7   Liquidation
Chapter 9   Adjustment of Debts of a Municipality
Chapter 11   Reorganization
Chapter 12   Adjustment of Debts of a Family Farmer with Regular Annual Income
Chapter 13   Adjustment of Debts of an Individual with Regular Income

Relief under the Bankruptcy Code falls within one of two categories, liquidation, which is covered by Chapter 7 of the Bankruptcy Code, and rehabilitation, which is covered by Chapters 9, 11, 12 and 13 of the Bankruptcy Code. Chapters 1, 3, and 5 of the Bankruptcy Code set forth rules and procedures for both liquidation and rehabilitation actions.

All bankruptcy matters are heard in federal bankruptcy courts. Once a bankruptcy petition is filed, that particular bankruptcy court has jurisdiction over all of the property of the subject of the petition, referred to in the Bankruptcy Code as the debtor. The bankruptcy court will have jurisdiction over all of the property of the debtor without regard to its location.

Each bankruptcy court is under the authority of a U.S. district court. This is because federal bankruptcy judges are appointed to 14 year terms as opposed to the life tenure granted to federal district judges under Article III of the U.S. Constitution. Congress chose to empower federal bankruptcy judges with limited special powers, as opposed to making them Article III federal judges. An appeal from the decision of a bankruptcy court is taken to the federal district court. An adverse ruling from the district court can be appealed to the U.S. Circuit Court of Appeals for that federal circuit. Unless a court has ruled that part of the Bankruptcy Code is unconstitutional, the U.S. Supreme Court will hear bankruptcy appeals from the circuit courts at its discretion. In most cases, the U.S. Supreme Court will not review bankruptcy court decisions.

A. The Debtor

A debtor can be an individual, partnership, corporation, or municipality. The debtor must reside in the United States or have its domicile, place of business or property in the United States.

Any individual, partnership, or corporation is eligible for liquidation under Chapter 7 of the Bankruptcy Code except for railroads, domestic insurance companies, banks, or other lending institutions insured by the FDIC. Any debtor eligible for liquidation under Chapter 7 may also be eligible for reorganization under Chapter 11 except for stockbrokers and commodity brokers which are limited to special provisions under Chapter 7. Railroads are eligible for reorganization under Chapter 11, but not for liquidation under Chapter 7. The insolvencies of banks, savings and loans, and insurance companies are governed by other state and federal statutes.

B. Commencing The Case— The Petition

Each bankruptcy action is commenced by the filing of a bankruptcy petition. A petition may be either voluntary or involuntary. A voluntary petition is filed by the debtor. An involuntary petition is filed by a creditor or group of creditors meeting certain requirements. Relief under Chapters 7, 11, 12, and 13 may be commenced by a voluntary petition. Relief under Chapters 7 and 11 may be commenced by an involuntary petition. There are no involuntary Chapter 12 or Chapter 13 petitions. Chapter 9 of the Bankruptcy Code, the adjustment of debts of a municipality, will not be discussed in this text.

I. THE VOLUNTARY PETITION

If a debtor desires to obtain relief under the provisions of the Bankruptcy Code, a debtor must begin the case by filing a voluntary petition. A voluntary petition must be filed with the clerk of the bankruptcy court for that district on forms prescribed by the bankruptcy court. A voluntary petition must contain the following information:

1. A list of the secured and unsecured creditors.
2. A statement of the financial affairs of the debtor.
3. A list of all property owned by the debtor, including property claimed by the debtor to be exempt from creditors' claims.
4. A statement of current income and expenses.

The bankruptcy petition and all other forms must be accurate and signed by the debtor under oath. Concealing assets or providing false information to the bankruptcy court is a federal crime.

If the court finds the voluntary petition to be proper, the filing of the petition itself will constitute an "order for relief."

2. THE INVOLUNTARY PETITION

An involuntary petition is filed by creditors of the debtor in an attempt to force the debtor into bankruptcy. Remember that a Chapter 12 or Chapter 13 case cannot be commenced through an involuntary petition. Certain requirements must be met prior to filing an involuntary petition. The requirements depend upon the number of creditors that have claims against the debtor.

If the debtor has 12 or more creditors, it takes at least 3 creditors having unsecured claims totaling an aggregate of at least $5,000 to join in the involuntary petition.

If a debtor has less than 12 creditors, any one creditor having a claim of at least $5,000 may file an involuntary petition against the debtor.

After the petition and summons are served upon the debtor, the debtor has 20 days to object to the involuntary petition. If the debtor fails to object, the court will enter an order for relief. If the debtor files an objection within the time limit, the court will hold a hearing and enter an order for relief if it discovers either of the following to be true:

1. The debtor is generally not paying its debts as they become due (unless such debts are the subject of a bona fide dispute). This is known as equitable insolvency. This is one of the few situations where the court employs a definition of insolvency other than balance sheet insolvency; or
2. A receiver, assignee or custodian took possession or was appointed to take charge of substantially all of the debtor's property within 120 days prior to the filing of the petition. If this occurs, an irrefutable presumption exists that the debtor is unable to pay its debts as they mature.

If the court enters an order for relief, the debtor must provide all of the information to the court as if the debtor had filed a voluntary petition. Information must be presented under oath.

Because an involuntary petition could potentially destroy a debtor's business and reputation, the Code provides that any person filing a petition in bad faith may be liable to the debtor for court costs, attorney's fees, punitive and other damages.

3. THE AUTOMATIC STAY

The automatic stay is one of the most important features of the Bankruptcy Code. The exact moment a petition is filed, the automatic stay goes into effect. The filing of a petition "stays" or prevents further efforts by creditors to collect debts or enforce obligations of the debtor. It also stays any legal proceedings currently pending as well as the creation, perfection or enforcement of any liens upon the debtor's property, except purchase money security interests perfected within the grace period.

Any party knowingly violating the automatic stay is subject to paying damages, including attorney's fees. Violators may also have to explain their actions to the bankruptcy judge whose court is charged with enforcing the automatic stay.

The automatic stay generally continues until the case is closed or dismissed, or the debtor is granted or denied a discharge. Upon a creditor's request, the court may terminate or otherwise modify the automatic stay. This is advantageous for secured creditors who want to foreclose upon the debtor's property. If more money is owed against the collateral than it is worth, the property has no residual value to the unsecured creditors. In these situations, courts will grant a secured party relief from the automatic stay as to that particular piece of property only, permitting the secured creditor to repossess or otherwise foreclose upon the collateral.

V. Liquidation

The important provisions and mechanisms affecting bankruptcy liquidations under Chapter 7 of the Bankruptcy Code are presented below. Unless otherwise stated in the section describing Rehabilitations under Chapters 11, 12, and 13, the same procedures and mechanisms apply to them as well.

A. The Trustee

Soon after the court enters an order for relief, an interim or provisional trustee is appointed to preside over the debtor's property until the first meeting of the creditors. At the first meeting of the creditor's, either a permanent trustee is elected or the interim trustee becomes the permanent trustee. The trustee is charged with the duty of collecting the debtor's property, reducing it to cash and distributing it to the creditors according to the priorities established in the Bankruptcy Code.

B. The First Meeting of the Creditors

Within a reasonable time after the entry of the order for relief, the United States Trustee shall convene and preside at a meeting of the creditors. The United States Trustee may convene a meeting of the equity security holders. The Court may not preside at and may not attend any meeting of the creditors, including any final meeting of the creditors.

Unless excused by the Court, the debtor is required to attend the first meeting of the creditors and to submit to their questions as well as questions from the trustee. The debtor must respond under an oath to tell the truth. The debtor's petition may be dismissed or the debtor may be denied her discharge in bankruptcy if she fails to appear at the meeting when required or makes false statements under oath to the creditors or the trustee.

In order to preserve their claims, creditors are required to file proofs of claim with the clerk of the Bankruptcy Court. In most circumstances, this must be done within 90 days following the first meeting of the creditors. But, in Chapter 11 and certain other cases, the court will establish a later deadline for filing proofs of claim.

C. The Property of the Estate

Generally, at the time the petition is filed, all of the debtor's nonexempt assets become part of the bankruptcy estate. In addition, interests in certain property such as gifts, inheritances, divorce property settlements or life insurance proceeds to which the debtor became entitled within 180 days following the date of the petition, may or may not become part of the estate depending on other circumstances. Otherwise, property acquired after the date of the petition remains the debtor's property.

D. The Debtor's Exempt Property

The Bankruptcy Code recognizes the state law concept of permitting the debtor to exempt certain property from creditors' attachment and execution. It would not be logical to have a bankruptcy law providing relief for individual debtors without permitting them to protect certain personal assets or items needed for daily living. The Bankruptcy Code establishes federal exemptions for individual debtors but, the Code also permits each state the option of deciding to have its state exemption scheme applied to its residents seeking relief under the Bankruptcy Code. In fact, over two-thirds of the states have opted to have their state exemption laws applied to individual debtors residing in those states.

In those states not opting-out of the Bankruptcy Code exemption scheme, individual debtors are permitted to exempt the following property:

1. Up to $7,500 in equity in the debtor's residence and burial plot.

2. Interest in a motor vehicle up to $1,200.

3. The debtor's interest, not to exceed $200 in value in any particular item, or $4,000 in aggregate value, in household furnishings, household goods, wearing apparel, appliances, books, animals, crops, or musical instruments that are held primarily for personal, family or household use of the debtor or a dependent of the debtor.

4. The debtor's aggregate interest, not to exceed $500 in value, in jewelry held primarily for personal, family or household use of the debtor or a dependent of the debtor.

5. The debtor's aggregate interest in any property, not to exceed $400 in value, plus up to $3,750 of any unused amount of the exemption provided for under Paragraph 1.

6. The debtor's aggregate interest, not to exceed $750 in value, in any implements, professional books or tools of the debtor's trade or the trade of a dependent.

7. Any unmatured life insurance contract owned by the debtor, other than a credit life insurance contract.

8. Certain interests in accrued dividends or interest under life insurance contracts owned by the debtor.

9. Professionally prescribed health aids for the debtor or a dependent of the debtor.

10. The debtor's right to receive Social Security benefits, unemployment compensation, local public assistance, veteran's benefits, disability benefits, unemployment benefits or alimony, support or separate maintenance payments for the support of

Example. The Third National Bank loaned purchase money to Marge's Diesel Hut for engine blocks and parts for resale to the motor freight industry. As a part of the transaction, Marge's granted to the bank a purchase money security interest in the items purchased. Three days after Marge obtained possession of the items purchased with the loan proceeds, Marge filed for relief under Chapter 11 of the Bankruptcy Code. The bank had yet to perfect its interest. But, so long as it perfects before the expiration of the grace period, the bank's security interest will be valid and superior. ▢

the debtor or any dependent of the debtor.

11. The right to receive certain personal injury awards and other awards arising out of accidents or crimes.

E. The Powers of the Trustee

I. IN GENERAL

The trustee is required to collect the nonexempt assets of the estate and reduce them to cash for distribution to the creditors. In order to accomplish this, the Bankruptcy Code gives the trustee certain powers. First, the trustee has the rights of a lien creditor in all property of the estate from the date the petition was filed. The trustee is also considered a bona fide purchaser for value of the debtor's nonexempt property. This means that with respect to personal property, the bankruptcy trustee will prevail against an unperfected security interest or a party with lien rights who has not properly recorded its lien. The trustee will also prevail against a mortgagee who hasn't filed its mortgage against the debtor's real property.

The message to lenders is clear. Failure to take steps to comply with the law for protection of the creditor's interest in the collateral, whether by filing a document with a public official or by other means of perfection, will cause a secured lender to lose its priority in the collateral to the bankruptcy trustee.

There is a minor exception. Recall that a secured creditor who has a purchase money security interest in a particular piece of collateral has a grace period during which it may file its financing statement. This grace period is usually a 10 day period beginning from the date of the debtor's receipt of the collateral. Some states have extended that period to as long as 30 days. What happens if a bankruptcy petition is filed during the grace period? Bankruptcy law will yield to the UCC in this situation so long as the secured creditor perfects the purchase money security interest before the grace period expires.

2. THE TRUSTEE'S AVOIDING POWERS

The trustee has the power to set aside certain transactions that occurred prior to the filing of the petition. These powers are known as the "trustee's avoiding powers." They are so named because the trustee has the power to declare void certain transactions as described below.

The trustee may take any action that the debtor could have taken to recover money if a defense exists that would make the transaction voidable. Therefore, if the trustee can establish that the debtor could have avoided the transaction due to fraud, duress, incapacity or mutual mistake, the trustee has the power to declare the transaction void and recover any consideration paid by the debtor for the estate. Any recovery of valuable property will ultimately benefit the creditors of the estate.

As presented in the opening of this chapter, the Bankruptcy Code was designed to promote fairness in the distribution of the debtor's assets to the creditors. One of the problems creditors face as a debtor edges closer to bankruptcy is the debtor exhausting assets to pay certain creditors, but not others. Often payments are made to creditors who are related to the debtor or who otherwise can provide benefits to the debtor after the completion of the bankruptcy. These types of transfers are known as "preferential transfers" because the transfer "prefers" one creditor over another. The Code specifically empowers the trustee to avoid certain preferential transfers.

In order for the trustee to establish the existence of a voidable preference, she must prove each of the following:

1. The transfer was made to or for the benefit of a creditor;
2. The transfer was made for or on account of an "antecedent debt." This is a debt owed by the debtor prior to the date of the transfer in question;
3. The debtor was insolvent when the transfer was made. For these purposes, the debtor is presumed to have been insolvent during the 90 day period immediately preceding the filing of the petition;
4. The transfer was made within 90 days immediately preceding the filing of the petition except in cases which the creditor was an insider, and then the trustee is empowered to question all insider transfers during for one year preceding the petition. Insiders include relatives, general partners, officers, directors and controlling shareholders of corporations, and corporations controlled by the debtor; and
5. The creditor received more as the result of the transfer than it would

have received under a Chapter 7 proceeding (liquidation).

A preferential transfer is not a fraudulent conveyance. A preferential transfer can be the lawful payment of an existing debt. The debtor's equity is not reduced following a preferential transfer. The debtor is merely reducing assets that could have been used to benefit all creditors in exchange for the reduction of a liability owed to one particular creditor.

Both the debtor the creditor may challenge the trustees attempt to avoid what appears to have been a preferential transfer by rebutting the presumption that the debtor was insolvent at the time of the transfer. One of the elements of a voidable preference is that the debtor must have been insolvent at the time the transfer was made. The debtor or the creditor can challenge the presumption that the debtor was insolvent during the 90 days immediately preceding the filing of the petition. If a party challenging the trustee's action can prove that the debtor was not insolvent at the time of the transfer, the transfer is not avoidable as a preference.

Another exception to the trustee's power to avoid a transaction as a preference is to demonstrate that the transaction represented a contemporaneous exchange for new value. This is a situation in which a creditor extends additional loan proceeds to a debtor in exchange for the debtor pledging additional collateral to support the new loan. But, if the debtor pledges additional assets as collateral to support existing debts, without getting new loan proceeds or something of equivalent value, the new pledge of collateral can be set aside as avoidable preference.

In addition, payments for services rendered within 10 to 15 days prior to the payment of the current consideration are not usually deemed preferences. Therefore, if a creditor receives a payment in the ordinary course of business, such as a payment for electrical service, the payment cannot be recovered as a

Example. Assume that Ken Worthy owed $10,000 each to five different banks. But, the Loan Star National Bank had always been his favorite. Ken desired to maintain good relations with Loan Star. Ken had $12,000 of assets remaining to repay his creditors. Therefore, on June 1, he repaid the $10,000 owed to the Loan Star National Bank. On July 15, Ken filed a petition for relief in the Bankruptcy Court under Chapter 7. Ken had only $2,000 in his bankruptcy estate to pay creditors.

The transfer to the Loan Star National Bank was a preferential transfer subject to the trustee's avoiding powers. It was a preferential transfer because it was made to a creditor, on account of a previously existing debt while Ken was insolvent, the transfer was made within 90 days immediately preceding the filing of his petition and Loan Star received more than it would have received under a Chapter 7 liquidation had the transfer not been made. □

voidable preference. Additionally, in a case filed by an individual debtor whose debts are primarily consumer debts, the trustee will not be able to establish a voidable preference for transfers of any property by the debtor to a creditor up to a total value of $600.

If the debtor has transferred property, as opposed to cash, to a creditor, the trustee has the power to recover that particular asset. But, if that asset has subsequently been sold to an innocent purchaser for value, the property cannot be recovered by the trustee. The trustee's remedy will be to recover cash from the creditor equal to the fair market value of the property transferred.

3. AVOIDANCE OF FRAUDULENT TRANSFERS AND CERTAIN LIENS

The trustee has the power to avoid fraudulent transfers occurring within one year before the date of the filing of the petition. The Code's treatment of fraudulent conveyances is similar to that found in the Uniform Fraudulent Conveyances Act.

The trustee has the power to set aside transfers made by the debtor with the actual intent to hinder, delay or defraud creditors. The trustee may also invalidate transfers where the debtor received less than a reasonably equivalent value for the transfer, so long as the debtor (1) was insolvent when the trans-

fer was made or became insolvent as a result of it, or (2) was engaged in a transaction or about to engage in a transaction for which its remaining property would be unreasonably small capital, or (3) intended to incur debts beyond its ability to repay them.

The trustee is also permitted to avoid any lien that was not enforceable against the debtor on the date of the petition or enforceable against a bona fide purchaser for value.

F. Distribution of the Property of the Estate

1. CREDITOR'S CLAIMS

Notice of the bankruptcy proceeding is sent by the bankruptcy court to all creditor's listed on the debtor's schedule of creditors. In order to receive a distribution from the estate, a creditor is required to file a proof of claim. Shareholders may also file a proof of interest.

Once filed, a proof of claim will be automatically allowed unless contested by the trustee, the debtor or another creditor. If that occurs, a hearing will be held to determine the validity of the claim. But, some claims will be denied or limited as a matter of law. They are:

1. The claim will be disallowed to the extent it is unenforceable against the debtor or the debtor's property.

2. The claim will be disallowed to the extent it represents an interest accruing after the petition was filed.
3. Claims for property taxes will be disallowed to the extent that the tax claim exceeds the value of the debtor's interest in the land.
4. Claims for services rendered by the debtor's attorney or an insider are allowed only to the extent of the reasonable value of those services.
5. Claims for post-petition alimony, maintenance, or child support are disallowed. But, these debts cannot discharged under bankruptcy. These obligations can be satisfied from the debtor's post-petition assets.
6. Claims by the debtor's landlord for future rent on a lease terminated in the bankruptcy proceeding will be limited.
7. Claims of the debtor's employees for future compensation due under employment contracts will be limited.
8. Federal tax claims resulting from the debtor's late payment of state unemployment taxes are disallowed.

2. PRIORITY OF PAYMENT

The Bankruptcy Code establishes the order that the various classes of creditors will be paid. Each class must be paid in full before the next class in priority can receive any payment. If there are not sufficient proceeds available to pay a class in full, then each member of the class must be paid in proportion to the size of its claim.

Prior to reducing the assets of the estate to cash and distributing it, the secured creditors must be satisfied. A secured creditor may be partially secured and partially unsecured. A secured creditor is secured to the extent of the collateral's value. To the extent that a creditor's claim exceeds the value of the collateral, the claim will be deemed unsecured. If the value of the asset securing a claim exceeds the value of the claim, the asset will be sold and the secured claim will be satisfied. The remaining proceeds will be placed into the general assets of the bankruptcy estate.

After the secured creditors are satisfied, the Code establishes the following system of priorities for payment of the unsecured claims.

1. The administrative expenses related to representing and managing the bankruptcy estate, including the fees of professionals, such as attorneys and accountants.
2. In an involuntary bankruptcy, the unsecured claims arising in the ordinary course of the debtor's business after the filing of the petition, but before the granting of an order for relief or the appointment of a trustee.
3. Claims of employees for wages earned within 90 days before the filing of the petition up to $2,000.
4. Unsecured claims for contributions to employee benefit plans resulting from services rendered within 180 days before the filing of the petition, limited to $2,000 times the number of employees covered by the plan.
5. Claims by farmers and fishermen up to $2,000, against debtor operators of grain storage or fish storage or processing facilities.
6. Unsecured claims up to $900 based on money given to the debtor prior to bankruptcy in payment for property or services not delivered or rendered.
7. Certain taxes owed for a period of 3 years prior to the filing of the petition.

Any property remaining is paid to satisfy the general unsecured claims of the creditors. Unless these claims can be paid in full, which is almost never the case, payment must be made on a pro-rata basis. In the unlikely situation that the general unsecured claims can be paid in full and assets remain, the remainder will be remitted to the debtor.

In situations where the debtor has no assets, the creditors listed on the debtor's bankruptcy schedule will be notified of this and will be instructed not to file a claim. In "no asset" cases, the unsecured creditors will receive nothing at all.

A consumer holding collateral may file an intention to "reaffirm the debt" and keep the collateral. This often occurs when an individual debtor has had major financial reverses but still wants to retain her house or car pledged as collateral. If the debtor chooses to do this, she must continue making payments to the secured creditor and conform completely to the terms and provisions of the contract. If the debtor defaults, the creditor may resort to any lawful remedy, including repossessing or foreclosing upon the collateral.

G. Discharge of Debts and Exceptions

From a creditor's perspective, the purpose of bankruptcy is to effect equitable treatment of the claims. While from the debtor's view, the bankruptcy law is designed to give the debtor a "fresh start," free of the claims of the creditors listed on the debtor's schedule of debts. A discharge in bankruptcy releases the debtor from any further liability on the debts listed by the debtor on her bankruptcy schedules. The discharge will be granted unless the court or a party raises a legal basis for denying it.

A discharge in bankruptcy voids most judgements against the debtor. The discharge prevents creditors from commencing or continuing any legal proceeding or other act to collect a discharged debt. This prohibits further collection efforts, including telephone calls, letters and personal contacts.

Not all debtors will receive a discharge. And even if a debtor receives a discharge, certain debts may be excepted from the discharge. If a debtor is denied a discharge, all collection efforts, including those with the assistance of a court of law, may proceed against the debtor. This means all of the debtor's nonex-empt assets may be seized to satisfy the claims of creditors. If a particular debt is excepted from the discharge, the creditor owning that claim may pursue collection of that claim without any restriction placed upon it by the bankruptcy court.

I. CERTAIN DEBTORS NOT DISCHARGED

Unless a creditor or the trustee in bankruptcy objects to the discharge and establishes a ground for denying the discharge, the Code provides a discharge to the debtor. The grounds for objecting to a discharge are generally based upon the debtor's dishonesty or lack of cooperation in the bankruptcy proceeding. If such an objection is made, the court will hold a hearing to determine if a reason exists to support a denial of the debtor's discharge. Specific grounds for denying a debtor's discharge include:

1. The debtor is not an individual. Under Chapter 7, corporations and partnerships are ineligible for discharge. They may obtain relief under Chapter 11 or terminate the organization under state law.

2. The debtor made a fraudulent conveyance of property, either before or after the case was commenced.

3. The debtor concealed, destroyed, falsified or failed to keep or preserve financial books and records from which the debtor's financial condition or business transactions could be ascertained.

4. The debtor knowingly and fraudulently: (a) made a false oath or account, (b) presented or used a false claim, (c) received consideration for acting or failing to act in connection with the bankruptcy, or (d) withheld financial books and records from the bankruptcy trustee.

5. The debtor failed to explain to the satisfaction of the court any loss or defi-

ciency of assets necessary to meet liabilities.

6. The debtor refused to obey a lawful order of the court, failed to respond to a question based upon the privilege of self incrimination after having been granted immunity, or failed to testify or respond to material questions approved by the court when self incrimination was not involved.

7. The debtor committed any of the acts specified in paragraphs 2-6 above in connection with a separate bankruptcy case involving an insider within one year prior to the debtor's bankruptcy petition.

8. The debtor signed a written waiver of discharge with the court's approval after the order for relief was entered.

9. The debtor had been granted a discharge in a case commenced within six years before the date of the filing of the petition.

2. REVOCATION OF DISCHARGE

Upon the request of the trustee or a creditor, a discharge previously granted may be revoked if the requesting party can prove that the discharge was obtained through fraud, that the debtor knowingly and fraudulently retained property belonging to the estate or the debtor failed to obey an order of the court.

3. CERTAIN DEBTS WILL NOT BE DISCHARGED

Even if the debtor is granted a discharge, the Code provides that certain prepetition debts will survive the discharge and may be collected against the debtor's post-petition assets. Those debts not discharged include:

1. Claims for back taxes accruing within 3 years prior to bankruptcy.

2. Claims against property or money obtained by the debtor under false pretenses or by false representation.

3. Claims that the debtor did not list in his bankruptcy schedules.

4. Claims based on fraud or misuse of funds by the debtor while he was acting in a fiduciary capacity or claims involving the debtor's embezzlement or larceny.

5. Alimony and child support.

6. Claims based on willful or malicious conduct by the debtor toward another person or property of another.

7. Certain fines and penalties payable to governmental units.

8. Certain student loans, unless payment imposes an undue hardship on the debtor and the debtor's dependents.

9. Consumer debts of more than $500 for luxury goods or services owed to a single creditor incurred within 45 days of the order for relief. The debtor may rebut this presumption if he can prove that any debts reasonably incurred to support the debtor or his dependents should not be classified as luxury goods or services.

10. Cash advances totalling more than $1,000 as extensions of open-end consumer credit obtained by the debtor within 20 days of the order for relief. This is another category in which the debtor will have an opportunity to rebut the presumption that the claim is per se non dischargeable.

11. Judgments or consent decrees awarded against a debtor as the result of the debtor's operation of a motor vehicle while legally intoxicated.

VI. Rehabilitation of the Debtor— Chapters 11, 12 and 13

Under many circumstances, the debtor's ability to repay its creditors will be greater if the debtor is permitted to reorganize and operate, as opposed to being liquidated. This is because an operating entity often has a going concern value that is greater than the sum of its individual assets. Consider for instance, a manufacturing company that has been in existence for 20 years. The company has established goodwill among its customers, suppliers, and the business community. There is inherent value in having a customer base and having an established logistical network for the receipt of raw materials and the shipment of the finished product. The value of those organizational tools and network structures are not individual assets that may be auctioned at a public sale. Should the manufacturing concern face a short term economic problem preventing it from meeting its current obligations, liquidation would not be in the best interests of the creditors if the company could be reorganized into a viable organization. The going concern value of the company as reorganized will ultimately benefit the creditors. The primary goal of reorganizing a debtor is the maximization of the creditors' recovery.

Chapter 11 of the Code deals with reorganization of debtors in general while Chapters 12 and 13 are specialty reorganization chapters. Chapter 12 governs exclusively debtors qualifying as family farmers with regular annual incomes. Chapter 13 governs the adjustment of debts of individuals with regular incomes.

In all cases, a reorganization involves the adoption of a plan of rehabilitation altering some or all of the claims of the unsecured creditors, such as reducing them, converting them into other forms of debt or equity, or extending the period of payment. Under Chapter 11, the rights of secured creditors may be affected, but not adversely prejudiced. The rights of corporate shareholders may be reduced or destroyed under a corporate reorganization plan.

At any time while a Chapter 7 case is pending, whether it be voluntary or involuntary, a debtor has an absolute right to convert the case to a Chapter 11, 12, or 13 proceeding if it can otherwise qualify under the Chapter selected and the case has not been converted from another form in the past. This assures that the debtor is given an opportunity to repay his debts if he is able. If a rehabilitation plan is unsuccessful, the case may be converted by the debtor, or in some circumstances, by his creditors, to a Chapter 7 case.

Unless otherwise stated, the procedural mechanisms, such as the automatic stay, apply to rehabilitation cases.

A. Reorganization under Chapter 11

Chapter 11 is the most common technique used to rehabilitate corporations or other large commercial debtors. A Chapter 11 case may be initiated by a voluntary petition or an involuntary petition. Involuntary petitions must meet the same criteria as an involuntary petition under Chapter 7. A court may, upon the request of the trustee or a creditor, hold a hearing to determine whether a Chapter 7 case should be converted into a Chapter 11 case. In addition, a debtor may convert a Chapter 7 case into a Chapter 11 case.

I. THE DEBTOR IN POSSESSION

One of the most significant differences between Chapter 11 and Chapter 7 is the management of the property of the estate. In a Chapter 11 case, the property is usually managed by the debtor, as opposed to the trustee. This is known as "the debtor in possession." If the debtor is in possession, no trustee will be appointed. The debtor in possession has the rights and powers of the trustee as well as the responsibility of performing the duties of the trustee. This means that the debtor in possession has the power and duty to avoid preferential transfers, to set aside fraudulent conveyances and to disaffirm executory contracts not valuable to the estate.

The debtor in possession must fulfill her powers and duties in the same manner as an independent trustee. If any party in interest can prove to the court that the debtor in possession is not carrying out her duties according to the proper standards, including demonstrating the existence of fraud, dishonesty, incompetence or gross mismanagement, the court can remove the debtor in possession and appoint a trustee. The court may also remove a debtor in possession and appoint an independent trustee if the court finds that such a move would be in best interests of the creditors, shareholders, or other interested parties. The court also has the power to appoint an independent examiner to investigate any allegations of fraud, dishonesty, misconduct or other irregularities prior to removing a debtor in possession and appointing an independent trustee.

Often, a Chapter 11 case involves extremely large corporations with thousands of creditors. In such a case, the court is required to appoint a committee of creditors holding unsecured claims. The court may also appoint committees representing other classes of creditors or shareholders. Creditor's committees usually consist of persons holding the seven largest claims against the debtor of the type represented by the committee. These committees perform various functions, such as consulting with the trustee or the debtor in the possession regarding administration of the case, investigating the debtor's conduct, participating in the formulation of a reorganization plan and requesting the appointment of a trustee or examiner.

2. THE PLAN

Chapter 11 requires the development and confirmation of a plan that will return the debtor to solvent operation. The plan must be fair and equitable; and must:

1. Classify the claims of creditors and other interests into like classes.
2. Specify how each class will be treated under the plan. The Code requires that each member within a class be treated equally.
3. Set forth an adequate means for being put into effect.

During the first 120 days following the filing of the petition, the debtor has the exclusive right to file a plan of reorganization. If the debtor does not file a plan of reorganization within that time, or fails to get creditor consent for the plan within the first 180 days, any party to the bankruptcy, including creditors, may propose a plan of reorganization.

Once a plan has been developed and proposed, each class of creditors must vote on it. Classes that are not impaired under the plan, that is, their rights are not adversely affected, are deemed to have approved the plan.

The Code requires the proponents of a plan to prepare a written disclosure statement that must be approved by the court. It must contain information adequate to enable the members of each class to make an informed judgement about the plan.

To be accepted by a class of creditors, the plan must be approved by those holding at least 2/3 in dollar amount and more than 1/2 of the number of allowed claims within the class. To be accepted by a class of equity holders, persons holding at least 2/3 in dollar amount of a given class of equity security must approve the plan. Any class receiving nothing under the plan will be deemed to have automatically rejected the plan.

Following the vote on the plan, the court will hold a hearing for the confirmation of the

> **Example.** Assume a debtor has an existing lease for the space it occupies. The debtor in possession or trustee has the power to disaffirm the remaining portion of the lease without the fear of being sued for breach of contract. This is advantageous for entities that have entered into speculative lease agreements.
>
> During the real estate boom of the early 1980's, many businesses entered into office and facility lease agreements with escalating lease rates in anticipation of real estate prices continuing to climb at a constant rate. In many major cities, real estate prices dramatically fell in the middle and late 1980's. This left many business organizations locked into long term lease agreements with lease payments 4 to 5 times greater than the prevailing market rate. ☐

plan. In most cases, the court will confirm the plan if it has been proposed in good faith, each class of claimants has either accepted the plan or has not impaired under the plan, and the additional technical requirements set forth in the Code have been satisfied.

3. CRAM DOWN

Chapter 11 provides for a mechanism to prevent, in some circumstances, a faction of dissatisfied claimants from obstructing the confirmation of the plan. Under the Code, even if a class rejects the plan, the Court may confirm the plan if it finds that the plan does not discriminate unfairly and is fair and equitable with respect to the impaired class's interests. In order to effectuate a cram down, the "absolute priority rule" must not be violated. The absolute priority rule states that a class must be paid in full before the next junior class in priority receives anything under the plan. If a plan is in compliance with the absolute priority rule, and at least one impaired class votes to accept the plan, the court will confirm the plan, permitting the cram down so long as the plan does not discriminate unfairly and is fair and equitable with respect to each impaired class that rejected it. Dissident classes are protected in cram downs because the Code requires that each class must still receive what it would have received in the event of a Chapter 7 liquidation.

If the plan is confirmed, the rights and liabilities are established for all claimants, even those claimants who voted against the plan.

4. DISAFFIRMING EXECUTORY CONTRACTS

The debtor in possession or trustee has the power to disaffirm most executory contracts to which the debtor is a party. An executory contract is a contract that has not been fully performed.

The debtor in possession's power to disaffirm executory contracts became an important issue to labor unions. Some businesses employed this power as a tool to break collective bargaining contracts with labor union. Because a labor contract is an executory contract until it expires, a debtor in possession could file for bankruptcy under Chapter 11 and immediately disaffirm the labor agreement under the Code as originally enacted. In response to this, the bankruptcy Code was altered with respect to the power to disaffirm executory labor contracts. The Code now requires the debtor to propose modifications to the labor agreement for consideration by the union. The Code requires that these modifications be presented to the labor union in good faith. The labor union is entitled to examine the debtor's relevant financial information to evaluate the proposal. If the union fails to accept the proposed modification without good cause, the trustee or debtor in possession may reject the remainder of the contract.

5. ADEQUATE PROTECTION FOR SECURED CREDITORS

Secured creditors who have properly filed real estate mortgages or perfected interests in goods will defeat the claims of a bankruptcy trustee or debtor in possession. But under Chapter 11, the rights of secured creditors may be affected. In a reorganization, the debtor in possession has the power to sell or lease property that is the subject to a security interest. Remember that while the automatic stay is in effect, a secured creditor or real property mortgagee cannot take action to recover the collateral. Often the collateral is necessary to the debtor for an effective reorganization. An airline attempting to reorganize could not effectively operate if all of its planes had been repossessed by a secured lender. Consider that a manufacturing concern could not operate if its factory building had been foreclosed upon by its real estate lender.

By the same token, the Code places an important emphasis on protecting the rights of secured creditors. To enforce this concept, the Code requires the debtor provide the secured party with "adequate protection" of its interest in the collateral while enforcement efforts are prevented by the automatic stay. While the Code does not specifically define adequate protection, it does state a number of ways adequate protection can be provided to the secured party. One method is to require cash payments; or additional or replacement liens on the property of the estate to compensate the secured party for any decrease in value of the collateral resulting from either the delay in being able to enforce its rights or the debtor's use of the property. Adequate protection may also be provided by granting such other relief that will provide the secured party with the "indubitable equivalent" of its interest in the collateral.

If the debtor fails to provide adequate protection, the secured creditor may request that the court lift the automatic stay and permit the secured party to exercise its rights and remedies against the collateral. It is essential that a plan of reorganization not adversely affect the value of any secured party's claim. The court will not approve the plan if any secured party can demonstrate to the court that the plan will decrease the value of its secured claim without providing it adequate protection.

B. Rehabilitation under Chapter 13

This is often called the "wage earner" chapter. It applies only to individuals who have regular income and owe unsecured debts of less than $100,000 and secured debts of less than $350,000.

If a debtor under Chapter 13 has a separate business, the business debt or business operations will not be affected by an individual's Chapter 13 case. A Chapter 13 may be commenced only by the debtor. There are no involuntary Chapter 13 petitions. A Chapter 7 debtor may convert her proceeding to a Chapter 13 case if she can qualify under Chapter 13.

Under Chapter 13, the debtor retains possession of all of the property of the estate until the court orders otherwise. But, a trustee will be appointed to oversee the debtor's activities and progress under the plan. Unlike Chapter 7, the property of the estate will include non-exempt assets owned by the debtor prior to the petition as well as certain property acquired and earnings received by the debtor after the petition was filed.

1. THE PLAN

Chapter 13 is less complex than Chapter 11 with respect to formulation of a plan. Only the debtor may file a Chapter 13 plan which must at least:

1. Provide for submission to the trustee of whatever portion of the debtor's future income is needed to implement the plan;
2. Provide for full payment of claims entitled to priority; and
3. Provide identical treatment of all claims within a particular class.

A plan may call for complete or partial payment of all existing debts. The time for payment may not exceed 3 years unless the court approves a longer term. But, the longest repayment term that a court may approve is 5 years.

Creditors do not vote to accept or reject a Chapter 13 plan. The court alone decides on its approval. If the trustee or an unsecured creditor objects to the plan, the court cannot approve it unless the court finds that the value of the property distributed is at least equal to the amount claims, or that all of the debtor's disposable income to be received during the three year plan period will be applied to making payments to creditors.

After a debtor completes all of the payments under a Chapter 13 plan, the debts are discharged, except for child support, alimony and a few special types of debt.

Once a plan is confirmed, the debtor must make the plan's payments to the trustee. The trustee is responsible for paying the creditors according to the terms of the plan. The debtor must start making payments under the plan within 30 days after the plan is filed. Once the payments under the plan are completed, the debtor will be discharged from all of the debts covered by the plan.

2. THE ADVANTAGES OF A CHAPTER 13 DISCHARGE

Chapter 13 is an efficient vehicle for consumers desiring debt relieF. It offers a number of advantages over Chapter 7. A Chapter 13 discharge can include claims that the debtor fraudulently incurred debt and claims resulting from malicious or willful injury. This would not be possible under Chapter 7. Therefore, a Chapter 13 discharge can be extremely beneficial to certain debtors over the provisions of a Chapter 7 discharge.

The hardship provision under Chapter 13 does not exist under Chapter 7. In addition, a Chapter 13 debtor can generally retain property that has been pledged as collateral and require secured creditors to continue financing the debt. Chapter 7 requires the debtor to pay cash in an amount equal to the lesser of the loan balance or the fair market value of the collateral to each secured creditor deprived of its collateral. Moreover, a Chapter 13 plan can be approved over the objection of a creditor.

A Chapter 13 discharge can be revoked within one year if it was obtained by fraud. A common challenge made by creditors against Chapter 13 debtors is that the plan was not proposed in good faith.

C. Rehabilitation under Chapter 12

During the 1970's and early 1980's, American farmers employed increasing levels of debt to finance their operations. Unfortunately, in the early 1980's the prices for many farm products unexpectedly and drastically fell as the result of political forces and changes in the international marketplace. To make things worse, interest rates were at record high levels. These factors resulted in staggering financial losses for farming operations. Many family farmers financed their increasing levels of debt with their farmland as collateral. The depressed market prices led to record defaults on farm loans. This in turn, led to a record number of farm foreclosures. The overwhelming level of farm foreclosures led to a collapse in the price of farmland, which fed the downward spiral of the agriculture economy.

The foreclosure sale of family farms that had been in the same family for multiple generations was a disturbing picture for many small communities as well as for those states depending upon farming for economic stability. The farm foreclosures also disturbed those who hold the American tradition of the family farm as an important cultural value.[2]

Congress responded to the plight of the family farmer in 1986 by adding Chapter 12 to the Bankruptcy Code. It is entitled "Adjustment of Debts of a Family Farmer with Regular Annual Income." Under this Chapter, a "family farmer" is defined generally as an individual (or individual and spouse) engaged in farming operations who (1) does not have debts exceeding $1.5 million, (2) has at least 80 percent of the total fixed debt arising out of a farming operation owned or operated by the debtor and (3) derives at least 50 percent of his gross income is derived from the farming operation.

In addition, a partnership or corporation may qualify as a debtor under Chapter 12 if (1) its total debt falls under the $1.5 million limit, (2) at least 80 percent of its total fixed debt arises out of a farming operation owned or operated by the debtor, (3) more than 80 percent of the debtor's assets are related to the farming operation and (4) more than one-half of its stock or equity is owned by members of the same family who conduct the farming operation.

Chapter 12 closely resembles Chapter 13 because it was modeled after Chapter 13. Prior to the enactment of Chapter 12, many farmers desired to seek relief under Chapter 13 but had debt limits exceeding the Chapter 13 limits.

Under Chapter 12, a debtor files a plan of reorganization within 90 days after the petition is filed. The confirmation hearing must be concluded within 45 days after the plan is filed. At the hearing the court will confirm the plan if it meets the standards similar to those applied under Chapter 13. Under the plan, the secured creditors must ultimately receive payments in at least the amounts of their collateral values. In addition, all of the farmer's disposable income for the 3 years following the confirmation of the plan (or longer if the court approves) must be applied to repaying the creditor's claims. Chapter 12 defines disposable income as income received less amounts needed to support the farmer and to continue the farming operation. Upon completing the payments under the plan, the scheduled debts are discharged.

Secured creditors complain that Chapter 12 is unfair to them because under Chapter 11, a debtor is required to put up adequate protection for the secured party if the debtor desired to continue to use the collateral. Adequate protection is usually calculated as lost opportunity costs to the secured party. As a general rule, the debtor is required to pay an amount equal to the projected interest earnings on a sum of money equal to the value of the property that the debtor wishes to keep using. But, Chapter 12 defines adequate protection as an amount equal to the reasonable rental value of the property. Keep in mind that rental prices for land in a depressed farm economy are often significantly lower than the interest that could be earned on the money if the land were sold at public auction.

Chapter 12 is scheduled to be automatically repealed on October 1, 1993 unless Congress takes affirmative action to extent its life.

* * *

Problems

1. Dan Dawson, doing business as Dawson Fashions, is worried about an involuntary bankruptcy proceeding being filed by his creditors. His net worth using a balance-sheet approach is $8,000 ($108,000 assets—$100,000 liabilities).

---

2. The economic troubles of family farmers became the subject of numerous national network television news stories as well as at least one popular rock song and accompanying music video by John Cougar Mellencamp. Numerous telethons and other fund raisers were organized for the purpose of assisting family farmers in economic trouble.

However, his cash flow is negative and he has been hard pressed to meet current obligations as they mature. He is, in fact, some $12,500 in arrears in payments to his creditors on bills submitted during the past two months.

(a) What are the current requirements for a creditor or creditors filing an involuntary petition in bankruptcy and could they be satisfied in this situation?

(b) Will the fact that Dawson is solvent in the bankruptcy sense result in the court's dismissing the creditors petition if Dawson contests the propriety of the filing of a petition? (Modified from A.I.C.P.A. Nov. 81-4a.)

2. Davis owns a ship in which he repairs electrical appliances. Two months ago Electrical Supply Company sold Davis, on credit, a machine for testing electrical appliances and obtained a perfected security interest at that time to secure payment of the balance due. Davis' creditors have now filed an involuntary petition in bankruptcy against him. What is the status of Electrical Supply?

a. Electrical Supply is a secured creditor that has the right, if not paid, to assert its rights against the machine sold to Davis to enforce its claim.

b. Electrical Supply must surrender its perfected security interest to the trustee in bankruptcy and share as a general creditor of the bankrupt's estate.

c. Electrical Supply's perfected security interest constitutes a preference and is voidable.

d. Electrical Supply must elect to resort exclusively to its secured interest or to relinquish it and obtain the same share as a general creditor. (Modified from A.I.C.P.A. May 78-1 (23) and May 79-1 (22).)

3. On January 10, Davis gave Cantrell a mortgage on his office building to secure a past-due $40,000 obligation which he owed Cantrell. Cantrell promptly recorded the mortgage. On March 15, a petition in bankruptcy was filed against Davis. The trustee in bankruptcy desires to prevent Cantrell from qualifying as a secured creditor. In seeking to set aside the mortgage, which of the following statements is correct?

a. The mortgage cannot be set aside since it is a real property mortgage and recorded.

b. Even if the mortgage is set aside, Cantrell has a priority in respect to the office building.

c. The mortgage can only be set aside if the mortgage conveyance was fraudulent.

d. The mortgage can be set aside even if was taken with no knowledge of the fact that Davis was insolvent in the bankruptcy sense. (Modified from A.I.C.P.A. May 78-1(25).)

4. Disco Records, Inc., was in dire financial condition which was widely known in the relevant business community. Disco's liabilities exceeded its assets by approximately $200,000. Jolly Plastics, Inc., one of Disco's creditors, was pressing Disco to pay $30,000 of overdue accounts. Disco decided to mortgage or sell its warehouse to improve its cash position, provide funds to forestall creditors, and permit it to work out its financial difficulties.

Disco first approached several banks and attempted to mortgage the property. However, the banks would only loan an amount equal to 50% of the value of the property. The maximum funds that Disco could obtain from a bank was $30,000 which was not enough to forestall bankruptcy. Disco abandoned this approach.

Disco then placed the property on the market. The property was listed with several brokers on a non-exclusive basis and was advertised in the local papers. Jolly learned of the proposed sale and, because of unique advantages of the property to Jolly, offered $62,500. This was $2,500 more than any other prospective purchaser had offered. The purchase price consisted of cancellation of the $30,000 overdue debt and $32,500 in cash.

The sale was consummated on August 1. On the following October 14, a petition in bankruptcy against Disco was duly filed by a group of its aggrieved creditors. The trustee in bankruptcy has attacked the sale of land as a voidable preference. Will the trustee prevail? (Modified from A.I.C.P.A. Nov. 78-2b)

5. D owned a store building in which he carried on a retail appliance business. D sustained financial reverses, became insolvent in the bankruptcy sense on May 1, remained insolvent thereafter, and was adjudged a voluntary bankrupt on a petition filed September 10.

(a) On June 1 S, one of D's regular suppliers, received from D an order for certain TV sets for $4,000 on the usual terms of 2/ 10 net 30. At this time S had reason to believe that D was insolvent. (1) S refused to sell to D except for cash. D agreed and on June 24, S delivered the TV sets to D, and D paid S the agreed $4,000. What right would the trustee have against S? Explain. (2) S refused to sell to D without some security. D agreed and on the date stated below S delivered the TV sets to D, and D dated, signed, and gave S a writing promising to pay $4,000 in 30 days and stating that a security interest in the described TV sets would remain in S until the full price was paid. When D was adjudged bankrupt, he had not paid S and still had in stock in his store the TV sets received from S. (a) The security agreement was dated June 2. S filed a financing statement the same day. As between the trustee and S who would have superior interest in the described TV sets? Explain. (b) The security agreement was dated July 5. S filed a financing statement the same day. Answer the same question as in (a) above. (c) The security agreement was dated June 2. S filed a financing statement on July 5. Answer the same question as in (a) above. (d) Same facts and question as in (c) above, except that on the stated dates S had no reason to believe D was insolvent.

(b) On April 15 S, one of D's regular suppliers delivered certain TV sets for D for $4,000 payable 2/ 10 net 30. When D did not pay, S sued and obtained a judgment against D. (1) S obtained the judgment against D on June 1, but did nothing further. After the bankruptcy adjudication of September 10, what would be the status of this judgment

if, when S obtained the judgment, (a) he had no reason to know that D was insolvent? (b) he knew that D was insolvent? Explain. (2) S obtained the judgment against D on July 1, but did nothing further. Same additional facts as immediately above. Answer the same questions.

6. On February 1, D borrowed $1,000 from C, and signed and gave to C a one-month note for that amount with interest at the rate of 6 percent per year. The note contained the following provision: "I hereby waive the benefits of the present and any future bankrupt law that may be passed by the United States." On the following April 1, D was adjudged bankrupt. In final settlement of the bankruptcy proceeding all general creditors, including C, received 10 percent on their final claims, and D received a discharge in bankruptcy. Seven months after completion of the bankruptcy proceeding, D inherited a large sum of money. C thereupon sought to collect the balance of the note from D, and upon D's refusal to pay, sued D.

(a) How much, if anything, could C collect? Explain.

(b) Other facts remaining the same, assume that one month after completion of the bankruptcy proceeding, D in writing promised C that he would pay C the balance of the note within six months. How much, if anything, could C collect in his lawsuit against D? Explain.

7. A bankrupt who has voluntarily filed for and received a discharge in bankruptcy

(a) Will receive a discharge of any and all debts owed to him as long as he has not committed a bankruptcy offense.

(b) Can obtain another voluntary discharge in bankruptcy after five years have elapsed from the date of the prior discharge.

(c) Must surrender for distribution to the creditors amounts received as an inheritance if the receipt occurs within 180 days after filing of the petition.

(d) Is precluded from owning or operating a similar business for two years. (A.I.C.P.A. May 83-1(23).)

8. Skidmore, doing business as Frock & Fashions, is hopelessly insolvent. Several of his aggressive creditors are threatening to attach his property or force him to make preferential payments of their debts. In fairness to himself and to all his creditors, Skidmore has filed a voluntary petition in bankruptcy on behalf of himself and Frock & Fashions. An order for relief has been entered (i.e. he has been adjudged bankrupt).

Skidmore's bankruptcy is fairly straightforward with the following exceptions:

(1) Skidmore claims exemptions for his summer cottage and for his home.

(2) Morse, a business creditor, asserts that commercial creditors have a first claim to all Skidmore's property, business and personal.

(3) Walton seeks a denial of Skidmore's discharge since Skidmore obtained credit from him by use of a fraudulent financial statement.

(4) Harper claims a priority for the amount owed him which was not satisfied as a result of his resorting to the collateral securing his loan.

(a) What are the principal avoiding powers of the trustee in bankruptcy?

(b) Discuss in separate paragraphs each of the various claims and assertions stated above. (A.I.C.P.A. Nov. 83-3a).

9. Under the Bankruptcy code, one of the elements that must be established in order for the trustee in bankruptcy to void a preferential transfer to a creditor who is not an insider is that

(a) The transferee-creditor received more than he would have received in a liquidation proceeding under the Bankruptcy Code.

(b) Permission was received from the bankruptcy judge prior to the trustee's signing an order avoiding the transfer.

(c) The transfer was in fact a contemporaneous exchange for new value given to the debtor.

(d) The transferee-creditor knew or had reason to know that the debtor was insolvent. (A.I.C.P.A. May 84-1(18).)

10. Davis has been involuntarily petitioned into bankruptcy under the liquidation provisions of the Bankruptcy Code. After reducing Davis' non-exempt property to cash, the following expenses and unsecured claims of creditors remain:

Expenses

Fees incurred to recover property belonging in the bankrupt's estate $9,000
Costs necessary to sell the property of the estate $6,000

Unsecured Claims:

Wage claims of Edwards, earned as an employee of Davis within 61 days of the filing of the bankruptcy petition $3,000
Income taxes for the two years immediately preceding the filing of the bankruptcy petition $80,000

(a) If the cash available for distribution is $12,000, what amounts will be distributed for expenses?

(b) If the cash available for distribution is $25,000, what amount will be distributed for the income tax claims? (Modified from A.I.C.P.A. Nov. 84-1(26 & 27).)

11. On July 1, Debtor, a sole proprietor operating a drugstore, was involuntarily petitioned into bankruptcy by his creditors. At that time, and for at least 60 days prior thereto, Debtor was unable to pay his current obligations and also had a negative net worth. Prior to the filing of the petition Debtor made the following transfers:

(1) May 17—Paid an unsecured creditor the full $7,500 outstanding on a loan obtained from the creditor on April 10.

(2) June 6—Gave a mortgagee a mortgage on his home for a loan made to Debtor on June 4 which they intended to be a secured loan.

(3) June 16—Paid the electric bill for the month of May which was incurred in Debtor's business. The bill was received by Debtor on June 4 and had a June 18 due date.

At the time the petition was filed, Debtor owned a rental warehouse and was involved in a divorce proceeding. The trustee in bankruptcy has informed Debtor that the Debtor's estate will include the following non-exempt property:

(1) Rents received from July 1 through November 1 on the warehouse.

(2) Property received on October 10 as a result of the Debtors' final divorce decree.

(a) Discuss whether the trustee in bankruptcy can properly avoid or set aside the three transfers made by Debtor.

(b) Was the trustee correct by including in the Debtor's estate rents on the warehouse and the property received as a result of the final divorce decree. (Modified from A.I.C.P.A. May 85-5)

Real Property

Real Property

I. Definition and Classification

A. Definition

Real property generally includes land and whatever is growing on or permanently attached to the land. Personal property, on the other hand, generally refers to things which are moveable, things which are not attached to the land. For example, a house and the land on which it was constructed is real property, but the furniture in the house is personal property. Real property also consists of certain rights derived from the land based upon the classification, interest or estate that the owner has in the land. If, for example, an individual owns a tract of mountain land outright (in fee simple absolute), he has the right to sell it; however, if the owner leased the land, his tenant would only have the right to occupy it for the duration of the lease. At the outset, therefore, it is important not only to understand what real property is, but also what rights co-exist with the land based upon the classification of one's interest or estate in the land.

B. Classification of Estates

Historically, the classification of an interest or estate in land dates back to the feudal period in England when social status was determined by the extent of an individual's ownership interest in the land. Those estates which were compatible with the dignity of a freeman were called freehold estates, the duration of which was for at least a life in being. If the estate endured for less than a life, it was called a non-freehold estate.

1. FREEHOLD ESTATES

Freehold estates can be categorized into various groups based primarily upon the extent and duration of the estate owner's interest in the land. It is beyond the scope of this chapter to discuss all the forms of freehold estates and their various characteristics; however, several of the more important ones are (1) fee simple absolute; (2) fee simple determinable; (3) fee simple subject to a condition subsequent; and (4) life estate.

Fee Simple Absolute

A fee simple absolute is the largest estate, in terms of its owner's rights, known to the law. The owner of a fee simple absolute estate can (within the confines of zoning and other law that may affect the land) use, abuse, have exclusive possession of, take the fruits of, and dispose of, by deed (inter vivos) or by will (at death), his land. The estate is most commonly created by deed where the conveyancing language will read "to B" or "to B and his heirs." Under common law, the words "and his heirs" had to be part of the conveyancing language for B to get a fee simple absolute, otherwise B would get only a life interest and the remainder would revert to the grantor. However, under modern law, most states consider simply "to B" sufficient, since it is the intent of the parties that matters.

Fee Simple Determinable

A fee simple determinable, sometimes called a base or qualified fee, is in reality a fee simple absolute created to continue until the happening of a stated event. For example, G conveys a fee simple absolute estate "to B, as long as the land is used for recreational purposes." B receives a fee simple until such time as he discontinues the specified use. The important characteristic of this estate is that the instant it is no longer used for the intended purpose, it automatically reverts back to G, the grantor. G does not have to take any positive action for the reversion to occur. Incidentally, even though the land is used for recreational purposes, G still has an interest in the land. Since there is a possibility he might get the land back in the future, the estate he retains is called a possibility of reverter. Because the fee simple determinable estate is subject to a condition, it clearly does not carry with it the same rights as a fee simple absolute. Its use is restricted, and hence it is something less than the largest estate.

Fee Simple Subject to a Condition Subsequent

A fee simple subject to a condition subsequent is similar to a fee simple determinable in all respects except that, upon the happening of the stated event, the estate will continue in B until G physically reenters and repossesses the land or brings legal action to have B removed. Therefore, the language necessary to create such an estate is "to B, but if the land is used for anything other than recreation purposes, G has the right to reenter and repossess the land." The language must include words of reentry and repossession for a fee simple subject to condition subsequent to arise. (Again note that G retains the possibility of a reverter as long as the land is used for recreational purposes.)

Life Estate

A life estate, as the words indicate, is created for the life of someone, perhaps a tenant in possession, perhaps someone other than the tenant. The conveyancing language would simply be "to B for life." B has the right to use the land and dispose of his life interest therein, but he cannot commit waste or injure G's reversionary interest. B also has the right to exclusively possess the land subject, however, to G's right to come on the land to collect rent, make essential repairs and, in short, to do anything necessary to protect his reversionary interest. In general, B can use the land in the same way as if he were a fee simple owner, except that the corpus must be left reasonably intact for the owner of the reversion, G, or remainder (someone other than G) interest.

2. NON-FREEHOLD ESTATES

Non-freehold estates are those which endure for less than a life. They generally arise out of a landlord-tenant relationship (discussed more fully later in this chapter) and, as such, are classified according to the duration of the lease. For example, an estate for years arises when an owner-landlord leases his land to a tenant for a definite period of years; an estate from year to year arises when an owner-landlord leases his land to a tenant for one year where, in the absence of notification by either party, the lease renews itself annually; or a tenancy at will arises when an owner-landlord leases his land to a tenant for an indeterminate duration at the will of either party where termination will occur at any time without notice by either party.

II. Contracts to Sell Real Property

Under the statutes of frauds in the various states, a contract to sell real estate is not fully enforceable against the seller unless sufficiently evidenced by a writing signed by the seller or by his agent whose authority is in writing.

As soon as an enforceable agreement to sell real estate is entered into, a property interest in the described real estate passes to and vests in the buyer. Since legal title is still vested in the seller, the property interest which vests in the buyer is frequently referred to as an *equitable* title or ownership. The exact nature of the respective legal and equitable interests varies somewhat among the states. In many states:

1. Sufficient real estate interest vests in the buyer so that, after formation of the contract but before its performance (that is, before transfer of legal title to the buyer):

(a) Should either or both parties die, the seller's interest passes to his personal property heirs, the buyer's interest to his real estate heirs.

(b) Should either or both parties marry, the seller's newly acquired spouse has no potential dower (or curtesy) interest in the property. In many states, the buyer's newly acquired spouse likewise has no potential dower (or curtesy) interest, until the buyer obtains full legal title.

(c) Should the property be accidentally damaged or destroyed through no fault of either party, the loss falls on the buyer. Any casualty insurance the seller may be carrying is held for the benefit of the buyer.

(d) Should a judgment be entered against the buyer, the judgment creditor obtains a lien against the property in the amount of the purchase price paid at that time. This lien, like any other judgment lien, will continue for the statutory period and then expire unless the judgment creditor renews the judgment on the record.

2. Sufficient real estate interest remains in the seller so that, in the absence of an express agreement to the contrary, the seller's right either to possession or to rents and profits continues until the seller transfers full legal title to the buyer.

Usually the transfer of any interest in land becomes effective:

1. As between the parties—when the transfer agreement is entered into;

2. As to a later third person (acquiring an interest for value without actual knowledge of the prior interest)—when something is done on the land (for example, the transferee assuming exclusive and readily apparent occupancy of the land) or on the public record affecting land titles, sufficient to give notice of the first transferee's interest.

The practice in many states is for most land-purchase contracts to be performed within a fairly short time; therefore, they are usually not recorded. However, if the buyer pays a substantial sum before he is to receive legal title under the contract, or if the buyer distrusts the seller's honesty or solvency, the buyer should consult his lawyer about having the land-purchase contract recorded, especially if the buyer is not immediately assuming exclusive and readily apparent occupancy of the land.

III. Co–Ownership

A. Definition and Introduction

While a contract always requires two persons, one on each side of the agreement, nothing prevents more than two persons from joining together in the same contract. For example, in a contract to purchase certain property, two persons (or even more than two) can join together on one side of the contract, both (or all) binding themselves to purchase the property from the seller. When several persons join as buyers, they all acquire rights and obligations under the contract. Whether the co-buyers must be joined together as co-parties when a lawsuit is brought to enforce the contract is a procedural question of concern to lawyers. The important point being emphasized here is that several persons acting in concert can acquire rights as co-owners (and undertake obligations) just as readily as one person can.

When the property in question is real estate, note that a definite distinction exists between co-owners and adjoining owners. If A and B co-own a piece of land with two identical buildings, each owns an undivided one-half interest in the total property, comprising the land and both buildings. On the other hand, if A and B are adjoining owners of, for example, a two-unit connected or row dwelling building, A owns one of the row homes and B the other. A and B are not co-owners of the entire structure. Each is a separate owner of one of the units, just as if the two units were not physically connected. They are owners of nothing more than the common wall which forms one side of each of the two homes.

The several principal types of co-ownership of property are: joint tenancy, tenancy in common, tenancy by entireties, tenancy in partnership, and community property. Tenancy in partnership is the form of co-ownership held by persons who are business partners. It is best considered as a part of partnership law and is briefly discussed in Chapter 19. Community property is a form of co-ownership which developed under the civil law rather than the common law. Community property systems have been adopted by statutes in a few western and southwestern states; in all but these few states community property is not a recognized form of property co-ownership in this country.

Co-ownership rights first originated in connection with real estate, and while some states restrict co-ownership to real estate, most states now recognize that some or all of the common-law types of co-ownership can apply both to real estate and to personal property, including in the latter both tangible items of property (like an automobile), quasi-tangible items (like stock in a corporation), and intangible rights to sue and enforce contracts (for example, to collect a money debt).

That persons are married does not mean that they are co-owners of all of their property. Although married, a person can nevertheless be the separate or sole owner of property, and if it is personal property, he or she will have full power to transfer title without his or her spouse joining in the transfer or consenting to it. While real estate can also be solely owned, its transfer is restricted. Since early common law days it has been considered desirable as a matter of policy to grant to a widow an interest not only in property owned by her husband at the time of his death, but also in any real estate (real estate only, not personal property) owned by him at any time during the marriage. Common law also recognized a similar interest in a surviving widower. At common law the interest of a surviving wife was called "dower," that of a surviving husband, "curtesy." In modern times, statutes in many states provide somewhat the same rights to surviving spouses. (Usually the extent of the surviving spouse's statutory interest will vary from a fractional interest to total ownership, depending upon the number and relationship of other heirs left by the deceased spouse.) In some states it is possible for a husband or wife to transfer his or her individually owned real estate without the joinder of the other spouse so long as fair and adequate consideration is received. Therefore, a purchaser should consult his lawyer before buying land from a married person unless that person's spouse also signs the deed.

A surviving spouse's right in certain property cannot be greater than the interest which the deceased spouse held in that property. If a creditor with a bona fide claim against a hus-

Example. The title to certain land was in John Smith, as sole owner. Ten years after acquiring the land, John married Mary. The year following his marriage, John signed a deed transferring his land to A. Adams. Mary did not sign the deed. Twenty-five years after this transfer John died, survived by his widow Mary. When John died the land was owned by D. Davis, having been successively transferred by Adams to Brown, Brown to Carter, and by Carter to Davis.

In many states, an ownership interest in the land would vest in Mary upon John's death. If Davis wished to continue as sole owner of the land he would have to buy Mary's interest at her price. (Whether Davis would have any right to recover for his loss from Carter, Brown, or Adams, or from John's estate, would depend upon the type of contract made in the various deeds.) On the other hand, if Mary along with John had signed the transfer to Adams, Mary would have given up this possible interest. ☐

* * *

Example. John signed an enforceable contract to sell certain land to a buyer, the deed to be delivered in two months. One month later John married Mary. A month after the marriage, John signed and tendered a deed to the buyer who refused to pay unless Mary also signed.

Mary would have no interest or possibility of interest (that is no dower interest) and could be enjoined from asserting any interest in the event she should survive John. As soon as a written contract for the sale of land is signed, an interest in the property passes to the buyer (see Chapter 22). Although the seller still has the legal title, not sufficient property interest is left in the seller for dower (or curtesy) to attach in favor of a spouse acquired after the contract date. ☐

band has the sheriff levy on the husband's real estate, the ensuing sheriff's sale will pass the husband's title free from any dower claim of his wife.

B. Common Forms of Co–Ownership

I. JOINT TENANCY

A feature which the law calls the "right of survivorship" is the chief characteristic of a joint tenancy under the common law. The title of joint tenants is considered as having a singleness or oneness because it is created and vested in the owners by a single transfer. Upon the death of one joint tenant, the title remains as a single entity vested in the surviving co-owner (or co-owners). Because of this singleness-of-title theory, a surviving spouse has no dower or curtesy interest in property owned by the deceased spouse and a third person as joint tenants (unless, under statutes in some states, creation of the joint tenancy involved a transfer of property or money which had previously been solely owned by the deceased spouse during the marriage).

To term this a "right" of survivorship is somewhat of a misnomer. It is a result of this form of co-ownership rather than an irrevocable *right*. The singleness of title can be terminated by the act of one of the tenants without the consent of the other (or others). To the extent that the oneness of title is terminated, there is no longer a joint tenancy and, therefore, no longer the survivorship feature. For example, if A and B inherit property as joint tenants and still hold title in that manner when A dies, the entire title will vest in B. However, if A transfers his interest to T, a third person, the oneness of title ends since T's title vests in him at a different time than did B's. T and B are co-owners as tenants in common. Should T die, his interest will pass to his heirs.

B will continue to have his original interest but no more (unless he is T's heir).

Any property interest which a person has a right to transfer can be attached by his creditors. Suppose A and B are joint tenants of certain property, and a creditor with a judgment against A has the sheriff levy on A's interest in the co-owned property and sell it at sheriff's sale. The sale will terminate the joint tenancy, and the purchaser at the sheriff's sale will become a co-owner with B, the type of coownership being a tenancy in common.

The survivorship feature of a joint tenancy terminates only if the singleness of title is terminated before the death of a co-owner. Suppose that A and B are joint tenants of certain property and A dies, leaving a will stating that his interest in the property is to pass to T. Since a will does not take effect until death, it is not effective to end the singleness of title of A and B *before* A's death. Since the singleness of title exists at the time A dies, B will own the entire interest.

2. TENANCY IN COMMON

A tenancy in common is the usual type of ownership unless the parties are husband and wife. Statutes in many states declare that if two or more persons (other than husband and wife) are co-owners, they are tenants in common unless they expressly manifest an intention to take title as joint tenants. If A and B purchase land and wish to take title as joint tenants (assuming that the law of their state recognizes joint tenancies), they will usually have the deed read, "to A and B as joint tenants with the right of survivorship and not as tenants in common."

The chief differences between joint tenancies and tenancies in common are:

1. Tenants in common can own unequal interests. Because of the singleness-of-title theory, joint tenants are of necessity equal co-owners so long as they remain joint tenants. While tenants in common are presumed to be equal owners unless they indicate oth-erwise, it is possible for their interests to be unequal, in any ratio that they expressly indicate.

2. There is no right of survivorship in a tenancy in common. If A and B are tenants in common of certain property and A dies, A's interest passes to his heirs; B will continue to own the fractional interest he held before A's death but will have no greater interest—unless he is A's heir.

3. TENANCY BY ENTIRETIES

In the many states which continue to recognize this common law form of co-ownership, persons can be tenants by entireties only if they are actually husband and wife when they become co-owners. If co-owners are not actually husband and wife when they acquire title to certain property, their later marriage will not of itself convert them into tenants by entireties. If a transfer of title specifies that the transferees are husband and wife (and they actually are), they are usually presumed to own as tenants by entireties unless they expressly indicate their intent to co-own in some other way (for example as tenants in common).

The singleness-of-title theory applies to a tenancy by entireties, with the following results:

1. *Survivorship.* Just as with joint tenancy, upon the death of one tenant by entireties the entire title automatically and immediately vests in the survivor.

2. *Continuance.* At common law, unlike a joint tenancy, a tenancy by entireties cannot be changed or split by the act of either co-owner alone, nor can it be split by claimants who are creditors of only one of the co-owners, so long as the co-owners remain husband and wife. By statute in many states a divorce will change a tenancy by entireties into a tenancy in common. Businessmen frequently use tenancies by entireties to exempt certain of their assets from the claims of business creditors.

Example. A husband and wife own certain property as tenants by entireties. A creditor obtains a judgment against the husband.

In a state which recognizes common law tenancies by entireties, the creditor has no right at all against the property, while the wife lives and the parties are not divorced. The creditor can proceed only against property owned individually by the husband—if he has any. ☐

However, a debtor is not permitted to transfer his assets in a way that will defraud his creditors. Suppose that a house is titled solely in the name of a husband. Presumably when creditors extend credit to him they know and rely upon the fact that they can attach the real estate. The husband cannot effectively put the property beyond the reach of his creditors unless he retains other assets sufficient to pay all of his obligations. If a husband transfers title from himself to himself and his wife as tenants by entireties and retains insufficient individually owned assets to meet all of his obligations, the transfer is fraudulent as to creditors, and the creditors can have the transfer canceled. Suppose, however, that the husband is solvent when the entireties title to certain property arises, but is insolvent when he makes payment on the property. In the few states in which such cases have been litigated (chiefly Michigan and Pennsylvania), the courts have reached opposite conclusions. In Pennsylvania the status of the property is determined by the husband's financial condition at the time the entireties title is created. If the husband is solvent then, the property is immune from the claims of his individual creditors even though he is insolvent when he makes payments, while under the Michigan view, any payments which the husband makes after he becomes insolvent are voidable by his creditors.

The different forms of co-ownership and the characteristics applicable to them can be summarized in table 30.1.

IV. Transfers of Title

A transfer of the legal title to real estate is accomplished by a written instrument called a "deed."

A sale of real estate does not always include a warranty or guaranty of title by the seller. This differs from the law regarding sales of goods. Through his act of selling *goods*, a seller is considered as impliedly warranting that he is transferring clear title to the buyer. No such warranty is implied from the act of transferring *land*. If a warranty of title is to accompany the transfer of land, it must arise from appropriate language expressly used in the deed. The deed may expressly state the terms of a warranty, or may instead contain language which some statute declares gives rise to a warranty.

A warranty to defend title is the most common warranty used in modern real estate conveyancing. There are two types of such warranties, general and special.

General Warranty. A standard form of this warranty commonly used in some states reads:

And the said grantor, his heirs, executors and administrators, does hereby covenant and agree to and with the said grantee, his heirs and assigns, that the said grantor, his heirs and assigns, all the above, together with the above mentioned and described premises, unto the said grantee, his heirs and assigns, against the said grantor and his heirs and assigns, and against all and every other person or persons whomsoever lawfully claiming or to claim the same shall and will

Example.   John Smith purchased a home for himself and his family, paying $1,000 down and financing the balance of $10,000 through a mortgage payable in monthly installments over the next ten years. He was solvent at the time, title to the premises was taken in the names of "John Smith and Mary Smith, his wife," and the mortgage was signed by both husband and wife. Beginning the fourth year thereafter, John began falling behind in payments to the grocer from whom he obtained groceries on credit, but John continued to purchase from that grocer for the next several years. During this time John continued making regular payments on the mortgage so that it was completely paid off by the end of the tenth year. The payments came entirely from John's earnings. In February of the eleventh year Mary became seriously ill and was not expected to live much longer. In an attempt to put the home beyond the reach of John's creditors (especially the grocer) after Mary's death, John and Mary in March signed and recorded a deed transferring the property to their son for $1. Mary died in July, after which John continued in possession of the house, living in it just as though it was still his home. In August the grocer obtained a judgment against John for the unpaid balance of the grocery bill, interests, and costs, a total of $4,000, proved that John had been continuously insolvent since the fourth year of the mortgage, and brought an action to have the transfer to the son canceled .

Under the Pennsylvania view the grocer would not be entitled to the requested decree and would have no right to collect any part of his judgment from the transferred property. John was solvent when the entireties title was acquired. While the marriage continued with both parties alive, the entireties property was not subject to the claims of creditors of one of the parties. The husband's creditors would have rights only if upon the death of the wife, the husband survived, still owning the property. A debtor has no legal obligation to assure that this mere possibility of an interest is preserved for the benefit of his creditors. Since the husband's creditors had no claims against the property before Mary died, they would have no grounds to complain when the husband and wife gave the property away.

On the other hand, under the Michigan view the creditor could attach so much of the value of the house as equaled the amount of mortgage payments which the husband made after he became insolvent. ▢

---

warrant and forever defend by these presents.

Special Warranty. A standard form reads as above with the last few lines changed to read, " . . . person or persons whomsoever lawfully claiming or to claim the same by, through, or under him, shall and will warrant and forever defend by these presents."

By making this promise to warrant and defend, the grantor promises to pay for any loss suffered by the grantee or any later owner of the property, as a result of a prior claim which arose.

1. (Special warranty) while the grantor owned the property; or
2. (General warranty) while the grantor owned the property and also at any time before the grantor owned the property.

Statutes in some states provide that if a deed uses the word "grant" or the word "convey," either word is considered as stating what amounts to a special warranty.

If a deed states no express warranty, and does not include a statutory equivalent of a warranty, then no warranty accompanies the transfer of the property. A common form for a

TABLE 30.1 CHARACTERISTICS OF CO-OWNERSHIP

Type of Co-Ownership	Survivorship	Disposal Allowed: During Life	Disposal Allowed: At Death	Subject to Individual Debts
Joint Tenancy	X	X		X
Tenancy by Entireties	X			
Tenancy in Common		X	X	X

deed making no warranty at all (commonly called a "quitclaim deed") reads in part:

> The said grantor, for and in consideration of the sum of One Dollar lawful money of the United States, to him in hand paid by the said grantee, at and before the enseating and delivery of these presents, the payment and receipt whereof is hereby acknowledged, has remised, released, and quit claimed, and by these presents does remise, release, and quit claim into the said grantee and to his heirs and assigns forever, all that certain piece of land situated in the City of _____, County of _____, in the State of more particularly described as follows: . . ."

A grantee should promptly record his deed, in order to protect his interest against third persons who deal with the grantor in the justified belief that the grantor still owns the property.

V. Real Estate Liens

A "lien" is a claim held by one person against the property or property interest of another person. The most important liens which may exist against real estate are: (1) mortgage liens, (2) judgment liens, and (3) mechanic's liens.

A. Mortgage and Judgment Liens

1. MORTGAGE DEFINED

A creditor desiring security for payment of an obligation may obtain from his debtor ownership, title, or a security interest in certain of the debtor's property until the obligation is paid. Generally in such an arrangement the parties intend that the debtor remain in possession at least until he defaults under the obligation. Such a transfer or pledge of title as security for an obligation is a *mortgage*. A *chattel mortgage* is a security interest in personal property, and is covered by the Uniform Commercial Code (see Chapter 27). When the term "mortgage" is used alone, it usually refers to a real estate mortgage.

Mortgages may be classified as *purchase money* and *nonpurchase money*. A purchase money mortgage secures credit extended to enable the debtor to purchase the property which is the subject of the mortgage. A purchase money mortgage usually has certain priorities over other liens.

The document forms used in a mortgage transaction vary in different states. In some states, forms similar to those developed at early common law are still used. The common-law instruments are the result of early common-law history, and nowadays are not considered by the courts as meaning literally what they say. A cardinal rule for many modern lawyers in drafting legal papers is to write exactly, clearly, and briefly what is meant. The common-law mortgage forms disregard this rule entirely. Nevertheless, since the forms have been working satisfactorily for hundreds of years (over which time they have been thoroughly litigated), and since procedural statutes have been drafted according to these forms, a practicing lawyer has very little inducement to attempt to simplify them on his own initiative.

The common-law forms for a mortgage transaction consist of two instruments. One evidences the obligation and is usually called the "bond" or "judgment note." The other instrument, termed the "mortgage," creates a security interest in the real estate which is the subject of the mortgage transaction. The mortgage instrument is recorded to protect the security interest of the mortgage holder.

The common-law bond and mortgage forms for a $5,000, five year, 15 percent mortgage may be briefly outlined as follows. (It should be emphasized that these are only *outlines*; the forms in actual use are considerably longer and contain a number of additional provisions not included or referred to here. Note that, as is the practice in some states, the bond is for double the actual amount of the mortgage debt.)

BOND

D. Davis, as debtor, is bound to C. Carter, as creditor, in the sum of $10,000, signed and sealed this date.

The condition of this obligation is that if the debtor shall pay to the creditor, five years from date, the sum of $5,000 together with interest at the rate of 15 percent per year, then this bond shall cease and be forever void; otherwise it shall remain in full force and effect.

[A confession of judgment provision is usually included in states where valid.]

(*signed*) D. Davis   **SEAL**

MORTGAGE

Whereas D. Davis, as debtor, by bond of this date is bound to C. Carter, as creditor, in the sum of $10,000, conditioned for the payment five years from date of $5,000 together with interest at the rate of 15 percent per year.

In consideration of and to secure said debt, the debtor grants and conveys to the creditor the following described land: [then is written a description of the mortgaged land, copied from the debtor's deed]

Provided nevertheless that if the debtor pays the creditor according to the conditions of the above mentioned bond, then these presents shall cease and be null and void.

(*signed*) D. Davis   **SEAL**

2. DURATION OF LIEN

In general, a mortgage lien becomes effective between the parties as soon as they sign their agreement to that effect, and remains effective until barred by a statute of limitations. As to a third person who acquires an interest in a piece of land without actual knowledge of a prior mortgage, the mortgage is usually effective only from the date it is recorded. A properly recorded mortgage lien usually continues effective as to the mortgaged land until the mortgage holder receives payment or agrees to release that land from the mortgage lien. On the other hand, while a judgment lien also becomes effective from the date entered on the record, it will continue as an effective lien for only a limited time—namely the statutory period (for example five years in Pennsylvania)—after which it expires as a lien unless renewed on the record. Usually, if renewed before expiration of the statutory period, the lien continues from the time originally obtained; if renewed after expiration of that period, the lien is effective only from the date of renewal. This limited span of life refers to the judgment's *lien* on real estate. Usually no statute of limitations applies to the judgment itself; it continues as a collectible obligation until paid.

Real Property

3. MULTIPLE LIENS

If a mortgage is already on record when a judgment becomes a lien against the debtor's real estate, the judgment is, of course, secondary in claim to the mortgage. The mortgage-holder has the right to realize on his lien unhampered by the judgment, while any attempt by the judgment creditor to realize on his judgment will be subject to the prior mortgage. A sheriff's sale on a prior lien will divest (that is, remove as a claim against the property) any later lien against the real estate (except real estate taxes which usually remain liens until paid). In most states, a sheriff's sale on a later lien will not affect a prior lien.

4. REMEDIES OF MORTGAGE HOLDER

State statutes prescribe the remedies available to the creditor when the debtor fails to pay his mortgage obligation. Usually a creditor has one or more of three possible remedies:

1. Sometimes a creditor has the right to obtain possession or control of the mortgaged premises. The creditor then applies the net rents and profits to the mortgage debt and when the obligation is fully paid, restores the property to the debtor.

2. The creditor can obtain a judgment against the debtor on the obligation which the mortgage secures, that is, on the note or bond. Once the creditor obtains a judgment he may proceed like any other judgment creditor with a levy and sheriff's sale. The judgment is a lien on the mortgaged property from the effective date of the mortgage lien, and is a lien on other realty owned by the debtor in that county from the date the judgment is obtained.

3. The creditor can foreclose the mortgage. He does this by suing and obtaining a judgment for foreclosure which is then followed by a sheriff's sale of the mortgaged property. This is a limited type of judgment, effective as to the mortgaged property only; entry of judgment for foreclosure does not give the credi-

tor a lien or right to levy on any other of the debtor's property. After the mortgaged property is sold at sheriff's sale, the debtor's interest in the property is completely cut off (foreclosed). If the foreclosure sheriff's sale fails to realize the full amount of the mortgage obligation, the creditor can usually still avail himself of the second remedy described above.

5. DEFICIENCY JUDGMENT STATUTES

A sheriff's attachment and sale under any real estate lien results in the sale of the attached property to the highest bidder, regardless of how small the bid is. Therefore, the attaching creditor should be present or represented at the sheriff's sale to prevent another person's buying the property for too low a price. Since the proceeds from the sale (after payment of taxes and costs—and employees if entitled to priority) are paid to the attaching creditor, up to the amount of his claim, the creditor can bid up to that amount and (with the above exceptions) not have to make an actual payment. If no other bids are received, the creditor can buy the property for taxes and costs, and the sale will be recorded as yielding nothing toward satisfaction of the creditor's judgment. Many states have statutes affording a debtor some protection against an overly greedy creditor. Such statutes usually apply when the judgment creditor, who initiates an attachment and sheriff's sale of his debtor's real estate, bids for and buys the property himself for less than the amount of his judgment. Under some statutes, the creditor's judgment is nevertheless considered fully paid and satisfied unless within a certain time (e.g., six months) after the sale, the creditor initiates a proceeding to have the court determine and declare the fair value of the realty as of the time of sale to the creditor. Although the sheriff's sale did not actually realize the amount of the court-declared fair value, this amount will be credited to the judgment. If the fair value is less than the amount of the judgment, the creditor may proceed with a

806

levy and sheriff's sale to collect from other of the debtor's property. If the fair value equals the amount of the judgment, the creditor's judgment is considered fully paid and satisfied. If the court-declared fair value exceeds the amount of the judgment, the creditor usually has no obligation to pay the amount of the overage to the debtor since such an excess was not actually realized at the sheriff's sale.

6. TRANSFER OF MORTGAGED PROPERTY

Title Acquired by Grantee

When a debtor sells property upon which there is a properly recorded mortgage, the title acquired by the grantee is subject to the mortgage. That the grantee has no personal knowledge of the mortgage is immaterial.

Liability of Grantee

Especially if the mortgaged property has depreciated so that upon foreclosure it does not realize the amount of the obligation, a question may arise as to whether the creditor can recover the deficiency from the grantee. The answer depends upon the contract between the debtor and the grantee, which is usually evidenced by the type of mortgage-reference provision contained in the deed. The two principal types of mortgage-reference provisions are (1) a statement that the transfer is subject to the mortgage, and (2) a statement that not only is the transfer subject to the mortgage, but also that the grantee is assuming and agreeing to pay the mortgage. The usual effect of such provisions can be summarized as follows:

1. If the grantee expressly assumes personal liability:

(a) *Right of the creditor against the grantee.* The creditor, as a third party beneficiary of the debtor-grantee contract, can recover the full amount of the obligation from the grantee.

(b) *Right of the creditor against the debtor.* The mortgage is security for an obligation personally incurred by the debtor, and no matter what happens to the mortgaged property, the debtor remains liable until the creditor receives full payment for the obligation, or until the creditor (by a legally enforceable agreement) expressly releases the debtor. As with the assignment of contracts generally (see Chapter 11), a delegation to the grantee of the duty of performance does not release the original obligor even though the creditor acquires the alternative right to collect from the grantee.

(c) *Right of the debtor against the grantee.* Whatever amount of the mortgage obligation the debtor is forced to pay, the debtor can in turn recover from the grantee by virtue of their agreement.

2. If the grantee does not expressly assume personal liability:

(a) *Right of the creditor against the grantee.* The grantee has no personal liability to the creditor.

(b) *Right of the creditor against the debtor.* As explained above, the debtor's personal obligation to the creditor is not affected by whether or not the grantee assumes the mortgage obligation.

(c) *Right of the debtor against the grantee.* Even though the grantee does not expressly assume the obligation (and therefore incurs no personal liability to the creditor), if the debtor and grantee take the amount of the mortgage obligation into account and deduct it in determining the selling price, the grantee has an implied obligation to reimburse the debtor for whatever of the mortgage obligation the creditor collects from the debtor.

B. Mechanics' Liens

Practically all states have statutes authorizing mechanics' liens. The term "mechanic" is somewhat of a misnomer, since such statutes apply to real estate only. Mechanic's lien statutes assume that if a person's labor or material has improved or added to the value of land it is fair that he should have a claim against the land for his compensation. In theory, therefore, the claim is against the land itself rather than against the owner of the land personally.

Although there is considerable variation among the states as to details, mechanic's lien statutes fall into two general classes, known respectively as the "New York system" and the "Pennsylvania system." In general, under a New York system statute, the lien which may be obtained against real estate is limited to the amount which the owner still owes under his construction or repair contract. The lien obtainable under a Pennsylvania system statute is not so limited; a lien may be obtained even though the owner of the land has fully paid the price due under the construction or repair contract.

Statutes vary as to persons having a right to obtain mechanics' liens. Such persons may include:

1. An architect with whom the owner of land contracts for overseeing or supervising construction or repair of a building.

2. A builder with whom the owner contracts for construction or repair of a building on his land.

3. A subcontractor with whom the builder in turn contracts for performance of a portion of the construction or repair contract.

4. A materialman or supplier who furnishes either to the owner or to the builder, supplies or materials used in the construction or repair of a building.

An authorized person may obtain a mechanic's lien against certain real estate by filing a claim in the proper public office. The right to obtain a mechanic's lien may be waived by agreement. In some states, the right of any person (including subcontractors and materialmen) to obtain a mechanic's lien may be barred by an express agreement to that effect entered into by the owner of the land and the builder if (1) the subcontractor or materialman has actual notice of the agreement, or (2) the agreement is properly recorded before the start of work on the premises or otherwise within the period specified in the statute. It may seem strange that an agreement between the owner and builder can affect a subcontractor or materialman who is not a party to the agreement, and prevent either of them from obtaining a mechanic's lien. However, this is no more strange than the remainder of the Pennsylvania system statute, which permits a subcontractor or materialman (1) to obtain a lien without a lawsuit, (2) against the property of a person who is not otherwise the lienor's debtor.

VI. Landlords and Tenants

In any discussion of the rights and duties of landlords and tenants, two legal principles predominate: (1) for a person to become a tenant of certain premises, he must have an agreement or contract with the landowner (landlord), and (2) such an agreement grants to the tenant a real estate interest in the rented premises.

Since the landlord-tenant relationship is contractual, the usual contract rules apply, including those pertaining to offer and acceptance, excuse or nonexcuse, etc. Except as otherwise required by the statute of frauds, the contract (commonly called a "lease") may be express or implied, oral or written. As is discussed in Chapter 9, most statutes of frauds require a lease for longer than a specified duration to be evidenced by a signed writing in order to be enforceable. When the parties use a written lease, frequently they choose a standard printed form suitable for their state. Such printed forms are usually prepared by or for landlords and lean heavily in their favor.

Because a tenant has a real estate interest, he is quite like an owner of the rented premises for the duration of the lease. However, because his ownership interest is limited in duration, he must refrain from causing permanent injury to the premises, or otherwise harming the premises in any way that will continue to affect the premises after expiration of the leasehold period. Such harmful conduct by a tenant is called "waste."

A roomer in a rooming house or a guest in a hotel is a lodger rather than a tenant. The parties to a lodging agreement do not intend to vest in the lodger a right of exclusive possession, one of the chief attributes of a real estate interest.

If an entire building is leased to a tenant, his interest includes not only the building but also the land upon which it stands. If an apartment or an office in a building is leased, the tenant has a real estate interest in that portion of the building but no interest in the land. It would be impractical to consider that occupants of different portions of a single building have interests in sections or slices of the land upon which the building stands, or interests in portions of the air space over the surface of the land.

The legal theory that a landlord-tenant relationship is both a contract relationship and a land relationship is especially apparent in the common-law rules concerning possession, condition of premises, and remedies.

A. Right of Possession

By the act of leasing, a landlord impliedly warrants (unless expressly stated otherwise) that the tenant will have exclusive possession of the leased premises, uninterrupted either by the landlord himself or by a third person having a claim or interest enforceable against the landlord.

If some third person has a properly recorded title or interest which at the time of leasing is effective against the landlord, that interest will also be effective against the tenant and superior to his interest. In turn, the tenant will have a breach of warranty claim against the landlord for any damages resulting from the tenant's being disturbed or dispossessed by the superior interest—unless at the time of leasing the landlord disclosed the existence of the third person's interest and expressly stated that he was leasing subject to that interest.

Unless the lease provides otherwise, the landlord himself may not disturb the possession of the tenant except to inspect for waste. If the landlord unjustifiably disturbs the tenant, the landlord is liable for damages. If the landlord's intrusion is sufficient to interfere with the tenant's beneficial use of the premises, the tenant has the right to move out and terminate his obligation to pay rent. In many states a tenant thus evicted by conduct of the landlord can recover damages in addition to terminating his rent obligation; in other states the tenant thus evicted is excused from paying rent, but he has no right to recover damages unless, in addition, the landlord is guilty of fraud or contractual bad faith (for example, by causing the tenant's eviction with a deliberate intent to disaffirm the lease and resume possession).

A landlord may expressly reserve in the lease a right of entry for certain stated purposes. Printed form dwelling leases frequently contain a provision such as the following:

> The right to label said premises for sale or rent, and also the right of the landlord to enter upon any portion of the same at all times (accompanied by other parties, if so desired by the landlord) to examine into their condition or for the purpose of making repairs or improvements or showing the premises with the view of renting or selling the same is expressly conceded by the tenant.

If a tenant is disturbed by a third person who does not have a superior interest and does not represent the landlord, the tenant can recover damages from the intruder but not from the landlord.

B. Deterioration, Damage, or Destruction of Premises

I. BEFORE COMMENCEMENT OF THE LEASEHOLD TERM

If, between the time of contracting and the time for commencement of the leasehold term, the premises are substantially damaged or destroyed through no fault of either party, the ordinary contract rule as to excuse applies, and both parties are excused from the contract.

2. AFTER COMMENCEMENT OF THE LEASEHOLD TERM

Lease of Entire Building

Landlord's Obligation. Under the common-law rules, a landlord, through the act of renting, does not by implication warrant either that a building is usable for the tenant's purposes or for any purpose, nor that the building is tenantable or will remain so. In general, unless expressly agreed otherwise, the only obligation of the landlord as to condition of the premises is to warn the tenant of any weaknesses or defects (1) which constitute an unreasonable risk of personal injury to the tenant or to some other person on the premises with permission from the tenant, and (2) which are actually known to the landlord at the time of leasing, and (3) which the landlord can reasonably expect will not be discovered by the tenant upon ordinary inspection. All three conditions must be present for the landlord to be held liable.

Tenant's Obligation. 1. *Obligation to Pay Rent.* If a rental building deteriorates, is damaged, is destroyed, or is otherwise not usable by the tenant, the tenant still has the land interest for which he has agreed to pay the rent stated in the lease. Therefore, under the common-law rules which are still followed in many states, a casualty to the premises will not excuse a tenant from his obligation to pay rent. That the landlord receives reimbursement from his casualty insurance and refuses to repair or rebuild is usually immaterial; that the casualty resulted from a concealed defect in the building (for example, defective wiring causing a fire) is usually immaterial, unless the defect was actually known to the landlord at the time of leasing. Note that this is little more than an application of the ordinary contract rule, to the effect that a person will usually not be excused from his contract merely because an unforeseen event reduces the value of what he has obtained under the contract or even renders it worthless for his purposes (see Chapter 10).

2. *Obligation to Repair or Rebuild.* A tenant is obliged to make ordinary repairs of a minor nature such as are necessary to prevent greater damage to the rented building. For example, the tenant must replace a broken window or at least cover over the opening, but he would not have to replace a faulty roof, because, unless he agrees otherwise, a tenant is not obliged to rebuild or to repair major damage—although he must continue to pay rent.

A tenant may be obligated to make major repairs if he so agrees in the lease. A provision similar to the following is often included in printed form leases:

> The tenant agrees to keep and preserve the premises in good order, and at the expiration of the term of this lease, to peaceably and quietly surrender and yield up the premises in as good order and condition as the same shall be in at the time of taking possession— reasonable use and wear only excepted.

In some states such a provision is construed as obligating the tenant to make repairs no matter how major, and even to rebuild in case of total destruction. If so obligated, the tenant has the benefit of any casualty insurance held by the landlord. If the lease exceptions are expanded to include an "act of God," the tenant is still not adequately protected. He will be liable for destruction caused by an accidental fire not the fault of either party, unless the fire resulted from an unexpected natural force, like a bolt of lightning. If the landlord is agreeable, the tenant should have the exception further expanded to include "reasonable use, wear, and damage from fire or other agency not caused by the tenant." Or the tenant should realize the magnitude of his obligation and take out his own casualty insurance.

Lease of an Apartment

If an entire building is not leased to a certain tenant, the landlord is considered as implying a promise to keep in reasonably safe condition the portions of the building not leased (such as the roof, common corridor and stairway, and outside walls). The tenant may recover damages resulting from the landlord's negligent failure to maintain or repair these portions, and a casualty sufficient to prevent the tenant's beneficial use of the portion leased to him will free the tenant from further payment of rent. However, in many states, the landlord has no obligation concerning a condition of disrepair arising *within* an apartment after leasing—unless (as is especially true in larger cities), a city ordinance requires a landlord to maintain multiple-tenanted premises in a certain specified state of repair.

C. Holding Over

If a tenant continues in possession after expiration of his lease, he is said to be "holding over." Generally, regardless of the tenant's actual intent or what he says, his act of holding over constitutes an offer to the landlord to extend or renew the lease. The landlord can if he wishes reject the offer and have the tenant evicted, or he can accept the offer. If by words or conduct the landlord indicates acceptance, a new contract is formed renewing the lease.

The duration and continuity of the renewed lease may differ from that of the expired lease. Otherwise (except for such that clearly do not apply), all of the terms, agreements, conditions, and waivers contained in the expired lease also apply to the renewed lease.

I. DURATION

If the expired lease is for one year or longer, the renewed lease is usually considered as being for one year. If the expired lease is for a period shorter than a year, generally the renewed lease is for an equal period.

2. CONTINUITY

States differ as to whether the renewed lease is a definite term lease or a continuously renewing lease (usually called a "periodic lease"). In many states, holding over with the consent of the landlord creates a continuously renewing or periodic lease (unless the original lease provides otherwise). The chief difference is that upon expiration of a definite term lease (unless expressly agreed otherwise), the tenant's right to occupy the leased premises terminates, even though the landlord gives the tenant no advance notice to that effect. On the other hand, a periodic lease (year-to-year, month-to-month, etc.) is effective and binding on the parties for the leasehold term, and in addition, renews automatically for another term, unless the landlord gives the tenant proper advance notice to leave, or (in most states) the tenant gives the landlord previous notice of his intent to move.

A periodic tenancy, discussed here as arising when the tenant holds over with the landlord's consent, may also be created by an express agreement of the parties, by an oral lease extending longer than the statute-of-frauds period, or by a lease which fails to specify any duration. In the latter case, the term of the periodic tenancy equals the time interval used by the parties in stating the rent obligation.

D. Eviction

That a tenant's legal right to occupy certain premises has expired, does not necessarily mean that the tenant will promptly leave the premises. If a tenant holds over a lease for a

Example. L leased certain described premises to T, effective July 20, 1985. The lease agreement said nothing concerning notice to quit or notice of intent to leave, and said nothing as to duration. Assume that the applicable state law required three-months' notice to terminate a year-to-year tenancy, and thirty-days' notice to terminate a periodic tenancy shorter than year-to-year, and that holding over created a periodic tenancy.

1. The agreed rent was $50 per month, payable in advance.

(a) Assume that on August 17, 1985, L decided he wished T to move out, or T decided he wished to move. T's right to occupy would end at midnight August 19, 1985, without any prior notice to quit. Likewise if T quit the premises before midnight August 19, 1985, he would have no further obligation to pay rent, even though he gave no prior notice of his intent to leave.

(b) Assume that T continued to occupy and pay rent without any new arrangement, and that on April 28 of the present year, L decided he wished T to move out, or T decided he wished to move. The earliest L could end T's right to occupy would be midnight June 19, and L would have to give T thirty-days' notice before that date. Likewise (in most states) T would be obligated to pay rent until midnight June 19; to end his obligation on that date T would have to move out by then, after giving L thirty-days' prior notice of his intent to leave.

2. The agreed rent was $600 per year payable in monthly installments in advance .

(a) Assume that on July 12, 1986, L decided he wishes to move out, or T decided he wished to move. T's right to occupy would end at midnight July 19, 1986, without any prior notice to quit. Likewise, if T quit the premises before that time, he would have no further obligation to pay rent, even though he gave no advance notice of his intent to leave.

(b) Assume that T continued to occupy and pay rent without any new arrangement, and that, on April 28 of the present year, L decided he wished T to move out or T decided he wished to move. The earliest L could end T's right to occupy would be at midnight July 19 of next year, and L would have to give T three-months' notice before that date. Likewise (in most states), T would be obligated to pay rent until midnight July 19 of next year; to end his obligation on that date, T would have to move out by then after giving L three-months' prior notice of his intent to leave. ☐

definite term (and the lease does not expressly require notice to quit), the tenant's legal right to occupy ends upon expiration of the term. If the tenant holds under a periodic tenancy, his right to occupy ends upon expiration of his current term if the landlord has given the required notice before then. If a tenant refuses to leave even though his right to stay has terminated, the landlord must take additional steps to have the tenant removed. The landlord may bring the type of lawsuit (usually called ejectment) available to any owner of real estate when another person is wrongfully in possession. This type of lawsuit is available whether the wrongful possessor is a former tenant or instead is a trespasser who never had permission to occupy. However, such a lawsuit, requiring a full-scale trial, is usually too slow and costly to be a fully adequate remedy for a landlord. Many states have statutes which provide special landlord dispossession actions, speedier and less costly than a standard ejectment lawsuit. Sometimes standard form leases contain a provision authorizing entry of a judgment by confession in an action of ejectment. In states where judgment by confession is valid, this is the simplest and speediest remedy; in many such cases the landlord can have the sheriff forcefully remove the tenant about a week after the start of the proceeding.

E. Collection of Overdue Rent

As the law of landlord and tenant slowly evolved following the abolition of the feudal system, two kinds of remedies gradually arose under which a landlord could collect overdue rent: (1) a contract lawsuit against the tenant to enforce his lease agreement to pay, and (2) a proceeding relating to the real estate itself, under which the landlord could take possession of any goods on the premises, even goods belonging to persons other than the tenant. The latter remedy (known as "distress," "distraint," or "landlord's levy") has been abolished or modified by statute in most states, but is still retained in some states.

* * *

Problems

1. S and B entered into a written contract under which S agreed to sell and B to buy a certain, described house and lot for $20,000, payable $1,000 with the signing of the agreement, the balance on the settlement date one month later, at which time S was to give B a deed for the property. S had fire insurance on the property in the amount of $12,000. S made no assignment of this insurance to B, and the agreement between S and B contained nothing relative to damage or destruction of the premises. Two days later, through no fault of either party, an accidental fire completely destroyed the house. S collected $12,000 from the insurance company but made no attempt to rebuild the house. On the settlement date, S tendered to B a deed for the premises and demanded the balance of the purchase price. B in turn demanded return of the $1,000 he had paid upon signing of the agreement. S sued B, and B counterclaimed against S. What result?

2. S entered into a written contract with B for sale by S and purchase by B of certain premises for $25,000, payable in stated installments, B to have the right of possession immediately and to obtain a deed upon completion of the contracted payments. No public recording was made of the contract. B took up residence on the premises and was still living there six months later when C obtained a judgment against S for $10,000. By this time B had paid $20,000 on the purchase price. When C had the sheriff levy on the premises, he learned for the first time about the contract of sale. What right would C have against the premises? Explain.

3. Andrew Adams' rich uncle died owning a number of pieces of real estate. In the uncle's will, three of these properties were properly and fully described and left as follows:

First property: "to Andrew Adams and Bernard Brown, equally as tenants in common."

Second property: "to Andrew Adams and Mary Adams, his wife, as tenants by entireties."

Third property: "to Andrew Adams and Charles Carter, equally, as joint tenants with the right of survivorship and not as tenants in common."

Neither Brown nor Carter was related to Adams.

(a) Assume that Adams became insolvent before his uncle's death, and remained insolvent thereafter. Two years later, one of Adams' creditors obtained a judgment against Adams and wished to collect his claim from the above properties. (1) As to the first property, would the creditor have the right to proceed against (a) the entire title; (b) a one-half interest; (c) some other fractional interest; (d) no interest? (2) As to the second property, select one of the four choices listed above. (3) As to the third property, select one of the four choices listed above

(b) Assume that Adams remained fully solvent at all times and, when he died two years after his uncle's death, he left enough money to pay all debts and taxes, and in his will left the three properties to his two sons, Robert and William Adams. (1) As to the first property, after Andrew Adams' death, would Bernard Brown own (a) the entire title; (b) a one-half interest; (c) some other fractional interest; (d) no interest? (2) As to the second property, would Mary Adams own (a), (b), (c) or (d) (select one of the four choices listed above)? (3) As to the third property, would Charles Carter own (a), (b), (c), or (d) (select one of the four choices listed above)?

4. Dambres is considering purchasing Blackacre. The title search revealed that the property was willed by Adams jointly to his children, Donald and Martha. The language contained in the will is unclear as to whether a joint tenancy or a tenancy in common was intended. Donald is dead and Martha has agreed to convey her entire interest in Blackacre to Dambres. Under the circumstances, will Dambres end up owning all of Blackacre? (Modified from A.I.C.P.A., May 80-26.)

5. J obtained a judgment against A who owned and occupied certain premises, but J did nothing further to enforce the judgment until later. One year after J obtained his judgment, A sold and transferred the property to B using a special warranty deed with no exceptions. One year later B sold and transferred the property to C using a special warranty deed with no exceptions, and a year later C, in turn, sold and transferred to D using a general warranty deed with no exceptions. Each purchaser paid full value and recorded his deed the same day he bought the property. Assume that under the applicable state law, judgment liens were valid for five years. Four years after obtaining the judgment, J had the sheriff levy on the premises. This was the first that B, C, and D knew of J's judgment. J released the property from the levy when D paid J $3,000, the amount then owing on the judgment. Would D have a legal right to collect $3,000 from A; from B; from C? Explain.

6. On February 1, X obtained a $2,000 judgment against B. Thereafter, on March 1, B entered into a written contract with S agreeing to purchase a large tract of potentially oil-bearing land owned by S. Upon signing the contract, B paid S $1,000 and contracted to pay S $4,000 more on the settlement date two weeks later and to give S a six-month mortgage for $20,000, the balance of the price. The parties carried out the contract and the new deed and mortgage were recorded on March 15. Thereafter, on April 1, B sold and transferred the property to C by special warranty deed which stated that the transfer was "under and subject to a $20,000 mortgage given to S on March 15 of this year." On April 15, Y obtained a $7,000 judgment against C. On May 1, C sold and transferred the property to D by special warranty deed which stated that the transfer was "under and subject to a $20,000 mortgage given to S on March 15 of this year, which the grantee hereof assumes and agrees to pay." By the time S's mortgage came due on September 1, drilling for oil had been abandoned as hopeless. When the mortgage was not paid, S instituted foreclosure proceedings and the property was sold at sheriff's sale for $5,000, its then fair value.

(a) When the foreclosure proceedings were instituted, a dispute arose among X, Y, and S as to who held a valid lien against the land, and if more than one lien existed, what the order of priority was. How would the dispute be settled? Explain.

(b) For the portion of the mortgage remaining unpaid, would S have a right to collect from B; from C; from D? Explain.

(c) From whom could Y collect the unpaid portion of this judgment? Explain.

7. On April 1, S, the owner of a lot, contracted with a builder for construction of a house on S's lot, according to certain plans and specifications, the builder to supply, perform, and supervise all labor, materials, and landscaping, and complete the house ready for occupancy. By the contract S agreed to pay the builder $20,000 at stated intervals as the work progressed. The builder completed construction on August 1, on which date S made the final contract payment and moved into the house. On August 3, S received a surprise promotion and transfer to another state. S immediately engaged a real estate broker to negotiate a sale of the home for a commission of 5 percent. The broker's efforts induced B to buy. On August 10, S and B signed a contract for the sale and pur-

chase of the home for $23,000, and B engaged a lawyer to search the title. Nobody told the lawyer that the building was of recent construction. The lawyer gave B a written certificate dated August 20, stating that he had searched the records of title and found a good record title in S. On the same day B paid S the agreed purchase price, S signed and gave B a special warranty deed and paid his broker the agreed commission, B's lawyer had the deed recorded, and B moved into the house. On August 25, S and B each received from a supplier a letter stating that the builder still owed $4,000 for materials purchased for and used in construction of the house, and demanding payment. Shortly thereafter, the builder was adjudged a voluntary bankrupt, and, on September 1, the supplier filed a mechanic's-lien claim against the property. With considerable vehemence, arguments raged concerning liabilities to the supplier and to each other of S, B, B's lawyer, and the real estate broker. Who could recover how much from whom? Explain.

8. O, the owner of a business building, mortgaged the premises to a bank as security for a $20,000 loan payable in five years, and the bank promptly recorded the mortgage. Three years later T was looking for a suitable location for his business. Liking O's building, T entered into a written agreement with O, leasing the premises for ten years. The lease did not mention the mortgage, and T had no actual knowledge of it. T went into possession and spent over $5,000 redecorating and fixing up the premises in a way suitable for T's business. T expected to recoup this amount from his business profits during the next ten years. Two years later the mortgage came due, and when O failed to pay, T and the bank each for the first time learned of the other's interest. The bank started foreclosure proceedings on the mortgage. What were the relative rights of the bank and T as to each other and as to O? Explain .

9. By written agreement L leased to T a certain house and lot for one year, beginning April 1, at a yearly rental of $600 payable in monthly installments in advance. T took possession and, on August 20, a fire not the fault of L or T destroyed the house and T moved elsewhere. T's last rental payment was made according to the lease on August 1, for that month. Neither L nor T had fire insurance.

(a) There was no provision in the lease pertaining to damage to or destruction of the premises. (1) L made no effort to have the house rebuilt, but in April of the following year, L sued T for rent. State how much, if anything, L was entitled to recover from T. Explain. (2) Upon L's demand, T refused to have the house rebuilt. L rebuilt it to its previous condition and sued T for the expense. Was L entitled to recover? Explain.

(b) The only provision in the lease pertaining to damage to or destruction of the premises read: "At the end of the term the premises shall be delivered up in as good condition as at the commencement of the term, ordinary wear and tear and unavoidable damage by fire, tempest, and lightning excepted." (1) and (2) Same additional facts and questions as in (1) and (2) above.

(c) The only provision in the lease pertaining to damage to or destruction of the premises read: "T shall keep the premises in repair and at the expiration of the term of this lease, T shall return the premises in as good order and condition as the same shall be in at the time of taking possession, reasonable use and wear excepted." (1) and (2) Same additional facts and questions as in (1) and (2) above.

10. L leased to T an apartment in an apartment building, for one year, at a stated rental, and T moved in. Three months later the tenant occupying the apartment directly above T's reported to the landlord that the drain was partially clogged and draining very slowly. The landlord said that he would have the drain fixed. However, he failed to do so and, shortly, the drain became completely clogged. Water overflow leaked through the ceiling in T's apartment, causing a large section of plaster to come loose and fall, damaging some of T's furniture. What rights would T have as to the damaged furniture and as to the unsightly condition of the ceiling? Explain.

815

11. By written agreement, L leased to T a certain house and lot for a term of one year from November 1, 1986, at a yearly rental of $1,200 payable in monthly installments in advance. The written lease provided: "T will take good care of the premises while occupying the same, surrendering the premises, without notice, to L at the end of the term or any extension thereof, in as good condition as he received the premises, reasonable wear and tear and accidental damage or destruction excepted; should T remain in the rented premises by consent of L, after expiration of the term, or any extension thereof, said term shall be presumed to have been extended or further extended for a period of one year and so on from year to year, upon and under the same terms, conditions, and limitations as are herein provided and expressed." On August 15, to the present year L sold the premises to B and assigned to B all right, title, and interest in the lease, together with rentals due on and after September 1. T was notified of the sale, and, beginning September 1, paid rent to B. On October 1 B notified T to quit at the expiration of his current term. T refused to move and on November 2, B sued to recover possession. Would B be entitled to recover? Explain.

31

Gifts and Inheritance

Gifts and Inheritance

ONE WAY IN WHICH PROPERTY is frequently transferred, or property interests created, is by gift, made either during the lifetime of the transferor or upon his death (through inheritance). A decedent's heir who inherits certain property interests receives what might be called a "deathtime" gift. Making a death gift by means of a last will and testament is, of course, quite different from making a lifetime gift. A bequest or legacy in a will does not become effective or vest any right in the legatee until the testator (the signer of the will) dies because a will can be revoked by the testator anytime before he dies. On the other hand, an unrestricted living gift during the donor's lifetime is usually made with an intent to vest a right in the donee immediately, or in the near future, and once it is made, it cannot be revoked.

I. Gifts

Although there is considerable difference between a contract to transfer property and a gift of the property, there is also a marked policy similarity. If a person expresses an intent to transfer something of value to another—whether he intends the transfer to be made now or later—the law will not enforce the intent unless there is "something" in addition to the bare intent. In the case of a contractual promise, this "something" is consideration or a legally recognized equivalent of consideration (see Chapter 6). In the case of a gift, this "something" is delivery or a legally recognized equivalent of delivery. It is a rule of policy, therefore, that for a gift to be legally effective and enforceable, two elements are required, (1) a present intent to make a gift, and (2) a delivery of the subject matter of the gift, or a legally recognized equivalent of delivery.

A. Present Intent

To make a valid gift, the donor must intend that ownership or an interest in the subject matter of the gift is to vest in the donee immediately. An intent that ownership is to pass at some future time either forms a contractual promise—which is not enforceable in the absence of consideration or its equivalent or is a will, which (for most purposes) must be in writing, and is not effective until the donor dies.

B. Delivery or its Equivalent

An actual physical transfer of the subject matter of the gift is obviously an effective delivery.

Legally recognized equivalents of delivery include:

1. The donor's delivering to his intended donee (or to some third party to turn over to the donee) possession of something, which to some extent gives the donee (and to the same extent deprives the donor of) control over the subject matter of the gift.

2. The donor's making a contract with a third person (or institution for the benefit of the donee), sufficient to vest an enforceable interest in the donee.

818

Example. On March 29, a woman who owned some valuable diamond jewelry was taken from her home to a hospital where she died on April 1. As she was leaving her house, the woman said to an impartial witness: "I have given my diamonds to Nancy, my niece, and if anything happens to me, she is to have them." After the woman's death, the court appointed an administrator to pay her debts and distribute her property to her heirs. The administrator demanded the diamonds from Nancy and when she refused to surrender them, sued to recover possession.

The administrator would recover. The intent expressed by the owner was not to make a present gift but rather for ownership to vest in Nancy in the future. Therefore no valid gift was made. This was an oral will which in most states is not valid or effective to transfer valuable property.

Written Instrument Evidencing an Obligation or Interest. If an obligation owed to a creditor is evidenced by a written instrument signed by the debtor, the creditor can usually make a valid gift of the obligation (presuming he manifests an intent to make a present gift), by delivering the written instrument to the donee or to someone for the donee. Valid gifts of promissory notes and corporate bonds are often made in this way. Likewise, the delivery of a signed stock certificate to the donee or to someone for the donee (with intent to make a present gift) accomplishes an effective gift.

Valuables Stored in a Safe-deposit Box. Generally, if the subscriber to a safe-deposit box delivers the key to another person with the intent to make a present gift of the contents, an effective gift is made. If the subscriber has another key and thus retains access to the box, some courts have said that delivering one of two keys will not make an effective gift of the contents of the box. Sometimes these courts base their conclusion on insufficiency of delivery; sometimes, the conclusion is more accurately based on the lack of a clear manifestation of an intent to make a present gift. If the evidence shows that nothing more was said or done by the subscriber, his delivering one of his two keys is more indicative of his appointing the recipient of the key as his agent than of making an outright gift.

Money in a Bank Account. Usually the presentation of the deposit book issued by a bank is required to make withdrawals from a savings account but not from a checking account. Generally, therefore, delivery of a savings deposit book, with donative intent, makes a gift of the amount in the account, while delivery of a checking account deposit book does not accomplish a gift. If a donor makes a gift of a check drawn on his checking account, even if the check is drawn for the entire balance in the account, the donor nevertheless still has power to stop payment on the check. Therefore, no effective gift of money takes place until the check is paid by the bank, or until the check is transferred to a holder in due course. Much litigation has arisen involving joint bank accounts. Suppose that Arthur Adams opens a joint bank account in the names of Arthur Adams and Bernard Brown, or Adams changes his one-name account to a joint account by adding Brown's name—in either case Adams being the source of all the money deposited in the account. Frequently such a joint account has a survivorship provision— the money is to be paid to the survivor of the two parties. Generally, Adams will maintain a joint account for one of two reasons: (1) to enable Brown as Adams' agent to have access to the funds for the benefit of Adams or his estate; or (2) to make a gift to Brown of one-half of the money that Adams deposits in the account, and, upon Adams' death, of all of the

Example. If John Jones gave $10,000 to each of his five children and $100,000 to his wife, the total amount of the gifts ($150,000) would not be subject to federal gift. It is possible for a donor to 'split' his gift with his or her spouse. A 'split' gift occurs when a spouse consents to apply his or her annual $10,000 exclusion to a gift made by a donor spouse. Thus, in the above example, John Jones could give each of his five children $20,000 gift tax free if his spouse consented to the gift. □

money. Courts in the various states differ as to the factors relied upon in determining whether an agency or a gift is intended. In some states, the courts have said that (continuing the Adams-Brown example) Adams' designating the account as a joint account merely indicates that Brown is Adams' agent. In this connection, it is usually immaterial whether the account is an "and" or an "or" account. However, the same courts are inclined to say that if, in addition, Adams and Brown both sign a signature card clearly stating that the account goes to the survivor, an effective gift is made to Brown.

C. Federal Gift Tax Implications

Anytime a gift is made, one of the primary considerations a donor must take into account is the federal gift tax which is assessed against the fair market value of the property transferred. For federal gift tax purposes, a gift includes a transfer of real or personal property for less than full and adequate consideration in money or money's worth. Thus, if Arthur Adams entered into an agreement with his son Andrew to sell Blackacre to Andrew for $50,000, when its fair market value was $75,000, for federal gift tax purposes, a gift of $25,000 has been made.

Federal gift taxes, similar to federal individual income taxes, are marginal-progressive in nature. They range from 18 percent on the first $10,000 of taxable gifts to 55 percent on taxable gifts made from 1984 to 1992 and 50 percent on taxable gifts made in 1993 and years thereafter in excess of $2,500,000. The

upper limit has been phased in under the Economic Recovery Act of 1981 as amended by the Tax Reform Acts of 1984 and 1987. The same rates apply to estates.

In computing the federal taxable gift, two important federal gift tax provisions are worth noting:

1. A donor is entitled to an annual federal gift tax exclusion of $10,000 per year per donee; and

2. A donor is entitled to an unlimited federal gift tax exclusion to his or her spouse.

Federal law also provides for a credit called a unified credit to offset federal gift and estate taxes. The credit must be used and is first applied against lifetime gifts. Any unused credit is then applied against federal estate taxes. The amount of the credit is $47,000 in 1981 and is phased in to $192,800 in 1987 and years thereafter. For example, the marginal rate on a gift of $600,000 in 1991 is $192,800, thus the gift would pass entirely gift tax free if made in 1991 (assuming no previous gifts were made), but there would be no credit left over to offset federal estate taxes.

II. Inheritance

A. Introduction and Historical Background

Inheritance of property is entirely statutory. As the United States Supreme Court stated a number of years ago:

> While the laws of all civilized States recognize in every citizen the absolute right to his

own earnings, and to the enjoyment of his own property, and the increase thereof, during his life, except so far as the State may require him to contribute his share for public expenses, the right to dispose of his property by will has always been considered purely a creature of statute and within legislative control.... Though the general consent of the most enlightened nations has, from the earliest historical period, recognized a natural right in children to inherit the property of their parents, we know of no legal principle to prevent the legislature from taking away or limiting the right of testamentary disposition or imposing such conditions upon its exercise as it may deem conducive to public good.[1]

The general objectives of inheritance statutes are *primarily* to accomplish the distribution of a decedent's property through a practical and workable system, and in conformity with the public interest; and *secondarily*, so long as consistent with the primary objective, to make distribution in accordance with a decedent's expressed desire or in a way that approximates what the decedent would probably have desired had he expressed an intent. In order that a decedent's wishes can be accurately determined, inheritance statutes are vigilant against the risk of forged and fraudulently altered wills, and accept as valid only what can be clearly shown to be a genuine expression of the decedent's intent.

A will is an effective direction given by an owner of property, stating how his property is to pass upon his death. The maker of a will is referred to as the *testator*; when he dies, he is said to have died *testate*. A person dying without a valid will dies *intestate*. A person may be testate as to some of his property and intestate as to other; in other words a will may be valid although it does not include all of a testator's property. Frequently when a bank account is opened, the card which the depositor

is requested to sign contains a statement naming the person to whom the account is to be paid upon the depositor's death. Often, this is an effective will for the amount remaining in the account when the depositor dies.

Usually, soon after the testator's death, his will is submitted to the proper judicial officials together with satisfactory evidence that it is the testator's genuine and valid will. Such evidence usually consists of the testimony of persons who saw the decedent sign the will, or who are acquainted with the testator's signature and believe that the signature on the offered will is genuine. If the document which is offered as a will is challenged or contested, its validity must be determined by a trial court. Upon satisfactory proof that an offered will is genuine and valid, a decree to that effect is issued. The will is then said to be proved or "probated." Frequently, a testator will name in his will the person (or institution, such as a bank) by whom he desires his estate to be administered. Upon probate of the will the testator's nominee will be appointed executor. Under supervision of the court, the executor gathers together the testator's assets, pays his debts, and distributes the balance of the estate to the proper parties. Statutes provide a certain order of priority for payment of creditors when estates are insolvent.

If a decedent dies intestate, and court administration of his property is desirable or necessary, a party having a proper interest in the decedent's property can request the court to appoint an administrator for the decedent's estate. The administrator's duties are much the same as those of an executor.

Obviously the appointment of an administrator is not necessary for every person who dies. If nothing is to be gained or accomplished through the administration of a decedent's estate, there is no need to incur the expense. Settlement by agreement among a decedent's family will sometimes suffice, for example, with a small estate consisting of property easily transferred by delivery. If a decedent leaves

---

1. *United States v. Perkins* 163 U.S. 625, 16 S. Ct. 1073, 41 L. Ed. 287 (1896).

goods of more than nominal value, or real estate, it is usually wise for his survivors to consult a lawyer as to the necessity of formal administration of the estate. If the lawyer considers administration unnecessary, the parties should enlist the lawyer's services to properly accomplish a family settlement. Participants in a family settlement must be sure that funeral and burial expenses, all other enforceable debts, and inheritance taxes are paid before dividing the decedent's property. Heirs are not personally liable for a decedent's debts. However, if there is no formal administration of a decedent's estate, each heir who receives a share thereby becomes liable for any of the decedent's unpaid debts, up to the value of the property received.

Statutes in many states provide for short and inexpensive administration of small estates. Also, when wages or salary are owed to a decedent, statutes frequently permit the employer to make payment to certain designated survivors, without the necessity of any administration proceedings.

Since the settlement of estates usually takes a year or longer, statutes in most states provide for some sort of a monetary allowance to the family of a decedent. In theory, a family allowance is a gratuity given by the law to assist the decedent's family to obtain its needs without waiting for complete administration of the estate. Usually, therefore, the right to a family allowance is not affected by whether the decedent dies testate or intestate, or whether his estate is solvent or insolvent. Apparently to further expedite payment of the allowance, some statutes (1) do not require proof of need, (2) grant the allowance to either a surviving husband or wife if a member of the same household with the decedent at the time of his death, and (3) if no spouse who was a member of the same household survives the decedent, grant the family allowance to the decedent's child or children who were members of the same household as the decedent—regardless of the age, dependency, or marital status of the child. With the exception of a family allowance, only the net amount of a decedent's estate, after payment of all costs of administration, debts, and taxes, can pass to the heirs.

In order to prevent too much delay in settling estates, statutes in many states give a decedent's creditors a certain period of time within which to file claims. If a creditor fails to claim within the specified time (for example, one year after advertisement of the appointment of the executor or administrator), then, while the creditor's claim is still enforceable against any of the decedent's property not yet distributed, the creditor has no rights against the decedent's representative personally or against heirs to whom the decedent's property has already been distributed. In some states this rule applies to a creditor whose claim is unmatured, contingent, or both, and whether or not the creditor has actual knowledge of the decedent's death.

If a property owner and one of his heirs both sustain fatal injuries in an accident, the descent of property will depend upon which one survives the other, even for only a moment. If both die before someone arrives at the scene, an attempt to determine the respective times of the deaths may involve highly speculative medical guesses. A number of states have avoided the problem by adopting the Uniform Simultaneous Death Act. A few of the provisions of this act may be summarized as follows:

When the title to or inheriting of property depends upon priority of death, and there is no sufficient evidence that the persons died otherwise than simultaneously, the property of each person is disposed of as if he had survived, except as otherwise provided by will.

When there is no sufficient evidence that two joint tenants or tenants by the entireties have died otherwise than simultaneously, the property so held is distributed, one-half as if one had survived, and one-half as if the other survived. With an appropriate change of the

Example. When Andrew Brown died, a metal file box was found in his office containing various insurance policies, receipts, and a will dated about twenty years before Andrew's death. The will had been written by an attorney and signed at the end by Andrew Brown in the presence of the attorney and his secretary, both of whom signed as witnesses. As originally written and signed, the chief portion of the will read: "I give, devise, and bequeath unto my beloved brother Charles Brown, his heirs and assigns forever, all my property, real, personal, and mixed, of what nature or kind soever, and wherever the same may be found at the time of my death." When the will was found after Andrew's death, the words, "brother, Charles," had been crossed out in ink and immediately above the deletions, in ink of the same shade as that used to make the deletions and apparently in Andrew's handwriting, were written the words, "nephew, David." Andrew had never married and his parents were both dead. At one time Andrew had a brother Charles and a sister Evelyn. About ten years before Andrew's death, Charles died, survived by his widow and son, David. Andrew had been very close to Charles and his family, had made his home with them, and continued to do so after Charles' death. As the boy David grew up, Andrew took him into the trucking business which Andrew owned and operated. Andrew's sister Evelyn was married, lived in a distant part of the country, and for the past fifteen years before Andrew's death, the only contact between Evelyn and Andrew was the mutual exchange of Christmas cards. Presumably, Andrew made the above-quoted changes in his will after Charles' death. When Andrew died, Evelyn claimed one-half of Andrew's estate.

Was the will as changed a valid will? Clearly not. After a person dies, the law must protect his estate against forged and altered wills. The way to prove the genuineness of a will is either through a witness who saw the testator proclaim and sign the document as his will, or through recognition of the testator's handwriting. When handwriting is in question, the way to prove its authorship is to compare the questioned writing with writing admitted to be genuine. The most individual part of a person's writing is his signature. The signature, therefore, is taken as the best test of the genuineness of a will. The changes in Andrew's will could have been made by someone else. The best test—a signature—was not added after the changes. Therefore the document as changed was not a valid will.

Was the will as originally written still in effect? This question involves a very arguable and complex legal concept. In the case upon which this example is based, the court said that apparently Andrew lined out the words in the will with an intent to cancel them. Therefore, the will as originally written was canceled and no longer in effect.

Conclusion: Andrew died without a valid will, and under the intestacy statutes his property would be divided into two parts, one part passing through the deceased Charles to David, the other half passing to Evelyn.

Irony: While the death of a will beneficiary before the testator will usually cancel any provision in favor of the deceased beneficiary, statutes frequently provide that a will provision will not lapse if the named beneficiary was a close relative of the testator and leaves a child or children. If Andrew had kept his inexperienced fingers off the will, David would have inherited everything. But when Andrew tried, without expert advice, to change the will, he completely defeated his intent.

fraction, the same formula applies if property is owned by three or more joint tenants.

Although the inheritance statues of the various states differ widely in many details, there is considerable uniformity in the general pattern they follow. As an example of one state's inheritance pattern, some of the chief provisions of the Pennsylvania statutes (and court decisions interpreting them) will be summarized. No attempt is made here to cover all of the details and exceptions that make up the Pennsylvania inheritance scheme. It cannot be too strongly emphasized that the entire subject of wills and decedent's estate is complex. Writing a will, even a simple one, should, if at all possible, be left to skilled legal technicians.

B. Outline of Pennsylvania Inheritance Scheme

I. DISTRIBUTION BY WILL

Who May Make a Will

Any person of sound mind, eighteen years of age or older may make a will.

Form and Execution of a Will

A will must be in writing and signed by the testator at the end. Any writing after the testator's signature is not part of the will and does not affect it. The statute specifies procedures for signing by mark if the testator is unable to sign his name, and for someone signing for the testator, if the testator is unable to make a mark.

In addition to the testator's signature, most states (Pennsylvania excluded) require the signatures of two (or sometimes three) witnesses. Such signing or "subscribing" witnesses need not read the will or be familiar with its contents; they merely observe the testator sign the document after he tells them that it is his will.

Revocation of a Will

A *codicil* is a change which is added to an existing will; to be valid, the testator must sign at the end of the codicil.

A will or codicil in writing cannot be revoked or altered otherwise than: (1) by some other will, codicil, or other writing signed at the end and provable in the same manner as a will; or (2) by being burnt, torn, canceled, obliterated, or destroyed, with the intent and for the purpose of revocation, either by the testator himself, or if by another person, at the testator's direction and in the presence of two other persons.

Modification by Circumstances

Divorce. If a testator is divorced after making a will, all provisions in the will in favor of or relating to his spouse become ineffective for all purposes.

Marriage. If a testator marries after making a will, the surviving spouse will receive his or her intestate share unless the will provides for a greater share.

Birth or Adoption. If a testator fails to provide in his will for his child born or adopted after making the will, the failure may be intentional, or instead (as so often is the case) may be the result of the testators delay in modifying his will. If it does not appear from the will that the omission was intentional, the legislatures of many states feel it to be sound policy to assume that the testator procrastinated and to modify his will accordingly. Under the Pennsylvania formula, the testator's property which passes to his or her surviving spouse (taking either under or against the will) is first deducted. Then, if any of the testator's estate remains, the after-born (or after-adopted) child receives from this property the share he would receive if the testator had died unmarried and intestate. A child in existence when the will was made takes only the share (if any) provided in the will.

Slaying. If a person participates as a principal or as an accessory before the fact in the willful and unlawful killing of the testator, he or she will not receive any of the benefits to which he or she might be entitled in testator's estate.

Spouse's Dissent. Except for his (or her) surviving spouse, a testator may disinherit any heir. No matter how closely related the parties are, it is not necessary that the testator specify any nominal amount for the disinherited person, nor mention the one being disinherited, nor give any reason. In fact, it is usually better for the testator not to state any reason in the will. A testator who is considerably aggravated with the ne'er-do-well he is disinheriting and proceeds to say why in his will may lay his estate open to a libel suit when the will is published.

A testator cannot disinherit his (or her) spouse. The spouse is entitled to take a certain share, in spite of the will (commonly called "taking against the will"). The share received by a spouse who takes against a will is described later as part of the topic, "Distribution Not by Will."

Rules of Interpretation

The following are some of the rules which help to determine the meaning of words used in a will.

In construing a bequest or devise to a person described by relationship to the testator rather than by name: (1) any person adopted before the death of the testator is considered the child of his adopting parent and not the child of his natural parent; (2) an illegitimate person is considered the child of his mother and not of his father, unless the parents later marry and thus legitimate the child.

Ordinarily, if a beneficiary dies before the testator, any devise or bequest in favor of the beneficiary is considered to have lapsed. However, even though a beneficiary (whether named or indicated by relationship) dies before the testator's death: (1) a devise or bequest to a child or other issue of the testator will not lapse, if the indicated beneficiary leaves issue surviving the testator; (2) if the property in question would not otherwise pass to the testator's spouse, a gift to the testator's brother, sister, or child thereof will not lapse, if the indicated beneficiary leaves issue surviving the testator. In either of these situations the gift for the indicated beneficiary, instead of lapsing, will pass to his or her issue.

Unless the contrary is stated or implied in the will in question,

1. If a beneficiary is not named but rather is designated as "child" or "children" (of the testator or of some other person), the gift is presumed to be intended for whoever fits that designation at the time the bequest or devise vests or is to be paid.

2. If a beneficiary is not named but is designated as "wife" (of the testator or of some other person), the gift is presumed to be intended for the person who was wife at the time the will was written.

If after the family allowance and debts are paid, insufficient property remains to pay all devises and bequests, the testator's heirs take in the following order:

1. Any specific devise or bequest to the testator's spouse is paid.

2. Then if property remains, any specific devise or bequest to the testator's issue is paid. If all within this class cannot be paid in full, payment is prorated.

3. Then if property remains, payment is made on any specific devise or bequest in favor of someone other than the testator's spouse and issue. Payments are prorated if necessary.

4. Then if property remains, any general devise or bequest is paid with payment prorated if necessary.

2. DISTRIBUTION NOT BY WILL (INTESTATE SUCCESSION)

The term "issue" includes all lineal descendants—child, grandchild, great-grandchild, etc., while the term "child" is limited to the first degree of descendancy.

Share of Surviving Spouse

1. As to real and personal property interests owned by a decedent at the time of death:

(a) If not included in a will, the share of the surviving spouse is as follows: (1) the entire intestate estate if there is no surviving issue or parent of the decedent; (2) the first $30,000 plus one-half of the balance of the intestate estate if there is no surviving issue of the decedent but he is survived by a parent or parents or if there are surviving issue of the decedent all of whom are issue of the surviving spouse also; and (3) one-half of the intestate estate if there are surviving issue of the decedent, one or more of whom are not issue of the surviving spouse. If there is partial intestacy, any property received by the surviving spouse under the will shall satisfy the $30,000 allowance mentioned in (2) above.

(b) If included in decedent's will, but his or her surviving spouse chooses to take against the will, the surviving spouse is entitled to a one-third interest in decedent's estate.

2. As to interests transferred by decedent during marriage:

(a) If the decedent retained a power to revoke or use all or part of what he (or she) transferred, to that extent, the surviving spouse may treat the transfer as a testamentary disposition (that is, like a will) and take against it. There is an exception: the spouse has no right to take against any contract of life insurance purchased by the decedent.

(b) As to real estate transferred by decedent during marriage: If a surviving spouse did not join in the deceased spouse's conveyance of real estate, then upon the decedent's death, an ownership interest in the transferred real estate will vest in the surviving spouse unless it was transferred for adequate consideration.

Forfeiture of Spouse's Right. A surviving spouse is barred from (1) taking against decedent's will or other testamentary disposition, and/or (2) taking an intestate share of a decedent's property, if, for at least one year prior to the death of the decedent, the surviving spouse willfully neglected or refused to perform the duty to support to other spouse, or willfully and maliciously deserted the other spouse.

Share of Others than Spouse

The share of decedent's estate to which the surviving spouse is not entitled, or the entire estate if there is no surviving spouse, descends:

1. To the issue of the decedent. If no issue survives the decedent, then
2. To the decedent's parents, or to his parent if only one is still living. If no parent survives the decedent, then
3. To the issue of each of the decedent's parents: If no issue of either of the decedent's parents survives the decedent, then
4. If at least one parent of either the decedent's mother or father is living, then half of the property goes to that grandparent (or if the other grandparent on that same side also still lives, to both), and the other half of the property goes to the grandparent or grandparents on the other side; or, if both are dead, to decedent's uncles, aunts, or their children on that other side. If none of these survive, this half goes with the first half. If no grandparent survives the decedent, then
5. To the decedent's uncles, aunts, or their children. If none of the above described persons survives the decedent, then
6. To the Commonwealth of Pennsylvania.

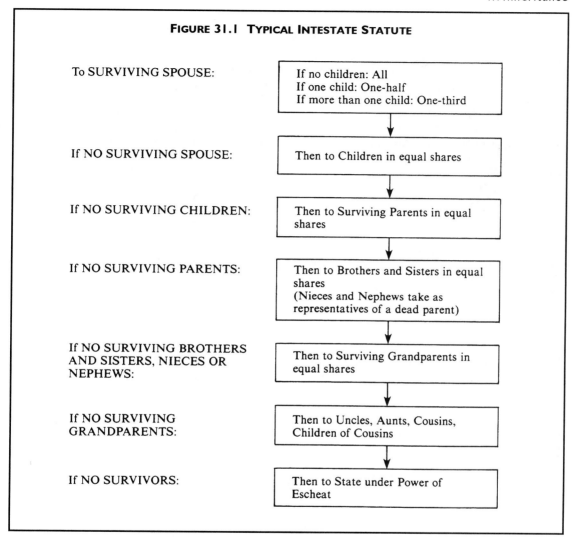

FIGURE 31.1 TYPICAL INTESTATE STATUTE

To SURVIVING SPOUSE:

> If no children: All
> If one child: One-half
> If more than one child: One-third

If NO SURVIVING SPOUSE:

> Then to Children in equal shares

If NO SURVIVING CHILDREN:

> Then to Surviving Parents in equal shares

If NO SURVIVING PARENTS:

> Then to Brothers and Sisters in equal shares
> (Nieces and Nephews take as representatives of a dead parent)

If NO SURVIVING BROTHERS AND SISTERS, NIECES OR NEPHEWS:

> Then to Surviving Grandparents in equal shares

If NO SURVIVING GRANDPARENTS:

> Then to Uncles, Aunts, Cousins, Children of Cousins

If NO SURVIVORS:

> Then to State under Power of Escheat

Figure 31.1 illustrates the order of descent and distribution under a statute that is similar but not identical with the Pennsylvania scheme.

Degree of Relationship. If the heirs (other than a spouse) who are entitled to inherit are all in the same degree of relationship to the decedent, all share equally. If the heirs (other than a spouse) entitled to inherit the dece-

dent's property are in different degrees of relationship to the decedent, the living heir in the nearest degree of relationship to the decedent fixes the level at which distribution is calculated. The decedent's estate is then equally divided by the number of lines of heirs at that level, either living, or if dead survived by issue. A share passes to each living heir at that level; for any heir at that level who is dead, his share passes to his issue. If any deceased heir has more than one issue in the same degree of relationship, they divide equally the share that comes down the line of the deceased heir.

Half Blood. No distinction is made between heirs of the whole and those of the half blood.

Tenancy Taken. When real or personal property is inherited by a husband and wife together, they take as tenants by the entireties.

C. Federal Estate Tax

When an individual dies, the fair market value of assets the decedent owned at death is subject to a federal estate tax; i.e., a tax levied on the privilege of transferring property at death. The amount of the tax is identical to the federal tax on lifetime gifts. Thus, as previously discussed, the marginal-progressive estate tax rates have a lower limit of 18 percent and an upper limit for years 1993 and thereafter of 50 percent. In addition, the unified estate and gift tax credit that has not been applied to lifetime gifts, will be applied as a credit against federal estate taxes.

In computing federal taxable estate, it is worth noting that any amount which passes to a surviving spouse is a deduction known as the marital deduction. Thus, if a decedent spouse left his entire estate to the surviving spouse, it would be entirely tax free for federal estate tax purposes. The special provision applies only to a surviving spouse and no other beneficiaries.

* * *

Problems

1. One paragraph of a will, signed in 1934, read: "I bequeath to the Chicago Trust Company the sum of $50,000, in trust to invest and to pay the income monthly to my nephew, Nathan, for and during the term of his natural life, and upon his death, to pay the principal amount of said trust to his wife and children share and share alike." From 1930 to 1936 Nathan was living with his wife, Ivy, and their two children, Andrew and Betty. In November, 1936, Nathan and Ivy were divorced, Nathan retaining custody of the children. In 1940 Nathan married Jane and at the time of his death some years later, he was survived by his widow Jane, by Andrew and Betty, and also by Carol and David, children of Nathan and Jane. Ivy also remarried shortly after the divorce and when Nathan died, was living in a distant community. How should the trust fund be distributed? Explain.

2. When D died, he left to survive him the persons listed below. His net estate for distribution to heirs (after payment of all costs, debts, taxes, and allowances) was $30,000. For each of the following, determine how this amount should be distributed:

(a) D's survivors: widow, brother, two nieces (daughters of D's deceased sister) and a daughter-in-law (widow of D's deceased son).

(b) D's survivors: all specified in Part (a) plus D's father.

(c) D's survivors: all specified in Part (b) plus a son.

(d) D's survivors: all specified in Part (c) plus two grandchildren (children of D's deceased daughter).

(e) D's survivors: widow and one cousin (son of D's deceased uncle).

3. Andrew White, seriously ill and advised by his doctor that he was about to die, called to his bedside in his home an old friend and neighbor, and his housekeeper, neither of whom was related to Andrew. In the presence of disinterested witnesses Andrew handed his friend a corporate bond having a value of $4,000, saying, "This is yours." Then Andrew gave his housekeeper the key to his safe-deposit box saying, "When I die, the contents of the box will belong to you." Andrew died the following day. The safe-deposit box contained $8,000 in cash. In addition to the bond and cash, Andrew left other personal property of the

value of $24,000, after deducting costs, debts, and taxes. Andrew died intestate, survived by: Bernard White, an adopted child of one of Andrew's deceased brothers; Carrie White, Bernard's mother; David White, the illegitimate child of Andrew's deceased sister; Edward White, a half-brother; Frank and George White, sons of another of Andrew's deceased brothers; and Hanna White, the mother of Frank and George. How should Andrew's estate be distributed? Explain.

4. When Andrew White died, he left a will dated 1957 which read in part: "I devise and bequeath to my wife, Alice, such portion of my estate which is required by law but no more. The balance of my estate I devise and bequeath to my children and their heirs." In 1958, the only child of Andrew and Alice died in infancy. In 1959, Andrew and Alice adopted Bernard White, Andrew's adult brother, as their child. In 1960, Charles White was born to Andrew and Alice. Bernard died in 1961, survived by his widow Dona. When Andrew died, he was survived by Alice, Charles, and Dona. At the time of Andrew's death, he and Alice had $10,000 in a joint bank account which they held as tenants by entireties. Andrew's other property, after liquidation and payment of all costs, debts, taxes, and family allowance, amounted to $30,000. How should Andrew's estate be distributed? Explain.

5. When Harry Smith died, a paper was found in his safe-deposit box. It was written in the decedent's handwriting and, in its entirety, read:

"Last Will and Testament, December 1, 1945. I, Harry Smith, give and bequeath unto my wife, Mary Smith, the sum of $10,000 and to my son, Robert Smith, the rest, residue, and remainder of my estate."

In 1948, Harry and Mary were divorced. In 1950, Harry married Janet, but in 1951 Janet left Harry without good reason and never returned. At the time of Harry's death several years later, his former wife, Mary, was alive. He was survived by his widow, Janet; his son, Robert; a daughter, Ruth; and two grandchildren, Samuel and June, children of a son, Archie, who had predeceased Harry. The grandchildren lived with their mother,

Sara, the widow of Archie. All of decedent's children were born prior to 1945. The estate of Harry consisted entirely of personal property. After all allowances, administration expenses, debts, and taxes were paid there was a balance for distribution of $45,000.

(a) Should the written instrument quoted above be probated? Explain.

(b) Other facts remaining the same, assume that decedent died intestate. How should his estate be distributed? Explain.

(c) Other facts remaining the same, assume that decedent left a valid will reading the same as the above-quoted instrument. How should his estate be distributed? Explain.

(d) Other facts remaining the same, assume that decedent left a valid will reading the same as the above-quoted instrument except that it did not contain the name "Mary Smith." How should his estate be distributed? Explain.

(e) Other facts remaining the same, assume that decedent left a valid will dated 1950, reading the same as the above-quoted instrument with Janet as the named wife. How should his estate be distributed? Explain.

6. Why might a donor make a substantial gift to a donee even though gift taxes are assessed? How and why is the federal gift tax definition of a gift different from the common law definition.

The Constitution of the United States of America

WE THE PEOPLE OF THE UNITED STATES, in Order to form a more perfect Union, establish Justice, insure domestic Tranquility, provide for the common defence, promote the general Welfare, and secure the Blessings of Liberty to ourselves and our Posterity, do ordain and establish this Constitution for the United States of America.

Article I

SECTION I

All legislative Powers herein granted shall be vested in a Congress of the United States, which shall consist of a Senate and House of Representatives .

SECTION 2

The House of Representatives shall be composed of Members chosen every second Year by the People of the several States, and the Electors in each State shall have the Qualifications requisite for Electors of the most numerous Branch of the State Legislature.

No Person shall be a Representative who shall not have attained to the Age of twenty five Years, and been seven Years a Citizen of the United States, and who shall not, when elected, be an Inhabitant of that State in which he shall be chosen.

Representatives and direct Taxes shall be apportioned among the several States which may be included within this Union, according to their respective Numbers, which shall be determined hy adding to the whole Number of free Persons, in-

cluding those bound to Service for a Term of Years, and excluding Indians not taxed, three fifths of all other Persons. The actual Enumeration shall be made within three Years after the first Meeting of the Congress of the United States, and within every subsequent Term of ten Years, in such Manner as they shall by Law direct. The Number of Representatives shall not exceed one for every thirty Thousand, but each State shall have at Least one Representative; and until such enumeration shall be made, the State of New Hampshire shall be entitled to choose three, Massachusetts eight, Rhode Island and Providence Plantations one, Connecticut five, New York six, New Jersey four, Pennsylvania eight, Delaware one, Maryland six, Virginia ten, North Carolina five, South Carolina five, and Georgia three.

When vacancies happen in the Representation from any State, and Executive Authority thereof shall issue Writs of Election to fill such Vacancies.

The House of Representatives shall choose their Speaker and other Officers; and shall have the sole Power of Impeachment.

SECTION 3

The Senate of the United States shall be composed of two Senators from each State, chosen by the Legislature thereof, for six Years; and each Senator shall have one Vote.

Immediately after they shall be assembled in Consequence of the first Election, they shall be divided as equally as may be into three Classes. The Seats of the Senators of the first Class shall be vacated at the Expiration of the second Year, of the second Class at the Expiration of the fourth Year, and of the third Class at the Expiration of the sixth Year, so that one third may be chosen every second Year; and if Vacancies happen by Resignation, or otherwise, during the Recess of the Legislature of any State, the Executive thereof may make temporary Appointments until the next Meeting of the Legislature, which shall then fill such Vacancies.

No Person shall be a Senator who shall not have attained to the Age of thirty Years, and been nine Years a Citizen of the United States, and who shall not, when elected, be an Inhabitant of that State for which he shall be chosen.

The Vice President of the United States shall be President of the Senate, but shall have no Vote, unless they be equally divided.

The Senate shall choose their other Officers, and also a President pro tempore, in the Absence of the Vice President, or when he shall exercise the Office of President of the United States.

The Senate shall have the sole Power to try all Impeachments. When sitting for that Purpose, they shall be on Oath or Affirmation. When the President of the United States is tried, the Chief Justice shall preside: And no Person shall be convicted without the Concurrence of two thirds of the Members present.

Judgment in Cases of Impeachment shall not extend further than to removal from Office, and disqualification to hold and enjoy any Office of honor, Trust, or Profit under the United States; but the Party convicted shall nevertheless be liable and subject to Indictment, Trial, Judgment, and Punishment, according to Law.

SECTION 4

The Times, Places and Manner of holding Elections for Senators and Representatives, shall be prescribed in each State by the Legislature thereof; but the Congress may at any time by Law make or alter such Regulations, except as to the Places of choosing Senators.

The Congress shall assemble at least once in every Year, and such Meeting shall be on the first Monday in December, unless they shall by Law appoint a different Day.

SECTION 5

Each House shall be the Judge of the Elections, Returns, and Qualifications of its own Members, and a Majority of each shall constitute a Quorum to do Business; but a smaller Number may adjourn from day to day, and may be authorized to compel the Attendance of absent Members, in such Manner, and under such Penalties as each House may provide.

Each House may determine the Rules of its Proceedings, punish its Members for disorderly Behavior, and, with the Concurrence of two thirds, expel a Member.

Each House shall keep a Journal of its Proceedings, and from time to time publish the same, excepting such Parts as may in their Judgment require Secrecy; and the Yeas and Nays of the Members of either House on any question shall, at the Desire of one fifth of those Present, be entered on the Journal.

Neither House, during the Session of Congress, shall, without the Consent of the other, adjourn for more than three days, nor to any other Place than that in which the two Houses shall be sitting.

SECTION 6

The Senators and Representatives shall receive a Compensation for their Services, to be ascertained by Law, and paid out of the Treasury of the United States. They shall in all Cases, except Treason, Felony and Breach of the Peace, be privileged from Arrest during their Attendance at the Session of their respective Houses, and in going to and returning from the same; and for any Speech or Debate in either House, they shall not be questioned in any other Place.

No Senator or Representative shall, during the Time for which he was elected, be appointed to any civil Office under the Authority of the United States, which shall have been created, or the Emoluments whereof shall have been increased during such time; and no Person holding any Office under the United States, shall be a Member of either House during his Continuance in Office.

SECTION 7

All bills for raising Revenue shall originate in the House of Representatives, but the Senate may propose or concur with, Amendments as on other Bills.

Every Bill which shall have passed the House of Representatives and the Senate, shall, before it become a Law, be presented to the President of the United States; If he approve he shall sign it, but if not he shall return it, with his Objections to the

House in which it shall have originated, who shall enter the Objections at large on their Journal, and proceed to reconsider it. If after such Reconsideration two thirds of that House shall agree to pass the Bill, it shall be sent together with the Objections, to the other House, by which it shall likewise be reconsidered, and if approved by two thirds of that House, it shall become a Law. But in all such Cases the Votes of both Houses shall be determined by Yeas and Nays, and the Names of the Persons voting for and against the Bill shall be entered on the Journal of each House respectively. If any Bill shall not be returned by the President within ten Days (Sundays excepted) after it shall have been presented to him, the Same shall be a Law, in like Manner as if he had signed it, unless the Congress by their Adjournment prevent its Return in which Case it shall not be a Law.

Every Order, Resolution, or Vote, to which the Concurrence of the Senate and House of Representatives may be necessary (except on a question of Adjournment) shall be presented to the President of the United States; and before the Same shall take Effect, shall be approved by him, or being disapproved by him, shall be repassed by two thirds of the Senate and House of Representatives, according to the Rules and Limitations prescribed in the Case of a Bill.

SECTION 8

The Congress shall have Power To lay and collect Taxes, Duties, Imposts and Excises, to pay the Debts and provide for the common Defence and general Welfare of the United Sates: but all Duties, Imposts and Excises shall be uniform throughout the United States:

To borrow Money on the credit of the United States;

To regulate Commerce with foreign Nations, and among the several States, and with the Indian Tribes;

To establish an uniform Rule of Naturalization, and uniform Laws on the subject of Bankruptcies throughout the United Sates;

To coin Money, regulate the Value thereof, and of foreign Coin, and fix the Standard of Weights and Measures;

To provide for the Punishment of counterfeiting the Securities and current Coin of the United States;

To establish Post Offices and post Roads;

To promote the Progress of Science and useful Arts, by securing limited Times to Authors and Inventors the exclusive Right to their respective Writings and Discoveries;

To constitute Tribunals inferior to the Supreme Court;

To define and punish Piracies and Felonies committed on the high Seas, and Offenses against the Law of Nations;

To declare War, grant Letters of Marque and Reprisal, and make Rules concerning Captures on Land and Water;

To raise and support Armies, but no Appropriation of Money to that Use shall be for a longer Term than two Years;

To provide and maintain a Navy;

To make Rules for the Government and Regulation of the land and naval Forces;

To provide for calling forth the Militia to execute the Laws of the Union, suppress Insurrections and repel Invasions;

To provide for organizing, arming, and disciplining, the Militia, and for governing such Part of them as may be employed in the Service of the United States, reserving to the States respectively, the Appointment of the Officers, and the Authority of training the Militia according to the discipline prescribed by Congress;

To exercise exclusive Legislation in all Cases whatsoever, over such District (not exceeding ten Miles square) as may, by Cession of particular States, and the Acceptance of Congress, become the Seat of the Government of the United States, and to exercise like Authority over all Place purchased by the Consent of the Legislature of the State in which the Same shall be, for the Erection of Forts, Magazines, Arsenals, dock-Yards, and other needful Buildings;—And

To make all Laws which shall be necessary and proper for carrying into Execution the foregoing Powers, and all other Powers vested by this Constitution in the Government of the United States, or in any Department or Officer thereof.

SECTION 9

The Migration or Importation of such Persons as any of the States now existing shall think proper to admit, shall not be prohibited by the Congress prior to the Year one thousand eight hundred and eight, but a Tax or duty may be imposed on such Importation, not exceeding ten dollars for each Person.

The privilege of the Writ of Habeas Corpus shall not be suspended, unless when in Cases of Rebellion or Invasion the public Safety may require it.

No Bill of Attainder or ex post facto Law shall be passed.

No Capitation, or other direct, Tax shall be laid, unless in Proportion to the Census or Enumeration herein before directed to be taken.

No Tax or Duty shall be laid on Articles exported from any State.

No Preference shall be given by any Regulation of Commerce or Revenue to the Ports of one State over those of another; nor shall Vessels bound to, or from, one State be obliged to enter, clear, or pay Duties in another.

No Money shall be drawn from the Treasury, but in Consequence of Appropriations made by Law; and a regular Statement and Account of the Receipts and Expenditures of all public Money shall be published from time to time.

No Title of Nobility shall be granted by the United States; And no Person holding any Office of Profit or Trust under them, shall, without the Consent of the Congress, accept of any present, Emolument, Office, or Title, of any kind whatever, from any King, Prince, or foreign State.

SECTION 10

No State shall enter into any Treaty, Alliance, or Confederation; grant Letters of Marque and Reprisal; coin Money; emit Bills of Credit; make any Thing but gold and silver Coin a Tender in Payment of Debts; pass any Bill of Attainder, ex post facto Law, or Law impairing the Obligation of Contracts, or grant any Title of Nobility.

No State shall, without the Consent of the Congress, lay any Imposts or Duties on Imports or Exports, except what may be absolutely necessary for executing it's inspection Laws; and the net Produce of all Duties and Imposts, laid by any State on Imports or Exports, shall be for the Use of the Treasury of the Untied States; and all such Laws shall be subject to the Revision and Control of the Congress . No State shall, without the Consent of Congress, lay any Duty of Tonnage, keep Troops, or Ships of War in time of Peace, enter into any Agreement or Compact with another State, or with a foreign Power, or engage in War, unless actually invaded, or in such imminent Danger as will not admit of delay.

Article II

SECTION 1

The executive Power shall be vested in a President of the United States of America. He shall hold his Office during the Term of four Years, and, together with the Vice President, chosen for the same Term, be elected, as follows:

Each State shall appoint, in such Manner as the Legislature thereof may direct, a Number of Electors, equal to the whole Number of Senators and Representatives to which the State may be entitled in the Congress; but no Senator or Representative, or Person holding an Office of Trust or Profit under the United States, shall be appointed an Elector.

The Electors shall meet in their respective States, and vote by Ballot for two Persons, of whom one at least shall not be an Inhabitant of the same Sate with themselves. And they shall make a List of all the Persons voted for, and of the Number of Votes for each; which List they shall sign and certify, and transmit sealed to the Seat of the Government of the United States, directed to the President of the Senate. The President of the Senate shall, in the Presence of the Senate and House of Representatives, open all the Certificates, and the Votes shall then be counted. The Person having the greatest Number of Votes shall be the President, if such Number be a Majority of the whole Number of Electors appointed; and if there be more than one who have such Majority, and have an equal Number of Votes, then the House of Representatives shall immediately choose by Ballot one of them for President; and if no Person have a Majority, then from the five highest on the List the said House shall in like Manner choose the President. But in choosing the President, the Votes shall be taken by States, the Representation from each State having one Vote; A quorum for this Purpose shall consist of a Member or Members from two thirds of the States, and a Majority of all the States shall be necessary to a Choice. In every Case, after the Choice of the President, the Person having the greater Number of Votes of the Electors shall be the Vice President. But if there should remain two or more who have equal Votes, the Senate shall choose from them by Ballot the Vice President.

The Congress may determine the Time of choosing the Electors, and the Day on which they shall give their Votes; which Day shall be the same throughout the United States.

No person except a natural born Citizen, or a Citizen of the United States, at the time of the Adoption of this Constitution, shall be eligible to the Office of President; neither shall any Person be eligible to that Office who shall not have attained to the Age of thirty five Years, and been fourteen Years a Resident within the United States.

In Case of the Removal of the President from Office, or of his Death, Resignation or Inability to discharge the Powers and Duties of the said Office, the same shall devolve on the Vice President, and the Congress may by Law provide for the Case of Removal, Death, Resignation, or Inability, both of the President and Vice President, declaring what Officer shall then act as President, and such Officer shall act accordingly, until the Disability be removed, or a President shall be elected.

The President shall, at stated Times, receive for his Services, a Compensation, which shall neither be increased nor diminished during the Period for which he shall have been elected, and he shall not receive within that Period any other Emolument from the United States, or any of them.

Before he enter on the Execution of his Office, he shall take the following Oath or Affirmation: "I do solemnly swear (or affirm) that I will faithfully execute the Office of President of the United Sates, and will to the best of my Ability, preserve, protect and defend the Constitution of the United States."

SECTION 2

The President shall be Commander in Chief of the Army and Navy of the United States, and of the Militia of the several States, when called into the actual Service of the United States; he may require the Opinion, in writing, of the principal Officer in each of the executive Departments, upon any Subject relating to the Duties of their respective Offices, and he shall have Power to grant Reprieves and Pardons for Offenses against the United States, except in Cases of Impeachment.

He shall have Power, by and with the Advice and Consent of the Senate to make Treaties, provided two thirds of the Senators present concur; and he shall nominate, and by and with the Advice and Consent of the Senate, shall appoint Ambassadors, other public Ministers and Consuls. Judges of the supreme Court, and all other Officers of the United States, whose Appointments are not herein otherwise provided for, and which shall be established by Law; but the Congress may by Law vest the Ap-

pointment of such inferior Officers, as they think proper, in the President alone, in the Courts of Law, or in the Heads of Departments.

The President shall have Power to fill up all Vacancies that may happen during the Recess of the Senate, by granting Commissions which shall expire at the End of their next Session.

SECTION 3

He shall from time to time give to the Congress Information of the State of the Union, and recommend to their Consideration such Measures as he shall judge necessary and expedient; he may, on extraordinary Occasion, convene both Houses, or either of them, and in Case of Disagreement between them, with Respect to the Time of Adjournment, he may adjourn them to such Time as he shall think proper; he shall receive Ambassadors and other public Ministers; he shall take Care that the Laws be faithfully executed, and shall Commission all the Officers of the United States.

SECTION 4

The President, Vice President, and all civil Officers of the United States, shall be removed from Office on Impeachment for, and Conviction of, Treason, Bribery, or other high Crimes and Misdemeanors.

Article III

SECTION 1

The judicial Power of the United States, shall be vested in one supreme Court, and in such inferior Courts as the Congress may from time to time ordain and establish. The Judges, both of the supreme and inferior Courts, shall hold their Offices during good Behaviour, and shall, at stated Times, receive for their Services a Compensation, which shall not be diminished during their Continuance in Office.

SECTION 2

The judicial Power shall extend to all Cases, in Law and Equity, arising under this Constitution, the Laws of the United States, and Treaties made, or which shall be made, under their Authority;—to all Cases affecting Ambassadors, other public Ministers and Consuls;—to all Cases of admiralty and maritime Jurisdiction;—to Controversies to which the United States shall be a Party;—to Controversies between two or more States;—between a State and Citizens of another State; between Citizens of different States;—between Citizens of the same State claiming Lands under Grants of different States, and between a State, or the Citizens thereof, and foreign States, Citizens or Subjects.

In all Cases affecting Ambassadors, other public Ministers and Consuls, and those in which a State shall be a Party, the supreme Court shall have original Jurisdiction. In all the other Cases before mentioned, the supreme Court shall have appellate Jurisdiction, both as to Law and Fact, with such Exceptions, and under such Regulations as the Congress shall make.

The Trial of all Crimes, except in Cases of Impeachment, shall be by Jury; and such Trial shall be held in the State where the said Crimes shall have been committed; but when not committed within any State, the Trial shall be at such Place or Places as the Congress may by Law have directed.

SECTION 3

Treason against the United States, shall consist only in levying War against them, or, in adhering to their Enemies, giving them Aid and Comfort. No Person shall be convicted of Treason unless on the Testimony of two Witnesses to the same overt Act, or on Confession in open Court.

The Congress shall have Power to declare the Punishment of Treason, but no Attainder of Treason shall work Corruption of Blood, or Forfeiture except during the Life of the Person attainted.

Article IV

SECTION I

Full Faith and Credit shall be given in each State to the public Acts, Records, and judicial Proceedings of every other State. And the Congress may by general Laws prescribe the Manner in which such Acts, Records and Proceedings shall be proved, and the Effect thereof.

SECTION 2

The Citizens of each State shall be entitled to all Privileges and Immunities of Citizens in the several States.

A Person charged in any State with Treason, Felony, or other Crime, who shall flee from Justice, and be found in another State, shall on Demand of the executive Authority of the State from which he fled, be delivered up, to be removed to the State having Jurisdiction of the Crime.

No Person held to Service or Labour in one State, under the Laws thereof, escaping into another, shall, in Consequence of any Law or Regulation therein, be discharged from such Service of Labour, but shall be delivered up on Claim of the Party to whom such Service or Labour may be due.

SECTION 3

New States may be admitted by the Congress into this Union; but no new State shall be formed or erected within the Jurisdiction of any other State; nor any State be formed by the Junction of two or more States, or Parts of States, without the Consent of the Legislatures of the States concerned as well as of the Congress.

The Congress shall have Power to dispose of and make all needful Rules and Regulations respecting the Territory or other Property belonging to the United States; and nothing in this Constitution shall be so constructed as to Prejudice any Claims of the United States, or of any particular State.

SECTION 4

The United States shall guarantee to every State in this Union a Republican Form of Government, and shall protect each of them against Invasion; and on Application of the Legislature, or of the Executive (when the Legislature cannot be convened) against domestic Violence.

Article V

The Congress, whenever two thirds of both Houses shall deem it necessary, shall propose Amendments to this Constitution, or, on the Application of the Legislatures of two thirds of the several States, shall call a Convention for proposing Amendments, which, in either Case, shall be valid to all Intents and Purposes, as part of this Constitution, when ratified by the Legislatures of three fourths of the several States, or by Conventions in three fourths thereof, as the one or the other Mode of Ratification may be proposed by the Congress; Provided that no Amendment which may be made prior to the Year One thousand eight hundred and eight shall in any Manner affect the first and fourth Clauses in the Ninth Section of the first Article; and that no State, without its Consent, shall be deprived of its equal Suffrage in the Senate.

Article VI

All Debts contracted and Engagements entered into, before the Adoption of this Constitution shall he as valid against the United States under this Constitution, as under the Confederation.

This Constitution, and the Laws of the United States which shall be made in Pursuance thereof; and all Treaties made, or which shall be made, under the Authority of the United States, shall be the supreme Law of the Land; and the Judges in every State shall be bound thereby, any Thing in the Constitution or Laws of any State to the Contrary notwithstanding.

The Senators and Representatives before mentioned, and the Members of the several State Legislatures, and all executive and judicial Officers, both of the United States and of the several States, shall be bound by Oath or Affirmation, to support this Constitution; but no religious Test shall ever be required as a Qualification to any Office or public Trust under the United States.

Article VII

The Ratification of the Conventions of nine States shall be sufficient for the Establishment of this Constitution between the States so ratifying the Same.

Amendment I [1791]

Congress shall make no law respecting an establishment of religion, or prohibiting the free exercise thereof; or abridging the freedom of speech, or of the press; or the right of the people peaceably to assembly, and to petition the Government for a redress of grievances.

Amendment II [1791]

A well regulated Militia, being necessary to the security of a free State, the right of the people to keep and bear Arms, shall not be infringed.

Amendment III [1791]

No Soldier shall, in time of peace be quartered in any house, without the consent of the Owner, nor in time of war, but in a manner to be prescribed by law.

Amendment IV [1791]

The right of the people to be secure in their persons, houses, papers, and effects, against unreasonable searches and seizures, shall not be violated, and no Warrants shall issue, but upon probable cause, supported by Oath or affirmation, and particularly describing the place to be searched, and the persons or things to be seized.

Amendment V [1791]

No person shall be held to answer for a capital, or otherwise infamous crime, unless on a presentment or indictment of a Grand Jury, except in cases arising in the land or naval forces, or in the Militia, when in actual service in time of War or public danger; nor shall any person be subject for the same offence to be twice put in jeopardy of life or limb; nor shall be compelled in any criminal case to be a witness against himself, nor be deprived of life, liberty, or property, without due process of law; nor shall private property be taken for public use, without just compensation.

Amendment VI [1791]

In all criminal prosecutions, the accused shall enjoy the right to a speedy and public trial, by an impartial jury of the State and district wherein the crime shall have been committed, which district shall have been previously ascertained by law, and to be informed of the nature and cause of the accusation; to be confronted with the witnesses against him; to have compulsory process for obtaining witnesses in his favor, and to have the Assistance of Counsel for his defense.

Amendment VII [1791]

In Suits at common law, where the value in controversy shall exceed twenty dollars, the right of trial by jury shall be preserved, and no fact tried by jury, shall be otherwise reexamined in any Court of the United States, than according to the rules of the common law.

Amendment VIII [1791]

Excessive bail shall not be required, nor excessive fines imposed, nor cruel and unusual punishments inflicted.

Amendment IX [1791]

The enumeration in the Constitution, of certain rights, shall not be construed to deny or disparage others retained by the people.

Amendment X [1791]

The powers not delegated to the United States by the Constitution, nor prohibited by it to the States, are reserved to the States respectively, or to the people.

Amendment XI [1798]

The Judicial power of the United States shall not be construed to extend to any suit in law or equity, commenced or prosecuted against one of the United States by Citizens or another State, or by Citizens or Subjects of any Foreign State.

Amendment XII [1804]

The Electors shall meet in their respective states, and vote by ballot for President and Vice-President, one of whom, at least, shall not be an inhabitant of the same state with themselves; they shall name in their ballots the person voted for as President, and in distinct ballots the person voted for as Vice-President, and they shall make distinct lists of all persons voted for as President, and of all persons voted for as Vice-President, and of the number of votes for each, which lists they shall sign and certify, and transmit sealed to the seat of the government of the United States, directed to the President of the Senate;—The President of the Senate shall, in the presence of the Senate and House of Representatives, open all the certificates and the votes shall then be counted;—The person having the greatest number of votes for President, shall be the President, if such number be a majority of the whole number of Electors appointed; and if no person have such majority, then from the persons having the highest numbers not exceeding three on the list of those voted for as President, the House of Representatives shall choose immediately, by ballot, the President. But in choosing the President, the votes shall be taken by states, the representation from each state having one vote; a quorum for this purpose shall consist of a member or members from two-thirds of the states, and a majority of all states shall be necessary to a choice. And if the House of Representatives shall not

choose a President whenever the right of choice shall devolve upon them, before the fourth day of March next following, then the Vice-President shall act as President, as in the case of the death or other constitutional disability of the President.—The person having the greatest number of votes as Vice-President, shall be the Vice-President, if such number be a majority of the whole number of Electors appointed, and if no person have a majority, then from the two highest numbers on the list, the Senate shall choose the Vice-President; a quorum for the purpose shall consist of two-thirds of the whole number of Senators, and a majority of the whole number shall be necessary to a choice. But no person constitutionally ineligible to the office of President shall be eligible to that of Vice-President of the United States.

Amendment XIII [1865]

SECTION 1

Neither slavery nor involuntary servitude, except as a punishment for crime whereof the party shall have been duly convicted, shall exist within the United States, or any place subject to their jurisdiction.

SECTION 2

Congress shall have power to enforce this article by appropriate legislation.

Amendment XIV [1868]

SECTION 1

All persons born or naturalized in the United States, and subject to the jurisdiction thereof, are citizens of the United States and of the State wherein they reside. No State shall make or enforce any law which shall abridge the privileges or immunities of citizens of the United States; nor shall any State deprive any person of life, liberty, or property, without due process of law; nor deny to any person within its jurisdiction the equal protection of the laws.

SECTION 2

Representatives shall be apportioned among the several States according to their respective numbers, counting the whole number of persons in each State, excluding Indians not taxed. But when the right to vote at any election for the choice of electors for President and Vice President of the United States, Representatives in Congress, the Executive and Judicial officers of a State, or the members of the Legislature thereof, is denied to any of the male inhabitants of such State, being twenty-one years of age, and citizens of the United States, or in any way abridged, except for participation in rebellion, or other crime, the basis of representation therein shall be reduced in the proportion which the number of such male citizens shall bear to the whole number of male citizens twenty-one years of age in such State.

SECTION 3

No person shall be a Senator or Representative in Congress, or elector of President and Vice President, or hold any office, civil or military, under the United States, or under any State, who having previously taken an oath, as a member of Congress, or as an officer of the United States, or as a member of any State legislature, or as an executive or judicial officer of any State, to support the Constitution of the United States, shall have engaged in insurrection or rebellion against the same, or given aid or comfort to the enemies thereof. But Congress may by a vote of two-thirds of each House, remove such disability.

SECTION 4

The validity of the public debt of the United States, authorized by law, including debts incurred for payment of pensions and bounties for services in suppressing insurrection or rebellion, shall not be questioned. But neither the United States nor any State shall assume or pay any debt or obligation incurred in aid of insurrection or rebellion against the United States, or any claim for the loss or emancipation of any slave; but all such debts, obligations and claims shall be held illegal and void.

SECTION 5

The Congress shall have power to enforce, by appropriate legislation, the provisions of this article.

Amendment XV [1870]

SECTION 1

The right of citizens of the United States to vote shall not be denied or abridged by the United States or by any State on account of race, color, or previous condition of servitude.

SECTION 2

The Congress shall have power to enforce this article by appropriate legislation.

Amendment XVI [1913]

The Congress shall have power to lay and collect taxes on incomes, from whatever source derived, without apportionment among the several States, and without regard to any census or enumeration.

Amendment XVII [1913]

The Senate of the United States shall be composed of two Senators from each State, elected by the people thereof, for six years; and each Senator shall have one vote. The electors in each State shall have the qualifications requisite for electors of the most numerous branch of the State legislatures.

When vacancies happen in the representation of any State in the Senate, the executive authority of such State shall issue writs of election to fill such vacancies: Provided, That the legislature of any State may empower the executive thereof to make temporary appointments until the people fill the vacancies by election as the legislature may direct.

This amendment shall not be so construed as to affect the election or term of any Senator chosen before it becomes valid as part of the Constitution.

Amendment XVIII [1919]

SECTION 1

After one year from the ratification of this article the manufacture, sale, or transportation of intoxicating liquors within, the importation thereof into, or the exportation thereof from the United States and all territory subject to the jurisdiction thereof for beverage purposes is hereby prohibited.

SECTION 2

The Congress and the several States shall have concurrent power to enforce this article by appropriate legislation.

SECTION 3

This article shall be inoperative unless it shall have been ratified as an amendment to the Constitution by the legislatures of the several States, as provided in the Constitution, within seven years from the date of the submission hereof to the States by the Congress.

Amendment XIX [1920]

The right of citizens of the United States to vote shall not be denied or abridged by the United States or by any State on account of sex.

Congress shall have power to enforce this article by appropriate legislation.

Amendment XX [1933]

SECTION 1

The terms of the President and Vice President shall end at noon on the 20th day of January, and the terms of Senators and Representatives at noon on the 3d day of January, of the years in which such terms would have ended if this article had not been ratified; and the terms of their successors shall then begin.

SECTION 2

The Congress shall assemble at least once in every year, and such meeting shall begin at noon on the 3d day of January, unless they shall by law appoint a different day.

SECTION 3

If, at the time fixed for the beginning of the term of the President, the President elect shall have died, the Vice President elect shall become President. If the President shall not have been chosen before the time fixed for the beginning of his term, or if the President elect shall have failed to qualify, then the Vice President elect shall act as President until a President shall have qualified; and the Congress may by law provide for the case wherein neither a President elect nor a Vice President elect shall have qualified, declaring who shall then act as President, or the manner in which one who is to act shall be selected, and such person shall act accordingly until a President or Vice President shall have qualified.

SECTION 4

The Congress may by law provide for the case of the death of any of the persons from whom the House of Representatives may choose a President whenever the right of choice shall have developed upon them, and for the case of the death of any of the persons from whom the Senate may choose a Vice President whenever the right of choice shall have devolved upon them.

SECTION 5

Sections 1 and 2 shall take effect on the 15th day of October following the ratification of this article.

SECTION 6

This article shall be inoperative unless it shall have been ratified as an amendment to the Constitution by the legislatures of three-fourths of the several States within seven years from the date of its submission.

Amendment XXI [1933]

SECTION 1

The eighteenth article of amendment to the Constitution of the United States is hereby repealed.

SECTION 2

The transportation or importation into any State, Territory, or possession of the United States for delivery or use therein of intoxicating liquors, in violation of the laws thereof, is hereby prohibited.

SECTION 3

This article shall be inoperative unless it shall have been ratified as an amendment to the Constitution by conventions in the several States, as provided in the Constitution, within seven years from the date of the submission hereof to the States by the Congress.

Amendment XXII [1951]

SECTION 1

No person shall be elected to the office of the President more than twice, and no person who has held the office of President, or acted as President, for more than two years of a term to which some other person was elected President shall be elected to the office of President more than once. But this Article shall not apply to any person holding the office of President when this Article was proposed by the Congress, and shall not prevent any person who may be holding the office of President, or acting as President, during the term within which this Article becomes operative from holding the office of President or acting as President during the remainder of such term.

SECTION 2

This article shall be inoperative unless it shall have been ratified as an amendment to the Constitution by the legislatures of three-fourths of the several States within seven years from the date of its submission to the States by the Congress.

Amendment XXIII [1961]

SECTION 1

The District constituting the seat of Government of the United States shall appoint in such manner as the Congress may direct:

A number of electors of President and Vice President equal to the whole number of Senators and Representatives in Congress to which the District would be entitled if it were a State, but in no event more than the least populous state; they shall be in addition to those appointed by the states, but they shall be considered, for the purposes of the election of President and Vice President, to be electors appointed by a state; and they shall meet in the District and perform such duties as provided by the twelfth article of amendment.

SECTION 2

The Congress shall have power to enforce this article by appropriate legislation.

Amendment XXIV [1964]

SECTION 1

The right of citizens of the United States to vote in any primary or other election for President or Vice President, for electors for President or Vice President, or for Senator or Representative in Congress, shall not be denied or abridged by the United States, or nay State by reason of failure to pay any poll tax or other tax.

SECTION 2

The Congress shall have power to enforce this article by appropriate legislation.

Amendment XXV [1967]

SECTION 1

In case of the removal of the President from office or of his death or resignation, the Vice President shall become President.

SECTION 2

Whenever there is a vacancy in the office of the Vice President, the President shall nominate a Vice President who shall take office upon confirmation by a majority vote of both Houses of Congress.

SECTION 3

Whenever the President transmits to the President pro tempore of the Senate and the Speaker of the House of Representatives his written declaration that he is unable to discharge the powers and duties of his office, and until he transmits to them a written declaration to the contrary, such powers and duties shall be discharged by the Vice President as Acting President.

SECTION 4

Whenever the Vice President and a majority of either the principal officers of the executive departments or of such other body as Congress may by law provide, transmit to the President pro tempore of the Senate and the Speaker of the House of Representatives their written declaration that the President is unable to discharge the powers and duties of his office, the Vice President shall immediately assume the powers and duties of the office as Acting President.

Thereafter, when the President transmits to the President pro tempore of the Senate and the Speaker of the House of Representatives his written declaration that no inability exists, he shall resume the powers and duties of his office unless the Vice President and a majority of either the principal officers of the executive department or of such other body as Congress may by law provide, transmit within four days to the President pro tempore of the Senate and the Speaker of the House of Representatives their written declaration and the President is unable to discharge the powers and duties of his office. Thereupon Congress shall decide the issue, assembling within forty-eight hours for that purpose if not in session. If the Congress, within twenty-one days after receipt of the latter written declaration, or, if Congress is not in session, within twenty-one days after Congress is required to assemble, determines by two-thirds vote of both Houses that the President is unable to discharge the powers and duties of his office, the Vice President shall continue to discharge the same as Acting President; otherwise, the President shall resume the powers and duties of his office.

Amendment XXVI [1971]

SECTION I

The right of citizens of the United States, who are eighteen years of age or older, to vote shall not be denied or abridged by the United States or by any State on account of age.

SECTION 2

The Congress shall have power to enforce this article by appropriate legislation.

Appendix

B

The Uniform Commercial Code

The Uniform Commercial Code[1] consists of 10 Articles as follows:

1. GENERAL PROVISIONS
2. SALES
3. COMMERCIAL PAPER
4. BANK DEPOSITS AND COLLECTIONS
5. LETTERS OF CREDIT
6. BULK TRANSFERS
7. WAREHOUSE RECEIPTS, BILLS OF LADING AND OTHER DOCUMENTS OF TITLE
8. INVESTMENT SECURITIES
9. SECURED TRANSACTIONS: SALES OF ACCOUNTS, CONTRACT RIGHTS AND CHATTEL PAPER
10. EFFECTIVE DATE AND REPEALER

Article I
General Provisions

PART I
SHORT TITLE, CONSTRUCTION, APPLICATION AND SUBJECT MATTER OF THE ACT

§ 1-101. SHORT TITLE.

This Act shall be known and may be cited as Uniform Commercial Code.

---

1. Adopted in 52 jurisdictions; all 50 States, although Louisiana had adopted only Articles, 1, 3, 4, and 5; the District of Columbia, and the Virgin Islands.

§ 1-102. PURPOSES; RULES OF CONSTRUCTION; VARIATION BY AGREEMENT.

(1) This Act shall be liberally construed and applied to promote its underlying purposes and policies.

(2) Underlying purposes and policies of this Act are

(a) to simplify, clarify and modernize the law governing commercial transactions;

(b) to permit the continued expansion of commercial practices through custom, usage and agreement of the parties;

(c) to make uniform the law among the various jurisdictions.

(3) The effect of provisions of this Act may be varied by agreement, except as otherwise provided in this Act and except that the obligations of good faith, diligence, reasonableness and care prescribed by this Act may not be disclaimed by agreement but the parties may by agreement determine the standards by which the performance of such obligations is to be measured if such standards are not manifestly unreasonable.

(4) The presence in certain provisions of this Act of the words "unless otherwise agreed" or words of similar import does not imply that the effect of other provisions may not be varied by agreement under subsection (3).

(5) In this Act unless the context otherwise requires

(a) words in the singular number include the plural, and in the plural include the singular;

(b) words of the masculine gender include the feminine and the neuter, and when the sense so indicates words of the neuter gender may refer to any gender.

§ 1-103. SUPPLEMENTARY GENERAL PRINCIPLES OF LAW APPLICABLE.

Unless displaced by the particular provisions of this Act, the principles of law and equity, including the law merchant and the law relative to capacity to contract, principal and agent, estoppel, fraud, misrepresentation, duress, coercion, mistake, bankruptcy, or other validating or invalidating cause shall supplement its provisions.

§ 1–104. CONSTRUCTION AGAINST IMPLICIT REPEAL.

This Act being a general act intended as a unified coverage of it subject matter, no part of it shall be deemed to be impliedly repealed by subsequent legislation if such construction can reasonably be avoided.

§ 1–105. TERRITORIAL APPLICATION OF THE ACT; PARTIES' POWER TO CHOOSE APPLICABLE LAW.

(1) Except as provided hereafter in this section, when a transaction bears a reasonable relation to this state and also to another state or nation the parties may agree that the law either of this state or of such other state or nation shall govern their rights and duties. Failing such agreement this Act applies to transactions bearing an appropriate relation to this state.

(2) Where one of the following provisions of this Act specifies the applicable law, that provision governs and a contrary agreement is effective only to the extent permitted by the law (including the conflict of laws rules) so specified:

Rights of creditors against sold goods. Section 2–402.

Applicability of the Article on Bank Deposits and Collections. Section 4–102.

Bulk transfers subject to the Article on Bulk Transfers. Section 6–102.

Applicability of the Article on Investment Securities. Section 8–106.

Perfection provisions of the Article on Secured Transactions. Section 9–103.

§ 1–106. REMEDIES TO BE LIBERALLY ADMINISTERED.

(1) The remedies provided by this Act shall be liberally administered to the end that the aggrieved party may be put in as good a position as if the other party had fully performed but neither consequential or special nor penal damages may be had except as specifically provided in this Act or by other rule of law

(2) Any right or obligation declared by this Act is enforceable by action unless the provision declaring it specifies a different and limited effect.

§ 1–107. WAIVER OR RENUNCIATION OF CLAIM OR RIGHT AFTER BREACH.

Any claim or right arising out of an alleged breach can be discharged in whole or in part without consideration by a written waiver or renunciation signed and delivered by the aggrieved party.

§ 1–108. SEVERABILITY.

If any provision or clause of this Act or application thereof to any person or circumstances is held invalid, such invalidity shall not affect other provisions or applications of the Act which can be given effect without the invalid provision or application, and to this end the provisions of this Act are declared to be severable.

§1–109. SECTION CAPTIONS.

Section captions are parts of this Act.

**PART 2
GENERAL DEFINITIONS AND
PRINCIPLES OF INTERPRETATION**

§ 1–201. GENERAL DEFINITIONS.

Subject to additional definitions contained in the subsequent Articles of this Act which are applicable to specific Articles or Parts thereof, and unless the context otherwise requires, in this Act:

(1) "Action" in the sense of a judicial proceeding includes recoupment, counterclaim, set-off, suit in equity and any other proceedings in which rights are determined.

(2) "Aggrieved party" means a party entitled to resort to a remedy.

(3) "Agreement" means the bargain of the parties in fact as found in their language or by implication from other circumstances including course of dealing or usage of trade or course of performance as provided in this Act (Sections 1–205 and 2–208). Whether an agreement has legal consequences is determined by the provisions of this Act, if applicable; otherwise by law of contracts (Section 1–103). (Compare "Contract".)

(4) "Bank" means any person engaged in the business of banking.

(5) "Bearer" means the person in possession of an instrument, document of title, or certified security payable to bearer or indorsed in blank.

(6) "Bill of lading" means a document evidencing the receipt of goods for shipment issued by a person engaged in the business of transporting or forwarding goods, and includes an airbill. "Airbill" means a document serving for air transportation as a bill of lading does for marine or rail transportation, and includes an air consignment note or air waybill.

(7) "Branch" includes a separately incorporated foreign branch of a bank.

(8) "Burden of establishing" a fact means the burden of persuading the triers of fact that the existence of the fact is more probable than its non-existence.

(9) "Buyer in ordinary course of business" means a person who in good faith and without knowledge that the sale to him is in violation of the ownership rights or se-

curity interest of a third party in the goods buys in ordinary course from a person in the business of selling goods of that kind but does not include a pawnbroker. All persons who sell minerals or the like (including oil and gas) at wellhead or minehead shall be deemed to be persons in the business of selling goods of that kind. "Buying" may be for cash or by exchange of other property or on secured or unsecured credit and includes receiving goods or documents of title under a pre-existing contract for sale but does not include a transfer in bulk or as security for or in total or partial satisfaction of a money debt.

(10) "Conspicuous": A term or clause is conspicuous when it is so written that a reasonable person against whom it is to operate ought to have noticed it. A printed heading in capitals (as: NON-NEGOTIABLE BILL OF LADING) is conspicuous. Language in the body of a form is "conspicuous" if it is in larger or other contrasting type or color. But in a telegram any stated term is "conspicuous". Whether a term or clause is "conspicuous" or not is for decision by the court.

(11) "Contract" means the total legal obligation which results from the parties' agreement is affected by this Act and any other applicable rules of law. (Compare "Agreement".)

(12) "Creditor" includes a general creditor, a secured creditor, a lien creditor and any representative of creditors, including an assignee for the benefit of creditors, a trustee in bankruptcy, a receiver in equity and an executor or administrator of an insolvent debtor's or assignor's estate.

(13) "Defendant" includes a person in the position of defendant in a cross-action or counterclaim .

(14) "Delivery" with respect to instruments, documents of title, chattel paper, or certificated securities means voluntary transfer of possession .

(15) "Document of title" includes bill of lading, dock warrant, dock receipt, warehouse receipt or order for the delivery of goods, and also any other document which in the regular course of business or financing is treated as adequately evidencing that the person in possession of it is entitled to receive, hold and dispose of the document and the goods it covers. To be a document of title a document must purport to be issued by or addressed to a bailee and purport to cover goods in the bailee's possession which are either identified or are fungible portions of an identified mass.

(16) "Fault" means wrongful act, omission or breach.

(17) "Fungible" with respect to goods or securities means goods or securities of which any unit is, by nature or usage of trade, the equivalent of any other like unit. Goods which are not fungible shall be deemed fungible for the purposes of this Act to the extent that under a particular

agreement or document unlike units are treated as equivalents.

(18) "Genuine" means free of forgery or counterfeiting.

(19) "Good faith" means honesty in fact in the conduct or transaction concerned.

(20) "Holder" means a person who is in possession of a document of title or an instrument or a certificated investment security drawn, issued, or indorsed to him or his order or to bearer or in blank.

(21) To "honor" is to pay or to accept and pay, or where a credit so engages to purchase or discount a draft complying with the terms of the credit.

(22) "Insolvency proceedings" includes any assignment for the benefit of creditors or other proceedings intended to liquidate or rehabilitate the estate of the person involved.

(23) A person is "insolvent" who either has ceased to pay his debts in the ordinary course of business or cannot pay his debts as they become due or is insolvent within the meaning of the federal bankruptcy law.

(24) "Money" means a medium of exchange authorized or adopted by a domestic or foreign government as a part of its currency.

(25) A person has "notice" of a fact when

(a) he has actual knowledge of it; or

(b) he has received a notice or notification of it; or

(c) from all the facts and circumstances known to him at the time in question he has reason to know that it exists.

A person "knows" or has "knowledge" of a fact when he has actual knowledge of it. "Discover" or "learn" or a word or phrase of similar import refers to knowledge rather than to reason to know. The time and circumstances under which a notice or notification may cease to be effective are not determined by this Act.

(26) A person "notifies" or "gives" a notice or notification to another by taking such steps as may be reasonably required to inform the other in ordinary course whether or not such other actually comes to know of it. A person "receives" a notice or notification when

(a) it comes to his attention; or

(b) it is duly delivered at the place of business through which the contract was made or at any other place held out by him as the place for receipt of such communications.

(27) Notice, knowledge or a notice or notification received by an organization is effective for a particular transaction from the time when it is brought to the attention of the individual conducting that transaction, and in any event from the time when it would have been brought to his attention if the organization had exercised

due diligence. An organization exercises due diligence if it maintains reasonable routines for communicating significant information to the person conducting the transaction and there is reasonable routines for communicating significant information to the person conducting the transaction and there is reasonable compliance with the routines. Due diligence does not require an individual acting for the organization to communicate information unless such communication is part of his regular duties or unless he has reason to know of the transaction and that the transaction would be materially affected by the information.

(28) "Organization" includes a corporation, government or governmental subdivision or agency, business trust, estate, trust, partnership or association, two or more persons having a joint or common interest, or any other legal or commercial entity.

(29) "Party", as distinct from "third party", means a person who has engaged in a transaction or made an agreement within this Act.

(30) "Person" includes an individual or an organization (See Section 1–102).

(31) "Presumption" or "presumed" means that the trier of fact must find the existence of the fact presumed unless and until evidence is introduced which would support a finding of its non-existence.

(32) "Purchase" includes taking by sale, discount, negotiation, mortgage, pledge, lien, issue or re-issue, gift or any other voluntary transaction creating an interest in property.

(33) "Purchaser" means a person who takes by purchase.

(34) "Remedy" means any remedial right to which an aggrieved party is entitled with or without resort to a tribunal.

(35) "Representative" includes an agent, an officer of a corporation, or association, and a trustee, executor or administrator of an estate, or any other person empowered to act for another.

(36) "Rights" includes remedies.

(37) "Security interest" means an interest in personal property or fixtures which secures payment or performance of an obligation. The retention or reservation of title by a seller of goods notwithstanding shipment or delivery to the buyer (Section 2–401) is limited in effect to a reservation of a "security interest". The term also includes any interest of a buyer of accounts or chattel paper which is subject to Article 9. The special property interest of a buyer of goods on identification of such goods to a contract for sale under Section 2–401 is not a "security interest", but a buyer may also acquire a "security interest" by complying with Article 9. Unless a lease or consignment is intended as security, reservation of title thereunder is not a "security interest" but a consignment is in any event subject to the provisions on consignment sales (Section 2–326). Whether a lease is intended as security is to be determined by the facts of each case; however, (a) the inclusion of an option to purchase does not of itself make the lease one intended for security, and (b) an agreement that upon compliance with the terms of the lease the lessee shall become or has the option to become the owner of the property for no additional consideration or for a nominal consideration does make the lease one intended for security.

(38) "Send" in connection with any writing or notice means to deposit in the mail or deliver for transmission by any other usual means of communication with postage or cost of transmission provided for and properly addressed and in the case of an instrument to an address specified thereon or otherwise agreed, or if there be none to any address reasonable under the circumstances. The receipt of any writing or notice within the time at which it would have arrived if properly sent has the effect of a proper sending.

(39) "Signed"" includes any symbol executed or adopted by a party with present intention to authenticate a writing

(40) "Surety" includes guarantor.

(41) "Telegram" includes a message transmitted by radio, teletype, cable, any mechanical method of transmission, or the like.

(42) "Term" means the portion of an agreement which relates to a particular matter.

(43) "Unauthorized" signature or indorsement means one made without actual, implied or apparent authority and includes a forgery.

(44) "Value". Except as otherwise provided with respect to negotiable instruments and bank collections (Sections 3–303, 4–208 and 4–209) a person gives "value" for rights if he acquires them

    (a) in return for a binding commitment to extend credit or for the extension of immediately available credit whether or not drawn upon and whether or not a charge-back is provided for in the event of difficulties in collection; or

    (b) as security for or in total or partial satisfaction of a pre-existing claim; or

    (c) by accepting delivery pursuant to a preexisting contract for purchase; or

    (d) generally, in return for any consideration sufficient to support a simple contract.

(45) "Warehouse receipt" means a receipt issued by a person engaged in the business of storing goods for hire.

(46) "Written" or "writing" includes printing, typewriting or any other intentional reduction to tangible form. [Amended in 1962, 1972 and 1977.]

§ 1–202. PRIMA FACIE EVIDENCE BY THIRD PARTY DOCUMENTS.

A document in due form purporting to be a bill of lading, policy or certificate of insurance, official weigher's or inspector's certificate, consular invoice, or any other document authorized or required by the contract to be issued by a third party shall be prima facie evidence of its own authenticity and genuineness and of the facts stated in the document by the third party.

§ 1–203. OBLIGATION OF GOOD FAITH.

Every contract or duty within this Act imposes an obligation of good faith in its performance or enforcement.

§ 1–204. TIME; REASONABLE TIME; "SEASONABLY".

(1) Whenever this Act requires any action to be taken within a reasonable time, any time which is not manifestly unreasonable may be fixed by agreement.

(2) What is reasonable time for taking any action depends on the nature, purpose and circumstances of such action.

(3) An action is taken "seasonably" when it is taken at or within the time agreed or if no time is agreed at or within a reasonable time.

§1–205. COURSE OF DEALING AND USAGE OF TRADE.

(1) A course of dealing is a sequence of previous conduct between the parties to a particular transaction which is fairly to be regarded as establishing a common basis of understanding for interpreting their expressions and other conduct.

(2) A usage of trade is any practice or method of dealing having such regularity of observance in a place, vocation or trade as to justify an expectation that it will be observed with respect to the transaction in question. The existence and scope of such usage are to be proved as facts. If it is established that such a usage is embodied in a written trade code or similar writing the interpretation of the writing is for the court.

(3) A course of dealing between parties and any usage of trade in the vocation or trade in which they are engaged or of which they are or should be aware give particular meaning to and supplement or qualify terms of an agreement.

(4) The express terms of an agreement and an applicable course of dealing or usage of trade shall be constructed wherever reasonable as consistent with each other; but when such construction is unreasonable express terms control both course of dealing and usage of trade and course of dealing controls usage trade.

(5) An applicable usage of trade in the place where any part of performance is to occur shall be used in interpreting the agreement as to the part of the performance.

(6) Evidence of a relevant usage of trade offered by one party is not admissible unless and until he has given the other party such notice as the court finds sufficient to prevent unfair surprise to the latter.

§ 1–206. STATUTE OF FRAUDS FOR KINDS OF PERSONAL PROPERTY NOT OTHERWISE COVERED.

(1) Except in the cases described in subsection (2) of this section a contract for the sale of personal property is not enforceable by way of action or defense beyond five thousand dollars in amount or value or remedy unless there is some writing which indicates that a contract for sale has been made between the parties at a defined or stated price, reasonably identifies the subject matter, and is signed by the party against whom enforcement is sought or by his authorized agent.

(2) Subsection (1) of this section does not apply to contracts for the sale of goods (Section 2–201) nor of securities (Section 8–319) nor to security agreements (Section 9–203).

§ 1–207. PERFORMANCE OR ACCEPTANCE UNDER RESERVATION OF RIGHTS.

A party who with explicit reservation of rights performs or promises performance or assents to performance in the manner demanded or offered by the other party does not thereby prejudice the rights reserved. Such words as "without prejudice", "under protest" or the like are sufficient.

§ 1–208. OPTION TO ACCELERATE AT WILL.

A term providing that one party or his successor in interest may accelerate payment or performance or require collateral or additional collateral "at will" or "when he deems himself insecure" or in words of similar import shall be construed to mean that he shall have power to do so only if he in good faith believes that the prospect of payment or performance is impaired. The burden of establishing lack of good faith is on the party against whom the power has been exercised.

§ 1–209. SUBORDINATED OBLIGATIONS.

An obligation may be issued as subordinated to payment of another obligation of the person obligated, or a creditor may subordinate his right to payment of an obligation by agreement with either the person obligated or another creditor of the person obligated. Such a subordination does not create a security interest as against either the common debtor or a subordinated creditor. This section shall be construed as declaring the law as it existed prior to the enactment of this section and not as modifying it. Added 1966.

Note: This new section is proposed as an optional provision to make it clear that a subordination agreement does not create a security interest unless so intended.

Article 2
Sales

PART I
SHORT TITLE, GENERAL CONSTRUCTION AND SUBJECT MATTER

§ 2–101. SHORT TITLE.

This Article shall be known and may be cited as Uniform Commercial Code–Sales.

§ 2–102. SCOPE; CERTAIN SECURITY AND OTHER TRANSACTIONS EXCLUDED FROM THIS ARTICLE.

Unless the context otherwise requires, this Article applies to transactions in goods; it does not apply to any transaction which although in the form of an unconditional contract to sell or present sale is intended to operate only as a security transaction nor does this Article impair or repeal any statute regulating sales to consumers, farmers or other specified classes of buyers.

§ 2–103. DEFINITIONS AND INDEX OF DEFINITIONS.

(1) In this Article unless the context otherwise requires

(a) "Buyer" means a person who buys or contracts to buy goods.

(b) "Good faith" in the case of a merchant means honesty in fact and the observance of reasonable commercial standards of fair dealing in the trade.

(c) "Receipt" of goods means taking physical possession of them.

(d) "Seller" means a person who sells or contracts to sell goods.

(2) Other definitions applying to this Article or to specified Parts thereof, and the sections in which they appear are:

"Acceptance". Section 2–606.

"Banker's credit". Section 2–325.

"Between merchants". Section 2–104.

"Cancellation". Section 2–106(4).

"Commercial unit". Section 2–105.

"Confirmed credit". Section 2–325.

"Conforming to contract". Section 2–106.

"Cover". Section 2–712.

"Entrusting". Section 2–403.

"Financing agency". Section 2–104.

"Future goods". Section 2–105.

"Goods". Section 2–105.

"Identification". Section 2–501.

"Installment contract". Section 2–612.

"Letter of Credit". Section 2–325.

"Lot". Section 2–105.

"Merchant". Section 2–104.

"Overseas". Section 2–323.

"Person in position of seller". Section 2–707.

"Present sale". Section 2–106.

"Sale". Section 2–106.

"Sale on approval". Section 2–326.

"Sale or return". Section 2–326.

"Termination". Section 2–106.

(3) The following definitions in other Articles apply to this Article:

"Check". Section 3–104.

"Consignee". Section 7–102.

"Consignor". Section 7–102.

"Consumer goods". Section 9–109.

"Dishonor". Section 3–507.

"Draft". Section 3–104.

(4) In addition Article 1 contains general definitions and principles of construction and interpretation applicable throughout this Article.

§ 2–104. DEFINITIONS: "MERCHANT"; "BETWEEN MERCHANTS"; "FINANCING AGENCY".

(1) "Merchant" means a person who deals in goods of the kind or otherwise by his occupation holds himself out as having knowledge or skill peculiar to the practices or goods involved in the transaction or to whom such knowledge or skill may be attributed by his employment of an agent or broker or other intermediary who by his occupation holds himself out as having such knowledge or skill.

(2) "Financing agency" means a bank, finance company or other person who in the ordinary course of business makes advances against goods or documents of title or who by arrangement with either the seller or the buyer intervenes in ordinary course to make or collect payment due or claimed under the contract for sale, as by purchasing or paying the seller's draft or making advances against it or by merely taking it for collection whether or not documents of title accompany the draft. "Financing agency" includes also a bank or other person who similarly intervenes between persons who are in the position of seller and buyer in respect to the goods (Section 2–707).

(3) "Between merchants" means in any transaction with respect to which both parties are chargeable with the knowledge or skill of merchants.

§ 2–105. DEFINITIONS: TRANSFERABILITY; "GOODS"; "FUTURE" GOODS; "LOT"; "COMMERCIAL UNIT".

(1) "Goods" means all things (including specially manufactured goods) which are movable at the time of identification to the contract for sale other than the money in which the price is to be paid, investment securities (Article 8) and things in action. "Goods" also includes the unborn young of animals and growing crops and other identified things attached to realty as described in the section on goods to be severed from realty (Section 2–107).

(2) Goods must be existing and identified before any interest in them can pass. Goods which are not both existing and identified are "future" goods. A purported present sale of future goods or of any interest therein operates as a contract to sell.

(3) There may be a sale of a part interest in existing identified goods.

(4) An undivided share in an identified bulk of fungible goods is sufficiently identified to be sold although the quantity of the bulk is not determined. Any agreed proportion of such a bulk or any quantity thereof agreed upon by number, weight or other measure may to the extent of the seller's interest in the bulk be sold to the buyer who then becomes an owner in common.

(5) "Lot" means a parcel or a single article which is the subject matter of a separate sale or delivery, whether or not it is sufficient to perform the contract.

(6) "Commercial unit" means such a unit of goods as by commercial usage is a single whole for purposes of sale and division of which materially impairs its character or value on the market or in use. A commercial unit may be a single article (as a machine) or a set of articles (as a suite of furniture or an assortment of sizes) or a quantity (as a bale, gross, or carload) or any other unit treated in use or in the relevant market as a single whole.

§ 2–106. DEFINITIONS: "CONTRACT"; "AGREEMENT"; "CONTRACT FOR SALE"; "SALE"; "PRESENT SALE"; "CONFORMING" TO CONTRACT: "TERMINATION"; "CANCELLATION".

(1) In this Article unless the context otherwise requires "contract" and "agreement" are limited to those relating to the present or future sale of goods. "Contract for sale" includes both a present sale of goods and a contract to sell goods at a future time. A "sale" consists in the passing of title from the seller to the buyer for a price (Section 2-401). A "present sale" means a sale which is accomplished by the making of the contract.

(2) Goods or conduct including any part of a performance are "conforming" or conform to the contract when they are in accordance with the obligations under the contract.

(3) "Termination" occurs when either party pursuant to a power created by agreement or law puts an end to the contract otherwise than for its breach. On "termination" all obligations which are still executory on both sides are discharged but any right based on prior breach or performance survives.

(4) "Cancellation" occurs when either party puts an end to the contract for breach by the other and its effect is the same as that of "termination" except that the cancelling party also retains any remedy for breach of the whole contract or any unperformed balance.

§ 2–107. GOODS TO BE SEVERED FROM REALTY: RECORDING.

(1) A contract for the sale of minerals or the like (including oil and gas) or a structure or its materials to be removed from realty is a contract for the sale of goods within this Article if they are to be severed by the seller but until severance a purported present sale thereof which is not effective as a transfer of an interest in land is effective only as a contract to sell.

(2) A contract for the sale apart from the land of growing crops or other things attached to realty and capable of severance without material harm thereto but not described in subsection (1) or of timber to be cut is a contract for the sale of goods within this Article whether the subject matter is to be severed by the buyer or by the seller even though it forms part of the realty at the time of contracting, and the parties can by identification effect a present sale before severance.

(3) The provisions of this section are subject to any third party rights provided by the law relating to realty records, and the contract for sale may be executed and recorded as a document transferring an interest in land and shall then constitute notice to third parties of the buyer's rights under the contract for sale.

PART 2
FORM, FORMATION AND READJUSTMENT OF CONTRACT

§ 2–201. FORMAL REQUIREMENTS; STATUTE OF FRAUDS.

(1) Except as otherwise provided in this section a contract for the sale of goods for the price of $500 or more is not enforceable by way of action or defense unless there is some writing sufficient to indicate that a contract for sale has been made between the parties and signed by the party against whom enforcement is sought or by his authorized agent or broker. A writing is not sufficient because it omits or incorrectly states a term agreed upon but the contract is not enforceable under this paragraph beyond the quantity of goods shown in such writing.

(2) Between merchants if within a reasonable time a writing in confirmation of the contract and sufficient against the sender is received and the party receiving it has reason to know its contents, it satisfies the requirements of subsection (1) against such party unless written notice of

objection to its contents is given within ten days after it is received.

(3) A contract which does not satisfy the requirements of subsection (1) but which is valid in other respects in enforceable

(a) if the goods are to be specially manufactured for the buyer and are not suitable for sale to others in the ordinary course of the seller's business and the seller, before notice of repudiation is received and under circumstances which reasonably indicate that the goods are for the buyer, has made either a substantial beginning of their manufacture or commitments for their procurement; or

(b) if the party against whom enforcement is sought admits in his pleading, testimony or otherwise in court that a contract for sale was made, but the contract is not enforceable under this provision beyond the quantity of goods admitted; or

(c) with respect to goods for which payment has been made and accepted or which have been received and accepted (Sec. 2-606).

§ 2–202. FINAL WRITTEN EXPRESSION: PAROL OR EXTRINSIC EVIDENCE.

Terms with respect to which the confirmatory memoranda of the parties agree or which are otherwise set forth in a writing intended by the parties as a final expression of their agreement with respect to such terms as are included therein may not be contradicted by evidence of any prior agreement or of a contemporaneous oral agreement but may be explained or supplemented

(a) by course of dealing or usage of trade (Section 1-205) or by course of performance (Section 2–208); and

(b) by evidence of consistent additional terms unless the court finds the writing to have been intended also as a complete and exclusive statement of the terms of the agreement.

§ 2–203. SEALS INOPERATIVE.

The affixing of a seal to a writing evidencing a contract for sale or an offer to buy or sell goods does not constitute the writing a sealed instrument and the law with respect to sealed instruments does not apply to such a contract or offer.

§ 2–204. FORMATION IN GENERAL.

(1) A contract for sale of goods may be made in any manner sufficient to show agreement, including conduct by both parties which recognizes the existence of such a contract.

(2) An agreement sufficient to constitute a contract for sale may be found even though the moment of its making is undetermined.

(3) Even though one or more terms are left open a contract for sales does not fail for indefiniteness if the parties have intended to make a contract and there is a reasonably certain basis for giving an appropriate remedy.

§ 2–205. FIRM OFFERS.

An offer by a merchant to buy or sell goods in a signed writing which by its terms gives assurance that it will be held open is not revocable, for lack of consideration, during the time stated or if no time is stated for a reasonable time but in no event may such period of irrevocability exceed three months; but any such term of assurance on a form supplied by the offeree must be separately signed by the offeror.

§ 2–206. OFFER AND ACCEPTANCE IN FORMATION OF CONTRACT.

(1) Unless other unambiguously indicated by the language or circumstances

(a) an offer to make a contract shall be construed as inviting acceptance in any manner and by any medium reasonable in the circumstances;

(b) an order or other offer to buy goods for prompt or current shipment shall be construed as inviting acceptance either by a prompt promise to ship or by the prompt or current shipment of conforming or nonconforming goods, but a shipment of nonconforming goods does not constitute an acceptance if the seller seasonably notifies the buyer that the shipment is offered only as an accommodation to the buyer.

(2) Where the beginning of a requested performance is a reasonable mode of acceptance an offeror who is not notified of acceptance within a reasonable time may treat the offer as having lapsed before acceptance.

§ 2–207. ADDITIONAL TERMS IN ACCEPTANCE OR CONFIRMATION.

(1) A definite and seasonable expression of acceptance or a written confirmation which is sent within a reasonable time operates as an acceptance even though it states terms additional to or different from those offered or agreed upon, unless acceptance is expressly made conditional on assent to the additional or different terms.

(2) The additional terms are to be construed as proposals for addition to the contract. Between merchants such terms become part of the contract unless:

(a) the offer expressly limits acceptance to the terms of the offer;

(b) they materially alter it; or

(c) notification of objection to them has already been given or is given within a reasonable time after notice of them is received.

(3) Conduct by both parties which recognizes the existence of a contract is sufficient to establish a contract for sale although the writings of the parties do not otherwise establish a contract. In such case the terms of the particular contract consist of those terms on which the writings of the parties agree, together with any supplementary terms incorporated under any other provisions of this Act.

§ 2–208. COURSE OF PERFORMANCE OR PRACTICAL CONSTRUCTION.

(1) Where the contract for sale involves repeated occasions for performance by either party with knowledge of the nature of the performance and opportunity for objection to it by the other, any course of performance accepted or acquiesced in without objection shall be relevant to determine the meaning of the agreement.

(2) The express terms of the agreement and any such course of performance, as well as any course of dealing and usage of trade, shall be construed whenever reasonable as consistent with each other; but when such construction is unreasonable, express terms shall control course of performance and course of performance shall control both course of dealing and usage of trade (Section 1–205).

(3) Subject to the provisions of the next section on modification and waiver, such course of performance shall be relevant to show a waiver or modification of any term inconsistent with such course of performance.

§ 2–209. MODIFICATION, RESCISSION AND WAIVER.

(1) An agreement modifying a contract within this Article needs no consideration to be binding.

(2) A signed agreement which excludes modification or rescission except by a signed writing cannot be otherwise modified or rescinded, but except as between merchants such a requirement on a form supplied by the merchant must be separately signed by the other party.

(3) The requirements of the statute of frauds section of this Article (Section 2–201) must be satisfied if the contract as modified is within its provisions.

(4) Although an attempt at modification or rescission does not satisfy the requirements of subsection (2) or (3) it can operate as a waiver.

(5) A party who has made a waiver affecting an executory portion of the contract may retract the waiver by reasonable notification received by the other party that strict performance will be required of any term waived, unless the retraction would be unjust in view of a material change of position in reliance on the waiver.

§ 2–210. DELEGATION OF PERFORMANCE; ASSIGNMENT OF RIGHTS.

(1) A party may perform his duty through a delegate unless otherwise agreed or unless the other party has a substantial interest in having his original promisor perform or control the acts required by the contract. No delegation of performance relieves the party delegating of any duty to perform or any liability for breach.

(2) Unless otherwise agreed all rights of either seller or buyer can be assigned except where the assignment would materially change the duty of the other party, or increase materially the burden or risk imposed on him by his contract, or impair materially his chance of obtaining return performance. A right to damages for breach of the whole contract or a right arising out of the assignor's due performance of his entire obligation can be assigned despite agreement otherwise.

(3) Unless the circumstances indicate the contrary a prohibition of assignment of "the contract" is lo be construed as barring only the delegation to the assignee of the assignor's performance.

(4) An assignment of "the contract" or of "all my rights under the contract" or an assignment in similar general terms is an assignment of rights and unless the language or the circumstances (as in an assignment for security) indicate the contrary, it is a delegation of performance of the duties of the assignor and its acceptance by the assignee constitutes a promise by him to perform those duties. This promise is enforceable by either the assignor or the other party to the original contract.

(5) The other party may treat any assignment which delegates performance as creating reasonable grounds for insecurity and may without prejudice to his rights against the assignor demand assurances from the assignee (Section 2–609).

PART 3
GENERAL OBLIGATION AND CONSTRUCTION OF CONTRACT

§ 2–301. GENERAL OBLIGATIONS OF PARTIES.

The obligation of the seller is to transfer and deliver and that of the buyer is to accept and pay in accordance with the contract.

§ 2–302. UNCONSCIONABLE CONTRACT OR CLAUSE.

(1) If the court as a matter of law finds the contract or any clause of the contract to have been unconscionable at the time it was made the court may refuse to enforce the contract, or it may enforce the remainder of the contract without the unconscionable clause, or it may so limit the application of any unconscionable clause as to avoid any unconscionable result.

(2) When it is claimed or appears to the court that the contract or any clause thereof may be unconscionable the

parties shall be afforded a reasonable opportunity to present evidence as to its commercial setting, purpose and effect to aid the court in making the determination.

§ 2–303. ALLOCATIONS OR DIVISION OF RISKS.

Where this Article allocates a risk or a burden as between the parties "unless otherwise agreed", the agreement may not only shift the allocation but may also divide the risk or burden.

§ 2–304. PRICE PAYABLE IN MONEY, GOODS, REALTY, OR OTHERWISE.

(1) The price can be made payable in money or otherwise. If it is payable in whole or in part in goods each party is a seller of the goods which he is to transfer.

(2) Even though all or part of the price is payable in an interest in realty the transfer of the goods and the seller's obligations with reference to them are subject to this Article, but not the transfer of the interest in realty or the transferor's obligations in connection therewith.

§ 2–305. OPEN PRICE TERM.

(1) The parties if they so intend can conclude a contract for sale even though the price is not settled. In such a case the price is a reasonable price at the time for delivery if

(a) nothing is said as to price; or

(b) the price is left to be agreed by the parties and they fail to agree; or

(c) the price is to be fixed in terms of some agreed market or other standard as set or recorded by a third person or agency and it is not so set or recorded.

(2) A price to be fixed by the seller or by the buyer means a price for him to fix in good faith .

(3) When a price left to be fixed otherwise than by agreement of the parties fails to be fixed through fault of one party the other may at his option treat the contract as cancelled or himself fix a reasonable price.

(4) Where, however, the parties intend not to be bound unless the price be fixed or agreed and it is not fixed or agreed there is no contract. In such a case the buyer must return any goods already received or if unable so to do must pay their reasonable value at the time of delivery and the seller must return any portion of the price paid on account.

§ 2–306. OUTPUT, REQUIREMENTS AND EXCLUSIVE DEALINGS.

(1) A term which measures the quantity by the output of the seller or the requirements of the buyer means such actual output or requirements as may occur in good faith, except that no quantity unreasonably disproportionate to any stated estimate or in the absence of a stated estimate to any normal or otherwise comparable prior output or requirements may be tendered or demanded.

(2) A lawful agreement by either the seller or the buyer for exclusive dealing in the kind of goods concerned imposes unless otherwise agreed an obligation by the seller to use best efforts to supply the goods and by the buyer to use best efforts to promote their sale.

§ 2–307. DELIVERY IN SINGLE LOT OR SEVERAL LOTS.

Unless otherwise agreed all goods called for by a contract for sale must be tendered in a single delivery and payment is due only on such tender but where the circumstances give either party the right to make or demand delivery in lots the price if it can be apportioned may be demanded for each lot.

§ 2–308. ABSENCE OF SPECIFIED PLACE FOR DELIVERY.

Unless otherwise agreed

(a) the place for delivery of goods is the seller's place of business or if he has none his residence; but

(b) in a contract for sale of identified goods which to the knowledge of the parties at the time of contracting are in some other place, that place is the place for their delivery; and

(c) documents of title may be delivered through customary banking channels.

§ 2–309. ABSENCE OF SPECIFIC TIME PROVISIONS; NOTICE OF TERMINATION.

(1) The time for shipment or delivery or any other action under a contract if not provided in this Article or agreed upon shall be a reasonable time.

(2) Where the contract provides for successive performances but is indefinite in duration it is valid for a reasonable time but unless otherwise agreed may be terminated at any time by either party.

(3) Termination of a contract by one party except on the happening of an agreed event requires that reasonable notification be received by the other party and an agreement dispensing with notification is invalid if its operation would be unconscionable.

§ 2–310. OPEN TIME FOR PAYMENT OR RUNNING OF CREDIT; AUTHORITY TO SHIP UNDER RESERVATION.

Unless otherwise agreed

(a) payment is due at the time and place at which the buyer is to receive the goods even though the place of shipment is the place of delivery; and

(b) if the seller is authorized to send the goods he may ship them under reservation, and may tender the documents of title, but the buyer may inspect the goods after their arrival before payment is due unless such inspection is inconsistent with the terms of the contract (Section 2–513); and

(c) if delivery is authorized and made by way of documents of title otherwise than by subsection (b) then payment is due at the time and place at which the buyer is to receive the documents regardless of where the goods are to be received; and

(d) where the seller is required or authorized to ship the goods on credit the credit period runs from the time of shipment but postdating the invoice or delaying its dispatch will correspondingly delay the starting of the credit period.

§ 2–311. Options and Cooperation Respecting Performance.

(1) An agreement for sale which is otherwise sufficiently definite (subsection (3) of Section 2–204) to be a contract is not made invalid by the fact that it leaves particulars of performance to be specified by one of the parties. Any such specification must be made in good faith and within limits set by commercial reasonableness.

(2) Unless otherwise agreed specifications relating to assortment of the goods are at the buyer's option and except as otherwise provided in subsections (1)(c) and (3) of Section 2–319 specifications or arrangements relating to shipment are at the seller's option.

(3) Where such specification would materially affect the other party's performance but is not seasonably made or where one party's cooperation is necessary to the agreed performance of the other but is not seasonably forthcoming, the other party in addition to all other remedies

(a) is excused for any resulting delay in his own performance; and

(b) may also either proceed to perform in any reasonable manner or after the time for a material part of his own performance treat the failure to specify or to cooperate as a breach by failure to deliver or accept the goods.

§ 2–312. Warranty of Title and Against Infringement; Buyer's Obligation Against Infringement.

(1) Subject to subsection (2) there is in a contract for sale a warranty by the seller that

(a) the title conveyed shall be good, and its transfer rightful; and

(b) the goods shall be delivered free from any security interest or other lien or encumbrance of which the buyer at the time of contracting has no knowledge.

(2) A warranty under subsection (1) will be excluded or modified only by specific language or by circumstances which give the buyer reason to know that the person selling does not claim title himself or that he is purporting to sell only such right or title as he or a third person may have.

(3) Unless otherwise agreed a seller who is a merchant regularly dealing in goods of the kind warrants that the goods shall be delivered free of the rightful claim of any third person by way of infringement or the like but a buyer who furnishes specifications to the seller must hold the seller harmless against any such claim which arises out of compliance with the specifications.

§ 2–313. Express Warranties by Affirmation, Promise, Description, Sample.

(1) Express warranties by the seller are created as follows:

(a) Any affirmation of fact or promise made by the seller to the buyer which relates to the goods and becomes part of the basis of the bargain creates an express warranty that the goods shall conform to the affirmation or promise.

(b) Any description of the goods which is made part of the basis of the bargain creates an express warranty that the goods shall conform to the description.

(c) Any sample or model which is made part of the basis of the bargain creates an express warranty that the whole of the goods shall conform to the sample or model.

(2) It is not necessary to the creation of an express warranty that the seller use formal words such as 'warrant" or "guarantee" or that he have a specific intention to make a warranty, but an affirmation merely of the value of the goods or a statement purporting to be merely the seller's opinion or commendation of the goods does not create a warranty.

§ 2–314. Implied Warranty: Merchantability; Usage of Trade.

(1) Unless excluded or modified (Section 2–316), a warranty that the goods shall be merchantable is implied in a contract for their sale if the seller is a merchant with respect to goods of that kind. Under this section the serving for value of food or drink to be consumed either on the premises or elsewhere is a sale.

(2) Goods to be merchantable must be at least such as

(a) pass without objection in the trade under the contract description; and

(b) in the case of fungible goods, are of fair average quality within the description; and

(c) are fit for the ordinary purposes for which such goods are used; and

(d) run, within the variations permitted by the agreement, of even kind, quality and quantity within each unit and among all units involved; and

(e) are adequately contained, packaged, and labeled as the agreement may require; and

(f) conform to the promises or affirmations of fact made on the container or label if any.

(3) Unless excluded or modified (Section 2–316) other implied warranties may arise from course of dealing or usage of trade.

§ 2–315. IMPLIED WARRANTY: FITNESS FOR PARTICULAR PURPOSE.

Where the seller at the time of contracting has reason to know any particular purpose for which the goods are required and that the buyer is relying on the seller's skill or judgment to select or furnish suitable goods, there is unless excluded or modified under the next section an implied warranty that the goods shall be fit for such purpose.

§ 2–316. EXCLUSION OR MODIFICATION OF WARRANTIES.

(1) Words or conduct relevant to the creation of an express warranty and words or conduct tending to negate or limit warranty shall be construed wherever reasonable as consistent with each other; but subject to the provisions of this Article on parol or extrinsic evidence (Section 2–202) negation or limitation is inoperative to the extent that such construction is unreasonable.

(2) Subject to subsection (3), to exclude or modify the implied warranty of merchantability or any part of it the language must mention merchantability and in case of a writing must be conspicuous, and to exclude or modify any implied warranty of fitness the exclusion must be by a writing and conspicuous. Language to exclude all implied warranties of fitness is sufficient if it states, for example, that "There are no warranties which extend beyond the description on the face hereof."

(3) Notwithstanding subsection(2)

(a) unless the circumstances indicate otherwise, all implied warranties are excluded by expressions like "as is", "with all faults" or other language which in common understanding calls the buyer's attention to the exclusion of warranties and makes plain that there is no implied warranty; and

(b) when the buyer before entering into the contract has examined the goods or the sample or model as fully as he desired or has refused to examine the goods there is no implied warranty with regard to defects which an examination ought in the circumstances to have revealed to him; and

(c) an implied warranty can also be excluded or modified by course of dealing or course of performance or usage of trade.

(4) Remedies for breach of warranty can be limited in accordance with the provisions of this Article on liquidation or limitation of damages and on contractual modification of remedy (Sections 2–718 and 2–719).

§ 2–317. CUMULATION AND CONFLICT OF WARRANTIES EXPRESS OR IMPLIED.

Warranties whether express or implied shall be construed as consistent with each other and as cumulative, but if such construction is unreasonable the intention of the parties shall determine which warranty is dominant. In ascertaining that intention the following rules apply:

(a) Exact or technical specifications displace an inconsistent sample or model or general language of description.

(b) A sample from an existing bulk displaces inconsistent general language of description.

(c) Express warranties displace inconsistent implied warranties other than an implied warranty of fitness for a particular purpose.

§ 2–318. THIRD PARTY BENEFICIARIES OF WARRANTIES EXPRESS OR IMPLIED.

Note: If this Act is introduced in the Congress of the United States this section should be omitted. (States to select one alternative.)

ALTERNATIVE A

A seller's warranty whether express or implied extends to any natural person who is in the family or household of his buyer or who is a guest in his home if it is reasonable to expect that such person may use, consume or be affected by the goods and who is injured in person by breach of the warranty. A seller may not exclude or limit the operation of this section.

ALTERNATIVE B

A seller's warranty whether express or implied extends to any natural person who may reasonably be expected to use, consume or be affected by the goods and who is injured in person by breach of the warranty. A seller may not exclude or limit the operation of this section.

ALTERNATIVE C

A seller's warranty whether express or implied extends to any person who may reasonably be expected to use, consume or be affected by the goods and who is injured by breach of the warranty. A seller may not exclude or limit the operation of this section with respect to injury to the person of an individual to whom the warranty extends. As amended in 1966.

§ 2–319. F.O.B. AND F.A.S. TERMS.

(1) Unless otherwise agreed the term F.O.B. (which means "free on board") at a named place, even though used only in connection with the stated price, is a delivery term under which

(a) when the term is F.O.B. the place of shipment, the seller must at that place ship the goods in the manner provided in this Article (Section 2–504) and bear the expense and risk of putting them into the possession of the carrier; or

(b) when the term is F.O.B. the place of destination, the seller must at his own expense and risk transport the goods to that place and there tender delivery of them in the manner provided in this Article (Section 2–503);

(c) when under either (a) or (b) the term is also F.O.B. vessel, car or other vehicle, the seller must in addition at his own expense and risk load the goods on board. If the term is F.O.B. vessel the buyer must name the vessel and in an appropriate case the seller must comply with the provisions of this Article on the form of bill of lading (Section 2–323).

(2) Unless otherwise agreed the term F.A.S. vessel (which means "free alongside") at a named port, even though used only in connection with the stated price, is a delivery term under which the seller must

(a) at his own expense and risk deliver the goods alongside the vessel in the manner usual in that port or on a dock designated and provided by the buyer; and

(b) obtain and tender a receipt for the goods in exchange for which the carrier is under a duty to issue a bill of lading.

(3) Unless otherwise agreed in any case falling within subsection (1)(a) or (c) or subsection (2) the buyer must seasonably give any needed instructions for making delivery, including when the term is F.A.S. or F.O.B. the loading berth of the vessel and in an appropriate case its name and sailing date. The seller may treat the failure of needed instructions as a failure of cooperation under this Article (Section 2–311). He may also at his option move the goods in any reasonable manner preparatory to delivery or shipment.

(4) Under the term F.O.B. vessel or F.A.S. unless otherwise agreed the buyer must make payment against tender of the required documents and the seller may not tender nor the buyer demand delivery of the goods in substitution for the documents.

§ 2–320. C.I.F. AND C. & F. TERMS.

(1) The term C.I.F. means that the price includes in a lump sun the cost of the goods and the insurance and freight to the named destination. The term C. & F. or C.F. means that the price so includes cost and freight to the named destination.

(2) Unless otherwise agreed and even though used only in connection with the stated price and destination, the term C.I.F. destination or its equivalent requires the seller at his own expense and risk to

(a) put the goods into the possession of a carrier at the port for shipment and obtain a negotiable bill or

bills of lading covering the entire transportation to the named destination; and

(b) load the goods and obtain a receipt from the carrier (which may be contained in the bill of lading) showing that the freight has been paid or provided for; and

(c) obtain a policy or certificate of insurance, including any war risk insurance, of a kind and on terms then current at the port of shipment in the usual amount, in the currency of the contract, shown to cover the same goods covered by the bill of lading and providing for payment of loss to the order of the buyer or for the account of whom it may concern; but the seller may add to the price the amount of the premium for any such war risk insurance; and

(d) prepare an invoice of the goods and procure any other documents required to effect shipment or to comply with the contract; and

(e) forward and tender with commercial promptness all the documents in due form and with any indorsement necessary to perfect the buyer's rights

(3) Unless otherwise agreed the term C. & F. or its equivalent has the same effect and imposes upon the seller the same obligations and risks as a C.I.F. term except the obligation as to insurance.

(4) Under the term C.I.F. or C. & F. unless otherwise agreed the buyer must make payment against tender of the required documents and the seller may not tender nor the buyer demand delivery of the goods in substitution for the documents.

§ 2–321. C.I.F. OR C. & F.: "NET LANDED WEIGHTS"; "PAYMENT ON ARRIVAL"; WARRANTY OF CONDITION ON ARRIVAL.

Under a contract containing a term C.I.F. or C. & F.

(1) Where the price is based on or is to be adjusted according to "net landed weights", "delivered weights", "out turn" quantity or quality or the like, unless otherwise agreed the seller must reasonably estimate the price. The payment due on tender of the documents called for by the contract is the amount so estimated, but after final adjustment of the price a settlement must be made with commercial promptness.

(2) An agreement described in subsection (1) or any warranty of quality or condition of the goods on arrival places upon the seller the risk of ordinary deterioration, shrinkage and the like in transportation but has no effect on the place or time of identification to the contract for sale or delivery or on the passing of the risk of loss.

(3) Unless otherwise agreed where the contract provides for payment on or after arrival of the goods the seller must before payment allow such preliminary inspection as is feasible; but if the goods are lost delivery of the doc-

uments and payment are due when the goods should have arrived.

§ 2–322. DELIVERY "EX-SHIP".

(1) Unless otherwise agreed a term for delivery of goods "ex-ship" (which means from the carrying vessel) or in equivalent language is not restricted to a particular ship and requires delivery from a ship which has reached a place at the named port of destination where goods of the kind are usually discharged.

(2) Under such a term unless otherwise agreed

(a) the seller must discharge all liens arising out of the carriage and furnish the buyer with a direction which puts the carrier under a duty to deliver the goods;

(b) the risk of loss does not pass to the buyer until the goods leave the ship's tackle or are otherwise properly unloaded.

§ 2–323. FORM OF BILL OF LADING REQUIRED IN OVERSEAS SHIPMENT; "OVERSEAS".

(1) Where the contract contemplates overseas shipment and contains a term C.I.F. or C. & F. or F.O.B. vessel, the seller unless otherwise agreed must obtain a negotiable bill of lading stating that the goods have been loaded on board or, in the case of a term C.I.F. or C. & F., received for shipment.

(2) Where in a case within subsection (1) a bill of lading has been issued in a set of parts unless otherwise agreed if the documents are not to be sent from abroad the buyer may demand tender of the full set; otherwise only one part of the bill of lading need be tendered. Even if the agreement expressly requires a full set

(a) due tender of a single part is acceptable within the provisions of this Article on cure of improper delivery (subsection (1) of Section 2–508); and

(b) even though the full set is demanded, if the documents are sent from abroad the person tendering an incomplete set may nevertheless require payment upon furnishing an indemnity which the buyer in good faith deems adequate.

(3) A shipment by water or by air or a contract contemplating such shipment is "overseas" insofar as by usage of trade or agreement it is subject to the commercial, financing or shipping practices characteristic of international deep water commerce.

§ 2–324. "NO ARRIVAL, NO SALE" TERM.

Under a term "no arrival, no sale" or terms of like meaning, unless otherwise agreed,

(a) the seller must properly ship conforming goods and if they arrive by any means he must tender them on arrival but he assumes no obligation that the

goods will arrive unless he has caused the non-arrival; and

(b) where without fault of the seller the goods are in part lost or have so deteriorated as no longer to conform to the contract or arrive after the contract time, the buyer may proceed as if there had been casualty to identified goods (Section 2-613).

§ 2–325. "LETTER OF CREDIT" TERM; "CONFIRMED CREDIT".

(1) Failure of the buyer seasonably to furnish an agreed letter of credit is a breach of the contract for sale.

(2) The delivery to seller of a proper letter of credit suspends the buyer's obligation to pay. If the letter of credit is dishonored, the seller may on seasonable notification to the buyer require payment directly from him.

(3) Unless otherwise agreed the term "letter of credit" or "banker's credit" in a contract for sale means an irrevocable credit issued by a financing agency of good repute and, where the shipment is overseas, of good international repute. The term "confirmed credit" means that the credit must also carry the direct obligation of such an agency which does business in the seller's financial market.

§ 2–326. SALE ON APPROVAL AND SALE OR RETURN; CONSIGNMENT SALES AND RIGHTS OF CREDITORS.

(1) Unless otherwise agreed, if delivered goods may be returned by the buyer even though they conform to the contract, the transaction is

(a) a "sale on approval" if the goods are delivered primarily for use; and

(b) a "sale or return" if the goods are delivered primarily for resale.

(2) Except as provided in subsection (3), goods held on approval are not subject to the claims of the buyer's creditors until acceptance; goods held on sale or return are subject to such claims while in the buyer's possession .

(3) Where goods are delivered to a person for sale and such person maintains a place of business at which he deals in goods of the kind involved, under a name other than the name of the person making delivery, then with respect to claims of creditors of the person conducting the business the goods are deemed to be on sale or return. The provisions of this subsection are applicable even though an agreement purports to reserve title to the person making delivery until payment or resale or uses such words as "on consignment" or "on memorandum". However, this subsection is not applicable if the person making delivery

(a) complies with an applicable law providing for a consignor's interest or the like to be evidenced by a sign, or

(b) establishes that the person conducting the business is generally known by his creditors to be substantially engaged in selling the goods of others, or

(c) complies with the filing provisions of the Article on Secured Transactions (Article 9).

(4) Any "or return" term of a contract for sale is to be treated as a separate contract for sale within the statute of frauds section of this Article (Section 2–201) and as contradicting the sale aspect of the contract within the provisions of this Article on parol or extrinsic evidence (Section 2–202).

§ 2–327. Special Incidents of Sale on Approval and Sale or Return.

(1) Under a sale on approval unless otherwise agreed

(a) although the goods are identified to the contract the risk of loss and the title do not pass to the buyer until acceptance; and

(b) use of the goods consistent with the purpose of trial is not acceptance but failure seasonably to notify the seller of election to return the goods is acceptance, and if the goods conform to the contract acceptance of any part is acceptance of the whole; and

(c) after due notification of election to return, the return is at the seller's risk and expense but a merchant buyer must follow any reasonable instructions.

(2) Under a sale or return unless otherwise agreed

(a) the option to return extends to the whole or any commercial unit of the goods while in substantially their original condition, but must be exercised seasonably; and

(b) the return is at the buyer's risk and expense.

§ 2–328. Sale by Auction.

(1) In a sale by auction if goods are put up in lots each lot is the subject of a separate sale.

(2) A sale by auction is complete when the auctioneer so announces by the fall of the hammer or in other customary manner. Where a bid is made while the hammer is falling in acceptance of a prior bid the auctioneer may in his discretion reopen the bidding or declare the goods sold under the bid on which the hammer was falling.

(3) Such a sale is with reserve unless the goods are in explicit terms put up without reserve. In an auction with reserve the auctioneer may withdraw the goods at any time until he announces completion of the sale. In an auction without reserve, after the auctioneer calls for bids on an article or lot, that article or lot cannot be withdrawn unless no bid is made within a reasonable time. In either case a bidder may retract his bid until the auctioneer's announcement of completion of the sale, but a bidder's retraction does not revive any previous bid.

(4) If the auctioneer knowingly receives a bid on the seller's behalf or the seller makes or procures such a bid, and notice has not been given that liberty for such bidding is reserved, the buyer may at his option avoid the sale or take the goods at the price of the last good faith bid prior to the completion of the sale. This subsection shall not apply to any bid at a forced sale.

PART 4
TITLE, CREDITORS AND GOOD FAITH PURCHASERS

§ 2–401. Passing of Title; Reservation for Security; Limited Application of This Section.

Each provision of this Article with regard to the rights, obligations or remedies of the seller, the buyer, purchasers or other third parties applies irrespective of title to the goods except where the provision refers to such title. Insofar as situations are not covered by the other provisions of this Article and matters concerning title became material the following rules apply:

(1) Title to goods cannot pass under a contract for sale prior to their identification to the contract (Section 2–501), and unless otherwise explicitly agreed the buyer acquires by their identification a special property as limited by this Act. Any retention or reservation by the seller of the title (property) in goods shipped or delivered to the buyer is limited in effect to a reservation of a security interest. Subject to these provisions and to the provisions of the Article on Secured Transactions (Article 9), title to goods passes from the seller to the buyer in any manner on any conditions explicitly agreed on by the parties.

(2) Unless otherwise explicitly agreed title passes to the buyer at the time and place at which the seller completes his performance with reference to the physical delivery of the goods, despite any reservation of a security interest and even though a document of title is to be delivered at a different time or place; and in particular and despite any reservation of a security interest by the bill of lading.

(a) if the contract requires or authorizes the seller to send the goods to the buyer but does not require him to deliver them at destination, title passes to the buyer at the time and place of shipment; but

(b) if the contract requires delivery at destination, title, passes on tender there.

(3) Unless otherwise explicitly agreed where delivery is to be made without moving the goods,

(a) if the seller is to deliver a document of title, title passes at the time when and the place where he delivers such documents; or

(b) if the goods are at the time of contracting already identified and no documents are to be delivered, title passes at the time and place of contracting.

(4) A rejection or other refusal by the buyer to receive or retain the goods, whether or not justified, or a justified revocation of acceptance revests title to the goods in the seller. Such revesting occurs by operation of law and is not a "sale".

§ 2–402. RIGHTS OF SELLER'S CREDITORS AGAINST SOLD GOODS.

(1) Except as provided in subsections (2) and (3), rights of unsecured creditors of the seller with respect to goods which have been identified to a contract for sale are subject to the buyer's rights to recover the goods under this Article (Sections 2–502 and 2–716).

(2) A creditor of the seller may treat a sale or an identification of goods to a contract for sale as void if as against him a retention of possession by the seller is fraudulent under any rule of law of the state where the goods are situated, except that retention of possession in good faith and current course of trade by a merchant-seller for a commercially reasonable time after a sale or identification is not fraudulent.

(3) Nothing in this Article shall be deemed to impair the rights of creditors of the seller

(a) under the provisions of the Article on Secured Transactions (Article 9); or

(b) where identification to the contract or delivery is made not in current course of trade but in satisfaction of or as security for a pre-existing claim for money, security or the like and is made under circumstances which under any rule of law of the state where the goods are situated would apart from this Article constitute the transaction a fraudulent transfer or voidable preference.

§ 2–403. POWER TO TRANSFER; GOOD FAITH PURCHASE OF GOODS; "ENTRUSTING".

(1) A purchase of goods acquires all title which his transferor had or had power to transfer except that a purchaser of a limited interest acquires rights only to the extent of the interest purchased. A person with voidable title has power to transfer a good title to a good faith purchaser for value. When goods have been delivered under a transaction of purchase the purchaser has such power even though

(a) the transferor was deceived as to the identity of the purchaser, or

(b) the delivery was in exchange for a check which is later dishonored, or

(c) it was agreed that the transaction was to be a "cash sale", or

(d) the delivery was procured through fraud punishable as larcenous under the criminal law.

(2) Any entrusting of possession of goods to a merchant who deals in goods of that kind gives him power to transfer all rights of the entruster to a buyer in ordinary course of business.

(3) "Entrusting" includes any delivery and any acquiescence in retention of possession regardless of any condition expressed between the parties to the delivery or acquiescence and regardless of whether the procurement of the entrusting or the possessor's disposition of the goods have been such as to be larcenous under the criminal law.

(4) The rights of other purchasers of goods and of lien creditors are governed by the Articles on Secured Transactions (Article 9), Bulk Transfers (Article 6) and Documents of Title (Article 7).

PART 5
PERFORMANCE

§ 2–501. INSURABLE INTEREST IN GOODS; MANNER OF IDENTIFICATION OF GOODS.

(1) The buyer obtains a special property and an insurable interest in goods by identification of existing goods as goods to which the contract refers even though the goods so identified are nonconforming and he has an option to return or reject them. Such identification can be made at any time and in any manner explicitly agreed to by the parties. In the absence of explicit agreement identification occurs

(a) when the contract is made if it is for the sale of goods already existing and identified;

(b) if the contract is for the sale of future goods other than those described in paragraph (c), when goods are shipped, marked or otherwise designated by the seller as goods to which the contract refers;

(c) when the crops are planted or otherwise become growing crops or the young are conceived if the contract is for the sale of unborn young to be born within twelve months after contracting or for the sale of crops to be harvested within twelve months or the next normal harvest season after contracting whichever is longer.

(2) The seller retains an insurable interest in goods so long as title to or any security interest in the goods remains in him and where the identification is by the seller alone he may until default or insolvency or notification to the buyer that the identification is final substitute other goods for those identified.

(3) Nothing in this section impairs any insurable interest recognized under any other statute or rule of law.

§ 2–502. BUYER'S RIGHT TO GOODS ON SELLER'S INSOLVENCY.

(1) Subject to subsection (2) and even though the goods have not been shipped a buyer who has paid a part or all of the price of goods in which he has a special property

under the provisions of the immediately preceding section may on making and keeping good a tender of any unpaid portion of their price recover them from the seller if the seller becomes insolvent within ten days after receipt of the first installment on their price.

(2) If the identification creating his special property has been made by the buyer he acquires the right to recover the goods only if they conform to the contract for sale.

§ 2–503. Manner of Seller's Tender of Delivery.

(1) Tender of delivery requires that the seller put and hold conforming goods at the buyer's disposition and give the buyer any notification reasonably necessary to enable him to take delivery. The manner, time and place for tender are determined by the agreement and this Article, and in particular

(a) tender must be at a reasonable hour, and if it is of goods they must be kept available for the period reasonably necessary to enable the buyer to take possession; but

(b) unless otherwise agreed the buyer must furnish facilities reasonably suited to the receipt of goods.

(2) Where the case is within the next section respecting shipment tender requires that the seller comply with its provisions.

(3) Where the seller is required to deliver at a particular destination tender requires that he comply with subsection (1) and also in any appropriate case tender documents as described in subsections (4) and (5) of this section.

(4) Where goods are in the possession of a bailee and are to be delivered without being moved

(a) tender requires that the seller either tender a negotiable document of title covering such goods or procure acknowledgment by the bailee of the buyer's right to possession of the gods; but

(b) tender to the buyer of a non-negotiable document of title or of a written direction to the bailee to deliver is sufficient tender unless the buyer seasonably objects, and receipt by the bailee of notification of the buyer's rights fixes those rights as against the bailee and all third persons; but risk of loss of the goods and of any failure by the bailee to honor the non-negotiable document of title or to obey the direction remains on the seller until the buyer has had a reasonable time to present the document or direction, and a refusal by the bailee to honor the document or to obey the direction defeats the tender.

(5) Where the contract requires the seller to deliver documents

(a) he must tender all such documents in correct form, except as provided in this Article with respect to bills of lading in a set (subsection (2) of Section 2–323); and

(b) tender through customary banking channel is sufficient and dishonor of a draft accompanying the documents constitutes non-acceptance or rejection.

§ 2–504. Shipment by Seller.

Where the seller is required or authorized to send the goods to the buyer and the contract does not require him to deliver them at a particular destination, then unless otherwise agreed he must

(a) put the goods in the possession of such a carrier and make such a contract for their transportation as may be reasonable having regard to the nature of the goods and other circumstances of the case; and

(b) obtain and promptly deliver or tender in due form any document necessary to enable the buyer to obtain possession of the goods or otherwise required by the agreement or by usage of trade; and

(c) promptly notify the buyer of the shipment.

Failure to notify the buyer under paragraph (c) or to make a proper contract under paragraph (a) is a ground for rejection only if material delay or loss ensues.

§ 2–505. Seller's Shipment Under Reservation.

(1) Where the seller has identified goods to the contract by or before shipment:

(a) his procurement of a negotiable bill of lading to his own order or otherwise reserves in him a security interest in the goods. His procurement of the bill to the order of a financing agency or of the buyer indicates in addition only the seller's expectation of transferring that interest to the person named.

(b) a non-negotiable bill of lading to himself or his nominee reserves possession of the goods as security but except in a case of conditional delivery (subsection (2) of Section 2–507) a non-negotiable bill of lading naming the buyer as consignee reserves no security interest even though the seller retains possession of the bill of lading.

(2) When the shipment by the seller with reservation of a security interest is in violation of the contract for sale it constitutes an improper contract for transportation within the preceding section but impairs neither the rights given to the buyer by shipment and identification of the goods to the contract nor the seller's powers as a holder of a negotiable document.

§ 2–506. Rights of Financing Agency.

(1) A financing agency by paying or purchasing for value a draft which relates to a shipment of goods acquires to the extent of the payment or purchase and in addition to its own rights under the draft and any document of title securing it any rights of the shipper in the goods including the right to stop delivery and the shipper's right to have the draft honored by the buyer.

(2) The right to reimbursement of a financing agency which has in good faith honored or purchased the draft under commitment to or authority from the buyer is not impaired by subsequent discovery of defects with reference to any relevant document which was apparently regular on its face.

§ 3–507. EFFECT OF SELLER'S TENDER; DELIVERY ON CONDITION.

(1) Tender of delivery is a condition to the buyer's duty to accept the goods and, unless otherwise agreed, to his duty to pay for them. Tender entitles the seller to acceptance of the goods and to payment according to the contract.

(2) Where payment is due and demanded on the delivery to the buyer of goods or documents of title, his right as against the seller to retain or dispose of them is conditional upon his making the payment due.

§ 2–508. CURE BY SELLER OF IMPROPER TENDER OR DELIVERY; REPLACEMENT.

(1) Where any tender or delivery by the seller is rejected because non-conforming and the time for performance has not yet expired, the seller may seasonably notify the buyer of his intention to cure and may then within the contract time make a conforming delivery.

(2) Where the buyer rejects a non-conforming tender which the seller had reasonable grounds to believe would be acceptable with or without money allowance the seller may if he seasonably notifies the buyer have a further reasonable time to substitute a conforming tender.

§ 2–509. RISK OF LOSS IN THE ABSENCE OF BREACH.

(1) Where the contract requires or authorizes the seller to ship the goods by carrier

(a) if it does not require him to deliver them at a particular destination, the risk of loss passes to the buyer when the goods are duly delivered to the carrier even though the shipment is under reservation (Section 2–505); but

(b) if it does require him to deliver them at a particular destination and the goods are there duly tendered while in the possession of the carrier, the risk of loss passes to the buyer when the goods are there duly so tendered as to enable the buyer to take delivery.

(2) Where the goods are held by a bailee to be delivered without being moved, the risk of loss passes to the buyer

(a) on his receipt of a negotiable document of title covering the goods; or

(b) on acknowledgment by the bailee of the buyer's right to possession of the goods; or

(c) after his receipt of a non-negotiable document of title or other written direction to deliver, as provided in subsection (4)(b) of Section 2–503.

(3) In any case not within subsection (1) or (2), the risk of loss passes to the buyer on his receipt of the goods if the seller is a merchant; otherwise, the risk passes to the buyer on tender of delivery.

(4) The provisions of this section are subject to contrary agreement of the parties and to the provisions of this Article on sale on approval (Section 2–327) and on effect of breach on risk of loss (Section 2–510).

§ 2–510. EFFECT OF BREACH ON RISK OF LOSS.

(1) Where a tender or delivery of goods so fails to conform to the contract as to give a right of rejection the risk of their loss remains on the seller until cure or acceptance.

(2) Where the buyer rightfully revokes acceptance he may to the extent of any deficiency in his effective insurance coverage treat the risk of loss as having rested on the seller from the beginning.

(3) Where the buyer as to conforming goods already identified to the contract for sale repudiates or is otherwise in breach before risk of their loss has passed him, the seller may to the extent of any deficiency in his effective insurance coverage treat the risk of loss as resting on the buyer for a commercially reasonable time.

§ 2–511. TENDER OF PAYMENT BY BUYER; PAYMENT BY CHECK.

(1) Unless otherwise agreed tender of payment is a condition to the seller's duty to tender and complete any delivery.

(2) Tender of payment is sufficient when made by any means or in any manner current in the ordinary course of business unless the seller demands payment in legal tender and gives any extension of time reasonably necessary to procure it.

(3) Subject to the provisions of this Act on the effect of an instrument on an obligation (Section 3–802), payment by check is conditional and is defeated as between the parties by dishonor of the check on due presentment.

§ 2–512. PAYMENT BY BUYER BEFORE INSPECTION.

(1) Where the contract requires payment before inspection non-conformity of the goods does not excuse the buyer from so making payment unless

(a) the non-conformity appears without inspection; or

(b) despite tender of the required documents the circumstance would justify injunction against honor under the provisions of this Act (Section 5–114).

(2) Payment pursuant to subsection (1) does not constitute an acceptance of goods or impair the buyer's right to inspect or any of his remedies.

§ 2–513. BUYER'S RIGHT TO INSPECTION OF GOODS.

(1) Unless otherwise agreed and subject to subsection (3), where goods are tendered or delivered or identified to the contract for sale, the buyer has a right before payment or acceptance to inspect them at any reasonable place and time and in any reasonable manner. When the seller is required or authorized to send the goods to the buyer, the inspection may be after their arrival.

(2) Expenses of inspection must be borne by the buyer but may be recovered from the seller if the goods do not conform and are rejected.

(3) Unless otherwise agreed and subject to the provisions of this Article on C.I.F. contracts (subsection (3) of Section 2-321), the buyer is not entitled to inspect the goods before payment of the price when the contract provides

(a) for delivery "C.O.D." or on other like terms; or

(b) for payment against documents of title, except where such payment is due only after the goods are to become available for inspection.

(4) A place or method of inspection fixed by the parties is presumed to be exclusive but unless otherwise expressly agreed it does not postpone identification or shift the place for delivery or for passing the risk of loss. If compliance becomes impossible, inspection shall be as provided in this section unless the place or method fixed was clearly intended as an indispensable condition failure of which avoids the contract.

§ 2–514. WHEN DOCUMENTS DELIVERABLE ON ACCEPTANCE; WHEN ON PAYMENT.

Unless otherwise agreed documents against which a draft is drawn are to be delivered to the drawee on acceptance of the draft if it is payable more than three days after presentment; otherwise, only on payment.

§ 2–515. PRESERVING EVIDENCE OF GOODS IN DISPUTE.

In furtherance of the adjustment of any claim or dispute

(a) either party on reasonable notification to the other and for the purpose of ascertaining the facts and preserving evidence has the right to inspect, test and sample the goods including such of them as may be in the possession or control of the other; and

(b) the parties may agree to a third party inspection or survey to determine the conformity or condition of the goods and may agree that the findings shall be binding upon them in any subsequent litigation or adjustment.

PART 6
BREACH, REPUDIATION AND EXCUSE

§ 2–601. BUYER'S RIGHTS ON IMPROPER DELIVERY.

Subject to the provisions of this Article on breach in installment contracts (Section 2–612) and unless otherwise agreed under the sections on contractual limitations of remedy (Sections 2–718 and 2–719), if the goods or the tender of delivery fail in any respect to conform to the contract, the buyer may

(a) reject the whole; or

(b) accept the whole; or

(c) accept any commercial units or units and reject the rest.

§ 2–602. MANNER AND EFFECT OF RIGHTFUL REJECTION.

(1) Rejection of goods must be within a reasonable time after their delivery or tender. It is ineffective unless the buyer seasonably notifies the seller.

(2) Subject to the provisions of the two following sections on rejected goods (Sections 2–603 and 2–604),

(a) after rejection any exercise of ownership by the buyer with respect to any commercial unit is wrongful as against the seller; and

(b) if the buyer has before rejection taken physical possession of goods in which he does not have a security interest under the provisions of this Article (subsection (3) of Section 2–711), he is under a duty after rejection to hold them with reasonable care at the seller's disposition for a time sufficient to permit the seller to remove them; but

(c) the buyer has no further obligations with regard to goods rightfully rejected. (3) The seller's rights with respect to goods wrongfully rejected are governed by the provisions of this Article on seller's remedies in general (Section 2-703).

§ 2–603. MERCHANT BUYER'S DUTIES AS TO RIGHTFULLY REJECTED GOODS.

(1) Subject to any security interest in the buyer (subsection (3) of Section 2–711), when the seller has no agent or place of business at the market of rejection a merchant buyer is under a duty after rejection of goods in his possession or control to follow any reasonable instructions received from the seller with respect to the goods and in the absence of such instructions to make reasonable efforts to sell them for the seller's account if they are perishable or threaten to decline in value speedily. Instructions are not reasonable if on demand indemnity for expenses is not forthcoming.

(2) When the buyer sells goods under subsection (1), he is entitled to reimbursement from the seller or out of the proceeds for reasonable expenses of caring for and selling them, and if the expenses include no selling commis-

sion then to such commission as is usual in the trade or if there is none to a reasonable sum not exceeding ten percent on the gross proceeds.

(3) In complying with this section the buyer is held only to good faith and good faith conduct hereunder is neither acceptance nor conversion nor the basis of an action for damages .

§ 2–604. Buyer's Options as to Salvage of Rightfully Rejected Goods.

Subject to the provisions of the immediately preceding section on perishables if the seller gives no instructions within a reasonable time after notification of rejection the buyer may store the rejected goods for the seller's account or reship them to him or resell them for the seller's account with reimbursement as provided in the preceding section. Such action is not acceptance or conversion.

§ 2–605. Waiver of Buyer's Objections by Failure to Particularize.

(1) The buyer's failure to state in connection with rejection a particular defect which is ascertainable by reasonable inspection precludes him from relying on the unstated defect to justify rejection or to establish breach

(a) where the seller could have cured it if stated seasonably; or

(b) between merchants when the seller has after rejection made a request in writing for a full and final written statement of all defects on which the buyer proposes to rely.

(2) Payment against documents made without reservation of rights precludes recovery of the payment for defects apparent on the face of the documents.

§ 2–606. What Constitutes Acceptance of Goods.

(1) Acceptance of goods occurs when the buyer

(a) after a reasonable opportunity to inspect the goods signifies to the seller that the goods are conforming or that he will take or retain them in spite of their nonconformity; or

(b) fails to make an effective rejection (subsection (1) of Section 2–602), but such acceptance does not occur until the buyer has had a reasonable opportunity to inspect them; or

(c) does any act inconsistent with the seller's ownership; but if such act is wrongful as against the seller it is an acceptance only if ratified by him.

(2) Acceptance of a part of any commercial unit is acceptance of that entire unit.

§ 2–607. Effect of Acceptance; Notice of Breach; Burden of Establishing Breach After Acceptance; Notice of Claim or Litigation to Person Answerable Over.

(1) The buyer must pay at the contract rate for any goods accepted.

(2) Acceptance of goods by the buyer precludes rejection of the goods accepted and if made with knowledge of a non-conformity cannot be revoked because of it unless the acceptance was on the reasonable assumption that the non-conformity would be seasonably cured but acceptance does not of itself impair any other remedy provided by this Article for non-conformity.

(3) Where a tender has been accepted

(a) the buyer must within a reasonable time after he discovers or should have discovered any breach notify the seller of breach or be barred from any remedy; and

(b) if the claim is one for infringement or the like (subsection (3) of Section 2–312) and the buyer is sued as a result of such a breach he must so notify the seller within a reasonable time after he receives notice of the litigation or be barred from any remedy over for liability established by the litigation.

(4) The burden is on the buyer to establish any breach with respect to the goods accepted.

(5) Where the buyer is sued for breach of a warranty or other obligation for which his seller is answerable over

(a) he may give his seller written notice of the litigation. If the notice states that the seller may come in and defend and that if the seller does not do so he will be bound in any action against him by his buyer by any determination of fact common to the two litigations, then unless the seller after seasonable receipt of the notice does come in and defend he is so bound.

(b) if the claim is one for infringement or the like (subsection (3) of Section 2–312) the original seller may demand in writing that his buyer turn over to him control of the litigation including settlement or else be barred from any remedy over and if he also agrees to bear all expense and to satisfy any adverse judgment, then unless the buyer after seasonable receipt of the demand does turn over control the buyer is so barred.

(6) The provisions of subsections (3), (4), and (5) apply to any obligation of a buyer to hold the seller harmless against infringement or the like (subsection (3) of Section 2–312).

§ 2–608. Revocation of Acceptance in Whole or in Part.

(1) The buyer may revoke his acceptance of a lot or commercial unit whose non-conformity substantially impairs its value to him if he has accepted it

(a) on the reasonable assumption that its nonconformity would be cured and it has not been seasonably cured; or

(b) without discovery of such non-conformity if his acceptance was reasonably induced either by the difficulty of discovery before acceptance or by the seller's assurances.

(2) Revocation of acceptance must occur within a reasonable time after the buyer discovers or should have discovered the ground for it and before any substantial change in condition of the goods which is not caused by their own defects. It is not effective until the buyer notifies the seller of it.

(3) A buyer who so revokes has the same rights and duties with regard to the goods involved as if he had rejected them.

§ 2–609. RIGHT TO ADEQUATE ASSURANCE OF PERFORMANCE.

(1) A contract for sale imposes an obligation on each party that the other's expectation of receiving due performance will not be impaired. When reasonable grounds for insecurity arise with respect to the performance of either party the other may in writing demand adequate assurance of due performance and until he receives such assurance may if commercially reasonable suspend any performance for which he has not already received the agreed return.

(2) Between merchants the reasonableness of grounds for insecurity and the adequacy of any assurance offered shall be determined according to commercial standards.

(3) Acceptance of any improper delivery or payment does not prejudice the aggrieved party's right to demand adequate assurance of future performance.

(4) After receipt of a justified demand failure to provide within a reasonable time not exceeding thirty days such assurance of due performance as is adequate under the circumstances of the particular case is a repudiation of the contract.

§ 2–610. ANTICIPATORY REPUDIATION.

When either party repudiates the contract with respect to a performance not yet due the loss of which will substantially impair the value of the contract to the other, the aggrieved party may

(a) for a commercially reasonable time await performance by the repudiating party; or

(b) resort to any remedy for breach (Section 2–703 or Section 2–711), even though he has notified the repudiating party that he would await the latter's performance and has urged retraction; and

(c) in either case suspend his own performance or proceed in accordance with the provisions of this Article on the seller's right to identify goods to the contract notwithstanding breach or to salvage unfinished goods (Section 2-704).

§ 2–611. RETRACTION OF ANTICIPATORY REPUDIATION.

(1) Until the repudiating party's next performance is due he can retract his repudiation unless the aggrieved party has since the repudiation cancelled or materially changed his position or otherwise indicated that he considers the repudiation final.

(2) Retraction may be by any method which clearly indicates to the aggrieved party that the repudiating party intends to perform, but must include any assurance justifiably demanded under the provisions of this Article (Section 2–609).

(3) Retraction reinstates the repudiating party's rights under the contract with due excuse and allowance to the aggrieved party for any delay occasioned by the repudiation.

§ 2–612. "INSTALLMENT CONTRACT"; BREACH.

(1) An "installment contract" is one which requires or authorizes the delivery of goods in separate lots to be separately accepted, even though the contract contains a clause "each delivery is a separate contract" or its equivalent.

(2) The buyer may reject any installment which is non-conforming if the non-conformity substantially impairs the value of that installment and cannot be cured or if the nonconformity is a defect in the required documents, but if the non-conformity does not fall within subsection (3) and the seller gives adequate assurance of its cure the buyer must accept that installment.

(3) Whenever non-conformity or default with respect to one or more installments substantially impairs the value of the whole contract there is a breach of the whole. But the aggrieved party reinstates the contract if he accepts a non-conforming installment without seasonably notifying of cancellation or if he brings an action with respect only to past installments or demands performance as to future installments.

§ 2–613. CASUALTY TO IDENTIFIED GOODS.

Where the contract requires for its performance goods identified when the contract is made, and the goods suffer casualty without fault of either party before the risk of loss passes to the buyer, or in a proper case under a "no arrival, no sale" term (Section 2–324) then

(a) if the loss is total the contract is avoided; and

(b) if the loss is partial or the goods have so deteriorated as no longer to conform to the contract the buyer may nevertheless demand inspection and at his option either treat the contract as voided or accept the goods with due allowance from the contract price for the deterioration or the deficiency in quantity but without further right against the seller.

§ 2–614. SUBSTITUTED PERFORMANCE.

(1) Where without fault of either party the agreed berthing, loading, or unloading facilities fail or an agreed type of carrier becomes unavailable or the agreed manner of delivery otherwise becomes commercially impracticable but a commercially reasonable substitute is available, such substitute performance must be tendered and accepted.

(2) If the agreed means or manner of payment fails because of domestic or foreign governmental regulation, the seller may withhold or stop delivery unless the buyer provides a means or manner of payment which is commercially a substantial equivalent. If delivery has already been taken, payment by the means or in the manner provided by the regulation discharges the buyer's obligation unless the regulation is discriminatory, oppressive or predatory.

§ 2–615. EXCUSE BY FAILURE OF PRESUPPOSED CONDITIONS.

Except so far as a seller may have assumed a greater obligation and subject to the preceding section on substituted performance:

(a) Delay in delivery or non-delivery in whole or in party by a seller who complies with paragraphs (b) and (c) is not a breach of his duty under a contract for sale if performance as agreed has been made impracticable by the occurrence of a contingency the nonoccurrence of which was a basic assumption on which the contract was made or by compliance in good faith with any applicable foreign or domestic governmental regulation or order whether or not it later proves to be invalid.

(b) Where the causes mentioned in paragraph (a) affect only a part of the seller's capacity to perform, he must allocate production and deliveries among his customers but may at his option include regular customers not then under contract as well as his own requirements for further manufacture. He may so allocate in any manner which is fair and reasonable.

(c) The seller must notify the buyer seasonably that there will be delay or non-delivery and, when allocation is required under paragraph (b), of the estimated quota thus made available for the buyer.

§ 2–616. PROCEDURE ON NOTICE CLAIMING EXCUSE.

(1) Where the buyer receives notification of a material or indefinite delay or an allocation justified under the preceding section he may by written notification to the seller as to any delivery concerned, and where the prospective deficiency substantially impairs the value of the whole contract under the provisions of this Article relating to breach of installment contracts (Section 2 612), then also as to the whole,

(a) terminate and thereby discharge any unexecuted portion of the contract; or

(b) modify the contract by agreeing to take his available quota in substitution.

(2) If after receipt of such notification from the seller the buyer fails so to modify the contract within a reasonable time not exceeding thirty days the contract lapses with respect to any deliveries affected.

(3) The provisions of this section may not be negated by agreement except in so far as the seller has assumed a greater obligation under the preceding section.

**PART 7
REMEDIES**

§ 2–701. REMEDIES FOR BREACH OF COLLATERAL CONTRACTS NOT IMPAIRED.

Remedies for breach of obligations or promise collateral or ancillary to a contract for sale are not impaired by the provisions of this Article.

§ 2–702. SELLER'S REMEDIES ON DISCOVERY OF BUYER'S INSOLVENCY.

(1) Where the seller discovers the buyer to be insolvent he may refuse delivery except for cash including payment for all goods theretofore delivered under the contract, and stop delivery under this Article (Section 2–705).

(2) Where the seller discovers that the buyer has received goods on credit while insolvent he may reclaim the goods upon demand made within ten days after the receipt, but if misrepresentation of solvency has been made to the particular seller in writing within three months before delivery the ten day limitation does not apply. Except as provided in this subsection the seller may not base a right to reclaim goods on the buyer's fraudulent or innocent misrepresentation of solvency or of intent to pay.

(3) The seller's right to reclaim under subsection (2) is subject to the rights of a buyer in ordinary course or other good faith purchaser under this Article (Section 2–403). Successful reclamation of goods excludes all other remedies with respect to them.

§ 2–703. SELLER'S REMEDIES IN GENERAL.

Where the buyer wrongfully rejects or revokes acceptance of goods or fails to make a payment due on or before delivery or repudiates with respect to a part or the whole, then with respect to any goods directly affected and, if the breach is of the whole contract (Section 2–612), then also with respect to the whole and undelivered balance, the aggrieved seller may

(a) withhold delivery of such goods;

(b) stop delivery by any bailee as hereafter provided (Section 2–705);

(c) proceed under the next section respecting goods still unidentified to the contract;

(d) resell and recover damages as hereafter provided (Section 2–706);

(e) recover damages for non-acceptance (Section 2–708) or in a proper case the price (Section 2–709);

(f) cancel.

§ 2–704. SELLER'S RIGHT TO IDENTIFY GOODS TO THE CONTRACT NOTWITHSTANDING BREACH OR TO SALVAGE UNFINISHED GOODS.

(1) An aggrieved seller under the preceding section may

(a) identify to the contract conforming goods not already identified if at the time he learned of the breach they are in his possession or control;

(b) treat as the subject of resale goods which have demonstrably been intended for the particular contract even though those goods are unfinished.

(2) Where the goods are unfinished an aggrieved seller may in the exercise of reasonable commercial judgment for the purposes of avoiding loss and of effective realization either complete the manufacture and wholly identify the goods to the contract or cease manufacture and resell for scrap or salvage value or proceed in any other reasonable manner.

§ 2–705. SELLER'S STOPPAGE OF DELIVERY IN TRANSIT OR OTHERWISE.

(1) The seller may stop delivery of goods in the possession of a carrier or other bailee when he discovers the buyer to be insolvent (Section 2–702) and may stop delivery of carload, truckload, planeload or larger shipments of express or freight when the buyer repudiates or fails to make a payment due before delivery or if for any other reason the seller has a right to withhold or reclaim the goods.

(2) As against such buyer the seller may stop delivery until

(a) receipt of goods by the buyer; or

(b) acknowledgment to the buyer by any bailee of the goods except a carrier that the bailee holds the goods for the buyer; or

(c) such acknowledgment to the buyer by a carrier by reshipment or as warehouseman; or

(d) negotiation to the buyer of any negotiable document of title covering the goods.

(3) (a) To stop delivery the seller must so notify as to enable the bailee by reasonable diligence to prevent delivery of the goods.

(b) After such notification the bailee must hold and deliver the goods according to the directions of the seller but the seller is liable to the bailee for any ensuing charges or damages.

(c) If a negotiable document of title has been issued for goods the bailee is not obliged to obey a notification to stop until surrender of the document.

(d) A carrier who has issued a non-negotiable bill of lading is not obliged to obey a notification to stop received from a person other than the consignor.

§ 2–706. SELLER'S RESALE INCLUDING CONTRACT FOR RESALE.

(1) Under the conditions stated in Section 2–703 on seller's remedies, the seller may resell the goods concerned or the undelivered balance thereof. Where the resale is made in good faith and in a commercially reasonable manner the seller may recover the difference between the resale price and the contract price together with any incidental damages allowed under the provisions of this Article (Section 2–710), but less expenses saved in consequence of the buyer's breach.

(2) Except as otherwise provided in subsection (3) or unless otherwise agreed resale may be at public or private sale including sale by way of one or more contracts to sell or of identification to an existing contract of the seller. Sale may be as a unit or in parcels and at any time and place and on any terms but every aspect of the sale including the method, manner, time, place and terms must be commercially reasonable. The resale must be reasonably identified as referring to the broken contract, but it is not necessary that the goods be in existence or that any or all of them have been identified to the contract before the breach.

(3) Where the resale is at private sale the seller must give the buyer reasonable notification of his intention to resell.

(4) Where the resale is at public sale

(a) only identified goods can be sold except where there is a recognized market for a public sale of futures in goods of the kind; and

(b) it must be made at a usual place or market for public sale if one is reasonably available and except in the case of goods which are perishable or threaten to decline in value speedily the seller must give the buyer reasonable notice of the time and place of the resale; and

(c) if the goods are not to be within the view of those attending the sale the notification of sale must state the place where the goods are located and provide for their reasonable inspection by prospective bidders; and

(d) the seller may buy.

(5) A purchaser who buys in good faith at a resale takes the goods free of any rights of the original buyer even

though the seller fails to comply with one or more of the requirements of this section.

(6) The seller is not accountable to the buyer for any profit made on any resale. A person in the position of a seller (Section 2-707) or a buyer who has rightfully rejected or justifiably revoked acceptance must account for any excess over the amount of his security interest, as hereinafter defined (subsection (3) of Section 2–711).

§ 2–707. "Person in the Position of a Seller".

(1) A "person in the position of a seller" includes as against a principal an agent who has paid or become responsible for the price of goods on behalf of his principal or anyone who otherwise holds a security interest or other right in goods similar to that of a seller.

(2) A person in the position of a seller may as provided in this Article withhold or stop delivery (Section 2-705) and resell (Section 2–706) and recover incidental damages (Section 2–710).

§ 2–708. Seller's Damages for Non-Acceptance or Repudiation.

(1) Subject to subsection (2) and to the provisions of this Article with respect to proof of market price (Section 2-723), the measure of damages for non-acceptance or repudiation by the buyer is the difference between the market price at the time and place for tender and the unpaid contract price together with any incidental damages provided in this Article (Section 2-710), but less expenses saved in consequence of the buyer's breach.

(2) If the measure of damages provided in subsection (1) is inadequate to put the seller in as good a position as performance would have done then the measure of damages is the profit (including reasonable overhead) which the seller would have made from full performance by the buyer, together with any incidental damages provided in this Article (Section 2–710), due allowance for costs reasonably incurred and due credit for payments or proceeds of resale.

§ 2-709. Action for the Price.

(1) When the buyer fails to pay the price as it becomes due the seller may recover, together with any incidental damages under the next section, the price

(a) of goods accepted or of conforming goods lost or damaged within a commercially reasonable time after risk of their loss has passed to the buyer; and

(b) of goods identified to the contract if the seller is unable after reasonable effort to resell them at a reasonable price or the circumstances reasonably indicate that such effort will be unavailing.

(2) Where the seller sues for the price he must hold for the buyer any goods which have been identified to the contract and are still in his control except that if resale be-

come possible he may resell them at any time prior to the collection of the judgment. The net proceeds of any such resale must be credited to the buyer and payment of the judgment entitles him to any goods not resold.

(3) After the buyer has wrongfully rejected or revoked acceptance of the goods or has failed to make a payment due or has repudiated (Section 2-610), a seller who is held not entitled to the price under this section shall nevertheless be awarded damages for non-acceptance under the preceding section.

§ 2–710. Seller's Incidental Damages.

Incidental damages to an aggrieved seller include any commercially reasonable charges, expenses or commissions incurred in stopping delivery, in the transportation, care and custody of goods after the buyer's breach, in connection with return or resale of the goods or otherwise resulting from the breach.

§ 2–711. Buyer's Remedies in General;

Buyer's Security Interest in Rejected Goods.

(1) Where the seller fails to make delivery or repudiates or the buyer rightfully rejects or justifiably revokes acceptance then with respect to any goods involved, and with respect to the whole if the breach goes to the whole contract (Section 2–612), the buyer may cancel and whether or not he has done so may in addition to recovering so much of the price as has been paid

(a) "cover" and have damages under the next section as to all the goods affected whether or not they have been identified to the contract; or

(b) recover damages for non-delivery as provided in this Article (Section 2–713).

(2) Where the seller fails to deliver or repudiates the buyer may also

(a) if the goods have been identified recover them as provided in this Article Section 2–502) or

(b) in a proper case obtain specific performance or replevy the goods as provided in this Article (Section 2- 716).

(3) On rightful rejection or justifiable revocation of acceptance a buyer has a security interest in goods in his possession or control for any payments made on their price and any expenses reasonably incurred in their inspection, receipt, transportation, care and custody and may hold such goods and resell them in like manner as an aggrieved seller (Section 2-706).

§ 2-712. "Cover"; Buyer's Procurement of Substitute Goods.

(1) After a breach within the preceding section the buyer may "cover" by making in good faith and without unreasonable delay any reasonable purchase of or contract to

purchase goods in substitution for those due from the seller.

§ 2–713. BUYER'S DAMAGES FOR NON-DELIVERY OR REPUDIATION.

(1) Subject to the provisions of this Article with respect to proof of market price (Section 2–723), the measure of damages for non-delivery or repudiation by the seller is the difference between the market price at the time when the buyer learned of the breach and the contract price together with any incidental and consequential damages provided in this Article (Section 2-715), but less expenses saved in consequence of the seller's breach.

(2) Market price is to be determined as of the place for tender or, in cases of rejection after arrival or revocation of acceptance, as of the place of arrival.

§ 2–714. BUYER'S DAMAGES FOR BREACH IN REGARD TO ACCEPTED GOODS.

(1) Where the buyer has accepted goods and given notification (subsection (3) of Section 2–607) he may recover as damages for any non-conformity of tender the loss resulting in the ordinary course of events from the seller's breach as determined in any manner which is reasonable.

(2) The measure of damages for breach of warranty is the difference at the time and place of acceptance between the value of the goods accepted and the value they would have had if they had been as warranted, unless special circumstances show proximate damages of a different amount.

(3)In a proper case any incidental and consequential damages under the next section may also be recovered.

§ 2–715. BUYER'S INCIDENTAL AND CONSEQUENTIAL DAMAGES.

(1) Incidental damages resulting from the seller's breach include expenses reasonably incurred in inspection, receipt, transportation and care and custody of goods rightfully rejected, any commercially reasonable charges, expenses or commissions in connection with effecting cover and any other reasonable expense incident to the delay or other breach .

(2) Consequential damages resulting from the seller's breach include

(a) any loss resulting from general or particular requirements and needs of which the seller at the time of contracting had reason to know and which could not reasonably be prevented by cover or otherwise; and

(b) injury to person or property proximately resulting from any breach of warranty.

§ 2–716. BUYER'S RIGHT TO SPECIFIC PERFORMANCE OR REPLEVIN.

(1) Specific performance may be decreed where the goods are unique or in other proper circumstances.

(2) The decree for specific performance may include such terms and conditions as to payment of the price, damages, or other relief as the court may deem just.

(3) The buyer has a right of replevin for goods identified to the contract if after reasonable effort he is unable to effect cover for such goods or the circumstances reasonably indicate that such effort will be unavailing or if the goods have been shipped under reservation and satisfaction of the security interest in them has been made or tendered.

§ 2–717. DEDUCTION OF DAMAGES FROM THE PRICE.

The buyer on notifying the seller of his intention to do so may deduct all or any part of the damages resulting from any breach of the contract from any part of the price still due under the same contract.

§ 2–718. LIQUIDATION OR LIMITATION OF DAMAGES; DEPOSITS.

(1) Damages for breach by either party may be liquidated in the agreement but only at an amount which is reasonable in the light of the anticipated or actual harm caused by the breach, the difficulties of proof of loss, and the inconvenience or nonfeasibility of otherwise obtaining an adequate remedy. A term fixing unreasonably large liquidated damages is void as a penalty.

(2) Where the seller justifiably withholds delivery of goods because of the buyer's breach, the buyer is entitled to restitution of any amount by which the sum of his payments exceeds

(a) the amount of which the seller is entitled by virtue of terms liquidating the seller's damages in accordance with subsection (1), or

(b) in the absence of such terms, twenty per cent of the value of the total performance for which the buyer is obligated under the contract or $500, whichever is smaller.

(3) The buyer's right to restitution under subsection (2) is subject to offset to the extent that the seller establishes

(a) a right to recover damages under the provisions of this Article other than subsection (1), and

(b) the amount or value of any benefits received by the buyer directly or indirectly by reason of the contract.

(4) Where a seller has received payment in goods their reasonable value or the proceeds of their resale shall be treated as payments for the purposes of subsection (2); but if the seller has notice of the buyer's breach before reselling goods received in part performance, his resale is subject to the conditions laid down in this Article on resale by an aggrieved seller (Section 2–706).

§ 2–719. Contractual Modification or Limitation of Remedy.

(1) Subject to the provisions of subsections (2) and (3) of this section and of the preceding section on liquidation and limitation of damages,

(a) the agreement may provide for remedies in addition to or in substitution for those provided in this Article and may limit or alter the measure of damages recoverable under this Article, as by limiting the buyer's remedies to return of the goods and repayment of the price or to repair and replacement of non-conforming goods or parts; and

(b) resort to a remedy as provided is optional unless the remedy is expressly agreed to be exclusive, in which case it is the sole remedy.

(2) Where circumstances cause an exclusive or limited remedy to fail of its essential purpose, remedy may be had as provided in this Act.

(3) Consequential damages may be limited or excluded unless the limitation or exclusion is unconscionable. Limitation of consequential damages for injury to the person in the case of consumer goods is prima facie unconscionable but limitation of damages where the loss is commercial is not.

§ 2–720. Effect of "Cancellation" or "Recession" on Claims for Antecedent Breach.

Unless the contrary intention clearly appears, expressions of "cancellation" or "rescission" of the contract or the like shall not be construed as a renunciation or discharge of any claim in damages for an antecedent breach.

§ 2–721. Remedies for Fraud.

Remedies for material misrepresentation or fraud include all remedies available under this Article for non-fraudulent breach. Neither rescission or a claim for rescission of the contract for sale nor rejection or return of the goods shall bar or be deemed inconsistent with a claim for damages or other remedy.

§ 2–722. Who Can Sue Third Parties for Injury to Goods.

Where a third party so deals with goods which have been identified to a contract for sale as to cause actionable injury to a party to that contract.

(a) a right of action against the third party is in either party to the contract for sale who has title to or a security interest or a special property or an insurable interest in the goods; and if the goods have been destroyed or converted a right of action is also in the party who either bore the risk of loss under the contract for sale or has since the injury assumed that risk as against the other;

(b) if at the time of the injury the party plaintiff did not bear the risk of loss as against the other party to the contract for sale and there is no arrangement between them for disposition of the recovery, his suit or settlement is, subject to his own interest, as a fiduciary for the other party to the contract;

(c) either party may with the consent of the other sue for the benefit of whom it may concern.

§ 2–723. Proof of Market Price: Time and Place.

(1) If an action based on anticipatory repudiation comes to trial before the time for performance with respect to some or all of the goods, any damages based on market price

(Section 2–708 or Section 2–713) shall be determined according to the price of such goods prevailing at the time when the aggrieved party learned of the repudiation.

(2) If evidence of a price prevailing at the times or places described in this Article is not readily available the price prevailing within any reasonable time before or after the time described or at any other place which in commercial judgment or under usage of trade would serve as a reasonable substitute for the one described may be used, making any proper allowance for the cost of transporting the goods to or from such other place.

(3) Evidence of a relevant price prevailing at a time or place other than the one described in this Article offered by one party is not admissible unless and until he has given the other party such notice as the court finds sufficient to prevent unfair surprise.

§ 2–724. Admissibility of Market Quotations.

Whenever the prevailing price or value of any goods regularly bought and sold in any established commodity market is in issue, reports in official publications or trade journals or in newspapers or periodicals of general circulation published as the reports of such market shall be admissible in evidence. The circumstances of the preparation of such a report may be shown to affect its weight but not its admissibility.

§ 2–725. Statute of Limitations in Contracts for Sale.

(1) An action for breach of any contract for sale must be commenced within four years after the cause of action has accrued. By the original agreement the parties may reduce the period of limitation to not less than one year but may not extend it.

(2) A cause of action accrues when the breach occurs, regardless of the aggrieved party's lack of knowledge of the breach. A breach of warranty occurs when tender of delivery is made, except that where a warranty explicitly extends to future performance of the goods and discovery of the breach must await the time of such performance the cause of action accrues when the breach is or should have been discovered.

(3) Where an action commenced within the time limited by subsection (1) is so terminated as to leave available a remedy by another action for the same breach such other action may be commenced after the expiration of the time limited and within six months after the termination of the first action unless the termination resulted from voluntary discontinuance or from dismissal for failure or neglect to prosecute.

(4) This section does not alter the law on tolling of the statue of limitations nor does it apply to causes of action which have accrued before this Act becomes effective.

Article 3
Commercial Paper

PART I
SHORT TITLE, FORM AND INTERPRETATION

§ 3–101. SHORT TITLE.

This Article shall be known and may be cited as Uniform Commercial Code–Commercial Paper.

§ 3–102. DEFINITIONS AND INDEX OF DEFINITIONS.

(1) In this Article unless the context otherwise requires

(a) "Issue" means the first delivery of an instrument to a holder or a remitter.

(b) An "order" is a direction to pay and must be more than an authorization or request. It must identify the person to pay with reasonable certainty. It may be addressed to one or more such persons jointly or in the alternative but not in succession .

(c) A "promise" is an undertaking to pay and must be more than an acknowledgment of an obligation.

(d) "Secondary party" means a drawer or endorser.

(e) "Instrument" means a negotiable instrument.

(2) Other definitions applying to this Article and the sections in which they appear are:

"Acceptance". Section 3- 410.

"Accommodation party". Section 3-415.

"Alteration". Section 3-407.

"Certificate of deposit". Section 3–104.

"Certification". Section 3–411.

"Check". Section 3–104.

"Definite time". Section 3–109.

"Dishonor". Section 3–507.

"Draft". Section 3–104.

"Holder in due course". Section 3–302.

"Negotiation". Section 3–202

"Note". Section 3–104.

"Notice of dishonor". Section 3–508.

"On demand". Section 3–108.

"Presentment". Section 3–504.

"Protest". Section 3–509.

"Restrictive Indorsement". Section 3–205.

"Signature". Section 3–401.

(3) The following definitions in other Articles apply to this Article:

"Account". Section 4–104.

"Banking Day". Section 4 104.

"Clearing House". Section 4–104.

"Collecting Bank". Section 4–105.

"Customer". Section 4–104.

"Depositary Bank". Section 4–105.

"Documentary Draft". Section 4– 104.

"Intermediary Bank". Section 4–105.

"Item". Section 4–104.

"Midnight deadline". Section 4–104.

"Payor Bank". Section 4–105.

(4) In addition to Article I contains general definitions and principles of construction and interpretation applicable throughout this Article.

§ 3–103. LIMITATIONS ON SCOPE OF ARTICLE.

(1) This Article does not apply to money, documents of title or investment securities.

(2) The provisions of this Article are subject to the provisions of the Article on Bank Deposits and Collections (Article 4) and Secured Transactions (Article 9).

§ 3–104. FORM OF NEGOTIABLE INSTRUMENTS; "DRAFT"; "CHECK"; "CERTIFICATE OF DEPOSIT"; "NOTE".

(1) Any writing to be a negotiable instrument within this Article must

(a) be signed by the maker or drawer; and

(b) contain an unconditional promise or order to pay a sum certain in money and no other promise, order, obligation or power given by the maker or drawer except as authorized by this Article; and

(c) be payable on demand or at a definite time; and

(d) be payable to order or to bearer.

(2) A writing which complies with the requirements of this section is

(a) a "draft" ("bill of exchange") if it is an order;

(b) a "check" if it is a draft drawn on a bank and payable on demand;

(c) a "certificate of deposit" if it is an acknowledgment by a bank of receipt of money with an engagement to repay it;

(d) a "note" if it is a promise other than a certificate of deposit.

(3) As used in other Articles of this Act, and as the context may require, the terms "draft", "check", "certificate of deposit" and "note" may refer to instruments which are not negotiable within this Article as well as to instruments which are so negotiable.

§ 3–105. WHEN PROMISE OR ORDER UNCONDITIONAL.

(1) A promise or order otherwise unconditional is not made conditional by the fact that the instrument

(a) is subject to implied or constructive conditions; or

(b) states its consideration, whether performed or promised, or the transaction which gave rise to the instrument, or that the promise or order is made or the instrument matures in accordance with or "as per" such transaction; or

(c) refers to or states that it arises out of a separate agreement or refers to a separate agreement for rights as to prepayment or acceleration; or

(d) states that it is drawn under a letter of credit; or

(e) states that it is secured, whether by mortgage, reservation of title or otherwise; or

(f) indicates a particular account to be debited or any other fund or source from which reimbursement is expected; or

(g) is limited to payment out of a particular fund or the proceeds of a particular source, if the instrument is issued by a government or governmental agency or unit; or

(h) is limited to payment out of the entire assets of a partnership, unincorporated association, trust or estate by or on behalf of which the instrument is issued.

(2) A promise or order is not unconditional if the instrument

(a) states that it is subject to or governed by any other agreement; or

(b) states that it is to be paid only out of a particular fund or source except as provided in this section.

§ 3–106. SUM CERTAIN.

(1) The sum payable is a sum certain even though it is to be paid

(a) with stated interest or by stated installments; or

(b) with stated different rates of interest before and after default or a specified date; or

(c) with a stated discount or addition if paid before or after the date fixed for payment; or

(d) with exchange or less exchange, whether at a fixed rate or at the current rate; or

(e) with costs of collection or an attorney's fee or both upon default.

(2) Nothing in this section shall validate any term which is otherwise illegal.

§ 3–107. MONEY.

(1) An instrument is payable in money if the medium of exchange in which it is payable is money at the time the instrument is made. An instrument payable in "currency" or "current funds" is payable in money.

(2) A promise to order to pay a sum stated in a foreign currency is for a sum certain in money and, unless a different medium of payment is specified in the instrument, may be satisfied by payment of that number of dollars which the stated foreign currency will purchase at the buying sight rate for that currency on the day on which the instrument is payable or, if payable on demand, on the day of demand. If such an instrument specifies a foreign currency as the medium of payment the instrument is payable in that currency.

§ 3–108. PAYABLE ON DEMAND.

Instruments payable on demand include those payable at sight or on presentation and those in which no time for payment is stated.

§ 3–109. DEFINITE TIME.

(1) An instrument is payable at a definite time if by its terms it is payable

(a) on or before a stated date or at a fixed period after a stated date; or

(b) at a fixed period after sight; or

(c) at a definite time subject to any acceleration; or

(d) at a definite time subject to extension at the option of the holder, or to extension to a further definite time at the option of the maker or acceptor or automatically upon or after a specified act or event.

(2) An instrument which by its terms is otherwise payable only upon an act or event uncertain as to time of occurrence is not payable at a definite time even though the act or event has occurred.

§ 3–110. PAYABLE TO ORDER.

(1) An instrument is payable to order when by its terms it is payable to the order or assigns of any person therein specified with reasonable certainty, or to him or his order, or when it is conspicuously designated on its face as

"exchange" or the like and names a payee. It may be payable to the order of

(a) the maker or drawer; or

(b) the drawee; or

(c) a payee who is not maker, a drawer or drawee; or

(d) two or more payees together or in the alternative; or

(e) an estate, trust or fund, in which case it is payable to the order of the representative of such estate, trust or fund or his successors; or

(f) an office, or an officer by his title as such in which case it is payable to the principal but the incumbent of the office or his successors may act as if he or they were the holder; or

(g) a partnership or unincorporated association, in which case it is payable to the partnership or association and may be indorsed or transferred by any person thereto authorized.

(2) An instrument not payable to order is not made so payable by such words as "payable upon return of this instrument properly indorsed."

(3) An instrument made payable both to order and to bearer is payable to order unless thc bearer words are handwritten or typewritten.

§ 3–111. PAYABLE TO BEARER.

An instrument is payable to bearer when by its terms it is payable to

(a) bearer or the order of bearer; or

(b) a specified person or bearer; or

(c) "cash" or the order of "cash", or any other indication which does not purport to designate a specific payee.

§ 3–112. TERMS AND OMISSIONS NOT AFFECTING NEGOTIABILITY.

(1) The negotiability of an instrument is not affected by

(a) the omission of a statement of any consideration or of the place where the instrument is drawn or payable; or

(b) a statement that collateral has been given to secure obligations either on the instrument or otherwise of an obligor on the instrument or that in case of default on those obligations the holder may realize on or dispose of the collateral; or

(c) a promise or power to maintain or protect collateral or to give additional collateral; or

(d) a term authorizing a confession of judgment on the instrument if it is not paid when due; or

(e) a term purporting to waive the benefit of any law intended for the advantage or protection of any obligor; or

(f) a term in a draft providing that the payee by indorsing or cashing it acknowledges full satisfaction of an obligation of the drawer; or

(g) a statement in a draft drawn in a set of parts (Section 3–801) to the effect that the order is effective only if no other part has been honored.

(2) Nothing in this section shall validate any term which is otherwise illegal.

§ 3–113. SEAL.

An instrument otherwise negotiable is within this Article even though it is under a seal.

§ 3–114. DATE, ANTEDATING, POSTDATING.

(1) The negotiability of an instrument is not affected by the fact that it is undated, antedated or postdated.

(2) Where an instrument is antedated or postdated the time when it is payable is determined by the stated date if the instrument is payable on demand or at a fixed period after date.

(3) Where the instrument or any signature thereon is dated, the date is presumed to be correct.

§ 3–115. INCOMPLETE INSTRUMENTS.

(1) When a paper whose contents at the time of signing show that it is intended to become an instrument is signed while still incomplete in any necessary respect cannot be enforced until completed, but when it is completed in accordance with authority given it is effective as completed.

(2) If the completion is unauthorized the rules as to material alteration apply (Section 3–407), even though the paper was not delivered by the maker or drawer; but the burden of establishing that any completion is unauthorized is on the party so asserting.

§ 3–116. INSTRUMENTS PAYABLE TO TWO OR MORE PERSONS.

An instrument payable to the order of two or more persons

(a) if in the alternative is payable to any one of them and may be negotiated, discharged or enforced by any of them who has possession of it;

(b) if not in the alternative is payable to all of them and may be negotiated, discharged or enforced only by all of them.

§ 3–117. INSTRUMENTS PAYABLE WITH WORDS OF DESCRIPTION.

An instrument made payable to a named person with the addition of words describing him

(a) as agent or officer of a specified person is payable to his principal but the agent or officer may act as if he were the holder;

(b) as any other fiduciary for a specified person or purpose is payable to the payee and may be negotiated, discharged or enforced by him;

(c) in any other manner is payable to the payee unconditionally and the additional words are without effect on subsequent parties.

§ 3–118. AMBIGUOUS TERMS AND RULES OF CONSTRUCTION.

The following rules apply to every instrument:

(a) Where there is doubt whether the instrument is a draft or a note the holder may treat it as either. A draft drawn on the drawer is effective as a note.

(b) Handwritten terms control typewritten and printed terms, and typewritten control printed.

(c) Words control figures except that if the words are ambiguous figures control.

(d) Unless otherwise specified a provision for interest means interest at the judgment rate at the place of payment from the date of the instrument, or if it is undated from the date of issue.

(e) Unless the instrument otherwise specifies two or more persons who sign as maker, acceptor or drawer or indorser and as a part of the same transaction are jointly and severally liable even though the instrument contains such words as "I promise to pay."

(f) Unless otherwise specified consent to extension authorizes a single extension for not longer than the original period. A consent to extension, expressed in the instrument, is binding on secondary parties and accommodation makers. A holder may not exercise his option to extend an instrument over the objection of a maker or acceptor or other party who in accordance with Section 3–604 tenders full payment when the instrument is due.

§ 3–119. OTHER WRITINGS AFFECTING INSTRUMENT.

(1) As between the obligor and his immediate obligee or any transferee the terms of an instrument may be modified or affected by any other written agreement executed as a part of the same transaction, except that a holder in due course is not affected by any limitation of his rights arising out of the separate written agreement if he had no notice of the limitation when he took the instrument.

(2) A separate agreement does not affect the negotiability of an instrument.

§ 3–120. INSTRUMENTS "PAYABLE THROUGH" BANK.

An instrument which states that it is "payable through" a bank or the like designates that bank as a collecting bank to make presentment but does not of itself authorize the bank to pay the instrument.

§ 3–121. INSTRUMENTS PAYABLE AT BANK.

Note: If this Act is introduced in the Congress of the United States this section should be omitted.

(States to select either alternative)

ALTERNATIVE A

A note or acceptance which states that it is payable at a bank is the equivalent of a draft drawn on the bank payable when it falls due out of any funds of the maker or acceptor in current account or otherwise available for such payment.

ALTERNATIVE B

A note or acceptance which states that it is payable at a bank is not of itself an order or authorization to the bank to pay it.

§ 3–122. ACCRUAL OF CAUSE OF ACTION.

(1) A cause of action against a maker or an acceptor accrues

(a) in the case of a time instrument on the day after maturity;

(b) in the case of a demand instrument upon its date or, if no date is stated, on the date of issue.

(2) A cause of action against the obligor of a demand or time certificate of deposit accrues upon demand, but demand on a time certificate may not be made until on or after the date of maturity.

(3) A cause of action against a drawer of a draft of an indorser of any instrument accrues upon demand following dishonor of the instrument. Notice of dishonor is a demand.

(4) Unless an instrument provides otherwise, interest runs at the rate provided by law for a judgment

(a) in the case of a maker, acceptor or other primary obligor of a demand instrument, from the date of demand;

(b) in all other cases from the date of accrual of the cause of action.

PART 2
TRANSFER AND NEGOTIATION

§ 3–201. TRANSFER; RIGHT TO INDORSEMENT.

(1) Transfer of an instrument vests in the transferee such rights as the transferor has therein, except that a transferee who has himself been a party to any fraud or illegality affecting the instrument or who as a prior holder had notice of a defense or claim against it cannot improve his position by taking from a later holder in due course.

(2) A transfer of security interest in an instrument vests the foregoing rights in the transferee to the extent of the interest transferred .

(3) Unless otherwise agreed any transfer for value of an instrument not then payable to bearer gives the transferee the specifically enforceable right to have the unqualified indorsement of the transferor. Negotiation takes effect only when the indorsement is made and until that time there is no presumption that the transferee is the owner.

§ 3–202. NEGOTIATION.

(1) Negotiation is the transfer of an instrument in such form that the transferee becomes a holder. If the instrument is payable to order it is negotiated by delivery with any necessary indorsement; if payable to bearer it is negotiated by delivery.

(2) An indorsement must be written by or on behalf of the holder and on the instrument or on a paper so firmly affixed thereto as to become a part thereof.

(3) An indorsement is effective for negotiation only when it conveys the entire instrument or any unpaid residue. If it purports to be of less it operates only as a partial assignment.

(4) Words of assignment, condition, waiver, guaranty, limitation or disclaimer of liability and the like accompanying an indorsement do not affect its character as an indorsement.

§ 3–203. WRONG OR MISSPELLED NAME.

Where an instrument is made payable to a person under a misspelled name or one other than his own he may indorse in that name or his own or both; but signature in both names may be required by a person paying or giving value for the instrument.

§ 3–204. SPECIAL INDORSEMENT; BLANK INDORSEMENT.

(1) A special indorsement specifies the person to whom or to whose order it makes the instrument payable. Any instrument specially indorsed becomes payable to the order of the special indorsee and may be further negotiated only by his indorsement.

(2) An indorsement in blank specifies no particular indorsee and may consist of a mere signature. An instrument payable to order and indorsed in blank becomes payable to bearer and may be negotiated by delivery alone until specially indorsed.

(3) The holder may convert a blank indorsement into a special indorsement by writing over the signature of the indorser in blank any contract consistent with the character of the indorsement.

§ 3–205. RESTRICTIVE INDORSEMENTS.

An indorsement is restrictive which either

(a) is conditional; or

(b) purports to prohibit further transfer of the instrument; or

(c) includes the words "for collection", "for deposit", "pay any bank", or like terms signifying a purpose of deposit or collection; or

(d) otherwise states that it is for the benefit or use of the indorser or of another person.

§ 3–206. EFFECT OF RESTRICTIVE INDORSEMENT.

(1) No restrictive indorsement prevents further transfer or negotiation of the instrument.

(2) An intermediary bank, or a payor bank which is not the depositary bank, is neither given notice nor otherwise affected by a restrictive indorsement of any person except the bank's immediate transferor or the person presenting for payment.

(3) Except for an intermediary bank, any transferee under an indorsement which is conditional or includes the words 'for collection", "for deposit", "pay any bank", or like terms (subparagraphs (a) and (c) of Section 3–205) must pay or apply any value given by him for or on the security of the instrument consistently with the indorsement and to the extent that he does so he becomes a holder for value. In addition such transferee is a holder in due course if he otherwise complies with the requirements of Section 3 302 on what constitutes a holder in due course.

(4) The first taker under an indorsement for the benefit of the indorser or another person (subparagraph (d) of Section 3–205) must pay or apply any value given by him for or on the security of the instrument consistently with the indorsement and to the extent that he does so he becomes a holder for value. In addition such taker is a holder in due course if he otherwise complies with the requirements of Section 3–302 on what constitutes a holder in due course. A later holder for value is neither given notice nor otherwise affected by such restrictive indorsement unless he has knowledge that a fiduciary or other person has negotiated the instrument in any transaction for his own benefit or otherwise in breach of duty (subsection (2) of Section 3–304).

§ 3–207. NEGOTIATION EFFECTIVE ALTHOUGH IT MAY BE RESCINDED.

(1) Negotiation is effective to transfer the instrument although the negotiation is

(a) made by an infant, a corporation exceeding its powers, or any other person without capacity; or

(b) obtained by fraud, duress or mistake of any kind; or

(c) part of an illegal transaction; or

(d) made in breach of duty.

(2) Except as against a subsequent holder in due course such negotiation is in an appropriate case subject to rescission, the declaration of a constructive trust or any other remedy permitted by law.

§ 3–208. REACQUISITION.

Where an instrument is returned to or reacquired by a prior party he may cancel any indorsement which is not necessary to his title and reissue or further negotiate the instrument, but any intervening party is discharged as against the reacquiring party and subsequent holders not in due course and if his indorsement has been cancelled is discharged as against subsequent holders in due course as well.

PART 3
RIGHTS OF A HOLDER

§ 3–301. RIGHTS OF A HOLDER.

The holder of an instrument whether or not he is the owner may transfer or negotiate it and, except as otherwise provided in Section 3–603 on payment or satisfaction, discharge it or enforce payment in his own name.

§ 3–302. HOLDER IN DUE COURSE

(1) A holder in due course is a holder who takes the instrument

(a) for value; and

(b) in good faith; and

(c) without notice that it is overdue or has been dishonored or of any defense against or claim to it on the part of any person.

(2) A payee may be a holder in due course.

(3) A holder does not become a holder in due course of an instrument:

(a) by purchase of it at judicial sale or by taking it under legal process; or

(b) by acquiring it in taking over an estate; or

(c) by purchasing it as part of a bulk transaction not in regular course of business of the transferor.

(4) A purchaser of a limited interest can be a holder in due course only to the extent of the interest purchased.

§ 3–303. TAKING FOR VALUE.

A holder takes the instrument for value

(a) to the extent that the agreed consideration has been performed or that he acquires a security interest in or a lien on the instrument otherwise than by legal process; or

(b) when he takes the instrument in payment of or as security for an antecedent claim against any person whether or not the claim is due; or

(c) when he gives a negotiable instrument for it or makes an irrevocable commitment to a third person.

§ 3–304. NOTICE TO PURCHASER.

(1) The purchaser has notice of a claim or defense if

(a) the instrument is so incomplete, bears such visible evidence of forgery or alteration, or is otherwise so irregular as to call into question its validity, terms or ownership or to create an ambiguity as to the party to pay; or

(b) the purchaser has notice that the obligation of any party is voidable in whole or in part, or that all parties have been discharged .

(3) The purchaser has notice that an instrument is overdue if he has reason to know

(a) that any part of the principal amount is overdue or that there is an uncured default in payment of another instrument of the same series; or

(b) that acceleration of the instrument has been made; or

(c) that he is taking a demand instrument after demand has been made or more than a reasonable length of time after its issue. A reasonable time for a check drawn and payable within the states and territories of the United States and the District of Columbia is presumed to be thirty days.

(4) Knowledge of the following facts does not of itself give the purchaser notice of a defense or claim

(a) that the instrument is antedated or postdated;

(b) that it was issued or negotiated in return for an executory promise or accompanied by a separate agreement, unless the purchaser has notice that a defense or claim has arisen from the terms thereof;

(c) that any party has signed for accommodation;

(d) that an incomplete instrument has been completed, unless the purchaser has notice of any improper completion;

(e) that any person negotiating the instrument is or was a fiduciary;

(f) that there has been default in payment of interest on the instrument or in payment of any other instrument, except one of the same series.

(5) The filing or recording of a document does not of itself constitute notice within the provisions of this Article to a person who would otherwise be a holder in due course.

(6) To be effective notice must be received at such time and in such manner as to give a reasonable opportunity to act on it.

§ 3–305. RIGHTS OF A HOLDER IN DUE COURSE.

To the extent that a holder is a holder in due course he takes the instrument free from

(1) all claims to it on the part of any person; and

(2) all defenses of any party to the instrument with whom the holder has not dealt except

(a) infancy, to the extent that it is a defense to a simple contract; and

(b) such other incapacity, or duress, or illegality of the transaction, as renders the obligation of the party a nullity; and

(c) such misrepresentation as has included the party to sign the instrument with neither knowledge nor reasonable opportunity to obtain knowledge of its character or its essential terms; and

(d) discharge in insolvency proceedings; and

(e) any other discharge of which the holder has notice when he takes the instrument.

§ 3–306. RIGHTS OF ONE NOT HOLDER IN DUE COURSE.

Unless he has the rights of a holder in due course any person takes the instrument subject to

(a) all valid claims to it on the part of any person; and

(b) all defenses of any party which would be available in an action on a simple contract; and

(c) the defenses of want or failure of consideration, nonperformance of any condition precedent, nondelivery, or delivery for a special purpose (Section 3–408); and

(d) the defense that he or a person through whom he holds the instrument acquired it by theft, or that payment or satisfaction to such holder would be inconsistent with the terms of a restrictive indorsement. The claim of any third person to the instrument is not otherwise available as a defense to any party liable thereon unless the third person himself defends the action for such party.

§ 3–307. BURDEN OF ESTABLISHING SIGNATURES, DEFENSES AND DUE COURSE.

(1) Unless specifically denied in the pleadings each signature on an instrument is admitted. When the effectiveness of a signature is put in issue

(a) the burden of establishing it is on the party claiming under the signature; but

(b) the signature is presumed to be genuine or authorized except where the action is to enforce the obligation of a purported signer who has died or become incompetent before proof is required.

(2) When signatures are admitted or established, production of the instrument entitles a holder to recover on it unless the defendant establishes a defense.

(3) After it is shown that a defense exists a person claiming the rights of a holder in due course has the burden of establishing that he or some person under whom he claims is in all respects a holder in due course.

PART 4
LIABILITY OF PARTIES

§ 3–401. SIGNATURE.

(1) No person is liable on an instrument unless his signature appears thereon.

(2) A signature is made by use of any name, including any trade or assumed name, upon an instrument, or by any word or mark used in lieu of a written signature.

§ 3–402. SIGNATURE IN AMBIGUOUS CAPACITY.

Unless the instrument clearly indicates that a signature is made in some other capacity it is an indorsement.

§ 3–403. SIGNATURE BY AUTHORIZED REPRESENTATIVE.

(1) A signature may be made by an agent or other representative, and his authority to make it may be established as in other cases of representation. No particular form of appointment is necessary to establish such authority.

(2) An authorized representative who signs his own name to an instrument

(a) is personally obligated if the instrument neither names the person represented nor shows that the representative signed in a representative capacity;

(b) except as otherwise established between the immediate parties, is personally obligated if the instrument names the person represented but does not show that the representative signed in a representative capacity, of if the instrument does not name the person represented but does show that the representative signed in a representative capacity.

(3) Except as otherwise established the name of an organization preceded or followed by the name and office of an authorized individual is a signature made in a representative capacity.

§ 3–404. UNAUTHORIZED SIGNATURES.

(1) Any unauthorized signature is wholly inoperative as that of the person whose name is signed unless he ratifies it or is precluded from denying it; but it operates as the signature of the unauthorized signer in favor of any person who in good faith pays the instrument or takes it for value.

(2) Any unauthorized signature may be ratified for all purposes of this Article. Such ratification does not of itself affect any rights of the person ratifying against the actual signer.

§ 3–405. IMPOSTORS; SIGNATURE IN NAME OF PAYEE.

(1) An indorsement by any person in the name of a named payee is effective if

(a) an imposter by use of the mails or otherwise has induced the maker or drawer to issue the instrument to him or his confederate in the name of the payee; or

(b) a person signing as or on behalf of a maker or drawer intends the payee to have no interest in the instrument; or

(c) an agent or employee of the maker or drawer has supplied him with the name of the payee intending the latter to have no such interest.

(2) Nothing in this section shall affect the criminal or civil liability of the person so indorsing.

§ 3–406. NEGLIGENCE CONTRIBUTING TO ALTERATION OR UNAUTHORIZED SIGNATURE.

Any person who by his negligence substantially contributes to a material alteration of the instrument or to the making of an unauthorized signature is precluded from asserting the alteration or lack of authority against a holder in due course or against a drawee or other payor who pays the instrument in good faith and in accordance with the reasonable commercial standards of the drawee's or payor's business.

§ 3–407. ALTERATION.

(1) Any alteration of an instrument is material which changes the contract of any party thereto in any respect, including any such change in

(a) the number or relations of the parties; or

(b) an incomplete instrument, by completing it otherwise than as authorized; or

(c) the writing as signed, by adding to it or by removing any part of it.

(2) As against any person other than a subsequent holder in due course

(a) alteration by the holder which is both fraudulent and material discharges any party whose contract is thereby changed unless that party assents or is precluded from asserting the defense;

(b) no other alteration discharges any party and the instrument may be enforced according to its original tenor, or as to incomplete instruments according to the authority given.

(3) A subsequent holder in due course may in all cases enforce the instrument according to its original tenor, and when an incomplete instrument has been completed, he may enforce it as completed.

§ 3–408. CONSIDERATION.

Want or failure of consideration is a defense as against any person not having the rights of a holder in due course

(Section 3–305), except that no consideration is necessary for an instrument or obligation thereon given in payment of or as security for an antecedent obligation of any kind. Nothing in this section shall be taken to displace any statute outside this Act under which a promise is enforceable notwithstanding lack or failure of consideration. Partial failure of consideration is a defense pro tanto whether or not the failure is in an ascertained or liquidated amount.

§ 3–409. DRAFT NOT AN ASSIGNMENT.

(1) A check or other draft does not of itself operate as an assignment of any funds in the hands of the drawee available for its payment, and the drawee is not liable on the instrument until he accepts it.

(2) Nothing in this section shall affect any liability in contract, tort or otherwise arising from any letter of credit or other obligation or representation which is not an acceptance.

§ 3–410. DEFINITION AND OPERATION OF ACCEPTANCE.

(1) Acceptance is the drawee's signed engagement to honor the draft as presented. It must be written on the draft, and may consist of his signature alone. It becomes operative when completed by delivery or notification.

(2) A draft may be accepted although it has not been signed by the drawer or is otherwise incomplete or is overdue or has been dishonored .

(3) Where the draft is payable at a fixed period after sight and the acceptor fails to date his acceptance the holder may complete it by supplying a date in good faith.

§ 3–411. CERTIFICATION OF A CHECK.

(1) Certification of a check is acceptance. Where a holder procures certification the drawer and all prior indorsers are discharged .

(2) Unless otherwise agreed a bank has no obligation to certify a check.

(3) A bank may certify a check before returning it for lack of proper indorsement. If it does so the drawer is discharged.

§ 3–412. ACCEPTANCE VARYING DRAFT.

(1) Where the drawee's proffered acceptance in any manner varies the draft as presented the holder may refuse the acceptance and treat the draft as dishonored in which case the drawee is entitled to have his acceptance cancelled.

(2) The terms of the draft are not varied by an acceptance to pay at any particular bank or place in the United States, unless the acceptance states that the draft is to be paid only at such bank or place.

(3) Where the holder assents to an acceptance varying the terms of the draft each drawer and indorser who does not affirmatively assent is discharged.

§ 3–413. CONTRACT OF MAKER, DRAWER AND ACCEPTOR.

(1) The maker or acceptor engages that he will pay the instrument according to its tenor at the time of his engagement or as completed pursuant to Section 3–115 on incomplete instruments.

(2) The drawer engages that upon dishonor of the draft and any necessary notice of dishonor or protest he will pay the amount of the draft to the holder or to any indorser who takes it up. The drawer may disclaim this liability by drawing without recourse.

(3) By making, drawing or accepting the party admits as against all subsequent parties including the drawee the existence of the payee and his then capacity to indorse.

§ 3–414. CONTRACT OF INDORSER; ORDER OF LIABILITY.

(1) Unless the indorsement otherwise specifies (as by such words as "without recourse") every indorser engages that upon dishonor and any necessary notice of dishonor and protest he will pay the instrument according to its tenor at the time of his indorsement to the holder or to any subsequent indorser who takes it up, even though the indorser who takes it up was not obligated to do so.

(2) Unless they otherwise agree indorsers are liable to one another in the order in which they indorse, which is presumed to be the order in which their signatures appear on the instrument.

§ 3–415. CONTRACT OF ACCOMMODATION PARTY.

(1) An accommodation party is one who signs the instrument in any capacity for the purpose of lending his name to another party to it.

(2) When the instrument has been taken for value before it is due the accommodation party is liable in the capacity in which he has signed even though the taker knows of the accommodation.

(3) As against a holder in due course and without notice of the accommodation oral proof of the accommodation is not admissible to give the accommodation party the benefit of discharges dependent on his character as such. In other cases the accommodation character may be shown by oral proof.

(4) An indorsement which shows that it is not in the chain of title is notice of its accommodation character.

(5) An accommodation party is not liable to the party accommodated, and if he pays the instrument has a right of recourse on the instrument against such party.

§ 3–416. CONTRACT OF GUARANTOR.

(1) "Payment guaranteed" or equivalent words added to a signature mean that the signer engages that if the instrument is not paid when due he will pay it according to its tenor without resort by the holder to any other party.

(2) "Collection guaranteed" or equivalent words added to a signature mean that the signer engages that if the instrument is not paid when due he will pay it according to its tenor, but only after the holder has reduced his claim against the maker or acceptor to judgment and execution has been returned unsatisfied, or after the maker or acceptor has become insolvent or it is otherwise apparent that it is useless to proceed against him.

(3) Words of guaranty which do not otherwise specify guarantee payment.

(4) No words of guaranty added to the signature of a sole maker or acceptor affect his liability on the instrument. Such words added to the signature of one of two or more makers or acceptors create a presumption that the signature is for the accommodation of the others.

(5) When words of guaranty are used presentment, notice of dishonor and protest are not necessary to charge the user.

(6) Any guaranty written on the instrument is enforceable notwithstanding any statute of frauds.

§ 3–417. WARRANTIES ON PRESENTMENT AND TRANSFER.

(1) Any person who obtains payment or acceptance and any prior transferor warrants to a person who in good faith pays or accepts that

(a) he has a good title to the instrument or is authorized to obtain payment or acceptance on behalf of one who has a good title; and

(b) he has no knowledge that the signature of the maker or drawer is unauthorized, except that this warranty is not given by a holder in due course acting in good faith

(i) to a maker with respect to the maker's own signature; or

(ii) to a drawer with respect to the drawer's own signature, whether or not the drawer is also the drawee; or

(iii) to an acceptor of a draft if the holder in due course took the draft after the acceptance or obtained the acceptance without knowledge that the drawer's signature was unauthorized; and

(c) the instrument has not been materially altered, except that this warranty is not given by a holder in due course acting in good faith

(i) to the maker of a note; or

(ii) to the drawer of a draft whether or not the drawer is also the drawee; or

(iii) to the acceptor of a draft with respect to an alternation made prior to the acceptance if the holder in due course took the draft after the acceptance, even though the acceptance provided "payable as originally drawn" or equivalent terms; or

(iv) to the acceptor of a draft with respect to an alternation made after the acceptance.

(2) Any person who transfers an instrument and receives consideration warrants to his transferee and if the transfer is by indorsement to any subsequent holder who takes the instrument in good faith that

(a) he has a good title to the instrument or is authorized to obtain payment or acceptance on behalf of one who has a good title and the transfer is otherwise rightful; and

(b) all signatures are genuine or authorized; and

(c) the instrument has not been materially altered; and

(d) no defense of any party is good against him; and

(e) he has no knowledge of any insolvency proceeding instituted with respect to the maker or acceptor or the drawer of an unaccepted instrument.

(3) By transferring "without recourse" the transferor limits the obligation stated in subsection (2)(d) to a warranty that he has no knowledge of such a defense.

(4) A selling agent or broker who does not disclose the fact that he is acting only as such gives the warranties provided in this section, but if he makes such disclosure warrants only his good faith and authority.

§ 3–418. FINALITY OF PAYMENT OR ACCEPTANCE.

Except for recovery of bank payments as provided in the Article on Bank Deposits and Collections (Article 4) and except for liability for breach of warranty on presentment under the preceding section, payment or acceptance of any instrument is final in favor of a holder in due course, or a person who has in good faith changed his position in reliance on the payment.

§ 3–419. CONVERSION OF INSTRUMENT; INNOCENT REPRESENTATIVE.

(1) An instrument is converted when

(a) a drawee to whom it is delivered for acceptance refuses to return it on demand; or

(b) any person to whom it is delivered for payment refuses on demand either to pay or to return it; or

(c) it is paid on a forged indorsement.

(2) In an action against a drawee under subsection (1) the measure of the drawee's liability is the face amount of the instrument. In any other action under subsection (1) the measure of liability is presumed to be the face amount of the instrument.

(3) Subject to the provisions of this Act concerning restrictive indorsements a representative, including a depositary or collecting bank, who has in good faith and in accordance with the reasonable commercial standards applicable to the business of such representative dealt with an instrument or its proceeds on behalf of one who was not the true owner and is not liable in conversion or otherwise to the true owner beyond the amount of any proceeds remaining in his hands.

(4) An intermediary bank or payor bank which is not a depositary bank is not liable in conversion solely by reason of the fact that proceeds of an item indorsed restrictively (Sections 3–205 and 3–206) are not paid or applied consistently with the restrictive indorsement of an indorser other than its immediate transferor.

PART 5
PRESENTMENT, NOTICE OF DISHONOR AND PROTEST

§ 3–501. WHEN PRESENTMENT, NOTICE OF DISHONOR, AND PROTEST NECESSARY OR PERMISSIBLE.

(1) Unless excused (Section 3-511) presentment is necessary to charge secondary parties as follows:

(a) presentment for acceptance is necessary to charge the drawer and indorsers of a draft where the draft so provides, or is payable elsewhere than at the residence or place of business of the drawee, or its date of payment depends upon such presentment. The holder may at his option present for acceptance any other draft payable at a stated date;

(b) presentment for payment is necessary to charge any indorser;

(c) in the case of any drawer, the acceptor of a draft payable at a bank or the maker of a note payable at a bank, presentment for payment is necessary, but failure to make presentment discharges such drawer, acceptor or maker only as stated in Section 3–502(1)(b).

(2) Unless excused (Section 3–511)

(a) notice of any dishonor is necessary to charge any indorser;

(b) in the case of any drawer, the acceptor of a draft payable at a bank or the maker of a note payable at a bank, notice of any dishonor is necessary, but failure to give such notice discharges such drawer, acceptor or maker only as stated in Section 3–502(1)(b).

(3) Unless excused (Section 3–511) protest of any dishonor is necessary to charge the drawer and indorsers of any draft which on its face appears to be drawn or payable outside of the states, territories, dependencies, and possessions of the United States, the District of Columbia and the Commonwealth of Puerto Rico. The holder may

at his option make protest of any dishonor of any other instrument and in the case of a foreign draft may on insolvency of the acceptor before maturity make protest for better security.

(4) Notwithstanding any provision of this section, neither presentment nor notice of dishonor nor protest is necessary to charge an indorser who has indorsed an instrument after maturity.

§ 3–502. UNEXCUSED DELAY; DISCHARGE.

(1) Where without excuse any necessary presentment or notice of dishonor is delayed beyond the time when it is due

(a) any indorser is discharged; and

(b) any drawer or the acceptor of a draft payable at a bank or the maker of a note payable at a bank who because the drawee or payor bank becomes insolvent during the delay is deprived of funds maintained with the drawee or payor bank to cover the instrument may discharge his liability by written assignment to the holder of his rights against the drawee or payor bank in respect of such funds, but such drawer, acceptor or maker is not otherwise discharged.

(2) Where without excuse a necessary protest is delayed beyond the time when it is due any drawer or indorser is discharged.

§ 3–503. TIME OF PRESENTMENT.

(1) Unless a different time is expressed in the instrument the time for any presentment is determined as follows:

(a) where an instrument is payable at or a fixed period after a stated date any presentment for acceptance must be made on or before the date it is payable;

(b) where an instrument is payable after sight it must either be presented for acceptance or negotiated within a reasonable time after date or issue whichever is later;

(c) where an instrument shows the date on which it is payable presentment for payment is due on that date;

(d) where an instrument is accelerated presentment for payment is due within a reasonable time after the acceleration;

(e) with respect to the liability of any secondary party presentment for acceptance or payment of any other instrument is due within a reasonable time after such party becomes liable thereon.

(2) A reasonable time for presentment is determined by the nature of the instrument, any usage of banking or trade and the facts of the particular case. In the case of an uncertified check which is drawn and payable within the United States and which is not a draft drawn by a bank the following are presumed to be reasonable periods within which to present for payment or to initiate bank collection:

(a) with respect to the liability of the drawer, thirty days after date of issue whichever is later; and

(b) with respect to the liability of an indorser, seven days after his indorsement.

(3) Where any presentment is due on a day which is not a full business day for either the person making presentment or the party to pay or accept, presentment is due on the next following day which is a full business day for both parties.

(4) Presentment to be sufficient must be made at a reasonable hour, and if at a bank during its banking day.

§ 3–504. HOW PRESENTMENT MADE.

(1) Presentment is a demand for acceptance or payment made upon the maker, acceptor, drawee or other payor by or on behalf of the holder.

(2) Presentment may be made

(a) by mail, in which event the time of presentment is determined by the time of receipt of the mail; or

(b) through a clearing house; or

(c) at the place of acceptance or payment specified in the instrument or if there be none at the place of business or residence of the party to accept or pay. If neither the party to accept or pay nor anyone authorized to act for him is present or accessible at such place presentment is excused.

(3) It may be made

(a) to any one of two or more makers, acceptors, drawees or other payors; or

(b) to any person who has authority to make or refuse the acceptance or payment.

(4) A draft accepted or a note made payable at a bank in the United States must be presented at such bank.

(5) In the cases described in Section 4–210 presentment may be made in manner and with the result stated in that section.

§ 3–505. RIGHTS OF PARTY TO WHOM PRESENTMENT IS MADE.

(1) The party to whom presentment is made may without dishonor require

(a) exhibition of the instrument; and

(b) reasonable identification of the person making presentment and evidence of his authority to make it if made for another; and

(c) that the instrument be produced for acceptance or payment at a place specified in it, or if there be none at any place reasonable in the circumstances; and

(d) a signed receipt on the instrument for any partial or full payment and its surrender upon full payment.

(2) Failure to comply with any such requirement invalidates the presentment but the person presenting has a reasonable time in which to comply and the time for acceptance or payment runs from the time of compliance.

§ 3–506. TIME ALLOWED FOR ACCEPTANCE OR PAYMENT.

(1) Acceptance may be deferred without dishonor until the close of the next business day following presentment. The holder may also in good faith effort to obtain acceptance and without either dishonor of the instrument or discharge of secondary parties allow postponement of acceptance for an additional business day.

(2) Except as a longer time is allowed in the case of documentary drafts drawn under a letter of credit, and unless an earlier time is agreed to by the party to pay, payment of an instrument may be deferred without dishonor pending reasonable examination to determine whether it is properly payable, but payment must be made in any event before the close of business on the day of presentment.

§ 3–507. DISHONOR; HOLDER'S RIGHT OF RECOURSE; TERM ALLOWING RE-PRESENTMENT.

(1) An instrument is dishonored when

(a) a necessary or optional presentment is duly made and due acceptance or payment is refused or cannot be obtained within the prescribed time or in case of bank collections the instrument is seasonably returned by the midnight deadline (Section 4–301); or

(b) presentment is excused and the instrument is not duly accepted or paid.

(2) Subject to any necessary notice of dishonor and protest, the holder has upon dishonor an immediate right of recourse against the drawers and indorsers.

(3) Return of an instrument for lack of proper indorsement is not dishonor.

(4) A term in a draft or an indorsement thereof allowing a stated time for re-presentment in the event of any dishonor of the draft by nonacceptance if a time draft or by nonpayment if a sight draft gives the holder as against any secondary party bound by the term an option to waive the dishonor without affecting the liability of the secondary party and he may present again up to the end of the stated time.

§ 3–508. NOTICE OF DISHONOR.

(1) Notice of dishonor may be given to any person who may be liable on the instrument by or on behalf of the holder or any party who has himself received notice, or any other party who can be compelled to pay the instrument. In addition an agent or bank in whose hands the instrument is dishonored may give notice to his principal or customer or to another agent or bank from which the instrument was received.

(2) Any necessary notice must be given by a bank before its midnight deadline and by any other person before midnight of the third business day after dishonor or receipt of notice of dishonor.

(3) Notice may be given in any reasonable manner. It may be oral or written and in any terms which identify the instrument and state that it has been dishonored. A misdescription which does not mislead the party notified does not vitiate the notice. Sending the instrument bearing a stamp, ticket or writing stating that acceptance or payment has been refused or sending a notice of debit with respect to the instrument is sufficient.

(4) Written notice is given when sent although it is not received.

(5) Notice to one partner is notice to each although the firm has been dissolved.

(6) When any party is in insolvency proceedings instituted after the issue of the instrument notice may be given either to the party or to the representative of his estate.

(7) When any party is dead or incompetent notice may be sent to his last known address or given to his personal representative.

(8) Notice operates for the benefit of all parties who have rights on the instrument against the party notified.

§ 3–509. PROTEST; NOTING FOR PROTEST.

(1) A protest is a certificate of dishonor made under the hand and seal of a United States consul or vice consul or a notary public or other person authorized to certify dishonor by the law of the place where dishonor occurs. It may be made upon information satisfactory to such person.

(2) The protest must identify the instrument and certify either that due presentment has been made or the reason why it is excused and that the instrument has been dishonored by nonacceptance or nonpayment.

(3) The protest may also certify that notice of dishonor has been given to all parties or to specified parties.

(4) Subject to subsection (5) any necessary protest is due by the time that notice of dishonor is due.

(5) If, before protest is due, an instrument has been noted for protest by the officer to make protest, the protest may be made at any time thereafter as of the date of the noting.

§ **3–510.** EVIDENCE OF DISHONOR AND NOTICE OF DIS-
HONOR.

The following are admissible as evidence and create a
presumption of dishonor and of any notice of dishonor
therein shown:

(a) a document regular in form as provided in the
preceding section which purports to be a protest;

(b) the purported stamp or writing of the drawee,
payor bank or presenting bank on the instrument or
accompanying it stating that acceptance or payment
has been refused for reasons consistent with dishonor;

(c) any book or record of the drawee, payor bank, or
any collecting bank kept in the usual course of business which shows dishonor, even though there is no
evidence of who made the entry.

§ **3–511.** WAIVED OR EXCUSED PRESENTMENT, PROTEST OR
NOTICE OF DISHONOR OR DELAY THEREIN.

(1) Delay in presentment, protest or notice of dishonor is
excused when the party is without notice that it is due or
when the delay is caused by circumstances beyond his
control and he exercises reasonable diligence after the
cause of the delay ceases to operate.

(2) Presentment or notice or protest as the case may be is
entirely excused when

(a) the party to be charged has waived it expressly or
by implication either before or after it is due; or

(b) such party has himself dishonored the instrument
or has countermanded payment or otherwise has no
reason to expect or right to require that the instrument be accepted or paid; or

(c) by reasonable diligence the presentment or protest cannot be made or the notice given.

(3) Presentment is also entirely excused when

(a) the maker, acceptor or drawee of any instrument
except a documentary draft is dead or in insolvency
proceedings instituted after the issue of the instrument; or

(b) acceptance or payment is refused but not for want
of proper presentment.

(4) Where a draft has been dishonored by nonacceptance
a later presentment for payment and any notice of dishonor and protest for nonpayment are excused unless in
the meantime the instrument has been accepted.

(5) A waiver of protest is also a waiver of presentment and
of notice of dishonor even though protest is not required.

(6) Where a waiver of presentment or notice or protest is
embodied in the instrument itself it is binding upon all
parties; but where it is written above the signature of an
indorser it binds him only.

PART 6
DISCHARGE

§ **3–601.** DISCHARGE OF PARTIES.

(1) The extent of the discharge of any party from liability
on an instrument is governed by the sections on

(a) payment or satisfaction (Section 3– 603); or

(b) tender of payment (Section 3–604); or

(c) cancellation or renunciation (Section 3–605); or

(d) impairment of right of recourse or of collateral
(Section 3–606); or

(e) reacquisition of the instrument by a prior party
(Section 3–208); or

(f) fraudulent and material alteration (Section 3–
407); or

(g) certification of a check (Section 3–411); or

(h) acceptance varying a draft (Section 3–412); or

(i) unexcused delay in presentment or notice of dishonor or protest (Section 3-502).

(2) Any party is also discharged from his liability on an instrument to another party by any other act or agreement
with such party which would discharge his simple contract for the payment of money.

(3) The liability of all parties is discharged when any party
who has himself no right of action or recourse on the instrument

(a) reacquires the instrument in his own right; or

(b) is discharged under any provision of this Article,
except as otherwise provided with respect to discharge for impairment of recourse or of collateral
(Section 3–606).

§**3–602.** EFFECT OF DISCHARGE AGAINST HOLDER IN DUE
COURSE.

No discharge of any party provided by this Article is effective against a subsequent holder in due course unless he
has notice thereof when he takes the instrument.

§ **3–603.** PAYMENT OR SATISFACTION.

(1) The liability of any party is discharged to the extent of
his payment or satisfaction to the holder even though it is
made with knowledge of a claim of another person to the
instrument unless prior to such payment or satisfaction
the person making the claim either supplies indemnity
deemed adequate by the party seeking the discharge or
enjoins payment or satisfaction by order of a court of
competent jurisdiction in an action in which the adverse
claimant and the holder are parties. This subsection does
not, however, result in the discharge of the liability

(a) of a party who in bad faith pays or satisfies a
holder who acquired the instrument by theft or who

(unless having the rights of a holder in due course) holds through one who so acquired it; or

(b) of a party (other than an intermediary bank or a payor bank which is not a depositary bank) who pays or satisfies the holder of an instrument which has been restrictively indorsed in a manner not consistent with the terms of such restrictive indorsement.

(2) Payment or satisfaction may be made with the consent of the holder by any person including a stranger to the instrument. Surrender of the instrument to such a person gives him the rights of a transferee (Section 3–201).

§ 3–604. Tender of Payment.

(1) Any party making tender of full payment to a holder when or after it is due is discharged to the extent of all subsequent liability for interest, costs and attorney's fees.

(2) The holder's refusal of such tender wholly discharges any party who has a right of recourse against the party making the tender.

(3) Where the maker or acceptor of an instrument payable otherwise than on demand is able and ready to pay at every place of payment specified in the instrument when it is due, it is equivalent to tender.

§ 3–605. Cancellation and Renunciation.

(1) The holder of an instrument may even without consideration discharge any party

(a) in any manner apparent on the face of the instrument or the indorsement, as by intentionally cancelling the instrument or the party's signature by destruction or mutilation, or by striking out the party's signature; or

(b) by renouncing his rights by a writing signed and delivered or by surrender of the instrument to the party to be discharged .

(2) Neither cancellation nor renunciation without surrender of the instrument affects the title thereto.

§ 3–606. Impairment of Recourse or of Collateral.

(1) The holder discharges any party to the instrument to the extent that without such party's consent the holder

(a) without express reservation or rights releases or agrees not to sue any person against whom the party has to the knowledge of the holder a right of recourse or agrees to suspend the right to enforce against such person the instrument or collateral or otherwise discharges such person, except that failure or delay in effecting any required presentment, protest or notice of dishonor with respect to any such person does not discharge any party as to whom presentment, protest or notice of dishonor is effective or unnecessary; or

(b) unjustifiably impairs any collateral for the instrument given by or on behalf of the party or any person against whom he has a right of recourse.

(2) By express reservation of rights against a party with a right of recourse the holder preserves

(a) all his rights against such party as of the time when the instrument was originally due; and

(b) the right of the party to pay the instrument as of that time; and

(c) all rights of such party to recourse against others.

PART 7
ADVICE OF INTERNATIONAL SIGHT DRAFT

§ 3–701. Letter of Advice of International Sight Draft.

(1) A "letter of advice" is a drawer's communication to the drawee that a described draft has been drawn.

(2) Unless otherwise agreed when a bank receives from another bank a letter of advice of an international sight draft the drawee bank may immediately debit the drawer's account and stop the running of interest pro tanto. Such a debit and any resulting credit to any account covering outstanding drafts leaves in the drawer full power to stop payment or otherwise dispose of the amount and creates no trust or interest in favor of the holder.

(3) Unless otherwise agreed and except where a draft is drawn under a credit issued by the drawee, the drawee of an international sight draft owes the drawer no duty to pay an unadvised draft but if it does so and the draft is genuine, may appropriately debit the drawer's account.

PART 8
MISCELLANEOUS

§ 3–801. Drafts in a Set.

(1) Where a draft is drawn in a set of parts, each of which is numbered and expressed to be an order only if no other part has been honored, the whole of the parts constitutes one draft but a taker of any part may become a holder in due course of the draft.

(2) Any person who negotiates, indorses or accepts a single part of a draft drawn in a set thereby becomes liable to any holder in due course of that part as if it were the whole set, but as between different holders in due course to whom different parts have been negotiated the holder whose title first accrues has all rights to the draft and its proceeds.

(3) As against the drawee the first presented part of a draft drawn in a set is the part entitled to payment, or if a time draft to acceptance and payment. Acceptance of any subsequently presented part renders the drawee liable thereon under subsection (2). With respect both to a

holder and to the drawer payment of a subsequently presented part of a draft payable at sight has the same effect as payment of a check notwithstanding an effective stop order (Section 4–407).

(4) Except as otherwise provided in this section, where any part of a draft in a set is discharged by payment or otherwise the whole draft is discharged.

§ 3–802. EFFECT OF INSTRUMENT ON OBLIGATION FOR WHICH IT IS GIVEN.

(1) Unless otherwise agreed where an instrument is taken for an underlying obligation

(a) the obligation to pro tanto discharged if a bank is drawer, maker or acceptor of the instrument and there is no recourse on the instrument against the underlying obligor; and

(b) in any other case the obligation is suspended pro tanto until the instrument is due for or if it is payable on demand until its presentment. If the instrument is dishonored action may be maintained on either the instrument or the obligation; discharge of the underlying obligor on the instrument also discharges him on the obligation.

(2) The taking in good faith of a check which is not postdated does not of itself so extend the time on the original obligation as to discharge a surety.

§ 3–803. NOTICE TO THIRD PARTY.

Where a defendant is sued for breach of an obligation for which a third person is answerable over under this Article he may give the third person written notice of the litigation, and the person notified may then give similar notice to any other person who is answerable over to him under this Article. If the notice states that the person notified may come in and defend and that if the person notified does not do so he will in any action against him by the person giving the notice be bound by any determination of fact common to the two litigations, then unless after seasonable receipt of the notice the person notified does come in and defend he is so bound.

§ 3–804. LOST, DESTROYED OR STOLEN INSTRUMENTS.

The owner of an instrument which is lost, whether by destruction, theft or otherwise, may maintain an action in his own name and recover from any party liable thereon upon due proof of his ownership, the facts which prevent his production of the instrument and its terms. The court may require security indemnifying the defendant against loss by reason of further claims on the instrument.

§ 3–805. INSTRUMENTS NOT PAYABLE TO ORDER OR TO BEARER.

This Article applies to any instrument whose terms do not preclude transfer and which is otherwise negotiable within this Article but which is not payable to order or to bearer, except that there can be no holder in due course of such an instrument.

Article 4
Bank Deposits and
Collections

PART I
GENERAL PROVISIONS AND DEFINITIONS

§ 4–101. SHORT TITLE.

This Article shall be known and may be cited as Uniform Commercial Code—Bank Deposits and Collections.

§ 4–102. APPLICABILITY.

(1) To the extent that items within this Article are also within the scope of Articles 3 and 8, they are subject to the provisions of those Articles. In the event of conflict the provisions of this Article govern those of Article 3 but the provisions of Article 8 govern those of this Article.

(2) The liability of a bank for action or non-action with respect to any item handled by it for purposes of presentment, payment or collection is governed by the law of the place where the bank is located. In the case of action or non-action by or at a branch or separate office of a bank, its liability is governed by the law of the place where the branch or separate office is located.

§ 4–103. VARIATION BY AGREEMENT; MEASURE OF DAMAGES; CERTAIN ACTION CONSTITUTING ORDINARY CARE.

(1) The effect of the provisions of this Article may be varied by agreement except that no agreement can disclaim a bank's responsibility for its own lack of good faith or failure to exercise ordinary care or can limit the measure of damages for such lack or failure; but the parties may by agreement determine the standards by which such responsibility is to be measured if such standards are not manifestly unreasonable.

(2) Federal Reserve regulations and operating letters, clearing house rules, and the like, have the effect of agreements under subsection (1), whether or not specifically assented to by all parties interested in items handled.

(3) Action or non-action approved by this Article or pursuant to Federal Reserve regulations or operating letters constitutes the exercise of ordinary care and, in the absence of special instructions, action or non-action consistent with clearing house rules and the like or with a general banking usage not disapproved by this Article, prima facie constitutes the exercise of ordinary care.

(4) The specification or approval of certain procedures by this Article does not constitute disapproval of other procedures which may be reasonable under the circumstances.

(5) The measure of damages for failure to exercise ordinary care in handling an item is the amount of the item reduced by an amount which could not have been realized by the use of ordinary care, and where there is bad faith it includes other damages, if any, suffered by the party as a proximate consequence.

§ 4-104. DEFINITIONS AND INDEX OF DEFINITIONS.

(1) In this Article unless the context otherwise requires

(a) "Account" means any account with a bank and includes a checking, time, interest or savings account;

(b) "Afternoon" means the period of a day between noon and midnight;

(c) "Banking day" means that part of any day on which a bank is open to the public for carrying on substantially all of its banking functions;

(d) "Clearing house" means any association of banks or other payors regularly clearing items;

(e) "Customer" means any person having an account with a bank or for whom a bank has agreed to collect items and includes a bank carrying an account with another bank;

(f) "Documentary draft" means any negotiable or non-negotiable draft with accompanying documents, securities or other papers to be delivered against honor of the draft;

(g) "Item" means any instrument for the payment of money even though it is not negotiable but does not include money;

(h) "Midnight deadline" with respect to a bank is midnight on its next banking day following the banking day on which it receives the relevant item or notice or from which the time for taking action commences to run, whichever is later;

(i) "Properly payable" includes the availability of funds for payment at the time of decision to pay or dishonor;

(j) "Settle" means to pay in cash, by clearing house settlement, in a charge or credit or by remittance, or otherwise as instructed. A settlement may be either provisional or final;

(k) "Suspends payments" with respect to a bank means that it has been closed by order of the supervisory authorities, that a public officer has been appointed to take it over or that it ceases or refuses to make payments in the ordinary course of business.

(2) Other definitions applying to this Article and the sections in which they appear are:

"Collecting bank" Section 4 105.

"Depositary bank" Section 4–105.

"Intermediary bank" Section 4–105.

"Payor bank" Section 4 105.

"Presenting bank" Section 4–105.

"Remitting bank" Section 4--105.

(3) The following definitions in other Articles apply to this Article:

"Acceptance" Section 3–410.

"Certificate of deposit" Section 3–104.

"Certification" Section 3 411.

"Check" Section 3–104.

"Draft" Section 3–104.

"Holder in due course" Section 3–302.

"Notice of dishonor" Section 3–508.

"Presentment" Section 3–504.

"Protest" Section 3–509.

"Secondary party" Section 3–102.

(4) In addition Article 1 contains general definitions and principles of construction and interpretation applicable throughout this Article.

§ 4-105. "DEPOSITARY BANK"; "INTERMEDIARY BANK"; "COLLECTING BANK"; "PAYOR BANK"; "PRESENTING BANK"; "REMITTING BANK".

In this Article unless the context otherwise requires:

(a) "Depositary bank" means the first bank to which an item is transferred for collection even though it is also the payor bank;

(b) "Payor bank" means a bank by which an item is payable as drawn or accepted;

(c) "Intermediary bank" means any bank to which an item is transferred in course of collection except the depositary or payor bank;

(d) "Collecting bank" means any bank handling the item for collection except the payor bank;

(e) "Presenting bank" means any bank presenting an item except a payor bank;

(f) "Remitting bank" means any payor or intermediary bank remitting for an item.

§ 4-106. SEPARATE OFFICE OF A BANK.

A branch or separate office of a bank [maintaining its own deposit ledgers] is a separate bank for the purpose of computing the time within which and determining the place at or to which action may be taken or notices or orders shall be given under this Article and under Article 3.

Note: The brackets are to make it optional with the several states whether to require a branch to maintain its own deposit ledgers in order to be considered to be a separate bank for certain purposes under Article 4. In some states "maintaining its own deposit ledgers" is a satisfactory test. In others branch banking practices are such that this test would not be suitable.

§ 4–107. Time of Receipt of Items.

(1) For the purpose of allowing time to process items, prove balances and make the necessary entries on its books to determine its position for the day, a bank may fix an afternoon hour of two P.M. or later as a cut-off hour for the handling of money and items and the making of entries on its books.

(2) Any item or deposit of money received on any day after a cut-off hour so fixed or after the close of the banking day may be treated as being received at the opening of the next banking day.

§ 4–108. Delays

(1) Unless otherwise instructed, a collecting bank in a good faith effort to secure payment may, in the case of specific items and with or without the approval of any person involved, waive, modify or extend time limits imposed or permitted by this Act for a period not in excess of an additional banking day without discharge of secondary parties and without liability to its transferor or any prior party.

(2) Delay by a collecting bank or payor bank beyond time limits prescribed or permitted by this Act or by instructions is excused if caused by interruption of communication facilities, suspension of payments by another bank, war, emergency conditions or other circumstances beyond the control of the bank provided it exercises such diligence as the circumstances require.

§ 4–109. Process of Posting.

The "process of posting" means the usual procedure followed by a payor bank in determining to pay an item and in recording the payment including one or more of the following or other steps as determined by the bank:

(a) verification of any signature;

(b) ascertaining that sufficient funds are available;

(c) affixing a "paid" or other stamp;

(d) entering a charge or entry to a customer's account;

(e) correcting or reversing an entry or erroneous action with respect to the item.

PART 2
COLLECTION OF ITEMS:
DEPOSITARY AND COLLECTING BANKS

§ 4–201. Presumption and Duration of Agency Status of Collecting Banks and Provisional Status of Credits; Applicability of Article; Item Indorsed "Pay Any Bank".

(1) Unless a contrary intent clearly appears and prior to the time that a settlement given by a collecting bank for an item is or becomes final (subsection (3) of Section 4–211 and Sections 4–212 and 4–213) the bank is an agent or subagent of the owner of the item and any settlement given for the item is provisional. This provision applies regardless of the form of indorsement or lack of indorsement and even though credit given for the item is subject to immediate withdrawal as of right or is in fact withdrawn; but the continuance of ownership of an item by its owner and any rights of the owner to proceeds of the item are subject to rights of a collecting bank such as those resulting from outstanding advances on the item and valid rights of setoff. When an item is handled by banks for purposes of presentment, payment and collection, the relevant provisions of this Article apply even though action of parties clearly establishes that a particular bank has purchased the item and is the owner of it.

(2) After an item has been indorsed with the words "pay any bank" or the like, only a bank may acquire the rights of a holder

(a) until the item has been returned to the customer initiating collection; or

(b) until the item has been specially indorsed by a bank to a person who is not a bank.

§ 4–202. Responsibility for Collection; When Action Seasonable.

(1) A collecting bank must use ordinary care in

(a) presenting an item or sending it for presentment; and

(b) sending notice of dishonor or nonpayment or returning an item other than a documentary draft to the bank's transferor [or directly to the depositary bank under subsection (2) of Section 4–212] *(see note to Section 4-212)* after learning that the item has not been paid or accepted as the case may be; and

(c) settling for an item when the bank receives final settlement; and

(d) making or providing for any necessary protest; and

(e) notifying its transferor of any loss or delay in transit within a reasonable time after discovery thereof.

(2) A collecting bank taking proper action before its midnight deadline following receipt of an item, notice or payment acts seasonably; taking proper action within a rea-

sonably longer time may be seasonable but the bank has the burden of so establishing.

(3) Subject to subsection (1)(a), a bank is not liable for the insolvency, neglect, misconduct, mistake or default of another bank or person or for loss or destruction of an item in transit or in the possession of others.

§ 4–203. EFFECT OF INSTRUCTIONS.

Subject to the provisions of Article 3 concerning conversion of instruments (Section 3–419) and the provisions of both Article 3 and this Article concerning restrictive indorsements only a collecting bank's transferor can give instructions which affect the bank or constitute notice to it and a collecting bank is not liable to prior parties for any action taken pursuant to such instructions or in accordance with any agreement with its transferor.

§ 4–204. METHODS OF SENDING AND PRESENTING; SENDING DIRECT TO PAYOR BANK.

(1) A collecting bank must send items by reasonably prompt method taking into consideration any relevant instructions, the nature of the item, the number of such items on hand, and the cost of collection involved and the method generally used by it or others to present such items.

(2) A collecting bank may send

(a) any item direct to the payor bank;

(b) any item to any non-bank payor if authorized by its transferor; and

(c) any item other than documentary drafts to any nonbank payor, if authorized by Federal Reserve regulation or operating letter, clearing house rule or the like.

(3) Presentment may be made by presenting bank at a place where the payor bank has requested that presentment be made.

§ 4–205. SUPPLYING MISSING INDORSEMENT; NO NOTICE FROM PRIOR INDORSEMENT.

(1) A depositary bank which has taken an item for collection may supply any indorsement of the customer which is necessary to title unless the item contains the words "payee's indorsement required" or the like. In the absence of such a requirement a statement placed on the item by the depositary bank to the effect that the item was deposited by a customer or credited to his account is effective as the customer's indorsement.

(2) An intermediary bank, or payor bank which is not a depositary bank, is neither given notice or otherwise affected by a restrictive indorsement of any person except the bank's immediate transferor.

§ 4–206. TRANSFER BETWEEN BANKS.

Any agreed method which identifies the transferor bank is sufficient for the item's further transfer to another bank.

§ 4–207. WARRANTIES OF CUSTOMER AND COLLECTING BANK ON TRANSFER OR PRESENTMENT OF ITEMS; TIME FOR CLAIMS.

(1) Each customer or collecting bank who obtains payment or acceptance of an item and each prior customer and collecting bank warrants to the payor bank or other payor who in good faith pays or accepts the item that

(a) he has a good title to the item or is authorized to obtain payment or acceptance on behalf of one who has a good title; and

(b) he has no knowledge that the signature of the maker or drawer is unauthorized, except that this warranty is not given by any customer or collecting bank that is a holder in due course and acts in good faith

(i) to a maker with respect to the maker's own signature; or

(ii) to a drawer with respect to the drawer's own signature, whether or not the drawer is also the drawee; or

(iii) to an acceptor of an item if the holder in due course took the item after the acceptance or obtained the acceptance without knowledge that the drawer's signature was unauthorized; and

(c) the item has not been materially altered, except that this warranty is not given by any customer or collecting bank that is a holder in due course and acts in good faith

(i) to the maker of a note; or

(ii) to the drawer of a draft whether or not the drawer is also the drawee; or

(iii) to the acceptor of an item with respect to an alteration made prior to the acceptance if the holder in due course took the item after the acceptance, even though the acceptance provided "payable as originally drawn" or equivalent terms; or

(iv) to the acceptor of an item with respect to an alteration made after the acceptance.

(2) Each customer and collecting bank who transfers an item and receives a settlement or other consideration for it warrants to his transferee and to any subsequent collecting bank who takes the item in good faith that

(a) he has a good title to the item or is authorized to obtain payment or acceptance on behalf of one who has a good title and the transfer is otherwise rightful; and

(b) all signatures are genuine or authorized; and

(c) the item has not been materially altered; and

(d) no defense of any party is good against him; and

(e) he has no knowledge of any insolvency proceeding instituted with respect to the maker or acceptor or the drawer of an unaccepted item.

In addition each customer and collecting bank so transferring an item and receiving a settlement or other consideration engages that upon dishonor and any necessary notice of dishonor and protest he will take up the item.

(3) The warranties and the engagement to honor set forth in the two preceding subsection arise notwithstanding the absence of indorsement or words of guaranty or warranty in the transfer or presentment and a collecting bank remains liable for their breach despite remittance to its transferor. Damages for breach of such warranties or engagement to honor shall not exceed the consideration received by the customer or collecting bank responsible plus finance charges and expenses related to the item, if any.

(4) Unless a claim for breach of warranty under this section is made within a reasonable time after the person claiming learns of the breach, the person liable is discharged to the extent of any loss caused by the delay in making claim.

§ 4–208. SECURITY INTEREST OF COLLECTING BANK IN ITEMS, ACCOMPANYING DOCUMENTS AND PROCEEDS.

(1) A bank has a security interest in an item and any accompanying documents or the proceeds of either

(a) in case of an item deposited in an account to the extent to which credit given for the item has been withdrawn or applied;

(b) in case of an item for which it has given credit available for withdrawal as of right, to the extent of the credit given whether or not the credit is drawn upon and whether or not there is a right of charge-back; or

(c) if it makes an advance on or against the item.

(2) When credit which has been given for several items received at one time or pursuant to a single agreement is withdrawn or applied in part the security interest remains upon all the items, any accompanying documents or the proceeds of either. For the purpose of this section, credits first given are first withdrawn.

(3) Receipt by a collecting bank of a final settlement for an item is a realization on its security interest in the item, accompanying documents and proceeds. To the extent and so long as the bank does not receive final settlement for the item or give up possession of the item or accompanying documents for 4–211. Media or Remittance; Provisional purposes other than collection, the security inter-

est continues and is subject to the provisions of Article 9 except that

(a) no security agreement is necessary to make the security interest enforceable (subsection (1)(a) of Section 9–203); and

(b) no filing is required to perfect the security interest; and

(c) the security interest has priority over conflicting perfected security interests in the item, accompanying documents or proceeds.

§ 4–209. WHEN BANK GIVES VALUE FOR PURPOSES OF HOLDER IN DUE COURSE.

For purposes of determining its status as a holder in due course, the bank has given value to the extent that it has a security interest in an item provided that the bank otherwise complies with the requirements of Section 3–302 on what constitutes a holder in due course.

§ 4–210. PRESENTMENT BY NOTICE OF ITEM NOT PAYABLE BY, THROUGH OR AT A BANK; LIABILITY OF SECONDARY PARTIES.

(1) Unless otherwise instructed, a collecting bank may present an item not payable by, through or at a bank by sending to the party to accept or pay a written notice that the bank holds the item for acceptance or payment. The notice must be sent in time to be received on or before the day when presentment is due and the bank must meet any requirement of the party to accept or pay under Section 3–505 by the close of the bank's next banking day after it knows of the requirement.

(2) Where presentment is made by notice and neither honor nor request for compliance with a requirement under Section 3–505 is received by the close of business on the day after maturity or in the case of demand items by the close of business on the third banking day after notice was sent, the presenting bank may treat the item as dishonored and charge any secondary party by sending him notice of the facts .

§ 4–211. MEDIA OR REMITTANCE: PROVISIONAL AND FINAL SETTLEMENT IN REMITTANCE CASES.

(1) A collecting bank may take in settlement of an item

(a) a check of the remitting bank or of another bank on any bank except the remitting bank; or

(b) a cashier's check or similar primary obligation of a remitting bank which is a member of or clears through a member of the same clearing house or group as the collecting bank; or

(c) appropriate authority to charge an account of the remitting bank or of another bank with the collecting bank; or

(d) if the item is drawn upon or payable by a person other than a bank, a cashier's check, certified check or other bank check or obligation.

(2) If before its midnight deadline the collecting bank properly dishonors a remittance check or authorization to charge on itself or presents or forwards for collection a remittance instrument of or on another bank which is of a kind approved by subsection (1) or has not been authorized by it, the collecting bank is not liable to prior parties in the event of the dishonor of such check, instrument or authorization.

(3) A settlement for an item by means of a remittance instrument or authorization to charge is or becomes a final settlement as to both the person making and the person receiving the settlement

(a) if the remittance instrument or authorization to charge is of a kind approved by subsection (1) or has not been authorized by the person receiving the settlement and in either case the person receiving the settlement acts seasonably before its midnight deadline in presenting, forwarding for collection or paying the instrument or authorization, at the time the remittance instrument or authorization is finally paid by the payor by which it is payable;

(b) if the person receiving the settlement has authorized remittance by a non-bank check or obligation or by a cashier's check or similar primary obligation of or a check upon the payor or other remitting bank which is not of a kind approved by subsection (1)(b), at the time of the receipt of such remittance check or obligation; or

(c) if in a case not covered by subparagraphs (a) or (b) the person receiving the settlement fails to seasonably present, forward for collection, pay or return a remittance instrument or authorization to it to charge before its midnight deadline, at such midnight deadline.

§ 4–212. RIGHT OF CHARGE-BACK OR REFUND.

(1) If a collecting bank has made provisional settlement with its customer for an item and itself fails by reason of dishonor, suspension of payments by a bank or otherwise to receive a settlement for the item which is or becomes final, the bank may revoke the settlement given by it, charge back the amount of any credit given for the item to its customer's account or obtain refund from its customer whether or not it is able to return the items if by its midnight deadline or within a longer reasonable time after it learns the facts it returns the item or sends notification of the facts. These rights to revoke, charge-back and obtain refund terminate if and when a settlement for the item received by the bank is or becomes final (subsection (3) of Section 4– 211 and subsections (2) and (3) of Section 4–213).

[(2) Within the time and manner prescribed by this section and Section 4–301, an intermediary or payor bank, as the case may be, may return an unpaid item directly to the depositary bank and may send for collection a draft on the depositary bank and obtain reimbursement. In such case, if the depositary bank has received provisional settlement for the item, it must reimburse the bank drawing the draft and any provisional credits for the item between banks shall become and remain final.]

Note: Direction returns is recognized as an innovation that is not yet established bank practice, and therefore, Paragraph 2 has been bracketed. Some lawyers have doubts whether it should be included in legislation or left to development by agreement.

(3)A depositary bank which is also the payor may charge-back the amount of an item to its customer's account or obtain refund in accordance with the section governing return of an item received by a payor bank for credit on its books (Section 4–301).

(4) The right to charge-back is not affected by

(a) prior use of the credit given for the item; or

(b) failure by any bank to exercise ordinary care with respect to the item but any bank so failing remains liable.

(5) A failure to charge-back or claim refund does not affect other rights of the bank against the customer or any other party.

(6) If credit is given in dollars as the equivalent of the value of an item payable in a foreign currency the dollar amount of any charge-back or refund shall be calculated on the basis of the buying sight rate for the foreign currency prevailing on the day when the person entitled to the charge-back or refund learns that it will not receive payment in ordinary course.

§ 4–213. FINAL PAYMENT OF ITEM BY PAYOR BANK; WHEN PROVISIONAL DEBITS AND CREDITS BECOME FINAL; WHEN CERTAIN CREDITS BECOME AVAILABLE FOR WITHDRAWAL.

(1) An item is finally paid by a payor bank when the bank has done any of the following, whichever happens first:

(a) paid the item in cash; or

(b) settled for the item without reserving a right to revoke the settlement and without having such right under statute, clearing house rule or agreement; or

(c) completed the process of posting the item to the indicated amount of the drawer, maker or other person to be charged therewith; or

(d) made a provisional settlement for the item and failed to revoke the settlement in the time and manner permitted by statute, clearing house rule or agreement.

Upon a final payment under subparagraphs (b), (c), or (d) the payor bank shall be accountable for the amount of the item.

(2) If provisional settlement for an item between the presenting and payor banks is made through a clearing house or by debits or credits in an account between them, then to the extent that provisional debits or credits for the item are entered in accounts between the presenting and payor banks or between the presenting and successive prior collecting banks seriatim, they become final upon final payment of the item by the payor bank.

(3) If a collecting bank receives a settlement for an item which is or becomes final (subsection (3) of Section 4-211, subsection (2) of Section 4-213) the bank is accountable to its customer for the amount of the item and any provisional credit given for the item in an account with its customer becomes final.

(4) Subject to any right of the bank to apply the credit to an obligation of the customer, credit given by a bank for an item in an account with its customer becomes available for withdrawal as of right

   (a) in any case where the bank has received a provisional settlement for the item,—when such settlement becomes final and the bank has had a reasonable time to learn that the settlement is final;

   (b) in any case where the bank is both a depositary bank and a payor bank and the item is finally paid,—at the opening of the bank's second banking day following receipt of the item.

(5) A deposit of money in a bank is final when made but, subject to any right of the bank to apply the deposit to an obligation of the customer, the deposit becomes available for withdrawal as of right at the opening of the bank's next banking day following receipt of the deposit.

§ 4-214. INSOLVENCY AND PREFERENCE.

(1) Any item in or coming into the possession of a payor or collecting bank which suspends payment and which item is not finally paid shall be returned by the receiver, trustee or agent in charge of the closed bank to the presenting bank or the closed bank's customer.

(2) If a payor bank finally pays an item and suspends payments without making a settlement for the item with its customer or the presenting bank which settlement is or becomes final, the owner of the item has a preferred claim against the payor bank.

(3) If a payor bank gives or a collecting bank gives or receives a provisional settlement for an item and thereafter suspends payments, the suspension does not prevent or interfere with the settlement becoming final if such finality occurs automatically upon the lapse of certain time or the happening of certain events (subsection (3) of Section 4-211, subsections (1)(d), (2) and (3) of Section 4-213).

(4) If a collecting bank receives from subsequent parties settlement for an item which settlement is or becomes final and suspends payments without making a settlement for the item with its customer which is or becomes final, the owner of the item has a preferred claim against such collecting bank.

PART 3
COLLECTION OF ITEMS: PAYOR BANKS

§ 4-301. DEFERRED POSTING; RECOVERY OF PAYMENT BY RETURN OF ITEMS; TIME OF DISHONOR.

(1) Where an authorized settlement for a demand item (other than a documentary draft) received by a payor bank otherwise than for immediate payment over the counter has been made before midnight of the banking day of receipt the payor bank may revoke the settlement and recover any payment if before it has made final payment (subsection (1) of Section 4-213) and before its midnight deadline it

   (a) returns the item; or

   (b) sends written notice of dishonor or nonpayment if the item is held for protest or is otherwise unavailable for return.

(2) If a demand item is received by a payor bank for credit on its books it may return such item or send notice of dishonor and may revoke any credit given or recover the amount thereof withdrawn by its customer, if it acts within the time limit and in the manner specified in the preceding subsection.

(3) Unless previous notice of dishonor has been sent an item is dishonored at the time when for purposes of dishonor it is returned or notice sent in accordance with this section.

(4) An item is returned:

   (a) as to an item received through a clearing house, when it is delivered to the presenting or last collecting bank or to the clearing house or is sent or delivered in accordance with its rules; or

   (b) in all other cases, when it is sent or delivered to the bank's customer or transferor or pursuant to his instructions.

§ 4-302. PAYOR BANK'S RESPONSIBILITY FOR LATE RETURN OF ITEM.

In the absence of a valid defense such as a breach of a presentment warranty (subsection (1) of Section 4-207), settlement effected or the like, if an item is presented on and received by a payor bank the bank is accountable for the amount of

   (a) a demand item other than a documentary draft whether properly payable or not if the bank, in any case where it is not also the depositary bank, retains the item beyond midnight of the banking day or receipt without settling for it or, regardless of whether it is also the depositary bank, does not pay or return the item or send notice of dishonor until after its midnight deadline; or

(b) any other properly payable item unless within the time allowed for acceptance or payment of that item the bank either accepts or pays the item or returns it and accompanying documents.

§ 4–303. When Items Subject to Notice, Stop-Order, Legal Process or Setoff; Order in Which Items May Be Charged or Certified.

(1) Any knowledge, notice or stop-order received by, legal process served upon or setoff exercised by a payor bank, whether or not effective under other rules of law to terminate, suspend or modify the bank's right or duty to pay an item or to charge its customer's account for the item, comes too late to so terminate, suspend or modify such right or duty if the knowledge, notice, stop-order or legal process is received or served and a reasonable time for the bank to act thereon expires or the setoff is exercised after the bank has done any of the following:

(a) accepted or certified the item;

(b) paid the item in cash;

(c) settled for the item without reserving a right to revoke the settlement and without having such right under statute, clearing house rule or agreement;

(d) completed the process of posting the item to the indicated account of the drawer, maker or other person to be charged therewith or otherwise has evidenced by examination of such indicated account and by action its decision to pay the item; or

(e) become accountable for the amount of the item under subsection (1)(d) of Section 4–213 and Section 4–302 dealing with the payor bank's responsibility for late return of items.

(2) Subject to the provisions of subsection (1) items may be accepted, paid, certified or charged to the indicated account of its customer in any order convenient to the bank.

PART 4
RELATIONSHIP BETWEEN PAYOR BANK
AND ITS CUSTOMER

§ 4–401. When Bank May Charge Customer's Account.

(1) As against its customer, a bank may charge against his account any item which is otherwise properly payable from that account even though the charge creates an overdraft.

(2) A bank which in good faith makes payment to a holder may charge the indicated account of its customer according to

(a) the original tenor of his altered item;

(b) the tenor of his competed item, even though the bank knows the item has been completed unless the bank has notice that the completion was improper.

§ 4–402. Bank's Liability to Customer for Wrongful Dishonor.

A payor bank is liable to its customer for damages proximately caused by the wrongful dishonor of an item. When the dishonor occurs through mistake liability is limited to actual damages proved. If so proximately caused proved damages may include damages for an arrest or prosecution of the customer or other consequential damages. Whether any consequential damages are proximately caused by the wrongful dishonor is a question of fact to be determined in each case.

§ 4–403. Customer's Right to Stop Payment; Burden of Proof of Loss.

(1) A customer may by order to his bank stop payment of any item payable for his account but the order must be received at such time and in such manner as to afford the bank a reasonable opportunity to act on it prior to any action by the bank with respect to the item described in Section 4–303.

(2) An oral order is binding upon the bank only for fourteen calendar days unless confirmed in writing within that period. A written order is effective for only six months unless renewed in writing.

(3) The burden of establishing the fact and amount of loss resulting from the payment of an item contrary to a binding stop payment order is on the customer.

§ 4–404. Bank Not Obligated to Pay Check More Than Six Months Old.

A bank is under no obligation to a customer having a checking account to pay a check, other than a certified check, which is presented more than six months after its date, but it may charge its customer's account for a payment made thereafter in good faith.

§ 4–405. Death or Incompetence of Customer.

(1) A payor or collecting bank's authority to accept, pay or collect an item or to account for proceeds of its collection if otherwise effective is not rendered ineffective by incompetence of a customer of either bank existing at the time the item is issued or its collection is undertaken if the bank does not know of an adjudication of incompetence. Neither death nor incompetence of a customer revokes such authority to accept, pay, collect or account until the bank knows of the fact of death or of an adjudication of incompetence and has reasonable opportunity to act on it.

(2) Even with knowledge a bank may for ten days after the date of death pay or certify checks drawn on or prior to

that date unless ordered to stop payment by a person claiming an interest in the account.

§ 4–406. CUSTOMER'S DUTY TO DISCOVER AND REPORT UNAUTHORIZED SIGNATURE OR ALTERATION.

(1) When a bank sends to its customer a statement of account accompanied by items paid in good faith in support of the debit entries or holds the statement and items pursuant to a request or instructions of its customer or otherwise in a reasonable manner makes the statement and items available to the customer, the customer must exercise reasonable care and promptness to examine the statement and items to discover his unauthorized signature or any alteration on an item and must notify the bank promptly after discovery thereof.

(2) If the bank establishes that the customer failed with respect to an item to comply with the duties imposed on the customer by subsection (1) the customer is precluded from asserting against the bank

(a) his unauthorized signature or any alteration on the item if the bank also establishes that it suffered a loss by reason of such failure; and

(b) an unauthorized signature or alteration by the same wrongdoer or any other item paid in good faith by the bank after the first item and statement was available to the customer for a reasonable period not exceeding fourteen calendar days and before the bank receives notification from the customer of any such unauthorized signature or alteration.

(3) The preclusion under subsection (2) does not apply if the customer establishes lack of ordinary care on the part of the bank in paying the item(s).

(4) Without regard to care or lack of care of either the customer or the bank a customer who does not within one year from the time the statement and items are made available to the customer (subsection (1)) discover and report his unauthorized signature or any alteration on the face or back of the item or does not within three years from that time discover and report any unauthorized indorsement is precluded from asserting against the bank such unauthorized signature or indorsement or such alteration.

(5) If under this section a payor bank has a valid defense against a claim of a customer upon or resulting from payment of an item and waives or fails upon request to assert the defense the bank may not assert against any collecting bank or other prior party presenting or transferring the item a claim based upon the unauthorized signature or alteration giving rise to the customer's claim.

§ 4–407. PAYOR BANK'S RIGHT TO SUBROGATION ON IMPROPER PAYMENT.

If payor bank has paid an item over the stop payment order of the drawer or maker or otherwise under circumstances giving a basis for objection by the drawer or maker, to prevent unjust enrichment and only to the extent necessary to prevent loss to the bank by reason of its payment of the item, the payor bank shall be subrogated to the rights

(a) of any holder in due course on the item against the drawer or maker; and

(b) of the payee or any other holder of the item against the drawer or maker either on the item or under the transaction out of which the item arose; and

(c) of the drawer or maker against the payee or any other holder of the item with respect to the transaction out of which the item arose.

PART 5
COLLECTION OF DOCUMENTARY DRAFTS

§ 4–501. HANDLING OF DOCUMENTARY DRAFTS; DUTY TO SEND FOR PRESENTMENT AND TO NOTIFY CUSTOMER OF DISHONOR.

A bank which takes a documentary draft for collection must present or send the draft and accompanying documents for presentment and upon learning that the draft has not been paid or accepted in due course must seasonably notify its customer of such fact even though it may have discounted or bought the draft or extended credit available for withdrawal as of right.

§ 4–502. PRESENTMENT OF "ON ARRIVAL" DRAFTS.

When a draft or the relevant instructions require presentment "on arrival", "when goods arrive" or the like, the collecting bank need not present until in its judgment a reasonable time for arrival of the goods has expired. Refusal to pay or accept because the goods have not arrived is not dishonor; the bank must notify its transferor of such refusal but need not present the draft again until it is instructed to do so or learns of the arrival of the goods.

§ 4–503. RESPONSIBILITY OF PRESENTING BANK FOR DOCUMENTS AND GOODS; REPORT OF REASONS FOR DISHONOR; REFEREE IN CASE OF NEED.

Unless otherwise instructed and except as provided in Article 5 a bank presenting a documentary draft

(a) must deliver the documents to the drawee on acceptance of the draft if it is payable more than three days after presentment, otherwise, only on payment; and

(b) upon dishonor, either in the case of presentment for acceptance or presentment for payment, may seek and follow instructions from any referee in case of need designated in the draft or if the presenting bank does not choose to utilize his services it must use diligence and good faith to ascertain the reason for dishonor, must notify its transferor of the dishonor and of the results of its effort to ascertain the reasons thereof and must request instructions.

But the presenting bank is under no obligation with respect to goods represented by the documents except to follow any reasonable instructions seasonably received; it has a right to reimbursement for any expense incurred in following instructions and to prepayment of or indemnity for such expenses.

§ 4–504. PRIVILEGE OF PRESENTING BANK TO DEAL WITH GOODS; SECURITY INTEREST FOR EXPENSES.

(1) A presenting bank which, following the dishonor of a documentary draft, has seasonably requested instructions but does not receive them within a reasonable time may store, sell, or otherwise deal with the goods in any reasonable manner.

Article 5
Letters of Credit
(Omitted)

Article 6
Bulk Transfers
(Omitted)

Article 7
Warehouse Receipts, Bills of Lading and Other Documents of Title
(Omitted)

Article 8
Investment Securities
(Omitted)

Article 9
Secured Transactions: Sales of Accounts and Chattel Paper

Note: The adoption of this Article should be accompanied by the repeal of existing statutes dealing with conditional sales, trust receipts, factor's liens where the factors is given a non-possessory lien, chattel mortgages, crop mortgages, mortgages on railroad equipment, assignment of accounts and general statutes regulating security interests in personal property.

Where the state has a retail installment selling act or small loan act, that legislation should be carefully examined to determine what changes in those acts are needed to conform them to this Article. This Article primarily sets out rules defining rights of a secured party against persons dealing with the debtor, it does not prescribe regulations and controls which may be necessary to curb abuses arising in the small loan business or in the financing of consumer purchases on credit. Accordingly there is no intention to repeal existing regulatory acts in those fields by enactment or re-enactment of Article 9. See Section 9-203(4) and the Note thereto.

PART I
SHORT TITLE, APPLICABILITY AND DEFINITIONS

§ 9–101. SHORT TITLE.

This Article shall be known and may be cited as Uniform Commercial Code—Secured Transactions.

§ 9–102. POLICY AND SUBJECT MATTER OF ARTICLE.

(1) Except as otherwise provided in Section 9 104 on excluded transactions, this Article applies

(a) to any transaction (regardless of its form) which is intended to create a security interest in personal property or fixtures including goods, documents, instruments, general intangibles, chattel paper or accounts; and also

(b) to any sale of accounts or chattel paper.

(2) This Article applies to security interests created by contract including pledge, assignment, chattel mortgage, chattel trust, trust deed, factor's lien, equipment trust, conditional sale, trust receipt, other lien or title retention contract and lease or consignment intended as security. This Article does not apply to statutory liens except as provided in Section 9–310.

(3) The application of this Article to a security interest in a secured obligation is not affected by the fact that the obligation is itself secured by a transaction or interest to which this Article does not apply. Amended in 1972.

§ 9–103. PERFECTION OF SECURITY INTEREST IN MULTIPLE STATE TRANSACTIONS

(1) Documents, instruments and ordinary goods.

(a) This subsection applies to documents and instruments and to goods other than those covered by a certificate of title described in subsection (2), mobile goods described in subsection (3), and minerals described in subsection (5).

(b) Except as otherwise provided in this subsection, perfection and the effect of perfection or non-perfection of a security interest in collateral are governed by the law of the jurisdiction where the collateral is when the last event occurs on which is based the assertion that the security interest is perfected or unperfected.

(c) If the parties to a transaction creating a purchase money security interest in goods in one jurisdiction understand at the time that the security interest attaches that the goods will be kept in another jurisdiction, then the law of the other jurisdiction governs the perfection and the effect of perfection or non-perfection of the security interest from the time it attaches until thirty days after the debtor receives possession of the goods and thereafter if the goods are taken to the other jurisdiction before the end of the thirty-day period.

(d) When collateral is brought into and kept in this state while subject to a security interest perfected under the law of the jurisdiction from which the collateral was removed, the security interest remains perfected, but if action is required by Part 3 of this Article to perfect the security interest,

(i) if the action is not taken before the expiration of the period of perfection in the other jurisdiction or the end of four months after the collateral is brought into this state, whichever period first expires, the security interest becomes unperfected at the end of that period and is thereafter deemed to have unperfected as against a person who became a purchaser after removal;

(ii) if the action is taken before the expiration of the period specified in subparagraph (i), the security interest continues perfected thereafter;

(iii) for the purpose of priority over a buyer of consumer goods (subsection (2) of Section 9–307), the period of the effectiveness of a filing in the jurisdiction from which the collateral is removed is governed by the rules with respect to perfection in subparagraphs (i) and (ii).

(2) Certificate of title.

(a) This subsection applies to goods covered by a certificate of title issued under a statute of this state or of another jurisdiction under the law of which indication of a security interest on the certificate is required as a condition of perfection.

(b) Except as otherwise provided in this subsection, perfection and the effect of perfection or non-perfection of the security interest are governed by the law (including the conflict of laws rules) of the jurisdiction issuing the certificate until four months after the goods are removed from that jurisdiction and thereafter until the goods are registered in another jurisdiction, but in any event not beyond surrender of the certificate. After the expiration of that period, the goods are not covered by the certificate of title within the meaning of this section.

(c) Except with respect to the rights of a buyer described in the next paragraph, a security interest, perfected in another jurisdiction otherwise than by notation on a certificate of title, in goods brought into this state and thereafter covered by a certificate of title issued by this state is subject to the rules stated in paragraph (d) of subsection (1) .

(d) If goods are brought into this state while a security interest therein is perfected in any manner under the law of jurisdiction from which the goods are removed and a certificate of title is issued by this state and the certificate does not show that the goods are subject to the security interest or that they may be subject to security interests not shown on the certificate, the security interest is subordinate to the rights of the buyer of the goods who is not in the business of selling goods of that kind to the extent that he gives value and receives delivery of the goods after issuance of the certificate and without knowledge of the security interest.

(3) Accounts. general intangibles and mobile goods.

(a) This subsection applies to accounts (other than an account described in subsection (5) on minerals) and general intangibles (other than uncertificated securities) and to goods which are mobile and which are of a type normally used in more than one jurisdiction, such as motor vehicles, trailers, rolling stock, airplanes, shipping containers, road building and construction machinery and commercial harvesting machinery and the like, if the goods are equipment or are inventory leased or held for lease by the debtor to others, and are not covered by a certificate of title described in subsection (2).

(b) The law (including the conflict of laws rules) of the jurisdiction in which the debtor is located governs the perfection and the effect of perfection or non-perfection of the security interest.

(c) If, however, the debtor is located in a jurisdiction which is not a part of the United States, and which does not provide for perfection of the security interest by filing or recording in that jurisdiction, the law of the jurisdiction in the United States in which the debtor has its major executive office in the United States governs the perfection and the effect of perfection or non-perfection of the security interest through filing. In the alternative, if the debtor is located in a jurisdiction which is not a part of the United States or Canada and the collateral is accounts or general intangibles for money due or to become due, the security interest may be perfected by notification to the account debtor. As used in this paragraph, "United States" includes its territories and possessions and the Commonwealth of Puerto Rico.

(d) A debtor shall be deemed located at his place of business if he has one, at his chief executive office if he has more than one place of business, otherwise at his residence. If, however, the debtor is a foreign air carrier under the Federal Aviation Act of 1958, as amended, it shall be deemed located at the designated office of the agent upon whom service of process may be made on behalf of the foreign air carrier.

(e) A security interest perfected under the law of the jurisdiction of the location of the debtor is perfected until the expiration of four months after a change of the debtor's location to another jurisdiction, or until perfection would have ceased by the law of the first jurisdiction, whichever period first expires. Unless perfected in the new jurisdiction before the end of that period, it becomes unperfected thereafter and is deemed to have been unperfected as against a person who became a purchaser after the change.

(4) Chattel paper.

The rules stated for goods in subsection (1) apply to a possessory security interest in chattel paper. The rules stated for accounts in subsection (3) apply to a non-possessory security interest in chattel paper, but the security interest may not be perfected by notification to the account debtor.

(5) Minerals.

Perfection and the effect of perfection or non-perfection of a security interest in which is created by a debtor who has an interest in minerals or the like (including oil and gas) before extraction and which attaches thereto as extracted, or which attaches to an account resulting from the sale thereof at the wellhead or minehead are governed by the law (including the conflict of laws rules) of the jurisdiction wherein the wellhead or minehead is located.

(6) Uncertificated securities.

The law (including the conflict of laws rules) of the jurisdiction of organization of the issuer governs the perfection and the effect of perfection or non-perfection of a security interest in uncertificated securities.

Amended in 1972 and 1977.

§ 9–104. TRANSACTIONS EXCLUDED FROM ARTICLE.

This Article does not apply

(a) to a security interest subject to any statute of the United States, to the extent that such statute governs the rights of parties to and third parties affected by transactions in particular types of property; or

(b) to the landlord's lien; or

(c) to a lien given by statute or other rule of law for services or materials except as provided in Section 9–310 on priority of such liens; or

(d) to a transfer of a claim for wages, salary or other compensation of an employee; or

(e) to a transfer by a government or governmental subdivision or agency; or

(f) to a sale of accounts or chattel paper as part of a sale of the business out of which they arose, or an assignment of accounts or chattel paper which is for the purpose of collection only, or a transfer of a right to payment under a contract to an assignee who is also to do the performance under the contract or a transfer of a single account to an assignee in whole or partial satisfaction of a preexisting indebtedness; or

(g) to a transfer of an interest in or claim in or under any policy of insurance, except as provided with respect to proceeds (Section 9–306) and priorities in proceeds (Section 9–312); or

(h) to a right represented by a judgment (other than a judgment taken on a right to payment which was collateral); or

(i) to any right of set-off; or

(j) except to the extent that provision is made for fixtures in Section 9–313, to the creation or transfer of an interest in or lien on real estate, including a lease or rents thereunder; or

(k) to a transfer in whole or in part of any claim arising out of tort; or

(l) to a transfer of an interest in any deposit account (subsection (1) of Section 9–105), except as provided with respect to proceeds (Section 9–306) and priorities in proceeds (Section 9–312).

Amended in 1972.

§ 9-105. Definitions and Index of Definitions

(1) In this Article unless the context otherwise requires:

(a) "Account debtor" means the person who is obligated on an account, chattel paper or general intangible;

(b) "Chattel paper" means a writing or writings which evidence both a monetary obligation and a security interest in or a lease of specific goods, but a charter or other contract involving the use or hire of a vessel is not chattel paper. When a transaction is evidenced both by such a security agreement or a lease and by an instrument or a series of instruments, the group of writings taken together constitutes chattel paper;

(c) "Collateral" means the property subject to a security interest, and includes accounts and chattel paper which have been sold;

(d) "Debtor" means the person who owes payment or other performance of the obligation secured, whether or not he owns or has rights in the collateral, and includes the seller of accounts or chattel paper. Where the debtor and the owner of the collateral are not the same person, the term "debtor" means the owner of the collateral in any provision of the Article dealing with the collateral, the obligor in any provision dealing with the obligation, and may include both where the context so requires;

(e) "Deposit account" means a demand, time, savings, passbook or like account maintained with a bank, savings and loan association, credit union or like organization, other than an account evidenced by a certificate of deposit;

(f) "Document" means document of title as defined in the general definitions of Article 1 (Section 1–201), and a receipt of the kind described in subsection (2) of Section 7–201;

(g) "Encumbrance" includes real estate mortgages and other liens on real estate and all other rights in real estate that are not ownership interests;

(h) "Goods" includes all things which are movable at the time the security interest attaches or which are fixtures (Section 9–313), but does not include money, documents, instruments, accounts, chattel paper, general intangibles, or minerals or the like (including oil and gas) before extraction. "Goods" also includes standing timber which is to be cut and removed under a conveyance or contract for sale, the unborn young of animals, and growing crops;

(i) "Instrument" means a negotiable instrument (defined in Section 3–104), or a certificated security (defined in Section 8–102) or any other writing which evidences a right to the payment of money and is not itself a security agreement or lease and is of a type which is in ordinary course of business transferred by delivery with any necessary indorsement or assignment;

(j) "Mortgage" means a consensual interest created by a real estate mortgage, a trust deed on real estate, or the like;

(k) An advance is made "pursuant to commitment" if the secured party has bound himself to make it, whether or not a subsequent event of default or other event not within his control has relieved or may relieve him from his obligation;

(l) "Security agreement" means an agreement which creates or provides for a security interest;

(m) "Secured party" means a lender, seller or other person in whose favor there is a security interest, including a person to whom accounts or chattel paper have been sold. When the holder of obligations issued under an indenture of trust, equipment trust agreement or the like are represented by a trustee or other person, the representative is the secured party;

(n) "Transmitting utility" means any person primarily engaged in the railroad, street railway or trolley bus business, the electric or electronics communications transmission business, the transmission of goods by pipeline, or the transmission or the production and transmission of electricity, steam, gas or water, or the provision of sewer service. (2) Other definitions apply to this Article and the sections in which they appear are:

"Account". Section 9–106.

"Attach". Section 9–203.

"Construction mortgage". Section 9–313(1).

"Consumer goods". Section 9–109(1).

"Equipment". Section 9–109(2).

"Farm products". Section 9–109(3).

"Fixture". Section 9–313(1).

"Fixture filing". Section 9–313(1).

"General intangibles". Section 9–106.

"Inventory". Section 9–109(4).

"Lien creditor". Section 9–301(3).

"Proceeds". Section 9–306(1).

"Purchase money security interest". Section 9–107.

"United States". Section 9–103.

(3) The following definitions in other Articles apply to this Article:

"Check". Section 3–104.
"Contract for sale". Section 2–106.
"Holder in due course". Section 3–302.
"Note". Section 3–104.
"Sale". Section 2–106.

(4) In addition Article 1 contains general definitions and principles of construction and interpretation applicable throughout this Article.

Amended in 1966, 1972 and 1977.

§ 9–106. DEFINITIONS: "ACCOUNT"; "GENERAL INTANGIBLES".

"Account" means any right to payment for goods sold or leased or for services rendered which is not evidenced by an instrument or chattel paper, whether or not it has been earned by performance. "General intangibles" means any personal property (including things in action) other than goods, accounts, chattel paper, documents, instruments, and money. All rights to payment earned or unearned under a charter or other contract involving the use or hire of a vessel and all rights incident to the charter or contract are accounts. Amended in 1966, 1972.

§ 9–107. DEFINITIONS: "PURCHASE MONEY SECURITY INTEREST".

A security interest is a "purchase money security interest" to the extent that it is

(a) taken or retained by the seller of the collateral to secure all or part of its price; or

(b) taken by a person who by making advances or incurring an obligation gives value to enable the debtor to acquire rights in or the use of collateral if such value is in fact so used .

§ 9–108. WHEN AFTER-ACQUIRED COLLATERAL NOT SECURITY FOR ANTECEDENT DEBT.

Where a secured party makes an advance, incurs an obligation, releases a perfected security interest, or otherwise gives new value which is to be secured in whole or in part by after-acquired property his security interest in the after-acquired collateral shall be deemed to be taken for new value and not as security for an antecedent debt if the debtor acquires his rights in such collateral either in the ordinary course of his business or under a contract of purchase made pursuant to the security agreement within a reasonable time after new value is given.

§ 9–109. CLASSIFICATION OF GOODS; "CONSUMER GOODS", "EQUIPMENT", "FARM PRODUCTS"; "INVENTORY".

Goods are

(1) "consumer goods" if they are used or bought for use primarily for personal, family or household purposes;

(2) "equipment" if they are used or bought for use primarily in business (including farming or a profession) or by a debtor who is a non-profit organization or a governmental subdivision or agency or if the goods are not included in the definitions of inventory, farm products or consumer goods;

(3) "farm products" if they are crops or livestock or supplies used or produced in farming operations or if they are products of crops or livestock in their unmanufactured states (such as ginned cotton, woolclip, maple syrup, milk and eggs), and if they are in the possession of a debtor engaged in raising, fattening, grazing or other farming operations. If goods are farm products they are neither equipment nor inventory;

(4) "inventory" if they are held by a person who holds them for sale or lease or to be furnished under contracts of service or if he has so furnished them, or if they are raw materials, work in process or materials used or consumed in a business. Inventory of a person is not to be classified as his equipment.

§ 9–110. SUFFICIENCY OF DESCRIPTION.

For purposes of this Article any description of personal property or real estate is sufficient whether or not it is specific if it reasonably identifies what is described.

§ 9–111. APPLICABILITY OF BULK TRANSFER LAWS.

The creation of a security interest is not a bulk transfer under Article 6 (see Section 6–103).

§ 9–112. WHERE COLLATERAL IS NOT OWNED BY DEBTOR.

Unless otherwise agreed, when a secured party knows that collateral is owned by a person who is not the debtor, the owner of the collateral is entitled to receive from the secured party any surplus under Section 9–502(2) or under Section 9–504(1), and is not liable for the debt or for any deficiency after resale, and he has the same right as the debtor

(a) to receive statements under Section 9–208;

(b) to receive notice of and to object to a secured party's proposal to retain the collateral in satisfaction of the indebtedness under Section 9–505;

(c) to redeem the collateral under Section 9– 506;

(d) to obtain injunctive or other relief under Section 9–507(1); and

(e) to recover losses caused to him under Section 9–208(2).

§ 9–113. SECURITY INTERESTS ARISING UNDER ARTICLE ON SALES.

A security interest arising solely under the Article on Sales (Article 2) is subject to the provisions of this Article except that to the extent that and so long as the debtor does not have or does not lawfully obtain possession of the goods

(a) no security agreement is necessary to make the security interest enforceable; and

(b) no filing is required to perfect the security interest; and

(c) the rights of the secured party on default by the debtor are governed by the Article on Sales (Article 2).

§ 9–114. CONSIGNMENT.

(1) A person who delivers goods under a consignment which is not a security interest and who would be required to file under this Article by paragraph (3)(c) of Section 2–326 has priority over a secured party who is or becomes a creditor of the consignee and who would have a perfected security interest in the goods if they were the property of the consignee, and also has priority with respect to identifiable cash proceeds received on or before delivery of the goods to a buyer, if

(a) the consignor complies with the filing provision of the Article on Sales with respect to consignments (paragraph (3)(c) of Section 2–326) before the consignee receives possession of the goods; and

(b) the consignor gives notification in writing to the holder of the security interest if the holder has filed a financing statement covering the same types of goods before the date of the filing made by the consignor; and

(c) the holder of the security interest receives the notification within five years before the consignee receives possession of the goods; and

(d) the notification states that the consignor expects to deliver goods on consignment to the consignee, describing the goods by item or type.

(2) In the case of a consignment which is not a security interest an in which the requirements of the preceding subsection have not been met, a person who delivers goods to another is subordinate to a person who would have a perfected security interest in the goods if they were the property of the debtor.

Added in 1972.

PART 2
VALIDITY OF SECURITY AGREEMENT AND RIGHTS OF PARTIES THERETO

§ 9–201. GENERAL VALIDITY OF SECURITY AGREEMENT.

Except as otherwise provided by this Act a security agreement is effective according to its terms between the parties, against purchasers of the collateral and against creditors. Nothing in this Article validates any charge or practice illegal under any statute or regulation thereun-

der governing usury, small loans, retail installment sales, or the like, or extends the application of any such statute or regulation to any transaction not otherwise subject thereto.

§ 9–202. TITLE TO COLLATERAL IMMATERIAL.

Each provision of this Article with regard to rights, obligations and remedies applies whether title to collateral is in the secured party or in the debtor.

§ 9–203. ATTACHMENT AND ENFORCEABILITY OF SECURITY INTEREST; PROCEEDS; FORMAL REQUISITES

(1) Subject to the provisions of Section 4–208 on the security interest of a collecting bank, Section 8–321 on security interests in securities and Section 9–113 on a security interest arising under the Article on Sales, a security interest is not enforceable against the debtor or third parties with respect to the collateral and does not attach unless:

(a) the collateral is in the possession of the secured party pursuant to agreement, or the debtor has signed a security agreement which contains a description of the collateral and in addition, when the security interest covers crops growing or to be grown or timber to be cut, a description of the land concerned;

(b) value has been given; and

(c) the debtor has rights in the collateral

(2) A security interest attaches when it becomes enforceable against the debtor with respect to the collateral. Attachment occurs as soon as all of the events specified in subsection (1) have taken place unless explicit agreement postpones the time of attaching.

(3) Unless otherwise agreed a security agreement gives the secured party the rights to proceeds provided by Section 9–306.

(4) A transaction, although subject to this Article, is also subject to . . . *, and in the case of conflict between the provisions of this Article and any such statute, the provisions of such statute control. Failure to comply with any applicable statute has only the effect which is specified therein.

Amended in 1972 and 1977.

Note: At * in subsection (4) insert reference to any local statute regarding small loans, retain installment sales and the like.

The foregoing subsection (4) is designed to make it clear that certain transactions, although subject to this Article, must also comply with other applicable legislation.

This Article is designed to regulate all the "security" aspects of transactions within its scope. There is, however, must regulatory legislation, particularly in the consumer field, which supplements this Article and should not be repealed by its enactment. Examples are small loan acts, retail installment selling acts and the like. Such acts may provide for licensing and rate regulation and may prescribe particular forms of contract. Such provisions should remain in force despite the enactment of this Article. On the other hand if a retail installment selling act contains provisions on filing, rights on default, etc., such provisions should be repealed as inconsistent with this Article except that inconsistent provisions as to deficiencies, penalties, etc., in the Uniform Consumer Credit Code and other recent related legislation should remain because those statutes were drafted after the substantial enactment of the Article and with the intention of modifying certain provisions of this Article as to consumer credit.

§ 9–204. After-Acquired Property; Future Advances.

(1) Except as provided in subsection (2), a security agreement may provide that any or all obligations covered by the security agreement are to be secured by after-acquired collateral .

(2) No security interest attaches under an after-acquired property clause to consumer goods other than accessions (Section 9–314) when given as additional security unless the debtor acquires rights in them within ten days after the secured party gives value.

(3) Obligations covered by a security agreement may include future advances or other value whether or not the advances or value are given pursuant to commitment (subsection (1) of Section 9–105).

Amended in 1972.

§ 9–205. Use of Disposition of Collateral Without Accounting Permissible.

A security interest is not invalid or fraudulent against creditors by reason of liberty in the debtor to use, commingle or dispose of all or part of the collateral (including returned or repossessed goods) or to collect or compromise accounts or chattel paper, or to accept the return of goods or make repossessions, or to use, commingle or dispose of proceeds, or by reason of the failure of the secured party to require the debtor to account for proceeds or replace collateral. This section does not relax the requirements of possession where perfection of a security interest depends upon possession of the collateral by the secured party or by a bailee.

Amended in 1972.

§ 9–206. Agreement Not to Assert Defenses Against Assignee; Modification of Sales Warranties Where Security Agreement Exists.

(1) Subject to any statute or decision which establishes a different rule for buyers or lessees of consumer goods, an agreement by a buyer or lessee that he will not assert against an assignee any claim or defense which he may have against the seller or lessor is enforceable by an assignee who takes his assignment for value, in good faith and without notice of a claim or defense, except as to defenses of a type which may be asserted against a holder in due course of a negotiable instrument under the Article on Commercial Paper (Article 3). A buyer who as part of one transaction signs both a negotiable instrument and a security agreement makes such an agreement.

(2) When a seller retains a purchase money security interest in goods in the Article on Sales (Article 2) governs the sale and any disclaimer, limitation or modification of the seller's warranties.

Amended in 1962.

§ 9–207. Rights and Duties When Collateral is in Secured Party's Possession.

(1) A secured party must use reasonable care in the custody and preservation of collateral in his possession. In the case of an instrument or chattel paper reasonable care includes taking necessary steps to preserve rights against prior parties unless otherwise agreed.

(2) Unless otherwise agreed, when collateral is in the secured party's possession

(a) reasonable expenses (including the cost of any insurance and payment of taxes or other charges) incurred in the custody, preservation, use or operation of the collateral are chargeable to the debtor and are secured by the collateral;

(b) the risk of accidental loss or damage is on the debtor to the extent of any deficiency in any effective insurance coverage;

(c) the secured party may hold as additional security any increase or profits (except money) received from the collateral, but money so received, unless remitted to the debtor, shall be applied in reduction of the secured obligation;

(d) the secured party must keep the collateral identifiable but fungible collateral may be commingled;

(e) the secured party may repledge the collateral upon terms which do not impair the debtor's right to redeem it.

(3) A secured party is liable for any loss caused by his failure to meet any obligation imposed by the preceding subsections but does not lose his security interest.

(4) A secured party must use or operate the collateral for the purpose of preserving the collateral or its value or pursuant to the order of a court of appropriate jurisdiction or, except in the case of consumer goods, in the manner and to the extent provided in the security agreement.

§ 9–208. Request for Statement of Account or List of Collateral.

(1) A debtor may sign a statement indicating what he believes to be the aggregate amount of unpaid indebted-

ness as of a specified date and may send it to the secured party with a request that the statement be approved or corrected and returned to the debtor. When the security agreement or any other record kept by the secured party identifies the collateral a debtor may similarly request the secured party to approve or correct a list of the collateral.

(2) The secured party must comply with such a request within two weeks after receipt by sending a written correction or approval. If the secured party claims a security interest in all of a particular type of collateral owned by the debtor he may indicate that fact in his reply and need not approve or correct an itemized list of such collateral. If the secured party without reasonable excuse fails to comply he is liable for any loss caused to the debtor thereby; and if the debtor has properly included in his request a good faith statement of the obligation or a list of the collateral or both the secured party may claim a security interest only as shown in the statement against persons misled by his failure to comply. If he no longer has an interest in the obligation or collateral at the time the request is received he must disclose the name and address of any successor in interest known to him and he is liable for any loss caused to the debtor as a result of failure to disclose. A successor in interest is not subject to this section until a request is received by him.

(3) A debtor is entitled to such a statement once every six months without charge. The secured party may require payment of a charge not exceeding $10 for each additional statement furnished.

PART 3
RIGHTS OF THIRD PARTIES; PERFECTED AND UNPERFECTED SECURITY INTERESTS; RULES OF PRIORITY

§ 9–301. PERSONS WHO TAKE PRIORITY OVER UNPERFECTED SECURITY INTERESTS; RIGHTS OF "LIEN CREDITOR".

(1) Except as otherwise provided in subsection (2), an unperfected security interest is subordinate to the rights of

(a) persons entitled to priority under Section 9–312;

(b) a person who becomes a lien creditor before the security interest is perfected;

(c) in the case of goods, instruments, documents, and chattel paper, a person who is not a secured party and who is a transferee in bulk or other buyer not in ordinary course of business or is a buyer of farm products in ordinary course of business, to the extent that he gives value and receives delivery of the collateral without knowledge of the security interest and before it is perfected;

(d) in the case of accounts and general intangibles, a person who is not a secured party and who is a trans-

feree to the extent that he gives value without knowledge of the security interest and before it is perfected.

(2) If the secured party files with respect to a purchase money security interest before or within ten days after the debtor receives possession of the collateral, he takes priority over the rights of a transferee in bulk or of a lien creditor which arise between the time the security interest attaches and the time of filing.

(3) A "lien creditor" means a creditor who has acquired a lien on the property involved by attachment, levy or the like and includes an assignee for benefit of creditors from the time of assignment, and a trustee in bankruptcy from the date of filing of the petition or a receiver in equity from the time of appointment.

(4) A person who becomes a lien creditor while a security interest is perfected takes subject to the security interest only to the extent that it secures advances made before he becomes a lien creditor or within 45 days thereafter or made without knowledge of the lien or pursuant to a commitment entered into without knowledge of the lien.

Amended in 1972.

§ 9–302. WHEN FILING IS REQUIRED TO PERFECT SECURITY INTEREST; SECURITY INTERESTS TO WHICH FILING PROVISIONS OF THIS ARTICLE DO NOT APPLY.

(1) A financing statement must be filed to perfect all security interests except the following:

(a) a security interest in collateral in possession of the secured party under Section 9–305;

(b) a security interest temporarily perfected in instruments or documents without delivery under Section 9–304 or in proceeds for a 10 day period under Section 9–306;

(c) a security interest created by an assignment of a beneficial interest in a trust or a decedent's estate;

(d) a purchase money security interest in consumer goods; but filing is required for a motor vehicle required to be registered; and fixture filing is required for priority over conflicting interests in fixtures to the extent provided in Section 9–313;

(e) an assignment of accounts which does not alone or in conjunction with other assignments to the same assignee transfer a significant part of the outstanding accounts of the assignor;

(f) a security interest of a collecting bank (Section 4–208) or in securities (Section 8–321) or arising under the Article on Sales (see Section 9–113) or covered in subsection (3) of this section;

(g) an assignment for the benefit of all the creditors of the transferor, and subsequent transfers by the assignee thereunder.

(2) If a secured party assigns a perfected security interest, no filing under this Article is required in order to con-

tinue the perfected status of the security interest against creditors of and transferees from the original debtor.

(3) The filing of a financing statement otherwise required by this Article is not necessary or effective to perfect a security interest in property subject to

(a) a statute or treaty of the United States which provides for a national or international registration or a national or international certificate of title or which specifies a place of filing different from that specified in this Article for filing of the security interest; or

(b) the following statutes of this state; [list any certificate of title statute covering automobiles, trailers, mobile homes, boats, farm tractors, or the like, and any central filing statute.]; but during any period in which collateral is inventory held for sale by a person who is in the business of selling goods of that kind, the filing provisions of this Article (Part 4) apply to a security interest in that collateral created by him as debtor; or

(c) a certificate of title statute of another jurisdiction under the law of which indication of a security interest on the certificate is required as a condition of perfection (subsection (2) of Section 9–103).

(4) Compliance with a statute or treaty described in subsection (3) is equivalent to the filing of a financing statement under this Article, and a security interest in property subject to the statute or treaty can be perfected only by compliance therewith except as provided in Section 9–103 on multiple state transactions. Duration and renewal of perfection of a security interest perfected by compliance with the statute or treaty are governed by the provisions of the statute or treaty; in other respects the security interest is subject to this Article.

Amended in 1972 and 1977.

§ 9–303. WHEN SECURITY INTEREST IS PERFECTED; CONTINUITY OF PERFECTION.

(1) A security interest is perfected when it has attached and when all of the applicable steps required for perfection have been taken. Such steps are specified in Sections 9–302, 9–304, 9–305, and 9–306. If such steps are taken before the security interest attaches, it is perfected at the time when it attaches.

(2) If a security interest is originally perfected in any way permitted under this Article and is subsequently perfected in some other way under this Article, without an intermediate period when it was unperfected, the security interest shall be deemed to be perfected continuously for the purposes of this Article.

§ 9–304. PERFECTION OF SECURITY INTEREST IN INSTRUMENTS, DOCUMENTS, AND GOODS COVERED BY DOCUMENTS; PERFECTION BY PERMISSIVE FILING; TEMPORARY PERFECTION WITHOUT FILING OR TRANSFER OF POSSESSION

(1) A security interest in chattel paper or negotiable documents may be perfected by filing. A security interest in money or instruments (other than certificated securities or instruments which constitute part of chattel paper) can be perfected only by the secured party's taking possession, except as provided in subsections (4) and (5) of this section and subsections (2) and (3) of Section 9–306 on proceeds.

(2) During the period that goods are in the possession of the issuer of a negotiable document thereof, a security interest in the goods is perfected by perfecting a security interest in the document, and any security interest in the goods otherwise perfected during such period is subject thereto.

(3) A security interest in goods in the possession of a bailee other than one who has issued a negotiable document therefor is perfected by issuance of a document in the name of the secured party or by the bailee's receipt of notification of the secured party's interest or by filing as to the goods.

(4) A security interest in instruments (other than certificated securities) or negotiable documents is perfected without filing or the taking of possession for a period of 21 days from the time it attaches to the extent that it arises for new value given under a written security agreement.

(5) A security interest remains perfected for a period of 21 days without filing where a secured party having a perfected security interest in an instrument (other than a certificated security), a negotiable document or goods in possession of a bailee other than one who has issued a negotiable document therefor

(a) makes available to the debtor the goods or documents representing the goods for the purpose of ultimate sale or exchange or for the purpose of loading, unloading, storing, shipping, transshipping, manufacturing, processing or otherwise dealing with them in a manner preliminary to their sale or exchange, but priority between conflicting security interests in the goods is subject to subsection (3) of Section 9–312; or

(b) delivers the instrument to the debtor for the purpose of ultimate sale or exchange of presentation, collection, renewal or registration of transfer.

(6) After the 21 day period in subsections (4) and (5) perfection depends upon compliance with applicable provisions of this Article.

Amended in 1972 and 1977.

§ 9–305. When Possession by Secured Party Perfects Security Interest Without Filing

A security interest in letters of credit and advices of credit (subsection (2)(a) of Section 5–116), goods, instruments (other than certificated securities), money, negotiable documents, or chattel paper may be perfected by the secured party's taking possession of the collateral. If such collateral other than goods covered by a negotiable document is held by a bailee, the secured party is deemed to have possession from the time the bailee receives notification of the secured party's interest. A security interest is perfected by possession from the time possession is taken without a relation back and continues only so long as possession is retained, unless otherwise specified in this Article. The security interest may be otherwise perfected as provided in this Article before or after the period of possession by the secured party.

Amended in 1972 and 1977.

§ 9–306. "Proceeds"; Secured Party's Rights on Disposition of Collateral.

(1) "Proceeds" includes whatever is received upon the sale, exchange, collection or other disposition of collateral or proceeds. Insurance payable by reason of loss or damage to the collateral is proceeds, except to the extent that it is payable to a person other than a party to the security agreement. Money, checks, deposit accounts, and the like are "cash proceeds". All other proceeds are "non-cash proceeds".

(2) Except where this Article otherwise provides, a security interest continues in collateral notwithstanding sale, exchange or other disposition thereof unless the disposition was authorized by the secured party in the security agreement or otherwise, and also continues in any identifiable proceeds including collections received by the debtor.

(3) The security interest in proceeds is a continuously perfected security interest if the interest in the original collateral was perfected but it ceases to be a perfected security interest and becomes unperfected ten days after receipt of the proceeds by the debtor unless

(a) a filed financing statement covers the original collateral and the proceeds are collateral in which a security interest may be perfected by filing in the office or offices where the financing statement has been filed and, if the proceeds are acquired with cash proceeds, the description of collateral in the financing statement indicates the types of property constituting the proceeds; or

(b) a filed financing statement covers the original collateral and the proceeds are identifiable cash proceeds; or

(c) the security interest in the proceeds is perfected before the expiration of the ten day period.

Except as provided in this section, a security interest in proceeds can be perfected only by the methods or under the circumstances permitted in this Article for original collateral of the same type.

(4) In the event of insolvency proceedings instituted by or against a debtor, a secured party with a perfected security interest in proceeds has a perfected security interest only in the following proceeds:

(a) in identifiable non-cash proceeds and in separate deposit accounts containing only proceeds;

(b) in identifiable cash proceeds in the form of money which is neither commingled with other money nor deposited in a deposit account prior to the insolvency proceedings;

(c) in identifiable cash proceeds in the form of checks and the like which are not deposited in a deposit account prior to the insolvency proceedings; and

(d) in all cash and deposit accounts of the debtor in which proceeds have been commingled with other funds, but the perfected security interest under this paragraph (d) is

(i) subject to any right to set-off; and

(ii) limited to an amount not greater than the amount of any cash proceeds received by the debtor within ten days before the institution of the insolvency proceedings less the sum of (1) the payments to the secured party on account of cash proceeds received by the debtor during such period and (2) the cash proceeds received by the debtor during such period to which the secured party is entitled under paragraphs (a) through (c) of this subsection (4).

(5) If a sale of goods results in an account or chattel paper which is transferred by the seller to the secured party, and if the goods are returned to or are repossessed by the seller or the secured party, the following rules determine priorities:

(a) If the goods were collateral at the time of sale, for an indebtedness of the seller which is still unpaid, the original security interest attaches again to the goods and continues as a perfected security interest if it was perfected at the time when the goods were sold. If the security interest was originally perfected by a filing which is still effective, nothing further is required to continue the perfected status; in any other case, the secured party must take possession of the returned or repossessed goods or must file.

(b) An unpaid transferee of the chattel paper has a security interest in the goods against the transferor. Such security interest is prior to a security interest asserted under paragraph (a) to the extent that the transferee of the chattel paper was entitled to priority under Section 9–308.

(c) An unpaid transferee of the account has a security interest in the goods against the transferor. Such security interest is subordinate to a security interest asserted under paragraph (a).

(d) A security interest of an unpaid transferee asserted under paragraph (b) or (c) must be perfected for protection against creditors of the transferor and purchasers of the returned or repossessed goods.

Amended in 1972.

§ 9–307. PROTECTION OF BUYERS OF GOODS.

(1) A buyer in ordinary course of business (subsection (9) of Section 1–201) other than a person buying farm products from a person engaged in farming operations takes free of a security interest created by his seller even though the security interest is perfected and even though the buyer knows of its existence.

(2) In the case of consumer goods, a buyer takes free of a security interest even though perfected if he buys without knowledge of the security interest, for value and for his own personal, family or household purposes unless prior to the purchase the secured party has filed a financing statement covering such goods.

(3) A buyer other than a buyer in ordinary course of business (subsection (1) of this section) takes free of a security interest to the extent that it secures future advances made after the secured party acquires knowledge of the purchase, or more than 45 days after the purchase, whichever first occurs, unless made pursuant to a commitment entered into without knowledge of the purchase and before the expiration of the 45 day period. Amended in 1972.

§ 9–308. PURCHASE OF CHATTEL PAPER AND INSTRUMENTS.

A purchaser of chattel paper or an instrument who gives new value and takes possession of it in the ordinary course of his business has priority over a security interest in the chattel paper or instrument

(a) which is perfected under Section 9–304 (permissive filing and temporary perfection) or under Section 9–306 (perfection as to proceeds) if he acts without knowledge that the specific paper or instrument is subject to a security interest; or

(b) which is claimed merely as proceeds of inventory subject to a security interest (Section 9–306) even though he knows that the specific paper or instrument is subject to the security interest.

Amended in 1972.

§ 9–309. PROTECTION OF PURCHASERS OF INSTRUMENTS, DOCUMENTS AND SECURITIES

Nothing in this Article limits the rights of a holder in due course of a negotiable instrument (Section 3–302) or a holder to whom a negotiable document of title has been duly negotiated (Section 7–501) or a bona fide purchaser of a security (Section 8–302) and the holders or purchasers take priority over an earlier security interest even though perfected. Filing under this Article does not constitute notice of the security interest to such holders or purchasers.

Amended in 1977.

§ 9–310. PRIORITY OF CERTAIN LIENS ARISING BY OPERATION OF LAW.

When a person in the ordinary course of his business furnishes services or materials with respect to goods subject to a security interest, a lien upon goods in the possession of such person given by statute or rule of law for such materials or services takes priority over a perfected security interest unless the lien is statutory and the statute expressly provides otherwise.

§ 9–311. ALIENABILITY OF DEBTOR'S RIGHTS: JUDICIAL PROCESS.

The debtor's rights in collateral may be voluntarily or involuntarily transferred (by way of sale, creation of a security interest, attachment, levy, garnishment or other judicial process) notwithstanding a provision in the security agreement prohibiting any transfer or making the transfer constitute a default.

§ 9–312. PRIORITIES AMONG CONFLICTING SECURITY INTERESTS IN THE SAME COLLATERAL

(1) The rules of priority stated in other sections of this Part and in the following sections shall govern when applicable: Section 4–208 with respect to the security interests of collecting banks in items being collected, accompanying documents and proceeds; Section 9–103 on security interests related to other jurisdictions; Section 9-114 on consignments.

(2) A perfected security interest in crops for new value given to enable the debtor to produce the crops during the production season and given not more than three months before the crops become growing crops by planting or otherwise takes priority over an earlier perfected security interest to the extent that such earlier interest secures obligations due more than six months before the crops become growing crops by planting or otherwise, even though the person giving new value had knowledge of the earlier security interest.

(3) A perfected purchase money security interest in inventory has priority over a conflicting security interest in the same inventory and also has priority in identifiable cash proceeds received on or before the delivery of the inventory to a buyer if

(a) the purchase money security interest is perfected at the time the debtor receives possession of the inventory; and

(b) the purchase money secured party gives notification in writing to the holder of the conflicting security interest if the holder had filed a financing statement covering the same types of inventory (i) before the date of the filing made by the purchase money secured party, or (ii) before the beginning of the 21 day period where the purchase money security interest is temporarily perfected without filing or possession (subsection (5) of Section 9–304); and

(c) the holder of the conflicting security interest receives the notification within five years before the debtor receives possession of the inventory; and

(d) the notification states that the person giving the notice has or expects to acquire a purchase money security interest in inventory of the debtor, describing such inventory by item or type.

(4) A purchase money security interest in collateral other than inventory has priority over a conflicting security interest in the same collateral or its proceeds if the purchase money security interest is perfected at the time the debtor receives possession of the collateral or within ten days thereafter.

(5) In all cases not governed by other rules stated in this section (including cases of purchase money security interests which do not qualify for the special priorities set forth in subsections (3) and (4) of this section), priority between conflicting security interests in the same collateral shall be determined according to the following rules:

(a) Conflicting security interests rank according to priority in time of filing or perfection. Priority dates from the time a filing is first made covering the collateral or the time the security interest is first perfected, whichever is earlier, provided that there is no period thereafter when there is neither filing nor perfection.

(b) So long as conflicting security interests are unperfected, the first to attach has priority.

(6) For the purposes of subsection (5) a date of filing or perfection as to collateral is also a date of filing or perfection as to proceeds.

(7) If future advances are made while a security interest is perfected by filing, the taking of possession, or under Section 8–321 on securities, the security interest has the same priority for the purposes of subsection (5) with respect to the future advances as it does with respect to the first advance. If a commitment is made before or while the security interest is so perfected, the security interest has the same priority with respect to advances made pursuant thereto. In other cases a perfected security interest has priority from the date the advance is made.

Amended in 1972 and 1977.

§ 9–313. Priority of Security Interests in Fixtures.

(1) In this section and in the provisions of Part 4 of this Article referring to fixture filing, unless the context otherwise requires

(a) goods are "fixtures" when they become so related to particular real estate that an interest in them arises under real estate law

(b) a "fixture filing" is the filing in the office where a mortgage on the real estate would be filed or recorded of a financing statement covering goods which are or are to become fixtures and conforming to the requirements of subsection (5) of Section 9–402

(c) a mortgage is a "construction mortgage" to the extent that it secures an obligation incurred for the construction of an improvement on land including the acquisition cost of the land, if the recorded writing also indicates.

(2) A security interest under this Article may be created in goods which are fixtures or may continue in goods which become fixtures, but no security interest exists under this Article in ordinary building materials incorporated into an improvement on land.

(3) This Article does not prevent creation of an encumbrance upon fixtures pursuant to real estate law.

(4) A perfected security interest in fixtures has priority over the conflicting interest of an encumbrancer or owner of the real estate where

(a) the security interest is a purchase money security interest, the interest of the encumbrancer or owner arises before the goods become fixtures, the security interest is perfected by a fixture filing before the goods become fixtures or within ten days thereafter, and the debtor has an interest of record in the real estate or is in possession of the real estate; or

(b) the security interest is perfected by a fixture filing before the interest of the encumbrancer or owner is of record, the security interest has priority over any conflicting interest of a predecessor in title of the encumbrancer or owner, and the debtor has an interest of record in the real estate or is in possession of the real estate; or

(c) the fixtures are readily removable factory or office machines or readily removable replacements of domestic appliances which are consumer goods, and before the goods become fixtures the security interest is perfected by any method permitted by this Article; or

(d) the conflicting interest is a lien on the real estate obtained by legal or equitable proceedings after the security interest was perfected by any method permitted by this Article.

(5) A security interest in fixtures, whether or not perfected, has priority over the conflicting interest of an encumbrancer or owner of the real estate where

(a) the encumbrancer or owner has consented in writing to the security interest or has disclaimed an interest in the goods as fixtures; or

(b) the debtor has a right to remove the goods as against the encumbrancer or owner. If the debtor's right terminates, the priority of the security interest continues for a reasonable time.

(6) Notwithstanding paragraph (a) of subsection (4) but otherwise subject to subsections (4) and (5), a security interest in fixtures is subordinate to a construction mortgage recorded before the goods become fixtures if the goods become fixtures before the completion of the construction. To the extent that it is given to refinance a construction mortgage, a mortgage has this priority to the same extent as the construction mortgage.

(7) In cases not within the preceding subsections, a security interest in fixtures is subordinate to the conflicting interest of an encumbrancer or owner of the related real estate who is not the debtor.

(8) When the secured party has priority over all owners and encumbrancers of the real estate, he may, on default, subject to the provisions of Part 5, remove his collateral from the real estate but he must reimburse any encumbrancer or owner of the real estate who is not the debtor and who has not otherwise agreed for the cost of repair of any physical injury, but not for any diminution in value of the real estate caused by the absence of the goods removed or by any necessity of replacing them. A person entitled to reimbursement may refuse permission to remove until the secured party gives adequate security for the performance of this obligation. Amended in 1972.

§ 9–314. ACCESSIONS.

(1) A security interest in goods which attaches before they are installed in or affixed to other goods takes priority as to the goods installed or affixed (called in this section "accessions") over the claims of all persons to the whole except as stated in subsection (3) and subject to Section 9–315(1).

(2) A security interest which attaches to goods after they become part of a whole is valid against all persons subsequently acquiring interests in the whole except as stated in subsection (3) but is invalid against any person with an interest in the whole at the time the security interest attaches to the goods who has not in writing consented to the security interest or disclaimed an interest in the goods as part of the whole.

(3) The security interests described in subsections (1) and (2) do not take priority over

(a) a subsequent purchaser for value of any interest in the whole; or

(b) a creditor with a lien on the whole subsequently obtained by judicial proceedings; or

(c) a creditor with a prior perfected security interest in the whole to the extent that he makes subsequent advances if the subsequent purchase is made, the lien by judicial proceedings obtained or the subsequent advance under the prior perfected security interest is made or contracted for without knowledge of the security interest and before it is perfected. A purchaser of the whole at a foreclosure sale other than the holder of a perfected security interest purchasing at his own foreclosure sale is a subsequent purchaser within this section.

(4) When under subsections (1) or (2) and (3) a secured party has an interest in accessions which has priority over the claims of all persons who have interests in the whole, he may on default subject to the provisions of Part 5 remove his collateral from the whole but he must reimburse any encumbrancer or owner of the whole who is not the debtor and who has not otherwise agreed for the cost of repair of any physical injury but not for any diminution in value of the whole caused by the absence of the goods removed or by any necessity for replacing them. A person entitled to reimbursement may refuse permission to remove until the secured party gives adequate security for the performance of this obligation.

§ 9–315. PRIORITY WHEN GOODS ARE COMMINGLED OR PROCESSED.

(1) If a security interest in goods was perfected and subsequently the goods or a part thereof have become part of a product or mass, the security interest continues in the product or mass if

(a) the goods are so manufactured, processed, assembled or commingled that their identity is lost in the product or mass; or

(b) a financing statement covering the original goods also covers the product into which the goods have been manufactured, processed or assembled.

In a case to which paragraph (b) applies, no separate security interest in that part of the original goods which has been manufactured, processed or assembled into the product may be claimed under Section 9-314.

(2) When under subsection (1) more than one security interest attaches to the product or mass, they rank equally according to the ratio that the cost of goods to which each interest originally attached bears to the cost of the total product or mass.

§ 9–316. PRIORITY SUBJECT TO SUBORDINATION.

Nothing in this Article prevents subordination by agreement by any person entitled to priority.

§ 9–317. SECURED PARTY NOT OBLIGATED ON CONTRACT OF DEBTOR.

The mere existence of a security interest or authority given to the debtor to dispose of or use collateral does not impose contract or tort liability upon the secured party for the debtor's acts or omissions.

§ 9–318. DEFENSES AGAINST ASSIGNEE; MODIFICATION OF CONTRACT AFTER NOTIFICATION OF ASSIGNMENT; TERM PROHIBITING ASSIGNMENT INEFFECTIVE; IDENTIFICATION AND PROOF OF ASSIGNMENT.

(1) Unless an account debtor has made an enforceable agreement not to assert defenses or claims arising out of a sale as provided in Section 9–206 the rights of an assignee are subject to

(a) all the terms of the contract between the account debtor and assignor and any defense or claim arising therefrom; and

(b) any other defense or claim of the account debtor against the assignor which accrues before the account debtor receives notification of the assignment.

(2) So far as the right to payment or a part thereof under an assigned contract has not been fully earned by performance, and notwithstanding notification of the assignment, any modification of or substitution for the contract made in good faith and in accordance with reasonable commercial standards is effective against an assignee unless the account debtor has otherwise agreed but the assignee acquires corresponding rights under the modified or substituted contract. The assignment may provide that such modification or substitution is a breach by the assignor.

(3) The account debtor is authorized to pay the assignor until the account debtor receives notification that the amount due or to become due has been assigned and that payment is to be made to the assignee. A notification which does not reasonably identify the rights assigned is ineffective. If requested by the account debtor, the assignee must seasonably furnish reasonable proof that the assignment has been made and unless he does so the account debtor may pay the assignor.

(4) A term in any contract between an account debtor and an assignor is ineffective if it prohibits assignment of an account or prohibits creation of a security interest in a general intangible for money due or to become due or requires the account debtor's consent to such assignment or security interest.

Amended in 1972.

PART 4
FILING

§ 9–401. PLACE OF FILING; ERRONEOUS FILING; REMOVAL OF COLLATERAL.

First Alternative Subsection (1)

(1) The proper place to file in order to perfect a security interest is as follows:

(a) when the collateral is timber to be cut or is minerals or the like (including oil and gas) or accounts subject to subsection (5) of Section 9–103, or when the financing statement is filed as a fixture filing (Section 9–313) and the collateral is good which are or are to become fixtures, then in the office where a mortgage on the real estate would be filed or recorded;

(b) in all other cases, in the office of the [Secretary of State].

Second Alternative Subsection (1)

(1) The proper place to file in order to perfect a security interest is as follows:

(a) when the collateral is equipment used in farming operations, or farm products, or accounts or general intangibles arising from or relating to the sale of farm products by a farmer, or consumer goods, then in the office of the . . . in the county of the debtor's residence or if the debtor is not a resident of this state then in the office of the . . . in the county where the goods are kept, in addition when the collateral is crops growing or to be grown in the office of the . . . in the county where the land is located;

(b) when the collateral is timber to be cut or is minerals or the like (including oil and gas) or accounts subject to subsection (5) of Section 9–103, or when the financing statement is filed as a fixture filing (Section 9–313) and the collateral is goods which are or are to become fixtures, then in the office where a mortgage on the real estate would be filed or recorded;

(c) in all other cases, in the office of the [Secretary of State].

Third Alternative Subsection (1)

(1) The proper place to file in order to perfect a security interest is as follows:

(a) when the collateral is equipment used in farming operations, or farm products, or accounts or general intangibles arising from or relating to the sale of farm products by a farmer, or consumer goods, then in the office of the . . . in the county of the debtor's residence or if the debtor is not a resident of this state then in the office of the . . . in the county where the goods are kept, and in addition when the collateral is crops growing or to be grown in the office of the . . . in the county where the land is located;

(b) when the collateral is timber to be cut or is minerals or the like (including oil and gas) or accounts subject to subsection (5) or Section 9–103, or when the financing statement is filed as a fixture filing (Section 9–313) and the collateral is goods which are or are to become fixtures, then in the office where a mortgage on the real estate would be filed or recorded;

(c) in all other cases, in the office of the [Secretary of State] and in addition, if the debtor has a place of business in only one county of this state, also in the office of . . . of such county, or, if the debtor has no place of business in this state, but resides in the state, also in the office of . . . of the county in which he resides.

Note: One of the three alternatives should be selected as subsection(1).

(2) A filing which is made in good faith in an improper place or not in all of the places required by this section is nevertheless effective with regard to any collateral as to which the filing complied with the requirements of this Article and is also effective with regard to collateral covered by the financing statement against any person who has knowledge of the contents of such financing statement.

(3) A filing which is made in the proper place in this state continues effective even though the debtor's residence or place of business or the location of the collateral or its use, whichever controlled the original filing, is thereafter changed.

Alternative Subsection (3)

[(3) A filing which is made in the proper county continues effective for four months after a change to another county of the debtor's residence or place of business or the location of the collateral, whichever controlled the original filing. It becomes effective thereafter unless a copy of the financing statement signed by the secured party is filed in the new county within said period. The security interest may also be perfected in the new county after the expiration of the four-month period; in such case perfection dates from the time of perfection in the new county. A change in the use of the collateral does not impair the effectiveness of the original filing.]

(4) The rules stated in Section 9–103 determine whether filing is necessary in this state.

(5) Notwithstanding the preceding subsections, and subject to subsection (3) of Section 9–302, the proper place to file in order to perfect a security interest in collateral, including fixtures, of a transmitting utility is the office of the [Secretary of State]. This filing constitutes a fixture filing (Section 9–313) as to the collateral described therein which is or is to become fixtures.

(6) For the purposes of this section, the residence of an organization is its place of business if it has one or its chief executive office if it has more than one place of business.

Amended in 1962 and 1972.

Note: Subsection (6) should be used only if the state chooses the Second or Third Alternative Subsection (1).

§ 9–402. FORMAL REQUISITES OF FINANCING STATEMENT; AMENDMENTS; MORTGAGE AS FINANCING STATEMENT.

(1) A financing statement is sufficient if it gives the names of the debtor and the secured party, is signed by the debtor, gives an address of the secured party from which information concerning the security interest may be obtained, gives a mailing address of the debtor and contains a statement indicating the types, or describing the items, of collateral. A financing statement may be filed before a security agreement is made or a security interest otherwise attaches. When the financing statement covers crops growing or to be grown, the statement must also contain a description of the real estate concerned. When the financing statement covers timber to be cut or covers minerals or the like (including oil and gas) or accounts subject to subsection (5) of Section 9–103, or when the financing statement is filed as a fixture filing (Section 9–313) and the collateral is goods which are or are to become fixtures, the statement must also comply with subsection (5). A copy of the security agreement is sufficient as a financing statement if it contains the above information and is signed by the debtor. A carbon, photographic or other reproduction of a security agreement or a financing statement is sufficient as a financing statement if the security agreement so provides or if the original has been filed in this state.

(2) A financing statement which otherwise complies with subsection (1) is sufficient when it is signed by the secured party instead of the debtor if it is filed to perfect a security interest in

(a) collateral already subject to a security interest in another jurisdiction when it is brought into this state, or when the debtor's location is changed to this state. Such a financing statement must state that the collateral was brought into this state or that the debtor's location was changed to this state under such circumstances; or

(b) proceeds under Section 9–306 if the security interest in the original collateral was perfected. Such a financing statement must describe the original collateral; or

(c) collateral as to which the filing has lapsed; or

(d) collateral acquired after a change of name, identity or corporate structure of the debtor (subsection (7)).

(3) A form substantially as follows is sufficient to comply with subsection (1):

Name of debtor (or assignor) ....

Address ....

Name of secured party

(or assignee) ....

Address ....

1. This financing statement covers the following types (or items) of property:

(Describe) ....

2. (If collateral is crops) The above described crops are growing or are to be grown on:

(Describe Real Estate) ....

3. (If applicable) The above goods are to become fixtures on *

*Where appropriate substitute either "The above timber is standing on...." or "The above minerals or the like (including oil and gas) or accounts will be financed at the wellhead or minehead of the well or mine located on.... "

(Describe Real Estate) .... and this financing statement is to be filed [for record] in the real estate records. (If the debtor does not have an interest of record) The name of a record owner is ....
....

4. (If products of collateral are claimed) Products of the collateral are also covered.

(use whichever is applicable	Signature of Debtor (or Assignor)
	Signature of Debtor Secured Party (or Assignee)

(4) A financing statement may be amended by filing a writing signed by both the debtor and the secured party. An amendment does not extend the period of effectiveness of a financing statement. If any amendment adds collateral, it is effective as to the added collateral only from the filing date of the amendment. In this Article, unless the context otherwise requires, the term "financing statement" means the original financing statement and any amendments.

(5) A financing statement covering timber to be cut or covering minerals or the like (including oil and gas) or accounts subject to subsection (5) of Section 9–103, or a financing statement filed as a future filing (Section 9–313) where the debtor is not a transmitting utility, must show that it covers this type of collateral, must recite that it is to be filed [for record] in the real estate records, and the financing statement must contain a description of the real estate [sufficient if it were contained in a mortgage of the real estate to give constructive notice of the mortgage under the law of this state] . If the debtor does not have an interest of record in the real estate, the financing statement must show the name of a record owner.

(6) A mortgage is effective as a financing statement filed as a fixture filing from the date of its recording if

(a) the goods are described in the mortgage by item or type; and

(b) the goods are or are to become fixtures related to the real estate described in the mortgage; and

(c) the mortgage complies with the requirements for a financing statement in this section other than a recital that it is to be filed in the real estate records; and

(d) the mortgage is duly recorded.

No fee with reference to the financing statement is required other than the regular recording and satisfaction fees with respect to the mortgage.

(7) A financing statement sufficiently shows the name of the debtor if it gives the individual, partnership or corporate name of the debtor, whether or not it adds other trade names or names of partners. Where the debtor so changes his name or in the case of an organization its name, identity or corporate structure that a filed financing statement becomes seriously misleading, the filing is not effective to perfect a security interest in collateral acquired by the debtor more than four months after the change, unless a new appropriate financing statement is filed before the expiration of that time. A filed financing statement remains effective with respect to collateral transferred by the debtor even though the secured party knows of or consents to the transfer.

(8) A financing statement substantially complying with the requirements of this section is effective even though it contains minor errors which are not seriously misleading. Amended in 1972.

Note: Language in brackets is optional.

Note: Where the state has any special recording system for real estate other than the usual grantor-grantee index (as, for instance, a tract system or a title registration or Torrens system) local adaptations of subsection (5) and Section 9–403(7) may be necessary. See Mass. Cen. Laws Chapter 106, Section 9–409.

§ **9–403.** What Constitutes Filing; Duration of Filing; Effect of Lapsed Filing; Duties of Filing Officer.

(1) Presentation for filing of a financing statement and tender of the filing fee or acceptance of the statement by the filing officer constitutes filing under this Article.

(2) Except as provided in subsection (6) a filed financing statement is effective for a period of five years from the date of filing. The effectiveness of a filed financing statement lapses on the expiration of the five year period unless a continuation statement is filed prior to the lapse. If a security interest perfected by filing exists at the time insolvency proceedings are commenced by or against the

debtor, the security interest remains perfected until termination of the insolvency proceedings and thereafter for a period of sixty days or until the expiration of the five year period, whichever occurs later. Upon lapse the security interest becomes unperfected, unless it is perfected without filing. If the security interest becomes unperfected upon lapse, it is deemed to have been unperfected as against a person who became a purchaser or lien creditor before lapse.

(3) A continuation statement may be filed by the secured party within six months prior to the expiration of the five year period specified in subsection (2). Any such continuation statement must be signed by the secure party, identify the original statement by file number and state that the original statement is still effective. A continuation statement signed by a person other than the secured party of records must be accompanied by a separate written statement of assignment signed by the secured party of record and comply with subsection (2) of Section 9 405, including payment of the required fee. Upon timely filing of the continuation statement, the effectiveness of the original statement is continued for five years after the last date to which the filing was effective whereupon it lapses in the same manner as provided in subsection (2) unless another continuation statement is filed prior to such lapse. Succeeding continuation statements may be filed in the same manner to continue the effectiveness of the original statement. Unless a statute on disposition of public records provides otherwise, the filing officer may remove a lapsed statement from the files and destroy it immediately if he has retained a microfilm or other photographic record, or in other cases after one year after the lapse. The filing officer shall arrange matters by physical annexation of financing statements to continuation statements or other related filings, or by other means, that if he physically destroys the financing statements of a period of more than five years past, those which have been continued by a continuation statement or which are still effective under subsection (6) shall be retained.

(4) Except as provided in subsection (7) a filing officer shall mark each statement with a file number and with the date and hour of filing and shall hold the statement or a microfilm or other photographic copy thereof for public inspection. In addition the filing officer shall index the statement according to the name of the debtor and shall note in the index the file number and the address of the debtor given in the statement.

(5) The uniform fee for filing and indexing and for stamping a copy furnished by the secured party to show the date and place of filing for an original financing statement or for a continuation statement shall be $ . . . if the statement is in the standard form prescribed by the [Secretary of State] and otherwise shall be $ . . . plus in each case, if the financing statement is subject to subsection (5) of Section 9–402, $ . . . The uniform fee for each name more than one required to be indexed shall be $ . . . The se-

cured party may at his option show a trade name for any person and an extra uniform indexing fee of $ . . . shall be paid with respect thereto.

(6) If the debtor is a transmitting utility (subsection (5) of Section 9–401) and a filed financing statement so states, it is effective until a termination statement is filed. A real estate mortgage which is effective as a fixture filing under subsection (6) of Section 9–402 remains effective as a fixture filing until the mortgage is released or satisfied of record or its effectiveness otherwise terminates as to the real estate.

(7) When a financing statement covers timber to be cut or covers minerals or the like (including oil and gas) or accounts subject to subsection (5) of Section 9–103, or is filed as a fixture filing, [it shall be filed for record and] the filing officer shall index it under the names of the debtor and any owner or record shown on the financing statement in the same fashion as if they were the mortgagors in a mortgage of the real estate described, and, to the extent that the law of this state provides for indexing of mortgages under the name of the mortgagee, under the name of the secured party as if he were the mortgagee thereunder, or where indexing is by description in the same fashion as if the financing statement were a mortgage of the real estate described. Amended in 1972.

Note: In states in which writings will not appear in the real estate records and indices unless actually recorded the bracketed language in subsection (7) should be used.

§ 9–404. TERMINATION STATEMENT.

(1) If a financing statement covering consumer goods is filed on or after . . ., then within one month or within then days following written demand by the debtor after there is no outstanding secured obligation and no commitment to make advances, incur obligations or otherwise give value, the secured party must file with each filing officer with whom the financing statement was filed, a termination statement to the effect that he no longer claims a security interest under the financing statement, which shall be identified by file number. In other cases whenever there is no outstanding secured obligation and no commitment to make advances, incur obligations or otherwise give value, the secured party must on written demand by the debtor send the debtor, for each filing officer with whom the financing statement was filed, a termination statement to the effect that he no longer claims a security interest under the financing statement, which shall be identified by file number. A termination statement signed by a person other than the secured party of record must be accompanied by a separate written statement of assignment signed by the secured party of record complying with the subsection (2) of Section 9–405, including payment of the required fee.

If the affected secured party fails to file such a termination statement as required by this subsection, or to send such termination statement within ten days after proper demand therefor, he shall be liable to the debtor for one hundred dollars, and in addition for any loss caused to the debtor by such failure.

(2) On presentation to the filing officer of such a termination statement he must note it in the index. If he has received the termination statement in duplicate, he shall return one copy of the termination statement to the secured party stamped to show the time of receipt thereof. If the filing officer has a microfilm or other photographic record of the financing statement, and of any related continuation statement, statement of assignment and statement of release, he may remove the originals from the files at any time after receipt of the termination statement, or if he has no such record, he may remove them from the files at any time after one year after receipt of the termination statement.

(3) If the termination statement is in the standard form prescribed by the [Secretary of State], the uniform fee for filing and indexing the termination statement shall be $ . . ., and otherwise shall be $ . . ., plus in each case an additional fee of $ . . . for each name more than one against which the termination statement is required to be indexed. Amended in 1972.

Note: The date to be inserted should be the effective date of the revised Article 9.

§ 9–405. ASSIGNMENT OF SECURITY INTEREST; DUTIES OF FILING OFFICER; FEES.

(1) A financing statement may disclose an assignment of a security interest in the collateral described in the financing statement by indication in the financing statement of the name and address of the assignee or by an assignment itself or a copy thereof on the face or back of the statement. On presentation to the filing officer of such a financing statement the filing officer shall mark the same as provided in Section 9–403(4). The uniform fee for filing, indexing and furnishing filing data for a financing statement so indicating an assignment shall be $ . . . if the statement is in the standard form prescribed by the [Secretary of State] and otherwise shall be $ . . ., plus in each case an additional fee of $ . . . for each name more than one against which the financing statement is required to be indexed.

(2) A secured party may assign of record all or part of his rights under a financing statement by the filing in the place where the original financing statement was filed of a separate written statement of assignment signed by the secured party of record and setting forth the name of the secured party of record and the debtor, the file number and the date of filing of the financing statement and the name and address of the assignee and containing a description of the collateral assigned. A copy of the assignment is sufficient as a separate statement if it complies with the preceding sentence. On presentation to the fil-

ing officer of such a separate statement, the filing officer shall mark such separate statement with the date and hour of the filing. He shall note the assignment on the index of the financing statement, or in the case of a fixture filing, or a filing covering timber to be cut, or covering minerals or the like (including oil and gas) or accounts subject to subsection (5) of Section 9–103, he shall index the assignment under the name of the assignor as grantor and, to the extent that the law of this state provides for indexing the assignment of a mortgage under the name of the assignee, he shall index the assignment of the financing statement under the name of the assignee. The uniform fee for filing, indexing and furnishing filing data about such a separate statement of assignment shall be $ . . . if the statement is in the standard form prescribed by the [Secretary of State] and otherwise shall be $ . . ., plus in each case an additional fee of $ . . . for each name more than one against which the statement of assignment is required to be indexed. Notwithstanding the provisions of this subsection, an assignment of record of a security interest in a fixture contained in a mortgage effective as a fixture filing (subsection (6) of Section 9–402) may be made only by an assignment of the mortgage in the manner provided by the law of this state other than this Act.

(3) After the disclosure or filing of an assignment under this section, the assignee is the secured party of record. Amended in 1972.

§ 9–406. RELEASE OF COLLATERAL; DUTIES OF FILING OFFICER; FEES.

A secured party of record may by his signed statement release all or a part of any collateral described in a filed financing statement. The statement of release is sufficient if it contains a description of the collateral being released, the name and address of the debtor, the name and address of the secured party, and the file number of the financing statement. A statement of release signed by a person other than the secured party of record must be accompanied by a separate written statement of assignment signed by the secured party of record and complying with subsection of (2) of Section 9–405, including payment of the required fee. Upon presentation of such a statement of release to the filing officer he shall mark the statement with the hour and the date of filing and shall note the same upon the margin of the index of the filing of the financing statement. The uniform fee for filing and noting of such a statement of release shall be $ . . . if the statement is in the standard form prescribed by the [Secretary of State] and otherwise shall be $ . . ., plus in each case an additional fee of $ . . . for each name more than one against which the statement of release is required to be indexed. Amended in 1972.

§ 9–407. INFORMATION FROM FILING OFFICER].

(1) If the person filing any financing statement, termination statement, statement of assignment, or statement of

release, furnishes the filing officer a copy thereof, the filing officer shall upon request note upon the copy the file number and date and hour of the filing of the original and deliver or send the copy to such person.]

[(2) Upon request of any person, the filing officer shall issue his certificate showing whether there is on file on the date and hour stated therein, any presently effective financing s.atement naming a particular debtor and any statement of assignment thereof and if there is, giving the date and hour of filing of each such statement and the names and addresses of each secured party therein. The uniform fee for such a certificate shall be $ . . . if the request for the certificate is in the standard form prescribed by the [Secretary of State] and otherwise shall be $ . . . Upon request the filing officer shall furnish a copy of any filed financing statement or statement of assignment for a uniform fee of $ . . . per page.]

Amended in 1972.

Note: This section is proposed as an option provision to require filing officers to furnish certificates. Local law and practices should be consulted with regard to the advisability of adoption.

§ 9–408. FINANCING STATEMENTS COVERING CONSIGNED OR LEASED GOODS.

A consignor or lessor of goods may file a financing statement using the terms "consignor," "consignee," "lessor," "lessee" or the like instead of the terms specified in Section 9–402. The provisions of this Part shall apply as appropriate to such a financing statement but its filing shall not of itself be a factor in determining whether or not the consignment or lease is intended as security (Section I 201(37)). However, if it is determined for other reasons that the consignment or lease is so intended, a security interest of the consignor or lessor which attaches to the consigned or leased goods is perfected by such filing. Added in 1972.

PART 5
DEFAULT

§ 9–501. DEFAULT; PROCEDURE WHEN SECURITY AGREEMENT COVERS BOTH REAL AND PERSONAL PROPERTY.

(1) When a debtor is in default under a security agreement, a secured party has the rights and remedies provided in this Part and except as limited by subsection (3) those provided in the security agreement. He may reduce his claim to judgment, foreclose or otherwise enforce the security interest by any available judicial procedure. If the collateral is documents the secured party may proceed either as to the documents or as to the goods covered thereby. A secured party in possession has the rights, remedies and duties provided in Section 9–207. The rights and remedies referred to in this subsection are cumulative.

(2) After default, the debtor has the rights and remedies provided in this Part, those provided in the security agreement and those provided in Section 9–207.

(3) To the extent that they give rights to the debtor and impose duties on the secured party, the rules stated in the subsections referred to below may not be waived or varied except as provided with respect to compulsory disposition of collateral (subsection (3) of Section 9–504 and Section 9–505) and with respect to redemption of collateral (Section 9–506) but the parties may by agreement determine the standards by which the fulfillment of these rights and duties is to be measured if such standards are not manifestly unreasonable:

(a) subsection (2) of Section 9–502 and subsection (2) of Section 9–504 insofar as they require accounting for surplus proceeds of collateral;

(b) subsection (3) of Section 9–504 and subsection (I) of Section 9–505 which deal with disposition of collateral;

(c) subsection (2) of Section 9–505 which deals with acceptance of collateral as discharge of obligation;

(d) Section 9–506 which deals with redemption of collateral; and

(e) subsection (1) of Section 9–507 which deals with the secured party's liability for failure to comply with this Part.

(4) If the security agreement covers both real and personal property, the secured party may proceed under this Part as to the personal property in accordance with his rights and remedies in respect of the real property in which case the provisions of this Part do not apply.

(5) When a secured party has reduced his claim to judgment the lien of any levy which may be made upon his collateral by virtue of any execution based upon the judgment shall relate back to the date of the perfection of the security interest in such collateral. A judicial sale, pursuant to such execution, is a foreclosure of the security interest by judicial procedure within the meaning of this section, and the secured party may purchase at the sale and thereafter hold the collateral free of any other requirements of this Article. Amended in 1972.

§ 9–502. COLLECTION RIGHTS OF SECURED PARTY.

(1) When so agreed and in any event on default the secured party is entitled to notify an account debtor or the obligor on an instrument to make payment to him whether or not the assignor was theretofore making collections on the collateral, and also to take control of any proceeds to which he is entitled under Section 9–306.

(2) A secured party who by agreement is entitled to charge back uncollected collateral or otherwise to full or limited recourse against the debtor and who undertakes to collect from the account debtor or obligors must pro-

ceed in a commercially reasonable manner and may deduct his reasonable expenses of realization from the collections. If the security agreement secures an indebtedness, the secured party must account to the debtor for any surplus, and unless otherwise agreed, the debtor is liable for any deficiency. But, if the underlying transaction was a sale of accounts or chattel paper, the debtor is entitled to any surplus or is liable for any deficiency only if the security agreement so provides. Amended in 1972.

§ 9–503. SECURED PARTY'S RIGHT TO TAKE POSSESSION AFTER DEFAULT.

Unless otherwise agreed a secured party has on default the right to take possession of the collateral. In taking possession a secured party may proceed without judicial process if this can be done without breach of the peace or may proceed by action. If the security agreement so provides the secured party may require the debtor to assemble the collateral and make it available to the secured party at a place to be designated by the secured party which is reasonably convenient to both parties. Without removal a secured party may render equipment unusable, and may dispose of collateral on the debtor's premises under Section 9–504.

§ 9–504. SECURED PARTY'S RIGHT TO DISPOSE OF COLLATERAL AFTER DEFAULT; EFFECT OF DISPOSITION.

(1) A secured party after default may sell, lease or otherwise dispose of any or all of the collateral in its then condition or following any commercially reasonable preparation or processing. Any sale of goods is subject to the Article on Sales (Article 2). The proceeds of disposition shall be applied in the order following to (a) the reasonable expenses of retaking, holding, preparing for sale or lease, selling, leasing and the like and, to the extent provided for in the agreement and not prohibited by law, the reasonable attorneys' fees and legal expenses incurred by the secured party;

(b) the satisfaction of indebtedness secured by the security interest under which the disposition is made;

(c) the satisfaction of indebtedness secured by any subordinate security interest in the collateral if written notification of demand therefor is received before distribution of the proceeds is completed. If requested by the secured party, the holder of a subordinate security interest must seasonably furnish reasonable proof of his interest, and unless he does so, the secured party need not comply with his demand.

(2) If the security interest secures an indebtedness, the secured party must account to the debtor for any surplus, and, unless otherwise agreed, the debtor is liable for any deficiency. But if the underlying transaction was a sale of accounts or chattel paper, the debtor is entitled to any

surplus or is liable for any deficiency only if the security agreement so provides.

(3) Disposition of the collateral may be by public or private proceedings and may be made by way of one or more contracts. Sale or other disposition may be as a unit or in parcels and at any time and place and on any terms but every aspect of the disposition including the method, manner, time, place and terms must be commercially reasonable. Unless collateral is perishable or threatens to decline speedily in value or is of a type customarily sold on a recognized market, reasonable notification of the time and place of any public sale or reasonable notification of the time after which any private sale or other intended disposition is to be made shall be sent by the secured party to the debtor, if he has not signed after default a statement renouncing or modifying his right to notification of sale. In the case of consumer goods no other notification need be sent. In other cases notification shall be sent to any other secured party from whom the secured party has received (before sending his notification to the debtor or before the debtor's renunciation of his rights) written notice of a claim of an interest in the collateral. The secured party may buy at any public sale and if the collateral is of a type customarily sold in a recognized market or is of a type which is the subject of widely distributed standard price quotations he may buy at private sale.

(4) When collateral is disposed of by a secured party after default, the disposition transfers to a purchaser for value all of the debtor's rights therein, discharges the security interest under which it is made and any security interest or lien subordinate thereto. The purchaser takes free of all such rights and interests even though the secured party fails to comply with the requirements of this Part or of any judicial proceedings

(a) in the case of a public sale, if the purchaser has no knowledge of any defects in the sale and if he does not buy in collusion with the secured party, other bidders or the person conducting the sale; or

(b) in any other case, if the purchaser acts in good faith.

(5) A person who is liable to a secured party under a guaranty, indorsement, repurchase agreement or the like and who receives a transfer of collateral from the secured party or is subrogated to his rights has thereafter the rights and duties of the secured party. Such a transfer of collateral is not a sale or disposition of the collateral under this Article. Amended in 1972.

§ 9–505. COMPULSORY DISPOSITION OF COLLATERAL; ACCEPTANCE OF THE COLLATERAL AS DISCHARGE OF OBLIGATION.

(1) If the debtor has paid sixty per cent of the cash price in the case of a purchase money security interest in consumer goods or sixty per cent of the loan in the case of an-

ther security interest in consumer goods, and has not signed after default a statement renouncing or modifying his rights under this Part a secured party who has taken possession of collateral must dispose of it under Section 9–504 and if he fails to do so within ninety days after he takes possession the debtor at his option may recover in conversion or under Section 9–507(1) on secured party's liability.

(2) In any other case involving consumer goods or any other collateral a secured party in possession may, after default, propose to retain the collateral in satisfaction of the obligation. Written notice of such proposal shall be sent to the debtor if he has not signed after default a statement renouncing or modifying his rights under this subsection. In the case of consumer goods no other notice need be given. In other cases notice shall be sent to any other secured party from whom the secured party has received (before sending his notice to the debtor or before the debtor's renunciation of his rights) written notice of a claim of an interest in the collateral. If the secured party receives objection in writing from a person entitled to receive notification within twenty-one days after the notice was sent, the secured party must dispose of the collateral under Section 9–504. In the absence of such written objection the secured party may retain the collateral in satisfaction of the debtor's obligation. Amended in 1972.

§ 9–506. DEBTOR'S RIGHT TO REDEEM COLLATERAL.

At any time before the secured party has disposed of collateral or entered into a contract for its disposition under Section 9–504 or before the obligation has ben discharged under Section 9–505(2) the debtor or any other secured party may unless otherwise agreed in writing after default redeem the collateral by tendering fulfillment of all obligations secured by the collateral as well as the expenses reasonably incurred by the secured party in retaking, holding and preparing the collateral for disposition, in arranging for the sale, and to the extent provided in the agreement and not prohibited by law, his reasonable attorney's fees and legal expenses.

§ 9–507. SECURED PARTY'S LIABILITY FOR FAILURE TO COMPLY WITH THIS PART.

(1) If it is established that the secured party is not proceeding in accordance with the provisions of this Part disposition may be ordered or restrained in appropriate terms and conditions. If the disposition has occurred the debtor or any person entitled to notification or whose security interest has been made known to the secured party prior to the disposition has a right to recover from the secured party any loss caused by a failure to comply with the provisions of this Part. If the collateral is consumer goods, the debtor has a right to recover in any event an amount not less than the credit service charge plus ten per cent of the principal amount of the debt or the time price differential plus 10 per cent of the cash price.

(2) The fact that a better price could have been obtained by a sale at a different time or in a different method from that selected by the secured party is not of itself sufficient to establish that the sale was not made in a commercially reasonable manner. If the secured party either sells the collateral in the usual manner in any recognized market therefor or if he sells at the price current in such market at the time of his sale or if he has otherwise sold in conformity with reasonable commercial practices among dealers in the type of property sold he has sold in a commercially reasonable manner. The principles stated in the two preceding sentences with respect to sales also apply as may be appropriate to other types of disposition. A disposition which has been approved in any judicial proceeding or by any bona fide creditor's committee or representative of creditors shall conclusively be deemed to be commercially reasonable, but this sentence does not indicate that any such approval must be obtained in any case nor does it indicate that any disposition not so approved is not commercially reasonable.

Article 10
Effective Date
and Repealer

(Omitted)

Article 11
(Reporter's Draft)
Effective Date
and Transition
Provisions

(Omitted)